THE OXFORD HISTORY OF
THE CHRISTIAN CHURCH

Edited by
Henry and Owen Chadwick

Church and Society in Eighteenth Century France

VOLUME 1

THE CLERICAL ESTABLISHMENT AND ITS
SOCIAL RAMIFICATIONS

JOHN McMANNERS

CLARENDON PRESS · OXFORD
1998

Oxford University Press, Great Clarendon Street, Oxford OX2 6DP
Oxford New York
Athens Auckland Bangkok Bogota Bombay Buenos Aires
Calcutta Cape Town Dar es Salaam Delhi Florence Hong Kong Istanbul
Karachi Kuala Lumpur Madras Madrid Melbourne Mexico City
Nairobi Paris Singapore Taipei Tokyo Toronto Warsaw
and associated companies in
Berlin Ibadan

Oxford is a registered trade mark of Oxford University Press

Published in the United States
by Oxford University Press Inc., New York

© John McManners 1998

The moral rights of the author have been asserted

First published 1998

British Library Cataloguing in Publication Data
Data available

Library of Congress Cataloging in Publication Data
The church in eighteenth-century France / John McManners.
(The Oxford history of the Christian Church)
Includes bibliographical references.
Contents: 1. Clergy and people—2. Church, power, and politics.
1. Catholic Church—France—History—18th century. 2. France—
Church history—18th century. I. Title. II. Series.
BX1529.M36 1998 282'.44'09033—dc21 97-47458
ISBN 0-19-826905-6

1 3 5 7 9 10 8 6 4 2

Typeset by Regent Typesetting, London
Printed in Great Britain on acid-free paper by
Bookcraft (Bath) Ltd., Midsomer Norton

To Sarah

ACKNOWLEDGEMENTS

The editors of this Series generously allowed me to make an idio-syncratic, maverick contribution, and encouraged me to write at my own length and pace. The Delegates of Oxford University Press courageously accepted the enormous book which I finally presented. Thereafter, all concerned at the Press have exceeded the bounds of duty in assisting me: Hilary O'Shea, Editor for Theology and Classics, Elizabeth Alsop who set in train the processes of pro-duction, and Enid Barker who sportingly came out of retirement to bring the work to conclusion when Elizabeth moved to new fields of endeavour in London, Jean van Altena the copy editor, Judith Colleran the proofreader, and Meg Davies who compiled the index. To all I am deeply grateful. I am also especially indebted to friends who read over, with critical and discerning eyes the chapters falling within the areas of their research: Robin Briggs (Chs. 30, 31), Scott Mandelbrote (Chs. 33, 44), Margaret Bent (Ch. 15), John Rogister (Chs. 39, 40, 41), Nigel Aston (Chs. 48, 49, 50). Chapter 21, difficult to write, was read by Richard Fargher, Robert Darnton, and Nicolas Cronk—they saved me from many an error, though I suspect they will not be entirely happy with the final version. Finally, I must express my thanks to All Souls College, where I have been granted an academic home since retiring from the chair of Ecclesiastical History. Successive secretaries have typed my ill-written manuscripts in their various recensions, and Margaret Lord has completed the task with a blend of intuition and accuracy. For the final proof-reading the college enabled me to employ Genevieve Hawkins, famous in the Faculty of Modern Languages for her expertise. Here in All Souls I have found friendship and intellectual companionship, with many an opportunity to discuss the problems of interpreting the French eighteenth century. It has been a rare privilege, making the fourteen years since I retired the happiest of my life.

J.M.

CONTENTS

ABBREVIATIONS

PRIMARY SOURCES

D'Argenson	R.-L. de Voyer, marquis D'Argenson, *Journal et mémoires*, ed. E. J. B. Rathery (9 vols., 1859–67).
Bachaumont	L. P. de Bachaumont, Pidanset de Mairobert, and Mouffle d'Angerville, *Mémoires secrets pour servir à histoire de la République des lettres en France* (36 vols., 1779–89).
Barbier	E.-J.-F. Barbier, *Chronique de la Régence et du règne de Louis XV, 1718–1763* (8 vols., 1857–8).
Grimm	F.-M. Grimm, *Correspondance littéraire, philosophique et politique*, ed. M. Tourneux (16 vols., 1871–80).
Guyot	P.-J. Guyot, *Répertoire universel et raisonné de jurisprudence civile, criminelle, canonique et bénéficiale* (64 vols., 1775–83, + 14 vols. supp. 1786).
Luynes	C.-P. d'Albert, duc de Luynes, *Mémoires du duc de Luynes sur la cour de Louis XV*, ed. L. Dussieux and E. Soulié (11 vols., 1860–5).
Marais	M. Marais, *Journal et mémoires*, ed. M. de Lescure (4 vols., 1863).
Métra	L.-F. Métra *et al.*, *Correspondance secrète, politique et littéraire* (18 vols., 1781–90).
P.V. Ass.	*Collection des procès verbaux des Assemblées générales du clergé de France* (10 vols., 1767–78).
Saint-Simon	Louis de Rouvroy, duc de Saint-Simon, *Mémoires* (21 vols., 1829).
Saint-Simon (Pléiade)	Louis de Rouvroy, duc de Saint-Simon, *Mémoires*, ed. G. Truc, Pléiade (9 vols., 1950).
Voltaire, *Corresp.*	Voltaire, *Correspondance*, ed. Th. Besterman (101 vols., Geneva, 1953–65). References to this edition unless stated otherwise. *Correspondance*, new augmented edition by Th. Besterman (135 vols., Paris, 1963–77).
Voltaire, *Œuvres*	François-Marie Arouet, Voltaire, *Œuvres complètes*, ed. L. Moland (52 vols., 1877–85).

Abbreviations

PERIODICALS

Am. Hist. Rev.	*American Historical Review* (Washington)
Amis Chinon	*Les Amis du vieux Chinon: Bulletin* (Chinon)
Anal. cist.	*Analecta cisterciensia* (Rome)
L'Anjou hist.	*L'Anjou historique* (Angers)
Ann.	*Annales. Économies. Sociétés. Civilisations.* (Paris)
Ann. Acad. Mâcon	*Annales de l'Académie de Mâcon* (Mâcon)
Ann. Bourgogne	*Annales de Bourgogne* (Dijon)
Ann. Bretagne	*Annales de Bretagne et des pays de l'Ouest* (Rennes)
Ann. Clermont-Ferrand	*Annales de Clermont-Ferrrand* (Clermont-Ferrand)
Ann. dém. hist.	*Annales de démographie historique* (Paris)
Ann. Est	*Annales de l'Est* (Nancy)
Ann. Haute-Provence	*Annales de Haute-Provence* (Dijon)
Ann. hist. Rév. fr.	*Annales historiques de la Révolution française* (formerly *Revue historique de la Révolution française*) (Paris)
Ann. internat. crim.	*Annales internationales de criminologie* (Paris)
Ann. Malte	*Annales de l'Ordre souverain militaire de Malte* (Rome)
Ann. Midi	*Annales du Midi* (Toulouse)
Ann. Normandie	*Annales de Normandie* (Caen)
Ann. rév.	*Annales révolutionnaires* (Société des études robespierristes) (Paris)
Ann. Soc. Cannes	*Annales de la Société scientifique et littéraire de Cannes et de l'arrondissement de Grasse* (Cannes)
Ann. Soc. Rousseau	*Annales de la Société Jean-Jacques Rousseau* (Geneva)
Ann. Soc. Saint-Malo	*Annales de la Société d'histoire et d'archéologie de l'arrondissement de Saint-Malo* (Saint-Malo)
L'Année canonique	*L'Année canonique* (Inst. cath. fac. de droit canonique, Paris)
Arch. Église Alsace	*Archives de l'Église d'Alsace* (Strasbourg)
Arch. Hist. Soc. Jesu	*Archivum Historicum Societatis Jesu* (Rome)
Arch. juives	*Archives juives*
Bibl. École Chartes	*Bibliothèque de l'École des Chartes* (Paris)
Le Bugey	*Le Bugey* (Belley)
Bull. Acad. delph.	*Bulletin (mensuel) de l'Académie delphinale* (Grenoble)
Bull. ann. Cluny	*Bulletin annuel des amis de Cluny* (Dijon)
Bull. Auvergne	*Bulletin historique et scientifique de l'Auvergne* (Clermont-Ferrand)

Bull. Belley	*Bulletin d'histoire et d'archéologie du diocèse de Belley* (Bourg-en-Bresse)
Bull. Com. Nîmes	*Bulletin du Comité de l'art chrétien de Nîmes* (Nîmes)
Bull. Com. Paris	*Bulletin du Comité d'histoire et d'archéologie du diocèse de Paris* (Paris)
Bull. Comm. Seine-et-Oise	*Bulletin de la Commission des antiquités et des arts de Seine-et-Oise* (Versailles)
Bull. Diana	*Bulletin de la Diana* (Montbrison)
Bull. Fac. cath. Lille	*Bulletin des Facultés catholiques de Lille* (Lille)
Bull. Féd. Franche Comté	*Bulletin de la Fédération des sociétés savantes de Franche Comté* (Besançon)
Bull. Hist. Med.	*Bulletin of the History of Medicine* (Baltimore)
Bull. litt. ecclés.	*Bulletin de littérature ecclésiastique* (Institut catholique: Toulouse)
Bull. Lyon	*Bulletin historique du diocèse de Lyon* (Lyon)
Bull. méms. Soc. Côtes-du-Nord	*Bulletin et mémoires de la Société d'émulation des Côtes-du-Nord* (Saint-Brieuc)
Bull. méms. Soc. Ille-et-Vilaine	*Bulletin et mémoires de la Société archéologique du département d'Ille-et-Vilaine* (Rennes)
Bull. Soc. Aube	*Bulletin (mensuel) de la Société académique d'agriculture, sciences, arts et belles-lettres du département de l'Aube* (earlier *Mémoires*) (Troyes)
Bull. Soc. Basses-Alpes	*Bulletin de la Société scientifique et littéraire des Basses-Alpes* (Digne)
Bull. Soc. Bayonne	*Bulletin (trimestriel) de la Société des sciences, lettres et arts de Bayonne* (Bayonne)
Bull. Soc. Borda	*Bulletin (trimestriel) de la Société de Borda* (Dax)
Bull. Soc. Bretagne	*Bulletin de la Société d'histoire et archéologie de Bretagne* (Rennes)
Bull. Soc. Draguignan	*Bulletin de la Société d'études scientifiques et archéologiques de Draguignan* (Draguignan)
Bull. Soc. Drôme	*Bulletin de la Société d'archéologie et de statistique de la Drôme* (Valence)
Bull. Soc. Eure-et-Loire	*Bulletin de la Société archéologique et historique d'Eure-et-Loire* (Chartres)
Bull. Soc. Gers	*Bulletin de la Société archéologique, historique, littéraire et scientifique du Gers* (Auch)
Bull. Soc. Guyenne	*Bulletin de la Société des Bibliophiles de Guyenne* (Bordeaux)
Bull. Soc. Hautes-Alpes	*Bulletin de la Société d'études historiques, scientifiques et littéraires des Hautes-Alpes* (Gap)
Bull. Soc. hist. mod.	*Bulletin de la Société de l'histoire moderne* (Paris)
Bull. Soc. hist. prot. fr.	*Bulletin de la Société de l'histoire du protestantisme français* (Paris)

Bull. Soc. Meuse	*Bulletin des Sociétés d'histoire et archéologie de la Meuse* (Bar-le-Duc)
Bull. Soc. Montargis	*Bulletin de la Société d'émulation de l'arrondissement de Montargis* (Montargis)
Bull. Soc. Morbihan	*Bulletin (mensuel) de la Société polymathique du Morbihan* (Vannes)
Bull. Soc. Morinie	*Bulletin historique de la Société des antiquaires de la Morinie* (earlier *Mémoires*) (Saint-Omer)
Bull. Soc. Nantes	*Bulletin de la Société archéologique et historique de Nantes et de la Loire-Inférieure* (Nantes)
Bull. Soc. Normandie	*Bulletin de la Société des antiquaires de Normandie* (Caen-Rouen)
Bull. Soc. Oise	*Bulletin de la Société académique d'archéologie, sciences et arts du département de l'Oise* (Beauvais)
Bull. Soc. Orléanais	*Bulletin (trimestriel) de la Société archéologique et historique de l'Orléanais* (Orléans)
Bull. Soc. Orne	*Bulletin de la Société historique et archéologique de l'Orne* (Alençon)
Bull. Soc. Ouest	*Bulletin de la Société des antiquaires de l'Ouest et des Musées de Poitiers* (earlier *Mémoires*) (Poitiers)
Bull. Soc. Paris	*Bulletin de la Société de l'histoire de Paris et de l'Île-de-France* (Paris)
Bull. Soc. Pau	*Bulletin de la Société des sciences, lettres et arts de Pau* (Pau)
Bull. Soc. phil. vosgienne	*Bulletin de la Société philomatique vosgienne* (Saint-Dié)
Bull. Soc. Sarthe	*Bulletin de la Société d'agriculture, sciences et arts de la Sarthe* (Le Mans)
Bull. Soc. Seine-et-Marne	*Bulletin de la Société d'archéologie, sciences, lettres et arts du département de Seine-et-Marne* (Meaux)
Bull. Soc. Sens	*Bulletin de la Société archéologique de Sens* (Sens)
Cahiers hist.	*Cahiers d'histoire* (Lyon: universities of Clermont, Lyon, and Grenoble)
Cahiers hist. enseign.	*Cahiers de l'histoire de l'enseignement* (Rouen)
Cahiers Bazadais	*Les Cahiers du Bazadais* (Bazas)
Cahiers Vitrezais	*Les Cahiers du Vitrezais: revue historique, archéologique et littéraire des Hauts de Gironde* (Paris)
Cath. Hist. Rev.	*The Catholic Historical Review* (Washington)
Chron. Port-Royal	*Chroniques de Port-Royal* (Paris)
Church Hist.	*Church History* (Chicago)
Cîteaux	*Cîteaux, commentarii cistercienses* (Achel)
Coll. cist.	*Collectanea cisterciensia* (Rome)

Comptes Soc. Clermont-en-Beauvaisis	Comptes rendus et mémoires de la Société archéologique et historique de Clermont-en-Beauvaisis (Clermont-en-Beauvaisis)
Divus Thomas	Divus Thomas, commentarium de philosophia et theologia (Plaisance)
Eng. Hist. Rev.	English Historical Review (London)
Ensembles d'Écoles	Ensemble d'Écoles supérieures et Facultés catholiques (Fédération universitaire et polytechnique de Lille) (Lille)
Études rurales	Études rurales (École des Hautes Études) (Paris)
Études XVIIIᵉ siècle	Études sur le dix-huitième siècle (Univ. libre, Brussels)
Eur. J. Population	European Journal of Population (Amsterdam)
Eur. St. Rev.	European Studies Review (European History Quarterly) (London)
Fr. Hist.	French History (Oxford)
Fr. Hist. St.	French Historical Studies (Raleigh, NC)
Fr. St.	French Studies (Oxford)
Genava	Genava (Geneva)
Hist. J.	The Historical Journal (Cambridge)
L'Information hist.	L'Information historique (Paris)
JAMS	Journal of the American Musicological Society (Richmond, Va.)
J. Eccles. Hist.	Journal of Ecclesiastical History (London)
J. hist.	Journal historique
J. Interdisc. Hist.	Journal of Interdisciplinary History
J. Mod. Hist.	Journal of Modern History (Chicago)
J. Ren. Mod. St.	Journal of Renaissance and Modern Studies (Nottingham)
Lettres romanes	Lettres romanes (Louvain)
Maison-Dieu	La Maison-Dieu (Centre de Pastorale liturgique: Paris)
Mélanges sc. relig.	Mélanges de science religieuse (Lille)
Méms. Acad. Besançon	Mémoires de l'Académie des sciences, belles-lettres et arts de Besançon (Besançon)
Méms. Acad. Lyon	Mémoires de l'Académie des sciences, belles-lettres et arts de Lyon (Lyon)
Méms. Acad. nat. Angers	Mémoires de l'Académie nationale des sciences, arts et belles-lettres d'Angers (Angers)
Méms. Acad. nat. Caen	Mémoires de l'Académie nationale des sciences, arts et belles-lettres de Caen (Caen)
Méms. Acad. nat. Dijon	Mémoires de l'Académie nationale (impériale) des sciences, arts et belles-lettres de Dijon (Dijon)
Méms. Acad. nat. Metz	Mémoires de l'Académie nationale des sciences, arts et belles-lettres de Metz (Metz)

Méms. Acad. nat. Toulouse	*Mémoires de l'Académie nationale des sciences, inscriptions et belles-lettres de Toulouse* (Toulouse)
Méms. Comm. Côte-d'Or	*Mémoires de la Commission des antiquités de la Côte-d'Or* (Dijon)
Méms. Soc. Alais	*Mémoires et comptes rendus de la Société scientifique et littéraire d'Alais* (Alais)
Méms. Soc. Aube	*Mémoires de la Société académique d'agriculture, des sciences, arts et belles-lettres du département de l'Aube* (later *Bulletin*) (Troyes)
Méms. Soc. Bretagne	*Mémoires de la Société d'histoire et d'archéologie de Bretagne* (later *Bulletin*) (Rennes)
Méms. Soc. Cambrai	*Mémoires de la Société d'émulation de Cambrai* (Cambrai)
Méms. Soc. Carcassonne	*Mémoires de la Société des arts et des sciences de Carcassonne* (Carcassonne)
Méms. Soc. Côtes-du-Nord	*Mémoires de la Société d'émulation des Côtes-du-Nord* (Saint-Brieuc)
Méms. Soc. Doubs	*Mémoires de la Société d'émulation du département du Doubs* (Besançon)
Méms. Soc. Marne	*Mémoires de la Société d'agriculture, commerce, sciences et arts du département de la Marne* (Châlons-sur-Marne)
Méms. Soc. Morinie	*Mémoires de la Société des antiquaires de la Morinie* (later *Bulletin*) (Saint-Omer)
Méms. Soc. Nord	*Mémoires de la Société centrale d'agriculture, sciences et arts du département du Nord* (Douai)
Méms. Soc. Orléans	*Mémoires de la Société d'agriculture, sciences, belles-lettres et arts d'Orléans* (Orléans)
Méms. Soc. Ouest	*Mémoires de la Société des antiquaires de l'Ouest* (later *Bulletin*) (Poitiers)
Méms. Soc. Paris	*Mémoires de la Société de l'histoire de Paris et de l'Île-de-France* (later *Bulletin*) (Paris)
Méms. Soc. Rambouillet	*Mémoires de la Société archéologique de Rambouillet* (Rambouillet)
Méms. Trav. Fac. cath. Lille	*Mémoires et Travaux des Facultés catholiques de Lille* (later *Bulletin*) (Lille)
Mentalités	*Mentalités: histoire des cultures et des sociétés* (Paris)
Le Monde alpin	*Le Monde alpin et rhodanien* (Nyons)
La Montagne Sainte-Geneviève	*La Montagne Sainte-Geneviève et ses abords: Société historique et archéologique du Ve arrondissement* (Paris)
Music & Letters	*Music & Letters* (Taunton)
Neophilologus	*Neophilologus* (New York)
Nice hist.	*Nice historique* (Nice)

Nouv. Rev. Champagne et Brie	*La Nouvelle Revue de Champagne et de Brie* (earlier, just *Revue*) (Châlons-sur-Marne)
Pays d'Auge	*Le Pays d'Auge* (Lisieux)
Population	*Population* (Paris)
Provence hist.	*Provence historique* (Marseille)
Province du Maine	*La Province du Maine* (Le Mans)
Rev. Alsace	*Revue d'Alsace* (Strasbourg)
Rev. Anjou	*Revue de l'Anjou* (from 1880; earlier titles included *Maine-et-Loire* and *Maine*) (Angers)
Rev. Auvergne	*La Revue d'Auvergne* (Clermont-Ferrand)
Rev. Bas-Poitou	*Revue de Bas-Poitou* (Fontenay-le-Comte)
Rev. belge phil. hist.	*Revue belge de philologie et d'histoire* (Brussels)
Rev. bénédictine	*Revue bénédictine* (Abbey of Maredsous, Belgium)
Rev. Bordeaux	*Revue historique de Bordeaux et du département de la Gironde* (Bordeaux)
Rev. Champagne et Brie	*Revue de Champagne et de Brie* (revived as *Nouvelle*) (Châlons-sur-Marne)
Rev. Clergé fr.	*Revue du Clergé français* (Paris)
Rev. Comminges	*Revue de Comminges* (Toulouse)
Rev. études juives	*Revue des études juives* (Société des études juives) (Paris)
Rév. fr.	*La Révolution française* (Paris)
Rev. Gascogne	*Revue de Gascogne: Bulletin de la Société historique de Gascogne* (Auch)
Rev. Gévaudan	*Revue du Gévaudan, des Causses et des Cévennes* (Mende)
Rev. Haute-Auvergne	*Revue de la Haute-Auvergne* (Société des lettres, sciences et arts de la Haute-Auvergne) (Aurillac)
Rev. hist.	*Revue historique* (Paris)
Rev. hist. armée	*Revue historique de l'armée* (Paris)
Rev. hist. droit fr.	*Revue historique de droit français et étranger* (Paris)
Rev. hist. ecclés.	*Revue d'histoire ecclésiastique* (Louvain)
Rev. hist. écon. sociale	*Revue d'histoire économique et sociale* (earlier *Annales*) (Paris)
Rev. hist. Église Fr.	*Revue d'histoire de l'Église de France* (Paris)
Rev. hist. litt. Fr.	*Revue d'histoire littéraire de la France* (Paris)
Rev. hist. missions	*Revue de l'histoire des missions* (Paris)
Rev. hist. mod. contemp.	*Revue d'histoire moderne et contemporaine* (Paris)
Rev. hist. religions	*Revue de l'histoire des religions* (Paris)
Rev. hist. théâtre	*Revue d'histoire du théâtre* (Paris)
Rev. internat. enseign.	*Revue internationale de l'enseignement* (Paris)
Rev. Libournais	*Revue historique et archéologique du Libournais* (Libourne)

Rev. Lyon	*Revue d'histoire de Lyon* (Lyon)
Rev. Mabillon	*Revue Mabillon* (Ligugé)
Rev. Maine	*Revue historique et archéologique du Maine* (Le Mans)
Rev. monde cath.	*Revue du monde catholique* (Paris)
Rev. mus.	*Revue musicale* (Paris)
Rev. Nord	*Revue du Nord* (Paris)
Rev. quest. hist.	*Revue des questions historiques* (Paris)
Rev. Rouergue	*Revue du Rouergue* (Rodez)
Rev. sc. hum.	*Revue des sciences humaines* (Lille)
Rev. sc. philos. théol.	*Revue des sciences philosophiques et théologiques* (Paris)
Rev. Soc. Villiers-sur-Marne	*Revue de la Société historique de Villiers-sur-Marne et de la Brie française* (Villiers–sur–Marne)
Rev. Socs. Haute-Normandie	*Revue des Sociétés savantes de Haute-Normandie* (Rouen)
Rev. Versailles	*Revue de l'histoire de Versailles et de Seine-et-Oise* (Versailles)
Rev. Vivarais	*Revue historique, archéologique et scientifique du Vivarais* (Annonay)
Soc. sav. hist. arch.	*La Société savoisienne d'histoire et d'archéologie: Mémoires et documents* (Chambéry)
St. 18th C. Culture	*Studies in Eighteenth-Century Culture* (Cleveland)
S.V.E.C.	*Studies on Voltaire and the 18th Century* (Voltaire Foundation, Oxford)
Theol. Zeitschrift	*Theologische Zeitschrift* (Basel)
Trav. Acad. nat. Reims	*Travaux de l'Académie nationale de Reims* (Reims)
XVIIIᵉ Siècle	*Dix-huitième Siècle* (Paris)
XVIIᵉ Siècle	*Dix-septième Siècle: Bulletin de la Société d'études du XVIIᵉ siècle* (Paris)
Yale Fr. St.	*Yale French Studies* (New Haven)

THE THEME

This book attempts to give a picture of the religious life of the people of eighteenth-century France, to recapture the atmosphere of the times, and to appreciate the beliefs, aspirations, hopes, and fears of four generations. It is written out of interest and sympathy, adopting the approach of the portrait painter rather than that of the clinical diagnostician, aiming for friendly realism rather than morbid analysis. To be fair, and if erring, erring on the side of generosity, presentation in detail is required; individuals and groups come out less well in history written in broad generalizations. Their justification lies in the small print of the historical record rather than in the formal pages. This approach fits with the methodology which the nature of the subject imposes, for the enormous wealth of the Gallican Church, its alliance with the State, and its close, almost symbiotic, integration with the social order mean that it cannot be treated as a self-contained unit. There is no escape from exploring the detailed context of how everything worked (taxation, property holding, the legal system, the hierarchy of classes) and how everyone lived (customs, communities, families, sociability). The history of the Church cannot be separated from the history of society generally.

The constant pressure of worldly interests influenced almost everything that happened in the life of the Church; one of the driving themes in these studies, religious vocation and allegiance among both clergy and laity, is no exception. The century provides many examples of dramatic renunciations, saintly conduct, and sacrificial dedication—glimpses of souls destined to break through all the webs of self-interest in the human situation in any age. But giving realistic consideration to allegiance to the Church and the call to serve it in the material circumstances of the day, with rewards to be won and social status to be achieved, vocation appears in a more complex, variant form, a mutation to be judged by adjusted criteria. The choice of the monastic life took place against the background of families making arrangements for the careers and maintenance of their children. Candidates called to the parochial ministry were considering it as a career, useful to their family and giving opportunities for local leadership. The aristocratic monopoly of bishoprics is explained by the dynastic policies of noble families, the policies of the Crown, and the protocol of Versailles, and something of a justification becomes apparent when the secular and social obligations of bishops are reviewed. These are obvious examples among many. With the interdependence of Church and society a dimension of ambiguity creeps into reflections on religious motivation. It could be that in what follows the emphasis has leaned too far towards material factors, for just as the Devil has the best tunes, so the affairs of the world provide the historian with better evidence than fervour and devotion.

Yet inspiration is only seemingly devalued by being seen in its worldly milieu. In subtle ways self-interest operates in Church affairs everywhere, in whatever social environment; in an age of ecclesiastical wealth and power it is simply more evident. Saints and fanatics excepted, motivation is rarely single-minded, and it is the mark of a civilized mind to follow an ideal yet be conscious of worldly advantages, and to know when they ought to be repudiated and when they may be accepted. Sacrificial certainty driving to its goal evokes admiration, but sympathy is more readily accorded to routine, ambiguous, or provisional commitments, sometimes managing to transcend personal gain, sometimes transmuting it into opportunity, or, taking the easiest path, accommodating it into a workable compromise.

Under the *ancien régime*, we find clerics who are totally cynical, some scandalous to boot; but there are many more who are paradoxically edifying—unbelievers meticulously fulfilling their duties, dubious characters who change course, routine careerists, believers without enthusiasm who refuse to let the side down, and a multitude of good men and women drawn to the Church for both self-interested reasons and the desire to serve it, who would be astonished if asked to distinguish between the two.

As the picture of Church life builds up, a pattern of development becomes apparent. The old social order was evolving, and stirrings of division and discontent demonstrated that it had to change more rapidly to avert disaster. As the royal government creaked on towards eventual bankruptcy, the archaic machinery of the Gallican Church was slowing down every initiative for pastoral efficiency: benefice law put a premium upon guile and influence; the confusions of diocesan and parochial structure handicapped the clergy in coping with shifts of population; and the chaotic conventions of rule in so many of the monastic orders made reforming schemes illusory.

It was becoming evident that the nobility would have to surrender its privileges, voluntarily or under pressure from the Crown or, if the crust of tradition and order cracked, in revolutionary turmoil. Nowhere was this more certain than in the Church, where the build-up of the challenge to aristocratic monopoly gained apostolic force when a corpus of theological arguments came in to reinforce those from natural law, with the curés as propagandists and leaders. Opposition to the riches and exemptions of ecclesiastics was growing. While the scepticism of the Enlightenment did not endanger the Church in the short term—it was a spectacular firework display on the horizon—the earthy realities of anticlerical feeling accumulated over questions of taxation, tithe, church fees and rates, leasehold and feudal dues—envy was intensified by oppressiveness. Stories of luxurious living and idleness, the hypocrisy and uncharitable bitterness of the Jansenist–Jesuit struggle, and revulsion against the persecution of the Protestants influenced public opinion (with Rousseau as its prophet) to separate the Christianity of the gospels from the claims of the institutional Church. The standard arguments from divine ordinance, the Scriptures, and immemorial tradition in defence of clerical wealth and privilege sounded hollow.

Yet in many ways, this was the golden age of the French Church. An increasing number of bishops, some showing little zeal in their own lives, strove to improve standards among their clergy. Never before had the parish priests been so moral and well educated, and never before or since had they been drawn from such reputable families and enjoyed so much respect. Never had there been so many Easter confessions and communions, and so many laymen living lives of well-informed belief and pious practice. The work of religious institutions in education and care for the sick reached a new level of dedication and expertise. Liturgical observances were conducted with unsurpassed splendour, and church music achieved a unique professional sophistication. But this was the mellow autumn season adorning the landscape with rich colours before the leaves began to fall and winter came. And this golden age had a contradiction at its heart. The clergy, so many of them touched with Counter-Reformation zeal, were trying to enforce the austerities of piety on the confraternities, pilgrimages, and manifold traditional observances of the people; by so doing they were hastening the breakdown of mass conformity. They were unwilling to accept the compromises with the world on which the Gallican Church's monolithic splendour rested.

The four generations of this century were the last to profit by—

and be oppressed by—the majestic worldly greatness of the Gallican Church and the (at least nominal) deference of authority to other-worldly principles resulting from the accumulated understandings between religion and power which had tamed barbarism and given Europe its distinctive Christian civilization. A new order was coming in by stealth and osmosis, then, finally, in a brutal cataclysm. In it, the injustices of the past were swept away, and injustices more logically based replaced them. As the reverberations of the clash of ideals, the interventions of circumstance, and the play of individual ambitions fade into retrospect, at the core of the Revolution is seen a vast seizure and transfer of property, the patrimony of the Church that had underpinned so many vocations, kept so many decent families in the fashion to which they were accustomed, and enabled the kings to tie in the feuding aristocracy to the service of the nation. Shorn of its wealth and the influence and temptation which wealth brings, and with the old routines of conformity shattered by war and social overturn, the Church was to become a minority group following more closely its divine inspiration, but with its authority confined to its own voluntary adherents, while the State and the majority went their way with only fading nuances of religion to direct consciences and restrain conduct. Though the sphere of individual opportunity and general liberty has been widened, to the benefit of so many, the old decencies and certainties have decayed, and there is no way back to them. There is always a price to pay for freedom.

I

CHURCH AND STATE

I

THE CORONATION:
REFLECTIONS ON THE
ALLEGIANCE OF THE CLERGY

I

On Friday, 9 June 1775, Louis XVI came to Reims for the *Sacre*, the ceremony of his coronation. The civilian militia paraded outside the city gates, where the provincial governor, the duc de Bourbon, and the municipal officers in scarlet gowns met him. The king changed over from his huge travelling coach to a gala carriage, all glass, paintings, and embroidery, surmounted by plumes. Salvoes of artillery were fired, and the bells pealed, as he was escorted to the cathedral square between the ranks of the Gardes Françaises in their blue, white, and red uniforms.[1] The bishops of the ecclesiastical province, led by the archbishop of Reims, Cardinal La Roche-Aymon, met Louis in the shadow of the vast ornate façade of the cathedral. The cardinal was old and feeble, but he had girded himself to preside over the ceremonies of the coming days, when an archbishop of Reims was the most prestigious figure in France after the king. A mediocre and compliant man ('on ne se brouille pas avec moi'[2]), he had risen to monopolize the greatest ecclesiastical offices and sinecures Versailles could confer: *grand aumônier du Roi*, holder of the *feuille des bénéfices* and the titular abbacy of Saint-Germain, as well as the prelacy of Reims. The king knelt before the bishops to receive aspersion with holy water and to kiss the gospel book. A Te Deum was sung, then the royal cortège adjourned to the episcopal palace for loyal harangues. On the Saturday evening, the king attended a sermon. With apostolic rigour and fashionable reformist zeal, Boisgelin, archbishop of Aix, preached on the duties of rulers; Louis commended him, though the Court did not allow his liberal sentiments to be published.[3]

The coronation took place on 11 June, Trinity Sunday. The Gothic aspect of the cathedral interior was masked by tapestry draping the pillars, by statues and ornaments, and by a lofty woodwork of Corinthian orders with richly gilded fluting and grooving, encasing the walls of the choir. Above the royal throne was a cupola of violet velvet drapery. An orchestra of a hundred players was concealed behind the altar. The canons of Reims were in their stalls, for they had a prescriptive right to their own places. On the epistle side of the choir were packed ministers of state, high ecclesiastics, and nobles of the robe; on the gospel side, peers, marshals of France, and wearers of the cordon bleu. The duc de Croÿ made a quick check to ensure that no one had manœuvred into a higher place than his rank justified: 'qu'il n'y avait point d'embarras pour le rang'.[4] Ensconced among the reverend canons was the 21-year-old Charles-Maurice, abbé de Périgord, on the first stage of an ecclesiastical career forced on him by his family because of his lameness. His uncle, the coadjutor of Reims, had arranged a canonry for him five weeks before, barely a month after he had been made a subdeacon.[5] In his memoirs, the young abbé says nothing about the *Sacre* except that the festivities gave him the opportunity to cultivate the friendship of three influential ladies of the Court.[6] Within fifteen years of hearing the king at Reims swearing to defend the privileges of the Church, Charles-Maurice, now bearing the name of Talleyrand and bishop of Autun, was to propose the sale of ecclesiastical property in the revolutionary assembly, and within thirty years he was to wear the splendid habit of *Grand Chambellan* at the coronation of Napoleon, and to parade in the same office at the coronation of the last Bourbon king twenty-one years later still.

Everyone was in place by 7 o'clock in the morning. Then, a procession set off down the newly constructed covered way to the archbishop's palace to bring back the king—the *grand maître des cérémonies*, the canons of Reims, players of music, and the bishops of Laon and Beauvais. The precentor of the cathedral hammered on the door. 'Que demandez-vous?' 'Nous demandons le roi.' 'Le roi dort.' But at the third time of asking—'Nous demandons Louis XVI que Dieu nous a donné pour roi'—the door was opened.[7]

The king in a silver cloak over a crimson shirt and wearing a black velvet hat adorned with diamonds was brought to the cathedral and set before the altar. Holy water was sprinkled over him, and the prayer was said: 'God almighty and eternal, who hast elevated to the kingdom thy servant Louis, grant that he may ensure the good of his subjects in all the course of his reign, and never depart from the paths of justice and of truth.'[8]

The *Veni Creator* was sung while the archbishop of Reims proceeded to the cathedral porch to meet the procession of the *Sainte*

Ampoule.[9] The holy oil for the king's anointing, brought down from heaven by a dove at the prayer of Saint-Rémy for the baptism of Clovis, was kept in the *Sainte Ampoule*, a tiny crystal flask silvered inside and carried, for safety's sake, in a golden holder shaped like a dove, enamelled white with red beak and claws. The revered object was brought to the cathedral by the *grand prieur* of the abbey of Saint-Rémy, riding a white horse and dressed in a golden cope. He was sheltered by a canopy borne aloft by the four *chevaliers de la Sainte Ampoule* (vassals of fiefs of the abbey), and at each corner rode the *barons otagers*, hostages for the safe return of the flask, dressed in cloth of gold, each escorted by a groom. Ahead of the *grand prieur* went his monks in white albs and the Minims with their cross, and ahead of them marched a military escort of musketeers with their band, and first of all, a rustic guard of the men of the parish of Le Chesne, dressed in blue, wearing gaiters, with cockades and oak leaves in their hats, muskets on shoulder. This was their peculiar privilege, for their ancestors in the village had preserved the *Sainte Ampoule* from destruction in the Hundred Years War.

The coronation service began with the king taking the oaths. He promised to 'preserve the canonical privilege, law and justice due' to the 'bishops and the churches committed to their charge', to preserve all Christian people in peace, to prevent rapine and iniquity, to be merciful and equitable in judgement, and to do all in his power 'to exterminate, in all lands subjected to my rule, the heretics declared to be so by the Church (*nommément condamnés par l'Église*)'.[10]

The bishops of Laon and Beauvais then asked the congregation if it received its king, and respectful silence ensued; Louis then took the oath to preserve the two great orders of chivalry—that of the Saint-Esprit and that of Saint-Louis—and to enforce the edicts against duelling (a solemn gesture against aristocratic lawlessness introduced by Louis XIV).

The king had made his promises, and he was now invested with the first instalment of the panoply of office.[11] The spurs (which came from the early days of the Capetian monarchy), the sword (supposedly that of Charlemagne, though the oldest part, the hilt, with two winged heads guarding the tree of life, dated only from the eleventh century), the long sceptre (surmounted by an effigy of Charlemagne, though dating only from the High Middle Ages), lay on the altar. Between coronations, these regalia were kept in the Parisian abbey of Saint-Denis, whose abbot was in proud attendance, standing by his treasures. The senior lay peer affixed the spurs, and the archbishop girded on the sword, after solemnly consecrating it to noble deeds. The king held it, drawn, while an anthem was sung; thereafter it was borne before him by a nobleman for the rest of the ceremony.

Kneeling on a vast carpet of violet velvet scattered with golden fleurs-de-lis, the king received the seven unctions. A drop of resin from the *Sainte Ampoule* was taken out on a golden needle and mixed with the *sainte chrême*, the oil used in the cathedral for baptisms, confirmations, and ordinations. What was left on the paten after the ceremony was returned to the flask, so the supply of the sacred balm would continue to be available at the coronations of kings of France for all time.[12] The six ecclesiastical peers stood around; the archbishop of Reims, assisted by the bishop of Laon, administered the unctions; the prelates of Beauvais, Langres, Châlons, and Noyon arrayed their monarch in a tunic and dalmatic, vestments of a priestly type. Then came the unctions on the palms, unctions appropriate for a bishop. The great ermine-braided mantle was thrown over the king's shoulders, and he was then given the remaining symbols of office: the sceptre, the ring, and the *main de justice*.

It was time to call in the laity. The Garde des Sceaux invited the lay peers to assemble, summoning them for the occasion under the archaic titles of dukes of Normandy, Burgundy, and Aquitaine, and counts of Toulouse, Flanders, and Champagne—evoking the memories of the war lords who had built the West in distant centuries, oddly contrasting with the present luxurious generation: the king's two brothers, and the duc d'Orléans and his son the duc de Chartres, and the prince de Condé and his son the duc de Bourbon.[13]

Then came the actual coronation. The archbishop of Reims took the crown from the altar and placed it on the royal brow. All the peers, ecclesiastical and lay, gathered round and put out a hand to steady it. Crowned and vested with the garments and insignia of office, Louis moved off to his throne. As he sat there, the archbishop, now mitre-less, paid him the homage of a kiss and cried 'Vivat rex in aeternum!'—a cry which was echoed by all the peers. This was the signal for unrestrained public rejoicing. The air thundered with fanfares of trumpets, the crash of artillery, and the pealing of all the bells of the city, and the great doors of the cathedral were flung open to let the people surge in to catch a glimpse of their ruler on his throne, adorned with the diadem of Charlemagne.[14] Among them (or was he stranded in the throng in the streets outside?) was an ugly 16-year-old playing truant from school at Troyes; on his return, he was to write a well-informed essay on the *Sacre* for his teacher, an early venture into eloquence by Georges-Jacques Danton.[15]

There were lengthy prayers, and the Te Deum was sung, a prelude to the celebration of the coronation mass—dramatically, a quiet anticlimax to the ceremony; spiritually, the true heart of it. The king recognized his insignificance and mortality by taking off his crown when the gospel was read; then the Church received him into the circle of its chosen ministry by giving him communion in both kinds, a prerogative of the clergy.

As the royal procession left the cathedral, hundreds of little birds were released from their cages to flutter under the vaults, and the heralds scattered commemorative medals among the people.

Though the comte d'Artois and some libertine nobles had laughed and gossiped,[16] the overwhelming impression was one of splendour, dignity, and rejoicing, a vast pageant of national loyalty. As she saw her husband crowned, Marie Antoinette had broken down and wept. It was astonishing, she reflected, that the king should be so received by his people only two months after starvation had driven so many to riot; we must work for their happiness, she wrote to the empress, her mother. It had been a day she would never forget. 'Je sais bien que je n'oublierai de ma vie (dût-elle durer cent ans) la journée du Sacre.'[17] The royal couple were drawn together: Louis by the sight of her tears, Marie Antoinette by the vision of his great calling; but the attraction lasted but a day, and desire failed.

Cardinal La Roche-Aymon, sustained through the rigours of the long ceremonial by coffee and stimulants, ended the day feeling fine. Solicitously, the king asked him if he was tired. 'O non, Sire! prêt à recommencer'; a fatuous answer which delighted the courtiers for long afterwards.[18]

From henceforth, Louis, the Lord's anointed, was endowed with the power of healing the victims of scrofula. Renan was to exaggerate when he described the 'touching' for 'the king's evil' as the 'eighth sacrament', but it was true enough that the monarch, once crowned, was regarded as the channel of divine mercy (he could act only if he was in a state of grace and had received communion). Three days after the *Sacre*, on 14 June, a procession[19] set off for the abbey of Saint-Rémy, a procession with a military flavour—the Musketeers, the Swiss Guards, the *Chevaux-légers*, and the Royal Pages, with Louis on his famous horse 'Vainqueur' (a corpulent young man, but a fearless horseman, he looked his best in the saddle). The Benedictines of Saint-Rémy had gathered a multitude of sufferers from miles around into various hospitals awaiting the great day—there were many, alas, for the tumours massed behind ears and under jaws were the effect of malnutrition. The scrofulous were gathered together in the open air, 1,000, perhaps 2,000 of them. The task of touching was repulsive. The royal person was protected, in so far as the head of each scrofulous person was held by a doctor, and the supplicants' hands were clasped within the gloved hands of the captain of the Guard, but the day was hot and the vast assembly stank. Louis was relieved to complete the exhausting round and wash in vinegar and water scented with orange blossom.[20]

The message of the *Sacre* was: the king's power comes from God. His servants only open the door to the summons to attend the cathedral when the formula is used 'whom God has given us for king'. The symbols of office (the spurs excepted) are handed over by the ecclesiastical peers; even the sword is a gift from God. More than this, the king is a sacerdotal figure. The anointings, the priestly vestments, the reception of the Sacrament in both kinds, the gift of healing, and perhaps some minor details—the hands of the bishops outstretched to steady the crown, the sceptre as long as a bishop's pastoral staff—all imply that he belongs to the ranks of the clerical estate, those whose peculiar vocation comes intensely, uniquely, and directly from Heaven. Being called by God and instituted by God's servants, however, brings special obligations; the sovereign solemnly swears to preserve the privileges of the ecclesiastical order and to suppress heresy. Throne and altar are allied and interdependent. The prayers,[21] a richly layered historical accumulation, place the monarch in the lineage of Abraham, Moses, David, and Solomon: called by God, favoured by God, and exercising power in the shadow of the divine authority. The manifold intercessions have a threefold emphasis. First, the king is exhorted to fulfil his obligations, and God is implored to help him to do so. Louis is told that he must govern his passions, set a good example, and be magnanimous. May he be a defender of the Church, a 'munificent patron' of ecclesiastical foundations; may he drive out 'false Christians, enemies of the name of Jesus Christ and heretics'. To all, he must give impartial justice, and he must wreak vengeance on the unjust. To the 'princes and seigneurs' of his realm, he must be 'liberal and kind', but his most especial solicitude must be shown to the poor, pilgrims, widows, and orphans. Secondly, the Church reciprocates by calling down on the king the blessings of Heaven, in this life and the next. No fewer than twelve prayers ask for the boon of eternal felicity in the afterlife. But an equal number ask for the overthrow of his enemies in this (including the famous archaic supplication for the strength of the rhinoceros). Six petitions ask for the king to be granted a long life; others ask that he be granted forgiveness for his sins, be delivered from infirmity, and that his descendants may reign for long after him. Thirdly, the prayers ask for material blessing to be shed upon the people of the kingdom. There are several references to the blessing of peace, one specific appeal for the multiplication of population, and two appeals (in the words of the blessings in the Old Testament) for the dew of heaven, the fatness of the earth, and an abundance of corn and oil for the consolation of the people.

The *Sacre* was too solemn a national institution to be ridiculed, but anticlericals and lawyers were not prepared to allow the clergy to make capital out of the manifestly religious implications of the ceremonies. A journalist heaved a sigh of relief when he described how the lay peers were finally summoned to come forward: 'here is the moment when the clergy ceases to attribute to itself the right of conferring unlimited power on the king.' To his disillusioned eye, the unctions and the arrayal in sacerdotal vestments constituted the supreme moment for clerical pretensions—'symbols by which the order of clergy seeks, no doubt, to prove it is united to the royal power'.[22] He was right; the unctions could imply a certain subordination of the monarch—as the Epistle to the Hebrews had said, 'the less is blessed of the better'. And in France, as distinct from England, it was accepted that the king could not exercise his healing touch until he became the Lord's anointed.[23] Laymen, therefore, preferred not to enthuse over this aspect of the liturgical observances. Scholars, in the safe obscurity of Latin, had doubts about the provenance of the *Sainte Ampoule* and the story of the dove.[24] Voltaire could not see how 'a few drops of oil' made any difference to an essentially secular ceremony[25]—in fact, the clergy did not claim that they did in so far as the rights of sovereignty were concerned.[26]

Those who had reservations about the unctions went even further in their scepticism about the magical touch of kings.[27] Saint-Simon has a story, untrue and evilly sardonic, about Mme de Soubise being the mistress of Louis XIV, yet dying from scrofula. Montesquieu was ironical in the *Lettres Persanes*; the *Encyclopédie* expressed disbelief; Voltaire urged the French monarchs to follow the example of William of Orange and renounce the claim to work miracles.[28] At the beginning of the reign of Louis XV the formula was indeed changed, from the absolute 'Dieu te guérit' to the hopeful 'Dieu te guérisse', and from 1739 onwards, Louis XV's private life ensured that he was disqualified from exercising healing powers. On Christmas Day 1736 he communicated and touched for the king's evil according to usage; the next Christmas, 'illness' provided an excuse to do neither. His last Easter duty was performed in 1738, and there was scandal at Eastertide in 1739 when he did not call the scrofulous to appear before him.[29] Thus there was a gap of thirty-six years before Louis XVI touched the sick after his coronation. Three or four certificates about people he had cured were welcomed at Versailles, but it is doubtful if he convoked any further ceremonies of healing.

To the lawyers, the essential, decisively anticlerical point about the coronation was: whatever else the clergy bestowed upon the monarch in the name of God, they certainly did not make him king. From the end of the thirteenth century, the legal beginning of a royal reign was dated from the accession, not from the *Sacre*.[30] Skilfully taking the ceremonies as a whole and avoiding precise language so as to give little opportunity for magnifying the role of the Church, chancelier d'Aguesseau defined what he supposed were the religious implications: 'Kings protest publicly before the altar that it is by God that they reign . . . the people, receiving the king in a fashion (*en quelque manière*) from the hands of God, are more disposed . . . to revere and obey him, not only by motives of fear or hope, but by a sentiment and principle of religion.'[31] Similarly, the *Encyclopédie*, welcoming the legal point that the king ruled already by his birth and right of succession, treated the *Sacre* as a picturesque parable to instruct the multitude. 'Doubtless, the object of this pious ceremony is to teach the people, by a striking spectacle, that the king's person is sacred, and threats against his life are forbidden because, as the Scripture says of Saul, he is the *Lord's anointed*.'[32]

Apart from minimizing the importance of the religious aspects of the *Sacre* in general, on two specific points men of the Enlightenment accused the clergy of impropriety. One concerned an omission—deliberate or accidental we cannot know—from the traditional usages.[33] After the two bishops had asked the congregation if it received its king, the silence that ensued ought to have been followed by the announcement of the Archbishop of Reims: 'quia populus acclamavit te, te sacro regem'—a formula transmitted from prelate to prelate since Saint-Rémy. A substantial volume published later in the year, *Le Sacre royal, ou les droits de la nation française reconnus et confirmés par cette cérémonie*, declared that the omission was engineered by a 'party of reaction', a conspiracy which included the higher clergy. Other pamphleteers took up the theme: the monarchy, they argued, was founded on a social contract, to which the people in general gave formal assent. There were similar sentiments in the account of the *Sacre* given by a radical journalist at the point where he described how the peers, lay and ecclesiastical, put out their hands to touch the crown—'a truly noble and expressive allegory, but one which would be much more appropriate if delegates of the people also joined in supporting the crown with the same allegorical implication'.[34]

The second point of criticism concerned the maintenance of a traditional observance which enlightened opinion regarded as no longer civilized—the oath to extirpate heresy. In the space of the three generations since Louis XIV, the persecutions had died away, and the law courts had found ways and means of—virtually—giving civil rights to Protestants.[35] Turgot urged the young king to take a revised form of coronation oath: 'I promise God and my people to govern my kingdom with justice according to the laws; never to wage war except in a just and indisputable cause; to employ all my authority to maintain the rights of each of my subjects; and to work all my life to render them as happy as is in my power.'[36] Louis was sympathetic, but in the end he dared not do it—he mumbled the offensive formula almost inaudibly. The Assemblies of Clergy continued their hollow exhortations for action against heretics; 'under the government of a monarch', they argued, 'troubles are practically always inseparable from the diversity of religious opinions', and the coronation oath was 'the foundation of public peace', with its obligations to 'enforce morality and protect religion'.[37] When, in 1787, the long overdue grant of civil rights to Protestants was made, the clergy mostly acquiesced, though there were protests that Louis had betrayed his mission and broken his promises. In January 1788 the bishop of Dol scandalously used the opportunity of a Breton delegation to Versailles to denounce his sovereign to his face. Constantine, Theodosius, and Charlemagne, he declared, would have convoked a national council of the Church before embarking on a measure 'that threatened the collapse of the arches of the sanctuary'.[38]

II

The interdependence of Church and State, rehearsed in the *Sacre* once in a lifetime, was continually demonstrated anew in the multitudinous official ceremonies of the *ancien régime*. The great occasions of secular rejoicing were marked by the solemn chanting of the Te Deum. This fourth-century hymn of praise and credal affirmation

had been drawn out of its devotional and liturgical context to be
made the propaganda manifestation of the monarchy. From the late
fourteenth century it had been central in the coronation ceremony,
and thereafter it became the general official observance of the cities
of France when rejoicing for fortunate occasions in the life of the
royal family and, above all, for military victories. In Toulouse, the
Te Deum was prescribed (with all the magistrates and great ones of
the city processing into the cathedral to hear it) on seventy-two
recorded occasions between 1738 and 1780. Only nine of these
were religious events (a new archbishop welcomed, a new saint
canonized, a new relic acquired, or a new altar consecrated); nineteen concerned the royal family (ten being to give thanks for the
king's recovery of health, seven for royal births); thirty-seven were
celebrations of military victories (including three peace treaties).[39] In
the heady days of the early Revolution, when the Nation and the
Law were being co-opted with the monarchy into the triple symbol
of patriotic ardour, the Te Deum remained indispensable. At the
festival of the Federation on 14 July 1790, everywhere in France it
was sung as the local community gathered to take the new civic oath
at the 'autel de la patrie'. It took another year before the pageant
masters of the Revolution conceived of national rejoicing in purely
secular terms with a pagan, neo-classical décor.

By contrast, in times of national disaster, dearth, defeat, royal
illness, the Church was called on to recite services of liturgical
penitence, and to invite the faithful to fervent intercessions. Thus,
the joys and sorrows of the royal family can be chronicled from the
liturgical record of the Parisian churches. On 11 September 1729,
Louis XV went to Notre-Dame to give thanks for the birth of the
dauphin, and all chapters, parishes, and religious communities
processed to the cathedral, and from thence to the Sainte-Chapelle,
to worship before its prestigious relic, the fragment of the True
Cross. Churchmen reminded the laity that only eleven months
before, the Queen had paid her first visit to Notre-Dame to pray for
a male heir. The collapse of the popularity of Louis XV can be
documented in the attendances at the intercessions for his recovery
from illness. In 1744, the whole capital came, and when he was pronounced out of danger, every guild commissioned a Te Deum, the
coal heavers outdoing all rivals by hiring the municipal oboes
and trumpets. In his last illness, thirty years later, hardly anyone
attended the intercessions or prayed before the relics of Ste
Geneviève, displayed for the purpose. As with the monarch, so with
the institutions which, under him, regulated society. When the law

courts reassembled after the vacation, proceedings began with a mass, the *messe rouge* of the parlement of Paris, so called because the lawyers wore their scarlet and ermine. If there had been an involuntary vacation because the magistrates had been exiled by the king, the *messe rouge* would be celebrated before they administered justice again; great was their delight on such an occasion, on 1 December 1732, when the verse for the day was Isaiah 1: 26: *Restituam tuos judices*: 'I will restore thy judges as at first, and thy counsellors as at the beginning; afterwards, thou shalt be called the city of righteousness, the faithful city.'[40] The terms and examinations of the universities, the commemorative days of individual faculties, municipal elections, the opening of a new building or bridge, the laying of the keel of a warship, the blessing of the colours of a regiment—the whole official life of the country was marked by religious observances. The directors of the most unpopular of the instruments of government were the most scrupulous about paying deference to God. The lease of the Ferme Générale of the taxes always ended with an article according alms to the poor, 'and that it might please God to bless this Association, a mass shall be said every day in the chapel of the *Hôtel des Fermes* at Paris, paid for at the ordinary tariff'.[41]

The celebration of this alliance of Church and State, so evident in ceremonies, was a commonplace of ecclesiastical eloquence. The people were brought to obedience by the teachings of religion, and the Church was preserved in safety under the shadow of the secular power: 'God subjects peoples to the authority of kings and the authority of kings ought to keep the peoples submissive to God,' said the Jesuit Charles de Neuville preaching before Louis XV: 'Religion is the support of the throne, and the throne gives protection to religion.'[42] As the century progressed, it became injudicious for the clergy to define this 'protection'; liberal journalists were outraged when ecclesiastical obituarists, short of other material to praise Louis XV, instanced in his favour the censorship of irreligious books and the penalizing of Protestants.[43] Preachers used extravagant language in expressing loyalty to the hereditary monarchy of France. 'Vous êtes des Dieux,' said Bossuet of kings,[44] though the context in which he said it hardly gave monarchs cause for complacency. The pastoral letters of bishops might stray over the borderline which separated sycophancy from blasphemy—like using New Testament phrases about the incarnation of the Saviour to greet the birth of a new royal prince.[45] Unconditional loyalty to the person of the monarch was expressed in the oath of allegiance taken by a bishop: he would not take part in any treasonable design 'and if any such comes to my notice, I will make it known to your Majesty'.[46] The law-books define what was involved; the only case in which the secret of the confessional could be violated was when a crime of 'lèze majesté au premier chef' was involved.[47]

Looked at from a doctrinal point of view, loyal rhetoric wandered furthest from orthodoxy in the routine assertions so commonly found, that religion would fail if it did not have the support of the monarchical State. Massillon had declared: 'Religion grows feeble and collapses . . . wherever civil harmony is destroyed.'[48] 'I will not separate religion from the State,' said Archbishop Boisgelin to Louis XVI in December 1790, 'nor the State from your person, because religion and the State fall with the king.'[49] These statements were leaving a great truth unsaid: the Church had an eternal mission, and if the secular order fell or the State lost its monarchical organization, the Church would go on. Even as Boisgelin spoke, the time was rapidly approaching when churchmen would be obliged to dig into the unspoken assumptions behind their political theory and adjust to a world in revolution; essentially, it was public order that was sacred, and a *de facto* government had to be obeyed. The mystique of royal sovereignty was real enough, but fragile. Churchmen did not say that the quasi-sacerdotal status received by kings at their coronation was the origin of their sovereignty, though it 'rendered their power more acceptable to the subjects and less dangerous to themselves'.[50] Power had a divine origin, but this did not mean that God gave it as a peculiar personal gift to the ruler; power came from God in his general activity as creator: he made man of a nature demanding life in society, and life in society demanded a final secular authority. 'In all this', Suarez had said, 'there is no divine action distinct from creation.' The greatest French theologian of the century, Bergier, in his *Quelle est la source de toute autorité?* (1789), ridiculed theories of political contracts made among men who had sprung up from the earth as isolated individuals; in reality, God created men with reciprocal rights and duties from the beginning. There was an original social nexus, and from it systems of government had arisen; we must accept them, since 'the harshest of governments is a lesser evil than anarchy'. The ideal is the 'conservation of the people', not their 'absolute liberty', a dream of 'an imaginary happiness which no nation has ever enjoyed since the creation'.[51] The argument from anarchy is strong, but ambiguous so far as monarchy is concerned. Any port will do if the storm is wild enough.

The raw, utilitarian antithesis between anarchy and government which underlay the Christian doctrine of obedience was an argument of last resort, to be drawn on in desperate, revolutionary days. The divinity that hedged a king implied some sense of more direct divine election. This election was more often assumed than defined. An attempt to do so was made, at the end of the seventeenth century, by Quesnel the Jansenist, arguing on Thomist lines and anxious to show that the authority of Louis XIV had nothing to fear from his party; what he said was the quintessence of current orthodoxy, though more logically put.[52] Essentially, he appealed to the operation of the providential hand of God in history. A king may be elected; 'this instinct by which a multitude of persons of different temperaments agree to choose a man to command them and by which they focus their choice on a single man . . . can only be regarded as a singular effect of the guidance of God, who holds in his hand the hearts of all men'. Another way a monarch may achieve power is by conquest in a just war, for all peoples, even pagans, accept God as 'the sovereign arbiter of battles'. But there is a third way, superior to the others: 'legitimate succession', as in France. The caprice of peoples, cabals, and violence can vitiate an election, and a tyrant with an army of barbarians can win a war. God may not be actually operating in a particular election or on a particular battlefield. But children are always a gift of God, and he sends to kings the heirs destined to succeed them in their sovereignty. 'This way of entering into authority is more excellent, and it imitates . . . the manner in which the Son of God received from his Father all his power and authority, by way of birth; for God the Father, engendering the Son, communicates to him all that is in his own essence.' Hereditary government also resembles the rule of God, as it is eternal. And in whatever way a king comes to rule, whether by election, battle, or—more surely—by legitimate succession, he is 'God's minister', as St Paul said, and as Aquinas taught. There was, of course, a difficulty. As in any view of the workings of Providence, there was a twilight area where the divine purpose seemed to falter. An election might be fraudulent or a victory mere brute force; as for hereditary monarchy, what of a barren queen or an imbecile or vicious heir? These were further examples of crisis, where the theologians had to fall back on the argument from anarchy to maintain the obligation of obedience. France, however, was fortunate: a thousand years of monarchy were evidence to demonstrate the long-continuing providence of God underlying the accidents of history.

There had once been a time when the Church had obeyed—or suffered beneath—an alien and unsympathetic government only because the alternative was anarchy; churchmen, said the archbishop of Tours, in a speech to the General Assembly of the Clergy in 1745, had then appeared in the courts of emperors only to defend their conduct and, maybe, face martyrdom. 'Since Constantine and Clovis', however, these unhappy days had ended, and the two powers were 'in firm alliance'.[53] When they reflected on the role of the temporal power in this alliance, the clergy, like the magistrates, held that the king, though absolute, was not arbitrary. Bossuet had listed the obligations of kings: to obey Christian precepts, observe the fundamental laws of France, protect the Church, and defend the poor.[54] As a mere man, no better than all the others, the ruler ought to be 'submissive to [the prelates] in the order of religion' and open-hearted towards the miseries of his fellows. Both the human being and the wearer of the crown were under the shadow of the judgement of God. The language of adulation addressed by churchmen to kings was generally ambiguous. The phrase 'Ye are gods' in Bossuet's great Palm Sunday sermon (1662) comes from Psalm 82, in which God speaks to unjust judges: 'Ye are gods . . . nevertheless ye shall die like men and fall like one of the princes.' Ironically, the orator thunders on: 'Oh gods of flesh and blood, gods of dust and mud', you will die, and what is godlike and continuous is your authority. 'The man dies, it is true, but the king, as we say, never dies, the image of God is immortal.'[55] It was hardly a declaration of the divine right of kings.

But there were no earthly sanctions against the misdemeanours of a sovereign. Bossuet's 'Ye are gods' was less a declaration of adoration, than a threat of mortality and the judgement of the next world, allied to an admission of impotence on the part of the subject in this. A Christian could remonstrate and, even, disobey if he was prepared to be struck down, but he was not entitled to revolt. Even as late as 1663, the Sorbonne had defended the possibility of launching an ecclesiastical excommunication against a tyrant. But the need for an assured principle of order in society was pressing all the while towards a doctrine of non-resistance: memories of the murders of Henri III and Henri IV and the civil wars of the sixteenth and seventeenth centuries were never far from the minds of Frenchmen. The Third Estate of the Estates General of 1614 had advanced the proposition: kings could not be deposed by the Church, and subjects could not be released from their oath of allegiance. This declaration was accepted by the Assembly of Clergy of 1682 as the first of its Four Gallican Articles, which were to be taught in all universities, colleges, and seminaries.[56] The Assemblies of Clergy in 1750 and 1756 renewed the formal statement that Christians are not entitled to revolt against duly constituted authority; this was said categorically, without reservations admitting the marginal possibility of tyrannicide which could be found in Aquinas and which for long had been included in Christian political theory.

The doctrine of non-resistance had nothing to do with absolutism: France was not a 'despotisme à la Turque'. The actors in the pageant of the *Sacre*—from the peers ecclesiastical and lay to the abbots of Saint-Rémy and Saint-Denis, from the canons of Reims down to the humble peasants of Le Chesne—played their parts by traditional right and privilege. It was a demonstration of how France was a monarchy hedged around by convention and vested interest. As Jean Bodin had said long ago, his country was not ruled by a 'seigniorial monarchy' or a tyranny, but by a royal or legitimate one, in which 'natural liberty and the natural right to property are secured to all'.[57] The lesson was enhanced by the spectacle of the monarch taking solemn oaths before he was crowned—though Louis XV held he had taken them 'to God alone', implying that only Heaven could call him to a reckoning. Though they did not claim that any sublunary authority could enforce accountability upon the king, the parlements certainly disagreed with this view of the coronation oaths—they were taken 'to the nation'.[58] Furthermore, the jurists were prepared to elaborate the royal obligations. They held that, in addition to the coronation oaths, there were other 'fundamental laws'—concerning the succession to the Crown, the age at which the king ceased to be a minor, the exact time when his reign began, the Catholicity of the monarchy, and the inviolability of the Crown demesne. More vaguely, they talked of the traditions and 'maximes du royaume'— for example, laws should be published in due form, and officials should not be dismissed without due process. From time to time they tried to add the parlement's right to register royal edicts and remonstrate against them. (Louis XV flatly denied this in 1766.) This claim to a role of verification and criticism was given a wider justification by the theories of Montesquieu; in 1766 Joly de Fleury declared that traditional corporations within the State were indispensable to liberty—'it is of the essence of a monarchy that there be intermediary bodies'.[59] The struggle of the parlement of Paris with the Crown throughout the eighteenth century was, in a sense, the attempt of the magistrates to establish themselves as the intermediary body which was the interpreter of a set of fundamental understandings between monarch and people, more especially since the Estates General no longer met. Their claims, it has been said, were 'a middle term in the development of the idea of national sovereignty'.[60]

The parlements formulated a version of liberty, but this idea was not their monopoly. After the coronation of Louis XVI, a journalist described the popular anger at the omission of the question to the people asking if they accepted Louis as their king. 'However vain and derisory this formula today, there is great disapproval of the fact that the Clergy, for whom this pious spectacle seems especially designed, should have ventured on its own initiative to cut out this particular part and preserve only that which especially concerns its own interests.'[61] *Le Sacre royal, ou les droits de la nation française reconnus et confirmés par cette cérémonie* (1775) pointed to the announcement which the bishops had omitted from the ritual as confirmation of the idea that the monarchy was founded on a social contract; other pamphleteers followed, taking the same line. These writers were not intending to preach revolution. They deplored Louis XV's attempt to abolish the parlements, and they were anticlerical, wanting to give power a rational and mundane origin, not a divine one. True, there was a 'republicanism' abroad at the end of the *ancien régime*; but it was, in reality, a cult of devotion to the ideal of liberty and patriotism under the monarchy. Its manifestation at the beginning of the Revolution was the idolizing of one of those far distant and dubiously relevant heroes of the Roman history taught in the *collèges*: Lucius Junius Brutus, who fought against Tarquin. He it was who figured in David's picture exhibited in September 1789 and in Voltaire's play revived in Paris in November 1790.[62]

Like the magistrates of the parlements, the clergy claimed to have the right to collaborate with and guide the monarchy; nor did the fresh breeze of liberty that was blowing towards the end of the *ancien régime* leave them indifferent. But the jurists who were so fond of fundamental laws, traditions, maxims, and intermediary bodies to hedge in the royal absolutism had no enthusiasm for lending the benefit of these concepts to churchmen. 'C'est l'Église qui est dans l'État, et non pas l'État dans l'Église.'[63] An *arrête* of the parlement of Paris in September 1731 defined the relationship of the two powers.

The temporal power, established directly by God, is absolutely independent of all other powers . . . it is not the business of the ministers of the Church, under whatever pretext, teaching or otherwise, to fix the boundaries God has placed between the two powers, and . . . the canons and regulations that the Church is entitled to make do not become laws of the State except in so far as they are endowed with the sovereign's respectable authority . . . To the temporal power alone belongs the jurisdiction which has the right to employ visible and exterior force to compel obedience by the subjects of the King. The ministers of the Church are accountable to the King, and in case of abuse, to the law courts, for the exercise of the jurisdiction which they hold from the King and, even, for the exercise of the power they hold directly from God, in anything which might endanger public safety, the laws or the maxims of the Kingdom.[64]

The temporal power, then, was autonomous, supreme in its own sphere, and the sole judge of the extent of its own dominion. Customary boundaries between the two powers could always be revised by the secular ruler; the Church was a ship with an ecclesiastical pilot who did the everyday navigation, but there was a captain in charge of security who would intervene if there was trouble aboard which might lead to shipwreck.[65] 'All exterior and public authority is but an emanation of the power (of kings). The Crown is the source of all magistracy, political, civil and ecclesiastical.'[66] Thus, according to the standard law dictionary, 'the rank, precedences, property, possessions, rights, prerogatives and privileges of the clergy are held solely from the generosity, the piety and will of the sovereigns'.[67]

These sweeping views of secular pre-eminence were invoked against the pretensions of churchmen in general and of the Roman Curia in particular, in an uncompromising fashion. The Church was regulated by canon law (the collection which Pope Hadrian II had given to Charlemagne, the canons assembled by Gratian, the decretals of Gregory IX, and so on), but only in so far as these prescriptions were not contrary to the liberties and usages of France and the ordinances of her kings. Constitutions of popes of the last 300 years were not binding, and new papal bulls needed letters of confirmation from the king (issued after due examination by the parlements)—a rule reaffirmed by the parlement of Paris in 1703, 1716, 1764, and 1765.[68] Every Maundy Thursday the Pope reissued the thunderous bull *In coena Domini*, proclaiming the immunities of ecclesiastics, their jurisdictions, and their properties. Not a word of this was valid in France; nor was the kingdom subject to the decrees of the Holy Office or of the Congregation of the Index. The Crown had the oversight of the use of all ecclesiastical property and, maybe, had a right in reserve to pronounce on its very existence. The king named to 'all the prelacies of the kingdom', not, as the Pope might imagine, by virtue of the Concordat, but as 'founder, donor, suzerain and protector'.[69]

To enforce these Erastian maxims against the clergy, one of the ploys of the lawyers was to undermine them with pious deference; they served a master whose kingdom was not of this world: God would look after them, so no one else need bother. This was the principle behind the verdicts in lawsuits in the first half of the century about 'la cause de Dieu'; evidence of a vow before God to give money to a hospital, or of an entry in a parish register promising to pay for a new pulpit, was not an argument at law—only a last will and testament was enforceable against the heirs.[70] The same device helped to whittle down the precedence enjoyed by ecclesiastics as members of the First Estate.[71] Servants of another world, they were accorded first place because for long people had admired their virtues; there was always an impropriety, then, in any attempt to enforce a priority which was not freely offered. The Crown was the fountain of honour, of course, and Louis XIV's edict of 1695 gave the dignitaries of chapters precedence over presiding officers of law courts, and canons over ordinary magistrates. The lawyers, however, interpreted the sovereign's will restrictively: only cathedral chapters were meant; the 'second order' clergy, curés, and the like were excluded, and the *cour des comptes* of Montpellier by tradition took pride of place over the cathedral of that city, and so on.[72]

Readers of Montesquieu, converted to the necessity of intermediary powers to prevent monarchy becoming despotism, might have encouraged the clergy to think of themselves in this mediating role. The dauphin, son of Louis XV, was said (by Père Griffet) to have derived this lesson from *L'Esprit des lois*: 'le pouvoir du Clergé y est très convenable; il sert de borne au despotisme sans y opposer de violence'.[73] But the lawyers reserved this task for the parlements, and tended to subject ecclesiastics to the will of the sovereign.

The evolution of the lawyers towards a view of monarchy as absolute yet hedged with restrictions, open to remonstrance and criticism yet never endangered by armed resistance, had run parallel with the thinking of the clergy. So far, churchmen and magistrates were in agreement, though each side would have claimed the leadership in remonstrance and presenting the case for the people. The lawyers were also in agreement with the Assembly of Clergy's statement of 1765: 'within the alliance of temporal and spiritual, each power is sovereign and absolute in what concerns it'.[74] But the point of disagreement came with the question: 'who defines the boundaries within which this sovereign and absolute sway is exercised?' In the last resort, the clergy were not prepared to leave the definition in the hands of the secular power. Their case was squarely put by the Assembly of 1765 in its 'Exposition of the rights of the Spiritual Power'. They agreed that the sovereign could examine religious institutions from their temporal side and admit or not admit them,[75] and they conceded that the secular authority had a special interest in ecclesiastical property, though with two provisos: first, such property was 'legitimately acquired',[76] so was protected by the same safeguards which private individuals and corporations enjoyed, and second, there were sanctifying circumstances of biblical warrant and charitable obligations which the State was obliged to respect. (Even so, in practice, pleading sanctity could not get churchmen out of contractual obligations—a test case was settled by ordinance of the parlement of Paris in 1603 establishing the right of a bell-founder whose bill had not been paid to confiscate the bells from the steeple, even though they had been solemnly consecrated.[77]) But doctrine, morals, and the administration of the sacraments the clergy declared to be exclusively within the spiritual sphere. On such matters, a bishop could not be restrained from speaking freely: 'silence can never be imposed on those whom God has instituted as his spokesmen'—so much for the royal resort to a 'law of silence' in September 1754. The secular power was never entitled to suspend the execution of the judgements of the Church. Though external circumstances concerning the administration of the sacraments might have major secular repercussions, the lay courts could not intervene:[78] they could not determine, for example, if consent had been given to a marriage. Nor could they rule a refusal of communion to be a deprivation of individual rights or an actionable defamation of a citizen—'the refusal of the most august of our sacraments can never be within the competence of the civil authority'. This ill-considered and unrealistic proclamation of clerical authority was promptly suppressed by the parlement of Paris, while the king, anxious to extract a substantial subsidy from the ecclesiastical Assembly, made haste to annul the parlement's pronouncement—without, of course, endorsing that of the clergy. There was a storm of controversy.[79] The canonists, Le Paige and Maultrot, reaffirmed the right of the magistrates to 'guarantee citizens in the possession of the exterior advantages enjoyed by all Christians'. Jansenist pamphleteers, long accustomed to extracting questions of 'fact' from the domain of spiritual infallibility, enlarged the sphere of the secular power, by listing the matters of 'fact' which the prince was entitled to decide, like interpreting ambiguities of language, verifying the correct performance of canonical procedures, and, indeed, ruling what was fact and what was doctrine in the first place. Other polemicists were ruthlessly anticlerical. There was Richer (*De l'autorité du Clergé et du pouvoir du magistrat politique sur l'exercice des fonctions du ministère* (2 vols., 1766)), the marquis de Puységur

(*Discussion intéressante sur la prétention du clergé d'être le premier ordre d'un état*, 1767), and Cerfvol (*Du droit du souverain sur les biens fonds du Clergé et des moines*, 1770). Christians are pilgrims on the earth on their way to another country, was Richer's theme. The prince examines their beliefs and, if satisfied, makes a contract with them guaranteeing them safe conduct through his dominions. Bound by this contract, churchmen cannot innovate in doctrine—cannot, say, add a bull like *Unigenitus* to the original declaration of belief which has been verified. Further, being responsible for good order, the temporal sovereign imposes rules on the travellers for their journey; their conduct was likely to be better in future, for example, if he decided to legalize divorce among them, to order their priests to marry, and confiscate ecclesiastical property. The idea of selling off the landed domain of the Church appealed to Puységur and Cerfvol, the marquis because the clergy are 'strangers in the world', Cerfvol because of the precepts of the gospel—we are ordered to sell all we possess and give to the poor, and if the rest of us cannot realistically do this, the ordained ministers at least should obey. In his *Défense des Actes du Clergé de France* (1769), Le Franc de Pompignan, bishop of Le Puy, made something of a reply to the Gallican canonists, but he could only express panic and foreboding at the theorizing of Richer; there was a design, he said, to subject religion to the State along the lines of English Erastianism or, worse still, Rousseau's 'Civil Religion'.

The arguments of the clergy in defence of their rights were feeble by the standards of the Enlightenment, but respectable by those of the law-books. They cited 'authorities', specific texts from the New Testament and from the Fathers. There was the charge to 'teach all nations', 'to bind and to loose', and to speak in Christ's name—'he that heareth you heareth me'. St Paul was cited as evidence that the Holy Spirit had established bishops 'to govern the Church of God'. There were citations from Ambrose, Gregory Nazianzus, Pope Gelasius, and a few other writers, and Charlemagne's dictum that those who did not show submission to their pastors were hardly likely to be faithful to him.[80] Churchmen were conscious, however, that the sort of precedents capable of transforming sweeping Dominical charges into mundane practical authority were thinly spread. The Assembly of 1775 complained of the failure of historians and canonists to make full use of the laws of the first Christian emperors, 'so favourable to episcopal jurisdiction and to religion. It is astonishing that they have been regarded as foreign to the Gallican Church.'[81] The Assembly did not say how this relevance could be established. The instinct of the lawyers had been right: if they loaded the Church with praise as a virtuous institution proclaiming a 'kingdom not of this world', it would not be easy for bishops to claim final authority in matters which had a tincture of secular involvement.

What the Church needed was a Montesquieu, a genius who could ally erudition with theoretical speculation to justify the Church's position in society and its claims against the temporal power. Fénelon, relativist, utilitarian, pessimistic, ready to argue from first principles rather than Scripture,[82] could have done it; but his dreams of a Church freed from State control and a State liberalized by aristocratic councils and estates were removed from reality and, mostly, confined to private circulation. At the end of the *ancien régime*, Loménie de Brienne, in his *Mémoire sur les Assemblées Provinciales*, faced the Church's problem and adapted the ideas of Montesquieu and Fénelon towards a solution. The argument from being the First Order in the State was dead, and he avoided using it. Before Sièyes said it, the idea was current that the Third Estate was, in fact, the foundation of the nation. Of the Tiers État the marquis de Mirabeau had said, 'celui-ci comprend tout le reste, et quel reste! . . . Ce reste est tout de fait, et rien de droit.'[83] And in a pamphlet of 1787, the genealogist Maugard declared: 'There are two principal Orders in the State, the Nobles, which include the Clergy because their privileges are almost identical, and the People.'[84] Loménie de Brienne recognized the validity of these two observations, and combined them into a theory giving the clergy a lofty political role. In a popular State, he said, everyone claims to be equal, and in a despotism the ruler forces them to be so. These are unsatisfactory forms of government. France is fortunate in being a monarchy founded on 'honour'; 'les grands', the great ones of the land, inspired by this principle, defend the people from the abuses of authority, and uphold the throne against the fickleness of the people. So, in setting up the new provincial assemblies, there must be a clear recognition of distinctions of rank. True, in accordance with the spirit of the times, the Tiers État must have more than a third of the representation, and voting must be in common. 'Je repousse absolument les délibérations par ordres.' But the presidency must be given to 'les grands', and they must give leadership. These great ones are defined as the nobles and the clergy—all the clergy, irrespective of birth or rank. 'Properly speaking, there are only two Estates in France, nobles and non-nobles.' The merits of the clergy, their good education, their hard work, their 'attachment to authority by interest and duty', their friendship with the people, their willingness to tell the truth to the king, and the 'excellency of their functions' generally give them the right to noble privileges and to belong to 'the great', the leadership cadre of the nation.[85]

This was a defence of the claims of churchmen purely on Enlightenment principles, but it was unrealistic in treating the clergy as a unified body standing solemnly by to play its role in the new constitutional arrangements. In any deliberative assembly, if the lower clergy had representatives, they would sooner or later discover that their place was not with 'les grands', but with the people.

2

THE RELIGION OF VERSAILLES

I

Isolated from the real life of their people within the crowded, unhygienic splendours of Versailles, the kings of France had two preoccupations besides ruling: to maintain decorum and to keep boredom at bay. Nine thousand soldiers provided pomp and security. Among the 6,000 civilian officials and servants were 200 ecclesiastics. There were as many grooms in the stables, and almost as many musicians in the *musique du Roi*; for hunting and theatrical performances vied with religious ceremonies as the chief pastimes. The greatest ecclesiastic of all was the *grand aumônier*, his office 'almost as ancient as the monarchy itself'.[1] He walked on the king's right in processions, attended (though he did not always say) the prayers at the royal *lever* and *coucher* and the grace at meals, baptized the royal children, and conducted the nuptials of princes and princesses of the blood (always in the presence of the curé of Versailles, for no one, however great, could infringe the rights of parish priests). By virtue of his appointment, he was a commander in the most honourable of all the orders of chivalry, the Ordre du Saint-Esprit. Without having to make the profession of faith or to produce his proofs of nobility, he joined the 100 greatest nobles in the land and the eight other ecclesiastics whom the king delighted to honour, and wore the prestigious cordon bleu (for knights, the riband ran from the right shoulder across to the sword guard; for prelates, the cross, with its dove and fleurs-de-lis, hung on a blue ribbon around the neck).[2] The memoirs and correspondence of courtiers are full of envious yearnings and conspiracies to gain promotion to this inner circle of the great.[3] There were revenues and patronage attached to the *grande aumônerie*,[4] but these could hardly matter to one who would already be a bishop, a cardinal, and the holder of at least one rich abbey *in commendam* (in 1789 aristocratic court chaplains held no fewer than eighty-three abbeys between them).[5] Early in the eighteenth century the Rohan family, which had made the see of Strasbourg its fief, seemed to have appropriated the *grande aumônerie* as family property also; but in 1756 their monopoly was broken. In the beginning of the reign of Louis XVI they rescued it, though with difficulty—the story of how this was done being a good illustration of the way in which great families treated ecclesiastical office as a perquisite of birth.[6] The comtesse de Marsan, sister of the prince de Soubise, persuaded Louis XV to promise the reversion of the office to her cousin, Prince Louis de Rohan, coadjutor of Strasbourg, and when Louis XVI ascended the throne, persuaded him to renew his grandfather's promise. Marie Antoinette hated Louis de Rohan (believing him to have written to Mme du Barry ridiculing her mother, the empress); she insisted that the king change his mind. When Cardinal de la Roche-Aymon, the *grand aumônier*, finally died, there was a tremendous confrontation between the king and the comtesse de Marsan; she won, Rohan receiving the office, though on condition that he would resign after two years if he still was not wanted. The question did not arise, since in his naïve and unprincipled attempt to win the queen's favour, Cardinal Louis de Rohan was implicated in the diamond necklace scandal and was banished from court, Montmorency, bishop of Metz, succeeding as the chief of the chaplains to the Crown.

Next in the ecclesiastical hierarchy at Court was the *premier aumônier du Roi*, whose chief duty was to greet the king when he arrived at his place in chapel, take his hat, and hand it to the *aumônier de quartier*.[7] The importance of the office was that it gave access to the monarch, the fountain of promotion. For this reason, and from pride and royalist principles, the bishops competed for it. Like so many offices, this was bought and sold (the price was 300,000 livres, and the salary was 12,000, so there was an average return on the investment).[8] Under the jurisdiction of this 'first' chaplain were eight other *aumôniers du Roi*, serving in pairs for a quarter of the year. They gave the king communion, marked the brows of royalty with ashes on Ash Wednesday, said the prayers at the *lever* and *coucher* and the grace at formal meals, and were present at the king's daily mass, holding his hat, not entitled to take it from him, but with the privi-lege (absolute except as against the *grand aumônier*) of giving it back directly. Their perquisites were 300 livres and meals at a special table, and their offices changed hands at about 30,000 livres.[9] Parallel to them, though less distinguished, were the chaplains of the queen and of other members of the royal family. These were offices suited to bishops. Of the daughters of Louis XV, Mme Victoire had the bishop of Evreux as her *premier aumônier*, Mme Sophie the bishop of Chartres, while Mme Adélaïde, appointing a chaplain in 1772, could not find an existing diocesan bishop, so had to settle for the grant of a title of bishop *in partibus* for her candidate (that is, an episcopal title attached to some ancient city in lands now ruled by infidels). She insisted he must not be given 'one of those names which give rise to jesting'. The Roman chancellery wanted 'Paphos', but in the end he got 'Pergame'. Eight years later, the comte d'Artois wanted his chaplain elevated, and the foreign minister wrote to the ambassador in Rome: 'organize it, Monseigneur, so they do not resurrect the title of "Paphos"'. This great diplomatic matter was resolved, and the abbé Gaston became bishop of Terme in Cappadocia.[10] In addition to this crowd of chaplains to the royal family with episcopal titles resonant with the splendours of Nestorian Christianity, there was also the *maître de l'oratoire du Roi*, a priest with no functions, but with the right to a place near the monarch's prayer-desk in the chapel and to a salary of 4,800 livres; in 1746, gossips of the Court were delighted to recount how the abbé d'Oppede had sold the office to the abbé Honolstein for 80,000 livres, having bought it five years previously for half the price.[11] Below these were minor clergy acting as assistant chaplains, sacristans, acolytes, chaplains to the military establishment and to the stable grooms—there were even two concerned with the spiritual welfare of the employees of the *venerie*, the department organizing the royal hunts.

Louis XV inherited and—with occasional variations—followed the daily routine of religious observances which Louis XIV had imposed on the Court: formal prayers before rising, informal ones after breakfast, mass at noon (Louis XIV had changed to 10 a.m. in his later years, but his successors changed back to midday), evening prayers following the afternoon's hunting or promenades, and prayer in bed after supper late at night.[12] There were also special observances. On Maundy Thursday, both the king and the queen, in separate ceremonies, washed the feet of a selected band of deserving poor: the *Miserere* in fauxbourdon was followed by a sermon and the *grand aumônier* pronouncing an absolution and a blessing, while after the washing, dukes and duchesses presented the poor with dishes chosen from the Lenten menu, fried carp and the like.[13] On Good Friday, the courtiers would come forward individually for the adoration of the Cross—the officiant, deacon and subdeacon, the royal confessor and chaplains, then the king himself, followed by the laity in descending order of rank.[14] Versailles had its own deferential additions to liturgical practice. When the queen was to receive communion, she chose a Host to be consecrated from a box containing many which was proffered to her; immediately after the reception, the celebrant would take a gilded cup of wine from a servant, the *premier maître d'hôtel* would taste it, then it would be presented to Her Majesty to drink; at the end of the service, the celebrant would place the end of his stole on the queen's head while he read the Gospel according to St John. (There were variants when the king or the dauphin communicated.[15]) On ordinary days, the royal couple would hear mass from their elevated tribune facing the high altar; on great festivals their chairs were on the level, but on a velvet carpet fringed with gold.[16] The greatest in the land were called on to play their role in liturgical observances; dukes would be required to hold the communion cloth before the dauphin when he received the sacrament,[17] and the queen nominated ladies to take the collection on festival days. In April 1746, Mme de Pompadour proudly confided to the duchesse de Luynes that she expected to be named for this duty at Easter: 'tout le monde dit que je quêterai le jour de Pâques'. But the long-suffering queen passed her over.[18]

The religion of the palace was closely connected with the 'royal parish' of Notre-Dame of Versailles, in which, strictly speaking, the king was a parishioner. Louis XIV had established the Lazarists in the cure of the growing town in 1674, giving them the abbot's share of the revenue of the abbey of Saint-Rémy of Sens, and the building of the new church began in 1684. Two years later, the abbé Hébert was brought from ruling the seminary at Arras to be curé, an austere man who, before he became a bishop in 1704,[19] had organized the parish pastorally and integrated it with the life of the Court. Royal generosity, generally at the expense of some ecclesiastical foundation, and the great growth of population made Notre-Dame of Versailles one of the most splendid parishes in the kingdom by the 1780s. There were 55,000 souls within its boundaries; the *fabrique* had a revenue of 36,000 livres; and in the presbytery, with its extensive gardens and library, no fewer than twenty-three priests resided.[20] On occasion, the king would attend the parish church. It was here, certainly, that he ought to perform his Easter duty; in his pious later years, Louis XIV communicated there every Easter (one of his five annual communions).[21] In 1722, Louis XV made his first Easter communion there, and in 1738, his last.[22] More usually, it was when a Te Deum was being sung for a national occasion, or when the annual Corpus Christi procession took place, that a royal party came to the parish. On 11 September 1729, the king was there to give thanks for the baptism of the dauphin; the royal music came to provide the accompaniment, and the churchwardens invested in 200 candles (the vergers had to start lighting at five in the evening to be ready for the Te Deum at six).[23] The Corpus Christi procession was a regular engagement. That of 4 June 1744 was noted for the anarchical display of the variegated colours of the ladies' parasols—someone had forgotten to prescribe uniformity.[24] In 1759, the parish used for the first time the new canopy of crimson velvet fringed with gold and worked with scriptural subjects in silken embroidery—it cost 90,000 livres; the king did what was expected of him, and gave 14,000 as his personal contribution.[25]

From time to time, the curé would attend at the château. When there was a dearth, the king was the first person to apply to for alms. The ladies of the court supported a charitable association in the parish of Notre-Dame (as also in that of Saint-Louis, the other, newer parish in town); the king paid for a physician (*chirurgien des pauvres*) in each, and sent to both curés regular gifts of firewood from the royal demesne.[26] When, in 1777, the parish set up a manufactory of lace to provide employment for poor children, the maréchal de Mouchy persuaded Louis XVI to endow it with 3,000 livres of annual income.[27] At the same time, the queen extended a standing invitation to the curé of Notre-Dame to attend, alms bag in hand, at 7 p.m. on Sundays at the Salon de Paix, where her weekly gambling sessions were held.[28] Before play began, Marie Antoinette would go round with the bag—'Pour les pauvres, s'il vous plaît'. The ladies gave 6 livres, and the men 24, enough usually being taken to pay for the maintenance of a hundred families in the coming week.

There were times when the curé entered the palace as of right, armed with his parish registers to record royal baptisms, funerals, and weddings. When the future Louis XVI married Marie Antoinette, after the nuptial mass the *grand aumônier* took the register from the hands of the curé and presented it to Louis XV, who signed as first of the witnesses—last of all came the signature of the humble parish priest.[29] Ceremonies which took place in other royal châteaux would, of course, come under the jurisdiction of the appropriate local curé. When Louis XV married Marie Lecsynska in the chapel of Fontainebleau, the curé of Fontainebleau was there with his register.[30] Similarly, when the dauphin, son of Louis XIV, died of smallpox in 1711, the fear of infection was so great that an *ad hoc* funeral procession went off to Saint-Denis by night with the coffin in an ordinary carriage, and the curé of Meudon had the dangerous honour of riding up front along with the official court chaplain.[31]

When a courtier was dying, the Holy Sacrament and the consecrated oils had to be sent for from the parish church. On Sunday, 29

June 1740, Mme de Sourches collapsed; the king left his evening
meal to go to the parish, and led the procession which brought the
Holy Sacrament; after the administration, he returned with the curé
and attended Benediction before recommencing his supper.[32] In
February 1752, when Madame, Louis XV's daughter, was dying, the
viaticum was administered by her *premier aumônier*, the bishop of
Meaux. But the prelate took over the ciborium from the curé, who
had brought it in procession, dukes bearing the canopy over it, and
the royal family, escorted by lackeys with torches, walking before.
When extreme unction was administered, again the bishop sent for
the parish priest, who brought the holy oils from their niche in his
church.[33] Mme de Pompadour died at the palace, and was buried in
Paris at the Capuchins of the Place Vendôme, but her funeral service
took place in the parish of Notre-Dame. Her coffin was taken from
her apartments near the king to her private mansion in Versailles,
and thence, in a procession with her forty-two servants, to the parish
church (this chronology is important, as it absolves Louis XV from
the charge of heartlessness; he wept on the freezing balcony when
she was first taken away—'voilà les seuls devoirs que j'ai pu lui
rendre'. If he asked how long the procession would take to reach
Paris, it was at the time of the departure from the parish church two
days later).[34]

Being a parishioner of Notre-Dame of Versailles, the monarch
was a member of the flock of the archbishop of Paris. The confessors
chosen by the king and queen were approved by the archbishop, and
permission to infringe the strict rules of fasting in Lent came by way
of the curé, who transmitted the diocesan ordinances. When, on
national occasions, the royal family went to Paris for services of
intercession or rejoicing, arrangements had to be made with the
chapter of Notre-Dame, the canons of Sainte-Geneviève, or whoever else was concerned.[35] But routine ecclesiastical matters within
the palace were regulated by the *grand aumônier*, free from diocesan
interference: there was always a possibility of dispute, for it was
impossible to exclude the ordinary altogether. In 1710, when the
new chapel was finished, Noailles, the archbishop, won the right to
consecrate it, to the chagrin of Cardinal de Janson, the *grand
aumônier*.[36] There was always a problem whenever the prelate of the
see of Paris was deemed worthy to become a member of the Ordre
du Saint-Esprit: he would have to come to the royal chapel for
investiture, and he would wish to have his cross carried before him,
and as this signified pre-eminent jurisdiction, the *grand aumônier*
would never accept it. The solution adopted in 1747 was to allow

the cross, but to put a note in the registers of the Order that this was 'without prejudice' to the conflicting claims.[37]

The affair of the archbishop's cross was typical. Prickliness about precedence was an occupational disease of courtiers, and religious ceremonies were the same as any others where pride was concerned. Under the Regency, the dukes warred against slights on their superiority—that was why those who did not have indispensable duties to perform at the coronation of Louis XV stayed away.[38] Thereafter, they boycotted the Maundy Thursday foot-washing (*la Cène*) of the king: some of them went instead to the queen's. In 1746, they boiled over with rage because the boy duc d'Antin, merely for the fun of it, carried the king's dishes to the poor; they blamed his mother for letting him out that morning. In the following year, however, the ducal claim was recognized, and they turned up at the *Cène*, not without disputes about seniority among themselves, however.[39] At royal funerals, the ducal interest mustered again to outmanoeuvre the princes of Lorraine, the Rohans, and the Bouillons, to be first in splashing holy water on the coffin.[40] At the funeral of the maréchal d'Estrées in 1737, to defeat the claim of the marshals to walk 'as a corporate body' close behind the coffin and to have the holy water precedence, the dukes got to the church of Saint-Sulpice early to monopolize the front seats; the marshals persuaded the vergers to move their chairs in front of the intruders; two dukes therefore pushed into the narrow gap between the distinguished soldiery and the sanctuary balustrade, upon which the maréchal de Noailles rushed off to find the curé and forbid any aspersions with holy water whatever.[41] Since their claims were so grievously flouted, in November 1744 the marshals stayed away from the funeral of the maréchal de Chaulnes, all except one, who was a close relative.[42]

The clergy were as competitive as the lords temporal in these ceremonial feuds and forays. In 1723, in view of the continual contests between prelates for the seats of honour, the king directed that the *grand maître des cérémonies* or his deputy must always be present in the chancel of whatever church the royal family were attending to check that due order was being observed; only when all was calm was he to go to the sacristy to escort the officiant to the altar. Rules create new possibilities of infringement, of course; in 1746, at the anniversary service for Louis XIV at Saint-Denis, the clergy accused the *grand maître* of disrespect by failing to advise the celebrant that the service could begin.[43] When he attended mass, the king would kiss the gospel book, which was held out to him—not by the celebrant, but by the senior bishop present.[44] In 1745, the Court, assembled in the cathedral of Notre-Dame in Paris, was delighted to hear Louis XV rejecting the gospels proffered by the *aumônier de quartier*: 'Ce n'est point à vous, c'est à M. le cardinal d'Auvergne.'[45] There were complexities, however. If the celebrant was himself a bishop, he yielded place to no one, and in 1748 Cardinal de Rohan added tricky provisos giving precedence within the episcopate to cardinals and to the *grand* and *premier aumôniers*.[46] Cardinals, entitled to more exalted feuds than other prelates, had their own running battle with the king, for they claimed the royal prerogative of wearing purple mourning instead of black. Louis XIV, nettled because he had mistaken the purple-draped sedan-chair of Cardinal de Bouillon for his own, deprived them of their singular privilege;[47] but in 1746 they were still clinging to it. In July of that year, when the Court was in mourning for the wife of the dauphin, they refused to put drapes on their carriages or chairs since the prohibition of purple was still being maintained.[48]

Cardinals were secure in their superiority over the episcopate generally, though bishops who sat on folding chairs at royal funeral services would not concede to them the right to repose on more solid seats with high backs.[49] And there were six bishops who enjoyed the status of peers of France with special duties to perform in the coronation, and they would not yield place to red hats and Roman titles. When Dubois, the regent's low-born minister, was made a cardinal, their rage was boundless. If he comes to the parlement for a royal *lit de justice*, said Clermont-Tonnere, bishop and comte of Noyon and peer, 'I will throw him from the upper seats to the lower ones, whatever may be the consequences, and I'll be aided and abetted by the lay peers, with whom measures have been concerted'.[50] No doubt wisely, Dubois never came. Lower down the scale, the chaplains haunted the *premier aumônier* over the right to say the royal grace; they conceded his pre-eminence, but what if he was late and the *aumônier de quartier* had already launched on the *Benedicite* which was the prelude to the grace proper? And the queen's chaplain in his turn would insist on taking over the grace on the days when the queen's kitchen staff were serving the king's dinner because the Court had just returned from Fontainebleau.[51] In their turn, the *aumôniers* were being pressed by the minor chaplains on their staff, anxious not to have to give way if they had once begun to say a grace in the presence of the royal family.[52] When the future cardinal Fleury became chaplain to the wife of the dauphin, an Oratorian father told him: 'assotissez votre esprit et endurcissez votre coeur'.[53] Everyone knew that these contests were unfitting for good men or men of intelligence, yet the ethos of a hierarchical society and the obsession with proximity to the monarch ensured that they continued, with minds stupefied and hearts hardened.

Sermons were preached before the king at Christmas, Easter, Pentecost, the feasts of Our Lady, All Saints' Day, the *Cène* on Maundy Thursday, and in two complete courses, one for Advent (on the four Sundays) and one, much longer, for Lent (on the Sundays and two other days each week).[54] The regent, to lighten the burden on the boy king—not to mention himself—had reduced the Lenten course to Sundays only (hence, the *Petit Carême*), but the Court soon returned to three sermons a week.[55] In 1751 Louis XV fixed the Lent weekdays as Tuesdays and Thursdays, when he did not hunt, and in his reign the practice became firm of always holding the sermons in the chapel at Versailles—Louis XIV having wandered around to Fontainebleau, Saint-Germain, the Palais Royal, and the two chapels of the Louvre.[56] The payment to the Court preacher, 1,500 livres for Advent and double for Lent,[57] was considerable, and the king sometimes added a pension. But there were more glittering possibilities: a successful preachment might be a stepping-stone to an abbey, or even a bishopric. Certainly, the performance was much discussed at Court afterwards: Père Neuville excelled at portraiture but was voluble and monotonous; Père Chapelin was sound in doctrine but wooden in gesture; Père Teinturier had authority but slipped into familiarity; Père Laugier had a fine presence and a sonorous voice, but lacked discretion.[58] The preacher was supposed to begin with a 'compliment' to the highest-ranking member of the royal family present. Finding apposite phraseology was difficult. Inadequate praise was not to be thought of, but too much would be in poor taste. The humble Capuchin who walked from Montfort to preach at the queen's Maundy Thursday in 1742 and walked back afterwards had no fewer than four compliments to the queen and another to the king; no one approved of this prophet from the wilderness so gauchely sycophantic.[59] The curé who spoke of French conquests in November of the same year found he had struck a false note;[60] so too did the Jesuit who compared the dauphin to Solomon ten years later.[61] And what if, contrary to expectation, the king failed to turn up? A provident preacher would have a reserve compliment to the queen up his sleeve, but if she caught the royal cold and stayed away as well, he was not likely to be ready for the dauphin.[62] Canon Boismont was particularly unlucky. He arrived to preach before the queen on

Maundy Thursday 1748, only to be whisked away to give his discourse before the king (the Cordelier nominated for the *Cène du Roi* having failed to appear).[63] Louis XV received no encomium that day: if the good canon had prepared an alternative compliment, it was downwards, without a thought that his sermon might be promoted.

After a compliment to the monarch, it was allowable to censure him. 'Let him vanquish his passions to merit the true glory, which is the happiness of the saints'[64] was an easy, oblique way of doing it. In his Lenten course of 1734, Père Teinturier urged the king to supervise his ministers and to go out and command his armies (it was said that Fleury was behind this exhortation, wishing to push his young master into accepting responsibility).[65] Père Griffet in 1751 thundered against adultery, and Mme de Pompadour trembled.[66] Three years later, another Jesuit, Laugier, denounced Louis XV's idleness and extravagance, and at Easter, instead of talking of the Resurrection, spoke of the duties of the great towards religion.[67] Two years after that, the abbé de Boismont drew a sharp contrast between the life of the Court and the way of true Christianity.[68] At the very end of Louis XV's reign, in 1773, came the most sensational censure of all, the abbé de Beauvais describing Solomon, weary of pleasures, turning to 'les vils restes de la licence publique', generally taken to be a reference to Mme du Barry.[69] 'Tell me, Richelieu,' said the king to that other notorious womanizer of the century, 'it seems that the preacher threw quite a number of stones into your garden.' 'Yes, Sire, and some thrown with such vigour that they bounced almost into the park of Versailles.'[70] Sophisticated presentation and emphasis were needed to bring these sorts of censures within the conventions of the Court. Laugier was exiled for his pains, while the abbé de Beauvais was rewarded with a bishopric, even though he was not of noble birth (true, it was a miserable little diocese amidst wild mountains). Eleven days after his promotion was announced, he preached again, and was in honour bound to demonstrate that he had not been bought off. 'Sire, my duty as a minister of the Gospel of truth is to tell you that your people are unhappy, that you are the cause, and that no one dare tell you.' And, he said, using the threat of Jonah, 'in 40 days Nineveh will be destroyed.' (In fact, 40 days later, Louis XV died.)[71] A journalist, reflecting on the 'vigorous and astringent style' which had earned the abbé de Beauvais the see of Senez, described how the abbé Rousseau, preaching before the king in February 1774, had imitated him, 'with a holy courage, as the devout will have it, but with cynicism, in the view of the courtiers'.[72] He was prepared to take the risks, in the hope of the reward.

Court sermons were, indeed, feats of apostolic brinkmanship: the preacher was expected to censure, but could he do it without vulgar disrespect? From the early seventeenth century, there had been a tradition of 'political eloquence' associated with the pulpit. 'There are occasions,' said Guéret's handbook of 'eloquence' in 1666, 'rare it is true, but necessary none the less, when nothing ought to confine the preacher's zeal, when he is permitted to say all, and when, rather than risk betraying the cause of God, he must pay no regard to the majesty of the king or to his sovereign authority.'[73] Louis XIV had set the seal of his majestic approval on this convention of sophisticated candour: 'the preacher has done his duty, it is now for us to do ours'.[74] The abbé Soldini, confessor to the dauphin, the future Louis XVI, looked with suspicion on the tradition of the Court sermon, and he warned his royal penitent not to encourage preachers either in their compliments or in their criticisms of the king. The sermon, his view seemed to be, should be emancipated from this unhealthy, ritualistic fixation on the doings of a single man. 'Let each take to himself what is personal to him in a sermon and not concern himself with what is relevant only to others.'[75] When, eventually, the dauphin was crowned as Louis XVI, the preachers no longer had an obvious royal target, but they could always—maybe with implied censure—exhort the king to repress irreligious propaganda and to alleviate the miseries of the people. The abbé Maury's sermon at the *Cène du Roi* in 1778 was one of the masterpieces of the new fashion of *bienfaisance* and *sensibilité*—even the useless comte d'Artois was reputed to know it by heart. Significantly, one of the *aumôniers du Roi* told Maury that he ought to have hammered the philosophes as well. 'Vous oubliez, M. l'abbé', was the reply, 'que je prêchois sur la charité.'[76]

Princes and princesses of France had their confessors whose names were published in the *Almanach royal*.[77] These confessors had established posts with a substantial salary and individual perquisites—two horses, as available, for the queen's, and four for the king's entirely under his own control.[78] Even for royalty, the established rules giving diocesan bishops the power of pastoral oversight could not be waived: the keeper of the king's conscience had to have the licence of the archbishop of Paris to hear confessions in the diocese. In 1722,[79] when Claude Fleury, a learned and conciliatory Gallican, became too old to carry on, Cardinal Noailles for more than a year refused to grant powers to his successor, Taschereau de Linières, no doubt because he was a Jesuit. This put the Court to great inconvenience. Linières was transferred to the Jesuit house at Pontoise, under the jurisdiction of the archbishop of Rouen, and when the king made his confession before his First Communion, he had to go outside the diocèse of Paris to Saint-Cyr, under the authority of the compliant bishop of Chartres. So long as he held the office, the confessor had the monopoly of the royal conscience, unless illness prevented him from acting—Louis XIV had been able to fulfil his Easter duties, mistresses and all, because this was the season of the year when a tactical indisposition incapacitated Père La Chaize. When, in 1757, Louis XV was stabbed by Damiens, he received immediate absolution from the first priest available, then again from Desmaretz, his official director of conscience.[80] Louis XIV had established the custom of having Jesuits in the office, and with Père Linières in the reign of his successor, the Jesuit monopoly began again, with Peyrusseau succeeding from 1743 to 1753, and Desmaretz thereafter. When the Jesuits were banned in France, Louis XV turned for a confessor to a curé reported to be their protégé.[81] So did his pious daughters, Mesdames Adélaïde, Victoire, and Sophie, who put themselves under the direction of the abbé Madier, curé of Saint-Séverin, a pupil of the Society of Jesus whose bitter warfare against his Jansenist parishioners had earned him three years' exile from the parlement of Paris. In 1774, his duties at Court were interrupted because he had refused the Sacraments to a dying Jansenist and had no alternative but to flee again from the wrath of the vengeful magistrates—leading a procession of four carts laden with his furniture, to save it from confiscation by the agents of the law.[82]

Under the Bourbons, the 'two powers' at Court, according to Montesquieu, were 'the mistress and the confessor'.[83] In Louis XIV's earlier years, the first power had prevailed, and his Jesuit directors incurred reproach for their feebleness, Père La Chaize being unkindly named 'la chaise de commodité'. To avoid further accusations of laxity, the confessors of Louis XV were stern about his sexual liaisons. When the king fell ill while with the armies at Metz in August 1744, Père Peyrusseau allied with the Jansenistically inclined bishop of Soissons, Fitz-James, to ensure that the duchesse de Châteauroux and her sister were sent away before the last sacraments were administered.[84] Long after Louis XV had ceased to have sexual relations with Mme de Pompadour, Père Desmaretz refused to allow him to take communion so long as she remained at Court. 'If the Jesuits were Molinists on this point under Louis XIV,' said Bernis, 'they are Jansenists in our time.'[85]

What passed between monarch and confessor we cannot know directly, but we may guess that political matters rarely entered into their discussions. Aquaviva, general of the Jesuits, in 1602 had laid down a realistic rule for those of his Order called to direct the consciences of kings: they could draw attention to abuses coming to their notice, but 'take care not to meddle in political affairs'. In the eighteenth century, when the ideal of religious toleration was winning over educated opinion, this rule was reinforced by the memory of the confessors who had broken it: the fanatical haters of Protestants pushed into office at Court by the Guise faction during the Wars of Religion, the two Jesuits who had encouraged the young Louis XIV to detest Calvinists and Jansenists, and even Père La Chaize, colourlessly detached rather than culpable. Le Tellier, keeping the royal conscience at the end of the reign, the implacable foe of Cardinal Noailles and Jansenism, could not possibly have been the malevolent desperado he appears to be in Saint-Simon's demonological gallery; but the odium he had incurred was a warning to his successors to stick to the rules of Aquaviva. Certainly, once the Sun King was gone, the *feuille des bénéfices* was taken out of the confessor's domain, and from henceforth he was excluded from decisions on the award of ecclesiastical promotions.

By the time of Louis XVI, the confessor was outside the political sphere altogether. There was nothing for court gossips to seize on; in the previous reign, the exclusion of the monarch from communion had been standing evidence of the working of the discipline of the confessional, but Louis XVI's sexual life was blameless, and open scandal ceased. As the duc de Berry before his accession, the future king[86] had been schooled in the wisdom of Fénelon by his director of conscience, the abbé Soldini, drawing from the *Télémaque* lessons of political guidance based on the fundamental principle of justice. But it was understood that these indicated no more than broad lines of thinking, and that the confessor would not intervene if specific political issues came up. Soldini's notes show the points of personal conduct he insisted on: conjugal fidelity, avoiding reading literature hostile to the Church, directing the royal hunt away from sown fields, abstention from the theatre, but compensation by enjoying hunting, cards, and dice to the full. A few months after his penitent came to the throne, the good abbé died, and his successor was Poupart, curé of Saint-Eustache, simple and virtuous, living all the while in his parish and never appearing at Court except for his private sessions with the king. By contrast, there was a throw-back to the discredited tradition of meddling in politics in the person of Marie Antoinette's confessor, the abbé Vermond, doctor of the Sorbonne and former *grand vicaire* of Loménie de Brienne at

Toulouse, an intriguer in the corridors of Versailles. The king had no director to steel his weak will in affairs of State, and the queen had no mentor to curb her frivolity.

II

The royal chapel at Versailles provided a fitting setting for the curiously formalized religion of the Court.[87] The fourth chapel on the site, it was a creation of Louis XIV, begun in 1698 by Mansart and finished in 1710 by Robert de Cotte, the two greatest architects of the day. All the eminent sculptors of the end of the reign contributed, except Girardon, who was too old, and Coysevox, who was entirely occupied in providing nymphs and river-gods for the gardens of Marly. The exterior was adorned with sculptures and bas-reliefs, and the interior, in bright, white stone, with paintings, marbles, gilt, and bronzes. The more sombre aspects of the Christian message were muted. The three ceiling paintings—the descent of the Holy Spirit by Jouvenet over the royal tribune, the Father in his glory by Noël Coypel in the centre, and Delafosse's Resurrection on the far side—were triumphalist, and the bas-relief by Coustou on the high altar, of the dead Christ on the knees of his mother, was overwhelmed by the Gloire designed by Van Clève. Around the chapel were bas-reliefs which constituted a 'Way of the Cross', from the foot-washing and the Last Supper to Gethsemane, the trials before Annas and Pilate, Peter's repentance and the descent from the Cross; but the sheer agony of the Crucifixion was absent, and there were attendant angels with floating drapery and cloud-borne cherubim. 'It is a Way of the Cross of a particular kind,' it has been said, 'in which the artist proceeds by discreet allusions, avoiding giving offence to the eyes of a fastidious Court.'[88] Royal symbols abounded. The monogram of Louis XIV and the armorial bearings of France filtered the light through the windows. There were fleurs-de-lis and cartouches bearing the royal arms. The royal tribune was more prominent than the altar; at each end there was a sort of pagoda of gilded wood set in a semi-circular projection—the king knelt in the left-hand one, the queen in the right. According to La Bruyère, on occasion,

the great nobles formed a vast circle at the foot of the altar and stood, backs towards the priest and the holy mysteries, their faces turned towards their King, who is seen kneeling in a tribune, and to whom they seem to be directing all their mind and all their heart. This usage, you can hardly avoid realizing, implies a sort of subordination, for the people seem to be worshipping the prince, and the prince worshipping God.[89]

This was under Louis XIV, of course; the forms remained, but lost their intensity of meaning under his successor.

The ceremonies which rolled on daily in the chapel combined exactitude with boredom and irreverence. Louis XIV had put the imprint of discipline on the religious observances of his Court as upon all others. Though idle and inclined to informality, Louis XV continued to be exacting so far as the routine of his chapel was concerned. 'The rites and ceremonies of the Church, the details of the Calendar are rather too often the subject of his conversations,' said the duc de Luynes; 'you can't imagine the degree to which he is well informed on these matters.'[90] The tradition continued under Louis XVI. There was no question of the royal family postponing mass when the launching of the Montgolfier balloon on 19 September 1783 had reached its crucial stage: everything had to be delayed until Marie Antoinette came back from the chapel to the terrace and Louis to the balcony with his telescope.[91] One of the sticklers for religious punctilio was the king's brother, the comte de Provence, in this resembling his royal grandfather. 'That's not how you ought to begin,' he said, when the *grand aumônier* was baptizing one of the royal children; 'the first thing to ask is who are the father and mother—that's what the *Rituel* prescribes.'[92] No doubt he was also gaining satisfaction from dragging in an allusion to the rumours about the conduct of Marie Antoinette. The king's other brother, the comte d'Artois, played the fool at the coronation;[93] it was he, too, who 'sniggered indecently and made the king laugh' in chapel on the day of Necker's dismissal.[94] Versailles was a machine in perpetual motion, producing recurrent patterns of boring magnificence. 'Always the same pleasures,' said a lady at the Court of Louis XIV, 'always at the same times, always with the same people.'[95] Behind the façade was a world of confusion and dirt: courtiers crammed into attics, servants sleeping in sheds and stables, rogues who cut the gold fringes from the curtains, and pilferers who took provisions from the kitchens and ice from the storage pits.[96] Louis XV, whose design for living was to separate Louis de Bourbon from the king of France,[97] built himself an independent life doubly insulated from harsh realities by being hidden away within the hollow shell of splendid ceremony.[98] After a public *coucher* with the standard prayers in the official bed in the *chambre de parade* where Louis XIV had died, he went off to the Petits Appartements; in the morning, his valet woke him, and he went through the empty rooms, over the balustrade and back into the official bed; the door to the Œil de Bœuf was then opened, and the courtiers flooded in, led by the *grand aumônier* to preside over morning prayers. The chapel was part of the official external ceremonial in which everyone had his hierarchical place, a sham which everyone endured while real life went on elsewhere. 'When I return from Versailles,' said a courtier, 'I sometimes stop in the street just to watch a dog gnawing a bone'[99]—this at least was a real happening.

How should a Christian conduct himself in this artificial, heartless environment, where religious observances rolled on in a routine that for so many had no personal relevance? A casuistry of the Christian at Court had been subtly developed in the circle of Fénelon in the reign of Louis XIV, but, for laymen at least, the formula was simple: to follow Soldini's advice, to apply the gospel precepts to one's own life and leave others to do what they conceived to be their duty. In practice, there were two ways of psychological adjustment. One was to follow the daily observances of religion in the royal circle with exactitude, seeking the inner meaning behind the routine; this was the way of the pious duc de Luynes. The other was to serve the king in all the details of Versailles, but to be, as it were, a spiritual *émigré* and find religious reality outside the system. This was Saint-Simon's way. His spiritual mentor had been Rancé, and he found his peace in retreats at La Trappe in Holy Week, and in Easter sojourns on his estates at La Ferté. His sole true happiness was with his wife: they were joined in bonds of affection as strong as the iron bands which he prescribed to rivet their coffins together for ever. He was one of those who hated Versailles, but could think of nothing else, even when away from it in his later years—a classic case of one of the La Bruyère characters 'que la Cour ne rend pas contents, mais qu'elle empêche de l'être ailleurs'.[100] His mind was full of the affairs of Versailles, but he was apart from its life. He detested the official religious policies which persecuted Jansenists and Protestants; he repudiated the amusements—he did not gamble, hunt, or woman-ize, and early on he gave up dancing; though he sought formal honours, he refused to do what everyone else did and ask for pensions and sinecures—what was called 'faire des affaires'. He saw everything, but it was not a world which involved his own Christian destiny among striving fellow sinners. Hypocrisy ruled, everyone was masked, and he watched for the single false move that betrays meanness of the soul. His hatreds were more than un-Christian; they

were perversely Augustinian. His enemies, described with 'demonological verve', were predestined to evil; there was no forgiveness
for them—not from him after thirty years, not from God in all
eternity.[101]

There was one person who took the religious ceremonies of the
Court with unspiritual, downright literalness—and who believed
above all in forgiveness: Louis XV. He was obsessed with death. If
he passed a cemetery, he wished to know if there were any newly
dug graves. 'This is the King's way,' said Mme de Pompadour; 'he
loves to talk about death.'[102] 'It often happened', said the duc de
Croÿ, 'that the King would speak only of sudden death, of the
prayers said over the dying and so on.'[103] He tormented others with
the fears that tormented him. 'Look at his colour'—this said within
the hearing of the subject—'his liver is obstructed, he has only a
month to live.'[104] 'Beware of that nosebleed,' he observed to someone else; 'at your age it is the forerunner of apoplexy.'[105] His macabre
insensitivity met its match with the aged marquis de Souvré. 'Where
do you wish to be buried?' 'At your feet, Sire.'[106] This obsession with
death reflected the strict logic of Louis' religion. He took literally the
Christian doctrine of instant forgiveness available to the penitent,
even at the very last moment,[107] and gave himself up to womanizing.
'He had made a calculation on the matter,' said the duc de Croÿ,
'and thought that, provided at death he repented and received the
sacraments, these [sexual immoralities] were unimportant things . . .
He counted always on the last minute, on a good *peccavi* to cover
everything amiss.'[108] The formal religion of the chapel at Versailles
was, then, all the religion that Louis XV had, but within its narrow
unspiritual limits, he was sincere. He was an official believer, conforming to all the routines,[109] a deliberate sinner keeping in touch
until the dread moment when he would have to break through to
the interior meaning. From 1738, he made no Easter communion.[110]
On his system, the great danger he ran was the sudden onset of death
without time for amendment (he was panic-stricken in 1773 when
the marquis de Chauvelin dropped dead at the card-table; they
pacified him with the story that there had been a flicker of pulse
when conditional absolution was given).[111] A nice calculation would
be required to judge when an illness was sufficiently serious to
warrant sending for the ministrations of the Church, for to promise
amendment of life, then to recover health and relapse into
immorality, would be a serious affair, casting new doubts on the
scheme of a planned conversion which was dubious enough already.
When, in 1744, the king fell ill when he was campaigning with the

armies, the reigning mistress, the duchesse de Châteauroux, had to be sent away;[112] when, in 1757, Damiens stabbed the king, it was touch and go whether Mme de Pompadour would be dismissed.[113] Her case was peculiar, in that sexual relations with Louis had ceased, and for a year she had been deep in conversations with the Jesuit Père Sacy, going with the queen (as a lady-in-waiting) to mass every day,[114] fasting, encouraging Voltaire to compose a verse translation of the Psalms,[115] writing to her husband offering to return to him (no doubt aware that he would not dare to accept).[116] She remained the king's companion and was not admitted to the sacraments until 1764, when she was dying; once she had received the viaticum, Louis could visit her no more.[117]

As between supporters of the official mistress and the familiars of the queen, there was, inevitably, a polarization of court groupings. Marie Lecsynska, Louis XV's consort, was deeply pious; the Pope rewarded her with the golden rose, and the courtiers complained of the inconvenience caused by her interminable devotional obser-vances.[118] Her meditations before a skull, said to be that of Ninon de l'Enclos, set a fashion for the ladies; a be-ribboned death's head, illuminated from within, became an ornament for dressing-tables.[119] Of the royal children, the dauphin, fat and idle, was given to ostentatious genuflections and open censure of his father's pleasures, though he fell into infidelities himself in due course.[120] Of the daughters, Mme Louise became a Carmelite nun, and the other three—Mesdames Adélaïde, Sophie, and Victoire—lived in a severe court of their own (puritanical except where food was concerned),[121] and won public appreciation for their devotion to religion. In February 1752, they not only stopped their carriage outside the church of Saint-Roch in Paris as the Holy Sacrament went by, they got out and knelt in the mud—'Ah! les adorables princesses!'[122] It was about this time, in the early 1750s, that a *parti dévot* began to form, ostensibly giving allegiance to the pious members of the royal family.[123] Marie-Louise-Geneviève de Rohan-Soubise, widow of the comte de Marsan, and the duc de Vauguyon (both bearing respon-sibilities for the education of the dauphin's children) were of the cabal, and among 'ces vilains dévots' D'Argenson also mentions the maréchal de Duras, the prince de Conti, the bishops around the Court, and Père de la Tour, the principal of the *collège* Louis-le-Grand; they put up the Jesuit Dumas as Lent preacher in 1752 to be eloquent on the theme of David and Bathsheba, hoping to oust Pompadour. Meanwhile, the marquise was trying to persuade Père de Sacy to admit her to communion; had she succeeded, the *dévots* would have been outmanœuvred. As it was, said the gossips, she took her revenge by allying with Choiseul to ruin the Jesuits.[124]

The new alignment of court factions at the end of the reign showed how little piety had to do with the politics of the *dévots*, for the comtesse de Marsan and the duc de Vauguyon became supporters of Mme du Barry, the new mistress. To them, it was more important to go along with Richelieu and d'Aiguillon to oust Choiseul and reduce the importance of the Austrian princess he had brought to France, than to demonstrate for rectitude.[125] Mme du Barry had been a high-class prostitute before she met the king;[126] Mme Adélaïde would have nothing to do with her, and joined the circle of Marie Antoinette.[127]

In 1774, when Louis XV was struck down by smallpox, the Court was divided into bitter factions over the question of confession, communion, and sending away Mme du Barry. Once the mistress had gone, she could never come back, and the alignment of forces at Versailles would be radically changed under a 'converted' king if he happened to survive.[128] The dissolute maréchal de Richelieu threatened curé Maudoux, the confessor, to try to keep him away from the royal bedside, and offered to obtain a cardinal's hat for the archbishop of Paris if he would only mind his own business. 'If you want to preside over a confession,' he said, 'listen to mine and you will learn of such sins as you never heard of before.' The devout party wanted to get Mme Louise, the king's Carmelite daughter, to come to the rescue, but hers was a closed Order and she could not leave her convent. The *grand aumônier* failed to stand up to the maréchal, and the bishop of Carcassonne rebuked him. On the eighth day of his illness, Louis made his own decision, sent for the abbé Maudoux, and confessed. The Holy Sacrament was brought from the parish; the ciborium was carried by the *grand aumônier*, the clergy of parish and chapel going before, the royal family and the courtiers following, all with lighted candles. The French guards lined the courtyard and the Swiss the staircase, their drums beating the retreat. Louis received communion holding the crucifix which Mme Louise had sent him.[129] The *grand aumônier* came to the door of the room to announce: 'Gentlemen, the King charges me to tell you that he asks pardon of God for having offended him and for the scandal he has caused among his people; if God gives him his health again, he will occupy himself in penitential exercises, in the maintenance of religion, and the relief of his people.'[130] Richelieu cursed. Two days later, the holy oils were brought, and extreme unction given.[131] By then, the king's face was swollen and encrusted beyond recognition—a 'bronze mask'. He lasted two more hours and then died: 'the most courageous death you would ever see', said the duc de Croÿ, 'and a very Christian one'.[132] The bishops had a difficult task composing their pastoral letters for the occasion.[133] Some spoke of the 'good king', more of his 'penitence'. The bishop of Lodève said he would not 'betray his ministry' by 'portraying vice without its deformity'. The final destiny of this prince, said the bishop of Alais, 'is concealed from our eyes by an impenetrable veil'. According to Voltaire, the curé of Neuilly preached a funeral sermon that was better than all the rest. Louis, he said, 'would have paid his debts if he had had the money'; he built the bridge at Neuilly, and he had a valet 'to whom I owe the appointment to my benefice'.[134] It was a fair summary of the duties of monarchs of the *ancien régime*: to do some public works and confer many private favours, to maintain the hierarchy of society, and to manœuvre along the fringes of bankruptcy.

III

The principal resource available to the king to do favours to individuals was the immense wealth of the Gallican Church. By the Concordat of 1516, the Crown appointed to the bishoprics (except Strasbourg, which remained in theory elective)[135] and to the headship of the great abbeys, more than 800 in number. Various other benefices—canonries, cures, and chapels—were disposed of by the Crown by rights of patronage and customs of a pre-emptive kind.[136] Such benefices as did not carry with them the cure of souls could be conferred on those nominal ecclesiastics whose sole qualification was the tonsure; the office of abbot of a great monastery, for example, was a dignity held *in commendam* with no obligations beyond supervising the arrangements that drew off something like a third of the revenue of the house. It was also customary for the king to allocate pensions to named individuals, to be deducted from the revenues of a bishopric or monastery. The list of current vacancies in this manifold patronage available to the Crown was called the *feuille des bénéfices*; a great deal of the intrigue, the ecclesiastical politics, and, indeed, the genuine piety of the Court swirled in a whirlpool around this notorious list. It was one of the principal reasons why the great nobles demonstrated their loyalty by dancing attendance at Versailles.

A foreign envoy at the court of Louis XIV in 1690 referred to the right to present to the benefices in the *feuille* as 'one of the most splendid possessions of the Crown'. Families which gave distinguished service in war, in the administration of justice, in finance, or at Court, he said, were rewarded by ecclesiastical promotion for their sons, 'without a penny coming out of the Treasury'.[137] This was only part of the story, of course. The Church had to be kept going as an administrative organization, if not as a spiritual one, so attention had to be given to ability; there were parties within the Church which lobbied for positions of authority, just as there were political cabals and aristocratic alliances pushing for influence or perquisites. There was, too, the matter of the king's conscience. If there was one sin for which damnation was sure, said the handbooks of the confessional, it was the conferring of ecclesiastical benefices for worldly motives. A monarch who was truly pious, as was Louis XVI, would be restrained by painful scruples; a monarch who was a notorious womanizer, as were Louis XIV and Louis XV, did well not to tie a second, major weight to his soul to drag it down to Hell.

Louis XIV began in 1661 by using a *conseil de conscience*, consisting of his confessor, the *grand aumônier* and three other bishops, to advise him on Church appointments.[138] As its members died off, they were not replaced, and the king and his confessor ran the business alone, except for a period in the 1690s, when Desmarais, bishop of Chartres, was taken on as an extra adviser. During his final illness Louis refused to make any further nominations. 'Mon père', he told Le Tellier, his confessor, 'I find myself burdened enough already by the large number of nominations to benefices that I have made during my reign; I fear greatly that I have been misled in the choice of candidates recommended to me, concerning which I may, very soon, have to render my account before the judgement of God.'[139]

After the Sun King's death, under the regent Orléans and subsequently, up to 1732, ecclesiastical appointments were discussed in a *conseil de conscience* of prelates. Two different sorts of anecdote are told about the attitude of the regent himself. A churchman with heavy debts appealed for a bishopric, without whose revenues, he said, 'I'll be dishonoured'. 'Better you than me,' said Orléans. To a canon who boasted that he was 'of episcopal timber', the reply came: 'Eh bien, when they start making wooden bishops, I won't fail, *monsieur*, to mention your name to the king.'[140] As against these tales of honesty, there is one of the regent announcing, over his morning cup of chocolate: 'the King has just signed the *feuille*; the Jansenists ought to be pleased with me this time, for I've given all to Grace and nothing to merit.'[141] There is no necessary contradiction between these two aspects of anecdotal evidence; the duc d'Orléans hoped, maybe, that the best man would be found on most occasions by the deliberations of the *conseil de conscience*, provided a corrupt promotion could be made when it suited his personal interests. The most notorious of his appointments without merit were those of Dubois, and after him, of the abbé de Saint-Albin, his illegitimate son by the actress Florence, to the wealthy see of Cambrai—in the wake of the saintly and sophisticated Fénelon. Parisian gossips rejoiced in scandals like this. The regent, they also noted, kept the abbey of Hautevillers in his family, because its lands produced the best champagne, and the bishop of Rennes moved to Nantes, thus tripling his income, after frequenting the company of the Regent's valet. And why did a Prussian diplomat enjoy a pension from the bishopric of Verdun, and a notorious gambler be given 2,000 livres a year from an abbey, having belatedly remembered that he had been tonsured in his youth?[142]

The regent died in December 1723, and after a brief interval of rule by the duc de Bourbon, Fleury, the king's tutor and a bishop, took over the administration in the summer of 1726. A few months later he was made a cardinal, as an enhancement of his authority and to give him precedence in the council. A long new era of stability began. Its outward symbol was the complex old ceremonial routine of the days of Louis XIV, interrupted from 1715 to 1722 when the Court had moved to Paris and the fountains ran dry and the trees withered at Versailles, but now restored amidst all its ancient splendours. Fleury took over the *feuille des bénéfices* himself, and made ecclesiastical appointments with the collaboration of the *conseil de conscience*—at least in theory—for six years or so. After that, he relied solely on the advice of M. Couturier, the superior of the seminary of Saint-Sulpice. As a churchman, Fleury paid due regard to merit in his promotions, and as an orthodox churchman, due regard to the exclusion of Jansenists. In a century famous for its insolent wit, the reply of the frivolous abbé de Bernis to the octogenarian cardinal was remembered. 'You will never receive an ecclesiastical benefice so long as I live!' 'Eh bien, Monseigneur, j'attendrai.'[143] By the standards of the *ancien régime* it might have been assumed that Fleury's nephew, the abbé Henri de Rosset de Ceilhas would be a certainty for the vacant bishopric of Lodève; the town and the chapter were supposed to be asking for him, and the archbishop of Narbonne pressed for his appointment: 'act with an urgency that recalls the elections of the Early Church', he wrote quaintly, recommending this piece of nepotism. Pons de Rosset, chevalier de

Rocozals, maréchal de camp, the candidate's brother, wrote to Fleury on 27 April 1732:

I can certify to you truthfully that he has piety and a great love for the poor, virtues he has inherited from your family. I noticed also that, since his return from Paris, he applies himself greatly to the reading of the Holy Scriptures. Your Eminence once honoured me with the confidence that you had heard that he allowed his subordinates to lead him. Since he has an excellent nature and is full of kindness, some enemy of his has ascribed this ridiculous trait to him. I know for a fact that if Your Eminence deemed it right to honour him with the dignity of a bishop, he would choose a grand vicaire and a chaplain who would edify the public by their morals and would be very knowledgeable.[144]

(In short, he is the twit of the family, but we'll get him good advisers.) Fleury turned him down. 'I pay more attention to looking for candidates suitable to serve the Church efficiently than to helping my own family.' Nevertheless, it was no disadvantage to be related to the cardinal-minister. Two great-nephews of Fleury eventually became archbishops.[145]

Fleury died in 1743. Tencin, a worldly prelate living down a seamy past, but strictly orthodox and with a head for business, was spoken of as a candidate to hold the *feuille*, and thought he had got it when the cardinal, approaching death, offered 'to do something' for him—but it was only to get him into the Academy.[146] The *feuille* went instead to Boyer, bishop of Mirepoix, a Théatin monk who had risen from obscurity by the lucky accident which had made him confessor to the duchesse de Lévis. He was an honest man, who imposed tests on candidates for bishoprics: interviews with a curé of Paris, reforming a nunnery, presiding over a difficult general-chapter of a monastic Order.[147] He excluded Jansenists, of course, leading D'Argenson to call him 'a persecutor for bagatelles' who put 'the Constitution *Unigenitus* above the Gospel'.[148] His ruthless orthodoxy apart, he was probably as fair as the pressures and prejudices of Versailles allowed. On the one hand, D'Argenson accused him of favouring the great nobles;[149] on the other, Bernis said that he did not even know the names of the pre-eminent aristocratic families—'he did not like the *noblesse*, and preferred to be deceived by men of obscure family'.[150] Louis XV, now his own master, 'worked' with Boyer on the *feuille*, and was said by the pious duc de Luynes to be conscientious in awarding benefices. 'I do not give bishoprics to either name or favour,' wrote Louis in 1764, 'but to those who, I believe, can do the most for religion and towards the peace of the kingdom—though I'm far from being infallible.'[151]

After Boyer, for two years, 1755–7, the *feuille* was held by old La Rochefoucauld, the worthy archbishop of Bourges, and on his death, it was transferred to Jarente, bishop of Digne. Unlike his two predecessors, Jarente was essentially a politician. He established himself at Versailles, and his new diocese, Orléans, saw him but rarely. Mlle Guimard, the dancer, was rumoured to be his mistress. (She was thin: 'Je ne conçois pas comme ce petit ver à soie n'est pas plus gras; il vit sur une si bonne feuille'.[152]) The papal nuncio hesitated to believe this and other stories: 'in this country, people easily pass adverse verdicts on those against whom a prejudice has formed'.[153] The prejudice, no doubt, arose from the gossip of Versailles. The king and Choiseul played practical jokes on their minister of the *feuille*; Louis had him knocked up in the middle of the night to order him to send to Orléans for some jars of the local marmalade for his daughters (the story comes with comic trimmings—'the Archbishop of Paris must have died', the search for the episcopal spectacles, the king's daughters have drawn a sedan chair on the letter). Choiseul sent two actresses dressed as abbés to call on him to ask for benefices and to claim the kiss of peace.[154] The *dévots* at Court decried Jarente's nominations for ecclesiastical office. 'He took the opposite line to his predecessor who wanted an exemplary clergy attached to religion,' said the dauphin; 'M. de Jarente chose too many people like himself.'[155] This reputation lingered on after his fall. A pamphleteer described him as 'an amiable and voluptuous brigand who spent more time in arranging a supper party than in appointing to a bishopric'.[156] In fact, his appointments were no worse than Boyer's; his worldliness was manifested chiefly in his favouring conciliatory candidates for the episcopate rather than harshly orthodox anti-Jansenists.

Jarente had been the nominee and agent of Choiseul; on Choiseul's fall and exile at the end of 1770, his position at Court became precarious, and he lost the *feuille* on 20 March 1771. He was succeeded by the highest-ranking prelate of the kingdom, La Roche-Aymon, archbishop of Reims, abbot of Saint-Germain, *grand aumônier* of France, soon to be made cardinal. His greatness had arisen, it was said, from a lifetime of servility—to Choiseul, then to Mme du Barry, then, after the accession of Louis XVI, to Maurepas. 'The triumph of mediocrity', said Mme du Deffand, wondering how he had contrived to do it 'without merit, without backers and, so to speak, without intrigue'.[157] The courtiers conspired to see the fatuous side of his universal pliability. 'On ne se brouille pas avec moi'—'Nobody falls out with me,' he said. According to the abbé de Véri, when Maurepas dominated in politics, La Roche-Aymon took up residence in the minister's study and in his wife's salon, and 'obeyed them in everything in the awarding of benefices'. Yet, said Véri, 'the choices he made for benefices were always good ones. The silence he has maintained among the clergy is evidence of his wisdom.'[158] The best way to end the feuds and divisions in the Gallican Church was to let politicians direct ecclesiastical appointments.

In 1777, Yves-Alexandre de Marbeuf, bishop of Autun, succeeded to the *feuille*.[159] He was known to have been strict about promotions in his diocese, getting his advisers to prepare lists of well-qualified *vicaires* to be recommended to the attention of lay patrons. As minister, he retained the bishop of Senez, himself a famous preacher, to report on sermons in the capital, and he tried to prohibit the accumulation of abbeys (he set an example by twice giving up an abbey on promotion to a better one, though it is true that he finished up with Ourscamp, enormously lucrative). Louis XVI, solidly insisting on sound morals as a basic qualification, backed him in providing Cambrai with its first good bishop since Fénelon, and in excluding Loménie de Brienne from the see of Paris ('the archbishop of Paris must at least believe in God'). The abbé de Bourbon, illegitimate son of the previous monarch, had fourteen bishops present when he said his first mass at Saint-Magloire, but no promotion from the *feuille* followed.[160] Yet Marbeuf's administration was savagely attacked in a series of pamphlets, the *Lettres secrètes*, between 1781 and 1784, and the truth was that his appointments were no better than anyone else's had been. The affairs of the *feuille* went best when the political direction at Versailles was firm: a king making appointments knowing that the price of dishonesty was eternal damnation, or a minister anxious to keep Church affairs decent and uncontroversial. Louis XVI was weak; Marie Antoinette and her *lecteur*, the abbé de Vermond, intervened too often to obtain rewards for the ecclesiastics of her circle,[161] while the aristocrats around the Court were more insistent than ever upon their perquisites from the wealth of the Church.[162]

On 4 August 1789, Marbeuf stepped down to give way to Le Franc de Pompignon, archbishop of Vienne. The *feuille* was now in the hands of a pious character who gave up his archbishopric because he had to live at Versailles. Under him, for the second time in the century, an episcopal see went to a commoner, with the elevation of the learned Asseline to Boulogne. By now the old system of appointments was nearing its end: by the Civil Constitution of the

Clergy, dioceses were to coincide with the new political units, the *départements*, and the departmental electors were to choose their bishops.

The history of the *feuille des bénéfices* is unedifying. In mid-century, D'Argenson thought it would be better to withdraw the custody of this famous list from ecclesiastics, and leave it to a lawyer from the Royal Council—just as the Ministry of War always worked better when a civilian was in charge, rather than a professional soldier.[163] Multitudes strove to attract the attention of the holder of the *feuille*, with servility, sanctimonious zeal, *bonhomie*, or insouciance according to their rank in society. 'There is no seigneur at court, however great he may be', reported the papal nuncio in 1766, 'who has not need of this prelate (Jarente) for the benefit of his relatives and friends.'[164] An indispensable qualification to be the dispenser of Crown patronage was the ability to devise a suave letter of refusal to the mighty. Thus Jarente wrote to the duchesse d'Ayen in 1750 concerning his failure to find a benefice for the abbé Saint-Just:

I am sure that I can justify myself to you whenever you are free to listen and to allow me to explain my position to you. I lament my situation: I am like a miserable debtor who owes more than he has money available to pay. Time is the only remedy, and I flatter myself that in due course it will demonstrate to you the respectful attachment with which I have the honour to be, Madame.[165]

On 15 August 1780, Turgot wrote to the duchesse d'Enville to tell her that he was going to see Marbeuf on the following day 'to find out if he has done something for those he promised to help. I have little hope that he has'—he had deceived people before.[166] Ordinary ecclesiastics presented themselves humbly in the antechambers of the minister of the *feuille*. A down-at-heel abbé, an ex-Cordelier forced into a friary by his parents and secularized after they died, wrote to Voltaire begging him to provide some verses congratulating La Roche-Aymon of the *feuille* on being made a cardinal: it might be a way to win a benefice and move to more salubrious quarters than his present lodgings above the pastry cook's opposite the rue des deux portes Saint-Sauveur.[167] In 1757, Canon Le Gouz of Dijon abandoned his quest for a supplementary benefice to finance his long stays in Paris. Jarente had taken over the *feuille*; and having buttered up the two previous holders, Le Gouz was unwilling to start again with a third. 'I am tired of supplicating and sweeping the floors of these disposers of Church property with the hem of my cassock. So I don't think that I'll go to clean up the spittle from the antechamber of the bishop of Digne with my clerical mantle.'[168] A pamphleteer described the scene in Marbeuf's waiting-room:

Picture it: a bizarre collection of monks, abbés, curés, soldiers, women. All these people are asking for bread. 'Pension!' 'Abbey!'. The words circulate and echo resoundingly from every mouth. Monseigneur has promises and consolations for everyone. 'M. le chevalier', he says to a respectable-looking soldier, 'these are hard times, don't get impatient, everything will work out'. 'M. le curé, you know my intentions: use them as a pillow for your repose, and believe me, the moment of happy awakening is not far away. I foresee . . . yes, go along, don't worry'. 'Mon cher abbé, you are displeased, and so am I. The Queen is getting hold of everything, I control nothing. But leave it to me, I have my plan . . . good day to you, be discreet and count on my help.'

Sometimes, the suppliants were so numerous that he could not give them this individual attention, and had to embark on an edifying collective oration before sending them away for another day.[169]

The system worked better than might have been expected. Whether it was the royal confessor, a *conseil de conscience*, the cardinal-first minister, a severe ex-monk, a cynical political churchman, some prestigious old archbishop, or a conscientious diocesan that held the *feuille* did not seem to make much difference. Probably things went best when there was a firm hand on the helm at Versailles, with the king or his chief political adviser well aware of direct personal responsibility. No doubt political designs would then be important, but what could be more wisely political than the desire to make appointments to pacify feuds between churchmen and to improve the climate of relations between clergy and laity? It was better than seeking out austere zealots who would reform with lofty insensitivity. The Church was rich, and there were sinecures and pensions enough to placate the lukewarm, vocationless, or useless sons of the aristocracy, to support government business, promote learning, and gratify local worthies. Bishoprics and other important offices with cure of souls were mostly awarded—within the system of aristocratic monopoly that prevailed at Versailles—with regard to merit and the interests of the Church. Any system of running ecclesiastical preferment, however honest the electoral procedures, whatever prayerful or charismatic formulas are prescribed or spontaneously invented, ends up looking frayed and finger-marked when the human aspects of rivalry and manipulation are detected. At Versailles, this human side was unashamedly evident, and anticlericals had easy fun mocking the strange detours of the workings of the Holy Spirit. But we have to remember that the men of the eighteenth century took the Church seriously, at once as an instrument of temporal rule, a socially necessary institution, and the intermediary of personal salvation. It is obvious to us how they pushed for families and friends; but we do not so easily understand the psychological restraints within which their pursuit of self-interest operated.

3

THE WORKING OF THE
CHURCH–STATE ALLIANCE

When a Church becomes rich and powerful, it is infiltrated by the world. For the most part without hypocrisy, individuals realize their ambitions within it, and without undue cynicism, the State makes use of ecclesiastical wealth, personnel, and prestige. The Church gains from the recruitment of ability and the support of secular force in its labours, while it loses in so far as its mission of conversion becomes a routine, its mysteries social observances, and its moral teaching a utilitarianism with supernatural sanctions. Religious perfectionists regret this, but a religion white hot and purified can never be a creed of the majority. Reformations and renewals will revive the traditions of sanctity in the Church, but a powerful established religion infiltrated by the world may yield more quiet decency in human behaviour and, perhaps, a greater sum of human happiness. In the nature of things, in the alliance of Church and State the secular power will be the gainer, for it is bent on achieving immediate and realizable ends, while the spiritual power is aiming for a perfection never attainable in this life, and looks to a mysterious eternal destiny. But there is always a reciprocity, and the balance of advantage is ever changing. In the eighteenth century, behind all the archaic complexities and convolutions of the relationship, the balance was tilting inexorably in favour of the secular power, and as events unfolded, it began to look as if the swing was irreversible.

I *Ecclesiastics in State Service*

During the eighteenth century, three First Ministers of the Crown were ecclesiastics. It was a question of making use of available talent. Dubois was a libertine, Fleury a man of piety, and Loménie de Brienne a sceptic; but all were outstanding for ability and tireless efficiency, and all three, in the tradition of Richelieu and Mazarin, were rewarded with the red hat of a cardinal. There never was a

clash of loyalties. With Dubois, there hardly could have been, for the
only moral anchor in his life was his friendship with the regent;
Fleury, however, was passionately devoted to papal orthodoxy, and
Brienne was a partisan of the Church whose doctrine he hardly
believed. Yet they put the interest of the king above all others. It
was a French and Gallican attitude. When Vergennes, devout to the
point of scrupulosity, was Foreign Minister, his chief clerk wrote of
him: 'the clergy counted him in the number of the pious, but they
dared not propose anything to him which tended to put the altar on
the level of the throne'.[1]

This Gallican devotion to the monarch encouraged the king to
turn to ecclesiastics when recruiting diplomats: again, a question of
enlisting talent where it could most obviously be found. Talleyrand,
who enjoyed a shady success in both careers, analysed the reasons
why churchmen make good ambassadors: they are used to dialectic
and detecting the nuances of argument; they have the confessor's art
of finding out secrets and keeping them; they enjoy ceremony and
protocol; they know all about women, yet have no wives.[2] Louis
XIV had used cardinal-prelates as envoys—d'Estrées to Bavaria,
Forbin-Jansen to Poland, Bonzi to Rome—but in the eighteenth
century there were few appointments of this kind, the notable
exceptions being Rohan, sent on a brief, glittering, and incompetent
foray to Vienna, and Bernis, making a long sojourn at Rome, where,
he said, he 'kept the French inn at the crossroads of Europe' and
gave lavish receptions—significant in the development of the Italian
ice-cream trade. Perhaps Louis XV refrained from choosing great
prelates because he suspected they would be too concerned in
lobbying for a cardinal's hat, whether by the favour of Rome or on
the nomination of a Catholic sovereign—certainly, this was why he
refused to make Bernis his ambassador to Poland.[3] But churchmen
of lower pretensions were still frequently employed in the diplomatic service. Through some contact, probably with a French
cardinal, they might be invited into the mission to Rome, like the
abbé Dufour, a *grand vicaire* of Angers, who was employed by the
Foreign Ministry from 1760 to 1767 to report on various cardinals of
the papal Curia.[4] Others made a deliberate choice of a diplomatic
career, putting the Church behind them except for its rewards.
Bernis did this, refusing Massillon's offer to make him a *grand vicaire*
because he felt no pastoral vocation; the bishop, he said, approved of
his honesty, and 'counselled me to devote myself to foreign affairs,
saying I would have great success in a career as a negotiator'.[5] This
was also the choice of the abbé Véri, doctor of the Sorbonne, canon

of Narbonne, *grand vicaire* of Bourges, a certain candidate for a bishopric. In 1756, he changed course: 'je quitta tout à fait la carrière ecclésiastique'.[6] He was appointed an *auditeur de Rote*, the representative of the French king on a Roman tribunal concerned with boring diplomatic and judicial affairs, an office with the virtue of attracting rich benefices to its holder. In 1772 he came back to Paris 'to enjoy the considerable fortune in benefices that this employment had procured for me'. Thereafter he could saunter round Versailles, a confidant of royalty, giving judicious advice on matters unimportant. His career is an example of another reason why churchmen were welcome in royal service: they were paid from ecclesiastical revenues. The abbé de Pomponne (1669–1756), ambassador to Venice and envoy extraordinary to other Italian states, enjoyed the revenue of two abbeys, one, Saint-Médard at Soissons, prodigiously rich.[7] The abbé de Ville (1701–74), an ex-Jesuit, graduated from tutor to the sons of the French representative in the United Provinces, to cipher clerk, chargé d'affaires, and ambassador; then from 1748 for long he was the *premier commis* at the Foreign Ministry, running the administration and co-ordinating information. His rewards were extensive monastic revenues and the episcopal title of 'bishop of Tricomium'; in his leisure he published translations of English political treatises and, remembering he was a churchman, edited Fénelon's spiritual writings.

The revenues of the Church also supported another sort of public servant, though not directly in the service of the Crown, the *conseillers clercs* of the highest law courts, the so-called sovereign courts. In each parlement, a number of magisterial posts (six in the parlement of Bordeaux, twelve in that of Paris) were reserved for clerics, who might be in priestly orders or, with dispensation, in minor orders or just tonsured. By background they had lower social standing than the nobles of the robe who were the lay *conseillers*, but they came from families of note, none the less.[8] The famous abbé Pucelle was a commoner, but his father was a wealthy *avocat*, and his mother a daughter of the maréchal de Catinat. They were more learned than their lay colleagues, and it was the longer time they spent in acquiring educational qualifications as much as their lower social origins which accounted for their average age on appointment being higher—28 years, 6 months, as against 22 years, 7 months, in the parlement of Paris. Their families had bought the office for them, and they drew a revenue from its perquisites. But all had other resources: for example, the abbé Salabery was chairman of the committee running the financial and legal affairs of the duc de

Penthièvre, though his efforts over seven years did not save this great nobleman from bankruptcy. Most important of all, in every case, however, was money from the Church. There were the abbatial monies held *in commendam*: Salabery had the abbey of Coulombes in the diocese of Chartres, while Voltaire's portly and philanthropic nephew the abbé Mignot, who walked unpretentiously every day to the *grand chambre* of the parlement and spent his nights in writing inaccurate history, drew 4,000 livres a year from the abbey of Scellières—the refuge where he took the body of his illustrious uncle for burial, to the rage of those clergy who had been looking forward to seeing the great philosophe denied a Christian resting-place. Probably more of the *conseillers clercs* found their ecclesiastical income from canonries, certainly in Paris, with the special privilege of being able to draw the fruits of their prebends *in absentia*. The chapter of Notre-Dame challenged this right in 1771, but the Royal Council reaffirmed it. Sometimes, though rarely, a *conseiller clerc* moved on into the direct service of the Crown: during the eighteenth century the parlement of Paris lost two of them to the diplomatic service, three to the corps of the *maîtres des requêtes*, one to membership of the Conseil d'État, and another to the great office of controller-general (the sinister, unbelieving abbé Terray). For the most part, however, they stayed with the parlement for life. With their learning, clerical status, and expertise, they provided leaders for the tiny 'Jansenist' clique on the magisterial benches—the abbé Chauvelin, 'coryphée tour à tour du théâtre et du jansénisme', and, above all, the choleric and eloquent abbé Pucelle. Both as magistrates and as churchmen, these clerical lawyers were self-consciously dignified. Pierre de Laffayart, who took up the theatre and had a comedy performed, was an aberration from type to be gossiped about. Laffayart's play was a flop: the title, *Le Fat*, was unfortunate—'a man never knows himself well enough to produce a convincing self-portrait', said Piron.

From the court at Versailles to a provincial workhouse, all government and municipal institutes had their chaplains, ranging from splendid gilded clerics in lofty office to threadbare abbés called in when needed. The observances of religion, available and indeed compulsory for the sick and poor in institutions, extended also to the prisons. When, in 1789, the Bastille was stormed and pulled down by enthusiastic volunteers, three priests lost their lodgings and employment, and were awarded pensions by the Crown as compensation.[9] As they were as numerous as the prisoners, presumably most of their work was with the garrison. And when the State executed a criminal, the clergy were present on the scaffold.[10] The confessor came to the prison cell to hear the last confession—under regulations which, strictly speaking, were incompatible with the Church's doctrine of forgiveness. Absolution was not given unless the criminal revealed the names of his accomplices (the Capuchins were said to err on the side of mercy here), and communion and extreme unction were withheld. This was because the death penalty was normally carried out on the day of the sentence, and 'it was not fitting to unite the adorable Body of Jesus Christ to a body soon to be subjected to loathsome indignities'. In 1788, the delay of a month between sentence and execution was decreed; yet the rule concerning the viaticum was not changed, and three of the *cahiers* of the clergy in 1789 complain of this. The confessor would accompany the condemned man on the cart on the way to execution, presiding when, at the portals of the cathedral he knelt to ask pardon of God, the king, and justice, and on the scaffold would stay with him to the end; if it was breaking on the wheel, he offered the crucifix to kiss as the agony intensified. On rare occasions, a hardened sinner refused the ministrations of religion; in 1755, the heroic smuggler Mandarin sent away the solicitous friar as 'too fat for a man who preaches penitence', and in 1784 two murderers turned their backs on the priest to address the executioner: 'c'est à vous que nous avons affaire'. There was a sanction to encourage an edifying conformity on the scaffold, for the executioner might shorten the agony of breaking or burning by merciful strangulation; when, in 1721, the bandit Cartouche was on the wheel, the executioner failed to act, and it was the confessor who ordered one of the guards to pull the rope tight. In 1781, a lawyer proposed that priests should be withdrawn from these scenes of cruelty, as the criminals blasphemed and the spectators cursed the confessor as if he was in league with the judges. But it was more usual to admire the clergy who performed such grim duties. 'I saw him embrace the wretch,' says Restif of such a one, 'devoured with fever, as infected as the dungeons from which he was taken, covered in vermin. And I said to myself, "O religion, here is your triumph."'

In the army and navy, chaplains were indispensable, for it was a maxim that discipline and morals require religion, and men who by profession were required to die for their king had a right to spiritual consolation before the final moment. The idea of sudden death as the easiest way was counterbalanced by the fear of dying unshriven. When the duchesse de Longueville heard her soldier-son had been killed, she did not ask if his end had been painless. 'Ah, mon cher fils! Est-il mort sur-le-champ? N'a-t-il pas eu un seul moment? Ah mon Dieu, quel sacrifice!'[11] A bishop dedicating regimental standards declared that 'the penance of blood' could wash away the stain of sin, but this dispensation to soldiers was not to be presumed on, and a man must make his peace so far as he could beforehand; this was provided for in the chaplain's prayers before battle, ending with the pronouncing of the general absolution.

From the early seventeenth century, most warships had chaplains, the Capuchins serving on the ships of the line and the Lazarists, directed to the duty by Vincent de Paul, on the galleys. Richelieu called on the Jesuits to take over service in the fleet, and one of them, Père Georges Fournier, a professor of mathematics at the *collège* of La Flèche, became an *aumônier de la marine*, and in 1643 published a famous treatise, *Hydrographie, contenant la théorie et la pratique de toutes les parties de la Navigation.*[12] At the end of the century, royal regulations made it mandatory for all warships to have chaplains, as well as merchant ships on long voyages. To provide priests for these duties, Louis XIV set up three seminaries: one, inadequately endowed, at Rochefort (1683) under the Lazarists, the others at Brest and Toulon under the Jesuits (1686). The training programmes were—officially—relentless. At Rochefort there was a year's probation followed by three years' instruction, with a daily schedule running from 5 a.m. to 9 p.m., the entire waking hours being filled with liturgical observances, meditation, self-examination, and lectures, except for two breaks of one and a half hours each for meals and recreation. In 1701 the shipping regulations were codified with a realistic proviso: the rules about chaplains were to apply only to vessels with a crew of thirty or more.[13] Even so, the bishops of the seaboard dioceses of Vannes, Saint-Malo, La Rochelle, Coutances, Bayonne, and Bordeaux protested to the king that it was impossible to find priests in the numbers required. The salary laid down in 1701 for the chaplain of a merchant ship was 30 livres a month, with meals at the captain's table;[14] this was not enough to attract candidates, and those who volunteered, said the bishop of Coutances, were motivated 'rather by libertinage than by piety'.[15] No single Order came forward to devote itself to the pastoral care of sailors, most of the *aumôniers* on the galleys being Lazarists, on the other ships Lazarists, Capuchins, Récollets, Jesuits, and seculars, some of them in flight from normal ecclesiastical discipline, though not always the worse for that. The hardships and dangers of life afloat deterred recruitment. Many of those going on a long voyage would not return. A warship patrolling the Atlantic and Indian oceans for four years between 1780 and 1784 lost 228 out of its crew of 430, only thirty of them killed in battle.[16] The conditions were appalling, especially in the galleys, with their oarsmen in chains—criminals, Turkish prisoners of war, and victimized Protestants. A chaplain hearing the confessions of the sick did so in a cavity three feet high in the poop, with his penitents lying in their excrement and covered in vermin, and all around were scenes of savagery—it was the selective flogging of Protestants which led the abbé Bion to renounce his chaplain's role and flee to Geneva to become a Calvinist.[17] Though the French Company of the Indies had the resources to pay well to fulfil its obligation to send a priest out with every argosy, sometimes a ship had to sail without one, and in 1766 the directors applied to the Irish seminary at Nantes for volunteers. At Saint-Malo in the 1730s, 2,600 fishermen left every year for the Newfoundland banks, and only sixteen priests accompanied them, and at the end of the *ancien régime* there were 3,700 fishermen and only six chaplains available.[18]

There were picturesque ceremonies when a ship was commissioned, solemn blessings according to the *Rituel* of the particular maritime diocese (all based on Pope Paul V's liturgy of 1614) with the inevitable references to Noah and the ark and Christ walking on the waters. When a vessel returned from a long voyage, there would be a high mass with Te Deum in the parish church, and while the crew roistered in port, they would be the target of mission sermons by the local Jesuits or Capuchins or, in Brittany, by the Montfortians. These interesting liturgical and evangelistic occasions were monopolized by the coastal clergy, and the *aumônier* would take over when the ship left port—if he had obeyed the rules, he would have observed a retreat of ten days beforehand to prepare himself. At sea, he had to say daily prayers before the mainmast, offering thanks for preservation, making an act of dedication for the day's work, and praying for the ship's company to be given strength to overcome temptation, especially the sin of cursing and swearing, and ending with the psalm for the king, *Domine salvum fac regem*. An effort would be made to observe the great feasts of the Church—for the Fête-Dieu, a procession round the decks and the firing of a cannon salvo. If a sailor fell gravely ill, the chaplain would take the Sacrament to him, observing regulations to ensure decorum: the Host must be in a ciborium or decent box, not openly on the paten, and a sailor with lantern and handbell would go before, while the officer of the watch would ensure that all members of the crew, Protestants included, removed their hats and knelt as the procession passed. A funeral would require a requiem mass with a *De profundis* and *Libera*, and if it was the captain who had died, there would be volleys of musket-shots and the firing of a single cannon. Before battle, or when the sky was lowering with imminent storm, the chaplain would offer prayers, recite the *Confiteor*, and give the assembled crew a general absolution. According to Fournier, they could be sure of God's forgiveness at these desperate moments, for penitence is sincere in proportion to the grimness of the danger— not a view the theologians generally accepted. The captain of a warship would also expect his chaplain to add a word to encourage his men to fight bravely. Before an engagement in the American War of Independence, the chaplain of the *Astrée* gave a famous oration in a single sentence: 'Mes amis, tous les braves gens vont au paradis, et tous les jean-foutres en enfer'.[19] On shipboard, all faced the same perils and had to contrive to live together. If the *aumôniers* were suspect to the bishops safe on dry land as reckless characters wearing lay dress on board and going along with a modicum of drink and swearing, it may be that, according to their lights, they did their duty.

As with the navy, so with the army, the royal government provided military chaplains, in time of war paying them realistically, more than the clergy ministering to the crews of ships. In the artillery and infantry, about 700 livres a year was given, calculated on a daily basis; this was the wage of a sergeant and rather better, for there was a superior ration allowance—a total income about equal to one of the poorer curés on the *congrue* (the official stipend for a parish priest who did not draw the tithe).[20] In the cavalry and dragoons, the salaries were slightly less. But in peacetime, the chaplains serving in the infantry and artillery were on half pay, while those in the mounted regiments got nothing at all. There was no retirement pension, a notable disadvantage, for bishops distrusted clergy who had been associated with the military[21] and were reluctant to collate them to parochial benefices. The government mooted the idea of a levy on ecclesiastical property to provide larger and more regular salaries, but nothing was done.[22] Some colonels, however, especially those recruiting in Lorraine and the Auvergne, raised money to pay much more, offering as much as 2,000 livres a year, with a retirement pension after thirty years' service. Under Richelieu, it was the Jesuits and a few Capuchins who had served with the armies; by the eighteenth century, chaplains came from a variety of backgrounds, though most of them were Récollet friars. In a *Mémoire abrégé sur les aumôniers de l'infanterie française* (1782), the duc de Mortemart, colonel of the regiment of

Lorraine, said that the priests who took service with the infantry 'seem to be drawn from the lowest class of clergy, at best useless, and sometimes a nuisance because of their ignorance and lack of morals'. The remedies he proposed were higher salaries to attract better men and the setting up of a seminary in a garrison town like Metz or Strasbourg to give a three-year course to ordinands destined for the army, with lessons in theology reinforced by history, geography, draughtsmanship, and fortification. As he said, it was not just the poor quality of the *aumôniers* giving cause for concern; they were also too few, only a hundred or so in all the infantry regiments in peacetime.[23]

When the puritanical comte de Saint-Germain had been Minister for War (1775–7), a seminary had indeed been set up, in concert with the archbishop of Paris, but it had lasted for only a few years.[24] Apart from the zealous minister himself, both government officials and churchmen thought enough had been done when the army had a minimum of formal liturgical offices and opportunities for every soldier to go shriven to his grave. Had there been genuine enthusiasm for the seminary, there would have been unions of benefices and diversion of monastic revenues sufficient to guarantee its success. The government similarly parsimoniously refused to make provision for retired soldiers—officers who were awarded the cross of St Louis received a small pension, and a few rankers obtained an abusive 'corrody' at the expense of a monastery; but most left the army without any means of support. There was, however, a splendid exception to the government's meanness, an institution where a selected group of officers and men lived in comfort for the rest of their lives—Louis XIV's prestigious foundation of the Invalides, a showpiece for the rest of Europe to admire.[25] The inmates lived well, with prodigious provision of bread, meat, and wine, comfortable quarters, and smart uniforms (blue coat and grey breeches, the officers having red facings and linings to the coats and silver braid stripes of rank). Thirty sisters of St Vincent de Paul administered the institution and supervised the care of the sick. As a result of good food and comfort, the inmates lived long: the average age of death in the last three years of the *ancien régime* was between 65 and 69 years of age.[26] The price paid by the retired warriors for their ease and distinction was conformity to a strict religious regimen—they were all Catholics, for after the revocation of the edict of Nantes, Protestants were excluded. They had to be present at mass and vespers on Sundays and saints' days, and at morning and evening prayers daily. If their knowledge was deemed insufficient, they could be summoned to a catechism session. To be allowed a day pass or longer leave, they had to show a *billet de confession* and a certificate of Easter communion. Two months in a punishment cell was the penalty for swearing, and expulsion for a second offence. Realistically, eight bouts of drunkenness were allowed, but once the quota was exceeded, the offender was transferred for a year to the grim institution for disciplining libertines, the criminally insane, and prostitutes, the Bicêtre. To what extent was this puritanical and pious life-style enforced? The twenty-six Lazarist priests of the original establishment were reduced in numbers by subsequent economies, and by the reign of Louis XVI they were down to five—though of the chapel musicians, the precentor, organist, and four choirboys were retained. The *pension* in which the clergy lived was in confusion, running deeper and deeper into debt and haunted by minor clerics of Paris who insinuated themselves to get cheap quarters. Probably, the clergy did little more eventually than keep the routine liturgical services going and hear Easter confessions. But a tourist in 1713 reported that at every hour of the day in the chapel of the Invalides there were numerous old soldiers sunk in reflective prayer.[27] If the compulsory piety was observed in a perfunctory fashion, there were some who sought the consolations of religion as they remembered the cruelties of war.

Soldiers were notoriously immoral, proverbially corrupting the inhabitants of any town where they were stationed. The chaplains despaired of making much impression on them in peacetime, and had the reputation of performing the necessary formalities of religion in a minimal fashion—rushing the men of a whole battalion through their individual confessions in a single morning, pronouncing rapid-fire absolutions like a series of 'bonjours'.[28] If the troops were to be converted, it would be by the descent of teams of Jesuits, Lazarists, or Capuchins on evangelistic missions. Commanding officers did not mind their *aumôniers* compressing spirituality into brusque formalities—what they especially required in quiet periods was for them to liaise with the local authorities to agree measures to keep the prostitutes away, lest the unit be decimated by venereal disease. On the march, when crossing the boundary of a diocese, the chaplain would be sent to call on the bishop, whether French or foreign, to request formal permission—always given—to enter his territory.[29] When battle was imminent, the army chaplains, like their colleagues at sea, had to conduct prayers and pronounce a general absolution, ending with a harangue to inspire courage.[30] These would-be encouraging talks were unpopular, so it was safest to keep them brief. One ran: '*Enfants de guerre*, though your hearts are filled with proud courage, humble yourselves before the Lord, for it is he alone who gives victory.' There is more than one version of the story about the lieutenant-colonel cutting the sermon short: 'Soldiers! M. l'abbé means to say, there is no salvation for cowards, *en avant!*'—or, as a variant, 'Vive le Roi!' Once the battle was joined, the *aumônier* was 'to hold himself available during the fighting to help the wounded and dying'. Perhaps he would find his post with the *hôpital ambulant* keeping up close to the firing line, or he would be sent back to one of the field ambulances in third echelon.[31] At the Battle of Fontenoy, the main hospital had a chief surgeon with thirty assistants, ten apothecaries, sixty-six male nurses, and eleven chaplains, eight being Récollet friars. The hospital routine included a mass in the morning and prayers at night followed by a round of the wards; all Catholic soldiers were required to make their confession every three days. The chaplains buried those who died, recording their names in a register, and were responsible for sending death certificates to the family and to regimental headquarters. François de Chennevières, the inspector-general of military hospitals, published a four-volume study of their working in 1742, in which he declared that the chaplains 'acquitted their duties to the general edification'. Perhaps the duc de Mortemart's unfavourable verdict concerned the peace-time conduct of the chaplains, while François de Chennevières was referring to them amid the grim butchery of the hospitals as the casualties were brought in. With all their faults, they measured up to the decisive test of war.

When we catch a glimpse of individuals, they appear worthy, maybe eccentric, though it is true that evidence tends to survive about those who in some way distinguished themselves. It is true also that those of ability had often been driven unwillingly into a military career, having through no fault of their own lost their niche in the ecclesiastical establishment—Jansenists ousted by the government, orthodox pursued by the parlements, Jesuits seeking employment after the destruction of their Order. Dom Pierre Toussaint, a Benedictine of the Congregation of Saint-Vanne and teacher at one of their *collèges*, was imprisoned for eleven months in the citadel of Verdun (no doubt for Jansenism); on coming out, he rehabilitated himself by serving as a chaplain in an artillery regiment for six years, then became principal of the *collège* at Metz.[32] J.-B.-J. Adent was a mendicant who got himself secularized and served two years in a parish, then ten years as a chaplain to the Languedoc dragoons, moving on to become a curé by the resignation of the previous incumbent in his favour; during the Revolution, he was elected a councillor of the district at Versailles.[33] Nicolas Segretier, curé of Meung-sur-Loire, on the orders of his bishop, refused the last sacraments to a dying Jansenist and had to flee from the wrath of the parlement of Paris. In 1756, he became *aumônier* to the duc de Beauvillier in the campaign in Germany, having two narrow escapes from cannon-balls, one passing so close that the wind of it paralysed his left leg for a month, the other spattering him with soil when it hit the ground. When the duke was wounded and a prisoner, he stayed with him, and when his master died, he took the sad news back to the family and stayed some months with the duchess—finally venturing back to his parish again.[34] The abbé Robin, chaplain to a regiment in Canada, came back to France, and in 1781 published an account of his American explorations and a brochure on free-masonry, then became *aumônier* to the vicomte de Noailles, the colonel of a cavalry regiment—Noailles set up a 'club' for his officers with books and newspapers available, and made Robin its presiding welfare officer.[35] The colonels of regiments were young aristocrats of the Court arrived directly into higher commands by a combination of privilege and purchase. Their personal chaplains, like Segretier and Robin, moved in loftier circles than the Récollets lower down under the orders of the hard-bitten professional officers, mostly poor provincial nobles, who ran the real work of the army, and the surgeons, who hacked away in the field hospitals. Even so, when battle was joined, cannon-balls and musket-shots were no respecters of persons.

II *Marriage and Parish Registers*

In high religious theory, the Church alone had the right to prescribe rules for marriage—affirmed in a papal brief of 1788 condemning Jansenist views recently put forward at a synod in Italy. To most appearances, this was the case in France. The clergy called the banns, perhaps checking on the degree of Christian instruction of the affianced pair, and conducted the ceremony. The laws of the Church determined the relationships within which marriage was allowed, and defined the impediments, citing the code of the Old Testament, equated, from its origin in remote antiquity, with natural law. It was not just immemorial custom which suggested the rules must be 'natural', for the theologians argued that the obligation to marry outside the family clan extended the boundaries of friendship and charity: exogamy was part of the social machinery prescribed by God for achieving the Christian aim of 'goodwill towards men'. The prohibited degrees were wider then than now, and the clergy added to them the impediment of 'spiritual affinity': that is, the relationship between godparent and godchild. This could not be justified from the code of the Old Testament, and came only marginally under the rubric of the expansion of the sphere of charity. Voltaire made fun of its illogicality: his noble savage is unable to marry the charming girl who converted him to Christianity, as she had unthinkingly stood sponsor for him at his baptism. The best that could be done to justify the prohibition was to cite the danger of undue influence, the possibility of misusing a duty of pastoral oversight to forward the desires of the flesh and social ambitions. These multitudinous restrictions on choice of partner caused hardship to many, especially in isolated rural communities, so there was a stream of applications for dispensations, giving a great deal of business to diocesan officials and the ecclesiastical courts.

But while marriage was the work of God joining a man and woman in unbreakable union, the institution was also the bedrock of the social order, ensuring the continuation of the race in a disciplined fashion and the transmission of property through the generations. As such, the State claimed a right of regulation, in the process necessarily treating marriage not as a sacrament, but a contract. Government legislation guaranteed the rights of the heads of households in setting a late age before parental prohibition could be overridden by the two contracting parties; there was a legal procedure (the *rapt de séduction* charge) to give respectable families protection against matrimonial adventurers; the law courts investigated the validity of marriages in suits concerning inheritance; the legal systems of the various provinces apportioned the control of the joint property and dowry between husband and wife; the secular courts as well as the ecclesiastical could pronounce a decree of separation when a marriage had foundered; the king could intervene by *lettre de cachet* in matrimonial relations where the honour of a family was concerned. The philosophes, concerned to diminish the importance of the clergy in the lives of individuals and in the community, put marriage firmly in the control of the State, making the contribution of the Church an optional extra.[36] Voltaire stated the case clearly in the *Dictionnaire philosophique*: 'Marriage is a contract by natural law (*droit des gens*); the Roman Church has made a sacrament of it. But the contract and the sacrament are two very different things: the one has civil consequences, the other qualifies for the blessings of the

Church.' Two legal treatises of mid-century (1753 and 1760) provided an array of learned arguments to support the Voltairean inference from the nature of things.

The basic principles of the theologians could be used to justify both the high ecclesiastical view of marriage as a sacrament and the secular view of marriage as a contract. The three ends of marriage, as St Augustine had defined them, were mutual self-giving, the procreation of children, and the sacramental union signifying the union of Christ with his Church. Everything else followed from the mutual self-giving. The celebrants of the sacrament were the man and woman themselves, their mutual consent and sexual congress constituting the marriage in the eyes of God. The Jansenists[37] used these principles to argue that the final word in marriage regulations, even where the prohibited degrees of affinity were concerned, should rest with the secular sovereign. In 1676, Jean de Launoy took this as a typical instance in which, in a Christian nation, the prince is the Church's agent for executive action. In Jansenist circles in the eighteenth century, the argument was given a full theological development. It is not the actions of the Church which make a union indissoluble, for St Paul had declared marriages with infidels to be valid, and in the first eight centuries in the West and the first ten centuries in the East, validity had not depended on the ministrations of the clergy. Thus the State was entitled to take the essence of marriage to be contractual and to regulate it accordingly.

Given that the free consent and self-giving of the two parties created the union in the eyes of God, provided the consent and self-giving could be established by evidence, the marriages of heretics and pagans were valid. The case of Protestants in France was odd, for Louis XIV had imposed the intolerant fiction that they did not exist, so it was Catholic marriage for them or nothing. Protestants who married before their own pastors risked the future of their children if rapacious Catholic relatives went to law to claim the inheritance. As the century went on, the law courts revolted against this manifest injustice by twisting every possible circumstance to disqualify the suit of the would-be plunderers. Protestant marriages were made legitimate in 1787; meanwhile, at mid-century, the great test for the liberal principle of the theologians arose. A Jew of Alsace, proclaiming his conversion to Christianity, maintained that his Jewish marriage was now null, so he was free to marry again in a true Christian union.[38] Two Parisian curés were approached and refused to call the banns, declaring his previous union with its two children to be permanent in the eyes of God. The archbishop backed them.

The parlement of Paris took the side of the convert, and when he was baptized on 10 August 1752, magistrates of the Court were among his godparents. The archbishop, regarding the conversion (given the design to marry again) as fraudulent, banned the curé who administered the baptism, to the rage of the parishioners, whom he had served faithfully for thirty-three years. The parlement denounced the episcopal sentence, on the ground that a parish priest is the sole judge of applications for baptism. On 7 November 1754 the front of theological principle was breached when the *officialité*, the court of the bishop of Strasbourg, was persuaded to declare the Jewish marriage null. With this verdict in hand, the new convert proposed to remarry in the diocese of Soissons; the bishop, Mgr Fitz-James, austere and Jansenistically inclined, turned him down, and reversed the Strasbourg decision. The *appel comme d'abus* went to the parlement of Paris, but the magistrates at last listened to the opinions of theologians and the cry of natural justice: a non-Christian marriage celebrated in good faith was declared indissoluble.

During the Revolution a multitude of cases arose to establish this finding.[39] The exiled bishops at first tried to argue that a marriage before one of the Constitutional Clergy was invalid, but they knew theological principle was against them, and they had to retreat; indeed, they conceded that even a union contracted in the presence of a municipal officer was valid—though, with a certain failure of logic, they added the proviso: so long as resort to a priest was not possible. The bishop of Langres, followed by other bishops and approved by Rome, urged Christians who wished to be faithful to orthodoxy as against the State-sponsored Constitutional Church, to marry before their own priests and register the event with the municipal officials, as Protestants had done under the 1787 edict. On the side of the new revolutionary government, the recognition that marriage was simply a contract came from a report by the canonist Durand de Maillane to the Assembly concerning a petition of the actor Talma against the refusal of the curé of Saint-Sulpice to call his banns because of his profession. The State, the report argued, is concerned only with the contract; the sacrament needs other dispositions, and is no affair of the legislator. Even so, no action was taken until 20 September 1792, when the Legislative Assembly, on the last day of its existence, legalized divorce and laicized the *état civil*—the keeping of the registers of births, marriages, and deaths. A Jansenist lawyer of the *ancien régime*, still writing on legal subjects in 1800, summed up the situation: marriage is established as a contract ruled by civil law, and not a sacrament; yet there still remains a distinction between unions Christians accept as made by the mutual consent of the two parties, and those they themselves celebrate within the Church with a specific dedication to the God of Christianity.

Church and State had a mutual interest in keeping permanent records of marriages. The clergy needed them for pastoral purposes and to prevent unions within the prohibited degrees, while the lawyers of the royal tribunals had to have formal documentation available to supervise the structure of family relationships and the transmission of rights to property. As ever, the government put the expense and effort on somebody else. In 1569, the curés were ordered to keep registers of births and baptisms and to deposit them from time to time at the *greffe*, the record office of the nearest royal law court.[40] In 1579, the regulation was extended to include marriages and deaths. The question of expense was clarified in 1667: the churchwardens (*fabriques*) of parishes had to provide two registers, one to stay in the parish archives, the other to be sent to the clerk of the magistrates. To extract State profits from these trans-actions over and above having other people pay for them, absurd offices were created for sale with the nominal duty of filing the information. The curés fulfilled their responsibilities with a mini-mum of zeal. They would fail to hand the copy to the royal court, or mislay their parish version. Often, their entries were full of erasures and unsigned corrections, or, indeed, were illegible altogether. The law-books cited the 'affaire Bouteville', a lawsuit turning on an undecipherable marginal note concerning a marriage. Why was it, asked the author of a legal handbook, that notaries deposited such well-written documents at the *greffe*, while the clergy are guilty of culpable carelessness: 'why are the children of this world wiser than the children of light?'[41] An answer was not far to seek: the notaries pocketed fees, and the curés got nothing. A register with its parchment leaves and official stamps was expensive (15 livres for a big town parish and 3 to 6 livres for a small country one); the lawyers were presented with their copy at the expense of the parishioners, who also had to pay a fee to the clerk who numbered the pages.[42] A curé might amuse himself by chronicling local events in his parish copy of the register,[43] but he was unenthu-siastic about acting as the unpaid servant of the government.

A royal declaration of 9 April 1736 tried to compel efficiency by laying down stern regulations.[44] A register was to cover a single year only. A month before the year began, the curé had to obtain two of them, one with stamped leaves, one with plain; both were to be taken to the nearest royal jurisdiction for checking and pagination. Blanks must not be left, and loose leaves must not be inserted. Entries must be precisely dated. Baptisms are to be verified with the signature of the priest, the father, and a godfather, weddings with those of the curé and two witnesses. At the end of each year, the stamped version was to be taken to the *greffe*. (Religious houses were also to keep separate registers of accessions to the noviciate and of professions; in each case a duplicate had to be kept to be handed in at the registry of the law court every five years.) The curés of Paris leagued together to sign no fewer than three successive protests against these regulations. Granted, a simple record was indispensable, but they saw no need for these bureaucratic elaborations. For one thing, they had not the time to do this amount of paperwork. Often, they had ten marriages a day, and, approaching Advent and Lent, when marriages were forbidden, twenty-five to thirty. Baptism parties arrived at the church unannounced, and a curé who thought he was turning out to baptize one child might find as many as eight with parents and godparents lined up waiting. To get the details of these ceremonies and the names of the witnesses was difficult enough, but to have to make a copy for the lawyers was a vexatious addition. Besides, depositing these records at the *greffe* left the secrets of families open to ill-intentioned curiosity, and the new precision of entry increased the danger. No longer could curés fudge the date of a marriage 'for the honour of families'—pre-nuptial conceptions would be obvious, illegitimate children would stand out from the others, and hasty, renewed ceremonies to cover up a wedding which some technicality had nullified would leave a jarring memorial. These complaints against the lust for accuracy and the frank justifications of pastoral subterfuges were unacceptable to the government, which insisted on compliance, though it was not until the end of July 1738 that all the parishes of the capital had conformed to the declaration and bought their double registers.

There was improvement, but scandal still occurred. In a comic lawsuit in 1768, a girl wanting to marry had to go to court to prove her sex, since her baptismal certificate, by some 'étourderie de sacristan', had her down as a boy.[45] Isolated errors became unusual; if something went wrong it was when some curé, worn out or drifting into irresponsibility in some rural backwater, gave up the struggle altogether. In such a case there had to be laborious interrogations of all the inhabitants to reconstitute the missing registers. The little town of Guémené in Brittany was pastorally served by the collegiate church of Notre-Dame-de-la Fosse. In 1774, the chapter decided that the canon in residence must sign the registers as correct every day before he left the sacristy: 'Otherwise, we will inevitably find ourselves back in the position of having to run round the town as we used to, to remedy omissions.'[46] Some of the *cahiers* of the clergy in 1789 admitted all was not well, and asked for remedial measures, perhaps sending round specimen entries for imitation.[47] At least one lay *cahier* asked for the recording of births, marriages, and deaths to be taken from the clergy and put in the hands of public officials, which in fact was what happened, marriage becoming a civil contract. The old monarchy had treated it as such without being willing to find the money to secularize the registration process.

III *Police Procedures and Religious Conformity*

'Que la Religion est le premier et le principal objet de la Police; que dans tous les temps les soins en ont été confiez aux deux Puissances, la spirituelle, et la temporelle.' So said Delamare's *Traité de la Police*.[48] The State had to support religion by its laws, its law courts, and their penalties, since 'the punishments at the disposal of the ministers of religion are not severe enough to vanquish the indocility of human nature'. There was an age-long justification for the use of coercion, since the Church was assumed to have inherited the privileged position of the synagogue in the Old Testament. True, Delamare concedes, for three centuries the Christian gospel was preached without the aid of the secular power, but as Chrysostom had said, this was a dispensation of Providence to demonstrate the ability of true religion to make its way in a hostile world independently of all human aid. Thereafter, the partnership of Church and State was renewed, to the benefit of mankind and the saving of souls. St Augustine, in controversy with the Donatists, had established the legitimacy and necessity of this alliance. Such was the theory of Church–State relationships in the standard handbook of police procedures of eighteenth-century France.

In practice, what ought the police to do to assist religion in its mission? We can obtain an answer to this question by abstracting the relevant points from Delamare's review of the duties of the *commissaires examinateurs* who are the 'eyes' of the Parisian magistrates.[49] For the moment we are not concerned with their collaboration with churchmen in enforcing the laws against Protestants or in suppressing immorality—they also had specific duties concerning the supervision of outward religious practice. They were to arrest perpetrators of acts of blasphemy and sacrilege. On Sundays and great feasts of the Church they were to roam at large to prevent commercial activities, and to close down wine bars, tennis courts, and theatres during the hours of divine service. In Lent, they had to watch the butchers' shops to spy out illicit sales of meat, and pop into cafés and hostelries ready to prosecute if meat dishes were being served. When a major religious procession was to take place, they were to go round ordering householders to decorate their street. In short, they were to protect religion against insult and outrage, and to ensure a decent outward conformity to Catholic customs and discipline.

During the sixteenth century, with religious warfare raging, the offence of blasphemy became more heinous than it had been.[50] So much so that it passed out of the jurisdiction of the ecclesiastical courts and was taken over by the secular magistrates, whose punishments reflected the hatred aroused by those who not only insulted God, but also destroyed the national unity. Yet, grave as it was taken to be, blasphemy was not a sin of interest to the casuists—it was too obvious, and not a matter for finely tuned distinctions. The standard manual of Pontas has no entry 'blasphème', and its readers would have to seek under 'jurer' or ponder on the single example given under the general heading of 'péché'.[51] In 1666, Louis XIV issued an edict defining the crime and setting a scale of punishments for it—possibly provoked to do so by the scandal aroused by a scene in Molière's *Don Juan* (soon suppressed) where the hero gives money to a poor man to induce him to curse God. The edict said that blasphemy consisted in insults proffered to God, the Eucharist, the Blessed Virgin, and the saints, and was punishable with fine and imprisonment for the first four offences; for the fifth, with exposure in the pillory from eight in the morning to one o'clock in the afternoon on a Sunday or holiday; for the sixth, by branding with a hot iron on the upper lip, for the seventh on the lower; for the eighth, by amputation of the tongue. In the nature of the case, detection of the full accumulation of successive offences was unlikely, and the magistrates were not enthusiastic about enforcing the law on every occasion. From 1700 to 1790, only ninety-one cases came on appeal to the parlement of Paris.[52] Though the law-books have an example of the exaction of the full, final penalty by the parlement in 1724, this was as a prelude to an execution by burning, indicating that the offence had been committed in association with the more serious crime of sacrilege; probably, it was only with the occurrence of such a combination of insults to religion that the extreme penalty for

blasphemy was invoked.[53] The army had its own peculiar savage prescription, laid down by a declaration of 1681, renewed in 1727: the
piercing of the tongue with a hot iron, a variant punishment
designed to leave the offender still capable of shouting a warning or
giving a command.[54] The threat of the burning iron does not seem
to have had much influence on the proverbially outrageous language
of military men. 'To give themselves a lively and cavalier style and
air,' said the bishop of Lodève in 1749, 'many Christians among the
soldiery adopt the affectation of swearing in God's name; and many
others, in all walks of life, try to supplement their lack of facility and
inventiveness in conversation by the profane use of this adorable
name.'[55]

The punishments for sacrilegious crimes were horrendous. This
was an age when authority, lacking effective machinery for law
enforcement, used exemplary penalties in a sort of 'calculus of deter-
rence', culminating in breaking on the wheel for crimes which
seemed to threaten the social order, with a longer or shorter time of
agony prescribed before merciful strangulation was allowed.[56] In this
graduated tabulation of terror, the maintenance of the hierarchy of
society was taken into account: unbelievable torments were inflicted
on Damiens in 1757 because he had lifted his hand against the king,
and the penalty for stealing a mere handkerchief within the sacred
precincts of the parlement of Paris was branding and three years in
the galleys.[57] This sort of special and odious protection was afforded
to religion. A declaration of 4 May 1724 allowed sentences of up to
lifetime slavery in the galleys for thefts in churches.[58] These were
ordinary thefts—say, by pickpockets, or by the ingenious rogues
who extracted money from offertory boxes with flat pieces of wood
and glue.[59] Sentences to the galleys tended to range from two to
twelve years.[60] Outside churches, there were various sorts of conduct
which the courts might treat as sacrilegious on the way to inflicting
savage punishment. The man who fired a pistol at a crucifix in
Reims in 1725 had his hand cut off and was burned at the stake—
'he made a religious end under the ministrations of a friar of the
Cordeliers', the local annalist recorded.[61] The year before, at
Charolles, Angélique Lombard, a vagabond convicted of having had
herself baptized several times (no doubt as a fund-raising technique),
was condemned to the *amende honorable*, branding with a fleur-de-lis
mark on the left shoulder, floggings at four street corners, and perpetual banishment.[62] By contrast, one 'Popo' in the village of
Sennely in 1758, who insulted the curé, turned his back on the
Sacrament, beat his wife, and 'had carnal knowledge of her on the

public square', was condemned only to burning a candle as a gesture of repentance[63]—clearly, the court had taken his inebriation to be a mitigating circumstance.

Drunken frolics apart, sacrilegious crimes were most often committed in the course of thefts of church plate and silver. Sometimes, the thieves were guilty of a double sacrilege when they stole or profaned the reserved Sacrament in the course of their depredations—as did the soldier who made away with a golden ciborium during the great fire of Rennes in 1720.[64] The revulsion aroused by such crimes inspired the various foundations of devotions 'for the reparation of the insults proffered to Our Saviour Jesus Christ in the Holy Sacrament of the Altar'; a curé of Paris in 1724 gave no less than 4,000 livres for this purpose.[65] And this was why the police of Paris from time to time held special sessions with the *premier président* of the parlement concerning the growing number of thefts from churches.[66] The penalty for stealing 'sacred vases with profanation' was the cutting off of the right hand and burning at the stake. In 1714 (a priest),[67] in 1768 (three thieves),[68] and in 1781 (a burglar of Amiens)[69] were executed in this way on the orders of the parlement of Paris. When such thefts 'with profanation' took place, there was sometimes a suspicion—spoken of in a whisper—that the ultimate sacrilege had been committed, the deliberate appropriation of a consecrated Host for use in the ceremonies of black magic. (There was such a case among the garrison at Lille in 1713, ending with three soldiers burned and one shot; fifty years later a solemn procession of expiation was held to mark the 'jubilee', as it were, of this disgrace to the city.)[70]

What was the good of these cruel punishments? In *L'Esprit des Lois*, Montesquieu coolly contrasted the practice of Catholic Europe with that of ancient Rome, where stealing sacred vases from a temple was treated as simple theft.[71] If there is an incident which constitutes an offence to religion, the proper penalties are not those imposed by the secular magistrates on ordinary criminals, but exclusion from public places of worship and from the society of faithful believers. And the magistrate should assess the outward action only; whatever sacrilege is committed in secret is a matter between the offender and God alone. Mere men cannot avenge the majesty of God: 'il faut honorer la Divinité, et ne la venger pas'.[72] No doubt Voltaire believed the same, but he found more fun in emphasizing the ridiculous side of official conformity, yet sardonically recommending it. What is blasphemy in Rome and Notre-Dame of Loretto, he says, is piety in London, Amsterdam, Berlin, and Berne,[73]

and what is holy in Tibet is contemptible in China. No matter—
when the Grand Lama orders his subjects to kiss a gold-wrapped
dollop of his excrement, they ought to obey, though the emperor of
China, independent and outside his boundaries, will rightly throw
the ludicrous contraption into his privy.[74] In fact, the magistrates of
France, while accepting the principle that it was futile to attempt to
'avenge the Divinity',[75] were still prepared on occasion to enforce
hand-chopping and burning. There can be little doubt of their
motivation. Whether they cared for Catholic belief or merely
respected the established customs of their country, like Voltaire, they
all regarded religion as an essential part of the hierarchical structure
of society; they feared all sacrilegious acts as subverting the decencies
and deference that helped to preserve the stability of the social
order.[76]

So long as sacrilege was regarded as a threat to public order, anticlericals had only limited opportunities to denounce the secular
cruelties exercised on religion's behalf—until the execution of the
chevalier La Barre in 1766 horrified the enlightened opinion of
Western Europe. This young man was brought before the court of
the *sénéchaussée* of Ponthieu in October 1765 on suspicion of being
implicated in the mutilation of a crucifix on the bridge at Abbeville.
The investigation failed to prove his complicity in this particular act
of sacrilege, but established the truth of other charges: he had kept
his hat on in the presence of the Sacrament, had sung outrageous
songs, possessed dangerous books, had made the sign of the cross
with obscene remarks, and parodied the priestly actions of consecration at mass.[77] He was sentenced to the standard preliminary tortures
that preceded an execution (to extract an avowal and the names of
accomplices), to have his tongue torn out, and to be decapitated;
when all this was over, the corpse was to be burned. The parlement
of Paris confirmed the sentence on 4 June 1766, and it was carried
out on 1 July, in front of an immense crowd that had poured in from
twenty leagues around and had waited a night and most of a day in
the rain. The *question* (crushing the legs between planks by driving
in wedges) was applied at five in the morning, and the decapitation
took place at five in the evening (the executioner merely simulating
the tearing out of the tongue). Clerical fanaticism had little to do
with the tragic outcome; it was essentially an affair of legal red tape,
corruption, and confusion.[78] M. de Belleval, a legal official of
Ponthieu, had pressed the case against La Barre as a personal
vendetta (the chevalier had been provided with a home by his
cousin, the abbess of Willancourt, and his presence in her house had

broken off her old friendship with Belleval—a miserable provincial feud worthy of inclusion in *Madame Bovary*). La Barre, unlike his partner in riot, d'Etallonde, who fled and became an officer in the Prussian army, had failed to do the usual thing and run away—had he done this, he would have been executed in effigy, and the affair would have been forgotten. The parlement of Paris had put on a special show of ferocious zeal to counterbalance the anticlerical reputation it was enhancing by attacking the Jesuits. The clergy had tried to stop the execution; the diocesan bishop[79] had asked for commutation to life imprisonment (the papal nuncio said that in Rome a year in gaol would have sufficed), and the Assembly of the Clergy of France asked for clemency.[80] The *procureur général* of the parlement had prepared an order to suspend the execution, but it was never sent—the bureaucrats of the scaffold delayed on 1 July from early morning to evening expecting it would arrive.

The cruel death of La Barre gave Voltaire yet another of his great anticlerical opportunities. He was eloquent on the laws which punished mere deviations from 'the dominant opinion' of the nation as if they were crimes of poisoning or parricide. It was absurd for the clergy to erect a crucifix on a bridge where it formed a temptation to every drunken reveller.[81] The bishop, who had presided at a ceremony of expiation when he had described the insult to the sacred figure as 'worthy of the most extreme punishments which this world affords', was blamed for inflaming public opinion, so that a single malicious judge (Belleval) and two stupid ones (a pig dealer and a nonentity) had been influenced to pass a viciously cruel sentence.[82] Voltaire had done some legal research, and he doubted whether this and most other executions for sacrilege were legitimate: the royal ordinance of 1682 spoke of 'sacrilège joint à la superstition', and this surely meant the profanation of Christian objects for the purpose of sorcery, and nothing more. His conclusion was that of Montesquieu, though he chose to quote Vauvenargues: 'ce qui n'offense pas la société n'est pas du ressort de la justice'.[83] The sole task of the police was to protect society—he implied that religion must stand or fall by the allegiance it can win in free intellectual debate.

In a work published in 1686, a parish priest of a rigorist turn of mind listed the activities appropriate for Sunday and other religious festivals. The faithful must attend mass and vespers and hear a sermon. In what time remained, they were recommended to attend the observances of churches other than their own and to visit the sick and the poor.

They may also see their friends or pay necessary social calls, go for walks, converse in an edifying way on the Christian instruction they have received, read some useful books (if they know how to read, otherwise get others to read to them), . . . enjoy sober and moderate repasts, . . . and even play games or indulge in other relaxations, provided these . . . are respectable and fitting to their station in life, and that they do not involve any dubious circumstances.[84]

The law of the land would hardly enforce such worthy activities, but the legislator did his best to circumscribe profane pastimes and to limit the 'dubious circumstances' which curé Thiers feared. Restrictions concerning Sundays and feast-days had been laid down by royal ordinances of 1560 and 1579 and various edicts of Louis XIV (renewed by the parlement of Paris in December 1734); these prohibitions were codified in the major police ordinance of 30 April 1778.[85] Work was forbidden, except when ecclesiastical authority certified a particular task as necessary: there were, however, various customary exemptions in which the necessity was regarded as permanently established. Though the actual baking of bread had to take place on a weekday, loaves could be sold on Sundays, provided the shop was shut to outward appearances. The *pâtisseurs* were allowed to stay open, for holidays were their principal trading times, but they had to close at Easter, Pentecost, All Saints, and the feast of St Laurent, their patron.[86] Barbers could wield their razors after divine service finished (presumably because they had once been surgeons); butchers could sell meat in the hot weather from the first Sunday after Trinity to the first Sunday in September, inclusive. Most judicial proceedings were null if conducted on a Sunday (the agents-general of the clergy in 1722 demonstrated the rule by getting the Royal Council to cancel a writ served on a curé of Rouen by a local monastery). By contrast, assignations to justice of a whole community were always served on Sundays at the end of Sunday mass or vespers, for that was when most people were there to hear the bad news. Barges[87] carrying grain to Paris passed down the waterways continuously, except during the four most solemn feasts of the year, for the provisioning of the capital was too vital a matter to risk any delay. For similar reasons, the parlement of Paris tended to allow millers to work on holy days, and in a case of 1765 accepted the plea that a shop could stay open to sell articles of necessity.[88] At Versailles, Sceaux, and a few other places near Paris, weekday markets were allowed to stay open when they fell on saints' days, though the archbishop in 1787 prevented the fair of Brie-Comte-Robert from gaining this privilege.[89] As for harvest time in the countryside, a sensible parish priest would try to accommodate the needs of his peasants, though maybe not so sweepingly as Restif's curé Pinard, who advanced the hour of mass, cancelled the sermon, and said that the schoolmaster and a few old people would be a sufficient congregation for vespers. 'Bind up your sheaves in this sunny weather,' he said; 'the people subject to the law of Moses were not allowed to violate the Sabbath in this way, but you, children of the regeneration, are free from the letter that killeth . . . God imposes one duty: that is, to love Him.'[90]

It was unrealistic to attempt to close wine bars, cafés, theatres, billiard saloons, and tennis courts all day on Sundays; besides, the authorities were well aware that men congregating on a holiday might resort to activities more dangerous to public order than getting drunk, watching entertainments, or playing games. The law therefore closed places of refreshment and amusement only during the hours of divine service.[91] At these times, dances were also forbidden, on pain of a fine of 500 livres and confiscation of the musical instruments.[92] If a new recreation was devised, the local authorities would regulate it as, in the summer of 1781, the *capitouls* of Toulouse banned the launching of a Montgolfier balloon on St Stephen's Day, on penalty of a fine of 1,000 livres for non-compliance. 'The curiosity to see the ascent of the balloon whose manœuvres will take a long time, might divert the people from fulfilling the acts of worship required by religion.'[93] It was customary to hold the threat of large fines over the heads of potential offenders. In 1719, the assizes of the seigneurial court of the village of Franxault in Burgundy ordained a penalty of 100 livres for serving drinks to customers during church time: the actual fines levied varied from 10 to 50 livres.[94] Police intervention against untimely Sunday drinking was quite frequent. The parish priest might insist on it, as he did at Bouzigues in 1744; twenty or so local inhabitants were found regaling themselves in the bar of one Goudard as the strains of the Magnificat resounded from the church—the customary fine of 3 livres went to the fund for the upkeep of the light before the Holy Sacrament.[95] In the Paris area, the parlement itself sometimes judged an indictment, with exemplary punishment resulting, but mostly, Sunday drinking cases were dealt with by the *chambre de police*, whose chief other task was to fine citizens who failed to sweep the street outside their doorstep.[96] The number of cases dealt with diminished in the early years of the century, but began to rise from 1725, with a still greater increase after 1740. By contrast, in 1755, the standard fine was reduced from 2 livres per customer detected to 1 livre, 10 sous, while the fine for failure to sweep the street doubled, from 2 livres to 4 livres. Nor did renewed drinking infringements attract heavier penalties, and there was no closing down of the premises of habitual offenders.[97] One might infer that the police were becoming more efficient—or officious—but that the actual offence was becoming less seriously regarded. The fine for illegal Sunday drinking was settling down into a sort of licence fee.

No doubt there were pious folk who observed Sunday with the piety that curé Thiers recommended, and others who at least liked to appear respectable. A cobbler of Chartres called on by an ecclesiastic (a future archbishop) for an urgent shoe repair on a Sunday professed to be scandalized.[98] Perhaps his trade had special pretensions. 'We aren't like the *canaille* and the dregs of the populace who employ Sundays and feast-days in going for walks and amusing themselves at fairs and assemblies, in wine bars and country inns,' said a pamphlet in defence of the shoemaker's profession; 'for our part, we are occupied solely on those days in doing useful work in churches, as bell-ringers, making the offering of *pain bénit*, and supervising the letting of chairs.'[99] The peasants sometimes worked on Sundays, sometimes enjoyed the holiday, according to the weather, the season, local tradition, and the character and exigencies of their curé;[100] town artisans would have less latitude, but be more influenced by the degree of their necessity. But clearly absenteeism from work was the rule—and it did nothing to increase the incidence of practices of piety.

Early in the century, a mission preacher complained of 'the false idea of most contemporary Christians that it suffices to have attended Holy Mass to be able to be free to employ all the rest of the day in business, amusement and idleness'.[101] In 1722, the parlement of Rennes described the typical Sunday of the lower orders as consisting of 'impious conversations in cemeteries' (being places of general resort near the church), wandering from wine bar to wine bar, playing boule and billiards during the hours of divine service, and indulging in 'execrable oaths and swearing'.[102] Things were presumably getting worse, for after a whole century of silence on the matter, the Assembly of the Clergy of France began to complain, in 1755, of the failure 'to sanctify Sundays'. 'In the past, disobedience was carefully concealed . . . now it shows itself openly.'[103] English travellers to France were struck by the light-hearted fashion in which the day of rest was enjoyed across the Channel. In 1776, Thomas Bentley took a drive through the Bois de Boulogne to Saint-Cloud and back. 'The most striking thing we saw here and all the way', he said,

was the immense crowds of people and the manner of their Sunday amusements. Many kinds of shops were open as on other days; everybody was
taking the air in their holiday clothes; close to the terrace leading to the
gardens of St Cloud under the shade of a grove a large party of young men
and women clean and decently dressed were dancing country dances and
minuets of three couples alternately with all the ease and decorum of a
genteel assembly. Multitudes were sitting upon the terrace conversing and
enjoying the open air; in the woods of Boulogne as we returned back we
observed many small parties enjoying themselves under the shade of the
trees and dancing away.[104]

Bentley's naïve enthusiasm for the innocent recreations of the
people was not shared by the philosophes; with them, the dominant
view was: if only the lower orders could be dissuaded from amusing
themselves on Sundays and, indeed, not be pressed overmuch to go
to church, they would be able to add an extra day of toil per week
to increase the national wealth. Reforming bishops had reduced the
number of saints of dubious authenticity: Turgot and the *Encyclopédie*
wanted further retrenchments in the calendar in the name of
utility.[105] A petition of the labouring classes to the king in 1770 asked
for 'permission to work'—this was a concoction of Voltaire,[106] who
could not abide idleness and was repelled by vulgar swilling in
taverns. This had been one of the abbé de Saint-Pierre's remedies for
the ills of France: fill Sundays with work and educational lectures as
well as church-going, to leave no time for drinking.[107] A pamphleteer of 1789 renewed the proposal, asking for secular Sunday schools
teaching law, anatomy, and botany to the ignorant multitude, alongside the usual catechism classes.[108] It is refreshing to turn from these
improving schemes to Necker, who saw no reason for the poor to
work an extra day since, sadly, their employers would pay them the
same subsistence wages whatever extra efforts they made. As it was,
on one day in the week they dressed like other citizens and did as
they pleased, enjoying the brief illusion of freedom. 'Et moi aussi,'
they could say, 'je suis libre.'[109]

One of the tasks of the police was to enforce outward conformity to
the Lenten fast, keeping a watch more particularly on butchers'
shops and eating-houses. A Parisian police ordinance of January 1768
clarified some details. An innkeeper serving meat dishes (for
foreigners and people with special authorizations) had to have a

document specifying the permission of his curé and countersigned
by the lieutenant-general of police, and he had to serve the privileged few at a separate table. A dignified police official, *L'exempte de
la compagnie du prévôt de l'île de France*, was authorized to visit the
houses of princes and *grands seigneurs* and to confiscate illegal joints
from their kitchens.[110] Strictly speaking, eggs were banned in Lent,
though most bishops issued an annual pastoral letter authorizing
them. This relaxation only gradually became established in the stern
diocese of Paris. There had been no more than two instances in sixty
years, when, early in 1729, a tremendous frost extracted the jealously
guarded privilege; Parisians rejoiced to find it was not cancelled
when the thaw came unexpectedly quickly.[111] Thereafter, permis-
sions became frequent—in 1731, 1732, 1735, then three years
running from 1739 to 1741, then nine consecutive years from 1745
to 1753.[112] A solemn ritual was followed by the civil and ecclesiastical powers when such relaxations were being sought: the municipal
authorities would draw up a petition, using the conventional
formula, 'vu la misère des temps' (which meant that bad weather or
famine was rendering the provisioning of the capital difficult); the
lieutenant-general of police would support this, referring the application to the parlement, which would send a deputation to the archbishop.[113] When the prelate had issued his pastoral letter giving
permission, the magistrates would pass on an *arrêt* authorizing the
execution of the episcopal decree, just to show the supremacy of the
temporal power.[114] In 1754, all was confusion, since parlement and
archbishop were at war with each other. Seeing that the magistrates
were so busily engaged in encroaching on spiritual matters, said the
old duchesse de Villars, she was asking the *premier président* of the
parlement for his permission to eat eggs that year.[115]

Individuals could be exempted from fasting, provided they had an
ecclesiastical authorization, generally given on the production of
medical evidence. The profits on the sale of meat to such privileged
folk were supposed to go to charity. The bishop would fix the
prices,[116] and in provincial towns a single butcher would be named,
le boucher de carême, who paid a fine to the local hospitals. In Paris,
the *hôtel-Dieu* had the privilege of overseeing the meat trade in Lent
and made 50,000 livres a year from it: this was the compensation
decreed by the Crown in 1774 when the monopoly was ended.[117] In
desperate times—famine or terrible weather—an episcopal ordinance might even allow meat to everyone. In Lorraine in 1720, with
no vegetables available, the price of eggs soaring, and butter said to
have lost its nourishing qualities, 'la crainte de voir les maladies

succéder à la disette' led to the authorization of meat four days in the week.[118] The first such general permission in Angers was given in January 1766, for every day 'up to and including Maundy Thursday'; for a whole month the Loire had been frozen so hard that horsemen could gallop across the ice.[119] In the same harsh year, the archbishop of Toulouse[120] allowed meat on three days in the week—for the first time within living memory, said a local annalist. The two prelates concerned, Jacques de Grasse and Loménie de Brienne, were suspected of having no serious Christian beliefs; no doubt they had more reasons than one for welcoming the opportunity to be generous to the shivering population of their dioceses.

The Lenten fast was an easy target for the anticlericals of the Enlightenment. It was a burden devised by churchmen, they pointed out, having nothing to do with the essence of religion in general or with the teachings of the founder of Christianity in particular. Christ did not forbid omelettes to his apostles, said Voltaire; on the contrary, he advised them, whatever city they entered, to 'eat such things as they set before you'.[121] Jesus fasted for forty days in the wilderness, a lawyer speculated; the Israelites wandered in the desert for forty years; the Flood lasted forty days; and Nineveh was allowed forty days in which to repent: perhaps Lent is a commemoration of one of these times, without—it is implied—a great deal of relevance to modern conditions.[122] Voltaire did not mind if the State imposed a sort of political Lent—it was, indeed, a civilized idea to stop the fearful carnage of animals for once in a year—but where was the authority of the Church in such a matter? In 1769, Jean-Baptiste Cloots (later to call himself 'Anacharsis'), a boy of 14 who was being educated in Paris, led his schoolboy companions astray with prohibited Lenten fare by using the standard anticlerical argument: 'to do an action which is in itself innocent, and which becomes criminal only because it is prohibited, is not to sin, so long as one cannot discover whether or not the prohibition emanates from a legitimate tribunal'.[123] In any case, said Voltaire, the Lenten discipline of the clergy was suspect because of the manifest inequality of the sacrifices they were trying to impose on the different classes of society. While the rich were eating their way to salvation with sole and salmon, turbot and sturgeon, the poor were deprived of such miserable scraps of meat as might come their way, and were dependent on special permission to eat eggs and butter—what else had they got to nourish them and make their black bread and chestnuts palatable?[124] It was one of the high points of the year for Parisian anticlericals when the post brought in the

Lenten pastoral letters of various bishops from the provinces—full of thunders of the Last Judgement and the Great Abyss, or of massive learning from the New Testament and the Fathers, leading usually to a splendid anticlimax as conclusion: authorizing the eating of cheese and butter—nay, even, of eggs—in the forthcoming forty days. If one of these publications survives, what will our descendants make of it in 2,000 or 3,000 years time, asked the *Correspondance littéraire* of the pastoral of the archbishop of Lyon in 1768. 'Ils se casseront la tête pour découvrir la liaison et la logique de ces idées.'[125] To what extent was the fast of Lent observed? It was commonly said that the austerities of the penitential season were endured only by the poor. According to the Lenten pastoral letter of the archbishop of Sens in 1779, the rich often obtained medical certificates allowing them to eat what they liked.[126] This was the fashionable thing to do. 'Look at our bourgeois citizen and his wife in their (draper's) shop, observing Lent strictly,' said the Jesuit Père Croisset in his *Parallèle des mœurs de ce siècle et la morale de Jésus-Christ* (1727); 'their fortune changes . . . and scarcely has the tape measure dropped from their hands than you see them putting on airs like people of quality and asking for dispensations from fasting.'[127] This class distinction was observed even in the kitchens of the Bastille: on the first Friday of his imprisonment, Marmontel gloomily ate the meatless meal provided, not knowing that it had been meant for his servant.[128] In any case, there were plenty of succulent dishes within the rules, for those who could afford them. Lent was the season to have tubs of fresh butter sent in from the countryside,[129] and to ensure plentiful supplies of fish and water birds (the test of an allowable fowl was: did the gravy remain uncongealed after fifteen minutes?—so a bishop gravely advised Mme Victoire, Louis XV's pious but comfortable daughter[130]). The peasant, whose existence is a perpetual Lent anyway, said Voltaire, awaits episcopal permission to eat his farmyard eggs, while the bishop himself looks forward to expensive dishes of soles.[131] Certainly, things were well organized at Versailles. 'A ray of grace has descended on us,' wrote the duc de la Vallière in April 1756; 'we fasted for three days a week during the whole of Lent, but on condition that we suffered no deprivations.'[132] Preachers were well aware that those with money and leisure could organize an attractive Lent for themselves: an occasional walk in a procession (a penitent's garb was no disadvantage to a good-looking woman),[133] extra time in bed to recuperate from privations, and food more delicately cooked and served than usual. 'For some—God grant there are none in my congregation today,' thundered the Oratorian

Surian, 'Lent is a more agreeable time, in a sophisticated way, than the other seasons of the year.'[134]

In the second half of the eighteenth century, contemporaries recorded a widespread decline of scruples about fasting in Paris, and the beginnings of a decline in Angers.[135] Mercier in the 1780s describes how the police of the capital had relaxed their vigilance: when he was a boy, they had confiscated the dinner sent to the prince de Condé from his private kitchens to the tennis court in the rue Mazarine, and a citizen taking broth to an ailing friend on a Friday did well to conceal it in a hat box; now, the butchers' shops openly sold meat without hindrance.[136] The king, however, still intervened to stop outrageous violations of decency by the great: the lavish subscription dinner organized by certain courtiers in 1776 for the first Thursday in Lent was whipped away and given to the poor of the parish of Saint-Roch (as it had cost five louis a head, the wits called it 'le repas des Chevaliers de Saint-Louis'[137]). In spite of the gulf between rich and poor, there was a sense in which the social life of Paris constituted a unity; there were occasions when the irreligious ostentation of the great provided a celebration of revolt for everyone. Such was the promenade of Longchamps which became a fashion in the last two decades of the *ancien régime*. It began with excursions through the Bois-de-Boulogne, on the Wednesday of Holy Week, Maundy Thursday, and Good Friday to hear *Tenebrae* sung by the nuns at the abbey of Longchamps—young bloods rode there on horseback, and the ladies in their carriages. The abbey, which had rejoiced in its fame and fortified its choir with opera singers, soon changed its policy in accordance with the solemnity of Lent, but the promenade had become an institution.[138] The rich vied in their splendour, the others crowded to watch them, and the police turned out in force to keep order, the city watch lining the streets from the Place Louis XV to the Porte Maillot, and the *maréchaussée* patrolling the woods beyond. The chief competition in ostentation was among the *filles entretenues* of court nobles and financiers. Mlle Guimard the dancer, 'la belle Damnée', won in 1768 with her invented coat of arms, supported by Graces and surmounted by cherubs, painted on the doors of her carriage.[139] In 1774, two dancers (one the mistress of the Spanish ambassador) scored off all other rivals by having no fewer than six horses pulling their carriages; the next year, Mlle Duthé tried the same gambit, adding blue morocco harness adorned with polished steel, and got hooted for ostentation;[140] in 1780, the daughter of the duchesse de Mazarin, pulled by four greys caparisoned in crimson silk, had to brook com-

parisons with a *fille* in a porcelain carriage and another who had the
distinction of the duc de Chartres riding alongside her all the way.[141]
In 1787, Mlle Rozalie of the Comédie-Italienne misbehaved so
badly in the parade that the lieutenant of police sent her to the prison
of For l'Évêque, where the young seigneurs of the Court visited her
and she took charitable collections for the release of debtors, which
made her universally popular.[142] Such were the subjects of Holy
Week gossip in Paris.

Concerning fasting and ordinary people, while there is a broad
assumption that they unenthusiastically gave some compliance, we
cannot hope to know what happened in their houses. Yet, oddly
enough, we do know about their reactions to the Church's precepts
to abstain from sexual intercourse in penitential seasons. Counting
backwards from dates of birth, we can infer[143] that sexual activity was
at its minimum in the early autumn (through preoccupation with
harvesting and sheer exhaustion) and in Lent (presumably principally
for religious reasons), while it was at its maximum in spring, once
Lent was over. Advent was not respected (though in French Canada
it was), but the rule of abstention in Lent was still taken seriously—
and in a branch of enjoyment which escaped the surveillance of the
police. It was, no doubt, natural to resort to—or to applaud—
brinkmanship in words and gestures banned by the police in association with the clergy, to find ways of enlivening Sunday with profane
merriment, to evade the austere regulations of penitential seasons,
and to laugh at the irreligious and anticlerical gestures of *grands
seigneurs* and philosophes. But to the mass of people who enjoyed no
privacy for reflection or devotion and owned so very little they
could offer as a gift, the Church's call to self-denial as a spiritual
exercise and a self-offering struck a chord of human need and led to
a degree of conformity to ecclesiastical discipline which was the
result neither of the coercion of the mind by habit nor the outward
act by the police. The flavour of this sort of conformity is rarely
evoked by the handbooks of spirituality read by the leisured classes
or in statistics of conduct; the historian is grateful for a glimpse of it,
even if he can only guess at its significance.

IV *The Church and Law Enforcement*

Just as the police powers of the State protected the observances of
religion, so the Church was expected to second the officers of the
State in the enforcement of the laws. Though the ecclesiastical courts

exercised jurisdiction over clerics, in the last resort royal jurisdiction could take over—the *appel comme d'abus* was the decisive weapon of the lay magistrates to defeat the pretensions of churchmen. The king's writ ran against all persons and in all places of his dominions. The ancient right of sanctuary was lost to the churches and convents of France—a criminal could be arrested in a church just as anywhere else.[144] It is true that there remained some oases of feudal jurisdictions in the cities, often enough owned by collegiate churches, in which the municipal police did not operate in non-criminal matters, though they were being taken over by the civic authorities whenever opportunity offered. This is what happened to the *sauvetés* of Saint-André and Saint-Seurin at Bordeaux at the end of the *ancien régime*.[145] Until then, under the lax policing of the canons, gambling dens and unpleasant and dangerous industrial establishments like iron foundries and tanneries had flourished, and dubious women had plied their trade in the very cloisters of the chapters and in the capitular prisons. There was a 'sanctuary' of a sort in Paris, the *enclos du Temple*, belonging to the knights of Malta, who had inherited it from the Templars. In this 'lieu d'asile', ordinary criminals could be arrested, but debtors, duellists, and writers who had fallen foul of the censorship were safe, provided they entered their names and the reason for their application for sanctuary in the register kept by the *bailli* of the Order. Gudin, friend of Beaumarchais, fled there in 1778, pursued by the police for verses satirizing the parlement Maupeou; he lived there together with Mme de Goodville, who had taken refuge in the Temple to escape her creditors, and they amused themselves by writing lampoons on the great, sending them to the lieutenant of police with their compliments.[146]

The clergy had no immunity from criminal prosecution and could not offer asylum to others; they could, however, give advice and comfort in the confessional under the seal of absolute secrecy. But the secular authorities, in every circumstance outside the confessional, expected the clergy to co-operate in law enforcement. They regarded the parish priests as having the duty of making government legislation known to their people, and ancient ordinances of the kings had laid on the curés the duty of reading out official announcements during the Sunday mass, when all the parishioners would be assembled.[147] The law courts also demanded the publication of their verdicts in significant cases, and the great came to insist on having notices read warning the public to respect their rights—as when a boundary dispute had been settled in their favour. The clergy, concerned to elevate the Sacrament of the altar to a pinnacle of reverence, challenged the old ordinances and established customs. Bishops directed curés[148] to limit notices during the mass to listing ecclesiastical feasts and fasts and the foundation masses for the coming week, relegating anything else to after the post-communion prayers or, better still, to the porch or churchyard after the congregation had left the church. In the case of a private announcement, let the individual concerned hire a notary or *huissier* to read out his notice, instead of imposing on the clergy. (Truth to tell, in the depths of the country curés did not regard such notices as a nuisance, especially where they charged a small fee for them, a practice continuing all through the century.) These episcopal rules were given official standing by the royal edict of 1695, freeing the curés from any obligation to mention private affairs, and the declaration of 1698 extended this to all secular affairs, even if the business of the king was concerned.[149] Curés were still subjected to pressure by local magistrates and nobles, and no doubt often yielded for the sake of a quiet life, but if they complained to the agents general of the clergy at Paris, they could be sure the Royal Council would intervene on the side of the Church. In 1742 the parlement of Pau ordered a curé to read out a newly surveyed documentation of the boundaries and feudal rights of the 'sieur de Capdeville'; a year later, the council cancelled the parlement's ruling.[150] Five years later, another case was won against the Maîtrise des Eaux et Forêts of Dôle. In 1775, a curé of the diocese of Chartres successfully defied the *chambre des comptes* which was demanding publication of its arbitration settling the boundaries of the royal forest of Senonches.[151] About this time, the parlement of Toulouse tested the established jurisprudence deriving from the edicts of 1695 and 1698 by demanding the reading of a verdict, alleging the subject to be morals and religion. The magistrates, who had sentenced three girls to death for concealing their pregnancies, so that their babies died, wanted the judgement widely disseminated as a warning to others. The agents-general of the clergy defeated the claim using an interesting new argument: granted the Church had the duty of assisting to maintain public morality, it was improper to do so by dishonouring private families by naming them in the house of God. Yet the idea that the clergy had to read out government regulations in church was deeply ingrained, and in 1789, the National Assembly, determined to claim for itself the full sovereign rights of the old monarchy, prescribed the reading of its decrees at *prône*. Local authorities, full of revolutionary self-importance, began to do the same. 'They are assimilating our ministry to that of town criers,' complained the bishop of Senez.[152]

When Church property was to be sold, however, the assembly recognized that it would be indecent for curés to have to read from the pulpit the list of ecclesiastical lands and buildings for auction, though there were anticlerical local authorities reluctant to recognize the incongruity.

There was a peculiar kind of public announcement detested by the clergy even more than the reading of government edicts; though it concerned secular business, it could not be excluded from the parish mass, for its essence was the proclamation of a threat of ecclesiastical penalties. The *monitoire*[153] was an injunction of the Church, issued on the request of a secular magistrate, ordering all Christian people to reveal whatever they might know about the circumstances and perpetrators of a particular criminal act, under pain of excommunication. The lawyers held certain crimes to be especially suitable for investigation in this fashion: the suppression of a last will and testament or the concealment of possessions in the inheritance; fraud, more especially fraudulent bankruptcy; usury; monopolistic conspiracy to force up prices—all involving clandestine manœuvres. Other suitable offences were those in which the perpetrators were known but no one would give evidence, as when cattle had broken through hedges and trampled a sown field or had been surreptitiously grazed on a meadow. A rumour of a duel, condoned by certain sections of public opinion, but held to be a threat to society by the government, was considered to be eminently worthy of investigation, and the procedures for obtaining a *monitoire* were made correspondingly easier. But in every case, the will of the secular court had to prevail: the *officiel*, the legal registrar of a diocese, had to comply with the request of the lay judge on pain of seizure of his property. The ecclesiastical courts could also resort to the *monitoire*, the standard examples being simony or the illegitimate appropriation of the title to a tithe by a layman. There were safeguards, however. A court, lay or ecclesiastical, could not embark on a 'fishing expedition': the judges must have made arrangements to prosecute or at least have a 'plainte répondue' before them, indicating that a civil case would be pursued. Offences concerning movable property were excluded, as were evasion of taxes or customs duties (there was also a papal ruling, not accepted in France, excluding small sums of money).[154] Except in cases of adultery, the names of individuals could not be mentioned in a derogatory fashion. Doctors and midwives had no obligation to proffer information (it went without saying that confessors could not do so); servants could not incriminate their masters; and the relatives of a criminal up to the fourth degree were free to remain silent.

When a *monitoire* was called for, the curé had to publish it on three successive Sundays, giving a certificate of performance to the *officiel* or to the lay tribunal; if any revelations were made to him as a result of the proclamation, he forwarded them to the court in a sealed envelope. Some diocesan *Rituels* provided a formula for a *monitoire* in which the excommunication was automatically incurred after a stated lapse of time (in the diocese of Bâle, it was thirty days, except for a murder, when it was three days only).[155] Or the *Rituel* might provide for the separate pronouncement of the excommunication, possibly in two stages of increasing gravity. The final step would be the proclamation of the *aggrave* (sometimes called the *réaggrave*), the major excommunication, consignment to total damnation. This could be done with sinister ceremonies—a white baptismal robe trampled under foot, a crucifix or a lighted candle thrown down; perhaps a coffin would be brought into the nave as stage scenery for the fulmination, then taken out and put on a bonfire, with two priests each throwing six stones (two and six being numbers short of the ecclesiastical golden norm, three and seven). While the flames roared, Psalm 109 would be recited: 'let Satan stand at his right hand. When he shall be judged, let him be condemned, and let his prayer be turned into sin. Let his days be few and another take his office. Let there be no man to pity him, nor have compassion on his fatherless children.'

These macabre, archaic thunders often enough failed to produce revelations. The excommunication of named persons for known transgression[156] (rarely possible in France except for open and continuous adultery) could be effective, as incurring social ostracism, but it was unlikely that undetected people whose only crime was to keep their own counsel would tremble. Officials and men of property using the *monitoire* in an attempt to break through the popular conspiracy of silence rarely succeeded. Year after year the municipality of Angers[157] uselessly had the clergy calling for the names of the scoundrels who broke up seats on the public promenades and damaged trees to get fuel in winter—the freezing poor were leagued together to survive. In 1736 the parlement of Brittany used the *monitoire* in an attempt to prevent the filling in of the ditches and the pulling down of the fences of a nobleman who had enclosed the common land at Plourivo; the peasants erected a gallows and dug a grave at its foot, with the notice 'It is here we will bury those who talk'—no one did.[158] A *monitoire* in the diocese of Gap led to the women of the parish pulling the priest out of his pulpit, tearing his cassock, throwing away his wig, and beating him with the processional cross, for they feared his anathemas might do damage to the crops.[159] Some *monitoires* were not only futile, but frivolous. Everyone except the victims enjoyed the lampoons circulating in provincial towns against the great; why should the terrors of Hell be invoked against the jester who put out a broadsheet ridiculing the canons of Reims, the satirist who described in verse the follies of the élite of Angers at a pretentious ball, the artist at Séez who painted a poster denouncing a local physician adorned with a border of knives dripping blood?[160] When anathemas were effective, it was because the criminals were well-known rogues without local sympathy, as at Auxerre in 1739, when Pierre Fleury, his wife, and three accomplices were identified as the nocturnal thieves who had stolen the iron grilles over cellar entrances, and were duly flogged, branded, and banished.[161] If a *monitoire* had the justification of being directed at a grave crime executed by stealth—a man killed by a pistol shot in an empty street in Paris,[162] musket balls fired through the windows of an unpopular seigneur,[163] the many revenges taken by arson in the countryside—almost by definition the chances of finding the criminal were small. Yet the law courts were happy to requisition the thunders of the Church, however useless, for it was a demonstration that the magistrates were at least doing something, expressing some concern. For their part, the clergy felt they were degrading their office and the majesty of religion by evoking superficial and superstitious *frissons* of terror demonstrably ineffective.

There were simple parish priests in remote places who entered into the spirit of these thunderous performances and improved them with threatening discourses, adding transformation into werewolves to the prescribed liturgical penalties.[164] But the better-educated and those in touch with urban opinion could do no other than regard the proceedings as theologically dubious and verging on the ridiculous, so they dissociated themselves as far as possible, and did no more than the bare minimum to conform to the law. This was more particularly so after the storm broke over the unjust condemnation of the Protestant Calas, in which the *monitoire* was revealed as the instrument of prejudiced judges; the magistrates of Toulouse had used it to ask for information about the 'assassins' of Marc-Antoine Calas, excluding the possibility of what really happened—suicide.[165] 'A monitoire can be a proscription,' Voltaire was to say.[166] This was the beginning of the road to the vicious verdict condemning Marc-Antoine's father to breaking on the wheel on the ground that he had murdered his son to prevent him converting to the Roman faith. In addition to high principle and the odium of the Calas affair, there

was also a material consideration to encourage clerical resentment.
Here was yet another instance of the clergy being obliged to work
for derisory remuneration in State service, to the profit of the
lawyers.[167] The registrar of a lay tribunal ordering a *monitoire* got a fee
of 30 sous, and his clerk 10 sous. The curé, who went through the
repeated ceremonies, wrote the certificate, copied down the evidence, and forwarded it, in the process making himself ridiculous
and, possibly, unpopular, got the same as the clerk, 10 sous. When
in Brittany the parish priests leagued together to ask a fee of three
livres, the magistrates of the parlement (who exacted considerable
épices from litigants) described their request as 'sordid avarice'. There
was also the matter of pride, of the dignity of the office of pastor, of
the majesty of the ceremonies of religion. Judging by their *cahiers* in
1789, this is what piqued the curés most. They were ashamed to see
'the sword of excommunication being unsheathed in executing the
sentence of a village judge', and angered at 'the frivolity and indis-
cretion with which *monitoires* are ordered, sometimes for absurd
reasons'.[168] 'Is it decent for the Church', asked the clergy of
Clermont-Ferrand, 'to be obliged, at the discretion of a simple
seigneurial judge, to deploy all the most formidable weapons in its
armoury, sometimes for matters bordering on the ridiculous?'[169]

4

THE WEALTH OF THE CHURCH

The Gallican Church was enormously wealthy. In the seventeenth century, envious estimates had accused churchmen of monopolizing a quarter of the wealth of the kingdom, more than the king, who enjoyed only a ninth.[1] According to more sober guesses at the beginning of the Revolution, ecclesiastics disposed of a total income twice as large as the yield of the basic land tax, the *taille*; if this was so, though not quite as rich as the Crown, the Church was not far from it. These splendid revenues were derived from two sources: property on the one hand and tithe on the other. Probably, tithe brought in rather more, but the balance between tithe and landed estates varied throughout France. There was an infinity of local differences and one broad, overwhelming contrast: in the North, where there were vast tracts of ecclesiastical property, tithe played a lesser part than in the South, where in some dioceses, it was the primary and indispensable support of the clergy. It formed three-quarters of their revenues in the dioceses of Albi, Castres, and Lavaur. The canons of the cathedral of Toulouse and the bishop of Pamiers would have been in penury without it.[2] Where the impact of ecclesiastical riches on public opinion is concerned, it is difficult to generalize about the estates of the Church, since they were so unevenly distributed throughout the country. More comprehensive statements can usually be made about tithe. Therefore, in this chapter, these two sources of income will be considered separately.

Though in some respects such separate consideration will bring clarity, it will also distort the picture. Those who paid were more concerned about the total amount dragged from their pockets than about the headings under which the various levies were made. The peasant who looked enviously on the broad acres of some great abbey and, maybe, paid rents and feudal dues to it was also paying tithe to churchmen. The total burden could be heavy. In one village in the mid-eighteenth century, where there were 62 houses and 240 inhabitants, with a gross income of 11,000 livres, the clergy took 2,400, the seigneur 1,900, and direct royal taxation 1,975. In another, of 212 houses and 630 inhabitants, with a gross income of

24,000 livres, the corresponding figures were 4,700, 4,150, and 4,230.[3] The clergy were making away with a fifth of the produce of the parish; the 'establishment' generally, including the clergy, with half. These are the sophisticated calculations of a modern historian, but the peasant, isolated and ignorant as he was, knew how much he harvested and who got what. This was his fate, accepted with bitterness.

A consideration of his lot may serve as a warning. In our fashionable enthusiasm for the study of nuances of social structure, we should never lose sight of the sheer oppressiveness of the *ancien régime*. It requires an effort of the imagination to understand how these unjust arrangements were stolidly and fatalistically accepted from below, and imposed, with only rare tremors of conscience, from above: the gilded world of Versailles, the crystalline salons of the Enlightenment, the rich and varied liturgical, spiritual, social, and cultural activities of the Gallican Church can be regarded, if we so wish, as self-contained subjects for historical study, taking for granted the complex underpinning of law, tradition, and coercion holding together the system of tribute that paid the bills. In this chapter on the wealth of the Church, we clamber, as it were, amid the joists and beams of this multifarious underpinning. The temptation is to hasten out of the obscurity up to the Church itself, that great autonomous institution, with its organization, its clergy, its role in society, its aspirations towards eternity. For the most part, indeed, the nature of the evidence available obliges us to do so. Yet, groping on the under-side of ecclesiastical history, we come into touch with rural France, and with the peasants, the vast majority of the population. Their role was to pay. Along rutted lanes, paths through cornfields, and sheep tracks in the mountains, we meet continually a multitude of weather-beaten figures, a spectacle of broken teeth, gnarled hands, rags, clogs, coarse woollen stockings, and homespun cloaks. These folk not only support the Church; they constitute it and justify its existence. If we can discover how they believed and felt, and what charity and hope religion brought into their living and their dying, this would be the quintessential ecclesiastical history—a history which, alas, will largely remain unwritten, though on a plane not accessible to terrestrial historians it is recorded and will not be forgotten.

I *Property*

According to Barbier, the early eighteenth-century diarist, a third of the whole territory of France was in ecclesiastical hands.[4] A cynical and irreverent *avocat*, he delighted in anticlerical exaggeration. When, at the beginning of the Revolution, it was a question of proposing the sale of the sacred acres to pay off the State debt, estimates of the assets to go to auction varied from 60 to 170 million. Talleyrand who, as a bishop, a former *agent général* of the clergy, a financial expert, and the deviser of the great spoliation, was likely to be well informed, spoke of 80 million. Lavoisier, both a scientist and one of the financiers collecting the taxes, thought 70.[5] In 1750, the reforming minister Machault, designing to subject the Church to ordinary taxation, had done sums coming to a higher total than even the most reckless estimates of 1790. He had probably been relying on documents in the royal archives which are now lost, the records of the *Économat*, the department in charge of the collection of the revenues of abbeys of royal foundation and bishoprics during vacancies, for the benefit of the Crown. Starting with the value of these opulent benefices and multiplying to take cognizance of the others would account for his figure being unreasonably high.[6] In fact, the quest for a reliable global assessment was hopeless. Agriculturally based revenues were subject to steep fluctuation; good or bad weather, good or bad management, could make all the difference. Few incomings were clear profit—there were always repairs to be done, pensions to be paid, obligations to be fulfilled. The estates of the Church were leased and sublet in various fashions according to the changing policies of institutions and the coming and going of personalities, while the true value of leases was obscured by the custom of giving unrecorded gratifications to proprietors at each renewal. And whatever government has ruled, Frenchmen have never willingly entrusted details of income and possessions to its agents. One can take it as a rule that the almanacs of the eighteenth century understate the revenues of bishoprics by at least 50 per cent. Efforts within the Church to get correct figures— for the diocesan list of benefices, the *pouillé*, for example—had only limited success, for clerical taxation in detail was as repugnant to the individual benefice holder as government exactions were to the Church in general.

Historians of our own century, with the documentation of the Revolutionary inventories, estimates, and sales available, have, with a great deal of burrowing in series Q of departmental archives, worked out the proportion of land held by the Church in particular areas. By the conflation of such studies, reasonably reliable calculations have been made applying to the whole cultivated area of France—somewhere between Henri See's 6 per cent and Georges Lefebvre's 10 per cent.[7] This average, like all averages, conceals variations—in this case, very great ones. Churchmen owned much more property in the towns than in the countryside. A third of the area of the cities of Toulouse and Rennes belonged to them, while all around Revel, near Toulouse, they had only 3.02 per cent, and in 130 rural parishes in the Rennes–Fougères–Vitré area, only 3.41 per cent.[8] Ecclesiastical property was also much more extensive in the North than in the South. In the plain of Picardy and around Laon and Cambrai, it totalled 30–40 per cent,[9] in the diocese of Arras, 19 per cent.[10] Here was tremendous wealth, obvious at first glance to the most hasty tourist; Thomas Bentley, posting from Calais to Paris in 1776, was astonished to see no châteaux or mansions of the gentry, 'but magnificent abbeys and churches everywhere, especially in Artois, which seems to be the paradise of the monks'.[11] Going south and west, the picture changed. Around Sens, the figure was 12 per cent,[12] in Touraine 10 per cent,[13] in the intendancy of Limoges 3 per cent,[14] in the *bocage* country of the West, in Quercy[15] and in the diocese of Auch, around 2 per cent.[16] Not surprisingly, the clergy of Auch fought hard to conserve every jot of tithe income. In Béarn, the clergy's share of the land was minute (0.003 per cent), chiefly consisting of gardens belonging to curés.[17]

Peasant anticlericalism might be supposed to be a collective passion which grows more bitter in proportion to the amount of ecclesiastical property in and around the parish. There would obviously be less provocation to envy in the Breton canton of Fougerai, with only one acre in each thousand belonging to priests,[18] than in Saint-André-de-la-Marche in the Angevin Vendée, where the figure was one in three, or in the little town of Montfaucon nearby, where a third of the inhabitants were paupers and two-thirds of the land belonged to the curés or to religious houses.[19] Yet, while there is truth in this broad generalization, there are distinctions to be made. The peasant assessed the quality of land with a professional eye, well aware of differences in value, and of the amount of labour that each patch would require to earn a living. Around Sens, the best arable land seemed to have fallen to the clergy and the nobles, and the clergy predominated in the ownership of forests and meadows—forests supplying the timber and firewood which were in short supply and requiring little labour, and meadows usually taken to be worth double or triple the same area under the cultivation of cereals.[20] Around Paris, where churchmen owned 14 per cent of the soil, their wealth was more manifest and more censured because some great religious institutions owned conspicuous blocs: the abbey of Saint-Denis was seigneur in seven parishes, the chapter of Sainte-Croix d'Orléans in five, Notre-Dame of Paris in three, and the Dames de Saint Cyr in fourteen. Here, there was also a sort of guilt by association, since Court nobles and magistrates of the parlement had bought up seigneuries, often with hunting rights in mind, over the years. (The prince de Condé had twelve, the prince de Conti, fourteen). Extensive clerical domains looked like part of the conspiracy of the great against the poor.[21] So it was in the Mauges area of Anjou. The wretched peasants had only 18 per cent of the land, but it was not the clergy (with 5.13 per cent) who stood in the way; the nobles had 60 per cent, and the bourgeoisie 17 per cent. Yet in 1789, the *cahiers* were virulently anticlerical, unanimously denouncing tithe and clamouring for the suppression of religious houses.[22]

As a rule, throughout the eighteenth century, the profits of landowners were rising, slowly in the first half of the century, rapidly after 1760. In Metz, there were four great abbeys of the Benedictine congregation of Saint-Vanne; we have figures for the rise in the revenues of three of them between 1766 and the beginning of 1789. Rounded off to the nearest thousand they are: a rise from 25,000 livres to 63,000 livres, from 24,000 to 65,000, and from 16,000 to 50,000.[23] Similarly, we have figures for the rise in the abbot's income in three of the four Benedictine abbeys of the congregation of Saint-Maur in the diocese of Sens between 1753 and 1789: in one it tripled, in another quadrupled, and in the third it remained stationary.[24] Studies of three great abbeys in the West (Saint-Aubin of Angers, Saint-Georges of Rennes, and Saint-Sauveur of Redon) show a slow rise from 1720 to 1760, then an explosive expansion in the reign of Louix XVI; Saint-Aubin doubled its income.[25] The lands of such well-endowed institutions often consisted of sizeable farms (some being *métairies* run by tenants on a share-crop basis), and these would be grouped into 'domains'; the abbey of Saint-Vincent at Le Mans owned fifty-five farms divided into six domains.[26] Around Tours, where such a major agricultural unit was called a 'terre' or a 'lieu', the basilica of Saint-Martin owned 'le lieu des Ligneries' in the parish of Charentilly, comprising a seigneurie with a clutter of feudal dues, seven farms, ponds, and a fulling mill; at the Revolution, the entrepreneur who leased the whole concern, one Bourreau, tried to buy it, but was outbid by a bourgeois of Tours.[27]

Property of this kind was conveniently disposed for exploitation on the large scale, and the holders—normally, abbeys, bishops, or chapters—were accustomed to negotiate leases with businessmen like Bourreau, who would sublet the land and organize the collection of the disparate revenues. Given the increasing opportunities for profit, there was no lack of takers, and this 'farming' of Church property (as of the tithe) was one of the surest ways for an enterprising monied family to move up into the higher reaches of finance and towards the purchase of noble status.

No doubt this was the most effective method for ecclesiastical institutions to improve their income, but ordinary folk regarded the monopoly of the capitalist *fermier* as a social evil:[28] arable land was turned into pasture, buildings were demolished, subtenants squeezed, local traditions broken, and local charitable obligations ignored. About a third of the peasants had not enough land of their own to live on; they had less than the standard five hectares regarded as the minimum plot to grow enough grain to feed a family. Many others had not a great deal more. These folk survived by day-labouring, practising part-time trades, grazing an animal on the common, following the harvesting round to get temporary reaping jobs, by vagabondage and outright begging; it was 'an economy of make-shifts'.[29] Ideally, their best resource was to find a complaisant landowner who was willing to lease out a small plot for a not too severe rent. And often enough, there was fragmented property of this kind available, belonging to chapters, parish priests, and parish vestries rather than to monasteries—odd fields, houses, gardens, and orchards which had been given by pious donors to pay for masses, to support a chapel, a confraternity, or some religious observance. In the district around Caudebec, where ecclesiastical property constituted only slightly over 5 per cent of the total cultivated land, its patchwork nature can be inferred from the fact that there was at least one item to reckon in no fewer than 132 out of 136 parishes.[30] In the Sarthe, we find a curé who has twenty-four separate plots, and another with no fewer than fifty.[31] Not all were suitable for leasehold, of course. Putting a tenant into a vineyard could be bad business, since he might let the vines run on to become woody, realizing quick profits but ruining long-term prospects.[32] Curés tended to use their local knowledge to cultivate their land with hired labour; on the other hand, vestries (*fabriques*) preferred to auction the leases to the highest bidder, which saved the churchwardens trouble and pleased the villagers. All in all, when there were small plots, there was a likelihood that some would be available for letting, and this is what the rural folk wanted. It was not so much the amount of property held by ecclesiastics, as the use they made of it, which determined peasant attitudes. Prelates and abbeys leasing out their estates in large units to capitalist contractors were hated, and even curés were frowned on if they insisted on tilling the odd field belonging to their benefices.[33] A parish containing lots of corners of land leased out at old traditional rents was one which agricultural reformers and the big entrepreneurs would condemn as backward and unproductive but for the mass of peasants it was ideal. Where approximations to this ideal existed, the sale of church lands at the Revolution swept them away.

It was a maxim in rural society that churchmen ought to lease their property to the laity. 'It is scandalous, and against both civil and canon law', says a *cahier* in 1789, 'that a priest, a curé should become a merchant. Let them be compelled to lease out their possessions, except those necessary to and dependent upon their dwellings.'[34] 'Let the clergy be no longer permitted to administer their property,' says another; 'this is incompatible with their ministry. In future, let their leases be put up to auction under the supervision of the nearest royal magistrate, and let these auctions be public. The people of the commonality, in taking over these leases, will find in them resources to enable them to bring up their families.'[35] The lust for leasehold was universal. The poor could not feed themselves without more land, and the richer sort saw handsome profits to be made from the bigger units. When Church property was sold under the Revolution, the successful bids at the auctions were normally well in excess of the official estimated prices, which had been calculated on the value of the leases.[36] One might conclude that most churchmen could probably have extracted more from their tenants if they had insisted on the strict market price and kept it up to date. In Artois, Picardy, and around Laon, and no doubt in some other places, the leases of ecclesiastical property had become virtually hereditary possessions within certain families; whether by customary deference or because of intimidation, rivals did not come forward to compete at renewal time.[37] When a tenant got into difficulties as a result of a natural disaster, or even from miscalculation, ecclesiastical institutions were more likely to be generous than secular landlords. Such had been the old days in Lorraine, said a report of 1790 looking back nostalgically:

The canons of Nancy had kept the ancient usage of according reductions and compensations to their leaseholders. Often enough, under these canons of former times, tenants who, by the terms of their leases were formally excluded from such remissions, nevertheless asked for them and got them as before. These reductions often saved them from ruin. That is one of the reasons why cultivators prefer to manage the lands of the clergy rather than those of the proprietors; among those who go bankrupt you rarely find one of the tenants of the clergy.[38]

When deploring the failure of eighteenth-century churchmen to devote more of their wealth to charity, we too easily overlook the hidden, almost involuntary contributions which an easygoing and decent tradition imposed on them.

The property of a benefice was vulnerable to depredation: an unscrupulous cleric might neglect repairs or anticipate revenues. There were, therefore, legal safeguards to protect future holders against present ones. Thus priority was given to repairs as against the claims of ordinary creditors—a precaution much to the disadvantage of tradesmen, money-lenders, and other laymen who had been too trusting. When that dubious prelate, Jacques de Grasse, bishop of Angers, died, the new bishop, Mgr Couet du Vivier de Lorry, was left with 100,000 livres worth of repairs to do and only half that amount available from the sale of the furniture of his predecessor. This was bad news for the baker, who had not been paid for years, and the good lady who owned the butcher's shop near the palace. That 'petit livre particulier que la demlle Coudray tenait exprès pour M. De Grasse' showed 1,891 livres, 10 sous, and 9 deniers owing; one fears she got none of it.[39] Another safeguard against depredation was that leases granted by benefice holders were automatically annulled on the death or resignation of the titular. Economic thinkers condemned this rule as a hindrance to efficient agriculture, since farmers on a precarious tenure are unlikely to embark on major improvements. Talleyrand, making a show as a man of progress, did not fail to elaborate the point in his speech of 10 October 1789, proposing the sale of the property of his Order.[40] In their *cahiers* the peasants took a more personal view of the disadvantage, and alleged sharp practice. In the *bailliage* of Amiens, eighty families had been evicted because the holders of two abbeys happened to resign simultaneously.[41] The inhabitants of Givry-sur-Aisne (near Reims) claimed to have seen many examples of a tenant losing his lease just as he was about to reap his first crop.[42] In fact, it was not easy to turn out a tenant: such ruthlessness would meet with *mauvais gré*—wilful damage, concerted local hostility.[43] Provided there were funds available to meet the extra costs of renewing the lease, eviction was hardly likely. But these costs were considerable because of the way the leasehold system operated. It was customary to draw up an agreement for a term of nine years or so, adding little or nothing to the annual rent which was specified, as this would attract a heavier State registration tax, but exacting a substantial lump sum as a sort of signing fee, the so-called *pot de vin*. This was a single, non-returnable payment. Thus, if a benefice fell vacant before the term prescribed in its lease, the tenant had paid excessively for a short tenure, while the departing benefice holder (or if he had died, his heirs) would be rejoicing in bearing off a comfortable, disproportionately large lump sum. So the strategic time to migrate from one benefice to another was shortly after the renewal of the leases. When this happened, there would be dark suspicions locally that the move at this particular moment was not an accident. The titular abbot of Saint-Jean at Amiens offered the tenants of his six large farms advantageous leases for the term of their individual lives—on condition of a substantial signing fee, of course. It was 'perfidious generosity' said the *cahier* of La Chaussée de Picquigny. 'Never was a proposal more enthusiastically accepted. Immediately, leases changed hands for the consideration of a *pot de vin*. What then did M. de Crillon (the abbot) do? In that very same year he resigned his abbey into the hands of the king to obtain a richer one'—and the tenants had to fork out all over again to conclude leases with his successor. This was a notable case of injustice, and M. de Crillon's victims went to law, with what result we know not.[44] It was not entirely impossible for an enlightened benefice holder to contrive a longer lease which was not cancelled, but the procedures were difficult, and examples are rare.[45] The broad picture over rural France is one of peasants, rich and poor, yearning to get hold of Church lands on leasehold, yet anxious not to pay the full economic rent, and complaining bitterly when the gamble over the initial outlay on signing a lease turned out unluckily for them.

Tocqueville approved of a land-owning clergy.[46] The possession of agricultural property would prevent them from becoming otherworldly, and would keep them in practical daily contact with their people; the Church, a popular institution, would be able to stand for liberty against tyrants and bureaucrats. One may argue about whether the political results he anticipated followed; but it is true that the clergy of eighteenth-century France came quite near to his specifications. Some curés had a good deal of land attached to their benefices. Of 352 parishes in the Sarthe, in only 15 was the parish priest limited to a simple garden, and in only 60 more did he have less than the five hectares which could feed a family. In 165 he had between 10 and 29 hectares, and in 37 between 30 and 50, while one had quite an estate, 200 hectares. About half the total also had a vine-yard, and there were some who held additional benefices whose revenue came from agricultural property nearby.[47] But even those curés who had no land to till or to lease were still tied up with the success or failure of the harvest if they drew all or a portion of the tithe. Thus France was full of priests who were knowledgeable about agriculture, in touch with their parishioners and the life of the countryside, looking at the weather, the progress of the crops, the health of the cattle, and the state of the market with the expert and apprehensive eye of the peasants. In his *Essai d'éducation nationale* in 1763 La Cholotais listed the secular expertise he required of a curé; he must know something of medicine and law, and above all must be well informed on methods of improving cultivation and on the art of surveying. When, in the second half of the century, the vogue for theorizing about agricultural improvements swept the country, and agricultural societies were founded, the clergy were prominent in their membership. Chief of them was the abbé François Rozier, who published a solid textbook on botany for the Royal Veterinary School in 1766, and won the first prize of the Royal Agricultural Society of Limoges in 1770 and that of the Society of Lyon in 1787. After publishing on 'the fermentation of wine and the best way to make eau-de-vie', on the cultivation of hemp and of rape (and how to 'extract an oil with the bad taste and disagreeable odour refined out of it'), from 1781 he began publishing a vast *Cours complet d'agriculture théorique, pratique, économique et de médecine rurale et vétérinaire* which had reached volume 8 by 1789.[48] At the invitation of the Royal Bureau of Agriculture of Le Mans, in 1769, Froger, a local curé, published his *Instructions d'agriculture et d'économie, pour les habitans de la campagne*. It was a moralizing book to encourage country people to read, and to convert them to the ethic of work, including useful tips like: in bad weather, don't be idle, clean out the stables and repair the hedges.[49] Humble curés tried their hand at essays for prize competitions, like the incumbent of a parish near Vienne who, early in 1789, submitted to the Agricultural Society of Paris his reflections on the introduction of potatoes. Baked in the oven with milk, salt and pepper, he said, they were 'mana' last winter, and they fattened the pigs 'd'une manière prodigieuse'.[50] No prize for these anecdotes; the Society preferred scientific analyses like those of the abbé de Commerell who, from just across the Alsace border, sent in his *mémoire* on the wastefulness of leaving land fallow, and was already well known for his brochure 'on the cultivation, use and advantages' of mangel wurzels as a last resort in times of crop failure—printed and reprinted by the government.[51] Many a monastery, and, even, parish priest, gained fame as improvers of vintages. The best vineyards around Beaune belonged to the monks of Citeaux,[52] and the best ones near Barr to the Antonists (producing the famous wine, the story ran, which Cardinal de Lorraine had dispensed to the Fathers of the Council of Trent to persuade them to vote on his side).[53] The authoritative guide to the wine-growing areas around Bordeaux was published by a cleric, the abbé Baurein, in 1784–6.[54] The curé of Cantenac (Médoc) sold 25,000 livres worth of wine annually in mid-century,[55] and the Benedictine monks of the abbey of Sainte-Croix exported their product to the abstemious Sons of the Prophet in the Levant in bottles labelled 'Eau minérale de Sainte-Croix'.[56]

Some of the great abbeys and bishoprics progressed from the ownership of extensive woods to becoming proprietors of iron-smelting furnaces: the bishops of Châlons, Évreux, Langres, Saint-Pol-de-Léon (the latter in a company with six nobles as associates), the chapter of the cathedral of Besançon, the abbeys of Clairvaux, Chalôns, and so on.[57] This natural progression from timber merchant to iron master is illustrated in the adventures of the Benedictines of Liessies in Hainault. The owners of smelting furnaces there were in a ring to keep down the price of fuel, so the monks refused to sell wood to them and set up their own ironworks. A great lawsuit ensued. Dom Gérard, who detested being away from home, lived miserably in Paris to prosecute it, doling out cheeses and snuff-boxes (and once the carcase of a whole wild boar) as bribes, and flourishing a statement signed by his abbot offering 2,000 écus to the lawyer who could win the case. The case was indeed won, and the monks kept their furnace, but Dom Gérard died in the capital away from his comfortable cell.[58] The clergy were as interested as the laity in schemes to enhance their profits. From 1719 the Discalced Carmelites of the rue de Vaugirard in Paris were exploiting their urban site by building five mansions for letting; in 1728 the Comte de Rottembourg took one, followed in his tenure by the Sicilian ambassador and by the princess de Croÿ, who entered on a nine-year lease at 7,000 livres a year.[59] A more picturesque venture into commercial enterprise is recorded by a traveller in the South. The abbey of Sylvanes had a thermal spring on its territory; when a medical report in 1772 praised the water as beneficial for those in ailing health or of a melancholy temperament the monks borrowed money to construct two pools and twenty guest-rooms, with further additions in 1786. A constant procession of well-off invalids came to stay, sent by the prestigious Medical Faculty of Montpellier.[60] To understand the clergy of eighteenth-century France and their place in society, we must remember, for better and for worse, their zestful entanglement in agricultural, commercial, and financial activities. Sometimes, these involvements could discredit their spiritual mission and their local standing. Not everyone approved of the curé of Franche Comté who 'appears at fairs among the pigs like a dealer'; much worse was the one who loaned money to the peasants at an interest of 30 per cent a month and had labourers working in his fields on Sundays and saints' days.[61] Property owning at once identified the clergy with lay society and alienated them from it. The occasional curé who was censured in the *cahier* of his parishioners, or the abbey more frequently denounced, had not usually been guilty of notable meanness or oppression. They had, however, transgressed some psychological boundary, and had done what was legal for everyone rather than what was considered fitting for ecclesiastics. Churchmen who were proprietors had special obligations, mostly of an informal and unenforceable kind, concerning fair rents, traditional procedures, debts, arrears, litigation, almsgiving. And, as we have seen, the greatest of all these half-understood obligations, so far as the mass of ordinary folk in the countryside was concerned, was that of making land available to the laity for leasehold on reasonable terms and in small lots.

So far we have considered the ownership of land in eighteenth-century France as if it was absolute property in our modern sense, even though the patterns of landholding were fantastically complicated. In fact, however, most property was in some way subject to feudal obligations, and part of the vast inheritance of the Gallican Church was its feudal dues from lands it did not own, but were within its fiefs and seigneuries. This sort of proprietary right did not come within Tocqueville's definition of an ownership which improves social relationships; on the contrary, he considered the survival of feudal obligations as destructive of respect between those who levied them and those who paid them. They had arisen as tributes to powerful lords in return for protection; now the king's writ ran in all the land, their justification was ended. As a simplified model of how feudalism still operated in the age of the Enlightenment we may imagine a village which has a nobleman (or a prelate or an abbey) as its seigneur. The lord of the manor's lawyers will attend to hold 'assizes', and though the Crown had taken away most of the powers of feudal justice, the villagers could be fined small sums and ordered to do various chores (like sweeping their chim-neys, ringing the church bells in thunderstorms, or appointing a communal herdsman). The seigneur would announce in his court the date fixed for harvesting or grape gathering (starting earlier him-self to get in first for hiring labour), and his legal assessors could impose their will in disputes concerning his rights (the inhabitants having a routine, but expensive, resort of appeal to royal courts). The lord's agents would collect various dues, like the *cens*, or quit rent, generally small but important as proof of feudal dependence, or tributes in kind such as chickens or eggs, and sometimes, though rarely, an onerous levy on crops at harvest time (*champart*). The lord might enjoy exclusive hunting or fishing rights, or the right to keep pigeons protected by law from the guns of the folk whose crops they raided; he might have the monopoly of the stud bull, the mill, or the communal oven (*banalités*); he might levy a toll on a bridge or side-road. Of course, nothing was ever quite as simple as this under the *ancien régime*. There might be a seigneur haut justicier over the seigneur with peculiar rights (for example, to saw down and sell roadside trees in the area of his jurisdiction). Several seigneurs might rule in a single village, or several villages be compounded in a single seigneurie: there would be enclaves and detached fragments; there would be odd local dues peculiar to one area (consider some curious items in the mass of feudal incidents owed to the bishop of Lodève: a *droit de pulvérage* on flocks in transit, a fine paid by those who pierced doors or windows in the old city walls, a *droit de coupe* on strangers who brought grain into the city to sell—this latter exaction bought off by the city for 600 livres a year).[62] Furthermore, urban fiefs and overlordship differed in various respects from rural ones, more especially because their chief revenue was usually derived from *lods et ventes*, a stiff tax on every house sale.

In all this archaic structure of vexatious jurisdictions and dues, the Church was inextricably involved. An ecclesiastic whose revenues came from straightforward landowning was lucky; some were dependent on the feudal incidents which everyone hated. The bishop of Quimper (until an abbey was united to his see in 1782 to boost the revenues) had only about 4,000 livres a year from his estates; he had twice as much from tithe (unpopular always) and about 21,000 from secular jurisdictions and feudal dues (even more unpopular).[63] In the seventeenth century, two-thirds of the immense revenues of the see of Paris were derived from *lods et ventes* on the houses of 500 streets of the capital; in 1674 the archbishop gave up most of his manifold feudal jurisdictions for a limited compensation—a financial loss, but a great improvement in public relations.[64] A study of ten abbeys in Normandy shows that only a third of their total revenues came from agricultural property; two-thirds came from feudal dues and tithe[65]—how could these monks ever hope to be popular in the countryside? Certain cities seemed to be locked within a strait-jacket by the feudal jurisdictions of ecclesiastics. Reims was one of them.[66] The archbishop's *ban* covered the *cité*, the old Gallo-Roman centre, and the cathedral chapter ruled in the cloisters and in two 'cantons' within the episcopal segment and in two outside it; the abbeys of Saint-Rémy and Saint-Nicaise and the *hôtel-Dieu* all had their seigneurial courts, while an official of the cathedral, the *vidame*, had a peculiar jurisdiction over the saddlers, glass-blowers, coopers, and tinkers wherever they dwelt. The archiepiscopal tribunal, meeting twice weekly, had no fewer than twenty-three officials, though truth to tell, they were all part-time and doubled up in other seigneurial courts wearing different hats. By contrast, in the town of Angers,[67] it was the cathedral chapter, rather than the bishop, which enjoyed the splendour of feudal superiority. The cité was its fief. Here, the canons of Saint-Maurice levied the *cens* on all householders, and from time to time imposed disciplinary regulations on them, such as ordering them to have the street swept in front of their own doorstep. Tradesmen had to apply to the chapter for permission to put up their signs, and the property of persons who died without direct heirs fell to the cathedral by escheat. As a reciprocal obligation, the chapter had to pay for improvements like street lighting, and had to rear children who were abandoned within the fief. This feudal jurisdiction was reinforced (which was unusual) by a spiritual one, since the cathedral enjoyed episcopal powers in the enclave around its walls; it held synods to which it summoned its dependent curés, and its ecclesiastical court issued dispensations, as for marrying within the lower reaches of the prohibited degrees or for eating meat in Lent. There were fifteen other seigneurial courts in Angers, all dependent upon ecclesiastical jurisdictions.[68] The chief were the penurious chapters of Saint-Maurille and Saint-Martin, which levied *lods et ventes* at a fifteenth of the selling price of houses, a fluctuating revenue averaging out at about 3,000 livres a year for Saint-Martin and a third of this for Saint-Maurille. The canons, aware how bitterly this tax was hated, tried to ingratiate themselves with their victims by granting remissions of 25 per cent. This was all very well for Saint-Maurille, enjoying rents on twenty houses built on the site of its old cemetery; being poorer, the canons of Saint-Martin in 1783 called a halt to this customary rebate. 'The charges they are at in respect of their fiefs are many in number, and are constantly augmenting.' This was true. As many as twenty children might be abandoned to their care annually (most would die, of course, but the cost of signing on an adoptive parent was about 100 livres), while the expenses of administering justice were not negligible. It was unfortunate to be levying unpopular and unjustifiable dues and yet be able to enjoy barely half the yield.

As, towards the end of the *ancien régime*, feudal dues appeared more obviously unreasonable and were more widely decried, the value of those that had not been fixed as a precise sum of money became much greater. It has been estimated that the yield of *lods et ventes* doubled between 1760 and 1790.[69] Dues in kind, reckoned as a proportion of the crop, albeit at a small fraction, became well worth having. Since the late seventeenth century, antiquarian studies had been flourishing; now, delving in the archives became an occasion of profit. Technical handbooks were published on the art of checking on the past history and present legality of feudal incidents, and *feudistes* arose, professional researchers who were paid by results. One such was appointed by the chapter of Sainte-Radegonde of Poitiers in 1785: a *feudiste-géographe*, to be paid 2,000 livres a year for six years, and half of all sums he recovered.[70] In other places, ecclesiastics themselves reorganized their charters, and, as Richeprey observed, he had yet to come across a feudal investigator who published any discoveries which would benefit the peasants who had to pay.[71] Fortified by technical expertise, seigneurs began to make more use of their right to 'renew' the *terriers*, the documents showing the boundaries of properties and the nature of the obligations attached to them. The peasants hated having to find their share of the expense of these renewals, and they feared the 'declarations' which they had to make: if they overstated their extent, they would be fined; if they understated it, they might be taken at their word. In 1781 both the archbishop of Cambrai and his metropolitan chapter took out letters patent for the renewal of *terriers* on their lands, causing anger and unrest among the rural population of the diocese.[72] Three years later, the archbishop of Embrun initiated a series of lawsuits before the parlement of Grenoble in an attempt to establish his right to *lods et ventes* on certain allodial lands which had remained outside the feudal nexus.[73] Travelling in the South in 1780, Richeprey described the *corvées* (labour dues) of four days a year 'enforced with extreme rigour' by the abbey of Aubrac, and how, when the vassals were unable to pay a peculiar rent reckoned in salt and apples, the monks would demand an unreasonable sum in its place. At Trémouille, his inn was besieged by angry peasants led by a man with an axe—they thought he had come to demand arrears of the *commun de paix*, a twelfth-century tax originally paid to repair the damage done by wandering mercenaries and now providing some financial solace to the bishop of Rodez and other great personages.[74] There would have been riots at Reims in 1770 in any case, but a contributory factor was the archbishop's *droit de stellage*, an impost on all grain brought into the city for sale. The contractor who levied this tax on the bread of the people was entitled to ban all marketing of grain within four leagues of the city walls and to imprison those suspected of breaking the regulations. The prelate got 14,000 livres a year from his *droit de stellage*, and at least 14,000 livres worth of unpopularity with it.[75] There was deep-seated economic malaise behind the riots at Lyon in 1786, but one of the superficial causes which provoked the mob was the archbishop's attempt to collect the arrears on his *droit de banvin*, an impost on wine sales, which drove the owners of bars and taverns to put up their shutters.[76] When a riot is inevitable, both drink and lack of it are dangerous.

Ecclesiastical institutions, organized to survive in perpetuity, furnished with rich archives with literate custodians, and never forgetting a precedent, were regarded as permanent menaces to the ordinary carefree citizen. When in Angers in the 1770s the canons of Saint-Martin and of Saint-Maurille and the monks of Saint-Nicolas were all engaged in lawsuits over escheats, the opposition lawyers made the point: 'Your courts will resound with disputes of this kind, always burdensome to citizens of limited means, though the chapters of Angers, opulent feudal lords, count outlay on a lawsuit a mere nothing if it can bring them some pickings from their fiefs.'[77] Citizens of limited means, indeed, did well to count the cost before they challenged some ecclesiastical institution. The village community of Donchery challenged the prior of the local monastery (who was also the bishop of Nancy) over his feudal control of the village oven and lost, at a cost of 1,440 livres, 14 sous, 8 deniers. This episcopal prior was a difficult man—witness the affair of the bridge which the floods had swept away. As seigneur, he was supposed to 'repair' it, but he refused to do anything, as 'repair' did not mean 'replace'. The *cahier* of Donchery is full of complaints against this 'usurper', who 'relies on the right of the strongest'.[78] And even if a case was won, a village might impoverish itself in the process. When the villagers of Saint-Maurice-aux-Riches-Hommes won a lawsuit against their seigneur, the bishop of Châlons, with damages of 2,000 livres, they found that they owed their parish priest 3,500 livres for expenses for the thousand days he had spent away from home prosecuting the case. It was a sum almost as large as the community's annual payment in direct taxation.[79]

Anticlerical propagandists were glad to remind their readers how churchmen profited from feudal payments given to them in return for non-existent services which would have been incompatible with their pious vocation anyway. Historical excursuses, Velly's *Histoire de France* and Renauldon's *Traité historique et pratique des droits seigneuriaux*, traced the incongruous alliance of Christianity and feudalism to the superstition of the laity and the worldliness of priests. There was scope for irony in listing the more ridiculous feudal obligations, like the mythical *droit du seigneur*, supposedly arrogated at the time of the crusades, that epoch of misguided religious zeal and cynical designs of plunder.[80] But there was one actual and scandalous feudal survival which anticlerics relished above all: that was 'serfdom'. In fact, it was not personal servitude, but a mode of servile tenure chiefly concerned with inheritance, though none the less hated for that. In Brittany, on the lands of the abbeys of Rellec and Bégard, and in one or two other ecclesiastical jurisdictions in the diocese of Tréguier, it took the form of *quevaise*.[81] The tenant, the *quevaisier*, paid a heavy *champart* of one sheaf in seven. When he died, the youngest son inherited, followed by the other sons, then by the youngest daughter, provided they were resident on the property. If there was no direct heir actually present, everything fell to the seigneur. If the *quevaisier* sold out to escape from his onerous tenure, the lord collected a quarter of the selling price; if he ceased to cultivate the land, the lord could confiscate it after a year and a day. Though the abbey of Rellec had given up most of its *champart* (after a revolt in 1727, when the house was burned down) and had begun to relax the terms of escheat, allowing inheritances to go to collateral heirs, there was continued friction and ill will. In 1774, the monks had sixteen lawsuits against their *quevaisiers* pending before the parlement of Rennes, with others on the way up through their own feudal court.

As it happened, this survival of a servile tenure in Brittany remained a curiosity of the law-books; the great exposures of 'serfdom' came in revelations about the injustices suffered by the peasants on the lands of two abbeys in the Jura Mountains—the Benedictine houses of Luxeuil[82] and Saint-Claude. (The latter was secularized in 1742 to form a chapter of exclusively noble canons; but the monks stayed on for the term of their lives, forming a joint institution.) The vassals of these two great foundations held their land subject to 'mainmorte'. They needed the consent of their seigneur to marry outside the fief, and could bequeath their property only to direct heirs actually living at home with them. To shake off these obligations, a man had to make a *désaveu*, a formal surrender of all his possessions. There were approximations to this sort of servile tenure in Franche Comté, Bourgogne, the Auvergne, and the Nivernais.[83] From this latter province, in 1756, there arose an outrageous lawsuit to set all Paris talking: a citizen of the capital died, and an obscure nobleman from the country round Nevers came forward to claim his not-inconsiderable inheritance on the ground that the dead man's father had been one of his tenants long ago. The magistrates of the Châtelet threw out the claim amidst the applause of bourgeois opinion.[84] In 1770, Voltaire was called in to champion the 'serfs' of Saint-Claude, and he joined forces with their lawyer, M. Christin, who was pleading a suit on their behalf before the parlement of Besançon. Two years later, Christin published an account of his investigations into the documentation put forward by the abbey: the title, *Dissertation sur l'abbaye de Saint-Claude, ses chroniques, ses légendes, ses chartes, ses usurpations, et sur les droits des habitants de cette terre*, is self-explanatory. It was one of those revelations of the pious forgeries of distant 'gothic' times which so delighted the erudite wits of the Enlightenment. For his contribution, Voltaire published *La Voix du curé*.[85] A priest is installed in his new parish on the feast of St Louis, 1772, and is astonished when his wretched parishioners complain to him that they are serfs to the abbey of Saint-Claude. 'Est-ce qu'il y a des esclaves en France?' asks the man of God. How can this be? St Louis crusaded to deliver Christians from slavery, and the Pères de La Merci risk their lives daily on the Barbary coast to ransom them. Well, they had better send these good Fathers to ransom us, says the village patriarch. The curé then recounts the findings of his enquiry into this ancient abuse. The name *mainmorte* given to this tenure arose, he assures us, because in the Middle Ages, seigneurs expected to confiscate the chattels of their dead vassals, and if there was nothing to take, they showed their displeasure by cutting off a hand from the corpse as a trophy. If an unsuspecting outsider settled within the jurisdiction of Saint-Claude for a year and a day, for ever after his inheritance would be in danger from the monks, even if he migrated far away, for the abbey enjoyed the 'right of pursuit' against its vassals. A woman told him how the abbey had tried to deprive her of a legacy because she had broken the feudal rule and slept the first night after her marriage in the house of her husband, not of her father; evidence of the fact had been obtained by threats of excommunication against recalcitrant witnesses. The good curé has a vision of Christ upbraiding the cellarer of the monastery for his oppression. 'You were the suffering Church,' says the cellarer; 'we are the Church triumphant . . . We gave them the hope of heaven, so we took their land from them.' To protest, the curé calls on one of the canons of Saint-Claude and gets a friendly reception, for the newly created canons 'had not contracted that hardness of heart, that greed, that secret hatred of the human race' which the monastic way of life engenders. Two local lawyers and a nobleman who own seigneuries containing serfs have just volunteered to renounce their rights, and the canons would have wished to do the same. But they were outvoted by the surviving monks, who refused to abandon their archaic privileges.

Four years later, Voltaire returned to the attack, this time drawing up a petition on behalf of the serfs of the Bernardine monks of Chézery. As a result of the frontier changes of 1760, they had been transferred from Savoy and incorporated into France, thus just missing being enfranchised by the king of Sardinia's edict abolishing serfdom two years later.[86] This foreign example and the march of enlightened ideas prevailed at Versailles, and in 1779 Necker abolished the *droit de poursuite*. On Crown lands, where he was completely free to take action, he ended the tenure by *mainmorte* altogether. A few seigneurs followed suit, including the penurious missionary priests of Beaupré, but not the two great abbeys. Clermont-Tonnerre, abbot of Luxeuil, proclaimed liberal sentiments. For the thirty years he had held his office, he said in 1775, he had seen how his tenants were 'dull, indolent, discouraged, downtrodden, their fields neglected . . . while the inhabitants of free villages, their neighbours, are busy and hard-working'.[87] Even so, fourteen years later he had still got no further than approaching three of his twenty-two villages with proposals for change. In fact, the enthusiasm at Luxeuil and Saint-Claude for reform was conditional upon substantial compensation being offered, and this had not been forthcoming. By 1789, the outcry against *mainmorte* was general. In their *cahier*, the peasants of Saint-Claude still remembered the woman who had slept at her husband's the first night.[88] 'The possessors of fiefs, most of them ecclesiastics,' the *cahier* of the Jura area began, 'obstinately insist, despite your (Majesty's) paternal invitation, to keep in the chains of servitude more than a million Frenchmen'.[89] A curé of Franche Comté, Clerget, published a powerful 'Cry of reason' against serfdom: *Cri de la Raison ou examen approfondi des lois et des coutumes qui tiennent dans la servitude mainmortable 1,500,000 sujets du Roi.* If these figures of a million to a million-and-a-half serfs are near the truth, there must have been quite a number of seigneuries held by laymen or minor ecclesiastics in which the 'cry of reason' and the 'paternal invitation' of the monarch had been ignored. But the abbeys of Luxeuil and Saint-Claude were so rich that it was not unreasonable that they should bear the brunt of public reprobation. In the rural rioting of July 1789, the peasants of Luxeuil paid off old scores: the books from the library (did they include the 'chronicles, legends and charters' Christin had denounced?) were burned, and the contents of the cellars drunk by the angry *mainmortables*.[90]

In eighteenth-century France, the question of the theoretical justification of property was much discussed from *L'Esprit des Lois* onwards.[91] There were two views. Its origin may be seen as 'natural'—the physiocrats embraced this opinion, and the revolutionary Declaration of Rights was to consecrate it; or its origin may be seen as 'social'—this supposition is found in Montesquieu, Voltaire, and Rousseau. In the debates of the Revolution, Camus and Mirabeau drew the inference from the 'social' theory that property could be taken over by the nation in urgent cases. Other orators, not denying this proposition so far as corporate bodies are concerned, rejected its severities as regards individuals. On the whole, the legislation of the Revolution (as distinct from the practice of a war for survival) did not interfere with the proprietary rights of individuals, except to forbid long leases (protecting the owner against himself) and by putting mining rights at the disposition of the nation, instead of in the power of the owner of the surface. The theory of 'social' creation was reserved for application to the estates of the Gallican Church, auctioned to pay the nation's debts. But the way towards this great expropriation had been prepared by the long-standing policy of the French monarchy, pragmatic and authoritarian, and little concerned with social theory. According to the lawyers,[92] the clergy were *usufruitiers* of their property, not absolute owners, and Church lands were a special case, peculiarly subject to royal oversight and control. One aspect of this control concerned the protection of the Church, and of all the pious families who had contributed to its endowments, against the carelessness or rapacity of the present holders of benefices. This was done partly by the granting of privileges—the cancellation of leases on a change of titular, and repairs being a privileged debt—and partly by restriction, since ecclesiastical property could not be alienated without the king's agreement. There had to be an enquiry *de commodo et incommodo*, and if sale was recommended, the decision had to be authorized by the local judges of the Crown or, for great benefices, by letters patent registered in the relevant parlement.[93] In this fashion, the archbishop of Aix got permission to sell half of a huge fief in 1782, and about the same time, the bishop of Nevers, as abbot of Saint-Cyran, was allowed to grant permanent leases of four *métairies* belonging to his abbey; these concessions were made because the properties concerned were difficult to manage.[94] An ecclesiastic could not cut the woods of his benefice without letters patent duly registered, and inspectors of the Eaux et Forêts made visitations every fifteen years to check that no illegal timber felling had taken place.[95]

These official procedures of enquiry, letters patent, and magisterial verification were also obligatory for churchmen who wished to acquire new property. In addition, there was a *droit d'amortissement* levied on any extension or improvement made to existing possessions; repairs, the signing of a new lease, the changing of a building to a different use—almost any sort of amelioration was regarded as taxable.[96] It was a question here, not of protecting the Church, but of protecting the State and the laity against its aggrandizement. This restrictive code was fortified by the royal edict of August 1749,[97] which was the culmination of the process of tightening up the laws of mortmain. (The word had two meanings in France: the notorious servile tenure in the Jura and the more general meaning, found also in England, of legislation to relax the grip of the 'dead hand' of the Church.) The bishops were indignant at the edict of 1749. 'It seems', said the bishop of Angers, 'that churchmen are foreigners, and not the children and relatives of the King's subjects, and as if their income is not spent in the Kingdom, or used to help the other subjects of the King and the poor, and all of us who are subject to mortmain are depicted as men who have no other aim than getting hold of the property of the laity.'[98] D'Argenson was one of the few laymen who sympathized with episcopal complaints. 'It's always said the Church is too rich, but I don't see who this harms.'[99] The general view was that an enduring corporation which already had vast possessions, would expand continually unless limitations were maintained. This being so, permission to acquire new property was hardly ever granted; indeed, if churchmen applied for ordinary compensation for encroachments by the Crown, the Royal Council was reluctant to grant it.[100]

From regulation and restriction for reasons of social utility, it was a short step to ideas of a limited confiscation in cases of necessity.

Had ecclesiastical property been evenly distributed over the country, the claustrophobic sense of monopoly in certain areas would not have been so pervasive; had the patterns of landowning been less complex, occasions for conflict would have been fewer. The number of skirmishes was in proportion to the length and illogicality of the frontiers between the possessions of the clergy and those of the laity. Anyone with an improving scheme for a road, a canal, or a public building, or wanting to round off his heritage or expand his business, would be likely to run athwart some ecclesiastical property owner. Thus, when in 1772 the marquis de Pérusse proposed a scheme for settling Acadian refugees on his moorland acres in Poitou, the government inspection party asked for 630 *arpents* of the lands of the marquis, 2,400 belonging to the bishop of Poitiers, and 980 belonging to the abbey of Fontevrault.[101] Similarly, when space was cleared to show off the colonnade of the Louvre in 1756, and a site for new stables for the Poste aux chevaux (the mounted courier's department of the postal service) had to be found, almost inevitably, it was acquired from a monastery.[102]

This is what one would expect in Paris, a crowded city of half a million inhabitants in which there were thirteen great abbeys and two hundred other religious houses. Such was the multitude of ecclesiastical buildings, monastic and others, that in August 1792, the commissioners charged with the task of removing the ornaments and symbols of the *ancien régime* despaired of finding them all, and called for local assistance: 'comme il y a trop grand nombre d'églises à Paris, il faut que les Sections viennent à notre secours'.[103] What was true of the capital was true, *mutatis mutandis*, of nearly all the towns of France, great and small. Marseille with its 88,000 population had thirty-four monastic establishments; Toulouse, rather less than half its size, had forty-six; Grenoble, Troyes, Reims, and Douai, half the size again, had twenty-six, nineteen, seventeen, and twenty-eight respectively; Aix, with 10,000 inhabitants, had six monasteries and twelve nunneries.[104] This was the sort of disproportion to catch the eye of an English traveller; passing through Coutances, Wraxall observed that the place was 'large, but the convents form a considerable part of its size, and the religious of different Orders a great part of its inhabitants'.[105] And in all these places, in addition to the enclosures of monks and nuns, there were also collegiate and parish churches, hospitals, *collèges*, and chapels. The picture is the same when we go down byways to seek out the tiny towns, hardly worthy of the name, except for a core of a few prestigious buildings. Montreuil-sur-Mer with 4,000 residents had eight religious houses.

'As is well known,' said the municipal officers in 1780, 'the town is composed largely of ecclesiastics, nobles, army officers and legal officials, and the people are few in number and poor because it is impossible to carry on any sort of commercial activity.'[106] Avallon, of the same size, agreeably and loftily situated, its ramparts looking down on vineyards and woods below, had two parishes, four religious houses, and a *collège*.[107] Pontivy in Brittany, rather smaller, could be summed up as a social entity briefly: the duc de Rohan's castle overlooking everything, thirty-two rich families, the recteur and a confraternity of six priests, the houses of the Ursulines and the Récollets, and a *collège* where the sons of decent families were educated.[108] Clermont, a miserable squalid place built on inhospitable volcanic rock, had a chapter of canons, a *collège*, a monastery, and a nunnery for its 2,000 inhabitants.[109] This was the same size as Belley, and here there were no fewer than five religious houses and, being the seat of a bishop, a cathedral too.[110]

Given the ground plan of so many towns, it was not surprising that diplomatic incidents and boundary skirmishes over the issue of Church property were frequent; indeed, these conflicts often hardened into an institutionalized feud. The eighteenth century was the great age of municipal improvements: town councils engaged in demolishing ancient ramparts and opening up promenades and straight, sweeping avenues, constructing fountains and statues, naming and numbering streets, installing street lighting, and planting trees in regimented ranks in newly created squares.[111] Zealous aldermen in search of *lebensraum*, and of the commercial profits that would accrue from institutional expansion, were thwarted at every turn by the extensive property of churchmen. We can see how the tensions developed in Angers.[112] There, religious foundations were popularly supposed to own 'three-quarters of the town'. Half-empty monasteries hired out their staterooms for meeting-places for guilds, university faculties, and professional associations; rich laymen like the Englishmen Mr Swinfort and Milord Southwell rented abbatical mansions, as local citizens rented less prestigious houses; old ladies took rooms in convents, and artisans hired sheds to store their gear. 'The Church was shrinking back inside its territory, leaving a fringe of secular leaseholders on its boundaries.' The city fathers cast envious eyes on so many splendid façades, spacious gardens, and strategic building sites. At one time it was a question of opening up a pedestrian way, at another enlarging a square, at another finding storage space for municipal property. Greater issues were: finding a meeting-hall for an agricultural society (hopeless negotiations with the abbey of Saint-Aubin), a site for a botanical garden (unsuccessful pleas to the abbey of Saint-Serge), a building for a new boarding-school (Saint-Aubin again for both buildings and teachers, and no success), a foundling hospital (could the decayed friary of Lesvière be taken for such a charitable object?), a barracks (no fewer than seven monastic houses were considered for confiscation). Let the Augustinian friars retire into a corner of their large enclosure, leaving the rest for the soldiers: 'the greater good is that which turns to the profit of society in general. No corporation or community can be allowed to go on living in a property which is useless to it, and which is rendered profitless to the State by the mere fact of their retaining it.' Or let the Benedictines of Saint-Serge move out; their Order would still retain three houses in Angers: 'when it is a question of the general interest, an opulent congregation ought to be disposed to make sacrifices'.

Eloquence of this sort about the greatest happiness of the greatest number was the house style of aldermen the world over when they complained about the possessions of the clergy. Vannes was a decayed and ancient city, whose population of 14,000 consisted of 1,000 paupers at one end of the scale and 300 nobles, 62 secular priests, and 300 monks and nuns at the other.[113] 'Ours is a little town', the municipal officers lamented in 1769, 'whose every building is on the verge of tumbling down, surrounded on every side by superb monasteries which hardly leave room for traffic to get in and out of the place. The monasteries form . . . a chain which binds tightly a constricted city of gothic construction, with few viable streets and a polluted atmosphere. We breathe contaminated air . . . the monks enjoy spacious enclosures.'[114] Dijon was another archaic town, its skyline dominated by the thirty-two bell towers of its churches and monasteries, its affairs dominated by nobles of the robe and churchmen. It produced little: no less than 13 per cent of its population were domestic servants.[115] Once again, it was the clergy who were blamed for this backwardness. In 1786, the intendant (supporting the municipality's plan to drive a road through the convent of the Jacobins) wrote: 'In this town, where rents are so high, there could hardly be a more important improvement than to put land up for sale whenever this is possible, for the dead hand of churchmen controls over two-fifths of the area.'[116]

The concentration of ecclesiastical property in so many towns promoted anticlerical feeling. Public opinion was formulated in the urban milieu: here, instinctive and envious emotions were fostered and transmuted into the sort of logical coherence that could lead to legislative action in revolutionary times. When, however, early in the Revolution, the sale of ecclesiastical property was proposed, townsfolk suddenly realized that there was something to be said for the 'dead hand' of the Church after all. The chapters and abbeys whose walls and gardens blocked the avenues of municipal improvement were also owners of vast estates in the countryside, from whence they drew in wealth to be spent in the city. Artists, goldsmiths, organ builders, bell-founders, lawyers, and estate agents profited from their commissions; respectable families competed to have their sons accepted as choirboys or to find a place in the *collège* or, when they were older, to receive ecclesiastical sinecures; daughters with only limited dowries would go into nunneries; artisans, tradesmen, provision sellers, and candlemakers rejoiced in the steady custom of ecclesiastical institutions, and ordinary folk found employment as cooks and domestic servants, as well as bell-ringers, sacristans, and beadles. Churchmen were better employers than most, sometimes finding a niche for the infirm or simple-minded, and keeping on the aged after their real usefulness was over. What would happen when the sources of all this expenditure were auctioned off to private individuals—where would the buyers live, and whom would they employ? At Angers, there was a cry for some major law court, a barracks, or some other institution of central government to be established to replace 'the losses which the town must bear by the suppression of its religious houses, which are very numerous and which spend all their revenue here'.[117] Bayeux, with 10,000 inhabitants a third of the size of Angers, was even more dependent, economically, upon the Church.[118] On 11 November 1790 the municipality declared: 'The town of Bayeux is absolutely without commerce, without manufactures and without industry; it is a cathedral city, and as the ecclesiastics of this town were in a position to spend 400,000 to 500,000 livres here annually, this sum, distributed and spread around in the hands of tradesmen, constituted the greater part of the public fortune of the town.' As for the more notable citizens, 'the Church and the Bar were the only professional outlets for their children'.[119]

Two major reforms of the second half of the century drew attention to the unreasonable extent of ecclesiastical possessions. One was the setting up of the Commission des réguliers in 1768 to reform the monasteries. Its investigations concerned not only the usefulness and discipline of each house, but also the number of its inmates as compared with the size of its buildings and income. Numerous possibilities of suppressions and transfers of monastic population were considered; some were proposed, and a limited number carried out. The laity watched these proceedings with interest, and were sometimes consulted. For long, unions of benefices had been taking place at the behest of reforming bishops, always after an enquiry *de commodo et incommodo* in which parishes, municipalities, and other interested parties had a chance to state their views. To provide extra funds for an educational establishment, for a hospital, to increase the revenues of a poor bishopric, or to found an endowment for a new parish—for purposes like these, chapels and priories without cure of souls, or even the abbatial manse of an abbey would be annexed. Often, laymen approved of these transfers and sometimes clamoured for them, though not if the money was to go out of the area, or if local families were going to be deprived of ecclesiastical sinecures for their sons. With the advent of the Commission des réguliers, the laity were encouraged to reflect more generally on the endowments of nearby monasteries and on what better use might be made of them.

The other reform was the edict of 1776 ordering the removal of cemeteries from populated areas, a result of horror stories about crowded graveyards, with their open burial pits, and the campaign of medical experts for hygienic improvements, and of an increasing refinement of sensibility with deep psychological roots in the changing patterns of human relationships.[120] Parsimonious churchwardens and parish assemblies, reluctant to pay the heavy expenses of acquiring new land and walling and gating it, did their best to avoid compliance, and landowners were usually incensed at any proposal that they should sell any of their heritage to provide a site for a new cemetery. There was a customary rule of jurisprudence which allowed the confiscation, against compensation, of land needed for public use: the 'vente forcée pour utilité publique'. There was universal resentment among proprietors whenever any resort to this device was mentioned, so municipal authorities preferred to apply for permission to exercise it against the extensive acres of the Church, rather than against their fellow citizens. What could be more appropriate, they argued, when they were searching for a cemetery? The aldermen of Angers and of Tours were in correspondence, conspiratorially, on this subject.[121] There was a difficulty about this policy, however. Since, by the mortmain legislation, churchmen were prevented from acquiring new property with the compensation money they would obtain, a forced sale of land was a notable disadvantage to them. The parlements, on grounds of equity, generally ruled, if other things were equal, that the property of laymen must be taken. With this security at law, the Benedictines of Bar-sur-Seine and the Dominicans of Grenoble turned down requests for some of their land, and the nuns of the Visitation at Angers even refused to allow a path to a new cemetery site to run through their grounds.[122] The best chance of getting hold of an ecclesiastical site was to persuade the curé to give a field (if he had one) in return for the old cemetery as an eventual extension to his garden. The intendant of Limoges said, sardonically, that in his rural parishes, the translation of cemeteries never took place except when such a deal was possible between the curé and the churchwardens.

The arguments of anticlericals against a wealthy, property-owning Church were predictable. The philosophes cited the gospel prohibitions against the amassing of riches;[123] they searched the Middle Ages for the donations of superstitious kings under the influence of wily priests. The Church is 'always gathering, never giving': it prevents the circulation of wealth and the development of manufactures.[124] Wealthy corporations must always be subject to the law of public utility as interpreted by the State. Turgot's article 'Fondation' in the *Encyclopédie* insists on the interests of the present over the past; a donor cannot tie up his gift for ever, to the prejudice of the human race—'society does not always have the same needs'.[125] Lawyers proclaimed the rights of the State over the property of the Church; whether from reforming or Gallican motives, some churchmen did the same. Between 1755 and 1757, the Jansenist abbé Mignot published a six-volume treatise on 'the rights of the State and of the Prince on the property of the clergy', with a separate supplementary volume giving the history of the feud between Henry II of England and Thomas à Becket, archbishop of Canterbury, as a special case history concerning the overweening pretensions of churchmen. He denied that the clergy had any justification, natural or divine, for escaping ordinary taxation. Councils, he said, denounced those who usurped the sacred acres, but they never denied the right of the prince to use them for the good of his people.[126] Pamphleteers began to make practical proposals for action on these principles. In 1770 was published the *Droit du souverain sur les bien fonds du clergé*: let all Church lands be sold by the sovereign, and the clergy become 'pensioners of the State'.[127] Other pamphlets followed. A common theme is that parish priests, the most useful and deserving of the clergy, should be given their fair share of the endowments. The rest, more particularly the monks, should be reduced in numbers and should own less.[128] Here we come to the final, irrefutable challenge to the vast endowments of the Gallican Church. They were being

misapplied. They were divided among the clergy by the accidents of
history and the self-seeking of the influential, in an unequal fashion
which was against all possible interpretions of the gospels, and to the
serious detriment of the Church as an institution.

II *Tithe*[129]

According to informed observers, tithe brought in rather more
revenue to the Gallican Church than its landed property.[130] In 1784,
Necker estimated this traditional tribute of the laity to be worth 130
million livres a year; at the beginning of the Revolution, when such
calculations suddenly became relevant to schemes for staving off
national bankruptcy, estimates stood at 120–3 million.

In theory, the levy was a tenth of the crop; in practice, said Arthur
Young, it was less.[131] This was indeed the case in many areas; in
Maine, Berry, and Champagne, it averaged one-thirteenth, around
Orléans only one-thirtieth, even less in parts of Dauphiné and
Provence.[132] On the other hand, there were places where tithe
outran the fraction implied by its formal definition, reaching one-
seventh in Lorraine and one-eighth sometimes in Gascony. Such
cases of an unusually high proportion need analysis, however: they
may represent a composite levy, including other dues of a seigneurial
kind.[133] Local custom sometimes reduced the formal burden; there
were villages where it was understood that the curé must accept less
than his legal entitlement,[134] and others where the community was
accustomed to buy off the tithe by paying a lump sum annually. This
is what happened in the little town of Gap,[135] in two villages in
the diocese of Lodève, and commonly in mountain hamlets in
Auvergne, where the rugged terrain made direct collection difficult.[136] Where such commutations were made, the payers got off
lightly (and, according to a government tax official in 1778, their
land was always more efficiently cultivated).[137] Even so, when all
corrections have been made, there were wide disparities between the
highest fractions levied and the lowest, all the more illogical and
vexatious when they coexisted—as they often did—within a narrow
area, even in adjoining parishes.

Tithes were of various kinds, according to the produce on which
they were levied: the *grosses dîmes*, the 'great tithes', on the main
cereal crops; the *menues dîmes*, the 'small tithes', divided into the
dîmes vertes on vegetables and fruits and the *dîme de sang* on animals
and wool. Different provinces had different rules about what was

included under each heading, and within each category the tariff could vary.[138] There were places where there was a due paid to the clergy as an alternative to the tithe. In Brittany, it was a tax collected by recteurs on the inheritance of moveable property, the so-called *neûmes*.[139] In some parishes in the *bocage* country and coastal marches of Bas-Poitou, chiefly in the diocese of Luçon, the place of tithe was taken by the *boisselage*, an unjust levy paid at a fixed amount of grain by all households, irrespective of the extent of their property or of the state of the year's harvest (in fifteen parishes, it was a supplement to the tithe, not a substitute for it). When a royal edict of 1769 replaced the *boisselage* with a tithe at one-sixteenth, the inhabitants protested so vehemently that the reform was withdrawn (the rich liked the old system because they got off cheaply, the poor because it was so unjust that the curé dared not make them pay).[140] In some places, there was an extra little tithe over and above the usual ones, like the *prémice* occasionally found in Brittany and the diocese of Lodève (one sheep in every sixty or so, or a piglet from the first litter of the season).[141] Voltaire also cites the *droit de moisson* in Franche Comté, paid by villagers to their curé in parishes where the orthodox *grosses dîmes* had fallen into the hands of monastic houses.[142]

The tithes within a parish were often levied by several different tithe owners. They might include—though not always—the parish priest himself, a bishop, chapter, monastery, priory, or other ecclesiastical foundation, or, maybe, a layman. The *dîmes inféodées*, tithes held by lay proprietors, were an old-established anomaly, and the law was strict about them: to prove his title, a layman had to demonstrate no less than 100 years' prescription—hence, one of the few victories of the clergy over Voltaire. When he bought his seigneurie at Ferney, he inherited a *dîme inféodée*, coming to the lord of the manor from the Bernese confiscation of ecclesiastical property at the Reformation, but not recognized by the parlement of Dijon when the Pays de Gex came under French overlordship. In spite of influence at court and well-organized litigation, the patriarch of Ferney had to agree to an inglorious compromise with his curé. As ever, he made the best of his discomfiture, adjuring the warring factions of Geneva to make peace by instancing his own sweet reasonableness, meeting with his parish priest to settle their differences over a friendly glass of wine.[143] Strict though the law was, a goodly proportion of the tithe of France—perhaps a twelfth—was held by laymen; had this been exclusively in the hands of the seigneurs descended from the founders of churches, the position would have been easier to justify, but by dint of having been sold and subdivided, the *dîmes inféodées* had passed to all sorts of people[144]—they had become property, just as feudal dues were property. Tithes held by churchmen other than the parish priest were open to similar censures whenever, as was often the case, the bishops, canons, or monks concerned enjoyed excessive riches. More than a third of the curés of France were paid the officially pre-scribed dole, the *portion congrue*, by the holders of the great tithes; and throughout the century, their complaints about the misappropriation of ecclesiastical wealth became more insistent, and received increas-ing popular support.[145]

In many parishes, the division of the tithes had reached an astonishing complexity. In one place near Sedan, the curé was entitled to two-fifths, the prior of Donchery, the chapter of Reims, and the local seigneur to one-fifth each. In the nearby parish of Torcy, the curé had half, the prior of Donchery thirteen-thirty-seconds, another prior one-sixteenth, and a seigneur one-thirty-second.[146] In the little village of Courbesseaux in Lorraine, the curé collected a quarter, a seminary seven-twenty-fourths, an abbot five-twenty-fourths, a prior one-eighth, and two lay lords three-forty-eighths each.[147] In the diocese of Toulouse, of 109 parish priests who owned tithes, only three were the exclusive collectors; 60 had half shares, 29 had thirds, and so on.[148] Confronted with problems of division, some tithe owners made peace among themselves by adopting a system of rotation, whether chronological (the curé to levy every third year, his lay rival in the other two)[149] or geographi-cal (the parish divided into halves with the two tithe owners col-lecting in alternate years in each).[150] In the diocese of Châlons-sur-Marne and in odd places elsewhere, a custom of division prevailed which must surely have been invented by lawyers anxious for fees: the right of the *suite de fer*. The curé of a parish in which a farmer stabled his horses or oxen during the winter had a right to collect half the tithes (and the whole of the tithes on animals and wool) in fields of another parish where these animals were used to do the ploughing. There were conditions, however: the boundaries of the parishes must run alongside at some point; the plough must be able to cross the border without encountering a stream or other natural obstacle; and the farmer must be self-employed.[151] In a tiny parish near Reims, this right to 'follow the plough' was divided equally between the curé, another parish priest, and the cathedral chapter, with the two curés owing small fractions of their portion to three different monastic institutions.[152] A whole history of distrust and litigation lay behind these confusions. Yet the story of such labyrinthine arrangements was not always a sordid one. In one Angevin parish a simple tripartite division had prevailed until a great nobleman listened to the stirrings of conscience and complicated everything by giving a ninth of his third share to the curé, and an eighth of it to maintain a local chapel.[153]

Whether there were various tithe owners or just one, the whole business of collection might be leased to a *fermier*. Since prices tended to rise and leases to be traditional, an entrepreneurial family which established itself in the tithe-farming business was likely to do well.[154] Collecting for a modest nunnery, then on to service with more opulent institutions, and eventually farming the *taille* for the government—this was how Cardinal Fleury's family had climbed up into the world of finance in the seventeenth century.[155] The list of *fermiers* who undertook to collect the archbishop of Albi's tithes shows that it was not artisans or peasants who competed for the contracts, but merchants and entrepreneurs, one-third of them from Albi itself and the others from smaller towns. Frequently, in this area of France, within reach of the great canal crossing the whole country, it was the professional grain merchants who took up the collection; a typical case is at Calmont in 1770, where the auction stood at just over 6,000 livres—a grain merchant took it up in alliance with an innkeeper and two other local worthies who would oversee the collection for him.[156] In the diocese of Auch, a fifth of the contractors were peasants, but always the richer, 'les plus aisés', of their villages. Most of the rest were bourgeois, and, significantly, when collection became difficult because of 'strikes' of tithe payers towards the end of the *ancien régime*, it was the richer merchants and lawyers who were able to stay in competition for the contracts. In 1786, the archbishop of Auch farmed the whole of his tithes (in more than 300 parishes) to an *avocat* of Paris for the huge sum of 306,000 livres and 706 sacks of barley. It is easy to see why the auction of the tithes of the bigger tithe owners should so often be won by the better-off bidders. To sign a contract, often for half a dozen years ahead, was too risky a business for a family without substantial resources, and a single rich entrepreneur could afford to finance a lawsuit against selected individuals, and could settle the matter of a rebate from the tithe owner for unpaid sums in one comprehensive negotiation.[157] To make the peasants fork out, it was as well to have a man of influence accustomed to hobnobbing with lawyers, and if he lived out of the parish, so much the better for his peace of mind.

Instead of contracting out the collection, a tithe owner might decide to exercise a general oversight himself, but employ one or two professionals to share the odium of getting the produce safely into his barn. In Anjou, these characters, called *métiviers*, were substantially remunerated, retaining between a tenth and a sixth of all they garnered.[158] Even doing it oneself, collecting a tithe could be an expensive business. One curé, in a year when he took up 2,178 livres' worth of produce, reckoned that the operation had cost him 435 livres: engaging two labourers and plying them with wine, hiring carts and extra help to unload them, and getting in a threshing expert had run away with a fifth of his income.[159] This was a high proportion: according to an official record in the diocese of Clermont in 1763, the cost of collection was normally one-tenth.[160] In 1786, a curé of the diocese of Comminges complained to his bishop about the alacrity of his parishioners in joining his rejoicing on the day his sheaves came home; by tradition, he had to furnish twelve jars of wine, twelve pounds of matured cheese, and a dinner to the municipal officers—after deducting these expenses and other largesse which he had to furnish at Christmas and on All Saints' Day, and the wages of a vicaire, he was left with only 512 livres to live on.[161] Another peculiar obligation afflicted the tithe owners of Lorraine, who had to provide their villagers with stud animals, and these, like aldermen invited to a tithe banquet, had voracious appetites. At Montiers-sur-Saulx,[162] in the diocese of Toul, where the tithe was shared between the curé and two abbeys, by tradition the parish priest provided the ram, the abbey of Ecurey the bull, and the abbey of Montier-en-Der the boar. But in 1714 the Benedictines of Ecurey refused to pay for a bull and persuaded the local court to order the curé to contribute towards it as he alone drew the *menues dîmes*. A new curé appealed against the verdict, and obtained a legal ruling obliging all three tithe owners to pay equally towards all three animals. The monks, on appeal to the *bailliage* court, got the curé condemned to pay one-third towards the bull and to pay entirely for the ram and the boar. But in 1730 the parish priest finally turned the tables; the system of pre-1714 was restored, and the conspiratorial Benedictines, in addition to having to pay all the expenses of furnishing the bull, incurred costs and damages to the curé and the inhabitants.

But the owner of the *grosses dîmes* had obligations going far beyond the provision of cheese and wine, bulls and boars. Any tithe owner who drew the revenues to the exclusion of the curé had, as his first obligation, to pay the officially prescribed salary to the parish priest—the so-called *congrue*. The *gros décimateur*, whether he was the parochial minister or not, was also responsible for the repairs to the church, at one time solely responsible. The edict of 1695 limited this obligation to the chancel and the choir, an injustice to parishioners which was not entirely forgotten in the *cahiers* of 1789.[163] In addition, if the parishioners were poor, chalices, ornaments, and liturgical books had to be provided, possibly candles also, and laundry expenses. Royal edicts of 1771 and 1772 made these obligations more precise. By contrast, an edict of May 1768, purporting to excuse tithe holders from having to pay out more than a third of their annual profit on repairs, was sufficiently ambiguous in its wording to cause confusion.[164] There was, however, some safeguard for a parish priest, as distinct from other tithe owners: by tradition, he ought always to be left with a reasonable living wage.[165] Doubtful questions abounded, with corresponding scope for litigation. What redress was available if the tithe owner was the Crown, and the administrators of the royal demesne refused to provide 'what is necessary for the celebration of the holy mysteries'?[166] Could a parish sue for past negligence? In 1740, a village in Dauphiné went to law for arrears of candles back to 1672.[167] Did 'what is necessary' include the salary of a parish clerk, as the parlement of Toulouse was trying to prove in the mid-eighteenth century?[168] Did repairing responsibilities accompany the enjoyment of the *menues dîmes*? Generally not, and the matter was finally settled by a ruling of the Grand Conseil in 1748—a verdict which rescued a country curé who was being haunted by the archbishop of Cambrai and the chapter of Notre-Dame of Paris (no less) to contribute to chancel repairs on the strength of a miserable tithe on beans and lentils and a mere bushel of grain allotted to him from the great tithes.[169] Towers and spires were ruinously expensive: if the tower was over the nave, the parishioners had to pay, if over the choir or chancel, the tithe owners. But what of the tower at Guyancourt, with two supporting pillars on one side and two on the other? It took lawsuits from 1769 to 1775 to get to the common-sense solution of dividing the cost.[170] What if the tower fell, damaging the nave? In 1751, the spire of Mortagne in Poitou was blown down, and the Benedictine monks who tithed there refused to rebuild it, as 'unnecessary'. The parish went to law, alleging that it had been a landmark for travellers and a look-out post when the English had attacked La Rochelle; in the end, the Benedictines escaped their obligation on the aesthetic ground that the architecture had been Gothic, and therefore of dubious value.[171] The edict of 1695 had favoured tithe owners, but it had not repealed certain provincial customs benefiting parishes;

more especially, it had not changed the old jurisprudence of Flanders.[172] Here, the exploiter of the great tithes was responsible for the whole of the church building, and was obliged to allocate two years' revenue out of every six for the purpose. The parlement of Flanders repelled all manœuvres of the tithe owners to bring the province under the law of 1695; indeed, the magistrates went further, and in a series of lawsuits ruled that the salaries of curés and repairs to vicarages and churches were expenses which holders of the *grosses dîmes* had to pay, however much they exceeded the compulsory two years' contribution.

Where the tithe of a parish went to the curé, his people looked to him to give proportionately to the poor. Whether by Christian charity or by the pressure of public opinion, most parish priests did something—and in times of famine, a great deal. But what of the absentee chapters, monasteries, and laymen whose contractors' carts trundled off the sheaves or the wine jars at the appropriate harvest season? In some places, more especially in Dauphiné, the holder of the great tithe on cereals was, by custom, expected to hand over a fixed proportion to the curé for the poor.[173] In others, the courts had intervened to make custom into obligation. In this way, great abbeys had been saddled with compulsory alms; Lessay in Normandy, for example, was under the orders of the parlement of Rouen to pay 6,000–7,000 livres a year 'without prejudice to ordinary almsgiving as circumstances require, or to the exercise of hospitality'.[174] When farming out its estates, an ecclesiastical institution might impose a tariff of charity on its contractor—in this way, perhaps, losing credit for its generosity among local people at the time and among historians subsequently.[175] In various other ways, friendly gestures were made by tithe owners to their villages; the *collège* of Pélegri near Cahors had set up exhibitions limited to the children of the three parishes where it collected half the tithe.[176] But except in crises of dearth, and not always then, the absentee tithe owners were rarely generous. 'I haven't received a *sou* from anybody at all to help me to aid the destitute in my parish,' said a curé of Guyenne in 1789; 'not even from le sieur Thyerri, who draws the great tithe . . . which Thyerri I must leave to the judgement of his own conscience.'[177] An enquiry, towards the end of the *ancien régime*, by the archbishop of Rouen throughout his diocese, was full of such complaints: the great abbey of Bec gives 72 livres a year only, that of Jumièges nothing at all; 'the poor get more aid from the most insignificant of Protestant families than they do from a celebrated abbey which plunders 800 acres of my parish'. 'It appears to me to be simple justice', said another curé, 'that the holders of the *grosses dîmes* should contribute to helping their brethren, seeing they enjoy crops that have been fertilized by the sweat of the poor.'[178] Similar complaints abound in the *cahiers* of 1789. The villagers of Cumières, near Reims, had an ancient tradition that the tithe which they paid at one-eleventh had, long ago, been as little as one-sixtieth, until their ancestors, 'as honest and trusting as monks and ecclesiastics are sly and crafty', had agreed to an increased payment for the rebuilding of the abbey of Hautvilliers, an increase which had been illegally perpetuated. Even so, the abbey gave no alms. 'The abbot of Hautvilliers does nothing to help to pay for the expenses of religious services in Cumières. We tried to stir up his charity on behalf of the poor, but there has been no reply; his heart of bronze remains deaf—it hears only the chink of gold pieces.'[179]

The motivation to contest the levy of tithe was universal, and confusions and ambiguities providing grounds for litigation were legion.[180] Mines and quarries were exempt, so were woods, though under certain circumstances a major cut of trees became taxable. Fruit-trees were exempt in most of France, but were all chargeable in Gascony, and certain fruits in some other places. Why, in Auvergne, should hemp pay so generally and hay so rarely, and why, when new crops in that province were mostly exempt, did turnips and sainfoin occasionally slip into the tithe gatherer's net?[181] The produce of hunting escaped, so too of fishing, except in certain Norman ports. Crops cut before due time were free if used to feed the working animals, but not if used to fatten beasts for sale to butchers. An enclosed private garden adjoining a house was free, but not if it was newly created from land that had once been ploughed and sown. Needless to say, there were regulations to stop the laity enclosing whole fields and calling them gardens; logical in injustice, the parlement of Bordeaux allowed one size of garden to a man who ploughed with two oxen, and double this amount to one who ploughed with four. Private parks did not pay tithe, but if they were created from arable land, compensation had to be paid; Louis XIV gave annuities to curés and the abbey of Sainte-Geneviève when he created the Trianon park in 1668—these fell steadily in value, and were a cause of complaint in the eighteenth century.[182]

Odd local circumstances could intensify ill will and provide occasions for tragi-comic feuds and litigation. Not every village had an established, clear procedure for allocating the tithe owners' share—like Blairy in Burgundy, where each proprietor had to stack his sheaves in a straight row, so that the *dixmeur* could start counting at any one he chose and collect every thirteenth sheaf thereafter,[183] or Heuilley, where the payment was a fixed measure of grain according to the amount of land under cultivation, the area to be declared by the proprietor, with the curé having the right to challenge (surveyor's fees paid by the party which was mistaken).[184] In some places, the size of sheaves was argued about; in others, whether they were properly tied, whether the necessary warning of the harvesting date had been given, whether the sheaves had remained available long enough in the field for inspection.[185] What of new crops—clover, potatoes, maize? What of crops planted between rows of vines?[186] Who was to dictate which of two alternative local measures of grain should be used—like the bushel of Falaise, marginally bigger than that of Briouze?[187] What if a crop of rye had been harvested green to be used as ties for the bundles of ripe grain later on? What of windfall fruit, fallen to the ground before it was ripe?[188] One thing was sure; if the tithe owner let things slip, a precedent would be created against him, and what was allowed to one individual in one year would be demanded by everyone the next. In 1770, a canon of Saint-Omer sued a proprietor of Helfaut for tithe on a few tobacco plants; a derisory sum was involved, but the crop might have become significant in a few years' time.[189] And in any case, there was the whole principle of tithe to be upheld, so that even the most improbable windfall was worth pursuing. In 1747 the curé of Issy won a lawsuit before the parlement of Paris for 'la dîme des sangliers élevés dans les maisons'—the severe winter had driven wild boars into the village for refuge. 'It is true', said the lawyers, 'that there is no custom of tithing wild boars, but that is not an argument for saying the claim is unfounded because up to now there has been no custom of rearing wild boars in houses.'[190] It was important to seize the right moment for litigation, and also to choose the appropriate adversary. In 1788, a curé wrote to the abbot of the Cistercian abbey of La Ferté-sur-Grosne proposing a joint onslaught on 'le sieur Grassart', evidently a man of substance, who had been stirring up the parishioners to refuse a tithe which the abbey and the parish priest shared between them.[191] This was the strategy of staking everything on breaking through the enemy's centre. But it might be safer to begin with an attack on the flank, to pick off some miserable peasant, thus establishing a legal ruling to be used against the richer ones. The poor, we must remember, ran the danger of ruin if they contested a lawsuit, since they might have to pay the costs of the other side. In Voltaire's correspondence we read of the fate of five peasant families who foolishly disputed a tithe of 30 livres a year which came to them as a charity, in opposition to the grasping curé of Monëns, only to find themselves condemned to pay 1,300 livres in costs, including the curé's lodging and wine bills during the hearing of the case in Dijon.[192] In 1767, the recteur of Saint-Denoual noted in his journal that his tithe of one fleece from each flock invariably brought him in the most mangy specimens: 'on vole le Recteur en tout'. Though nobles were the meanest of all in this respect, he dissimulated his ire; the only way to proceed was to look out for a chance to cite before the *présidial* someone too poor to fight back, then to publish the sentence of the court (at a cost of ten écus, he notes gloomily), in the hope of frightening the others.[193]

One standard device for evading tithe which the richer cultivator could resort to was to change to a different crop—one which the lawyers recommended as having a chance to qualify for exemption. Thus Restif de la Bretonne's father, smarting at the rapacious forays of the bishop and canons of Auxerre among his corn sheaves, planted part of his non-ploughable hill terrain with vines, and in seven years was producing wine, a commodity not titheable by local custom.[194] M. de Goupillières, *directeur* of the Mint at Caen, was not so lucky. In 1734 he went down in person to his seigneurie of Saint-Hilaire to supervise the change of some arable land to pasture (catching a cold in the process), and wrote a smooth letter to the curé— 'Mon Révérend Père'—pointing out that he was within his legal rights since he had left two-thirds of his land under the plough. After four years of litigation, however, he was condemned to pay an annual compensation.[195] His lawyers had not done their homework. True, a declaration of 1657 protecting tithe owners against loss of revenue when meadows were created had never been registered, and the parlement and the Grand Conseil had ruled that a tithe owner could claim compensation only if he was losing more than a third of his revenue. But the essential point was—it was a third of the *whole* tithe from the parish which mattered; thus, landowners who were quick to create meadows might get away with it, but not the later ones.[196] In this same year, 1734, M. Grandjean de Lespine planted trees on a stretch of his arable land in Crevecœur-en-Brie. In this case the curé failed in his lawsuit as his losses, on all heritages taken together, still did not total a third.

Disputes of a like kind arose from government edicts[197] to encourage the extension of the area of cultivation by granting a limited suspension of tithe. In 1761, an exemption for ten years was offered for wasteland brought under the plough; three years later this was raised to fifteen. As for land reclaimed from marsh, this would enjoy an exemption of twenty years, with tithe thereafter pegged at the low figure of one-fiftieth. Foolishly, the clergy of the province of Guyenne protested. 'The saying, you must sow before you can reap, is unknown to them,' complained Quesnay, the physiocrat.[198] Most ecclesiastics were more enlightened, and saw these concessions as a source of future profit: a minor waiving of principle in the present, and an increase of revenue in the long run. The chapter of Notre-Dame of Paris and the clerical representatives at the estates of Brittany were willing to improve on the government's regulations and offer a twenty-one years' immunity in the areas where they tithed. But what was 'wasteland'? Inevitably, any weedy patch that had escaped the plough for a while was claimed to be such by its owners, so an *arrêt* of 1766 laid down a definition of forty years without cultivation. The Assembly General of the Clergy still had to go on protesting, however; the parlement of Bordeaux was allowing proprietors to plough waste without giving the tithe owner notice of intent, thus obliterating evidence of previous cultivation, while in the *landes* the sand performed the function anyway. And what of the crafty estate managers who ploughed up old-established meadows and switched some of their old titheable arable land to pasture in exchange? In Gascony and Quercy, it was the nobles who led the way in manipulating the code concerning wasteland and marshes to evade the tithe owner's levies; bourgeois entrepreneurs tended to be mixed up in the business of collection, and therefore sided with the clergy.[199] A Breton nobleman wrote to the controller-general in 1783 pointing out that the fifteen-year exemption granted in 1766 was now running out for many proprietors.

The peasant proprietor, the laboureur [no doubt it was convenient not to mention the drainers and enclosers among the nobility], panic-stricken, can already see the Church annexing the fruit of his toil, and is deciding to abandon the cultivation of land he had enclosed from the waste, and on which he has become agreeably accustomed to pay nothing more than taxes to the State.

Thus, he concluded, the king is going to lose revenue, simply because the clergy are being allowed an unearned windfall—was there not a royal edict in 1749 forbidding them to acquire new property, and what is tithe but property of a sort?[200]

Given this atmosphere of suspicion, fraud, and litigation, tithe was inevitably hated. It was all the more grudgingly paid when the peasant made comparisons. If he paid tithe at a high rate, he would compare his burden with the lighter burden borne by others. Of a

group of thirty-six parishes in Champagne,[201] twenty-one paid a
global sum equal to one-third of all State taxation levied, but four
paid fully two-thirds of the total exactions of the Crown—an enormous disparity. The peasants were narrowly confined, physically and
intellectually, within the boundaries of their village community, but
where paying out was concerned, they knew when they were being
unequally treated. In Brittany, where tithe in adjoining parishes
could vary from one-tenth to one-thirty-sixth, this was a general
complaint in the *cahiers*. That of the village of Comblessac asked for
some reduction in its one-twelfth, 'seeing that the parishes around
owe it only on the fiftieth or thirtieth sheaf, and their land is better
quality than ours'.[202] Another comparison to be made was with the
privileged few who escaped paying tithe altogether. A man whose
income consisted solely in an official salary or house rents would pay
nothing. Mills were exempt, and forests often escaped, and these
were mostly owned by the privileged classes. In Provence nobles
paid at a lower rate than commoners, even on non-noble lands
which they might have purchased. The Orders of Malta, Cîteaux,
Cluny, the Prémontrés, and the Chartreux held exemptions granted
to them by popes, though there was a developing jurisprudence in
the eighteenth century to limit their privilege. Oddly enough, some
Protestants in Alsace were not liable, since the lawyers of Louis XIV
had failed to list all provincial peculiarities that needed to be changed
on annexation.[203] And finally, there was the most devastating comparison of all, between the poverty of the payer of tithe and the
wealth of some great ecclesiastical institution which levied it—and if
this institution collected seigneurial or other dues locally as well, the
cumulative effect was overwhelming. Richeprey, touring the South,
investigating inequalities of the taxation system, noted the nuns of
Saint-Sernin (Rodez) tied up in lawsuits with a parish in which they
levied a *champart* of one-quarter or one-fifth along with the tithe.[204]
The cathedral chapter of Beauvais, in twelve parishes of its estates,
enjoyed a tithe and a *champart* which together took 18 per cent of
the peasants' crops; the *cahiers* of this area in 1789 overflow with
bitterness.[205]

The peasant, enviously reflecting on his misery, was well aware
that the true rate at which he paid his tribute to the Church was
always higher than the ostensible official figure. As the villagers of
Saint-André-du-Double in Périgord said in their *cahier*, they paid
twice over when they paid a tithe on potatoes, then another one on
the pigs that were fed on them; similarly when they paid on grain
used to feed chickens. Furthermore, they were not allowed to

deduct anything to cover the seed-corn which they planted.[206] This was an important point, for the yield of grain was often only one in four; that is, a tithe which appeared to be one-eighth would in fact be one-fifth.[207] Dupont de Nemours, drawing up the *cahier* of the Tiers État of his *bailliage*, declared that proprietors were paying as much as a third of their crop if all expenses were taken into account. 'You imagine, O complaining farmer, that it's one sheaf in ten they are taking out of your field,' said a pamphleteer of 1789, *L'Iniquité de la dîme*, 'Great is your error; they are taking one in five. Half of your crop goes in covering your advances, your cost of cultivation, your seed-corn.'[208] And an important item in this cost of cultivation was the manuring of the fields. Carting seaweed or the fragrant contents of municipal cesspits to the land was a toilsome expedient available only to those who lived near the sea-shore or suburbs. For the most part, the fields were fertilized by the dung-impregnated litter which had bedded the animals, more especially during the winter months. But straw was so often in short supply: 'la paille est toujours ce qui manque', said an agricultural reformer in a treatise of 1763.[209] To collect tithe 'au champ' instead of 'dans le sac' (that is, taking the stalk along with the grain) was a notable device of seigneurial oppression—used, for example, by a Catholic seigneur against a Protestant village in Alsace to force it to conversion.[210] Some of the parlements made regulations compelling tithe owners to sell back their straw to the inhabitants at low prices fixed by the local judicial officials.[211] This arbitrary intervention of the magistrates was not unreasonable. The least that wealthy chapters and monasteries could do was to refrain from hampering the cultivators who grew the crops which paid their tribute.

If tithe was collected by a contractor, it was likely that enforcement would be harsher, and if the contractor was from outside the village, no one was satisfied. The richer peasants saw a lucrative job escaping them, and the poorer saw wealth leaving the parish that might have provided them with employment or charity. In Flanders, by a cherished local custom, the job of collecting tithes was auctioned annually in separate details, enabling even humble peasants to have a chance to try their hand at this minor capitalist enterprise. By contrast, in the areas where the archbishop of Cambrai left his tithe collection in the hands of the manager who ran all his estates, there was a general clamour in the *cahiers* of 1789 for tithe to be farmed to parishioners only.[212] There was an exception—an illogical one—to this preference for a local contractor. Some parish priests held the tithe in their own hands and collected it: this was accepted as an inevitable evil, and it was satisfying, at any rate, to reflect that the profits stayed in the parish. But there were curés who did not enjoy the tithe, but who nevertheless volunteered to collect it, to obtain the contractor's percentage.[213] Thus, the abbey or chapter which had usurped the curé's true patrimony (for this was how everyone regarded it), and which now paid him a mere pittance, was able to make use of his local knowledge in levying its dues. What was worse, here was a man of God stepping out of his spiritual role to usurp a job which a layman of the parish might have hoped for. 'By taking holy orders, he had become the protector and father of the flock confided to his care; but he takes the bread from the hands of the hard-up individuals who used to collect the tithes, work which used to help them to earn a living and to pay their taxes'—this concerning the curé of Marche-Maisons near Alençon, in the village *cahier*.[214] Another variant of the pastor as professional collector is when he shared a tithe with others, drawing a fraction which, perhaps, was too small to be economically levied on its own. In this case, it was only common sense to offer to collect the lot and to arrange the share-out. In his memoirs, Marquis-Ducastel, curé of Sainte-Suzanne, describes how he inherited a comfortable arrangement of this kind, handing over two-thirds to the abbot of Evron, less 360 livres collector's charges. A new abbot, however, put the business into the hands of the city slickers—'intriguers from Laval'— who farmed his estates; Marquis-Ducastel lost something like 800 livres a year by having to hire a separate barn for storing his third.[215] He does not tell us what was the attitude of the parishioners of Sainte-Suzanne; there was no doubt about that of the inhabitants of Rumegies, in the diocese of Tournai, earlier in the century. Dubois, the curé, tells us how the abbey of Saint-Amand enjoyed a tithe of seven-hundredths in his parish, and he himself one of one-hundredth, a fraction too small to levy effectively; how in 1702 he bought the right to levy the abbey tithe as well as his own—'using the same collector, the same cart and the same efforts as before!' He soon wished he had not been so efficient.

On every side nothing was heard but threats—to burn him out, to kill him, to insult him, to drive him out of his cure. And even his best friends in the parish all made war on him. And unless God in his goodness touches their hearts, they will never pardon him! Indeed, if the curé had had the least inkling that he'd become so unpopular, he'd never have thought of taking over this tithe collecting.[216]

The lawyers who grew sleek by conducting the tithe suits of the

laity had accumulated theoretical and historical arguments; anticlericals in search of ammunition did not need to go further than the
law dictionaries. Was tithe of divine institution? In his edict of 1657,
Louis XIV had repeated this claim, but the parlement of Paris had
refused to register it. The lawyers insisted that here was a simple
tax 'for the maintenance of the ministers of the Church'.[217] True,
the Levites had enjoyed their tithes, as recorded in the books of
Leviticus and Numbers. But the Gallican Church was in a different
situation, having its own landed endowment. St Paul was much concerned about the maintenance of preachers of the gospel, yet he was
silent about this Levitical precedent; so too were the laws of the first
six centuries.[218] Christians, unlike Jews, are not obliged to pay a fixed
tribute, St Augustine had boasted. St Thomas Aquinas does not
accept the principle of divine institution. Indeed, the argument ran,
the variations in the rate at which tithe was levied suggest an accumulation of practical concessions rather than the imposition of a
theoretical obligation. The parlement of Franche Comté used these
arguments in 1725 to prevent a curé from levying tithe on a tiny
hamlet. Even though the rest of the parish paid, the inhabitants of
Boismurie were held to be exempt on grounds of prescription—they
had evaded payment for a long time. No tithe was levied in the early
centuries; the Eastern Church has never had it; it has not been paid
in India or America, said the parlement. Therefore it has arisen
purely by custom, and as it arose, so let it die, beginning maybe in
the hamlet of Boismurie.[219] Montesquieu added learning and Voltaire
irony to the concept of tithe as a purely human institution which the
law of the land could modify. Payment of a tenth among the Jews,
said Montesquieu, had been 'part of the plan of the foundation of
their republic', while in France it was a 'charge independent of
those involved in the establishment of the monarchy'. Before
Charlemagne, tithe was 'preached . . . but not established', and for
long after him payment was episodic. And tithe, as Charlemagne had
devised it, was divided between the bishop, the clergy, the church
building, and the poor. Since he had considered his gifts to the
Church less as a religious than as a 'political dispensation', there is
every reason to believe that the tithe is not exclusively for the
clergy; in its primitive allocation, half went to the church fabric and
the indigent.[220] Voltaire, as ever, had fun with the arrangements of
the Old Testament. The Levites tithed in the wilderness of Cades,
and Abraham gave to Melchizedek the tithes of Sodom; let us pack
off our modern tithe owners to collect their revenues in those distant, insalubrious places. This applies, however, only to the rich

monks and canons, who drink choice vintages, eat pheasant and par-
tridge, and sleep, not unaccompanied, on feather-beds; by contrast,
Voltaire laments (probably sincerely) the lot of the country curé
'obliged to dispute a sheaf of corn with his poor parishioners . . . to
be hated and to hate'. Surely, these unjust exactions do not spring
from the Christian gospel: 'did God come down to earth to award a
quarter of my income to the . . . abbot of Saint-Denis?' In northern
Europe, ministers of religion are paid from public funds, and everyone is happier.[221] These were hard words; even so, the clergy were
to be officially maintained. But why should this maintenance be
official? According to a more radical view—rarely found—the laity
should be left to contribute of their own free will. In his journal,
the abbé Véri explored the unavowed, subconscious cause of the
intolerance of the Gallican Church towards Protestants: the fear that
tithe would be lost. 'As soon as the exercise of religion is freely
allowed, each believer then ought to allot the tithe of his field to the
actual minister who exercises pastoral care over him.'[222] There is a
logical further step which Véri does not mention: unbelievers might
keep their crops for themselves; once this was allowed, their
numbers would be legion.

   Criticism of tithe on grounds of history or principle was
reinforced by solid economic arguments from the physiocrats. The
theories of this dominant school of French economic thinkers were
dubious enough; they were mistaken about the declining population; they oversimplified when they made agriculture the sole source
of real wealth; their theoretical insistence that grain must be allowed
to rise to its natural price level disregarded the misery of the
common people. But they saw clearly what was wrong with the
French countryside; as a result of conspicuous waste, heavy taxation,
tithe, and the purchase of offices, investment in agriculture was
inadequate. So they proclaimed a new slogan, 'the inviolability of
agricultural capital'[223]—much discussed by provincial agricultural
societies. The owner of land ought not to push up the farmer's lease
to the limit, ought not to pass on to him the unpredictable burden
of State taxation. The actual tiller of the soil should enjoy a surplus,
growing in proportion to the intensity of his own efforts, and which,
in every sense of the word, he would plough back into the business.
Tithe clearly was a major drain of capital away from the land, and a
discouragement to enterprise and to the extension of the area of
cultivation. To the peasants' complaint that the true fraction of the
crops taken was greater than the apparent one, the physiocrats added
a further argument. The costs of agricultural production were

greatest in the least fertile areas, so that their tithe absorbed a greater fraction of the net crop than elsewhere: it was a levy falling most heavily on the poor.

The arguments of lawyers, philosophes, and physiocrats were but dimly grasped in rural France. Yet the peasants understood perfectly the basic principle at issue. Tithes were meant to pay the parochial ministers, to maintain the church building, and keep divine service going; but they had been diverted to other purposes. Properly used, they ought to provide a liberal maintenance for the curé, leaving him well enough off to feed the poor in time of dearth, and freeing him from the need to collect surplice-fees at weddings and funerals. *Dîme* and *casuel* (tithe and surplice-fees) were linked in the minds of the peasants: given the burden of the one, the other was unjustified. Representatives of the community of Gignac in the diocese of Aix-en-Provence in 1775 described how they paid tithe to the tune of 2,000 livres a year, and all they got back was 200 livres to pay a priest so ignorant that he did not know how to baptize; they applied, therefore, to be allowed to keep their money and use it to build up a real parochial life.[224] The *cahier* of Rougeon (diocese of Blois) gave a ruthless summary of peasant grievances:

We lament to see our parish priests in abjection, misery and necessity, while . . . a horde of monks of various sorts, abbots and canons take away our tithe and swindle our curés out of what is their due. The [tithe owners] on whom the benefice depends do not blush to see our churches without books, linen, ornaments, and on the verge of falling down, and dirtier than stables. Let their riches be cut back, and let our churches and our curé—the inspiration and support of our families—be properly endowed. And let us hear no more of surplice-fees—the tithe is sufficient to pay for the administration of the sacraments.[225]

In the last twenty years of the *ancien régime*, a revolt against tithe was smouldering in the south of France. In 1775, the Assembly General of the Clergy of France accused the parlement of Toulouse of an underhand design to encourage refusal to pay the *menues dîmes*. According to the magistrates, these could only be demanded if there was a clear title or long prescription, with proof that at least two-thirds of the inhabitants had been paying over at least two-thirds of the area of the parish, and that all had been paying at precisely the same rate (variations would show that the tribute was voluntary). Furthermore, these details had to be established by the testimony of witnesses other than the actual collectors. Since these were impossible conditions, the government issued declarations to rescue the

clergy, declarations which the magistrates refused to register.[226] To
the assembly of the clergy of the ecclesiastical province of Auch in
1780[227] (one of the areas of France where tithe was levied at a high
rate), the archbishop reported widespread refusals to pay any more
than the literal tenth and to pay anything at all on maize, which was
regarded as a new and exempt crop. 'This revolt is winning support
from parish to parish, to the point that, if the approaching Assembly
General of the Clergy fails to act in this respect, or acts unsuccessfully, payments will become purely a matter of individual choice,
and refusals universal.' The parlement of Toulouse backed M. de
Saint-Géry's defiance of the bishop of Lectoure over the payment of
a tithe of two-seventeenths on millet, and other cases were on the
way. At another assembly of the clergy of his province in September
1782, the archbishop of Auch spoke of 'an evident conspiracy', with
500 lawsuits pending before the parlement, and little doubt as to
what the verdicts would be. The crisis came when the magistrates of
Toulouse considered the plea of the villagers of Mouchez, who had
refused to pay a tithe of four-thirty-firsts on wheat, offering to pay
at one-tenth. The curé had won his case when he cited the three
chief recalcitrants before the court of the *sénéchaussée* of Auch; but
on appeal, the parlement reversed this verdict in March 1781. From
then onwards there was a torrent of refusals. By December 1784,
more than half the parishes of Auch and Comminges were offering
to pay at a strict tenth and no more. The tensions are evident in the
complaints of the curés to the bishop of Comminges in 1786. They
spoke of 'fire' and 'fermentation' and 'visible' threats; the old days
when the tithe owners could be brusque with their peasants were
over—'il faut les traiter comme à des noces: de cette façon, ma
portion est toujours petite'.[228] Not surprisingly, the clergy backed
away from the desperate confrontation that seemed to be
developing. Instead of 500 lawsuits being prosecuted, possibly only
a dozen were fought through to a conclusion. Tithe owners avoided
coming to a legal crunch unless they were confident about their
documentary evidence; the curés urged the archbishop and chapters
to be moderate, and were themselves willing to negotiate. In most
places there was a 'transaction'; on the main cereal crops the payment was reduced to the strict one-tenth, and by way of compensation the clergy might be allowed peaceful possession of the *menues
dîmes* in areas where these had been contested.[229] Other sovereign
courts began to follow the example of Toulouse. In 1774, the parlement of Normandy declared that only the tithe on the four basic
grain crops, wheat, rye, barley, and oats, could be levied as of right:

tithes on all other crops were 'insolites': that is, proof of forty years' possession was required.[230] The parlement of Burgundy had been accustomed to decide cases in favour of tithe owners; from 1770, it tended to find against them, and in 1775 issued an *arrêt* modelled on that of Normandy.[231] These were years of rising prices and of agricultural diversification. From both these developments (somewhat paradoxically coinciding) the tithe owners were gaining an enhanced income. Hence, given the pervasive anticlericalism of the countryside, an envious alliance of magistrates and cultivators formed against them.

At first sight it seems astonishing that the reformers of the early years of the Revolution abandoned their original idea of confiscating tithe for the coffers of the State, and simply suppressed it, thus making a handsome present to all landowners at a time of national bankruptcy. Yet it is not difficult to see why the intention of 4 August 1789[232] was never carried into effect. For long, there had been a vast, undeclared conspiracy over the whole of France to evade and outwit the tithe holders. On this issue landowners had become pathologically conditioned to be deaf to reason and religion, and, if need be, to patriotism. The history of the guerrilla war against tithe waged for so long in the law courts is essential evidence in any study of rural anticlericalism in France. A formula for calculating its intensity in any particular area may be suggested. Start with a standard, inevitable figure, then adjust it slightly for the worse in years of very bad or very good harvests, when tithe becomes especially hated as either a confiscation of the bread of the poor or a theft from the profits of diligence and enterprise. To this, add extra points of discontent if an ecclesiastical institution holds the tithe to the exclusion of the curé, more points still if that institution is scandalously rich, and still more if it levies seigneurial dues on the same people from whom it takes tithe, and a substantial bonus if it gives only derisory alms locally. All this to be multiplied by a coefficient based on the rate at which tithe is levied as compared with other places. The suppression of tithe by the representatives of the nation went far beyond what was suggested in the *cahiers*, yet was entirely compatible with them. Tithe had lost all religious overtones and associations, and had become just a set of dues authorized by the State and levied by a minority of citizens on all the others. As Condorcet said, it was 'un véritable revenu indépendant de tout service religieux'.[233]

5

THE GENERAL ASSEMBLIES OF THE
CLERGY AND CLERICAL TAXATION

I

The clergy of France voted taxation to the Crown in their own elected assemblies. This independence, unique in the kingdom, was jealously defended. In the preface to the first volume of the collection of the minutes of past meetings, published in 1767, the status and rights of the 'first Order in the nation' are proudly asserted: 'accustomed to make its remonstrances to its august Sovereign, to bring before him its *cahiers* of grievances, to offer him the gifts which it levies independently—a right which is a precious survival of the Estates General (*reste précieux des États Généraux*)'. In these volumes of minutes, says the editor, 'you see the Assemblies of this illustrious corporation constantly conserving their forms and usages, as zealous to give their Sovereign glittering proofs of their fidelity and their affection, as courageous to defend the sacred rights of religion; in a word, participating in the majesty of the State and in the holiness of [ecclesiastical] Councils.'[1]

The assemblies, which eventually gave the clergy a degree of independence of the Crown, had arisen because the Church was taken into partnership with the monarchy as a collaborator in the extension of royal power over a divided country. The foundation of the alliance was the Concordat of 1516, by which the king named the bishops.[2] The Wars of Religion drew the interests of churchmen and administrators closer. After 1563, the Papacy, anxious to have the reforms of the Council of Trent implemented in France, connived at the strengthening of the Gallican hierarchy, since the Tridentine decrees, not officially accepted by the Crown, were adopted by reforming bishops in their dioceses. More prosaically, the king needed money. The clergy had paid *décimes* to him, with papal permission, from the twelfth century, but the royal ministers wanted the inflow of money made more systematic. On their side, churchmen, afraid that in desperate times the State might confiscate their property, were co-operative. Thus, labyrinthine financial transactions created a new and more predictable system of clerical taxation, and the assemblies of the Gallican Church with it.

The clergy liked to think of their right to vote their own taxation as the remains of the old national franchises which the other orders in the State had failed to defend, or as the recognition by the secular power of the just authority of the spiritual. In fact, their right was ensured by an immense structure of debt. The king found it easiest to borrow money by using the Church as an intermediary; the clergy were well organized, they did not default on payments, and rarely delayed them. The system began with the 'contrat de Poissy' of 1561,[3] by which they engaged themselves for the next sixteen years to redeem the royal domain lands pledged to the Hôtel de Ville of Paris. The government, finding life easier under this arrangement, contracted new loans to be serviced by annuities on the clergy, and the contrat de Poissy was renewed at ten-yearly intervals. At these times the assemblies maintained the fiction that they were not obliged to go on making payments on behalf of the State, but many bourgeois families came to depend on these *rentes*, and as is the way with debts, the creditors were concerned to keep going the arrangements which ensured their regular income. These *rentes de l'Hôtel de Ville de Paris* continued to be paid all through the seventeenth and eighteenth centuries.

The *rentes* were a matter of about 400,000 livres annually, which, comparatively speaking, was not a large sum. But the Assemblies of Clergy went on to contract new debts, partly because it would have been impossible to meet the exactions of Louis XIV without recourse to anticipations of revenue, but not without a quiet realization that the increase of indebtedness was a further guarantee of indispensability and of the sanctity of their independent arrangements. In 1689, the Great Monarch wanted 18 million for 43 years' arrears of the *droit d'amortissement*, the fines paid for extensions and improvements to ecclesiastical property; in 1693 it was 7 million in *amercements* for the illegal cutting of woods over the past twenty-four years. In 1710, Louis collected the immense sum of 24 million livres as a lump payment to buy off clerical liability to his new capitation tax. (In the end, the clergy did well out of this transaction; the capitation did not end when the war was over, but continued throughout the eighteenth century, so that for six years' purchase they had bought off a liability which would have totalled 310 million by 1789.[4]) The assemblies which borrowed in 1686 to set up a fund to aid in the conversion of Protestants went on to borrow more to meet the royal demands: five and a half million out of the twelve they had to raise in 1690, twenty-four for the capitation in 1710, eight million in 1711, and twelve in 1715. By the end of the reign, they were finding over 6,250,000 a year, of which nearly 4,000,000 was payment of interest on the debt.[5] This debt, augmented from time to time (and occasionally held in check by attempts to consolidate it), remained throughout the eighteenth century. It was more than the king would ever be able to pay off, and the interest went to creditors who knew that they were holders of the safest investment in France. 'Rien n'est mieux payé que ce qui est assis sur le clergé,' said the duc de Luynes in 1755.[6] In 1784, according to Necker, the annual payments of the clergy were 400,000 livres for the old *rentes* on the Hôtel de Ville of Paris, interest on the main debt of 134 million to the tune of 5,800,000, a sum of 4,100,000 designed to pay off some of the main debt, and 700,000 interest on borrowings by individual dioceses. When the Revolution came and the lands of the Church were to be sold, the debt which had to be taken over was more than 149 million. It was then seen how good the credit of the clergy had been, since 104 million of the loans were at the rate of 4 per cent, 37 million at 2 to 2½ per cent, and eight million at 5 per cent.[7]

Some organization for assessing individual dioceses, collecting taxes from the clergy, and paying them into the treasury of the central government would always have been necessary; indeed, lacking a single, recognized episcopal head, the Gallican Church needed a bureaucratic headquarters to act as a post office between bishops and a link between dioceses for the transaction of everyday financial and legal affairs. But it was the existence of the debt which encouraged the Crown to favour the rapid and complex development of such machinery. A meeting held in 1580[8] marks the beginning of regularly held and legally recognized assemblies of the clergy. For the first time, representatives of the rank and file were present, as well as bishops; details of ceremonies and voting procedures were fixed; and a system of correspondence from Paris to *syndics* in each diocese was established. The king promised to call such another assembly in ten years' time, and in the meantime he would not set up any other machinery to tax the clergy, and not ask for any other impositions beyond those already granted. These promises became common form, though when Louis XIV was on the throne, they meant less than might be supposed. He reserved the right to ask at any time for a benevolence, a *don gratuit*, which he did not count as ordinary taxation, and he did not brook argument in the assemblies about the amount of money he demanded. But under weaker successors, this would not always be so. And administrative machinery, as it increases in efficiency and complexity, engenders its own power to resist, whether by bureaucratic inertia or by the ability to mount concerted opposition and propaganda.

In its final form, the system of taxation had, as the base of the pyramid, the *bureaux des décimes* (also known, in various places, as *chambres des décimes* or *bureaux diocésains*). An edict of 1615 had ordered each diocese to establish such a committee, and gradually this was done, the dioceses of Brittany being late in complying (Saint-Malo in 1681, Nantes in 1682, Rennes in 1696).[9] These bureaux assessed all holders of benefices, and saw that the proceeds were used to pay the contribution laid upon the diocese by the Assembly of the Clergy, and to meet various diocesan expenses, including payment of interest on any local debts which had been incurred. In cases of disputed assessment, the bureau had power to settle definitively those involving no more than 20 or 30 livres. Complainants would be heard only if they had paid all past arrears and had put down the cash for half their current assessment, and if they produced statements of their revenues backed with document-ary evidence (if not honestly done, double tax was chargeable).[10] The bureau had a *syndic*, some prominent ecclesiastic with a head for business, who had oversight of the taxation and conducted the correspondence with the central organization in Paris—indeed, the letters patent of 1616 and 1626 made him a sort of official defender of the interests of the diocese. The actual work of collecting and accounting was in the hands of a lay expert, the *receveur diocésain*, who sent up the money to the *receveur général* in Paris.[11] Like so many offices in seventeenth-century France, these diocesan receiverships had been put up for sale by the Crown. An edict of 1719 made a clean sweep of these venal posts, and allowed bishops and their bureaux to make their own nominations. Alas, in 1723 the Assembly of Clergy itself, faced with the payment of a heavy *don gratuit*, asked the king to sell the receiverships again to raise 1,500,000 livres; most dioceses bought them, and incurred heavy debts in the process.[12]

The diocesan bureaux were supposed to be 'representative' of the clergy. But the election of members by benefice holders was rare. Sometimes the bishop named the people he wanted, sometimes the existing group co-opted others or had a right to approve the bishop's choices. Often, the selection was made within a cadre of understandings about which institutions or classes of clergy were entitled to a voice—the cathedral, other chapters, a great abbey, curés of the town, curés of the countryside, and so on. In a few places, parish priests had obtained strong representation: eight out of ten in Lectoure, four out of seven in Lescar, three out of six in Montauban. But such democratic arrangements were rare; in most dioceses the bureau was the closed preserve of the clerical oligarchy around the bishop and the cathedral. In 1789, the *chambre ecclésiastique* of Paris consisted of the archbishop, the dean and two canons of Notre-Dame (one being the *syndic*), a canon of Saint-Honoré, the abbot of the canons regular of Sainte-Geneviève, and a single curé.[13] At Angers, there were two canons of the cathedral, one deputy for the four Benedictine abbeys, one for the canons regular of the abbey of Toussaint, one for the two royal chapters of the town, one for the other collegiate churches, and two curés—and these latter, being chosen by the bureau itself, were staid and peaceable characters, not the firebrands of the parishes. It was 'le comité particulier des chanoines' said a pamphleteer in 1789, denouncing the injustices under which the parish priests laboured.[14] This was an extreme case, but a law-book of 1769 regarded canonical domination as general— its recommended standard formula was: the bishop, two deputies of the cathedral, two of other chapters, and two others.[15] Bishops might chafe under the constraints of the diocesan oligarchy. In 1745, the bishop of Saint-Flour appealed to the Assembly to rescue him: he presided over a bureau with a fluctuating composition of about twenty, his cathedral having two representatives, the collegiate churches one each, and various abbots and priors also attending. At his request, the membership was reduced to seven, elected by the diocesan synod.[16] More commonly, however, there was an alliance of bishops and canons against the parish clergy, with the curés show- ing a growing discontent at their subordination. In 1770, a dispute in the diocese of Troyes led to the Assembly of the Clergy laying down new guide-lines for the composition of bureaux; in addition to the bishop, there would be one representative each for the cathe- dral, the other chapters, the religious houses, holders of benefices without cure of souls, and the curés—all to be elected.[17] Some dioceses reformed themselves along these lines, and some were com- pulsorily reformed by orders of the Royal Council; most remained unchanged or only superficially altered—hence, a continuing cause for discontent among the lower clergy.

If benefice holders who disputed their assessment had been able to resort to the secular courts, the autonomous system of clerical taxa- tion would have become unworkable. There was nothing the magis- trates relished more than running down hierarchical authority in the

Church and posing as the defenders of persecuted individuals. But the Church enjoyed the advantage of having special tribunals, largely under its own control, to handle tax appeals, the *chambres supérieures des décimes* at Paris, Lyon, Toulouse, Bordeaux, Rouen, Tours, Aix, and Bourges.[18] To these, each diocese of the ecclesiastical province sent a deputy, named by its bishop (and the bishops themselves could attend, except when a case concerning one of their own clergy was being heard). A representative of the archbishop presided at meetings, normally weekly. There were also three legal members, chosen by the *chambre* itself from the *conseillers* of the chief court of the town where the sessions were held, generally a parlement. It was sometimes possible to choose lawyers who were also clerics by status, the so-called *conseillers clercs*; but as these were few in number, the legal assessors were generally laymen. This ingenious combination of hand-picked lawyers and churchmen was an excuse to exclude the parlements from meddling, and the authority of these *chambres supérieures* was so solidly established, the standard law dictionary affirmed, that it was exercised even over institutions which enjoyed the specific right of taking all their litigation directly to the Crown. True, the Royal Council, in the last resort, could reverse any judgment, but generally it was content to send complaints to the Assembly for a final ruling.

At the summit of the taxation pyramid was the General Assembly of the Clergy of France. Decennially, in the years ending with the numeral '5', there would be a *Grande Assemblée*, while half-way through the interval, in the year ending with '0', there would be a *Petite Assemblée*. Theoretically, the former was for making great decisions, the latter for 'verifying the accounts'; in practice, important matters could be transacted at either. Their composition was different: to the 'great' Assembly each ecclesiastical province sent four deputies, two being bishops and two of the 'second order'; to the 'small' Assembly, each province sent one bishop and one other. There could also be an *assemblée extraordinaire*, called for some urgent reason, with deputies elected in the same numbers as for the small assemblies. This did not exhaust the emergency machinery, since the king could always ask for the summoning of an *ad hoc* gathering of such bishops as happened to be available. These were originally called assemblies of 'prélats à la suite de la Cour', and later came to be called assemblies of 'prélats présents à Paris'—perhaps one can infer that under Louis XIV the bishops came to play the courtier at Versailles, while under Louis XV they came to the capital to transact business and enjoy society. In 1749, when Machault d'Arnouville tried to compel the clergy of the frontier provinces to register their property for eligibility to a *vingtième*; in 1752, when the parlement of Paris published an *arrêt* against the archbishop; and in 1767, when the magistrates banished three ecclesiastics and confiscated their goods (over the refusal of sacraments to Jansenists), such emergency meetings of prelates were held. In 1767, there were three cardinals, nine archbishops, and twenty-four bishops present. Anticlerical wits, as usual, expressed their astonishment that so many zealous chief pastors were on hand, instead of being far away saving souls in their dioceses.

The election of deputies to assemblies was done in two stages. Each diocese sent its bishop (or his representative) and one other benefice holder to an assembly of the archiepiscopal province. In theory the non-episcopal delegate was 'elected', but hardly so in practice. In Angers, it was the so-called general assembly of the diocese, consisting of twenty-three monks and canons of the town and only two curés;[19] in some places, the prelate took whom he pleased. So the provincial meetings were packed with aristocratic dignitaries and members of the ruling oligarchy of the dioceses. The Gascon clergy, for example, meeting in 1755 (not at Auch as usual, but in Dax to mark the consecration of the new cathedral there), consisted of the bishops of Dax, Aire, Oloron, Bayonne, Tarbes, and Couseran, and the archbishop of Auch; of representatives of the bishops of Lescar, Comminges, Lectoure, and Bazas; of vicars-general from Auch, Bayonne, Bazas, and Tarbes; of canons from Aire, Comminges, Dax, and Couseran; and a single parish priest from the diocese of Oloron. (In 1756 there was one curé, in 1758 three, in 1775 two.[20])

The elections finally made in the ecclesiastical provinces were solemn manœuvres to find prestigious openings for ambitious young aristocrats. In the Gascon electoral meetings, there was an agreed rotation (not always observed) among the bishops; as for the other benefice holders, it was a question of string-pulling by prelates and whispered interventions from high society. In 1758, 1760, and 1787 it was nephews of local bishops who were elected; almost invariably in the second half of the century, all the elected were vicars-general. In the whole of France, during the reign of Louis XV, there was only one deputy to the Assemblies of the Clergy of France who was a straightforward parish priest (and the case is doubtful). The system of vicars-general (*grands vicaires*) around each diocesan bishop, apprentices to administration who were regarded as entitled to a monopoly of episcopal promotion, became universal in

France about 1720; a corporation of servants of the Crown was evolving into a self-perpetuating oligarchy. This development was rapidly reflected in the composition of the assemblies.[21] In 1725, of the thirty-two deputies of the second order, twenty-two had studied in Paris, eighteen were vicars-general, twenty-three were relatives of bishops in office, and fifteen later became bishops themselves. After 1750, it was rare for a deputy to be elected who was not a *grand vicaire*; in the assemblies of 1755–88, of the total of 128, no fewer than 115 held this rank in the dioceses, and the rest were on their way to it. They were going up to Paris to meetings of a club of the bishops and their circle. This was why the parliamentary system of the Gallican Church was so formidable, bringing together homogeneous gatherings of proud aristocrats linked by family ties and social relationships, proud of their traditions and well capable of defending the privileges and mission of the Church. Though there were some idle passengers, most were zealous for the interests of the Church and State alike, competing to show statesmanlike qualities deserving of promotion and the approbation of their peers. 'Ambition there took all its forms', said Talleyrand cynically of their meetings, 'and all its distinguishing colours—religion, humanity, patriotism and philosophy.' But the oligarchical composition of the assemblies appealed less and less to the rank and file of the working clergy who were outside the magic circle of privilege. In the form of a letter to a country parson, a pamphleteer of 1789 complained bitterly after meeting 'a young abbé just off his school bench, with no experience of life, no moral fibre, who aspires to Court favour and who has influence operating helping him to rise—likely as not a stranger to the diocese whose deputy he claims to be'. His conclusion was: 'the curés consider these so-called Assemblies of the Clergy of France as coalitions of prelates and of aspirants to the episcopate'.[22]

Under Louis XIV, the assemblies were kept in tutelage. The king would exclude a deputy he disliked by a *lettre de cachet*, or would demand that someone he favoured be elected, and he insisted that the archbishop of Paris should preside. Things were different after the Sun King died: the assemblies gained independence and control of their own procedures. They settled whatever disputes arose concerning the election of deputies; during the reign of Louis XV there were only two or three cases of exclusion by royal pressure, and these brought about by indirect means. Indeed, overt intervention would be resisted. The Assembly of 1740 nullified the election of the archbishop of Sens because he had given his archiepiscopal assemblies the impression that the king had forbidden voting for two of his fellow prelates.[23] From 1715, there was a system of alternating presidents from a panel of four to eight bishops, with one of them taking the lead in the most important business. From the deputies of the Second Order, the Assembly elected the officials who ran the day-to-day programme: the *promoteur* and the secretary. Proceedings were confidential. It was a relaxation of the rule when, in 1758, it was decided to allow bishops who were not members to be told the results of deliberations, though there was to be no revelation of the opinions expressed by individuals. Work went forward in committees, whose members were nominated (with equal numbers of bishops and others) by the senior president, who sat on all of them, along with the two *agents généraux* of the clergy. One of these bodies handled the apportionment of the tax burden among the dioceses, another scrutinized the contracts for loans, another dealt with the current application from the Crown for a *don gratuit*, and another with the verification of the debts of individual dioceses. If matters came to a vote in the full Assembly, it was usually taken by ecclesiastical provinces, a system which helped to prevent the gathering fissiparating into petty factions and competing family clans. The sense of purpose which might be expected to inspire a group of churchmen was intensified by the social homogeneity—abusive though it was—of the membership of the assemblies. Continuity was maintained because of the re-election of various bishops—not always by reason of their ability, it is true, since longevity and tenure of a see in a province with few dioceses helped. In particular, the role of leadership fell to the archbishops: of a total of 736 episcopal deputations from 1690 to 1787, 105 fell to them—or, rather, to thirteen of them, for the prelates of Embrun and of Albi were generally passed over, since their sees were undistinguished, and Lyon was hardly ever represented because its incumbents' claim to 'primacy' was rejected by the rest of the episcopate. One archbishop, Vintimille of Aix and Paris, was the senior president at all meetings from 1726 to 1745, and La Roche-Aymon of Narbonne and Reims from 1760 to 1775.[24] Both were vilified by memoir writers, but not because of any deficiency of worldly perspicuity. A comfortable permanent meeting-place helped to create a feeling of continuity and assurance in the meetings of assemblies. All through the eighteenth century, the deputies congregated at the monastery of the Grands Augustins, which provided a discussion chamber, committee rooms, and a corner for a running buffet, where less formal exchanges took place over tea, coffee, chocolate, bread, and cold meats.[25]

Proceedings were conducted with a solemn, established ceremony which affirmed the dignity and enduring tradition of the clerical hierarchy. The sessions opened with the mass of the Holy Spirit, attended by prelates in rochets and purple capes and the other clergy in long mantles and clerical hats (*bonnets carrés*), with the prior and monks of the Grands Augustins in copes bearing incense and holy water. After the gospel, all present came forward in order of seniority to kiss the book, before returning to their places to listen to a sermon which was not without its references to the conjoined poverty and loyalty of the clergy of the Gallican Church. When, after four to five months of deliberation in the case of great assemblies and two to three months for the lesser ones, the proceedings came to an end, all the battles fought were precisely recorded, and the record made available to the clergy in general. A year or two after the closure, minutes of the assembly were published in full, as well as the report of the agents of the clergy. In addition, reference works were published which made the information by which the Church could be defended easily available to the ecclesiastical lawyers. There was a collection of all legislation and legal texts, the *Mémoires du Clergé* (first edition in two volumes, 1595, the last in twelve volumes, 1700–30), and a collection of the minutes of assemblies drawn up by subjects to facilitate reference to precedents (10 volumes, 1767–81).[26]

II

The effectiveness of the assemblies in maintaining the privileges of the clergy depended, to a great extent, on the work of a small but, by eighteenth-century standards, efficient bureaucracy. The *receveur général* who was in charge of the collection of the taxes was a substantial financier (Boswell visited the one in office in 1775—'the house has no very large room', he observed, 'but is set with mirrors and covered in gold'[27]). But he was not an entrepreneur like the farmers-general of the indirect taxes of the State, making advances, then doing well out of the collecting; he was, rather, an employee, closely supervised. Ever since the Assembly of 1725, when the enraged deputies had discovered that their receiver had left 2,000,000 livres invested in the *billets* of Law's Scheme (rapidly declining in value) while borrowing real money for expenditure,[28] constant checks were made. The agents of the clergy were given a statement of income and disbursements every six months. Full accounts were rendered every five years to the regular assemblies, and by a two-thirds majority the deputies could dismiss their receiver and appoint someone else.

Between meetings of assemblies, affairs were in the hands of the *agents généraux* of the clergy,[29] able young clerics of aristocratic distinction, who were exercising their talents to qualify for a bishopric. They held office for a term of five years, being richly rewarded with a salary, expenses, gratifications, and benefices, with the final award of episcopal promotion to look forward to at the end of their tour of duty. From the king, the agents received letters of appointment as *conseillers d'état*, which gave them the right to attend the judicial branch of the Royal Council and to speak there, though not to vote. (Typically of the age, there were regulations about the type of hat they had to wear, and on 18 October 1770 the chancellor had to take the abbé Dulau aside and instruct him not to wear the aggressively ecclesiastical *bonnet carré*.[30])

Behind the agents was a well-organized bureaucracy. Its members were adept at feathering their own nests—an investigation of 1742 complained of 'the adroit avidity' of certain 'calculators of taxes' and 'couriers' who had pushed their wages up by a factor of thirty in as many years.[31] They were equally efficient, however, in looking after the affairs of the clergy. In 1748, the whole system was formalized under the *Bureau de l'agence*, which was to supervise the archives, consult the clergy's lawyers, send circulars to dioceses, and receive news from diocesan *syndics* in return.[32] Half the secret of the Gallican Church's success in maintaining its privileges lay in these archives. In 1715, the vaulted room with the barred windows and locking cupboards was organized, with an official archivist in charge, an inventory of contents, and a register which had to be signed for any document taken beyond the doors.[33] The other half of the secret was the council of six lawyers which gave consultations on judgments published by the various parlements or the Royal Council concerning Church affairs. The agents expected the diocesan *syndics* to send in all information concerning lawsuits about tithe or clerical privileges. If there was a defeat for the clergy, the causes were analysed and, maybe, an appeal against it lodged with the ministers of the Crown; if a victory, the news was circulated so all dioceses could profit by using the same arguments. In 1783, the *syndics* were invited to send in reports concerning lawsuits every three months, and there were plans, two years later, for setting up officers in each parlement town to collect information more directly. Agents came and went, but the whole process of fact-finding and indexing went on in the

care of the *garde des archives*, M. de Beauvais, assisted in his latter years
by M. Duchesne, his son-in-law, who succeeded him in office in
1775.[34] This legal family deserves its place in the history of the
eighteenth-century Church alongside the great episcopal families,
like the Rohans and the Luynes.

From 1780 to 1785, the two agents were Talleyrand and the
abbé de Boisgelin de Kerdu. Effectively, the work was done by
Talleyrand, since Boisgelin, discredited by his liaison with Mme de
Cavanac, a former mistress of Louis XV, decided that he had already
lost his hope of a bishopric and took things easily. Thus, the great
diplomat served his apprenticeship manœuvring among bishops,
royal ministers, and courtiers on affairs of tithe, parish registers, and
unions of benefices. Now he was confronting Vergennes in defence
of ecclesiastical temporalities, now standing up to the archbishop of
Paris denying his right to call meetings of bishops over the heads of
the agents. The king was pressed for legislation to improve the lot
of the lower clergy by increasing the *congrue*,[35] to regulate the sale of
books, to define the number of 'walled' towns whose benefices were
reserved to graduates, to issue a declaration forbidding curés to
league together against their superiors. The government was persuaded to withdraw a declaration concerning entries in baptismal
registers which the parish priests had found unworkable. The parlements were persuaded to hasten the issue of letters patent confirming
loans and unions of benefices. Tricky legal points were investigated:
could a parlement lift a ban on a curé imposed by a bishop's diocesan court? Could a Jew of Colmar who had bought a seigneurie
exercise the rights of patronage that went with it? Could a neglected
meadow count as uncultivated land so that it escaped tithe when
ploughed for a grain crop? All along the line, the privileges of the
clergy had to be defended. Ecclesiastical property being inalienable,
the lands of the abbey of Chaalis could not be sequestrated for debt:
'we defended [the monks] with regret', said the agents, 'because it
seemed to us that they only invoked the privilege to protect themselves from being obliged to fulfil their obligations'.[36]

The agents were nominated by the ecclesiastical provinces in their
assemblies (as will be remembered, two deputies, one being the
bishop, came up from each diocese). There was an established rotation. In 1765, the provinces of Vienne and Bourges nominated one
agent apiece; in 1770 the provinces of Lyon and Bordeaux, and so
on at quinquennial intervals—Rouen paired with Toulouse, Tours
with Aix, Sens and Auch, Paris and Albi, Embrun and Arles, Reims
and Narbonne. These arrangements were the cadre within which

the forces of aristocratic and episcopal influence operated. In 1775, the province of Rouen elected Pierre-Louis de la Rochefoucauld Bayers; his uncle was archbishop of Rouen, and his brother was bishop of Beauvais, where he served as *grand vicaire*. Meanwhile the province of Toulouse elected Louis-François-Alexandre de Jarente de Sénas d'Orgeval, a vicar-general of the diocese of Toulouse and nephew of the bishop of Orléans. When they retired from office five years later, the first became bishop of Saintes, and the second became coadjutor of his uncle at Orléans.[37] In 1780, the choice of the province of Aix lighted upon the abbé de Boisgelin de Kerdu, nephew of the archbishop and a *grand vicaire* in his diocese. About the same time, the province of Tours was electing Talleyrand, nephew of the archbishop of Reims. As usual, these elections had been settled quietly off the record long ago. In June 1772, the bishop of Dol had been writing to Bareau de Girac, bishop of Rennes, as he had to various other episcopal colleagues, soliciting his vote for his younger brother, a vicar-general of Nantes—'assuming always that you have not as yet contracted an engagement to someone else'.[38] The effort was vain. Among the prelates of Tours, Angers, Rennes, Quimper, Nantes, Le Mans, Saint-Brieuc, Tréguier, Saint-Malo, Léon, and Vannes, a majority had formed for Talleyrand by the meeting of 1775, where the real decision had been taken. There was a more dramatic confrontation in 1788 in the assembly of the province of Sens. The archbishop there was pushing for the abbé d'Osmond, brother of one bishop and nephew of another, to the chagrin of the bishop of Auxerre, who was recommending his own nephew, the abbé de la Bintinaye, a *grand vicaire* of his other uncle, the archbishop of Bordeaux. At the actual meeting, the archbishop of Sens was absent, supposedly overcome by the 'heat', so Cicé, bishop of Auxerre, had to preside. But he gained no advantage from his position as chairman, for a letter arrived from Versailles declaring that the king wished d'Osmond to be chosen. So he was, but the days when the clergy knuckled under to Louis XIV were gone—the Assembly annulled the proceedings, and ordered the province of Sens to make new elections.[39] There were regulations to ensure that candidates for the post of agent were in priest's orders, actually beneficed within the province sponsoring them, holding a true benefice and not just a chapel without cure of souls, and having resided there for a year before the election.[40] These rules, except for the residence, were observed, since elections were foreseen for a long time ahead, and minor details of a benefice here or there were easily adjusted. These were key posts, and they were awarded by the play of family influence within the episcopate, tempered by obscure political pressures and a determination to see the affairs of the Church efficiently run and its privileges preserved.

III

With the aid of this efficient bureaucracy, the Assembly strove to reform the archaic system of assessing and levying clerical taxes. Since the diocese was the unit of assessment, the numerous confusions over boundaries and jurisdictions compelled the Assembly to decide from time to time which diocesan bureau had the taxing authority over particular benefices. Could the dioceses of Boulogne and Amiens impose levies on their enclaves lying in more recently conquered territories which had not been incorporated within the financial jurisdiction of the clergy of France?[41] The diocese of Clermont taxed the abbey of Chaise-Dieu, but could it include the dependent priory of Poussan in the Montpellier area?[42] Could Arras, with its abbey of Saint-Vaast, include the *prévoté* of Mesnil in the see of Dijon?[43] A more serious problem was the varying loads of debt which had been incurred by individual dioceses. To raise the money for the benevolences given to Louis XIV in 1710, 1711, and 1715, the dioceses had been allowed to borrow on their own account, with the hope that they would obtain a lower rate of interest locally. Thereafter, the Assembly centralized borrowing and forbade independent initiative, and in 1735 took in hand the task of trying to force the dioceses back to solvency. Four failed to send in returns of their indebtedness, nine were found to be making no effort to repay the borrowed capital, and seven were trying, but behindhand. In 1742, the Assembly ordered the submission of a return of indebtedness every six months, and from then onwards had a standing item in its proceedings: a statement classifying the dioceses into six categories, the bottom one consisting of the hopeless defaulters. According to changes in local circumstances, these categories showed variations, but the hard core of failures always included Rieux, Beziers, Agen, Grasse, Vence, and Senez. They were all poor areas, and the benefice holders of Beziers took a long time to recover from disastrous floods, as those of Agen from famine, and those of Vence from warfare, while those of Grasse and more particularly of Senez suffered from scandalous overcharging to clerical taxation for more than a century.[44]

Here, indeed, was the most intractable problem of all, the long-standing injustice of the assessment breakdown between dioceses. Up to 1755, the assemblies shared out the burden on the basis of proportionality established long ago in 1516, revised in 1641 and 1646. Everyone knew that the figures were unreasonable. The area south of the Loire was known to pay more in proportion to its resources compared with the provinces north of that river. In 1701, the archbishop of Arles suggested drastic action to rectify the balance. Let all benefice holders be constrained to make a declaration of income, with the diocesan bureau entitled, in case of fraud, either to levy a punitive quadrupled tax, or simply to confiscate the revenues of the suspect and award him a pension of the amount shown on his return. A commission of prelates from north of the Loire would visit the south to check on procedures, and another from the south would go northwards.[45] Such an inquisitorial proposal was too unsporting to be accepted under the *ancien régime*, and anomalies grew worse. The clergy, better educated and with more contacts, compared notes with each other across diocesan boundaries; the legend in Autun was that the misdemeanours of a sixteenth-century bishop had brought down double impositions on his collaborators as a punishment.[46] Yet it was not Autun that made the running in complaining to the Assembly in the first half of the eighteenth century; it was Comminges, Narbonne, Glandève, Embrun (in alliance with Grenoble, Gap, and Saint-Paul-Trois-Châteaux), Grasse, and Poitiers. A mistake made in 1670 had been perpetuated, said Comminges; non-existent benefices were being counted, said Narbonne; Embrun and its three allied dioceses had a story of being taxed in local florins until 1515, and a mistake then being made when translating florins into livres.[47] The Assembly granted no remissions, except to Glandève, declaring that everyone should wait until a completely new taxation table was drawn up. Sure enough, the Assembly's own enquiries revealed anomalies even more scandalous than those complained of: the poor and tiny diocese of Senez had been paying four times as much as it ought,[48] and the diocese of Albi, which had barely a tenth of the revenues of Paris, had been paying as much and more.[49]

The will-o'-the-wisp of a comprehensive revaluation of all benefices of the kingdom based on the declarations of the holders as supervised by the diocesan *syndics* flitted through the discussions of various assemblies.[50] In the end, by one means or another—incomplete information of this kind, a pilot scheme in eight dioceses, information from the Crown about the value of the 'consistorial benefices' which were administered by the royal demesne in vacancies—a new tax assessment schedule was devised.[51] The concept of taxable income as against actual income was introduced, benefices being divided into categories, paying more in proportion to greater resources, but less according to greater weight of pastoral responsibilities. Taking the taxable wealth of the whole Church as rather more than 31 million, the diocese of Paris was reckoned to be worth just under 2 million, and so on down to Senez at 15,000, Vence and Glandève at 8,000, and Belley at 6,312.[52] The new tables fell far short of absolute justice; in particular, the admirable theory of exacting less from clergy engaged in the pastoral ministry was not carried into practice as comprehensively as parish priests desired and deserved. But given the complexities of the *ancien régime* and the almost universal indifference to the concept of simple honesty, it was an astonishing achievement.

IV

Apart from running the taxation system, the Assembly took upon itself, as a major duty, the presentation of the grievances of the Gallican Church on the occasion of granting supply. The complaints were always marshalled and processed ready for discussion, because the agents and the bureaucracy had been continually in session as a clearing-house and a centre for legal advice for all the dioceses. Many cases of ecclesiastics unfairly treated by the law courts or royal officials were settled by the agents themselves: it was only the more intractable instances that came to a full Assembly to be made a subject of official protest.

In the second half of the century, the assemblies were much concerned with the attempts of the secular magistrates to relieve the laity of some of their traditional obligations. The parlements of Toulouse and Grenoble were transferring from communities to tithe owner the duty of furnishing candles and other necessities for divine service, and that of Grenoble was trying to extend to all tithe the principle of compulsory alms; the parlement of Provence wanted the clergy to pay more towards the repair of their vicarages.[53] The magistrates of Brittany were the leaders of this lay attack. In 1721 they had declared the curés to be responsible for all vicarage repairs, great or small, and their ordinance stood unchanged in 1762,[54] while in 1735 they had annulled the new table of fees for marriages and funerals published by the bishops of the province.[55] Wherever the boundaries between ecclesiastical and secular jurisdiction were uncertain, the magistrates were encroaching. The archiepiscopal *chambres supérieures des décimes* dealt with disputes about clerical taxation, but if a diocesan *receveur* ran off with the cash, were the lay courts entitled to adjudicate on the financial obligations of his sureties?[56] After due investigation of faith and morals, a bishop could refuse a priest a visa for a benefice; the secular courts claimed the right to check if the refusal was justified, and if not to award the temporalities.[57] In an unprecedented intervention in 1771, the parlement of Dijon even claimed to give canonical institution as well.[58] Only the Church could lift the obligations of monastic or marriage vows; true, but the parlements argued that the civil consequences of these vows followed only upon genuine consent, and the fact of that 'consent' was a matter for purely lay enquiry.[59] Curés disciplined by their bishops could use the procedure of *appel comme d'abus* to go before the parlements; the judges might make the diocesan legal officials liable to damages for 'calumny',[60] or even lift the ecclesiastical censure altogether. Thus, in 1730, the Jansenist curé of Saint-Barthélemy in Paris, interdicted by his archbishop, was carrying on in his parish under warrant of the magistrates, 'giving invalid absolutions . . . and saying sacrilegious masses', said the Assembly.[61] This was just one of the incidents in the Jansenist furore, coming to its crisis with the Assembly's letter to the king of 20 June 1752; in denouncing the *arrêt* of the parlement forbidding the refusal of the sacraments to opponents of the bull *Unigenitus*, this letter claimed, with the full rigour of the Dominical texts, that the words of bishops are the words of Christ, and what they bind on earth is bound in heaven.[62]

The encroachments of the parlements fitted into a general pattern of developing anticlericalism which haunted the assemblies from the middle of the century. In 1745, the alarm was sounded against the illegal assemblies of Protestants and the marriages conducted by their pastors. The king was reminded of the Calvinists' 'love of a liberty that is the enemy of all authority', and was asked to enforce the laws against them, a request which was repeated in 1750 and 1775.[63] At the Assembly of 1750, the alarm was sounded against irreligious publications, especially the letters *Ne repugnate vestro bono*, on the theme of the social uselessness of the clergy.[64] Fifteen years later, it was the leading works of Voltaire and Rousseau that were condemned.[65]

In 1775, the theme of discussion was 'the decline of religion'. The Assembly refrained from lamentations about the propaganda of the philosophes, and took a practical view of the causes: there was a shortage of suitable vocations to the ministry, because of the high cost of an education lasting to the age of 24, the poverty of life on the *congrue*, the long wait for promotion, and the lack of adequate provision for retirement. The plan therefore was to confiscate benefices without cure of souls and to suppress the minor clergy of cathedrals, using the funds made available to provide free educational places, improved salaries, and official retirement pensions. Once these pensions were organized, the system of a resigning curé appointing his successor could be ended; bishops would gain more control over patronage, and would be able to encourage ability with promotion.[66]

This last proviso was typical: the assemblies were devoted to maintaining and increasing the power of the bishops. Abbeys like Cluny and cathedral chapters like Saintes, which enjoyed episcopal jurisdiction over certain parishes, were narrowly watched;[67] so too were curés who claimed the right to act collectively or to challenge the jurisdiction of their bishop.[68] In 1762, the proposal to delate the curés of Sées to the Royal Council was passed 'by acclamation'.[69]

Even so, it is remarkable how these gatherings of aristocrats fought for the Church as an institution against their own social class. Their brothers and cousins found sinecures in the Order of Malta and the Order of Saint-Lazare, but the prelates of successive assemblies waged war on these two abusive institutions. They opposed the knights of Malta's claims for freedom from tithe, for burials in their own chapels, for honorific distinctions in parish churches, for exemption for curés under their patronage from episcopal visitations.[70] The manœuvres of the Crown, from 1762 onwards, to reinforce the endowments of Saint-Lazare with the property of the decadent Order of Saint-Ruf and of the canons regular of Saint-Antoine met with unsparing condemnation. Must the clergy pay for 'the opulence and grandeur' of an institution that was 'of no sort of utility to the Church?', they asked. When the comte de Provence became grand master, increasing royal pressure compelled the clergy to offer something—but they did so with an ill grace, 'more by condescension than by justice', they bitterly minuted.[71]

V

In 1765, to forestall the condemnation by the Assembly of an injudicious pastoral letter he had written, the bishop of Alais argued that these gatherings were 'purely economic'. They were convoked solely to vote taxation to the Crown and to administer the financial affairs of the Church. If this had been true, the Gallican Church would have lived in administrative chaos, and, what is more, would not have been able to speak with a single voice in matters of doctrine and morals. Ideally, the forum for such pronouncements ought to have been a national council of bishops, but the Crown would not allow such a body to meet. The promise that some great doctrinal pronouncement by the Gallican episcopate would shed a vicarious splendour on the throne, as Nicaea had given lustre to the diadem of Constantine,[72] sounded unconvincing at Versailles. Requests for the convocation of provincial councils to deal with Jansenist bishops[73] were turned down—except for a meeting of the province of Embrun, which turned out to be a disreputable affair, not to be repeated. If the traditional councils of the Church were banned, however, there was an alternative—as the Assembly pointed out at length to the bishop of Alais. 'The right to teach and instruct is inseparable from the person of bishops and, far from diminishing their rights, their meeting together serves to give new force to their pronouncements.'[74] True, a bishop can be *judged* only by a provincial council, but when a pastoral letter has been published outside the individual diocese, it becomes a matter to be dealt with by the whole episcopate. The strict logic of this argument would demand that a doctrinal pronouncement of an Assembly should come from its episcopal members alone, and, indeed, this was what the procedures ensured. Deputies of the 'Second Order' were excluded from the settlement of matters of doctrine and morals unless their right to speak for the bishops of their province was explicitly stated in their letters of appointment. Conversely,[75] when such matters were discussed, bishops who were not members of the Assembly could attend. Thus at an extraordinary Assembly of forty-nine prelates in 1713–14, 'as only matters concerning doctrine were to be discussed, and not temporal affairs', the retired bishops of Avranches and of Tulle were present and signed the proceedings.[76] Normally, prelates took precedence according to the rank of their see, but in the Assembly they sat in order of the date of their consecration.[77] It was, as it were, a reminder that the worldly honours that went with ecclesiastical office were irrelevant: it was the interests of religion that were the essential concern of the delegates.

With this sort of justification, assemblies made the sort of pronouncements on doctrine and morals that might more appropriately have come from a national council of the episcopate. In the seventeenth century, the decrees of Trent, which had been refused

endorsement by the Crown, were described, independently, as 'rules
and oracles of the Church'. In 1700, various propositions of relaxed
morality had been censured. A pastoral letter on the Jansenist issue
for adoption in all dioceses was circulated five years later; nine years
after that a statement on the doctrine of grace was issued. In 1765,
all bishops were recommended to foster the cult of the Sacred Heart
(the queen's favourite devotion); and, in the course of the century,
applications were made to the Pope for the canonization of Mme
Chantal, François Régis, Mère Agnès of Saint-Catherine de Lauzet,
and Alain de Solmniac.[78] The Assembly of 1770 decided to sponsor
its own venture into apologetics, issuing an *Avertissement* on 'the
dangers of unbelief', followed five years later by another on 'the
advantages of the Christian religion'.

The word 'catechism' is absent from the index of the collections
of minutes. Maybe, as has been suggested, this is evidence of lack of
interest in popular religion, but with so many diocesan catechisms
available, and with orthodox and Jansenist controversialists lying in
wait on either hand to pounce on any offending word, the deputies
may be forgiven for letting sleeping dogs lie.

VI

Seen from Versailles, the whole point of the convocation of an
Assembly was to obtain a vote of money.[79] Louis XIV established—
almost—his right to have what he demanded without question. His
don gratuit of 1665 was the last which was held up by discussion.
Then, the royal commissioners had to present themselves three
times, on the last occasion laying on the table the drafts of the edicts
the clergy were demanding, before the grant was approved.
Thereafter, the Great Monarch's absolute will prevailed: he received
his vote 'without difficulty', or 'at once', as the minutes record. Even
so, he renewed promises of exemption from ordinary taxation; when
a *don gratuit* of 8 million was voted in 1711, it was recorded that the
clergy would never have to pay to a *dixième*—'exempt in perpetuity
. . . whatever may happen'. After the death of Louis XIV, supply was
no longer automatic. The Crown proceeded as if it would be, but
the Assembly always deliberated before agreeing, and might—just
possibly—refuse if the privileges of ecclesiastics were threatened. In
1725, an edict proclaiming the levy of a new tax, the *cinquantième*,
blandly included everyone, 'privileged or unprivileged . . . ecclesiastics or seculars'. The clergy had been in this situation before, in

1710–11 at the time of Louis XIV's *dixième*, and once again they managed to obtain a royal declaration exempting them. But it was a real fight and a real triumph this time. No supply was voted, and no arrangements to pay the *rentes* to State creditors were made at the 1725 Assembly, and a new one had to be called in the following year.[80] The declarations then extracted (for a *don* of 5 million) promised freedom from all ordinary taxes for the clergy in perpetuity, even if royal legislation specifically included them. Thereafter, amid the harsh demands of war, the clergy demonstrated patriotism—12 million in 1734, 10 million the next year, 3½ million in 1740, 12 million in 1742, 15 million in 1743, 11 million in 1747, and 16 million in 1748. But in May 1749, the controller-general, Machault, inserted yet another sinister preface in an edict establishing a *vingtième*—there would be 'no exceptions . . . all proprietors or *usufruitiers*, nobles or commoners, privileged or non-privileged' would pay. *Usufruitiers* presumably meant the clergy, and to establish the point circuitously, Machault ordered the *clergé étranger* (that is, of provinces annexed since 1561) to register their possessions with the *directeurs* of the *vingtième*. When, in the following year, Louis XV asked the Assembly for 7,500,000 livres, there was an outcry. D'Ormesson's speech[81] of application spoke of 'obligation', and he made formal the demand for declarations of clerical revenues, as well as revealing that the government was proposing to liquidate the debt of the clergy—no doubt as a first step in curtailing their financial autonomy. 'Our conscience and our honour', the Assembly told the king, 'will not permit us to consent to changing into an obligatory tribute a contribution which can only be the offering of our devotion.' The bishops of Languedoc forbade the intendant of their province to approach officials of their dioceses for tax information;[82] the aged bishop of Verdun published an open letter to the controller-general which was a masterpiece of sentimental obduracy;[83] the bishop of Grenoble rushed into print a three-volume defence of clerical immunities;[84] while the bishop of Metz excommunicated the intendant who was trying to extract clerical declarations.[85] The government unleashed a swarm of pamphleteers,[86] Voltaire included. 'Antichrist has come: he has sent numerous circular letters to the bishops of France, in which he has had the audacity to treat them as Frenchmen and subjects of the king.'[87] The clergy stood firm. 'On this occasion', said D'Argenson, 'the lower clergy . . . were absolutely solid with the higher, something never seen before,' and he refers to threats of putting the land under an interdict or, more practically, demanding the summoning of the

Estates General.[88] In the end, the king gave way: there was no hope of supply from the Church unless he did. Because he had capitulated, the Assembly demonstrated its generosity in 1755, and because of the war, further grants were made at an extraordinary Assembly three years later, and also in 1760 and 1762. A proposal to include ecclesiastics in a land census and their apparent inclusion in the edict of December 1764 on the taxation of *rentes* led to a new battle of wills; the long Assembly of 1765 withheld a third of the subsidy requested until these threatening proposals were withdrawn.[89] Large grants were made in 1770, 1772, and 1774; then Calonne's new designs against clerical immunities led to a further part-refusal of supply in 1785. Finally, in 1788, the clergy led the way in forcing the bankrupt king to call the Estates General. Only 1,800,000 livres of the 8,000,000 demanded was voted, and the remonstrance of the clergy of 15 June 'lifted the aristocratic revolt on to a new plane of dignity and universality'.[90] They had clung all the while to their unique privilege of voting their own taxation, they said, not for selfish reasons, but as custodians of 'the remains of the old national franchises'. The whole nation ought to follow their example and reclaim its rights, so long in abeyance. 'The glory of your Majesty is, not to be king of France, but king of Frenchmen, and the heart of your subjects is the finest of your domains.'

The downright refusal of supply was, however, abnormal. Usually, the demands of the Crown were granted by dignified, formal stages.[91] The clergy would go to Versailles to 'harangue' the monarch, then six members of the Council would come to the Grands Augustins on a courtesy visit. A few days later, the same six would return bearing the actual royal demand. The president of the Assembly would reply, saying how hard-up his constituents were, and how difficult it would be to find the sum required; the councillors would then retire into an adjoining room and wait for the reply, which was usually given on the same day. All the while, of course, less formal discussions had gone on in the committees with the government officials concerned. Seen from the *salle des séances* of the Grands Augustins, the point of all that was happening was to proclaim clerical grievances alongside the grudging vote of the funds demanded. Thus, at the extraordinary Assembly of 1782,[92] after the bishop of Senez had preached on Exodus 35: 29, 'omnes obtulerunt donaris', saying that paying up was a patriotic duty, the deputies proceeded to complain of the oppressions of the parlement of Toulouse on tithe owners, of the parlement of Rennes on the bishop and cathedral chapter of Saint-Malo, of the intendant of the *généralité* of

Caen who was trying to make the clergy pay towards the upkeep of roads, of the duc d'Orléans who was demanding payment of a feudal obligation, *foi et hommage*, from the lands of the Church within his *apanage*, of laymen who were evading tithe by switching areas of cultivation, of a peculiar new fraud concerning ecclesiastical benefices arising from a gap in the legislation on the subject, of the scoundrels who were circulating the works of Voltaire and Rousseau free of charge, and under the cover of night were throwing copies over the garden walls of nunneries. An Assembly also had a good deal of formal business to transact. The agents of the clergy would make their report, describing how the central bureaucracy had handled the matters which had arisen since the last meeting; the *receveur-général* would present his accounts, and there would be cases concerning disputed tax assessments coming up from the *chambres supérieures des décimes*. As befitted churchmen, there were charitable allocations to be made, 10,000 livres or so, partly from common funds and partly by the deputies forgoing four days' salary. In 1770, an extra 10,000 was found to give to the lieutenant of police of Paris for the families of those killed in the panic stampede at the fireworks for the marriage of the dauphin. There were pensions to be awarded to converted Protestant ministers, funds to a few favoured enterprises like missions to the Levant or seminaries at home, and gratifications to the authors of books defending religion. Less disinterested gifts were made to lawyers who had given consultations, and dignified rewards were proffered to great personages who had been helpful, in the form of 'bourses de jetons', purses of specially minted medallions.

VII

The subsidies voted by the Assemblies of the Clergy were not the only contributions made by churchmen to the State. Payments also came in from the so-called *clergé étranger*,[93] who were within the kingdom, but were not represented in the Assemblies and not subject to its assessments. The contrat de Poissy of 1561 applied only to the dioceses existing at that time; provinces united to France afterwards did not qualify for inclusion, though exceptions were made for Béarn and Navarre. Thus there was a separate taxation system for the provinces of Artois, Flanders, Hainault, Alsace, Franche Comté, Roussillon, and eventually for Lorraine. The clergy of Roussillon bought off royal taxes by the payment of agreed subscriptions. In Flanders, Artois, and Hainault, where the provincial estates voted taxation to the Crown, the clergy joined with the laity in paying their share. In Alsace,[94] ecclesiastical lands acquired after the Treaty of Munster of 24 October 1648 were liable to ordinary taxation, and lands held from before that date which were not directly cultivated by the benefice holder paid half tax. Capitation was due, though it was a special tax in Alsace, devoted to maintaining the *curés royaux*, the priests of the new parishes set up in Protestant areas. This levy could be heavy: in 1735 the bishop of Strasbourg paid 9,480 livres, nearly double his clerical taxation for that year. In addition, the Alsatian clergy, from time to time, paid a *don gratuit*. 'If the Government has been good enough to call their contributions a "free gift",' said a committee of clergy in 1788, 'it is a favour that makes no difference, for nothing could be further from being voluntary.' Even so, the dioceses of Alsace assessed themselves and, like the assemblies in the Grands Augustins, made difficulties about the level of contribution expected of them. The diocese of Bâle in 1735 audaciously offered only 3,500 livres; after a struggle it had to pay 20,000. Negotiations were complex. There were five dioceses in Alsace: Strasbourg and Bâle extensive, Spire, Besançon, and Metz smaller, and all having other parishes outside the province, and indeed, outside France altogether, under their jurisdiction. Five sets of arguments in dioceses which were not exclusively French and which were in fortress zones frequently suffering the ravages of war meant that the government could not be too exigent. In any case, in all the more recently acquired provinces the Crown was inclined to be lenient to woo the inhabitants. So the *clergé étranger* in Alsace and elsewhere escaped lightly. According to Necker, their income was about a fifth of the income of the clergy of France, but they paid only an eleventh part of the taxation voted by the general assemblies at the Grands Augustins. In 1749, Machault d'Arnouville attempted to compel the *clergé étranger* to furnish details of their possessions to the collectors of the *vingtièmes*, intending to subject them to ordinary taxation. The clergy of France held up supply until the government withdrew its claim, and the *clergé étranger* continued to pay at its modest rate until the Revolution came to absorb all individuals and corporations into a national taxation system.

When well-informed contemporaries estimated the amount that churchmen paid to national taxation, they included the votes of the *clergé étranger*; Necker, for example, put their contribution at 940,000 annually (though he was not including the capitation and the land which fell under the half-tax regulations). But there were other exactions of the Crown which were not normally included in the calculations. In times of war when the country faced defeat, the silver of churches could be requisitioned to be melted down to pay the armies. Louis XIV so ordered in 1689,[95] and Louis XV in 1759. Churches could retain such objects as were necessary for the decent performance of divine service, or to pay off debts. During the Seven Years War, some bishops obeyed Louis XV's orders with excessive zeal, instructing their curés to retain only the communion plate and a crucifix; the king had to issue new instructions authorizing the retention of everything necessary for divine service.[96] On Christmas Eve 1759, a curé of the diocese of Le Mans noted wryly that such sacrifices were not for his parishioners: 'as we have only what is necessary, indeed, not even that, we sent nothing'.[97] An extension of this emergency principle was the obligation for monasteries to receive within their walls aged or wounded soldiers, the 'oblats'. This was commuted by the Crown into a money tax. No doubt the change was to the relief of monks who cared for piety and decorum; what pleased the king was that something like a quarter of a million came in annually to the Treasury.[98] Then, there were the more indirect and stealthy impositions of the Crown. The absolute monarchy of France roared like a lion when demanding its heavy taxes, and as they were never enough, roamed like a jackal to find pickings to make up the deficit. From time to time, the dioceses, like municipalities, found that they had to buy up offices created by the Crown, or run the risk of ignorant practitioners confusing their affairs. That was why the diocese of Angers in 1778–9 paid good money to rescue the posts of apostolic notaries from the ordinary notaries, not being willing to leave applications and promotions in the hands of those unskilled in benefice law.[99] The State levied its fees on every legal transaction, and these were innumerable in a landowning Church in a litigious century. More especially, the government drew money from the clergy through its mortmain and leasehold legislation. When land came into the possession of an ecclesiastical foundation, there was a loss of secular taxation revenue to the Crown and of succession dues to the seigneurs; so compensation had to be paid. As far as the lord was concerned, churchmen might pay him *lods et ventes* one year in twenty, or they might designate 'un homme vivant, mourant et confisquant' whose death (or felony) would be taxable. For the State a compensation known as *amortissement* was paid. In November 1724 a royal edict regulated this as one-fifth of the capital value of 'noble' lands and one-sixth of that of commoners. The ruthless edict of 1749[100] made it difficult for the Church to acquire any new property at all, and what it did acquire (for example, by feudal escheat) had to be sold within a year and a day. But the *fermiers* of the royal demesne counted almost any change made in the use of ecclesiastical property as subject to the payment of *amortissement*: the rebuilding of a burnt-out house, unless it was precisely identical with the old one, unions of benefices, buildings acquired for charitable purposes, legacies in the form of annuities—all these were held to be chargeable. In 1774, one particular injustice in this programme of exactions was removed: canons and other churchmen who chose to live in smaller rented lodgings would not be charged on the leasing of their official houses. There was a catch, however—they would have to pay the *droit de nouvel acquêt*, one year's revenue out of every twenty.[101] The tax farmers of the State also collected a fee on the signing of a lease; ecclesiastics were obliged to make formal contracts before notaries, instead of evading taxation by agreements under private seal and signature. The law, perhaps, had not been clear; at least, in 1740 the Assembly paid the Crown 120,000 livres to buy off the arrears of the *droit de contrôle* which so many benefice holders had failed to render.[102] This did not prevent the intendant of Limoges, however, from charging the monks of Grandmont the usual tax on all the leases they had contracted privately since 1731.[103] Some of the demands of the *fermiers* of the tax were far-fetched indeed, and the wrath of the Assembly was correspondingly intensified: the documents establishing the dowries of nuns were held as chargeable,[104] and even curés who cultivated their own lands or gathered their own tithes were challenged to fork out on the leases that they *ought* to have been making.[105]

Did the Church of France pay its fair share of national taxation? We have seen how, quite apart from clerical subsidies freely voted, the government also extracted money indirectly under various pretexts—though it might be said that these harassments were the lot of most Frenchmen. The abbé Véri[106] argued that the *taille* and capitation paid by the contractors who farmed ecclesiastical property should also be taken into consideration; after all, these entrepreneurs took their expenses into account when bidding for their leases. What adjustments to total figures ought to be made for indirect payments of various kinds it is impossible to say. Thanks to the confusion of French finances, it is just as difficult to give exact figures for the total national burden. So only an impressionistic answer can be given on the question of 'fairness'. The monies levied by the general assemblies and by the *clergé étranger* during the reign of Louis XV averaged nearly 5 million a year, but this broad figure conceals a remarkable escalation of payments. In 1725–34, the clergy were making an annual contribution of 2,686,620; in 1765–74, of 7,352,108; in a period during which the State budget rather more than doubled, the clergy budget tripled.[107] According to Necker, in 1784 the Church was paying rather more than 10,000,000 a year; it is estimated that in the next few years the figure rose to between 16,000,000 and 18,000,000.[108] Sénac de Meilhan, an intendant in the latter years of the *ancien régime*, thought that 17,000,000 a year would have been a fair amount.[109] Thus, the Church was hardly paying its appropriate share earlier in the century, but came to be doing so in the reign of Louis XVI. As a different method of reckoning 'fairness', we might turn from comparing grand totals and look at the proportion of income paid by individual clerics as against, say, what provincial nobles paid. 'It is certain that no secular person pays as much as ecclesiastical property does,' said the abbé Véri in 1780. 'The tax demanded from benefice holders runs at a sixth or a fifth or even a quarter of the revenues of abbeys and at a twelfth, a tenth or an eighth for bishops and curés.'[110] True, assessments as between individual clerics were often unjustly calculated, giving undue favour to the great; even so, a modern calculation of the payments (after the tax reform of 1760) by eighty abbeys shows they did indeed pay a quarter to a sixth, while of thirty-nine bishops, sixteen paid over a tenth and thirteen between a tenth and a fifteenth.[111] This is more than nobles or many of the bourgeois paid. Significantly (once again, Véri points this out), the clergy, however grudgingly, almost always gave the ministers of the Crown the sum they demanded. No doubt, like the provincial estates which paid by *abonnement*, they got favourable terms because their credit was good and they could borrow to produce money quickly. Even so, had they been under-paying outrageously, one imagines that government pressure would have been more ruthless and disputes more frequent. The refusals of the clergy were in defence of their privileged independence, rather than to challenge the particular sum of money demanded. The general willingness of churchmen in their *cahiers* in 1789 to pay ordinary taxation (provided they remained an Order in the State) has been taken, rightly, as evidence of their affinities with the Third Estate and of their patriotism. But it was also evidence of their common sense: they knew they had little to lose, financially, by the change.

VIII

Lay society envied the privileges of churchmen, and was inclined to suppose—however unjustly—that they did well out of them. A hard-pressed taxpayer would see how ecclesiastics were exempt from the payment of *franc fief* (a due levied on commoners who bought noble land), from the *corvée* (forced labour, generally on the roads), the billeting of soldiers, local payments towards roads and bridges, taxes to pay off the debts of towns and provinces, and from municipal charitable levies. The lands of ecclesiastical benefices escaped tax when cultivated directly—an exasperating example would be to see a cleric selling off in bulk the wine from his vineyard exempt from the *aides*, the internal customs duties. An ecclesiastic rejoiced also in exemption on the patrimonial lands which came to him in direct succession, provided, once more, that he cultivated them directly; also on whatever property brought in the small income representing his clerical 'title', the sum needed to qualify for ordination. An envious onlooker on these accumulations of privilege might overlook the severe restrictions which, in fact, were applied to clerical immunities. Tenants who leased ecclesiastical lands paid ordinary taxation. So too did clerics on all property coming to them by collateral succession, or which they had purchased. And even that coming by direct succession could only be cultivated directly (and thus be privileged) if it lay in the actual parish of domicile; otherwise it had to be leased out to laymen subject to the *taille*. The tax farmers and officials were always hovering, ready to swoop. They argued that the possession of a benefice, as well as ordination, was a necessary condition to enjoy the immunity on patrimonial lands,[112] and if a cleric took up a lay occupation, he was conscripted forthwith for lay burdens like the *corvée*.[113]

The arguments of the laity for subjecting the clergy to ordinary taxation are found classified and enumerated in the treatises of the Gallican lawyers, who kept every precedent and every philosophical—and even theological—consideration handy for use to defend the purses of the laity. They were much the same arguments as were used to justify taking Church property in time of national emergency. A typical discussion would begin with a learned—and slanted—historical excursus.[114] In the earliest centuries, churchmen had held their possessions in common; in the fourth and fifth centuries they had divided them into four parts, with the poor and church buildings having a quarter each. Since then, laymen had been compelled to over-endow the Church by threats of excommunication and by superstitious preachments,[115] and accumulations of wealth had fallen into the hands of prelates and great abbeys. In short, we have now travelled a long way from the golden days when the austere missionary Church deserved a privilege like exemption from taxation. But in fact, the exemption had arisen along with the misapplication of the income. When the Franks conquered the Gauls, they freed the clergy from personal servitude, but not from ordinary taxation.[116] The immunity of clerics arose in the tenth century, and was maintained by the claim that the Church depended on the Pope alone.[117] The French State had never accepted this proposition, and the bull *In Coena Domini* of 1536, excommunicating those who taxed ecclesiastics without papal permission, had never been published in the kingdom. What dependence on Rome meant can be seen by looking at the unedifying causes for which popes had levied subsidies from their clergy—for crusades, onslaughts on heretics, campaigns against Christian princes, and even against rival popes.[118] Far better, like the Assembly of the Clergy in 1715, volunteer to support the king in defence of his frontiers.[119] The historical excursus would, throughout, be tailored to demonstrate how ecclesiastical immunities had arisen because of custom—by accident, not by divine right and scriptural tradition. Comparison would help here; look across the Channel to England, where the parsons pay taxes in the same way as everyone else. 'Rien n'est plus juste.'[120] Churchmen, it was always said, had the usufruct of their possessions rather than absolute ownership. The point could be taken a stage further. Their usufruct entitled them to draw an 'honest subsistence', no more; the surplus they were obliged to administer for the benefit of the poor. Church property, therefore, was 'the patrimony of the poor', who were the true, though passive owners.[121] In essence, a benefice is the right to preach, confess, and say mass, and its endowment is 'a fund that the Church has confided [to the holder] to employ for pious uses, and more especially to help the local poor'.[122] As patterns of social existence change, these various funds for pious uses need to be reallocated, and the Church authorities can do this. But who verifies that it is properly done, who checks that the subsistence taken is limited to what is 'honest', and who protects the rights of the poor? As these are questions of 'distributive justice' in society, the answer is clear: the secular sovereign must do so because he alone has the oversight of the whole social structure. 'The State is not in the Church, but the Church is in the State, which existed before it and which received it into its protection.'[123] The claim of the sovereign is double, for 'we must not confound the clergy with the Church . . . the Church is the assembly of the faithful under their legitimate pastors'.[124] The sovereign speaks for the mass of the faithful, as it were within the Church, just as he offers the Church his protection, as it were from outside it. 'Let every soul be subject to the higher powers,' says St Paul (Romans 13: 1; Titus 3: 1; cf. Peter 2: 13). St Augustine and St Ambrose say the same. Churchmen enjoying vast collective revenues need the protection of the secular arm more than other people,[125] and the gospels enjoin them to live austerely and humbly. They are, as Louis XIV observed, 'free from the dangers of war, from the wastefulness of luxury and the burden of rearing families'.[126] Therefore, they must contribute on an exceptional scale to the needs of the State and of society. And, as simple arithmetic shows, the less they pay, the more will have to come from the pockets of the laity.[127]

One of the arguments of the clergy in defence of their immunities was the need to preserve the dignity and independence of their ministry. Custodians of public morality who have the duty of rebuking sinners should not have to keep looking over their shoulders fearing the malice of the local notables and officials who assess and collect taxation.[128] Anticlericals had a ready reply: the whole independent assessment system of the clergy was run in the interests of a narrow oligarchy. Curés on the *congrue* were legally liable to pay up to 50 livres from 1690, and 60 from 1715, at a time when their pittance was only 300 a year.[129] The other curés were paying a seventh or an eighth of their income, in spite of all the pious platitudes about the indispensability of their ministry and their charitable obligations. By contrast, bishops tended to slip out of the net of strict accountability.[130] The automatic rebate of 6,000 livres to cardinals was at least according to a rule, but in the mid-eighteenth century some astonishing figures were current, which could be possible only by downright tax evasion: the bishop of Le Mans paying 1,050 livres on an income of 30,000, and his confrère at Verdun 180 on 60,000. Jacques de Grasse of Angers died in 1782 owing 16,000 from long ago, money that was never recovered.[131] Next after bishops in the hierarchy of underpayment came the canons of cathedrals, mostly aristocrats—in mid-century, those of Dijon and Besançon were paying about 1 per cent, those of Le Mans 5 per cent.[132] Reform of these abuses was slow. Benefice holders were ordered to make declarations of revenue to their diverse bureaux in 1727 and again in 1751. From this information the Assembly worked out a plan (accepted in 1760) for dividing benefice holders into eight categories of progressive taxation, taking into account both income and the usefulness of particular offices to the Church. This ought to have done much to reform abuses, but not everyone honoured the new prescriptions. A curé of Angers in 1785 accused the new bishop of paying less than a seventh of what he owed,[133] and the bishop of Quimper almost halved his contribution by having his episcopal estates and commendatory abbey assessed separately, thereby avoiding the higher rates of tax.[134]

All over France, tax officials, intendants, and municipal officers lay in wait, in a half-formulated anticlerical conspiracy, to trap the clergy into paying secular taxation. In the proceedings of the extraordinary Assembly of 1782[135] we hear of the benefice holders in the *généralité* of Caen, who had weakly agreed to pay a tax for the repair of the port of Grandville, because it was only for five years, and who were now being inscribed on the contribution rolls for works on the river banks. There was a bridge at Mareuil-sur-Ay (Champagne) for whose repair the curé was being charged 183 and a convent of nuns 1,650 livres. A curé of the diocese of Bourges was being compelled by the *fermiers* of the *gabelle* to buy the standard quantity of salt obligatory for commoners. 'Most often', the Assembly records, 'they attack our immunities in the persons of a few poor ecclesiastics who have no influence and are isolated from the advice they need to be able to defend themselves . . . one or two examples suffice to create a precedent.' The estates of Bresse (which came under French rule in 1601) were ordering the local clergy to pay to a *vingtième*, despite the fact that the Royal Council had ruled in 1626 that they must pay 3,000 livres annually to the clergy of France. The Assembly agreed to defend them, provided their contribution to clerical taxation was brought up to date and doubled. The estates of Provence were asking clergy and nobles to pay sixty-seven years' arrears of a local tax, having decided, belatedly, that they were liable.

Above all, there was the two-centuries-old feudal conspiracy by the Crown and the holders of royal *apanages* (in this case the duc d'Orléans and the comte d'Artois) to extract *foi et hommage, aveu et dénombrements*.[136] If they did such homage for their temporalities, the clergy would have fees to pay, and would render themselves liable to other feudal exactions. The dispute is worth lingering over, for it reveals with the sharpness of caricature the sort of rules of the game which governed the relations of Crown and Church in matters of taxation. For long—at least since 1674—churchmen had got away with evasive action, and from 1725 each Assembly had obtained a declaration of *surséance*—a stay of execution. The Assembly of 1750 had presented to it a masterly legal memorandum proving its case, but craftily decided to postpone publishing it, given that passions were then running so high against clerical privileges; instead, another request for a five years' *surséance* was made.[137] In 1775, aware that the sands were running out, the Assembly put on a brave face and asked the king to name commissioners from his Council to adjudicate; a committee of bishops was set up to prepare the clergy's brief, and to this the abbé Bouquet and the ecclesiastical lawyers brought a mountain of documents.[138] In 1782, the king announced that the stay of execution already granted to 1785 would be the last: the Council would then judge the issue definitively on the basis of evidence submitted by the clergy, on the one hand, and by the inspector-general of the royal domain, on the other.

   The memoranda of the two parties, published in 1785,[139] provide contrasting views of State and society. On the royal side, the king is said to enjoy a universal right of seigneurie, filling all empty spaces in his kingdom wherever feudal authority is not evident; this is the meaning of 'nulle terre sans seigneur'. Also, as 'Chef de la Police', the monarch can enter anyone's territory to inspect, and as the enforcer of public order he guarantees the property of each of his subjects as against all the others. The 'liberty' the clergy ask for is that of 'a naked savage'. The lawyers of the Assembly reply that most Church property goes back to the days before feudalism was invented, days of piety when a ruler would have considered it sacrilegious to impose any obligations on the free gifts of land he made to the Church. Feudal tenures arose because of the weakness of the monarchy; there is no reason to believe that kings now made their gifts to religion in a feudal way, unless they specifically stated that they were doing so. And to demonstrate that this was not done, the clergy produced thousands of documents. They contrast their evidence with the inspector of the domain's generalities—he is proclaiming a theory of absolutism, within which he is confusing sovereignty with suzerainty; he has no historical proofs. Laymen, like churchmen, rely on the complex documentation of the past to establish their ownership and their rights, so 'the interest of the Clergy is the interest of all citizens'. It was a curious, archaic controversy which was still unresolved when Church lands were finally put up for auction in the Revolution. In the form of a historical debate, it summed up the contrast between the starkness of theories of royal absolutism and State power dating from Louis XIV, and the *ancien régime*'s peculiar concept of liberty as a matter of tradition and privilege, however abusive. And in another form it restated the hypothesis which was to lead to the great Revolutionary confiscation: that the clergy were *usufruitiers* of their riches, and not absolute proprietors. All roads of anticlerical debate seemed to lead in the end to this single proposition—a dry legal formula which summed up the instinctive suspicion and envy of lay society confronted by an institutional alliance of immense material wealth and lofty spiritual ideals.

PART II

THE RELIGIOUS ESTABLISHMENT

6

DIOCESES

I

In 1789, there were 130 dioceses in France.[1] Of these, 123 were grouped into twenty-eight provinces under the metropolitan jurisdiction of archbishops; the archbishop of Tours had eleven suffragans, his colleague at Sens only three—there was no uniformity. The seven other dioceses had their metropolitans outside France, for the kings had extended their borders while the ecclesiastical structure remained the same when all foreign secular authority had been annihilated. Metz, Toul, Verdun, Nancy, and Saint-Dié responded to the German see of Trier, and Strasbourg to that of Mayence, and Perpignan to Tarragona in Spain. This total of the 130 dioceses of the Gallican Church does not include Corsica, even though the island was ceded to France in 1768. Three of its dioceses were under the jurisdiction of the archiepiscopal see of Genoa, and the other was under Pisa, the last remnants of the Italian connection.[2] Though the bishops of Avignon, Carpentras, Cavaillon, and Vaison are occasionally heard of in French history, they bore no allegiance to Versailles, since they belonged to a papal enclave surrounded by French territory—an enclave occasionally occupied by the French kings, but always returned. Another bishopric mentioned as identified with French soil was that of Bethléem—the title, awarded independently by the Pope, was attached to a hospital building near Clamecy in the Niverais.[3] Just as metropolitan sway over French bishops was exercised by German and Spanish archbishops, so too French archbishops were the official ecclesiastical superiors of foreign prelates outside the national territory: Embrun was the metropolitan see of Nice; Cambrai of Namur and Tourai; Besançon of Bâle and Lausanne; and Vienne of Annecy and Saint-Jean de Maurienne.

There were extreme disparities in the size of dioceses. Rouen, with 1,385 parishes, outstripped all the others. Six had between 700 and 800 (Bourges, Sens, Dax, Clermont, Le Mans, Autun); another five had between 500 and 700 parishes (Limoges, Metz, Cambrai,

Reims, Langres). By contrast, there were tiny dioceses, mostly clustered in the South, the creation of popes who were either strengthening local church organization against the Albigensian heresy or accumulating votes on their side in some future Council to deal with the great Avignon schism. The tiniest of all were the six dioceses of Toulon, Orange, Mirepoix, Agde, Vence, and Senez, with between twenty and thirty parishes each. A bishop of a small diocese often, but not always, found himself in a provincial backwater. It was so at Senez; the episcopal town consisted of 177 houses and the cathedral—it was better to abandon the episcopal palace and lodge at Castellane, where there was a population of nearly 2,000 and pilgrims came through town to visit the sanctuary of Notre-Dame-du-Roc.[4] The town and cathedral of Glandève (a diocese with fifty-five parishes) existed no more, having been swept away in a flood; the bishops' palace still stood, but was deserted for Entrevaux two miles away, where there were 1,500 inhabitants and a cathedral whose canons were poorer than the poorest artisans, and could afford only two choirboys.[5] By contrast, there was the diocese of Toulon, consisting of only twenty parishes, but serving the naval port and dockyard, and Marseille, with thirty-eight parishes but centred on one of the biggest commercial ports of Europe.

The oddness and irregularity of the diocesan framework of ecclesiastical France were matched by the internal complexities of the individual dioceses. What appeared to be a boundary on a map[6] was not necessarily the limit of a bishop's visitation tours—he might have to go further afield to inspect parishes forming enclaves in other dioceses. In 1622, the archdiocese of Paris had been carved out of that of Sens, but the parishes of the rural deanery of Champeaux, allotted to Paris, were surrounded by the territory remaining under Sens. The bishop of Lisieux had two 'exemptions' to look after, parishes in the dioceses of Bayeux and Rouen.[7] Dol, in Brittany, was a bizarre example of geographical confusion. Of the ninety-six parishes, forty-nine were clustered round the episcopal city; the rest were enclaved elsewhere (three in the diocese of Rennes, twenty-three in Saint-Malo, eleven in Tréguier, four in Rouen).[8] Minor absurdities of boundary drawing were legion, slicing farms, seigneuries, and villages in two—like the town of Morlaix, which was half under the bishop of Léon and half under his colleague of Tréguier.

Along the frontiers of France, the complexities of ecclesiastical structure were of international importance, a concern of national foreign policy. Metropolitan authority was nominal, so the supremacy of German and Spanish archbishops over French bishops rarely presented problems. More significant difficulties arose where royal conquests had bitten deep into the territories of external dioceses, so that foreign prelates ruled over parishes under French secular sovereignty. The bishops of Ypres and of Tournai were in this position; indeed, the latter had the greater part of his clergy inside the boundaries of France. In 1789, these two splendid prelates, Charles-Alexandre d'Arberg, count, and Guillaume Florentin de Salm-Salm, prince, of the Holy Roman Empire, imposed their greatness on the clerical electors of their French areas, and so were able to present themselves as deputies to the Estates General of 1789. On 20 July the National Assembly annulled their elections and sent them packing.[9] The prince-bishop of Spire had forty-five parishes in Alsace, French by right of conquest. It was a rule of the Gallican monarchy to exclude foreign jurisdictions from operating in France without royal consent—even if the Pope himself was concerned; foreign bishops with parishes within the kingdom were required to set up separate *officialités* (ecclesiastical courts) for them, locally based. In 1749, the sovereign court of Colmar, at the instance of Versailles, took notice that the prince-bishop had failed to do so, and declared his jurisdiction in Alsace suspended.[10] Another foreign prelate with a multitude of parishes in Alsace was the prince-bishop of Bâle.[11] History had made his position interestingly anomalous. Because of the Reformation he had lost Bâle, his nominal episcopal city, and ruled from Porrentry; his metropolitan was the French archbishop of Besançon. His diocese consisted of twelve deaneries, six in Switzerland and six in Alsace. The Alsatian deaneries (totalling 237 parishes), rejoicing in resonant names (*ultra colles Ottonis, citra colles Ottonis, inter colles,* Sundgau, Masevaux, and Rhenum), were ruled by 'chapitres ruraux', which had their own coats of arms and were under the presidency of parish priests elected by their fellows. Since the patronage of benefices was unchanged by the conquest, some of the curés were presented to their livings by German noblemen, even Protestant ones; alongside them, however, the Crown had filled gaps in the parochial system with 'curés royaux', paid by the State and appointed, like secular officials, by the intendant. The system ran very largely independently of the prince-bishop at Porrentry, and in any case, he was expected to appoint a suffragan for the French part of his diocese. In the 1780s, this was Gobel, son of a Gallican lawyer of Alsace, an intriguer who was to finish up as the constitutional bishop of Paris during the Revolution. In 1786, he began his apprenticeship to ambition by laying information against the morals of the bishop of Bâle in the hope of getting a diocese separated off for himself. But changing ecclesiastical boundaries was no easy matter; what minister at Versailles could have done it for the sole reason that a bishop, making a visitation of a nunnery, had ordered singing and dancing to the music of a flageolet played by his registrar?[12]

The south-east frontier was more complex still. Here, the jurisdictional problem was the other way round, French bishops having parishes within the sovereignty of the dukes of Savoy. In Savoy itself, the diocese of Grenoble ruled a sizeable *décanat* centring on Chambéry, and the diocese of Belley had the thirty parishes of the so-called Petit-Bugey; in the comté of Nice, the dioceses of Senez, Embrun, Vence, and Glandève all had parishes—Glandève had thirty, more than it possessed in France itself.[13] At Nice and at Chambéry, the dukes of Savoy had *sénats*, courts equivalent to the French parlements and resembling them in being determined to defend the secular power against ecclesiastical encroachments and foreign interference. They claimed the right to confirm all nominations to benefices or offices made by the French bishops, gave permission or refused it for visitations of monasteries or for laymen to appear as witnesses before ecclesiastical courts.[14] The fiscal officers of the dukes, equally vigilant, confiscated the revenues of episcopal sees during vacancies, in so far as they arose from the territories of Nice and Savoy, and did not hasten to restore them when a new bishop was appointed.[15] At various times in the century France and Savoy made treaties involving the simplification of their borders. In 1713, Senez and Embrun had to surrender their parishes; in 1760, by the Treaty of Turin, Vence did so—but there was no change for Glandève. This was the treaty dividing in two the town of Pont-de-Beauvoisin, with the curious proviso that the Lenten sermons paid for by the municipality must be given on either side of the border in alternate years. In 1779, a deal was done allowing Savoy to have its own separate diocese at Chambéry independent of Grenoble; but the thirty parishes of the Petit-Bugey remained in the diocese of Belley, even though Charles Emmanuel III offered Versailles the French parishes of his diocese of Geneva in exchange. Pastoral concerns were all very well, but a fragment of ecclesiastical jurisdiction was a diplomatic lever worth retaining to gain advantages in future negotiations.

II

A map of the ecclesiastical dioceses with all their complexities is difficult to draw. One of the total structure of France, civil, ecclesiastical, and traditional, defies representation, and needs to be stored in a computer. The ecclesiastical system was not geared into the various secular systems, and, for that matter, these secular arrangements rarely fitted into each other. There were the traditional provinces, some with and some without provincial estates, and those with estates having peculiar administrative and taxation arrangements. There were the royal administrative areas, the *généralités* under *intendants* and their sub-units under the *subdélégués*; the judicial areas of appeal with hierarchies of courts going up to the various parlements; specialist courts quite apart from all these intervened to take off litigation concerning various subjects—some concerned with taxation, some with the seaports, some with customs duties, some with 'rivers and forests', others with commercial transactions. There were the various odd boundary lines within which *gabelles*, *octrois*, and local taxes were levied; there were policing areas separating the town *archers* from the countryside *maréchaussée*; seigneuries and other feudal units had their fiscal and judicial activities, and there were meaningless areas where obsolete officials by purchase did nothing importantly. All these systems operated independently. Sometimes there was a fitting together, but even then the coincidence was never exact. It was commonly said that the 'dioceses' of Languedoc were units of both spiritual jurisdiction and civil administration, with the bishop playing a dominant role in the secular business. True, but the civil and religious boundaries were only approximately the same.[16] The secular diocese of Uzès was the ecclesiastical one, with the addition of seventeen parishes owing spiritual allegiance to the papal bishop of Avignon. Similarly, Nîmes had Beaucaire and six rural parishes belonging to the archbishop of Arles. The estates of Toulouse, with the archbishop presiding, ran the secular affairs of the diocese minus part of the episcopal city itself.

In some areas, all is multilayered confusion, so that the working of accident in history seems to have been perverse. The province of Périgord had two dioceses, Périgueux and Sarlat; administratively, it was also divided into two *élections*; but there was no correspondence between these ecclesiastical and secular units.[17] The 210 parishes of the province of Roussillon centred around Perpignan, where the bishop had his seat; yet, while he had most of the parishes, he did not have all, four other bishops outside the province being involved, including a Spanish bishop who had twenty-five of them. If a bishop had an administrative dispute or a lawsuit, he might have to fight his battle in duplicate or triplicate.[18] The bishop of Quimper had fourteen *subdélégués* of the intendant in his diocese, three of them being responsible for other areas outside it; there were ten *sénéchaussées* (royal courts of first instance), appeals from three of them going outside the diocese to the episcopal towns of other bishops, Vannes and Rennes. The bishop of Tarbes presided over the estates of the province of Bigorre, with 201 of his 294 parishes within the provincial boundaries. But ninety-three of his parishes belonged to other territorial units: twenty-five to the vicomté de Nébouzan, seven to the Pays des Affites, six to the comté de Pardiac, and seventeen to the province of Béarn. The others were in the valleys of the Pyrenees where the mountain folk ruled themselves in village assemblies, paying more attention to their big local proprietors than to government officials, and having more affinities with the Spaniards grazing their flocks on the high pastures than with the French of the plains.[19] The bishop of Autun had two parlements to reckon with, Paris and Dijon, and two intendants, one based at Dijon, the other at Moulins; in addition, there was the complication of his eighty-four parishes within the quasi-independent comté of Charolais, and twenty others within the boundaries of the dioceses of Châlons and Mâcon.[20]

III

To bring some degree of logic into the diocesan structure, it might have seemed that the first step was to unite some of the tiny bishoprics clustered in the South. The difficulties in putting through a union were almost insuperable.[21] Local interests would muster to defend the *status quo*. The prestige of the episcopal city, employment, and expenditure with local tradesmen were involved; aristocratic families would have had the bishopric earmarked as an appointment for one of their sons. The legal procedures for a union ground along slowly. By the canonical rules the metropolitan and the neighbouring bishops had to be consulted, as well as their collegiate chapters; to this the secular lawyers added the proviso that the 'consent of the people' ought to be sought, whatever that might mean. Then the Pope had to approve and issue his bulls. And in any case, a double vacancy had to be contrived, holding one see under an administrator until the other fell available. It was easier to carve new units out of the excessively large dioceses: this would enlist local pride and aristocratic ambition, rather than alienating them. The advantages were obvious: from sprawling cumbersome areas more manageable pastoral units would be fashioned. On these grounds of pastoral efficiency the new dioceses of Paris (1622), Albi (1675), and Blois (1697) were created.[22] A different motive operated when Alais was detached from Nîmes in 1694, since Nîmes had been a diocese of modest size; the two new units were small indeed—eighty-four and eighty-eight parishes. Here was the devastated fortress country of the Protestants of the Cévennes, isolated in their mountains and embittered by their forced conversion—closer episcopal supervision was deemed to be needed to attempt to make their Catholicism real.[23] For over a century Langres, with 619 parishes, had seemed ripe for division, with Dijon the obvious new episcopal city and the existing archdeaconry of that name furnishing convenient boundaries. After six years of negotiations with Rome, bulls were received in April 1731 detaching 135 parishes (together with nineteen from Besançon in a rounding-off exercise) to form the new unit. The abbey of Saint-Etienne became the new cathedral, and its abbatial revenue supplied the basis of an episcopal income, with supplements from other monasteries. The difficulties inherent in establishing an entirely new administration were alleviated by the choice of Jean Bouhier, son of a magistrate of the parlement of Dijon and already dean of the Sainte-Chapelle there.[24] His legal expertise was called on again in 1741 when the new diocese of Saint-Claude was created, joining eighty-one parishes from Lyon and seven from Besançon. Heroically, at the age of 76, Bouhier accepted a translation to become the first bishop. He completed the organization and published statutes in a synod in 1743, then resigned to take a well-earned rest, which turned out to be brief. The town of Saint-Claude, with a rich abbey whose church provided a cathedral and whose abbatial revenues endowed the bishopric, was an excellent centre for episcopal administration for an area not easily accessible from Lyon. There was, however, a hidden agenda behind this new creation. The monks of the abbey, aristocrats living in comfort in independent little houses around their great church, were haunted by fears of reform: as they submitted to the king in 1691, 'if they lived in the rigour of a more severe rule, it would be difficult to find persons of quality—such as they are and always have been—who would wish to join'. Hence, they applied to be transformed into secular canons, and the change was part of the deal when the new diocese was formed. Far from being grateful for their conversion to canons of a cathedral, the ex-monks made life difficult for the inex-perienced young bishop who succeeded tough old Bouhier.[25]

The huge diocese of Toul would long ago have been divided if pastoral considerations had ruled; but it straddled France and Lorraine, so politics prevailed. The dukes of Lorraine wanted their territories liberated from the jurisdiction of the French bishop by the creation of new dioceses at Nancy and Saint-Dié; the French king, unwilling to relinquish any levers of influence outside his boundaries, refused. In 1737, however, Lorraine fell to Stanislas, father of the French queen, and in 1766 reverted to France altogether. Now, Louis XV saw no objection to change—indeed, he saw advantages in pleasing the Lorrainers by letting them have their own bishops. In 1773, when the see of Toul fell vacant, he appointed a new prelate, brought from the poor see of Senez with the express provision that he agreed to sacrifice some of his territory. The cathedral chapter of Toul made difficulties; it was bought off by being granted 'noble' status, together with some extra endow-ments from monastic revenues, precedence over the chapters of Nancy and Saint-Dié (now to be elevated to cathedrals), and, not least, a mark of sartorial distinction for its canons. The canons of Saint-Dié had been given the right to wear a pectoral cross by Stanislas, but now Toul would out-vie them utterly, with an eight-pointed cross in gold and enamel, adorned with a fleur-de-lis and the figure of St Stephen, to be suspended round the neck on a red ribbon edged with purple. In 1777, papal briefs established the two new dioceses (Toul still had 645 parishes left). There was rejoicing in Lorraine and complaints in France. Some ecclesiastical business left the city of Toul. There were wrangles about which catechisms and liturgical books should be used, and news came of Saint-Dié and Nancy ousting the saints of Toul from their observances in favour of their own. Struggles for precedence among the clergy of the diocese of Nancy prevented the new bishop from organizing it into arch-deaconries and rural deaneries. Two rural deans of Toul who had lost parishes from their jurisdiction embarked on lawsuits. The feather-bedding canons of Toul were regarded as traitors and pilloried as 'crucimanes'.[26]

By this readjustment of ecclesiastical boundaries and jurisdictions, the Crown was strengthening its power on the borderlands of the kingdom. It had been a subsidiary motive for creating Dijon and Saint-Claude earlier. In the 1780s another borderland project was mooted, a new diocese with Lille as the episcopal city. This was never done.[27] The last new creation before the Revolution was

Moulins, carved out of Autun (forty-seven parishes), Clermont (ninety), and Bourges (eighty). Here was a case where Louis XVI broke the rules of procedure to enforce speedy change, perhaps because of his concern for pastoral efficiency, perhaps because the case for the reform seemed so obvious, Moulins already being a major administrative centre, the seat of an intendant ruling a vast *généralité*, and of one of the new provincial assemblies. The archbishop of Bourges and his cathedral chapter and the chapters of Autun and Clermont registered opposition, and the bishop of Mâcon delayed his verdict. Even so, with only the bishops of Autun and Clermont agreeing, on 17 April 1788 the king signed the decree for the new diocese, and named the abbé Gallois de La Tour, dean of the chapter of Moulins, as the first bishop. Only on 27 April did the government ask for the Pope's consent.[28] There was ample material here for those endless lawsuits characterizing the *ancien régime*, but the Revolution intervened, and the National Assembly redrew the entire map of France, making new administrative units, the *départements*, and making all the dioceses conform to them. Among the motives of the vast majority of bishops for rejecting the Civil Constitution of the Clergy, here is one whose importance has been understated. By canon and civil law and by tradition, the universal change of all the diocesan boundaries by mere legislative fiat was an astonishing innovation.

IV

Amid all these complexities of structure, what held the Gallican Church together? It was a church with a highly developed sense of identity, and its aristocratic bishops were bound together in an oligarchical esprit de corps. Even so, there was no central direction, and the Crown was determined this would remain so. Though the Pope had authority in morals and doctrine, his rescripts could not be published in France without royal permission. National councils were not called, and provincial councils were rare. The eighteen archbishops had their ecclesiastical courts of appeal from the courts of the dioceses of their province, and certain rights of precedence when meetings were held to choose deputies to the Assembly General of the Clergy, but the rank-and-file bishops would not allow them any meaningful inherent superiority. On 10 January 1734, the archbishop of Narbonne, as president of the estates of Languedoc, had his cross carried before him at a Te Deum in

Montpellier. Colbert, the local bishop, began a lawsuit against him. The other bishops backed Colbert, even though he was a Jansenist under the ban of Versailles. On 30 October Massillon wrote to him:

The enterprise of Mgr de Narbonne concerns the whole episcopate. If it is allowed to stand it constitutes an overthrow of our rules, leaving us little more than the title of delegates of our metropolitans in our diocese. Established as bishops by the authority of Jesus Christ and not that of the Roman pontiff, they (the metropolitans) form with us a single united episcopate which we, as individuals, share with them.[29]

The most prestigious archbishopric of all was Paris. With 472 parishes it was far from being the biggest, but its revenues were immense, its population enormous, and the archbishop had all the great, from the king downwards, within his pastoral responsibilities. 'By your office you are not only charged with the care of the diocese of Paris, but also of the whole clergy of the Church of France,' wrote the bishop of Châlons to his brother, promoted to the capital.[30] 'Every archbishop of Paris', wrote a canon of Notre-Dame at about the same time, 'who has guile and style (*manège et élévation*) and who applies himself to win people's hearts, will always be considered as head of the Gallican Church, and the court will show him deference, even if not well disposed to him'.[31] But during two long reigns, those of Louis-Antoine de Noailles and Christophe de Beaumont, the see was held by a prelate who was head of a minority faction, the one of Jansenists, the other of ultramontanes. The patience of the Court wore thin with both of them, and in the end Versailles was using the ancient claims to 'primacy' of Lyon to end disputes in the diocese of Paris over the head of its intransigent archbishop.

In fact, seven archbishops claimed the title of 'primat'.[32] Bordeaux and Narbonne were simply 'primat', Bourges 'primat des Aquitaines', Lyon 'primat des Gaulles', Reims 'primat de Gaule-Belgique', Vienne 'primat des primats', which appeared to outrange all the others, but in fact meant nothing. Except in the case of Lyon, this claim to superior authority was largely unrecognized and rarely invoked. It might mean that there was a court to deal with appeals from the courts of the archbishops, or the possibility to intervene to grant a visa for a benefice if all other means of filling it had been blocked by legal obstacles; thus, in 1745, the archbishop of Bourges, using his claim to have the last word in jurisdiction in all the dioceses of Aquitaine, allowed the abbé Lahitère to proceed to a canonry in the cathedral of Aire—his provisions from Rome having been turned down by the local bishop and the archbishop of Auch.[33]

The archbishop of Lyon enjoyed the title of 'primat des Gaulles' from the bull of Pope Gregory VII of 1079; the lawyers defined his primatial jurisdiction as extending over the archbishops of Sens, Tours, and Paris and all bishops in the area of the jurisdiction of the parlement of Paris. A royal decree confirmed his precedence in 1661, on the occasion of the marriage of Louis XIV. Bull and decree notwithstanding, the archbishops of Sens, Tours, and Rouen always resisted these claims. At the end of the seventeenth century, after bitter words about precedence had been exchanged in the royal chapel, the archbishop of Lyon went to law against his colleague of Rouen, and lost with costs. In 1707, the Pope and the Royal Council confirmed the metropolitan of Normandy in his claim to independence.[34] For all its importance, however, Paris was firmly under the metropolitan jurisdiction of Lyon—it was just a question of whether the king would allow it to be exercised. When Cardinal Noailles refused to publish *Unigenitus* in 1714, Louis XIV was assured by his lawyers that the primate of Lyon could intervene by issuing three summations and, failing compliance, publish the bull in the diocese of Paris himself.[35] The weary king refused to stir up more trouble. From mid-century, it was a question of dealing with the fanatical intransigence of Archbishop Christophe de Beaumont. In 1758, the Royal Council got the new archbishop of Lyon, Montazet, to annul a decree of Beaumont prohibiting the nuns of La Miséricorde, faubourg Saint-Marceau, from electing a mother superior. Fresh from this triumph, Montazet published his *Lettre de M. l'archevêque de Lyon, Primat de France, à M. l'archevêque de Paris* (1760) setting forth his rights, changing 'Gaules' to 'France' to head off those who might doubt the scope of ancient phraseology. In 1765, Montazet was called in to validate the uniting of certain benefices to the *collège* of Louis-le-Grand, since Beaumont was refusing to co-operate because he objected to the expulsion of the Jesuits. In the same year the curé of Saint-Sulpice resigned, and the patron named one of the vicaires to succeed him. Beaumont rejected the nomination, Lyon gave the necessary provisions, and Beaumont therefore interdicted the new man from ministerial functions. Pastoral chaos at Saint-Sulpice was avoided by M. de Lau, the old curé, withdrawing his resignation and winning a lawsuit before the Grand Chambre for restitution to his altar and vicarage. About the same time the abbé Couvret moved into a canonry at Notre-Dame by resignation of the previous incumbent; at the instance of the parlement of Paris the archbishop of Lyon provided the visa, Beaumont refusing it, and the canons leaguing together to send the new man to Coventry.[36]

These contentious affairs of appointments, jurisdiction, and precedence were of great concern to the prelates, but in the last resort they did not involve the leadership of the Gallican Church. If this was found anywhere it was in the assemblies of the clergy convoked by the Crown for taxation purposes. In these meetings, the role of leadership which the archaic claims to 'primacy' did nothing to confer, fell to the archbishops—or rather, to those of certain sees who were able and willing to conduct high political business. Half the deputies from the ecclesiastical provinces were bishops, with the metropolitans predominating (of 736 deputies from 1690 to 1788, 205 were of archiepiscopal rank). Those of Albi, Embrun, and Lyon were hardly ever present (Lyon because the claim to primacy roused general suspicion), and Reims was represented only from 1766 to 1776, when La Roche-Aymon, dominant at Court, held the see. The metropolitans of the great and populous sees of Paris, Rouen, and Bourges were always there, so too those of Narbonne and Toulouse, who *ex officio* played a major secular role, as well as an ecclesiastical one, in the South.[37] Except from 1701 to 1716, when the archbishop of Paris was president, this high dignity fell to the senior archbishop present, who thus became the leading negotiator for the clergy with the ministers of the Crown and the magistrates of the parlement. Since the assemblies were indispensable to the monarchy for the voting of money, the prelates made them a forum for formulating the policies and grievances of the Gallican Church and pressing its demands upon the government. Continuity came from the two agents-general and their bureaucracy running business in the intervals between the quinquennial meetings. As so often under the *ancien régime*, ways of getting things done were found outside the archaic structures and hierarchies.

V

By ancient custom, dioceses (the episcopal town apart) were divided into the major administrative units of archdeaconries, *archidiaconés*. A small diocese might have two or, even, just one, but the correlation with geographical extent, population or number of parishes was distant. Reims and Quimper (517 and 263 parishes) each had two. Of dioceses with between 700 and 800 parishes, Autun had four,

Sens five, Le Mans seven, Bourges eight; the 1,385 parishes of Rouen were shared between only six *archidiaconés*. In their turn these major units were divided into deaneries, sometimes called 'rural deaneries' (*doyennés*, sometimes called *ruraux*, sometimes *champêtres*). There were other names for the deaneries—*archiprêtrés* was common; around Albi they were *claveries*, around Cahors and Comminges *congrégations*, around Rodez *voyages*. 'All this variety of names refers to exactly the same thing', said a writer in the *Mercure géographique* of 1678.[38] There was little logic beyond that of history in the size and number of these variously named groupings of parishes. In the diocese of Paris, each of the three *archidiaconés* was divided into two *doyennés*; the four *archidiaconés* of Autun had ten, six, five, and four *archiprêtrés* respectively; Reims had thirteen *doyennés* in one group and ten in the other; Quimper had three in one and two in the other. As ever, there were oddities and exceptions. In Paris, the parishes of the Cité, the island, and the right bank of the Seine were in the *archiprêtré* of La Madeleine, and the left bank and the south in that of Saint-Séverin, neither of those two units being within the scope of any of the *archidiaconés*. There was also in the Paris diocese a *doyenné* of Champeaux which was in Brie but not in the jurisdiction of the archdeacon of that name; nor was it in that of either of the other two, the *grand archidiacre* and the *archidiacre-de-Josas*.[39]

An archdeacon was generally a canon of the diocesan cathedral; he might receive the emoluments of a simple canon or have additional allowances as well; he might enjoy precedence among the dignitaries of the chapter or not.[40] In some cases, he was entitled to make ancient and unpopular exactions—the *droit de déport* (taking up to a year's revenue from a benefice in a vacancy) or the *droit de dépouille* (the right to certain perquisites on the death of a curé—his best bed, cassock, surplice, and horse, or a fee in lieu thereof).[41] The bishop appointed an archdeacon with the agreement of the cathedral chapter. The archdeacon's duties differed from diocese to diocese: according to the standard law dictionary of the day, 'usage and possession are the only rules to consult to know the rights of the different *archidiacres*'.[42] But whether his powers were extensive or limited, they could be broadly defined as exercising jurisdiction in the name of the bishop and conducting the visitation of parishes by his authority. If he descended on a parish in formal visitation, he was entitled to levy a fee, one which the local people were inclined to regard as excessive, considering that they did not wish to be visited anyway, but which appeared trivial to the recipient. One hamlet in Brittany had fifteen houses, and the parish priest had an income of

900 livres; another had ninety-six houses and the curé drew 1,000 livres; when the archdeacons (of Evreux and of Ouche) came on visitation, their fees were 7 livres, 7 sols, 6 deniers, in one case and 3 livres, 15 sols in the other. It was custom which fixed these sums, disproportionate between the two places and with the church-wardens paying most of the fee in the first case and the curé paying most in the second.[43] The *droit de visite* had originally consisted of the right to a good dinner, this having been generally commuted to a money payment. With the proverbial rapacity which medieval satirists attached to his office, the archdeacon of Rennes in 1718 tried to exact both the fee and the dinner; the *présidial* found for him, but the parlement overturned the verdict on appeal.[44] One of the demands of the curés of Le Mans in their *cahier* of 1789 was to be visited only by their bishops, never by the archdeacon—evidence that archidiaconal visitations still took place, but also for their unpopularity.[45]

Bishops were disinclined to work through archdeacons. Once appointed, they remained ensconced in their niches, maybe growing old in exactions or idleness. In spite of the potential importance of their office, they could dispose of it by resignation, as with any other benefice. Between 1760 and 1763 the three archdeacons of Lisieux named their successors in this way. A bishop might thus be confronted by a chief administrator he could not trust, or even face a dynasty growing accustomed to rule. Therefore, whether as zealous reformers, dictatorial aristocrats, or even as slothful prelates wanting a quiet life, the bishops turned against the archdeacons. From the end of the seventeenth century the bishops undercut their arch-deacons' privileges and their role as visitors of the parishes in their archdeaconry. This was possible, for by law an archdeacon could not follow up his visitation by publishing ordinances or disciplining erring curés—all he could do was to report to diocesan head-quarters.[46] In 1741, the bishop of Langres issued orders to his archdeacons, putting them in their place; he wanted more detailed reports from them, but they were 'to observe and not to issue orders', except in emergency.[47] Three years later, in his synodal statutes, the bishop of Boulogne instructed his archdeacons to make annual visits 'in the places where we cannot go in person'— their role was supplementary. Also, he laid visitation duties more emphatically and directly upon his rural deans, giving them wide powers to absolve reserved cases, bless church ornaments, distribute the consecrated oils for use in baptism and extreme unction, and fill vacant cures with temporary incumbents.[48]

True, there were dioceses where the archdeacons remained active throughout the eighteenth century—Sées, for example. Under the reign of scandalous and negligent prelates, like Jarente at Orléans or Grimaldi at Noyon, archidiaconal visitations within the areas of their jurisdictions are the only ones we hear of. After the death of Noailles in 1729, visitations in the diocese of Paris were irregular, which left the way open for the archdeacon in the cathedral of Notre-Dame to emerge in a flurry of activity in the 1760s. Zealous bishops—Colbert at Montpellier, all those who ruled the tiny see of Orange, the occupants of the see of Nantes after 1746—did all their own visitations. When circumstances or inclination persuaded bishops to delegate, they were free to choose any of their clergy: to investigate the state of a chapel, for example, they might call in a neighbouring parish priest. In some dioceses, they bypassed the archdeacons and called on the rural deans to act. In Montpellier after Colbert, Berger de Charancy, a great visitor himself, used them (*archiprêtres*, as they were termed) to do 'verifications' as a follow-up to ordinances he had issued concerning a particular parish. His successor, in addition to travelling round himself, used the *archiprêtres* more widely, not only for verifications but also to make the visitations in the first place. Then came Raymond de Durfort (1766–74), not very active himself, but using the *archiprêtres* everywhere (with a resort to *grands vicaires* from 1770 to 1772). Malide (1774–91) continued the policy, though doing a great deal of the travelling himself. In the dioceses of Metz, Rodez, and Reims this same turning to rural deans is evident. But it was more usual to turn to a *grand vicaire*. When archdeacons are found on visitation tours, it is usually by virtue of a commission of *grand vicaire* rather than by their own authority—like Nicolas-Joseph de Paris, archdeacon of Pithiviers and vicar-general of bishop Fleuriau d'Armenonville at Orléans, right-hand man of his bishop and his assistant in constant visitations, and later his successor in the bishopric.[49] In the diocese of Langres in the first half of the eighteenth century, the bishops ordered visitations by both archdeacons and rural deans; by 1733, they were relying more on the rural deans; in the second half of the century they turned to their *grands vicaires*.[50] That cynical master of efficient administration, Loménie de Brienne, used *grands vicaires* exclusively in his archdiocese of Toulouse. It was the way to break through local torpor and assert episcopal authority.[51]

The *grands vicaires* were agents of the bishop pure and simple, commissioned to exercise jurisdiction in his name over the whole diocese, and revocable at will. If the see fell vacant, their powers lapsed at once.[52] Their office was unpaid, and they lived on some abbey held *in commendam* or canonry or ecclesiastical sinecure—whatever their patron was able to find for them. Throughout the eighteenth century, their numbers increased. There were six at Lisieux in 1717, nine in 1788; three at Rennes in 1710 and six in 1779; four at Bordeaux in 1730 and twelve in 1789. The importance of the office increased as the Crown came to choose its bishops from their number, after mid-century, almost exclusively. By 1725, half the non-episcopal deputies to the assemblies of clergy were *grands vicaires*; by 1750 practically all were.[53] The standard explanation for their multiplication is the Crown's insistence on administrative experience in a diocese as a qualification for the episcopate, leading to a rush of aristocratic candidates for the office and to the willingness of the aristocratic bishops to gratify their friends by appointing more of them. Even so, if there were extra passengers being added to the ship, the importance of key members of the crew was increasing, and the bishops needed more *grands vicaires* to help them run their dioceses.

The *doyens ruraux*, *archiprêtres*,[54] and so on were the bishop's confidential men in the oversight of a group of parishes. Even if, as was sometimes the case, they were put up by the archdeacon or proposed by election by their fellow curés, they were appointed by the bishop and revokable by him. The extreme limits of what their episcopally defined powers could be were listed by Bishop Roquette of Autun in 1690; they could absolve reserved cases in the confessional; if sent by the bishop, they could conduct a visitation; or they could go informally into parishes to help, for example, in training a schoolteacher or a catechist. If the bishop wanted to hold a synod, they would do the organization. Also—and this was probably their most important duty—they were to write to the bishop every three months to inform him of the state of the parishes and to report on any scandals. The commission of a rural dean would state specifically that it lasted only 'tant qu'il plaira à l'évêque', only so long as the bishop pleased.[55] There was thus no reason to distrust them (unlike the archdeacons), and in a well-organized diocese the bishop and his *grands vicaires* would make great use of them.

VI

Every diocese had its ecclesiastical court, the *officialité diocésaine*. Appeals could be made from its jurisdiction to the court of the archbishop of the province, the *officialité métropolitaine* (or *archiépiscopale*).

Where a *primat* had effective rights, as had the archbishop of Lyon, there was the theoretical possibility of taking a case further to the *officialité primatiale*. The system seemed straightforward, but nothing ever was under the *ancien régime*. There were *officialités* attached to ecclesiastical institutions other than dioceses: the chapter of Notre-Dame and the two Sainte-Chapelles at Paris, the cathedral of Saintes, the cathedral at Orléans all had their courts for the use of a dozen to a score of dependent parishes.[56] There was also a fossilized relic of one in the little town of Villedieu-les-Poêles serving the citizens and those of the nearby Villedieu-lès-Bailleul. For long, its legal personnel consisted only of the curé, and by 1782, he had ceased to act. The local people were angry at having to go further afield for dispensations to marry within the prohibited degrees, and in 1785 confusion ensued when a husband and wife petitioned for separation, one going to the *officialité* of Coutances, the other to that of Rouen.[57] The parlements would have no dealings with ecclesiastical courts located outside the boundaries of their jurisdictions; so where a diocese was divided between the spheres of different parlements, the bishop was obliged to have a second *officialité*, known as an *officialité foraine*, away from his episcopal city and on the other side of the dividing line.[58] Thus, while the dioceses of Autun, Limoges, Toul, and Sées had ecclesiastical courts near their cathedrals corresponding with their local parlements (Dijon, Bordeaux, Nancy, and Rouen), they had others corresponding with the parlement of Paris at Moulins, Gueret, Bar-le-Duc, and Mortagne. The dioceses of Lyon, Puy, and Tarbes were within the areas of different parlements, but the king had granted them exemption from the rule, since there was no subsidiary town of sufficient importance to house a law court. An archbishop was under the same constraints as an ordinary bishop: he had to duplicate his *officialité métropolitaine* if any of the dioceses of his province ran into the jurisdiction of other parlements. Thus, the archbishop of Bordeaux had an *officialité métropolitaine foraine* at Poitiers covering appeals from his suffragan dioceses of La Rochelle, Poitiers, and Luçon to correspond with the parlement of Paris. In two dioceses, without any explanation from conflicting areas of secular jurisdiction, an additional *officialité* just happened to exist: the bishop of Bayeux had an extra one at Caen, and the bishop of Coutances had two, at Saint-Lô and Vallogne.[59] Scattered around the frontiers were also the ecclesiastical courts of the foreign bishops who had parishes within France, as the archbishop of the papal enclave of Avignon had for the seventeen parishes under his ecclesiastical jurisdiction in Languedoc.[60] Similarly, outside France were the *officialités* of the French bishops who exercised pastoral sway over parishes in Nice, Savoy, and Germany; staffed by local lawyers, they figure only marginally in the history of the Gallican Church.

In addition to his main ecclesiastical court, a bishop had to have a diocesan registry.[61] Though this would probably be housed in the same building or, certainly, nearby, it was, strictly speaking, a royal institution, the clerk being a layman and a crown employee. Here, copies of all letters of ordination, signification of degrees to patrons, minutes of the taking possession of benefices, and so on had to be filed. All this documentation had to be on expensive government-stamped paper: in the first instance, this was a taxation office, though it also served as a place of ecclesiastical record, whose archives might well have to be consulted by the lawyers of the *officialité*.

The minimum staff for an *officialité* consisted of the *official* (that is, the judge) himself, the *promoteur* (the investigator and prosecutor), and their *greffier* (clerk). The *official* had to be a priest with a degree in law or theology and not belonging to a religious order (with the curious exception of any monk who came from the abbey of Fécamp).[62] Like as not, he would be a canon, probably of the cathedral. The *promoteur* had an unpleasant role to play, for he faced the inevitable difficulties of all those who have the duty of exercising discipline in society. As the learned abbé Bexon, refusing the office in the diocese of Toul, observed: if he reported the faults of the clergy to the bishop, he would be 'regarded as a hard man, perhaps even a persecutor', while if he failed to do so, the bishop would regard him as 'culpably tolerant'. There were other dangers too, for the secular judges would not countenance an 'odious inquisition' into the morals of the laity, and he was liable for damages if he challenged those of an ecclesiastic without convincing evidence.[63] In a populous diocese, additional staff were needed. Paris had a deputy for the *official*, two for the *promoteur*, and an administrative back-up of four attorneys, an usher, and a beadle. The *officialité métropolitaine*, with a different *official* and *promoteur*, used the same administrative services, so the meetings were set on Tuesdays and Fridays, with the diocesan court on Wednesdays and Saturdays. Taking into account the *officialités* of the cathedral, the Sainte-Chapelle, and the other Sainte-Chapelle out at Vincennes, the court of the cathedral chapter for its jurisdiction over elementary schools, the feudal court of the archbishop's *duché-pairie*, and the *bailliage du Banc du Chapître de l'Église de Paris* dealing with civil and criminal cases in and around the cathedral, the lawyers of the capital did well out of the affairs of the Church.[64]

The scope of ecclesiastical courts was wide in appearance, but in practice was constrained within strict boundaries set by the Crown and the secular magistrates. Crimes and offences against public order were matters for the lay judges: not just murder, rape, sodomy, and the like, but also offences which had ecclesiastical contexts—aggravated blasphemy, sacrilege, fighting in a sacred building, a priest marrying people outside his own parish, and so on.[65] Otherwise, priests, deacons, subdeacons, and monks were, as 'clercs', exempt from the lay courts—the summary justice of the *prévots des maréchaux* and the routine justice of the *présidiaux*. Quite often, however, a crime like murder would be dealt with conjointly by both lay and ecclesiastical justice, whether because an accused clerk exercised his right to insist on a dual review, or because the bishop issued letters of vicariate to enable the lawyers to proceed this way.[66] The broad immunity of clerks in civil cases was also subject to limitations: the clerk had to be the defendant, not the accuser, and the matter must not concern property, commerce, the payment of servants' wages, precedence in public places, and the interests of the Crown.[67] In some provinces, local custom also left the clergy open to a civil suit, as in Normandy, where the 'clameur de haro' could be raised. If two ecclesiastics were in litigation against each other, it might seem as if the ecclesiastical courts would have a monopoly—true, except where wills, church benefactions, the light before the reserved Sacrament, pew rents, the election of churchwardens, fights in church, the keeping of registers, the delineation of boundaries, and the sacking of vergers were concerned. The administration of the sacraments and the burial of the dead were the affairs of the clergy, but the secular magistrates were watchful all the same, for what if a lay parishioner was being insulted by a public refusal? Vows of religion were, more than any other matter, an exclusive affair of the *officialité*, but in these cases, as indeed in any others, there could always be the invocation of the *appel comme d'abus*, the final weapon by which the clergy could be defeated.

Much of the business of an ecclesiastical court concerned applications for dispensations to marry within the prohibited degrees, and these were numerous, for in small places everyone was related to all the others, and the prohibitions were extensive, including 'spiritual affinity', which precluded godparents from marrying their godchildren. The secular courts, however, monopolized marriage cases where the actual fact of the marriage was disputed, where promises had been broken, abduction was alleged, where dowries and inheritances were concerned. There was no divorce, the only remedy for marital breakdown being a decree of judicial separation, 'séparation de corps et d'habitation'. Generally, the petition would come from the wife, the husband having more severe means of getting rid of his wife if she had offended. She would usually go to the secular judges, who had the means to enforce their verdict and any settlement arising from it. But it was possible to go to the ecclesiastical court instead; this took advantage of the fact that canon law treated men and women as equal, adultery by either party being grounds for separation (though it is true that a woman would be sent to a convent for two years if she was the guilty party). In the diocese of Cambrai (probably because of the idiosyncratic character of the legal system there), the *officialité* was the court handling all these affairs, three-quarters coming from the wives, a tenth from the husbands, and a tenth being joint applications. The average number of separations decreed annually from 1737 to 1774 was nine—clearly, for most people marriage was simple and final, not a matter to take before lawyers.[68]

The power of the ecclesiastical courts was limited. They could not impose temporal penalties, though canonical penalties could be severe enough for a clerk, ranging from excommunication, interdiction from ministerial functions, deprivation of benefice, or imprisonment in a monastery. Laymen, without preferments or functions to be abrogated, could adopt a cavalier attitude to the fulminations of ecclesiastical judges. In most dioceses, the *officialité* no longer had a functioning prison, though at Lyon recourse could be made to the state fortress of Pierre en Cize, and at Paris there were cells in a tower in the first courtyard of the episcopal palace. In all the eighteenth century, no one was imprisoned in the gaol of the *officialité* at Montpellier—a dank underground cellar in the cloisters without a lock on the door. The laity were rarely prepared to co-operate with the diocesan lawyers when they went about their enquiries. In 1747, the bishop of Agde sent his *official* and *promoteur* to Celle to investigate allegations against a curé; there was a riot, the police would not help, and a magistrate who came down from Béziers interrogated witnesses and condemned the two ecclesiastical officers for defaming a worthy parish priest.[69] The sort of case an *officialité* could handle was the 'tumultuous incident' in the collegiate church of Saint-Géry in Cambrai in 1758. It concerned the chairs, the property of the chapter. When the curé was taking a catechism class, Michelle Noral, a lady of 50, the *chaisière*, burst in and tipped the children from their seats. The *promoteur* summoned witnesses, promising to make up the loss of their wages when attending the court. Noral said that Canon Mallet had ordered her to stack the chairs in a side chapel, and she had not understood the curé's protests because 'he spoke to her in Latin'. We do not know the verdict, but the *promoteur* asked for her to have to pay the costs and apologize to the curé in the presence of two witnesses.[70] To deal with a more serious case, a conjoint procedure of ecclesiastical and secular courts was needed if the penalty was to be severe. The priest who interrupted the sermon of the curé of Saint-André in Paris, declaring him to be preaching Luther and Calvin, was sentenced by the *official* to a period of prayer and fasting in a seminary, but the Châtelet insisted on a ceremony of reparation, a fine of 500 livres, and a five-year banishment from the city.[71] The affair in 1765 of the sermon of curé Papin of the village of Ormesson was more complex. The marquis d'Ormesson had pulled down the old church, which obstructed the entrance to his château, and built a new one, exhuming the bodies from the churchyard by warrant of the archbishop of Paris—Papin was accused of denouncing this as sacrilege. The *bailliage* court, alerted by the parlement of Paris, took up the case; the *officialité* intervened on grounds of clerical privilege, had Papin borne off to the ecclesiastical prison, and interrogated the witnesses, who turned out to have been prompted about the sermon by the marquis's estate manager. The *official* in a court reinforced by two canons of Notre-Dame and two barristers ordered the curé to a seminary for a month; the *bailliage* court fined him 10 livres for the poor of the parish. In short, he had been condemned by two jurisdictions, probably unjustly, and because a great nobleman was concerned; but his punishment was so light, it verged on acquittal.[72]

Given the cumbersome nature of conjoint procedures and the halting inefficiency of denunciations before the *officialité*, a bishop proposing to discipline an erring cleric would incline to short-circuit the old ways and act by the authority of the royal edict of 1698 giving him power to send a priest to a seminary for a period of penitence. The most common offenders were alcoholics, who would be sent to do a 'spiritual retreat' for forty days or so. Causing a public scandal in other ways (as losing money at tric trac to an officer of the garrison at Le Mans) might incur a longer period. For fornication, the customary rigours of the seminary might be supplemented by the humiliation of a public penance—like reciting the synodal ordinances and decretals on clerical conduct in front of the assembled ordinands before dinner on Fridays and dining on bread and water afterwards.[73] For graver breaches of discipline a *lettre de cachet* would be solicited from Versailles to send the offender to some

house of correction, like those run by the Frères des Écoles
Chrétiennes or the rigorous seminary of La Délivrande at Bayeux, or
the Bon Sauveur at Caen, whose nuns had disciplined prostitutes
before being changed to the task of taking in delinquent clergy. The
ancient structures of rule in France were falling into desuetude, and
new central officials had taken over, like the royal intendants running the *généralités*. In the same way, in the Church the episcopal
grands vicaires were doing the administering and inspecting which had
once been the prerogatives of the archdeacons, and bishops were
using arbitrary removals to seminaries and imprisonment by *lettres de
cachet* to root out scandal from the clerical estate without resort to the
cumbersome old *officialités*.

VII

The diocesan seminary[74] was the creation of the Counter-
Reformation, prescribed by the Council of Trent. In the course of
the seventeenth century, most bishops made an effort to comply
with the conciliar order. Finance was the problem. The initial
impetus might come from a pious donation of a site; thereafter, there
would be a continual search for benefices for union with the foundation. In theory, a bishop could tax his clergy to maintain the seminary, but this course was unpopular—'Why could not Monseigneur
find an abbey to annex?' was the cry. This search for 'unions' went
on all through the eighteenth century—an abbey was taken over by
Evreux in 1740, a priory in 1773 and an abbey in 1779 at Lisieux, an
abbey at Bayeux in 1781. These confiscations involved ruthless
utilitarian vandalism, demolishing the monastic church and buildings
and selling the fittings and debris.[75] There was also the problem of
finding endowments to provide maintenance grants for the poorer
students—150 livres a year for each of them was needed. Some
seminaries ran a *camérie*, a sort of cheap lodging-house (at Valonges,
a bed and soup twice a day for 3 livres a month).[76] Most, however,
shrank from this threadbare expedient, destructive of a common
spirit, and accepted only those who could pay or could win a
scholarship, whether by competition or favour. A seminarist accepting a *bourse* often had to undertake not to work outside the diocese
without the bishop's permission.[77] Thus, the number of grants
available from the seminary endowments was a significant factor in
the pastoral efficiency of the whole surrounding area.
    According to the interpretation of the intentions of the Council

of Trent and within the constraints of financial possibility, the concept of a seminary varied, both in the aims of the original foundation and the use to which it was eventually put. A royal declaration of 1698 summarized the wisdom built up by experience: bishops were ordered to set up a *grand séminaire* training and testing ordinands, and a *petit séminaire*[78] educating boys from the age of 12 as a preparatory school. These little seminaries, an invention of Vincent de Paul, had come late upon the scene, the first outside Paris being established by the bishop of Beauvais in 1648. New foundations were still being made in the late eighteenth century—at Boulogne in 1780, Toulouse and Oloron in 1784. Yet even by 1789, nearly half the dioceses were without one. From early on, these schools had two objects, often pursued in parallel. One was to provide boys with a basic education in the humanities, either by in-house teaching or by sending them to the local *collège* for most of their classes. The other was to enable boys of poor families to aspire to the priesthood. The content of the curriculum would correspond to the nature of the basic aim. In the one case, it would stop short at the end of philosophy, which completed the cycle of the humanities; in the case of the poor students, it would carry on with theology afterwards. Living cheaply at the little seminary, they could complete their formal theology, then move to the big seminary for their final instruction in pastoralia and the techniques of the ministry. Or, as a variant, some theology could be studied in both institutions; at Périgueux it was scholastic theology in the first, and moral theology, for three years, in the second. Not everyone who attended a little seminary or lodged there while attending a *collège* would go on to ordination, and some pupils were accepted who never had that intention. Most fathers, however, would not ask this privilege for their sons if they could afford to pay for education in a *collège*. Little seminary teaching concentrated on logic, metaphysics, and moral philosophy with only a reduced role for mathematics and physics. The range of prescribed authors was narrow; according to the abbé Carrel's *Science ecclésiastique* (1700), pagan authors ought to be avoided altogether. Courses were in Latin and were taught by way of dictation. Learning went at a snail's pace; one pupil remembered how a month went by reviewing the different definitions of 'philosophy'. But at least there was progress throughout the century; in spite of the fulminations of the parlement and the University of Paris, Cartesianism was winning, evident in the Latin courses of philosophy printed for Toul in 1769 and for Lyon in 1785.

There were 153 *grands séminaires* in France in 1760, and 130 in

1789, the main reason for the reduction in numbers being the expulsion of the Jesuits.[79] Half a dozen of the tiny dioceses had never managed to establish one, and another five dioceses had done so but had lost them by financial collapse—in the case of Mâcon, by fire destroying the buildings. On the other hand, a few dioceses had several, the precise count depending on the definition—three at Toulouse, four at Rouen, Rodez, and Lyon, and from eight to eleven in Paris. Outside this total of diocesan seminaries there were also some specialist institutions of the same kind. The Missions Étrangères had a small house in the rue du Bac in Paris training clergy for work in Canada and the Antilles. Up to 1786, when it went bankrupt, there was an English college in Paris, rue des Postes, drawing its students chiefly from the English school at Douai.[80] There was a similar Scottish institution in the rue des Fossés Saint-Victor. For the Irish, there were seminaries at Bordeaux, Nantes, Toulouse, Douai, Lille, and, especially, in Paris, the collège des Lombards, rue des Carmes, with an annexe of new buildings in the rue du Cheval-Vert put up by Laurence Kelly in 1770.[81] The mendicant orders also had houses devoted to the education of Irish friars in various countries; in France, there were Capuchin establishments at Bar-sur-Aube and Vassey and a Franciscan one at Boulay in Lorraine.[82] For the four Irish professors who taught at the Lombards and their French superior, the system was scandalous. The abbé Vaubrun and professor John Bourke protested to Rome in 1733, and the abbé de Nicholay renewed their complaints anonymously in mid-century. The Irish bishops insisted on ordaining their men before they left Ireland to study in France (presumably so that they could eke out a living by saying masses), and they showed no restraint over numbers. Consequently, said Bourke, there was a multitude of priests in Ireland 'without any function but to say mass, marry young couples and empty barrels'.[83] Scattered around France there were many others, some footloose adventurers, others useful to the bishops because willing to work in grim and lonely places where French priests were reluctant to stay. In Paris, there were 250 of them, most not living in the *collège* and some misbehaving. But pleas to Rome to suspend Irish ordinations for a while and to transform the Lombards into a genuine seminary for ordinands, not a lodging-house for unemployed priests, fell on deaf ears, though the Pope closed the Irish noviciates for friars from 1751 to 1773 and divided the Lombards into two sections, one for priests and one for ordinands. The Irish bishops remained incorrigible in their policy of ordaining; in the eyes of the hard-pressed Irish theologians in Paris trying to set up a dignified seminary, they were 'no better than a pack of cowboys'.[84]

There were also some special seminars to train penniless young men up to the priesthood, generally with the aim of directing them (like some of the Irish) to difficult areas. The seminary of Saint-Charles at Lyon was the prototype. In imitation of this successful venture, in 1740 the bishops of Grenoble, Viviers, Valence, and Gap collaborated to found a similar house at Grenoble to produce clergy for the remote mountain areas of the frontier.[85] In the diocese of Avranches there were experiments on a lesser scale with 'rural seminaries'. Paris, where young men from the provinces gravitated hoping to find a way into the priesthood, became a centre for such initiatives. In 1633, the Séminaire des Trente-Trois was founded, the title referring to the thirty-three years of the life of Christ, spent on earth in penury. Later in the seventeenth century, a student of Saint-Sulpice, François Chansiergues, founded a club for poor clerks lodging in the capital; they earned a living by copying sermons, giving tuition, walking in funeral processions, and doing other odd jobs on the fringes of the clerical world, supported each other, and worked together as best they might to qualify for ordination. Another student, the Breton abbé Poullart, bought a house in which he gave shelter to some of these poor clerks; by 1703 there were twelve of them, and soon their numbers had risen to seventy, and the Congrégation du Saint-Esprit was founded, inhabiting a seminary proper in the rue des Postes. Other communities of this kind sprang up, the so-called *Séminaires de la Providence*.[86] Archbishop Noailles and the wealthy curé of Saint-Jacques de la Boucherie, Louis de Marillac (son of a *maître des requêtes*), intervened, and united these ventures with the Chansiergues group to form the Seminary of Saint-Louis, the curé giving a house, and the prelate endowing forty free places.[87]

The *grands séminaires* in the dioceses were controlled by the local bishops, who prescribed the courses of study, appointed the *directeurs*, and made the final decisions about accepting individual candidates for ordination. Most bishops had confided the running of their seminaries to religious Orders; in 1760, a third of the total, sixty, were under the Lazarists, thirteen under the Eudistes (mostly in Normandy), fourteen under the Doctrinaires, fourteen under the Oratorians, twenty under the Sulpicians, and thirty-two under the Jesuits. Though each group of *directeurs* had its individual style, the establishments they ran were very much alike in discipline and atmosphere. But, according to what the diocese expected of them,

there were *grands séminaires* of various kinds, though different functions might be fulfilled together in the same institution. The simplest
case was a house of strict quiet discipline where the final preparation
for ordination was made. It was assumed that those entering had
already completed their quinquennium elsewhere—that is, two years
of philosophy and three years of theology. The synodal ordinances
of a bishop describe how this time of preparation must be spent:
prayer, meditation, and spiritual reading for the cultivation of the
inner life, acquiring the art of preaching and facility at plainchant,
learning the rules of the Church about the administration of the
sacraments and the customs and statutes of the diocese, analysing
problems of casuistry for application in the confessional. Some
episcopal regulations prescribe how the time before entrance to the
seminary must be spent. At Tarbes,[88] during the five years of study
of philosophy and theology at the local *collège*, the prospective ordi-
nand, living at home or in lodgings, was to wear clerical bands on
weekdays to mark out his vocation; on Sundays he had to attend
services in the cathedral or the church of Saint-Jean; and twice a year
he had to submit to an examination conducted by a *grand vicaire*, a
professor of the *collège*, and a *directeur* of the seminary—this to last
three days, with the closing session held in public. Thereafter, twelve
months' attendance at the seminary was required, spread over two
years. In other dioceses, the obligatory time of preparation for ordination was variously prescribed, but in roughly the same pattern—a
certain time for the subdiaconate, another for the diaconate, another
for the priesthood. In 1729, the bishop of Sées laid down eight
months for the first, one for the second, one for the third. If he did
not ask more, he said, it was because 'the faculties of the greater part
of the ordinands are too mediocre'. And he ordered them all to
buy the abridged version (it was four volumes all the same) of the
theology of Poitiers; they were forbidden to sell it or to lend it to
others.[89] At Paris, the preparation times were nine months, three
months and three months; at Bayeux three, six, and three, all to be
spread over three years; at Autun three, two, and three.[90] At Dol, the
patriarchal Urbain d'Hercé, becoming bishop in 1767, was horrified
to find that only three months altogether was needed; he immediately increased it to seven, with a vacation break in the middle
followed by an examination. His seminarists all had to dine in his
dining-hall and when they reached the subdiaconate, at his own
table—here, they were expected to marvel at their bishop's ability to
recite from memory the odes of Horace and the psalms between
courses.[91]

Most of the diocesan seminaries were organized to provide more than this minimum preparation for ordination.[92] They would accept ordinands who had completed their humanities to do from two to four years of theology; sometimes they would take over philosophy from the humanities curriculum as well. The teaching might be given exclusively by the *directeurs*—this is how the Lazarists and Sulpicians liked to have it; or some of it might be given externally, especially in the earlier years, the students attending at the local *collège* or, if there was one, the university. Each diocese had its pattern of study, though the bishop would not necessarily insist on a particular individual following the whole of it. At Nevers,[93] there were four years of theology with the first two studied externally; at Poitiers two years of philosophy then two years of theology. At Angers, the seminarists went once a day to a lecture in the Faculty of Theology of the university, but were otherwise taught by their own masters. The seminary of Larressonne in the diocese of Bayonne from 1747 allowed its students leave of absence to affiliate to a Spanish university.[94] Bordeaux had its seminary of Saint-Raphael, a place of severe spiritual discipline; here for five or six years a student would attend classes at the Jesuit *collège*, and after passing his examinations transferred to the séminaire des Ordinands for the prescribed months of pastoralia and retreat before the priesthood.[95] The working of the system in the diocese of Rouen is illustrated in the story of Jean-Marie Absolom Lebay's progress to holy orders. He was from a peasant family, and paid his way through the Oratorian *collège* at Dieppe by spare-time tutoring (his efforts brought on a nervous breakdown, from which he was rescued by an English doctor, who cured him and then committed suicide). He ended up with four prizes, including the one for 'diligence'. He got a place in the seminary of Saint-Nicaise at Rouen—number seventeen out of eighteen candidates; had it not been for the local curé who knew the *directeurs*, he might not have made it. He was there for five years, doing one of philosophy and one of physics externally at the *collège*, and three years of theology internally. At the end of the first year he received the tonsure, at the end of the second minor orders, at the end of the third the subdiaconate and the diaconate— this committed him to celibacy. He was 22 years of age when he left, having two years to wait before he would be old enough for ordination to the priesthood. Three months teaching in a *pensionnat* proved intolerable, due to the long hours and the embarrassment of being shorter in stature than all the pupils. He then became manager of a small saltpetre and gunpowder factory. After 'a not very rigorous examination' he was ordained priest in 1785, and earned a meagre living as a *prêtre habitué* at home. He was a vicaire when the Revolution came; not until 1819 did he become a curé—in his native village.[96] For someone without influence, it had been a slow and penny-pinching progress.

By definition, seminaries were austere places. Lay critics called them 'prisons', 'noviciates for monks', 'barracks for galley-slaves'. Drunk or immoral clergy sent there for a period of discipline did not need a special regimen—it existed already. Priests who found themselves penniless at the end of their working days and who were not in dioceses like Paris, Langres, or Rouen where prescient bishops had set up rest-homes for them, dreaded having to join the ordinands—being 'buried in the darkness of your seminary', as some of them complained to the bishop of Lisieux.[97] The fare was solid and simple; though, as one who endured it observes, it was the seminarists from poorer families who had never fed well who led in complaining.[98] The received wisdom was to prevent familiarity among the students and reduce conversations to a minimum, the ideal represented in the new buildings at Viviers in 1777, a series of cells opening into galleries around a central hall, so that all the doors could be under surveillance.[99] Confession once a week to one of the *directeurs* was the rule; there was no escape to confessors in town. Apart from the Parisian houses attended by great aristocrats and, towards the end of the century, Saint-Nicolas du Chardonnet, scandal or slackness is rarely reported. An isolated instance of cards and drinking at midnight could happen anywhere. Wigs and hair powder, more and more creeping into acceptance, were harmless fashions. The seminarist sent down for reading *L'Esprit* in chapel and another rusticated for possessing works of J.-J. Rousseau, the billiard-players at Caen, the chapel orchestra at Toulouse which struck up the 'March of the Bandits' when the procession moved into the stalls, might win our approval rather than our censure.[100]

According to philosophes and Jansenists, seminaries were haunts of ignorance and superstition. Some clergy who had passed through the system complained of the lack of intellectual content. There was all about the shape of tonsures, genuflexions and ceremonies, and the old canons of the Church, said one, and nothing of St Paul and the gospels.[101] Another, wanting to set up an academy of preaching, complained of the absence of the study of patristic texts: 'on donne trop de temps à former les cœurs et pas assez à former l'esprit'.[102] Yet the opposite objection is found—too much time spent on theological controversy: 'a young candidate who in his examinations is able to give effective replies to all the sophisms of heresy and impiety passes, and is judged capable of directing the consciences of 300 country folk who have never heard of Luther or Calvin, Jansenius or Quesnel'.[103] In fact, intellectual qualifications were secondary in a seminary education. 'The bishops send their ecclesiastics to us', said Jean Bonnet (dd. 1735), superior-general of the Lazarists, 'not to make teachers of theology out of them, but just curés and vicaires capable of instructing and directing the faithful.'[104] The framework of each day was prayer in the morning and evening, mass at 11 a.m. when those who had been out to lectures came back, and an hour's meditation according to the Salesian, Ignatian, or Oratorian methods as systematized in handbooks by Beuvelet in 1657 and Bussée in 1700. There was training for preaching, with the emphasis on clarity and simplicity; sermons corrected by the *directeurs* were tried out in the chapel with the object of enabling each seminarian to build up a corpus of twenty to thirty to take out when he left for parish work. The catechist's art was learned either in front of a seminary audience pretending to be children or a real class. Ceremonies were studied in Beuvelet's manual (1654), which took account of the rituals of the various dioceses as well as the Roman. The choreography of the liturgy and its manual actions were rehearsed, a wooden doll being used in simulated baptisms. Plainchant was studied with careful tuition, very often from outside experts. There was also a good deal of study of casuistry and the duties of the priest in the confessional. As the century progressed, the time spent in some of these exercises was curtailed (meditation was reduced to half an hour, and chanting became less important); even so, the subjects of pastoral value remained the core of the curriculum.

If the length and solidity of the textbooks specially produced for seminary use are an indication, there was every intention of giving students an exhaustive survey of moral and dogmatic theology.[105] Given the menace of Jansenism, bishops prescribed the reading lists, sometimes even commissioned the writing of the manuals themselves. The Jansenist volumes of Louis Habert were progressively outlawed, and most seminaries came to rely on the theology of Poitiers (1708), then that written by Tournely in sixteen volumes (1725–39) as later revised by Collet and abridged by him and others. Though these works were anti-Jansenist, they were Gallican, holding that infallibility required the assent of a majority of the bishops. They were also rigorist as regards the confessional. The theology of Lyon (1780) moved on from episcopal Gallicanism towards clerical democracy, the view that the unanimous collaboration of all the pastors, parish priests included, was required for infallibility. What was lacking in the vast systematization of these volumes was Church history, the direct study of the text of the Bible, and the drawing out of apologetical arguments to confront the thought of the Enlightenment. Improvements came in the course of the century.[106] In place of edifying stories, real Church history was read in the refectories and came into class work; the New Testament was read morning and evening and commented on in discussion groups; while from the *De vera religione* which Collet added to his abridgement of Tournely in 1751, every theological textbook came to have an apologetical section. Bailly's two-volume *Tractatus* (1758) of such arguments arranged for the use of seminaries had the unusual virtue of analysing, in a well-informed way, what the sceptical writers actually were saying.

If it was a question of the minimum course of seven to twelve months to pass through the stages to ordination, very little intellectual ground could be covered. The abbé de Mondran found his year at Toulouse (in the 1730s) unsatisfying: 'in the short space of a year they hurried along, accumulated subjects were passed in review as rapidly as through a magic lantern'.[107] He had not suffered too much himself, since he already had his *baccalauréat* in theology. Here is the difficulty when generalizing about the intellectual content of seminary courses. A priest who had received no more than the minimum training of a year obviously knew little about intellectual problems. But most had spent more than that, sometimes a great deal more, on theology. If this had taken place exclusively in the seminary, the teaching may have had a deadening effect, for the old custom of dictating endlessly to pupils carried on long after it was officially frowned upon: the idea being to send out the clergy of the future with a set of theology *cahiers* as well as a clutch of sermons.[108] But more and more, enlightened ideas were prevailing; *conférences*, discussion groups, were becoming the approved method of teaching, and the need to sharpen the weapons of Christian apologetics was bringing in a liberal and critical spirit in place of the old lapidary affirmations. There were so many combinations of theological study: in the seminary alone and for varying periods of time up to four years, in conjunction with a *collège* or with a university, and in the minority of seminaries duly affiliated to a university, in courses which would lead to a university degree. In this case, the value of the study depended a great deal on which university it was and at what stage the student left—at the *maîtrise* of arts, the *baccalauréat* of theology, the *licence* of theology, or the doctorate. Like most organizations in eighteenth-century France, the seminary system was full of illogicalities and confusions, but candidates for ecclesiastical office manœuvred their way through it with the help of such influence as they could muster, and got as much qualifying learning as they needed for the fulfilment of their ambitions.

We need to know more about the *directeurs* of the seminaries. If they were secular priests, the rewards of the Church rarely came their way. Christophe de Lalane, who ran the seminary at Langres from 1738 to 1745, then that of Quebec, and finished up as superior at Dax and a *vicaire général* of the diocese, was rewarded by the gift of an abbey only at the age of 60.[109] If they were members of an Order, they had been chosen from the learned and austere minority among their colleagues. Though they were nominated to their way of service by authority, they remained, in the best sense of the word, volunteers, for Lazarists, Doctrinaires, and Oratorians, all in their different ways, had taken vows which might be binding on the interior conscience, but were not enforceable against them by secular or canon law if they chose to leave.[110] Theirs was a vocation requiring the abandonment of the companionship and comforts so many pastoral or monastic duties afforded, though it brought wide contacts with the parish priests of a diocese, including austere friendships of a sort. When the clergy of France were confronted with the oath to the revolutionary Civil Constitution of the Clergy, it was often the *directeurs* of their local seminary to whom they turned for advice. In the dark days of the Terror the dominant figure in the Gallican Church and the keeper of its conscience was M. Emery, who had ruled the seminaries of Orléans, Lyon, and Angers before taking over at Saint-Sulpice—a man who rose at four in the morning to meditate and wore hair shirts and iron bracelets, and gave them as presents to his friends.[111] Free from bias towards the spirit of the *ancien régime* or rancour against the Revolution, and with the insight of clear logic and unshakable rectitude, he advised the persecuted clergy on their attitude towards the various revolutionary oaths. Those who had ridiculed the seminaries as dens of logic—chopping casuistry and wrangles over unreal contingencies—could not have guessed that national events would catch up with the exercises of the classroom.

7

THE BISHOPS: ARISTOCRATIC VOCATIONS

I

The king nominated to all the bishoprics of France.[1] The Pope had granted the right by the Concordat of 1516. According to one school of Gallican lawyers, the treaty covered the dioceses in provinces subsequently annexed; this was not agreed at Rome, but as the Pope conceded the right in separate instruments, the dispute made no difference to the exercise of the royal power. In theory, if the titular of a French see died while visiting Rome, the right of appointing a successor would lapse to the Pope—a contingency which fortunately did not arise to trouble the diplomats and lawyers of the eighteenth century. The one other apparent exception to the patronage of the Crown was the continuing right of the cathedral chapter of Strasbourg to elect its bishop, but in practice, the canons always accepted the name sent to them from Versailles.

By the Concordat, the king's power of choice was limited to sons of Catholic parents, of at least 27 years of age (by canon law it was 30), who had studied at a famous university and had obtained the *licence* in theology or in law, including canon law. The formal procedures of appointment were solemn and measured.[2] The king signed three letters—to the Pope, the 'Cardinal Protector' of French affairs in Rome, and the ambassador there. The bishop-to-be had to go to the nuncio in Paris to fill in an 'information de vie et de mœurs' of twenty searching questions, and to his own diocesan bishop to make a profession of faith before him and to sign an 'information' concerning the see to which he was nominated. He then sent these three documents and the king's three letters to a *banquier expéditionnaire en Cour de Rome*. The *banquier* went to the French ambassador to get his *expediatur* on the royal letter to the Pope, then took it to the Datary for the Roman bureaucracy to process it and send it onwards. Armed with his own royal letter, the Cardinal Protector would give notice to the first Consistory meeting that occurred of his intention to propose the candidate at the next session (the *Préconisation*). At the following Consistory the proposition was put, the cardinals gave their advice, and the Pope thereafter ordered the nine bulls to be sent to France, the most important being the provisions to the bishop-to-be and the authorization to one or more bishops to consecrate him.

There were ample opportunities in the process for objections to be made to the candidate's morals, beliefs, or fitness. Before this process had begun, there had been the original enquiry made before he had been ordained priest (this had been a problem with Dubois, for Archbishop Noailles refused to give his *licet*, and in the end the archbishop of Rouen had been persuaded to degrade himself and do so). The nuncio had the duty of checking the *information de vie et de mœurs* by taking opinions from two leading churchmen—in the case of Talleyrand, Dugnani obtained certificates of moral conduct from Thémines, bishop of Blois, and Barral, the coadjutor of Troyes.[3] The diocesan bishop could challenge the profession of faith, the cardinals could make enquiries between Consistories and advance objections, and, finally, the bishops authorized to consecrate could refuse. Yet the system rolled on without these opportunities being taken or, if they were, without making any difference. Good men combined with worldly men to operate it. The devout Massillon tried to persuade Noailles to give Dubois his *licet*, then was one of the three prelates who consecrated the crafty and dissolute minister to the episcopate.[4] How did his mind work, and the minds of others like him, when facing candidatures which, by any standard, were unacceptable? Tronson, the severe head of Saint-Sulpice, wrote to Colbert, the great minister of Louis XIV, on 29 August 1679, in reply to his formal enquiry whether his second son, aged 25 and just out of seminary, might be consecrated as coadjutor archbishop of Rouen. 'With all the sincerity I can muster', said Tronson, 'there is nothing in him to make him unsuitable . . . and he can render the Church service.'[5] So the boyish Jacques-Nicolas in the following year was consecrated 'archbishop of Carthage' and coadjutor of the most splendid see in France; there were thirty-six bishops at the ceremony and six who were nominated but not yet in office—'there were no more at the Council of Nicea,' said Mme de Sévigné. Tronson's carefully worded recommendation had meant, quite simply: it was in the interest of the Gallican Church to serve the political designs of the State: the king's will must prevail.

II

If the Church is to be in servitude, said a seventeenth-century Jansenist, it had better be to secular princes than to ecclesiastics: 'I prefer to see bishoprics given by the Court of France than by that of Rome.'[6] In an established Church, there is no reason why the secular power should not appoint bishops as good as those ecclesiastics might elect for themselves, or ecclesiastical authority impose. The ruler and his ministers have nothing to gain and much to lose by making appointments which churchmen would regard as falling short of the best available. But there is always the problem of the constituency which the government wishes to please. The theoretically absolute monarchy of France, though becoming more responsive to public opinion throughout the eighteenth century, was primarily looking for approval to the aristocracy: Versailles, where the nobles glittered around the king in self-interested subordination, was the heart and symbol of the monarchy's power. Oversimplifying, it can be said that the nobles had yielded up their anarchical local domination in return for bribes offered by the Crown, and the source for the bribes was the wealth and splendour of the Gallican Church.

In 1516, at the time of the Concordat, of the 102 bishops in place, ninety were nobles (sixty being of a lineage going back to 1400), four were commoners, and the remaining eight are of uncertain status.[7] The aristocratic predominance carried on to the Revolution: of the 1,416 nominations from 1516 to 1789, 1,227 were nobles, 62 were commoners, and the exact status of the remaining 127 has not been determined. Half of the commoners and those who may possibly have been so obtained their sees during the Wars of Religion, from 1560 to 1588, when the grip of the Crown was faltering. Within these broad figures of aristocratic monopoly, however, two major changes had taken place, imposed by the Crown to promote royal power and administrative efficiency, and to aid the Gallican Church in its religious mission. In the early sixteenth century, the noble prelates were occupying sees in areas where their families were dominant, no fewer than seventy-two of them established in place by virtual inheritance, members of dynasties. Royal policy, ruthlessly pushed ahead by Richelieu, was to break these family chains of succession, and appoint bishops to dioceses away from their family sphere of influence. Louis XIV firmly established this principle, the last dynastic see to be liberated being Senlis in 1702; he did, however, allow exceptions for newly annexed territories and areas where knowledge of the local language was desirable. Le Camus, bishop of Grenoble from 1671 to 1702, noted the effect of this change on the standing of the bishop in the local community: 'a bishop is usually a man fallen from the skies into the midst of a province where he finds no support, no help; monks, chapters and parlement continually cause him difficulties, officials never put themselves out to assist him'.[8] It meant the bishop was now entirely a king's man, an agent of the royal power on which he was dependent.

The second major change in the character of the episcopate imposed by royal policy was to insist that nobles who sought to rule dioceses must make themselves professionally qualified to do so. The stipulation of the Concordat concerning the *licence* was enforced, and in the reign of Louis XIV it became understood that the degree had to be taken at the Sorbonne; from 1700 the custom arose of residing at Saint-Sulpice for part of the time. From 1680, Louis XIV was also making it a rule that an apprenticeship in the office of *grand vicaire* was necessary: from 1660 to 1690, seventeen of the forty-seven nominations had held these administrative posts in the dioceses, then from 1690 to 1715, seventy-six out of 107; after 1730, this qualification became routinely indispensable. The scandal of very young bishops, 'évêques à la bavette', was ended. From 1589 to 1623, the average age on appointment was 35; thereafter it became about 40. In the eighteenth century, few appointments were made under the age of 30—the abbé de Saint-Albin, the illegitimate son of the regent, taking the see of Cambrai at 25 was an outrageous exception to all the rules. Vacancies in the episcopate were few, and they became fewer as the prelates, a long-lived class to start with, began to live longer still. In the eighteenth century, the average age of death was between 65 and 70, and the number of vacancies was just over five a year, declining at the end of the *ancien régime* to three and a half. There were always going to be many more aspirants than successful candidates. The noble families enjoying the virtual monopoly of the royal patronage—say, 300 of them, for 793 of the 1,416 nominations from 1516 to 1589 were from 269 families—knew exactly what qualifications had to be gained by their sons, what the chances of an appointment were, and how long the time of waiting was likely to be.

Among the 300 families, the pattern of recruitment changed somewhat as the years went by. There are various ways of categorizing the nobility of France, none comprehensive, all overlapping and subject to exceptions. Going by genealogy, there were the newly ennobled, the established nobles with four generations to prove it, and the *nobles de race*, the feudal families tracing their descent back to 1400 and earlier and entitled to be presented at Court. Looking at the caste by function, there were nobles of the Court and high administration, the magistrates of the parlements and other sovereign courts (the 'robe'), and the provincial nobles. Looking at the nobility on the scale of wealth, the provincial nobles fragment into contrasting groups, from rural squires forced into penury by the operation of the inheritance laws, to well-off landed families and, even, splendidly affluent ones, living on their fiefs. There was also, on the fringe of the nobility, a penumbra of rich families, holders of important municipal offices, successful bourgeois who had purchased estates, spoken of technically as 'living nobly', and rated as noble by local opinion. In the eighteenth century the *nobles de race* were the favourites for the bishoprics, and for the most important ones. Of the bishops of 1789, ninety-nine were from old feudal families, eighty of them having proceeded to 'the honours of the Court'. Authentic documentation going back to the High Middle Ages had enormous force in society; there are stories of it, unsupported by wealth or connections, opening the way to high office—a bishop of Mende taking refuge from a thunderstorm in the hovel of a penurious squire and happening to ask to see the family title-deeds, with the result that one son came to command a regiment and another became a vicar-general.[9] Among the prelates of 1789 there was such a case. Jean-Baptiste Chabot, bishop of Saint-Claude, had been a curé until he found his family *preuves* and had them verified by Chérin, the court genealogist, thus making himself eligible to rise to the top of the ecclesiastical hierarchy. The thirty-one prelates of 1789 who lacked the cachet of great antiquity mostly had lineages going back for at least two centuries, and those whose ancestral tree had shallower roots were of undeniable distinction. The family of Couet du Vivier de Lorry (Angers) had risen in high administration before being recognized as noble in 1675. Courtois (Belley) was from a family acquiring instant transmissible nobility early in the eighteenth century by paying the immense sum required for the office of *secrétaire du roi*; since then it had provided three generals for the armies of the king. Chaumont de la Galaisière (Saint-Dié) had as a grandfather a rich grain merchant from the Low Countries who had loaned money to Louis XIV; he became naturalized in France in 1720, and bought nobility as a *secrétaire du roi*; his son, the bishop's father, had become intendant of Lorraine and married the daughter of Controller General Orry. Two of the prelates of 1789 (both appointed in 1771) came from the penumbra of families regarded as noble though they lacked the documentation.[10] Le Quien de Neufville (Dax) had relatives in high positions in the army and the administration, but the family *preuves* were 'lost'; the best that could be done was to point to the grandfather recognized as noble in Portugal. Hachette des Portes was of the rich patrician merchant class of Reims, holders of high municipal office—wealth and distinction enough to enable him to proceed to the minor see of Glandève.

In the eighteenth century, appointments to the episcopate from families of the Court and high administration declined, from 25 per cent or more under Louis XIV to 18 per cent after 1726. One possible reason was the rising incidence of birth control in the highest echelons of society: there were fewer sons in search of an establishment. There was a decline too in the representatives of the nobles of the robe.[11] This class had provided the intelligent and moral heart of the Jansenist movement, and the powers that be in Church and State were excluding Jansenists from all influential ecclesiastical posts. When vacancies occurred in the dioceses where the opposition to *Unigenitus* was centred—Paris, Boulogne, Tours, Orléans, Meaux, Nantes, Montpellier, Aix, and Senez—strictly orthodox prelates were appointed. By 1740, there were no Jansenist bishops left. Not surprisingly, then, there were fewer religious vocations among the sons of the magistrates. Throughout the century, the parlement of Paris battled against the Crown on political, as well as religious, issues. One of the penalties the king could impose was to look elsewhere for his bishops: in the reign of Louis XVI, all appointments from the robe were from the provincial parlements. It is easier to define the classes within the nobility which were providing fewer recruits to the episcopate than to generalize about those producing the majority, for outside Court, higher administration, and robe, the caste was complex and heterogeneous. But broadly speaking, they were very often 'provincial' nobles, mostly of old feudal families and enjoying substantial incomes from landed estates and with a long tradition of military service.[12]

In the reign of Louis XIV, commoners—given brilliant abilities or membership of a family coming to the king's notice in his domestic service—could still hope to become bishops. Even so, in some circles their birth was held against them. Saint-Simon, with his fanatical cult of ancestry, refers to them in savage terms—'an ill-bred pedant from the dregs of the populace', and the like. One, who became bishop of Dax, then of Périgueux, was said 'to have been born a beggar (*gueux*), lived as a beggar and wanted to die as a beggar (*périr gueux*)'. In 1712, Paris heard how Hébert, bishop of Agen, had received an official rebuke: 'they wrote to him as if he was a scoundrel (*faquin*) just because he is not a *grand seigneur* and has been curé of Versailles. He replied as a bishop should, briefly, precisely.'[13] According to one calculation (there is room for small divergencies), from 1682 to 1700 sixteen commoners entered the episcopate, from 1700 to 1743 only nine. Thereafter, up to 1789, there was only one, appointed in 1774, a very special case. The abbé de Beauvais,[14] son of an *avocat* pleading before the parlement of Paris, was 43 years of age, the greatest preacher of his generation, adored by the king's pious daughters, who pressed for his elevation. He was also well thought of by the higher clergy, for his uncle was the lawyer presiding over the office of the agents-general, the key man in advising the Assembly of Clergy how to resist encroachments on clerical privileges. The bishopric they gave him was Senez, consisting of thirty parishes among barren mountains, with a tiny income. The promotion, in fact, put him to great inconvenience, as he struggled to run his diocese and to travel back and forth to Paris to fulfil preaching engagements; after nine years he resigned and joined the staff of Archbishop Juigné in the capital. The abbé Maury, preaching in 1775, thundered against the 'blind prejudice' of those who talked of the new bishop of Senez with condescension as one of the 'hommes de fortune', 'while, on the contrary, they are the only bishops for whom fortune has done nothing'. It was an isolated breakthrough for talent.

In 1790 France was ruled by the National Assembly, and the future of the episcopate was in doubt. Le Franc de Pompignan, the honest old archbishop of Vienne, had become minister of the *feuille* (and had shown remarkable scrupulosity in resigning his see to do so). The bishopric of Boulogne fell vacant, and, in the dying months of the old order, another commoner was appointed, Jean-René Asseline, aged 48, a brilliant scholar who held the chair of Hebrew at the Sorbonne and for long had been a *grand vicaire* of the diocese of Paris.[15] The story goes that his low birth was argued against his elevation (he was a son of a domestic servant of the Orléans family), but Louis XVI merely asked, 'a-t-il autant de vertus qu'on l'assure?' He was consecrated in time to publish a pastoral letter against the Civil Constitution of the Clergy, and to be evicted from the see he so well deserved and which had come to him so late.

III

Anticlerical orators of the Revolution were to declaim against the selection of bishops under the *ancien régime* as a matter of Court intrigue, with valets and mistresses as intermediaries. In the nature of the old society, Court influence counted. There were families under the king's eye as notable servants of the Crown. Dillon, archbishop of Narbonne, was the son of a lieutenant-general and had two brothers killed in the wars: a passport to promotion in the Church was brothers who risked their lives. Others came to notice as they acquired a contact at Versailles: Boisgelin, archbishop of Aix, had a brother who married a matron of honour to the royal princesses and joined his wife doing official duties in their household. In the next reign, Marie Antoinette and her circle radiated favouritism.[16] The abbé d'Agoult, disqualified from promotion because of his weakness for the ladies, was absolved by his links with her friends Breteuil and the Polignacs, and became bishop of Pamiers in 1787. Since La Tour du Pin Montauban, bishop of Nancy, chaplain to the queen, was refused the prestigious office of tutor to the dauphin, Marie Antoinette got him compensated with the rich see of Auch. Nobles who stayed away from Versailles needed a lucky accident to bring them to this sort of preferential notice. Hercé is said to have got Dol in 1767 because of a meeting with the duc d'Aiguillon when the estates of Brittany convened at Nantes, where for long he had run the diocese for his bishop; Gabriel Cortois de Quincey, archdeacon of Dijon, became bishop of Belley in 1751 because he out-argued an *esprit fort* in the stage-coach going to Paris, with a Théatin monk in the corner seat who turned out to be Boyer, minister of the *feuille*.[17]

But when the king 'worked', as the phrase went, with his minister, there were other pressures to take into account, more ecclesiastical in their nature, at least in their veneer. The bishops, and especially the archbishops, constituted a web of influence, and the system of qualifying as *grands vicaires* on their staffs gave them additional opportunities for liaising together in a sort of selection process. Of the episcopal generation of 1789,[18] twenty-three had an episcopal uncle as patron, four an episcopal brother, others had brothers marrying the nieces of bishops or more distant connections of relationship or friendship. The bishops in place were pushing members of their family (and pushing each other's), but they were also concerned about the dignity of their order, anxious to see it fortified with outstanding talent. They knew all the possible candidates and selectively groomed them for royal consideration.

There were, of course, dioceses and dioceses. The great nobles
wanted the most splendid sees for their sons, if not immediately,
then certainly by promotion. And the assessment of splendour
began, though it did not end there, with sheer material considerations: some bishoprics conferred enough to live on by the standards
of a modest country estate owner, others conferred riches on a scale
only enjoyed by grandees of the Court—and there were many
gradations of income between. About 1760, according to the
Almanach Royal, Paris was worth over half a million livres, and
Strasbourg and Metz were prodigiously rich. Around 80,000 livres
were Arras and Verdun, around 50,000 livres Vabres, Lodève, Dol,
Fréjus, Mirepoix, and Marseille. The poorest of all was Vence, at a
mere 12,000 livres. Two vague generalizations are possible: the very
tiny sees tended to have small incomes, and most of the sees in the
North were rich, while most in the South were poor—a contrast
reflecting the very different productivity of the two areas. Those
rewards did not correspond to either status or responsibilities.
Vienne was an archbishopric, but worth only 29,000 livres, Langres
of peerage rank was worth less still. Condom, Agen, and Lectoure
were dioceses of about equal size, but Condom had double the
income of either of the others. Everyone, including candidates for
episcopal promotion, used the *Almanach* when discussing incomes,
since it was at least broadly reliable in putting sees in order of
profitability, but it was assumed that the figures were much too low.
From the gossip of the time, Taine inferred that multiplication by
two would not be excessive. It is safer, however, to assume that it
was mostly the poorer bishoprics which were greatly understated.
An astonishing case is Troyes, down in the *Almanach* of 1789 as
worth 14,000 livres, but according to figures submitted by the
bishop himself in October 1790, really worth 68,068 livres, 6 sols
(a degree of precision arousing doubts). Early in the century, the
Assembly of Clergy, anxious to establish true figures for taxation
purposes, collected returns from the individual bishops, a method
which had never worked in France. Given that the incomes were
complex in derivation and fluctuating in yield, there was inevitably
cautious understatement in offering a figure likely to become permanent. Finally, the agents-general hit upon a surer way, examining
the accounts held in the *Régie des Economats*, the organization
collecting the revenues of bishoprics during vacancies. A good deal
depended, however, on when the vacancy had occurred, how long
it lasted, and how long the principal leases had been in unrevised
operation. Short of a detailed investigation of the financial archives

of a bishopric (where available), exact statements are impossible. One thing, however, is sure: episcopal incomes rose greatly in the course of the eighteenth century, a rise beginning about 1730 and becoming rapid after 1760.[19] It was dioceses like Strasbourg, Chartres, La Rochelle, and Rodez, where rents from land were the core of the income, which did best. The leases of the bishop of Chartres doubled from 1742 to 1770, and doubled again from 1770 to 1780. In so far as the facts were known, none of this would endear the bishops to their flocks and to those of their curés who lived on modest tithes or, worse still, on the *congrue*, with its belated and meagre augmentations.

The king and his minister of the *feuille* organized the patronage of abbeys in conjunction with that of bishoprics. A bishop would expect abbeys *in commendam* to supplement his income, the great aristocrats in the wealthy sees because they were great, the lesser nobles in the poorer sees because they needed the money. It was the great who received the most and the most promptly. Etienne Saint-Jean de Prunières became bishop of Grasse in 1753, and drew its income of 14,000 livres, as the years went by accumulating pensions of 9,000 livres extra; not until 1788 did he get an abbey, and it was worth only 5,000 livres a year.[20] Among his contemporaries, Montmorency-Laval at Metz with fifteen times his episcopal income had a further 60,000 livres from abbeys.[21] Cardinal Dominique de la Rochefoucauld, archbishop of Rouen from 1755, had an income from his see of 172,000 livres and the abbey of Cluny worth almost as much; nevertheless, in 1778, the abbey of Fécamp came his way.[22] These lofty noblemen had no doubts about their right to collect such vast revenues from the Church, though there were unwritten rules to add a veneer of decency. The income of the archbishop of Paris was so great that it was understood he needed no supplements; also, when one of the very lucrative monastic prizes fell to a bishop, he would feel obliged to throw back into the Versailles pool of benefices the smaller ones he had accumulated. This was a rule that Dubois, a vulgar adventurer, did not accept: he wrote to the Pope explaining why he deserved the extra abbey which had just been awarded to him—Richelieu had had twenty and Mazarin twenty-two, while he still had no more than eight.[23] A proper bishop would be more decorous in flouting the canonical ordinances against pluralities—provided the limited number of abbeys he retained yielded substantial revenues.

Behind this system of granting favours graded according to aristocratic standing and Court influence, a royal policy of a broader kind was operating, working towards political and ecclesiastical ends.[24] The king could modify a bishop's revenues in three ways: increasing them by adding an abbey or a grant of a pension from some ecclesiastical source, or diminishing them by deducting a pension. These devices were used in concert to maintain an equilibrium. A bishop already provided richly with abbeys who was moved up to a wealthier see might keep his abbeys but find the Crown had deducted pensions from his new income. A prelate who accepted translation to a poorer see to suit royal policy could expect to have the difference promptly made up. Long and valuable service would be recognized: for one, there would be an automatic increase as pensioners died off; for another, the Crown might offer an additional abbey. Apart from Vence and Saint-Paul-Trois-Châteaux, always left in poverty, the very lowest episcopal incomes were pushed up to a more dignified level. Also, certain sees, some rich, some not, were marked down for special consideration: the half-dozen most influential archbishoprics, the six conferring the title of peer, and the frontier sees of Strasbourg, Metz, and Verdun, where the completion of the annexation policy involved granting favours.

The *noblesse de race* had the greatest chance of obtaining the wealthy sees, and, for other reasons, they had a virtual monopoly of certain dioceses. The five 'foreign' dioceses—Besançon, Cambrai, Saint-Omer, Strasbourg, and Metz—carried with them princely titles in the Holy Roman Empire, so it was unthinkable to give any of them to an ordinary candidate—unless it was Dubois, of course. There were also the six carrying with them the rank of 'peer', three as 'counts' and three as 'dukes'. There were others, perhaps as many as twenty in number, for which lofty status was desirable, as there were numerous noble families in the diocese, who would look down on a prelate of inferior lineage.

In a minority of dioceses, there were reasons why the king, at least sometimes, would consider appointing a local candidate. Backers of a particular candidate would argue that the neighbours had a great affection for the family and wanted someone they knew.[25] And it was axiomatic that a bishop would enjoy exercising his splendid office among familiar faces; the minister of the *feuille*, if making such an appointment, would be sure to put a courteous cliché about it in his letter: 'I thought this place would be doubly agreeable to you, in that it puts you in the neighbourhood of your family.'[26] Knowledge of the local dialect was important for some areas: it was impossible, for example, to preside over the estates of Béarn without speaking Basque, so a man of the province had to be found for Lescar. This was certainly a consideration, though not an overriding one, when appointing to the bishoprics of Provence. Brittany was an ambiguous case. For pastoral efficiency, Breton was desirable, but experience had shown that anyone appointed from within the province would soon become involved in the tumultuous political agitations of the nobles. As a result, 'foreigners' were appointed to the important sees of Nantes, Saint-Malo, and Vannes throughout the eighteenth century, while Bretons got the less important ones of Tréguier, Saint-Pol-de-Léon, and Quimper.[27]

A different set of considerations operated when the minister of the *feuille* looked away from the demands of royal policy and the preference of the dioceses and considered the effect a particular nomination would have on the structure of the episcopate as a whole. An archbishop of Paris must be capable of giving leadership to the Gallican Church and must therefore be experienced (there was surprise when Beaumont went there after only a few years at Bayonne).[28] Somewhere on the episcopal bench, there ought to be an expert theologian—a factor which helped the rise of Languet de Gergy, the great polemicist against Jansenism. Looking at the scene more broadly, it was important to keep the age structure of the episcopate constant, with readily predictable possibilities of operating promotions and bringing in new blood at reasonably spaced intervals. When a bishop died young, there seems to have been a preference for appointing a young successor; when old, an older one.[29] This helped to keep the age and career pattern uniform, and to compensate dioceses for an unexpectedly short term of office by awarding the possibility of a longer one.

From time to time the king would consider the possibility of transferring a prelate to another see. In strict old-fashioned parlance, a bishop was 'married' to his see and ought to stay with his people for life, though in the eighteenth century it was a 'Jansenist' sentiment to proclaim it. By contrast, in Court circles, such moves were cynically regarded as simple matters of calculation of personal interest. On 21 April 1758 Bernis was advising the comte de Choiseul that his brother should accept the first vacancy: 'this will be the bridge towards the first great see which falls vacant afterwards'.[30] A few days later, news of the death of the archbishop of Tours arrived, and Bernis was trying to get it for the abbé de Choiseul—or, if the archbishop of Albi was moving over to take it, Albi would do. On 13 May it was a question of Evreux, and the idea was to persuade the bishop of Toul to take it, leaving Toul available. 'But the great point is to make the abbé de Choiseul a bishop. The king has promised not to leave him languishing in a minor see.' On 16 May, it was definitely Evreux: 'I won't congratulate you,' wrote Bernis, 'it's a simple stepping-stone.'

This correspondence comes from a Court intrigue in the circle of Mme de Pompadour; most translations were more decorously arranged and for better reasons. The vast disparities in wealth and importance meant that there was a ready-made ladder for promotion. As the bishop of poor and mountainous Glandève said in 1790, 'surely these translations can be regarded as the recompense for a laborious life spent in harsh surroundings offering no consolations but those we can hope to find in the fulfilment of our ministry'.[31] A vast and prestigious archbishopric like Rouen had to be ruled by a senior and experienced administrator—its five incumbents from 1709 to 1789 had served their apprenticeship in smaller bishoprics.[32] Conversely, individuals marked out by their great abilities needed to be moved to spheres of wider opportunity—thus Champion de Cicé and Loménie de Brienne staged at Condom and Rodez before taking over the great responsibilities of Bordeaux and Toulouse. And then, of course, there were always men of families of great distinction who could not be left to 'languish' low down in the hierarchy—bishop of Saint-Omer in 1775 at the age of 35, of Carcassonne three years later, and archbishop of Bourges ten years later still, this was an appropriate run of promotion for a son of the military aristocracy of the Court, Jean-Antoine Auguste de Chastenet de Puységur. On rare occasions (there was a case in 1719, and another in 1788) an episcopal appointment was resigned before it was taken up, as a more splendid see suddenly became available.

By contrast, there were prelates who refused the king's offer of promotion.[33] Belsunce, hero of the plague of Marseille, turned down Laon in 1723 and Bordeaux in 1729; the bishops of Limoges and Uzès refused offers in 1750 and 1754, preferring their peace of mind among people who were devoted to them. The saintly bishop of Orange agreed to move to Grenoble in 1788, then changed his mind. It might have appeared that Henri de Fleury, who left Tours for Cambrai in 1775, was drawn by the lure of the high income, yet originally he had refused, wishing to stay at Tours where for twenty-three years he had been happy. The king made him go, to give Cambrai a break from its series of worldly bishops—'you must accept, Fénelon has not yet been replaced'.[34] Some of the poorer bishoprics got the name of 'sièges de passage', but this was simply because of the accident of dates of vacancy; if there was no candidate of great family or conspicuous ability ready to begin his progress

over the 'stepping-stones', an appointment would be made of someone who might well stay there for life. During the century, Valence
had one episcopal reign of forty-five years, Pamiers of forty-six,
Carcassonne of fifty; in 1789, the bishop of Grasse had ruled for
thirty-seven years, of Bazas for forty-three, Saint-Paul-Trois-
Châteaux for forty-six, Saint-Dié for forty-seven; of the 130 bishops
of 1789, thirty-six had received translations, generally after a decent
interval of about ten years.[35] With the disparities between dioceses,
most bishops had an eye to promotion; there were important sees to
which the Crown had to move up experienced administrators; there
were some great families whose sons could not be left to 'languish'.
Given these factors, it is surprising that translations were the exception rather than the rule.

IV

Problem III Aristacus, an abbé of high birth and distinguished merit,
solicits a bishopric, desiring to serve the church usefully.
Reply He can not desire the office of bishop with the elevation to such a
high dignity in mind, without rendering himself guilty of ambition or presumption; he cannot desire it aiming to be honoured and respected, or to
become rich, without rendering himself guilty of ambition or avarice. In
addition, it is not enough to have a pure intention to be able to desire a
bishopric without sin; he must have all the virtues that the Apostle prescribes for a bishop.[36]

These episcopal virtues prescribed by St Paul were: to be vigilant,
sober, blameless, hospitable, apt to teach, and not to be a brawler or
a striker—the Pauline proviso about being the husband of one wife
having been tightened up subsequently by a presumably superior
authority. As for the right to solicit a bishopric, most casuists would
have said this was not allowed in any case, even by attempting to
give an impression of worthiness so as to be noticed for promotion.
Tronson of Saint-Sulpice called Fénelon to penitence when he was
made tutor to the duc de Bourgogne. You did not seek it, but
maybe you took care to show yourself in a favourable light; 'on a
souvent plus de part à son élévation qu'on ne pense . . . personne ne
saurait s'assurer entièrement qu'il ne se soit pas appelé soi-même'.[37]
Given the severity of the casuists, how could a young aristocrat seek
a bishopric with a sincere purpose? There was a single narrow gap in
the wall of prohibitions through which he could drag his conscience.
One of the factors in the clerical vocation was to be 'called'. The

Church needed well-qualified men for its service, and those with an 'inclination' had a duty to consider seriously, when they were invited; indeed, there was an obligation to accept 'if the Pope or another legitimate superior orders'.[38] Humility, fear, distrust of the worldly manœuvres of relatives, were not legitimate grounds for refusing an authentic call.[39] The way bishops were appointed in eighteenth-century France involved recommendation by existing prelates, nomination by the king, and confirmation by the Pope. The system was corrupt, yet formally correct. A *grand vicaire* offered a diocese of his own could, in a fashion, justifiably say he was 'called'.

Yet the system contrived to call only aristocrats. 'If I thought that noble birth was the principal condition required for episcopal office,' said Cardinal La Roche-Aymon, when appointing the abbé de Beauvais to Senez, 'I would trample my pectoral cross under foot.'[40] His cross remained undamaged, so there must have been good arguments to placate his conscience. They would start from the general theories by which the nobility justified its privileges. According to the lawyers, noble rank was a creation of the king as the reward for great past services, especially upon the battlefield—petitioners for royal favour in the Church and elsewhere would cite the members of their family who had died in their country's wars. There was also the argument, most strongly advanced in La Roque's *Traité de la noblesse* (new edn. 1735), that there was an inherent superiority of soul in certain families, transmitted in their 'semance'; there might be unfortunate accidents, but they did not vitiate the principle of a class inherently worthy to rule in Church and State. However, beyond the theorizing about worthiness derived from past generations, there was a basic proposition referring to the present: the episcopate was a secular institution with a crucial political role and social responsibility as well as a system for governing the Church. The simple apostolic days were gone for ever. The eighteenth-century view of the change was summed up by an English preacher in 1760: 'though the apostles for wise reasons were chosen from among men of low birth and parentage, yet times and circumstances are so changed that persons of noble extraction by coming into the Church, may add strength and ornament to it'.[41] This was the establishment view in France as well; it was the philosophes and revolutionary reformers who, somewhat disingenuously, recalled how Matthew and Luke were not called 'Monseigneur', and how a true Christian bishop, white of hair, furrowed of face, rustic staff in hand, would tramp round the lanes visiting his parishes.[42] In fact,

Matthew, Luke, and perambulating patriarchs could not have run an eighteenth-century diocese: collected the complex revenues, organized clerical taxation, directed the ecclesiastical courts, presided over provincial estates and the boards of hospitals and charities, out-faced intendants, parlements, military governors, municipal authorities and the powerful local nobility in defence of their clergy and the interests of the Church. It was to do tasks like this that the aristocratic aspirants to bishoprics were appointed.

Among the families accustomed to receiving bishoprics for their sons, vocation was a concept accepted with a nod, then left to the particular individual, who, no doubt, tended to think of it occasionally but not obsessively. In practice, young men of these families had a choice between two main careers, the Church and the armed forces. A stock figure in eighteenth-century literature is the younger son of a penurious noble house having to choose between them. An unpleasant mother in one of Marmontel's *Contes moraux* tells her second son: 'your father's fortune was not so considerable as was imagined; it will scarce suffice to settle your elder brother. For your part, you have simply to decide whether you will follow the career of benefices or of arms, whether you will have your head shaved or broken, whether you will take orders or a lieutenancy of infantry.'[43] In real life, the victims of such decisions are sometimes found looking back sadly on the mistake they had made: 'if I had taken the path of the Church, what tribulations, what toils I'd have spared myself,' says a soldier; a monk writes to his soldier brother of 'the fearful misery and harsh slavery to which I am reduced in this abominable monastery where schemes of ill-considered ambition have dragged me' (he finished up an abbot with comfortable apartments and his private town house).[44] But the young aspirants to the episcopate were not driven by necessity: their families were, for the most part, rich. It was not a question of pushing the youngest sons for bishoprics; the eldest inherited, of course, but it was the *second* son who was encouraged to follow an episcopal destiny, the preferred option for the prestige of the family. Of the bishops of 1789, sixty-one were second sons (twenty-one the second and last); twenty-four were third sons, ten fourth sons. These were families with long traditions of service—ninety-seven of these bishops had five generations of unbroken ecclesiastical service preceding them, forty-three of them having had bishops among their number. They were proud to serve the king, whether providing colonels of regiments or rulers of dioceses.

Occasionally, a young man who had originally chosen the army would change his mind and seek ordination. After the Peace of Utrecht, Antoine-Pierre de Grammont left his colonelcy at the age of 28, and from 1735 he was a worthy archbishop of Besançon, succeeding his uncle. A very different case was Paul-Albert de Luynes, a colonel of infantry in 1719 at the age of 16; a brother-officer struck him, he refused to fight a duel, and his termagant mother ordered him either to avenge the insult or be ordained. He was bishop of Bayeux in 1729 and archbishop of Sens in 1753, a wealthy, decent, and simple prelate who got up early to attend the parish church when the Court was at Fontainebleau, and read to peasant congregations the homilies he had written in his seminary, warning them against velvet cushions and other trappings of luxury.[45] Of the bishops of 1789 Saint-Pol-de-Léon had been a captain in the Queen's regiment, leaving after the Peace of Aix-la-Chapelle; Soissons had been a musketeer, Périgueux a captain of artillery. Waiting in the wings, but deprived of great ecclesiastical promotion by the Revolution, were Guillaume-Jean-François Souquet de Latour, who left the *école militaire* of Beaumont-en-Ange and was ordained in 1789, and Guillaume-Honoré Rocques de Montgaillard, who had been crippled by an accident at the *école militaire* of Sorèze and was about to become a *grand vicaire* of Champion de Cicé.[46] About this time, Chateaubriand was thinking of an ecclesiastical career, but decided against, perhaps because his mother was afraid of having a scandalous priest in the family. He became a second lieutenant in the regiment of Navarre, and in December 1788 took the tonsure, not intending to proceed further as an ecclesiastic, but to qualify for an income as a knight of Malta: 'An abuse, no doubt, in the ecclesiastical order,' he wrote, 'but a useful arrangement in the political order of the old constitution.'[47]

The recipients of privilege can easily convince themselves that it is merited. The great aristocratic families talked of the bishoprics with easy, possessive familiarity—discussed the income, the agreeableness of the house, the distance from Paris, the chances of getting a better see later on. A mother paints an attractive picture of clerical life to a third son: time in a seminary in Paris, then pensions and abbeys, chaplain to the king, agent-general of the clergy, a bishop at 30, 'et enfin le plus riche de la famille'.[48] Another mother gives her son an intensive education so that he can rise in the Church and rescue the straitened family fortunes, rebuild the family château, and, perhaps, emulate the greatness of her grandfather, Secretary of State to Louis XIV—Loménie de Brienne realized her ambitions.[49] A grandmother presents her 15-year-old grandson to Morellet, who is to be his tutor: 'he is destined to become a bishop; you have to ensure he passes his *licence* in theology'. Bishoprics and abbeys were underpinnings of the family structure—the policy of the La Rochefoucaulds as Saint-Simon defined it: one son for inheriting all the property and marrying, the girls and younger sons remaining celibate and living off ecclesiastical revenues. 'I am old,' said a crudely frank seventeenth-century nobleman; 'I am not rich, I have many children, my duty as a father is to preserve them from want by placing them advantageously.' As for fitness for episcopal office, he did not see how this came into it. 'If my son has not got the qualities required to govern a diocese, he will always be able to have capable ecclesiastics around him whose counsels he will faithfully follow.'[50]

Once a son had gained the necessary academic qualifications and become a *grand vicaire*, the family would mobilize to hasten on the final promotion. At the age of 30, in 1760, Pierre-Augustin Godert de Belbeuf became *grand vicaire* of Verdun.[51] His brother, *procureur général* of the parlement of Rouen, took charge of his candidature. The bishop of Verdun wrote plausibly, saying he was pressing the case, but information came suggesting these recommendations were lukewarm. So the archbishop of Rouen was persuaded to give Pierre-Augustin the grand vicariate of Pontoise. In 1767, the bishop of Lescar wrote to say that his colleague at Tarbes had just died— 200 leagues away, but an agreeable niche. Jarente, minister of the *feuille*, wrote encouraging letters to Rouen, until in 1771 he sent a final note of regret saying he had just been dismissed. Finally, in 1774, Avranches was offered. It had been a long haul of fourteen years. The campaign for Jean-de-Dieu-Raymond de Boisgelin was run by his father, a *président à mortier* of the parlement of Brittany, an operation conducted with a blend of cynicism and sincerity.[52] Strings were pulled through the prince de Soubise and Mme de Pompadour to get an abbey, and great was the disappointment when four years went by without success. Then the abbey came, and another four years of lobbying ensued until the see of Lavaur was offered. The intriguing *président à mortier* genuinely wanted his son to be a good Christian, and he was not unaware of the fact that being seen to be one might help on the promotion. 'I expect a great deal of a son who has voluntarily embraced such a respectable state; I hope that he will have religion, morals and application to the studies relating to his profession, rather than to *belles lettres*, which adorn only the mind and which often corrupt the heart.' This to the 20-year-old student. Then, two years later, at the time of the subdiaconate: 'the public expects edification of you. You have ambition, but it must always be subordinate to religion; you will reap the fruits in this world and the next.' So he did—at least in this world. In 1780, as archbishop of Aix, Boisgelin had an income of 219,000 livres from the Church, as against a family pittance of 27,000 livres.

In these operations to obtain an episcopal promotion, a relative in episcopal orders (generally an uncle) could be invaluable—to offer an appointment as *grand vicaire*, to use influence with other bishops towards an election as agent-general of the clergy, to put in a good word with the minister of the *feuille*. The way this family patronage worked may be considered in the careers of some of the related prelates who occupied sees in 1789. The two Rohans, glittering names from the highest reaches of the Court, did not need such recommendations, and they proceeded as of right to hold the wealthy sees of Strasbourg and Cambrai in unworthy splendour. The two Duplessis d'Argentré had come up their separate ways, Jean-Baptiste getting Sées by his Breton connections, while Louis-Charles, brought up by a relative, the bishop of Limoges, inherited the see when Mgr de Coeslosquet resigned it to become tutor to the dauphin and, as such, having Court influence to fix his own successor.[53] Of the three La Rochefoucaulds, all conscientious rulers of dioceses, Dominique (archbishop of Albi in 1747, then of Rouen in 1759) had been helped in his career by an uncle who was archbishop of Bourges; in his turn he helped two brothers of another branch of the family, François-Joseph becoming bishop of Beauvais in 1772, Pierre-Louis of Saintes in 1781 (after serving as vicar-general at Beauvais under his brother).[54] The eldest of the Champion de Cicé became bishop of Troyes in 1758, and took his brother as vicar-general; the one was promoted to Auxerre in 1777, the other got Rodez as his first bishopric in 1770. When La Roche-Aymon died in 1777, his great see of Reims went automatically to the nephew he had established as his coadjutor, Alexandre-Angélique de Talleyrand-Périgord; in his turn, the new archbishop looked after his nephew, the Talleyrand who was to become notorious, making him a canon of Reims and arranging his election as agent-general of the clergy. This patronage, proven administrative ability, and a letter from Talleyrand's dying father to the king finally brought the bishopric of Autun.

As the example of Reims in 1777 showed, a bishop might exercise enough influence to ensure his nephew the succession to the diocese. The bishop of Oloron, who died in 1735, was followed by his nephew; the nephew, promoted to Auch in 1741, was followed

by his great-nephew; the chain was broken in 1783 by an outsider—
who was nephew and *grand vicaire* to Loménie de Brienne.[55] The case
of Gilbert de Montmorin de Saint-Herem coming to the see of Aire
in 1723 was an unusual variant, as he was inheriting from his father,
who had left the army and taken holy orders after the death of his
wife.[56] The certain way to ensure succession was to persuade the
king to allow the nephew or other favoured relative to become
coadjutor bishop. In 1788, Barral took over Troyes and Jarente
d'Orgeval took over Orléans in this way, and in the same year
Loménie de Brienne had his 25-year-old nephew consecrated as
'archbishop of Trajanopolis' and coadjutor of his archidiocese of
Sens, a family contrivance broken by the Revolution.

A bishop was not likely to be able to foster the career of a nephew
who had no talent, but he could give him experience and a chance
to display such talent as he might possess, more especially by
engineering his election as a representative of the ecclesiastical
province to the Assembly General of the Clergy, or better still, as
one of the two agents-general. To get this ultimate opportunity, the
patronage of a bishop hardly sufficed—it needed an archbishop in
the family. The ecclesiastical provinces were paired and took their
turns in electing on a rota of forty years, the electing body being the
metropolitan assembly of two deputies from each diocese meeting
under the presidency of the archbishop. Thus in 1775, Rouen chose
Pierre-Louis de la Rochefoucauld, nephew of the archbishop, and
Toulouse chose François-Alexandre de Jarente, nephew of the
bishop of Orléans and protégé and *grand vicaire* of the presiding archbishop. In 1780, Tours elected Talleyrand by influence exercised
from Reims, and Aix the abbé de Boisgelin de Kerdu, nephew of
the archbishop. Talleyrand, more slowly than he would have
wished, reached the episcopate, but the abbé de Boisgelin had to be
content with rich abbeys because he was caught in the bedroom of
Mme de Cavanac and fought her angry husband, parrying the fire
shovel with the tongs.

V

When, for whatever reasons, a young nobleman had decided he had
a vocation to the episcopal state, he had to work to qualify himself
for selection: that is, to carry through university studies to the point
of obtaining the *licence*, and to serve an apprenticeship to diocesan
administration as a *grand vicaire*.

By the standards of the day and in formal qualifications, the bishops were well educated. Of the 130 ruling the dioceses in 1789, all were *licenciés* of a major university, except two Bretons whose academic careers had stopped at the *baccalauréat* and Cardinal Bernis, who had risen through Court favour and the diplomatic service. Of the *licenciés*, all except seven had qualified at Paris (between 1755 and 1760, the examination of theses at the Sorbonne had been suspended, so some candidates had moved out to Reims or Orléans). The degrees were mostly in theology, though a third of them were in law (with canon law included).

The first academic hurdle to be negotiated was the *maîtrise-ès-arts*, the examination being taken at the completion of the final two years of philosophy at a *collège* affiliated to the university. In these Parisian institutions, the future bishop sat on the classroom benches with contemporaries destined for the highest offices in Church, Government, and Law. In mid-century, at the Collège du Plessis, six future bishops were together—in later life they were to rule the sees of Saint-Dié, Noyon, Strasbourg, Bordeaux, Cambrai, and Lyon.[57] The three years after the *maîtrise* were devoted to theology, the candidates either going back to their *collèges* to lodge or moving on to a seminary, generally that of Saint-Sulpice. This was the point at which a family was well advised to hire a tutor: Le Tonnelier de Breteuil, the future bishop of Rennes, studying theology at the Collège de Lisieux from 1705 to 1709, was coached by M. Langlois, who was paid a fee of 1,000 livres a year.[58] There was an oral examination on five subjects: the attributes of God, the Trinity, the angels, and two others chosen by the candidate, and a thesis, the *tentative*, examined in public in a five-hour session by ten doctors. The subjects prescribed may give an impression of restricted horizons of study, though in practice, speculation could range widely; a candidate defending a thesis on, say, the angels, would make it a starting-point for a polemic against atheists and materialists who had aired their sceptical doubts about such aspects of the faith.[59] A satisfactory performance gained the *baccalauréat en théologie*, opening the way to the *licence*, requiring at least two more years' study of theology. The candidate now had to enrol in the society of the Sorbonne or of Navarre or take the status of *ubiquiste*; he had to proceed to the subdiaconate, which brought the obligation of celibacy; he had to be present at all public examinations of theses and be prepared to join in the questioning, and had to attend the lectures of the professors, taking down the information they dictated and writing it up in *cahiers* handed in for inspection at the end of the course. There were two oral examinations, one on Aquinas, the other on Church history, and three theses had to be sustained: the 'minor' on the sacraments (with a six-hour viva), the 'major' on the Bible and ecclesiastical history (ten hours), and the 'sorbonique' on the Incarnation and grace (twelve hours). Success in the *licence* was virtually equivalent to a doctorate; true, a further thesis had to be sustained before the *bonnet* was awarded, but this was a formality—as the abbé Baston said, it was a question of 'paying 600 livres and a ceremony'. Some bishops proceeded to the doctorate (twenty-five of the 130 of 1789 had done so), but most stayed at the *licence*, the officially prescribed qualification for the highest offices in the Church.

Stories of painless degrees given for fees or favour come mainly in the first half of the century from provincial universities and in the Faculties of Law and Medicine (though Jean-Antoine de Tinseau, who became bishop of Belley in 1745, had obtained a doctorate at his local university of Besançon at the age of 15).[60] By 1750, the theological training of the episcopate had come to be centred in Paris, and was decorous according to the regulations. True, as everywhere in France, the university gave deference to those of aristocratic birth, but it was a formalized deference, obvious to every eye and deceiving no one, and falling short of obsequiousness except in the case of sons of the very greatest families of the Court.[61] In the awarding of places in the *licence*, the first went to the candidate with the longest genealogy, and the next three to those named in the Sorbonne and Navarre as the most distinguished, the real list of academic merit beginning at number five. Granting the initial abuse, it was honestly done. The longest genealogy meant what it said: the son of a penurious Gascon squire whose line went back to the Crusades came first on one occasion, with the son of a *grand seigneur* postponing his graduation so as not to have to come after him.[62] Aristocrats with good results chose to figure in places five, six, and seven, preferring to be recognized as intelligent rather than parading ancestry. François-Joseph Partz de Pressy (later bishop of Boulogne) took the *licence* in 1738 at number five, so did Pierre-Louis Leyssin (later archbishop of Embrun) in 1748, as also Loménie de Brienne in 1752. Loménie de Brienne's thesis, sustained on 30 October 1751, was a masterpiece of brinkmanship, winning the highest award from the examiners, yet pleasing the audience by incorporating the epistemology of Locke and a view of divine action in history appropriate to the ideas of the Enlightenment. A conservative theologian, alarmed by the abbé de Prade's notorious thesis of November of the same year, accused Brienne of being in the same plot to insinuate unbelief into the Faculty of Theology.[63] Clearly, there were nobles who were academic high-flyers, and there were others who had their theses compiled by their tutors and who hired substitutes to copy the lecture notes (presenting them with the handsome binding and laudatory title-page which always won the approval of the professors).[64] Yet, so dull was the teaching and so hidebound the procedures of the Sorbonne, that coaching by tutors was a superior way to learning, and the sleek young men on their way to bishoprics had all the pride of their ancestry to inspire them to try to shine before the fashionable audiences which came to their *soutenances*. At the end of the *ancien régime* the curés challenged the bishops as members of an aristocratic caste, but it was no longer justifiable to add to the charge the accusation of ignorance of theology; about one in ten parish priests had the *licence* or the doctorate, the standard episcopal qualification.

Provincial seminaries tried, however inefficiently, to give their ordinands a grounding in pastoralia, the casuistry of the confessional, and the practices of the spiritual life. To what extent did the future bishops receive this formation? In the second half of the century, 60 per cent of them lived from three to seven years of their period of academic study in the seminary of Saint-Sulpice, and these were probably subjected to more discipline than those who went elsewhere. With Louis Tronson as superior at the end of the seventeenth century, Saint-Sulpice had been—so far as he could make it—an austere place. His correspondence shows him banning wigs, the wearing of slippers in chapel, the drinking of wine undiluted with water, and imposing one and a half hours of meditation daily, fasting three days a week, and the wearing of hair shirts on one of them. The sending down of offenders, he said, gave him more joy than welcoming new recruits, as it proved he was carrying out reforms. In truth, he was always trying to enforce reforms and never succeeding, and after his death, Saint-Sulpice went downhill. The reasons were partly inherent in the peculiar nature of the institution itself. Unlike other seminaries, it was not under the jurisdiction of the diocesan bishop, being under the abbey of Saint-Germain-des-Prés; nor were its recruits mainly from the diocese, most of them coming from elsewhere in France. It was a metropolitan centre with a reputation as the place to attend with a successful career in mind.[65] Central control met with obstacles, for Saint-Sulpice was a federation of houses rather than one. Around the Grand Séminaire were La Maison des Philosophes in the rue Pot de Fer, the Robertins in the Impasse Féron, and, from 1738, the community which came to be called the Collège de Laon, while there was a country house at Issy, and further country retreats there and at Vaugiraud for the affiliated branches.[66] As Saint-Sulpice became the recognized gateway to the episcopate, more aristocratic recruits came in; they required extensive accommodation, brought their own furniture, and were attended by their own servants. Cardinal Fleury's patronage of the Sulpicians was dangerous: he made Issy his favourite residence, so the place became a resort for high society, and the seminarists, who went there once a week and for a period of several weeks in summer lost the sense of separation from the world. Under the weak rule of M. Couturier and M. Le Gallic, the aristocratic ordinands broke down the disciplinary code. Le Gallic was kept awake at night by explosive charges fired at random round the house, and the crowning indignity came at the Corpus Christi procession of the district, when the students cut the rope of a canopy, trapping him under the collapsing canvas. Talleyrand recounts how his liaison with a pretty young actress passed without rebuke from the directors—'the abbé Couturier had taught them the art of closing their eyes . . . and not reproaching a Seminarist destined for archbishoprics'.[67] Belatedly, reform came in 1782 when M. Emery arrived as superior.[68] The first explosion that was perpetrated led to twenty-five expulsions. Theatrical productions ended in the Grand Séminaire and were discouraged in the Robertins and Laon. But in matters of life-style rather than discipline, he often had to put up with expressing disapproval and finding it had little effect. The elaborate hair-styling that went on, especially on the night before an ordination, could not be suppressed, though Emery defined 'sin' as beginning when 'deux ou trois étages' were built up, and he urged the frequenters of the *perruquiers* to consider if their action was one they could offer to God for his glory, as one deserving of reward on the Day of Judgement.

The life of a seminary is not truly reflected in the scandalous incidents recorded by gossip writers; even in the decadent days, there were intelligent discussion groups, more useful than the course at the Sorbonne, said the abbé Baston;[69] there was the daily round of liturgical observances and of meditation (at mid-century reduced to half an hour). The directors were known to report on the suitability of their charges for ordination, which was a restraint on excesses, if not on comfortable living. Most candidates for high office in the Church would have learned about ecclesiastical routines and gained a familiarity with the practices of piety. According to Bernis, the

Sulpicians concentrated on 'little things' concerning 'conduct'. Saint-Simon spoke of them as excelling in 'minutiae and useless puerilities'—severe criticisms, but on the other side of the divide to those of laxity. What was wrong with the training of the future bishops was its atmosphere rather than its deficiencies. They had their valets and the comfortable life-style to which they were accustomed. They were not at one with their fellow seminarists, just as, when they came to rule dioceses, they were not at one with their curés. They had served no apprenticeship to humility.

After the *licence* and ordination to the priesthood, the next step for the episcopal aspirant was to negotiate an appointment as a *grand vicaire*. An uncle or some family friend would issue the invitation, though it might be better to move out of the family circle if some prelate could be found who was high in favour at Court or ruled over a more prestigious diocese. At Rouen in 1756–60, no fewer than six future bishops were serving together as *grands vicaires* (this includes one who had the quasi-independent archidiaconal administration of Pontoise). According to ill-disposed critics, these apprentices to the episcopate were gilded drones, just filling in time until a vacancy came their way. 'C'est une dérision qui fait gémir,' said the abbé Barruel in 1789; 'our bishops have eight, ten, twelve or twenty *grands vicaires*; two or three, at most, work; the others hardly ever appear—yet these are the only ones who aspire to bishoprics and get them.'[70] In an obvious sense, Barruel's picture is true to life, for a bishop who valued his peace of mind would hardly confide his administration to young men newly arrived from the Sorbonne—he would have a few professionals doing it, like Jullien Lailler, who was vicar-general, *official*, archdeacon, and superior of the seminary all in one at Coutances from 1676 to 1725, or Louis Daignan de Sendat (dd. 1764), who ran the diocese of Auch for fifty years under three archbishops, one a complete absentee and the others there only intermittently.[71] Some of these professionals were indigenous to the diocese, often from families of local distinction, chosen because of their ability from parochial curés or canonries; others came in from outside with the bishop when he first arrived, having been his tutor or one of the directors of his seminary in Paris. They would form the effective administrative stiffening in the corps of *grands vicaires*. Champion de Cicé at Bordeaux had two of them, along with his nephew and two sons of *grands seigneurs*; Boisgelin at Aix had four, along with eleven young aristocrats; Bernis at Albi had two out of a dozen. Under the haughty and distant Montmorency-Laval at Metz the diocese was run by the abbés Bertin and Ravaut and by Henri de Chambre d'Urgons (who was made suffragan bishop in 1780), while the other ten *grands vicaires* looked on or were absent.[72]

Yet Barruel's condemnation of the system is only half justified. It was a manifest abuse to allow aristocratic candidates to walk into the office of *grand vicaire* with little or no pastoral experience; no doubt some of these young men took more time away from the diocese than was reasonable, and sought out what amusements provincial society afforded—perhaps introducing Parisian taste by organizing concerts or demonstrating the new sport of hot-air ballooning.[73] Yet it does not follow that they were not learning their trade by association with the bishop and his professionals. Béthisy de Mézières, bishop of Uzès from 1779, ran his diocese with four *grands vicaires*, all nobles; he had two in charge of the rural parishes, one of the town parishes and all charitable initiatives, the other of the seminary, retreats, *conférences ecclésiastiques*, missions, and all the monasteries— they came to a weekly staff meeting at 9 a.m. every Wednesday.[74] The apprenticeship served by many bishops was real. Indeed, circumstances like a frequently absent bishop or one in poor health sometimes pushed them into performing episcopal duties long before they got dioceses of their own. Thus François d'Andigné went to Dax in 1733 after ten years running Luçon as vicar-general, and Urbain de Hercé went to Dol in 1767 after being in charge at Nantes for thirteen years. The picture of the aristocratic *grand vicaire* idling away his years of waiting is untrue to human nature. These were active young men anxious to distinguish themselves. La Fare, who became bishop of Nancy in October 1787, had been a *grand vicaire* at Dijon under a distant relative, and here he became *syndic* of the diocese (that is, in charge of clerical taxation and correspondence with the agents-general in Paris), a member of the local Académie des sciences, arts et belles-lettres (succeeding Voltaire), dean of the Sainte-Chapelle of Dijon, a deputy to the Assembly General of the Clergy, *élu général du Clergé des États de Bourgogne* (that is, one of the committee running the affairs of the province in the intervals of the triennial meetings of the estates), and was summoned to Paris in 1787 as one of the Notables—quite an accumulation of distinctions and responsibilities for a man in his early thirties.[75]

The average time spent as a *grand vicaire* before promotion to the episcopate was ten years, not enough in circumstance or time span to gain pastoral insight, but adequate to master the details of administration and command. There is every reason to suppose that most of them took the business of learning seriously, whether from vocation, pride, or (except for the sons of the very greatest families) prudence, for the Crown took pastoral considerations seriously, and with vacancies occurring at the rate of only six to four a year, many candidates were going to be disappointed.

8

THE BISHOPS: WORLDLY
GREATNESS

I

What sort of men were brought to the bishoprics by the operation of royal choice and these aristocratic vocations? They had poise and a social viability enabling them to look impressive and act forcefully in their great office, and the system ensured they were reasonably learned and trained in diocesan administration. Anticlericals censured the favouritism by which they were appointed, and watched them narrowly to detect the vices typical of their aristocratic origins—they were generally accused of slackness about residence in favour of a life-style centred in the capital and Versailles, of haughtiness and spendthrift display, and, in snide allegations rather than circumstantial accusations, of sexual adventures in breach of their oath of celibacy and ordinary Christian duty.

One of the most obvious obligations of a pastor was to reside in the midst of his flock. The Council of Trent had defined an absence of more than three months without good cause as mortal sin, and authorized metropolitans to act against offenders. Royal declarations and edicts had reaffirmed the prescriptions of canon law, the edict of 1695 ordering the parlements to watch for absentees and report them to the *chancelier*, whose sanction would be the confiscation of temporalities. The law was clear, and there was machinery to enforce it, but it was not obeyed. 'I know of dioceses more . . . presbyterian than Scotland,' said D'Argenson in 1748, though he gave only one example of episcopal absence.[1] But a multitude of illustrations was forthcoming in 1764, when the parlement of Paris, acting in the spirit of the edict of 1695, published a list of prelates currently living in Paris with their addresses: about a quarter of the Gallican episcopate was there.[2] Two years later, without giving any figures, the papal nuncio reported that there were always too many bishops in the capital—they came to intrigue for better sees, he said, or to enjoy society.[3] In 1784, Louis XVI issued a circular, through

Breteuil, the new minister for the Maison du Roi, instructing the bishops to seek permission before absenting themselves from their dioceses. The abbé de Veri complained against this infringement of protocol, for this was really a matter for the *chancelier*; even so, he agreed that urgent action was needed, as no fewer than sixty bishops were renting houses in Paris.[4] As the wits were accustomed to observe, the Gallican Church could act quickly in a crisis, a quorum of bishops always being available for an emergency meeting at a few hours' notice. The *cahiers* of 1789 reflect the common opinion: 51 per cent of the *bailliage* meetings of the Tiers État, 38 per cent of the nobles, and 24 per cent of the clergy complain of episcopal non-residence.

There are a few examples throughout the century of absentees so blatant that they no longer scandalize, since they are vocationless prelates, given rank and emoluments in the Church for purely secular reasons, like Saint-Albin at Cambrai and—the most notorious case of all—Cardinal Polignac, diplomat, member of the three great Parisian academies, a handsome figure adorning high society, who died in 1741, archbishop of Auch for fifteen years without ever having been there. There were others, supposed to be in real command of their dioceses, whose absences were so frequent or prolonged as to be inexcusable by any standards. There was Jacques de Grasse, who died without sacraments in 1782, having run his diocese of Angers for twenty-four years chiefly from his Parisian lodgings. The story goes that after a long journey from Paris the day before, he stayed in bed and refused to conduct an ordination—until turned out by M. Emery, the austere superior of the seminary: 'a stay in Paris which does not appear to have been necessary and which ought to have finished earlier does not constitute a valid excuse; the clergy will not understand such a dereliction of duty'.[5] Louis-Jacques de Chapt de Rastignac, a well-loved archbishop of Tours for eighteen years, suddenly changed when disappointed in his hope of promotion to the see of Paris, and became an 'absentee monarch' for the next nine years.[6] There are numerous cases of bishops not normally given to absence, who had not hastened to take up their duties after they were consecrated, having family affairs to settle and preparations to make. An extreme example was Le Tonnelier de Breteuil, appointed to Rennes in October 1723, consecrated only in July 1725, and making his entry into his episcopal city on 7 June 1726; before 8 December, he was back in Versailles.[7] This custom of initial delay went on until the end of the century. In the early days of the Revolution, in 1790, Carcassonne still waited to catch a glimpse of its chief pastor, consecrated in October 1788, and in January 1791, when the bishops were on the verge of being displaced, Valence had not seen the prelate consecrated to serve the diocese fifteen months before.[8] If one adds to these two invisible men two established bishops who were also absent from Embrun and Saint-Brieuc[9] (one for the last three years, the other for five), they form an odd group of characters, presumably of political sense if not of religious conviction, who stayed away from their posts of responsibility when the whole future of the nation was being decided. The standard period of delay for taking over a see was something like a year. This was the period of waiting imposed on their expectant flocks by Jean de Caulet,[10] punctilious and miserly, going to Grenoble (1725–7); by the haughty Montmorency-Laval[11] going to Metz (1761–2); Christophe de Beaumont, pious, charitable, and intolerant, going to his first see of Bayonne (1741–3); Boisgelin, administrator and reformer, going to his first see of Lavaur (1764–5); and Jacques d'Audibert de Lussan,[12] a dedicated pastor, going to Bordeaux (1744–5). With their various virtues and vices, they seemed to regard this length of time as defensible.

While half the *cahiers* of the Tiers État condemned episcopal absenteeism, only a quarter of those of the clergy did so. It may be significant also that the clerical editors of the *Nouvelles ecclésiastiques*,[13] keeping a baleful eye on the conduct of all in authority in the Church, found no more than nine cases between 1769 and 1790. It could be that informed opinion about episcopal duties distinguished between necessary and self-indulgent absences. By canon law an ecclesiastic was entitled to take time off to visit his family, and by royal policy, bishops were planted away from their homes. Members of the Académie would feel they had to attend at least some meetings, and they had to be present when it was their turn to give a panegyric. Peers would be urged by their lay fellows to attend the parlement of Paris to defend the rights of their order. The minister of the *feuille* had to be at Versailles, and the ambassador to the Holy See (often a bishop) at Rome. Election by the ecclesiastical province as a deputy to the Assembly General of the Clergy was an obligation to be fulfilled, just as invitations from provincial estates to go on deputations to Versailles could hardly be refused. And even prelates who were not presidents of diocesan or provincial estates had sometimes to go to the centre of affairs when their people needed an advocate to ask for tax remissions or other favours. It could be time-consuming—two sojourns of a year each at Paris to get a subsidy for dredging the harbour at Fréjus.[14] Such was the nature of the social

order that serving the royal family in affairs of conscience or ceremonial was a duty outranking all others, and at any one time as many
as a dozen bishops might be chaplains at Court. Nicolas de Saulx-
Tavannes, the most genial of pastors, was promoted to Rouen, the
most responsible see in France, in 1734; three years later he became
chaplain to the queen, who insisted he accompany her everywhere.
By the standards of the day he was singularly honoured: on any
rational view, the last twenty years of his life were wasted.

No doubt the excuse of necessary business was often misused,
whether by the inflation of a small issue or by lingering over an
important one. Jean de Caulet of Grenoble spent a long time in Paris
prosecuting a lawsuit worth little more than 1,000 livres a year to
his episcopal income, blandly excusing his conduct to Fleury by saying: 'a bishop discredited (presumably by losing a legal battle) is a
bishop rendered useless'. Boisgelin,[15] justifiably an absentee during
frequent negotiations with the government on behalf of the estates
of Provence, had his private apartments and chapel in the mansion
of the comtesse de Grammont near Versailles, and was able to attend
the Academy fifty times in fourteen years. The argument of necessity had become elastic. The intense focusing of political life at
Versailles and of civilization and culture at Paris constituted a powerful attraction, a lure to draw the ambitious, the sociable, and the
intellectually sophisticated. The only way to defeat the temptation,
Le Camus decided, was to cease all correspondence with the centre,
asking no news and receiving none, cutting himself off amidst his
mountains. Massillon yielded to the temptations of Academy and
political involvement after his consecration, spending twenty
months in Paris and only six in his diocese of Clermont. Then he
made the break. Apart from a Court funeral sermon in 1723, he
remained in the Auvergne for the twenty-one years still left to him.[16]

The anticlerical stereotype of a bishop of the *ancien régime*
included a mistress, and if no candidate for the post could plausibly
be named, often enough a niece or widowed sister-in-law living in
the palace would be put in the category of suspects. Like most
stereotypes, this one throve on a few startling examples. The
Regency—that period of astonishing immorality among the great—
provided the most blatant cases of vocationless characters favoured
from the centre of power, who were contemptuous alike of religious
obligations and public opinion. There was Dubois, whose most
respectable liaison was with Mme de Tencin, ex-nun, novelist, and
'political whore' of the period; Saint-Albin, the regent's bastard,
whose mistress was to be the famous Mme O'Brien de Lismore,

coveted by the king;[17] and Phélypeaux, bishop of Lodève—he lived openly with women, says Saint-Simon, and boasted he did not believe in God, and 'all this was forgiven him for his name was Phélypeaux'.[18] There was also the sad case of the unbalanced abbé de Beauvilliers, named bishop of Beauvais in 1713, spending his first five years as a penitential anchorite, then falling in love with a woman and living as her inseparable companion. In the end he was forced to resign, compensated with an abbey, and finally interned in the monastery of Cîteaux.[19] Outrageous cases like these are hard to find later, though anticlerical sniping went on. D'Argenson in 1750 has a story of a bishop of Troyes giving a dubious lady a pair of earrings made from an altar ornament, and of a hoax letter from a 'widow' to the bishop of Chartres which led him to endow an allowance for her illegitimate child—'les histoires galantes sur les évêques les déshonorent à perpétuité'.[20] Even so, in 1766 the papal nuncio praised the bishops in his secret report as 'for the most part of good morals and praiseworthy conduct'.[21] In fact, what liaisons there were, were discreet, even if well known, as Jarente's with Mlle Guimard. The successor to the Regency stereotype-makers was Cardinal Rohan, bishop of Strasbourg, whose handsome, elegant figure glittered disastrously for Church and State through the reign of Louis XVI.[22] All Paris knew him, prouder of his cordon bleu than of his pectoral cross, striding between the ranks of his liveried lackeys, driving off to his mistress in the Chaussée d'Antin, the leafy suburb where the courtiers and bankers built houses for their secret pleasures. In 1782, he was shamed by association with his brother, who went bankrupt for a vast sum, bringing ruin to hundreds of minor creditors; in 1783, he himself was investigated by the parlement over shady transactions with the property of hospitals which he held in trust as chief chaplain to the king; in 1785, disguised as a musketeer, he met a woman he thought was the queen in a wood near Versailles, and was conned into buying a one-and-a-half-million-livres diamond necklace which vanished—as 'Cardinal Collier', he was tried before the parlement for treasonable culpability.

This is an example of a butterfly *grand seigneur* ensconced unworthily in ecclesiastical office, expected by all to live in mindless worldliness and not disappointing them. In other cases where anti-clerical gossip alleges furtive misbehaviour, it is not easy to find convincing evidence. There were plenty of vague general smears. A courtesan specializing in masochism says she has had the honour of whipping the highest ranks of the clergy, magistracy, and finance;[23]

a bishop gives a lift to a notorious brothel-keeper when her cab is damaged in a collision with his carriage—this does him great honour, since most of his colleagues would have known her and avoided becoming ridiculous.[24] *La Chasteté du clergé dévoilée* (1790), when all inhibitions were lifted from the pens of journalists, produced information, supposedly from the police files, about delinquent clergy, but only one out of about 200 bishops in the period covered was included. The police had said that the carriages of Jarente and Loménie de Brienne were driven too fast to be tailed, and the editors remarked that the bishops naturally would not be found out because they misbehaved at home, without needing to frequent the bordels. The *cahiers* of 1789 complain of the worldliness of bishops, but do not allege sexual immorality against any specific individual. The accusations of pamphleteers, when capable of being verified, look shaky. The story about the wife of the coachman of the comte d'Artois was ascribed to the bishop of Meaux, then transferred to his colleague of Chartres; a story which could well be true of the new bishop of Pamiers was told of his predecessor, who died in 1786 at the age of 84. For long, Conzié of Arras was supposed to have fought a duel for the affections of his mistress, disarming his opponent; rather disappointingly, it turns out to have been a fabrication.[25]

Looking at all episcopal sin, sexual and other, and making a grand total of the guilty men, the chief inquisitors of the day, puritanical or anticlerical, did not find a great deal to report.[26] Between 1760 and 1790, the *Nouvelles ecclésiastiques* found twenty sinners and five saints; of the newsletters, Bachaumont's censure 28 of the 130 prelates of 1789, and Lescure's have reservations about 36, the most extreme being another allegation of a duel—against an angry husband. Perhaps a dozen of the generation of 1789 were unworthy of their high office, and of these half a dozen were scandalous figures to boot. A special case deserving of sympathy is La Font de Savine of Viviers,[27] of brilliant talents but unstable character, giving lavish entertainments yet dreaming of a life of Rousseauistic simplicity, neglecting to say mass for months and leaving his valet to read the breviary for him, then falling into fits of devotion and spending days on his knees. The others of the six were vocationless *grands seigneurs*. Dillon, archbishop of Narbonne,[28] lived most of the year at his château of Hautefontaine near Paris, where there were balls, concerts, and hunting thrice a week. 'No swearing today,' he told his guests when the worthy bishop of Montpellier paid a visit. It was a household, said his niece in later years, 'where the rules of religion were daily violated'. Even so, he was most attentive to his duties as a secular administrator. Little can be said on behalf of the 'Cardinal Collier' and his cousin, Prince Ferdinand de Rohan-Guéménée of Cambrai, who lived in Paris leaving his suffragan, Millancourt, bishop of 'Aymeles', to run his diocese, or of Montmorency-Laval of Metz, spending his time in local high society and with the officers of the garrison, and too proud to speak to his parochial clergy. The sixth member of the scandalous group is unique in his total cynicism, playing the system with remorseless self-interest, without respect for the office of bishop or pride in exercising it. Talleyrand[29] was consecrated to the see of Autun on 16 January 1789. His story at the time and subsequently was that his family forced him into the Church: 'I am lame, a younger son, there is no way of escaping my destiny.' But probably he was a willing accomplice, driven by ambition; after all, he would go to the chapel of the Sorbonne to dream before the tomb of Richelieu. A career as *grand vicaire* to his uncle, the archbishop of Reims, and a brilliant tour of office as agent-general of the clergy provided solid qualifications, though promotion came slowly because of the hostility of the queen and a dearth of vacancies. There was never a pretence at a moral life, only a judicious discretion in gambling in closed clubs and liaisons, well known but never flaunted. With the Estates General approaching, Talleyrand was determined to be elected a deputy—the times being what they were, this was the only way to move into the loftiest political circles. The election campaign of the new bishop of Autun among his clergy was a masterpiece of diplomacy and hypocrisy.[30] An unctuous pastoral letter told how he was moved by the last moment of happiness of his dying father at the news of his promotion, how in a retreat he had decided to devote himself to his diocese—he was a 'public man' now, and public men have no rights, only duties; he praised the curés for succouring the poor during the harsh months of winter, and begged for their prayers; like St Paul writing to the Romans, he had a great longing to come to them. And on 12 March he did indeed arrive in his episcopal city. During the next twenty days he was seen frequenting churches and walking in the garden reading his breviary; he had his clergy to dinner, with Lenten fish brought daily on the stage-coach from Lyon, and he urged them to profit by the practice of mental prayer. On a reforming programme including the defence of church property, he was elected on 2 April. On Easter Day ten days later he left Autun without appearing at the cathedral services, and never came there again except in 1802, when his carriage broke down as he was passing through on diplomatic business.

Few bishops were scandalous figures, but an aura of worldliness hung around many more of them, lending credence to gossip. Even those who were frugal in their private lives lived in a splendid décor, and there were others, those who were often found in Paris, who had an aristocratic disdain for affecting to be better than they were, extending to an inclination to brinkmanship, refusing to conform to conventional suppositions about their role. Boisgelin expressed the irresponsible theme in verse:

> Et moy, j'ay le plaisir qu'a tout homme d'Église,
> Quand, ne pouvant pécher, au moins il scandalise.

While praising the conduct of the majority, the nuncio regretted that 'the severity of the observance of the canonical rules' was declining among them; the aged archbishop of Reims, he said, was 'a man of exemplary sanctity', yet he lived 'suivant l'usage d'ici et de la Cour'—true to his vocation, but not a man set apart, fitting in easily with the world of the courtiers.[31] 'In high society,' said Mercier twenty years later, 'you do not meet exaggerated characters . . . the magistrate, the bishop, the soldier, the financier, the courtier seem to have annexed the traits of each other's characters. There is no dominant colour, only nuances.'[32] The evolution of episcopal portraits from the seventeenth century shows a succession of generations following the prevailing fashion, without insistence on their status as churchmen.[33] They go along with lay society in abandoning the beard, then, under Louis XIV, they reduce the moustache to a thin line, then they become clean-shaven. They wear the everyday habits of their ecclesiastical rank, but not their mitres, and they display the coat of arms of their family, adorning it with the episcopal hat (with three tassels, rising to four for an archbishop and five for a cardinal). The memoir writers enjoyed collecting stories[34] showing them mixed up in comparatively blameless but incongruous pleasures—putting on a firework display at which a cardinal's hat was blown off, attending a ballet of animals (in this case leaving before the vulgar spectacle was completed). The Church's unreasonable ban on the theatre was breaking down, and in a box reserved for them at Mme de Montesson's private performances, Brienne, Champion de Cicé, Dillon, Talleyrand, and a few others could be found; two bishops are noted as attending a dubious play put on in secret in Trudaine's salon.[35] So too with the traditional canons prohibiting hunting. There had always been prelates devoted to the chase, with their dogs for chaplains, as Mme de Sévigné said.[36] They were fewer in the eighteenth century, though Grimaldi of Le Mans became notorious for thundering on horseback on a Sunday through a village procession of the Virgin. In a revealing witticism, Dillon replied to Louis XVI's complaint that he hunted himself but forbade the pastime to his clergy: 'Sire, my vices come from my ancestry, my curés' vices are their own.'[37] High birth, he is saying, confers immunity from the constraints imposed upon ordinary people, even if they arise from the laws of the Church.

These men were proud, a pride giving a curious, almost blatant insouciance to their failure to live up to their state as representatives of the mission of Christianity. But with the pride of their race came independence, courage, and generosity. When, against their worldly greatness, is set their activity as 'fathers in God', we can see how the vices coming to them from their ancestry were counterbalanced by the virtues.

II

To maintain his life-style and perform his duties, a bishop had to organize the collection of revenues—of the see and from his abbeys —from a variety of sources. From the start, he would need some expert *homme de confiance*, possibly coming from his family estates, to survey the position and advise him, and he would probably end up by employing one or more local capitalists as 'farmers' doing the collecting, whether on a fixed lease or for a percentage. Two contrasting dioceses illustrate the scope of possible problems. The vast riches of Strasbourg[38] were drawn from land—the domain and château of Saverne, estates, vineyards, huge tracts of forest, mining rights, and isolated farms in places well outside the diocesan boundaries; by contrast, Auch, also rich, drew only 6 per cent of its revenue from land; 94 per cent came from tithes in hundreds of parishes. The income of Toulouse and Cahors was predominantly from tithes, Embrun entirely so. Another source of income, sometimes associated with land ownership, sometimes not, was feudal dues. Quimper drew 20,000 livres from such seigneurial incidents as against only 8,000 livres from tithes and 4,000 livres from land.[39] Paris was the beneficiary of profits flowing in from the network of archaic feudal units which underlay the bustling scene of urban redevelopment and suburban expansion. In 1674, the archbishop had been deprived of his temporal jurisdiction in twenty-five seigneuries covering 500 streets, but he had received compensation and had the fiefs of Grange-Batelière and Poissy and the duchy of Saint-Cloud.[40]

Along with ancient levies, some bishops also presided over ventures of the modern kind: iron foundries brought profits to Evreux and Langres, and the most productive foundry in Brittany, at Paimpont, was jointly owned by the bishop of Saint-Pol-de-Léon and six noblemen.[41] Great possessions provided continual occasions for churchmen to incur odium, and they always constituted a problem of conscience—as the Jansenist Colbert of Montpellier put it, refusing to follow worldly men in their methods meant prejudicing the rights of one's successors.[42] Most bishops did the obvious thing, and left it all to their estate agents.

The initial expenses in becoming a bishop were considerable. Vestments, mitre, and ring were costly, and even an everyday habit would run to 300 livres or so—and they were required in black, in red, and in purple.[43] The bulls from Rome—unless as a concession they were gratis—had to be paid for. There was no relationship between the revenues of the see and the charges: Autun paid twice its annual income, and Strasbourg paid a tenth. At the installation in the royal chapel, the *suisses* and the musicians shared out 500 livres, even if the ceremony was transferred elsewhere.[44] Then the episcopal palace had to be furnished, the general procedure being to make an offer for the furniture of the previous incumbent. Negotiations with the heirs could be difficult. At Alet, in August 1764, bill-stickers and drummers toured the town announcing the sale, and offers and counter-offers succeeded until, in March 1765, Mgr de Chantérac, the new man, bought it all, library included, for 41,900 livres, 10 sols, 3 deniers (an exact sum indeed!).[45] Talleyrand, going to Autun in 1789, bought his predecessor's effects; when dunned for the money in September 1790, he coolly replied: 'the times we live in and present circumstances as well as the uncertainty of the future are obsessing everyone's minds—it is impossible to occupy oneself with personal affairs'.[46] There would be more trouble with the heirs over repairs. It was not just the palace and the buildings on the estates, there were also the towers and chancels of the churches in the parishes where the see owned the tithes. The bishop taking over at Dax in 1733 had lawsuits before the local *sénéchaussée* and the parlements of Pau and Bordeaux until, in the end, there was arbitration by the bishop of Lescar, and 6,000 livres was handed over.[47] At Dol in 1767, the income of the see was 18,000 livres, and the repairs stood at 55,000 livres. The situation of the poor see of Glandève in 1771 was so hopeless that the king stepped in and paid for the repairs, as neither the bishop who had just retired through ill health nor his successor could ever have settled the bill.[48] One of the resounding lawsuits of the century was Cardinal de Polignac versus the heirs of the previous archbishop of Auch but one, who had died in 1712 leaving 170,000 livres to the poor, 12,000 livres to the cathedral for a silver statue of St Augustine and nothing for repairs. According to the estimate, these stood at 400,000 livres. The Grand Conseil heard the case, Polignac in attendance every day in full episcopal regalia. He lost, and the court ordered the confiscation of a third of his revenues annually to pay off the debt.[49]

Once a bishop's revenues were coming in smoothly and he had cleared the initial debts he had incurred, his family would expect him to assist its poorer members. Certainly, those with no establishment of their own might come and live in the palace. Orphaned nieces and nephews were taken in, unmarried or widowed sisters or nieces would come, taking over the supervision of the household, sometimes usefully and winning local praise for charitable works as well.[50] Or there could be scandal. Mme Dusage, niece of Cordorcet, bishop of Auxerre, had her portrait painted with a ridiculous hairstyle featuring a ship in full sail, and shouted from her window at passers-by, soldiers included, inviting them to come up and see if it did her justice.[51] There were occasions when a major financial contribution was needed, the obvious ones being a dowry for a young woman or the purchasing of command of a regiment for a young man. At a dinner party in 1787 the marquis de Bouillé was declaiming against the clergy when the archbishop of Narbonne reminded him that his uncle, the bishop of Autun, had bought him his regiment. 'Un arrangement de famille': 'yes, an arrangement by which he paid everything.'[52] According to severe moralists, only money coming from the family could be applied to family needs, but the general view was that contributions from ecclesiastical income were in order during the donor's lifetime—legacies were a different matter. 'You know my principles,' said Boisgelin, archbishop of Aix, 'be rich to be useful, be rich without costing the State anything.'[53] By being useful, he meant giving his two sisters 300,000 livres each as a dowry, at the expense of the Church.

A bishop had to employ a numerous staff. Tronson, the austere head of the seminary of Saint-Sulpice, in 1683 was asked to prescribe what expenditures were morally justifiable to figure in episcopal accounts. His reply was puritanical.[54] A bishop could spend his private fortune on pleasures, provided he was generous to the poor and there was no display; he must not use revenues coming to him from the Church. He was not entitled to entertain the great—say, the magistrats of the parlement. If he wanted to win respect, let him

give alms. Nor was he entitled to employ musicians: if he wanted
recreations, there were 'walks and conversations with a few people
of learning and piety'. Yet, along with this impractical rigorism,
numerous servants are listed as indispensable. At the top of the
hierarchy were the chaplain, the 'gentleman secretary', and the *maître
d'hôtel*; then there was a surgeon, five lackeys for the bishop, and one
for the secretary, two *valets de chambre* and an extra one for the *maître
d'hôtel*, a cook, a turnspit, and two kitchen boys, a cellar man, a
furniture maintenance carpenter, an odd-job boy, a stable man, and
an unspecified number of grooms. The minimum list has obvious
omissions, like gardeners, outside maintenance men, and, as seen in
the bishop of Alet's inventory of 1763, a porter and a seamstress
(*couturière-lingère*). Nor has Tronson allowed for caretakers in residences other than the palace.

   The main residence of a bishop was in his episcopal city, probably
alongside the cathedral, and there was almost always a country
house, from two to nine leagues away, where he would, like as not,
spend the hotter months of the year, from Easter to All Saints' Day.
The bishops of Clermont and Tarbes had rural châteaux with
panoramic views of distant mountains; the archbishop of Albi could
relax in the gardens and orangery of the Petit Lude away from the
vast, grim, thirteenth-century fortress which was his residence in
town. For the see of Carcassonne there was the country retreat at
Vallelier, surrounded by rectangular sheets of water and fountains;
for Rouen the château de Gaillon with a fine billiard-room and a
chapel as big as a church; for Rennes the manor-house at Bruz; for
Besançon the château de Guy; for Dol the château des Ormes;
mansions at Andard for Angers, at Noslon for Sens, at Germiny
l'Évêque for Meaux; the bishops of Strasbourg had the vast palace
out at Saverne. The bishops of Alet had no country seat, but they
were accustomed to move in summer to a separate lodging rented
from the canons—it was on the south of the cathedral with views
across the river to the mountains. The archbishop of Paris spent most
of his time away from the stench and throngs of the capital at his
château of Conflans set in superb gardens designed by Le Nôtre, its
fountains kept playing by a hydraulic machine pumping in the water
across a wooden bridge of three arches.[55] A very great prelate could
maintain—probably rent—a town lodging in Paris, though none
were as splendid as the hôtel de Rohan of the bishops of Strasbourg,
adorned with landscapes by Boucher and its vast stables surmounted
by Le Lorrain's bas-relief of the horses of Apollo.

   The eighteenth-century bishops were great builders. Brand-new palaces in the elegant classical style went up at Lodève, Alais, Viviers, Dol, Carcassonne, Agen, Bordeaux, Lombez, Coutances, Belley, and Saint-Papoul, and there were embellishments and improvements almost everywhere. Enormous sums were expended. Mgr de Salignac de la Mothe Fénelon of Lombez died in 1787, heavily in debt because of his outlay on stones and mortar, and in 1790 the see of Carcassonne was still paying interest of 30,000 livres a year on sums borrowed by Mgr de Bézon to erect a new palace in place of the towers in the old *cité* which had housed his sixty-nine predecessors.[56] The country houses were also rebuilt or embellished anew. Having restored his town residence, Cardinal de Luynes in 1759 practically demolished the château of Nolson to add suites of rooms in the modern style, then went on to do the same at his manorhouse of Brienon.[57] Another cardinal, Choiseul of Besançon, spent a million livres on the château de Guy; another, Rohan of Strasbourg, rebuilt Saverne on a scale which afforded (so it was said) 700 beds for the guests who came to his hunting parties. Cardinal Bissy, Bossuet's successor at Meaux, did not do much at Germiny l'Évêque, but he replaced the iron railings so the new ones could be crowned with a cardinal's hat, like the enamelled one he had erected near the altar in the cathedral.[58] The last bishop of the diocese before the Revolution adorned the gardens behind these cardinal-hatted railings with figurines of bagpipe players, dancing swains, and nymphs, 'bought in the faubourg Saint-Antoine at Paris', said a critical tourist, 'and seeming to me unworthy of the country house of a bishop'. Stories of aristocrats using their influence to get roads rerouted to improve the amenities of their country seats abound in eighteenth-century France, and the anecdotes include some churchmen. The archbishop of Rouen[59] got the lane leading to the village of Gaillon diverted away from his kitchen garden, and the bishop of Mende intrigued to get improved access to his château, and found himself censured by Necker and the archbishops of Bordeaux and Toulouse, and having to give an account of his doings to the provincial estates of Haute Guienne.[60]

The 'building mania' has been censured as a spendthrift hobby unsuitable for churchmen. Yet zealous, pastorally minded prelates indulged in it as well as the worldly ones—Jean-Georges Souillac at Lodève, Cardinal de Luynes at Sens, François Renaud de Villeneuve Forcaliqueiret at Viviers, Gabriel Cortois de Quincey at Belley, Charles Lefèvre de Quesnoy at Coutances. There were worse ways of laying out a sizeable income than in building for posterity and using the best available architectural and artistic talent to adorn the episcopal city. Many a town in France is indebted to the good taste of these eighteenth-century prelates whose handsome buildings now house the *mairie*, the prefecture, the museum, or the archives. Since medieval buildings had been converted in the sixteenth century for more social living, enough time had elapsed for major repairs and improvements to be needed again (unless the work had been done already in the seventeenth century, as at Aix). The palace at Rennes[61] was constricted between the cathedral and two narrow streets, having no outlook and only a tiny courtyard and a sunless little garden. Not surprisingly, Mgr Bareau de Girac in 1770 moved to the abbatial mansion of a suppressed abbey nearby, set in the midst of spacious grounds, and adapted it for himself and his staff. When Souillac took over at Lodève in 1732, there was no episcopal residence, as the Protestants had destroyed it long ago—he expended his own fortune in building another.[62] The château of Saverne had been burnt down—that was why Rohan had to rebuild it, though he was not compelled to do so in such a sumptuous fashion.[63] At Lombez, La Mothe Fénelon had not much choice about going into debt, for his five-storey palace with its tottering spire was becoming dangerous and had to be demolished.[64] Charles Lefèvre de Quesnoy, doctor of the Sorbonne, was a sober prelate who had been vicar-general of the diocese of Coutances for twelve years before succeeding to the bishopric in 1757. A few expensive years later he was at his ease in his new palace—the chapel walls decorated with gilded bronzes, his library resplendent with tapestries and rich bindings, his bedroom in crimson velvet and gold fringings and adorned with pictures of Our Lady, allegories of the four seasons, and his own recently painted portrait. He was proud of his building achievements: he had, he said, provided work for those who needed it, rather than 'feeding the idle'.[65] In the context of his time it was a valid argument: people expected their bishop to spend his wealth locally—provided he did this, only bilious anticlericals would have grudged him his splendour. With one proviso: as a cliché of the Gallican lawyers had it, 'the wealth of the Church is the patrimony of the poor'—a bishop must give generously to the material needs of his flock.

III

Aristocratic privilege, allied to reasonable abilities and good fortune, gained promotion to a bishopric, and episcopal office, once gained, was a passport to additional distinctions, privilege leading to more privileges.

Peculiar honours and resounding titles went with certain sees—to rule at Strasbourg, Metz, or Cambrai was to be a prince of the Holy Roman Empire with the dignity of 'altesse sérénissime', at least until 1754, when the princes of the blood royal protested and got the title suppressed within the French territories.[66] Six bishoprics conferred peerages on their holders—Reims, Laon, and Langres with the status of 'duc', Beauvais, Châlons, and Noyon with that of 'comte'. In a similar category came the archbishop of Paris, though with a different justification, being a 'conseiller d'honneur né', a distinction he shared with the abbot of Cluny.[67] These eight ecclesiastics, together with the princes of the blood royal and the thirty-two lay ducs with peerage status had the right to sit in the parlement of Paris when they chose to do so, and to have their lawsuits judged there (though the bishop of Beauvais faced challenges on his claim from the magistrates of his local *présidial*).[68] The peerage bishops, proud of their distinctions, made common cause with the lay peers to defend them; more especially, the three episcopal ducs were solid with the thirty-two others. In September 1715, during a wrangle in the parlement after the death of Louis XIV, the archbishop of Reims was put up by his colleagues to make a protest to the regent; to his chagrin he realized afterwards that he had inadvertently conceded a point in his discourse, calling Orléans 'Monseigneur', while a peer of France should merely say 'Monsieur'.[69] When the *premier président* of the parlement refused to take off his hat when asking the ducs for their opinions (in the trial of the duc de la Force in 1721), the archbishop of Reims held a meeting in his Parisian lodgings to try to invalidate the whole proceedings.[70] At the ball for the marriage of Marie Antoinette some derogation to the precedence of the ducal peers was proposed (for diplomatic reasons to placate pretensions of courtiers from Vienna); the bishop of Noyon was chosen to take a protest to Versailles.[71] Sometimes the ecclesiastical peers ran into dilemmas peculiar to their standing as churchmen—how, for example, did they stand when a cardinal claimed to come before the peers at a meeting of the Royal Council?—and if that cardinal was Dubois?[72] The right to have lawsuits exclusively heard before the parlement had potential disadvantages. In 1731, the magistrates were proposing to call the peers to join them in trying the bishop of Laon for a fanatical pastoral letter. Was it wise to claim the right to be tried by a court of bishops alone, waiving the peerage privilege?[73] It made tactical sense in the circumstances, but it would be undermining an immunity from ecclesiastical process which might be useful on other occasions.

Under the *ancien régime*, the great were as proud of undeserved honours as of those they had merited—titles and decorations served as a confirmation of the splendour of their lineage and their high standing in royal favour. A prelate with claims to intellectuality, or who was well enough connected to become a court chaplain or tutor to royal children, would consider he had a claim to belong to the Academy, and would begin appropriate intrigues. 'This ambition to be of the Academy is very strange in a great lord,' said Piron in 1749, 'but I find it almost scandalous in a bishop.'[74] In this year, Paul-Albert de Luynes, who had ruled the see of Bayeux for the last fourteen years and was destined to greater things still in Church and at Court, was pushed by the royal advisers in preference to Voltaire. Apparently, the archbishop of Narbonne had been asked to allow his name to go forward, but had refused to stand against such a distinguished man of letters. Boyer, bishop of Mirepoix, who was running the royal patronage, was blamed for the whole affair. 'The Academy, the King, and the public,' said Voltaire, 'destined me to succeed Cardinal Fleury as one of the 40. Boyer was against it, and at last, after ten weeks' search, he found a prelate to fill the place of a prelate, in conformity to the ecclesiastical canons.'[75] Thirteen years later, the retired bishop of Limoges, Jean-Gilles de Coetlosquet, was elevated to the ranks of the immortals before Diderot. In a sense, these elections were demonstrations of the established social order, putting religious belief before scepticism. Duclos, the permanent secretary of the Academy, had a difficult time balancing between his friends the philosophes and the *dévots* and courtiers who accused him of plotting against religion, hence his famous *coup* in the election of 1763, when he, D'Alembert, and two others of the irreligious party illegally retained their black balls to prove that they had not voted against a churchman, the abbé de Radonvilliers.

Connoisseurs of literary curiosities rejoiced when the *éloge* of a dead academician or of a newly elected one had to be given by a member of the opposite party. Archbishop Languet of Sens, obliged to welcome Nivelle de la Chaussée, the sentimental dramatist, praised his plays for reading only, not for actual performances, when actors and actresses might be the occasion for erotic imaginings in the minds of the audience.[76] When, later on, he had to receive Marivaux, he reflected on his shortcomings, style included. Surely Marianne is more interesting, said the wits, than the prelate's heroine, Marguerite-Marie Alacoque.[77] Eleven years later, in 1754, Gresset, welcoming D'Alembert, levelled the score by satirical observations on the episcopate in referring to the achievements of the previous holder of the chair, the bishop of Vence. The temper of the times changed, however, and Archbishop Boisgelin, elected in 1776, gave an oration worthy of a philosophe, exhorting churchmen to study science and literature to defend religion, and praising republicanism, for a Cicero would be impossible under a monarchy.[78]

As princes of the Empire, as peers in the parlement, and as members of the Academy, some bishops achieved national standing; all of them, however, were splendidly predominant within the walls of their episcopal city. A new bishop was not consecrated in his diocesan cathedral, but in the royal chapel at Versailles or, sometimes, in the chapel of the Sulpicians at Issy. Before he went to his episcopal city, he had been consecrated by representatives of his fellow bishops to be one of their number, and had taken the oath of allegiance to the king, and the oath to obey the Pope. Thus he came to his people as the king's man, accepted by the hierarchy of the Church. His reception in his new home was marked by ceremonies symbolizing both his elevation as the representative of the Crown and of the universal Church, and also of his acceptance into a tightly knit, hierarchical local society, where all had their due place and, in their different ranks, their peculiar privileges. The representatives of all corporations and interests came to render deference to their new pastor—but with the implication he must recognize and respect their rights.

The municipal officers would be the first to present themselves (though local custom might allow some of the clergy to get in a brief gesture before them). At Paris, the archbishop had to stage for a night at the abbey of Saint-Victoire before entering town; here he was met by the *prévôt des marchands* and the aldermen.[79] At Grenoble, on the preliminary day, the clergy would come to the episcopal palace in the morning and the *consuls* of the town in the afternoon; that night, the sky was red with bonfires paid for by the municipality. The *jurats* of Bordeaux went out to the harbour of Blaye to greet their new prelate, then sailed down the estuary with him in the *maison navale*, a specially commissioned vessel decorated with damask, silks, and tapestries. (In 1781, to save money, they all came in from Blaye in an ordinary brigantine.) Everywhere, the seigneurs who held fiefs in town would present themselves to offer fealty and to escort the bishop into his cathedral—in Paris, they had the right leg bared in token of homage. In return, they had their perquisites, like the option to take away a piece of silver from the ensuing banquet. An archbishop of Auch prevented the baron de Montaut from collecting his souvenir, and ran into a lawsuit costing him 5,000 livres damages.[80] The second day of the observances at Grenoble was marked by the successive arrival of all the officers of the minor courts of justice and representatives of the notaries and *procureurs*, deputations from the parlement and the *chambre des comptes* (these specially honoured, as the bishop went out to meet them as they descended from their carriages), the officers of the artillery school, and the administrators of the *hôpital général*. On the day of the actual installation, the dean and canons and the guilds and confraternities escorted the bishop, with the *consuls* carrying the canopy held over his head. On the following day, in the chapter house, the canons took their oath of fidelity one by one, and were rewarded by a dinner that night in the palace.[81]

These courtesies, deferential but hinting at latent tensions, foreshadowed the future relations of bishop and municipality. A town expected its prelate to represent the interests of the citizens against the intendant, the provincial governor, the taxation officials, and the courtiers at Versailles; they would petition him to intervene, and generally he would do so.[82] A resident bishop would meet with approval, even if slack in performing his duties, for he would be spending money and providing employment locally. There was anger in Fréjus when Mgr du Bellay (1739–60) transferred his residence to Draguignan, and when Mgr de Bausset (1766–91) proposed to move the seminary also. Luckily, both prelates felt guilty, and encouraged by his predecessor from retirement in Paris, Mgr de Bausset moved back to Fréjus and won a bonus of applause by persuading the government to give funds for dredging the harbour.[83] The *consuls* of Carcassonne were gratified that their bishop was building a new palace in the lower town, but not when they discovered they might have to pay for repairs to the old one—they succeeded in evading the obligation.[84]

Whether present or absent, almost every bishop inherited conflicts with his municipality arising from his ancient status of seigneur of the town and 'haut, moyen et bas justicier'. In this capacity, he might have the right to levy archaic dues, like those on the measuring scoops for selling grain at the market, piercing doors and windows in the old city walls, while he might have the outright ownership of the ramparts with their potentially valuable building sites.[85] Equally contentious were rights to confirm mayor and aldermen in their offices or even to appoint some of them, or to sit, whether in person or by deputy, on the town council, perhaps taking the chair. At Albi, an episcopal officer presided over the *conseil politique* (the six *consuls*) and the *conseil renforcé* (the *consuls* and twenty-four oligarchically elected representatives).[86] At Béziers, the bishop named two of the *consuls*, and his *viguier* intervened in council meetings.[87] At Mende, he named all the *consuls* and various other officers, a range of powers angrily described by the citizens in January 1789 as 'feudal anarchy allowed to subsist by Richelieu because it favoured his creature, bishop de Marillac'. Half the aldermen of Cambrai had been named by the archbishop; the right had lapsed, but when Léopold-Charles de Choiseul arrived in 1766, he got letters patent restoring it by the influence of his brother, the royal minister. Once the fortunes of politics had removed his powerful influence at Versailles, the municipality demanded the restoration of its independence. These sorts of feuds could go on and on as a matter of routine. But some were settled amicably. In 1746, the archbishop and city of Reims suspended their rivalry to combine to defeat the government's plan for a new system of representation on the municipal council—each side stood to lose privileges.[88] The *consuls* of Nîmes in 1779 withdrew their opposition to the bishop sitting on their council, and he reciprocated by buying pumps for the fire brigade and paying a dole to unemployed workers—he was recorded officially as having 'conferred innumerable benefits on the town'.[89] A wrangle at Beziers about the right to supervise the taking of oaths by officials was ended by getting the intendant to mediate, 'recognizing that nothing is more disagreeable for the community than being in dispute with its bishop'. Mgr Armand-Claude de Nicolai, who had proposed the mediation, said he 'regretted going to law against his people', and cemented the new happy relations by refraining from exercising his right to send an officer to preside over the council—his *viguier* never attended again.[90]

These feuds are not properly interpreted as power struggles. A prelate who wanted his way in the affairs of a town could work through influence in high places: he did not need to be involved in the mêlée at council meetings. What was at stake was honour and precedence. So too with disputes with that splendid lofty figure the provincial military governor and with the rather ordinary *lieutenant du roi* of the city—about the way a seat faced in the cathedral, the right to be consulted on the date fixed for a Te Deum.[91] Bordeaux was a scene of disobliging measures (including the hiring of a flute-player to follow the archbishop everywhere, drawing attention to the company he kept) until in 1775 the prelate and the military governor made their *Traité de conventions de politesse et d'honnêteté*.[92] There were similar clashes between the palace and the local law courts. In 1726, the parlement of Brittany censured its *premier président* because he made a visit to the new bishop instead of waiting for the installation—he had 'compromised the dignity of parlement'. Three years later, after various quarrels, the magistrates scored off their bishop by rushing out of church after a Te Deum to light the bonfires before he could get out to wield the torch.[93] In 1743, the judges of the *présidial* at Auch showed their opinion of their Father in God by refusing to kneel at his benediction at the feast of the Assumption. 'A genoux là bas', cried Mgr de Montillet, and he took litigation right up to the Royal Council to ensure future compliance.[94] What in a later age looks like expensive and trivial one-upmanship, under the *ancien régime* was an expression of the ethos of the social order, held together by tradition, hierarchy, and deference, real and effective only because everyone was determined to retain his due place in it, whatever scandal or litigation ensued.

IV

In his memoirs, Talleyrand divided bishops into 'the very pious', 'the administrative specialists', and 'the worldly'. He himself belonged to the last two categories. The phraseology he used was common currency in the later years of the *ancien régime*. The term 'évêque administrateur' had become a cliché of discourse, used as a censure. 'An administrative bishop', said a pamphleteer, 'is a sort of hybrid, half sacred, half profane, who, under the livery of sanctity, exercises a philosophic apostolate, whose object is to purge France of all defects of government; he is a man inspired by the spirit of public philanthropy, aiming to demonstrate that in the last resort the sole religion of the State is the pursuit of the general happiness.'[95] Earlier, Le Franc de Pompignan, the virtuous bishop of Puy (later archbishop of Vienne), had described the 'prélats administrateurs' as a new phenomenon, a danger to the Church; later on, he himself was to accept a major administrative and political role.[96] In 1783, the bishop of Lombez said it was important to keep these dubious characters out of the great sees: he hoped La Luzerne would not be promoted from

Langres to Auch because 'he is a man of fashionable theories (*un homme à système*), one of our administrative bishops of the school of the philosophes'.[97]

Though both anticlericals and churchmen cried shame at men of God absorbed in worldly administration, the ruler of a diocese had always had secular duties to perform. This was evident in the number of public welfare enquiries involved in episcopal visitation tours, in the duty of chairing the committees running hospitals and other charitable institutions, and occasionally in taking the lead in enforcing government legislation. The royal declaration of 1776 ordering the closure of unhygienic cemeteries would never have been effective without the bishops intervening with ordonnances interdicting so many of the old urban burial grounds.[98] These predominantly secular duties simplified the problem of vocation for young men of the right social standing who wished to gain distinction and remuneration in the service of the State. Ordination was one option among the others. Turgot, who studied at the Sorbonne with Champion de Cicé, gave way to scruples which others found easy to push out of the conscious mind, and abandoned an ecclesiastical career; he was unable, he said, 'to resign myself to wearing a mask all my life' (and was also hopelessly in love with a charming beauty). Champion de Cicé became a leading administrative prelate, and Turgot intendant of Limoges. When complaints arose about the *évêque administrateur*,[99] it was not because the phenomenon was new, but because attitudes were changing. There was a growing awareness of the incongruity of the traditional alliance between sacred and secular. The ideas of the Enlightenment, the vortex from which the gales of reform were blowing, were a strange blend of quasi-Christian humanism and anticlericalism. The pious suspected prelates who adopted them, however selectively, and the philosophes had a vested interest in keeping this complex of ideas as their own monopoly.

Administratively, France fell into two very different areas. In rather more than two-thirds of the kingdom, the division into *généralités* and rule by intendants had taken over from the old traditional organization. In the remaining third, the provinces in the South and along the frontiers, provincial estates survived, levying taxation to meet the demands of the Crown and to pay for local needs. These estates were ramshackle bodies with traditional membership, varying from place to place, but always on oligarchical lines. Their clerical representatives were from the upper ranks of the hierarchy. In the Cambrésis, it was the bishop, six deputies of the metropolitan chapter, seven of the other chapters, and three abbots; in Burgundy, the bishops, the dean, and one canon from each chapter, and the heads of the most important abbeys; in the Mâconnais, the bishop, a representative of the cathedral chapter, and another of the noble canons of Saint-Pierre, and the abbots of Cluny and of two other great monasteries (a delegation of parish priests could attend at the *chambre du clergé* of Mâcon, but they were not allowed to vote). The nine bishops of Brittany, a canon of each of their cathedrals and the thirty-seven abbots of monasteries attended the estates of Brittany; in Languedoc the twenty-three bishops only, and in Provence the three bishops.

The part played by nobles (sometimes defined as 'nobles holding fiefs') varied from place to place. Of the many entitled to attend in the Cambrésis, only about a dozen did so, while in Brittany, a horde of penurious squires turned up, lured by the expectation of free drink when authority sought their votes; in Languedoc only twenty-three could attend, and in Provence, two. The representatives of the Third Estate, the commoners, were all aldermen or other members of the oligarchies ruling the towns. There was no representation of the countryside and the ordinary urban population. However, contrary to the general ethos of society, the structure and voting procedures of the most important estates gave a certain independence, or, indeed, priority to the commons. In Brittany, there were three chambers, and vote was by order. In the Mâconnais, each of the three chambers sent a representative to sit in the *chambre des élus triennaux*, in which the important business was transacted, and if it was a matter of taxation, the representative of the Third Estate had the casting vote. The estates of Béarn were unique in having only two houses, the clergy and nobles sitting together in one, leaving the commons in the other free to press their independent policies. The twenty-three bishops and the equal number of nobles of Languedoc sat in a common assembly with the forty-six deputies of the commons, and the vote was by head—united, the commons could not be defeated. In Provence, the three bishops and two nobles were similarly outweighed. The nobles of Provence intrigued to change the balance of power, and in October 1787 persuaded the government to re-establish the medieval form of the estates in which the aristocracy enjoyed numerical predominance. The parlement of Aix ordered the citizens to illuminate their houses in rejoicing, an astonishing example of the blindness of the privileged classes on the eve of the Revolution.

All these provincial assemblies were under episcopal presidency.

An exception up to 1766 was the Cambrésis,[100] and to mark their displeasure, the archbishops of Cambrai for long had ostentatiously stayed away. Then came Léopold Charles de Choiseul, strong in the backing of his brother the minister, and he obtained letters patent entitling him to take the chair at both the general assembly and the standing executive committee. The estates of Foix were under the bishop of Pamiers, of Bigorre under the bishop of Tarbes, of Béarn under the bishop of Lescar (or, in his absence, his colleague of Oloron), of the Gévauden under the bishop of Mende, of Artois under the bishop of Arras. The assemblies of the extensive province of Burgundy were presided over by the bishop of Autun, not without challenges to his authority, for his colleague of Chalon-sur-Saône had claims, and when Dijon became an episcopal see, there was a third competitor in the field.[101] And the presidential role was essentially political, very obvious at Mâcon; here the prelate was rarely seen at the *chambre du clergé*, but always took the chair at the dominating *chambre des élus*, where, except in taxation matters, he enjoyed the casting vote.[102] The estates of Brittany were tumultuous rebellious assemblies, and the Crown expected the bishops to manipulate votes for government policy. This made the task of the bishop of Rennes, normally in the presidential chair, a miserable one. Succeeding a prelate who had got himself translated to another see in despair, Bareau de Girac from 1770 ran the estates with general approval, but only because he took the side of the province against the royal officials—once he turned to the side of the Court, his position became hopeless: the only way for royal business to pass, it was said, was for the bishop of Rennes to pretend to be against it.[103] In Provence, the archbishop of Aix, provided he was conciliatory, could run the province from his chairman's position by wooing the votes of the dominant commons. The deliberations in Languedoc were directed by the archbishop of Narbonne or, in his absence, the archbishop of Toulouse; when appointing to the latter see, the king's advisers looked for someone who could handle the business of the estates and in due course proceed to Narbonne and inherit the presidency.[104]

Languedoc was peculiar in having numerous political assemblies operating individually in broad financial subordination to the estates. The vast province was divided into twenty-three 'civil dioceses', roughly, but not exactly, coinciding with the ecclesiastical units; in each, there was an assembly, the *assiette*. Immediately after the estates concluded their annual session, these *assiettes* met in each episcopal city under the direction of their bishops; each had a standing committee (the *comité de direction*) with the bishop in the chair, and through this organization he could run the affairs of the secular diocese, with the proviso that in matters financial, the decisions had to be verified by the estates of Languedoc. Thus the prelates of the province—and more especially those who ruled in the important dioceses of Narbonne, Toulouse, Lodève, Lavaur, Agde, Uzès, Saint-Pons, and Albi—had major secular responsibilities, and when the king had to fill one of these bishoprics, he had to look for candidates of proven administrative ability. From the king's point of view, the role of the presiding bishop in the estates of the various provinces was to ensure that the subsidies to the central government were duly voted; seen from the side of the provinces, he had the duty of intervening at Versailles to moderate the royal demands. On becoming archbishop of Aix in 1770, Boisgelin[105] got the estates of Provence to make him their standing representative in Paris—he welcomed the excuse to be so often in the capital, but his first foray there was certainly profitable, sending back a decree of the Royal Council remitting 150,000 livres on the province's payment to the salt tax. The estates commissioned half a dozen paintings by Vanloo as a tribute of gratitude. Later, he got the government to reduce its subsidy demands by the amount the province had already given as a loan to help in the Seven Years War, and he obtained a grant to meet two-thirds of the cost of a new Palais de Justice in Aix. When in 1782, the *intendant de la marine* at Toulon set up a bakery in the arsenal to cut the profits of the bakers in town, the archbishop rushed off to Court on behalf of his needy and kneading constituents. The cultivation of influence at Versailles by their bishops also served the people of Mâcon well, for without it they would have lost their estates altogether. The powerful estates of Burgundy were bent on absorbing minor assemblies around the periphery of their province; the comté de Charollais lost its independence in this way in 1751, and the Mâconnais was scheduled to be next. Bishop Henri de Valras, already successful in obtaining a reduction in the government's taxation demands, now obtained a promise that the estates of the Mâconnais would remain for his own lifetime. He died in 1763, but his successor, Gabriel-François Moreau, stayed on in Paris negotiating until the Burgundian plotters were again thwarted.[106]

No doubt many bishops enjoyed these involvements in high politics and the opportunity to linger in Parisian society; yet there were probably as many who preferred the quietness of provincial life or were zealous to concentrate on pastoral duties, and found jolting up by coach to the capital a burden. Witness the misadventures of

Urbain de Hercé of Dol, dragged out of his pious and comfortable routine by the estates of Brittany to be the mouthpiece of Breton grievances at Versailles. He was there in 1773 protesting against infractions of provincial liberties and excessive taxation, and two years later he read to the Court a memorandum against the oppressive conscription to the militia doing coastguard service. In 1782 he was back to register protests about taxation. Four years after, he presided over the estates in the absence of the bishop of Rennes, and was rewarded by the king with an abbey *in commendam*, which did nothing to soften his courageous outspokenness. Indeed, in the same year he was back at Versailles, and in January 1788 he appeared before the king with a Breton deputation to protest against the edict giving a very limited toleration to Protestants. 'The arches of the sanctuary are shaken,' he thundered—a great monarch like Constantine, Theodosius, or Charlemagne would have called a national council on an issue of this importance. He was exiled to his diocese, but was back at Court in July denouncing the royal measures of discipline against the parlement of Rennes—'edicts flatly contrary to our rights . . . registered by military force without the consent of the estates, the magistrates exiled, the courts rendered idle, the Temple of Justice profaned'.[107] He got back to his palace just in time for Christmas. The Breton nobles spoke of their bishops as pliable agents of royal absolutism, yet they were glad to push one forward to face royal displeasure by expressing their grievances at Versailles.[108]

What credit should go to the president of the executive committee of a local authority for improvements made during his tenure of office? This was a time when the enlightened classes were enthusiastic for public works, whether improvements to communications to facilitate trade and the movement of grain in times of shortage, or beautifying cities with prestigious architecture. Some of the bishops received praise for what was done under their chairmanships—Mgr de Bonneval, the last bishop of Pamiers, for road building in the Pyrenees, Mgr de Fumel for driving boulevards and avenues through the medieval walled city of Lodève, Loménie de Brienne of Toulouse for the digging of the canal du Midi, Boisgelin of Aix for the Malemort–Terrasson canal. A bishop of Castres built roads through difficult mountain country, introduced the potato ten years before Parmentier recommended it, and set up a cotton factory; a bishop of Sisteron devised irrigation schemes ('the fathers curse me but the children will bless me'); at Fréjus, it was the calling in of engineers to drain the marshes; at Agde, the promotion of the silk industry; at Saint-Pons, the bishop had the nursery for mulberry trees (for free distribution) set up near his country house—'so I can keep an eye on it'. Loménie de Brienne at Toulouse became famous throughout Europe for his remarkable 'philosophic' pastoral letter of 1774 to the farmers of his countryside in a time of cattle plague. He explained how the disease had originated in untanned hides imported from Guadalupe through Bayonne, ordered the killing of diseased animals, promising compensation from the estates (and, indeed, partly from himself), and forbade the old custom of bringing the herds together to be blessed by the parish priest—precautions, not prayer, would bring the infection to an end. This circular was published in the *Journal politique*, and was widely read in France and beyond.[109]

The trouble with fame of this kind, however, was that tax payers, expecially those who were not gaining prestige or profit from the innovations, were reluctant to pay for them. In Languedoc in 1789 the nobles complained, 'it is the bishops who settle public taxation, and they do not bear the burden of it', and a pamphleteer asked what good were all the fine roads of the province, 'more use to the prelates in their six-horse carriages than to the peasants with their carts'. 'You are not men,' the diatribe concluded, 'not citizens, but slaves of the archbishop of Narbonne.'[110] In Provence, the anger of the commons against the revival of the old form of the estates was boundless. Archbishop Boisgelin, who originally promoted this reactionary *coup*, now changed tack and asked for a doubling of the representatives of the Third Estate. The government refused, and it looked as though the selection of deputies to the approaching Estates General of the nation might fall into the hands of the privileged classes dominating the revised form of the provincial estates. The idea was swept away in a storm of popular discontent. Boisgelin, now swimming strongly with the tide, announced the desire of his clergy to surrender their taxation privileges.[111] Cardinal Bernis, archbishop of Albi, for long had been away from these tumults, living in splendour in Rome as French ambassador. But in the old days when he had presided over the estates of the Albigeois, he had made a remarkable statement of concern for the peasant majority unrepresented by anybody anywhere. 'The price of a single feast where boredom reigns,' he said, 'would feed a family of peasants for a year.' To tax these poor people, who have no property but their labour, to pay for the adornment of the province, would be 'sacrilegious theft'. 'Gentlemen, as Christians we are all brothers, as men we are friends, members of the same citizen body.'[112]

Archbishop Boisgelin regarded himself as 'the first Minister of Provence'. Why should he not go further? Given proven ability and favour at Court, anything was possible. There was a tradition of ecclesiastical diplomats—d'Estrées, Forbin-Janson, Polignac. They were fewer after Louis XIV, but there were two glittering examples. At Vienna, Rohan upheld French grandeur with outrageous ostentation, winning the favour of all the ladies except the two who would matter to him—the Empress and her daughter Marie Antoinette. In the last twenty years of the *ancien régime*, Bernis, archbishop of Albi, was at Rome, 'keeping the inn of France at the crossroads of Europe', rejoicing in seeing the cardinals flocking in to enjoy his ice-cream and in brilliant negotiations to settle minutiae—when the Revolution came, his procrastination and reactionary prejudices were to usher his king to disaster. But it was possible to rise higher than embassies. France had never been so great as when it was ruled by cardinals—Richelieu, Mazarin, and Fleury. They had been strong and subtle, and (though it was treasonable to say so) they had avoided the war-like excesses of Louis XIV which brought the country to starvation. Dubois was in the series of political cardinals, but he did not count in the same way; he had been an upstart who accumulated prestigious ecclesiastical ranks to atone for being the son of an apothecary. When the façade of absolutism cracked and Louis XVI began his experiments towards introducing an element of consent into government with the Notables and the Provincial Assemblies, Boisgelin, Champion de Cicé, and Loménie de Brienne pushed themselves forward in the role of administrative bishops willing to use their acquired skills in leading France into a new era of liberal monarchy. Brienne, who was said to have had these great ambitions from the start, 'étudiant la théologie comme un Hibernois pour être évêque et les *Mémoires du cardinal Retz* pour être homme d'État', was the one who arrived to play the role of a Richelieu, a Mazarin, or a Fleury—too late for France, for events were out of control; too late for himself, for he was already beyond enjoying power, tormented with eczema and pulmonary consumption, coughing blood. A bishop—Richelieu—had built up the absolutism of the monarchy, and a bishop finally presided over its approaching dissolution.

9

THE BISHOPS: FATHERS IN GOD

I

To fulfil his pastoral duties effectively, a bishop needed to know his diocese. The traditional aid to understanding and investigation was the diocesan *pouillé*, the annotated list of benefices. Such documents were notorious for their inaccuracy, though in the eighteenth century there were greater efforts at updating; at Aix, new editions were prepared in 1708, 1730, 1768, and 1781.[1] Good maps also became available. The French Academy produced a superb engraved map of the *généralité* of Paris in 1678; from this, a version covering the diocese was extracted. Soon afterwards came a map of the diocese of Coutances by Hariette de la Pagerie, and Bossuet commissioned one for Meaux in 1698—it included the basic patterns of relief, afforestation, and cultivation, the boundaries of parishes, rural deaneries, and archdeaconries, with symbols showing roadside calvaries and the sites of the ruined Protestant chapels. Eight years later Cardinal Noailles commissioned a Parisian revision from the geographer Besson; at the same time, the bishop of Le Mans sent a technically expert priest and one of his archdeacons to make a cartographical survey of his diocese. Their final production was broadly accurate, except for the area around Laval, where the inhabitants gave false data as they thought they were being assessed for taxation. Cartographers now did brisk business, Delisle (dd. 1720), the most famous of them, compiling maps for several dioceses.[2] In 1732, the bishop of Lisieux adopted the system which was to become the common practice of all cartographers, ecclesiastical and secular, asking the curés to co-operate in measurements and listing topographical details, thus circumventing the duplicity of the laity. Towards the end of the *ancien régime*, prelates with a bent for administration, some zealous pastors, some zealous only for efficiency, adopted the use of such questionnaires to their clergy to collect information for a diocesan dossier for easy reference.[3] This was done by Loménie de Brienne at Toulouse (1763), Champion de Cicé at Rodez (1770), Rohan-Guéménée at Bordeaux (1772),

Talleyrand-Périgord as coadjutor at Reims (1774), Rosset de Fleury at Cambrai (1778), Gain-Montagnac at Tarbes (1783), and Le Tonnelier de Breteuil at Montauban about the same time, and, in a most detailed fashion, by Eustache-Antoine d'Osmond at Comminges (1786). These might be simple enquiries, as at Cambrai, where they constituted a census of the number of communicants and the total number of inhabitants; or they could be comprehensive, perhaps unreasonably so. At Tarbes, there were many questions, but the form was simple, the curés having to fill in the blanks. Champion de Cicé showed his secular and humanitarian preoccupations in wanting to know especially about hospitals, schools, midwives, crops, trades, and economic resources; Osmond had a questionnaire of eight large pages, which irritated the curés, especially as they knew that the covert aim was to find out exact details of income for the purposes of clerical taxation. Some gave testy answers: about the extent of the parish—'You'd have to ask a geographer', about the total of the surplice fees (the *casuel*)—'Just work it out from my reply on the numbers of births, marriages and deaths'. Le Tonnelier de Breteuil was proud of the dossier he compiled, and had it bound in red morocco along with a couple of maps, and kept it in a pouch of purple silk embossed with his coat of arms.[4] Loménie de Brienne left his as it was—it filled seven volumes.

II

A bishop's relations with the people of his diocese was necessarily mainly indirect, through the parochial clergy whose pastoral labours he supervised. But there were two ways by which he was in direct contact with the laity: through his pastoral letters (*mandements*) and his visitation tours.

Every bishop, even an absentee, was expected to edify his diocesans quite frequently with a pastoral epistle, perhaps ordering his curés to read it to the faithful, perhaps leaving it to them to quote and summarize. Invariably, there was one for the beginning of Lent, awaited by all, not because of the eloquence of its call to penitence, but as defining what exemptions were to be granted to the fasting regulations. Eggs would normally be authorized, and in bad weather other foods would be taken off the prohibited list to make up for shortages. A pastoral letter would herald the calling of a synod, the issue of new liturgical books, a new catechism, or the publication of synodal statutes. In times of plague, drought, or storm, there would be calls for penitence to turn away God's wrath, and as time went on, among the catalogue of sins drawing down divine punishment, the spate of writings advocating scepticism and unbelief would receive a special censure. When Rome proclaimed a year of jubilee, the bishop would define the dates and details of the observances, and exhort to repentance and confession on the way to a good communion as against mere outward conformity with the jubilee requirements. For royal marriages, births, and deaths, the chief pastor of the diocese would express the loyal sentiments of his flock and urge all to join the Court in its mourning or celebration. When Louis XV died, in addition to patriotic rhetoric and reflections on the transitory nature of human grandeur, there were *mandements* insinuating fears for that womanizing monarch's eternal salvation. In time of war, in response to the king's request, calls for prayers for victory would be issued, and if victory came, a Te Deum of thanksgiving would be ordered in all the great churches. From mid-century, the episcopate began to use the pastoral letter as a vehicle to make public its corporate feeling on the dangers threatening the Church.[5] Archbishop Christophe de Beaumont's attack on the parlements in September 1756 evoked similar letters from sixteen of his episcopal colleagues, and there were other adherences to his renewed attack in October 1763, though three independent-minded Gallicans broke ranks and denounced it. The Assembly of Clergy's complaints against the rising literature of unbelief were taken up and elaborated in diocesan circulars, and from 1765, after the queen's appeal to the Assembly to promote the cult of the Sacré-Cœur, numbers of pastorals authorized and encouraged the devotion, Bishop Fumel of Lodève providing the prototype, which others copied or paraphrased.

Mandements were composed in orotund prose reinforced with the standard pious clichés which created the 'unction' approved by some and ridiculed by others, and their argument was supported by an array of learning—scriptural texts, the opinions of the Fathers, decisions of Councils, prescriptions of royal legislation. Not surprisingly, bishops called on their expert theologians to help with the drafting. The abbé Couet, a *grand vicaire* of Paris, was so pleased with an effort he wrote on behalf of Archbishop Noailles that he sent a copy to Voltaire, receiving *Marianne* in return: a pastoral and a tragedy, said Voltaire, combining to provide the world with comedy.[6] 'Have you read my *mandement?*' 'Et vous, Monseigneur?'[7] The authorship of pastoral letters was a never-failing subject of jest. Mgr should teach his secretary logic, for what he has produced 'is as stupid as if he had written it himself'.[8] An improved variant was to ascribe the sacred eloquence to some dubious literary hack. La Motte was supposed to have penned Tencin's denunciations of the Jansenist bishop Soanen. 'A remarkable fact,' said Voltaire, 'an archbishop condemns a bishop and it is an author of operas and comedies who pens the archbishop's censures.'[9] Pious folk collected pastoral letters to furnish arguments for the true faith against incredulity, and the wits sought them for their involuntary humour. Their archaic phraseology gave an agreeably comic flavour to the zoological distinction of aquatic creatures into flesh, fowl, and fish for Lenten purposes offered by a worthy bishop of Agde;[10] to the bishop of Marseille's denunciation of the clergy who attended the city's pleasure dome, the 'Wauxhall';[11] to Cardinal Rohan's pastoral from prison when he was under arrest for his shady activities in the diamond necklace scandal, comparing himself to 'St Paul in fetters'.[12] Equally collectable for connoisseurs was the 'philosophical' pastoral letter of Loménie de Brienne vetoing a pious practice on the principles of the Enlightenment: farmers were forbidden to bring their beasts together for benediction in a time of cattle plague, regarding the limiting of the spread of infection as more important than intercessions for divine intervention. The eighteenth century was the great age of pamphleteering, and the bishops' pastorals counted among their number. It was, said Marais in 1732, 'le siècle du papier et le siècle des mandements'.[13]

III

According to the Council of Trent, the bishop or his delegate was required to visit every parish at least every two years, but preferably annually.[14] Monasteries were to be exempt, being subject to their own visitations. A declaration of Louis XIV in 1696 had gone further than the Council, overriding the monastic claim to exemption. No doubt, as the Fathers of Trent had said, the aim of the episcopal tours of inspection was to extirpate heresy, maintain ecclesiastical discipline, and edify the faithful; royal legislation, especially a declaration of 1695, added specific points of secular importance: to examine the accounts of churchwardens, assess the adequacy of the curé's lodging, see to the decency of the cemetery, rectify errors in parish registers, and review the local schools, hospitals, and charities. The bishops were 'fathers in God', but so far as the State was concerned, they were also 'administrative inspectors'. A visitation to perform these duties was organized as the bishop thought fit, but the secular courts were prepared to intervene to protect the rights of the lower clergy and the laity. This could happen anywhere by the invocation of the *appel comme d'abus*, and in the jurisprudence of the parlement of Brittany, a group of parishes could not be convoked to a common meeting—the bishop of Léon was prevented from resorting to this economical method in 1735.[15]

The episcopal power of visitation could be delegated. In huge dioceses like Bourges and Rouen, this was inevitable, and in areas of difficult terrain or in seasons of bad weather, a bishop of advancing years or in poor health could advisedly send others to do the riding and walking. 'In addition to episcopal grace', said Le Camus of Grenoble, 'a mountain bishop needs the surefootedness of a chamois.' The last bishop of Dié, Mgr Plan des Augiers, visited from 1756 to 1778, preserving the record of his journeys in twelve *cahiers*. Not surprisingly, he gave up after these twenty-two years of peregrination, for away from the old Roman road Valence–Dié–Gap, his parishes were accessible only by bridle-paths he traversed by horse or mule.[16] A young man might enjoy such adventures. In the 1730s Mgr La Motte of Amiens was tramping the lanes of his diocese. 'I do not think that a four-horse carriage can ever give so great a pleasure as the freedom of the open road from which I so often profited,' he said in later years.[17] How an older man reacted is reflected in a letter of Souillac of Lodève in September 1735, after getting back to his fireside at night exhausted:

My legs, the muscles having been so severely punished, punished me in their turn. I had been obliged to go down the hill on foot by paths full of rocks and stones; add to that all the preaching, the detailed work of the inspections, the weight of the vestments, especially the heavy cope, not to mention the cross and mitre, which I had to walk in, sometimes over long distances, in a procession over broken paving stones.[18]

And in any case, bishops had duties to take them away from their dioceses and administrative responsibilities which at times were all-absorbing. There always had been compelling reasons to delegate, and this was being done in more organized fashion in the eighteenth century. Though the archdeacons sometimes carried on with their traditional role, more and more the prelates were handing over the visitation duties to their *grands vicaires* and to the rural deans, the latter probably the most efficient of all, in close touch with the local problems of the parishes on which they reported. So a general assessment of pastoral visitations must take account of the many taking place under delegated authority, with the certainty that the documentary record of many of these enquiries has long been lost.

For some dioceses our information is fragmentary.[19] The bishop of Lombez was on tour in 1764, 1777, and 1780, of Sarlat in 1737, 1753, and 1764; a single *tournée* is recorded for Tulle. For Condom, there are no archival minutes, but a letter of Alexandre-César d'Auteroche shows that he conducted a *tournée* in 1765. At Auch, the archbishop visited in 1754; we know, however, of one of his *archiprêtres* active in every parish of his rural jurisdiction annually from 1731 to 1742. Local annalists record with relish forays by their bishops and the ensuing alarms and confusions—incidents which otherwise we would not have heard about.[20] The pattern of the episcopate of Charles-Maurice Le Tellier at Reims (1671–1710) is of a certain number of inspections of his own, but the continuous routine being kept going by the rural deans; even so, the local record shows the archbishop coming six times to the hamlet of Etrépigny in twelve years—true, the curé was Meslier, posthumously to become notorious for his atheism, yet this was not known in his lifetime, and the Fathers, Malebranche, and Fénelon on his shelves proved his respectability.[21] Clearly, more visitations must have been taking place all over the country without ever being recorded.

A few scandalous prelates were little concerned with what went on in their dioceses, leading to complaints from their curés, not about being left alone, something most of them greatly desired, but because (unless there was a suffragan) there were few confirmations.[22] A Grimaldi who once, when driven to it, laid hands on 4,570 candidates in a single session, and a cardinal de Gesvres who did three visitations in forty years and held a confirmation at his palace once a decade were pastors whose flocks had only heard of their existence by hearsay, and, as the joke had it, were like the disciples in Acts 'who had not so much as heard if there be a Holy Ghost'. Yet significantly, visitations went on, whether episcopally conducted or by delegates, even when the head of the diocese was notorious for slackness or worldliness. Cambrai[23] was neglected after the death of Fénelon, and from 1716 to 1721, absentee prelates ruled. The next appointment was Charles de Saint-Albin, the loose-living illegitimate son of the regent, only 24 years of age. For two and a half years he postponed his arrival, but once he reached his episcopal city, he went out at once on a pastoral inspection, winning golden opinions by giving a threadbare old curé a pension of 100 livres. Cardinal Tencin of tarnished reputation, archbishop of Lyon at the end of his days, Mgr de Vauréal of Rennes, 'the handsomest man of his time' and active in the royal diplomatic service, Talaru de Chalmazel of Coutances, charitable but morally ambiguous, are all found visiting their parishes.[24] Others, neglecting the duty themselves, organized others to do it. There is evidence of the archdeacons and a canon conducting major inspections at least during the last ten years of Jarente's absentee episcopate at Orléans; Loménie de Brienne, constantly engaged in high government business, had his five vicars-general looking after every detail of pastoral administration in Toulouse. In 1767, Louis-André de Grimaldi, a byword for indifference to religious observances, arrived in Le Mans and organized his diocese into 'départements', each under a *grand vicaire*; they ruled, complained a curé, 'in little despotic empires—no reference to the bishop possible; he lived in inaccessible grandeur'.[25] Translated to Noyon in 1778, he inherited a system of delegation from his predecessor Charles de Broglie: a busy archdeacon visited continually, and he was left to continue his labours.[26]

By contrast, there were bishops, more numerous than the idle and the professional delegators, who regarded visitation as their inescapable duty and, sometimes, their pleasure. Early in the century there were fanatical workers like Le Peletier, who covered the whole diocese of Angers from 1693 to 1694, then went methodically around again in the next twelve years; his system was to lodge for a week in one place and go out from it to inspect a parish every day.[27] There was Charles Frézeau de la Frézetière, a tough ex-soldier, who stormed round 600 parishes of the diocese of La Rochelle in eight years.[28] Massillon began a general visitation of Clermont in 1721, taking nine years to complete, then another in 1730 taking five years, then in 1738 his third and last.[29] The diocese of Orléans, later to be so neglected by Jarente, was comprehensively covered under Fleuriau d'Armenonville (1706–33) by his *grand vicaire* Nicolas-Joseph de Paris; then as bishop himself Paris carried on all through his rule over the next twenty years (1733–53).[30] A bustling archdeacon had looked after Soissons for fifteen years until the arrival of Fitz-James in 1739—for the next twenty-five years he and the three archdeacons were continually active.[31] Much the same happened at Saint-Pol-de-Léon, where *grands vicaires* had done all the inspections for a decade, until La Marche arrived in 1772, and for the next eighteen years went out to the parishes every year himself.[32] Aristocrats of the highest lineage did not spare themselves. Cardinal de Luynes, in an episcopal career spanning three-quarters of the century, visited at Bayonne, then at Sens; the two brothers La Rochefoucauld were active at Beauvais and Saintes in the 1780s.[33] Juigné at Châlons-sur-

Marne travelled round all his parishes in his first eight years, then in 1772 began a second tour, this time sending a circular to his curés saying that all he would need was shelter—he was bringing cooks and provisions and invited them to dine with him. When translated to Paris, he could not continue such a demanding routine, but in his first year we find him inspecting the royal parish at Versailles.[34] Some zealous bishops were still pursuing their itineraries in extreme old age. La Motte of Amiens (1734–74) covered his whole diocese every five years, and at 85 was still carrying on. Baüyn of Uzès in 1774 issued a pastoral letter to say he was beginning his fourth general visitation at the age of 75, and listed twenty-six points on which he would require information. Jean de Dousset at Belley (1712–45) kept going until crippled by age and illness. Olivier Ségonde Kervilio completed eleven *tournées* of Tréguier in twenty-eight years, doing his last visitation in 1729 at the age of 86; his successor from 1731 completed ten tours in a dozen years, then collapsed exhausted in 1741, though two years later he was trying again.[35]

In some dioceses, the bishop's activity was intermittent. Jean de Caulet,[36] who ruled at Grenoble from 1725 to 1771, began with vigour, visiting sixty-nine parishes in 1728, fifty-two in the following year, then a gap while he attended the Assembly of Clergy in Paris, then ninety-six parishes in 1732 and seventy-six in 1733. At that point he stopped, and did not hold another general visitation until 1757. Perhaps, having familiarized himself with every hamlet in his mountainous diocese, he decided he would now administer from the centre, which was not unreasonable. La Rochelle was inspected by its bishop from 1729 to 1740; he then fell ill and did not go on tour for his remaining twenty-seven years.[37] Paris had a gap of sixty years after the death of Noailles, though there were archidiaconal tours of inspection. The pattern would change abruptly when a fervent bishop succeeded a slack one. At Alet yearly activity began when Charles de la Cropte de Chantérac took over (1763–89).[38] Gaspard de Jouffroy-Gonsans, succeeding Grimaldi at Le Mans in 1778, declared that he intended to visit every parish—'it is the only way to obtain the close union between pastor and flock . . . so much to be desired'. When he went to Fougerolles, no bishop had been there since 1744; at Landivy he confirmed 1,600 from four parishes amid a huge crowd 'who, within living memory, had never seen the bishop in this place'.[39]

There are other dioceses where the record of episcopal visitation is continuous for long periods.[40] The tiny dioceses of Senez and Orange were visited by their bishops all through the century. So too at Alais and Nîmes. On 6 March 1734, François d'Andigné entered Dax to be installed, and he began his first visitations on 21 November in winter weather. From then onwards, in his reign and under his two successors, the diocese was constantly visited up to the Revolution. The record is also extensive in Fréjus (to 1781), Vence (to 1779), and Grasse (to 1759). The big sees of Bordeaux, Langres, Montpellier, and Châlons were models of the working of the system throughout the century.[41] At Bordeaux, there was a change of emphasis in 1769, for after forty years' rule by prelates who regarded visitation, as one of them said, as 'their indispensable duty', under Rohan-Guéménée and Champion de Cicé *grands vicaires* took over, though there was a major archiepiscopal tour in 1787. Langres, visited from 1734 to 1789 by Mgr de Montmorin and Mgr de La Luzerne, was the scene of a not entirely successful experiment in 1741, an attempt to organize an independent assessment of the efficacy of the visitations by filtering the reports through a committee of experienced priests, the *bureau du gouvernement spirituel du diocèse*.[42] The severity and continuity of the visitations in the diocese of Montpellier were intensified by the tensions of the great ecclesiastical quarrel of the century. Colbert, as befitted the austere leader of the Jansenist cause, went everywhere in person; his successor, the ruthlessly orthodox Berger de Charancy (1738–48), followed his example—out of pastoral enthusiasm, rivalry with the achievements of his predecessor, and to smoke out Jansenists entrenched in the parishes. Raymond de Durfort (1766–74) delegated a far-ranging visitation policy to others, though he is found going to thirteen parishes himself in the course of the years 1769–71. Joseph-François de Malide (1774–90) kept the system going, but joined in frequently himself—there are records of his presence in 115 parishes.[43]

IV

'The 18th century was a great epoch for pastoral visitations.'[44] This was so, not only because of their frequency and continuity in many areas, but because the processes were becoming more sophisticated—organized delegation to vicars-general and rural deans, more attention to preliminary enquiries, to the dignity of the proceedings, to the follow-up for enforcement. In broad outline, there was a standard procedure built up through the years.[45] It was well known what documents had to be produced (in Clermont the diocesan *Rituel* listed them)—the inventory of possessions, the title-deeds to the property of the foundation, the accounts of the churchwardens, the confraternities, chapels, and hospitals, and the letters of priesthood of the clergy together with the warrants of their nomination to office, their authorization to preach, and, if absent from duty, a medical certificate. By the end of seventeenth century, it was established that the curé must also produce a filled-in copy of the diocesan questionnaire. Like so many pastoral innovations, the idea had come from Charles Borromeo, and the Assembly of the Clergy of France in 1579 had elaborated a list of questions along his lines; there was also a more detailed list in the treatise of the Italian monk Bartolomeo Gavanti. The circulation of a solemn pro forma to all the parishes came in at Clermont in 1620 and was rapidly adopted everywhere; soon it was printed, and the printed form was universal in the eighteenth century, although it came late to Limoges in 1730. In outline, the run of questions had become fixed, though additions and amendments were made from time to time. In the diocese of Clermont,[46] everything was unchanged from 1636 to 1789, except that an omission was made in deference to the ideas of the Enlightenment: the demand to name 'sorcerers, fortune-tellers— male and female—and others who weave spells' was dropped. In the diocese of Châlons-sur-Marne[47] in the early eighteenth century questions were added concerning parishioners who failed to perform their Easter duty and the 'dominant vices' of the population; at mid-century there were further additions asking about the provision of sermons and catechism classes, and whether steps were needed to deal with characters who frequented wine bars during the hours of divine service. Bordeaux began the century with thirty questions, soon dropping the one asking for details of the 'spiritual life' of the parish as a subject more suitable for private discussion between the priest and his bishop. In 1731, however, Mgr François Casaubon de Maniban sponsored a new model based on Italian practice,[48] with seventy paragraphs with their various subheadings making a total of 500 items, a document which, Mgr Louis d'Audibert de Lussan (1734–69) refined. No doubt there came a point when the multiplication of questions became self-defeating. Curé Nicolas Dumont of Villers-devant-le-Thour (500 communicants) told the archbishop of Reims in 1774, concerning the 'qualities and vices' of his parishioners: 'le caractère des habitants de Villers est à peu près celui des autres hommes'.[49]

There was a great deal to do on a visitation, so the bishop needed assistants. Bareau de Girac who, like all the bishops of Rennes in the century, rarely visited, when he did turn out, went in style—

coachman, outrider, lackey, *valet de chambre*, cook, a notary, and two priests. But the standard minimum formula was to take the domestic chaplain and a *grand vicaire*. Thus in 1748 the folk of Aubais in the diocese of Nîmes gathered to greet their prelate as he arrived with his vicar-general in a barouche drawn by two black mules, and the chaplain riding alongside on a white one.[50] The director of the seminary might be taken—he would probably have the advantage of personal knowledge of the parish priest in his earlier days.[51] The bishop of Mâcon in 1745–6 made an unusual addition to his party, one more characteristic of the seventeenth than the eighteenth century, taking the *promoteur* of his *officialité*, presumably a sinister gesture, as if offenders against morals were being noted down for prosecution.[52] According to the area and its dangers, whether of terrain or lawless inhabitants, a servant or more would be needed, a coachman, a groom, a lackey. These could be a nuisance. When the bishop of Agde was at Bouzigues in 1773, the town failed to give his retainers their tip, so they seized the *dais* (the canopy to shield the bishop, proudly carried in procession on its four poles by the churchwardens and two leading citizens). These, rather than miss their hour of glory, handed over the money.[53] A precisely similar episode over the 'pourboire au dais' is noted at Saint-Jeanret early in the century.[54] Characteristically of the age, the parishioners were subjected to an inspection at their own expense. The *pourboire* to the servants was part of a more general bill for entertainment—the notables of a little town borrowing 395 livres to make a splash,[55] those of a village modestly laying out 36 livres, recouped by a tax on farm animals, ten sols on a 'big beast', five on a pig, and two on a sheep.[56] There might be a fee, a *droit de procuration*, to be paid in lieu of entertainment, probably very small, 15 livres or so, the joint responsibility of clergy and laity.[57] The administrative assembly at Nîmes, the *assiette*, was accustomed to vote the bishop a lump sum to cover all the parishes at the beginning of his *tournée*—2,000 livres was given in 1787.[58]

In the seventeenth century, a bishop might well have been accompanied by a Jesuit or member of some other religious order as his preacher; the practice was dropped in the eighteenth century, though the bishop occasionally gave a sermon himself, not always being entirely comprehensible to rural congregations. Cardinal de Luynes once denounced the philosophes. 'You stupid girl,' said a mother to her daughter, 'falling asleep instead of listening to Monseigneur and learning about the lives of Saint Voltaire and Saint Rousseau.'[59] More often, the bishop was satisfied with celebrating a pontifical mass, perhaps with the offer of an indulgence to those who communicated. And he would hold a confirmation; peasants and their families from all around would gather, so a crowd of 500 or so was not unusual.[60] La Motte, bishop of Amiens, even when he was old, prolonged proceedings by interrogating candidates personally, 'resisting', as he said, 'the parents who are jealous when they see children of the same age accepted in preference to their own'.[61]

This would be embarrassing to some, but the dreaded moment for all came when the inquisitors began to inspect the church, the vicarage, and the cemetery. If the camouflage was seen through, the community would have to pay for repairs and improvements. A close scrutiny of the liturgical equipment[62] was sure to reveal faults which everyone had come to live with through usage, or put up with through parsimony—chalices, ciboriums, and pyxes to be regilded, tabernacles to be adorned and their locks repaired, the stoppers of the bottles for consecrated oil to be fitted properly, pictures to be cleaned, missing pages in the service-books replaced. Bishop La Motte always looked in the linen chest, for if the corporals used in the communion were grubby, 'to a believer in the Real Presence . . . this is worse than heresy, it is impiety'. He also specialized in the reverence due to the baptismal font; it was to be railed off, and the lid must be pyramidal, not flat, lest women attending divine service should seat their babies on it.[63] In some respects, however, a visitation might be welcome to curé and people, enabling them to bring the great to order and end the tyranny of their portentous pews obstructing the aisles.[64] The offenders, seigneurs (and sometimes the churchwardens themselves), could ignore ordinary complaints, but the bishop could order the sawing off of a foot or two and, indeed, total demolition if the documentation of the right to possess a pew was not forthcoming. A particularly searching enquiry was conducted at the church of Saint-Michel at Draguignan on 26 April 1763, by the bishop of Fréjus.[65] He ordered various pews to be shortened; the font was to be moved, since, where it was, 'little children are being exposed to draughts'; the five side altars would be interdicted unless 'within a month, counting from today' their pictures and steps were repaired. From these practical matters he moved to the local liturgical calendar, reducing the excessive use of the Holy Sacrament in processions and benedictions, forbidding nocturnal assemblies in the church, prescribing the exclusive use of the Roman rite, and requiring a low mass to be said after the Sunday high mass so that infirm people could attend. Then he dealt with the whole system of confraternities drawing the faithful away from the ordinary services in the parish church. The Pénitents survived, but were forbidden to frequent their chapels in the Easter fortnight or to have burials there; the other confraternities were reduced to three in number (the Holy Sacrament, the Rosary, and the Souls in Purgatory), and these were put under the control of the churchwardens and the sacristan.

Some adornments of the church might meet with disapproval as lacking in taste or conventional pious sentiment. The late seventeenth and early eighteenth centuries had been a time to get rid of dubious images—a St George looking like Perseus rescuing Andromeda, a Mary Magdalen in her finery as a courtesan.[66] Yet others had survived to catch the censorious eye later on—'a deformed and indecent statue' of Our Lady, a life-sized figure of a bucolic-looking Christ riding on an ass into Jerusalem, an image of St Martin on an unconvincing horse. An order to remove such objects would be made, always with the instruction to bury them in the churchyard—having been objects of piety to an earlier, naïve generation, they could not be reduced to secular firewood. A critical eye, wary of superstition, would be cast over relics. If the documents of authentication were inadequate and the stories concerning the saint were not edifying or reasonable, the bishop might order the removal of the fragmentary remains, or he might mercifully concede that an immemorial connection or the devotion of the parishioners could serve in lieu of formal correctness.[67] If the decision was removal, the bishop was well advised not to announce it until he was safely back in his palace; in 1721, Massillon opened the reliquary of the patron saint of one of his parishes, and was besieged in the sacristy by a mob and had his coach windows broken as he fled.[68]

Parishioners used every artifice to delay having to make repairs to the vicarage. Visitation time was the curé's opportunity to get authority on his side. If he convinced the bishop, the whole matter would be put to the intendant, who had the power to order a parish to hold a meeting to fix a rate to pay the building contractor—though, as a hard-headed layman, he was not likely to enforce an excessive degree of comfort at public expense.[69] By the edict of April 1695, the parishioners were also obliged to maintain the cemetery, especially the walls and gates.[70] In the first three-quarters of the century, when the great were buried inside the church and the rank and file piled in the *fosse commune* until it was filled, the graveyard was not the lonely spot for poetic reverie it subsequently became—cattle grazed, children played, men engaged in games of boule and hands of cards, and washing was hung out to dry. Reforming bishops objected to these profane activities, and if the church-wardens had not had the foresight to round up the beasts, expel the intruders, and hide the washing, episcopal censures would come their way. Far from wishing to make the burial ground an umbrageous romantic place, however, the bishops tended to order the sawing down of such trees as there were, since they gave shade to the gossips and the gamblers. By mid-century, a new consideration arose, a concern with hygiene, and the bishop of Saint-Papoul, anticipating the action of the government, interdicted a cemetery 'à cause de l'odeur'. A royal declaration of March 1776 banned burials in the churches, and ordered the setting up of new cemeteries in places where the old one had become a pestilential danger to the nearby inhabitants. In towns (though rarely in the countryside) this meant the reluctant parishioners might have to buy new land, hire a mason to wall it, and in addition still have to maintain the walls of the old graveyard for fifteen years—a heavy expense. Thus a new and sombre thunder-cloud hung over their heads at visitation time; if they failed to obey the royal orders or complied parsimoniously and nominally, they were sure to be brought to book when the inquisitors returned.

It was the curé's turn to tremble when the registers of the *état-civil* were called for—the records of births, marriages, and deaths.[71] The system ought to have been foolproof with copies of entries sent to the *greffe*, the record office of the nearest royal jurisdiction. In fact, the parish priests often did not bother to make these returns, and the idle officials did not bother to ask for them. In the parish, the register could be lost, damaged by fire or drips from a leaking roof, or gnawed by rats; through idleness, illness, or old age, some curés failed to fill them in anyway. In these circumstances, the best that could be done was to set in motion the process of individual declarations by which the record could be reconstituted.

This inspection over, the curé could breathe again and conduct his chief pastor to see the charitable institutions of the parish.[72] Was the schoolhouse big enough? Was there a schoolmaster, and was he properly paid? Was he competent? He might well be tested on the spot for numeracy and literacy. The midwife would be sent for. Had she qualifications, and if not medical ones, had she at least taken the ecclesiastical oath of her profession? If the parish had a *procureur des pauvres* or charitable bureau, the accounts would be checked, and if there was a hospital, it would be inspected. Here the bishop had the right to investigate, but he was on the borderline of his powers to issue orders; if things were wrong, he would have to invoke the secular authorities. There is a grim letter of Champion de Cicé, bishop of Rodez, to Necker in August 1780 describing the *maison de force* of Castelgaillard,[73] a sort of prison for vagabonds and beggars under the control of the intendant of Montauban. There were 200 men and women in a place built for 50, lying on rotting straw left unchanged for seven months, the living moving into the dirty sleeping places vacated by those who died; the surgeon was ignorant, and the gaoler brutal. The one redeeming feature was that in the course of the last year forty prisoners had escaped. For such an inspection, the bishop would ask some medical expert to join him. Mgr de Barral, bishop of Castres, indeed, was always accompanied by Dr Icard, the expert on inoculation against smallpox. By episcopal ordinance (perhaps of doubtful validity) he had declared this treatment obligatory on all children of his diocese, and those who were unwary enough to be around at visitation time were duly caught and given their 25 per cent chance to live longer.

The climax of a visitation was when the people were asked about the conduct of their curé, and he in turn was asked about theirs; normally, there were separate interrogations.[74] The tension was often less than might have been supposed, partly because from about 1730 the official assumption (unlike that of the seventeenth century) was that the clergy would be living moral lives, and partly because of the unspoken concordat between priest and parish to rub along together without getting into trouble with authority. Was the curé present at all the services? Did he give sermons, take catechisms, visit the sick, behave morally? Mostly, the parishioners expressed satisfaction, except over practical matters—he was asking for excessive improvements to the presbytery, he had taken possession of the church-wardens' accounts and would not return them. In Brittany, the parish elected two *témoins synodaux* as spokesmen, a system to throw up professional complainants. In the diocese of Tréguier they were hard put to find examples of sexual misdemeanours or violence, but they specialized in reporting drunkenness, with picturesque details of children fleeing from catechism and marriages held up for the taking of liquid refreshment. The curé who turned up drunk at visitation time at least had no defence to the charge. The bishop of Dol turned savagely on one malicious witness: 'I can see you are a *mauvais sujet*; think of your death, it is nearer than you imagine'—the man and his wife died within the week.[75]

When interrogated in his turn, the curé generally took care not to get others, or himself, into difficulties: 'Assez content'; 'Répond qu'il n'a pas lieu de s'en plaindre'; no one misses Easter Day, but ordinary Sundays are not so good—'répond qu'ils pourraient mieux l'observer'. If he wanted change, he would hope that authority would impose it without revealing where the proposal came from— like getting rid of the old *rituel* for conjuring away hailstones from the crops, the people being much attached to it and blaming the curé when it failed. He was unlikely to give the bishop the actual names of immoral parishioners—unless it was some ne'er-do-well whom nobody loved. In the eighteenth century, the emphasis of the questions changed to fit the reality of the answers likely to be given—the names of 'public sinners' were not asked for, but rather 'the dominant vices' of the community.[76] Some bishops, however, in the backwaters of the country, managed to carry on in the old rigorous ways. In Tréguier, the *promoteur* went round on the visitations, and held a sort of preliminary hearing of the ecclesiastical court on the spot for couples living in sin and applicants for judicial separation or marriage dispensations. In 1739, the bishop of Grasse banned dancing on the square in the shadow of the village cross: 'Christians should blush to resort to such divertissements before the symbol of our redemption.' Soanen, the Jansenist prelate of Senez, forbade parents to sleep along with their children or to have boys and girls in the same bed, and anathematized dancing and various folk observances of rural carnivals. But lay society was reacting against these archaic attempts to police morality by visitation ordinances. The parlement of Rennes in 1748 and the parlement of Rouen in 1768 suppressed pastoral letters of bishops because they included the usual questions about the morals of parishioners in their visitation programme.[77] By then, in most parishes, these enquiries were just a formality. What did survive, however, and indeed, became more important in the eighteenth century, was an old feature of the visitation which was very acceptable to the thought of the Enlightenment: the intervention of the bishop to reconcile feuds and wind up lawsuits by compromise.[78] Mostly, the episcopal arbitration, once offered, was successful. The bishop of Alet noted with surprise in his record of a visitation at Caudier in 1785 that he had failed to bring a lawsuit to an end.[79]

The findings of the bishop were recorded in the minutes of the visitation, and in the eighteenth century it became customary to issue separate ordinances specifically requiring the curé and parishioners to act, or exhorting the civil authorities (the intendant and the magistrates) to co-operate. *Grands vicaires* could also issue such injunctions, since they had full episcopal power by delegation; other clerics carrying out a visitation had to send the *procès-verbal* to the bishop, who would take action for enforcement. Given the bishop's power to discipline the clergy and to close churches by interdict, obedience was usually given, though in matters requiring the intervention of the civil authorities (like major repairs or police action against the keepers of wine bars) the episcopal complaint might receive only a nominal satisfaction. The best way to ensure compliance to ordinances was for visitations to be frequent. Thus the churchwardens of Saint-Julien de Courville, who were found neglecting their parish accounts by a visitation of 1755, were brought to book when the suffragan bishop of Reims arrived on another tour of inspection four years later and found they had still not managed to produce a record of their expenditure.[80] On rare occasions, a very strict bishop would follow up his visitation with a *contre-visite* a few months later. In September 1784 the bishop of Tulle published his visitation ordinances concerning various parishes he had covered in the summer and autumn months, saying he was allowing three months' grace for all concerned to put things in order; in February of the following year a vicar-general (the dean of the cathedral) went round on a tour of verification. This was unfortunate for the people of Lagarde, who had failed to put right the plank floor of their cloister, for the new inspection of their church revealed a need for some roof repairs which the bishop had missed.[81]

The eighteenth century had been a great epoch of episcopal visitation, but it was the last. The instrument was effective for dealing with outrageous scandals—clergy living in concubinage or riot, over-mighty laymen tyrannizing over the church; it was an excessive parade of authority to deal with minor cases. Life was becoming more civilized, and the conduct of churchmen more respectable. The seminaries had ensured that the clergy knew their professional duties, episcopal oversight and public opinion had brought them to conform to strict rules of conduct; catechism classes had given even the most ignorant laymen a concept of basic Christian duty. Coercing the laity into morality by clerical intervention had become an impossible dream—far from co-operating, the law courts would prevent it.[82] The printed pro formas filled in by the curés became an end in themselves, a substitute for the actual visitation; the bishop could stay at his headquarters with the basic file they provided and have the information cross-checked against the regular reports of the rural deans, coming in more reliably as communications improved. Pious critics of eighteenth-century religion have complained of the growing formalization of the visitation, its concentration on detailed 'practical' affairs. Truth to tell, the visitation was suitable only for dealing with the practical. If the fostering of spiritual needs and progress is the main duty of the bishop, it needs to take place in entirely different and non-inquisitorial circumstances—in long private conversations with individual priests or in clerical discussion groups, in sermons delivered on confirmation tours, and friendly visits totally unconnected with the search for shortcomings.

V

The formal method for a bishop to meet and direct his clergy was to assemble them in a diocesan synod; here, matters of common interest could be discussed, and the bishop could embody the findings—or impose his own—in statutes and ordinances. At Coutances, in 1744, a synod was convened to consider the *Rituel* newly drawn up by the diocesan liturgiologists. The curés, 300 of them, poured into town. There were few absentees, for the fine for remissness was stiff—3 to 5 livres to the poor. On the morning, the bishop took his place in the chapel of Saint-Lô in the cathedral; he was flanked by the archdeacons and rural deans, who had come up early to have preliminary discussions. One by one, the curés presented themselves in the episcopal presence. In the afternoon, the full synod met to consider the *Rituel*. It was approved, and very shortly afterwards was published. At two synods in earlier years the subjects considered (as revealed in the subsequently published ordinances) had concerned penitential discipline; in 1724, the necessity of having a confessional box in the church and hearing all confessions there, not elsewhere, was affirmed; in 1727, there was a review of the *cas réservés*—that is, sins too grave to be remitted by the curé on his own authority. Later, in 1761, the bishop reminded the synod of the rules prohibiting curés from employing young women as housekeepers and from drinking in wine bars. All this had been said before in earlier editions of the diocesan statutes, but copies of them had become rare, so those particular clauses needed to be reaffirmed.[83]

As in the diocese of Coutances, so also in that of Lodève, synods were frequent in the first half of the eighteenth century. In 1745, the bishop, having prepared a revised edition of the diocesan statutes, called a general synod, inviting all ecclesiastics who had cure of souls—not only the curés, but also the cathedral canons and the monks of the two Benedictine abbeys. In the morning, there was communion, a sermon, and prayer, ending with the *Libera* and the *De Profundis*. In the afternoon, all assembled at the episcopal palace for discussions which carried on into the following day, ending with a universal profession of the faith as laid down by the Council of Trent. By local custom, the synod ought to have elected the clergy's representatives on the diocesan bureau for assessment of clerical taxation, but in fact the bishop named them, and his choice was ratified (his successor was to exercise the same initiative at the synod of 1751). Forthwith, the *Statuts synodaux du diocèse de Lodève renouvelés et publiés dans le synod* were published, so swiftly that it was unreasonable to suppose that the two days of debate had made any difference. The volume bore the imprint of the bishop's Jansenist sympathies, excommunicating parishioners absent from mass for three consecutive Sundays, their sin solemnly listed as being on the *cas réservés*. As for lukewarm priests, the episcopal pastoral letter of the preface declared crudely that Christ was 'prêt à vomir de sa bouche tout prêtre qui ne paraît ni bien ni mauvais'.[84]

The calling of a synod was at the bishop's absolute discretion:[85] if he did not choose to call one—as at Montpellier from 1700 to 1724 and Auch from 1698 to 1727—there would be a gap in the series of meetings. There were none in the diocese of Nantes all century, and only three in that of Rennes after 1711—contrasting with frequent meetings convoked by the bishops of Saint-Malo and Dol. In the present state of our knowledge we cannot plot the incidence of synodal assemblies over the various dioceses, but it is sure that from mid-century they were dying out. At Lodève, they became infrequent. At Coutances, the numbers attending declined. From 1674 to 1712, of those invited, 70 per cent came; in a year of numerous absentees, like 1710, it was because of very bad weather. From 1726 to 1738, only 40 per cent of the parish priests turned up. Thereafter, synods faded out. The diocesan calendar still gave the dates for the meetings (in 1789 it was 28–9 April), but these were fossilized entries no longer observed. The *cahier* of the clergy of the *bailliage* of the Cotentin (which included the greater part of the dioceses of Coutances and Avranches) regretted the passing of the synods, and asked to have them back again. According to the regulations of the diocese of Paris, three separate synods were to meet annually. One was of the curés of the city and suburbs, under the presidency of the *official*, one of the rural curés under their archdeacons, and one of the whole diocese under the bishop himself. In fact, the last synod of the whole diocese was held in 1673, when a set of statutes was published.[86] Only the gatherings of capital and suburbs continued. The sixty curés attended well, the average number of absentees being a dozen. Their meeting of 1727 called on the bishop to summon the whole diocese (this was to protest against the bull *Unigenitus*), but the request was refused. When, in 1786, Archbishop Le Clerc de Juigné imposed a new *Rituel* it was never considered in synod; as a result, the canons of Notre-Dame refused to use it.[87]

One reason for the decline of synods was the rising temper of independence among the parish priests. The Jansenists encouraged the tendency; as they saw it, a bishop ought to convoke his curés at regular intervals, accepting their right to share in his authority and be co-regents of the diocese. The days of statutes going through on the nod were ended.[88] At Saint-Malo and Luçon in 1769 there were protests against the publication of new statutes in defiance of the will of the assembled clergy; at Rouen in 1783 there were complaints against the archbishop and his 'court of Zelanti'; at Rodez in the following year there were protests against 'dictation' from on high. If this was to be the new temper of synods, not surprisingly the bishops hesitated to hold meetings and invite challenges to their authority.

Yet, if this was their motive, they were being short-sighted; times were changing, and by judicious use of discussion in synod they could have transformed their relations with their clergy. Le Clerc de Juigné, who failed to revive the old general synod of Paris when he went there as archbishop, as bishop of Châlons-sur-Marne, from 1764, held synods in 1765 and 1766.[89] He forbore from hectoring his clergy about their conduct, merely reminding them to dress properly in cassocks, take care in making entries in their parish registers, and to refrain from hunting. He mentioned a few points about ceremonies which were far from obvious and where misconceptions could arise. The exposition of the Holy Sacrament was in order for the patronal festival, but not for the Sunday of the octave; there was no fee to the officiant at the funeral of a curé except the dead man's breviary; sin is officially possible only when a young person reaches the age of 7, a point to be borne in mind in any sermon at the funeral of a child; when several marriages are celebrated together, the final benediction must be given separately to each couple. And he invited his curés to let him have comments as to changes needed in a proposed new edition of the *Rituel*. There was nothing to offend the pride of the curés here, and, in a minor way, they were being treated as colleagues. A striking demonstration of episcopal solidarity with the lower clergy was given by Bishop La Luzerne of Langres when he held a long synod, from 27 August to 3 September 1783, the purpose being to consider the inadequacy of the *congrue*, the official salary for vicaires and non-tithe-holding curés. Against the opposition of the cathedral canons and the technical difficulties raised by the *grand archidiacre*,[90] he carried a proposal for new scales varying according to the numbers of houses in each parish, and he went off to Paris to ask for royal letters patent validating the increases in his diocese. His reform was overtaken by the royal edict of 1786 raising the *congrue*, though by considerably less. It is easy to see why he was popular with his curés.

There was a more obvious reason for the decline of synods than the reluctance of bishops to summon them. In the tiny dioceses, it was easy for the prelate to be in touch with his clergy without the necessity of calling them together—like Mgr du Tillet, last bishop of Orange, walking around the lanes, stick in hand and dog at heels. In dioceses with numerous clergy, the housing and entertaining of them all in one place was a difficult operation; in those of wide geographical extent or difficult terrain, travelling to the episcopal city was laborious. Significantly, when numbers at Coutances declined, it was the curés of the more distant archdeaconry who first gave up attending. Similarly, the general synod for the whole diocese of Paris lapsed while that of the capital alone continued. In fact, most dioceses were not suitable units for regular clerical meetings, a fact which was emphasized by the rise of new gatherings based on the rural deaneries, the *conférences ecclésiastiques*. This was not just a change of geographical area and numbers attending, but a change to a different objective, the continuation of the education of the parish priests beyond the basic stage they had reached in their seminaries. A typical *conférence* subject was the discussion of the problems of casuistry and pastoral care involved in the various *cas de conscience* inevitably arising to perplex the zealous confessor; a typical synodal subject was the necessity of a confessional box or the exact listing of the *cas réservés*. This contrast highlights the most essential of the reasons for the ending of the synods. The clergy were better behaved and better educated than ever before. Bishops edified them by circulating pastoral letters rather than by publishing synodal ordinances; the *cas réservés* were published in the breviary, and the instructions for the administration of the sacraments in the *Rituel*, so all had them handy. If, as was rare, a disciplinary intervention was needed, the bishop could use the powers vested in him by the edict of 1695 or ask for a *lettre de cachet*. Haranguing droves of clergy in a crowded assembly about their elementary duty was not only unnecessary, but old-fashioned, Jansenistic, shading into the comic. So the synods became fewer. The *Nouvelles ecclésiastiques* kept a lookout for them to give encouragement and approval, but between

1760 and 1790 found only fourteen dioceses in which they continued to meet.[91]

VI

The idea of discussion groups to educate the parish clergy had originated with Charles Borromeo and Vincent de Paul, and in the seventeenth century they sprang up in various dioceses, sometimes spontaneously, sometimes prompted by the teaching staff of the seminaries. In 1655, the bishop of La Rochelle formally ordered monthly discussions in each of his rural deaneries, and his lead was followed in other dioceses—Avranches, Bayeux, Lisieux, Coutances, Auch, Sens, Bordeaux.[92] The standard pattern was a monthly meeting seven times a year, omitting the season when bad weather made travelling difficult and the times of grain and wine harvest. Membership would consist of the curés of a rural deanery, though the grouping might be over a wider area if the bishop so prescribed. Under an active and severe prelate, the *conférences* could be regimented, almost inquisitorial affairs. As the system operated at Lodève,[93] all curés had to attend unless ill, very old, or required at the deathbed of a parishioner. Missing three meetings in a year incurred suspension from clerical functions. On the morning of the prescribed day, all had to be present by eight in the morning, on pain of a fine of three sols. There was mass at 9 a.m., then New Testament readings, followed by a frugal meal; in the afternoon, all had to appear formally dressed in cassocks and long cloaks to sing the *Veni Creator*, after which each curé produced his answer to the theological problem posed at the end of the last *conférence*. Some of these were read aloud, all listening silently, 'sans s'amuser à contester'. The moderator then read out the specimen answer prepared by the bishop or his theologians, and the clergy handed in their efforts to be sent off to the episcopal palace for official review. In 1733, the bishop instituted a new procedure, announcing in synod the theological questions for a year in advance, to encourage the curés to more serious study, and in 1738 he prescribed the form of the written answers: 'in a readable hand and on paper with a wide margin, so we can insert our comments'. In 1749, a further inducement to diligence was offered, since publication of the best answers began—they finally formed a series of four volumes, then another of five, mostly concerned with questions on the Scriptures, built up in a chronological series running through the Old Testament to the

New. Seeing the curés were at this time also required to come to synods and to an annual retreat, they must have felt themselves too enthusiastically supervised. In the diocese of Bordeaux,[94] the rural deans (there called *vicaires forains*) presided over the seven monthly *conférences* (*assemblées foraines*); they had to send to the archbishop an account of each meeting and attend collectively twice a year at the palace to give an account of their stewardship. The *assemblées* met in a different parish for each session, the local parish priest having to produce a meal for his colleagues, for which each paid 15 sols. There was low mass, high mass, a procession to the cemetery, and a sermon before lunch (eaten in silence while extracts from the New Testament were read). Then in the afternoon the *Veni Creator* and prayers, followed by four half-hour discussion periods (on a chapter of the Bible, on ecclesiastical duties, on moral theology, and on actual difficulties individuals had recently encountered in the confessional). Absentees were punished by having to send in written answers to the questions at the *conférence* they had missed.

Similar edifying sessions were prescribed for their clergy by reforming bishops in other dioceses. At Autun,[95] early in the century, the curés were ordered to assemble twice a year for discussions in the presence of their bishop and come to another two meetings in their local *archiprêtrés* under the rural dean. The synodal ordonnances of Carcassonne of 1713 impose fines for absence from the monthly *conférences*, the third offence involving a suspension of two months from clerical duties on weekdays. The bishop circulated advice to his clergy at their meetings on commercial problems in the confessional, judiciously balancing between the rights of masters and employees and advising on measures to take concerning issues of non-payment and defaulting creditors—a subject on which he was an expert, being a splendid aristocrat who had run up huge debts.[96] The synodal statutes of Amiens in 1736 ordered each rural dean to hold a 'chapter' of his parish priests twice a year.[97] In the diocese of Sens, the archbishop circulated an annual list of discussion questions, and there was complaint when the new prelate, arriving in 1753, set them at a more demanding intellectual level.[98]

Reports of *conférences* in the diocese of Coutances suggest a different atmosphere.[99] True, the formalities were there. Absentees were fined on a diocesan scale fixed in 1730, the discussions were serious, and the secretary forwarded the minutes to the bishop. Yet the curés were very willing to go—indeed, their meetings had begun in the mid-seventeenth century, with voluntary assemblies later taken over by the bishop and formalized. In the eighteenth century, for a while, meetings were fortnightly, though they finally became monthly. Some curés chose to attend in more than one rural deanery, and exempt curés (that is, those under the cathedral chapter, one in an enclave belonging to another diocese, and one in an independent *commanderie* of the Order of Malta) turned up to nearby meetings. The *conférences* had a cheerful communal spirit; a patron saint was nominated and duly honoured, masses were said for dead comrades, officers were democratically elected, and the whole gathering referred to itself as a 'republic'. This was a confraternity and a trade union as well as an officially sponsored discussion group. No doubt the Coutances evidence is a clue to what went on in other dioceses behind the official record; however severely a bishop might try to regiment the gatherings, there was a lot of good fellowship, renewal of friendships from seminary days, exchange of gossip and, indeed, of grievances. According to an embittered Jansenist curé of Poitou, they all had far too good a time. 'I seek out the society of persons of merit,' he sanctimoniously declared, 'as for those noisy gatherings where, under the name of *conférences* they assemble only to indulge in shameful and sometimes criminal excesses, I not only never liked them, but the first time I went to one I said quietly to myself—this will be the last.'[100]

Like the synods, the *conférences* began to decline, though there seems to have been a revival towards the end of the *ancien régime*: they began again in Toulouse in 1768 and in Lisieux in 1775.[101] Theological discussion month after month or quarterly would grow boring, and the curés, rising in social status, income, and educational qualifications, were becoming more sociable among themselves in informal ways, meeting to give lunch parties or to vie in the composition of verses and epigrams, or going off to some of the lay *sociétés de pensée* which were rising everywhere. If they wanted theological wrangles, they would have them privately among their friends, not in gatherings under episcopal supervision. Perhaps the growth of a radical temper among the parish priests disinclined the bishops to sponsor opportunities for the airing of dangerous opinions.

Indeed, the bishops were now inclining to favour yet another type of clerical meeting, one directed not to intellectual improvement, but to renewing and deepening the spiritual life of the individual by withdrawing for a few days into the seminary for prayerful exercises and silent contemplation away from the hassle of parochial business. According to a pious handbook of 1750,[102] the custom was established in a number of dioceses; according to another of 1770, in all of them.[103] Some bishops attempted to coerce their clergy to attend by withholding their power to hear confessions if they did not turn up at a retreat,[104] say, every two years; this had been the rule at Rennes and later at Dol.[105] Others encouraged them by keeping down the charge for board and lodging; at Le Mans in 1780 it was only 12 livres for nine days, and at Rouen about the same time it was entirely free.[106] The threats were a device of a bygone era, and the incentives did not work well. The rule in the dioceses of Amiens and Lisieux was a retreat every three years; in 1768, the bishop of Amiens complained that few curés and vicaires obeyed, 'even though it's only for a short time and not expensive'; in 1773, some of the curés of Lisieux went to the parlement by *appel comme d'abus* to have the obligation declared illegal.[107] The use of seminaries as places of discipline had given them sinister connotations, and the silence of retreat precluded the good fellowship which the *conférences* afforded. The curés, more and more imbued with the conviction of their independent status in the Church, were not happy to have their devotional lives policed as if they were monks obliged to pray by rote.

VII

Two factors conditioned the direct contacts and relationship between a bishop and his individual parish priests: one was the independent status of the curés, the other was their social inferiority.

While the bishop had power to discipline his clergy, this was only within the limits imposed by public opinion and the ever-watchful law courts with their procedure of the *appel comme d'abus*. The curés mostly did not need to fear their bishop; nor, for the most part, were they dependent on his favour. Except in a limited number of dioceses, the bishop had few parochial benefices to bestow, and his power to veto an appointment was limited and rarely used, for this could be done only on the ground of immorality, needing solid evidence to stand up before the secular magistrates, who were sure to be invoked. Nor had a bishop much chance to offer promotion to a better parish, and thus win support by fostering a lively anticipation of benefits to come. Even when a parish was in his gift, his plans for filling it might be thwarted by the operation of the 'resignation in favour', and by definition this right was most likely to be exercised in the important well-paid cures, those most worth having.

The prelates of a few dioceses were lucky. The archbishop of

Auch had more than four-fifths of the livings in his gift. Bordeaux, Tarbes, Saintes, Lodève, and Paris provided their rulers with the influence going with about half the appointments. But it was rare for more than a third of the parishes to depend on their chief pastor. This was the proportion at Alet. At Coutances, it was only 30 out of 489, 5 out of 145 at Saint-Pol-de-Léon, 12 out of 204 at Nîmes, 15 out of 213 at Strasbourg, 135 out of 1,460 at Rouen. The city of Paris,[108] as distinct from the whole diocese, is an example of the weakness of the archbishop's control; the patronage structure reveals one of the reasons why the clergy could so often be recklessly independent. Of the fifty-seven parishes, chapters appointed to sixteen, abbeys to thirteen, the University of Paris to three, the superior of Saint-Lazare to two, and one each were in the gift of the Grand Aumônier of France, the Grand Prieur of the Temple, the Order of Malta, the Oratory, and two of the curés. The archbishop had only seventeen parishes, and five of these were minuscule, only twenty to forty houses in each. Sainte-Marine had 'all 15 parishioners church-wardens', and only continued in existence, the story went, because the curé had the right to marry pregnant girls without their parents' consent, using wedding-rings made of straw. Of the nine huge populous parishes, only Saint-Paul, Saint-Germain-l'Auxerrois, and Saint-Eustache were in episcopal patronage; the others, Saint-Côme, Saint-Nicolas-des-Champs, Saint-Laurent, Saint-Étienne-du-Mont, Saint-Gervais, and Saint-Sulpice were outside the archbishop's gift. It was all very well to expect an archbishop to extirpate Jansenism: even if he could get rid of a curé, he had little control over who would become his successor.

The line between aristocrat and commoner ran clear through the Church of France, the offices of great emolument and distinction being monopolized by nobles. Closely examined, the line is blurred, for some families, especially those 'living nobly', were difficult to place, and some offices, like canonries, might be held by priests of differing social origins, depending on the need to have a sprinkling of efficient or learned practitioners appointed on merit. But so far as bishops are concerned, they were all on one side of the line, they were aristocrats: the curés were on the other, commoners (exceptions are so few that they can be ignored). From their youth, the bishops had expected to reach their great office because of their lineage; the curés knew that, however efficient or learned they were, they could never achieve elevation to the episcopate. The collaborators chosen by the bishop to run his diocese, the *grands vicaires*, were aristocrats, serving an apprenticeship to qualify for a mitre.

True, a prelate organizing to ensure his own peace of mind would do well to have a *grand vicaire* among the others who was an expert and not on the promotion ladder, some director of a seminary, a canon grown white-haired in pastoral duties. Mostly, however, the *grands vicaires* belonged to the bishop's own class and social circle. The dividing line was sharp, and the curés naturally resented it.

Yet the resentment, at least earlier in the century, should not be exaggerated. There was a fund of deference in society, and a sense of hierarchy in the Church working towards an acceptance of things as they were. And there was a respectable argument for aristocratic leadership: the head of a diocese had to be ready to outface the great to get justice for his people and his clergy. The curé of La Tour-Saint-Gélin in the diocese of Tours was harassed by his parishioners, led by the local seigneur, over tithes and payments for certain masses. In June 1777 a letter from his archbishop, Mgr de Conzié, arrived: 'Do not fear the threats made to you—insist on payment for your masses. If they raise a dispute in this matter, I will defend you. The same with your tithe; if they refuse to pay . . . whatever repugnance you have to start a lawsuit, I order you to do so, and I will be responsible for whatever legal means you have to employ.'[109] On Maundy Thursday 1779 the curé received from his archbishop a copy of the judgment of the parlement of Paris vindicating his case; no doubt he was glad to have an influential nobleman as his master. But progressively throughout the century, the curés, led by an intelligent and fiery minority, became more and more hostile to the subversion of the principle of the brotherhood of the ministry involved in the aristocratic monopoly. 'It is notorious . . . that the order of curés is totally excluded from the rewards your majesty bestows,' said one of their *cahiers* in 1789; 'it is an outrage, an injustice—we are disinherited.'[110]

Quite apart from the social gulf between them, there were good reasons why personal contact of a fulfilling sort between bishops and curés was limited. The sheer number of parishes in the bigger dioceses and the accumulation of courtly, secular and ecclesiastical administrative duties in many more left little time available for individual interviews. Also, the ethos of the hierarchical system tended to make all the opportunities for personal contact into formal, official occasions. In the synod, and at the visitation, the parish priest was, as it were, on parade, under test; even in the discussions of the *conférences* he was treated, often enough, as an examination candidate submitting his answers. It took a bishop of a particularly understanding and friendly nature to break through the obstacles of birth and the trammels of the system. Some followed the example of Fénelon and admitted curés to their table as occasion arose, even if it meant halting conversations about the price of pigs last market-day.[111] There were paradoxes: lack of fervour did not always go with aloofness, and virtue did not necessarily mean affability. Irreligious characters like Grimaldi and lazy ones like Couet du Vivier de Lorry were charming in personal intercourse when anyone managed to see them, while conscientious prelates like Thémines and Christophe de Beaumont never entertained their clergy. What was disastrous to relationships was not so much worldliness, but aristocratic *hauteur*. Boisgelin of Aix, a good administrator and an effective diocesan, was never likely to win the hearts of the men he described in a private letter as 'coarse, scruffy, ignorant; you'd have to be a lover of pestilential odours to enjoy the society of these mediators between heaven and earth'.[112] Montmorency-Laval, bishop of Metz from 1760, was a veritable caricature of obsessive pride—setting up a chapter for noble ladies, transforming his cathedral into a sanctuary for exclusively noble canons, entertaining army officers and nobles in his country château at Frascati, with never a thought of his lower clergy. As one of them said, 'his cold disdainful reserve withered the very hearts of the curés who dared approach him'. There was an inn on the road outside his park gates which did a good trade in providing meals for the curés who had come up to see him and needed refreshment before the long ride home.[113]

VIII

Bishops were judged, above all else, by their generosity to the poor. They intervened to try to protect their people from excessive taxation. 'If the pastors do not tell you about the misery of their flocks, who ever will?' wrote Massillon to Fleury.[114] They were acting as the voice of those who were allowed no voice of their own—as a bishop of Montauban said sardonically, denouncing the capitation tax, the poor have no say in what they have to pay, 'since people of wealth and consideration are normally at the head of public affairs'.[115] They were also watchful to ensure that the poor were not deprived of any of their traditional perquisites. When the maréchal de Richelieu, inveterate theatre-goer and seducer of ballet dancers, persuaded Louis XV to divert the poor-rate levied on theatre tickets to the adornment of the Opéra and the Comédie, archbishop Christophe de Beaumont stormed to Versailles to have the decision reversed.[116] The public expected these gestures, but they also expected the bishops to be forthcoming in their personal almsgiving. Local annalists knew exactly what sums they gave—one bishop of Nîmes gave donations totalling 43,000 livres to the Miséricorde over a period of five years, and his successor had a standing subscription of 300 livres a month.[117] Every act of meanness would be recorded, as the bishop of Grenoble giving only 12 livres a year to the collection for the hospital and, after a year of absence, having the gall to say 'he had given his alms in Paris'.[118] A curé would put a lapidary observation in his parish register: 'his liberality consisted in giving his zeal to God and nothing to men'. The Jansenist *Nouvelles ecclésiastiques* had its watch-dogs everywhere, and would make an ironical comment: 'by a perfection more than evangelical, neither his right hand nor his left know anything about his alms'.[119] But it seems that most bishops attempted to do their duty, though many fitted it in uneasily with maintaining their episcopal splendour and supporting members of their family. Some did a great deal more than any possible duty, having a strict rule of almsgiving verging on the prodigal, or giving recklessly with aristocratic indifference to accountancy. Every 30 December Mgr du Tillet of Orange checked his financial position, and on 1 January gave all the surplus to his curés for distribution to the needy.[120] Christophe de Beaumont, the archbishop of Paris who did so much harm to religion by his intolerance, gave away two-thirds of his vast income: at his death, more than 1,000 ecclesiastics and 500 nuns or women who had found refuge in convents were found to be his pensioners.[121] When he won half a million livres in a lawsuit, he gave it to Mme Necker, Protestant though she was, for her work for hospitals. His successor at Paris, Juigné, gave 100,000 livres a year, and handed over a great capital sum for rebuilding the *hôtel-Dieu* after it was destroyed by fire. Cardinal Dominique de la Rochefoucauld, with the revenues of the archbishopric of Rouen and the abbey of Cluny at his disposal, was spendthrift both on display and on charity, so much so that when he fled from France during the Revolution, he had to borrow for the journey.[122] At Dol, with its limited income, Urbain d'Hercé laid out his generosity with precise, patriarchal supervision. He lived simply, having his sister for housekeeper and refusing to put his servants into livery. Some of his savings he doled out to parishes and hospitals, some went on feeding his seminarists at his table, but the most part went in accordance with his principle that the poor do not need workhouses or medical attention but simply plenty of bread, meat, and wine. He subsidized the nuns of La Sagesse to run a daily soup kitchen, and always went there in person (or sent his sister or his brother, his vicar-general) to sample the cooking. On the Monday before Ash Wednesday the soup was replaced with a feast in the palace courtyard, followed by dancing.[123] His contemporary, the bishop of Alet, was another believer in hot broth, and the poor came daily to his palace with their bowls. There were others of the same generous disposition, like La Motte of Amiens (who told a convent of nuns, 'Never forget, what is given to you has been refused to the poor') and François-Renaud de Villeneuve of Montpellier, whose funeral in 1765 was interrupted by the throng struggling for relics of their 'saint'.[124]

A bishop, even one whose charities were routinely modest or thoughtlessly intermittent, in a crisis had to live up to his station and its duties, demonstrably so. A murrain strikes the herds—the bishop buys '7,000 horned cattle' as free replacements, or he offers to pay compensation to the farmers who are being ordered to destroy their diseased animals. In a famine he distributes 1,000 loaves every Sunday, or gives a sum of money, stands guarantor for a municipal loan to bring in grain from overseas, or contracts to feed so many hundred poor. The palace might be turned into a hospital in time of plague, or thrown open as a shelter for refugees from floods.[125] In desperate emergencies, there were bishops who sold their possessions and ran into debt. When the powder magazine at Abbeville blew up wreaking devastation all around, La Motte of Amiens sold even the altar silver of his chapel, and Henri-François Desnos auctioned his dinner plate in the severe winter of 1782–3. These are individuals from whom such gestures might have been expected, but there was also Bernis, worldly diplomat rather than pastor, who borrowed 150,000 livres for the victims of the great inundation at Albi in 1766.[126] In the terrible winter of 1788–9, stories come from every diocese about episcopal leadership in relief. Juigné at Paris sold his silver, gave 300,000 livres, then borrowed another 400,000 on the credit of his brother the marquis.[127] Palaces elsewhere were thrown open, bonfires kept blazing in their courtyards, food distributions made, large sums given and loaned to municipalities, hospitals, and *bureaux de charité*. The bishops recognized the obligation of overwhelming need, even if they were slow to react to everyday deprivations. Never had the old episcopate of France appeared so generous as on the eve of its ruin.

In times of great danger, the chief pastor of a diocese was expected not only to be ready to help the victims afterwards, but to be present sharing the risks. This spirit is epitomized in the conduct of Belsunce, the prickly and intolerant bishop of Marseille, in the great

plague of 1720.[128] On 25 May, the *Grand Saint-Antoine* sailed into
harbour with a cargo of bales of cotton from the Levant; in them
lurked the fleas carrying the plague. Once the dreaded tumours were
diagnosed, the prosperous citizens, about 10,000 of them, fled to
their country retreats. At the end of July, flight was no longer
possible, for the parlement of Aix ordered the closure of all exits
from the city. A cordon of soldiers shot or clubbed to death those
who tried to break through. By August 400 a day were dying: by the
beginning of September, 1,000. The *corbeaux* (mostly galley-slaves)
who carted the bodies away to mass graves had a life expectancy of
two days. Few ventured out into the corpse-strewn streets. Doctors
went round wearing hideous parrot-head masks filled with antiseptic
perfumes, their bodies totally swathed in waxed canvas robes, fend-
ing off passers-by and dogs with ten-foot poles. Belsunce made his
palace into a hospital, and went out daily with three confessors and
his household staff, giving alms and organizing the administration of
the last rites. It was no longer possible to obtain absolution in the
churches, as their porches were stacked high with corpses. Almost
every day, the bishop lost one of his confessors; when forty had died,
he feared that he himself might perish without the sacraments. On
14 September he had to move to the mansion of the chief magistrate, since it was impossible to get in and out of his palace without
clambering over rotting bodies half-eaten by dogs. He did not use
his carriage: the only time he rode anywhere, it was said, was when
he sat beside the drivers of the carts carrying the corpses to the
burial pits. On 1 November, with half the inhabitants dead, the
plague was abating rapidly, and the bishop walked barefoot to the
church of Saint-Ferréol and preached; on 31 December he processed
round the ramparts overlooking the desolate city. The plague was
over. Belsunce was a hero, and his enemies accused him of being
self-consciously so. But he refused the proffered rewards of translation to better bishoprics. He had not deserted his people when the
pestilence walked by noonday; he would not go now for enhanced
prestige and emoluments.

In the towns, with so many narrow streets, wooden houses, piles
of rubbish, and trade and industrial premises crowded in among the
inhabitants, and the houses in the richer quarters stuffed with stocks
of grain and fuel, fire was an ever-present hazard. At the end of the
ancien régime, bishops were active in setting up *bureaux de secours*: the
curés collected funds to form their reserves, and after an outbreak of
fire the leading citizens on the committee assessed the damage and
decided what level of compensation was possible—the bishop would

normally add to it himself. But he was expected to do more. When the alarm was given, it was his duty to turn out: unless the Capuchins or other mendicants had organized themselves as the fire brigade, there would be no professional expertise available, and not every city had gone to the expense of buying pumps. It was a question of forming a bucket chain, knocking down burning roofs and walls, and setting guards against looters. When a conflagration was out of control, the grim decision to demolish neighbouring houses to make a fire break might have to be taken. Leadership was needed, and exhortations to courage.[129] In the inferno that destroyed the whole centre of Rennes in December 1720, the soldiers of the garrison and townspeople were standing in despair; the bishop, the intendant, and a few leading citizens donned leather jackets and clogs to make symbolic efforts to beat out the flames as an example. On 30 December 1784, at a fire in Orange, Mgr du Tillet joined the bucket chain (and later made good all the losses suffered). Three bishops at least are recorded as heroes. Jarente, the morally dubious courtier who held the *feuille des bénéfices* during the ministry of Choiseul, had earlier, as bishop of Digne, led a fire-fighting foray. Juigné at Châlons performed a rescue at the risk of his life. When a child was shouting for help from a blazing building, Mgr d'Apchon of Dijon called on the bystanders to help, offering 100 louis as a reward. This was 2,000 livres, four times the annual wage of a skilled artisan, but there were no takers. So the bishop rushed in and brought out the child himself. It was a splendidly aristocratic performance. He demonstrated the valour of his class, but it was not for him to soil his hands with a menial heroic task if the lower orders would do it for money.

There was a general inquest into a bishop's fulfilment of his duty to the poor when the content of his last will and testament became known. During his life, there had been the conflicting demands of obligations to family and obligations to charity—now there was a final revelation where the priority lay. According to Le Camus, bishop of Grenoble, famous for pastoral zeal and tolerance to Huguenots, the laws of the Church required a bishop to give back to his family what he had received from it, and to the Church and to the poor whatever he had saved from his ecclesiastical revenues. In accordance with this principle he left his immense private fortune of over 1,000,000 livres to his two brothers and nephews and nieces; this left only 50,000 livres for other legacies, though in mitigation Le Camus noted that in his lifetime he had given 472,000 livres for ecclesiastical objects, mainly in repairs to his palace and country house.[130] A later bishop of Grenoble, Jean de Caulet, who died in 1771, left virtually everything, including his magnificent library, to his nephew the marquis de Grammont; the town hospital received only 1,000 livres. The city raised a subscription to buy the library, and the marquis did the decent thing and let it go at the cut price of 40,000 livres.[131] Another great family man was Cardinal Tencin, who left everything to his sister. The rectors of the hospital of Lyon threw on to the junk heap the marble bust of their late archbishop which they had commissioned in the hope of enlisting his gratitude.[132] Dubois, the minister of the regent, had built up an annual income which Saint-Simon estimated to have totalled 1,500,000 livres a year (including his bribes from England). His vast inheritance descended to his nephew, a canon, who gave it all to the poor, retaining only a sum of money to pay for a marble tomb for his uncle in the church of Saint-Honoré (the sculptor, perhaps maliciously, showed Dubois turned away from the altar, looking suspiciously towards the door).[133]

But Le Camus, in the interest of family, had distorted the 'laws of the Church'. They did not recommend the giving of a private fortune back to the family; they simply allowed it. The true ideal, the one which would ensure the psalmist's 'peace at the last', was to prefer the poor, to prefer them even to worthy ecclesiastical objects. Fléchier and Fénelon, who helped their nephews during life, made it clear to them that they could not expect anything by inheritance.[134] The examples of bishops who died nepotists to the last are outweighed by those who preferred pious works and the poor to the interests of their heirs. 'The *bureau des pauvres* is my universal legatee. I ask, indeed I order, that I be given a simple pauper's burial,' declared a bishop of Beauvais. An archbishop of Rouen forbade all adornments and armorial bearings on his tomb, and left all he possessed to his seminary of Saint-Louis, the refuge for the aged and infirm priests of his diocese.[135] A bishop of Châlons left 180,000 livres, only 10,000 of it to his relatives.[136] Of the rulers of the see of Lombez, Cône Roger, dying in 1710 at the age of 95, left everything to the hospital and the seminary. Charles de Maupeou, dying in 1751, left little, but all to the hospital. Jacques Richier de Cérisy, dying twenty years later, had made a judiciously balanced testament: relatives got 24,000 livres, his executor 3,000 livres; masses for his soul to the tune of 300 livres were ordered; his servants got 5,800; convents of nuns 6,900; the chapters of Rouen and Lombez 3,500 each; the cathedral 3,000 for ornaments; the schools of his diocese 2,000; the poor of his native place 1,600; the poor of Lombez 4,200; with a sum of 300 for such paupers as walked in his funeral procession. It was a suitable will for a Christian of the century: not too much on masses, fair to the relatives but not pampering them, reasonable to both ecclesiastical institutions and the poor. Perhaps, by the standards of the Enlightenment, there should have been more to the servants—Cardinal Charles-Antoine de la Roche-Aymon, archbishop of Reims, who left virtually everything to hospitals, was criticized for leaving only a year's wages to his staff. Alas! what Richier de Cérisy had not considered was his solvency. As so often happened, when his effects were realized, there was not enough money available, and all the legacies had to be halved.

No doubt one day historians will make a statistical analysis of all the testamentary dispositions of the bishops throughout the century. The final picture will be revealing, a comparative demonstration of how relatives, servants, pious works, ecclesiastical foundations and the poor were treated. Even so, conclusions as to the character and piety of individuals will not be easy to draw. Other disparate factors will have to be weighed. It was a precept of the casuists, especially the Jansenists, that almsgiving during life was more effective for salvation than distributions after death, so what had already been given must be set alongside the last gifts of all. For some, family obligations were overwhelming, for others, unimportant or already fulfilled. Some episcopal revenues were large, some very limited. And human nature is full of paradoxes. What of Cardinal de Gesvres, archbishop of Bourges, a notorious miser who for long had lived as a recluse, indifferent to what happened in his diocese? In 1744, at the age of 88 he died, leaving a huge fortune, including 293,000 livres cash in his coffers, and a store of gold. His will specified that it was all to go, in the first place, to fulfil his repairing obligations, then to endow the seminary and hospital, while his library was bequeathed to Saint-Germain-des-Prés. His relatives were to have his silver plate—nothing more.[137]

A minority of bishops had a saintly attitude towards wealth, being generous and charitable in the extreme. By contrast, a minority was generous only to immediate family. The majority between accepted their incomes and all the extras of pensions and abbeys, however excessive, without self-questioning, as their bounded right, and they spent profusely, whether in palace building, display, supporting relatives, or in charity; in a crisis, they would make spectacular charitable contributions. They did not doubt their own right to monopolize the great offices of the Church, and only late in the century did they take serious notice of the idea that they ought to pay ordinary taxation. They did not identify with the demand of the rising middle classes for careers open to talent and taxation fairly imposed on all. When they proclaimed the egalitarian commonplaces of gospel eloquence, as they did in sermons and pastorals, their favourite idea was the need to sympathize with those who had no property but their labour, nothing to sustain them but the sweat of their brows. They believed in their own privileges, and counterbalanced this complacency by taking up the cause of the disinherited. Theirs was an aristocratic attitude to wealth, tempered with Christian idealism, but motivated more by pride. In the early days of the Revolution, when ecclesiastical wealth was under universal scrutiny, a few of the bishops, the saints, were willing to abandon the greater part of it. In a pastoral of 7 March 1789 Tillet proposed ordinary taxation for all and the confiscation of two-thirds of the revenues of bishoprics and abbeys for five years to avoid any increase of tax burdens on the people. Men are equal, he said; 'we have the same Father in heaven, we are all descended from the same family tree, the same sun lights our path, we all descend equally into the tomb and we all appear before the same Judge'. Most of his colleagues, without such dramatic renunciations, refused to fight for their revenues: when they finally challenged the National Assembly, it was on an issue of principle, the right of the Church to be consulted about changes in its government. No doubt there was an element of instinctive tactical thinking in their conduct, but it corresponds to their aristocratic attitude to wealth: they accepted money without shame and spent it without restraint, but they were too proud to haggle about it.

10

PARISHES

I

By the eighteenth century, the parish boundaries of France had ceased to correspond to social realities and pastoral needs—in so far as they had ever done so. In towns, the population was illogically distributed. The migration of labour into a peripheral urban area had inflated one parish of Angers to 11,000 inhabitants, and one of Nantes to 25,000, whereas some of the others in these two cities had only a few hundred.[1] In Paris, Saint-Gervais, Saint-Merry, Saint-Paul, and Saint-Côme each had between 20,000 and 30,000 communicants; Saint-Étienne-du-Mont had 80,000, and Saint-Sulpice 90,000; by contrast, Saint-Opportune had 120, and Saint-Jean-de-Latran a few dozen.[2] There were great disparities in the extent of rural parishes. Though by law ten houses was the minimum, there were still official parishes in 1789 consisting of one or two houses alongside the presbytery;[3] some consisted of a mere hamlet and its fields; some were huge. A writer in the *Mercure géographique* in 1678 described examples in Brittany measuring five leagues by four, containing numbers of villages and twenty or more chapels apart from the main church. 'Each of these parishes has the aspect of a little province,' he says; 'the inhabitants speak of them as if they were separate and individual *pays*. Just as we talk of provinces, saying "in Brittany", "in Anjou", they say "in Quarantoy", "in Guer", "in Pimpoint".'[4]

Disparities in population and area were not the only illogicalities. Parish churches were rarely conveniently central—they might be on the very circumference. Perhaps two would stand right next to each other, as at Sablé, where the churches of Saint-Martin and of Notre-Dame were at opposite ends of a bridge over the river, with disputes about the ownership of the bridge and about sermons being interrupted by the peals of alien bells.[5] Boundaries zigzagged and curved. Here and there a parish had an enclave in the middle of another. In Paris, Saint-Étienne-du-Mont had enclaves at the Luxembourg and the Hôtel de Cluny, and Saint-Merry had the chapel of Jean-

Baptiste-de-Belleville, three kilometres away. The first accurate ecclesiastical map of the capital, drawn up on the orders of the archbishop in 1786, was said to reveal 'une mosaïque invraisemblable'.[6] Here, the explanation was that the boundaries were those of the medieval seigneuries of ecclesiastical institutions: distance had not hampered rent collecting as it did pastoral ministrations. But there could be more elevated explanations, as at Moulins, where the parish of Saint-Bonnet outside the walls had jurisdiction over a chapel and the houses around it in town, because in 1635 the curé had ventured there to minister to the plague-stricken.[7] In some places, the borderline between parishes was in dispute. In others, a dispute had been settled by the device of the '*alternatif*': a farm or hamlet would come under one curé in one year and under the other the next. Of the 274 parishes in the archdeaconry of Autun, thirty-eight had alternating areas on their boundaries—two had as many as six each, and in a few cases the rotation was among three parishes rather than two. Take-over date (generally on the feast of St Michael on 29 September or of St Martin on 11 November) was a time of pastoral confusion. In 1689, the curés alleged serious long-term effects, the folk concerned being 'like lost souls, without religion or fear of God'.[8] Another sort of alternation, less deadly to souls but vexing to bishops, was that of parishes oscillating between dioceses—as between Limoges and Périgueux.[9] Another variant of these cumbrous compromises was the system found in Normandy, of having more than one curé ruling in a parish. There is an example of three of them, each with his own sector to administer, with the supreme authority rotating at fortnightly intervals. In a parish under the bishop of Lisieux, there were four coequal parish priests, and the general statistics of that diocese showed the—at first sight—mysterious figures of 489 parishes and 522 curés.[10] Old disputes had been settled by creating a legacy of confusion for the future.

In some rural areas, traditional boundaries took no account of the difficulties of the terrain: curés might have to visit their people across marshes, ravines, or rivers. In those days of sudden floods and ill-repaired bridges, a river was regarded as the most sinister obstacle; a *cahier* of 1789 from Périgord, proposing reorganization, asked 'that no parish should extend to the far side of a river, for crossing is an inevitable cause of fatal accidents, whether to the pastors or to the parishioners'.[11] Another source of confusion was the way in which secular boundaries sometimes cut across ecclesiastical ones. The parish of La Tour Saint-Gélin was partly in the province of Touraine and partly in Poitou, with all its inhabitants claiming they were in

Poitou, as the *gabelle*, the odious salt tax, did not operate there.[12] The intendancy of Montauban was unique in that its 1,411 parishes and 1,179 village communities were separate entities, with the added complication that communities sometimes overlapped each other. The extreme cases at the ends of the spectrum were a parish which included seventeen communities as against a community including sixteen parishes. In 1782, an attempt was made to put all administrative business into the pattern of the parochial units, but with little success. Two years later, the intendant confessed that he was still baffled.[13] Not all these cross-divisions were inherited from distant times. In 1784–5, in their war against smuggling, the Farmers General of the taxes built a wall round Paris linking up the gates where customs duties were levied, cheerfully bisecting various parishes as they did so.[14]

Ecclesiastical reformers lamented the chaotic parochial structure, more especially in the towns, and exercised their ingenuity in plans for unions and separations. Sometimes they succeeded. In Paris, eight new parishes, mainly peripheral, were created in the seventeenth century, and three in the eighteenth.[15] There were two new creations in the diocese of Nîmes in 1772–3, and two in that of Boulogne in 1787.[16] But these were piecemeal tinkerings, the best that could be done in the circumstances. It was difficult to find new endowments. As ever, tithe owners would resist new burdens, and curés on modest incomes would rather stay overworked than be rescued by a reform that left them underpaid. When the bishop of Bayonne in 1776 ordered the separation of two villages which for long had coexisted uneasily within one parish, he felt constrained to add the proviso that the ruling would not come into effect until the pension of 600 livres paid by the curé to his predecessor was extinguished.[17] Local demands for reform would be countered by local objections to new expenditure. Though the bishop was not obliged to wait on anyone's consent, he had to hold a legal enquiry *de commodo et incommodo*, at which evidence was presented by interested parties.[18] The bishop of Oloron held such an enquiry in 1745 to consider the application of the hamlet of Sarrance, site of a prestigious pilgrim sanctuary, to be separated from the parish of Bedous. He decided that a new church must be built at Sarrance, and the intendant ordered a local levy of 3 livres a barrel of wine for twelve years to help to pay for it. The innkeepers were enraged, the owner of the proposed site refused to sell it, and the architect produced impossible plans. In the end, in 1760, the new church of Sarrance was consecrated, with the ruling that the curé of Bedous was to send a vicaire there to officiate, but that Easter communions and weddings were to be confined to the parish church. This system was unpopular, and in 1780 the inhabitants of Sarrance again asked to have a curé of their own. Another investigation *de commodo et incommodo* ensued, the petitioners having to pay more than 300 livres in expenses to a vicar-general, a legal official, and a clerk. The bishop decided to create the new parish, its pastor to be paid by the deduction of 500 livres a year from the tithes of Bedous. The curé refused to pay, and appealed to the secular courts, alleging that the whole independence movement at Sarrance had been inspired by the local family of Castéra plotting to create a new benefice which, in fact, had fallen to one of its sons. But by 1785, the incumbent of Bedous had lost his case, and the new parish became a reality at his expense.[19] A longer battle, lasting for more than a century, was waged to create the new parish of Boutonnet on the outskirts of Montpellier. The people of this village, it was argued in 1650, were in danger of dying without the sacraments, since they were far distant from the parish church and the city gates were locked at night. The cathedral chapter of Saint-Pierre held up progress until 1750, when a pastoral visitation by the bishop revealed that the population, recorded as 500 at an enquiry in 1687, had reached 1,500. At this point, the chapter gave way, but the seigneur took over the opposition role, as the site proposed for the new church was outside his seigneurie. Another site was chosen, but the cathedral chapter rejected it. And so it went on, until the revolutionary reorganization of the Church, when the new parish was created by annexing the chapel of the Récollets for general worship.[20] It took the Revolution, confiscating ecclesiastical property, abolishing tithes, instituting State salaries for the clergy, and replacing the rights of patrons by election, to make the redrawing of the old parochial boundaries possible.

II

By a deduction from the main technical terms in use, one might imagine that the parish in eighteenth-century France had a logical and effective administrative structure. There was the *assemblée générale* (the parish council, as it were), which was the final authority. It might well have an inner committee meeting more frequently, the *bureau ordinaire*. The executive officer was the *marguillier* (church-warden); his task was to pay the bills incurred in keeping the church and its services going, and to collect and administer the revenues of the parish, legally embodied in a corporate institution, the *fabrique* (vestry). This broad picture has its validity, but the detailed reality almost defies description by its complexity.

The responsibility of the assembly was defined by Potier de la Germondaye in his *Introduction au gouvernement des paroisses* (1777). (He uses the term 'général' for the assembly, as that was the customary title in Brittany, the province with which he was especially concerned.) 'Temporal government', he says, 'has as its objective the administration of the property and revenues of the *fabrique*, repairs to the church, the provision of vestments, books and sacred vases, and of all that is necessary for the celebration of divine service. This government is confided to the *général* of the parish.'[21] 'Général' and 'assemblée générale' have a democratic ring, but the trend of the century, especially in the towns, was to exclude ordinary people. Guyot's legal dictionary says that the general assembly (to be held twice a year) should consist only of 'persons of consideration'— nobles, judicial officers, *avocats*, ex-churchwardens, the solid citizens who are in charge of distributions to the poor, and notables (defined as inhabitants paying from 12 to 15 livres a year to the *taille* or the *capitation* taxes).[22]

He based his enumeration on formal decisions of the parliament of Paris for parishes in Orléans and in Nogent-sur-Marne in 1762 and 1763. He could equally have cited Angers, where the municipal officers, troubled by a caucus of the lower orders in their official parish of Saint-Michel du Tertre, obtained a 'wise regulation' of the parlement of Paris to exclude them. In 1766, the parish of Saint-Julien followed suit in adopting this oligarchical constitution, and by an ordinance of 1786, the parlement made it general for the whole of Anjou.[23] Early in the century, the magistrates of Brittany had limited the *général* to seventeen members, all legal officers and notables,[24] and those of Toulouse had imposed similar limitations later.[25] Even so, in some places, there were well-attended meetings. A town parish might boast many of the great within its boundaries; on 5 April 1778 at Saint-Gervais in Paris there were fifty-five present, including two *présidents* and two *conseillers* of the parlement, one of the *chambre des comptes*, three marquises, two counts, seven army officers, six *avocats*, nine doctors, one merchant, and d'Hozier, the court genealogist.[26] Conversely, in rural France a tendency to democratic attendance remained, if only because peasant villages could not throw up the galaxy of official talent which the regulations of the parlements prescribed.

Questions of eligibility to attend were complicated, because there were two other kinds of assembly in addition to that of the ecclesiastical parish; often enough, no distinction of any kind was made, but sometimes they were separate. In the village, the *grands jours* of the seigneurie might still be held, called together by the lord's legal officer; here, regulations about chimney sweeping and fire precautions were announced, and dates were prescribed for the beginning of harvesting, and appointments made to communal jobs like cowherd and goatherd. In many places in Burgundy, this meeting was separate from that of the ecclesiastical parish—a churchwarden, for example, would be described as having been elected 'à l'issue des grands jours'—that is, immediately after the seigneurial assembly had ended.[27] It was this separation of assemblies which one Bertrand was appealing to in 1738 in a dispute in the village of Pouilly (seventy-six houses). He accused the seigneurial legal officer of 'surprising' the assembly by introducing a proposal to finance improvements to a chapel, since, properly speaking, such a matter ought only to have been raised at an assembly held in the church. He was fined 10 livres for 'contempt', increased to 15 when he said 'Metté vingt'.[28] The other kind of assembly was one of all the inhabitants—the sort of gathering Sully had in mind when, early in the seventeenth century, he ordered the planting of two elm trees near church doors to give shade to its deliberations.[29] In Angers, the municipality called for meetings in the parishes to review the names of candidates for municipal office, to elect deputies to attend at the town hall when the new officers were installed, and to give an opinion on proposals for innovations which would affect the pockets of citizens, like the installation of street lamps or the founding of an orphanage.[30] In the North, around Cambrai and Lille, custom excluded the curé from any part in these gatherings.[31] In Lille, he was also excluded from the magistracy, and in 1699 the city fathers went so far as to try to prevent him concerning himself with official charity—'the curés ought to apply themselves principally to know the consciences of their parishioners rather than enquiring about their temporal necessities'.[32] In the diocese of Tarbes, the *assemblée générale* was the common gathering for the affairs of both the ecclesiastical parish and the community, and hence all householders were entitled to attend.[33] Elsewhere in the countryside the numbers present were sometimes high enough to show that the concept of wide involvement carried on; more especially there was a presumption that all householders could attend in matters involving the levy of a heavy rate.

Assemblies everywhere tend to do detailed work through committees, and, generally in parishes of some importance, the device of using a *bureau ordinaire* was becoming more frequent in the eighteenth century.[34] The parlement of Paris, at the request of various parishes, issued *arrêts* of authorization—for Saint-Jean-en-Grève in 1737, for Saint-Germain-en-Laye in 1739, for Nemours in 1763; the parlement of Rouen did the same for its whole area of jurisdiction in 1751. The usual formula for membership was the curé, the churchwardens and ex-wardens, and, in country areas, the seigneur. Meetings were generally to be fortnightly. In 1774, the curé of Givry-sur-Aine replied to a questionnaire of his bishop concerning the *bureau de fabrique*. Attending, he said, were himself, the warden in office, and three ex-wardens; the other parishioners did not want to come to the meetings (he implies that they could), but if a difficult decision was to be made, 'we ask those from whom we expect good advice and they come along'.[35] Regulations published by the government on 25 June 1787 proposed to systematize this arrangement and to get rid of lingering elements of democracy in the composition of the assemblies. The *assemblée générale* was to consist of the inhabitants paying at least 10 livres in taxation, and it was to set up a *conseil* of from three to nine members, with the curé and seigneur being there *ex officio*.[36]

In the parish assembly the curé had the place of honour and signed first, but the chief *marguillier* presided and had the casting vote.[37] The parish priest was not supposed to write the minutes or to have custody of them; if he made a proposal, he had to retire while it was discussed,[38] and meetings were to be held in the church or some other official place, and not in the presbytery.[39] Manifestly, in poor and illiterate communities, these rules were unlikely to be observed. The assembly was supposed to elect the churchwardens and officers to take charge of poor relief, and to appoint sacristans and schoolmasters; it approved the accounts and any unusual expenditure, and accepted foundation masses (provided the curé also agreed). The wardens or the *bureau* dealt with seating, burials, leases, invitations to visiting preachers, and other detailed matters.[40] From 1759 to 1782 the assembly of Saint-Pierre de Montsort in the province of Maine voted money to supplement the miserable yield of collections to support the vicaire and pay fees to visiting preachers, took over the repairs to the choir from the curé in return for his seating fees, suppressed pews and introduced chairs, arranged for paving the church floor and having the bell recast, and argued with the curé over church furnishings and the salaries of the sacristan and the vergers. This was a parish with well-attended meetings, as many as fifty people recorded as present on one occasion, and dissentients allowed to record their opposition: 'Je signe le présent, qui est que je m'oppose.'[41]

As we might imagine, discussion tended to centre on how to avoid spending money. The parish of Notre-Dame de Vitré, where the people were particularly mean towards their clergy, was confronted in 1776 with an expensive problem. The new curé, Béchu, was a giant, and no rochet or surplice in the sacristy would fit him. Gloomily, the *général* resigned itself to buying new ones, but imposed economy by ruling that linen would henceforward be provided for Sundays and high festivals only. Béchu scored by moving elsewhere two years later. The assembly tried to persuade him to buy the new vestments at current prices; if not, there was nothing for it but to have them made into surplices for choirboys.[42]

III

Every parish had a churchwarden responsible for the administration of its corporate property and revenues and for paying the costs of maintaining the church and its liturgical observances out of the proceeds. There might be from one to four wardens, but the actual handling of the money was always the responsibility of a single one of them. In theory, the parish assembly elected the wardens,[43] but where the assembly was not an oligarchy already, the right to vote was usually limited to 'notables' and higher taxpayers. Sometimes the *bureau* appointed, sometimes the outgoing man nominated his successor, sometimes the seigneur of the place had the dominant voice;[44] there were places where the curé said who it would be and that was an end to it.[45] In the diocese of Tarbes, the municipal officers, the *consuls*, succeeded to the wardenship when their tour of secular duty was over; the parlement of Toulouse wanted to make this a general rule within the area of its jurisdiction, but at least one bishop (Mirepoix) forbade it.[46] Given the method of selection and the desirability of literacy, numeracy, and solvency, churchwardens were taken from the more prosperous reaches of society; in towns, notaries, *procureurs*, and merchants are often found. The Parisian parish of Saint-Leu-Saint-Gilles always had four wardens in office, one a magistrate and three from the bourgeoisie, and there was a specific rule that no one exercising a mechanical art was eligible.[47] The financial status of the *marguilliers* of Saint-Médard may be deduced from the custom which constrained them to give a gift of 200 livres to the church on their retirement; the new pulpit installed in 1718 was paid for by six such contributions.[48] By contrast, in poverty-stricken rural areas the parish was lucky to find anyone remotely qualified to serve. If there was such a person, he might well hold office for life in default of a replacement. There were places where a single individual, for meagre fees, was cleaner, organ-blower, bell-ringer, gardener, and grave-digger, and was saddled with the responsibility of *marguillier* as well.[49] In the Auvergne, these comprehensive duties were not infrequently allotted to a woman—a *bailleresse*—until in 1768 the parlement of Paris forbade the practice.[50]

A churchwarden undertook a time-consuming job fraught with financial perils: a sensible man would try to evade it. When Louis XIV put up offices for sale, this was one for which he found no takers.[51] With the usual injustice of the *ancien régime*, nobles were exempt, though in great town parishes like Saint-Gervais at Paris they might condescend to accept the title of *marguillier d'honneur* and give aloof and dignified protection.[52] Exempt too were soldiers, *avocats*, and the holders of certain official posts. Anyone who had served as *marguillier comptable* (financially responsible warden) was entitled to refuse to accept a further term of office, even if he had moved to another parish.[53] Assemblies would resort to legal summonses to compel some recalcitrant citizen to serve, while the nominated victim would try to escape by producing medical certificates[54] or purchasing an office conferring exemption. The *général* of a Breton parish bitterly minuted of such a draft-dodger that he was far from being the most meritorious candidate and that they assumed that 'le sieur Lorin ne s'est pas trouvé digne de servir à l'église'.[55]

On the other hand, there were those who volunteered to be churchwardens—a few out of piety or public spirit, but most out of pride. To walk immediately after the clergy in processions, often preceding even the officers of justice, to appoint lay employees like vergers, choristers, *suisses*, and ringers, to name Lent and Advent preachers, draw up the roster of inhabitants for presenting the *pain bénit*, to talk about leases and investments with local bigwigs—all this made a man important and affirmed that he had arrived.[56] This was the decisive stage in the ascension of a *coq du village*: 'having been the accounting warden (*trésorier*), he's immediately named as *syndic* (the chief lay representative of the village); then he crowns his pate with an ample wig, swells proudly in his pew, argues over sacristy matters, persuading himself that the nave belongs to him more than to other parishioners, because he pays more than others towards its repairs'.[57]

A *marguillier* needed the consent of an assembly to spend more than a limited sum (generally 10 livres).[58] Cash and valuables were kept in a box in the sacristy with two or three locks: the warden, the curé, and, maybe, the seigneur's legal official kept the keys. These arrangements were well known to thieves, so any considerable sum in hand would be loaned out among solvent parishioners rather than hoarded. In 1776, the parlement of Rennes ordered parishes to have a man bedded down in the sacristy at night, ready to ring the bells if he was awoken by intruders. Accounts were supposed to be rendered to the assembly and, if notice was given, to the bishop or archdeacon when they came on visitation. Satisfactory records of receipts and expenditure were hard to come by. 'What I collected I put into a single pocket and when I paid out I took it from the same pocket'—an effective system which did not lend itself to documentation. A parish might put up with financial informalities if there was no one else capable of taking over, but if there were ex-wardens who had successfully given an account of their stewardship in the past, they would be sure to lead the clamour in the assembly for the 'verification' of their successors' accounts.[59] So too if parishioners had noticed any frivolous expenditure: *marguilliers* were not granted any entertainment allowance for 'collations and bottles'.

Relations between churchwardens and parish priests were better than might have been expected, perhaps because the lawyers had drawn the boundaries between spiritual and secular in parochial affairs with a fair degree of precision. The administration of the revenues of the *fabrique* was 'a purely lay and temporal affair'.[60] So too was the allocation of seating in the nave. Church furnishings were generally controlled by the laity; a curé, for example, could not exchange an old crucifix for a new one without permission.[61] On the other hand, the content of the liturgical services was the curé's affair; Saint-Germain-l'Auxerrois was unique in having the churchwardens prescribing the prayers to be said when the Holy Sacrament was exposed in a particular ciborium.[62] In some dioceses, there was disagreement about the *marguillier*'s oath on taking office, the synod ruling that it was to be said in the presence of the curé, the Gallican lawyers denouncing the practice.[63]

There were also disputes about the appointment and disciplining of the minor functionaries who assisted at the liturgical offices— sacking a choirboy or a verger could be a sensational affair in the depths of provincial France.[64] The tough tanners and tilers of the Parisian parish of Saint-Médard, deprived of their Jansenist curé, waged war against his successor, more particularly refusing to pay for

the *suisse* he had appointed to precede him in processions and protect him from insult. The churchwardens took the affair to the
Grand Conseil and won, and when a royal *lettre de cachet* reversed the
verdict, they went back to the Grand Conseil again.[65] The other
great cause of disagreement was the control of charitable distributions. The tensions found in many parishes are evident on a bigger
scale at Saint-Gervais in Paris from 1761, when the curé François
Feu died at the age of 90 after a reign of over sixty years. The
churchwardens were then free to speak out and demand the
appointment of a *trésorier des pauvres*. Up to then, the curé had dominated the pious lady who ran the general charitable fund and the
committee in charge of aid to poor families, while keeping in
his own hands the giving of alms to the 'pauvres honteux', the
respectable folk who did not wish anyone to know of their plight.
To ensure his control, Feu had abstracted from the parish archives
the documents concerning the legacies and other funds available for
charity. 'There will be general surprise', said his will, 'at finding in
my files a number of contracts in favour of the poor . . . Precautions
to safeguard their interests are good. God will enlighten my successor on this point, which is delicate.' His successor, indeed, carried
on as before. The wardens challenged the legality of the 'so-called
charitable assembly' he defiantly called in April 1773. The whole dispute went to the parlement, ending in 1780 with the curé being
awarded 2,000 livres legal costs against the parish.[66] There was a
growing desire among the laity to have a greater say in parochial
affairs—at least, so it seemed to the archbishop of Paris, who in 1772
complained to the Assembly of Clergy about the *marguilliers* who
ousted curés from their rights in the distribution of alms and in
the nomination of ecclesiastics to employment in churches. 'Such a
manner of proceeding', he said, 'is imperceptibly building up the lay
and secular power in the temporal administration of parishes upon
the ruins of ecclesiastical authority.'[67]

IV

The property and revenues of a parish church were corporately
embodied in the *fabrique*. This was an independent body, protected
by the law courts from the interference of bishops[68] and, like the
clergy, exempt from ordinary taxation, but paying dues levied on the
acquisition of new property.[69] Revenue came from diverse sources.
There would be small parcels of land—meadows, fields, enclosures,

houses—acquired higgledy-piggledy over the years from pious legacies.[70] Money bequeathed to pay for masses would be loaned out or invested with the Clergy of France. In some places, the curé had to hand over to the *fabrique* a portion of his tithe levies.[71] The pious made gifts in kind—a piglet or some flax; a lady would hand over a silk dress to make a new chasuble.[72] Collections[73] taken at church services or at the door yielded miserable sums, except where, as in Paris, Mercier saw pretty girls taking round the plate preceded by the *suisse* insistently banging his pike butt on the floor.[74] Door to door collecting, which yielded more, needed legal permission. The *troncs*, the offertory boxes in churches, were prominently displayed but brought in little, so that in some parishes the wardens did not bother to open them for years. Whatever could be put up for sale was sold—nuts or fruit growing in the cemetery, worn linen, posts of honour in confraternities, candle wax left over after ceremonies.[75] The *fabrique* owned 'ornaments' which were hired out to families for funerals—20 sols for silver candlesticks to take to the house and other small sums for candelabra on the altar, a black pall to cover the coffin, 'noms de Jésus' and 'têtes de mort'. There were special fees to pay for a burial space within the church building, and lesser fees for places outside, separate from the common burial pit.[76]

The living, like the dead, had to pay differential fees for their accommodation. Rents were charged for private pews, and chairs were hired out, usually through a contractor. The law looked after the interests of the poor, since the contractor had to leave standing room for those who were not his clients, and he was forbidden to charge for the parish mass on Sunday mornings.[77] In country places, seating revenue would be small, since pews were not expensive (maybe 3 livres entry fee and an annual payment of 3 sous a place), and few would wish to pay for a chair. In important town parishes, however, the income might be considerable, from 800 livres in the richest parish of Angers to 18,000 livres in a major Parisian one like Saint-Merry.[78] Official pews were limited to the *seigneur haut justicier* and the patron and, in a city, to the municipal officers in the parish where the town hall was situated (they were entitled to have the mayoral accommodation painted blue and adorned with fleurs-de-lis). Otherwise, the churchwardens disposed entirely of pew space; when a life concessionaire died, they were entitled—nay, obliged—to auction the amenity, though in the event of a tied bid, the heirs ought to have precedence.[79] In theory, there was no priority for nobles. The writer of a legal treatise applauded the system of the highest bidder: 'if people have to fight it out with hard cash, the

Church profits thereby, and he who is defeated by money alone will not consider himself vanquished so far as his honour is concerned.'[80] In practice, such philosophical resignation to defeat was rare. In 1727, the duc d'Uzès was trying to evict the municipal officers from their pew in the cathedral and put his own arms and livery upon it; in 1729 a wine-grower of Cormeilles sued the wardens for a pew which, he said, had always gone along with the house he had just purchased.[81] Frauds over payment were frequent. Families would rent pew space, then quietly expand it; others brazenly moved in without authorization, and might even rent to others the privilege they had usurped; others engraved fictitious names on the wood-work to evade payment, or moved the whole contraption out when payment time came round, then moved it back afterwards.[82]

Abuses of this sort, and the rising tide of sentimentality and theoretical egalitarianism, helped to make pews unpopular, but there was a more decisive argument against them: if the space was turned over to a contractor to hire out chairs, the income could be doubled.[83] In the royal parish of Notre-Dame at Versailles, in 1749, chairs yielded 8,000 livres, pews 1,143 livres, and as the latter belonged to some of the greatest in the land, change seemed impossible. But in 1753, the king authorized a reform of ruthless illegality, and on the night of 9–10 July the pews were carted away. 'Je ne comprends rien de cette destruction,' complained the duc de Luynes who had been paying 50 livres a year for his privilege. The parish did well, financially at least, out of the change; in 1778, the chairs yielded 13,000 livres.[84] The parish of Saint-Leu-Saint-Gilles in Paris followed suit a year later, once more with a nocturnal clearance. Only a stealthy *fait accompli* could avoid the lamentations and obstructions of influential families with their lackeys and attendant lawyers' clerks and notaries.[85]

Normally, the income from endowments and seating, charges for the 'ornaments' and for burials, and the yield of collections and boxes and pious donations sufficed to pay the expenses of the liturgical offices. Candles, books, linen, and vestments were needed; in some places the tithe owner had obligations in these respects, though the churchwardens were not always able to enforce them. The chief expense, however, would be the payment of employees. In those days of ecclesiastical wealth, no one performed an ecclesiastical function without being paid for it. Calculations were made with some precision: in 1735 the *porte-bannière* of Saint-Merry at Paris had his yearly wage raised from 4 livres, 10 sols, to 9 livres, because the new banner was heavier than the old.[86] A wealthy town parish would

employ a swarm of officials. The chief would be the sacristan, probably an ecclesiastic. In charge of the altar silver (depositing caution
money against loss or damage) and of the registers, and exercising
general oversight, sacristans were notoriously self-important. The
parish of Toussaint in Rennes had one who was too superior to
decorate the altars himself, a task which he delegated to his servant;
he ruled the church with a rod of iron, and demonstrated his power
by deliberately locking the churchwarden in the vestry.[87] Vergers
(*bedeaux, bâtonniers, massiers*) wore black gowns when on duty, and
bore wands of office when escorting the faithful to their places in
church and handbells when escorting them on their last journey to
the cemetery; they took round notices of parish assemblies and
morsels of the *pain bénit* to distinguished citizens; they might have
sweeping and ringing obligations and act as agents for the hire of
chairs, as well as such other duties as their contracts might prescribe
('mettre les draps mortuaires à sécher dans le cimetière' being a
curious instance).[88] The archetypal verger was at once pompous and
decrepit, since he was likely to hang on in office as long as his legs
would support him. By contrast, the *suisse* had to be a fine upstand-
ing figure, his uniform and halberd giving him a military air—the
suisse of Saint-Eustache became a general in the revolutionary
armies.[89] The bell-ringers, the *corbeaux* who bore the dead to their
graves, and the *fossoyeurs* who dug them were typecast in a different
fashion, as being addicted to alcoholic refreshment; the ringers had
to slake their thirst, the bearers clearly needed cheering up, and the
diggers qualified under both headings. Organists were a superior
category of employee, though they were rarely generously paid—
hence the common complaint that they wore out the instrument in
supplementing their income by teaching children to play and allowing unqualified adults to experiment, 'useless characters who fool
around with the keyboard and the bellows, stir up a great cloud of
dust and ruin the stops'.[90] As an alternative to an organist, a parish
might hire a player of the serpent, apparently an effective instrument
for leading the congregation in the simple singing of the Kyrie,
Gloria, Credo, Sanctus, and Agnus Dei. Or maybe, there would be
a choir. At Saint-Martin in Rennes the men were paid a mere 3
livres a year, at Sainte-Croix in Nantes, 50 livres. For this higher
wage they would have to be well turned out, 'frisé et poudré', be
punctual, open the doors for ecclesiastics, and undertake never to go
out in the streets in their surplices. Choirboys, in theory at least,
were subjected to an even stricter discipline.

   The lay employees of parish churches deserve their own sociological study. Though churchwardens were inclined to economize and appoint the least demanding applicant, certain families—as so often happened in eighteenth-century France—managed to corner these modest offices. A verger would be succeeded by his son or son-in-law, and children and grandchildren would be taken on as choirboys, thurifers, cross-bearers, and banner-carriers. These arrangements suited a conservative social order, and kept traditional liturgical observances and other routines going smoothly. Not everyone would know how to remove the stains of spitting and to put a gloss on marble paving. When the parishioners of Helfaut in 1753 laid blue and white marble slabs in their sanctuary, the wife of the verger was sent to Saint-Omer to find out the secret (on condition of a small gratuity) from the *suisse* of the cathedral.[91] Hereditary succession avoided the scandal of ex-employees of the Church falling into destitution in their declining years. When the *suisse* of Saint-Merry grew old, the wardens gave 200 livres to his son-in-law to pay his fees to become a master cobbler, on condition that he provided a home for his father-in-law and stood in for him when he was not well enough to perform his duties.[92] Nepotism took the place of retirement pensions.

This picture of swarming ecclesiastical employees in their cosy dynasties applies only to the big and wealthy town parishes, of course. In a poor rural parish one omni-competent person would ring the bells, dig the graves, clean the church, preside at its ceremonies; he might also be schoolmaster (or his wife schoolmistress). Where all were poor and ignorant, he might also be constrained to act as churchwarden as well, charged with the care of largely non-existent monies. But where the finances extended to paying extra bodies, they would surely be taken on. This was a labour-intensive society, with many people on the margin of survival, scraping together a living by odd jobs and makeshifts; the church had a duty to provide as many opportunities as possible. It was a society too where one of the major signs of success was conspicuous waste in the employment of numerous retainers: the parish church had its dignity to maintain, as much as any nobleman surrounded by his lackeys.

V

With its ordinary incomings and ordinary outgoings, a parish would carry on in approximate equilibrium, but rarely were there reserves in hand to meet a financial crisis. More especially, desperate

measures had to be taken when a major repair to the church building was required. While the tithe owner was responsible for the
chancel, the parishioners had to repair the nave (except in Flanders
and Artois where the tithe paid everything, and in Roussillon
where it contributed nothing). Short of some extraordinary source
of revenue, like getting permission to fell timber on communal
property or to confiscate the enclosures of those who had
encroached on it,[93] a rate would have to be levied. The bishop,
probably alerted by a visitation report, would issue an ordinance for
repairs; if this was ignored, he could close the building by interdict
as well as calling on the lay magistrates to intervene. Tension was
likely to arise between the curé and his flock: he would have to be
vigilant to ensure no corners were being cut in the repairing plans,
and sometimes he was also actively campaigning for improvements
to be incorporated into it—this would be resisted with grim determination.[94] The intendant had to be informed, as he gave permission
for the financial levy; his *subdélégué* would make an inspection and
supervise the auction of the contract in three sessions spaced at
intervals of three weeks.[95] All these proceedings were regarded with
dismay by the parishioners. Either they would turn up and raise
every possible objection, or they would stay away altogether,
leaving the intendant to proceed by arbitrary fiat against a solid wall
of non-co-operation.[96] Tight-fisted, suspicious, and unwilling to
commit themselves to corporate civil responsibility,[97] the peasants
did their best to avoid paying—hence, most country churches were
left in poor repair by a conspiracy of evasion. Visitation reports early
in the century retail stories of unpaved floors, tottering walls, and
intruding animals—dogs, maybe, making off with the bones of the
faithful from the tombs in the aisles.[98] In 1738, a curé of the diocese
of Saintes nearly died from the bite of an adder which had nested
in his tabernacle.[99] Conditions improved, but gradually. In mid-
century, fifty parishes of the diocese of Boulogne had no sacristies,
and in others, what passed for one was too damp to be used: 'on
est obligé de se revêtir à la vue du peuple, rien de plus indécent'.[100]
Even in the 1780s, reports of picturesque dilapidation are still found.
In one parish in Brittany, to stop the rats eating the altar cloths,
wooden covers had to be made with spaces for cats to circulate.[101] In
a church in Burgundy, most of the windows were broken, the door
did not fit, the roof leaked, and the communion rail was sagging.[102]
Neglect of repairs sometimes created a danger to life and limb. In
1756, a report on a country church said that 'most of the inhabitants
stay away from mass and the offices because they are afraid of being

engulfed in a collapse'. In the North, at the church of Saint-Nicolas in Braine, in April 1787, a beam of the framework of the tower fell close to the confessional, and the vicaire, a woman penitent, and the notary Petiteau who was waiting his turn to be shriven narrowly escaped being crushed.[103]

Such dangerous incidents were not unknown in cities, even in churches which were rich and famous. In 1739, chunks of plaster, big enough to be lethal, were falling from the ceiling of the Parisian church of the Madeleine, and six years later, creaks and groans in the high altar of Saint-Merry showed the supports worm-eaten, and the whole structure, statues, reliquary, and suspended tabernacle could have fallen at any minute.[104] There were casualties at Mâcon in 1759 in a wild rush for safety when the roof beams of the cathedral began cracking.[105] To be a regular worshipper in one of the six parishes of Besançon required fortitude.[106] The church of Saint-Donat, closed as unsafe in 1688, stood as a crumbling warning, until in 1769 it had to be demolished. On 25 February 1729, the spire of the cathedral fell, flattening two bays of the apse. In the following year, the church of Sainte-Brigitte was pulled down. The year after, the city council ordered the parishioners of the Madeleine to move their services to the chapel of the Cordeliers; the wisdom of the decision was demonstrated fifteen years later when the tower of their old church collapsed. It was as well they had not transferred to the precincts of the other friary in the town, since in 1752 the roof of the chapel of the Jacobins caved in. The parishioners of Saint-Jean-Baptiste, better organized than most, anticipated disaster, and repaired their tower in 1745–6, and on the eve of the Revolution were collecting money for a reconstruction of the entire building. Through long neglect, the splendid central church of Saint-Pierre, scene of all the municipal ceremonies, was in a parlous state; in 1727 the intendant reported it to be 'ready to collapse, perhaps at the very moment when this is least expected'. As this was the official parish, and Besançon was a garrison town, the local people expected help from the government, and they were, in fact, granted the sealing fees from the four so-called *chancelleries* of Franche Comté. The intendant wished to elaborate the reconstruction project, buying up houses to provide a new site for the church, and leaving a vast square for military parades. At 5 p.m. on 23 August 1729, a high-powered conference was held at the presbytery; the duc de Levy, the provincial governor, was there, the *premier président* of the parlement, the lieutenant-general of police, two municipal councillors, the curé, the churchwarden, two ex-wardens, the professor of law at the university, and an *avocat*. The intendant undertook to compel the house owners to sell at a valuation, and he offered financial help (in fact, the Royal Council sent 22,000 livres). Even so, the parishioners established their point: they could not legally be constrained to pay for the enlargement of a public square. This was the responsibility of the municipality, and in 1732 the intendant ordered the city fathers to buy up the houses as a matter of public utility. The contract for rebuilding the church was let at the huge sum of 156,699 livres, and on 5 July 1732 the archbishop consecrated the foundation-stone with pomp. Not everyone was satisfied. The three chaplains of Saint-Pierre complained that the new edifice would be too small, and offered 8,000 livres towards its enlargement, which offer, they said, was refused 'with invectives, arrogance and scorn'. By contrast, the municipality complained that it would be too large, and that the alignment of the façade was not parallel to the town hall. The parishioners complained of the cost; at an assembly in March 1741, presided over by the intendant in person, their rate was set at 8,000 livres a year for the next twenty years. In fact, ten years and 80,000 livres later, the work stopped with the walls twenty-five feet high. Nothing more was done until 1770, when three successive parish assemblies were held in the town hall, reaching an agreement to pay 10,000 livres annually for the next six years. In 1772, work was suspended again on the king's order. An architectural competition held by the academy of Besançon had thrown up new ideas, including an even bigger square with a statue of the monarch in the centre, and the parishioners of Saint-Pierre to be moved elsewhere—say, to the collegiate church of Saint-Paul. The municipality liked the idea of robbing Peter to transfer to Paul—or to the chapel of the Carmelites or the Benedictines: 'if we can clear a useful public square in place of a useless parish church, the opportunity must not be missed'. The parishioners replied that Saint-Paul was near the barracks, and therefore unsuited to the attendance of young women and children, while the streets leading to the Carmelites and Benedictines were impassable in winter. The archbishop agreed with them, and promised to persuade the government to sanction the financing of the completion of the new church of Saint-Pierre by a lottery (this was refused, since the state lotteries would suffer by competition). In 1779, with a new curé, a new archbishop, and a new Minister of War pushing for action, the rebuilding began again. The parish, in January 1785, agreed to borrow 30,000 livres and to tax itself at 8,000 livres annually for the next twelve years. Alas! in the following year, with the work nearing completion, a committee of architects, masons, and master carpenters declared the foundations insecure and the roof beams of dubious timber: the whole structure, they said, was dangerous. No doubt their minds were conditioned by the past history of church architecture in Besançon; time has vindicated the maligned building contractor, since his work survived intact into the twentieth century.

In spite of the reluctance of the mass of inhabitants to pay for propping up their parish churches, the eighteenth century, especially the latter half, was an age of restoration, improvement, and new building.[107] The authorities were becoming insistent in enforcing the old edict of 1661 concerning church repairs, and the growing sophistication of society was reflected in the desire of churchwardens in richer parishes to make a name for themselves by innovations in the current fashion, while the generosity of wealthy individuals could make up for the thrifty hostility of the majority—though it is true that wealthy benefactors were most often found in the more opulent parishes and their contributions were directed more to the creation of new splendours than to maintaining the old. But in a crisis, an aristocratic parishioner was expected to demonstrate his superiority by conspicuous giving. When the church of Bolbec had to be rebuilt after a fire in 1772, the duc de Charost was prominent in choosing an architect and exhorting to action, though when he gave only 10,000 livres of the 60,000 required, the parishioners were disillusioned. About the same time, the *premier président* of the parlement of Rouen presented the village near his country mansion with a brand-new church in elegant brick: with mixed motives and vastly more publicity, Voltaire had done the same for the parishioners of his estate. In country churches we hear of panelling, wainscot, gilding, paving, porches, and sacristies added, a roof of brick instead of the old timber, newly fashionable plastering and whitewashing, new altar-pieces in the ornate baroque style of the early century, and the new sobriety and elegance of the reign of Louis XVI.[108] The twelve churchwardens of Notre-Dame of Versailles, in attempting to give superior adornment to their church as befitted its royal connections, got into a famous lawsuit: their ornate new clock, costing more than 30,000 livres, would not go, but the parlement of Paris ordered payment in full to the maker—as if the chief purpose was to preach to the congregation about mortality, with the ability to tell the actual time a bonus.[109] In the great Parisian churches, the wardens spent lavishly. At Saint-Merry[110] the pews were thrown out (in a nocturnal foray to pre-empt objections), and the floor richly paved; the worm-eaten altar was replaced by a new one by the Slodtz brothers at the enormous price of 85,000 livres, and an even more expensive pulpit commissioned from Michel Slodtz (in 1753, the contract was to represent Error and Paganism overthrown amid the débris of pagodas, idols, and books; six years later, the ideas of the Enlightenment had had their effect, and the design was changed to a figure of Religion escorted by two angels with laurel wreaths). In the first half of the century Paris was agog with stories of the scandalous excesses of Languet, the curé of Saint-Sulpice, in raising money for the rebuilding of his church (including confiscating a piece of tableware wherever he dined to be melted down for his silver statue of the Virgin). 'He even managed to extract a subscription from the Pope,' said the wits, recording the laying of the foundation-stone of the new altar by the nuncio—in the end, the vast income from the royal lottery paid for the completion of the façade and the towers.[111]

A particular amenity of the church which could impose heavy and unexpected expenditure was the bell, or peal of bells; there was always a danger of a crack in the metal. The tithe owner might have to maintain the tower, but the *fabrique* was responsible for the bell, the timber framework supporting it, and the rope.[112] This was not unreasonable, for while bishops liked to issue ordinances against 'profane ringing', the bells were as much a lay institution as an ecclesiastical one. They pealed for military victories, royal occasions, and local celebrations. In times of invasion, fire, or other danger, they rang as a tocsin, and in areas favourable to smuggling as a warning that the customs officials were coming.[113] At the approach of thunderstorms, they were rung to ward off the dangerous lightning strike; the parlement of Paris, duly informed of the new discoveries about electricity, banned the practice in 1784.[114] Younger and more light-hearted parishioners liked to ascend the belfry to ring on festive occasions like the eve of St John's Day, All Saints, or Christmas—sometimes officially rewarded with bread and cheese or black pudding (*boudin*)[115] and sometimes unofficially fortified with strong drink. But for the sober respectable inhabitants, the less the bells rang the better: they were easily damaged, and costly to replace. This was one of the uncovenanted expenses of untoward celebrations. When Louis XVI went on solemn progress through Normandy in June 1787, and the 200 bells of Rouen were swung *en branle*, the most famous of them all, the 'Georges d'Amboise', 40,000 livres in weight, was cracked beyond redemption.[116] In October 1716 the parish assembly of Saint-Martin of the Breton town of Vitré looked back sadly on the activities of the 'gens de bonne volonté' who for 'le seul plaisir de sonner' had rung some extra peals; thanks to their zeal, one of the bells was cracked, and the *fabrique* was already in debt.[117] Frequent ringing might do more than break the bell—the tower itself might suffer damage. So argued the city fathers of Metz in 1745, hoping to persuade the cathedral to cease ringing the big 'Marie' (installed in a tower whose repairs were a municipal responsibility). The treasurer of the chapter tested the vibrations with 'a goblet full of red liquid'; none was spilt, so the canons decided to carry on as before, 'considering the fine effect that this bell produces'.[118]

When a recasting was necessary, every effort was made to find a patron who would spare the parish the expenditure. Affluent curés, 'seduced by the thought of passing on to posterity their names engraved on bronze', often made a gift to their church in this way.[119] When the new bell was blessed—'baptized' in popular parlance—a 'godfather' and 'godmother' were chosen from wealthy parishioners of the neighbourhood; for example, the parish of Avernay in 1729 had the marquis de Lhéry, commander of the garrison at Reims, and the abbess of the local abbey.[120] The sponsors would make a solid gift to the church; the curé and parish in return would give them gloves and sweetmeats, have their Christian names and coats of arms engraved on the bell, and, maybe, an entry in the parish register would record their right to 'the glorious title of benefactor of humanity'.[121] The parishes of Notre-Dame and of Saint-Louis at Versailles and that of Fontainebleau could hope to have the king and queen or other members of the royal family; their gifts would be a roll of cloth of gold (to drape the bell and make vestments afterwards, possibly worth as much as 25,000 livres) and a sum of money, from 300 to 600 livres.[122] The assembly of Saint-Martin at Vitré was dumbfounded when the local seigneur and his wife refused to act as godparents; to put pseudo-obsequious pressure on them, it sent the bell-founder to call and 'ask for their instructions' concerning their coat of arms which the bell was scheduled to bear.[123]

The *fabrique* was determined to get value for money when a recasting was necessary. There would be a strict contract, by which the bell was to be taken down, weighed, recast (with a specific price for any extra metal that was needed), a final exact weight would be specified, the tone would have to be harmonized with the other bells, and finally there would be the rehanging. The parish of Saint-Pierre of Montsort got all this for 120 livres;[124] another Angevin parish got a smaller bell recast by a travelling expert from Lorraine for 80 livres 4 sols, including the extra metal.[125] When the big bell of Saint-Jeannet in Provence had to be renewed in 1766 as a result of the activities of 'une troupe d'enfants qui sonnèrent plus qu'à l'ordinaire', the churchwardens economized by having an old cauldron, used by a confraternity to cook beans for charity soup, incorporated in the melting. It was a mistake, and the work had to be done again.[126] (Presumably the cauldron was copper; the eighteenth-century formula for bell metal was fifty parts pure copper, ten to twelve parts pewter or tin, and one part antimony.[127]) Things could go wrong: the process was dicey, and the bell-founders were, often enough, wandering adventurers with dubious credentials.[128] The parish of Helfaut had to have the same bell recast in 1750, 1770, and 1781 at a cost of about 1,000 livres a time.[129] At Saint-Jean de Luz the mould collapsed at the pouring, and a second founder had to be engaged to give a verdict on who was to blame and how to rescue the situation.[130] The great abbey of Chelles could afford to employ the best, yet in 1752, when the recasting of the first and third bells was complete, they were found to be greatly underweight and out of harmony; the founder, owing more by penalty clauses than was due to him, fled far from the province.[131] The air above the cities of France was full of the reverberation and tintinnabulation of a fanciful diversity of peals, recalling some to pious reflection, but worrying all by the thought of yet another levy on the pockets of householders.

Repairs to the presbytery were a lesser burden than repairs to the church, but an even more fertile source of acrimony.[132] Paradoxically, by being extended to cover every contingency, the legal regulations had multiplied occasions for litigation. Royal edicts laid down a minimum accommodation, but what amenities ought to be included in the definition of each room? The curé had to do the running repairs, and the parish the major ones; what if neglect of the former brought on a big bill for the latter? If no house was provided, or if the available house was uninhabitable during reconstruction, the curé had to be paid a lodging allowance of 60 livres a year (40 if there were fewer than 100 families in his care); if repairs would cost over 500 livres, the parish could ask to have the building demolished and simply pay the annual sum. Since such lodging payments always fell into arrears, curés generally insisted on a house, and normally got one. If the parish priest wanted a barn or stables, he had to pay for them himself. In 1749, a parish in the diocese of Reims added a barn to its vicarage, by mistake, in ignorance of the law; the wardens tried to persuade the curé to contribute, but he refused; the parish therefore put the barn up for auction; nobody wanted it, so the curé bought it for a mere 318 livres.[133] If an incumbent improved his presbytery at his own expense, the addition would ultimately become a repairing burden to his flock; hence, the intendant had to approve all new plans. In 1782, the intendant of Tours fined a curé 2,000 livres for spending 10,000 livres of his own money on unauthorized additions.[134] While the law clearly made the parish responsible for the presbytery, the laity occasionally suggested that an affluent cleric had at least a moral obligation not to insist on the letter of his rights; those who were learned could cite a decision of the Council of Rouen in 1231[135] and the continuing jurisprudence of the province of Flanders to support the argument.[136]

Given such opportunities for dispute and reproach, vicarage repairs were an inevitable focus for local anticlericalism. Once the curé mentioned his leaking roof or creaking beams in the parish assembly, a cloud of gloom and ill will descended. The inhabitants might refuse to discuss the matter, and fail to turn up at subsequent meetings;[137] they might argue that neglect of running repairs had caused the trouble or, conversely, that the presbytery was an oasis of comfort in the midst of their own miserable hovels, and needed nothing doing to it. If the curé resorted to the law, his parishioners might engage him for years in guerrilla warfare in the courts; it took the abbé Laugier thirteen years—from 1721 to 1734—to get a new presbytery from his parishioners of Saint-Jeannet, and in the end he also extracted 468 livres lodging allowance and the costs of his litigation.[138] In 1669, the parlement of Paris ordered a village in the diocese of Autun to pay the penal sum of 220 livres a year so long as there was no vicarage; the stubborn inhabitants were still paying in 1739.[139] With luck, a curé might be successful in invoking the arbitrary power of the intendant against the inhabitants, as at Bouzigues on the southern coast in 1770, where the community was peremptorily ordered to do 2,650 livres of repairs (decently, the curé voluntarily forwent 900 worth).[140] But generally, royal officials tended to be unsympathetic. 'The curés all want to be lodged like seigneurs,' complained a *subdélégué* in the second half of the century.[141] 'The curés ask too much,' said an intendant; 'in consequence I propose in future not to agree to anything beyond what is indispensable.'[142] The law courts and the Royal Council were strict about running repairs: unless a curé could demonstrate that he had been up to date with the 'réparations locatives', he had little chance of winning his case over the 'grosses réparations'. In the last resort, when a contract for doing the repairs had finally been made, the angry parishioners might threaten reprisals against the builders' men, or riot to keep them away from the decaying vicarage which was causing so much expense.[143]

Since running repairs were so important at law, an incumbent who was solicitous of the interests of his heirs would either do the work and keep evidence that he had done so, or—better still—make a contract with the churchwardens to pay a yearly sum (say, 30 livres) on condition the parish took over from him the 'réparations locatives'.[144] When a benefice holder died, his successor did well to call in surveyors and have an official list of dilapidations prepared, ready to go to law against the heirs. Meanwhile, the parish would ensure that seals were put on the dead man's furniture and his savings kept in legal custody until the responsibility for the repairs had been settled. In 1772, the curé of Belle-Isle in the diocese of Vannes died. His nephew and heir, a parish priest in the diocese of Le Mans, offered a lump sum to put the vicarage to rights. The wary parishioners were not to be bought off (it could be that a local contractor was hoping to overcharge a 'foreigner'). The nephew took the matter before the parlement of Rennes and finally got possession of his inheritance in 1775; he had a lump sum in cash, but the sale of the furniture barely covered his legal expenses.[145] With the injustice characteristic of the *ancien régime*, a vicarage of minimum standard had to be maintained, irrespective of the number of parishioners, their wealth, and the size of the endowments. The people would have wished, if other things had been equal, to see their priest well housed, and curés disliked being a burden—hence the ruthlessness of all concerned when an outsider arrived to claim a clerical inheritance.

The government of France, expert at centralizing power, was equally skilful at devolving financial liabilities. Parishioners, taxed for the State and tithed for the Church, were also responsible for the upkeep of church buildings and presbyteries. They did their duty under duress or with gloomy acquiescence, but they would go to any lengths to avoid an increase in the burden. Thus, when schemes of parochial reform were mooted, the universal clamour was for the cheapest variant. If a parish was to be divided, only the most essential and rudimentary new buildings were to be provided; if a union was proposed, the church and vicarage cheapest to maintain must be preserved, not the most convenient or prestigious. When Church and State progress majestically forward in harmony, on every side human nature furtively seeks escape routes and hiding-places, to avoid being implicated in their costly splendour.

II

THE CURÉS: SOCIAL ORIGINS,
INCOMES, MENTALITY

I *Social Origins*

In many areas of France, the curés were local men, born and bred in the diocese. Of the 273 parish priests of the diocese of Bologne in 1725, we know the place of origin of 268; only twenty-eight had come from outside, and ten of these were from the neighbouring diocese of Amiens.[1] Of the 730 ecclesiastics who answered the questionnaire of the archbishop of Reims in 1774, no fewer than 644 said they had been born under his jurisdiction;[2] Le Mans was such another diocese where the clergy were locally recruited.[3] In the dioceses of Beauvais,[4] Bazas, Lisieux,[5] Dol, Rennes, and Saint-Malo, about 25 per cent of the curés (or recteurs) were 'foreigners'; most of these, however, were foreigners from near at hand—the influx to serve under the three Breton bishops was mostly from other areas of Brittany, while of the fifty-nine outsiders of Lisieux, all but eight came from Normandy, no fewer than twenty-two of them from the single diocese of Bayeux.[6] This 'natural' pattern of local men occupying local benefices could only operate, of course, where ecclesiastical vocations were maintained at a reasonably high level, as they were in Normandy (source of one-eighth of the recruitment of the whole country) and the Massif Central (source of one-tenth). By contrast, there were signs of a decline in clerical vocations in the Loire Valley, Berry, the Orléanais, and much of the South.[7] Vocations also came in patterns which might vary sharply between one comparatively small locality and another; the bishop of Boulogne, for example, knew that his supply of priests came from around his episcopal city and the town of Saint-Pol, and not around Calais;[8] the bishop of Strasbourg knew that his was in central Alsace,[9] just as the bishop of La Rochelle would look towards the Mauges and the Gatine areas (though recruitment was evening up through-out the eighteenth century).[10] Depending on how these local patterns of vocations fitted into the official boundaries of ecclesiastical jurisdiction, contrasting situations in neighbouring dioceses were created: thus Valence always had candidates for its vacant posts and a surplus which was exported to help the contiguous diocese of Dié, usually in difficulties.[11] A small diocese lacking solid catchment areas for vocations was vulnerable, and it was not necessarily a sign of pastoral neglect if it became dependent on outsiders—as in Lodève in 1735, when thirty-two of the fifty-seven parishes had an imported curé.[12] These dissimilarities between clerical recruitment areas have been described as 'self-reinforcing', on the ground that where there were few vocations, parishes would be served by incoming priests of a lower calibre, lacking a knowledge of local dialect and custom, and thus incapable of eliciting more vocations from their flocks.[13] Yet things could and did change. So often, the patrons of livings— bishops, seigneurs, chapters, monasteries—were local persons and institutions, subject to the solicitations and pressures of neighbours, and therefore inclined to local men if they could be found. The practice of 'resignation in favour' worked in the same direction. A reforming bishop pushing for recruits and the teaching of a well-organized seminary would have their effect, and in the worldly and family context in which, so often, vocations were formed, discussions about locally available vacancies would in time create the will to fill them. In the mid-seventeenth century, half the priests ordained in the diocese of Vannes came from outside; by 1789, nearly nine out of every ten recteurs were local men.[14] In the diocese of Strasbourg, half the clergy in 1680 came from outside Haute-Alsace; in 1700, the situation was much the same, there being only fifty-one Alsatians among the 127 curés whose place of origin is known to us; by 1720, eight out of ten were Alsatians, and by 1760 virtually all of them. There had been a great onrush of vocations: the clergy 'multiply so strongly', complained a *grand vicaire* to the bishop in 1740, 'that I do not know where I can place them'.[15] At the beginning of the eighteenth century, the 213 parishes in the diocese of Gap were understaffed, but by 1760 there were too many priests for the employment available; by the 1780s, vocations had declined again, so that vicaires were brought in from Embrun, one of the dioceses like Valence which had a supply of priests for export.[16]

In the two areas, the city of Paris and the diocese of Bordeaux, where an influx of clergy from outside was most evident, there were special circumstances. In Paris, of the priests who took the oath to the Civil Constitution of the Clergy in January 1791 and gave their diocese of origin, two-thirds came from outside, especially from Normandy, that great reservoir of vocations.[17] The capital was a centre to which clerics came for education and where they stayed because of opportunity, and this immigration of churchmen corresponded to what was happening in lay society. Paris lived and expanded by drawing in its population from the provinces: marriage contracts in the faubourg Saint-Antoine and elsewhere show that 40 per cent of the bridegrooms were provincials by origin. According to the ecclesiastical census of 1772 in the diocese of Bordeaux, a third of the curés and half of the vicaires came from outside[18]—we may guess that the difference between these two fractions represents the degree of favouritism in promotion given to local men. It can be seen clearly in the town of Bordeaux itself, where the office of curé or vicaire was much sought after—nine of the fifteen curés were born in the city, two in other places in the diocese, and, indeed, there was only one who was entirely without local connections, while of the twenty-seven vicaires in town, sixteen were born there, and four in other places in the diocese—the rest had become 'naturalized', as it were, by serving elsewhere under the archbishop's jurisdiction before being promoted to a parish in his episcopal city.[19] One reason, no doubt, for the failure of the diocese to produce sufficient vocations was that the town itself, one of the great commercial centres of France, afforded a wider variety of lay careers for intelligent young men than the other provincial centres. Another reason was the dearth of attractive rural cures. There were so many parishes in the Landes so sunk in misery and poverty that only the most dedicated or desperate priests would have wished to go there. In 1731 the curé of Lamothe wrote to his archbishop saying that the clergy all around him wanted to leave, 'preferring serving as a vicaire elsewhere rather than being a curé in a place where you are too poor to pay a farm worker, where in winter you are cut off by floods and in danger of drowning whenever you go out, and where in the fine weather you are devoured by flies'.[20] Focused on its port, the Bordeaux diocese had the chance to import clergy from overseas as well as across its land boundaries: 15 in every 100 of its immigrant vicaires came from Ireland.[21]

In the Church, as everywhere in society, nobles gravitated towards well-paid and dignified offices—including the limited number of parochial cures that qualified for this description. The proportion of nobles among the secular clergy was small, perhaps 1 per cent overall,[22] and it was declining throughout the century. But in some areas, the average was greatly exceeded: 18 per cent in the diocese of Tréguier,[23] 15 per cent in that of Aix,[24] 5–10 per cent in Tarbes,[25] 6–12 per cent in Vannes (falling to 2 per cent after 1740),[26]

4 per cent in Lisieux,[27] 2 per cent in Reims.[28] The figures are highest where there were numerous families of poor nobles of the sword whose younger sons had little to inherit and only the Church and the army for a career. Normally one would expect to find nobles in the better sort of canonries, but parishes with a substantial income could also attract high birth. When reconstruction in Alsace greatly increased the value of a number of parochial benefices, the sons of some of the best families in the province came forward to possess them.[29] In Burgundy, Brazey-en-Plaine was one of those odd, lucrative cures where the priest was on the *congrue*, but had a substantial income from surplice-fees and pious foundations; in 1773, Pierre-Claude Perrot, 'écuyer, bachelier en droit, prêtre', son of a magistrate of the chambre des comptes of Dijon, resigned his canonry in the church of Saint-Jean in that city to possess it.[30] For almost a century, the rich cure of La Haye-Pesnel in Normandy was held by a succession of noblemen until in 1759 the monopoly collapsed and a peasant's son who had been vicaire there for twenty years was appointed—and the presbytery changed its appearance from a château to a farmhouse.[31] One would guess that there were attractions in the parish of Fontenay-le-Comte when we find it held in the second half of the eighteenth century by M. de Rémigioux, écuyer, seigneur de la Grégouillière.[32] And perhaps the most splendid parish in the whole kingdom was that of Saint-Sulpice in Paris, ruled from 1748 to 1778 by Jean Dulau d'Allemans, the son of a marquis.[33] Down in the South, in the diocese of Lescar, the Tristan family, *jurats* of the town of Pau, held the lucrative cure of Gan in family possession, as if it was yet another of their fiefs or vineyards. After forty years as curé, Henri de Tristan resigned in 1721 to his nephew Arnaud, who forthwith resigned to his brother Daniel, who remained in Paris for eight years before he actually undertook the duties. Thereafter, portly, witty, resplendent with gold snuff-box and gold-topped cane, and in wigs sent specially from Paris, he presided over his parish, hobnobbing with the bishop and the intendant, and attending the sessions of the estates of Béarn arrayed in his *veste de noblesse*.[34] In the diocese of Tréguier (18 per cent nobles in the ranks of the secular clergy), there were a dozen rich cures with incomes ranging from 2,400 livres to 4,000; these were held chiefly by nobles, the other parochial benefices, mostly poor, going to commoners.[35] In 1764, the necrology of the diocese published the names of priests who were nobles above those who were commoners. 'If they'd made a necrology at Rome in the year of the death of Saint Peter and Saint Paul,' a disgruntled curé wrote to the superior of the

seminary of Vannes, 'and if they'd put Paul first because he was a nobleman, the Christians would have been scandalized. They revered Peter the prisoner more than Paul the *gentilhomme*.'[36]

This did not mean that noble curés were admitted to office by the bishops without assessment of their worthiness. Marie-Hubert-Lénor d'Imbleval was refused the living of Saint-Germain-de-Clairefeuille by a *vicaire général* of the bishop of Lisieux in 1764, even though he had been a canon and a curé elsewhere;[37] Canon de Luzarches was turned down for the rich double parish of Saint-Laurent with Notre-Dame de Recouvrance at Orléans after doing a year's special study for an examination which he failed—though a cynic might point out that he was asked very elementary questions, and that after an appeal to the archbishop of Paris and a new examination, he finally succeeded.[38] By contrast, there were some nobles who accepted humble parish offices that might have gone to anyone. Charles-Sextus Ventré de la Touloubre, allied to the Vintimilles, the princes of Monaco, was a vicaire in various parishes of the diocese of Paris before becoming curé of Bièvres in 1789;[39] and the abbé D'Espouy, son of the *chevalier* of that name, was *archiprêtre* and curé of the miserably poor parish of Saint-Paul d'Oueil in the diocese of Comminges; as the vicarage was in ruins, he lived fifteen minutes' ride away in his château.[40] Probably, such aristocrats were as effective pastorally as most of their contemporaries, even if they were accustomed to make their flocks call them 'M. l'abbé' instead of 'M. le curé'.[41] The *cahier* of the village of Fougerolles accuses Jean-Baptiste Ouvrard de la Haye of being a hard man where tithes were concerned (he was on the fringe of the *noblesse*: his father owned three seigneuries, a brother was a magistrate in a *bailliage* court, and an uncle an *avocat* pleading before the parlement of Paris). With his comfortable revenue, his seven horses in the stables, and his ostentatious coat of arms in the church, he was proud and, maybe, harsh; but he employed extra vicaires at his own expense, and in the terrible winter of 1788 he maintained the poor by paying them (children included) for building a terrace and planting it with lime trees at the end of his rectory garden.[42] He was acting as nobles generally did, living ostentatiously with no sign of a social conscience in ordinary times, but generous in a crisis.

Though there were few nobles in the parochial ministry, their presence is evidence of the great dignity of the office of curé in popular esteem. The sons of affluent commoners might consider that the status compensated for the shortcomings of income. A coal, iron, and corn merchant of Saint-Florent-le-Vieil exhorted his son to weigh well the profits of the business before seeking ordination: 'Tu pourras amasser du bien dans mon commerce.' But Claude Robin's heart was set on the role of leadership the parochial office conferred—in 1752, he even permuted a canonry, after only six months' tenure, to become curé of Saint-Pierre at Angers.[43] Among the lesser bourgeoisie, there was a perpetual quest for 'notability', hence the expensive, ineradicable determination to buy office from the Crown, whether in a minor law court or tax office, or as a 'registrar' or 'controller' of something or other. A son safely in the Church served the same purpose, as well as guaranteeing his own future. Of the sons of an apothecary of Libourne, one followed the law and made his son, in his turn, a *conseiller* of the *présidial* and, in 1743, *maire*; the other became a country curé nearby—the family had done well for itself.[44] 'Often, in our milieu', said Thibaudeau, 'you choose between the Church and the law courts.' With embarrassing frankness, the abbé Baston describes his own decision. 'I had to choose one of three states of life: the Church, Medicine and the Bar. Well, wrangling wearied me, hence, no Bar. Illnesses scared me—hence, no Medicine. That left the Church.'[45] At the end of the *ancien régime*, there were signs that the rewards of parochial benefices were coming to be regarded as too meagre for the sons of the bourgeoisie, especially in an area of economic decline like Brittany, where families were feeling the pinch. In 1784–5 the bishop of Rennes drew up a memorandum on the decline of vocations in his episcopal city: 'the fathers of well-off families who can't hope to put their sons into canonries or the more considerable benefices, take care to discourage them from embarking on a long and expensive course of study and a career in which they'll have to live on a mere 200 livres for several years awaiting a parochial cure which might only give them 500 or 600'.[46] The same tendency was noted in the town of Nantes. In the neighbouring dioceses of Saint-Malo and Saint-Brieuc, however, there was a rise in sacerdotal recruitment—but it was from less well-off families. Here is a hint of the new nature of clerical recruitment which would prevail in the nineteenth century—from poorer classes of society, corresponding to the decline in the income and status of the curés.

Further down the social scale, below the bracket of lower bourgeoisie and the corresponding peasant group of self-sufficient farmers, among those who were respectable though without pretensions to notability, the security and dignity of the parochial ministry were the utmost boundaries of a father's ambition for his son. 'What are you going to do with the boy?' someone asks an artisan whose son is at *collège*. 'Ah! we'll see, he must begin by learning a bit of Latin; he can then take the cassock.' 'You are dedicating him to the ecclesiastical state?' 'Certainly, it's the best job there is; *Dominus vobiscum* never wanted for bread.'[47] But not all who aspired to the authority to pronounce the clerical blessing could get there. A boy had to be both clever and lucky to get the necessary education free of charge, and in any case the years of schooling and study were a loss of earning capacity to the family. And the clerical 'title', something like 100 livres of guaranteed yearly income, had to be found. For the mass of peasants (day-labourers or possessing only enough land to earn a bare subsistence) and for poor artisans and manual workers in towns, the prospect of a son in the ecclesiastical state was a distant one. These people could not afford to have a vocation. In 1780, the bishop of Saint-Pol-de-Léon complained that he was short of clergy because vocations were declining among the more prosperous families, and he could not think of a way to supplement 'the lack of resources of the parents whose children seek the ecclesiastical state, a disposition which we now find only among the most indigent classes'.[48] There are no day-labourers or *haricotiers* among the curés, says the historian of the Beauvais area—they are all from the milieu of shopkeepers, the literate classes, and the small peasant farmers.[49] The historian of the peasants of Burgundy notes the exclusion from the ministry of most of the subjects of his study; the clergy come from the ranks of the *petite bourgeoisie* and the better-off rural families.[50] A boy from a poor family sometimes broke through the barriers set by indigence by coming to notice as clever and receiving a bursary or help from a patron; his clerical title might be made up by help from pious well-wishers, subscriptions from relatives, the gift of a benefice, or the bishop agreeing to waive the obligation. The chances were better in the towns—more schools, the possibility of employment as a choirboy or server, more clergy and pious ladies who might be inclined to acts of charity. The best leg-up of all for the poor aspirant to orders was to have someone in the family who had already beaten the odds and achieved ecclesiastical office or connections. Antoine Plassard, who became curé of Saint-Vincent at Mâcon in 1746, was the son of an artisan; his chance had come as a choirboy in the church of Saint-Pierre where his uncle was an assistant priest.[51] The abbé Jallet, curé of Chérigné in Poitou, the tenth child of a gardener and only 5 years old when his father died, would never have been heard of had not his maternal uncle, the curé of Nanteuil, taken him in and educated him.[52] Bernier, a brilliant young man who became a vicaire at Angers in

1787, the son of a weaver of Daon-sur-Mayenne, owed everything to the fact that his mother was a schoolmistress and his father the local sacristan.[53]

A conspectus of the range of society from which the parochial clergy were recruited is seen in the curés of the town of Angers at the end of the *ancien régime* (they would be a more respectable group than the average, because of the requirement of a university degree for a benefice in a 'walled town'). Huchelou des Roches's father was a *conseiller de la Prévoté*, and his mother bore a name highly respected in the Angevin magistracy; Robin was the son of a wholesale merchant in a little market town; Boumard came from a family of agricultural middlemen who farmed scattered properties of ecclesiastical landlords; Bernier was the son of a country weaver; Gruget was one of the numerous children of a hard-pressed saddle maker.[54] In social status they ran from the minor 'robe' and officials to merchants, estate managers, and farmers, down to artisans.

These generalizations from examples are confirmed by the available statistics on a wider scale, though as these concern either all secular priests at a given time or candidates presenting themselves for ordination over a period, they do not reflect the composition of the parochial ministry exactly. Sons of distinguished families would usually, given the opportunity, choose to go to canonries in the better-endowed chapters, or to one of the odd offices in state employment or the legal profession which fell to ecclesiastics. Some priests became tutors or chaplains, while the unambitious might choose to remain as *habitués*, earning small fees by saying foundation masses. Probably, when we have general statistics of the class origin of the secular priesthood, we ought to assume that rather fewer from the top and bottom of the social range we are dealing with found their way into the parochial ministry.

Thanks to the bureaucrats of the Revolution drawing up lists of clergy (for taking oaths of loyalty or qualifying for pensions—or for exile or the guillotine), we can sometimes make a statistical generalization for the whole country without waiting for the exhaustive accumulation of local detail. Forty per cent of the priests of France in 1790 had been born in a town (defined as possessing at least 2,000 inhabitants).[55] There were great contrasts between dioceses, however; urban recruitment accounted for 10 per cent of the vocations of the diocese of Nantes, and for 78 per cent of those of the diocese of Orléans. Rural recruitment predominated in the mountain areas (Alps, Pyrenees, and the Massif Central), and also in Normandy, Brittany, the Boulonnais, and Bas-Poitou. It is important to remember, however, that the distinction between town and country in eighteenth-century France did not usually follow the boundary lines which historians like to draw between social groups; so many urban dwellers owned or managed country property, so many of the richer sort alternated between town and country houses, so many notaries and other sorts of lawyers lived in the countryside gathering feudal rents or managing the affairs of absentee landlords, so many peasants plied trades and were involved in cottage industries. In the diocese of Vannes,[56] half the vocations were those of the sons of *laboureurs*—that is, the better-off peasants who ploughed their own acres and had fully enough to live on. But very few of the other half came from the urban milieu. Artisans and shopkeeping families in the towns provided only 3–7 per cent of the ordinands (rising to 11 per cent in 1740); 7–10 per cent of the ordinands were sons of artisans and merchants living in villages and the countryside; 20–26 per cent were technically 'bourgeois' but chiefly from the rural bourgeoisie of notaries, seigneurial judges, and the like. If we are looking for priests with a 'peasant' mentality (a doubtful concept to isolate, as so many professional and urban people were closely in touch with rural affairs), the significant statistics are those of the *laboureurs*: 75 per cent in the diocese of Coutances, 61 per cent in Tréguier, 50 per cent in Vannes, 48 per cent in Boulogne, 25 per cent in Gap, 22 per cent in Lisieux, 19 per cent in Reims and 9 per cent in Luçon.[57]

Four of these dioceses have recently been studied in detail. For that of Boulogne[58] we know, roughly, the social standing of the families of 326 ordinands throughout the century (two-thirds of the total). After the *laboureurs* (157), it is the merchants of the three main towns of Boulogne, Calais, and Saint-Pol who produce the most vocations (52); next come the artisans of town and country— farriers, cobblers, bakers, tailors, etc. (37); there are 15 legal and official types (7 notaries, 2 *avocats*, 4 *procureurs*, 2 *greffiers*), and lower down are 3 surgeons, 5 innkeepers, and 4 cooks. There are no fishermen or sailors, and only five families of the poorer peasantry. In the diocese of Reims,[59] the *laboureurs* provided only one-fifth of the vocations, merchants one-third, *officiers* one-fifth, and a twentieth from schoolmasters and the medical profession. Artisans provided a higher figure than elsewhere (16 per cent), because Reims was a centre of cloth manufacture.[60] In the diocese of Lisieux, the *laboureurs* account for 21 per cent of the vocations, as against a large bourgeois recruitment—54 per cent merchants and another 20 per cent from a congeries of highly respectable groups (those 'living nobly' 4.5 per cent; *rentiers* 3 per cent; *officiers* 8 per cent; legal, medical, and professional 4.5 per cent). There were few artisans, only 4 per cent.[61] The impression gained from the figures of professions, trades, and contemporary classifications like 'notable', 'rentier', 'officier' should be verified, when possible, on the simpler, harsher scale of actual riches. We know that 71 per cent of the titles for ordination in the diocese of Lisieux and 87.5 per cent of those of Boulogne were paid up by the families of the ordinands—the others needed help of various kinds. Timothy Tackett's remarkable study of clerical recruitment in the diocese of Gap has improved on this sort of analysis.[62] From the rolls of the capitation tax he has drawn up an index showing the percentage of heads of household in each community assessed for tax at a lower rate than that of each priest's family. The results demonstrate that the ordinands came from the 'economic élite' of their respective communities; more than half came from families in the upper 15 per cent of taxpayers, and more than three-quarters from the upper 30 per cent. During the century, there was a shift in vocations from the south to the north of the diocese, and from bourgeois to peasant milieux. This does not affect the rule that vocations come from the more prosperous; as bourgeois ordinands became fewer, the rise in grain prices in Dauphiné from 1740 lifted more peasant families of the valley of the Drac in the north into the income bracket which favoured clerical vocations. Idealists may regret that the ministry of the Church had become the preserve of the respectable class of society, but it was the inevitable result of the work of the Catholic reformers. An educated clergy had to be paid for.

II *Income*

Concerning sources of income, the curés fell into two broad categories. In about a third of the parishes of France, the principal tithes were collected by a bishop, chapter, monastery, or seigneur, and the tithe owner paid the curé a fixed salary, the so-called *portion congrue*. The other two-thirds of the parish priests collected their own tithes, and these, together with whatever lands went with the benefice, were their main source of income. In some areas, these lands were extensive. In the Sarthe[63] (the diocese of Le Mans) no fewer than half the curés had ten or more hectares (this was the acreage which could maintain a peasant family of six, in a good year, assuming two-thirds of the area was left fallow); one in every ten had thirty or more hectares, and one in every thirty had fifty hectares or more. But the curés here were lucky; such extensive landholding was rare. Even so, almost everywhere, those who had an acre or two in addition to their garden were numerous, and to have something, however small in extent, was valuable—a resource for fruit and vegetables, chickens and eggs, grazing for a horse, an opportunity for pig keeping. There were, too, curés from the richer sort of families who inherited land, while those who accumulated savings might buy property as an investment.[64] The landed endowment of a parochial cure, where it existed, usually consisted of scattered fragments, subject to obligations (like foundation masses) and by custom rented out cheaply to local people: a curé was not likely to draw anything like the standard return which a private owner could have hoped for. The laity watched narrowly to keep the privileges of clerical agriculturalists to a minimum.[65] Exemption from the *aides* (internal customs duties on drink) applied only to wine produced on their actual benefices, and only when sold in bulk, while free entry through the *octroi* barriers at the gates of towns was granted only for foodstuffs for their personal consumption. In provinces of *taille réelle*, the laity tried hard to find evidence that the land exploited by the clergy had been originally owned by laymen, and thus subject to land tax; in Languedoc, where there was no limitation of date, and antiquity carried no prescription, such enquiries often ranged far back, with the enthusiastic co-operation of the Cour des Aides of Montpellier. In areas of *taille personnelle* (most of France), the curé's exemption was for a limited area, and only if he tilled the land himself—otherwise, his tenant had to pay the tax.[66] Hence, there were all sorts of agreements on the borderline of fraud between curés and the peasants who undertook to cultivate their acres, while the rest of the village, anxious to spread the burden of the *taille* on as many households as possible, was ruthlessly vigilant against them.

The curé landowner was certainly in touch with the life of his peasant parishioners. Too much so, occasionally, as when the wife of Pierre Perrachon put a sheep and a goat into the sown cornfield of the curé of Saint-Point, threatened him with a stick, and told the concourse of delighted spectators about his failure to find a 'p—' in the village and his resort to one at Mâcon.[67] The letters of curé Jacques Lorieul of the diocese of Lisieux are full of rural technicalities: the weather, the price of corn, ideas of agricultural improvement, a mare that cost 110 livres, the two cows calving, so there was milk to rear two pigs at a clear profit of 25 livres each, the butter safely stored for winter, and the surplus sold for 70 livres.[68] A pig also figures prominently in the correspondence of curé Barbotin writing back to his parish from the meeting of the Estates General at Versailles in 1789: bought to kill in December, the animal died, amidst the lamentations of his servant Catherine. Don't forget, he says, to cover the jasmine, the myrtles, and the little orange tree at the first sign of bad weather in October. At another time he is wanting to be sure the tulip bulbs are stored in their boxes; at another he is ordering the cutting of the bleached linen into bed sheets, leaving enough for Catherine to make herself a shift; sell the grain, he says, to local people only, but for cash down unless we really know the buyer.[69] No doubt, tenants often fell out with their clerical landlords—none the less, theirs was a relationship affording opportunities for generosity on the one hand and reciprocal good nature on the other. The curé of Rémalard in the diocese of Chartres in 1767 rented a house to a barber-wig maker for a nominal sum of money, two sugar loaves each of four livres weight, four bottles of brandy, a wig of ordinary quality once a year, and a free shave twice a week.[70] One hopes their frequent meetings were enlivened by the gossip and badinage usually associated with barbers' shops.

For most curés, tithe was the main source of income—more important than the lands of the benefice. It was commonly said that a tithe-owning priest was to be envied as compared with those miserably dependent on the *congrue*: this was generally, but not always the case, for tithes could yield anything from 10,000 livres a year and more to 300 and less. Often, what appeared to be enormously rich tithing benefices were not so in reality. For one thing, the curé had to be an effective man of business before all that was due to him was collected. The incumbent of Saint-Pierre d'Eyraud boasted in 1790 that he had been drawing 3,000 livres a year from half the tithe of his parish, whereas the other half, belonging to the chapter of Périgueux, yielded only 1,555 livres.[71] Sometimes, Christian charity or, failing that, mere self-preservation would indicate the inadvisability of being too efficient. There were so many legal pitfalls concerning different kinds of tithe and complicated divisions of the produce between tithe owners; a curé did well to take what he could get without controversy, rather than stirring up ill will and engaging in costly lawsuits. A parish priest in the diocese of Lyon described how his claim to a particular tithe might one day be contested, 'which would be disastrous for the benefice, that is why I conduct myself on this subject with the greatest kindness, and turn a blind eye to a lot of things'.[72] By law, even a very small tithe had to be gathered by an accredited agent, a *chercheur de dixmes*, who would claim a sheaf in every two dozen for his pains.[73] Collecting on a bigger scale meant hiring carts, horses, day-labourers, threshers— this might run away with a tenth or even a fifth or a quarter of the income.[74] One or two vicaires might have to be paid from the proceeds. There was, too, the obligation to repair the chancel of the parish church, possibly including an expensive tower or spire. When reformers complained of the inequalities in the remuneration of ministers, the curés, some with fat tithes, replied by drawing attention to their outgoings. One with a modest 1,712 livres in tithe paid 350 to a vicaire, and gave compulsory alms of 16½ bushels of barley to the poor.[75] Another with 2,050, said he paid a vicaire, and maintained two horses (his parish being extensive in area); in August, to collect his tithe, he hired four more horses and five men; he had to pay for repairs to his barn, winepress, and stables, and to subscribe a quarter (he had this proportion of the parish tithe) of the repairs to the choir, 'which is exposed to extraordinary gales of wind'—he also gave alms to 400 poor.[76] Another, with the splendid figure of 8,300 livres from lands and tithe, had only 3,937 left after paying expenses and the salary of two vicaires.[77] On the other side, we should remember the fringe benefits which come the way of those who deal in indispensable commodities: no doubt the curé and his household took out as much as possible for their own subsistence before the official calculations of income began.

We have considered elsewhere the complexities of the tithe system and the legal entanglements which ensued. Sometimes, curé would be set against curé, with lay society relishing the impropriety of the conflict. In May 1731, the wealthy and aristocratic curé of Gan in Béarn wrote to his neighbour, the abbé Pessarton, doctor of theology and curé of Rébénac, a letter which at least had the merit of abjuring hypocrisy.

I am grateful for the charity which prompts you to remind me that zeal for the house of God and the salvation of souls ought to be the unique solicitude inspiring a pastor who is charged with the oversight of the faithful. I will do all that is within me, *Monsieur*, to profit from your salutary exhortations, by conserving the flock that is committed to my care and vigilance and, if possible, augmenting its numbers. But setting aside for the moment the question of the glory of God, let us drop the mask, let us speak without disguise, using the language of truth. The spirit of all the letters which you have done me the honour to write to me, tends only to one single objective—to deprive me, under a lofty pretext, of the *novales* (tithes on new crops) of 14 or 15 houses in (the hamlet of) Haut-le-Gan, upon which you claim to have acquired a right dating from a mythical concordat which was made—if you are to be believed—in the Year of Grace 1711, between the bishop of Oloron, the late Mgr de Mesplas bishop of Lescar, and my late uncle.[78]

Curés in poorer circumstances could not afford to be so suave: in 1750 we find the *prieur-curé* of Vienne-la-Ville turning out, shotgun under arm and accompanied by his housekeeper, the schoolmaster and a few 'armed men', to repel the tithe collectors of the neighbouring parish.[79]

Disputes of curés with their flocks were legion. When to collect, how, what measures to use, the introduction of new crops, the changing of areas of cultivation—almost anything could lead to a lawsuit, and even the most irenical of pastors, willing to sacrifice his own income, had to remember that he was responsible for the interests of his successors. In an extreme gesture, one parish priest refused absolution to recalcitrant parishioners at Eastertide, leading to further resort to the courts for abuse of ecclesiastical power.[80] On the other side violence brooded. In a parish in Normandy, where there was a dispute over the straw of the tithe, the peasants near the vicarage marked their geese with a special sign so they could shoot those of the curé when they strayed on to their land;[81] in a parish near Puy de Dôme, after mediation by the *subdélégué* over payments on sheep had broken down, the horsemen of the *maréchaussée* who were sent in to coerce the inhabitants (by the cost of their billeting) had to flee for their lives.[82] Sometimes a curé was faced by a cynical alliance of seigneur and peasants refusing to pay, or the inhabitants leagued together to defeat him on a test case. The picture was unedifying; as Voltaire sardonically pointed out to the bishop of Annecy when the curé of Moens, near Ferney, won a tithe suit against his parishioners before the parlement of Dijon, Protestant pastors did not go to law against their people.[83]

In the *cahiers* of 1789, the peasants occasionally take their chance to censure the rapacity of their curé; he appropriates the straw which is essential for their manure;[84] his men throw the sheaves around to choose the biggest, and in so doing shake out some of the grain;[85] he comes round meanly in person checking the number of new-born calves.[86]

Of the fifth of the parish *cahiers* which propose the abolition or buying off of tithe, and the two-fifths wanting a reform of the system, most are concerned with tithes usurped by bishops, chapters, and monasteries: it would be a different matter if the curé, living in the place and responsible for its poor, was drawing all the income.[87]

This is what so many of them imply: even then, the parish priest's share of the harvest would always have been the subject of grumbling. 'These tithes', said the *cahier* of the parish of Thouai in Périgord, 'by their very nature compel us to look on our pastors, who are our friends and the consolers of our sorrows, as persons hostile to us, and expose them to the risk of being regarded as members of the class which oppresses the common people.'[88]

A tithe-owning curé might happen to be poor; the curés on the *congrue*, however, were officially so—unless they had fortuitous supplementary sources of income. The word *congrue*[89] was derived from an old adjective meaning 'expressed in exact terms': it had nothing to do with 'congruous', and it was certainly never congruous with the cost of living. Since the end of the sixteenth century, the king had fixed the amount which the holders of the great tithe had to give to their 'perpetual vicars'. In 1686, the figure was put at 300 livres a year, a small sum, but by the edict the *congruistes* also had a right to the *dîmes novales*, the 'new tithes' on wastelands brought under cultivation, and on crops newly introduced into the area (these were becoming important—the cultivation of maize, potatoes, beet, and tobacco was spreading). By a declaration of 17 May 1768, the government raised the payment to 500 livres, which was said to be the average price of 25 *setiers* of wheat; a sustained rise in grain prices was to lead to a further increase in the *congrue*. Counterbalancing the generosity, however, the declaration transferred the *novales* (including those the curés were already levying) to the holders of the great tithe. Perhaps this could be justified on grounds of administrative convenience, but it looked very much as though the higher clergy had foreseen how the expansion and diversification of agriculture was going to make the *novales* a gold-mine in the future. Grain prices did indeed rise. 'Le cas prévu', said the curés of Aurillac in Auvergne in May 1780, 'c'est-à-dire l'augmentation considérable dans le prix des graines est arrivé.'[90] A leisurely five years later, the abbés Talleyrand and Boisgelin, agents of the clergy, reported to the General Assembly of the Clergy of France in favour of a *congrue* of 700 livres, which was established by the edict of 2 December 1786.

Most *congruistes*, we may assume, drew the salary officially prescribed, but by no means all did so: eighteenth-century France was a patchwork of traditional agreements and exceptions. We find wretched priests who accepted less in consideration of a scrap of land which the tithe holder transferred to them.[91] In 1789, of twenty-four *congruistes* in the area around Rennes, at least seven were being underpaid,[92] and in the poverty-stricken Mauges area of Anjou most were drawing only 500–600 livres,[93] well short of the official figure—probably, the tithe holder was incapable of paying the full amount in many cases. Royal edicts fixing the *congrue* did not apply to the numerous parishes dependent on the Order of Malta; according to the knights, this was fair, since the Order paid the clerical taxation on its benefices, waived visitation fees, and, through its provincial chapters, was willing to vote special grants to needy incumbents.[94] If the instance of the curé of Pomerol, near Bordeaux, is typical, these special grants were a fable. The *congrue* here was 200 livres, raised to 300 in 1758 (the local *commandeur* of the Order drew 2,800 from the tithes of the parish). The curé who died in 1734 left verses complaining of his melancholy diet:

> Sans pain, sans vin de dîme
> Il vit d'une sardine

His successor, according to the magistrates of Libourne, who appealed on his behalf to the *commandeur*, lived solely on bread and water—they gave a certificate to this effect.[95] On the other hand, some *congruistes* drew more than their official salary. This might be the case when the curé was rendering some special services to his tithe owner, or because the latter was inclined to be generous. Thus, there were two curés at Chelles, ministering to their flocks in the shadow of the great abbey: one was quite well off from his lands and an annual grain payment from the nuns for saying their masses, and the other had 160 livres extra from leases over and above his 700 livres *congrue*.[96] When the Crown acquired the duchy of Châteauroux in 1741, the Conseil d'État awarded minor additions, ranging from 15 livres to 134, to the clergy of the seventeen parishes involved.[97] More usually, the *congruiste* who was getting more was benefiting from some old local agreement—on such a ground, the courts refused to allow the abbey of Eu to bring down one of its curés from his traditional 800 livres to the 500 of the 1768 edict.[98] By a series of 'transactions' with their canons, the thirty *vicaires perpétuels* of the chapter of Périgueux by 1790 had pushed their salaries well above the official 700 livres; according to their declarations in that year they were drawing on the average 1,354 each, which was only 313 short of the average for all the curés of the diocese.[99]

About 30 per cent of the curés of France were in receipt of the *congrue*. The figure, however, conceals wide local diversities. In seventeen of the larger dioceses for which exact figures are conveniently available,[100] there was a total of 7,694 parishes, and in 2,754 of them the priest was on the *congrue*. But in four of these dioceses, such unlucky salaried curés constituted a small minority—in Coutances (22 out of 295), Saint-Pol-de-Léon (9 of 120), Metz (30 of 397). The standard proportion of a third is found, roughly, in the huge dioceses of Bourges (222 of 792) and Limoges (209 of 868), and in Auch (74 of 262); the proportion is rather lower in Paris (137 of 470), Bordeaux (98 of 282), Reims (99 of 418), Rennes (38 of 142), and Oloron (47 of 149). In the remaining five dioceses, *congruistes* are over half the total—Clermont (410 of 800), Rodez (293 of 465), Tarbes (188 of 298), Gap (146 of 214), with Vienne having an almost exclusively salaried ministry (400 of 430). Just as areas of vast ecclesiastical property holding were the pacemakers for the accelerating movement of anticlerical envy among the laity, so too the regions where the *congrue* predominated tended to play a role of leadership in clerical discontent. In the latter years of the *ancien régime* Dauphiné was a centre of the agitation of the lower clergy: the percentage of *congruistes* in the seven dioceses of that province, as recorded by the Clergy of France in 1760, was: Vienne 93 per cent, Valence 41 per cent, Dié 61 per cent, Saint-Paul-Trois-Châteaux 74 per cent, Embrun 80 per cent, Grenoble 92 per cent, Gap 68 per cent.[101]

Whenever and wherever the *congruistes* complained, they were conscious of the solid backing of their parishioners. It was a general local interest to have the produce of the village fields sold to local people, and profits locally made used to provide employment and poor relief near at home. In a presentation of their case in 1755, the curés of Nîmes[102] begin by citing the standard arguments from inside the ecclesiastical structure: 'the tithe belongs to the curés by common law; its passing into other hands is a usurpation'; ecclesiastical revenues are held by those who do not do the work, 'most often they are cold spectators of the tribulations of the Church whose revenues they have monopolized'; the good of religion and the decencies of distributive justice demand reform. Then they go on to say that lay society is with them, 'the voice of the people', who have an interest in ensuring that their contributions are spent locally and provide the sort of wage to attract able clergy into the parochial office. A lay pamphleteer of 1786 did a precise calculation; suppress monasteries and chapters, confiscate their tithes, and share them out among the parish priests, and each curé would have an income of 1,428 livres, double the figure of the official *congrue* newly prescribed in that very year.[103]

All parish priests, whether tithe owners or *congruistes*, were

entitled to the income from the *casuel*, the surplice-fees for the performance of the occasional offices. A very small parish would not
yield much; in 1756, the curé of Épinay near Paris complained that
his thirty families provided him with only two funerals a year and a
marriage in every three or four. In two neighbouring parishes, with
incomes of over 1,000 livres a year, the *casuel* contributed 100 to
each; in another, nothing at all.[104] But in Gemeaux, a populous
village in Burgundy where the tithe yielded 600 to 700 livres, the
occasional offices brought 1,000 to 2,000 (the folk were generous
here; everyone joined in putting an offering for the celebrant on the
patten used in the nuptial mass).[105] There were town parishes where
the *casuel* was virtually the whole of the revenue—La Trinité at
Cherbourg (1,100 livres),[106] Saint-Gervais (8,000)[107] and Saint-Leu-
Saint-Gilles (3,900) at Paris.[108] The curé could not hope, of course,
to keep such large sums exclusively for himself, since he had to
provide for the minor ecclesiastics who helped him—unless, like the
curé of the cathedral at Bordeaux, he maintained his standard of
living by spending his entire time baptizing, marrying, and bury-
ing.[109]

The *casuel* was hated by the laity.[110] They had already paid for the
services of the clergy, they argued, through the tithe. Any extra
offering for the pastor should be purely voluntary, and so it had been
until custom hardened into obligation towards the end of the sixteenth century. At weddings amid the general hilarity and show-off
expenditure, an extra payment among the others could be handed
over with reasonable cheerfulness, but there was universal dissatis-
faction at the charges for funerals. It was intolerable that these sad
occasions should be a source of profit to the pastor of the flock. 'Is
it not sufficiently distressing for us to lose our relatives?' asked a
cahier of 1789; 'must the memory of our sorrows be renewed by a
bill for surplice-fees which is even more burdensome to us than the
crushing weight of official taxation?'[111]

Some of the diocesan tables of fees (drawn up by the bishops in
accordance with Louis XIV's edict of 1695) made concessions to the
Christian and common-sense principle that the tariff should take
into account the ability of a particular family to pay. The Autun
ordinance, which remained in force from 1706 to 1789, divided the
population into four classes, though their payments were not very
steeply differentiated, as the nobles, *avocats*, doctors, and *rentiers* of
the first class had to pay only double the fees imposed on the servants, day-labourers, and *menu peuple* of the fourth.[112] The Amiens
tariff of 1744[113] left baptisms free of charge (as was universal), and

charged ordinary folk 15 sols for *fiançailles* (ceremony of engagement to be married), with 1 livre, 5 sols, for the richer sort; the calling of banns cost 3 or 5 livres, and the nuptial benediction and mass was 1 livre, 4 sols, or 3 livres, 15 sols. As against these graded charges for supposedly equal access to the offices of the Church, funerals were differentiated according to the magnificence of the ceremonies on offer. An ordinary funeral cost 2 livres; there were four more expensive ones, culminating in a 'service très solennel à neuf leçons, vigiles à neuf leçons, convoi, enterrement, grandes commendations' at 12 livres, 15 sols, with extra charges if more than one priest attended, and for acolytes, cross-bearers, and so on.[114] Some of the occasional offices were optional, and the very poor, maybe, would have to do without them—the blessing of the nuptial bed at 10 sols plus 5 for the clerk and 3 for the attendant choirboy; blessing new houses at 10 sols, or beehives at 5.[115] This deprivation of spiritual and picturesque adjuncts to family life imposed on the poor was most grimly evident at the funeral of a child. An infant could be buried drably for 12 sols, but to have a mass of the Holy Angels, with white stole and the message of assured salvation, cost 2 livres, 5 sols, the price of three days' labour amid sheaves and furrows.[116]

A few curés tried to institute more sharply differentiated surplice-fees in their parishes to ease the burden on the poor.[117] One, in the diocese of Boulogne, tried the opposite tack, and to rescue them from humiliation, insisted on having the same service for all, in spiritual equality; this was unpopular, for the poor liked to see displays put on by their superiors.[118] Another curé tried to persuade the village to pay a fixed annual composition which would cover all households.[119] But more and more parish priests found it impossible to levy any sort of surplice-fees; some of their people were too poor to pay them, and all of them were recalcitrant. In 1728, a curé of Normandy described his parish: 150 households, two-thirds of the bread-winners being poor fishermen, and the State levying 800 livres a year in taxation—he could ask nothing, 'casuel néant'.[120] A parish priest wrote to the bishop of Grenoble in 1765 asking permission to retire to a religious community, so weary was he of struggling to exist on the *congrue*—as for the surplice-fees, he said, 'l'humanité répugne à tirer d'eux les moindres émoluments'.[121] Three of the replies of curés to the bishop of Comminges's comprehensive questionnaire of 1786 refer to fees of 100 livres or over (786, 400 shared with the vicaires, and 100), but for the most part, the sums are derisory, and some curés flatly state that it is out of the question to levy anything at all. 'Only a priest without heart or compassion could do so'; 'Surplice-fees are no longer customary'; 'Lost entirely'; 'For long extinct'; 'Practically destroyed'; 'nil, nil, nil'; 'It is an honorarium which will soon be remembered only as a name'; 'An odious and execrable word'; 'What profit can you draw from the *casuel* in a parish where the curé himself has to pay for the candles for a funeral?'; 'The dead are a surcharge on the curé'.[122]

When Church property was confiscated during the Revolution, the curés had to make declarations of their income. Since they were to be paid a basic rate and, if they had drawn more than this under the *ancien régime*, half the excess (excluding from the calculation the proceeds of the *casuel*), their statements naturally do not err on the low side. These declarations reveal a further source of income which some parish priests had enjoyed—a source not fully discussed in earlier controversies about clerical poverty. Every tonsured ecclesiastic was technically qualified to hold benefices without cure of souls, and those who were well connected accumulated a fair revenue in this way. Some of these, of course, were curés. A priest who was particularly learned or efficient might be favoured by interested patrons with gifts of chapels or priories, and with these to support him, might be persuaded to stay in some strategic parish even if its income was small. Of the seventeen curés of Angers,[123] four enjoyed 1,000 livres or more from such extra benefices. One, the curé of Saint-Aignan, a tiny parish in the centre of town, drew practically nothing by virtue of his parochial office, but had 1,500 livres from eight chapels. The curé of Sainte-Croix, with a basic income of 400 livres, was the titular of three chapels bringing in half as much again. Just as bishops were fortified by grants of abbeys *in commendam* by the Crown, so too the more favoured (and generally more able) curés had their supplementary resources.

Like everyone who was of respectable status in eighteenth-century France, the curés had their perquisites of office. In richer parishes, the offerings at the main mass of Easter might reach a fair figure—in the Breton countryside, said a report of 1781, they were scandalously solicited: 'a verger or choirman follows the recteur or curé who is administering the communion, and cries "Payez vos deniers pascaux! Pay your Easter dues!" Then everyone hastens to fumble in his clothing, most often in an indecent fashion, to get money out of his pocket or his purse to put on the collection plate.'[124] In some places, farmers who owned plough animals gave the curé one or two sheaves each on condition he read the Passion narrative daily 'from the feast of the Invention of the Holy Cross to the feast of its Exaltation'.[125] There were small payments for saying foundation masses (about one livre for a low mass and three times as much for the nine lessons, commendation, and high mass).[126] Perhaps there would be the candle ends left after the ceremonies of the First Communion and of Candlemas (not on other days, these belonged to the churchwardens).[127] Gifts dedicated on the high altar were supposedly the curé's, but not those on the minor ones.[128] Pious ladies might leave some contribution to the comfort of their pastor behind them in the confessional, and learned priests in university towns might draw fees for examining theses in the Faculty of Theology.[129] Some curés also managed to insist on the continuance of 'folkloric' levies which most people in the eighteenth century were now refusing to render—a tribute of eggs from the boys and girls making their First Communion, or of flax by those who attended mass on the day of Sainte-Barbe.[130]

In this complex, archaic social order, perquisites were offset by uncovenanted obligations—the many things the pastor had to pay for because there was no one else to do so. There were no retirement pensions; a parish priest who resigned contracted with his successor for a pension, normally a third of the income of the benefice. Bad harvests might be as disastrous for the priest as for the peasant parishioners. Just as his income fell, there would be more poor to be rescued from starvation, and if a pauper died, like as not, it would be the curé who paid for the shroud and the necessary minimum of four candles. A *casuel* of 8,000 and 1,200 livres in house rents made the curé of Saint-Gervais in Paris seemingly rich, but he complained that inescapable good works took away half his revenue—300 livres and 80 livres lodging allowance to maintain a priest at Pont-aux-Choux for catechisms; 100 for classes to educate young clerics; gratuities coming to 500 to assistant clergy for attending the offices of the church; lodgings for them, 1,000; to poor families, about 500; unpredictable sums to parish schools, and 54 to the Dames de la Charité who went visiting in the slums. 'I wanted to shake off this latter burden,' he naïvely recorded in 1762, 'but the universal outcry (*le soulèvement général*) obliged me to submit to it.'[131]

The difficulty of assessing the necessary outgoings of a curé is matched by the difficulty of finding out exactly what he had coming in originally. So often, the income was a composite affair. In his memoirs, curé Ducastel describes how by 1785 he had at last been awarded one of the plums of ecclesiastical preferment, the living of Marolles-les-Braults—6,500 livres from tithes farmed out, 350 from tithes in kind, a *métairie* (a farm leased on a crop-sharing basis) worth 922, an enclosure bringing in 260, and a field worth 126, assorted other lands worth 600, *casuel* and foundation masses worth 500.[132] Had he not told us all this, it is probable that some branch or other of his earnings would have been as impenetrable to the historian as it probably was to the diocesan bureau that assessed taxation. Contemporary attempts to state a global sum by the addition of disparate earnings were approximations, and loaded at that. The diocesan *pouillé*, the published list of benefices, always quoted much too low a figure, reflecting the amount the incumbents reluctantly admitted to be theirs in the face of overwhelming evidence. Conversely, the declarations of 1790, seeing it was a question of extracting the maximum salary from the government, were pushed as high as credulity would allow. The pension obtained by a resigning curé is probably the best guide of all; it would be a third of the total income, a figure arrived at after negotiation in which the new man had investigated the accounts to keep the figure down and the old one had used every argument to inflate it. In the diocese of Lisieux, the evidence from retirement pensions tends to add 25 per cent to the published figures of benefice income.[133] Even then, in a particular case, we may be mistaken. A candidate may have been willing to pay at a high rate because he knew his predecessor had not long to live, or because of affection for him, or because of sheer desperation to get the parish; the retiring curé may have been willing to accept less than his due because he was resigning to a close friend or relative, or to build up a good relationship—and in any case, the value of any extra benefices without cure of souls would not have entered into the calculation. In interpreting official figures of income without the aid of account-books or resignation pensions, the rule must be to increase the amount by at least a quarter, but with one proviso. The very lowest figures are more likely to be accurate. Everyone knew how much the *congrue* was, and there were few opportunities to augment it. Where the product of land or tithes was minute, there was little scope for improvement, and the priests who spent their lives in the poorest parishes were those who lacked the influence which obtained supplementary benefices. The curés who were officially poor were probably really so; those who were higher up the scale were richer than was given out, and progressively so as we ascend the published tabulations of incomes.

Another 'rule' of analysis for clerical revenues is: in spite of continual fluctuations, the rich curés will remain rich, and the poor ones poor. Where the land is productive and agriculture progressive, the income of the parish priest will share in the general prosperity—his acres will produce more, his leases go up, his tithes increase, his people will be more able to pay his surplice-fees, the money from foundations and pious gifts will increase, the priories and chapels nearest at hand to provide supplementary benefices will be more productive. If a curé was comparatively well-off under Louis XIII, it was likely that his successor would be so under Louis XV.[134] There was, then, an established geography of clerical incomes. The pattern varied in different parts of the country. Towards the end of the *ancien régime* there were few parish priests with less than 700 livres in Anjou (the Mauges area excepted), in the Sarthe, in the dioceses of Quimper, Nancy, and Metz.[135] By contrast, probably half the curés of the dioceses of Bordeaux, Dijon, Autun, Nîmes, Reims, Clermont, Rodez, Tarbes, and Gap did not rise much over the 700 mark.[136] This was principally because of the *congrue*, but not entirely so: of the 336 parishes of Bordeaux, 149 were in the poorest category, and there were only 98 *congruistes*.[137] In every diocese there were a few splendidly lucrative cures, the distant object of everyone's ambition: 4,000 livres seems to have been the point at which envy became universal.[138] In six areas for which comprehensive figures are available, the solid figure of 3,000 livres or above is found in a proportion of 1:7 in the most favoured, and 1:27 in the least favoured, with various intermediate ratios in the others.[139] Bordeaux, with its mass of poor incumbents, had twenty curés who drew over 3,000 livres, with two of them enjoying over 10,000. Most curés had an income of something between the 700 of the poor and the 3,000 of the prosperous; many between 700 and 1,200, fewer between 1,200 and 2,800, fewer still between 2,000 and 3,000. Everywhere there were illogicalities and inequalities. The richest curé of Anjou had over 7,000 livres, the poorest just over 400. A country rural dean of the diocese of Le Mans cites the incomes of the parishes of his deanery as five at 700 livres, nine at 700–1,000, seven at 1,000–2,000, and three over 2,000.[140] The curés of Saint-Sulpice and Saint-Eustache at Paris, said Mercier, drew more than some provincial bishops;[141] but some of the smaller parishes of the capital were just above the *congrue* level. In this comparison the weight of duties and the scale of income have some relationship, but this was unusual. A curé in the town of Dijon[142] with 400 communicants had an income rather larger than that of two colleagues who each had ten times the number, and in the countryside nearby a priest with a tiny flock had five times the income of another who served four times the population. These injustices, theoretically indefensible, did not cause as much bitterness as might be imagined. Social standing and influence and, less certainly, learning and ability, brought promotion to the

richer benefices, while supplementary chapels, which in some cases
added to the inequality, in others helped to rectify it. Envy was, no
doubt, a universal passion, but the arrangements of the Church
reflected the unjust arrangements of the social order, so that, revolutionary spirits apart, most curés' realistic expectations were realistically catered for.

It was an eighteenth-century commonplace—parishioners,
reforming ecclesiastics, philosophes, and anticlericals all echoed it—
that the curés were not given their fair share of the wealth of the
Church, and that many of them were underpaid.[143] This was true of
the priests who received the bare *congrue* or less. According to two
modern historians of the rural population,[144] 500 livres (700 after the
1786 edict) was a more than living wage, and this is undeniable in
comparison with the mass of the peasantry. It was more than double
the amount a novelist assumed would keep a wounded soldier—
board, lodging, and medical attention.[145] But it was not enough to
enable a curé to discharge his duties with dignity and to give alms to
the needy. The curé who saved enough from his *congrue* to have his
tombstone inscribed with a last protest, 'Dionisius Boutinot, Vixit
Pauper, et Pauper mortuus est', was telling the sober truth.[146] A *congruiste* of Dauphiné filled in the details, describing himself as wearing
coarse, ragged clothing, living on black bread, vegetables, milk, nuts,
and 'a few scraps of bacon', with no possibility of entertaining
respectable parishioners who called on him, or of helping the deserving poor.[147] Maybe he exaggerated; even so, the numerous contemporary estimates of an appropriate income for a curé ran a good deal
higher than 500 or 700 livres. Early in the century, the abbé de
Saint-Pierre thought these 'officers of morality' should have a minimum of 1,200.[148] In their *cahiers*, the favourite figure for the clergy
to ask is 1,500 (exactly what was proposed by the Tiers État at Auch
and Angoulême).[149] In the National Assembly in June 1790 the abbé
de Marolles, demonstrating his patriotic austerity, pared the figure
down to 1,040,[150] and the Assembly, trying to be fair but not
extravagant, decided to give a basic 1,200 livres plus half the extra
income individuals had earned under the *ancien régime*. This was not
a bad figure; a canon of Saint-Omer in 1781 said he could live well
and keep two servants on 1,200 livres,[151] though a country curé at the
time argued for a minimum of double this amount.[152] (These
estimates and proposals all concerned net income, without any
expenses concerning agricultural production or tithe collection.) It
all depended, of course, on what sort of dignity a curé was supposed
to maintain. While poor folk dressed in the motley cast-off clothing

of the better sort, or in threadbare family heirlooms, a curé had to be respectably turned out, and new clothing was expensive. One of them said he needed 12 livres a year for three pairs of shoes, 15 for three pairs of stockings, 8 for three shirts, 6 for gaiters and as much for a hat, 10 for clerical bands and neckwear and handkerchiefs—add two pairs of breeches yearly, a new cloak and a short cassock every three years, and wear and tear on the long cassock worn in church, and 100 livres a year was required.[153] A servant was indispensable and, in most parishes, a horse. In difficult terrain, two servants and two horses were needed, for in bad weather or at night, through swamp or on precipitous tracks, the curé needed a man riding with him and someone left at home to guard the presbytery from thieves.[154] Local prices varied. Clerical estimates of the cost of a servant ran from 60 to 200 livres (probably the former figure does not include food and clothing),[155] and of a horse from 100 to 200 livres (the latter figure no doubt includes the cost of an eventual replacement).[156] The curés of Orléans in 1773 put together a complete list of necessary expenses: food and wine, 600 livres; wood and candles, 200; dress and furnishings, 200; books and surplice, 60; horse, 100; a servant, 60; repairs, 30; spending money, 80; alms to the sick, 50—with a few other items, like clerical taxation, they reached a total of 1,340 livres. Four years earlier a curé of the diocese of Nantes had made an almost identical estimate, though pushed up to 1,800 livres because he asked for two servants and two horses.[157]

Bearing in mind what lay society expected of a curé, 1,500 livres seems a comfortable, reasonable income. Most parish priests got less. A tiny minority lived in grinding poverty, and about a quarter[158] of the total had half the desirable figure, which gave them a standard of living above the mass of the peasantry, but short of the necessary dignity of their office. Perhaps a third had more than 1,500, with some at the top of the scale enjoying real affluence. Since promotion recognized both ability and influence, the system, with all its injustices, tended to fulfil social expectations. What was resented by all the curés, however, was the grip of monasteries, chapters, and bishops on the tithes and lands of the Church, and when they complained, they knew lay society was solidly behind them. Their discontent was intensified by theological and legal theories exalting the role of the parish priest, combined with the humanitarian and utilitarian propaganda of the Enlightenment. When the *novales* were confiscated by the edict of 1768 and the news spread in the dioceses that the upper clergy were not paying their fair share of clerical taxation, resentment hardened into revolt. It was not just a question of an improved standard of living and distributive justice, it was also a struggle for status, and for a level of income that would make the more effective performance of professional duties possible, while reducing envious passions among the clergy themselves and improving social and charitable relations with parishioners. It was not often that those who wanted to be paid more could cite such unexceptionable social and religious arguments for their case.

III *Mentality*

Collet's *Traité des devoirs d'un Pasteur* (1758) lists the recommended composition of a parish priest's library.[159] Though the actual titles are updated, the span of coverage is that established in similar lists by three generations of reforming bishops.[160] The central items were the decrees and the catechism of the Council of Trent and the Bible. Collet proposed the newly published edition of the Council by the abbé du Petitchâteau, which had the advantage of annotations saying which points had been accepted in France and which not. Since, in these difficult days, women (no doubt Jansenistically inclined) study the 'petites notes' of M. de Saci in a design to embarrass their clergy with questions about the Scriptures, he recommended two or three solid biblical commentaries; not that a curé needs to know the details of Hebrew musical instruments—sufficient to study the sacred history in so far as it conveys moral lessons, and the Psalms, the Wisdom books, and the Prophets as evocative preludes to the New Testament. Another principal heading concerns the manuals of casuistry necessary for the guidance of souls in the confessional. In place of St Charles Borromeo, the old stand-by, Collet lists the dictionary of Pontas, the *Résolutions* of M. de la Paluelle, and the *Conférences* of Paris and Angers. A curé must also be knowledgeable in ecclesiastical law and in some branches of civil law—thus Fleury, Héricourt, and La Combe should be on his shelves—and he would do well also to make enquiries about the customary law of his particular province. For controversy with Protestants—a subject other lists were not much concerned with—there are authoritative authors (especially Bossuet), though Collet advised against going into too much detail about subjects like Purgatory: 'Keep to the promises of Christ to the Church because this fundamental point settles all the others.' Finally, there is spiritual reading. Strangely, Collet does not follow the usual custom of including St Thomas à Kempis and St François de Sales. Instead, he has Charles Demia,

Tronson, Massillon, Opstraet, Abelly, Boudon on prayer, and Père le Brun's explanation of the ceremonies of the mass. As usual in these bibliographies, he proposes whatever lives of the saints are conveniently available, and to these he adds a pious biography more relevant to the experience of ordinary people, *La Vie de Jacques Cochois, ou le bon laquais* (1696). The emphasis throughout is on what might be called 'applied theology'. The curé must know the rules the Church has prescribed and the details of ecclesiastical law; he must be able to explain difficulties in the Bible and to rehearse the arguments against heretics; he must deal effectively with moral problems in the confessional; while cultivating his own interior priestly life, he must also be versed in a spirituality adapted to composing sermons in which exhortation plays a more important part than explanation.

How many curés bought the books reformers so enthusiastically prescribed for them? At the end of the reign of Louis XIV, a priest with as many as a dozen volumes was a rarity in the west of France.[161] In the diocese of La Rochelle (worse than most, it is true), a single book on law, another on casuistry, a catechism, and a few sermon manuals were regarded as adequate—some priests did not even possess a New Testament.[162] Throughout the eighteenth century, a few rural curés can be found, financially hard up and with no pretensions to learning, whose ambitions had not strayed above this low, minimum level. A report of 1790 speaks of some as satisfied with an *ABC*, a catechism, a psalter, 'et quelques rares autres bouquins'; though, more optimistically, a similar report for another area gave the composition of the standard book shelf as the breviary, the proceedings of the Council of Trent, the synodical ordinances of the diocese, the theological *summa* of Collet or of Habert, some works of meditation and sermons, a handbook on tithe law, the *Mercure* for the news, and a cookery book.[163] Curés in towns were usually better provided; at the beginning of the century, a parish priest in the diocese of Paris was likely to own at least a hundred volumes.[164] Everywhere, in both town and country, there was rapid progress in the eighteenth century. In the West, of forty-five curés whose book holdings for the years 1725–30 are listed, thirty-three had at least twenty titles, and nineteen had over a hundred; after 1760, a similar sample suggests that three-quarters of the secular clergy had passed the 100 mark.[165] At the end of the *ancien régime* there were curés (their cases no doubt illustrating the happy coincidence of the solid learning of the incumbent and the substantial tithes of the benefice) who had impressive libraries—a Breton recteur with 1,225 books (at a time when the bishop of Nantes had only 78),[166] a curé of Sens who fled during the Revolution, leaving 2,170 volumes behind him.[167] Though we hear occasionally of Diderot's *Encyclopédie*, of works of Voltaire, essays on newly fashionable scientific experiments, and the like, the contents of these clerical libraries are rarely eclectic; most of the books are 'religious' and, indeed, figure generally on the Counter-Reformation lists—the Bible, casuistry and moral theology, liturgy, pastoralia, and devotion predominating.

Since the shelves of the parish priests contained so little about science, geography, secular history, or contemporary literary and philosophical debates, we might infer that the new specialized ecclesiastical culture and the new culture of lay society were diverging far apart.[168] Churchmen had broken free from the tyranny of the Latin literature of their college days, and become professional students of moral and pastoral theology; in the process, they were losing touch with the educated laity.

There is broad truth in this generalization, but reservations need to be made. It is only when books become comparatively inexpensive that a personal collection provides the historian with a guide to the mentality of the owner. A curé generally had enough to do to pay for his basic professional library—the solid volumes for reference and pastoral purposes which impressed the bishop or the archdeacon at visitation time. But no doubt, in his friendly contacts with the educated laity and in visits to the *cabinet littéraire* or lending library of his local town, he would come across more lively reading than the tomes solemnly listed as on his shelves when the testamentary executor came round after his funeral. We must distinguish too between being well read and being well informed. Curés who read few of the works of the Enlightenment often knew their content and purpose, none the less, from the literary journalism of the day. The standard reading for a curé who was a severe moralist and theologian, said one of the wits, is 'La Gazette et les Saints-Pères'—the *Gazette* and the ancient Fathers.[169]

There were two practical subjects on which society expected the clergy to use their reading for the general benefit—medicine and agriculture. Generally, doctors and surgeons were concentrated in towns, country areas being poorly served with professional medical advice. Apart from a few tips in the almanacs, the leaflets hawked by pedlars showed little interest in matters of health;[170] it seemed that the peasants relied on their old traditional remedies, or on advice from some local worthy, more especially from their parish priest.[171]

It was the curé's task to read from the pulpit the proclamations of the intendant concerning precautions to be taken in times of epidemic, and he would be in charge of the distribution of the medicines officially provided—'the peasant would put them in his soup and think them sweeter than honey because they cost nothing'.[172] 'Healing the body and the soul', one curé declared, 'are two ministries which the pastors ought to exercise simultaneously,' and another described himself as having been 'apostle, judge, surgeon, and doctor' to his people for thirty-four years.[173] Occasionally, we hear of a parson who had become a specialist. In 1775, four curés meeting in Le Mans had a theological argument so heated that one of them collapsed and died—the local chronicle laments that he was the only one in town who could treat maladies of the eyes.[174] Mostly, however, the role of the parochial minister was to be a general practitioner, and as such he was more closely in touch with the lives, and more particularly the deaths, of his people than we can easily imagine today.

As cultivating land, leasing it to others, or as tithe owners, country curés were knowledgeable about farming. They were expected to be, for this was an improving century, and the priest had a duty to read up on the latest agricultural improvements in the gazettes or government pamphlets and to pass on the advice to his peasant neighbours. In 1763, Duhamel du Monceau, the chief theoretician of agricultural reform, paid tribute to the clergy. 'A country curé, once the duties of his office have been completed, always has a certain amount of leisure. Many of them think that the best employment they can make of it is to instruct their parishioners in the useful practices which they have found set out in reliable books about agriculture.'[175] The royal societies of agriculture which sprang up in the second half of the century usually had a parish priest or two on their membership lists (along with more dilettante monks and canons), and the intendants were accustomed to ask the parish clergy for information or advice when there was an epidemic among the cattle or a plague of insects devouring the crops.[176] The abbé Froger, who ruled the parish of Mayer in the diocese of Le Mans and was a member of the Agricultural Society of Tours, in 1769 published his *Instructions d'agriculture et d'économie pour les habitans de la campagne*, a volume calculated to teach country folk to read, to improve their agricultural methods, and to reform their morals simultaneously. Hard work was his gospel: he urged the peasants not to spend too much time on devotional practices, but to please God by enthusiastically fulfilling the penance they had inherited from the curse on Adam; the sweat of their brows, he pointed out, would also make them rich.[177] Less dourly, he urged generosity to servants and kindness to children. Clearly he had read Rousseau, recommending breast-feeding, frequent changes of nappies, and loose, comfortable clothing for infants—and when they grew older, they were not to be frightened with stories about ghosts or witches.[178] By contrast, Louis-François Norbert de Pressac de la Chagnaye, curé of Saint-Gaudent in the Vienne, was a technical expert rather than a moralist; he published the results of his investigations into the medicinal properties of herbs, and denounced the wastefulness of common pasture and land left fallow—and won the gold medal of the Parisian Society of Agriculture in 1789.[179] Félix Armand, curé of Saint-Martin-en-Lys in the diocese of Alet, who introduced the potato to his parishioners, also gave them an easier road to market; he surveyed (by having himself lowered on a rope into the gorges) and directed the construction of the track to Quibajon, which reduced the journey time of muleteers from twelve hours to one. Later, he came to the notice of Napoleon: 'a pity he's a priest, I'd have made him a general'.[180] These practical activities were what the men of the Enlightenment expected of their clergy. When the bishop of Amiens sent young aspirants for parochial benefices to work in a mill to learn the latest techniques, a Parisian gazetteer applauded the spectacle of their black coats dusted with flour, evidence of time better spent than in 'theological speculation'.[181]

Another practical service which lay society expected of the curé—supposing he was sufficiently lettered—was to teach young people Latin, thus opening their way to places in the Church or the medical or legal professions. 'M. le curé continues zealously to teach Latin to nine or ten young people, and in so doing fulfils the wishes of Mgr the archbishop,' say the minutes of a ruri-decanal visitation in Normandy in 1775.[182] A surgeon's son near Perpignan, destined by his family for the medical profession, remembered how he was sent to the worthy curé of Canet, and within three years, he was translating Virgil.[183] This was one of the manifold uses of a relative in holy orders; thus Jean-Joseph Mounier of Grenoble, the future politician, was dragooned into literacy by the curé of Rives, an uncle he remembered as 'a severe, choleric pedagogue'.[184]

Some parish priests, holders of doctorates and men of serious learning, found a sphere for themselves in the faculties of theology of their local universities, attending the formal disputations for the examination of theses and the unplanned disputes which were the normal way the faculties were governed. 'Give me my money back and I'll hand in my doctorate', curé Robin of Angers was wont to cry when losing his temper at such meetings.[185] Pierre Buquet of Caen[186] even contrived to run the parish of Saint-Sauveur-du-Marché along with being librarian of the university, though there were those who disapproved of this demanding plurality. The more ambitious of the learned sought fame by publication. The two most distinguished theologians of the century, Cotelle de la Blandinière, author of the *Conférences* of Angers, and Bergier, author of the famous *Dictionnaire de théologie dogmatique*, came from the ranks of the curés, though in due course they were whisked off to prestigious canonries, the first to the cathedral of Blois, the second to Notre-Dame at Paris.[187] Less seriously learned figures found inspiration in their parishes for contributions to apologetics. Husson, a curé of the diocese of Toul, challenged Rousseau's confession of faith of the 'vicaire savoyard' with his *La Confession de foi d'un curé Lorrain* (sound, but too difficult for ordinary folk, said a colleague[188]), and Bernière in the diocese of Le Mans demonstrated the falsity of all non-Christian religions from the beginning of time in his *Élève de la raison et de la foi* (1771).[189]

For the most part, however, parish priests inspired with the passion for authorship preferred history to theology—more especially, local history. Among many minor antiquaries in the diocese of Angers there was one more significant figure, Rangeard, curé of Andard, the luminary of the local academy, who struggled to write the definitive history of Anjou, though he was manœuvred out of completing it by the dog-in-the-manger Benedictines of Saint-Maur. There was also curé Robin, who specialized in archaeology, tracing the line of the old Roman road and finally proving, to his own satisfaction, that his church of Saint-Pierre was senior in foundation to the cathedral. In every diocese[190] they had their counterparts—mostly less able—collectors of genealogical information or curious historical anecdotes, readers of papers about their antiquarian discoveries to local academies. According to some austere critics, a priest in the pastoral office ought to apply himself to higher things: to these, curé Robin gave the appropriate reply:

It was nearly always the . . . pastors of the people . . . the priests of the various nations, who transmitted to us the history of the most celebrated epochs and the most interesting events; and as for the time I spend, my writings are to me what social engagements are to others—they are my tric-trac, my games of draughts, my hands at cards.[191]

Even if he did not have ambitions as a historian, a curé still regarded himself as the repository of local traditions. After all, he kept the registers of births, marriages, and deaths. The curé of Souppes, near Montargis, made an index to these volumes from 1622 to his own day in the 1740s, so his parishioners could look up their ancestors and their family alliances. 'People want to know from whom they are descended,' he said, 'who their parents are and to have the evidence that they have been born in legitimate wedlock and are members of the Catholic faith, to know what became of their ancestors . . . and where their mortal dust reposes, and to see the names of the successive generations set down in these hallowed records.'[192] (Curé Froger knew of a more utilitarian reason for his parishioners to keep up with their parish registers: they would be ready to claim any inheritance which fell due to them.[193]) Historians are particularly grateful to the clergy who used their registers as a convenient place to record the significant events of their times. 'The 9 January 1709 it froze so hard that the sown grain was destroyed. The vines froze to the very roots . . . grain sold at 7 livres a measure and barley at 12.'[194] The weather, floods, thunderbolts, and hailstones are general in these chronicles. Robin, curé of Saint-Pierre of Angers, tells of the mild winter of 1758–9, 'like a continual spring', of the savage duration of the winter of 1766, when 'on Ash Wednesday, 12 February, we were still going to see the skaters on the meadow of Saint-Serge', and the great freeze of 1788–9, when carts and horses crossed the ice on the river, and of the following thaw, when the curé himself had to use a bridge of planks to get home after celebrating midnight mass on Christmas Eve.[195] Sometimes, the registers tell of the tribulations of famine—and sometimes, the hardships are daringly ascribed to government mismanagement. The outcome of a lawsuit might be recorded, one conducted by the parish priest himself, or perhaps by others. In 1726, a curé gleefully notes how the parlement of Dijon found in favour of his bishop against a league of eight senior curés embattled against the episcopal plan of reform.[196] Another specializes on catastrophe—a wolf terrorizes the parish in 1748, and an earthquake follows seven years later (a minor tremor radiating out from the great Lisbon disaster). 'Manus Dei fecit hoc ad correctionem nostram'[197]—something like this was the standard comment. Or some figure from the great world outside flashes like a meteor across the dull provincial sky: as in 1777, an Angevin tells how the Emperor Joseph II, brother of the queen, passed by, pausing only to change horses.[198] Or the great events of national life might suddenly irrupt into the local torpor; curé Robin tells how the news of the fall of the Bastille reached Angers, how there was a rush to the town hall to demand the formation of a militia, while the duc de Brissac, the military commander, dared not go out of his lodgings to inspect his troops.[199] One of the most assiduous of these clerical chroniclers is the naïve Antoine Plassard, curé of Saint-Vincent of Mâcon, who made a record of notable occurrences in his city from 1744 to 1767. Among those passing through was the Turkish ambassador, the artillery going to the war in Italy, and prisoners coming back from it, a chain-gang on the way to the Mediterranean galleys, a triumphal procession of friars displaying the emancipated slaves they had ransomed from the Barbary corsairs, and another of converted Chinese, and an alarming fairground 'satyr', no doubt an orang-utan. He records the death of a nobleman, and on the same line, 'the mortality among farm animals has been general this year'. There was a man who murdered his wife and was broken on the wheel before a prodigious crowd, a dog poisoner who was never caught, an ancient citizen who was fêted when he reached 104 until it was realized that he was using his father's birth certificate, a Capuchin preacher at the Carmelites who was too fat to get into the pulpit, and the picnic on an island in the lake given by M. de Lamartine at which three people were drowned when the boat overturned—a curious mid-eighteenth-century association between a Lamartine and 'le lac'.[200]

From gossipy entries in parish registers to journalism was a short step. At Troyes in 1776, when the disapproval of polite society drove the satirical *Éphémérides Troyennes* out of business, the respectable *Almanach de la ville de Troyes* which replaced it had the curé of Saint-Savine as co-editor.[201] A more lively publication of these latter years of the *ancien régime* was *L'Improvisateur* of Louis Sallentin, curé of Mouy in the diocese of Beauvais—Talleyrand is said to have enjoyed dipping into its pages. (More than once, the author warned his readers to be cautious about matrimony, but this did not stop him, in November 1793, at the age of 48, from marrying the young ex-nun who was the popular society of Clermont's goddess of liberty.[202]) Unless there was a royal postmaster living nearby,[203] the country priest would be the first man to turn to for the news, whether of war or of politics, or of the cultural achievements of the Enlightenment. If a Montgolfier balloon passed over, he would explain to the terrified peasants what it was,[204] and if he incautiously went on to declare that 'the whole thing is folly, because it will never be possible to travel through the air as on the water',[205] who can blame him? When an eclipse was expected to cause difficulties in the holding of divine service, the bishop's staff would send round a circular, and a curé with superior scientific knowledge might have a chance to show off to his parishioners that he knew better than a panicky *grand vicaire*.[206] From artificial respiration to recent techniques in midwifery, from electric shocks to mesmerism, the curé would be the local expert on matters scientific. No doubt a few of them took up scientific experiments as a hobby, after the fashion of the day—though whether the working model of the universe according to Ptolemy constructed by the curé of Viroflay in 1755 for the edification of the eldest son of the dauphin was science more than classical studies and craftsmanship is hard to say.[207]

Though freemasonry was under the ban of the Church, curés are found as members of lodges; they are not, however, as numerous as monks and canons. Whether a parish priest joined probably depended more than anything else on the attitude of his diocesan bishop. The bishop of Luçon being strict, the curé of Sables d'Olonne refused to say mass at the inauguration ceremonies of his local lodge. In 1770, the curé of Lunéville, under orders of the bishop of Toul, refused to say a requiem for the soul of a parishioner who was a mason—until the secular courts ordered him to do so.[208] By contrast, we find a parish priest prominent in the lodge of Montreuil-sur-Mer, and another in that of Alençon,[209] and the pastor of Chatellerault holding a solemn mass annually on St John's Day for the masonic fraternity, to which they came with drums, violins, and candles (until in 1753 the bishop of Poitiers intervened).[210] In country places, it was the clergy who had heard of Voltaire and Rousseau, and maybe approved of them, even if they misspelt their names in comments in their registers.[211] Of forty subscribers to the *Encyclopédie* on two lists in Périgord, twenty-four were curés, and of 253 subscribers on a list for Franche Comté there were nine country curés along with nine canons of Besançon.[212] Considering how few parish priests had incomes large enough to justify such a purchase, the number is significant. La Gorce's old-fashioned comment on these progressive, well-read clergy of the *ancien régime* as 'enlightened and blind . . . lacking any sense of the (dangers) of the future and closing their eyes in case they saw too much'[213] misunderstands the relations between the Church and society. The better-educated curés who acted as intellectual middlemen distinguished between literary merit and progressive ideas on the one hand and anticlerical propaganda and irreligious speculation on the other. In their own way, they condemned 'prejudices' and 'systems', and looked forward to the triumph of a respectable and conformist Enlightenment.[214] True, there were two parish priests who achieved notoriety as total unbelievers, and contributed to the clandestine manuscripts which circulated in the first half of the century—Meslier, who left behind him the atheistical testament so relished by Voltaire, and Guillaume, who made a learned study of the 'three impostors', Moses, Jesus, and Muhammad. Meslier wrote with bitter revolutionary zeal, but Guillaume, apparently, for distraction. 'A poor country curé, bored and like the ungrateful deer which eats the vine which conceals it from the hounds, he amused himself by writing a treatise to fit the title of the legendary one about which there had been so many rumours, the *De Tribus impostoribus*.'[215] The sceptical abbé in the camp of the philosophes is a common eighteenth-century phenomenon, but these are probably the only ones to be drawn from the ranks of the curés.

Inevitably, the parochial ministry added its routine quota to the official poetry of the century, the *éloges* of famous men or local worthies, celebrations of national occasions, odes to distinguished visitors—as also to the solemn theologizing versification typified in curé Charles-Hubert Saint-Just's *L'Athéisme détruit . . . ou l'homme évadé* and *Zo-andro-Théodicié, ou le système de la Nature*.[216] The critical comments on the government which were slipped into parish registers might also find expression in bitter verses, as in those of curé Légiste of Pomerol on the death of Louis XIV; an insomniac who wrote in bed to keep boredom at bay, he also produced Christmas carols, madrigals, and satires on monks and canons.[217] A crude lyricism is found in Jean-Claude Peyrot's *Poésies diverses, patoises et françaises* (1774) and *Les Quatre Saisons, ou les Géorgiques patoises* (1781), realistically depicting peasant life in the Rouergue, where his parish was situated. Though his verses were enlivened by burlesque details, the *Mercure de France* complained of him counting sheep one by one and spending whole pages on a fly or a blade of grass.[218] What the *Mercure* preferred from its curé contributors was pastoral verse in a moralizing vein on the innocence of the golden age and the vanity of riches; Jean-Jacques Rousseau copied some of these down with approval.[219] Most satisfying of all, though most ephemeral, were the light-hearted poems of curés on social occasions—an ode in praise of tobacco dedicated to a *grand vicaire* who enjoyed his snuff[220] and the invitations to dinner written in verse by the confraternity of country clergy to which Marmontel was lucky enough to be invited. 'Happy society of poets,' he said, 'where no one was envious, no one was difficult to please; where each was as satisfied with himself as with others, as if the circle had been wholly composed of Horaces and Anacreons.'[221]

To go beyond occasional verse or antiquarian discussions and produce a novel or a tragedy was a dangerous venture. This was to move up into a different league and attract the notice of the wits and reviewers of the capital. J.-J. Gautier, curé of Lande-de-Goult, got away with it. With 1,500 livres a year, only sixty households to care for, and his only link with civilization a track impassable to carriages, he lived a comfortable, lonely existence, which he enlivened by trips to the masonic lodge at Alençon and by writing. His *Essai sur les mœurs champêtres* (1787) was an idyllic picture of the life and leisure of a country parson; next came a pamphlet defending the right of his parishioners to collect wood from the Crown lands nearby; and then his *Jean le Noir ou le misanthrope* (1789), a picaresque novel imitating Voltaire. Provincial society applauded his publications, and, his ecclesiastical vocation abandoned, he finished up directing the chief establishment of secondary education at Alençon after the Revolution.[222] Curé Petit of Mont-Chauvet in Normandy was not so lucky. His was another tiny parish, with no one to talk to but the schoolmaster, who was 'only a peasant dressed in black' anyway. So he wrote his tragedy *David et Bethsabée*, published at Rouen in 1754. In the preface he explained why he had not put the bath-tub scene on stage, and to those who said his style resembled Corneille's, he replied that this was not because of any plagiarism on his part. Unfortunately, just as he was working on his second literary venture, a madrigal of 700 verses on his farm labourer putting his serving-girl in the family way, he met Diderot, who wickedly invited him to read his tragedy to a gathering of the philosophes at d'Holbach's, which he did portentously amid scenes of desperately stifled hilarity. Rousseau told him they were making a fool of him, but, undeterred, he published a second tragedy, *Balthazar*, saying in the preface that if Racine had not been willing to try again after a flop, he would never have written *Phèdre*; and he vanishes from history promising to write a third—'I am young, and I am courageous'.[223]

For every curé whose literary and intellectual ambitions are known to us, there must have been many others whose aspirations remain unrecorded, or, if recorded, have now been forgotten, and many more still whose horizons were limited to the performance of their pastoral duties and the enjoyment of such sociability and status as their parish afforded. Yet an impressionistic survey of the activities of a few is a pointer to the outlook of the whole class. In close touch with the ordinary life of their people through land, tithes, and fees on the one hand and, by contrast, charitable works on the other, the curés were also medical, legal, and agricultural advisers, educationalists, counsellors of families, custodians of local traditions and chroniclers of contemporary events, memorialists of occasions of public rejoicing or mourning, disseminators of news, official and unofficial, and of selective and censored information about the writings of the Enlightenment. The Counter-Reformation had revolutionized the education of the clergy, but the results were not what zealous reformers had expected. Instead of priests solidly grounded in the Scriptures, the Fathers and the masters of spirituality, knowledgeable in theology and skilled in the casuistry of the confessional, redoubtable controversialists against Protestants and unbelievers, preachers who would exalt ecclesiastical discipline and conformity, a race of socially active, well-informed, and picturesquely individualistic local leaders had been turned out. To be 'in the world, not of it' is an impossible ideal. The instrument is always affected by the material it works on.

> My nature is subdu'd
> To what it works in, like the dyer's hand;
> Pity me then, and wish I were renewed.

THE 'BON CURÉ'

I

Upon my word of honour, and speaking the simple truth, I say that if I
was to be born again, or if my youth could be renewed like that of the
eagle, I would never be anything other than a country curé—ministering
to the smallest of hamlets—which I would prefer to all the prelacies in the
universe . . . Shall we never see the dawn of the happy day which will
bring back the golden age of the Church, when the office of the country
parish priest will be held in the high esteem which it merits?[1]

So said Jean-Pierre Camus, bishop of Belley, in 1642, a churchman
exalting the pastoral office in the spirit of the Catholic reformers, and
a novelist echoing the literary tradition which magnified 'le bon
prêtre', the reconciler of family feuds, the rescuer of star-crossed
lovers, the moralistic commentator on the injustices of an unfeeling
world.

Eighteenth-century deists and philosophes inherited this tradition,
and praised the worthy parish priest—though with a difference.
Rousseau's Savoyard vicaire[2] yearned for a parish of his own, where
he would share the poverty of his people and reconcile them to their
lot; he would look after Protestants equally with Catholics, never
attempting to convert them, and would teach the ideals of the
gospels without too much concern about the narrower precepts of
the Church. 'Je ne trouve rien de si beau que d'être curé. Un bon
curé est un ministre de bonté comme un bon magistrat est un
ministre de justice.' To the philosophes, a real-life curé was an
appropriate butt for ridicule: Diderot was merciless about the curé of
La Chevrette's all-too expressive nose,[3] about 'le petit Croque-Dieu
de Sussy',[4] and the Norman parish priest who published an unfortunate tragedy about Bathsheba;[5] while Voltaire enjoyed the comic
enthronement of the curé of Courdimanche by a country house
party tricked out in paper hats and moustaches of soot.[6] But in theory
and officially, in the writings of the philosophes, the kindly country
curé was awarded enthusiastic praise. There was, however, one proviso: he had to be useful, advising his people on law, medicine, and

agriculture, and, said Voltaire sardonically, making sure that they kept on working in the fields on saints' days.[7] The same prescription for the good parish priest is given in La Chalotais's *Essai d'éducation nationale* (1763); being useful as a doctor, surveyor, and arbiter of disputes is what is required, not 'bad Latin, useless scholasticism and theological quarrels'.[8] Rousseau was not so crudely utilitarian, though he wanted his parish priest to concentrate on teaching moral conduct, not doctrine. 'I agree that you must teach them all the nonsense in the Catechism,' he told a friend who had just been appointed to a parish, 'provided that you teach them also to believe in God and to love virtue. Make them Christians, since you have to, but do not forget the more important, indispensable duty of making them honest folk.'[9] Nearer to the harsh and humdrum realities of peasant life, Restif de la Bretonne was more inclined to consider Christian belief as useful in a parish priest, though he conceded it was not essential. One of his heroes, Antoine Foudriat, curé of Saci, 'had all the moral virtues which make an *honnête homme*'; he was a perceptive adviser to families and a courageous defender of his people, winning a lawsuit for them against their oppressive seigneur. 'What was lacking in this pastor? . . . He was not a Christian . . . His brilliant imagination, his unfailing good taste, his sophisticated insight—all this inclined him, not towards an appreciation of Christianity, but rather to distance himself from it.' He was a materialist, a pantheist. 'Dieu ne fut pour lui que la Nature', and the religion which he taught officially was to him an unsociable faith which condemned pleasure and devalued intelligence. By contrast, Edmé-Nicolas, Restif's half-brother, curé of Courgis near Chablis, spent a great deal of time meditating on the Scriptures and the story of revelation, rising at three in the morning to do so; he said his mass at seven o'clock, then stayed in church kneeling at the altar, available to those who wished to come for advice. He was 'the father of all his parishioners, the arbiter of their differences, the consoler and helper of the sick'. He lived on a third of his 1,500 livres income, and gave the rest away. In winter, he arranged for loans of grain from the richer folk to the poorer, setting the example himself. Every week he visited every household; he organized free schools, and went in person into the fields to teach children who were obliged to go out to work. When his parish was swept by a great fire in 1749, he wrote letters and went off preaching to gather subscriptions for rebuilding the houses. When the bishop offered him a better living, he refused to move. His parishioners had one complaint against him: his sermons were too long.[10]

From a stock literary character, *le bon curé* had become a hero of the Enlightenment: his activities were a standing criticism of the rich and idle upper clergy, and a proclamation of the ideal of utilitarian, secular benevolence. The spiritual writers of the Counter-Reformation approved of the same practical achievements, but put them in a loftier, other-worldly context. Charles Demia's *Trésor clerical* (1694) described parish priests as 'les Sacrificateurs et adora-teurs de la divine Majesté pour les Paroissiens'; at the altar, they represent all their people in offering sacrifice and adoration to God.[11] The ceremonies for the installation of a curé emphasized this role of sacerdotal representation of the whole worshipping community: taking holy water and aspersing all present, kneeling before the crucifix, praying before the high altar and kissing it, opening the missal and reading from it, adoring the Holy Sacrament, intoning the Te Deum, giving the benediction with the Sacrament held aloft before returning it to the tabernacle, visiting the baptismal font, and ringing the bell as a signal for the ringers to embark on a full peal— all this as a prelude to the practical business of visiting the vicarage and having the local apostolic notary read the act of taking posses-sion to the assembled people at the main door of the church.[12] A law-book describes this representational role another way, looking westwards down the nave, as it were, instead of eastwards to the altar: the curé leads the faithful on their journey towards eternal life by ensuring that they fulfil all the precepts of revealed religion, more especially the reception of the sacraments. The State recognized this leadership function for its own purposes, since in administering the sacraments the curé 'assures and records the legal existence of all citizens'. Thus, 'in the eyes of both statesmen and Christians, the rank and office of curé cannot be other than infinitely respectable'.[13]

The dignity of the curé was enhanced by his security of tenure— perhaps we should say, all curés properly so called were secure. A *desservant*—a priest put in by the bishop to run a parish in a vacancy—could be dismissed.[14] The curés royaux of Alsace, holding benefices set up by the Crown in Protestant areas, were named by the royal intendant, invested by the bishop, and, if need be, removed by him.[15] There were also the so-called prieurs-curés, for the most part canons regular of the Order of Sainte-Geneviève (63 of the 400 parishes of the diocese of Angers were theirs, 60 of the 767 of the archdiocese of Sens, and most of those of the diocese of Uzés[16]). The triennial chapters of Sainte-Geneviève examined the evidence of superiors and visitors and drew up a list of priests suited for parochial office; once appointed, they were likely to remain, though they could be revoked by the head of their Order, provided he could demonstrate 'just cause' and had the agreement of his 'assistants' and the consent of the diocesan bishop. In the course of a Parisian dispute in 1747, a Jansenist parish priest ridiculed a prieur-curé as lacking in true authority—'since your abbot, in concert with M. the archbishop, can dismiss you at will, you are not a proper titular'.[17] As this gibe shows, the curés were proud of their security and independence. The machinations of the espiscopally dominated Assembly of the Clergy in 1682 and 1700 to abolish the parson's freehold failed. In theory, the ecclesiastical court of the diocese, the *officialité*, could hear a case against a scandalous curé and sentence him to confinement in a monastery; in practice, the secular courts were likely to overturn the sentence at the slightest hint of doubtful procedures. When, in the 1770s, the inhabitants of Marbaix appealed to the archbishop of Cambrai to get rid of curé Jean Philippe Denise, whose eccentricities were making worship impossible (he would say mass only in the afternoons, and when he did so, it was 'in a ridiculous and indecent manner'; he cursed the children at catechisms, and showed his backside to a complaining parishioner), the procedures were long-drawn-out and hesitant. In 1776, a coadjutor was appointed to take the main services, but after years of struggle, he found it impossible to carry on in face of the interruptions of Denise. So in January 1788, the *promoteur* of the diocese appointed a distinguished parish priest to conduct an investigation, and depositions were taken from twenty witnesses. In July, the *official*—he was an archdeacon and a canon of Cambrai—heard all the evidence again in person, together with some extra witnesses, and interrogated Denise himself for five days in August. The file was then handed to Deprez, professor of canon and civil law in the University of Douai, who advised the *official* that he had omitted to read certain legal warnings to Denise at the first interrogation. So the whole process started again on 3 September. Then, on 8 and 9 November, Denise and the witnesses were brought into confrontation. At last, it was possible to think of passing sentence, and the *promoteur* proposed six years' confinement in a monastery, with the recitation of the penitential psalms on Fridays. Professor Deprez declared the penitential provisions inappropriate for one who was mentally deranged, and drew the *official*'s attention to the need to have two graduates at law conjoined with him for passing judgment. On Christmas Eve 1788, the *official* held a final interrogation assisted by two luminaries of the parlement of Flanders, a *conseiller-clerc* (a magistrate who was also an ecclesiastic) and an *avocat*, and sentence was pronounced. It had taken twelve years to push poor crazy Denise into a monastery, and in February 1791, the municipality of Marbaix was panic-stricken at the thought that under the new order in France he would be let out to haunt their parish services once again.[18] Since legal procedures were so cumbersome, the only effective way for a bishop to get rid of a parish priest was to apply to the Crown to use the arbitrary device of a *lettre de cachet*.[19] Such an intervention, if granted, could be cruel enough; a litigious curé of the diocese of Saint-Dié was locked up by his bishop in various ecclesiastical internment centres from 1780 to 1789—at the *maison de force* of Maréville, the gaolers told him that he had been sentenced to an extra two years' imprisonment 'immediately after the dinner which ought to have been followed by his release'.[20] It was not easy, however, to get a *lettre de cachet*, the resort to it was unpopular, the intendant and his officials made careful enquiries before the Minister signed the order, and the law courts were watchful to strike a blow against oppressive prelates; it took the archbishop of Bordeaux three years to get rid of the outrageous curé of Saint-Bonnet, who, Sacrament in hand, had denounced a distinguished citizen whose tenants had refused to cart the vicarage firewood.[21] What a bishop could do more easily to discipline a parish priest was to invoke the royal edicts of 1695 and 1698, and send him for three months to a seminary. Even so, there were strict rules about procedures, and the secular magistrates could intervene by the process of *appel comme d'abus*; the law-books cite several cases of bishops being condemned to paying costs and damages for misuse of their powers.[22]

A curé enjoyed great independence in the exercise of his spiritual role. The mere fact of holding letters of appointment entitled him to hear confessions, preach, catechize, administer the last rites, and baptize within his parish. With some exceptions (exempt monasteries, emergencies, and so on) these were exclusive rights which others needed permission to exercise, and they were rights which were jealously guarded. Mostly, it was a question of defending them against the encroachments of monasteries, chapters, and the clergy of other parishes. The son of a courtier born in the parish of Saint-Roch was to be baptized in the royal chapel at Versailles by a great prelate: there was nothing for it but to have the curé of Notre-Dame of Versailles and the curé of Saint-Roch both present, important and arrayed in white stoles.[23] On his deathbed Cardinal Fleury confessed to a monk, but after solemn discussion, it was decided that only the parish priest of Fontainebleau could bring him the viaticum.[24] The archbishop of Paris's palace dominated the tiny parish of Sainte-Marine, but there was a grave legal scandal in 1732 when a priest other than the curé gave the episcopal *valet de chambre* the last rites.[25] Some monasteries had exemptions; even so, their servants had to be confessed, shriven, and buried by the parish priest.[26] If it was the bishop who trespassed on the powers of the parochial clergy, the law courts would intervene. Thus, in 1756, the curés of Auxerre routed their bishop, who was trying to claim the power to license them to catechize.[27] What a bishop could do was to prevent a curé from hearing confessions or preaching outside his parish, though an express individual prohibition had to be issued.[28] Since (curés within their own boundaries excepted) preaching and confessing needed episcopal warrant, the bishop in practice had a veto on the appointments of vicaires—a curé's theoretical right to choose his collaborators was not of much use unless they were granted powers from on high.[29] In short, a bishop could pin down an unsatisfactory parish priest (or one with whom he was in feud) within the duties of his own parish, keeping him out of the pastoral life of the rest of the diocese[30] and depriving him of vicaires. But to do more, and more especially to get rid of him, was difficult indeed.

Security of tenure and the consciousness of their standing in the local community encouraged the curés to proud independence. Inevitably, some were obsequious to aristocratic prelates; equally, some were truculent. A Breton recteur in 1778, accepting a proposal for arbitration put forward by his bishop, gratuitously observed, 'Je l'ai fait uniquement par religion et non en vue de vous obliger.'[31] Obviously, a parish priest with a large income and a large congregation was a man of importance. In Paris, there was a concentration of such clergy; they were, said a lawyer in 1757, 'universally esteemed and respected . . . celebrated in all the kingdom by their capacity, their talents and their education, so that to say "He is a curé of Paris" is equivalent to delivering a formal encomium on a man'.[32] These were the clergy described by an envious Jansenist in 1789 as elevating themselves above their fellows in the provinces 'by the distance between heaven above and earth beneath'.[33] Truth to tell, however, provincial curés tended to be just as proud. To the Parisian who was standing on his dignity as the pastor of the church of Saint-Médard, a provincial colleague from the archdiocese of Sens replied, 'Monsieur, it's the curé of Rocheplatte who is speaking to you. I think one is as good as the other.'[34] In 1750, the priest of the miserable hamlet of Chênhutte in Anjou went on a trip to Paris and a pilgrimage to Rome. To the footman who tried to exclude him from the royal dining-room at Versailles he protested, 'I am one of the king's men, I am a curé of his dominions, and I desire the honour of seeing him dine'—and he stayed to examine the gold plate and sample the dessert. At Rome, he declared openly that he would rather rule the parish of Chênhutte than be Pope.[35] The revolt of the lower clergy at the end of the *ancien régime* was less a protest of the harassed and browbeaten than of the proud, demanding further recognition of their status.

II

The second half of the seventeenth century and the first two decades of the eighteenth saw the moral reformation of the parochial clergy of France. 'If you compare the clergy in 1724 with those of the beginning of the seventeenth century', writes the historian of the diocese of La Rochelle, 'you see . . . that the Catholic reform had fashioned a new style of *bon prêtre*, which represents at once a sociological type, a spiritual ideal and a pastoral programme.'[36] Instead of exalting the priestly office in the abstract, the dignity of the priesthood was tied to the pastoral function and the responsibility for souls. The grinding poverty which had degraded so many parish priests was alleviated, and educational standards were transformed. (In more than one diocese, the links between clerical poverty and ignorance and dubious morality is evident in the visitation returns.[37]) As civilization advanced, the laity became more demanding: parishioners who had joked about their clergy's affairs with women and complained only about their financial exactions had tended to get the pastors they deserved.[38] Educated church-goers no longer regarded the priest as the mechanical performer of the sacramental actions: they looked to him for advice and example. The improvement is evident everywhere. Between 1622 and 1695, the boorish priests who did not even know the formula of absolution vanished from the countryside around Paris, and literate professionals took their place.[39] Complaints of concubinage had been numerous in the diocese of Autun in the mid-seventeenth century; but there are only half a dozen known cases in the eighteenth; the dubious curés of the episcopal town of Autun in 1689 had given way to excellent pastors forty years later.[40] Drunkenness was common in the diocese of Tréguier at the end of the reign of Louis XIV—toping in the sacristy, collapsing at catechisms, charging a bottle of eau-de-vie as the price of absolution: it was rare in the late eighteenth century.[41]

In the first half of the seventeenth century, the list of parish priests of the diocese of La Rochelle at any one time would include 10–25 per cent who had been under censure; in 1724, the figure was 5 per cent. The number of sexual offences remained much the same; it was drinking and brawling that were declining.[42] In a rural deanery near Rouen in 1682, a dozen out of the forty-seven clergy were noted as unsatisfactory (true, this was chiefly because of their ruthless litigation over tithes); after 1736, few clergy of the diocese of Rouen merited censure.[43] In 1682, of the 182 curés of the diocese of Strasbourg, 32 had been before the *officialité* at one time or another (a recent case was one who had melted down the *trésor* of his church to make ornaments for his mistress). Counting others who had been disciplined by archdeacons and rural deans, probably a quarter of the clergy were unsatisfactory. The chief offence was sexual misconduct—generally going to bed with the housekeeper on cold winter nights or when drunk. A report of 1697 said that all but twenty of the clergy were inadequate, and that none of them ever opened a book. But in the eighteenth century, most curés were well educated and well behaved. Between 1701 and 1720, there were fifteen sexual offences censured, nine between 1721 and 1740, and only four between 1741 and 1760.[44] Statistics from other places for the eighteenth century are equally reassuring. Of the 450 priests of the diocese of Quimper (263 of them ruling parishes), only half a dozen were removed from their charges in the last thirty years of the *ancien régime*.[45] In the 130 parishes of the Grand Vicariate of Pontoise, there were twenty-five disciplinary cases between 1680 and 1770; in 90 parishes around Dijon, there were a dozen cases between 1731 and 1789.[46] The secretary of the bishop of Toul, in notes he compiled on the parish priests of the diocese in 1773, put down three-quarters of them as good men; of the less impressive minority, the only ones whose offences approached scandal were a nobleman who did not know the language of his flock, and five accused of sexual misdemeanours—of these, one cleared himself before the law courts, and one was vouched for as being a faithful pastor notwithstanding.[47] The bishop of Nîmes's 'observations' of 1775 on the discipline of his clergy referred to their hunting, their application for dispensations to have under-age housekeepers, their abbreviation of catechisms and homilies, unauthorized absences, and wearing lay attire when travelling; he does not refer to more serious offences, and the only breach of the rules which was common was failure to attend the *conférences*, the bishop's improving discussion groups.[48] A similar set of notes drawn up by a vicar-general of the diocese of Valence in 1789 covering 277 clergy (100 being curés) contains hardly any cases of serious censure.[49]

Inevitably, among 30,000 parish clergy there would be some black sheep. In 1727, the *vicaire perpétuel* of La Coste in Provence was sentenced to be hanged for 'spiritual incest', seducing a female penitent;[50] in 1757, the curé of Ludres was condemned by the sovereign court of Lorraine to be burned for sodomy (he made an edifying speech to the parishioners before his execution, and pilgrimages were organized to the site of his execution).[51] Journalists never failed to report a sexual scandal; it was satisfying to find a cleric who added extra names to his baptismal registers and cuckolded the men he married.[52] Village gossips were always on the watch. If their curé was walking in the dusk with a woman, sure enough, it would be possible to say that 'plusieurs personnes les ont vu s'embrasser'.[53] A whisper of an ambiguous proposition in the confessional was hard to rebut; if the housekeeper at the presbytery became pregnant, the priest was the first suspect. A story from the diocese of Orléans told how one curé was blatantly cheerful at the news: 'that means a little *benedicamus* to act as server at my masses'.[54]

Any sign of affinity between a priest and a female parishioner, however innocent, would be noted—and, no doubt, the romantic abbé Pollin was not the only celebrant who sighed after a girl who attended his masses, yet never dared to speak to her.[55] If an incumbent was ruthless about his financial dues, his parishioners might be inclined to mention their suspicions in other respects at visitation time; as in 1783, the people of Bertincourt (Cambrai) accused curé Robert Coplo of dubious sexual relations, and 'il exige des droits insolites et exorbitants'.[56] Anticlericals found it easier to make dark hints in general terms than to give specific examples. The *cahier* of Vihiers says, 'there are many virtuous curés, but even these will concede that they certainly have colleagues who are not. Ask in country places and the folk will tell you things about the morals of many of their pastors that we dare not set down here.'[57] Occasionally, some scandalous story would come to light, when episcopal sanctions were taken and the offender was exiled to the seminary; in the diocese of Quimper, in 1757, a recteur was disciplined for his 'commerce très scandaleux avec la fille d'un marchand de sardines', and in 1785, a priest was revealed as having had an affair with the wife of a septuagenarian, while another felt it wise to flee from his parish and join the navy.[58] Yet, what is striking is the contrast between the very few formal accusations of sexual misconduct and the general enthusiasm to speculate, spy out, or joke about the possibilities. It seems that this was a matter in which the clergy knew they were being tested, and discipline was maintained.

That a cleric should compensate for his enforced celibacy by moderate addiction to some other pleasure was popularly approved; indeed, a curé was supposed to be a sociable character, and refusing a proffered glass could cause offence.[59] Occasionally, however, parishioners would delate their pastor at visitation time if he was a real drunkard or, maybe, if he tippled and they had financial grievances against him, making them more aware of his other failings. The curé whose legs gave way under him at the altar, another who wassailed continually, 'even after midnight', another who in an inebriated rage at vespers broke the processional cross on the back of an intruding dog were duly reported.[60] As for the character of the diocese of Autun who turned up tipsy at the synodal meeting of the clergy, he had indeed volunteered for the bread and water and the penitential psalms.[61] Bishops tended to be strict about drunkenness: the curé of the diocese of Sens who in 1770, under the influence, chanted the Pascal anthem at a funeral was fined 60 livres by the diocesan court and sent for two years to a seminary (though it is true that when summoned before the archbishop, he had over-fortified himself with restoratives beforehand).[62]

The vices of the country curé tended to be those of the peasants among whom he lived and whose agricultural labours he so often shared: over-indulgence at festivals or in rare times of abundance, going out hunting[63] in defiance of diocesan ordinances, coarse jesting, appearing at fairs, horse-trading and pig dealing, frauding and jostling with the scruffiest, perhaps even lending money at usurious rates.[64] An individual with peasant preoccupations yet vested with authority spiritual and temporal was subject to dangerous temptations—hence, sometimes, threats of refusal of communion to enforce payment of dues, and high-handed interventions to serve worldly ends. In the parish of Cirgues in the suburbs of Clermont, Mathieu Geneix, a graduate of the University of Paris, coveted the house and garden of old Payard as a site for a new vicarage. To evict him, he got his parishioners to divert a massive sluice of drain water into the cemetery, and to break down Payard's wall so that it swept on knee deep into his property. Whether it was divine retribution for this design on Naboth's vineyard, or simply ignorance of hydro-statics, he contrived to flood his church as well, and to ruin the 'sacred well of Abraham' which was its unique feature.[65] The violence and malice which often characterized peasant feuds were sometimes evident in the conduct of the pastor—ringing the bells in triumphal peals when an enemy left the parish, heaping cinders on to another who unsuspectingly presented himself at the altar rails during the Ash Wednesday ceremonies, turning out with a club or even a gun to lead a cohort of supporters (generally including the sacristan, schoolmaster, and the housekeeper with her broom) in a tithe war.[66] The militia fire at pigeons, interrupting a baptism—the curé rushes out, seizes a musket, and knocks down its owner. A vicaire wins at cards and punches his unlucky adversary because he insists on signing his note of indebtedness as 'argent de jeu'.[67] Half a dozen peasants put on a Christmas farce, *La Vie des trois roys*; the recteur judges it to be sacrilegious, goes down with his shotgun, and orders them to desist—Herod draws his sabre and is knocked flat by the priest with his gun butt, and the angry audience attack the presbytery.[68] These are the sort of incidents that enliven rural chronicles. Voltaire got a good deal of anticlerical mileage out of the curé of Moens's puritanical attempt to maintain morality by collecting a posse of parishioners from the local wine bar to chastise three young men who had gone to spend the night with a widow of bad reputation. The Sage of Ferney professed to be surprised when the neighbouring parish priests backed up their bellicose colleague: 'they claim they have a judicial right to beat their parishioners with sticks as granted by the First Lateran Council'.[69] What Voltaire does not emphasize is that the curé of Moens had the support of his people—he had only to call at the cabaret to be able to recruit his team of vigilantes. As often as not, a priest involved in affrays and subterfuges was collaborating with his parishioners rather than acting against them. Villages near the internal customs boundaries often engaged in smuggling, and it was not unknown for parish priests to cross over with a load, or to hide sacks of salt or boxes of tobacco in sacristies or behind altars.[70] Or, if not in actual collusion, they might conform to what was expected of them and do their best for smugglers on the run—maybe ring the bell as a tocsin to alert the countryside to the presence of enforcement officers,[71] or give shelter to fugitives. The dramatist Sedaine had a story of a curé who took provisions to two starving smugglers hiding in his confessional; he was given money for his poor-box and a roll of cloth, but died of remorse three weeks later.[72]

Examples of dubious curés become fewer as the century progresses, and the gossip about them comes to concern foibles, eccentricities, and pardonable self-indulgences, rather than vices. Slackness in dress, unbuttoned cassocks and the like (as befitted men without wives) was common.[73] Risqué jesting offended sensitive parishioners. 'He was renowned for his administrative skill, his wisdom and his morals,' says Cournot of his curé in Franche Comté, 'but that did not exclude from his conversation a certain Gallic wantonness (*certaines gaillardises gauloises*) which shocked us'.[74] Over-familiarity with liturgical observances led to irreverent incidents which, perhaps, gave more cause for amusement than censure, like curé Robin of Angers interrupting his sermon to give instructions about a leg of mutton for his supper that evening.[75] These were haphazard, unsqueamish days, and anticlericals could always take a solemn, reverent line to justify their censures. 'Curé Flollet and his vicaire both have a dog', says one censorious village official, 'which they take with them to the church. The dogs urinate against the pews and the altar, and even in the holy water stoup at the entrance to the chancel.'[76] Marmontel recounts a Limousin story of the curé at mass hearing the hunting dogs baying when they started the hare.

'Briffaut y est-il?'
'Oui, monsieur le curé.'
'En ce cas-là, le lièvre est f . . . . . Lavabo inter innocentes Manus meas.'[77]

A similar story of a conversation at mass is told of Pierre Guyart, curé of Lélanne, learned and lame, who translated all the works of Horace, did battle royal in the courts for a neighbouring village against its seigneur, and maintained the six orphan children of one of his nieces.

'Introibo ad altari Dei. Ta mère a-t-elle filé ma chanvre?'
'Nenni, M. le curé.'
'Tu lui diras qu'elle est une bougre de paresseuse.'
'Oh, pour ça, M. le curé, nenni, elle me battrai.'
'Si tu ne lui dis pas, je te rosserai: ainsi choisis et va ton train.'
'Ad Deum . . .'[78]

Another subject for amused and not too censorious gossip was the inclination of the clergy to be good trenchermen. Piron, a seigneurial official in the village of Aubais, chronicled enviously the gastronomic exploits of his curé. The *fermier* of the lands of the marquis gave a party in 1749, after which none of the guests ate for two days and the parish priest for even longer. Another prosperous citizen gave a collation in 1752 with 'lofty pyramids of meringues . . . very delicate, melting in the mouth'; 'the ladies, and principally the gentlemen of the clergy, did the most execution'. The next year the curé himself gave a dinner: pâté, turkey, two shoulders of lamb, a rabbit, and a salad, which seemed all the more gluttonous as Piron was not invited.[79] Occasionally, at the end of the *ancien régime*, we hear of clerical dining clubs: when it was his turn, Yves Besnard introduced his less sophisticated and poorer colleagues to the delights of having liqueurs with their coffee.[80] The curé of Lande-Fleurie was so pleased with himself after giving such an entertainment that he entered the menu (turbot, sole, and smaller fish) in his baptismal register: 'It is good that posterity should know we fared well and that wine was not lacking.'[81] His naïve pride suggests that this was a rare indulgence.

III

Parishioners did not wish their priest to be an austere man, and they would turn an indulgent eye on his little luxuries. What they expected from him was geniality and helpfulness and, to those who were poor, generosity. Generally, their expectations were fulfilled. Curés tended to live long,[82] and as often as not, stayed in the same parish. Over the years they got to know their people intimately. Their principal duty, it was universally agreed, was to visit their flocks, whatever the weather and the difficulties of the terrain. 'Autant de pas, autant de casse-cou', one curé told his bishop; it would take 'several hours', he said, to get to a shepherd who fell ill up in the summer pastures in the hills. There are places, said another, where in bad weather you have to pick your way on foot, not forgetting to make the sign of the cross and an act of contrition before venturing.[83] Conversely, members of the parish continually had to visit their curé. He officiated at births, deaths, and marriages, giving congratulations, consolation, and advice as required, and he had the official duty of recording these family events, together with the names of witnesses, details of trade or profession, of dispensations for consanguinity and so on.[84] Great was the expense and tribulation of establishing a new set of records if an inefficient or senile curé had neglected his duty.[85] These were documents of the utmost importance 'to the republic', said the standard legal handbook, 'and to establish the status of individuals and to maintain the peace of mind of families'.[86] The curé's signature was needed on all sorts of other documents. For some charitable distributions, those presenting themselves needed authentication of their need.[87] A nice story circulated in Paris in 1777 about an old man who used a certificate of poverty issued by the curé of Saint-Roch to get bread for his dog; when the fraud was detected, the curé sportingly paid himself to maintain the faithful hound.[88] Peasants who had been ruined by fire, flood, hail, theft, or fraud would ask their parish priest for *la pique*—their hard-luck story formally written down and signed as an authorization to go round begging. Chimney-sweeps and pedlars liked to carry one, forged if necessary, for use if trade was slack.[89] Sea bathing was supposedly efficacious to cure the bite of a mad dog, and victims begged their way to the coast, fortified by clerical attestations.[90] Some certificates were splendidly formal, issued by the bishop himself on the recommendation of the parochial clergy. 'Christophe de Beaumont, duc de Saint-Cloud, peer of France, Commander of the Order of the Saint-Esprit, *Proviseur* of the Sorbonne . . . archbishop of Paris, having reviewed the certificate of *le sieur* Brunet, a curé of our diocese . . .' and so on, allowing a named individual whose house had been burned down to beg for two months around Paris.[91] Those who, because of a supposed infirmity, were allowed to eat meat in Lent, sent down to the butcher's a document from the curé confirming that their case had been established. The wretched peasant who was nominated to collect the *taille*, the main land tax, was responsible to the government for the money owed by defaulters, but with a note from the parish priest he could recover the sum from the next year's assessment.[92] Certificates of good morals were required to be able to practise as a midwife and, indeed, were often asked for by employers. Thérèse, Rousseau's old mistress, had to have one before she could draw the pension awarded to her by the National Assembly in December 1790.[93] There was a story of two asses which bit each other, leading to a court case between their owners in which one of the parties turned up with the curé's certificate of previous good conduct for his animal.[94] A wet nurse applying to foster an orphan baby for one of the great hospitals had to arrive furnished with the attestation of her parish priest (giving name, husband's name and profession, moral standing of the family, age, health, number of children and date of birth of the last one), and a further clerical signature was required before she could draw her first payment.[95] When wolves plagued a district, it was customary for the intendant to offer a reward for every one killed; bounty hunters had to take the ears to the curé who would exchange them for the necessary certificate.[96]

In rural France, the presbytery was the main point of contact for the village with the outside world. Just as passing vagabonds knocked at the door for alms, so respectable travellers who could not find an inn would call there for refuge—customs or taxation officials who would be unwelcome elsewhere, a doctor coming over a long distance to give a consultation, a notary coming to draw up a contract, a honeymoon couple whose coach had lost a wheel (and were given dinner, a bed for the night, and the loan of the curé's horse the next day to get back to civilization).[97] At La Balme near Lyon, where there was a sacred grotto, the incumbent continually had the better sort of pilgrims calling for refreshments; 'on ne peut faire autrement que de les recevoir', he said, though he was glad to get to know some influential city people.[98] Government officials applied to the parochial clergy for statistical information—the numbers of vagrants, for example.[99] In 1770, the intendant of the Auvergne asked them to help him to produce a census of children; a rumour that they were to be kidnapped and sent to colonize Corsica led to threats of murder and arson if the parish priests sent in their returns.[100] When compiling his famous geographical dictionary, the abbé d'Expilly tried, with indifferent success, to get the clergy to supply him with demographical data from their registers, and in some dioceses, notably Lisieux, Bayeux, and Narbonne, the bishops allied with the scientists in an attempt to persuade the clergy to fill in geographical questionnaires and to take compass bearings for map-making projects.[101] In times of plague, the curé going round anointing the dying with drips of consecrated oil on the end of a long stick,[102] was the sole channel of communication to advise the outside authorities of the needs of the entrapped inhabitants. Had Turgot lasted longer in office, he might have systematized the role of the curés as government agents—when he had been intendant of Limoges, he said, he regarded them as his natural *subdélégués*.

Whether from spiritual contacts, official ones, or purely from sociability, the curé knew everyone within his boundaries—except in some of the teeming parishes in the great cities. Perhaps he kept an annotated register of his flock as prescribed by St Charles Borromeo, who had wanted an index of those capable of giving alms, those who could co-operate with information, the few suitable to be trained to form a spiritual élite, and, on the other hand, the recalcitrant sinners. In the second half of the seventeenth century the *Rituels* of at least a dozen dioceses ordered the keeping of such a register or notebook, and at least eight other dioceses followed suit in the eighteenth century. There was a difficulty, however, for the whole concept was suspect to the laity: in 1673, the bishop of Agen was taken to law before the parlement of Toulouse by the municipal officers of his episcopal town (abetted by the canons of the cathedral)—this sort of record, they said, 'threatened the repose, tranquillity and honour of families'. Certainly, if an index of sinners fell into the wrong hands, an action for defamation would arise; this was why one *Rituel*, in 1751, prescribed the use of cipher. Probably most curés regarded the keeping of such formal records as useless systematization, wasting time and in doubtful taste—few of these 'livres d'états des âmes' have survived.[103] In any case, whether he knew the people concerned or not, the curé would be the first to know of anyone in trouble. A village girl gets pregnant: he comes round to protect her from the wrath of her parents and, if necessary, to find her an alternative refuge.[104] If there are other girls in the family, he checks on the parental discipline.[105] The daughter of a magistrate of Grenoble is betrayed by the son of a newly rich official; her parish priest gets a respectable matron and a midwife to look after her, and extracts certificates of paternity and a promise to maintain the child from the seducer (a future member of the National Convention and a terrorist).[106] A girl being pushed unwillingly into a convent does well to appeal for help in her parish confessional.[107] A writer on politically sensitive subjects has documents he wants to put away safely: Mme d'Houdetot tells Jean-Jacques that the curé of Deuil will take charge of them with great discretion.[108] The daughter of a poor noble in the provinces has to write business letters to a rich *fermier général* in the capital: her parish priest composes them so skilfully for her that she is called to Paris with a view to marriage.[109] A young and pretty widow is entangled in legal difficulties, and an older widowed farmer with seven children who lives nearby is just the influential man she needs to protect her; the curé virtually orders him to marry her, and he never regrets it.[110] At Le Mans, a rich young man sends flowers and verses to the daughter of a *trésorier de France*; alas, a fall as a child has left him with an absurdly flattened nose, and he does not dare to propose—but the parish priest is at hand and puts the question for him.[111]

IV

In rural France, it was important for the curé to have good relations with the seigneur, both for his own comfort, and for the benefit of his people. 'The curé and the seigneur ought to be allies for the edification of the people,' said a solemn legal handbook.[112] No doubt, if only for worldly reasons, both parties had much to gain from such an alliance, and there were curés who did what they were told and lords of the manor who attended church services and listened attentively to sermons to set a good example. But within the very church building itself there were established occasions for quarrels, given that this was a society where precedence and inherited rights were cherished and only the poor were shy of litigation. 'If jurisprudence had not set limits to the ambition of men,' said a lawyer, 'everyone who was anyone in the parish would claim honorific recognition within the church'[113]—that is, the so-called 'droits honorifiques' or the 'honneurs de l'Église'. These privileges were accorded only to the patron and to the seigneur[114] (the two, not infrequently, were the same person). The patron presented to the benefice; he was also in a unique position in that, if he had fallen on hard times, he could demand alms as of right from the revenues of the church, getting something back of what his ancestors had given; he also had the right to be received in procession by the clergy (there was a procession for the seigneur only if he had the rank of prince). The comparative standing of patrons and seigneurs was debated by the lawyers: the former had obviously given most to the parish, but the latter, it was argued, represented the Crown.[115] But, broadly speaking, both had the right to the honours of the church, and the language of jurisprudence tended to use the heading of 'seigneur' to subsume both of them.

The curé wafted incense towards the seigneur at long range from the altar steps at mass, and at close range at vespers—provided always the clerks wearing surplices were incensed first, the lord was in his official pew, the calendar showed an incense day according to the diocesan *Rituel*, and it was not one of the special parochial days when the Holy Sacrament was exposed on the altar.[116] Needless to say, the courts had ensured that a parish priest who obtained permission to take over an incense day for an additional exposition of the Sacrament—whether as a pious innovation or as a manœuvre against secular authority—would have to render the duty to the seigneur on the following Sunday.[117] Another so-called major honour was the right to a seigneurial pew; but if this structure hampered the performance of divine service, the ecclesiastical authorities could move it—though the circumstances would always be a matter of argument; certainly, a curé was advised to wait until the archdeacon or bishop authorized this drastic action.[118] Another major honour was that the seigneur and his wife were to be recommended by name, and their children collectively, to the prayers of the congregation;[119] whether this was done with sincere feeling and the right inflection of voice was difficult to embody in legal rulings. The death of the lord was the occasion for his family to demand a special honorific recognition. The bell had to be tolled, possibly for a very long time. The coat of arms of the dead man could also be displayed, repeated round the building on a black band of paper or cloth—the so-called *litre funèbre*—or the heirs might even demand that the whole band be painted directly on to the walls.[120] The corpse would be buried in the sanctuary, possibly in a family vault; this privilege was retained for patrons, seigneurs, and curés only, in the hygienic legislation of 1776.[121] Aspersion with holy water was counted a 'minor' honour. A theologian argued that in this respect, 'with the exception of the bishop, everyone counts as *peuple* in their relation to the celebrant'.[122] Seigneurs disagreed,[123] taking the view that they ought to precede minor clerics who happened to wear surplices and might well be their gardeners or servants. The law was ambiguous, and as the curé could score by splashing holy water with excessive liberality, actions were as liable to contrary interpretations as the law itself. Another minor honour was precedence in the reception of the *pain bénit* distributed at the end of mass. One legal authority joined the theologians in saying there should be no recognition of ranks here, all being equal, as at the Eucharist, of which the *pain bénit* was the symbol.[124] Another, however, laid down the order of priority: clerks in surplices, the patron and his family, the seigneur and his, then all the faithful—though the church-wardens were not obliged to seek out the great in their private pews.[125]

These standard honours of the church, codified by decisions of the law courts, were without prejudice to other rights which might have been inherited. A *cahier* of 1789 from Provence complains of a ceremony of homage still exacted from the whole community: 'You see the curé on one side, and on the other more than 300 property owners, led by the *consuls* . . . taking liege homage on their knees, and bare headed.'[126] In Burgundy, at Bretenières, Bernard Garnier de Terreneuve, ex-captain of grenadiers, in addition to the usual honours, was entitled to have a churchwarden call on him to remind him of the hour of mass, and when he and his lady entered the church, 'all the parishioners must rise and salute them'.[127] In the church of Auxerre, the marquis de Chastellux was entitled to attend divine service in surplice and sword, plumed hat and spurs, with two dogs on the leash and a bird of prey on his wrist, 'and where he sits, there is a ring to tie up the dogs and a perch for the bird'. It is said, a diarist of 1722 records, that the marquis comes once a year to exercise his right lest it lapse—'cela est fort extraordinaire'.[128]

There were three reasons, said the curé of Saint-Denoual in the diocese of Saint-Brieuc, why a parish priest ought to be on good terms with his local seigneur. On principle, the representative of the founder of the church should be respected, while the parish and, more particularly, its poor continually need assistance (he himself had been given wood for rebuilding his church and 100 livres to buy seed-corn for the indigent after the dearth of 1768). Thirdly—a self-regarding reason—once the peasants see you are out of favour with the great, they will cheerfully make difficulties for you.[129] Another curé added a fourth reason of an entirely opposite nature. Around him were poor and illiterate nobles, prepared to marry a daughter to one of their farm labourers in lieu of wages, who came to the presbytery after church, accompanied by their families, to get a square meal in the name of their ancestors; they deserved to be treated generously by the clergy.[130] Supposing, however, that the lord of the manor were rich enough and well disposed, the curé had much to gain. He would have an ally in his charitable work; in the last years of the *ancien régime*, the marquis de Fayolle in Poitou was persuaded by his parish priest to found a charity workshop and to sell his stock of grain at low prices, 'imitating the conduct of Joseph when he was in charge of feeding the land of Egypt'.[131] Repairs to the presbytery might be done free of charge, and the church building improved. 'Ask what you will for the repair of your cure and I'll do it,' said a capitalist who had just leased a seigneurie; and he pulled down the ugly old church which masked the view from the château and built a new one (according to an English traveller, the gilded Christ in it was given the seigneur's features). True, this was Voltaire,[132] putting up his façade of sardonic respectability, though after all, he was merely demonstrating that he knew what was expected of him. On occasion, the curé would be invited to the château to dine. Collet's treatise on the duties of a pastor specifically warns against maintaining a diplomatic silence in face of the seigneur's luxurious living, 'so you can have a place marked down as yours at his table and the honour of joining the company of Mme la Comtesse'.[133] The marquis de Ferrières often had the curé of Poligny-en-Mirebalais to dinner; being a cultivated nobleman and engaged in writing a book on theism, he was glad to exchange ideas with a well-read ecclesiastic of a Jansenist turn of mind.[134] Another noble of Poitou, César de Marans, an army officer who was far from well off, had to put up with the parish priest at his table occasionally because his wife and mother-in-law would persecute him otherwise. On 11 January 1790 he noted in his diary, 'the recteur is coming to dine with us, Madame is deploying all her graciousness'.[135] Though the chapel of the château (where there was one) might be regarded by the parish clergy as a threat to their pastoral monopoly, the chaplain of the seigneur could be of assistance to them. At Aubais in the diocese of Nîmes, the chaplain was a great preacher, whether in standard French or in patois, a specialist at haunting the congregation with menaces of judgement in Advent.[136] Dubois de Fosseux, secretary of the academy of Arras at the end of the *ancien régime*, seems to have been the ideal seigneur so far as the clergy were concerned. He rebuilt the church of Fosseux, extracting 2,000 livres from the tithe owner, the abbess of Etrun, and lending the rest of the money himself. He would send the *Année littéraire* and the *Mercure de France* across to the presbytery when he had finished with them (Swift's 'gazettes sent gratis down and franked, for which the patron's duly thanked'), and frequently invited the curé to dinner. His charity was lavish, and curé Delebarre would send him a note if it was excessive: 'I've no need for soup this week'; 'as for the meat, it's not all distributed yet'. In winter, Dubois de Fosseux spent his time in his house at Arras, where he was a churchwarden of Sainte-Croix; the abbé Poche, who was the parish priest there and called himself 'votre curé d'hiver', enjoyed his friendship, receiving invitations to go out to the château of Fosseux in summer, and getting his shopping done for him when the great man was in Paris.[137]

In return for dinners, repairs, and charitable contributions, what could the curé offer? Through his daily contact with the peasants, he could smooth over difficulties—get agreement, for example, that a chaotic feast, 'vulgarly called *la Trippe*', need no longer be given by the lord, but could be bought off for an annual payment of 45 livres.[138] When the abbé Delebarre took over the parish in 1780, Dubois de Fosseux, who was often away on business and fulfilling cultural and literary engagements in Arras, took the opportunity of making him his home correspondent, sending regular letters describing how things were going in the village and on the estate.[139] The curé of Rémaugis in Picardy, who succeeded his uncle in office in 1783, was a trained lawyer who was taken by the marquis de Mailly as his estate agent for the lands around the village; continually pressed by the dowager marquise in Paris to send more money, and accused by the marquis of softness towards the peasants, he carried on for ten years until he was dismissed and left undisturbed in the fulfilment of his pastoral duties.[140] If the nobleman's family was pious and the parish priest was skilled in spiritual direction, there would be more respectable reasons for his being welcome at the château. With his eye for the wry practicalities of his ministry, curé Gautier cited the value of the confessional in persuading the lady of the manor to accord due marital rights to her henpecked husband, 'who never ceases to admire the powerful eloquence of his curé who brings about such a great transformation'.[141]

When curé and seigneur were at loggerheads, the lawyers rubbed their hands. Ringing the bells for forty days on the death of the lord or his lady seems excessive, but in 1743 the parlement of Toulouse settled a lawsuit by ordering this—and the covering of an ancestral bust in the church with the parish funeral pall (except when it was being used for another funeral, and in Holy Week and at Easter).[142] The courts had to decide whether the holy water sprinkler was to be presented to the seigneur so that he could asperge himself, or whether the clergy should do it for him; the latter was the right answer, leading to lawsuits about raps on the knuckles inflicted by this holy instrument, the spoiling of a new wig, and the soaking of guests.[143] Without permission, a lord would extend his pew as his family or finances expanded, making the route to the altar circuitous; without due warning, an angry curé would take an axe to a venerable seigneurial chair.[144] In 1733, the bishop of Autun enjoined the inhabitants of Arnay-le-Duc to demolish the pew of their seigneur— and he was the duke of Lorraine.[145] In 1775, the inhabitants of Villedieu-les-Poêles and their priest threw out the pew of the local *commandeur* of the Order of Malta and those of his officers, and set up a fine churchwarden's bench in their place.[146] One ingenious curé solved the problem of an offensive pew without wrecking it by filling the chapel where it was situated with barrels.[147] Sometimes, the intercessions for the lord's family were rendered with less than convincing sincerity; more directly insulting, the seigneur might be subjected to unflattering observations in the homily at mass.[148] The curé of Bonneville in 1774 read from the altar the documents of his lawsuit against the seigneurial family, describing its members as 'stupid clots' and 'comics'.[149] In 1756, the purchaser of the seigneurie of La Marte in Haute-Provence was welcomed to his new parish by the priest with fighting words—'No! I receive you as Augustin Pellicot, a merchant trading to Spain, and I'll never recognize you as the master of La Marte'.[150]

Both sides in these disputes had their pride. Even a charitable action by the lord could meet with disapproval if the curé's role as intermediary with the poor was not recognized. Stanislas de Clermont Tonnerre, taking over the seigneurie of Champlâtreux in the 1780s, unthinkingly got the old men of the parish to elect three of their number to distribute his alms of bread and meat; even though the curé nominated the poor families who received this largesse, he was displeased. 'Ce mode convient à la paroisse et déplut à M. le curé.'[151] Sophisticated nobles at feud with the clergy could quietly vanish from church services and hear mass in their private chapel (though bishops insisted that parishioners must not attend and that the lord and his family should make their Easter duty with the parish).[152] Rustic nobles would show their displeasure without finesse. In 1778 one is recorded as wearing his hat in church, whistling all the way as he walked to his seat in the chancel, and distracting the congregation by doing conjuring tricks.[153] Bad relationships might culminate in blows. We hear of an aged nobleman complaining of being bullied, and of a curé who set his dog on a *commandeur* of the Order of Malta, and conversely, of a parish priest hit with the butt of a musket, and another beaten up by the Negro lackey of the lady of the manor.[154] Some curés on principle had no time for nobles of any sort. 'They obstinately insist on treating the Third Estate like a race of slaves and beasts of burden,' said one; 'pastors ought not to keep company with nobles, their natural enemies,' said another.[155] Jean Roux, the parish priest of La Balme (the pilgrim sanctuary near Lyon), in 1769 recorded: 'How happy the curé will be after the death of M. de Boulieu! . . . Thank the Lord it will be the end of his race.' Five years later, the longed-for event occurred. 'Ah! how good it is to have the seigneur in the next world: he's at rest and so am I.'[156]

In 1789, complaints against the aristocracy became universal. A Norman curé called for the end of the 'servitude' of holy water and incense, a worldly annexation of honours due to God alone, and 'the cause of a multitude of ruinous and scandalous lawsuits'.[157] Another in Avranches denounced the local seigneur from the pulpit as an opponent of national regeneration, 'who has nothing of the man but the name'.[158] Nearby, in the Norman *bocage*, the peasants, in the July tumults, forced Mme de Grieu d'Enneval to give up the 3,000 livres costs she had won in a lawsuit over a pew.[159] The marquis de Villette wrote an open letter to his notary renouncing his feudal dues and declaring: 'No more masses at the château! Convert the foundation to benefit the poor, and we will attend the mass of the community. Sign on my behalf a renunciation of my pew, of holy water and, above all, of incense, an impertinent usage, an *ultramondaine* [sic] pantomime.'[160] But in some places, old habits of deference died hard. Municipalities in 1790 and 1791 were protesting against parish priests who continued to give individual aspersion with holy water to 'ci-devant seigneurs', and on 18 September 1792 a complaint was made that notables and *ci-devant* officers of seigneurial justice were having the *pain bénit* presented to them 'in distinguished morsels on an individual plate'.[161]

V

There was a popular feeling that the seigneur ought to be generous to the poor in the lands where he was gathering feudal dues and incidents, but all too often, the expectation went for naught, the lord of the manor being more concerned in saving up to spend his winters among the élite society of the nearest major town. But the curé's obligation to the poor was inescapable. They were his special responsibility: 'Giving alms is a duty of the rich, but for the curé it is a rigorous obligation. Whatever he takes from his benefice to spend upon himself beyond what is necessary, he is taking it from the poor.'[162] Beggars came to the door of the presbytery expecting alms as of right. 'I have to give daily hospitality to passers-by of every kind,' said a priest whose parish was at a crossroads.[163] Another was so poor, he said, that his parishioners expected nothing from him, but not so those from outside: 'strangers, not knowing the situation, believe that, as my house is a presbytery, they have the right to insist on help, and if they don't get it there are oaths, blasphemies, curses, and menaces of arson'.[164] As the bishop of Avranches said in the same year (1786), the more prosperous peasants should be grateful that their clergy divert dangerous visitors from their doors, the beggars who begin with supplications but end with threats; 'someone has to give them bread and soup . . . and it's the curés who provide it'.[165] The incumbents of the bigger Parisian parishes had substantial incomes and huge numbers of poor, to whom they were correspondingly generous—in personal terms, over and above the institutional charities, lay collections, and so on which existed in so many places.[166] In the dearth of 1725, Languet de Gergy of Saint-Sulpice sold his furniture to feed his parishioners (his ability to extract subscriptions from the rich was notorious: he made them support a muslin factory to provide employment, and when invited out to dine, he would take away the silver from his place to be incorporated in a statue of the Virgin he was planning—'Notre-Dame de vieille vaisselle').[167] In the 1770s curé Cochin of Saint-Jacques was also running a factory making linen; it promoted employment, and the product was made into shirts for the aged, 'having them first worn by the young people so that the material would be softened by usage'.[168] At the same time, the curé of the Madeleine was giving

3,000 livres a year of his own money to the poor.[169] When Élie de Beaumont, the celebrated barrister and publicist, in January 1778 sent eight partridges to the presbytery of Saint-Nicolas 'for the poor', the reply was devastating:

I suppose you think that I have inherited the ability of our divine Lord to multiply loaves and fishes . . . I have 20,000 poor . . . and I know of no anatomist who could perform the dissection necessary for a share-out . . . Reserve your delicate taste and refinement for your literary productions, and be more straightforwardly generous in your charitable offerings.[170]

In the countryside, when a family fell on bad times, a loan, a gift of seed-corn, or other alms would be likely to be forthcoming from the curé.[171] The peasant *cahiers* of 1789, even those tinged with anti-clerical bitterness, generally sing the praises of the parish priests— 'consolers of the miseries of the people', 'humble and virtuous ecclesiastics living in our midst and sharing our hardships'; 'if only their incomes could be raised to a level which corresponded to the generosity of their instincts'.[172] These sentiments reflect the memories of the recent conduct of the parochial clergy during the harsh winters of the last years of the *ancien régime*. In 1785–6, the recteur of Theix provided employment for the poor by paying them to repair two bridges: had he been the actual tithe owner, he told the intendant, he would have been able to do more.[173] The curé of Ailly-le-Haut-Clocher spent his patrimonial income of 800 livres a year entirely on feeding the hungry who flocked in from all around, especially from Abbeville, to take advantage of his generosity.[174] In the spring of 1787, in the Breton parish of Berné, plague arrived on top of hunger as a scourge of the inhabitants; 'the only man in the parish who is generous and a friend of humanity', said the local surgeon, 'is their pastor'; he had sold his table silver and was living only on rye bread so that he could help others.[175] Jallet, curé of Chérigné, was finding 24 livres a week himself to add to the contributions of a few richer parishioners to maintain the poor, and when he went up as a deputy to the Estates General, he gave all his stock of grain away.[176]

In crises of a different kind—some parochial lawsuit against a seigneur or other influential person, the curé was expected to give leadership, maybe to go off to the distant town for long sojourns with lawyers. When plague drew near, it was the clergy above all who had to stay in place when others fled; when other sorts of danger threatened, their people would look to them for leadership, heroism even. In the 1780s we hear of a curé of the Châlons area fording a river in flood sixteen times to carry infirm parishioners to safety,[177] and another of Lorraine who was lowered into a collapsing well to rescue a trapped bricklayer (he offered a reward first of all to anyone who would do it, and when there were no takers, went down himself).[178] From the later years of Louis XIV comes the remarkable story of the curé of a coastal village taking command when the English fleet loomed on the horizon, threatening invasion; he lined up the armed coastguards on the beach, and behind them had all the inhabitants, women and girls included, wearing red hats, and some mounted on horses, donkeys, and cows—giving the appearance, from a distance, of a force of infantry and cavalry.[179]

These of course are exceptional incidents—but they illustrate an atmosphere of relationships very different from the manifold tales of arguments about tithe or surplice-fees. In everyday contacts, in any case, a curé tended to have genial, albeit businesslike, relations with his people. Witness curé Barbotin's letters from the Estates General at Versailles to the priest who was looking after his parish in his absence. 'I haven't paid for the wood I bought from Jean-Baptiste Devaney. He owes me money and I owe him. I am persuaded that he is not well off. If you can give him a few écus, that would be fine.' 'There is no need to ask for a receipt from honest folk.' 'I must set an example in paying my debts.' Then, apropos of a small sum owed to him (Barbotin is not sure just how much it is): 'If he pays, accept it; if not, do not press him, because he can't be well off.'[180] Another glimpse of friendly relationships comes in an obituary notice in a parish register concerning a curé who had refurnished his church (which had been 'a real stable of Bethlehem'), and set up a fund to provide milk for children and to award an annual prize for 'wisdom and virtue' to a girl elected by the parish.

He fell ill at Fresney where he had gone to see his family, on 1 December 1780. Immediately he set off back to his parish . . . On arrival, knowing that he was dying, he solemnly received the sacraments on the fifth of the month, and died on the ninth at six in the evening, loved and regretted by all his people and especially by his successor, who had always been his friend.[181]

Another entry in a register gives a glimpse of an ancient, worthy curé in high serious mood:

Today, 8 June 1762, having taken possession of this parish on 8 June 1712, for 50 years I have lived and live still without trouble and in peace with all men. But I have every reason to fear the terrible judgements of God who has confided to me, over so long a period, the care of thousands of souls—

a perilous task. *Pasce oves meas!* He will demand a rigorous account of them from me. *Itaque miseremi mei vos saltem, amice mei, et orate.*[182]

We do well not to forget that the diverse and picturesque concourse of the curés of the *ancien régime,* however worldly or rumbustious some of them seem, consists of men who knew that they lived in the shadow of judgement.

COLLABORATORS OF THE CURÉ

I *Life at the Presbytery—the housekeeper*

Most curés were ill housed. The reason was simple: the parish had to provide the presbytery and do the major repairs, and the inhabitants were never willing to part with money. Royal ordinances specified what the minimum accommodation must be. In 1695, it was two rooms with fireplaces, a kitchen, barn, cellar, and stable; in 1776, this was improved to the standard kitchen, stable, barn, and cellar, a bedroom with a little 'cabinet', a study, and another room suitable for hospitality.[1] In bigger towns, the law was better observed than elsewhere; there were more parishioners, often, to pay the rates; there were more respectable people who had to be entertained; and ecclesiastical authority was nearer at hand to see that decency was maintained. In Angers, a parlour, a dining-room, and two to five other rooms with fireplaces are found.[2] In the limited number of country parishes where the curé drew fat tithes, his house was likely to correspond to his affluence, since successive generations of incumbents would have had the means to improve and extend at their own expense. At Chauffailles in the diocese of Mâcon, where from 1728 onwards for thirty years the curé had paid for a rebuilding programme, there was a walled garden, a 'pretty courtyard enclosed with walls and a gateway' with a brand-new barn and stable on one side, while the house had a vestibule with a decorated ceiling, a dining-room and a study, both panelled, and a stone staircase leading up to 'two handsome rooms, excellent accommodation', with two small bedrooms alongside them.[3] But in any case, even the most agreeable country vicarage was likely to resemble a farmhouse rather than a mansion. The one at Clohars-Carnoët in Brittany was supposed to be attractive, but this was chiefly because it offered barn, stable, dovecote, pigsty, winepress, bakery, and two cellars, one for wine and one for cider, all in good order.[4] In the poorer rural areas and in parishes with a small population, the curé often lived in something approaching squalor. The inhabitants would never agree that this was the case, of course; many were so much worse off than he was, and the few who were better off would have to pay a substantial rate if his house was to be improved. The curé of Flaxien in the diocese of Belley appealed to the intendant to enforce a rebuilding; he had, he said, no more than a kitchen, cellar, bedroom, and small study, with half the roof consisting of thatch in a dangerous condition. A small committee of the more important citizens, however, reported that he had one 'spacious, splendid room', together with three smaller ones—a study, a bedroom, and a spare room—'le tout en fort bon état'. The *subdélégué* reporting to the intendant complained that 'these gentlemen, the curés, all want to be lodged like seigneurs'.[5] Whatever the truth of the matter, one doubts that phrase 'all in good order'. Curés continually complained that their parishioners refused to concern themselves with the vicarage until it was actually falling down. 'My house lets in everything except light,' said one, and he went on to describe how one of his parish registers had been totally eaten by rats.[6] Another wrote a comic poem about the frogs which had taken up residence in the pools in his sitting-room, and how he had to keep moving his bed around to avoid drips from the ceiling.[7]

In 1786, the parish clergy of the diocese of Comminges had to report to their bishop just how they were lodged; making allowance for their natural bias and the fact that this was a poor diocese, their replies are revealing. Few were precise about their available space; one had eight rooms, four had two up and two down, one had two rooms, and one had a single chamber only. But some gave picturesque descriptions of their misery. 'I am in danger of being buried in the ruins of the old seigneurial castle.' 'A very simple presbytery: one room and a lean-to with a wooden roof and no walls; no means of locking up, and adjoining the cemetery; it's a house isolated from all others, where I have the dead as my only neighbours.' 'The presbytery of Cazeneuve is . . . uninhabitable—without a chimney, propped between two very old houses and in continual danger of collapse and, although it is on high ground, it's mainly subterranean, like a bottle that is immersed in a bucket of water to cool the wine.' Thus, the curé has to live elsewhere, at Saint-Elix, his subordinate church, 'the only place where he was able to find a room fourteen paces wide and eighteen paces long, and even so, having to keep his firewood, wine, grain and horse in eight different sheds'. 'The presbytery is a sewer and in a very bad state, badly situated and dangerously unhealthy because of damp.' 'The presbytery is much dilapidated, perched on a rock exposed to the storms—no comfort here; no stable, no hen-house, no garden; in a word, uninhabitable.'[8] These were among the worst cases, of course. The total statistics which came in to the bishop's office showed that sixty-four vicarages were in good repair (eleven having been rebuilt by parishes and six by the curés out of their own pockets), sixty needed major repair (of which half a dozen needed total reconstruction), and eleven were uninhabitable. There were, in addition, twenty-one pastors who simply had no house at all and lodged where they could (one had a single room in a house occupied by two families, 'which causes all sorts of unpleasantness'[9]).

In the official prescription of accommodation in a presbytery, nothing was provided for the housekeeper; if she lived in, she might well have to sleep in the kitchen. Some curés were looked after by a female relative. A family which made sacrifices to get a son into the priesthood expected some reciprocity; a widowed mother, an aunt, a sister[10] needed a home, just as a celibate priest needed a housekeeper—and the two necessities sometimes conveniently coincided. Orphaned nieces were a special problem; the wills of curés frequently include provision for them,[11] and Restif has a moving story about a parish priest who saved for years to accumulate dowries for two of them, then gave all the money to his parishioners to rescue them from starvation after a terrible fire.[12] When a niece came to live at the presbytery, there was lively interest in the village: maybe she was given to good works, or perhaps just embarrassingly ultra-pious; maybe she got pregnant or married some riotous husband[13]—or was she a niece at all? There was always scope for gossip.

But whether the housekeeper of the curé was a relative or—as was more likely—not, she was one of the most intriguing figures in the chronicles and mythology of rural France. Every diocese had its stern synodal statute devised to prevent young women from taking up this prestigious office—at least 40 years of age was a common formula, some even said 50.[14] Bishops tended to interpret the rules strictly; a relaxation granted because aged parents were present, as chaperones as it were, would be withdrawn when they died, and priests who were of advanced years themselves could rarely hope for indulgence, 'as if age ever took away concupiscence'.[15] Yet the rules were frequently infringed, often because it was simply impossible to find a suitable person within them. There were heavy farmyard chores[16] to do, as well as cooking and cleaning; the place had to be protected from insistent beggars and sinister prowlers;[17] there were messages to carry, often at a distance; and it was important for the housekeeper to get around the village gossiping, partly to report back about which way public opinion was moving,[18] and partly to drop appropriate hints in prosperous households about current needs in the presbytery. If he could afford it, a curé also needed a manservant, a *valet*[19] to do repairs, gather the tithes, thrash the grain, dig the garden, and groom the horse, and if this all-purpose handyman had a young wife who did the vicarage housekeeping, what could be more reasonable? If the age rule were strictly observed, the position might soon be reached when the curé was burdened with an ancient *gouvernante* who had to have a young maidservant to help her, whose labours she would grumpily supervise from her permanent chair at the fireside, from whence she would talk endlessly to all callers of 'the cows, of the vicaire, of the hens and of God, of the rosary and of werewolves, of the virtue of the scapulary against fevers and agues, and of apparitions of the dead, muttering an occasional enlivening chorus learned from some stupid mission preacher'.[20]

Gossip about the clergy jumping into bed with their housekeepers was inevitable and (as we have argued) largely unjustified in the eighteenth century, except in backward and isolated areas. Even so, relations between curés and their *gouvernantes* were necessarily close and often friendly; there were consultations about local problems, discussions about the advisability of accepting some preferred new benefice.[21] Curé Barbotin at the Estates General often thought of his Catherine and her husband back at home; he was concerned for her comfort, amused at her foibles, alarmed at her illness, and when the Revolution confiscated half his income, he promised to continue to support them: 'as long as I have bread to eat, I'll try to keep both of them'.[22] Direct questions about sexual morality, yes or no, are not the best way to understand these subtle relationships. Curé Jacques-Joseph Besse of Saint-Aubin (Avesnes) explained, long afterwards, to an investigating papal official, why he had married his housekeeper during the Revolution. She had served him for twenty-four years, refusing offers of marriage on the assumption that he would provide for her in her old age. Having a little land of his own, which he could not legally settle upon her unless she was his wife, he had married her. 'She was justified in relying on the uprightness of my heart!' He claimed that he had lived chastely before his marriage, but he could not help thinking that the rule of celibacy for the clergy was a mistaken one—and he wished things had been otherwise for him all those years ago.[23] This is a story about a long friendship, not to be frowned upon by the austere, or what is worse, treated with a wry Clochemerlian tolerance.

II *The vicaires*

As a rule of thumb in eighteenth-century pastoral calculations, the curé of a rural parish with 500 communicants needed a vicaire to help him.[24] There were other factors involved, of course: the extent and difficulty of the terrain, the availability of masses at the chapels of monasteries, seigneurs, or confraternities, the presence of *prêtres habitués* or tonsured clerks to give assistance, the age and health of the incumbent himself. A town parish was different: a compact population of three times the size could be served by a single pastor.[25] So far as a reasonable equation of population with clerical manpower was concerned, the traditional boundaries of parishes were often absurd, but the allocation of assistant clergy frequently helped to remedy the imbalance. Of the dozen town parishes of Angers, three tiny ones were served by the curé alone, and a fourth had a vicaire only because of the duties connected with the perpetual adoration of the Holy Sacrament at its altar. Six parishes had two vicaires each, and there were two others which were specially favoured with more. One was the splendid official parish of Saint-Michel du Tertre, in whose church the mayors had their pew and where the walls were lined with the tombs of the Angevin magistracy, and in whose narrow streets, amidst numerous dwelling-houses, the prison and most of the tennis-courts, billiard-saloons, gaming-houses, and inns of the city were found; here were four vicaires. There was also the huge working-class parish of La Trinité, with its 11,000 population, which had five.[26] For different reasons, the curé of Antibes in the diocese of Grasse had been allowed the same high number of assistants; though there were only 4,500 inhabitants, there was a large military garrison permanently stationed there, and the Crown, which collected the local tithes, was disposed to be generous in making provision for a peculiarly difficult pastoral situation.[27] In the huge parishes of Paris, curés presided over con-fraternities of bustling, ambitious vicaires as well as a multitude of *prêtres habitués*. Maybe they would operate as a team, as at Saint-Laurent, where the eccentric and charitable abbé Cottrell, a hypochondriac who never ventured outside in winter and was per-petually shouting 'Fermez-moi cette porte!', left one of his staff to arrange the complicated duty rosters;[28] maybe they would be allo-cated to particular districts, as in 1739 the curé of Saint-Germain-l'Auxerrois broke up his empire into nine sectors, each to be pastorally directed by one of the vicaires.[29] Often, such delegation of duties followed naturally from the geography of the parish, as at

Notre-Dame of Alençon, where the two vicaires were stationed at each of the two dependent churches.[30]

Ask in any parish, and almost everywhere curé and people would say how welcome a vicaire would be to give a helping hand—provided they did not have to pay for him. Usually, the tithe owner was responsible for the salary—that is, the curé himself or, if he was on the *congrue*, the person or institution which actually held the great tithes. There was an official *congrue* laid down for a vicaire: 150 livres, raised to 200 in 1768, to 250 in 1778, to 300 in 1784. The inhabitants, who might have to pay something if the tithe could not cover the cost, were in any case legally responsible for finding lodgings (though not furniture) for their vicaire;[31] in practice, they tended to expect the parish priest to put him up in the presbytery. Since a vicariate was not a benefice, the holder, strictly speaking, had to be in possession of the clerical 'title', which meant an extra 100 livres or so in addition to the *congrue*. Thus, towards the end of the *ancien régime*, one might assume that a vicaire with his free lodgings and *congrue* was securely above the poverty line, though far from well-off.

Having said this, we must remember that, as usual in eighteenth-century France, there were almost as many exceptions to the rule as examples confirming it. Sometimes, a parish contrived to have a vicaire without being able to offer the official salary; a mere pittance, backed up by permission to cultivate a piece of the common land, perhaps, or a fee for acting as village schoolmaster.[32] On the other hand, there might be something over and above the general *congrue*. A common ingredient in a salary, or a supplement to it, was an annual offering, often in kind, with the vicaire going from door to door to collect it. In Brittany, where the parlement had forbidden this embarrassing exercise, there were parishes where a local rate was levied in lieu, others where a few pious families came forward with voluntary donations, and mean ones where no supplement at all was offered.[33] Sometimes, an old custom or the proceeds of a legacy helped out—a tribute of butter as a reward for performing some monthly liturgical observance in one place,[34] a substantial fund yielding no less than 600 livres a year to the lucky vicaire in another.[35] The parish of Linselles in the diocese of Tournai got along comfortably with a vicaire who drew 335 livres a year from the local seigneur for acting as his chaplain, the community doing no more than adding a small supplement for saying a low mass every Sunday. But in 1742, the bishop refused to allow the doubling-up of seigneurial chaplain and vicaire to continue; the community, unwilling to add to its charges, hired a Capuchin cheaply to say the low masses; the angry curé got the bishop to ban the Capuchin from celebrating—and so it went on to 1750, when all was settled at the expense of the tithe owner.[36]

Here indeed was the general difficulty in obtaining a vicaire when one was needed: it was a new burden on the tithe owner, and he was unlikely to pay up cheerfully. Witness, for example, a battle of claim and counter-claim which took place in the early eighteenth century between the parish of Vaulx and the canons of Saint-Géry of Cambrai over the inhabitants' demand for a vicaire to serve the dependent chapel of Vraucourt. The parishioners said that some of them had to walk half a league to church, the canons said a quarter (and surely it was not reasonable to take into account everyone who was foolish enough to build a house on the fringes of the parish). Some people had to cross a dangerous stream; the canons asked why they did not build better bridges, and denied that anyone had ever died without the sacraments because of floods. The area is subject to warfare; if so, replied the canons, everyone runs away, so no clergy are needed. The curé said he needed help in hearing confessions; the canons agreed, seeing that he was away from the place half the time and was principally engaged in mending clocks. (Merely a hobby, replied the curé.) Finally, the archbishop's commissioners arrived, accompanied by a professional surveyor and an assistant to carry his instruments—the parish was measured out, and it was solemnly ruled that Vaulx and Vraucourt were so close together that a vicaire was not necessary, so the canons saved their money.[37] The diocesan ruling might not be the end of the matter; there were curés who went up to the parlement or even beyond to the Royal Council to extract a *congrue* to pay an assistant. When François-Antoine Drogy, doctor of the Sorbonne and a son of a minor family of the robe, took over the parish of Saint-Nicolas at Coutances in 1773, he found himself with 6,000 parishioners and only one vicaire, whom he had to pay himself out of a total income of 1,622 livres (*congrue*, surplice-fees, and foundation masses all included). He needed four helpers, let alone one, he told the bishop. Since he insisted on his point, the orders finally came down from Bayeux for the holding of the usual enquiry into 'the extent of the parish, the size of the population, and the difficulty of the roads'. When it appeared that the tithe-owning prelate was not likely to pay (there was a flaw in Drogy's case—there were fourteen *prêtres habitués* in his parish), he wrote around to his colleagues asking for advice. Gervais de la Prise, curé of Saint-Pierre of Caen, it turned out, was already suing the bishop before the parlement of Paris for just such a grievance. Wiser heads suggested a petition, backed by a few other parish priests, to the Assembly General of the Clergy, suggesting that some of the funds that maintained the *habitués* should be confiscated and turned from the support of 'drones' to the payment of genuine vicaires.[38]

According to handbooks of spirituality, the vicariate was a period of apprenticeship to pastoral expertise and the building-up of the interior life of prayer; according to the legal ones, it was an interval of manœuvre and intrigue to obtain a permanent benefice. Influence and contacts were important; indeed a newly ordained priest without them might not even find a suitable place as a vicaire for a while. Living at home or with friends he would say masses at 12 sols a time or walk in funeral processions at a rather higher fee, and preach the two or three sermons he had off by heart in parishes willing to offer him the proceeds of the collection. Out of this meagre income (it is the memoirs of the abbé Lesage, a priest of the diocese of Saint-Brieuc at the end of the *ancien régime*, which recount these details[39]), his first expenditure was to provide himself with the basic equipment of the wage-earning ecclesiastic, a watch, an umbrella, a good-quality long cassock, and a collection of cribs of sermon notes. Finally, a parochial vacancy would come his way—maybe just a *vicariat de tolérance* (helping out temporarily) or, much more satisfactory, a *vicariat fondé*, an established post.[40] Since the ultimate object was promotion, and a degree of subservience was inevitable, it was best (said a cheerfully cynical curé giving advice to junior clergy) to avoid taking up service under a young parish priest; he was likely to be proud and a hard taskmaster, and to have an old mother or aunt or young niece coming to live with him, so many unpredictable womenfolk to be humoured and placated. Failing an uncle or a friend of the family, look for some old parish priest with no relatives who has fallen out with his parishioners—just the man to leave you independently in charge and to nominate you as his successor when he decides to resign and take his pension.[41]

Vicaires moved around. Some posts were much more attractive than others—a better salary, more agreeable society, better chances of promotion. An assistant priest who made his mark as a pastor or a preacher, or who was well connected, would get his own parish quickly; one who was something of a failure might think it wise to start again somewhere else—indeed, he might be encouraged to do so. In the village of Aubais, in 1748, the abbé David left after four years, having accidentally shot the local surgeon in the leg when they were out hunting; the abbé Favre, a sentimental preacher beloved of the ladies, was called to higher things; Père de la Croix, a monk, arrived in 1757, but moved within the year to become an army chaplain; his successor, Clément, departed even more rapidly, being virtually hooted out of the church by the congregation.[42] Since only about half the rural parishes had a vicaire, the overall proportion of rural benefices to applicants was not unfavourable (from the massive documentation put together in the investigations of 1790, it seems that 20,500 vicaires were waiting for the deaths or resignations of 39,000 curés[43]). Thus, while much would depend upon circumstances and local supply and demand, promotion to a parish of one's own was not likely to be delayed more than ten years.[44] In 1766, a vicaire of Orléans wrote some comic verses addressed to his bishop (did he send them?), pronouncing himself ripe for becoming a parochial curé ('I am an expert at funerals,' he said; 'when I bury them, they don't come back'); he had been a subordinate for seven years, and clearly regarded this as over the average.[45] Even so, in every diocese we find priests who were stranded for ever in the vicariate. Some, it is true, might not aspire to go further. To be a senior vicaire in one of the great Parisian parishes was to be an ecclesiastic of some distinction—like the rotund abbé Jay, premier vicaire of Saint-Barthélémy as Mme Roland remembered him: severe of mien and a man of business, with a private income, two brothers successful notaries living nearby, and a horse-faced, aristocratic female relative running his household and laying on lavish dinners and agreeable parties at tric-trac.[46] Or there were the eccentrics deaf to the call of ambition—perhaps through innate diffidence or disciplined humility, or even through aristocratic pride. Chateaubriand never forgot how, as a boy, he was given an écu wrapped in a dirty piece of paper by his relative the abbé de Chateaubriand de la Guéronde—hefty, red-faced, with an unkempt wig, torn cassock, dirty shoes, holed stockings, plodding along with his big stick and muttering his matins; he was just a vicaire, but he had blown up the prince de Condé for insulting him by the offer of a tutorship in a ducal household.[47] But mostly, the unpromoted vicaire was a melancholy failure. Even if, over long years, he settled happily locally, what if a thrusting new curé arrived and sacked him?[48] And what happened when he was too old to carry on? A curé could always resign and keep a third of his income, but there was no such resort for the aged vicaire. Well-meaning bishops tried to set up institutions to receive them, but how could a parochial pastor settle down, in the company of fellow geriatrics, to 'a monastic type of life, meals only in the refectory, having to attend choir and sing the psalms, in a house in which there was a superior over him and porters in charge at the gates? He'd rather beg or starve.'[49]

III *The* prêtres habitués

Though the Church in France was like a hierarchical pyramid, with some footholds for ability and many more for birth and influence to assist ambitious climbers to work their way upwards, the analogy needs modification. At every level of the crumbling traditional monument there were horizontal side-tracks and devious openings and passages, leading to comfortable chambers, sunny niches, and convenient ledges, places where the modest, the unspiritual, or the ruthlessly ascetic cleric might decide to rest a while, or even to stay in perpetuity. Just as there were great aristocrats who were content with the unearned income of an abbey *in commendam* without hankering after a bishopric, so there were ordinary priests (large numbers of them—one estimate runs as high as 10,000[50]) content to live on the margins of the parochial structure, enjoying—for good or bad reasons—their leisure and independence. 'Immediately after his ordination,' it was said of one of these, 'he returned to his village and occupied himself with manual labour, digging the garden, chopping wood, scything grass, churning the milk, content to repeat his daily office every evening and to say a mass every Sunday in a private chapel.'[51] Curé Gauthier the essayist knew such a one—a big, leather-jacketed peasant type, spending all the week on his farm and giving no help to the curé except that he came in to say the early mass on Sunday mornings.[52] Others, perhaps with some private means or some small benefice without cure of souls, or maybe dependent entirely on what could be scraped together from ecclesiastical fees, hung around a particular church earning small sums from saying masses, helping in various ceremonies or undertaking some duties like those of sacristan. In the archdiocese of Besançon they were called *vicaires domestiques*, as distinguished from the genuine *vicaires canoniques*; elsewhere they went by the names of *obitiers, choristes, chapelains fondés, prêtres libres, familiers*, and, the most general name, *prêtres habitués*.

The big parishes of Paris were haunts of these supernumerary clergy. In the preliminary elections to the Estates General of 1789, in the fifty-two parishes of the capital, 600 'parish clergy' voted; there were 23 at Saint-Merry, 36 at Saint-Germain-l'Auxerrois, 62 at Saint-Nicolas-du-Chardonnet, 72 at Saint-Eustache, and 85 at

Saint-Roch. At Saint-Étienne-du-Mont there were 173, but this is a figure of a rather different kind, as it includes many academic teachers and students in holy orders.[53] Alternatively, an idea of the number of priests around in the capital can be gained by looking at the expense accounts of distinguished funerals. At Saint-Sulpice on 15 November 1785, the coffin of an aristocratic lady was accompanied by the curé, a vicaire, 'le vicaire des convois', 'le confesseur en robe et gants', and sixty other ecclesiastics, all paid for attending.[54] In the city of Bordeaux at the end of the *ancien régime* there were 77 priests belonging to the *sociétés de bénéficiers* which existed in eight parishes, and another 44 *prêtres habitués* (all these in priests' orders: there were also 108 deacons and subdeacons, sacrists, and tonsured clerks).[55] It was not always ancient foundations and legacies which provided the funds to maintain this pool of supplementary ecclesiastical labour. Versailles was a new town with a convent of Récollets, but no abbeys or collegiate churches and only one ancient parish; here, the royal parish of Notre-Dame (founded in 1682) had thirty priests available, the aristocratic parish of Saint-Louis (founded in 1754) had twenty-five, while Saint-Symphorien (founded in the late Middle Ages), which served the working-class population, had only four.[56] In some places, more especially in Brittany, there were towns and bigger villages which hired supernumerary priests, called *prêtres de chœur*; a vacancy was announced with the other notices at Sunday mass; candidates had to present a certificate of good morals, and were tested for vocal musical ability, and the winner would be appointed to office by the parish council.[57] Depending on the amount of surplice-fees available, they might earn from 30 livres a year in a rural place to up to 250 in a town, though not all towns were profitable places—only about 50 livres was available in Coutances or Cherbourg, and at Alençon it was said that their income would barely pay for the laundry of their surplices.[58]

An unbeneficed hanger-on was very much an ecclesiastical dogsbody; there were, however, certain *prêtres habitués* who held modestly dignified formal offices in their local church, living corporately in a sort of 'college' (probably presided over by the curé, just as a dean presided over a cathedral chapter), enjoying a recognized place in society and an income from some ancient foundation. Usually, the original founder had laid down the conditions of eligibility for membership; probably it was necessary to have been born in the town or in the actual parish, or to have parents of local lineage, or even to be 'founder's kin'. Such privileged little corporations were the *prêtres filleuls* and the *communalistes* found in various

churches in the dioceses of Saint-Flour and Limoges and, more especially, Clermont (129 communities there);[59] so also were the forty or
so communities of *mépartistes* in the dioceses of Autun, Mâcon,
Langres, Chalon-sur-Saône, and Dijon (there were five in the city of
Dijon itself).[60] There were also sixty colleges of priests under the
name of *familiarités* in Franche Comté,[61] and the *enfants prêtres* of
Mirecourt in Lorraine.[62] Cournot tells how his grandfather transferred his practice of notary to the little town of Gray in Franche
Comté specifically to ensure that his sons would qualify, if they so
desired, for such an ecclesiastical sinecure.[63] A family man had to be
far-sighted; a young priest who became one of the *filleuls* of Saint-
Gervais in Paris obtained entrance only after a long lawsuit—parishioners had priority for entrance, but he had been born prematurely,
while his mother was making a social call outside the boundaries. He
was lucky, won his case, and enjoyed 200 livres a year for life.[64] The
members of the communities naturally wished to limit the number
of entrants so as to leave more money for each of them in the distributions from the common fund. In 1752, the nine *filleuls* of
Montaigut (whose income was very low) sent a legal officer, a
huissier, to their curé to warn him formally that there were young
clerics of dubious qualifications seeking the priesthood solely to get
access to the revenues of their guild: let him not give any of them
attestations of good morals or certificates of belonging to the parish
until formal announcements had been made in church, so that
challenges could be made against them.[65]

In theory, a college of priests attached to a parish ought to have
been a boon to the curé: in practice, many parish priests did not find
this to be the case, and most would have wished to replace them
with proper vicaires. At the church of Saint-Pierre in Caen, there
were twelve *habitués* earning no less than 500 livres a year each;
resplendent in grey cloaks, they gave themselves the airs of canons.
At the beginning of the century, the curé went to law to try to
confiscate two of their places for vicaires; they always say they help
me, he complained, but when you ask one to preach, he has a sore
throat; to visit the sick, and he has an attack of cramp; to take a
catechism, and a fit of diarrhoea strikes him just when the class is
about to begin, and they are everlastingly away visiting sick relatives.
The bishop of Bayeux tried in vain to reform them. They remained,
said the curé in 1787, 'a swarm of useless and idle drones who eat
the honey of the bees'.[66] Nearby in Caen was the parish of Saint-
Nicolas with 10,000 population and only one vicaire; the four *obitiers*
and two other supernumerary priests were of little use, said the curé

in 1785. 'Only one occupies himself with pastoral duties. The others, being independent, spend their time in sheer idleness, or in forming cabals to defeat my best efforts, stirring up the parishioners and sounding the alarm at the least thing that displeases them.'[67] In the diocese of Clermont, where communities of *filleuls* flourished more than anywhere else, curés struggled continually against them; a parish priest on the *congrue* was sometimes financially worse off than they were, and one who was a newcomer found them entrenched with popular support, for they were by definition members of local families. In 1724, Bishop Massillon issued an ordinance against these 'idle priests who regard themselves as masters of the churches and . . . expend all their zeal in denying to the curés the rights which are essential to their office'; accordingly, he laid down rules giving curés and vicaires precedence at all ceremonies, and prescribing fines on *filleuls* for every absence from masses, vespers, and processions. In 1764, a later bishop of Clermont tightened these rules and imposed an examination for admission to the communities, in which the curé would have the decisive voice.[68] Occasionally, disputes between parish priests and corporations of *habitués* came up before the parlements, with varying outcomes, for the instinct of the magistrates to favour the pastoral ministry sometimes clashed with their devotion to ancient custom. The most successful case for the curés was one of 1766, when the parlement of Lorraine cracked down on the *enfants prêtres* of Mirecourt, subordinating them to the parish clergy, and even denying them corporate status.[69]

From the curé's point of view, the usefulness of a community of *habitués* depended very much on the degree of control he could exercise over its members. In the vast parish of Saint-Gervais in Paris, where sixty of them (freely recruited, though preference was given to candidates born within the parish) lived together in a sort of seminary under central discipline, they were indispensable. Curé François Feu, who resigned in 1699, left his substantial fortune to help to maintain them. During the reign of his nephew, namesake, and successor, however, the value of the investments maintaining the community collapsed, and the new man arriving in 1762 was in despair at having only thirty priests, inadequately paid at that, to keep going the manifold parochial activities.[70] But to control subordinates who had independent sources of income and could not be dismissed was difficult. The curé of Sainte-Feyre (diocese of Clermont) had a college of priests of which he was the head (enjoying a double share in their distributions), and they were formally his vicaires, doing ordinary parish duties. Even so, he was not happy with such permanently established and influential collaborators, and in 1723, 1735, and 1748 he went to law, unsuccessfully, to try to suppress their foundation.[71] In the little town of Ille in Roussillon, the curé seemed to have triumphed in 1736 when he got the ecclesiastical courts to order the local community of priests to provide him with two vicaires; in fact, by 1765, everyone wanted the end of the arrangement, for pastoral authority had disintegrated and the parish complained of having three heads instead of one.[72]

Ecclesiastical reformers looked coldly on footloose priests outside the official command structure, and the trend of the late seventeenth century was to replace *habitués* with vicaires wherever possible. In the diocese of La Rochelle there had been 110 *habitués* and 175 vicaires in 1648; by 1724 there were fewer than a dozen *habitués* and about 200 vicaires.[73] (These figures suggest that it was easier to get rid of abuses than to find the money for improvements.) The eighteenth century saw the decline of most of the colleges and communities of supernumerary priests—whether as a result of the hostility of the curés, the rigour of new regulations imposed by bishops, the decline of revenues by maladministration, or because of changes in the attitude of public opinion towards sinecures and clerical idleness. We have seen how the curé of Saint-Gervais lost half of his team of assistants. Most of the *mépartistes* of the diocese of Autun were gone by mid-century.[74] At Ille, the college which had thirty-one priests in 1732 was down to twenty-three in 1763;[75] at Sainte-Feyre, the income which had once maintained twenty priests was divided among eight in 1700, among two or three in 1750, until by 1790 there was only one to share with the curé.[76] In the first half of the century the *filleuls* of Notre-Dame of Aurillac were sixty-strong; by 1789 the number of their 'prebends' was halved, and some were unfilled.[77] At Treignac-sur-Vézéré in the Limousin the *prêtres filleuls* who had sixteen members in the mid-seventeenth century were down to three in 1700, and survived to 1789 with only one or two members.[78] The sixteen places of the *société de bénéficiers* of the parish of Saint-Michel in Bordeaux were mostly empty by the end of the *ancien régime*.[79] These were all communities in towns (albeit some of them were very small ones—2,000 inhabitants constituted a 'town' by the standards of the *ancien régime*); in other words, in the more sophisticated places where opinion was hardening against abuses. In the rural isolation of Raulhac-en-Caulades, however, the old ways were undisturbed, and in 1789 there was a community of eleven priests, all born in the parish and sons of fathers born there, sharing nearly 4,500 livres a year among themselves, adding to the income of their sinecure by commercial or agricultural work, and meeting from time to time to dine together—and, no doubt, to toast their generous fifteenth-century founder.[80]

The suppression of the colleges of the *prêtres habitués* by the Constituent Assembly in August 1790 was an inevitable reform: the Revolution did what bishops had been trying to do for more than a century. The chief result was that respectable, middling sort of families in provincial towns lost a comfortable resort of modest sinecures, and had to push their sons into the new bureaucracy. The Church was rid of a system which had encouraged dubious vocations, though it was also one which had provided opportunities for eccentric individuals to express themselves, sometimes with advantage to religion or society. The *prêtres habitués* ranged from peasant farmers, shopkeepers, idle young men who lived at home, and tired old men with private incomes who enjoyed the consideration accorded to ecclesiastics; to acolytes, sacristans, chaplains, and all the minor functionaries who kept the ceremonial life of the bigger churches going; to confessors, spiritual guides, and preachers; to students, tutors, scholars, and publicists. François de Chaffault, an *habitué* of Saint-Gervais, who made a will in 1714 leaving money to pay forty fellow priests ('only 40', he said modestly)[81] to walk in his funeral procession, had done well for himself by becoming chaplain to the duchesse d'Orléans. Pierre-Antoine Textoris of a solid family of Aurillac, which had often held municipal office, was a *prêtre filleul* there, and a tutor in a noble family and chaplain to a convent of nuns.[82] Michel-Claude Guibert of Dieppe, the son of an artisan, was ordained in 1721, and spent the rest of his days as an *habitué* of the church of Saint-Rémy, drawing a meagre 40 livres a year which he made up to 200 by saying masses and acting as chaplain to two local charitable institutions. In a long, laborious lifetime (he died in 1784 at the age of 87) he wrote a massive chronicle of the history of Dieppe, which earned him election to the academy of Rouen and nomination as a notable of his native town.[83] It does not become a fellow historian to complain too much of the abusive system which gave leisure for research and writing to a colleague and predecessor in the great tradition which we serve.

14

CANONS AND CHAPTERS

I

There were 130 cathedrals in France, one for each diocese. Strictly speaking, there were 131, for the diocese of Sisteron had two, the collegiate church of Forcalquier having the title of 'con-cathédrale'; in its choir there was an episcopal throne, and a new bishop had to come to the church to repeat his solemn entry and his oath.[1] There were lawsuits, but the parlement of Aix maintained the canons of Forcalquier in their rights. Most of the cathedrals were in towns of over 2,000 inhabitants; perhaps fifteen were in smaller places—Saint-Lizier in the Pyrenees was a hamlet, Vaison an encampment in a Gallo-Roman ruin. The diocese of Glandève had no cathedral in its episcopal town, a flood having swept it away, so there was a miserable substitute in the tiny town of Entrevaux. Rennes presented the unusual spectacle of a chapter without a church, as the cathedral had been destroyed in the great fire of 1720; rebuilding was proceeding intermittently, but by the Revolution the new walls were only five feet high.

The diocesan chapters were not the only collegiate churches: there were at least 500 others.[2] Some were rich and splendid, like Saint-Honoré in Paris and Saint-Martin in Tours, others were little more than seigneurial chapels founded to pray for the souls of the lords of some estate; between these extremes there were all sorts of variants. Because of the distribution of dioceses, the cathedrals were mainly in the South, while the other collegiate churches were concentrated in the richer North, above the Bordeaux–Valence line. Half of them were in places with over 2,000 inhabitants, though there were larger towns entirely without them—Le Havre, Dieppe, Fécamp, and, much larger still, over 20,000, Caen, Versailles, and Brest. A quarter of the collegiate churches were in episcopal cities: Lyon had eight, Soissons six (for only 8,000 people), Le Mans and Angers four, Reims and Marseille three, Paris thirteen. The cathedrals naturally claimed pre-eminence. Their chapters, they held, were 'the synod of the diocese' and the *de jure* council of the bishop.

By the eighteenth century, the bishops had become too powerful to be subjected to compulsory advice; even so, the cathedral would be a focus for diocesan affairs through the activities of individual canons—archdeacons, *grands vicaires*, the *official*, and the *promoteur*. And in a vacancy of the see, its chapter took over the administration of the diocese, holding synods, issuing pastoral letters, consecrating the holy oils, absolving reserved cases, supervising the ecclesiastical court, and (though this was disputed) instituting to benefices. The other chapters of the town, however, would make a point of not being too deferential. They had their corporate pride, and such singularities and distinctions as they possessed would be flaunted against their colleagues at the cathedral. A classic feud was seen in the diocese of Cambrai,[3] the chapters of Saint-Géry and Sainte-Croix against the metropolitan chapter over representation in the provincial estates. In 1786, a coalition of the two minor chapters with the abbots of great monasteries, the provincial nobles, and Court interests around Calonne obtained a royal ruling depriving the cathedral of its privileged position, so the metropolitan canons shook the dust of the estates of the Cambrésis off their feet and attended no more. In some episcopal cities, the cathedral's claim to dominate rang hollow in face of the sheer riches and splendour of a rival. In Bordeaux, Saint-Seurin was on a level with the metropolitan church, as was Saint-Sernin in Toulouse. The canons of Saint-Honoré in Paris were much richer than those of Notre-Dame. In Tours,[4] Saint-Martin eclipsed the cathedral; the king himself had the supreme title of 'abbé', and princes of the blood and dukes were honorary canons; the fifty-one prebendal stalls and the eleven for dignitaries attracted vast incomes, and the minor clergy of the foundation, benefice holders, and *prêtres habitués* were 271 in number, one-sixth of the total of priests in the entire archdiocese.

There was no fixed number of canons for the chapter of a collegiate church, and not even an agreed optimum number. Of the cathedrals, adding dignitaries to the total, there were 93 at Chartres, 84 at Laon, 62 at Tours, 50 at Autun and Auxerre, 49 at Le Mans, 40 at Clermont, 32 at Lyon, and fewer than 30 at Angers, Alet, Tarbes, Boulogne, and Strasbourg. In a provincial town with three or four collegiate churches, the streets of the old city could see the coming and going of something like a hundred canons—at Reims,[5] Notre-Dame had 73, Saint-Symphorien 22, Saint-Timothée 13, Saint-Balsamie 13. By contrast, in the small dioceses of the South, there were cathedrals where there were hardly enough clergy to keep the liturgical services going, and the bishop had to call in curés from the countryside to make up the numbers when he officiated pontifically.[6] The cathedral of Agde was an exception, having substantial endowments, and therefore able to employ 68 ecclesiastics, a third of them priests—in a diocese where there were only 25 curés and 15 vicaires.[7]

There were vast disparities between chapters in the level of canonical incomes, though it is difficult to give precise figures; these were not available to outsiders at the time, and have proved elusive since. The total revenue of the foundation is not always a guide to what individuals drew, since the number of stalls and the responsibilities of the chapter have to be taken into account. There were good years and bad years, depending on the harvest, efficiency of land management, the accidents governing feudal dues, and the outcome of lawsuits. A canon might rise in income as he grew more senior, and deans and dignitaries drew supplements, sometimes double. Figures put forward in the second half of the century for canonical incomes in the cathedrals show Metz, Nîmes, and Bordeaux at 5,000 livres and more; Uzès, Nancy, Tarbes, and Angers at 3,000; Reims, Langres, Périgueux, Agen, Saint-Brieuc, and Amiens between 2,000 and 3,000; Sarlat and Bazas at about 1,500; Sens and Rennes at 700 to 900. Quimper and Autun were poor foundations with a sharp differentiation of income internally, the junior canons scraping along miserably until they went up a few rungs on the ladder of seniority. In some of the tiny dioceses of the South, there were cathedrals with more debts than income, so canons at Gap, Digne, Rieux, and Glandève got virtually nothing.[8]

There were similar wide diversities in incomes in the other collegiate churches. At Saint-Honoré in Paris, Saint-Martin at Tours, and Saint-Caprais at Agen the rewards were far above those offered in most cathedrals. Many, without having such wealth, nevertheless provided a comfortable life-style. Such a foundation was the church at Ecouis, a little town in Normandy.[9] The twelve canons each had a little house with a garden, grouped together in an enclosure cut off from the world by a high wall and from the church by several ranks of lime trees; none of their prebends yielded less than 2,000 livres a year, and the dean drew double. They said the services, looked after the parish, met in chapter every Wednesday and Friday, and were the leaders of local society. On similar incomes, the canons of Saint-Sauveur at Metz lived a dignified existence in an urban milieu. In the province of Guienne, there were rural canons whose incomes were less than those of the poorest parish priests on the *congrue*—not surprisingly, at Génissac and Villandraut they were to be unanimous in supporting the revolutionary church settlement—they did not regret the passing of the old ecclesiastical order.[10] In the diocese of Autun, the prebends of Avenay yielded 1,000 livres a year, while at Aigueperse and La Pré-sous-Arcy the canons no longer drew any remuneration. They had virtually ceased to perform any duties, except that at La Pré-sous-Arcy they met to celebrate a high mass on the great feast-days—that is, until 1757, when their penniless foundation was suppressed.[11]

Collegiate churches too poor to keep their liturgical offices going, with their canons wandering the countryside to earn a living, were anathema to reforming bishops, while the revenues of some of the others might have been employed more usefully elsewhere in the Church. Suppression, however, was not easy. Pensions had to be allotted to the chapter members, and arrangements made for the pastoral care of local people and the continuance of the masses for the souls of founders and benefactors. While the canons might be happy to be pensioned off, the laity of the place might object, out of conservatism, fear of the obligations of repairing the church, the drying up of income for local tradesmen, and the loss of sinecures for their children. The obligatory legal procedures of *de commodo et incommodo* gave all interested parties a chance to state their opposition, and the episcopal decree of suppression needed letters patent of the king registered in the parlement of the relevant jurisdiction to be effective. A less contentious way of proceeding was to leave the foundation extant but to suppress some of the prebends. Thus the archbishop of Sens, in a campaign to bring order among his collegiate churches between 1759 and 1778, ended two of them altogether, took a post of dignitary and three canonries from another, eleven canonical stalls from another, and seventeen chapels attached to the foundation from another.[12] A chapter might itself appeal to the king to allow a reduction in the number of prebends, or to leave one of them empty for a term of years to pay for some unusual expenditure, say, on the organ.

From the point of view of a chapter, however, the ideal remedy for poverty was a 'union', an extra benefice without cure of souls absorbed into the foundation, and petitions would be made to the king, the bishop, or, if there was one, a lay patron to ask for such a prize.[13] It was difficult, for all the *collèges*, seminaries, and hospitals were competing for similar annexations. More difficult still, for entirely different reasons, were prospects of union of a more sweeping kind, the merger of two chapters. The canons on either side would insist on getting a good bargain, financially, or in honorific distinctions and precedences. Willy-nilly, there had to be an amalgamation at Montauban in 1739, for the cathedral of Saint-Martin and the collegiate church of Saint-Etienne had been destroyed by the Protestants in the Wars of Religion, and the king had paid for building a single church for both of them.[14] Susceptibilities were allayed by making it a federal union, each group retaining its own *mense* (property and income), with the provost of Saint-Martin the head of the united chapter and the dean of Saint-Etienne next in seniority, the balance being evened by making the sacristan of Saint-Etienne the *ex officio* curé of the town parish. Another successful union took place at Le Mans in 1743, the two royal collegiate foundations there amalgamating, Saint-Pierre de la Cour absorbing the Sainte-Chapelle du Gué de Maulny.[15] On 11 February the clergy of the two churches processed together in copes, transferring the reserved Sacrament permanently from the one church to the other, singing as they went, 'Ecce quam bonum et quam jucundum, habitare fratres in unum'. It was indeed good and joyful, though it had taken three years of tight negotiations. For success, the chapters to be united needed to be in the same town, thus minimizing local protests, and have ample resources to pool, or, failing that, be able to balance superior riches on one side against superior distinction on the other—in the way daughters of financiers were married off to sons of nobles. In accordance with these rules, in 1744 two unions to bolster the revenues of metropolitan chapters were agreed: Isle-Barbe joined the cathedral of Lyon,[16] and Saint-Germain-l'Auxerrois joined Notre-Dame of Paris. For the most celebrated church in the land, Notre-Dame was poor, its canons drawing barely 2,500 livres a year, while at Saint-Germain-l'Auxerrois it was three times this. It took eight years of argument, the churchwardens of the parish of Saint-Germain and representatives of the university leading the opposition. In the end, two royal councillors negotiated a compromise, by which canonries would be extinguished as their holders died, up to the point when all the prebends afforded a suitably large income—by 1789, a canon of Notre-Dame had 7,000 livres.[17]

By contrast with these successes, the archbishop of Sens ran into insurmountable obstacles when he tried to unite the collegiate churches of Bray and Val de Provins to his cathedral.[18] The pastoral benefits were manifest: the metropole was under-endowed, and priests were needed to transfer to the pastoral ministry. From 1756 to 1770 negotiations went on, the inhabitants of Bray and Provins raising a clamour—money would move away from town and be spent elsewhere, and fewer priests would be available to help in their

parishes. But the final rock of shipwreck proved to be the intransigence of the intended beneficiaries, the canons of Sens. By the proposed merger, the dignitaries of the two alien foundations would
assume places in the choir subordinate, it is true, to the metropolitan dignitaries, but in advance of ordinary canons—this, they said,
was 'revolting'. The archbishop sardonically replied that their pride
had cost them 450 livres a year each, a 50 per cent rise of income
thrown away.

Reform was slow, and all that could be done in the short term
was to reduce anomalies and scandals. So, throughout the century,
something over 600 chapters remained, containing perhaps 12,000
canons, a few very rich, many comfortably off, some living a
meagre and threadbare existence. Given the hierarchical nature of
the social order, the kind of appointments to the various canonries,
rich and poor, may easily be predicted. A study of the incomes of
the members of the twelve chapters of Guienne (including the extra
benefices they held, along with the emoluments of their stalls) shows
how the inegalitarian logic of the system operated: 'the canon con-
serves . . . a level comparable to that of the social group from which
he derives'.[19]

II

A candidate for a stall in a particular collegiate church would scrutin-
ize the canons in place, and wonder who would be the first to be
called to higher things, in this world or the next. 'It is time for
fortune to take an interest in my affairs,' wrote the abbé Siéyès,
'appearances are not favourable at the moment—all the canons are
in marvellous good health.'[20] If chance seemed to beckon, he had to
make enquiries to find where the power of appointment was vested,
and this might vary according to which stall was involved and at
what time of the year the vacancy occurred. Power to nominate
might lie with the king, the bishop, the chapter, or outside persons
or institutions, lay or ecclesiastical. If the chapter was the authority,
nomination might be by election, by the holder of a particular
prebend or, more likely, by the canon on duty, the 'canon of
the week'—variously known as the 'chanoine hebdomadier', the
'chanoine en aigle', the 'chanoine en semaine de chape', the 'tour-
naire', or the 'semanier'. Quite often, there was a system of alternating appointment: for example, the king might appoint in certain
months, and the chapter in others; or the division might come

between canonries conferring seats on the left of the choir and those on the right, or there might be a simple turn for turn. Since Nancy[21] was a diocese newly created in 1771, one might assume that the arrangements for its cathedral were those officially regarded as best—equal sharing between king and chapter, but with royal patronage for the office of dean and chapter election for the canon *écolâtre* in charge of teaching and education. Troyes and Sarlat had all canons episcopally appointed, Notre-Dame of Paris all but two; at Autun, all the stalls, the dean's included, went by capitular election; at Alet and Bazas bishop and chapter appointed in alternation. Among minor collegiate churches there were many where collation was made by the bishop on the presentation of a noble family; in the diocese of Bazas the twelve canons of La Réole, the twelve of Uzeste, and the ten of Casteljalux were seigneurially appointed. The variant possibilities may be illustrated from the diocese of Metz.[22] Saint-Sauveur had a provost, the nominal head, appointed by the Crown, an elected dean, and eleven canons chosen in half the year by the king and in the other half by the canon of the week. At Saint-Pierre le Grand, the provost was a royal nominee, and, once in office, he appointed the canons as vacancies occurred. The chapter of Gorce was established in the church and with the endowments of the old Benedictine abbey, and thus, for historical reasons, the canons were nominated by the commendatory abbot (in 1789, this was the papal nuncio Pamphili). At Mars-la-Tour the provost and the four canons held stalls under the patronage of the owners of neighbouring seigneuries.

Everywhere there was a patchwork diversity which time and custom had established. Yet even this was not the end of the story: there were various general legal rules in favour of privileged patrons or candidates qualifying for special priority, and these rules could intervene and override—there were the rights of the Crown and magistrates of parlement enforceable in certain contingencies, the months allocated to graduates, and the possibilities of permutation or resignation in favour.

In the quest for a canonry, the most important advantage was to have a relative already ensconced in the chapter. He might influence his colleagues in an election or, better still, confer a stall on his own authority if he was *en semaine* when the vacancy occurred.[23] More certainly however, the appointment would come from a resignation in favour—there seem to have been more of these for canonries than for parochial cures. Nepveu de la Manouillière, of a noble family of the province of Maine, had three relatives who were canons of Le

Mans, and in 1759, when he was 27, one of them resigned in his favour.[24] Observing the chapter from within, he records similar resignations in 1760, 1768, 1772 (the deanery), and 1776, and two permutations (1760, 1784). The 1776 appointment he recounts with disapproving relish. The abbé Savanne became a canon, even though, as the son of a bankrupt tanner, he was not welcome to the chapter. Canon Roger resigned his stall to him on condition of the usual pension and of an additional one from a rich and lonely widow, Mme de Nouans, who had taken up with Savanne and, indeed, paid him an allowance ('since she is horribly ugly, she has to pay dearly to get anyone to befriend her'). Eight years later she died, and Savanne inherited her fortune, which put him one up on his grudging and haughty colleagues. There were places where the transmission of stalls by resignation was so common that dynasties formed and a whole foundation consisted of closely connected local families—as at the cathedrals of Autun and Clermont and the collegiate churches of Draguignan, Beaucaire, and Chérolles.[25] The system was abusive, but not without advantage to the Church, as Massillon recognized when he took Jean-Baptiste de Champflour, who had inherited his canonry from one relative and the provostship from another, as his *grand vicaire*.[26] A man wielding great local influence could be useful to his bishop.

In some cases, merit alone won a stall: the bishop might want a collaborator to help with writing sermons and pastoral letters, look after diocesan legal or financial business, conduct visitations, perhaps as a *grand vicaire*; the chapter itself might want an expert theologian, a preacher, an expert on music. For most appointments, however, influence was the key, though exercised in diverse ways, whether at Versailles or locally, within the chapter or in the networks of family connections outside it. The broad general effect followed from the nature of the social order: well-endowed and prestigious chapters filled with nobles, and the deans and provosts of moderately important collegial churches tended to be noble also.

In the case of twenty-one chapters (in 1789) the system of preference to the aristocracy was systematized into monopoly—stalls were exclusively reserved for nobles. Those who enjoyed this privilege were not shamefaced about it; provincial families kept complaining that there were not more, and occasionally the king promoted an existing collegiate institution into the exclusive category. When the new diocese of Saint-Claude was created, the monks of the abbey of Saint-Pierre became canons of a 'noble' cathedral; in 1751 the bishop of Marseille made the old abbey of Saint-Victor into a collegiate church reserved for ancient families of Provence; in 1776 and 1777, the cathedrals of Toul and Metz were ennobled, though in the case of Metz, commoners with university degrees could still aspire to ten of the prebends, the five offices of dignitary and the twenty-eight other prebends being closed to them. Normally, four generations of nobility on both father's and mother's side were required; Besançon, where eight quarters were stipulated, had an escape clause admitting the sons of the more recently ennobled, provided they held a doctorate of theology or canon law. The genealogical documents (the *preuves*) had to be produced, and a defect would disqualify. Thus the abbé de Tencin was excluded from the chapter of Saint-Jean at Lyon; he gloated later when he went back there as archbishop: 'Lapidem quem reprobaverunt aedificantes, hic factus est in caput anguli'; a quick-witted canon capped the quotation with the next verse of the psalm, and honours were even: 'A Domino factum est istud; et est mirabile in oculis nostris.'[27] Aristocratic families arranging a marriage with a bride of the new nobility had to weigh the size of the dowry against the shortfall in genealogical qualifications to get privileged canonries for the sons. The disagreeable maréchal de Broglie used to reproach his wife because their marriage 'had closed the doors of the great chapters against the children'. 'The only doors I have closed to them are the doors of the poorhouse', she would reply.[28] When the comte de Horn was to be broken on the wheel for murder, Saint-Simon tried to get the penalty changed to beheading, not from merciful sentiments, but because 'the infamy would exclude the three following generations from any noble chapter'.[29]

Among these exclusive foundations, there was a hierarchy of splendour. Mende, Vienne, Saint-Dié, Bar-le-Duc, and Brioude were open to long genealogies without great supporting influence, while Besançon, Lyon, and Strasbourg were for the very great. The canons of Besançon, resplendent in violet cassocks and ermine-lined mantles, were rich; those of Saint-Jean of Lyon by comparison were poor (except for the abbeys they held *in commendam*, of course), but they were compensated by peculiar distinctions: the title of 'comte', the right to wear a mitre when officiating on feast-days, and, from 1745, membership of an order rejoicing in wearing an eight-pointed gold and enamel cross, the image of St John the Baptist in the centre and fleurs-de-lis and coronets radiating from it.[30] But Strasbourg stood high above all rivals. Its canons were princes of France or Germany, or at least counts of the Holy Roman Empire. In 1789, there were three Rohan, four Hohenlohe, one Croÿ, one

La Trémoille, two Trocheser, six Koenigsegs, and four Salm—
names famous throughout Europe.[31]

Outside the charmed circle of the 'noble' chapters, aristocratic
churchmen by preference sought a place in the greater cathedrals. At
Angers in 1789,[32] the dean and eleven canons were nobles, two from
the city itself, the rest from Anjou, Brittany, the Vendée, and
Normandy. Their families were of solid provincial standing, sending
sons into the Church, the Army, and the Law. Only two canons
were commoners, one the son of a tanner, one the former schoolmaster of the choirboys. Three other stalls provided an income for
absentees; two were in the royal household—a minor clerk in the
chapel at Versailles and a tutor to the pages of the Grande Écurie
du Roi; the third stall had been annexed by the rector of the
University of Paris using a peculiar professorial right, a procedure
some regarded as sharp practice. In the cathedral of Chartres,[33] with
ninety stalls to fill, half the canons were nobles (47 per cent from
1750 to 1759), and of the commoners, half were doctors of the
Sorbonne, some mostly concerned with university business in Paris,
some running the diocese for the bishop. A curé of the town
described the feud between the two parties:

one composed of men of high birth, the other of commoners, doctors or
at least, learned, who had got their canonries either by the operation of the
months reserved for graduates or because they were needed for their
learning or their usefulness. These two parties are at continual war, the one
side armed with disdain, the other with arguments. What sad effects the
distinctions between men cause—or, rather, their folly . . . Happily, blood
has never been shed. From time to time, though, common interest and
corporate feeling unite all the canons, nobles and commoners.

Falling short of the distinction and income of Angers and Chartres,
the cathedral of Saint-André at Bordeaux and the rival church of
Saint-Seurin had a lesser proportion of nobles, a quarter at the end
of the *ancien régime*.[34] The magistrates of the parlement and the
merchant patricians sought better things for their sons.

'Every little town', said Montesquieu, 'has one or two chapters
with small revenues . . . and from 10 to 20 or 30 places; if these
places were more considerable, the nobility would be interested in
them—being the only idle corporation in the kingdom, needing
property other than its own to maintain itself.'[35] Two qualifications
need to be made to this broadly true generalization. Nobles would
be interested in the office of dean, with its double emoluments and
priority of esteem. In Angers, there were five chapters altogether,

and in 1789 all the deans were of high birth. Also, in a province like Périgueux, where there were many penurious noble houses, candidates of long lineage might compete for even unimportant posts. Otherwise, the poor foundations were staffed by the sons of notaries, *avocats* and other lawyers, officials, merchants, and tradesmen. The bourgeoisie, like the aristocracy, had its sinecures; the more influential a middle-class family, the higher in the ecclesiastical scale of affluence and distinction its sons were likely to be found.

Influence was what counted, but it could only be exercised on behalf of candidates with the appropriate qualifications—or who were on the way to getting them. By ecclesiastical law, it was possible to hold a canonry and go no further in orders than the tonsure, but in the eighteenth century, very few held back from major orders, as to do so meant incurring the disapproval of the bishop and of colleagues and exclusion from the choir and a voice in chapter.[36] Nor was it possible any longer to take over a stall at an early age, or at least, to do this required untoward social pressure; in the two chapters of Bordeaux during the eighteenth century only six became canons before the age of 18, all of great families, four being of the nobility of the robe. Nine out of every ten canons of these two foundations were above the age of 20 when appointed, and the subdiaconate leading to the priesthood was necessary before emoluments could be drawn. Canons of cathedrals were often doctors of theology; half of those of the two great chapters of Bordeaux held this degree, while in the lesser collegiates most held the *maîtrise* or the *baccalauréat*. It was mostly the middling and lower bourgeoisie of town and countryside which could afford to educate its sons to this standard, and had contacts sufficient to warrant the hope that by doing so, it would be able to place them agreeably.

Only a fifth of the canons of the twelve chapters of Guienne moved on, and then rarely to higher promotions. A few applicants may have hoped to stage for a while until superior promotion came, but most were simply in search of an establishment for life, possibly one already noted by their family as appropriate and, with reasonable good fortune, obtainable.

III

Canons were following a career prescribed for them by family and society, their progress facilitated by influence—so much is easy to document. The inner spiritual yearning, the response to the divine call, the desire to serve religion and the Church, remain, for most of them, their individual secret. Perhaps they tended to be less idealistic in their vocation than the curés, given their generally greater income and less demanding pastoral obligations. In the second half of the seventeenth century one of them asked himself in verse what his motivation had been:

> Eus-tu d'autres motifs que ceux de la fortune
> Et ne la pris-tu pas, animé du plaisir
> D'avoir mieux de quoy vivre, avec plus de loisir?[37]

The only test he could apply was to examine his own conduct, putting out of his mind how he came by his canonry, and asking only what use he was making of it. For most churchmen of the past, this is the only test of vocation available to the historian.

By the eighteenth century, the conduct of most canons was respectable—gone were the scandal and indecorum associated with their name in earlier ages. True, there were occasional *déboires* to rejoice the anticlerical gossips—leaving for England with a nun, raping the bell-ringer's daughter, installing a lady in a house in the country[38]—but sexual lapses were rare, and only flight would save the serious offender from destitution of office and imprisonment in a house of penitential discipline. As with monasteries, so too the collegiate churches in out-of-the-way places could slide into misconduct through lack of supervision: the provost of Bourbon-Lancy sold the lead from the seigneurial coffins and the metal of the bells, and allowed his housekeeper to make skirts from old altar linen.[39] The clergy of Notre-Dame de la Fosse at Guémené-Guincamp in Brittany were so ill remunerated that they had to wander round seeking supplementary employment in local chapels; consequently, the chapter could not keep an eye on all its members, and in the end asked the bishop of Vannes to evict the abbé Thibaut, habitually drunk during divine service.[40] The typical sins of canons were less dramatic than those. A list of comic book titles circulating in Reims in 1758, probably written by a young canon of the cathedral, had the dean down as author of 'How to take off a calotte' (an ecclesiastical hat), and two of his colleagues as offering 'Detachment from the goods of this world' and 'How to speak about religion without having any'[41]—implying preoccupation with trivialities, worldliness, and hypocrisy as the shortcomings of chapter members. Almost everywhere the best-documented failings were slackness and irreverence in the performance of the liturgical offices. There are picturesque examples, but it is dangerous to generalize from them.

Bernard-Laurent Soumille, one of the minor clergy of Villeneuve, near Avignon, noted the lapses of the canons in his journal: 8 February 1737, they stayed late at dinner in the Benedictine monastery, so a minor clerk had to say the offices; 2 August 1757, there were no canons in the choir, only the dean and four assistant priests; 9 May 1769, only a single canon turned out for the Rogation procession, the morning being misty. Yet these are the only examples he found over thirty years, and of them he says 'chose extraordinaire', 'I have never seen anything like it'.[42]

Our knowledge of the failings of canons is well documented, because chapters collectively took measures to put things right. Here, a canon is noted in the registers for going hunting, there for wearing a red coat under his surplice for a wager, somewhere else for clearing his head at mass by taking a pinch of snuff.[43] In 1777, all was not well at Notre-Dame du Val in the town of Provins: one canon had falsified a register, another only attends matins in the first half of the year, and the dean cannot come to services because of a nervous illness—'that may be so, but it is all his own fault . . . with his daily indulgence in good cheer'.[44] We know all this because canon Brunet, in charge of chapter discipline, called on the bishop to intervene. In 1781, Canon Bexon wrote to his colleagues of the Sainte-Chapelle in Paris exhorting them to desist from irreverent conduct, 'talking to each other loudly and freely during the divine office . . . sustained conversations, prolonged dialogues . . . with an air of facility, indeed of gaiety, even of petulance . . . making it obvious the subject is profane'.[45] Cathedral chapters were generally decorous, being better organized and proud of their splendid display and music; they were also under the censorious eyes of the towns-folk, and if the bishop was strict and resident, under episcopal scrutiny as well. Fitz-James, bishop of Soissons, hearing that only four or five canons were going on the customary procession from the cathedral to the church of Saint-Crépin for the first vespers of the parochial feast, at the last chime of the bell joined in himself—there was a wild rush of the canons from their houses, so that thirty or more were present when the march reached its destination.[46]

If there was a besetting sin of canons, it was pride. In their intro-verted collegiate life they had resounding feuds with each other, like the dispute between the *trésorier* and the *chantre* of the Sainte-Chapelle in 1607, which provided the plot for Boileau's *Le Lutrin*. But more often it was a corporate pride, a pride turning against the whole outside world—bishop, curés, municipality, and other chapters. When a canon was installed, he presented a cope to the sacristy, endowed an anniversary mass, and gave tips to chapter employees; it marked the beginning of an allegiance, probably for life, to the institution with which he identified more and more as the years went by. Canons lived longer than most classes of society, most clergy even. In the two chapters of Bordeaux, where the average life expectancy was 65, in 1790, out of forty-six, thirty-one were over 50 years of age, and eleven were over 70. Old men grow set in their ways, cling to their distinctions, more and more take refuge in the life of the closed corporate society in which their lot has been cast. The daily ceremonial routine and the recurrence of processions and dignified observances instilled into the mind the importance of precedence and status, of privileges to be maintained out of piety for past generations, and in the interests of those to come after. There was a continual concern to prove and celebrate the antiquity of the foundation, the provenance and efficacy of the relics, the splendour of the architecture and music.

After pride, the next most insidious temptation was sloth.

> Les chanoines vermeils et brillants de santé
> S'engraissent d'une longue et sainte oisiveté,

said Boileau. His picture of canons in bed during matins and leaving minor clerks to sing the office while they dined was no longer true in the eighteenth century, but the accusations continued. Curé Meslier used the same phrase as Boileau: 'holy idleness'. It was a continual complaint of the curés that canons were well paid for doing little. Truth was, there was more to be done than was commonly supposed, and a great deal more that could usefully be done, though not obligatory. A canon's life-style was what he chose to make it.

IV

Canons had an obligation to reside. When first appointed, they had to keep residence for a fixed period (*la rigoureuse*), generally for eight months, to qualify for future payments. Thereafter, each foundation had its particular requirement, there being no necessary uniformity. The legitimacy of this diversity of regulations was confirmed in a lawsuit of 1749.[47] Five of the canons of Dreux decided to tighten up their rule and extend the minimum annual period to nine months; the other four objected and invoked the law. The courts ruled canonries to be temporal benefices, not subject to the laws of the

Church, and exempt from episcopal intervention except when the morals of an individual or the decency of the liturgical offices were in question; the obligations of residence were such as were laid down by the rules of the foundation, and the secular judges would interpret them. There were a few places where the rules were lax: the high and mighty canons of Strasbourg had to reside for a mere three months. In most places, the rule was six months. At the cathedral of Sens, it was stricter: six months qualified to receive the *gros fruits*, in the case of this penurious chapter, a mere 60 livres, staying on for a total of nine months qualified for the *grandes distributions*, about 600 livres.

Inevitably, some canons evaded the regulations. Court chaplains had an official right to enjoy an income without appearing to collect it, and men of great families whose influence overawed the chapter an unofficial one. A celebrated case was Pezé de Courtalvert[48] of an illustrious noble family of Maine, who died in 1771 at the age of 91, a canon of Nantes for fifty years while residing all the while in Paris (but did he in fact draw an income?—he also had two rich abbeys). Most canons, however, at least those in reputable foundations, were constrained to obey the rules: if they failed to keep residence, they drew no income. Nor was it possible to alleviate the burden of residence by missing the occasional service. A register was kept recording who was present on each occasion, sometimes with two entries, the one at the end to catch any who slipped away early. There was a tariff of fines for absences so noted, with extra to pay for great feast-days and a surcharge on officers with greater incomes. And 'absence' was defined: it began at the Gloria of the *Venite* at matins, and of the first psalm at vespers, and at the last Kyrie of mass. The registers bear witness to the sort of excuse needed to win an exemption.[49] 'M. Tardif, being in ill health, will not be fined (*picqué*) if he does not attend matins this winter'; a medical certificate accompanies permission to go to a thermal station to bathe for a skin eruption; two or three months are granted to an applicant who wishes 'to breathe the air of his native place'. Aristocratic birth did not exempt: even at Strasbourg a prince came in person to make application, even though as a court chaplain he might have stayed away with impunity. Nor did spiritual duties out of town: a preacher from Autun, much in demand in Paris, lost his *gros fruits* because he was away too long. The prevailing strictness is seen in the debate among the cathedrals of Normandy[50] on the question of absence for university study in the case of canons appointed (legally but abusively) before ordination. Avranches wished to know what the others did, firstly about dispensation from the *rigoureuse*, and secondly, once the *rigoureuse* was completed, did the absentee student just get the *gros fruits*, or was he allowed a share in the distributions as well? Evreux and Coutances allowed exemption from the *rigoureuse*, the others not (strictness on this point was probably general, for even the noble chapter of Lyon was unyielding here[51]). As to sharing in the distributions, Sées gave nothing, Bayeux said it all depended on circumstances, Lisieux allowed a proportion of the annual allowance of grain, Rouen gave a fixed 500 livres, Avranches only 100. All agreed on one point: if the favoured individual did not get ordained, he must be evicted from his canonry and, if possible, compelled to restore whatever income he had drawn.

A canon was expected to attend chapter meetings. Twice a year, there would be a general chapter, theoretically compulsory for all, whether in residence or not. A solemn mass of the Holy Spirit would open proceedings, followed by a sermon of exhortation behind closed doors, with the public excluded. The minor clergy would appear one by one for praise or blame, and the sittings would continue for two or three days, drawing up regulations on matters which had arisen during the past six months. Thereafter, there were the routine chapter meetings attended by those in residence, some-times once a week, more often twice. In a crisis, there would be a special emergency meeting, with the canons summoned by the pealing of the great bell. At Rouen, the chapter assembled for its regular sessions no fewer than three times a week, and, according to one of its members, the discussions were exemplary—'in 12 years . . . I never heard a disobliging word'.[52]

The liturgical round of the great collegiate churches consisted of the seven daily offices and high mass, with low masses shared out among canons and minor clerks. Strictly followed, this programme would have broken up the day to the point of preventing many other activities. In practice, however, the offices were usually grouped into three sessions: perhaps mass, matins, lauds, and prime between 4 and 6 a.m., tierce, none, and high mass beginning at 9 a.m., and vespers and compline at 2.30 p.m. Though convenient, this could still mean spending five or six hours a day in the cathe-dral, probably telescoping into about four, since amalgamation tends to mean abbreviation. The comfort of chapter life was greatly affected by the hour at which the first service was set. Matins at 6 a.m., as at Nancy, was a routine hardship, while set at 3 a.m. (and 1.30 in Lent and Advent) as at Clermont, it was a severe one. There was an oath dating back to 1367 at Notre-Dame of Paris, to attend matins at midnight;[53] there was no dispensation from the obligation, not even for illness or for the *chanoines jubilés* (over 50 years of age) who were excused the daylight offices. These nocturnal forays were bleak, so the canons wore their nightcaps, looking (as one of them remarked) 'like characters in a theatrical farce', though they left them behind on Christmas Eve, when the faithful crowded in to greet the Nativity.[54] Whether by night or by day, four to five hours was a long time to spend in a vast church in winter: rheumatism was the canons' occupational disease.

In addition to the daily round, attendance was required on special occasions, especially at processions. Some would be ordered by the bishop at times of national rejoicing or penitence and to intercede for favourable weather. At Angers[55] there were general processions of all churches on St Mark's Day, Palm Sunday, Ascension Day, and Corpus Christi, while the cathedral had its own observances on the first Sunday of the month and on nineteen other special days throughout the year. Other liturgical observances when the full attendance of available canons was required were those arising from the fraternal alliances of churches. The cathedrals of Le Mans and Angers were in such a 'society of prayer', and both had agreements with others outside France, Angers with Compostela, Le Mans with Paderborn. The minor chapters of Angers had their humbler alliances: Saint-Pierre with Saint-Maurille, and Saint-Laud and Saint-Martin with each other and with Saint-Pierre de la Cour of Le Mans. The obligations of these capitular confraternities included sending representatives to patronal festivals and attending certain joint processions; when news of the death of a canon of the other chapter arrived, the vespers of the dead were recited, and on the following day a requiem was celebrated.

At the ceremonies of processions and high festivals the canons were the cynosure of every eye, so much capitular time was spent discussing the details of dress, music, and choreography. Timings would be changed, processional routes altered, precautions laid down to prevent confusion; a note would be made in the registers even if such a conjunction of events would not recur until thirty years afterwards. The eclipse of the sun on 1 April 1764 did not catch the canons of France unawares. In the South, they could be proud of having put the service times forward to escape the darkness, but in the North, the eclipse turned out to be a mere passing shadow, and those who set out in procession armed with candles were chagrined to find they had made themselves ridiculous.[56] There were strict rules for dress, whether in the stalls or in the processions. There was a summer and a winter habit; in most collegiate churches the black cassock was the foundation garment, with the *aumusse* covering the shoulders in summer (a sort of hood lined with fur or grey or red material); in winter, there would be the *rochet* (an embroidered surplice with narrow sleeves), and over it the *chape* (a long black sleeveless garment, perhaps with trimmings of fur, silk, or velvet). For outdoor ceremonies, the standard dress would be enfolded in the *camail* (a hooded cloak of black cloth lined with crimson satin). The old ecclesiastical ban on wigs had been collapsing from the early years of the century, so a powdered *perruque* surmounted by the *bonnet carré* (the black box hat) would complete the canonical splendour. Each liturgical occasion had its prescribed variant of dress, and there was scope for quarrels between those who stood by tradition and others who wanted to change to something more colourful or prestigious. The canons of Notre-Dame of Paris[57] were accustomed to put aside their purple summer cassocks and change to cold weather habit at All Saints; so if there was a celebration of national rejoicing after that date, they would attend the Te Deum in black cassocks and capes. The older men were against change; the younger wanted to use the summer colour. Thanks to the king describing their appearance at the celebration for the birth of the dauphin (December 1781) as 'werewolves' and the discovery of a seventeenth-century precedent in the archives, the younger men prevailed, and at the next Te Deum they were all resplendent in purple. At Le Mans, the quarrel over dress was one chapter against another. The canons of Saint-Pierre de la Cour, already enjoying special finery for feast-days by royal *brevet*, in 1782 voted themselves into a new splendour for ordinary days, black velvet (silk in summer) with red buttons and laces. Inconsolable at this gesture of sartorial one-upmanship, the canons of the cathedral complained bitterly.

At some time in his career, a canon would have to take on administrative duties for his chapter—supervising the collection of rents, feudal dues, and tithes; drawing up accounts, paying over clerical taxation; prosecuting the inevitable lawsuits; negotiating with contractors over repairs and improvements; inventorying furniture and church ornaments. These affairs were time-consuming, not only because of the complexities of property holding, but also because they involved questions of public relations. Everywhere it was a story of tithe strikes, rent evasions, opposition to seigneurial justice by innkeepers, local notables or municipal authorities, wrangles with the heirs over the *lods et ventes* paid on houses when the owner died. The obviously efficient method of coping was to have a single practical expert and leave everything to him. In poor provincial chapters this was normal—a single *trésorier* who drew extra emoluments for his pains. Even so, there always had to be two separate allocations of property and resources: the *mense capitulaire* for the maintenance of the church, the paying of the choir, employees, and the liturgical expenses, and the *mense canonicale*, to pay the canons. These departments might well be under separate control. In some very poor foundations there was no choir and no staff beyond an all-purpose verger, and the *mense capitulaire*, probably called by the less imposing name of *fabrique*, had little revenue, sometimes none at all. Before Saint-Pierre de la Cour in Le Mans simplified its procedures in 1775, there had been three departments of revenue, not two: the *office de l'argenterie* for repairs, music, services, and clerical taxation; the *office des anniversaires*, paying the minor clergy, sacristan, and the fees for masses; and the *gros des prébendes mise en partition*, and within this office two separate groups of estates, one to pay each canon his *gros fruits*, the other providing the distribution for daily attendance at services. In the cathedral at Chartres,[58] the chapter collectively named the lay *fermiers* gathering the income of the *mense capitulaire*, and the rest of the property was divided into twenty-three prebends, each with possessions spread over the province of Beauce. Each prebend was allocated to a group of canons (averaging four each), the members having to hold the *régence* in turn for a year, naming the bailiffs and clerks, and with the obligation to tour round the property on personal inspections. Everywhere there were lawsuits: the chapter at Digne was bankrupted by them. The courts were leisurely and the law complex; a chapter did well to appoint one of its members to run all the litigation, a task in the cathedral of Langres falling to Didier-Pierre Diderot, brother of the *philosophe*. A literary connection like this brings the notice of history, and Didier-Pierre has deserved notoriety as intolerant; he should also be remembered, however, as efficient, austere, and recklessly charitable.[59]

Among the canon administrators, there was a special category of those concerned with helping the bishop to run the diocese. In the cathedral there would be the archdeacons, perhaps in place despite the bishop, or perhaps his welcome collaborators. There would be some of the *grands vicaires*, since they often acquired a canonry to provide for their establishment; the bishop was also likely to choose the *official* and the *promoteur* of his ecclesiastical court from the chapter members, or, if choosing them from outside, would look out for a canonry to reward them. During the vacancy of a see, often prolonged for a year or two owing to the leisurely way in which newly appointed prelates moved to take up their duties, the cathedral chapter ran the diocese. This meant appointing four canons as administrators, whether from the existing *grands vicaires* or others, and discussing a new range of affairs in chapter meetings. Since one perennial item of business, the search for ways and means to resist episcopal encroachments, would for the time being fall into abeyance, perhaps the average duration of debate was not too far exceeded.

According to the abbé Baston, canon of Rouen, 'the canonical life, when its duties are properly performed, absorbs the greater part of the day'.[60] A doctor of the Sorbonne and devoted to scholarly pursuits, he naturally put first in his list of possible duties preaching and teaching—in particular, training young men for the ministry of the Church. By royal edicts, renewed by Louis XIV in 1695, every cathedral had to reserve a prebend for a *théologal*, who was to preach every Sunday and give three lectures a week on the Scriptures. The rule was observed, with varying results. In one cathedral the canon *théologal* received presentations of table silver from his colleagues for his moving Lent and Advent courses; in another, the canons found his sermons unbearable (perhaps because the bishop had forced his appointment on them), and in face of their hostility, he hired a Capuchin to deputize in the pulpit.[61] Some cathedrals had another official post, the *écolâtre*, with responsibilities for education in the city or the diocese; at Notre-Dame in Paris he had the duty of inspecting the elementary schools of the capital.[62] In some provincial collegiate churches there would be an endowment called a *prestimoni*, the canon holding it receiving extra income for teaching local children.[63] In a university town, there would be chapter members active in the Faculty of Theology, some attending as doctors exercising their right to join in the examination of theses, others holders of chairs and giving lectures—professorial remuneration was so low that ecclesiastical benefices like canonries were needed to survive. In the cathedral of Angers a succession of such learned figures produced that vast compendium of rigidly orthodox theology, the *Conférences d'Angers*. These *conférences* were delivered as actual lectures; then, from 1703, publication began, reaching twenty-four volumes by 1758. The last in the line of the authors was Cotelle de la Blandinière, who in 1780 was given a pension by the Assembly of Clergy for his services. By then, he had moved from Angers to Blois, where he was a canon and archdeacon. From there, in 1785, at the age of 78, he added four new volumes defending the rights of bishops against the rising tide of agitation among the parish clergy.

A canon against the curés—this was to be expected, for chapters were under attack as appropriators of revenues which could have been better used to support the parochial ministry. Yet some canons were fully occupied in the pastoral ministry, whether holding the office of curé as an obligation of their stall, or elected to the office by their chapter, or informally, taking on the duties by preference or to gain an additional income.[64] At Bray, Brienon, and Saint-Julien-du-Sault in the diocese of Sens, the chapter ran the parish. In the diocese of Autun, there were three poor foundations where the dean was curé with one or two canons around him, while the rest were away eking out a living doing pastoral duties in the countryside. The parishes of Saint-Martin and Saint-Gengulf in Metz had a canon as their *ex officio* parish priest. So too at Paris at Saint-Merry, Saint-Sépulchre, Saint-Benoît, and Saint-Etienne-des-Gués, churches at once collegiate and parochial, where the cure of souls was the responsibility of the *chanoine chéficier*. The sacrist of Saint-Etienne of Montauban was curé; he was not one of the nine canons, but was much richer than any of them, with a lodging allowance and large surplice-fees on top of a canonical income. At Draguignan, the 6,000 inhabitants attended the church of Notre-Dame-et-Saint-Michel, with the curé as head of the chapter, having under him a *capiscol*, four canons, and two chaplains. Did he really rule the chapter? It appeared so, especially after the bishop's ruling of 1735 that he, and not the canon of the week, was entitled to administer the last sacraments to all members of the foundation. Even if there were no formal ties with a parish, a chapter was, in any case, a pool of talent from which help could come by invitation of the curé—to conduct missions and retreats, for example. Or an invitation might come from the laity, for confraternities and guilds chose ecclesiastics to conduct their liturgical services, and bringing in a canon as *prieur* would fortify the members with the presence of a local celebrity.

There was also the hearing of confessions, a duty high on Baston's list. These were the days when numerous clergy were required to man the confessionals, not only to help out in the parishes, but also to hear the frequent and obligatory confessions of nuns, the inmates of hospitals and workhouses, and schoolboys in the *collèges*. Canons as well as friars might be involved in these duties, though it was more usual for them to be invited to fulfil a more prestigious role as the *supérieur ecclésiastique* of a monastery, nunnery, or charitable institution. This office did not involve being the chaplain, confessor, or visitor (though any of these duties might be combined with it), but acting as a liaison officer with the bishop, and as an adviser and protector. Canon Moranges of the cathedral of Clermont was such a superior to two convents of nuns; Bishop Massillon praised his 'douceur et modération', and when he died, invited his brother, another canon, to succeed him.[65] The abbé Blain had held a stall in the cathedral of Rouen, resigned to become a curé, then got back into a canonry again, feeling 'more attracted to the life of prayer and contemplation'. Even so, he became adviser to the Sœurs du Sacré-Cœur at Ernemont six leagues out of town, the Hospitalières de Saint-François near at hand, and the Frères des Écoles Chrétiennes.[66] There can never be a history of the office of *supérieur ecclésiastique*, but it was significant in interlocking the tiny closed worlds of the religious communities of provincial towns, rendering them susceptible to undemonstrative guidance and capable of forming a common opinion on questions of the day in times of crisis.

There are two other entries on Baston's list of optional tasks: one, writing, is obvious; the other may sound incongruous. 'Several sit as judges in the magistrates' courts,' he says. These were the *conseillers-clercs*, clerics highly qualified in the law who had bought magisterial office and were useful to the tribunals for cases involving canon law and ecclesiastical issues. In every parlement there were a few of them, very often combining the office conveniently with a canonry; there were the colleagues of Baston in Rouen and there were others in Toulouse, Bordeaux, and Paris. Here, in the parlement of Paris, was one who won nation-wide fame, the abbé Pucelle, short of stature, purple and choleric of countenance, a fearless denouncer of the encroachments of the Crown. Others served in the hierarchy of courts next below the parlements, the *bailliages*, *présidiaux*, and *sénéchaussées*. In the *présidial* of Quimper was Canon Reymond, in trouble with the bishop in 1776 because he was president of the masonic lodge where his fellow magistrates foregathered.[67] At Villefranche, an ornament of the *sénéchaussée* court was Canon Dominique Roland (brother in law to the future heroine of the Girondins); not only that, but he won election to the local academy, was chaplain to the *hôpital général*, and the precentor of his church[68]—one canon at least who could not be described as idle.

Every major chapter could boast of one or two members who achieved fame, at least locally, as writers and modest intellectuals. Numerous canons engaged in antiquarian pottering, generally collecting anecdotes about their foundation or local affairs; the chapter archives would take them this far, but their libraries mostly lacked the books to move on to wider themes, and few canons had substantial private collections. A few serious attempts to write history were made. The abbé Montjoie of Notre-Dame, a *conseiller-clerc* at the parlement, published his *Curiosités de l'Église de Paris* in 1763; Du Temps, of Bordeaux, produced a survey of all the great benefices of the country in *Le Clergé de France* (1774), and a life of that hammer of the armies of Louis XIV, John, Duke of Marlborough; another from Bordeaux, Dubignon, in 1778 gave the world two volumes of *Considérations sur l'origine et les révolutions du gouvernement des Romains*, suitably critical of tyrants, since they were 'the fruit of solitude and unhappiness', written during eighteen months in the Bastille and three years of exile resulting from a quarrel with the bishop of Arras.[69] We hear of a specialist in oriental languages at Besançon, a promoter of a cure for paralysis by electric shocks at Sens, an inventor of a technique for reclaiming the *landes* by terracing with hurdles and planting pine trees at Bordeaux, and of versifiers both in Latin and French, including one who wrote 728 alexandrines on an intrepid journey on horseback by a canonical colleague all the twelve miles from Carrouges to Alençon.[70]

Some gained minor celebrity on the margins of the Enlightenment. At the end of the seventeenth century, Claude Nicaise of the Sainte-Chapelle of Dijon was a correspondent of all the scholars and wits of Europe, 'l'agent général de la république des lettres'.[71] About the same time Jules Bellet of Bordeaux published his novel of adventure, *Relation curieuse des voyages du sieur Montauban, capitaine des Flibustiers* (1698), and for thirty years more continued to pour out verses, studies on biology and climatology, speculations on the souls of animals, the nature of angels, fauns and satyrs in the Bible, and a practical treatise on the use of the divining rod. Canon Talbert of Besançon beat Rousseau for the Academy of Dijon prize: he described how inequality came with the Fall, yet still had to be accepted, 'quae sunt, a Deo ordinata sunt'—though religion will help us to bear it. The abbé Gaudet published four volumes on *L'Harmonie générale du Christianisme et de la raison* (1766), and about this time the abbé Trublet of Saint-Malo had taken over the role once filled by Claude Nicaise, and was the universal correspondent of the Republic of Letters.[72] At the end of the *ancien régime* there were three outstanding canonical intellectuals in Paris. Bergier, the theologian, was at Notre-Dame; so too was Mazéas, whose work on logic and mathematics won him election to the Royal Society of London and the Academy of Berlin. At the Sainte-Chapelle was Bexon, master of many languages, a technical publicist on agricultural methods, the writer of a history of Lorraine, and a major collaborator of Buffon, who encouraged his researches, appropriated them, and made no acknowledgement. Bexon's achievements, however, got him promotion within the Sainte-Chapelle to the dignity of *grand chantre*. It was here in 1784 that he opened a crate of mineralogical specimens and died through inhaling their poisonous dust, a martyr to science.[73]

Historical research was an excuse to get chapter permission to escape to Paris. At the beginning of 1789, Canon Lépine of Périgueux was there, working with the Benedictines of Saint-Germain-des-Prés during the day on the history of his province, and spending his nights at the theatre, even in Lent. He was given to good cheer, and had a figure to match. 'Take care not to add a name to the martyrology,' wrote a colleague; 'all that is needed is for the *poissardes* to take one look at you and decide that you are the cause of the high price of bread.'[74] Pascal Fenel de Darguy of Sens died in 1753, having had many a leave of absence from his chapter and grants from the archbishop and diocese to live in Paris and work on local history—he left a stack of notes and had not written a line. Typically of academic researchers, rather than being grateful, he resented having to do ordinary canonical duties: 'to compose history you need a more tranquil life-style, and chapter business wastes all my time'. Truth was, he mainly occupied himself competing for essay prizes, hoping to win election to the Academy of Inscriptions.[75]

Another constant visitor to Paris was Canon Le Gouz of the Sainte-Chapelle of Dijon.[76] At home, he said, people thought of him as wearing brocaded coats at the salons of duchesses, playing cards with the wives of farmers-general, and drinking champagne with opera girls. Yet his activities were blameless—to him the capital was a place for cultured ease and spiritual uplift. He listened to all the great preachers, sought out the churches with the finest music, wandered the quays browsing at bookstalls, and daily read a page of Latin, Greek, and Hebrew to keep up his linguistic skills. One of his favourite authors was Quesnel, whose Jansenist severities he found 'beautiful . . . you would have to be made of bronze not to be moved'. Even more he loved the Scriptures; beside them, all other writings were merely 'tittle-tattle', insubstantial nourishment, 'whipped cream'.

V

In a labour-intensive society devoted to ostentation, the ceremonies of the great churches were supported by a horde of minor ecclesiastics and lay employees, making their meagre living and enjoying their minor prestige on the fringes of a religion of outward show. At Bordeaux, Clermont, Orléans, Bourges, Saint-Martin of Tours, and elsewhere, at the summit of the hierarchy of this clerical underworld were the *chanoines semi-prébendés*. They were not real canons, being excluded from chapter meetings; they were paid little and worked hard, having to attend all the services. Everywhere, their ambition was to gain admission to the chapter, and nowhere did they succeed. Three tried at Clermont, in 1761, to manœuvre their way to recognition by insisting that, as 'canons', they could stay in their stalls to sing instead of going down to join the men of the choir. The chapter censured them, but did not punish them otherwise, since their leader had 'worn out his eyesight working in the library', and the other two were in poor health. Six years later, they revolted again; the parlement of Paris found against them, except that, in future, they were not to be insulted by being called 'the canon's serfs'.[77]

Below the *semi-prébendés* the *bas chœur* began. This consisted of ecclesiastics, mostly priests, who were permanently employed on salaries of from 300 to 600 livres a year—they would be called *chapelains hebdomadaires*, *prébendiers mineurs*, *prêtres bénéficiers*, or some such title. In a small place, there would be only four or so, in larger ones a dozen to thirty. Though all had to be available to sing the offices, walk in processions, do pastoral work, or whatever else was needed, some had specific offices and duties. At Notre-Dame[78] one was a *chevicier*, who had to sleep in the church as the night-duty priest, another a sacristan of masses, and a third the sacristan of the chapelle de la Vierge. The cathedral of Toulouse had two groups of clergy paid under collective endowments (four *prébendiers de la douzaine* and ten *prébendiers du vingt-quatre*—of which four were cantors and two epistle readers) and fourteen other *prébendiers* who were salaried independently. Care of the relics, of the ornaments for certain altars, of the functions taking place in a particular chapel, the oversight of a confraternity, keeping minutes of chapter meetings, or registers of attendances at services—these were tasks for which someone had to be given specific responsibility. There was never difficulty in filling the posts in the *bas chœur*, for every great church also had a pool of *prêtres habitués*, making a living by saying masses, walking in funeral processions, and doing other ecclesiastical odd jobs for which fees were forthcoming. They tended to consist of the very old and the very young, the old trying to survive with dignity in their retirement, the young hoping for promotion to *chapelain hebdomadaire*, or the grant of some small chapel in the foundation, or some lucky offer from outside. Some places had an endowed confraternity for the benefit of these *prêtres habitués*, as at the cathedral of Bordeaux, where there was the *Treizaine de Notre-Dame*, a group recruiting by co-option and paying small allowances to its members.[79]

The securely beneficed *chapelains hebdomadaires* came from the ranks of promoted choirmen and instrumentalists, ex-choirboys educated up to holy orders, sons of modest local families happy to have found a niche and intending to sojourn there for life, and, by contrast, young priests with ambition hoping to find contacts, possibly among the canons, to forward their careers. Those who chose to live and die in these minor posts were not necessarily untalented: they may have just wanted an undemanding existence. Bernard-Laurent Soumille,[80] *prêtre bénéficier* of Villeneuve, was a mathematician who published two treatises applying the calculus of probabilities to games of chance, another on an agricultural machine and how to work it, and another on his own invention of a hydraulic device. In his journal, he recounts the doings of his canons without envy; perhaps, having begun as a shepherd-boy and come to the notice of a kindly ecclesiastic by carving the alphabet on a tree, he felt lucky to have risen so far.

Not all the clergy of the *bas chœur* were so self-effacing. They battled for precedence among themselves and collectively to impose their claims upon their canons. At Villeneuve, they wanted the right to accompany the chapter to meet visiting bishops, and if this was not allowed, they would not go at all.[81] From 1767 to 1771, the canons of Toulouse were at law before the parlement against their senior *prébendier*,[82] while those of Dax were prosecuting similar cases before the parlement of Bordeaux, one being rather sinister, an affair of false keys to the sacristy cupboard. In 1783, an arbitration ended the Dax feud, leaving the canons supreme, though *prébendiers* who were dissatisfied were to be entitled to retire with generous life pensions of 600 livres a year.[83] As ever, these sorts of disputes were enlivened with comic and sacrilegious incidents. In 1745, the parlement of Paris ruled that *prêtres habitués* at Saint-Merry should be allowed to sit in the lower reaches of the stalls if there was room. In 1754, Canon Moussinet, enraged to see one of them exercising his right and sitting immediately below, 'smote him with a breviary in-quarto several times and in divers fashions, and using insulting terms. *D'où scandale!*[84] Moussinet, a canon of thirty-four years' standing, belonged to the Jansenists, and was the covert banker of their funds—but austere religious allegiance did not incline him to for-bearance where the rights of his chapter were concerned.

A great church also had a multitude of lay employees. The material possessions of the chapter were in the oversight of lawyers, registrars, bailiffs, collectors, and the like, little concerned with the liturgical life of the place, though often seen around on their legal and financial business. The maintenance of the fabric employed many others. Local tradesmen would be given the official title of capitular architect, mason, glazier, goldsmith, jeweller, clock-winder; major repairs would mean resort to contractors. Other laymen were employed to play their pompous role in the ceremonies of the church. Notre-Dame of Paris had three *suisses*, six vergers, five *francs sergents* and six *huissiers* (these latter two categories were probably employed chiefly in policing the cathedral square and keeping order in the court room of the feudal jurisdiction). Vergers were not equal: they had precedences and peculiar titles, various ornamented staves, chains, badges, and gowns. Some were specialists at outdoor proces-sions: Saint-Martin at Tours had a *pauvre de Saint-Martin* marching in all of them, a symbolic beggar, as it were, awaiting the saint's proverbial largesse.[85] Then there were the bell-ringers, sweepers, cleaners, and dog-catchers. It is difficult to know how their schedules of work were organized. Le Mans had a *sergent* who supervised everything from the bell-ringing to the chapter prison, appointing appropriate staff; he bought the office for a down payment of 1,400 livres, so presumably it was profitable—perhaps the sum was a sort of caution money. When he died in 1770, the canons did not replace him, but appointed a *suisse* and three vergers directly, at salaries of 300 livres each.[86] As was usually the case with ecclesiastical institu-tions, the lay employees lingered on long after their days of effective service were over. Vergers were proverbially tottering and venerable figures. When Church property was sold in the Revolution, there were many unimportant people who regretted the loss of their modest employment and status in the wasteful ostentatious days before the invention of liberty.

VI

The great chapters of France had clients and influence, but few real friends. In the cities, the townsfolk were ambivalent in their attitude. They were glad to see revenues sucked in from the countryside to be spent to the profit of urban tradesmen. In Chartres, about one in twenty of the 13,000 inhabitants directly or indirectly drew a living from the cathedral; when three deputies were elected by the commons to the Estates General of 1789, they were all *baillis*, legal and financial agents of the canons. But great possessions and privilege drew hatred. During the Revolution, Siéyès risked his liberal reputation to defend Church property, urging the Assembly to resist 'the bourgeois jealousy which torments the inhabitants of little towns against *M. le chanoine* and *M. le bénéficier*'. As a canon of Chartres, he knew. 'Here', writes the historian of the foundation, 'it seems that all the opposition to the abuses of the *ancien régime* had crystallized in concentration upon the cathedral chapter, regarded as the symbol of parasitism.'[87] Half the canons were nobles, and of the total, nobles and commoners together, two-thirds came from outside the province. The aristocracy was pushing ahead in preferment by virtue of birth, and foreigners were drawing incomes which might have gone to deserving local families. It was not easy for these newcomers to win acceptance in town, though the Herculean abbé Mitouflet, who could carry two sacks of grain at arm's length, was the toast of the wine bars. And this alien chapter controlled other posts coveted by local people, 213 parochial cures and 83 chapels of the diocese being in its patronage. As in so many places, there were disputes with the municipality over seigneurial jurisdictions and the nomination of aldermen. But envy was the undercurrent in society which swept on the tide of anticlerical feeling. As the notaries of the city observed in 1784 in one of their disputes with the chapter, they were 'citizens with limited incomes, fathers of families . . . working hard to maintain and educate their children', while against them were 'eighty benefice holders, rich without working for it, bachelors without dependants, indifferent to other people'.

Most cathedrals exercised a feudal superiority in parts of the episcopal city. By virtue of the rights of the fief, the chapter would exact *lods et ventes*, a charge of about a fifteenth of the price when a house within the jurisdiction was sold. The area directly adjacent to the church was usually under seigneurial control in a more direct sense, with the chapter exercising police powers to the exclusion of the civic authorities. Ordinances directing householders to clean the street outside their doors or to have their chimneys swept (to avoid fire hazards), everyday matters if emanating from the secular authorities, suddenly became tyrannical when issued by churchmen.[88] The fief of Saint-Seurin at Bordeaux was a *sauveté*, a sanctuary, a refuge for artisans escaping the yoke of the guilds, for criminals and prostitutes in flight from the municipal police, and entrepreneurs setting up fearful establishments in defiance of city regulations—tanneries, slaughterhouses, foundries, and even a gunpowder magazine. There were many complaints, including some from citizens who censured the spoil-sport canons for refusing to allow the traditional bull race to crash through their streets. The municipality, in alliance with the intendant, worked continually and, finally and belatedly, successfully, to subject the *sauveté* to the ordinary police.[89] Chapter property within the urban boundaries often enough occasioned disputes about eligibility to local taxation. The city of Béziers had been at law against the cathedral of Saint-Nazaire since the time of Saint Louis over such a question, in some years the costs running away with half the municipal budget. The case was before the *cour des aides* of Montpellier and the Royal Council in the 1770s; then the bishop mediated and, having failed, in 1778 called in his father, a distinguished lawyer, to devise a compromise. At this point, the documentation ends, though probably not the lawsuit.[90] Fairs and markets posed problems to relationships, for the square in front of the cathedral was generally the ideal location, and it was not always obvious who was entitled to authorize the market and to collect dues from the stall holders. In 1770, the law had to be invoked at Metz, for the city aldermen encouraged trading in the Place Saint-Etienne, and the canons had just paid for paving it.

Everywhere, there were quarrels about protocol and precedence. At Tréguier,[91] prominent citizens claimed the right to have the great bell of the cathedral tolled for family funerals, but they were reluctant to pay the 80 livres ringing fee. The mayor expected the celebrant at the high mass on Palm Sunday to come down to his pew and present him with a palm frond, and at the feast of the Purification with a candle—gestures resented by canonical pride and arguably incompatible with a high theological view of the Sacrament. What was the order of precedence in the Corpus Christi procession? The municipal oligarchy could not be denied its splendid pew in the nave, but was it entitled to have its coat of arms proudly emblazoned on it? In a society obsessed with rank and status, every provincial town had these running feuds. Expensive though they were, they had less effect on personal relationships than might be supposed—in a peculiar sense the participants saw themselves as putting on a comedy for public entertainment: self-affirming display by conspicuous waste through litigation. Yet they had their effect on the popular concept of religion, continually treating it as a pattern of formal observances, an everyday affair without mystical overtones.

Cathedral chapters were proud corporations. Just as they did battle with municipalities, so they would fight against bishops and any other churchmen whose pretensions exceeded, even fractionally, the rights which precedent gave them. Any ecclesiastic coming into their precincts, however lofty his station and solemn his mission, had to conform to the rules of the foundation. The bishop of Soissons, arriving at Reims in 1721 to conduct the funeral of the late archbishop, found he had to take an oath to the church of Reims before he was allowed to officiate.[92] When there was a royal visit to Notre-Dame, the canons lay in wait to repel the claims of chaplains from Versailles. The young king came in 1721 to give thanks for his recovery from illness; 'il y avait une dispute ecclésiastique', said a Parisian diarist, 'ce qui ne manque jamais d'arriver'—the *premier aumônier du roi* was there to say mass, but the canons excluded him from the high altar. The regent was called on for a ruling, and he transferred the mass to the chapelle de la Vierge. This was the arrangement enforced in 1743 when the dauphin came, and when his wife came four years later. On this latter occasion, the ecclesiastics of the Court brought bread, wine, and candles to the chapel, but the canons would not allow them to be used—it was their prerogative to furnish all the materials for a Eucharist in their church.[93]

When the ceremonies involved the diocesan bishop, the situation might be different, for he had certain rights which could not be gainsaid. While a cathedral was independent of ordinary episcopal jurisdiction, being directly under the Holy See, the bishop was entitled to have the last word on certain occasions and issues.[94] His approval was needed for major changes in the building and its seating arrangements, and burials could not be made in tombs in the chancel without his permission; he could nominate Lenten preachers, and prescribe the ceremonies for ordinations, the consecration of the sacred oils, and meetings of the diocesan synod. If there was a controversy about foundation masses, relics, or miracles, an episcopal ruling would settle the matter. A conciliatory bishop would consult his chapter about arrangements in its church, but a disobliging one could bustle through, enforcing his rights. Yet precedent could not cover every eventuality, so a prelate riding roughshod over his canons might take a fall in the law courts. As chief pastor, he might claim to adjust the time of services to make them more convenient for the laity, but at Rieux, the attempt led to litigation right up to the parlement and the Royal Council.[95] At Notre-Dame in Paris there were only seven days in the year when the archbishop had the right to officiate in the choir without chapter permission. He had not asked for it for the high mass of the jubilee of April 1751, so the sacristans refused him the communion plate; after a wrangle, he gave an undertaking that the occasion would not constitute a precedent, and the mass began two hours later.[96] A bishop was entitled to be saluted by the thurifer when the incense was swung and to have acolytes carrying candles before him; in 1722, the canons of Nîmes enquired of their colleagues at Carcassonne about the limits of these privileges—was he entitled to remain seated while being wafted with incense, was he allowed to put his coat of arms on the candlesticks? No, came the reply.[97] The archbishop of Rouen who swept down the aisle with a train-bearer carrying the tail of his robe was innovating—the dean in person forcibly pulled the robe away.[98] If a new edition of the breviary came out without consultation, the cathedral might refuse to use it, as happened at Lyon in 1774, because the minor changes inconvenienced those canons who said the responses by heart.[99] A chapter could not control the ceremonies for consecrating the sacred oils, but what if the whole prestigious ceremony was moved away to the seminary chapel? This breach with tradition occurred at Le Mans in 1760, the bishop alleging the handicap of his rheumatism. 'There were several extraordinary chapters held over this affair,' noted one of the canons, though in the end, the idea of a lawsuit was abandoned—after all, the prelate was 81 years of age, and his excuse was convincing.[100]

There were places where bishop and cathedral chapter became locked into a permanent feud. The canons of Saint-Maurice of Angers feared Mgr Jacques de Grasse without respecting him; they were super-orthodox, anti-Jansenist, and full of zeal, whereas he was a tough, unspiritual Gallican and Jesuit-hater, who neglected his diocese to live in Paris. On his rare forays into the cathedral, he ignored the canons' rules about dress, and when he issued pastoral letters, he did not consult them, and omitted to call them 'frères'. The chapter scored by neglecting to repair the gutters cascading water on to the leaking palace roof, and the bishop arranged for an increase in clerical taxation to fall on his inconsiderate neighbours (taxation to which he himself was a notorious defaulter). In 1760 and 1769, he rounded off the vendetta by allying with his parish priests to defeat the chapter on questions concerning the authorization of confraternities and representation on the municipal council.[101] At Lombez, early in the century, there was an accumulation of miserable disputes—about the provost's claim to a chair in the sanctuary, the episcopal dykes draining water away from the chapter's mill, the election of officials, the right to light the municipal bonfire on St John's Eve, and about the shadow cast by a wall. Later in the century there was a different kind of confrontation, with the bishop trying to reform the too-comfortable canons. In his Christmas allocution to them on 23 December 1782, Mgr Salignac de La Mothe Fénelon accused them of malicious gossip, even in the sacristy and when the sacred vestments were worn, and of sheer idleness. He begged them to engage in edifying reading or, even, just study profane history, and offered to lend them books.[102]

Yet estrangement was not always bitter. Lawsuits about precedence and privileges were the common coin of relationships in French society, and did not preclude an appreciation of their comic quality or co-operation on other matters. The seventeenth century had been the age of the great battles of bishops against chapters; their eighteenth-century disputes were skirmishes on the margins of power. Because the Crown had adopted the episcopate as an instrument of domination and direction, the cathedrals had lost any effective right to be institutions of counsel and co-administration in the dioceses. Indeed, this was one of the reasons for the genial torpor reigning in many a cathedral close: 'confined to a secondary role, the canons were driven to find solace in the agreeable idleness of a life without challenges'.[103] Some bishops liked that kind of existence too, and were not disposed to stir up trouble at their very palace gates. In Angers, Couet du Vivier de Lorry, idle but sympathetic, soon effaced the memories of Jacques de Grasse's bristling hostility. Grimaldi, worldly and genial, came to Le Mans in 1767; he encouraged his canons to adopt a more splendid ceremonial dress and to beautify their church, and he often came to celebrate there, and welcomed them to dine at his table.[104] As 1789 approached, the demands of the parish priests for a say in the government of the Church became vociferous, and bishops and canons drew together in a conservative alliance; their rivalry had been a luxury of privilege, to be abandoned when both sides were threatened from below.

The quarrels of chapters with bishops and municipal officers were conducted within the established order of things: the canons were censured, but not so as to challenge their *raison d'être*, their right to exist. This radical criticism came into the debate because of their intensifying feud with the parish clergy, and lay society was glad to annex the arguments overheard in the course of clerical disagreements. Those who had to work hard for their living, whether in the pastoral ministry or in the everyday toil of society, were instinctively united in suspicion of members of corporations enjoying the inestimable boon of leisure. 'Aquets messieurs lous chanoines . . . biben comme dos princes et n'a d'autres penes que de canta queque litanie,' said the Bordeaux fishwives. Their life, said curé Meslier, is 'la perfection de la sainte-oisiveté'.[105] Canons were well paid for doing nothing but sing responses: with this utilitarian criticism agreed on, what was needed was a demonstration that this easy mode of life was not of divine institution, and was not necessary to the Church.

The parish priests envied the canons of the great foundations their wealth, the splendour of their ceremonies, the multitude of assistant clergy they had orbiting around their ministrations. Some curés had cause, not only for generalized envy, but for specific resentment when a chapter was the *curé primitif* of their parish.[106] This meant that the chapter paid them a dole by way of salary, and exercised honorific rights within the parish church which were vexatious to the pride of both priest and people—notably, sending a representative to celebrate the high mass of Christmas, Easter, Pentecost, All Saints, and the patronal festival. There was a variant type of humiliating dependence when the parish shared the church building with the chapter. In these cases, it was general to find the canons monopolizing the high altar, the stalls, and the great peal of bells, while the curés celebrated and preached in bleak naves or inglorious side chapels, their offices announced by the tintinnabulation of an inferior bell. There were disputes and lawsuits, and from this milieu of strife arose the pamphlet attacks on canons which were to have so much effect on public opinion. These writings combined the rehearsal of particular grievances with the ecclesiology of the Richerist theologians to press the cause of the curés, part of a growing movement of clerical unrest in the eighteenth century.

Auxerre became a centre of agitation in the late 1760s, when 'letters' were published on the dignity of the curés as against the canons.[107] A few years later, the controversy was renewed by Canon Frappier, who made an astonishing challenge to the old jurisprudence of France, alleging the cathedral to be 'la Paroisse des paroisses', a church in which all townspeople were entitled to make their Easter communion, bypassing their parish of residence, and the dean to be the 'archiprêtre' enjoying powers over the curés. Curé

Saloman of Saint-Regnobert replied in his *Lettres d'un Auxerrois à M. Frappier, chanoine de l'église cathédrale* (1779).[108] He had looked up Frappier's learned references; most were incorrectly cited, and some were sheer invention—let him confine himself to his task of supervising the cathedral repairs, something requiring none of the qualities of the historian. The curés were instituted by Christ himself; they are responsible only to the bishop, not to the dean, and all the pastoral functions are theirs by right. They alone can administer the last sacraments to their parishioners, marry them, bury them, and, in cases of emergency, authenticate their last testaments in the presence of two witnesses. The canons cannot perform these duties, even for their own bell-ringers. 'What is a canon? A man of retreat, of prayer, of study . . . How glorious for canons thus to be associated with the functions of the Angels! . . . But with all this, they are not Pastors in the Church . . . nor are they charged with the direction of its affairs.'

The same arguments were put forward from Angers, where the churches of Saint-Pierre, Saint-Maurille, Saint-Laud, and Saint-Martin were in dual occupancy, with chapters lording it over parishes. The story of their disputes was publicized, locally, then finally nationally, by the abbé Robin, the bellicose and eccentric curé of Saint-Pierre. The money he inherited from his father, a wholesale merchant, gave him funds to prosecute lawsuits, and in achieving his doctorate at the University of Angers, he had accumulated sufficient learning to embark on researches into provincial history—to his own satisfaction, they proved that the curés of the town had the right to be called 'cardinals', the natural councillors of the bishop, and were entitled to accompany him when he celebrated pontifically. Not surprisingly, the parish priest of Saint-Pierre was the senior 'cardinal' of them all. For forty years curé Robin battled against his chapter: over his right to an honorary canonry, to take the funerals of relatives of canons, over the building of a house for the parish sacristan, the ownership of the title-deeds to the cemetery, the parish right of way through the sacristy, the ownership of a ciborium, and the control of a confraternity—a story he recounted in a volume of 200 pages published in 1785. Having set his tribulations in the context of the Richerist arguments about the superiority of the parish priests, he recommended the abolition of most of the chapters of the land—not all of them, for he was not declaring them useless: 'nothing so sanctifying as psalm singing'.

'Chapters are simple gatherings of hermits who continually try to aggrandize themselves . . . the status of a canon is a private one, with the sole aim of sanctifying those who embrace it.' This was the condemnation of the two chapters of the city of Bordeaux launched by the fifteen curés of the place in 1778.[109] By contrast, they argued that their own status was one of usefulness to others: they were 'dedicated to the service of the faithful, the public and society'. The chapters replied feebly, saying they were 'the mother churches', claiming their privileges from tradition, irrespective of the question of usefulness. In Chartres, a similar debate took place with greater asperity in 1789.[110] Curé Pierre-Nicolas Tabourier accused the cathedral of usurping property truly belonging to the parish clergy, and imposing its 'aristocratic' domination on a Church that was in origin 'republican'. An *avocat*, Janvier de Flainville, joined in with a call for immediate practical measures: the suppression of numerous canonries in the eighteen chapters of the diocese to improve the wages of the parish clergy—'12 canons less means the enrichment of 50 curés'.

The effect of these agitations was to leave the canons friendless in the crisis of revolutionary times. Smaller and poorer foundations in the countryside enjoyed some local tolerance, especially if they did parochial duties; but the great chapters in the towns were the subject of comprehensive censure, and it was in the towns that a politically effective public opinion was formulated. The king's government was encouraged, almost compelled, to weight the voting system for electing clerical deputies to the Estates General against the canons and in favour of the curés. In their protests, the chapters revealed how out of touch they were: they argued that, being 'distinguished corporations', they should be given power as against 'isolated individuals', and that since bishops, chapters, and great benefice holders had, collectively, twice the wealth of the curés, they should have commensurate voting rights[111]—in short, a new injustice to compound the old. To no avail—only ten canons were elected.

15

THE GREAT CHAPTERS:
ARCHITECTURE AND MUSIC

I

For long the cathedrals and great collegiates had been churches belonging to the canons, in that it was here they said their obligatory daily offices, and belonging to the people, in so far as they were a congeries of chapels and shrines devoted to the cult of saints and the observances of confraternities, sites for prestigious burials, and places of popular resort for secular purposes. In the seventeenth century there was a clerical take-over, the canons downgrading popular usages and looking on their churches as settings for triumphalist liturgical services. The principal role of the people was to be worshippers under ecclesiastical direction. In the monasteries, the round of daily offices was still directed to the improvement of the spiritual health of the clerks who performed them; in the collegiate churches, the edification of the worshipping laity was becoming the primary aim—here, they would find the pomp and dignity lacking in their parishes. As the canons of Bordeaux, writing in self-justification to the National Assembly in 1789, declared, 'le ministère habituel d'un chapitre est de présenter journellement au peuple le spectacle du culte public dans sa plénitude'. In public statements at about the same time they described their cathedral as 'a Gate to Heaven for the whole diocese' and their high mass as 'the daily sacrifice of the town and diocese'.[1]

Translated into practice, this meant sophisticated music and, especially at high mass, elaborate ritual and displays of rich vestments. The splendour of the worship of the great churches of France in the eighteenth century has rarely been surpassed. True, there were wrangles, insults, jostling for precedence, to add a note of comic incongruity. But this was the price paid for employing such a multitude of clergy and, on the many occasions of national and civic celebration, drawing a packed congregation of those who counted— provincial governors, military officers, municipal aldermen, magistrates of the law courts, notables, guildsmen, members of confraternities. 'It is astonishing that men bring their love of distinctions to the very steps of the altars—practically all treatises on this matter begin with this reflection,' says the standard law dictionary of the century; 'but those who have the right to these public honours must have them recognized in the churches, since under our constitution the people has no opportunity of gathering together elsewhere.'[2] So, sacred ground as it was, rank and standing in the hierarchy of society were maintained, and if it meant fisticuffs and lawsuits, so be it.

But whatever the intrusive incidents, the cadre of worship was dramatic, its choreography precise and measured, the vestments glittering, the display of gold and silver ornaments and reliquaries opulent. Picturesque traditional ceremonies survived to diversify standard routines. At Saint-Martin of Tours, the celebrant at high mass made his confession at the tomb of the saint while the choir sang the introit, and at the offertory, the deacon and subdeacon brought the bread and wine in procession to the altar, preceded by a verger with staff, two choirboys with candles, and two thurifers arrayed in copes. At matins on Easter Day at Angers, two ecclesiastics in dalmatics wearing gloves and red hats represented the mourning women and approached the long white curtains symbolic of the 'sepulchre'; the gospel words were read, and from the 'tomb' emerged the 'angels', two chaplains in copes bearing silver-mounted ostrich eggs and singing 'Alleluia, Resurrexit Dominus'; the choir responded 'Deo gratias, Alleluia', and the organ swept into the Te Deum. There were similar enactments on Easter Day at Troyes. Not all antique observances survived, for the eighteenth century was all the while imposing its sense of decency and order, expurgating versicles and ceremonies which might excite the mockery of the sophisticated. At Chartres in 1700, the chapter ended the installation of a 'boy bishop' on Holy Innocents' Day; in 1765, the release of a pigeon during the liturgy of Pentecost was abandoned—organizing the pigeon-man and keeping him sober had proved difficult, and the fluttering distracted the choirboys.[3] Then, alas, in 1784, the reformers suppressed the wearing of wreaths of flowers by the choir during the octave of Corpus Christi and the following Sundays to St John the Baptist's Day. Abandoning the flowers was unimaginative austerity, but most changes were judicious, so the traditional and the new were agreeably blended, the sombre vividness of medieval copes allied to the pale pastel colours and gold thread of the modern chasubles, the lofty gothic arches overhead, the gilded magnificence of the baroque high altars, and the rococo encased walnut of the pulpits below. It is in the context of this liturgical splendour combining old ceremonies with the new emphases of Counter-Reformation spirituality that the architectural demolitions and additions of the eighteenth-century canons should be evaluated.

II

'Vandalisme' was a word coined by Grégoire in a report to the Convention on 31 August 1794 (14 Fructidor, Year III) recommending official protection for the Roman inscriptions of Gaul. Then, and subsequently, it was used to censure the cultural devastation wreaked by the French Revolution, whether motivated by anticlericalism, hatred of aristocracy and monarchy, or by expedients to serve the war effort. By extension, it is used by art historians in love with the Middle Ages to describe the ruthless modification of their churches by the canons of the *ancien régime*—'le vandalisme embellisseur des chanoines'.[4] This is welcome to historians of the left, who relish the myth of monks and canons, blinded by their 'intransigent classicism',[5] waging a campaign to destroy the monuments of the Middle Ages—the argument *tu quoque* offered in mitigation of the crimes of the revolutionaries. In fact, these clerics of the old France, whatever demolitions were their responsibility, were far from being intransigent followers of a fashion or haters of things medieval. They were connoisseurs, aware of the nuances of competing artistic styles and (what is rarely conceded to them) churchmen with a spiritual and theological preoccupation with the ways in which art can serve religious ends.

True, they had in their minds a stereotype, evolved in the seventeenth century, of what a new-style church should look like, a concept sharply differing from the Gothic of the cathedrals they had inherited. Mansart's chapel of the Invalides embodies the ideal—the arching dome, the vast free-standing columns of the interior supporting a far-projecting entablature, and a high altar in black marble modelled on Bernini's baldachin in St Peter's at Rome. It was an amalgam of classical and baroque, according with the pervasive principle of the age, 'le bon goût'. On 6 September 1764, Parisians had the chance to see the definitive Enlightenment neo-classical version of the French style when the king laid the foundation-stone of the new church of the abbey of Sainte-Geneviève.[6] Soufflot, the architect, had on display a painted plaster model of the project: a cross-shaped building with four equal arms, lighted by forty-two large windows, a central dome under which the reliquary of the saint would repose, and an altar with a colossal *gloire* of angels set in one of the arms, and, outside, a vast colonnade. The central dome brought echoes of Byzantium, the Renaissance, and the baroque, and showed a rejoicing in technical expertise, an expertise that was incomplete, for in 1776 cracks began to appear in Soufflot's unfinished masterpiece. Since the continuing proceeds of the public lottery were to pay the bills, the architect planned a lavish interior, adorned with works from the chisels of Coustou and Houdon and the brushes of every distinguished metropolitan painter. The fame of the splendid building project resounded in the provinces. When the chief engineer for the province of Burgundy designed a new church for the little town of Givry in 1778, it was Soufflot's plan reduced to miniature.[7]

Yet, while the men of the eighteenth century had their peculiar ideal of ecclesiastical architecture, they were not blind to alternatives. In the arts, the Enlightenment proclaimed simple luminous principles while indulging in complex, eclectic, and exotic realizations. For architecture, Blondel's *Cours d'architecture* (1675–8) gave them their basic doctrine: to follow nature and reason, not fantasy. But they debated endlessly about what was natural and, even, what was reasonable. Were Gothic interiors 'natural' because (as was wrongly supposed) they tried to reproduce the effect of avenues of immense trees reaching skywards? Must columns be cylindrical because nature made nothing square? According to Blondel, the orders of architecture were permanently valid because derived from the proportions of the human body; the abbé Laugier, distrusting this abstract analogy, said they had been devised to show off exterior façades in sunlit climates.[8] The Quarrel of the Ancients and Moderns shook Blondel's dictum of seeking inspiration in classical antiquity and the Renaissance; it became a commonplace to say that the past could not bind the present—what progress could there be in the arts if everything had to be done by imitation? The canons of the eighteenth century were not trapped in classicism and the rules of Blondel. If they had in their minds a single directing principle, it was elegantly expressed by Voltaire:

> Simple en était la noble architecture,
> Chaque ornement en sa place arrêté
> Y semblait mis par la nécessité,
> L'art s'y cachait sous l'air de la nature,
> L'œil satisfait embrassait sa structure,
> Jamais surpris et toujours enchanté.[9]

This was how reason and nature worked in harmony: the utmost exercise of human ingenuity in detail creating a whole which appeared inevitable and hence, in a special sense, 'natural'.

Cathedral chapters did not instruct their architects with the gilded dome of the Invalides or the colonnade of Sainte-Geneviève in mind; nor were the architects single-minded enthusiasts for the modern idiom they had adopted. Astonishingly confident in their own sureness of artistic touch, they were nevertheless at one with the intellectual fashion of their age, which was discovering the splendour of the Middle Ages.[10] The Benedictines of Saint-Maur lauded the diligence of the monastic chroniclers, La Curne de Sainte Palaye the magnanimity of chivalry, the comte de Tressan the romance of the troubadours, and architects admitted the beauties of the Gothic style. In 1741, Soufflot produced a *Mémoire sur l'architecture gothique* for the Académie des Beaux-Arts of Lyon. He condemned the 'bizarre and chimerical ornaments of the Goths',[11] and regretted their excessive enthusiasm for sheer height and vertical lines; yet they were masters of light and shade, and erected buildings full of unexpected vistas and ravishing surprises. In 1775, the architectural theorist Laugier declared Gothic to be the best available style for churches: 'behind the mass of grotesque ornamentation which mars the effect, you sense a compelling, indefinable atmosphere of grandeur and majesty'.[12] An architect of Bordeaux in 1776 distinguished the intellectual appeal of the fashionable new architecture from the spiritual appeal of the medieval. 'By their prodigious height, our Gothic churches offer beauties missing from Saint-Sulpice, Saint-Roch and modern buildings in the Greek style. These, our intellect approves, but it is in the Gothic churches that our soul is moved and freed from bondage.'[13] There was praise, though always with a reservation, concerning the 'ornements'. They destroyed coherence, Montesquieu said: 'the confusion of ornaments fatigues . . . a Gothic building is a kind of enigma.'[14] Others found a lack of sophistication and propriety in the details themselves. A journalist in 1765 agreed that Gothic was splendid, but rejected it all the same, since 'its daring and lightness appear inseparable from its bad taste'.[15] Cochin the engraver, defending his friend Soufflot's plan for Sainte-Geneviève in 1770, explained why the Gothic style was not acceptable—'le mauvais goût des ornements'.[16] Through most of the century, this standard criticism prevailed. Yet by the 1780s, the climate of opinion was changing as the mood of pre-romantic reverie became fashionable. 'Medieval' ruins and tombs became features of the 'English garden', and at the Salon of 1785 artists were exhibiting paintings of mysterious Gothic interiors. 'A veritable Gothic revival'[17] was beginning. It was a tragedy that the revolutionary and Napoleonic era, inspired by Pompeii and Herculaneum, turned to the grim classicism of power and the style of ancient Rome.

The canons did not reject the architectural heritage of the Middle Ages. Repairs were made with a sense of the importance of avoiding incongruities. The cathedrals of Blois and Toulouse and the abbey church of Saint-Etienne at Caen were restored in the late seventeenth century in their original Gothic style, as was Strasbourg after the fire of 1759, and here, in the 1770s, additions along the outer walls for shops were done in an elaborate archaic pastiche. If accident destroyed a church, the rebuilding was likely to be a recreation of the past.[18] This happened at the abbey of Corbie, spires included, from 1701 to 1730, and at the abbey of Poissy, under the supervision of the king's architect, Robert de Cotte. The question of new style or old was fought out at Orléans, where the Huguenots had destroyed the cathedral.[19] Robert de Cotte repaired the skeleton of the portico in Gothic, but submitted a neo-Greek design for the nave, and there were some who looked forward to a fashionable imitation of the dome of the Invalides. But the canons and some influential citizens led by Bishop Fleuriau d'Armenonville in 1708 successfully appealed for royal consent to a plan in the original style by a local architect, Guillaume Hénault. It was his avowed aim to 'unite the Gothic to the Antique', and in this spirit Robert de Cotte refined the design before the rebuilding began.[20] It went on through the century, not without controversy, for under Trouard as architect, from 1769, there was danger of collapse, since the medieval techniques of thrusting heavy masses skywards had been only imperfectly mastered. The work was completed early in the nineteenth century, an uninspiring example of the Gothic revival devised before due time, in the era of the Enlightenment.

The canons appreciated the majesty and religious feeling of their Gothic heritage, but they were unhappy about 'le mauvais goût des ornements'. They wished to banish what was crude or grotesque and, even more importantly, what was superstitious, for theological as well as aesthetic considerations were involved. Burial vaults in churches were expressions of a naïve conviction that proximity to the altars could confer a priority on the Day of Resurrection, and they represented assertions of family pride as against Christian equality, so there was a bias towards getting rid of 'the gilded tombs of frail and sinful mortals'[21]—though this did not prevent the erection of some splendid eighteenth-century mausoleums with dramatic allegorical force. These grounds of challenge would not, of course, affect the tomb of Lazarus at Autun; but the canons destroyed it, partly because its twelfth-century design in the form of a church struck them as 'd'un gothique bâtard et de mauvais goût', but also because they were embarrassed at the story—how Lazarus, Martha, and Mary had sailed to Marseille, then travelled northwards. Superstition should be banished from the ornamentation of churches, and sound scholarship should prevail. Statues and paintings ought to conform to a proper understanding of biblical times (the disciples at the Last Supper should be reclining, not sitting, for example).[22] Pagan influences should be rejected: no nudes, no monsters, nothing 'capricious'. In this the Christian critics were saying much the same as Diderot from his unbelieving vantage-point: the infant Christ should not be Cupid minus wings, John the Baptist Ulysses in a sheepskin, Jesus a 'muscular bandit' like Hercules.[23] And Diderot and everyone else were quick to laugh if female saints had an aura of erotic charm.[24] The Last Judgement, a favourite subject on the western façades of churches, could be relied on to provide nudes and naïvetés and be all too literal—hence the fate of these sculptured assizes at Saint-Germain-l'Auxerrois, Notre-Dame, Angers, and Autun.

But theology intervened to do more than sanitize and exclude: it provided the driving principle for change, one which coincided neatly with the Voltairean ideal of noble simplicity and unity:

> Chaque ornement en sa place arrêté
> Y semblait mis par la nécessité . . .

This would come about when every detail led the eye to the devotional heart of Christian worship. In Counter-Reformation spirituality, devotion was brought to a central focus, away from the cults of minor saints and provincial traditions: God comes to earth, and the worshipping congregation comes together at the altar, in the Eucharist. The centre of the church must be the high altar, to be made overwhelmingly splendid in the fashion coming from Rome, with marble columns, a great baldachin, and a golden *gloire* of cloud-borne angels. This was the centre to which a new perspective would lead, uninterrupted by rood-screens, tombs, memorials, and clutters of statuary—the eye would rather be led up to it by delicately wrought grilles and polished marble floors. Down these vistas, the sunlight would stream, through new clear glass if necessary, suggesting a belief that was luminously reasonable, as against the mystery of the dim religious light.

A rich Benedictine abbey like Saint-Nicaise of Reims, with no one to please but its own inmates, could embark on these changes in a comprehensive programme. In 1772, when it was completed, Dom Philbert Leauté described what had been achieved.[25] The wooden medieval altar had been replaced with a new one in marble and bronze. The choir and the sanctuary leading up to it had been paved with red, grey, black, and white marble, so that a pattern of cubes was seen whichever way one looked at it. The windows had been reglazed in white glass, creating 'a wonderful effect'; then, since 'un vilain jubé gothique' interrupted 'the beautiful prospect of such elegant architecture', it had been demolished, together with the twelve-foot walls around the choir, which were replaced with grilles of wrought iron. Finally, from 1760 to 1765, new stalls and panelling were fitted.

Changes of this kind carried through by a brashly self-confident generation were bound to result in archaeological tragedies. At Sens, the Carolingian gold reredos was sent to the Royal Mint, and the altar where St Louis had married his queen was destroyed;[26] at Rouen the tombs of Richard Cœur de Lion and Charles V vanished, and the chapel in the episcopal palace where Joan of Arc was tried was rebuilt, albeit elegantly;[27] at Angers, the tomb of Duke René, hero of the province, and of his lady was evicted from the chancel, while tapestries of the fourteenth and fifteenth centuries were sold;[28] at Autun the tomb of Lazarus went; at Auxerre the gigantic statue of St Christopher was felled.[29]

Yet listing these disasters in an undifferentiated catalogue of crime is unjust. Changes were usually carried out piecemeal, over an extended period, beginning with the installation or, at least, the planning of a splendid new altar. The Slodtz brothers, at a cost of half a million livres, gave Soissons its new high altar with the great *gloire* towering over it; Servandoni, the architect of Saint-Sulpice, designed the Roman-type baldachin for Sens; when the fashion for the baroque was declining, in 1786, Sées built a severely classical altar with columns.[30] At Angers, the process of change began in 1699 with moving forward the altar in isolation, 'à la romaine', with handsome new paving leading up to it. Then, in 1757, the great baldachin on red marble columns was erected, with a flurry of cherubim supporting a gilded orb and crown. High mass at these altars was to be the focal point of Christian worship and the centre of architectural unity of the church, to which all perspectives tended. The parishioners of Saint-Étienne-du-Mont in Paris got rid of the rood-screen in 1740—it was, they said, 'a bridge whose presence interrupts the view of our Holy Mysteries'.[31] Five years later, the clergy of Saint-Germain-l'Auxerrois followed the same argument: the mass should not be concealed, but be 'a spectacle for the faithful'. Astonishingly, the prior of Saint-Denis dared to propose to the king the removal of the royal tombs in his abbey church. They are unsightly, he said, some of the effigies lacking hands and their crowns damaged. The new black and white marble paving could not be laid 'avec toute la symétrie de l'art' so long as they encumbered the floor; they impeded processions, and they made it impossible to see the celebrant at the altar.[32] The last was the strongest argument: a sweeping perspective was needed.

This was why the medieval rood-screens were doomed. At Reims, Beauvais, Angers, Bourges, Sens, Chartres, Puy-en-Velay, Tours, Limoges—indeed, almost everywhere—they were removed. There were degrees of ruthlessness in the operation: the canons of Chartres had the whole structure dismantled and the stones pounded into gravel to level the floor, except those adorned with bas-reliefs, which were incorporated into the paving; the bishop of Limoges ensured that his chapter rebuilt everything as it had been against the wall at the back of the nave. The canons of Amiens destroyed their screen, but refused to sacrifice their high-backed stalls to the view, since they were exquisitely carved, as if from fine wax. In some places the medieval work was replaced with a more delicately constructed barrier, one which broke up the view without obliterating it—a grille of ironwork in acanthus designs at Rieux, a row of Ionic pillars at Sens. A defence of rood-screens, *Dissertation sur les jubés*, had been published in 1688, an appeal to the quaint liturgical traditions of the Gallican Church: in their niches, arches, and pulpits, anointings, abjurations, and preachings had taken place, and soloists had been stationed there to alternate responses with the choir.[33] These precedents, referring to observances preceding the focusing of worship on the high altar, were little heeded. When some of the canons of Rouen fought against the majority of their colleagues in an attempt to preserve the old rood-screen, they argued from aesthetic and religious congruity, not from ancient practice.[34] The proposed replacement, they said, with its arches and Ionic columns, would clash with the Gothic surroundings; furthermore, the new project involved irreverence to the Holy Sacrament, since the tabernacle was to be housed in the pedestal of a statue. They were outvoted; the stone saints and Virgin were sold off to parish churches, and the new colonnade went up, consisting of six marble shafts of antique workmanship, plundered long ago from the ruins of Leptis Magna in North Africa.

The clear glass in the abbey of Saint-Nicaise had created 'a wonderful effect'. But this was not an innovation to be introduced lightly, since excessive sunlight could be an embarrassment—one parish church making the change had to buy curtains to keep the nave cool in summer. Most removals of stained glass were limited exercises. A damaged window might be glazed in clear, because replacement stained glass was hard to find; Pierre Le Vieil's *Traité pratique et historique de la peinture sur verre* was an advertisement for himself as the only successful practitioner of the art in Paris. If the scene depicted was theologically suspect or 'indecent', there was all the more reason to abandon it. Bernini had shown the way to direct the fall of light to intensify the impact of the sculptured dream, but few in France had followed him. Yet, if a new artistic masterpiece was installed, it would need illumination—clear glass was put in individual windows at Strasbourg and Notre-Dame in Paris to make the most of fashionable mausoleums by Pigalle. Above all, light had to be focused on the new high altars. Chartres from 1763 to 1789 was the supreme example. The fine range of sixteenth-century statuary round the choir was preserved and augmented; the thirteenth-century screen was replaced by a grille; the nearby pillars were encased in marble and stucco; and Bridan was commissioned to carve a colossal Assumption and bas-reliefs to frame the new altar of marble and gilded bronze. To show off this dramatic new liturgical centre-point, the stained glass of six of the famous windows was removed.[35]

The ideal of unity hymned by Voltaire and Blondel's doctrine of the 'bel ensemble' ran disastrously to seed in the second half of the century. Blondel's treatise had shown an incomprehension of the value, to both eye and imagination, of the sight of the natural building materials and their finish and graining: 'the nature of the materials ought not to matter; the beauty of the masses, the proportion of the parts and the unity of the whole are the first considerations.'[36] This sounds well until translated into practical terms as plaster and whitewash. Experts on these processes from Italy toured France, and at Metz, Meaux, Chartres, Angers, and various other places found cathedral chapters willing to hire them to complete the 'bel ensemble', obliterating the pattern of the stonework, engulfing ancient frescos, knocking off gargoyles and projections, and walling up niches and embrasures. Instead of the ornamental clutter distracting from the majesty of Gothic, there was now a modern fashion to degrade its splendour by a superficial contrivance. A process beginning intelligently with the building of splendid new baroque high altars finished up with unselective and damaging innovation which had lost any vestige of aesthetic or theological justification.

The architectural history of Notre-Dame in Paris reflects the differing motives intervening for change, whether improving or vandalizing. There was a revolutionary transformation early on, based on the idea of the centrality of the altar, followed by a period of repair and innovative restoration, then, finally, another of destructive incidents. From 1699 to 1725, under the direction of Robert de Cotte, a new high altar was built, and the rood-screen, the sculptured walls surrounding the choir, and various medieval tombs were swept away. Magnificent new choir-stalls in ornate woodwork (paid for by Canon La Poste) were substituted for the old; there were fifty-two high stalls and twenty-six low ones, their backs decorated with bas-reliefs and the pillars between the seats carved in foliated scrolls and the instruments of the Passion. Statues of the Virgin and of Louis XIII and Louis XIV were commissioned from Coustou and Coysevoix, to go at the east end. Under Cardinal Noailles as archbishop, the keynote was restoration, mostly at his expense. The southern rose window with Christ surrounded by saints, apostles, and the wise and foolish virgins was repaired and modified. The decrepit chapels of St Martin and St Anne were knocked into one under the invocation of St Louis, made resplendent in the modern style with a marble altar and two marble statues. Austere as he was, Noailles had his share of aristocratic pride, and the new chapel became his family burial vault. In 1741–3, Le Vieil drastically replaced some of the stained glass with clear. Thereafter the changes were episodic and destructive, getting rid of excesses of an unfashionable past. At Soufflot's instance the central pillar and statue of Christ were removed from the porch, ostensibly to allow canopies carried in procession to enter more easily.[37] In 1786, the colossal statue of St Christopher (ridiculed by the wits as 'un roi Gothique') was destroyed; the canons, facing the complaints of simple folk, pretended that a heavy beam from the scaffolding of a repairing operation had fallen on it. In 1787, capitals of columns and gargoyles which had become loose were knocked off and not replaced.[38]

The educated consensus of the day was with the canons in their ruthless programme of modernization. Mercier complained, not of the destruction of Gothic features, but of the clear glass and bright daylight. He had loved promenading in the shadows, trembling with solemn thoughts when the bells thundered in the gloom—the canons had ended 'that imposing obscurity' which arouses religious emotions. But this was in 1782, and he was reflecting the new mood of pre-romantic reverie; the men of the Enlightenment preferred to think of the divine as manifested in glittering light, not in twilight melancholy. To them, religious awe arose from the sight of the lofty grandeur of the Gothic framework. A French exile in Rome, devotee of neo-classicism as he was, took Notre-Dame as the perfection of spirituality in architecture, with its 'unshakable mass' allied to 'daring' and 'lightness' of construction.[39] It was the aspect of their inheritance which the eighteenth-century canons admired and, in their self-confident and reckless way, assumed they were enhancing.

III

The splendour of the liturgical offices required music, and the great chapters laid out large sums, in some cases as much as a quarter of the income of the foundation, on maintaining a choir backed up by the organ and half a dozen or more musical instruments. The routine minimum music for the daily offices remained the traditional Gregorian chant (the notation in black lozenges on four lines and spaces), sung in unison without accompaniment.[40] Dr Burney found this at Lyon, where the canons and choirboys sang together 'without organs or books', and he thought it was the usual weekday practice in most places.[41] In fact, however, monodic plainsong was coming to be reserved for days of penitence—fauxbourdon and polyphony were taking over.[42] In the seventeenth century, the canons of Sisteron, under a statutory obligation to be proficient in the 'ars musica', had won a lawsuit defining this as plainsong, since, said their lawyers, the four-part singing only began in the fifteenth century. But times had brought changes, and this legal judgement had since been reversed. On Sundays and, sometimes, weekdays, the offices, especially vespers and compline, were diversified by the addition of motets, while at Benediction there would be a motet and the brief psalm *Laudate Dominum omnes gentes* as an epilogue.[43] At high mass, there were full settings, including the Kyrie, Gloria, Credo, Sanctus, Agnus Dei, and Benedictus, and motets might be added after the Epistle and during the Offertory and the Consecration. Though some of the congregation attended principally to enjoy the music, the structure of the sacramental rite at least dominated the presentation. The churches did not follow the Royal Chapel in making the music an end in itself: the daily mass at Versailles was a low mass with a motet of a quarter of an hour or more running on until the beginning of the Consecration, then a brief motet during the Elevation and Post Communion, the whole choir finally joining in singing the *Domine salvum* for the preservation of the king.[44] It was 'a musically elaborate, but liturgically minimal, service'.[45] In addition to the continual liturgical round, every church had its traditional musical requirements for special occasions and seasons. Something original would be expected from the choir for the feast of the patron saint. In times of national danger the psalm *Deus judicium* would be sung, in times of rejoicing, a Te Deum.[46] The season of Lent required a certain austerity in the music, but it provided haunting candle-lit performances of *Tenebrae* with two or three voices. At Christmas, there were carols, perhaps locally composed ones, depicting each guild and community in town bringing picturesquely characteristic offerings to the manger; in Toulouse, the young men of the city wrote new ones every year, competing for the honour of theirs being chosen by the canons for performance by the cathedral choir.[47]

A great deal of music was required, and the *maître de musique* had to provide it. The choirmaster of a cathedral today chooses scores from a huge fund of ready-made, perfected music, taking an eclectic view over a whole range of differing styles and periods, from the elaborate naïveté and spontaneous lyricism of earlier ages to the formalities and brilliance of the grand styles, classical, baroque, romantic, modernist, experimental. The range of music available in eighteenth-century France was inevitably more limited. There were plainsong and traditional settings for psalmody and standard responses—the fauxbourdon accompaniment of Lassus and of Jean de Bournonville for the Gregorian chant had been in print since the early seventeenth century. The Parisian firm of Ballard published music, sometimes traditional (as in 1707, ten masses by Lassus), sometimes new, by French composers.[48] In the 1680s, by order of Louis XIV, it printed fifty motets by Lully and other composers of the Royal Chapel. Posthumous publication made the works of others available; when Michel-Richard de Lalande died in 1726, his widow published his forty motets, the glory of the newer music of Versailles.[49] There was also a good deal of manuscript material available. Chapters encouraged their *maîtres de musique* to deposit copies of their scores in the archives; an ex-choirboy who had risen to eminence would send a few of his pieces as a tribute of gratitude for the education he had received. In 1782, François Giroust, *surintendant de la musique du roi*, gave the chapter of Orléans manuscript copies of a dozen Magnificats in memory of his happy days as *maître de musique* there. A director of provincial music would not lightly make his materials available to rivals and plagiarists, but he would be glad to gain fame by publishing a few choice items, and his canons, not loath to become renowned by association, would vote him a 'gratification' in recognition. Some of their compositions touched greatness—like Gilles's requiem with its haunting splendour.[50] These *maîtres de chapelle* of the old France, said Prunières, deserve to be the subject of a major monograph rescuing them from oblivion—they lived in their distant provinces, yet they were rivals of Campra and Rameau, who had themselves shared their provincial life-style before being drawn to Paris and the Opera.[51]

Yet, while there was material available for direct use or adaptation, the canons of a great French church would choose their *maître de musique*, not only as choir trainer and conductor, but as composer, and they expected that his own works would be the mainstay of his repertoire. No doubt he would simplify or adapt from some of the examples from Paris and Versailles and plagiarize here and there, but his pieces would bear the imprint of his own craftsmanship, and be written to fit the resources available to him. The congregations of that day listened to the music of their church in a different fashion from those of our century. The writer of the score would be known to them, and he would be using the idioms of the current fashion. As they listened, they were at once more involved and more critical, more confident in their own judgement, yet more limited in their expectations than we are.

A *maître de musique* needed many qualities, but the indispensable one was the ability to compose. When filling a vacancy, the chapter of Chartres would invite a prospective candidate to come, expenses paid, to stay for a week. On the Sunday, he would put on the music for the services, and then spend the remaining time setting given passages of devotional writing to music.[52] The scores he produced would be examined by a committee of canons and their advisers. If a candidate was unable to come, the chapter, as a concession, might allow him to send a selection of his musical compositions for the committee's consideration. The church of Saint-Séverin at Bordeaux locked up its candidates for several days composing music for given proses then sent the finished efforts to Paris for review by experts.[53] In 1786, Notre-Dame of Paris systematized these sorts of tests into a formal competition, in which J.-F. Lesueur defeated the *maîtres de musique* of Arras, Meaux, Tours, and Orléans. The triumph went to his head, and he did not have a long reign. After making some startling innovations, he announced to the chapter that he was going to London to audition there; in fact, he never did set off for

England, but was away long enough for the chapter to decide to dismiss him (though one of the canons gave him lodging in his country house, where he settled down to write operas).[54]

The candidates in these competitions were not unknown to the chapters beforehand. Vacancies were advertised by sending personal letters to reputable *maîtres de musique* of other churches encouraging them to apply. The canons watched the progress of promising choir boys, encouraging them to write compositions for performance by the choir: these might be so impressive that promotion could come direct from senior boy, as happened to Louis Fromental at Rouen in 1728, on the strength of his six motets with full orchestration.[55] In other cases, when a boy's voice broke, he would be kept on as an instrumentalist or clerk in the *bas chœur* until he was ripe to take over. This was how Henri Hardouin became *maître* at Reims. After serving as a choirboy, he was given a place among the minor clergy with the income of a chapel to support him; in December 1748 he was ordained subdeacon, and in the following year, at the age of 22, he took charge of the music. Liège backed up the career of a promising boy in a similar fashion, sending him to Rome to study in 1728, giving him a benefice when he came back in 1731, so that he was available for final promotion seven years later.[56] A chapter might also keep in touch with an ex-choirboy who had gone elsewhere and won fame, then in due course appeal to his local connections and loyalties to urge him to return. The canons of the cathedral of Sainte-Croix of Orléans had followed the career of Charles Hérissé after he left in 1758 to become *maître de chapelle* at Meaux; they knew of his gold medal in the competition of 1770 for a motet for unaccompanied voices and of his mass for the patronal festival of his church, much talked of in Paris.[57] In 1776, they moved to capture him with 2,500 livres a year and a canonry *semi-prébendé*; when, eleven years later, Notre-Dame of Paris issued an invitation, they kept him by the award of a generous retirement pension.

Since there was keen competition for their services, the *maîtres de musique* were inclined to move frequently—there was always some better financial offer, some more prestigious choir to conduct, some more agreeable place to live, some disagreeable circumstance to escape from, or some whim to gratify. Chartres, rich and splendid, found it easy to poach established musicians, but difficult to keep them. After fifteen years' stability to 1722, there was a two-year tenure, followed by a major competition in 1724, with candidates from the cathedrals of Evreux, Le Mans, Orléans, Mantes, Cambrai, Saint-Quentin, Coutances, and Langres.[58] The man from Langres was appointed, but never came (he heard that he was the favourite for the succession at Notre-Dame in Paris). So the canons settled for the man from Evreux. After three years, he was offered Rouen, accepted, but changed his mind and stayed. When he died in 1731, a former choirboy of Chartres who had risen to direct the music at Orléans succeeded, but for him it was only a stepping-stone to Notre-Dame in Paris. When he left three years later, the canons appointed Dulac from Tours; he stayed for three years, then decided he preferred Tours after all. The *maître de musique* of Verdun came, but could not control the boys and was dismissed, though this did not prevent him from progressing to fame at Saint-Germain-l'Auxerrois and Notre-Dame. The next appointment, from Dijon, was also disastrous, and he was sent packing, not only ignominiously, but with a royal *lettre de cachet* excluding him from the diocese. Dulac changed his mind again, and was persuaded to return; four years later, in 1753, he was off to Rouen. A search among the churches of Paris turned up a replacement from Saint-Jean-en-Grève who proved hopelessly idle. There was another competition in 1756, and three ex-choirboys of Chartres, all *maîtres de musique* in other cathedrals, applied. Demongeot was chosen, and he presented the canons with a manuscript collection of his masses as a gesture of gratitude for the start in life they had given him. Five years later, Notre-Dame of Paris, that menace to the musical ambitions of provincial chapters, stole him away. Stability finally came with Lalande from Soissons. He stayed for twenty-four years, tormented with illness towards the end—when the Corpus Christi procession toured the city, he had himself carried round so that he could conduct at each 'station'. He died in 1785, and the canons, who had long foreseen the vacancy, were ready to bring in the *maître de musique* from Evreux.

If Chartres with its wealth could not achieve continuity, what chance had the poorer chapters? At Troyes, the canons paid too little, and expected too much. At mid-century, they dismissed one *maître de musique* because he got married, 'par décence pour l'église'.[59] The next one, brought from Sainte-Radegonde of Poitiers, lasted two years. Deroussy came from Sées, but the canons were outraged at his Te Deum for the birth of the dauphin; he failed to compose a complete musical setting, and had some of the verses 'sung in *chant sur le livre*', 'au lieu de faire exécuter de la grande musique'. He was dismissed; others were tried; none was satisfactory; so Deroussy was reinstated. His successor resigned in 1761 after only a year in office, chagrined at having had to make an apology to one of the canons for some gesture of insolence. The chapter resolved to train a replacement, and sent one of the minor clerks to Paris to study music; no sooner was he back than he married. The same expedient was tried again; the abbé Duval returned from Paris, was ordained priest, and took over the music. His ordination had disqualified him from marriage, but qualified him for ecclesiastical promotion, and he left to become a canon at Dôle. Confusion followed. A candidate from Rouen was rejected because he demanded a higher salary. The *maître de musique* of Evreux made no such demand and was appointed; immediately he arrived, he made an increase of salary a condition of staying. Three months later, in June 1788, he refused to live in the *maîtrise*, and was forthwith dismissed. The old chapter declined to its fall with a subdeacon arriving from Paris to take over a collapsing choir.

What inducements could a chapter offer to persuade a man to stay? Given an appropriate person who had taken holy orders, he might be offered a canonry. Troyes, Meaux, and Bazas resorted to this guarantee of permanency; by this means Bazas kept Jean Maurin for fifty-one years.[60] The canons of Reims, having had a fright when Chartres tried to tempt Hardouin away, made sure they kept him by giving supplements to his income. His basic salary of 1,500 livres and free board and lodging were augmented by 'gratifications', including payments when he published collections of masses. In 1756 they gave him a second chapel (worth 200 livres) and in 1779 a third (245 livres), and in 1776 they made him a canon of Saint-Balsamie (500 livres), a chapter in town whose prebends were in their gift.[61] As the years went by, however, a musician in the post at Reims would be less and less likely to leave, for here, once in a generation, the most prestigious musical celebration of all took place, the coronation. True, Hardouin came off second-best in the negotiations with the *chapelle du roi*, for on the Sunday when Louis XVI was crowned, the mass was the composition of Giroux, the royal *maître de musique*, who conducted in person, and the Te Deum was to a setting by Rebel, the *surintendant de la musique du roi*. However, at the vespers of the preceding Saturday, the choir of Reims was allowed to sing the psalms antiphonally with the choir from Versailles, and on the following Saturday, at the vespers when the king was installed as the Grand Master of the Ordre du Saint-Esprit, Hardouin and his musicians had the monopoly.

Chartres, a rich, huge chapter full of feuds and unpopular with the laity, could not keep its directors of music—probably, they found it difficult to integrate with local society. By contrast, Angers, a small chapter, happily united and meshed with the social life of the town, kept its musicians because they found recognition and struck roots in the place. Bachelier, appointed shortly after leaving the choir school, stayed for forty-eight years, and left only because he was given a canonry in the neighbouring church of Saint-Pierre. Three successors followed in fifteen years, then Voillement, brought from Troyes, stayed to the Revolution. The local newspaper praised his style, declaring him to have 'a place among the most distinguished composers of church music';[62] his advice and co-operation were sought for every musical occasion, and the amateur musicians of the town came to the cathedral to form an orchestra when he celebrated the first mass after his ordination in 1785. Three years later, Notre-Dame of Paris called him, setting him above forty-seven rivals (so it was said), but the adulation and companionship he had found in Angers and the guarantee of a retiring pension of 800 livres at the age of 50 sufficed to convince him that the grandeurs of the capital were overrated. Recognition and friendship probably did more to retain the services of a *maître de musique* than straightforward financial inducements, but, if there was a more prestigious choir to conduct and greater musical scope, the temptation to move became almost irresistible. That is why music was a migratory profession in eighteenth-century France.

IV

The number of choirboys employed by the great churches was comparatively small: ten was the standard formula, as at Reims, Angers, and Chartres; in Paris there were twelve at Notre-Dame, and eight at the Sainte-Chapelle; there were six at Bordeaux and Coutances. The quality of the voices was superb. Candidates were legion, and the search for outstanding talent relentless. For children of peasants, artisans, and lower-middle-class people, there was no better opportunity for a start in life; for parents, no greater pride than to see a son walking the street to the cathedral, resplendent in red cassock and black biretta (at Chartres), or in white cassock like the pope with purple cap and red cape (at Angers). Chapters combed the parishes of their dioceses, following up every rumoured discovery of perfect tone and timbre—raw, untutored quality was what mattered, for the most intensive training would be given. At Troyes, the *maître de musique* was allowed time off to tour the villages, and in 1774 the canons decided to have advertisements read at sermon time at mass in all the churches of the town for the six weeks before the examination. At Chartres, the *maître de musique* not only went round the parishes, but also kept up a wide correspondence, including writing to his colleagues running the music of other cathedrals and to the *musiciens du roi* at Versailles. This network of contacts was effective: in the eight years before mid-century, six boys were brought in from Paris and a few from further afield. It was a two-way traffic, for musicians from Versailles were sent to spy out outstanding talent in the provinces, and it was not easy to resist an invitation—or, indeed, an order—to move to the Royal Chapel.[63] The final decision at Chartres was made at an audition in the presence of the whole chapter. The boys arrived, escorted by their parents or their parish priest (travel expenses paid), and the winners were appointed for a year's probationary period, the chapter making a formal contract with the family. This involved leaving home and taking up residence, if all went well, for something like ten years, in the choir school (variously termed the *maîtrise*, the *psalette*, or, at Reims, the *Maison au Pélican*). (Ten years may seem long, but voices broke later in those days.) Such was the rivalry between chapters that the office of choirboy was one of the few worthwhile employments in eighteenth-century France which was awarded exclusively on the basis of ability, though a testimonial from, say, the duchesse de Choiseul, could make a difference if other things were equal.[64]

The boys were well cared for. The chapter would appoint representatives to exercise oversight: at Tours, it was the two canons living in the house facing the *psalette* with windows overlooking the playground; at Reims, the annually elected *chanoine maître de la prébende des enfants de chœur*; at Chartres, a committee of three canons; at Troyes, two with a third added if major decisions had to be taken. The *maître de musique* was required to live in the choir school and be responsible for the running of the place, with a couple of women servants to cook and clean. If he neglected his duties, the canon superiors would act quickly, as at Troyes in 1782, when they hired seminarists to take over. The accommodation would be spartan but spacious, much better than the boys could have hoped for at home. An inventory at Troyes shows a dormitory with eight beds, a study with a wooden table and benches and an altar with a white cloth, flowers, and brass candlesticks, together with a kitchen and two other rooms. The food was remarkable for an age when the poor so often went hungry and so rarely ate meat; one contract with parents specifies bread, meat, and wine at every meal. There was generous medical attention. At Toulouse in 1735, two boys with ringworm were sent twice a week in a sedan chair to the hospital for treatment, and wigs were purchased for them to hide the deformity; at Troyes in 1738, when a boy was sent home with an infectious disease, a doctor was commissioned to pay visits, and an allowance was made to his mother to provide meat to make 'beef tea'.

Choirboys received a thorough education, specialist, but not narrow. Latin, French, and catechism were taught by a *maître de grammaire*; at Chartres in 1780 this was a well-paid office—1,125 livres with an extra 200 for doubling up as 'épistolier' and fees for masses, a total income which many a curé would envy. The musical training extended far beyond reading music, voice production, and accurate singing; expert tutors were brought in to teach the boys to play instruments, the serpent, bassoon, double bass, and the newer-fashioned violin, perhaps with the proviso that the instrument would be theirs eventually. Harmony, counterpoint, and orchestration were taught, and the boys were encouraged to produce original compositions. They could submit a motet, or even a complete mass, to the chapter for performance on a feast-day; if accepted, there was the honour of celebrity on the occasion and a gratuity voted by the canons, perhaps 20 or 30 livres. At Chartres, a boy on leaving had a right to read a Latin oration to the chapter asking permission to have a final motet performed and to be allowed to conduct it—a request usually granted.

When a choirboy's voice broke, the chapter saw to his future. There was a 'trousseau' of clothing and a leaving payment, a basic sum with extras—accumulated fees for having sung in endowed services, or for general meritorious conduct. At Notre-Dame of Paris and the great parish of Saint-Eustache and at Chartres, the total was regularly 300 livres or more, at Toulouse and Troyes half as much. Apprenticeship fees were paid, and contracts with employers arranged. A superior performer might be invited to stay on as an instrumentalist, or the post might be offered as a means of temporary support until it was possible to seek audition as a choirman. Those who chose an ecclesiastical career would have some or all of their seminary expenses paid; the cathedral of Coutances had an endowment providing six scholarships (*bourses*) at the Collège d'Harcourt in Paris. Outstanding musical talent could win astonishingly rapid promotion. In 1727, Louis Fromental, senior boy at Rouen, presented his canons with half a dozen motets with full orchestral score: in the following year they appointed him their *maître de musique*.[65] Bernard Jumentier left Chartres at the age of 18 to take charge of the music at Senlis. After a few months he fell ill;

the canons of Chartres, who had already paid his travelling expenses, welcomed him back and maintained him until he recovered, when he went off to be *maître de musique* at Saint-Malo, later moving up to Coutances.

Given their good prospects and their superior lot among their contemporaries, choirboys worked hard and behaved well. The sanction of expulsion was rarely needed: a consistently 'mutinous and proud' individual, after being given a second chance, might have to go, so too the senior boy involved in 'un épouvantable scandale dans la maîtrise'. Even so, a chapter might offer to arrange an apprenticeship and give a small maintenance allowance on condition of attending catechism classes. Another sanction, less severe, was to withhold payment of some customary gift. In 1786, the Sainte-Chapelle cancelled the Easter pocket-money because of irreverence during the services, and on two occasions refrained from adding supplementary extras to the leaving grants of boys who had contrived to have masses of their composition performed without the permission of the chapter. But punishments were rare. The canons accepted the inevitability of a measure of original sin, and put up with a moderate degree of laughter, whispering, and 'the circulation of manuscript works whose content is unknown to the chapter'[66]— had they been confiscated, no doubt by now they would be given in a footnote to some study of the clandestine literature of the Enlightenment.

In return for their generosity, the canons required the utmost diligence. The day of a choirboy was packed with regimented activity, though perhaps no more so than was the lot of the pupils in the *collèges*. At Reims, prayers were said at 6 a.m., then there was the procession to the cathedral in cassocks, surplices, and hats, with cloaks in cold weather. Matins and lauds were then sung antiphonally, with the choir divided into two sections. Breakfast was at 7 a.m., then a music practice for the two masses following; after the masses, classroom work till noon. Dinner and a recreational break all took place in an hour. Then an hour's practice for vespers, sung at 2 p.m.; then classes until 7 p.m., with a short break for a snack. Supper and recreation occupied the hour from 7 p.m. to 8 p.m., followed by prayers with the singing of versicles. Thereafter, bed, though some might be allowed to stay up to copy music. There was a mid-week relaxation of this austere curriculum—a free afternoon on the Tuesday and a supervised walk after vespers on the Wednesday. At Coutances, Toulouse, and Notre-Dame of Paris the programme of a choirboy's life was equally stern (indeed, at

Coutances, everything began earlier, at 4 a.m. in summer and 5 p.m. in winter). There was hardly any home leave, though every church had its occasions of holiday celebration—a feast or an excursion. Notre-Dame had its annual day trip to Saint-Denis and another to Meudon, and Archbishop de Juigné added a third by his summer invitations to his palace and gardens at Conflans.

No doubt in the *maîtrise*, as in French society generally, the official regulations were much sterner than actual practice, with plenty of that collusive idleness between masters and pupils which can make school-days so agreeable. And the daily round of the liturgical offices was not as boring as might be thought. The music was continually varied, and everyone's turn came to sing a solo. There were ceremonial duties—carrying the processional cross or candles in their silver sconces, wielding the snuffer, swinging the incense (there would be a practice incense boat in the *maîtrise*), parading round the church or outside in processions, joining in a foray from the choir-stalls to chant a motet at the tomb of the founder, making an informal pilgrimage to sing a May carol at the bishop's palace. Churches had their seasonal observances, with the boys playing picturesque roles. In Holy Week at Chartres, after *Tenebrae*, they accompanied two canons to the altar and sang 'miserere nobis' as the canons intoned the Kyrie, and at 'factus obediens usque ad mortem', a single boy replied 'mortem crucis', then all lay prostrate on the paving stones until the dean gave the signal to leave by striking three times on his stall. On Holy Saturday at Troyes, after compline, the litanies of the Sacred Name of Jesus were sung by two boys kneeling in the aisle, the full choir in the stalls accompanying in fauxbourdon; then there was a procession, and after in the vestry there was 20 sous for every boy for his 'Easter breakfast'. There was an abundance of such quaint rituals, often supported by an endowment to provide pocket-money or a feast. There was rivalry to be chosen for the posts of honour and intrigues to avoid the boring ones, basking in praise when things went well and taking refuge in wry 'in jokes' when some would-be reverent observance ended in disaster. Though the work was hard and the hours long, life was always interesting for the choirboys of the *ancien régime*.

A choirboy whose voice broke well, retaining force and purity of tone, might well aspire to a career as a professional singer. His chapter might give him a grant to study music in Paris in lieu of paying for an apprenticeship, but it was not easy to move directly into the world of opera and the theatre; the staging-point post would have to be a period as a choirman in one of the great churches. Other boys,

with an ecclesiastical career in mind, might follow the same path and
serve as a church musician while studying. And in any case, to be a
choirman was a career in itself. At Angers, a *psalteur* could expect to
earn 900 livres a year, with the possibility of a house provided. At
Chartres in 1791, the salaries were said to run from 1,000 to 1,400
livres; since this was at a time when applicants for government
pensions tended to inflate their returns, no doubt the figure
included fees for singing anniversary masses, and also extras from the
foundation of 'Saint-Piat', a sort of prebend applied to supporting
the musical side of the cathedral's activities. Employment was
usually for life, with income continued in sickness and old age.[67] At
the Sainte-Chapelle in Paris there was no concept of retirement, for
when a choirman aged 67 asked for 'vétérance' so that he could miss
matins, the canons refused on the grounds that there was no precedent; however, they agreed to let him stay in bed in the early morning and mark him down as present. The same concession was made,
seventeen years later, to another weary applicant. Ecclesiastical
employment had its constraints, of course. The canons would not
allow their singers to perform in secular concerts unless the repertoire was dignified and had religious overtones. At Troyes, choirmen
were supposed to present a *billet* four times a year certifying they had
received communion; in 1783, the canons decided to enforce the
rule against those who had grown negligent.[68] Everywhere, chapters
had the right to impose fines for breaches of discipline. The registers
at Angers show deductions from salaries for unconventional dress in
church, insolence to a canon, absence from matins, slipping off to
the vestry before the end of the service, and for causing scandal by
'des conversations inutiles, souvent prolongées, même à haute
voix, et par leurs rires immodérés', a nice formula used in 1772 and
regarded as so appropriate that it was copied into the record when
fines were imposed again three years later.[69]

The number of choirmen, like the number of boys, was comparatively small—sixteen at Chartres, ten at Bordeaux, in very small
places only four. There was a great pool of talent to choose from,
especially from former choirboys already trained to musical expertise. But there was difficulty in recruiting good voices in the high
register—Toulouse, which at one time had one bass, two tenors, and
three countertenors, was a remarkable exception.[70] In 1749 a canon
of Troyes wrote from Paris to one of his colleagues: he had found a
tenor, and it was urgent to get him, as the bishop of Meaux was
making offers. He was an ex-opera singer, retired on an inadequate
pension. Somehow, and not very suitably, he had managed to get

ordained as a priest; his life was blameless, but he lacked intelligence and could not sight-read—he could only sing things he had studied the night before.[71] Nevertheless, his voice was strong and soaring. Seeing there was a demand for their services, the choirmen of the great churches constituted a mobile profession; outstanding talent always got better offers from outside, and tended to move round until local circumstances and friendships brought equilibrium. Some good performers did not accept contracts tying them down, but made themselves available for hire. In 1777, the *maître de musique* of Reims was looking for a tenor for a special occasion; he failed, but managed to get two good bass voices to come from Soissons. For major occasions, like the memorial service on the death of Louis XV, the Sainte-Chapelle of Paris would hire a dozen extra singers. The ecclesiastical musical world, in which everybody knew everyone else, constituted a sort of confraternity. A wandering singer of any quality was likely to be welcomed to join in the liturgical services while he was in town and be voted a gratuity by the canons when leaving, while a famous performer who was passing would offer to give a solo without reward—a nice question for the canons to decide: was he too distinguished to be offered an honorarium?

V

The development of French church music of the Enlightenment towards complexity, sophistication, and virtuosity owed something to sheer technological progress. From the beginning of the seventeenth century, there was a remarkable improvement in the precision and tone of musical instruments. The serpent, said to have been invented in 1590, was a development from various types of horn, bent to be shorter and more manageable, and was used to provide a heavy, rather raucous bass undercurrent. Cathedrals, which normally had two of them, had to look for senior choirboys well endowed with 'vent' and 'estomac' capable of blowing them. Le Cerf de Viéville, writing in 1705, described the serpent as 'privileged', since it was established in the churches by long usage.[72] Together with the organ (to keep the voices 'steady'), it had come to be regarded as the only allowable accompaniment for services 'around the altar'; then, he said, about twenty years earlier, strings had come in, being introduced into Notre-Dame of Paris by Campra. Even so, there were usually only two or three bass fiddles and a rather larger number of violins. As he wrote, all constraints had been abandoned in the

Royal Chapel at Versailles. At the baptism of the dauphin thirty-seven years earlier, the full orchestra of the Chambre and the trumpets and drums of the military establishment had been added to the chapel instrumentalists.[73] A provincial visitor to Versailles in 1699 was surprised to hear oboes and flutes dominating the cadences of the violins; however, he said, the effect was deeply religious: 'ils ne servirent qu'à m'élever le cœur vers Dieu'. With the example of the Royal Court and religious concerts in Paris shaping educated opinion, the idea that only certain instruments could be 'religious' faded. When the clarinet came from Saxony to the Opéra in mid-century, the greater churches adopted it soon afterwards.[74] As the canons of Notre-Dame said in 1786, when hiring a professional orchestra to support their music on solemn feast-days: 'Why must we have only reedy bassoons and lugubrious violins? By what fatality do the most melodious instruments come under an especial anathema?'[75] There was always the problem of expense, however. The cost of a full orchestra every day, or even every Sunday, would have been prohibitive.

The organ, always the indispensable accompaniment in churches, in the course of the seventeenth century had been improved into an instrument of rich and varied scope—there had been an increase in the number of manuals, the multiplication of reed-stops, the widening of the boundaries of resonance into a sonorous timbre, the multiplying of the facilities for embellishment in counterpoint and complex cadences. This elaboration of function was matched by proud display on the organ case: a show of flowers, cherubs, wreaths, fiery-crested urns, musical instruments, palm trees, St Cecilia with her spinet, and King David with his harp. In the seventeenth century the style of high fashion was white and gold, as in the royal chapel at Versailles, the Sainte-Chapelle and Notre-Dame at Paris, though later the richness of the natural wood was preferred to emphasize the delicacy of the carving.[76] Either way, it was a search for a visual pleasure to prefigure the charm of the music.

The seventeenth century had its great organ-builders; early, there was Valeran de Héman, who gave Rouen the splendid instrument on which Jean Titelouze, the composer, trained a whole school of church organists, and later, there was Alexandre Thierry who constructed the king's organ at Versailles.[77] In addition to the big names, in every little town there were workmen who could at least do repairs, and from their families came the great *facteurs d'orgues* of the eighteenth century: Clicquot, Dallery, Cavaillé. Clicquot, whose great individual achievements were the organs of Saint-Gervais

(1760), Saint-Sulpice (1781), and Poitiers (1790), did most of his other work in partnership with Charles Dallery, who had learned his trade from an uncle, a cooper of Amiens, who had exchanged the skills of barrel hooping for the mechanics of music. Together, Clicquot and Dallery built or repaired the instruments of Notre-Dame, Saint-Nicolas-des-Champs, Saint-Merry, and the Sainte-Chapelle, as well as doing numerous repairs—at the Royal Chapel and, in 1766, at the parish church of Versailles, where the organ had never been the same since 1730, when a thunderbolt had perforated the pipes with a multitude of little holes.[78] In the provinces, the Dupont family maintained the organs of the great churches of Lorraine. The area round Toulouse was the circuit of the Dominican friar Joseph Cavaillé and his assistant Frère Isnard—they rebuilt the cathedral organ, and repaired those of the parishes all around. Jean d'Angeville came to Angers from Paris in 1738 at the invitation of the chapter of Saint-Pierre; after working for this church, he was given the contract for renewing the cathedral instrument, and thereafter stayed in Anjou.[79] In like manner the Micot family, father and son, came from Paris to Bordeaux at the invitation of the canons of Saint-Seurin and then stayed on. The finest organ in town, however, was not their work—this was at the abbey of Sainte-Croix, completed in mid-century by one of its monks, the famous Dom Bedos, whose treatise, *L'Art du facteur d'orgues* (1766), became the indispensable handbook of contemporary expertise.[80]

Great *facteurs* were invited: lesser ones travelled round seeking commissions. Chapters and churchwardens examined their testimonials and made enquiries before signing a contract, but while doubts tormented their thrifty minds, if their church was bereft of music, there was a bias towards seizing the opportunity. In 1722 at Saint-Jean-de-Luz on the Spanish frontier, the notables committed 4,800 livres seeing that 'un entrepreneur horganiste estranger se trouve sur les lieux', and in 1755, another 1,500 livres because 'un facteur d'orgue de reputation est sur le lieu'.[81] When the work was finished, an expert would be called in to certify it; in 1722, the organist of the cathedral of Troyes earned a fee of 54 livres for going out to Ervy to make such a check.[82] The churchwardens of Saint-Jean-de-Luz made a mistake in 1722, for within eight years they had to call in an expert from far-away Paris to find out what was wrong, and on his recommendation brought in a *facteur* from the capital at a fee of 3,000 livres. The canons and parishioners of Saint-Michel of Draguignan in 1717 signed up an Italian who took their instrument to pieces then fled; seven years later they paid 2,000 livres to an expert from Marseille to put it together again.[83] The chapter of the cathedral of Orléans flatly refused to pay Adeline of Langres, for they had his repairs assessed by their own musicians and by the *maître de musique* and organist of Saint-Aignan and the organist of Saint-Paul, and they were united in condemnation.[84] The verdict of such a high-powered 'jury' (as the term went) had to be accepted. The wretched *facteur d'orgue* had to struggle on making readjustments, hoping he would not go bankrupt in the process—though he might try to shift the blame on to the conditions in which he had to work. The organist of the cathedral of Perpignan rejected the repairs made to a village organ; according to the *facteur*, the faults were the result of 'les déprédations des rats qui avaient gâté son ouvrage'.[85]

Organ playing, like organ building, was usually a family profession. Given the technicalities of the instrument and the difficulty of access, to become an accomplished performer needed the patronage of an established one: thus, Louis-Claude Daquin, the prodigy of the century, who played before Louis XIV in 1700 at the age of 6, was trained up to greatness by Louis Marchand of the Royal Chapel. A chapter might select a promising choirboy and send him to Paris for expert tuition, as the canons of Amiens did in 1780. Usually, however, skill was transmitted within the family circle. Organists, even if they took minor orders, generally stopped short of the subdiaconate and the obligation of celibacy; they married, and naturally wished to pass on their profitable expertise to their sons—and sometimes, their daughters.[86] Or there would be a nephew anxious to join the profession. Pierre-Claude Fourqueray, the son of an organist, came to Notre-Dame in 1761, and when he died eleven years later, his place was taken by his 27-year-old nephew, Nicolas Séjan. A father would negotiate to get his son appointed to some nearby church; Bainville, of the cathedral of Saint-Maurice at Angers, in 1773 suggested this to the canons of Saint-Pierre, offering to come over himself to play on great occasions—the young man, however, preferred to take his chance in Paris. Jean-Philippe Rameau, the future maestro of French opera, whose father was organist of the cathedral of Dijon, also chose to adventure on his own account; he played the violin with a travelling opera troupe, took employment as a church organist at Avignon and Clermont, then succeeded his father at Dijon briefly, before going back to Clermont by way of Lyon.[87] The canons of Clermont hoped to confine his wandering genius by a nine-year contract, but he haunted them with such barbarous music that they had to let him go to his destiny in Paris. In more conventional families, the young man would stay on as coadjutor, as it were, at the keyboard, in due course inheriting the succession. Louis Siret played for the cathedral of Troyes for fifty-one years, and on his death his son Nicolas took over for another half-century. Nicolas died in 1754, and was succeeded by the Joly brothers; after thirty years one of them was replaced by his son in the condominium. In Paris, centred on the church of Saint-Gervais, there was the resplendent Couperin dynasty. In the seventeenth century, Louis and Charles followed one another, with François their brother playing in other churches.[88] In 1685, at the age of 17, François II, the most famous of them all, took the inheritance. His father had died six years earlier, and the churchwardens paid Lalande to be *locum tenens* until the youngster grew up. Nicolas, a half-cousin of Couperin 'the Great', succeeded at Saint-Gervais in 1733. When he died fifteen years later, the succession fell to his son, Armand-Louis Couperin, who combined the duties with those at the churches of Sainte-Marguerite, Saint-Barthélemy, Saint-Merry, Saint-Jean-en-Grève, the Carmes-Billette, and the Sainte-Chapelle, with the addition, from 1755, of Notre-Dame; all the while he was also taking his turn, over a quarter of the year, at the Royal Chapel. One after the other, his two sons followed him at Saint-Gervais and the cathedral.

Armand-Louis Couperin was able to hold his collection of seven musical pluralities by playing himself in each church on its most important festivals and sending his wife and sons to deputize at others. This was a common practice. Guillaume-Antoine Calvière, a national celebrity praised in verses in the *Mercure*, reigned at Notre-Dame from 1730 to 1755, along with the Sainte-Chapelle, Saint-Germain-des-Prés, Sainte-Marguerite, and, from 1738, the Royal Chapel. The same practice is found in the provinces. The Joly brothers at Troyes, assisted by their sons and one of the wives, played for the cathedral and three parish churches, accumulating small fees and tied up in tricky contracts specifying when and where the two experts should play in person. The chapel at Versailles was an exclusive engagement, but here there were four organists, each in office for a quarter of the year, and free to play elsewhere at any other time. After the death of Calvière, Notre-Dame adopted the same system, simultaneously appointing Drouard de Bousset and Daquin (both of the Royal Chapel), Solange, and Armand-Louis Couperin. When Bousset died in 1760, Balbastre was brought in, fresh from his scandalous triumph of drawing such crowds to the midnight mass of Christmas at Saint-Roch that the archbishop had barred him from performing on this occasion in future.[89] Thanks to its adoption of fourfold appointments, from 1760 to 1772, the cathedral of Paris enjoyed the services of the two most sophisticated virtuosos of the century, vying with each other in their periods of duty, Daquin and Balbastre.

What was the role of the organ in church services? From contracts of the late seventeenth century it seems that it was commonly omitted from the weekday music of Lent and Advent, from Holy Innocents' Day, and a few other saints' days, but was necessary for all Sundays and major festivals.[90] Then, the organist was required to contribute at first and second vespers, matins, lauds, the evening *salut* and compline, and at high mass. For the mass, the instructions might be detailed, mentioning the Kyrie, Gloria, Sanctus, Benedictus, Agnus Dei, and the psalm *Domine salvum* (the patriotic addition for the safety and honour of the king). For the Elevation and Communion, an improvisation might be required as a devotional background, hence the warning that the tone must be one of solemnity. At the offices sung in plainsong, he was expected to subordinate his playing to the voices; he must not drown the chant, though he could 'alternate' with the choir and contribute 'interludes'. This is what Dr Burney found on his tour of France: the serpent was the essential accompaniment to the chant, the 'crutch for the voices to lean on', and the organ was used principally to play the melody before it was sung.[91] But what connoisseurs came to hear were the motets diversifying the offices with their elaborate harmonies and embellishments, and the Kyries, Glorias, and other set pieces of the masses, and here the organ might be used as the dominant or exclusive accompaniment. The two masses for organ by Couperin 'the Great', one for a parish, one for a convent, are masterpieces of virtuosity, 'to show off the instrument and the skill of the player', arabesques and dialogues of brilliant descriptive music anticipating Berlioz and Liszt.[92]

For church organists, the supreme moment came when they could improvise. Their skill became legendary. There were stories of contrivances to make an organ half-dismantled for repair sound complete, of panic caused by the tumultuous rendering of a battle scene, of the imitation of the song of a nightingale so convincing that vergers were sent to the upper galleries to expel the intruding bird. According to Mercier, the Parisian organists played ariettas and sarabands at the Elevation at mass, and at the Te Deum and vespers, hunting songs, minuets, sentimental airs, and rigadoons.[93] There is whimsical exaggeration here, and a hint of the journalistic predisposition to poses of moral rigorism. But outrageously brilliant improvisation was what the public wanted; there was no more

popular musical occasion in the capital than Daquin or Balbastre performing fantastic variations on the tunes of old carols—a Christmas
custom which had begun with Lalande in the chapel at Versailles.
Great players were surrounded by the incense of hero worship. A
parodist of La Bruyère's 'characters' describes them as they could be
seen and heard in the churches of Paris.[94] 'Benoît' with his cloak
slung negligently over his shoulder and his vast-brimmed hat, his
playing thunderous and decorative, but lacking in delicacy; he bows
low to his audience expecting an encore—he regards no praise as too
fulsome. 'Célestin' goes to the organ loft as to a sanctuary where
none but the perfect can enter, and when he comes down among
the throng, it is with eyes raised to heaven and voice choking with
emotion: 'Oh cher ami, merci!' Praise of his performance is not
enough, you must 'understand' it. Then there is the modern
organist admired by the great public, 'Rapido-Prestout', the acrobat
of the keyboards, the inventor of novelties. Alas! why can we not
exchange them all for 'Cromatius', forbidding in mien, playing only
noble and majestic music?

French musicologists have seen the exhibitionist dexterity of these
organists of the *ancien régime* as evidence of the decadence of the discipline, with the mastery passing to the Protestant North.[95] Perhaps
this amounts to saying little more than that in Germany the instrument was developed to be capable of a wider range, and that France
produced no Johann Sebastian Bach. With the advent of the
Revolution and its crude propagandist insistence on military and
patriotic themes, decadence—if such it was—became collapse.
Balbastre finished up playing improvisations on the 'Marseillaise' and
the 'Ça ira' at Notre-Dame, but at least, by doing so, he rescued the
organ from demolition by the de-Christianizers.

VI

What was the nature of the music which the canons so lavishly subsidized? Did they have an ideal and seek to impose it, or did their
musicians produce a dominant style which they accepted? Or was
there an evolution of style going on progressively, shaped by the
musicians under pressures from canons, other patrons, and educated
opinion generally?

The rules of the Church reflected the traditional puritanical
fear of the excessive passion aroused by music and of the worldly
pleasure it gave its hearers. A papal circular in 1749 repeated the

terms of the decree of Innocent XII of 1692 limiting music at mass to introit, gradual, offertory, Gloria, and Credo, and if anything more was added (for example, at the Elevation), it must be sober, perhaps a hymn of St Thomas Aquinas.[96] 'Fastidious repetitions' and 'confusions of voices' were banned. If there was instrumental music, it must be solemn, not theatrical; drums, trumpets, oboes, flutes, and harps were forbidden. Some of these rules for decorum had support from opinion in Europe. Dr Burney defined church music as 'grave and scientific compositions for voices only, of which the excellence consists more in good harmony, learned modulation and fugues upon ingenious and sober subjects than in light airs and turbulent accompaniments'.[97] But the whole tendency of the eighteenth century was towards throwing off those constraints. As Voltaire observed gleefully, 'Church music—it is a search for the pleasures of the senses in the observances of a religion established to fight against them.'[98]

What was happening in music, as in the arts generally, might be described, though over-dramatically, in an analogy borrowed from Spengler. The eighteenth century to Spengler was the mellow autumn of the West, an indefensible proposition outside his cyclical theory of history. But there was an autumn, one of vivid sunset splendour, the beginning of the end of the 1,300-year-old Christian culture of Europe. The arts were gaining their total independence, completing their emergence from the cocoon of religion which had formed and nourished them. Yet the organic connection still existed, and religion, in a sense, became worldly to accommodate the inspirations of the artists who served it. In music, looked at from one side, the relationship shows the world of secular music as parasitic. It was the ex-choirboys, church organists, and instrumentalists (and their children) who became the basses and tenors and conductors and musicians of the Opéra, the writers of the scores like Philidor, Grétry, and Rameau, the directors of the Royal Chapel like Lalande and Campra.[99] 'All the singers who have achieved any fame,' wrote Portalis to Napoleon in 1805, 'received their musical education in the *maîtrises*; in those days there were no other institutions to teach vocal music—not only did these old choir schools do the task well, but as everyone knew, there was no possible alternative.'[100] Nor was there when he wrote: the music for the Emperor's coronation was devised by two *maîtres de musique* of the *ancien régime*.

The churches provided the world with its musicians, and the world, by a reverse traffic, set its imprint upon the music of the churches, for better or for worse, according to the assumptions and prejudices of the critical listener. Among severe moralists, there remained lingering doubts about music for God's service being produced by worldly men and unbelievers. But by the eighteenth century, the civilized concept that superior artistic achievement in itself belongs to the divine inspiration running through creation[101] had more than half won acceptance. Certainly, it was rare for the life-style of a composer to be taken as a disqualification for his music. Secure in the favour of Louis XIV, Lully wrote the *grands motets* of the Royal Chapel, though well known to qualify, by membership of a ring of sodomists, for execution by burning.[102] André Campra's geriatric bohemian adventures were not in the reckoning when music was needed to grace the laying of the foundation-stone of the new altar of Saint-Sulpice by the papal nuncio in 1732.[103]

But what of the day-to-day performers? Were they allowed to combine their sacred duties with forays into the world, playing music to stir the passions, singing songs of profane amours? In 1734, the bishop of Montpellier urged the canons of his cathedral not to allow 'the musicians of the temple of the Lord to sing the praises of his Enemy in the place of his abode', that is, in a secular concert-hall.[104] Most chapters, however, would allow their choirmen and instrumentalists to accept outside engagements provided the repertoire was broadly concerned with religious themes. The cathedral of Saint-André at Bordeaux dismissed its German organist Franz Beck because he conducted in the theatre—the rival chapter of Saint-Seurin promptly signed him on as choirmaster.

The converse problem arose when outside professionals were hired to strengthen the church music on important occasions. Often, it was possible to do so without scandal, for singers from other churches might be available, as well as former choirmen who had left ecclesiastical service but came back occasionally to earn a supplementary income. It was different, however, when talent was hired from the theatrical world. The ecclesiastical ban on actors did not apply to opera singers, for they belonged to an institution under royal patronage.[105] Nevertheless, the logic of their immunity was not accepted by the strictest of moralists. The audience at a theatrical performance felt the thrill of passion, without having to bear its severe and salutary consequences.[106] The Sorbonne in 1693 expressed specific reservations where opera was concerned. In the inevitable love intrigue of the plot, temptation lurks—in the words, often enhanced by declamation, and in the appearance and gestures of the singers—while the music sweeps us away on a tide of unthinking emotion.[107] Yet, even as the doctors of theology made their pronouncements, the courtiers and the rich of Paris were flocking to the convents of the Feuillants and Théatins to hear *Tenebrae* sung by soloists of the Opéra, men and women.[108] Because they haven't added dancing as yet, asked La Bruyère, must we call the spectacle an office of the Church?[109] At the Jesuit church of Saint-Louis, the psalms of vespers were sung by professionals in fashionable town dress—the writer of a comparison of French and Italian music at the beginning of the century said that new arrivals at the Opéra regarded the invitation to Saint-Louis as their indispensable initiation ceremony.[110] Throughout the century, the tradition of sophisticated performances of *Tenebrae* continued at the abbey of Longchamps (except for a period when the archbishop of Paris banned them).[111] But the great collegiate churches of Paris, in spite of their rivalry, did not yield to the temptation of hiring professionals of the stage—that is, until Lesueur became *maître de musique* of Notre-Dame in 1786. He persuaded the chapter to bring in singers from the Opéra and a full orchestra for the four principal feasts of the calendar. The cathedral was crowded, but some of the canons panicked when the complaints of the devout came in.[112] In their deliberations, they finally decided to keep on the orchestra—indeed, the vote of money for the instrumentalists was doubled—but to discontinue having the opera singers.

Anyone employed by a church was liable to be dismissed for immorality—if it was known. Where outstanding talent was concerned, it was not necessary to be officious and inquisitorial.[113] As for church musicians being eaten up by pride, 'gaining fame . . . before the altars in the presence of Jesus Christ who lived a humble and inconspicuous life',[114] as one strict moralist said, no one cared about it; nor was there much support for the complaint that the cost of the music was excessive when so many were poor and the Church had other responsibilities. Truth was, church-goers rejoiced to hear displays of ostentatious virtuosity and sophisticated contests for excellence, and canons spent as much as they could afford to keep their church's musical reputation ahead of that of all their rivals.

The imprint of the world was set upon church music by the ambitions and ingenuities of the musicians, coupled with the operation of social and cultural pressures. High society and sophisticated taste in eighteenth-century France were dominated by two milieux, 'la Cour et la Ville', the royal court at Versailles, and the capital, Paris. This was so with church music, as with so much else. The dominant influence in fashion was the royal chapel at Versailles. It had unique resources. In mid-century, in addition to the organ, there was an

orchestra of fifty, which could be reinforced by other instrumentalists from the king's *musique de la chambre*.[115] There were thirty chaplains to sing the priestly parts of the offices, doing so in a rotation
around the calendar, and another four who were experts reserved for
the masses at the great festivals. The choirboys were double the
number at most of the great cathedrals—twenty of them. The chapel
coutumier allows us to glimpse them off duty, allowed to play skittles,
boule, and quoits but not to skate, fight, throw stones or snowballs,
and doomed to instant expulsion if found writing on walls.[116] There
were fifty-two men, nicknamed 'Grille Boudins', since one of them
was caught toasting a sausage on the incense burner during mass.[117]
The shortage of high tenors was overcome by sending promising
singers to be trained at the Opéra, and by importing castrati from
Naples.[118] The chapel calendar was divided into four quarters, each
with a different *maître de musique* in charge. The office, prestigious
and allowing the holder to enjoy employment in one of the major
churches of Paris for three-quarters of the year, was sought after by
leading musicians from the churches of the provinces; when there
was a vacancy, they presented themselves at Versailles to compete,
being locked up in solitary confinement for six days, producing
original compositions. They were expected to conform to, and
enhance, the existing tradition of court music, hence one quarter of
the year was 'le quartier des morts' devoted to performing the music
of former composers of the Royal Chapel.

The *motet à grand chœur* which came to prevail at Versailles had
reached its definitive form with Lully—vocal parts in infinite complexity, sometimes with double choirs responding to each other,
solos, duets, and trios with orchestral accompaniment, recitative
and declamation accompanied by organ and bass strings.[119] It was
unabashedly theatrical music, written by a libertine, yet touched by
surges of deep religious feeling. The motets and the gigantic Te
Deum with drums and trumpets represent only one aspect of Lully's
genius.[120] His Elevations for one or two voices, *De Profundis*, *O
Lacrimae*, and *Miserere* are moving—Mme de Sévigné said of the
Miserere there could be 'no other music in heaven'.[121] The tradition
of the *grand motet* created by Lully was taken over and refined by
Lalande; after his death in 1726 the court of Louis XV made the
Tuesday of every week a Lalande day, devoted to his compositions.[122] His widow published his forty finest motets, tremendous set
pieces with their battery of five-part singers and the orchestra sweeping on beyond the themes of the choir, violins rising in counterpoint
above the voices.

The theatrical colour and uninhibited resort to operatic devices which characterized the music of the Royal Chapel owed something to Italian influences, mediated through two of the fashionable churches of Paris. Towards the end of the seventeenth century, Paolo Lorenzani, an ultramontane musical adventurer, excluded from Versailles by the jealousy of Lully, became *maître de musique* of the Théatins, while Marc-Antoine Charpentier, an imitator and rival of Lully and a disciple of Carissimi, ruled at the Jesuits.[123] Visitors returning from Rome had brought back glowing accounts of the dramatic performances of the massed choirs hired by the French embassy to celebrate the annual feast of St Louis;[124] polite society could now hear the Italian style every day at home. The Opéra was another meeting-place for the syncretism of national styles, and its effect on church music was evident in the religious music of Campra. In 1694 he left Notre-Dame to write for the theatre, and twenty-nine years later he left the Opéra to become a *maître de musique* at the Royal Chapel, and there for ten years he added to the tradition of the *grand motet* of Lully and Lalande elements of drama and pathos as in the Italian mode.

All the while a dispute resounded between connoisseurs enamoured of Italy and patriots loyal to France. To both sides, it was more than a rivalry between musicians over questions of style. At the stage of the 'Querelle des Bouffons' in 1752–4, one writer set French against Italian as talent versus nature, vehemence versus naïveté, ornament versus the truth in its purity. If there was a philosophical question at stake, it concerned the original derivation of music—is it a rational principle of nature, or is it the spontaneous language of the emotions?[125] The antithesis was artificial and ended in absurdity: Rameau's *boutade* that he could set the *Gazette d'Hollande* to music, and Rousseau's solemn assertion that only simple song, without harmony or instruments, is legitimate.[126] The controversy was tangential to church music, except in so far as the validation of emotional expression was concerned. 'Church music ought to be expressive' said a writer in 1725; 'the passions of opera are cold when compared to those depicted in our church music.'[127] His words are a pointer to the fallacy of attempting to divide music, ecclesiastical and secular, into sharply differentiated compartments: the feelings of love, pathos, tragedy, and hope, inseparable from our human condition, are all we have as guides to these sentiments as offered to God. In this sense, the 'Italians' in the quarrel were offering the musicians grounds for a greater freedom of expression. Yet, while the theorists argued about the two rational styles, the musicians themselves were engaged in the more prosaic activity of borrowing whatever attracted them in the compositions of their rivals. In the preface to his book of cantatas (1708), André Campra said he had tried to combine 'the delicacy of French music and the vivacity of the Italian'.[128] So too François Couperin in *Les Goûts réunis* (1724)—he proposed to imitate the best modes of both schools.[129]

Seeing that on the great ecclesiastical feasts and penitential days of the Church secular music was inappropriate, if not illegal, high society in Paris had grown used to enjoying religious music on these occasions, performed with worldly éclat. There were Christmas carols at the duchesse du Maine's, devoutly sung, though concluding with verses likening the bright eyes of the hostess to the star of Bethlehem;[130] mass every Sunday in the chapel of the wife of the farmer-general La Popelinière, when Gossec played the violin and Rameau improvised on the organ;[131] the *Miserere* of Lalande and motets by Mondonville sung in Pompadour's salon on Holy Saturday and Easter Day, with the royal mistress one of the voices.[132] This idea of religious music as entertainment was systematized for the theatre-going public of Paris by the foundation of the *Concert spirituel* in 1725. At first, performances were confined to Holy Week when the theatres were shut, but soon they were extended to all major ecclesiastical festivals and to all the days from Palm Sunday to Low Sunday. The entrance fee was four livres, affordable to all but the ordinary majority, and there were seats for 800 in the audience. Like the Royal Chapel, the *Concert spirituel* drew in talent from the churches—a bass from the choir of Lille who came and stayed on to write for the theatre, a choirboy of the Sainte-Chapelle who played the violin and finally became *surintendant de la musique du Roi*.[133] In 1766 the organizers of the concert offered a gold medal for a setting for *Super flumina Babylonis*, and, faced with two brilliant entries, awarded an extra one; both were won by Giroust, who was thus tempted from the *maîtrise* of Orléans to Paris and the Court.[134]

Parisians flocked to the concerts to hear the productions of the highly developed religious music of the French school, the glory of the chapel of Versailles. Apart from Pergolesi, practically all the music was by French composers, mostly of the century, Lalande, Gilles, Gossec, and Mondonville being the favourites.[135] It was staged without inhibition, from the start using the full range of professional talent available. At the second concert there was a motet by Couperin with full orchestra, sung by the tall and graceful Mlle Antier of the Opéra, with violin and flute sonatas. In 1728, Courbois's *Omnes gentes plaudite manibus* crashed out with an accompaniment of trumpets and cymbals.[136] The linkage with the style of Versailles was accentuated when Mondonville, one of the royal *maîtres de musique*, became director of the concerts from 1755. With him, the repertoire of the *grands motets* (at which he himself excelled) was diversified by the introduction of the oratorio. Originating in Rome, the genre in France had begun with Charpentier—in 1703 it was defined as 'a species of sacred opera'. But there were few examples before mid-century—the idea of telling a story in vocal and orchestral form had been largely confined to the cantata, usually on a mythological theme with an idealized love interest, the genre of 'the embarkation for Cythère'.[137] Mondonville's *Les Israëlites à la montagne d'Horeb* in 1758 marked the inauguration of the oratorio as a fashionable form. In the following years oratorios figured as major items in many a *Concert spirituel*—the biblical incident presented over half an hour or so, the words in French, and the resources of the Opéra, the Royal Chapel, and the choirs of Parisian churches enlisted to make a sweeping dramatic performance.[138] The fashion was relished by the musicians as an opportunity for displays of virtuosity, and by the public, especially those who agreed with D'Alembert's philistine verdict that 'toute musique qui ne peint rien n'est que du bruit'.[139] The worldly nature of the nominally religious themes of the *Concert spirituel* seemed to be reaffirmed when Gossec became director in 1773, for he had risen (from the inevitable choir school) as master of the music of La Popelinière and the prince de Conti. Yet his religious compositions are sincere and convincing. Religion and the arts were going their separate ways, but it was still possible for musicians to turn from vividly secular subjects and the passionate emotions of the human condition to the rarefied yearnings of religion with unselfconscious mastery.

The music of the Royal Chapel and the *Concert spirituel* was the ruling style of the Church of France. Only wealthy chapters had the resources to perform these tremendous motets, masses, and Te Deums, and then only on special occasions. But the *maître de musique* could put on the many pieces not requiring a sizeable orchestra—motets and masses for voices only, Elevations, *Misereres*, and *Tenebrae*; they adapted others, pillaged some, and in their own compositions emulated them all. Echoes of Lully, Lalande, Campra, Charpentier, and Mondonville were heard in many a provincial cathedral, recognized by those of the congregation who could afford to winter in Parisian society. Musicologists have censured the loss of true religious feeling in the 'great vocal and orchestral frescos'[140] and the abandonment of liturgical prayers for para-liturgical exercises of musical virtuosity.[141] Yet is true religious feeling an absolute ever the same? Who can be sure what devices of art and music evoke it, whether in the past or in varying social and cultural milieux today? A pious canon of Dijon thought Mondonville's motets at the *Concert spirituel* 'superior to everything I ever heard in later music',[142] without a hint of censure on grounds of worldliness; and an English visitor to Saint-Germain-l'Auxerrois in 1776 was touched to the heart: 'I heard them chanting the service, which I think the finest and most sublime devotional music in the world. I was fixed fast in a fit of devotion.'[143]

16

MONASTIC WEALTH AND THE
SOCIAL ORDER

I

You can never cross the Pont Neuf without seeing a monk, a white horse, and a whore, ran the proverb—which was hard luck on the two ladies who stood there and saw the first two but could not find the third.[1] The assumption was that, wherever one turned, a monk would be in view—or if not a monk, a nun. Voltaire's sardonic examples of the characteristic features of the civilization of his day included them: 'man will always be what he is now; this does not mean to say, however, that there will always be fine cities, cannons firing shot of 24 lbs weight, comic operas and convents of nuns'.[2] Members of the religious Orders in their habits of black, white, brown, and grey were a feature of the scene in the streets, and everyone had a monk or a nun among their relatives. Profession in the monastic life was an obvious possibility, duly weighed by families reflecting on how they could find an establishment for their sons and, more particularly, for their daughters.

Thanks to the inventories of the Revolution and the pension registers afterwards, a reasonable estimate of total numbers in 1789 can be given: 26,000 monks and 56,000 nuns.[3] Thus, religious were more numerous than parish clergy, for there were something like 60,000 curés and vicaires. The distribution of monasteries over the country was uneven; there was a concentration of monks in the borderlands of Artois, Hainault, Flanders, and Lorraine, and in Basse-Provence and Basse-Languedoc, and comparatively few in most of central France. Paris, however, was an exception, for here there were 900 monks in thirty-eight houses and 2,500 nuns in a hundred houses, about one person in religious life for every 300 inhabitants of the capital. The vast network of monastic establishments all over France was partly the legacy of the pious founders of the Middle Ages, and partly the recent creation of the zeal of seventeenth-century reformers. Of the hundred houses of women in Paris, only eight were created before the seventeenth century, and only eight from the century's end to the French Revolution. In the diocese of La Rochelle, in 1648 there were 130–80 nuns in seven houses; in 1724 there were 430 in twenty-two houses. The new foundations concentrated on education and caring for the sick and the poor. Of the seven convents of La Rochelle in 1648, all were 'cloistered', separated from secular life, and five were devoted to contemplation; of the twenty-two three-quarters of a century later, only eleven were 'cloistered', and only seven contemplative.[4] For the most part, in the eighteenth century the education of boys was in the hands of the Jesuits, Oratorians, Doctrinaires, Lazarists, Frères des Écoles Chrétiennes, and of girls in the hands of the Ursulines, nuns of the Visitation, and other 'new' congregations. The Filles de la Charité, founded by St Vincent de Paul in 1633, had spread everywhere, devoting their lives to the care of the sick with unparalleled dedication. These new and active congregations were immune from the decline in monastic recruitment which took place in the second half of the eighteenth century. Indeed, for those concerned with nursing and the education of the children of the poor, this was a golden age of new foundations.[5]

The wealth of the monasteries had been accumulated in the Middle Ages. The great institutions which had served the development of civilization in those distant days and had grown rich in the process, by now were mostly resting in the shade, leaving the new foundations to endure the toil and heat of the day. There were exceptions both ways, but this was the general picture. Pressures operating in the eighteenth century helped to ensure that the rich grew richer and the poor were kept down. Landed property conferred a security which even maladministration could not entirely undermine. The tendency was for agricultural rents to rise; this was true of tithe also, and it was the medieval foundations generally which enjoyed it. The pattern was uneven: in the diocese of Sens the income of one abbey quadrupled, while that of another remained stationary. Yet the general tendency was firm. The revenues of Sainte-Croix of Bordeaux tripled between 1730 and 1790. Saint-Aubin of Angers had a steady, small rise from 1720 to 1760, then 'an extraordinary explosion of land rent', amounting to a doubling in the next thirty years.[6] And, given landed possessions, it was often possible to devise some new method of exploitation. The monks of Sainte-Croix, always in debt, set up a rope factory and three sugar refineries, and, like the Cistercians of Beaune and the Antonists of Bar, they developed their wine trade, exporting their *vin blanc* to the Muslim Levant in bottles labelled 'eau minérale de

Sainte-Croix'.[7] The Discalced Carmelites of the rue de Vaugiraud in Paris owned a strip of urban land on which they built five mansions, leasing them out at about 7,000 livres a year each.[8] In 1723, the Benedictines of Liesses, realizing that the iron masters of Hainault were in a ring to keep down the price of the wood they bought from the abbey, set up furnaces themselves. Poor Dom Gérard had to stay in Paris for three years directing the lawsuits which ensued, distributing cheeses, snuff-boxes, and cash (and once a whole wild boar) as presents. 'To me the town is a prison and solitude is paradise,' he wrote, and he died there before he knew his case was won.[9] The Cistercians of Silvanes took advantage of the thermal springs on their lands to set up a hotel and two bathing places, getting Dr Malrieu in 1722 to certify their waters as 'containing chlorine, iron and sulphur, suitable for delicate, emaciated and weak persons, invalids and all those suffering from melancholy'.[10] And in emergencies, like a collapsing building, it was possible to ask royal permission to have a felling of timber.[11]

It was different with the newer institutions whose income was not safely derived from land. Disaster befell many of them in 1720 with the bursting of the bubble of Law's Scheme. The borrowers, whether institutions or individuals, on whose payments of interest so many communities depended, rushed to pay off their debts in paper. The estates of Brittany did so, and ruined two convents of nuns in Rennes.[12] The abbess of Gomerfontaine, making an entry in her registers in December 1721, attached one of the worthless banknotes of Law as a warning to her successors.[13] The royal edict of Mortmain in August 1749, banning religious institutions from increasing their holdings of land, hedged in the newer monasteries from acquisitions which might have guaranteed their future; the same edict also limited monastic investment to the loans floated by the government, the Clergy of France, dioceses, towns, and provincial estates, and on these, the interest was 5 per cent, lowered to 4 per cent in 1760. Enquiries in some dioceses in the 1720s revealed the grinding poverty to which so many of the convents of nuns were subjected— as in the diocese of Autun, where the bishop reported that twelve of his eighteen houses were running at a loss, and two more were just breaking even.[14] In 1727, the Royal Council set up a Commission de secours to rescue poor houses, but it seems to have been more inclined to propose suppressions than to provide financial help.

Reliable figures for incomes of religious houses are hard to establish. The religious and their superiors always had reasons to conceal affluence, and sometimes poverty as well. In 1727, the Dominicans of Bordeaux, hoping for royal help, said they had a deficit of 3,000 livres a year; faced with a threat of suppression, they discovered a 6,000 livres surplus.[15] Some apparently brave rent rolls had heavy charges to meet, like repairs to churches in parishes where tithe was levied and payments of the *congrue* to dependent curés. Even so, lack of precision does not invalidate broad comparisons, and everywhere we see a yawning divide between the rich and the poor houses.

In the diocese of Metz there was a massive concentration of wealth in the four great abbeys of the Congregation of Saint-Vanne, two Cistercian abbeys, a house of Chartreux, another of Prémontrés, a house of canonesses, and the abbey of Benedictine nuns of Saint-Glossinde; outside this charmed circle, the monastic scene was one of subsistence revenues running down to sheer penury.[16] In the diocese of Quimper, seven abbeys of men averaged 28,000 livres each, one of nuns had 5,000, and all the other houses were about 1,000 livres or less.[17] The contrast was stark in the monasteries crowded together in a provincial town. In Angers, the landed estates coming down from the Middle Ages were held by three Benedictine abbeys of Saint-Maur and by Ronceray, a haven for nuns of aristocratic lineage. The canons regular of the abbey of Toussaint had pretensions to grandeur which their income hardly warranted, and the Benedictine house of Lesvière was bankrupt. Of the seven houses of mendicants, four managed austerely, while the Récollets, Capuchins, and Minims were literally beggars. The Lazarists (preaching missions) and the Oratorians (running the *collège*) had arrived in the seventeenth century and had little endowment, and the Frères des Écoles Chrétiennes, invaluable teachers, had come only in 1741. Twelve Orders of women had established their convents since 1600, and of these, only the Ursulines were well off, having got their investments in land. The sisters caring for the sick, impotent, and penniless in three huge charitable institutions were short of resources (though some medieval endowments had fallen to the *hôtel-Dieu*). Seven of the twelve convents had been ruined by Law's Scheme in 1720, and struggled thereafter to survive; two (one for converted Protestant girls, now a hostel, and another of fallen women) never really became solvent again.[18]

The monasteries were wealthy—riches disproportionately divided as between individual Orders and houses, with little relation to social usefulness or service to religion, excessive in comparison with the income available to support the parochial ministry, and constituting an absurd proportion of the resources of the nation. Great riches create envy, and their misuse gives excuse for confiscation. By the eighteenth century, in a quiet way this had already happened; a comprehensive system to redistribute monastic income had come into being, a system operated by the Crown in the interests of the aristocracy.

II

By the Concordat with Rome of 1516, the king named the abbots of most of the regular abbeys of men in his kingdom. Exceptions were the seven houses which were the headquarters of their Order, as were Cîteaux and Grandmont, the four chief Cistercian daughter-houses, and Sainte-Geneviève at Paris, whose right to elect was confirmed by letters patent in 1626.[19] Also, up to 1764, the Benedictines of Saint-Maur made triennial elections to five major abbeys, but in that year the parlement of Paris overturned their right and transferred the nominations to the Crown. In Hainault, Flanders, Artois, the Cambrésis, and Alsace, provinces incorporated in metropolitan France after the Concordat, election by the monks remained the rule.[20] On very rare occasions, the king, by arbitrary fiat, imposed a cardinal or a prince of the blood royal on one of them; in these cases, the parlement and estates of Flanders insisted that the bulls of appointment contain the phrase, 'for this time only and without constituting a precedent'. Any election by the monks was supervised by a royal commissioner, who had the power to exclude individuals from voting if they were not French subjects, and the king's final warrant of confirmation was required. A cardinal appointed to an abbey whose headship was theoretically reserved to a monk had no power in the affairs of the whole Order;[21] priories in France depending on monasteries in the Low Countries were not at the Crown's disposal, but those in the Low Countries depending on French houses were. But an accumulation of legal rulings had defined most of the cases, and on the *feuille des bénéfices* at Versailles there were something like 815 abbeys and 280 priories for the aristocracy to intrigue for, and quite a number of others if those of small value are included.[22]

Usually, the king appointed an ecclesiastic who was not a monk—an *abbé commendataire*, holding the abbacy *in commendam*, that is, having the title and the revenue without being qualified to perform the duties. By the canonical rules,[23] the person nominated had to be at least 23 years of age and accept the obligation to proceed to priestly orders within a year; he must recite the offices of the breviary daily and wear clerical dress. These rules were ignored. All an *abbé commendataire* needed by way of qualification was to have become technically an ecclesiastic by being tonsured—a lock of his hair snipped off by the bishop at any time from the age of 7. Once tonsured, it was possible to hold benefices which did not involve the cure of souls, without any question of an obligation to celibacy or restriction of profession (though once an ecclesiastical benefice was obtained, it was not possible to bear arms without either renouncing it or obtaining a papal dispensation). Run-of-the-mill applicants for an abbey would improve their chances of getting one—or at least one that was fairly rich—if they proceeded to the priesthood, taking 'les derniers engagements'.[24] But influential candidates were awarded vast abbatial incomes on the strength of the tonsure alone, without pretence of any other tincture of religion.

The richest abbeys went to the great aristocrats. The *Almanach royal* for 1789 records their names, families more prestigious than most of those listed as holding bishoprics: Tilly, d'Estrées, La Rochefoucauld, Rohan, Vintimille, Chabannes, Crillon, Montesquieu. There was no question of the rules prohibiting the accumulation of benefices applying—a courtier would look back nostalgically at the thrill of having begun his accumulation, 'my first abbey'.[25] True, if some huge benefice came along, it became only decent to surrender a few minor ones. When he was young and well thought of at Court because his two brothers had just distinguished themselves on the battlefield, the abbé de Broglie was given the abbey of Vaux-de-Cernay with 7,500 livres. Two years later, in 1714, another (worth 13,000 livres) came his way. Then, after being agent of the Clergy of France from 1710 to 1720, he was rewarded with another worth 30,000 livres.[26] The story went that he had recommended a certain wine to the regent and sent him a present of 300 bottles. After estimating the costs of the original purchase, storage, and transport, Orléans said, 'the total is just right: the abbey of Mont-Saint-Michel'. Twenty years afterwards, to the astonishment of the courtiers, the abbé retired from society to live in his abbatial mansion at Vaux-de-Cernay, where he daily attended the offices of the monks. Had he been converted, or was he just saving to pay his debts? Vaux-de-Cernay was only six leagues from Versailles, so he would not lack for sophisticated company. Broglie was a priest and a doctor of theology, a churchman who preferred not to be tied down in a bishopric. A better—indeed, the classical—example of an unspiritual aristocrat waxing rich on ecclesiastical funds is his contemporary, Louis de Bourbon Condé, comte de Clermont, son of the prince de Condé and Mlle Nantes, daughter of Louis XIV and Mme de Montespan. With such a lineage, bulls for abbatial appointments rained on his once-tonsured locks—Bec, Saint-Claude, Marmoutier, Saint-Nicolas-des-Champs, and two others by the age of 13, and one more to top up at the age of 23. He surrendered three of these when the immense revenues of Saint-Germain-des-Prés came to him in 1737.[27] Rumour had it that he now had 300,000 livres a year, though in fact he had more than double this. Authorized by the Pope to bear arms without renouncing his benefices, he played the general in the French armies. Galloping back from the rout of Crefeld, he met the officer in charge of the baggage train. 'Have you seen any fugitives?' 'Non, Monseigneur, vous êtes le premier.' His harem in Paris was recruited principally from the Opéra; Mlle Carmago was succeeded by Mlle Le Duc, notorious for her parade down the Bois de Boulogne in Holy Week, glittering with diamonds and in a blue and gold carriage drawn by six tiny horses. The nearest he came to performing an ecclesiastical function was to build a marble mausoleum for his pet monkey McCarthy.

Vast revenues drew high-born and scandalous applicants. But for the most part, the system worked more decently. Bishops were always awarded supplementary income, those from the poorer dioceses because they needed them, those from the richer because they were from the great aristocratic families which expected unlimited largesse. In a distribution of ten abbeys in April 1745, Louis XV gave four to bishops, two to canons, two to *grands vicaires*, one to the French representative at Rome, and one to an ecclesiastical courtier.[28] According to the examples chosen, the system was a realistic redistribution of monastic revenues for the benefit of the wider church, or a pool of undeserved sinecures for the aristocracy. In the second half of the century, of the three Benedictine abbeys of Angers, the richest, Saint-Aubin, was held by the bishop of Sées, whose see provided an inadequate income; Saint-Serge was a perquisite of the bishop of Angers, who was in the middle-income episcopal range; and Saint-Nicolas was one of several benefices held by the abbé de Mostuejouls, a court chaplain. The Mostuejouls illustrate the way in which aristocratic families provided for themselves by decorous inroads into ecclesiastical wealth: the eldest son inherited the estate, the second son was a chaplain at Versailles, the third was a canon of the exclusively noble chapter of Saint-Julien de Brioude, and a daughter was a noble canoness of Remiremont.[29] The abbé François-Xavier Talbert, *grand vicaire* of Lescars, won a dozen

academy prizes for essays and poetry, including the Academy of
Dijon award on the origin of inequality (he suppressed his printed
version when he read Rousseau's). Yet he was so poor that he had
to sell his prize medals to survive. Who, then, could begrudge him
the income from the priory of the Mont-aux-Malades at Rouen,
leaving him free to follow his vocation as a preacher, which took
him twice to Paris to deliver the prestigious panegyric of Saint-Louis
before the Academy?[30] By contrast, who could defend the abbatial
revenues of Saint-Vaast in Flanders going to Rohan, bishop of the
wealthy see of Strasbourg and *grand aumônier* to the king? They came
to 52,000 livres a year when he took over, and he went to law and
got much more. Yet in 1749, the broad acres of Saint-Vaast, accumulated over more than a thousand years, found no aristocrat willing to be abbot, and Dom Vigor de Briois, one of the monks, took
over. It was because the lofty spire of the abbey church, long
tottering, had finally collapsed in February 1741, demolishing the
roof of the chancel. Repairs, the responsibility of the abbot, would
cost 2,800,000 livres. Dom Briois died in 1780, having restored the
church and reorganized the monastic revenues. Another Rohan
took over the role of titular abbot, now that it was profitable again.[31]

It was an illustration of the power of the aristocratic grip on the
State that the king so generally gave away, by the *commende*, so much
of the revenues of the abbeys of his kingdom, for he had other means
of confiscating monastic wealth which operated in parallel and could
easily have been extended. Just as, by the *régale*, the Crown drew the
revenues of bishoprics during vacancies, in the same way, appointment to an abbey could be suspended, putting the abbot's income,
as the phrase went, 'aux économats'. Thus in 1745, it was agreed to
put several abbeys *aux économats* to pay for the rebuilding of the
parish church of Saint-Louis at Versailles, and in 1750, the 50,000
livres a year of the abbey of Ligny was annexed for repairs to other
parish churches.[32] The king's faithful subjects throughout the realm
kept asking him for a share of this windfall income for useful projects. Thus, the University of Angers in 1762 applied for extra
endowments for a *collège* to replace that of the Jesuits of La Flèche,
asking the king to 'grant, for a fixed number of years, priories and
other benefices which are under the *économat* or which might come
under it—this would be sufficient to fulfil the object we propose'.[33]
Abbeys also had to pay an annual tax, the *droit d'oblat* for the maintenance of the old soldiers in the Invalides.[34] Originally, an *oblat* was
a royal pensioner granted the right of free residence in a monastery,
and a few superannuated campaigners are still found enjoying this

privilege as late as the mid-eighteenth century. But for the most part, the tax had replaced the obligation of direct hospitality. As the boundaries of France extended, so the tax followed to other monasteries, being imposed on those of Lorraine in 1768. This was the year in which the levy was raised to 300 livres a year on institutions with incomes of over 2,000 (75 livres a year on those of under 1,000). It was a trivial fee for rich foundations, but onerous for poor ones. The king was also entitled to grant a pension to be levied on the income of a nominated religious house. Occasionally, the money was directed to a respectable ecclesiastical use, like Saint-Vaast having to furnish 3,000 livres a year to a convent of nuns in Tournai. More often, it was a matter of conferring personal favours, with the aristocracy ever watchful to pounce for the lion's share. The duc de Luynes kept noting in his diary the awards as they became known at Versailles:[35] the monks of Saint-Amand elect a new abbot, but the king takes the opportunity to slap 38,000 livres worth of extra pensions on their house in addition to the old ones; the abbé de Castries gets a Cistercian abbey, but 7,000 of his 20,000 livres revenue is already appropriated for pensions; a converted Swedish nobleman living in Rome is given 6,000 a year from Saint-Germain-des-Prés; M. de Saint-André for long has had a pension on an abbey in Flanders, yet he does not belong to any order of chivalry—how can he be regarded as sufficiently distinguished to qualify? The king's will was sufficient to guarantee the worthiness of the recipients to have the money of the Church, a guarantee that was not transferable. Thus the law-books rejoiced in the case of Charles Gabrielli, aged 11, in 1765 given a pension of 1,500 livres on a priory; being hard up, he sold it to a lady who wanted an investment income; but the monastery refused to pay her; the affair went up through the courts to the parlement, which cancelled the transaction as simony.[36]

Another, more drastic way in which monastic wealth was diverted to other uses was by 'union des bénéfices'.[37] There were safeguards: an enquiry *de commodo et incommodo* with the appearance of the interested parties, royal letters patent to be registered, and if the cure of souls was involved, the diocesan bishop to be asked for his consent. On the other hand, if the government was carrying on a programme of reform, the necessity for a 'union' was taken for granted, and the king could act by arbitrary fiat. If a new diocese was planned, the first thing was to look for an abbey church for the cathedral and its buildings for an episcopal palace.[38] A bishop in a poor see could expect an abbey *in commendam* to see him through, but he might also try to unite one of his abbeys to the see in perpetuity for the benefit of his successors. He could also try for a union to bolster the income of his seminary or some other diocesan institution. But it was not easy to override vested rights. In 1781, the archbishop of Lyon got the priory of Savignieu (Forez) for the Oratorian *collège* at Montbrison, but the holder of the *commende* had to keep his revenues for life.[39] Massillon at Clermont tried for years to get the Benedictine abbey of Ébreuil for a seminary, putting in his nephew as abbot, a Trojan horse within the defences; he failed, but his successor made the building into a hospital when the number of monks fell to four.[40] A union might involve the suppression of the monastic house concerned, or it might just be the abbot's revenue that was taken over—as at the abbey of Saint-Jean at Laon, where the abbatial manse was given in 1756 to the new chapel being built at the École Militaire.[41] Generally speaking, unions were devised to put monastic wealth to a better use, whether within the Church or on its margins; but aristocratic greed being what it was, it was not impossible for a useful institution to be wound up to finance a sinecure.[42]

A commendatory abbot generally contrived to get half and often more of the revenues of the institution on which he was imposed. Reports submitted by the monastic houses of Normandy between 1723 and 1727 show the immensely rich abbey of Fécamp yielding 140,000 livres a year to its abbot and 138,840 to the community, while typical submissions from more ordinary houses show figures of 30,000 to the holder of the *commende* and 10,000 to the monks, ranging down to 10,000 as against 1,200. There are few examples of the community retaining the larger share, and there are complaints from some of the priors that they are being penalized by the unrealistic assumption that an allocation of 350 livres per head per year is enough for monks to live on.[43] Voltaire, who had a specialist anticlerical line in crocodile tears, professed to lament 'the fearful lot of a monk whose house is rich', since he will continually compare his own 'misery' to the 'opulence' of the abbot and the officials, and enviously curse the day he took his vows.[44] In fact, the monks in many of the great abbeys lived in some splendour, and Voltaire was the first to notice it. Even so, it is true that the *commende* did reduce some houses to penury and compelled them to limit their intake. In most monasteries, there was an established threefold division of revenues,[45] the abbot and the monks each having a share, and a further allocation to the *tiers lot*, which covered the *charges*—that is, repairs and a whole diversity of routine expenditure. The division might be traditional, or agreed by negotiation (*partage à l'amiable*); at any time however, one of the parties could go to the law courts asking for a *partage judiciare*. This possibility helped to bring about an equilibrium, the side which was doing best out of present arrangements making concessions to avoid the hazards of a major redistribution. From the monks' point of view, the best arrangement was to persuade their abbot to accept a fixed pension and leave the administration to them—after all, they had the local knowledge to extract the best terms from farmers and building contractors. Under the Regency, the abbé Du Bos was given the abbey of Notre-Dame de Ressons (Rouen); he had the abbot's share and control of the *tiers lot*, but for a quiet life he gave it all up for a guaranteed 2,000 livres a year.[46] On the other hand, an abbot, if he could arrange for the care of the administrative details, was likely to extract more if he kept the *tiers lot* in his own hands or, indeed, kept everything. The Maurists of the abbey of Ferrières accepted a fixed annual sum of 9,000 livres, on which they lived reasonably well, but their abbot was pocketing three times as much in a good year and shamefully neglected their buildings.[47] When a *partage* took place, or adjustments were made to it, there were a multitude of legal precautions the monks had to take. Under certain conditions, lands allocated to their 'claustral offices', like cellarer, were exempt from the *partage*—if they could establish the documentation to prove the case; it was up to them to push into the *tiers lot* as many things as possible—the library, the porters' wages, clerical taxation, hospitality, as well as repairs, and the repairs needed to be defined, whether 'minor' or 'maintenance' or 'major', preferably all of them. Otherwise, they would receive letters like the one sent by the archbishop of Aix to his abbey of Montmorel in 1741, refusing to be responsible 'for all the panes of glass broken by neglect, for paving a church that never has been paved, and for rebuilding buildings burned down, not by fire from heaven, but by your imprudence'.[48] And there was the problem of keeping the holder of the *commende* to his contractual obligations. On the death or resignation of a titular, like as not there would be a backlog of neglected repairs, possibly even going back to his predecessor—not just the monastery buildings, but farmhouses, wells, mills, aqueducts, winepresses, and local churches all over the estates.[49] If the bill came to too much, the heirs would renounce the inheritance. The new man coming into the abbacy *in commendam* would have to weigh up the gamble: he had to manage to live long enough to begin to scrape up a profit from an estate in dilapidation.[50] The monks had the consolation, such as it was, of knowing that it was the new abbot who had to pursue the litigation against his predecessor or the heirs, but this did not seal the leak in their dormitory roof or prevent the revenue of the estates from declining. The good Maurists of Ferrières, having jogged along for thirty years on their 9,000 livres a year from the distant chaplain to the duc d'Orléans, in 1780 were faced with the imminent collapse of their buildings; their new abbot, the bishop of Pamiers, had to arrange for demolitions and raise a large mortgage.[51]

A commendatory abbot might go and live in his benefice. When Huet resigned the bishopric of Avranches in 1699, the Court gave him Fontenay, and he soon had his nephew there putting the abbatial mansion in order, right down to having the fountains playing and reliable locks on the cellar doors.[52] Or perhaps he would make his abbatial mansion a hostel for retired priests, or a country resort for his holidays. But mostly, he was an absentee. The hard-up Benedictines of Saint-Gildas of Rhuys in Brittany, accustomed to never seeing their nominal head, had long ago incorporated his house into their living quarters—great was their chagrin when, in 1740, the abbé de Villeneuve announced that he wanted to occupy it; they had to build him a new one.[53] But continued absence did not make an abbot any the less determined to maximize his income. If he allowed the monks to administer the property in consideration of a pension, it would be by a lease for a limited term, to be put up in line with increases in agricultural rents at the renewal. If the monks would not pay more, there would be threats of the law and the *partage judiciaire*. Sometimes, a succession of abbots went along quietly, with their incomes being gradually increased by agreement. François-Charles de Béringhen d'Armainvilliers agreed with the Maurists of Sainte-Croix of Bordeaux in 1713 for 7,000 livres; Montmorency-Laval in 1743 improved the figure to 9,000. Growing dissatisfied, in 1754, he asked for the *partage*, but proceedings at law were inconclusive, and he resigned the abbey when he became bishop of Metz in 1760. Buisson de Beauteville, bishop of Alais, agreed a new lease, increased in 1770 to 10,400 livres a year. Two more abbots followed, and under the second, a *vicaire général* of Rouen, a *partage* was conceded by mutual agreement in 1787; it was never carried out.[54] By contrast, there was often great acrimony. Claude de Saint-Simon at the age of 20, in 1716, got the abbey of Saint-Pierre at Jumièges; he promptly broke the old agreement dating back to 1545, and demanded payment for every tree cut down since that time, struck the cellarer with his cane, and forced him and the prior to take refuge in other Benedictine houses; he insisted that the abbey dig deep into its capital to build a splendid new dormitory adorned with his coat of arms; as a result, the community had to reduce its numbers, leaving the new building half empty.[55] Still, there were worse cases of exactions: there are examples of poor houses being forced to close altogether.[56]

The incidence of monastic wealth was so unjust that it was impossible to argue against the principle of redistribution. According to good churchmen like the abbé Fleury, the ecclesiastical historian, the most appropriate use for the vast monastic surpluses was to make better provision for the secular clergy. In so far as the *commende* did this and contributed to pastoral efficiency, even austere Jansenists approved of it, plurality of benefices included. The stern Jansenist bishop of Agde, who died in 1702, asked pardon in his last testament for having two abbeys: he had prayed for grace to surrender them, but never had, for he made good use of the revenues, and did not wish to let them fall into less scrupulous hands.[57] But the *commende* was used essentially to provide for the aristocracy, to give supplementary incomes to members of great families, whether or not in high ecclesiastical office, and to provide respectable support for the younger sons of provincial nobles. As such, local opinion condemned it, since money which should have been spent where it was earned, for the benefit of trade or to provide alms to the poor, was siphoned off and spent elsewhere, more particularly in Paris.[58] And more and more, the sheer unfairness of the aristocratic grip on the wealth of the country rankled. In 1773, a pamphlet, *De l'usage qu'il conviendroit de faire du revenu des abbayes qui sont en commende*, proposed the abolition of the whole system: let the monks run their own estates, and let the king oblige them to pay pensions to maintain poor clergy, hospitals, seminaries, and good works of every kind.[59] Here spoke the charitable and egalitarian sentimentality of the latter years of the *ancien régime*. Yet the opposing theory of the rights of the nobility continued to flourish—not those of the great aristocrats, which were indefensible—but those of the hard-up provincial nobles, especially in areas where the customary law prescribed the division of heritages, resulting in families of ancient lineage inexorably slipping downwards into the ranks of the peasantry. To rescue them, Cardinal Fleury had thought of turning over the income of Saint-Germain-des-Prés to form a cadet school. Barbier heard the news and, cynical and envious bourgeois as he was, welcomed it: he accepted that provincial nobles needed help to educate their children.[60] Another cardinal, Bernis, looking back on how important to him had been his admission to the noble chapter of Lyon, reflected how, had he been a royal minister longer, he would have taken a good deal of monastic revenues to found more noble chapters, both of men and of women—and he would have ensured better endowments for canonries for the old nobility as against the new, to free them from the necessity of accepting marriages with rich commoners.[61] The archbishop of Reims in 1787 wanted all communities of monks in his diocese to sacrifice an annual sum in perpetuity to provide for the sons of poor nobles—giving them places in *collèges* and cadet schools and settlement grants for a start in life—and the houses of nuns were to make similar sacrifices for the daughters. 'The nobility, according to the constitution of the State', he said, 'has not the resources of the bourgeoisie or the people.'[62] It was a remarkable statement, on the very eve of the Revolution, of the divine right of a social class to be subsidized to maintain its status.

III

An abbot holding by the *commende* could take solemn possession of his church,[63] kiss the altar, sit in the highest stall, be presented with holy water, and wafted with incense—and, if in priestly orders, could even wear a pectoral cross; not that these privileges were ever exercised by the vast majority of Crown appointees. But he was legally prohibited from having anything to do with the internal discipline of the monastery: this was in the charge of a claustral prior elected by the monks (though some bishops who held a *commende* in their own diocese tried to claim the right to appoint).[64] There was, however, one Order, half-monastic, half-chivalric, whose vast income was monopolized by the sons of the aristocracy in a different fashion—by taking the vows and performing the obligations, in this case, the duty of waging war against the infidel.

The knights of St John of Jerusalem, a crusading Order of Hospitallers dating from the end of the eleventh century, had their headquarters at Malta, their base for warfare against the Turks and the Barbary corsairs.[65] The king of France regarded them as under his protection, and as providing a training school for his navy; their estates all over the country also furnished incomes and pensions for his naval officers. However, the Order of Malta, commonly so called, was jealous of its international status.[66] Of the seven *langues* (or *nations*) into which it was divided, three were French (Provence, Auvergne, and 'France'), but the other four were Italy, Germany, Castille, and Aragon. Of the three grand masters elected from 1734 to 1775, two were Spaniards and one Portuguese, and when a

Frenchman was elected in 1775, he was Emmanuel de Rohan, who was not *persona grata* at Versailles, since he served the duke of Parma, his father having fled from France after being involved in the Breton conspiracy of 1720. The lands of the Order in France, with their accompanying feudal dues and ecclesiastical tithes, were divided among 263 *commanderies*; these were grouped into *grands prieurés*, and these in their turn were units within the three *langues*. By contract, State and ecclesiastical taxation were paid by lump sums on favourable terms, coming to less than 200,000 livres a year, and half a million had to go annually to headquarters in Malta. This left five and a half million livres to reward the knights who rose to occupy the *commanderies*.

To become a *chevalier de Malte* required a minimum of four quarters of nobility on both the paternal and maternal side. There were exceptions, though they were few. It was possible to join, without proofs of nobility, as a *servant d'armes* and be promoted for distinguished services. Such a one, an exception in every way, was the French artist Favray, who was invited to Malta in 1744 to decorate churches and paint portraits, and rather more than thirty years later was made a knight by grand master Rohan. Towards the end of the *ancien régime*, wealth also came to make a difference, and old families accustomed to providing for their sons in the *commanderies* complained of the newly ennobled creeping in.[67] A young aristocrat might join the Order as a page of the grand master at the age of 12 or, more usually, wait to the age of 17 or 18 and go to Malta as a *caravaniste*. Each *langue* had its *auberge*, all fine seventeenth-century buildings, and here the young men lived a collegiate existence, playing billiards, fighting duels, and swaggering in cafés in their uniform of white breeches and red coats with yellow facings, occasionally being called out for forays at sea in the galleys. Finally, with splendid ceremonies, came investiture as a knight of the Order of St John of Jerusalem. The vow of celibacy was optional. The silver and enamel cross of the Order, worn round the neck on a ribbon of black watered silk, had three branches for the majority of knights who chose to preserve the right to marry; for the austere minority it had four branches and a white cross sewn on to the coat on the left-hand side.[68] The idea of a gallant crusader who had renounced the pleasures of the world was one to haunt the imagination of the age of *sensibilité*. The chevalier d'Anceny who kills Valmont in the duel in the denouement of the *Liaisons dangereuses* goes back to Malta to observe his vows, live separated from the world, and try to forget. And in real life there was the romantic story of the chevalier de

Boufflers, vowed to celibacy, who in 1778, at the age of 40, met Eléonore, comtesse de Sabran, a love that endured.[69]

Five years after investiture, a chevalier was eligible for a *commanderie* in his own *langue*. This could come eventually by seniority, or by promotion, depending on the grand master, the local *grand prieur*, and on influences from Versailles. *Commanderies* varied greatly in income. In the *prieuré* of Saint-Gilles in the *langue* of Provence, there were fifty-five of them with an average income of 18,500 livres each, but while Valence was worth 26,000, Valdrôme was farmed, in 1782, for a mere 4,800—hence, it was usually occupied by a *servant d'armes*. Every five years or so, a visitation was supposed to be made, a 'visite d'améliorissement' to test if the knight in occupation was worthy to be moved to a more lucrative post. But promotion tended to come slowly. Gaillard d'Agoult was at Poël-Laval in Dauphiné from 1748 to 1780 with revenues which rose little higher than 8,000 a year before he was offered the *commanderie* of Beaulieu with more than double the income.[70] The knights had the reputation of being harsh landlords. This was partly because most of them collected two sets of impositions which were often levied by different people—feudal dues and ecclesiastical tithe, and partly because nobles tended to be more exigent than monks of the religious Orders proper. Gaillard d'Agoult, with one-third of his revenues in tithe and one-third in seigneurial incidents, was in perpetual dispute with the inhabitants of Dieulefit (half of them being Protestants), and two other communities where he administered property joined with them to oppose him in lawsuits. His was a poor *commanderie*, but the bailli de Mirabeau (father of the revolutionary), who enjoyed 60,000 livres a year from Sainte-Eulalie, levied *champart* at one sheaf in every four to seven, tithe at one in ten, and the *prémice* at one in six—or so his peasants told the traveller Richeprey.[71] So much for 'l'ami des hommes'.

Gaillard d'Agoult had a great uncle who was *grand prieur* of Saint-Gilles and a brother who was a *commandeur* at Valence. This was typical: seafaring families of the nobility looked to the Order of Malta to support their sons in their naval careers. It was natural for the reforming abbé de Saint-Pierre to include in his project for 'perpetual peace' a scheme for a European fleet to burn out the North African pirates, for he had two brothers and a cousin who were squadron commanders in the Mediterranean.[72] Pierre André de Suffren followed two paternal uncles to Malta, served in both the Maltese galleys and the French navy, and at his death was drawing 58,000 livres income from his three *commanderies*.[73] These and other *chevaliers de Malte* form a picturesque gallery of adventurers—living dissolutely on their *commanderies* or bombarding the ports of Algiers and Tunis, writing from their ships to Rousseau or defending Voltaire in a literary society, languishing in the Bastille for verses describing Mme de Pompadour as a 'bloodsucker', taking up botany, and proposing the colonization of Guiana.[74] The marquis d'Éguilles, the future champion of the Jesuits before the parlement of Aix, was a *caravaniste* at Malta in his youth, and jumped ship in Sicily in a fit of pious fervour, attempting to join a local house of friars.[75] Claude de Rouvray de Saint-Simon (nephew of the writer of the memoirs) began as an Augustinian friar, fled to England and married, then got into the Order of Malta (against all the rules), was the hero of a naval engagement, became a *grand prieur* and the possessor of four *commanderies* and ended up as a diplomat.[76] Thus, a crusading Order devoted originally to driving the infidels from Jerusalem became the support of the life-style of French noble families and a major contributor to the efficiency of the French navy. And to draw an income as a *commandeur* or a *grand prieur* did not preclude a chevalier from holding the revenues of an abbey *in commendam* as well. A call for public prayers addressed to all the *langue* of France resounded with sonorous titles which are also attributions of sources of income. 'Jean-Philippe, Chevalier d'Orléans, Grandee of Spain, Great Cross of the Order of Jerusalem, Grand Prieur of France, General of the galleys of the King, Lieutenant-General of the Seas of the Levant, Commendatory Abbot of the abbey of Saint-Pierre d'Auvilay . . .'[77] He was fitting out his flagship and maintaining his state from the endowments bestowed on the Church in the pious Middle Ages.

IV

It was even more difficult for the poorer nobles to provide for their daughters than for their sons. A young man could join the army, taking the *brevet* of lieutenant and hoping to rise to lieutenant-colonel or even to *maréchal de camp*, the highest of the genuine fighting ranks. There was also the navy, preferably by way of the Order of Malta. Though trade was banned by the so-called law of *dérogéance*, it was possible to manage the estates or the finances of some great man. Marriage, judiciously arranged, could create a comfortable establishment, trading rank for dowry. And there was always the Church, possibly going no further than the tonsure and the *commende*. The girls had nowhere to turn but marriage, and the difficulty here was that a dowry had to be given, not received. Otherwise, the Church was the indispensable resource, and this meant taking religious vows. But, for a favoured minority, by definition from the more distinguished families which needed the help least, there was a less demanding way of gaining support from ecclesiastical revenues. All over France, but particularly in Lorraine, Franche Comté, Alsace, Hainault, Flanders, and Brabant, there were chapters of noble canonesses, providing staging-points where girls could await the arrival of eligible men and, failing a suitable match, could stay on for the rest of their lives. Though there were some differences in their rules, a standard pattern was: an abbess with two or three dignitaries, all taking the vow of chastity, and *chanoinesses prébendées* holding stalls, who vowed to obey the statutes of the house but did not accept the obligation of chastity and could leave whenever they desired. These ladies had the right to name a 'niece' or 'coadjutrice', who would come and live there intermittently and eventually, if both parties so desired, inherit the prebendal stall. Such a chapter was, said the *Dictionnaire de Trévoux*, 'rather a seminary or a respectable retreat for girls awaiting marriage than one for those engaged in the service of God'. They have no duties, said a lawyer sardonically, but to sing the office of Our Lady, 'an occupation which has nothing difficult about it except monotony'. However, he did not disapprove. 'Today', he added, 'these chapters are regarded as more useful establishments and more reasonable ones than the greater part of other religious institutions.'[78]

To gain admission, at least four quarters of nobility on both sides of the family were required. There was a formal examination of documents: Mme de Genlis tells how, at the age of 7, on her way to be installed as a canoness of Alix, she had to wait a fortnight at Lyon until the check was completed.[79] The genealogist's verification was expensive, though once the certificate was obtained, successive children could all make use of it: of the Chateaubriands, Lucile became a canoness of l'Argentière, then of Remiremont, on the strength of the family's *preuves*; then both her brothers took the opportunity to exercise the right of being presented to the king at Court, and one of them used the documentation to join the Order of Malta (in September 1789, too late to be of use to him).[80] Even when the proofs of nobility were established, a place in a noble chapter was hard to find. The search began early, and if a girl reached the age of 12 without a promise, the father would begin to despair.[81] More than influence was normally required: it was impor- tant to find a canoness in office to act as sponsor to a 'niece' and eventually pass on the prebendal stall. At Épinal in Lorraine, Gabrielle de Spada was pushed in by ducal nomination in 1729 at the age of 15, and was named as abbess by the duke in 1735 (with a papal brief of authorization, for the canonical age was 30). When she died in 1784, she had insinuated no fewer than five of her relatives into the chapter.[82] Her successor, promoted from canoness, was Mme d'Argenteuil, and she brought in her actual niece, aged 14, to occupy the stall she was vacating. Looking back after the Revolution on these golden days of privilege, the niece gave the standard aristo-cratic explanation: her grandfather and her two maternal uncles were killed in battle—'the Church nourished, in the shelter of its altars, a small number of daughters of the most distinguished families which had shed their blood for the fatherland'.[83]

There could be no question of subjecting chapters of noble canonesses to monastic discipline: all the pressures of polite society would be exercised against it. When the bishop of Grenoble early in the century tried to reform the chapter of Montfleury, the nobles of the province protested:

The decent liberty which the aforesaid ladies have enjoyed up to the present has always been a powerful attraction to persuade girls to renounce the world and retire to this house . . . They would never think of enter-ing it if it was as frightful as the bishop of Grenoble prescribes by his ordinance, which would cause a notable prejudice to all the noble families of the province.[84]

Thus, life in these oases of quasi-ecclesiastical calm tended to be comfortable. In a few, there was scandal or rumours of scandal. The abbey of Sainte-Marie de Saint-Jean-le-Grand in the suburbs of Autun, where the inmates took no vows and came and went as they pleased, was notorious; Sainte-Marie de Saint-Andoche in the middle of town was similarly disorganized, but was more respectable, ever since the shock administered by the bishop in 1679, when he threw out trouble-makers and walled up the gates.[85] Two chapters in the diocese of Metz claimed to be exclusively under the jurisdiction of the Pope and continually engaged their bishop in litigation, until the king finally forbade them to fill any vacancies.[86] But scandal was the exception. If, in Franche Comté, Migette went on to 1789 without either community life or canonical rule, Baume-les-Dames, Notre-Dame de Battant, and Château-Chalon were decorous.[87]

Overwhelming pride and excessive comfort were the only charges which a severe moralist could make against most houses. It was, indeed, a splendid destiny to be abbess of Remiremont, by virtue of office a princess of the Holy Roman Empire, administering a revenue of over 300,000 livres, exercising jurisdiction in more than seventy-five towns and villages, patron of a hundred livings (on her death all these churches had to toll their bells for twenty-four days without stopping).[88] And it was, indeed, an unforgettable memory for a teenage girl awaiting marriage, to be installed as a canoness of Alix, received in the choir by the ladies in black silk and voluminous cloaks fringed with ermine, then proceeding to one's own house in the semicircle of gardens around the abbatial mansion, and savouring the title of 'countess'.[89] Mme de Chastenay recorded how she was received at Épinal in 1785. The twenty-one ladies preceded by the band of the garrison came to her aunt's house to fetch her. Then, in church, the questions: 'What do you seek, my daughter?' 'The bread and wine of Saint Goëry, to serve God and the Holy Virgin.' Then the biscuit and the wine, the arraying with the blue sash with its pendant cross, the ermine embroidered cloak and the black veil, with the singing of the Te Deum. Thereafter, for four or five days, nothing but balls and celebrations. Contemporaries relished the incongruity of girls playing the ecclesiastic. They noted the sister of the princesse de Montauban, Mme de Béthizy, a 'pretty canoness of Poussay', going out hunting with a musket (she fell, and it killed her), and Charlotte, sister of Président de Brosses of the parlement of Dijon at Neuville-les-Dames, 'a certain little canoness, lively and jaunty, who does not look as if she passes her time with her breviary'.[90]

Never had the French nobility schemed more ruthlessly to profit from the accident of birth than in its autumnal years, when privilege was withering into discredit. Of all their entrepreneurial efforts to annex the patrimony of the Gallican Church, the most effective was the institution of chapters of canonesses. Priests on subsistence wages said the liturgical offices, and the ladies (abbesses and dignitaries excepted) could spend most of the year elsewhere in the social whirl, looking for husbands. The royal government, which ought to have been channelling ecclesiastical surpluses to charity and education, was more concerned to satisfy aristocratic greed, and made a virtue of directing more church funds to the canonesses, as if it was a salutary reform. Neuville-les-Dames in the diocese of Belley shook off the control of the abbey of Cluny in 1710, keeping some of its lands, accumulated various priories, and in 1786 was given half the income of the abbey of Tournis; Louis XV had meanwhile conferred on the ladies the title of 'countess'.[91] In the diocese of Metz, a new chapter of ladies was founded in 1762 by annexing two old Benedictine foundations, the first abbess appointed being the sister of the royal minister Choiseul.[92] When the hospitaller Order of Saint-André-de-Viennois was suppressed in 1782, the canonesses of Vienne got its property, circumventing a plot to annex it by the Order of Malta.[93] About this time, Pierre-Louis de la Rochefoucauld, bishop of Saintes, backed by the local nobles, established a chapter of canonesses in his episcopal town, annexing the abbey of Benedictine nuns of Notre-Dame-hors-les-murs for the purpose. But he had reckoned without the formidable abbess, Mme de Parabère, daughter of the regent by his most famous mistress; by 1789 she had got the king to cancel his permission, and had the bells of her church rung for twelve hours in celebration.[94] In the same year, another noble chapter of women was created in the diocese of Saint-Flour from the abbey of Saint-Pierre de Blesle, which was already a foundation of nuns of exclusively distinguished birth, with the income of other benefices added.[95] The destruction of the privileges of the nobility and the closure of the monasteries were at hand, but the aristocratic pursuit of ecclesiastical money went on to the very end.

V

Abbeys and priories of women did not come under the Concordat, but the king had quietly arrogated to himself the right to appoint to great houses; in ineffectual protest, the Roman Daterie sent provisions omitting the reference to royal nomination and saving face by stating, imaginatively, that the nuns had elected in secret ballot by a two-thirds majority. Because of their limited revenues, most convents of nuns were outside the scope of the royal interest, so their superiors were elected or, according to varying traditions, nominated by bishops or by lay or ecclesiastical patrons. The Crown also exempted the Annonciades and certain other houses from its assumed right of appointment.[96] What interested the king and the courtiers of Versailles was, above all, the disposal of the splendid abbeys of France, with their broad acres and proud buildings. For example, there was Avenay, owning extensive vineyards in the wine country round Reims; from their profits, the church and monastery, destroyed in the fire of 1754, were rebuilt within six years. There was Notre-Dame de Jouarre, 'Jouarre-la-Noble, Jouarre-la-Riche'; one farm, seven plantations of woods, and a quarry were exploited directly, sixteen farms and many meadows were leased out and extensive tithes collected, yielding an income of 2,000 livres for every nun in residence.[97] Fontevrault, with even more extensive estates, employed a *sénéchal*, a *procureur fiscal*, and a *greffier* solely to collect its feudal dues, and one employee to levy tolls on barges passing through Saumur on the River Loire. Louis XV made the abbey even richer, exempting it and its farmers from all taxation as a reward for its nuns having brought up four of his young daughters.

Such proud and wealthy foundations were inevitably given an abbess from one of the great aristocratic families at Court. The normal rules which governed the pattern of life of nuns did not apply to these ladies. They changed the Order to which they belonged to take promotion, they would move from the headship of one house to another supposedly more distinguished, and not infrequently—normally by the device of coadjutorship—arranged for a relative to succeed them. Whether as aristocrats, nuns, or human types, these remarkable ladies deserve the attention of historians and demographers. They tended to live to a great age, and since they were sometimes very young when appointed, their reign could be prodigiously long. At Notre-Dame de Perrigne[98] in the province of Maine, Renée de Beaumanoir came to rule in 1691, transferring from the Order of Fontevrault. Her niece, Eléonore de Morell d'Aubigny, succeeded her, and was in office for nearly forty years, dying at the age of 78. Anne-Madeleine de Girard de la Chaume then ruled for twenty-seven years, dying at the age of 82. When the eccentric daughter of the regent resigned the abbey of Chelles in 1734, Anne de Clermont Gersen de Chartre followed, and was still in office fifty-five years later when the Revolution began.[99] An even longer reign was that of Charlotte-Julie de Boufflers, daughter of the *maréchal*, who at the age of 22 succeeded her aunt at Avenay in 1720, and fifty-six years later resigned in favour of a noble lady who had been held up for long as subprior in the royal abbey of Saint-Paul under the rule of her sister.[100] 'Jouarre-la-Riche', after being held successively by three ladies of the Rohan clan, fell out of the family grip when a niece destined to succeed died suddenly, and in 1738 Catherine-Henriette de Montmorin de Saint-Hérem became abbess; she was still there, aged 90 and thinking of retiring, when the Revolution came.[101] Hers was a family with a particular vocation to serve the Gallican Church, conjoined with the inclination to administer its property. Twenty-eight years earlier, after the death of her mother, her widowed father had become bishop of Aire. Her brother Gilbert succeeded to his bishopric and then in 1733 was translated to the richer one of Langres. Catherine and her elder sister Louise-Claire had meanwhile become nuns in the abbey of Clavas (Lozère) under their aunt as abbess. Louise-Claire succeeded at Clavas, then moved on three times to the abbatial manses of more distinguished houses, and finally in 1742 got the greatest prize of all, Fontevrault; here, her brother, the bishop of Langres, installed her.[102] Catherine became abbess of Cherenton (Cher) in 1737, and a year later moved up to the splendours of Jouarre. Here, in 1753, her sister from Fontevrault, grievously ill, came to join her for the last two months of her life. To this family, as for others, having an aunt or other relative in the office of abbess, acting as an initial protector and sponsor, was important. Witness the ill luck—temporary as it turned out—of Anne-Eléonore-Marie de Béthun d'Orval, who was put in an abbey under her aunt's care from the age of 3 and was professed at 16. When her aunt left to rule elsewhere, her fellow nuns persecuted her for ten years, until she went off to her sister, the abbess of Saint-Pierre of Reims; after fourteen years there, she herself became an abbess, and went to rule the Benedictines of Notre-Dame du Val de Gif.[103]

For good and for ill, the exercise of power came early to these lofty aristocratic ladies; perhaps its satisfactions helped to prolong their days. Their estates were well run and their farmers held to strict accountability. Their alms were limited—the doctor of Chelles was paid more than the poor of the village received in charity. Yet, true daughters of *grands seigneurs*, they ran their communities into debt if the maintenance of status demanded conspicuous expenditure. Their curés were kept in due subordination; no share of the monastic wealth came to augment their often meagre allowances, and they had to render attendance at processions and liturgical offices, which demonstrated the superiority of the nuns. Anyone, however exalted, who challenged the abbey's rights would be resisted in the law courts. Early on in the Regency, the abbess of Fontevrault waged a battle against the secular courts to try to prevent them judging the case of a nun accused of arson; the secular judges won, luckily for the nun, who was proved innocent, while her abbess had been intending to inflict life imprisonment on bread and water.[104] Then there was a dispute with the officers of the department of Eaux et Forêts of Poitou over the felling of some timber; then a lawsuit of thirteen years' duration against the duc de Châtillon over dues he exacted on sheep at the market (lost in the end because Richard the Lion-Heart was proved to have been on crusade at the date when he was supposed to have granted the exemption). Then another battle against the comte de Montsoreau, involving the papal documents giving him the right to go through the abbey premises every Easter Monday to visit the tomb of one of his ancestors.

An aristocratic lady established in the rule of an abbey did not regard herself as having forsaken the world: there would be coffee drinking and giving dinner parties for local notables and distinguished callers from the social round of Paris and Versailles. Gossip writers sometimes alleged sexual adventures, but the accusations were rare and lost nothing in the telling.[105] More often, complaints concerned excessive contributions to the maintenance of relatives. Sisters or sisters-in-law who came to the abbey to retire after the death of their husbands were one thing, young men of the family were another.[106] Life for the nuns of Notre-Dame d'Yerres (in the diocese of Versailles) under the last two abbesses was disrupted by worldly nephews, and at Willancourt near Abbeville, Mme de Bron gave accommodation to the chevalier La Barre, who had unsuitable friends and collected dangerous books—as his trial and condemnation to death revealed to the whole of France.[107] One of the scandals, though a touching one, under the Regency was the spectacle of the ex-*garde des sceaux* D'Argenson, in disgrace at Court, living in retirement at the convent of La Madeleine du Trainel in the faubourg Saint-Antoine, in the company of the abbess, Gilberte-Françoise Véri d'Arbonze de Villemont, his former mistress. Jesting with the novices and endless conversations with his old flame were his only pleasures—he was 'le sacristan de la Madeleine'.[108] Scandal could only go so far; except for the very greatest, a royal *lettre de cachet* would bring an end to it—as in 1773, when the abbess of L'Abbaye Blanche at Mortain was sent under police escort to the abbey of Clairet (Nogent-le-Rotrou). She had travelled around the countryside running up debts and brought herself to public notice.[109] Generally, life in the great abbeys was decorous, but it was always comfortable and, when income allowed, sometimes luxurious. There was splendour at Chelles under the regent's daughter, until she was converted, asked pardon of her nuns, and finally left her greatness to die in a Paris convent. Fontevrault gave a three-day hunting and picnic party every 1 September for the anniversary of its abbess, Sophie Gillette de Pardaillon d'Eperon.[110] At Jouarre, Mme de Montmorin de Saint-Hérem had her own *maître d'hôtel*, coachman, postilion, lackeys, chamber maids, and other servants; her nuns dined well, and drank wine brought from Champagne, and this after 1755 in a fine new refectory she built by demolishing the seventh-century cell of Sainte-Felchilde, the first abbess. It was a worldly

existence, yet Mme de Montmorin, as her nuns called her, wore a
hair shirt under her silks. The great nobles looked with satisfaction
on the provision available for their daughters, and the lesser nobles
on the lesser provision for theirs in less distinguished houses. The rest
of society could not be expected to have their enthusiasm. What
reflections arose among the inhabitants of Rest-sous-Montsoreau
when they found that Fontevrault had had a ditch specially dug to
prevent them exercising their right of felling an oak sapling for a
maypole in the abbey woods, or among those of the villages on the
banks of the Loire when they saw the boat go past flying the abbey
flag, bringing the coffee and other colonial luxuries tax-free from
Nantes?[111]

VI

Montalembert described the *commende* as the 'leprosy' of the monastic Orders. This is the indignation of a clerical historian of the nineteenth century—the monks with their sincere vocations, on the one
hand, and the aristocratic outsiders filching their revenues, on the
other. But the nobles—and, indeed, others lower in the social scale
in their turn—were gaining the use of monastic wealth, not only by
annexation, but also by infiltration, by taking monastic vows and
thereby finding an assured maintenance and niche in society. Like
everything else in eighteenth-century France, the process operated
along hierarchical lines. The monastic vocation was not general: it
was to a particular Order, and there were vast differences in life-
style. A Benedictine monk would live a collegiate life in one of the
great abbeys, dining on fish and poultry, taking relaxation at cards or
concerts of music, going on an annual holiday with a horse and an
allowance provided; a Capuchin friar, wearing the white hood of
poverty ('a mushroom on a dunghill'), went round begging. It looks
as though vocations of the Benedictine kind came from higher
classes in society than those of the Capuchin kind. But until we have
studies of recruitment, establishing the status of families by reference
to the rolls of the capitation tax, it will be difficult to be more
precise about the male religious Orders. As it happens, however, we
can go some way to categorizing the houses of women by drawing
inferences from the working of the system of the 'dowry'.

Dowries, forbidden by the Lateran Council of 1215 and the
Council of Trent, were authorized in France by the royal declaration of 28 April 1693, which limited them to houses of Orders

founded since 1600, except when the bishop allowed them because of the difficult financial position of a particular community.[112] Maximum figures, whether for lump sum payments, annual subscriptions, or gifts of furniture were also specified—limits which were usually ignored. The amounts normally required were well known, being published in the almanacs, though in negotiations between the convent bursar and the family, rebates might be granted, especially in the case of a candidate who had exceptional qualifications or important social connections. A *contrat de religion* was signed at the taking of the habit, coming into force on the day of profession two years later. The presumptive heirs had to agree, and sometimes all the nuns would vote on the admission and sign the contract.[113]

The payment of dowries could be a great burden to families. An ecclesiastic of Nantes who negotiated for a year before agreeing to pay 100 livres on behalf of his niece had a message for her inserted with the documents: 'let her remember her poor uncle who generously sacrifices his bare necessities for the good of her salvation'.[114] A country nobleman who was already paying 345 livres a year to the Ursulines of Lamballe for the support of his two aunts and another 150 for his sister, had to find a lump sum of 33,000 livres to get his daughter in—all he could do was borrow it. A good lady of Lamballe helped him by paying for the banquet which, by custom, he had to give to the nuns on the day of the profession. Another provincial noble, in Périgord, told his daughter that she would have to renounce her manifest vocation: 'for long my second daughter has been asking me to be allowed to become a nun, but I will never be in a position to be able to pay her dowry. Yet how happy I'd be if I could see one of my daughters settled for life in a convent.'[115] In times of economic hardship like the latter years of the reign of Louis XIV, recruitment to the Ursulines of Tarbes dried up—families could not afford the 2,300 livres which was their tariff.[116] The system carried on, unreformed, right to the Revolution. 'It is a crying abuse', said a *cahier* of 1789 from Périgord, 'that communities of women have got permission to exact heavy gifts in the form of dowries . . . which have become ruinous to families.'[117] In addition to the main charge, the indictment went on, they ask for the furniture of a room, the provision of robes and linen, a fee for the sacristy, and an admission banquet for the nuns, so that there are families still paying off debts to convents contracted eighty years ago.

A dowry of 1,000 livres in 1768 was exactly double what a royal edict had first prescribed as the annual salary of a parish priest, and more than three times the sum which a novelist quoted as enough to provide a wounded soldier with board, lodging, and medical attention for a year.[118] Ordinary peasant and artisan families could not afford such sums, so their daughters could only go into the few convents which asked no dowry, or if a special concession was made, for example, to a girl with a good singing voice; otherwise, the nearest they could get was to join a religious house as an unprofessed lay servant. The great abbeys were an aristocratic preserve, the ordinary convents a bourgeois one. An orator to the academy of Angers in 1770 put the situation with naïvely brutal frankness—the reason for the existence of so many religious houses in the town was 'to provide decent and honourable retreats for that numerous portion of the nation which is too well-bred to degrade itself by doing the humble tasks to which lack of income seems to condemn it'.[119]

Convents diverged widely in the amounts of money they demanded, and families had to place their daughters on the dowry scale at the points which they could afford. In Paris, the Cistercian Dames de Panthémont, whose nuns were all of noble birth and whose work was the education of girls of distinguished families, prescribed 7,000–8,000 livres. In this same bracket were the Bénédictines de la Présentation and the Ursulines (both keeping schools for daughters of the rich), the Carmelites of the Marais *quartier* (their other house in the faubourg Saint-Jacques charged less), Port-Royal, the Dames de l'Assomption of the rue Saint-Honoré, and the noble Dames du Saint-Sépulcre. A whole series of others followed. At the middle range were the Filles de Saint-Agnès, who took no permanent vows and taught the children of the poor in the *quartier* of the Halles—they charged 2,000 livres. And at the bottom of the scale came three convents which did not insist on a dowry at all: the Filles de Saint-Thomas de Villeneuve looking after prostitutes in their house of the Bon Pasteur, the Filles de la Croix, and the Bénédictines du Val-de-Grâce. In the houses of women in Angers at the end of the *ancien régime* we can see how hierarchy was recognized by everyone. The wealthy abbey of Ronceray was, in its own definition, 'for the poor noble ladies of Anjou and Maine'. It is doubtful if any were poor, but their aristocratic credentials had to be impeccable—only one girl from the town itself had ranked high enough to gain entry to its dignified splendours. For the outstanding families of local fame, the Visitation was the first choice, both for the education of daughters and for their final establishment as nuns. When little Sophie de Milscent began her school-days there in 1781, two of her aunts were members of the community, and she remembered how one of them waylaid the visiting bishop to give him a proud recital of their family genealogy. The Ursulines, both for schooling and for the monastic profession, came next in order. This completed the charmed circle: the rest of the convents came a good deal lower, though even the Bon Pasteur, a home for fallen women, asked a 1,000 livres dowry from its novices.

Parents of the appropriate social groups expected one or more of their daughters to become nuns as a matter of family policy. Providing a dowry for a suitable marriage was vastly more expensive than finding a monastic one; it was important to preserve the inheritance intact for the eldest male heir; they did not want to have too many grown-up children staying perpetually at home; they were concerned to give their daughters an assured status in life, and a secure refuge against the day when death broke up the family unit.[120] These motives, of course, did not preclude others: the desire to see their daughters usefully occupied, to preserve their virtue, and to foster their piety. The question inevitably arises: to what degree and in what forms was persuasion—or even compulsion—used? How often did children voluntarily desire for themselves what others desired for them? What was the spiritual content of vocations, the sense of responding to a divine call, as against complying with the mores and exigencies of society?

Novelists relished the theme of the forced vocation, dramatic and affording a chance to moralize—'to show fathers and mothers that they ought always to leave their children free to choose their own way of life', as the tragic story of *La Religieuse malgré elle* demonstrated.[121] There were three beautiful Tencin girls: two married without affection to escape the cloister; the youngest, Claudine-Alexandrine, forced to take vows, recorded her protest before notaries, and fought until she got a papal rescript releasing her; she then made up for lost time in a career of political, literary and erotic adventures under the Regency. There were no such consolations for Mlle de Brun, forced into the Madelonnettes of La Flèche by her father the marquis after her elopement with Henri de Mirabel in 1732. She was released from her vows when her father died fourteen years later and Henri de Mirabel came back, a hero, from the Emperor's war against the Turks. But she would not marry him, and died, sick and lonely, long afterwards, in the days of Napoleon.[122]

Crude compulsion of this kind was rare. Parents who pushed their children into convents were matched by others who enjoyed the company of their daughters and wished to keep them out. In 1747 and 1760 there were fathers and mothers applying to the court of the

Châtelet for legal injunctions to prevent their daughters from taking vows,[123] and in 1760 the marquise de Mirabeau refused to be present when her third girl was professed in the convent of Montargis.[124] Ecclesiastics who were friends of the family might sing the praises of the monastic state, but they were just as likely to give warnings against worldly or sentimental motivation. The marquise de Créquy remembered with gratitude how her aunt, an abbess, and her uncle, a bishop, backed her determination to stay in the world.[125] The procedures for admission to the religious life gave opportunities for refusal. At a preliminary enquiry, a novice had to state that her parents had not 'forced her, pressured her or solicited her'. At the vesture, when the decisive question was asked, a public refusal could be given; 'I want the key of the convent gate,' one courageous young woman is said to have replied.[126] At the final profession, there was still a possibility of refusal, though admittedly remote. And even when solemn vows were taken, there were five years within which protest could be made alleging coercion, longer, if the 'violence' had continued.[127] In the first instance, the bishop's legal registrar and the superior of the religious house sat together to study the objections; if they rejected them, the secular courts could intervene by *appel comme d'abus*.[128] In the view of the lawyers, the presumption was in favour of the applicant, for God does not want unwilling subjects, monasteries ought not to want unsatisfactory inmates, and, as for the family, inheritance problems are no more difficult than those presented when a man presumed dead returns from overseas.[129] The law-books give startling illustrations of the anti-monastic attitude of the courts—all concerning monks rather than nuns, perhaps because complaints from women were rare and their allegations less sensational. If constraint was proved, the verdict was severe on those who had exercised it. In 1769, the parlement of Paris fined a merchant and condemned him to pay 10,000 livres damages to his son, and confiscated the money he had given to a religious house for its co-operation. Even in apparently hopeless cases, the courts would rescue an individual on a technical formality. In 1763, the Grand Conseil awarded 30,000 livres compensation to the wife of an ex-Cistercian monk who had been arrested for fleeing from his Order and died in prison; there was also an equally heavy fine on the abbot of Clairvaux.[130] Ten years later, the parlement of Bordeaux released a friar from vows he had taken twenty-five years earlier. In both cases, the pretext was the unsatisfactory state of the registers of the original profession. Forcing an unwilling subject into a monastery was not as easy as novelists supposed. At the Revolution, when the doors of the religious houses were thrown open, the nuns generally wished to maintain their vocation. Making allowances for the difficulty of women deciding to start new lives, their loyalty suggests that they were in their convents willingly. Under Napoleon, 356 married nuns applied to Cardinal Caprara to have their status recognized. Of these, seventy said they had never had a true vocation, and of these fifty-five alleged family pressures, direct in the form of beatings and deprivation, indirect in wrangles over property and from the burden of sheer poverty. Though these were obvious excuses to put forward, comparatively few made use of them.[131]

Forced vocations were rare; even so, there was a general assumption among contemporaries that veiled pressures within the family operated. But it was a business not of compulsion, but of social conditioning. Girls, especially those who were plain or belonging to the group of one in every five marked by smallpox, or who knew that little or no dowry was available for them, had to make a realistic calculation of their chances of marrying and ask what the alternatives might be. Cardinal Bernis tells how his two sisters were destined for the cloister; the elder, who was beautiful, was rescued by the marquis de Narbonne-Pelet, who took her without a dowry; the younger, 'not good-looking, just good-hearted', refused to become a nun so long as her father insisted, then became one voluntarily.[132] With the dowry crucial and the class system rigid, disappointment in love was frequent, and for the sad in heart, the cloister was a refuge. This was where the star-crossed lovers in Mme de Tencin's novels ended. This simple theme achieved a degree of sophistication through the growing interest in the tragic story of Héloïse and Abélard—reading their letters in Bussy-Rabutin's translation and weeping over Colardeau's famous poem.[133] The abbé Prévost, whose romantic imaginings always had a rough, earthy foundation, warned young people against such sacrificial follies: 'when the mists of desire clear, you will find yourself alone, disconsolate, without help from God or man'. Sometimes, the family was responsible for a child choosing the religious vocation, not because of actual promptings, but simply because the parents' vices made life at home insupportable—a daughter fleeing from the threat of sexual abuse, a son fleeing from violence and cruelty.[134] Or a girl would become a nun when the family broke up after the death of a father, as happened with a daughter of Melfort, the Jacobite exile, and of André-Michel Ramsay, the Scottish adventurer.[135]

Going into a religious house was, often enough, going among friends, joining sisters and aunts and acquaintances who were there already. A girl who had attended school under the nuns might wish to stay on with the teachers she had known and trusted. It was not just family pressure which counted, but family tradition. In 1691, at the age of 12, the eldest daughter of the duc de Beauvilliers went to the convent of Montargis, and stayed on there as a nun. Six of her sisters followed, at ages ranging from 5 to 2, and all, like her, eventually took lifelong vows. An eighth girl of the family was also educated at Montargis, but left to marry her cousin, the duc de Mortemart; she had two daughters who were sent to the same convent to be educated, and they both died there as nuns in mid-century.[136] Those whose birth qualified them for entrance to prestigious abbeys might have to go far from home, but ordinary candidates for the religious life would be going to a nearby institution, well known locally and with a web of friendly contacts, even in Orders which had strict seclusion. Only in heartless families (generally the very great) were children in monasteries forgotten. Adrian de Bertier, marquis de Pinsaguel, had one daughter married and three in a convent; when he died in 1752, his will left 40 livres to each of the three nuns, 'not to be paid to their superior, but to my daughters', and when his wife the marquise died four months later, life annuities of 20 livres each came to them. Families thought in terms not so much of getting rid of children, as of finding them an establishment for life corresponding to the family dignity.

If it was a question of edging a son or daughter towards the religious life, parents could always find an ecclesiastic who would act as persuader, one of those 'accapareurs de conscience' with head on side and lowered eyes whom Mme Roland remembered with revulsion.[137] Theological treatises still put the celibate state above the married, and the contemplative life above the active. A learned Dominican drew an astonishingly selfish conclusion from these premisses and from the law of self-preservation: go into the religious life, he said, because it offers the maximum chance of salvation; 'assure your own happiness before working for that of a third party, where this can be done without injustice'.[138] An argument more in tune with eighteenth-century opinion was the appeal to duty to Church and to society. It was hardly one to win recruits to the male religious Orders, since men had so many opportunities to serve in the secular clergy and in the world in general, but it did apply to women, whose chief opportunity to serve the Church and, indeed, society through teaching and nursing, lay in religious houses. With this in mind, churchmen discussing the vocation of nuns sometimes got to the point when it seemed more natural to them for a girl to

choose the religious rather than family life—to stay in the world was
the course requiring an explanation. There is a revealing statement
in a handbook of spiritual direction of 1750. If a confessor finds a
novice who has joined a religious community for wrong reasons, or
even has been forced in, he must not attempt to get her out. There
must be a delay, to see if she may have, after all, a real vocation:
'it must not be assumed [she] is not called, for God uses various
methods to direct us to our destiny'. In such a case, the nuns would
exercise their utmost persuasion. One may doubt the novelist who
said they did so 'like soldiers finding a sort of consolation in getting
themselves companions in their misery',[139] and also doubt the tales of
their exercising compulsion, though there are examples of touting
for money from families anxious to have a daughter brought to take
the veil.[140] But there were plenty of arguments—not always elevated
ones: the dangers of childbirth, the harassments of family life, the
useful work to be done, the danger of 'shipwreck at the hour of
death'.[141] And attitude was more important than argument, and for
that we ought to turn to Marivaux's imaginative insight. The nuns
were kind; they called the novice's doubts 'temptations'; they
flattered her, and led her on until she became 'an uncomprehending
spectator' of her irrevocable engagement.[142] The collective will of
a friendly community could be persuasive, and the end proposed,
the ceremonies of vesture and profession, were picturesque and
moving—the candles, the chanting, the thrill of being the cynosure
of every eye, the farewells to the family, the crawling under the
funeral pall before the Te Deum thundered out; their uncompromising finality appealed to youth as a gesture of self-affirmation,
and their sombre undertones were haunting, exercising an attraction
Diderot understood, according with the 'profound melancholy'
which accompanied the awakening of sexual desire.

The monasteries of France in the eighteenth century show a
peculiar equilibrium between spiritual inspiration and social needs.
The aristocracy gained for its children the use of the great wealth
which had accumulated in ancient institutions, whether by blatant
annexation as in the *commende* or by infiltration as in the great abbeys
of women. Lower down the social scale, the bourgeoisie was
equally anxious to place its children. For boys, the opportunity was
one of many; for girls, the convents were indispensable establishments to provide security and an outlet for useful activity, and the
middle classes contributed by their dowries to keep the system
going.

Yet what is true as a general sociological description does not explain away the genuine spirituality of vocations. There were some startling renunciations of the world, and a great deal of dedication and devotion within the cadre of social conditioning. Spiritual inspirations do not exist in a void. 'Can molten gold be carried from place to place in anything but crucibles of iron and steel?' asked Friedrich Naumann, himself an exponent of charismatic religion. This chapter has been concerned with the base metal crucible, which the historian can describe with more evidence to hand than is available for the molten gold. Yet the gold was there.

17

THE RELIGIOUS VOCATION AND SOCIAL USEFULNESS: MEN

I

A wealthy monastery was a centre of consumption and expenditure. This was the argument used by municipal authorities when protesting against commendatory abbots annexing half the income and spending it far away. Certainly, a great abbey provided employment. This was more especially so in a century when there was lavish architectural reconstruction. In some places, a 'school' of artists and craftsmen gathered around the long-continued building works, their favourite themes and technical devices being evident in the churches and châteaux of the neighbouring countryside. The number of permanent servants, if funds allowed, was sure to be excessive. The eight monks of the Cistercian abbey of Pereigne in 1789 had two cooks, a baker, two porters, a brazier, a gardener, two cowherds, a boy to look after the guest-house, three women (housekeeper, sewing maid, and dairy maid), and an archivist with legal qualifications.[1] At this time the Grande Chartreuse had 100 monks and 300 servants. 'When the religious houses in France are suppressed,' said a visitor, 'this one will have to be left, because it is indispensable to support the surrounding countryside.'[2] One of the reasons for the multiplication of servants was the comfortable tradition that local families ought to be offered places for their children, not necessarily within the limits of sheer utility. It was a substitute for almsgiving. When the government found it had German immigrants on its hands (brought in to colonize Cayenne but never sent), it circulated the abbeys of Brittany to ask the monks to stretch their payrolls and find places for them.[3] Another reason for the numerous servants was the custom of keeping on old retainers beyond their usefulness. At the Cistercian abbey of Morimond in its latter years, the nine servants had been there for an average time of twenty-five years, and in this century, when medical experts and economists supposed a working man would be worn out by the age of 50, six of them were over 60 years of age.[4]

Anticlericals gave the monks little credit for their easy-going attitude to their employees: by the mercantilist principles of the day, it
was drones subsidizing subsidiary drones. It was also an anticlerical
commonplace to describe the monasteries as stingy with their almsgiving. This was the general view of the peasants on the estates on
which rich abbeys collected rents, feudal dues, or tithes. An enquiry
of 1775[5] in the Toulouse area showed the abbey of Saint-Sernin as
giving only 30 livres annually to one of the parishes where it collected tithe, and 35 to another (true, there was also another 35, being
the interest on a sum bequeathed to the poor by a former abbot).
The abbey of Moissac, enjoying a half share of a tithe of 3,600
livres in one of its parishes, was accustomed to give from 15 to 21
annually. Curés, often too poor to give to charity themselves, led
their people in complaints.[6] These cases are typical of many, but
there were exceptions. The tax expert Richeprey,[7] investigating in
the South, found a Cistercian house giving back as much as it
received from a feudal rent, though in an uncritical fashion—distributions at Christmas and Easter at a flat rate to everyone above 14
years of age irrespective of need. There were some canons regular
nearby who also gave generous alms in such a haphazard fashion that
the bishop of Rodez proposed to compel them to reform their
undiscriminating largesse. One of his curés wrote to him in alarm,
with a warning that the people had come to depend on these hand-
outs—'if *Votre Grandeur* proposes changes, I supplicate you to give
me a warning, so I can flee as fast as I can from the fury that will be
kindled; it's all very well to say that the authorities will repress
disturbances—in the first uprising nothing will be respected, and
whatever else happens, I'll be the unhappy victim.' As a general rule,
it was the parish in which a monastery was situated which received
significant charity, and the ones further away which were neglected.[8]
The village of Mézidan, with a house of the Congrégation de France
(Génovéfains) in its midst owing five-sixths of the land, declared in
1790 that it had become entirely dependent on the canons regular,
who employed six men directly, and provided the sick and the poor
with food, clothing, firewood, and medicines; now that the
monastery was being suppressed, the parishioners 'are reduced to the
greatest misery'.[9]

Even if they tended to show indifference to everyday poverty, it
was characteristic of monks (as also of bishops) to react with remarkable generosity in crises of famine or other natural disasters—finding
accommodation for a family whose house had been burned down,
giving food and seed-corn when the crops had been flattened by

hail, lending money to borrowers who might not be able to return it, selling grain at low prices in time of starvation.[10] There are plenty of stories of attacks on rural monasteries in the 'Grande Peur' of 1789, but 3,000 peasants formed a cordon round the abbey of Arrouaise in Artois to protect the supplies of grain which the monks were selling cheaply from being pillaged by alien marauders.[11]

Monasteries were expected to provide hospitality to travellers. The great abbeys welcomed fulfilling the obligation so far as visitors of quality were concerned. Towards the end of the century, the son of a duke records enjoying 'excellent fish' at one of them; Chateaubriand remembered a dinner of 'eggs, carp and an enormous pike'; the English traveller Wraxall boasted of 'a dinner of great elegance'.[12] The Cistercian abbey of Saint-Sulpice at Bugey, on a snow-swept ridge with only sullen peasants[13] for neighbours amid the mountain desolation, to the uninitiated might have been expected to be a meagre place to dine, but Brillat Savarin, a dedicated gastronome, was delighted to go there—he had a small amateur orchestra, and the monks invited him to provide the music for mass and vespers on St Bernard's Day. The musicians arrived in time to breakfast on vast chines of ham and veal and 'a paté as large as a church'; they dined on a variety of delicately cooked meats and vegetables, supported by liqueurs and coffee ('clear, aromatic and wonderfully hot'), and ended the day with mulled eau-de-vie, a speciality of the cellarer, brought into the refectory in procession to the cheers of the assembled monks.[14] Earlier, John Breval at Cîteaux had found the guest master hospitable and reluctant to let him go; the monastic estates, said Breval, 'were never failing Resources for game and fish, and their cellars fill'd with the best Growths of Burgundy from their own vineyards; Guests of the greatest condition shall never catch them unprepared'.[15] The best families of Nîmes and Montpellier came to regard the Cistercian abbey of Franquevaux as a holiday resort, spending a week or two in this agreeable 'lieu de villégiature'.[16] When exiled to provincial towns by royal command, magistrates of the parlement of Paris would apply to the more comfortable monasteries for accommodation, though they might have to buy their meals from an outside *traiteur*.[17] When the great wished to escape from court, their families and friends, and the places where they were known, they would seek apartments in a religious house—a noble fleeing from the reproaches of the heirs he had disinherited, a converted *roué* trying to rehabilitate himself, a courtier withdrawing from the world to prepare for death.[18] Ladies more frequently sought refuge in houses of nuns, but the same resource could be useful, whether to a spiritual or a worldly end, for men who could afford it.

What happened to less respectable folk who arrived at the gates of a monastery? It was impossible to entertain every vagabond, though the austere *pères* of Sept-Fons 'made bread and soup available to all who presented themselves'. The Carthusians, equally dedicated, had a policy of helping travellers after enquiry into their circumstances. At their house of Boserville in Lorraine,[19] between January 1788 and March 1789 they gave 6,524 livres in alms, including money to a shipwrecked Italian sailor, a Frenchman returning to Liège from Naples, a soldier begging his way to Gascony, and a larger sum of 62 livres to 'a marquis who had fallen into destitution'. The 'unknown man apparently about 70 years of age with grey hair and rotting teeth' who died on his way to the Carthusian house of Notre-Dame de la Verne in 1777 had been directed there by the local peasants with a boy to guide him.[20] But most great abbeys limited their charity to a regular dole of bread without enquiry into the circumstances of recipients, though in some places a certificate of indigence from the curé was required, thus confining the benefit to local people. Documentation concerning the provisional continuance of customary alms when monasteries were being closed in 1790 gives some idea of the amount of charity being offered. In the North, the abbey of Vicoigne distributed 56 big loaves a fortnight and 400 small ones, and 200 herrings on Good Fridays; another abbey gave 15 large loaves every Sunday.[21] More substantially, Fécamp provided bread to the value of 15,000 livres a year, and there were similar doles at Fontevraud, Saint-Wandrille, Jumièges, and Bec.[22] The poor would assemble to collect their portions at fixed times; the Benedictines of Paray-le-Monial rang their great bell on three days in the week and every day in Lent and Advent to convoke them.[23] These indiscriminate hand-outs met with no favour from the men of the Enlightenment. As the *cahier* of Honfleur said, 'the day of distribution is a holiday, the worker puts down his spade and his axe and reposes in the bosom of sloth'.[24] Complaints of this kind against the Benedictines of Lessay in Normandy came to the ear of the government, and the king ordered the ending of the bread doles and the diverting of the expenditure (one-fifteenth of the total income of the monks) to the deserving poor of the parishes where the abbey owned property.[25]

No doubt some monks took vows out of a desire for a life of idleness. But for many more, this anticlerical formula represents a half-truth: they wanted to lead a leisured existence with freedom to pursue their own interests, not easy in a society where tradition, hierarchy, and family constrained individuality. Thus, a monastery would contribute to local life according to the idiosyncratic inspirations of its members. Antiquaries in search of curious historical or archaeological details and intellectuals savouring the debates of provincial academies would profit from the neighbourhood of some abbey, more especially one of the Congrégation de Saint-Maur or that of Saint-Vanne; so too would enthusiasts for the new sentimental egalitarianism finding expression in the masonic lodges, and the political gossips who met to read the newspapers at booksellers' counters and in cafés. Being much concerned with the cultivation of their estates, there were monks who became agricultural experts, contributing to the deliberations of the agricultural societies of the 1770s and 1780s—like Dom Leronge, author of the *Principes du cultivateur*; Dom Le Gendre, who experimented with sowing different kinds of grain; and Dom Wartel, exponent of deep manuring.[26] Vine growers were indebted to the intelligent husbandry of the abbeys. Dom Pierre Pérignon, bursar of Saint-Pierre d'Hautvilliers for forty-seven years (he died in 1715), made various discoveries, not least of which was the formula for perfecting champagne.[27] The monastic zeal for book collecting and cataloguing soon turned to the new fashion for surveys of scientific information, and it became common for rich abbeys to have their natural history collections; the one at Clairvaux was surprisingly up to date when inventoried in 1791, containing specimens of tungsten (only discovered in 1780) and molybdenum (isolated in 1782).[28] Some of the religious made a name for themselves in engineering and invention. The great waterworks at Marly, the pumps for the Jardin des Plantes, and the fire hydrants for the Palais Royal were designed by the Carmelite Sébastien Truchet (dd. 1729), as well as pieces of medical equipment—artificial arms and hearing aids.[29] A contemporary Augustinian friar devised the machine to lift the floor of the Opéra to the height of the stage, thus providing a level dance arena for the *bal de l'Opéra*.[30] In 1747 André Féry, a Minim of Reims, following the engineering tradition of his Order, published his *Dissertation sur le projet qu'on forme de donner des eaux à la ville de Reims*. A canon of the city gave the money to realize the project, and two years later the hydraulic machine began lifting water to the top of a sixty-foot tower; by 1753, fountains were playing in the centre of town.[31] A design (never realized) of the amateur inventor the Cistercian Dom Ganthey was praised by the Academy of Sciences in 1783: he proposed to institute a speedy postal service by attaching packets of letters to arrows fired from post office to post office by powerful mechanical bows.[32] More usefully, Noel, a Benedictine of Reims, perfected the technique of grinding spectacle lenses; Louis XV had him brought to Saint-Germain-des-Prés to construct a superior microscope for the royal apartments at Versailles.[33] The world had infiltrated the cloisters, but the monks were integrated into the life of the world. The gap between what Christian moralists wrote about the monastic vocation and that vocation in practice had never been greater, yet the contrast was not entirely to the discredit of those who took their vows in accordance with the routine assumptions and expectations of their families and society.

II

A man suffering from stones in the urinary tract or captured at sea by the Barbary corsairs would look more favourably on the religious than most of his contemporaries. The Frères de Saint-Jean-de-Dieu ran the best hospitals in France, with the most skilful surgeons, including the chief expert on the extraction of stones, while the ransoming of Christian slaves of the North African coast was organized and financed by the Trinitaires and the Order of Notre-Dame-de-la-Merci. The members of these three Orders won unstinted praise from Voltaire, especially those who risked their lives and freedom in the bazaars and slave markets of Algiers, Tunis, and Morocco. 'Les religieux de la rédemption des captifs sont la plus belle institution monastique,' he wrote.[34] His praises should be extended to the Lazarist house in Algiers and the Franciscan convents in Marrakesh and Meknes.[35] Considered by the criteria of fervour and regularity, the Trinitaires[36] (also called Mathurins after their founder, Jean de Matha) and the religious of La-Merci came low in the table of respectability. They were both international organizations dating from the thirteenth century, but their French establishments had never come under effective control, whether from Rome or from their own chief houses in Paris, which, indeed, were as undisciplined as any. Many of the eighty houses of Mathurins were tenanted by only one or two individuals (out of the total of 300), who did parish work and took life easy. La-Merci,[37] with only sixteen houses, all very poor, was condemned to suppression by the Commission des réguliers though no one seemed interested in enforcing the sentence.[38] But if they were drifting into decadence, these two Orders really did raise ransom money, and considerable sums. The

Trinitaires made annual payments to Algiers of about 100,000 livres; they also worked in Tunis, Tripoli, Smyrna, Constantinople, Egypt, and Persia.[39] Their budget for 1729 showed receipts of 274,559 livres and ransom payments of 235,803. At the head of their fund raising was the *procureur général des captifs*, elected by the national chapter general. He appointed laymen to take charge of the various collecting areas (with the title of *commissaires généraux des quêtes*), and these *commissaires* found local wardens (*marguilliers*) who organized collections and sold mementos and badges, especially scapulars—ordinary ones very cheap, and the gold and silver embroidered ones at 20 sous.[40] A parish might have a confraternity of 'la Rédemption', whose members, in consideration of their collection efforts, were entitled to wear the white surtout with the red and blue cross of the Order. To avoid clashes with the similar activities of La-Merci, the government had divided France into spheres of influence, with the smaller Order having the eastern frontier and the South.[41] On occasion bishops would issue pastoral letters exhorting the faithful to generosity: in 1754 it was to build a chapel in the slave barracks at Algiers, where the old buildings were being demolished; in 1756 it was to ransom 200 slaves from Morocco, the bishop of Le Mans describing them as hungry, vermin-ridden, 'toiling under a sky of bronze', and in danger of being tortured into apostasy.[42] Since the Dey had made this transaction a condition of concluding a treaty with France, the king paid for fifty releases, the Assembly of Clergy voted 200,000 livres,[43] and the monks found the rest—not easy, for the cost ran at 3,000 to 4,000 a head.

The ransoming process had been reduced to routine, but it was precarious.[44] The religious, who had chapels in all the slave barracks, were in touch with the captives and decided which cases could most usefully be followed up. They had to put the money into Mexican or Sevillian piastres, or in goods like tea, or even bring Turkish galley-slaves for exchange, having to buy them at Malta or Leghorn, the king of France not being inclined to let them have his. The usual bribes and the Dey's 10 per cent cut had to be arranged. In emergency, monks had to become hostages for the completion of a deal. And their lives could always be endangered by some warlike incident at sea, some false move by the other Order, or the forays of some 'Scarlet Pimpernel' like Père Jehannot. The king was not generous. Even when ransoming 300 of his soldiers (in 1785) by direct negotiation through his consul at Algiers, he extracted 443,000 livres of the ransom of 639,000 from the two religious Orders. The wealthy knights of Malta were as mean, allowing two of their officers to languish as slaves from 1708 to 1715, hoping to push the monks into paying.[45] Protestant captives were not allowed the benefit of Catholic collections, but if their own churches put up the funds, the Mathurins would act for them. So too for the Americans: Jefferson in 1787 found that the Order could do a deal at a tenth of the price the Dey of Algiers was asking in formal diplomatic negotiations.[46]

When the returning ransom ships reached Marseille, there were celebrations, then the monks and their liberated captives proceeded northwards, repeating their triumphal observances in various towns, ending up in Paris. These were the occasions when the local confraternities basked in public esteem and their major collections were taken. The ceremonies were traditional, following the same pattern ever since the mid-seventeenth century. In Paris in 1641 the processions defiled through the streets from 23 to 26 May with drums and trumpets sounding—soldiers, the city watch, the brethren of the confraternity of Notre-Dame-de-Bonne-Delivrance barefoot and carrying candles, the Mathurin fathers in their white robes with the red and blue cross on the front, with palms in their hands, the former captives bearing the banner of the Order, escorted by children dressed as angels. On 26 May, after receiving communion at the hands of the general of the Order, the captives were finally sent home, furnished with a certificate and money for the journey. With occasional variations, these ceremonies were repeated in the eighteenth century, the heart of the symbolism (derived from the banner of the Mathurins) centring on the 'angels' leading the liberated Christian slaves—sometimes dressed in rags, revealing their sunburnt and lacerated backs—the festoons of ribbons held by the children representing their former fetters. If the royal family had contributed to their release, some of them would have to go in procession at Versailles, from the parish church to the royal chapel.[47] A problem for the monks was that their cast of actors might be depleted by ungrateful individuals sneaking off home during the northward progress. In 1717, a knight of Malta whose freedom had been purchased by 12,000 livres from the Trinitaires and 10,000 from La-Merci refused to process as soon as he set foot in Marseille. He was summoned by a formal legal injunction, but it seemed that the courts could not oblige him. At least, however, the legal process has left us his name, Louis de Castellan d'Esparron.[48] Since the ranks would be well thinned by the time Paris was reached, how could the monks demonstrate to the public how many rescues they had made? An anticlerical diarist at the end of the *ancien régime* accused them of hiring substitutes, 'men from the suburbs who play the same masquerade every year'. Captives, whether real or supposititious, and some of the religious yielded to the temptation of the drink they were offered on their triumphal march, occasioning frequent stops while they were sobered up.[49] To the Parisians, who had never known the fear of being pursued by the galleys of the Barbary corsairs, it was comic entertainment.

The Frères de la Charité de Saint-Jean-de-Dieu[50] came to France at the beginning of the seventeenth century (having been founded in Portugal two centuries earlier). By 1789 they had 355 brothers running thirty-six hospitals, with a total of 3,181 beds. Most of their houses had reasonable endowments, and a few were rich. Thus, at Paris their central hospital and noviciate had 180,000 livres a year, Charenton had 128,000, and their small convalescent home 16,000, which was enough for its sixteen beds. To maximize income, some of the establishments specialized in taking soldiers and sailors as patients—in particular, there were 215 at the Isle of Ré and 1,200 at Brest. The king paid, but he got a good bargain: the vast naval hospital at Brest had been run by private contractors at 5 livres a head; when the brothers took over, the tariff dropped to 20 sous. Charenton had fifteen beds providing treatment for workers injured in the local stone quarries, while the money came from the fees paid for 100 internees in the prison wing. In the hospitals which were well off, the brothers set standards of medical care unknown elsewhere. In their central hospital at Paris, sixty brothers, eight doctors and surgeons, and twenty-four lay servants looked after 200 patients —a very favourable ratio. The sick were one to a bed, each having slippers, dressing-gown, chamber-pot, urine bottle, water flask, and cup alongside, and they enjoyed good meals, ending with beef tea and calf's-foot jelly after supper. They were spread over six spacious wards, each with its altar surmounted by a picture—one was by Rubens, another by Le Brun. The curious visitor could watch the procession of thanksgiving after dinner, proceeding from the ward altar with cross and candles, aspersing the patients with holy water to the chanting of the *De profundis*: perhaps he would be allowed to see an operation conducted by one of the best surgeons of the day, whether hired layman or brother. Of the brothers, Frère Cosme was the most famous. Son and grandson of provincial surgeons, he had begun as a Feuillant novice, then transferred. His speciality was the stone, for which he invented an alternative operation for certain cases, one which did not need an incision.[51] Stories of his fearsome dexterity and eccentricities were legion: removing a stone of 26 ounces, four times as big as any before; interrupted by the wife of the maréchal de Muy so that the stone broke fatally under the slipping pincers;[52] seated in the choir opposite his parish priest, the curé speculating on how soon he would be able to say the requiem over the surgeon, and the surgeon wondering when he would get the curé's body for dissection.[53] His fanaticism to practise on corpses led to Diderot's tale: he was disconsolate when a man expected to die recovered—'mon cadavre!' he lamented, and was pacified only when they found him another one.[54]

Serving the king could bring the Frères de Saint-Jean-de-Dieu into unpleasant places—as to the four military hospitals in San Domingo.[55] True, they had privileges, including the ownership of several plantations, and they had a Negro labour force to man the wards. But in this place of steamy heat, mosquitoes, and 'putrid exhalations', clergy of every kind succumbed to worldly temptations—the authorities regarded even the Capuchins as useless. Of the garrison of 7,000, up to 2,000 might be in hospital at one time, and the soldiers were drunken, insubordinate patients. The brothers pressed the governor to cut alcohol supplies and encourage orange juice; the governor accused the brothers of treating their patients with cold contempt, even though 'as religious and as doctors and surgeons they have a double obligation to serve the sick'.[56] The model Parisian hospital was filled with respectable patients, for it required influence to gain admission—hence the suavity and sympathy of the nursing staff, an attitude not found in the sweating, brutalized wards of San Domingo.

The prison run by the Frères de Saint-Jean-de-Dieu at Charenton was one of a number of such *maisons de force* kept by religious Orders at the behest of the king. Although the prisoners were incarcerated by royal order, it was normally at the request of their families. Of the 1,287 *lettres de cachet* issued in Provence from 1745 to 1789, 1,052 had been solicited by relatives, while 67 were at the instance of the ecclesiastical authorities.[57] The register of a *maison de force* would record the reasons, as at Charenton on 4 July 1789, the recording brother noted the arrival from the Bastille of the 'comte de Sade', a royal prisoner from 1777 on the application of his family, the law courts having found him not guilty of poisoning and sodomy, but known to be a libertine and insane.[58] (Unfortunately, the marquis de Sade's correspondence does not give an impression of the place; he says he got little exercise and became fat, and was glad to get out on the following Good Friday.[59]) In 1790, the National Assembly, moved by a storm of liberal protest against *lettres de cachet*, decreed a census of the establishments where victims of these arbitrary orders were detained. The list included ten royal fortresses, like the Pierre-en-Scize at Lyon and the Château d'If of later Monte Cristo fame; there were eight houses of Cordeliers, three of the Écoles Chrétiennes, and four others. There were also eleven convents and thirteen establishments under lay administration listed for women. These were far from being all the religious houses used from time to time as places of internment, but the Assembly had probably been given a comprehensive list of those most formally organized for the purpose.[60] One of the motives for the action of the legislators had been indignation at the recital of terrible conditions at Charenton, including confinement in dark cells fifty feet underground. Inspectors from the municipality went there, and reported the horror stories to be unfounded. The prison was in two departments: one where the inmates lived in agreeable apartments and moved around freely in spacious gardens against a background of idyllic scenery, another for the confinement of dangerous lunatics, who were kept behind bars. But there were no subterranean cells, the food was good, and there were frequent changes of linen, 'whose good quality astounded us'. The brothers humoured their prisoners, held long conversations with them, and cooked their favourite dishes; according to the inspectors, the place was an advertisement for true Christianity. It was honest praise, for the same inspectors reported a certain harshness of the nuns of the nearby Val d'Osne towards the four mad women in their charge.[61]

As was usually the case with institutions of the *ancien régime*, some *maisons de force* were humane and well organized, some abysmally crude and inefficient—the presence or absence of a secure income and an effective chain of command making the difference. It was a rule that a prisoner got the treatment corresponding to the maintenance grant which was being paid for him. At the Cordeliers of Caen, lunatics at 150–250 livres fared meagrely; libertines subsidized to the tune of 300 or more could eat with the monks, and at 450 and above could have a private room. The Cordeliers of Limoges specialized in confining erring ecclesiastics, an unhappy place, as the payments on their behalf were small.[62] The chevalier de la Musse, put into the Frères de Saint-Jean-de-Dieu at Pontorson at the age of 71 to stop him marrying a prostitute, the son of a farmer-general in a monastery at Nancy for a scandalous publication, the son of another farmer-general in Saint-Lazare, then at Mont Saint-Michel, for defying his father, the abbé d'Espagnac at the Barnabites of Montargis ('une espèce de maison de correction et comme un séminaire') for financial speculation—these were offenders from the monied classes, and their lot was an easy one.[63]

Yet there were *maisons de force* which, irrespective of income, fell into scandal. At Mont-Saint-Michel, the religious, 'sovereign despots on their rock', would not allow local officials to enter to check on the welfare of the prisoners. This was not because dark cruelties were being perpetrated—the great wooden cage and the oubliettes of the Middle Ages were empty, gaped at by shuddering tourists.[64] The fault of the place was laxity, the gaolers joining with the prisoners in loose living. A young nobleman confined for debauchery laughed at his mother, who had sent him there: 'She thought she was putting me among saints whose good . . . example would operate my conversion. She was absolutely mistaken. It was with the religious that I got drunk, in the refectory, or in my room, to which they brought wine night and day to drink with me.'[65] There was no such revelry at the Cordelier house of Saint-Pierre de Canon in Provence,[66] where negligence and ill will ruled. The *gardien* was a drunkard, the bursar could not read, and the chaplain had affairs with peasant women, while the prison was in the hands of an outside contractor whose only object was profit. The detainees were dressed in rags and slept on straw, their staple food was soup and stale bread, and they were flogged for misbehaviour. The contractors paid an annual fee, which went to the Cordeliers of Marseille, a source of revenue which dried up when inspectors arrived in 1767 to investigate complaints. Institutions of the *ancien régime* tended to be run on a perverse application of the principle of the greatest good of the greatest number, irrespective of the welfare of their inmates. Thus at Saint-Pierre de Canon, where families got rid of disreputable relatives, the Cordeliers had a rural corner where useless friars could be posted, together with a small annual income for their provincialate, a local contractor provided employment and lined his own pockets—if lunatics and libertines suffered, perhaps it was what they deserved.

III

The nobles and bourgeois of eighteenth-century France were educated in *collèges* run by institutes founded under the influence of the Counter-Reformation: the Jesuits, the creation of Ignatius Loyola in 1534: the Pères de la Doctrine Chrétienne established in the Comtat Venaissin in 1592 by César de Bus, then spreading to France and Italy; the Oratorians, founded by Bérulle in 1611 on the model of the Italian Oratory of Philip Neri; and the Lazarists of Vincent de Paul, dating from 1625. Until their suppression, the Jesuits were the dominant educational force, running 151 *collèges* with numerous teachers.[67] Next came the Oratorians, with 72 *collèges* and 800 or so staff, with their centre of gravity in Anjou and Touraine; then the Doctrinaires, with 60 *collèges* and about 500 staff, their main sphere of action being the South. The Lazarists had 83 establishments, but these were mainly seminaries and centres for the preaching of missions.

In small country places there were other *collèges* staffed by secular priests hired by the municipal authorities. At Saint-Gaudens, there were three of these masters and—a luxurious extra—a professor of philosophy paid by the provincial estates of Nébousan. The number of these 'secular' schools increased greatly as a result of the expulsion of the Jesuits. By the edict of 27 February 1763, the vacated institutions were to be directed by boards of governors, the diocesan bishop to preside, and the members to be the *premier président* and *procureur général* of the local parlement, the two chief municipal officers, two co-opted notables, and the headmaster of the school.[68] The boards would hire teachers by inspecting certificates of degrees, competitive examination, or review of testimonials. Practically all the masters appointed by the system were clergy. In some places, the system would not work, partly because the lay governors insisted on pushing their own fancy educational ideas on teachers who had no time to implement them. 'Education is a matter in which the imagination can roam and everyone can draw up schemes for it,' said the bishop of Langres sardonically, 'and the bourgeoisie, who have nothing else to administer, are infinitely jealous to run that of the *collèges*.'[69] When lay control collapsed, the towns had to call upon the established ecclesiastical teaching institutes and forgo their opportunities for interfering. At Lyon,[70] from the start, the practised Oratorians were invited to take over to replace the Jesuits, and in the following years Tournon, Arras, Béthune, Tours, Agen, and finally, in 1786, Autun followed suit. A dozen *collèges* fell to the Doctrinaires. But efficient teachers were in short supply. The Oratorians accepted these apparently splendid new opportunities only with reluctance—they lacked numbers to expand effectively. At Lyon, where the Jesuits had stationed eighty-five priests, they could never muster more than sixteen replacements, and parents complained of over-large classes and superficial teaching.

The Oratorians and the Doctrinaires[71] did not take monastic vows: they remained secular clerics attached to their institute by *vœux simples*, temporary obligations. As the century progressed, more and more of the Oratorians chose to hold back from proceeding to the priesthood; at the end of the *ancien régime* the proportion of the *pères* to the *confrères* was one to six. From mid-century, the same process was operating among the Doctrinaires—they moved more slowly to the priesthood: 'on est toujours à temps de s'engager pour la vie'.[72] At their general chapter of 1776, the Doctrinaires abolished vows altogether, replacing them with a simple promise, a change welcomed unanimously in France, though rejected in Italy. Recruitment to both institutes was principally from the *moyenne bourgeoisie*.[73] While among the secular clergy generally, there was a strong minority—a quarter to a third—of ordination recruits from the sons of artisans (generally *maîtres*, not ordinary journeymen) and the more prosperous peasants, in the two teaching institutions there were virtually no representatives of artisan or peasant families up to mid-century, and few afterwards. Sons of merchants, doctors, surgeons, apothecaries, notaries, and bureaucrats were numerous, and as much as a third of the total consisted of sons of nobles of the robe and other magistrates and royal *officiers*, with the aristocracy of the parlements preferring the Oratory. These were men from well-off families who chose a demanding vocation, but with the intention of fulfilling it in comfort. Their teaching duties were arduous, and they would attend mass on Sundays and saints' days and attend prayers every morning and evening (the Doctrinaires abolished this latter obligation in 1783). Yet they retained their private incomes (under some supervision) and, perhaps, drew the profits from some ecclesiastical sinecure; they had their own furniture, fires—servants even—and moved freely in society, dining with the best local families and dressing elegantly, sometimes ostentatiously. One of the pupils of the Oratorians at Angers remembered Père Limonas, hair curled and powdered, frock-coat open to reveal the trim legs (set off in silk stockings) which were his pride: he was given to witticisms, and was prepared to accept an excuse for laziness if presented with a *bon mot*.[74] And no doubt the schoolboys of Nantes long remembered their professor of physics, Père Mouchet, who, to the accompaniment of cheers and salvoes, went up in a hot-air balloon on the evening of 14 June 1784, vanishing over the horizon and coming down an hour later near Chinon.[75] As France became a hive of political speculation in the last years before the Revolution, the place to go for news was an Oratorian *collège*. At Dieppe they took *L'Esprit des Journaux*, the *Gazette de Leyde*, and the *Mercure* (sharing the cost with two prominent citizens), to which in 1788 they added the

Courrier de l'Europe and the *Année littéraire*.[76] An administrative official of Nantes in January of that year complained that the masters of the *collège* were more concerned with the news from Paris than with their teaching: 'always promenading around in society, the hours they are obliged to spend in their class-rooms are sheer boredom to them'.[77] Unlike those pillars of papal orthodoxy, the Jesuits and the Lazarists, the Doctrinaires and the Oratorians were deeply marked by Jansenism. In 1725, 20 per cent of the members in each of these institutes were appellants against *Unigenitus*.[78] They were harassed into outward submission by royal commissioners vetting the attendance at general chapters and by bishops closing *collèges* and banning individuals from teaching. Defying authority on a point of conscience can be a first step towards political liberalism. Both institutes were open to the political ideas of the Enlightenment—it was Oratorian thinkers at the end of the seventeenth century who had proclaimed the equality of men in the state of nature and declared the power of kings to originate in delegation from the people, and not directly from God. These progressive schoolmasters welcomed the collapse of royal absolutism in 1789, the Doctrinaires proudly proclaiming, 'nous sommes citoyens avant d'être instituteurs'. Their support for the new order was evident in the numerous recruits they provided for the constitutional Church. When the destructive tide of revolution ebbed, they were leaders in the creation of a new educational system and in the restoration of provincial cultural life. Strange mutations can happen to ideals. It has always been a psychological problem to understand the minds of the ex-Oratorian terrorists. Billaud Varenne is easiest to comprehend, since he had left teaching and become a lawyer (though he always admired his old colleagues, and wanted national education to be put into their charge).[79] But Joseph Lebon, who taught Latin diligently at Beaune and gave half his exiguous salary to buy books for poor students, and Fouché at Arras, knowing Massillon's sermons by heart and half in love with Charlotte Robespierre—how did they come to degrade their sentimental egalitarianism into anti-Christian masquerades and wholesale massacres?[80]

In 1789, there were about 48,000 pupils in the various *collèges*, that is, one in fifty-two of the boys aged from 8 to 18.[81] The vast majority came from the families of the upper and middling bourgeoisie. At big centres of population like Lyon, there would be numerous representatives of nobles of the sword and of the robe.[82] At the fashionable Oratorian *collège* of Juilly, there were prestigious names: Adrien Duport, Alexandre de Beauharnais, Bonald, Louis de Narbonne,

Hérault de Séchelles, the Baron Clootz, and the two sons of Laborde, the court banker.[83] At Angers, where half the intake was from families of merchants and master artisans, there was a strong counter-balancing minority (36 per cent) of the sons of the municipal oligarchy and magistrates of the *présidial*. Much the same at Lille, magistrates and municipal officers providing 30 per cent.[84]

At the other end of the social scale, most ordinary families could not hope to send a son to a *collège*. *Bourses*—exhibitions—were not numerous, and many were reserved for pupils proceeding to an ecclesiastical career. The *collèges*, lacking endowments, were dependent on municipalities (and sometimes provincial estates) for funds. There were examples of generosity, for, after all, the governing hierarchy of towns tended to consist of 'old boys'—paying the salary of the masters at Toulon and Marseille when the bishop closed the classrooms, and at Le Mans paying enough to enable free pupils to be taken.[85] But often, the schoolmasters had to operate on a shoe-string budget. At Forcalquier in Provence in 1769, only a single teacher was left to take all the classes, the town having ended its financial aid because it objected to the bishop exercising his right to appoint the masters. The Doctrinaires at Gimont in 1758 and at Lectoure in 1770 had to go on strike to get their salaries.[86] The Oratorians of Angers in 1770 had an income of only 2,148 livres to pay nine teachers and five servants; at the same time debts forced their house at Saumur to close its boarding wing, and at Soissons to consider closing altogether.[87] Free places for all candidates of real merit was the ideal of both the institutes, but in practice, a *collège* had to charge fees running from 400 to 700 livres. And in any case, even a free place was not much good to a family living beyond walking distance of the classrooms; relatives in town or some patron, probably an ecclesiastic, who would offer free lodgings were needed. The sons of artisans who got through to secondary education all went into the Church, and so did the sons of most of the merchants. Peasants' representatives were few, except in tiny *collèges* in the remote countryside. If there was a substantial rural recruitment (as at Le Mans, where it was 15 per cent), it was the sons of the richer peasants, the *laboureurs*.[88] The financial standing of a family also tended to determine the length of the course of schooling. In theory, a pupil attended from the age of 7 to 14, starting at the 'fifth class', then on a year at a time to the 'second' at the age of 10, then 'rhetoric' and 'rhetoric renewed' and 'logic' and 'logic renewed'. In practice, except for the sons of richer families or boys going on to an ecclesiastical career, it was common to leave after completing the 'second'. By contrast, if their parents could afford it, some less able pupils might stay on, repeating an unsatisfactory year; it was not unusual to find young men of 19 still hanging round as students.[89]

In certain respects, it was impossible to treat rich pupils as equal to poor ones. In establishments with boarders, the rich would demand a room with a fire and, perhaps, a servant in attendance. When theatrical performances were staged, the heroic parts would have to go to sons of distinguished families—and in any case it was their parents who could afford to provide splendid costumes. But equality was observed in the classroom, where the competitive spirit was fostered by rivalry for class placings, by prize givings, public recitals of rhetorical compositions and Latin verses, and the upholding of theses. In these ways, a line was drawn between pupils on grounds of merit alone. Dulaure's guide-book to Paris in 1787 described the competitions in rhetoric at Juilly at six-weekly intervals as designed to show 'it is not riches or wealth, but only merit and talents which deserve consideration'.[90] This bridging of class barriers was a conscious aim of the Oratorians. When constrained to run military academies, they declared their intention to mix pupils doing ordinary courses with those on the military side, 'thus stifling the haughtiness which young nobles are all too easily disposed to confuse with elevation of soul, and induce them to consider from a just point of view all orders in society'.[91] In the last pre-revolutionary generation it became a commonplace to say that the educational system of the *collèges* had ended the external differences between nobles and richer commoners. 'The sons of merchants and bourgeois', said Restif de la Bretonne in 1773, 'have as polished an exterior as the great because they are brought up like them.'[92] Why, then, should privilege subsist? 'The old order made a crucial error,' said Danton.

I was educated by it as an exhibitioner at the Collège du Plessis. I studied with great nobles who lived with me on equal terms. My studies once finished, I had nothing . . . My former comrades turned their backs on me. The Revolution came. I—and all those like me—we threw ourselves into it. The *ancien régime* drove us to it by giving us a good education without opening any opportunity for our talents.[93]

The education given in the *collèges* was not 'religious' in broad intent, though each day was set in a religious cadre. At Juilly in 1720, there were prayers at 6 a.m., supper and evening prayer at 8.45 p.m.; everything between was study and classes, with little time off for recreation.[94] In the lay *collèges* which succeeded the Jesuit institutions, there was hardly any relaxation in the pattern of observances: prayers and half an hour's Bible study beginning at 6 a.m., mass at 10.30 a.m., evening prayers at 8.45 p.m. It was formal religion, part of the unquestioned social order.[95] True, in Rennes after the Jesuits, there were traditional survivals regarded as overstepping the boundaries of devotions appropriate for schoolboys. At the annual prize giving, the successful pupils processed through the city behind their teachers, did seven 'stations' in the seven chapels of the Jacobins, heard a sermon, then were regaled with strawberries and wine and were allowed to fill their pockets with apples, finishing with a visit to the chapel of the Virgin, to prostrate themselves before her statue. 'We—professing as we did a passionate enthusiasm for the eighteenth century—were sunk deep in the Middle Ages,' said Moreau de Jonnes.[96]

The daily religious routine was the structure holding together the introverted world of the *collège*. Within this closed social unit the hours of work were long, and periods of recreation were few; holidays were limited—perhaps one day a week and two weeks in summer. Ordinary life was shut out. The claustrophobic atmosphere was intensified by the nature of the instruction (at least in the early decades of the century). The materials on which the mind was exercised came from a vanished civilization, studied through the medium of a dead language, one, moreover, approached mainly in the form of extracts judiciously selected. There were no opportunities to range curiously in the classical epoch, turning up, no doubt, scandalous incidents, dangerous arguments, erotic verse. The artificiality of the proceedings was defended by vaguely, though not very obviously, religious arguments: the need to know the language of the liturgy and of the officially available version of the Bible, the edifying nature of the moral and patriotic incidents of pagan antiquity, the value of studying a conspectus of the utmost perfection to which natural religion can attain, to gain a point of departure for an appreciation of the blessings of the Christian revelation.[97] Besides, a degree of abstraction from everyday reality was useful to keep concupiscence out of the mind (a consideration annexed by reformers who wanted more time given to mathematics). Oddly, the more obvious argument of our day emphasizing the training of the mind by the study of a demanding subject, whatever its factual content, was little used, except in the cliché 'Latin leads to anything' used by old-fashioned fathers arguing with sons who could not see why they should flog through Latin grammar and write essays on the remorse of Nero or verses on the virtue of magnanimity.

From the end of the seventeenth century, change was in the air. It was implicit in the proposals for the education of royal pupils devised by Bossuet and Fénelon, in Locke's proposal to bring the Latin classics to life by the use of interlinear translations, in Rollin's *Traité des études* (1726) giving translation and commentary priority over theme and composition. The Quarrel of Ancients and Moderns, with the Moderns prevailing, brought into competitive focus the glories of seventeenth-century French literature: Racine equalled the Greek tragedians, and Molière was superior to the Roman comic playwrights. French had become the intellectual tongue of the civilized world, a language other nations had to learn—why should the youth of France spend its time learning a different one? From the abbé Fleury's *Choix des études* (1686), the idea was abroad that the classical languages were useless, except it might be a snobbish conversational gambit to remark how easily Greek can be forgotten.

The Oratorians were the first to put the new ideas into effect. They had two allegiances which drew them towards innovation. One was their sympathy with the Jansenist cause. Port-Royal had used simplified Latin grammars written in French, a new departure breaking with the myth of the school as a re-creation of a patrician assembly in ancient Rome. The other allegiance was to Cartesianism—this brought them under the censure of the University of Paris and of Louis XIV. The prohibition against teaching Cartesianism was not, as Mme de Sévigné supposed, damaging to them, at least in the long term. For one thing, the philosophical fashion changed, and the Oratorians with it; the cosmology of Descartes was replaced by Newton's, and his epistemology by Locke's and Condillac's. For another, the lesson that clarity of thought was the cardinal intellectual virtue had been assimilated, and could not be forgotten. What the official ban did was to strengthen the Oratorian tradition of resistance to authority. In another fashion, they followed Descartes, who, as a friend of Bérulle and a native of Anjou, their heartland, was their cult figure. He had written, not in Latin, but in French, to appeal to the ladies and to those who 'use their pure and natural reason' rather than relying on 'old books'. Why should not French educationalists do the same? Lamy, an Oratorian of Cartesian persuasion, in his *Entretiens sur les sciences* (1684), complained of the obscurantist education he had endured, taught as if his head was tied up in a sack, and whipped if he went in the wrong direction. He wished to dethrone Latin, its versification, dictation, and themes, and the Aristotelian scholasticism which seemed to be its natural accompaniment, and pleaded for the study of the sciences, especially mathematics and geometry. In a manuscript proposal of 1720, Père Hoobigant wanted to exchange Latin for French, his new key discipline to be, not mathematics, but history. True, he favoured working from translations of Plutarch and classical historians, and wanted more poetry to sharpen the imagination, inevitably blunted by the factual examples of history.

From the beginning of the seventeenth century, the Oratory taught Latin through French grammars, and gave translation priority over the composition of themes. By mid-century, French was dominant. At Troyes, of the forty-five essays read by the class of rhetoric from 1765 to 1766, only four were in Latin, and from 1757 all the theses of logic and physics were in French. It was a great thing for a boy to take home his thesis bound and adorned with the arms of the Oratory (two angels bearing a crown of thorns and a palm with an inscription to Jesus and Mary); the privilege was available to more of them now that the language barrier was down. The current of intellectual fashion was turning towards history—the Maurists and their researches, popular histories of France by Président Hénault and various Jesuits, Bossuet and, in a different fashion, Voltaire, making the sweep of universal history a theme for the imagination. The demand was for a study of events relevant to the eighteenth century, and a great deal of modern history came into the curriculum of the *collèges*. This turning to the 'real' and away from the artificial environment constructed out of sanitized fragments of classical antiquity also prompted the study of the sciences. The abbé Coyer's *Plan d'éducation publique* of 1770 was concerned with 'things'—the pattern of lines in geometry, maps, globes, machines, skeletons, plants, animals. After 1770 the proportion of time devoted to the sciences within the philosophy course rose from a third to a half and kept on increasing, more especially because the custom developed of leaving the philosophy in Latin and teaching the mathematics, physics, and astronomy in French.

The Doctrinaires were following the same path as the Oratorians. From the end of the seventeenth century, they made French the main language of teaching—after 1770, exclusively. By that time their set authors included Corneille, Boileau, La Fontaine, Gresset, J.-B. Rousseau (not Jean-Jacques), and Voltaire. Then, belatedly, Racine came in; no doubt his tragedies had been held back because of their intense undertow of sexuality. History and geography became central subjects. In 1771 the Doctrinaires were denounced by the University of Paris; they had abandoned Latin themes and versification, logic and metaphysics, it was said, putting in their place a heterogeneous jumble of history, geography, and other superficial and interesting subjects—they had sold out to the philosophes. The Doctrinaires accepted this as the ultimate accolade, though they proffered defensive reservations about Latin. Perhaps more than the Oratorians, the Pères de la Doctrine Chrétienne taught 'citizenship', the fashionable word which was to link the sentimentality of the *ancien régime* to the severities of the Revolution. They emphasized morality rather than dogma, focusing on the concept of 'vocation', the fulfilment of the duties of one's station, the most corrupting sin of all being idleness. Their philosophy of society was summed up in the *Traité d'éducation civile, morale et religieuse* (1789) of Père Corbin, the principal of their *collège* at La Flèche, a study of Christian vocation in its obligations towards the State, society, and the property and persons of fellow citizens.[98]

More closely examined, the reform of the syllabuses of the *collèges* was not as radical as the University of Paris and other angry traditionalists supposed. Not all the new subjects were regarded as entirely respectable: the visitor of the Oratorians calling at the *collège* of Condom in 1784 said that 'mercenaries' could be hired to teach the light-hearted subjects, with the actual members of the institute limiting themselves to 'scientific and Christian education'.[99] The Maurists at Sorèz, defending themselves against the University of Paris, said that it was only the stupid pupils who were excused Latin, the others having to do it for four hours a day. The Doctrinaires in 1789 were still using many extracts from Latin authors, even if studying them through the French language. Their favourite was Cicero; there was never any use of Seneca or Tacitus. No doubt these exclusions were for moral reasons, just as the Oratorians, advanced as they were, as late as 1776 and 1785 banned theatrical productions, a prohibition which most *collèges* ignored. Moral instruction was ruthlessly imposed on any sort of entertaining reading. Père Grozelier of the Oratory published fables in 1760 and 1768 to enliven the classroom—the 'enfant gâté' who was cruel to a sheep got a broken leg, and another maltreating a cat lost an eye; another, given to gluttony, perished miserably, having mistaken arsenic for sugar.[100] There was a rush to study history, but it was history in the old providentialist vein. The principal of the *collège* of Lille, the abbé Lefian, ordered by the committee of management in 1772 to reform the syllabus, pronounced history to be central, 'the ruler of men'; therefore, he said, we must study sacred history first of all, then go on to demonstrate 'how God gives his aid to nations that are just'.[101] In 1789, the

Doctrinaires at Aix taught their sixth class from Erasmus, La Fontaine, and Racine's *Phèdre*; they had a course on natural history (this year's subject being birds), and they taught some French history. Even so, they had plenty of dogma from Fleury's catechism; they covered the Old Testament from creation to Judges; they had a special theme from the New Testament in the early life of Jesus; and their national history was organized as a theme of apologetics, a quarry of evidence to demonstrate the working of God's judgements.[102] At the end of the *ancien régime* the old and the new jostled together in the teaching of the *collèges*—an education ostensibly given by churchmen for Christian ends, yet generally regarded by families as being 'moral' in intention rather than specifically Christian, and all the while being quietly secularized from within.

IV

The *collèges* provided a civilized basic education for pupils who were born to status and office, without too much nonsense about merit, and for those of lower social classes who hoped to rise through the Church or the lower reaches of the legal profession. What they did not offer was technical or vocational training; the method and content of their teaching were evolving, but too slowly to forestall the rise of competition. Well-off parents who distrusted the *collèges*, whether as too ruthless, too religious, or as lacking in practical usefulness, could resort to other schools which were multiplying at the end of the *ancien régime*, the *pensionnats*. A guide-book to Paris of 1787 listed no fewer than three in the grande rue de Passy alone, charging fees like 450 livres from the age of 4 to 10, and 700 from 10 onwards.[103] Some establishments of this kind were down-market, like the one Mercier attended, run by 'le père Tocquet', a portly figure in scarlet coat and black velvet breeches, a great wielder of the rod, and a fine singer who performed at the parish offices of Saint-Germain-l'Auxerrois. 'Père' was unusual, probably ironical; 'abbé' was the general title, but in either case, these managers of schools were—nominally, at least—ecclesiastics. Some establishments claimed to be select. 'Although this pensionnat', says the prospectus of the abbé Liébault at Dijon in 1776, 'is singularly suited to young noblemen who are destined for a military career, we nevertheless admit the sons of bourgeois and merchants.'[104] In the local newspaper he proclaimed a syllabus of languages, sciences, arts, mathematics (useful for war), dancing, fencing, riding, with Greek optional—for

600 livres a year, rising to 800 after the age of 10. The abbé Hazard, more exclusive still, made no concessions to the middle classes: he opened a school at Nanterre for nobles only—too often, he said, they have to go into a military career having been educated like bourgeois.[105] He was starting his venture at an unpropitious time—February 1789. The most lavish academy of all was probably the abbé Choquart's in Paris. Hugh Elliot, who was there with his brother and their tutor from England, describes how the school celebrated the feast of St Louis in 1765, the boys in their blue and silver uniforms engaged in Prussian drill and military manœuvres all day, then performing in a ballet at night in the illuminated gardens, with opera singers and fireworks to complete the entertainment.[106]

As these establishments proliferated, they poached pupils from the *collèges*. The University of Angers tried to get a municipal regulation limiting the number of *pensionnats* in town to eight, to rescue the Collège d'Anjou from decline. Similar measures at Nantes failed, and by 1788 the boarding-house of the Oratorians there was half empty.[107] In 1777, the abbé de Massannes, after twenty years' teaching in Sorèz, 'giving lessons on the whole range of human knowledge to the élite youth there', came to Grenoble and opened a *pensionnat* which had 100 pupils within a year. In despair, the *collège* had to open a house for boarders in competition, call in new teachers, and institute a reform of the curriculum.[108]

The *pensionnats* gave vocationally oriented education to the sons of families which could afford to pay substantial fees. There was, however, an institution of this name which also gave highly specialist instruction, but as a remarkable philanthropic gesture—the abbé de l'Épée's *pensionnat* in Paris for deaf and dumb children. A Portuguese Jew in Bordeaux had invented an ingenious method of teaching them; he was pensioned by the Crown and by his own Jewish community, but was not able to put his scheme into large-scale practice. This was done by Épée, who put his inheritance into creating a school for the deaf and dumb in Paris. It became famous, was visited by noble ladies, bishops, the papal nuncio, the Emperor Joseph II, and Gustavus III of Sweden, and finally received an annual grant from the king, and was given accommodation in an empty monastery. Épée's disciples went out to set up similar establishments in Vienna, Rome, and Angers. Archbishop Champion de Cicé sent the abbé Sicard to Paris to learn the teaching methods; he returned and set up an institute at Bordeaux, though before long he went back to Paris to take over the main house. Here was an example of religion combining with the Enlightenment concept of philanthropy to produce an organization in which the thrill of putting a new 'scientific' discovery into practice was allied to the moral satisfaction of helping a disadvantaged class.

Some of the new *pensionnats* were angling for customers from traditional military families. Warfare was becoming more technical, and in mid-century the government set up a new structure for training military cadets. There were two specialist schools—of artillery and engineering—and a central École Militaire in Paris offering 500 places to the sons of nobles. This central school was confided first of all to the Prêtres de la Mission; predictably, they proved too rigorous in imposing the observances of religion, so three doctors of the Sorbonne were called in to supervise the teaching.[109] The professors who served under them were nearly all ecclesiastics, but they were not allowed to adopt the style of 'abbé'. Berthelin, who taught mathematics, complained of the deprivation, for he was indeed 'an honorary canon of Saint-Denis at Douai'.[110] The arrival of the comte de Saint-Germain as Minister of War led to further expansion. He had risen as a mercenary in foreign service; he knew better than anyone how the face of warfare was changing; and he was determined to professionalize training. Under his reform, a cadet had to go for five years to one of twelve new academies in the provinces; then, at the age of from 13 to 15, he would move up to the École Militaire in Paris; thereafter, he would be sent either to the Artillery or to the Engineering School, or directly to his regiment. By 1785, these twelve new provincial academies had 2,775 cadets. A quarter of these were paid for by the king; of those paying for themselves, half were of noble birth.[111]

These academies were all run by religious Orders: six by the Benedictines of Saint-Maur, three by the Oratorians, one by the Minims, one by the canons regular of Notre-Sauveur, one by the Doctrinaires. The government's advisers had a field-day devising a syllabus, the abbé Batteux drawing up fifty-eight volumes which, fortunately, were ignored. The Maurists had already been experimenting with a new scheme of modern subjects, more especially Dom Victor Fougeras, prior of the abbey of Sorèze. Now, with a teaching unit of twenty-four monks and twenty lay associates, he was given the opportunity of setting up one of the provincial military academies.[112] Latin and Greek became optional, while modern languages, mathematics, French history up to contemporary times, music, and gymnastics became core subjects. Molière was declared to be a superior writer of comedy to Aristophanes, and extracts from Voltaire's *Henriade* were set texts. There was the inevitable religious instruction and practice: compulsory daily services, Fleury's *Caté-chisme historique*, and the study of sacred history from the Old Testament to the sixth century. In these military schools, more than in others, the imposition of religious routines was counter-productive. At Brienne, run by the Minims, the pupils placed bets on how long each friar would take to say the daily mass; some unpopular ones took twenty minutes, but Père Châtaux won approval by omitting the Credo and Gloria and finishing in five. The usual disputes between religious and their parish priest for pastoral oversight of the rites of passage took place, the curé of Brienne winning a legal ruling to have the boys compelled to make their First Communion in his church. The first one to be sent was the Corsican cadet Bonaparte.[113]

V

On the margins between the bourgeoisie on the one hand and peasants and artisans on the other was a whole class of ambitious families wanting a good education of a vocational kind for their children. What was on offer in the *collèges* and *pensionnats* was not suitable; nor could they afford it. At the same time, among enlightened churchmen there was an awareness that the imposition of religious routines in schools needed a new philosophy of Christian instruction to achieve dispositions more inward than mere conformity. In a paradoxical fashion, movement towards these two objectives was achieved by a new foundation, the Frères des Écoles Chrétiennes[114]—paradoxical because the original inspiration had a different orientation, and because the Frères allied ideas of the Enlightenment with reactionary attitudes of an intolerant kind. Jean-Baptiste de La Salle, their founder, was a saint in the mould of Rancé of La Trappe. An aristocrat, destined for an easy life off ecclesiastical revenues, a canon of Reims at the abusive age of 16, he was converted, gave up his canonry and his private fortune, and in 1648 formed a brotherhood to educate the children of the very poor. It was to be a ruthlessly religious education—attendance at mass daily, a period of recollection of God's presence in the course of every lesson, half an hour of religious instruction every day and one and a half hours on Sundays. His brethren were to be uncompromisingly orthodox, giving total obedience to the Pope and set in flint-like opposition to Jansenism. By 1700, the Frères des Écoles Chrétiennes were running elementary schools in five towns.

In the years following, up to his death in 1719, La Salle diversified the activities of his followers by organizing Sunday classes for adults in more advanced subjects, by giving technical training in seamanship to boys in Calais, and by setting up a boarding-school for the sons of middle-class tradesmen in Rouen, with a curriculum suited to their needs. Eventually, these departures from the original aim became the Frères' claim to educational originality and influence in society. There was a choice, in founding a new institute, between the usual permanent vows of monks and the 'simple', temporary vows taken by the Oratorians, and La Salle ingeniously combined the two systems in a way which at once encouraged recruitment while discouraging faint-hearted vocations. Up to the age of 25, a brother took renewable vows, after which time he could choose either to undertake the lifelong obligation (provided he had already served for three years) or to stay in the provisional status, retaining his freedom to leave. In fact, this freedom was frequently used: of the twenty-six postulants coming into the noviciate of Saint-Yon in 1720, fourteen eventually departed from the institute; of those of 1740, eighteen out of twenty-six left; of 1748, twenty-three out of thirty-three; of 1760, ten out of seventeen.[115] There was no assumption that piety was enough to make a teacher; a brother was never sent to a school to teach until he himself had been instructed in educational techniques.

The *petites écoles*, the free elementary schools—the original purpose of the institute—proliferated up to mid-century. An invitation would come from a diocesan bishop (always a strictly orthodox one), an investigator would be sent down from headquarters, and he would ensure that financial support was guaranteed—generally in the form of a fixed salary for each teacher; then a task force of qualified teachers would arrive, a house of residence would be set up for them, and from it they would go out to teach in schools in the adjoining parishes—four schools in Arras, for example, five in Tours. By 1747, the Frères des Écoles Chrétiennes had put down roots in eighty locations, with a total of about 800 teachers working; by 1779, they had a hundred residences and were teaching 30,000 pupils. By now, expansion was virtually over, though Loménie de Brienne brought them belatedly to Toulouse, confiscating monastic revenues for the purpose—the opening date was, inauspiciously, March 1789.

In some places the Frères elaborated their elementary schools to undertake the teaching of vocational specialities, such as hydrography at Vannes and Nantes and commerce at Boulogne—thus drawing to their classes children from families of higher social standing than would normally have been interested. However, the major technical training for careers—in navigation, horticulture, surveying, accounting, in shop, office, and government service which was to become the speciality of the Frères—was given in their *pensionnats*, boarding-schools, at Angers, Saint-Yon, Saint-Omer, Marseille, Maréville (Lorraine), Montpellier, Mirepoix, Nantes, and Reims. Three more *pensionnats* were opened later. These establishments had to be self-financing. Municipalities, dominated by the upper classes, were old boys' associations of the local *collège*, and they lacked enthusiasm for rival institutions bringing superior education to the lower orders. The central government would help only on its own terms, and what the king's ministers required were prisons, with reliable gaolers to take care of special offenders—*maisons de force*. Three of the *pensionnats* took up this unpleasing work as a sideline to the school, in this way gaining an income and official favour. This combination of roles proved disastrous for Maréville. The delinquent population rose to 500, more than double the number of pupils, and the school was disrupted from 1778 to 1783 by extensive building work. Finally, given an inefficient superior, in 1789 the place was described as fit only for closure. The other two *pensionnats* doubling up as *maisons de force* also suffered, though less grievously. There was a major prison revolt at Saint-Yon in 1774. Earlier, at Angers, 'writings, arms, ropes and files were smuggled in and riots ensued, several brothers being victims . . . and perishing from the ill-treatment they suffered'. Although a wealthy family might pay as much as 1,000 livres a year to have a member confined, most contributed less, and the king's standard payment was 100, so the profits were not great, and school fees still had to be charged, as in the other *pensionnats*. Usually, parents were asked to pay 400 livres together with twelve changes of linen; only a family which had risen as far as the lower middle class could afford this.

There was no shortage of applicants. Mathematics with trigonometry, algebra, and geometry, book keeping and commercial law and practice, horticulture, the maintenance of machinery, calligraphy, surveying, and other practical disciplines made it an eminently useful syllabus. Latin was banned; grammar was ruthlessly hammered in, but without going on to the frills of rhetoric. Teaching did not consist of long expositions, but in crisp questions and answers, and in doing things, rather than knowing how to do them. In the textbooks, the commonplaces of the old educational methods were kept as adornments, while the substance of the instruction was newly presented. Thus, the explanation of how to turn from adding, subtracting, multiplying, and dividing to fractions was well founded psychologically—slowly, step by step, retaining confidence all the while; this was balanced by the old clichés in praise of mathematics— Archimedes outwitting the besiegers by his calculations, St Jerome declaring numbers to have mystical powers, and the parables of the unjust steward and the talents demonstrating the importance of learning to add up bills and calculate interest.

A student in a *pensionnat* was subject to a regime of fanatical orthodoxy: not a suspect volume in the library, the daily routine including prayer, meditation, mass, litanies of the Child Jesus and the rosary before breakfast, self-examination, the *De Profundis* and the Angelus before dinner, and litanies of the Passion and St Joseph afterwards, with catechism at 6 p.m. taught from a version which, in spite of the commercial speciality of the teaching, flatly condemned loans at interest.

Yet, in spite of these rigours, there was a new spirit in the teaching, ultimately derived from Locke and Fénelon and, perhaps, from Rollin. It was set out in La Salle's *Conduite des écoles*, published in 1720, the year after his death, and refined and augmented by Frère Agathon, the greatest of the superior-generals, in his *Les Douze Vertus d'un bon maître, par M. de la Salle* (1785). These twelve virtues included some surprising ones, certainly by the standards of the day: silence, humility, and generosity. Relationships with pupils were to be friendly. There were to be no beatings. Punishment should strike at pride, by imposing a period on the dunce's stool or relegation to the bottom of the class. In impossible cases, a refractory pupil should be sent home. There were to be no satirical observations, no discouraging words, no sneaking to parents—at the most say, 'could do better'. A teacher was not just a distributor and imposer of information, but must have thought out the reasons behind every commonplace proposition, and devised ways to make his subject interesting. Allegiance to Christian principles and beliefs would come to children by slow, indirect processes; their instructors should use the method already familiar in prayer and meditation: first, inculcate the truth, then explain it, then seek to give it vital force in the soul.

There is always a gap between educational ideals and what actually happens in the classroom, and the sheer rigour of the cadre of religious routines accorded ill with La Salle's almost Rousseauistic theory of sympathetic relationships with the children. So the Frères were not welcome everywhere. Upper-class citizens who sent their sons to the *collèges* scorned an intolerant organization educating children of the lower orders above their station; some bishops, whether because of their tolerant disposition or their Gallicanism, did not want them in their dioceses; some families complained of an excessive discipline exercised by mental pressures: the Jansenist *Nouvelles ecclésiastiques* kept up a running commentary on every fanatical incident or moral lapse which occurred in their establishments. The Frères des Écoles Chrétiennes were an ambivalent organization, the last creation in France of the uncompromising Counter-Reformation, and the appropriator of Enlightenment ideals into the ecclesiastically dominated educational system of the country.

THE RELIGIOUS VOCATION AND
SOCIAL USEFULNESS: WOMEN

I

The work of educating children and caring for the sick and the poor in eighteenth-century France was performed, almost exclusively, by monastic and quasi-monastic institutions founded since the year 1500. Immense endowments had fallen to the monasteries in the Middle Ages, but the new inspirations to a wider social and religious service had, mostly, passed these houses by. The Orders which had arrived earliest had retired to the shade, and the later arrivals bore the burden and heat of the day, without hope of receiving the traditional equal penny.

The newer congregations and institutes, so often lacking in endowment, had to resort to continual shifts to keep going—charging for the services they rendered, or resorting to methods of raising money not always compatible with the highest monastic ideals. Convents of nuns faced especial difficulties, since they did not have the resorts of male communities of going out begging, undertaking parish duties, earning fees for saying masses and preaching. So they had to be calculating about the dowries novices brought with them, let out rooms to old ladies as boarders, make things for sale— tapestries, chair covers, sweets, cakes, liqueurs, medicines—and coax free consultations from doctors and lawyers and delay the payment of tradesmen's bills for years on end. If they managed to make investments, it was generally in *rentes*, contracts of loan bringing in a regular income of interest; under Law's Scheme, the sensational financial experiment of the Regency (1718–20), borrowers rushed to repay their debts in the depreciating paper which was compulsory tender, bringing many a convent to ruin.

In 1727, the government took action to deal with the chaos caused by the bankruptcies. A Commission de secours of four prelates and four *maîtres des requêtes* instituted a sweeping enquiry. The nuns faced a dilemma when furnishing information, for while disclosure of their poverty might bring assistance, it was more likely to result in a decree of suppression, or of union with another house. The many communities where pockets of Jansenist influence were found (the Cistercian and Benedictine convents, and those of the Annonciades, the Calvairiennes, the Visitandines, the Carmelites, and the Ursulines) were particularly alarmed, for the bishops might take their chance to root out the weeds of heretical influence in their dioceses. In fact, the bishops avoided drastic action because of the danger of stirring up lay protests; the disaffected nuns were quietly disposed of by exile to other communities and deprivation of the sacraments, a story of suffering which went unnoticed except in the pages of the *Nouvelles ecclésiastiques*. When it came to the crunch, no one wanted to face the local unpopularity which a ruthless reform would have incurred. Like the Commission des réguliers which forty years later enquired into the monasteries of men, the Commission de secours filled the archives with statistics and did little. Over a long period, fifty houses of Ursulines received a *lettre de cachet* forbidding the reception of novices (fifteen because of Jansenism), but in the end only twenty were suppressed—out of a total of 400. The multitude of poverty-stricken communities of women struggled on, most regaining a precarious solvency.

II

Girls of the upper classes were all educated by nuns, families sending them into different convents according to their position in the social hierarchy, with the fees charged acting as a regulator. In Paris, there were forty-three houses of nuns devoted to such educational work.[1] The daughters of the highest aristocracy would gather at the Abbaye-aux-Bois, rue de Sèvres. A family choosing the maximum tariff with a couple of women attendants might pay as much as 30,000 livres a year. Actresses from the Comédie-Française and dancers and singers from the Opéra paid regular visits to give instruction in the theatrical graces, and the pupils performed sophisticated ballets and plays. Girls from families of the robe and high finance were found in the Dames de Sainte-Marie, rue Jacques, a severely disciplined academy. Noble but not quite so rich girls and those of distinguished bourgeois status would aspire to the Dames de Panthémont, rue de Grenelle, at 800 livres a year, with an extra 200 to be admitted to the table of the abbess and a further 300 for the services of a *femme de chambre*.[2] There were similar fees at La Madeleine de Traisnel, rue de Charonne, the abbaye Saint-

Antoine, Port-Royal, and the Bénédictines du Saint-Sacrement, rue Cassette.

In expensive boarding establishments such as these, girls stayed until a husband was found for them. Mercier ridiculed the dramatists who put on stage young men making their 'declaration' to the girl they adored. 'Nothing could be falser and further from the practice of society . . . No one makes love to young ladies. They are shut up in convents until the day of their marriage. No one sees them alone.' The same, he adds, in bourgeois households with the daughters at home—they are never seen apart from their mothers. Protestations of love can be made only to *grisettes*, the pretty shop girls on their weekend off. Mercier was exaggerating: convent supervision was not as fierce, and young people not so lacking in ingenuity, as he implies. True, the high aristocracy, determined to clinch advantageous alliances in their select circle, tended to ignore the wishes of their daughters; a marriage might be hastened on, even though the bride was not of age to consummate it—in this case, she would go back to her convent after the ceremony, as happened in 1778 when Mlle de Choiseul and, later, Mlle de Bourbonne returned to the Abbaye-aux-Bois,[3] where, no doubt, they cut a splendid figure among the other envious *pensionnaires*. Lower down the social scale, and more and more throughout the century, there was a recognition by families of a daughter's right to be consulted and consent. As marriageable age approached, the convent school slipped unobtrusively into becoming a marriage agency, and the nuns, abandoning their traditional role of persuaders towards a religious vocation, moved into the role of advisers in worldly or sentimental choices. Occasionally, a young woman would be transferred by her family from her convent school to another sort of convent acting as a 'finishing school' to await her suitors, as Mirabeau's beautiful 13-year-old sister was moved from the house of the Benedictine nuns of Montargis to that run by nuns of Dominican allegiance. 'What is charming about this monastery', said her notorious brother, 'is that it is not in the least religious, and numerous ladies retire here for an agreeable social life.'[4] The marriage-agency role might be blatant; Barbier tells a grim story of young men crowding to a Parisian convent to meet an ugly girl supposed to have 30,000 livres a year— all the result of a cruel practical joke. There could, however, be something touching about the brides-for-sale system. In 1775 the comtesse de Brionne asked the abbess of Panthémont to find a wife for her friend, M. de Saint-Péravy, a magistrate of the parlement. The abbess addressed her *pensionnaires*: 'There is a gentleman with

40,000 livres a year and holder of a distinguished office who wants to marry one of you. I warn you he is not much to look at but he has a beautiful disposition.' The rich girls scoffed and a shy and pretty poor one was sure no one would want her; within a few days she was Mme de Saint-Péravy.[5] As a matrimonial agency, the system worked well enough, since everyone understood the rules. A rich planter in Guadeloupe, not finding suitable men on the island for his daughter, naturally sent her to a convent in France—at Bordeaux. Here, a relative advised her on how to make her choice: do not be impatient to escape the cloister; do not see one suitor too often, lest you get too attached to him too early; remember that the public will be judging your conduct as you make your choice.[6] So in the end, though it might be difficult, a young woman had her choice, or at least a liberty to refuse. A few, in the end, decided against marriage altogether, and without taking vows, stayed on comfortably as *pensionnaires* all their lives.[7]

There was speculation among watchers of protocol when the little daughters of Louis XV were to be sent to school, Cardinal Fleury insisting this must be done to avoid the expense of maintaining a separate household for them at Versailles. The Court rejected the gilded Parisian academies for daughters of the high aristocracy, and ensured that the 'filles de France' were kept aloof in their unique rank, taking little heed of their educational prospects, and none of their happiness. Aged 5, 4, 2, and 1 (a baby in arms), they were packed off to the abbey of Fontevrault eighty leagues away. Marie Adélaïde, aged 7, was lucky. Coached in a piteously worded entreaty, she threw herself at the king's feet and was excused from exile. In their seven years at Fontevrault, one of the girls barely managed to complete learning the alphabet, and another had a nervous breakdown from having to go to confession in the vault serving as the convent's burial place. The pious queen never went to visit them.[8]

Paradoxically, the king's daughters were ill brought up, while a superb, but severe education was available for girls at the one school which was a royal foundation, paid for by royal gifts and compulsory levies on other monasteries decreed by the Crown. Under the influence of Mme de Maintenon, Louis XIV had founded 'la communauté royale de Saint-Louis de Saint-Cyr' to educate 250 girls from poor noble families which had served the nation in war. The Dames de Saint-Louis began as a lay institute taking temporary vows, but in 1692 their vows were made permanent, and the community became a regular monastery under the rule of St Augustine.

The girls were at Saint-Cyr from the ages of 7 to 12, and could stay on until they were 20. They were dressed in severe uniforms; their days were full of classes and religious exercises; they were never allowed to go home; and their parents could come to see them only four times a year, and always in the presence of a nun. Under this strict regime, they were taught a great deal of practical expertise, more especially the art of household management, and it was a lament among country noblemen looking for diligent wives that the nuns so often persuaded their charges to stay in the religious life.[9] The 'filles de France' would have done a great deal better there than among the sycophantic and inefficient splendours of Fontevrault.

As in Paris, so on a lesser scale in the other towns, there was a hierarchy of convents educating fee-paying girls. Some nuns ran a formal school as their main activity—at the abbey of Saint-Georges at Rennes, the terms were 230 livres a year, sheets and towels not included, with the abbess guaranteeing personal attention to her pupils.[10] Others took boarders occasionally, according to their inclination and financial necessities. Strictly, the Visitandines were not supposed to teach; François de Sales had wished them to devote their lives to contemplation, though a particular convent might take in three or four girls who were known to have a precocious vocation to the monastic state. The daily routine prescribed by the Order was two meals a day, at 10 a.m. and 6 p.m., the first preceded by public confession of faults and eaten in silence (except on the eve of the Epiphany); there were two hours' recreation, all the rest of the time being spent in reciting the offices, spiritual reading, prayer, and meditation.[11] Within the intensity of this contemplative life, the Visitandine cult of the Sacred Heart of Jesus was born. But as time went on, the proviso allowing the taking of pupils considered to have the beginnings of a vocation to the cloister became the gateway for some of the nuns in some houses to become schoolmistresses. Convents of the Visitation were all autonomous, with no central direction to prevent them from following their own inclinations. The rules, in a way, facilitated the change, for François de Sales, to accommodate ladies of a delicate constitution, had abolished the night offices and prescribed a period of rest of two hours at noon: the routine of liturgical observances was not all-absorbing. The nuns were practically all from families of great distinction, and within their family circles there was always pressure to find places for girls to be educated under the charge of persons of their own station in life, in whose society they could safely grow up to marriageable age. It is remarkable how often a house of Visitandines had boarders who were nieces of nuns in the same establishment.[12] Educational activities also ensured recruitment. An analysis of the careers of the 403 Visitandines mentioned in the circular letters of the various houses from 1667 to 1789 shows how half of them had begun their connection with the Order as schoolgirls in its care: these convents for ladies of the highest social class were self-perpetuating.

In some houses, educational activities were a sideline to the contemplative life, taking a few girls on grounds of family relationship or potential vocation. In the diocese of Autun, at Moulins, Charolles, Paray-le-Monial, and Autun itself, the number of boarders at any one time was between seven and fourteen, a limited number, short of being a school. At Moulins, the implication that the little girls were presumed to be going to take the veil was emphasized by making them wear the habit of the Order, a resort to a parade of pious intention which did not please all parents.[13] On the other hand, a particular house might decide to move into education as its principal activity. At Angers, more than thirty boarders were taken, all from aristocratic or leading bourgeois families.[14] As befitted their station in life, the girls were taught singing, dancing, acting, and the social graces; the annual play was a social occasion for Angevin high society, and if some of the girls had to dress as men to complete the cast, no one minded—except the Jansenists, of course. The Visitandines' line on girls taking male parts did not include doubts about transvestism: what was to be avoided was amorous intrigue. Thus, in their convent at Beaune, when they drew lots for a play to celebrate the birthday of their mother superior, they rejoiced when the verdict fell on the *Mort de César*, an all-male heroic piece without sexual overtones. There remained the problem of a prologue to mark the occasion, and one of the nuns wrote to her cousin, Mme du Châtelet, who persuaded her lover, Voltaire, to write what was required, done in twenty minutes flat as he stood in the corner of the chimney-piece. It was an orthodox effusion, the philosophe asking the sisters to pray for him 'to the Master of all our imaginings'.[15]

By contrast with the Visitandines, the Ursulines were an Order specifically devoted to education.[16] Angela Merici, their Italian founder, had organized them as celibate schoolmistresses living in their own homes, and Charles Borromeo had brought them into community life under the modified rule of St Augustine. Pontifical bulls (as to the Ursulines of Toulouse in 1615) had praised them as a bulwark against heretics, and defined their duties as giving free education to girls, to include reading, writing, and needlework, though with the primary object of inspiring them to religious ardour. In the battle against heresy, they indeed played their part when Louis XIV's persecution forced Protestant girls of prominent families into convents for education. The bitter-sweet cruelty of persuasion which followed is unpleasant to imagine. On occasion it worked, and girls stayed on to take the veil: there was the strange case of Marguerite de Labouetière, who on her wedding-day fled to take refuge for ever in the Ursuline convent of Orthez, where her enforced school-days had been spent. As for free schooling, most houses made an effort to give some elementary instruction to the poor, but their essential role came to be the running of fee-paying boarding-schools. In towns where there was straight competition, the Visitandines, or the Clarisses, were likely to attract the most prestigious pupils; even so, the Ursulines stood high socially. At Rouen, a third of the intake came from families of nobles of the sword or of the robe. Even the snobbish girls at the Visitation of Angers were constrained to concede that the Ursuline school was 'exactly the same as ours, only less well run'.

'Increasing religious ardour', as prescribed by the papal directives, was a difficult formula to implement. Certainly, an Ursuline house took entire possession of a girl's life, reducing her connections with home to a minimum. The regulations of Paris in 1651 and 1705 allow no holidays: at Dijon, the vacation was a month. If the parents lived locally, they could visit their children in the convent parlour, or meetings at home would be allowed, though never staying overnight. The girls rose at 6 a.m. and attended a daily mass; on Sundays they also had the rosary, the office of the Virgin, the seven penitential psalms, and litanies of the saints; on Christmas Day they attended three masses. On the Friday of the week after Corpus Christi, there were religious celebrations all day, for this was the day to commemorate the visions of the Sacred Heart to Marguerite Marie Alacoque at Paray-le-Monial in 1673 and 1674. The nuns were adept at devising picturesque little ceremonies: the usage of the white veil for the First Communion is an Ursuline invention. The convent library would have the *Imitation*, St François de Sales's *Introduction*, and a few Jesuit works of spirituality, while the Order printed various handbooks of devotion for the use of its boarders, one of the favourite exercises being the renewal of baptismal promises. Catechism courses were held twice a day, at Angers all through the century from the same dog-eared notebooks dating from 1700. The nuns prepared 'abridgements' of Christian doctrine for use in teaching, generally using a quadripartite division: the Creed, the Pater Noster, the Ten Commandments, and the sacraments as the guide to the four dispositions leading to salvation—faith, hope, charity, and the doing of good works. Classes began and ended with prayer, and all who passed by the crucifix on the classroom wall paused to bow. How deep and affecting was the inner experience behind the accumulation of observances? According to an angry Jansenist, the Christian life was being 'reduced to a few external practices which they ally with the maxims of the world'.[17] Yet the magnetism to draw so many girls to choose the monastic vocation was there, and it was commonly said, whether in praise or blame, that convent education made a permanent imprint on those who were brought up in its religious regimentation.

Ursuline education was adaptable to local circumstances. There were 400 houses, each independent, with the sisters electing their mother superior annually. There was no imposition of syllabuses from central direction, and the bishops, who had the official disciplinary oversight, were little concerned with teaching programmes. Houses even drew up their own catechisms, or chose them from among those produced in various dioceses, and if there was a leaven of Jansenism in the place, there were some powerful examples from the pens of Jansenist theologians available. Convents had their educational specialities. All taught needlework, but Angers became a centre of rich embroidery from the time the first needlewoman of the queen arrived from Versailles to make her profession. In many places, the sisters made a great deal of local history and stories of the saints of the province, and they had a growing interest in the wider field of Church history and in the secular history of France. News of Ursulines working abroad—like Marie de l'Incarnation in Canada—encouraged them to add the reading of the Jesuit *Relations* to the curriculum. For its day, the Parisian rule-book was enlightened in its educational methodology. Like the Jesuits, the Ursulines were to organize their classes in competing groups, though of twelve instead of ten, *dizainières* instead of *décurions*. The teacher was 'to speak little but ask many questions', encouraging the pupils to 'move from . . . the known to the unknown'. The way to break into a new subject was to treat it 'historically', tracing its development. The peculiar difficulty of being supposed to offer free education, yet actually charging for it, was reflected in the calculated ambiguity with which teachers were directed to 'treat rich and poor pupils alike, but not to put girls of distinguished families near to the poor and dirty ones'. The regulations also had a puritanical paragraph forbidding 'indecent games, such as comedies and dances'. In the interests of a lively upper-class education, this prohibition was ignored. There were limits, of course; there was a great scandal in the late seventeenth century when an Ursuline convent near Grenoble put on a performance of *Tartuffe* in the choir of the chapel.[18] But 'speech-days' with sketches, ballets, pastorals, and burlesques written by the nuns and featuring local characters were universal. The rules were strict, the practice cheerfully individualistic. This being so, the quality of the education depended even more than is usually the case on the quality of the teachers. The Ursulines were recruited from the social groups, like the nobles of the robe, where intellectual families abounded. Among their number were a granddaughter of Malherbe, two sisters of Ménage, three aunts of Fénelon, a daughter of Jean Racine, the sister of Diderot (she was prouder of her brother the canon than of the *philosophe*), the sister of Buffon, and two aunts of Lamartine. As a result of the undercurrent of Jansenism in the Order, many of the sisters read historical and controversial books with serious attention—they knew their Nicole, Pascal, Bossuet, and the pulpit orators of the reign of Louis XIV. 'She made herself very proficient at teaching by the enlightenment she drew from prayer and the reading of good books,' said the obituary notice of one of the ladies of the Parisian house of Saint-Jacques. In the context of the times, it was as good a way of teacher training as any.

The Ursulines were the biggest teaching order of women, but there were innumerable other convents of various 'allegiances' scattered over the country, offering paying places for girls. The quality of the education varied, and families, unless they had precise local knowledge, made enquiries. A Carmelite friar in Paris replied to anxious parents: do not send your daughter to the nuns of Compiègne, 'they go in for silly ceremonies, they shear the girls' hair and give them ridiculous pet names'; send her rather to the abbey of Sainte-Austreberthe.[19] To what extent did this diversity of schools really fulfil the expectations of the public? According to Molière, the object of the education of girls was twofold: character formation, to ensure moral conduct, and training in household management.[20] Defenders of convent education were eloquent about moral purpose. 'What use are so many convents?' asks the sceptic. An orator at the Academy of Angers in 1770 replied: 'What use are they? ungrateful men. To rear for you good mothers of families, chaste and loyal spouses, vigilant housewives, women who are virtuous citizens. Can the sweet voice of Nature be heard amid the tumult and worldliness of your own homes . . .' and so on.[21] Yet, granting the priority of moral formation, should household management set the boundaries of feminine intellectual endeavour? It was as if, Mme de

Lambert complained, 'girls were a species apart, to be left in isolation, without any thought of the fact that they comprise half of the population . . . and that by them, families either rise or go down to destruction'.[22] Late in the century there were a few campaigners for total equality for women, Riballier and Condorcet in particular. But the main current of liberal feeling, from Fénelon to Rousseau, was to give equal rights, but not to equal things. Girls should be regarded as of equal importance to boys, though they should be trained essentially as wives and mothers and—a potentially far-ranging admission—as educators of the next generation of citizens. This meant that it was less the deficiencies of the content of feminine education which were challenged, as the very idea of the convent as the setting for the educational process. The eighteenth century saw a remarkable change in the status of women, associated less with the theoretical idea of equality than with their more effective contribution to the work of the world as civilization and economic life advanced and diversified, and with the discovery of the supreme value of 'femininity'—'a decisive mutation in the history of civilization'.[23]

In the context of this new view of women, the writers of the Enlightenment made a predictable attack on convent education. Girls, it was said, were deprived of knowledge of the real world. They emerge like cave-dwellers blinded when they step into the sunshine, said Fénelon. The man who presents himself at the convent grille on a reconnaissance for a marriage partner, even if he looks like a monkey, is welcomed as a deliverer—the view of Voltaire.[24] Grimm was savagely dismissive: according to him, girls are taught nothing of true virtue, honour or decency, for what they learn of these things is unconnected with reality; they are forced into the arms of a husband they do not love and subjected to his ruthless sexual demands; by reaction, they then throw off all the decencies themselves. Having been locked up without pleasure, said a great lady, they rush to seize it once it comes within their grasp: 'une fille qui n'a rien vu, se meurt de tout voir à la fois'.[25] These accusations (not all compatible one with another) invert the moral argument for convent education. The enclosed life is meant to inculcate Christian morality; in fact, it merely creates an ignorance of the world which encourages immorality. Both churchmen and philosophes talked of these matters with unimaginative solemnity, the first exaggerating the strictness of convent education and its benefits, the second exaggerating its unworldliness. Girls (and, for that matter, nuns) were neither so punctilious in pious observances nor so clueless about the facts of life as was supposed. Humourless commentators on education do not understand how children are resourceful enough to outwit the system and how they contrive to educate each other.

III

The communities of women devoted to education felt an uneasy obligation to make no distinction between rich and poor families. In practice, discrimination was inevitable, since the rich insisted on it, and the poor could not pay the fees. The Ursulines ought to have dispensed free education to all, but in the diocese of Autun, their communities charging minimum fees to poorer families (120 livres in 1720) found they were incurring a running deficit—and such a fee excluded half the population anyway.[26] So the general practice was to have a fee-paying school to which a few ordinary children were admitted free for reading and writing lessons. At Angers, the Ursulines claimed to teach such a free class of sixty: according to their enemies, the true figure was nearer twenty.[27] At Quimperlé, though it was hard to make ends meet, they took some peasant girls into their classes at no charge. Marie-Anne de Kervénozael, the aristocratic prioress, was a woman of principle; she refused to admit rich ladies as paying guests, even though her brother the marquis was dipping into his own fortune to save her house from bankruptcy, and in 1740 she roundly condemned those of her nuns who were using disparaging words to their penurious pupils and driving them away. In education, she said, peasants count as much as nobles.[28]

As a rule, however, the nuns who took lifelong vows and accepted the full obligation of the cloistered life were chiefly concerned with educating the daughters of fee-paying families.[29] Free education was given by the many new 'secular' institutes which arose in the seventeenth century, composed of dedicated women who took only 'simple' (temporary) vows, or no vows at all. There were varying degrees of formality in organization. Some women volunteering for teaching became tertiaries, members of the 'Third Order' of one of the existing older congregations—Dominicans, Capuchins, Récollets, Eudistes, and so on. The Carmelites of the diocese of Vannes drew up rules in 1670 for entry to this confraternity of service: to be over 30 years of age, unmarried, and enjoying economic independence—this necessarily limited recruits to reasonably well-off families.[30] There was no question of withdrawing from worldly affairs, though there was a rule to avoid the riotous celebrations accompanying weddings and baptisms unless the happy event concerned relatives. By the eighteenth century, numerous parishes of the diocese had Carmelite schoolmistresses, and some had a Dominican tertiary.

Most of the schoolmistresses, however, came from the new foundations which proliferated from 1660 onwards. These teaching institutes went by the names of 'Sœurs grises', 'Dames régentes', 'Filles de la Charité', 'Béates', or other names derived from those of their founders, or under the invocation of the names of Jesus, Our Lady, and various saints, and associated by designation with the particular towns in which they had originated.[31] The process continued in the eighteenth century. The Sœurs d'Ernemont[32] and the Sœurs de Saint-Paul of Chartres at the end of the seventeenth century were followed by the Filles de Saint-Paul at Tréguier (started in 1699, statutes drawn up in 1727),[33] the Congrégation de la Sagesse of Saint-Laurent-sur-Sèvre (1703), the Filles du Saint-Esprit of Plérin (1706), the Congrégation de la Providence of Evreux (1714), the Sœurs du Bon Sauveur of Caen (combining, not entirely incongruously, teaching children and prison visiting), the Institut des Sœurs de l'École of Toul (1720), the Sœurs de la Doctrine Chrétienne of Nancy, called the 'Vatelottes' after Canon Vatelot, their founder (1752). After the mid-century, innovation slackened, but in 1762 Jean-Martin Moye, a retired missionary from China, founded the Filles de la Providence in Lorraine, an inspirational group with little formal structure, to teach in rural parishes.[34] About the same time, the bishop of Langres, disappointed by the sloth of his three houses of Ursulines, decided to attach lay women, taking only annual vows, to one of them. The experiment succeeded, and by 1789 the educational work of all three houses was run by the sisters with informal vows.[35]

In contrast to what was happening in Orders where the nuns took solemn perpetual vows, recruitment to these congregations of temporary allegiance flourished in the eighteenth century. The Sœurs de Saint-Paul, founded in 1694 by a curé, and moving into Chartres to run a school and hospital in 1708, had fifteen houses by 1727 and fifty in 1780.[36] The best years for the Sœurs d'Ernemont were after 1750; for the Filles de la Providence of Rouen, 1730–9 and after 1760. The great expansion of the Filles de la Sagesse of Saint-Laurent-sur-Sèvre came after 1730, and, indeed, was still going on throughout the Revolution, in spite of the horrors of the Vendean civil war in the countryside which they served. In 1760, recruitment to such congregations constituted 11 per cent of women entering religious life in France: in 1789 it was 21 per cent.[37]

The proliferation of these new organizations to educate the children of the poor (and sometimes to nurse the sick as well) was possible because of a surge of vocations, a fruit of the inspiration of the piety of the Church of the Counter-Reformation and of a transformation of social relationships with the advance of civilization. Women of the aristocracy, once married, enjoyed great freedom; those of bourgeois families helped their husbands in shop and counting-house, and ran the business if their partner died. But women of lower social classes had few opportunities for working independently with recognized status. With the new foundations came their breakthrough. The initial impetus for recruitment and organization came, often, from zealous parish priests seconded by pious aristocratic ladies. In this way, the Congrégation de la Providence of Evreux began about 1700.[38] Curé Duvivier of the village of Caër set up a school with his sister Justine as the teacher; then came a legacy from a great lady of a family of the robe, another from an abbé, another from the curé of Thevray. Bishops, aware of the importance of a religious education for the mothers of the future, gave support, especially in Protestant areas. 'The education of girls', said the bishop of Dax about the crypto-Calvinist population of Orthez, 'is the only method we have of bringing the people to the true faith.'[39] Some prelates, weary of the multiplication of formal nunneries, wanted teachers with a minimum of institutional fuss and amenable to the direction of the parish priests; as the bishop of Cahors said in 1673, 'pious girls and widows' could do useful work and 'banish for ever from those who run such Christian schools all desire to form their own religious institutions and convents, as has sometimes happened'.[40]

Though formality and regulation were kept to a minimum, the drive of some formidable lady (generally of aristocratic family) at the centre often ensured continuity. Similarly, the setting up of a central 'seminary' to train the teachers (a device often used) would ensure high standards and a corresponding welcome in the parishes. Both factors were evident in the successful expansion of the Dames de Saint-Maur.[41] They began in the seventeenth century as the Filles maîtresses des écoles charitables du Saint-Enfant-Jésus, and in 1678 set up their seminary in Paris in the rue Saint-Maur. When Louis XIV revoked the edict of Nantes, there was a demand in the southern dioceses for teachers for the 'converted' Protestant girls, and twenty-seven new foundations were made there from 1681 to 1689. In 1719, the Rouen community became separate, under the title of the Sœurs de la Providence, while the main branch centred at Paris called itself the Dames de Saint-Maur. From 1719 to 1761 Catherine de Bossedon, of the high nobility of Auvergne, was superior, presiding over further expansion and outwitting the bureaucracy which denied her institute letters patent by passing on the property by private testament to individuals. At the Revolution, there were fifty-six schools with 500–600 sisters teaching in them.

The standard combination of founders—a curé and an aristocratic lady—was matched by another: the charismatic Christian propagandist and the lady who was his spiritual friend, like François de Sales and Jeanne de Chantal, Vincent de Paul and Louise de Marillac. The Filles de la Sagesse owed their origin to such an alliance. The organization of mission preachers set up by Louis-Marie Grignon de Montfort would never have been accompanied by an institute of women teachers and nurses but for the quiet persistence of Marie-Louise Trichet (Sœur Marie-Louise de Jésus), who carried on after her mentor's disorganized ventures at Poitiers and La Rochelle had foundered, and after his death in 1716 lived on for forty more years perfecting the work of his dreams.[42]

Numerous schools were run as a sideline by congregations whose primary duty was to nurse the sick. The Filles de la Charité of Vincent de Paul ran classes in annexes to municipal hospitals. In Paris, in twenty-five parishes they had houses as bases for sisters fulfilling the dual role of nurses and teachers. In Lorraine, the Congrégation de Saint-Charles had forty-six establishments of this kind. In the countryside, the resident sister of a teaching institute was expected to be a social worker in every sense of the word. A curé, rejoicing in the decision of the Filles de Notre-Dame to set up a school in his parish, listed the benefits he expected from the arrival of the sisters: they would 'help the poor, learn how to do (surgical) bleeding, study medicines and know how to make them, instruct poor children free of charge, teaching them not only to read and write but also the principles of religion, as well as how to work at a trade appropriate to their station in life, so they can subsequently earn their living'.[43] Since many of the men of the province spend half the year away from home as migratory labourers, he added, the education of girls was doubly important, as in the end, it was the mothers acting alone who brought up the children.

If the fulminations of bishops against mixed education had been effective, the sisters would have taught only girls, but in practice, only fanatical curés insisted on the rules. In his synodal charge of 1747, the bishop of Lectoure said his parish priests had assured him of the impossibility of realistically organizing the segregation of the sexes, so he could only hope that they would at least ensure 'that the boys do not place themselves promiscuously among the girls'.[44] For most children, attendance at school was of brief duration. According to the educational theorists of the day, children of the poor should not begin until the age of 7 or 8, and by then they were almost ready for apprenticeship or work in the fields. The Parisian parish of Saint-Étienne-du-Mont[45] was unusual in its regulation specifying two years, but this was only for those who showed signs of progress, otherwise six months was the limit; and the full curriculum was ambitious, including the reading of Latin as well as French. The emphasis of the schools was on 'moral' development, with many religious observances—the sign of the cross, prayers, catechism, attendance at mass, and learning to serve at the altar. Discipline and routine were the keynotes, not the cultivation of the imagination; as the abbé de Saint-Pierre defined education, it was 'to bring about the happiness of mankind by the inculcation of indispensable habits'. The regulations of schools and handbooks like Crousez's *Traité de l'éducation des enfants* (1722) show how reading was taught: it was a matter of being able to recite passages and learn them by heart. The content would be explained to the children to retain their interest, but teasing out the meaning for themselves was secondary; first, they would learn the passage, then they would go on to the recognition of individual letters, then individual words, then put the words together. Later in the century reformers tried to humanize the system, proposing to begin by teaching a vocabulary of 300 words, then proceeding to reading as essentially understanding; there were also experiments with manual aides to memory, like arranging alphabetical cards or setting type on toy printing presses.[46] Such luxuries were not for ordinary pupils. The typical school was stuck in the rut of a primitive methodology. This was inevitable, for classes were huge, sometimes a hundred strong. The sister from the religious institute would preside, making forays for testing, while a dozen or so *récitateurs*, chosen from the most forward pupils, would teach small groups. The air would be full of the drone of these different units monotonously chanting their lines.

In many places, especially in the towns, the sisters would economize on reading and writing time to teach girls a trade—spinning, or weaving. In Paris, the Filles de Sainte-Geneviève did something of everything—taught in schools, nursed the sick, conducted devotional meetings for women, and ran a *chambre de travail* to train girls for their first job. The Filles de la Providence of the capital taught orphans to make tapestries and ornate embroideries, including some commissioned by the palace of Versailles.[47] In Lyon, the ladies of a lay association, the Tiers Ordre féminin de la Trinité, had as their aim 'to teach manufacturing work to girls who have no dowry to get themselves a husband or to gain entry to a nunnery, so enabling them to subsist and keep them from the dire necessity which might bring their innocence to shipwreck'.[48]

On Sundays, the sisters would be called to the parish church to take catechism classes. The regulations of the Dames de Saint-Maur prescribed question-and-answer sessions to encourage children to 'generous emulation', with their parents invited to attend to add solemnity to the rivalry. As for the sisters themselves, they were 'forbidden to give themselves airs as preachers'.[49] Another, more interesting duty was incumbent on the Sœurs d'écoles of Châlons-sur-Marne; they were to go in their formal grey dresses to the *veillées*, the evening social gatherings of women, where sewing and knitting were accompanied by gossip and folk-tales—if possible, they were to introduce catechism competitions and the singing of pious canticles.[50] As ever under the *ancien régime*, a place had to be found for social misfits in religious institutions, however incongruously. In Angers, the house of La Providence at one time was charging a fee of 200 livres to one family for teaching their daughter sewing, to another for looking after a mad girl and to another for looking after a kleptomaniac. Or, at the other end of the scale, an institute might be required by the government to move into more sophisticated teaching and set up a boarding-school. In 1775, the king transferred the revenues of a suppressed house of Cordeliers to the Dames de Saint-Maur, to enable them to set up an academy for daughters of impoverished nobles' families around Toulouse—it ended up with eighteen sisters and twenty servants looking after a hundred girls—even so, there was a free class for the daughters of ordinary people.[51]

Some of the educational institutes remained small. The Migamionnes, founded in the Parisian parish of Saint-Nicolas-du-Chardonnet, expanded to no more than four parishes in the nearby countryside. The Sœurs de Sainte-Anne (Saumur), the Sœurs de l'Enfant Jésus (Reims), and the Sœurs de la Croix (Lavaur) had from fifty to a hundred teachers; the Sœurs de la Chapelle-Riboul (Evron) had eighty-nine schools and more schoolmistresses; the Sœurs de la Doctrine Chrétienne (Metz) and the Filles de la Charité (Nevers) had more; and the Filles de la Sagesse in their heyday had 941 schools. In some dioceses, women hastened to take the opportunity of this new kind of religious and social service; in others, where the practices of church life and devotion were lukewarm, vocations were few. It was not easy for enterprising bishops or ambitious superiors of institutes to switch teachers into the barren areas, for local knowledge was important, and in many places familiarity with the patois was indispensable. About 1780, in the diocese of Tarbes only 3 per cent of the parishes had a significant number of girls in their schools; in the dioceses of Albi, Castres, and Lavaur, the figure was 6 per cent; in Arles, 60 per cent. The variations in these figures were chiefly—though not entirely—due to the incidence of vocations to teaching duties.[52]

Girls had the best chance of becoming literate in the towns.[53] In Grenoble, there were five free schools for them, with four convents also taking external pupils; in Paris, there were innumerable elementary schools—the canon-precentor of Notre-Dame had inspection rights in 334 of them, 167 reserved for girls. In some cities— Clermont, Riom, Moulins, Aurillac, Puy, and Lyon—there were more elementary places for girls than for boys. The classes in towns were often large, so the number of women in the various teaching institutes must be multiplied by a large factor to estimate the number of children taught. As the duration of a pupil's school career tended to be brief, there was a rapid turnover—many received some education, albeit superficial. And the sum total of the modest instruction available is not exhausted by a survey of the teaching sisters. Parishes hired lay teachers, men and women (though at starvation rates of pay); curés and vicaires taught children of favoured families, or boys and girls who seemed promising candidates for a religious vocation; elder sisters back from service in urban households and tired old uncles back from the wars passed on the rudiments of literacy they had picked up. The old assumption that the vast majority of girls of the poorer classes received no formal education was an unjustified deduction from the contrast between the numbers of women who could sign their names as compared with men. Writing was not put high on the list of feminine educational priorities; moral and religious instruction, sewing and other handicrafts, and reading of simple pious manuals and folk-tales were the essentials, and in these respects, the sisters of the new institutes served them well.

IV

Schoolgirls were not the only boarders accepted by convents; if the nuns had sufficient accommodation, they might let it out to ladies seeking a retirement home or a refuge.[54] It was a way to make money—perhaps the nuns would build a special annexe for boarders, or adapt the mansion of the abbess if it was spacious. At Rennes, almost all the communities of women were in this business. The Carmelites, whose rule forbade *pensionnaires*, with an income of only 4,000 livres could not afford to obey it, and by 1789 were drawing 10,000 a year from forty paying guests. By taking a rich boarder in the seventeenth century, the Ursulines had added to their enclosure an attractive house; the contract specified that Mme du Chastellier de la Thébaudais who gave it had to have her private parlour, a space in the garden to grow flowers, oranges from the orangery, and the right to name a novice to be accepted without a dowry. The Calvairiennes, who made a similar contract about the same time, found it a disastrous bargain, for the lady had huge debts, and as her heirs, the nuns were liable; in 1780 they were still being sued by creditors.

A lady who took rooms in a convent might be doing so for temporary convenience, as during the months her husband was away with his regiment, or for a period of retreat, perhaps to recover after a bereavement.[55] Or it might be for a space of meditation before a major event in her life—girls sometimes went in for a few weeks before their First Communion.[56] A long lease on an apartment might be part of a plan to economize, as with the widowed duchesse de Choiseul trying to pay off her husband's debts, or the marquise de Créqui saving up for her children.[57] A permanent lease was a standard resort of ladies wanting a refuge in old age or, at the end of a stormy life, seeking a period of detachment to prepare for death.[58] Taking residence in a particular convent might be a device to achieve social cachet, hence the applications to get into the Parisian house of l'Assomption when Mlle Alexandrine, Mme de Pompadour's daughter, went there.[59] A lady pursued by malicious gossip might become a monastic boarder to pre-empt a veneer of respectability, like the princesse de Talmont going to the nuns of Saint-Joseph in the rue Saint-Dominique while she carried on a prestigious liaison.[60] A maltreated wife awaiting the parlement's decree of separation was supposed to keep a low profile while proceedings lasted; the Filles de l'Union Chrétienne, rue Saint-Denis, specialized in exercising discretion in these cases.[61] More dramatically, the mistress of some great nobleman might retire to break off the affair, as Mlle Ménard in flight from the duc de Chaulnes. M. de Sartine, the lieutenant of police, got the abbé Duguet to negotiate a place for her and her daughter in the Cordelières of the rue l'Oursine. He did this by pretending she was a relative; she left after a fortnight, and the good abbé looked ridiculous.[62] The mother of M. Prévot called on Mlle Basse, a dancer at the Opéra, and pleaded with her to abdicate her hold over her son so that he could make an advantageous marriage: the girl generously retired to a convent to leave her lover free.[63]

There was a strange underworld of relationships in the life of boarding-houses. The paying guests could fall out with the nuns or with each other, perhaps dragging the nuns into their quarrels. Such bitterness arose in a community at Fécamp in 1738 that the house was banned from taking more *pensionnaires*, and one of them, Mme Diggs, an Englishwoman, was expelled.[64] There were special difficulties when the paying guests were there reluctantly, banished from the world by a royal *lettre de cachet*. The king rarely paid the fees, the family asking for the reclusion order being responsible. The four houses at Paris usually used by the authorities for this purpose occasionally refused to accept 'des personnes trop décriées', insisting on a direct order from the archbishop before they would comply.[65] There were mysteries. Who was 'Milady' in the Benedictine abbey at Pontoise (a house of English nuns of noble lineage). She had been sent there, willingly, by a *lettre de cachet* requested by the great Soubise family, and she wrote unrevealing letters of brooding melancholy.[66] Parents would use the royal authority to discipline an erring daughter, it could be, unjustly—Marie de Massol was released from the Ursulines of Châtillon because the nuns took her part. Catherine de Beauzeville was not so lucky: she was incarcerated in 1747, took unwilling vows six years later, and in 1789 was still trying to get free.[67] There was a standard legal procedure for dealing with an adulterous wife. She was put in a convent for two years wearing secular dress, during which time her husband could recall her. If not, she had to stay for life, observing the rules like a nun, without being one, though if her husband died, she could get out if someone wanted to marry her.[68] The comte de Choiseul-Stainville, who had married a girl twenty-five years his junior, put up with her gallantries until she began an affair with an actor who had been a *garçon perruquier*. As she was setting off to a fancy-dress ball, she was bundled into a carriage and sent to the Filles de Sainte-Marie at Nancy, never to emerge, her fortune sequestrated for her two daughters.[69] Protestant husbands envied Catholics this grim resource for establishing domestic peace: in 1789 the consistories of Alsace asked for the restoration of their old right to pronounce divorces, 'since they have not the convents available for the confinement of women who are adulterous or lacking in circumspection'.[70] Lacking in circumspection—clearly there could be reasons other than adultery, for example, spendthrift folly. Indeed, there was a presumption that a woman separated from her husband ought to withdraw from society. On this ground, Louis XVI ordered the princesse de Monaco into a religious house: 'quand une femme ne vit pas avec son mari, elle ne doit pas vivre dans le monde'.[71] In the lawless days of the Regency, a retreat into seclusion might be in the woman's best interests. There was a guard of fifty soldiers at the monastery of Port-Royal in Paris in 1723 when the princesse de Conti was boarding there, lest the prince should try to kidnap her. He was wanting to force her to sign a deed of separation by which she would live in a convent for four years (moving to a different house if there was a fire or an outbreak of smallpox), but with the obligation to come back home if the couple's two sons died, staying for long enough to provide another heir.[72] These sorts of social arrangements provided novelists with convenient tragic denouements. 'Mme d'Archenes is still in a convent, where she was sent for having incurred the resentment of a man in high office and for having brought disgrace upon her husband.'[73] Mme de Tourval, betrayed, dies in the same religious house and in the very room where she had slept as a schoolgirl.[74] Real life could be stranger than fiction, as the adventures of the Mirabeau family showed. The marquis, the so-called 'Ami des Hommes', with a wife, daughter, and son incarcerated at the same time, broke a record: 'vous avez donc entrepris de peupler les couvents?' And Sophie de Malroy, marquise de Monnier, thrown into a nunnery by her injured husband, found consolation with the son (the revolutionary Mirabeau), who settled in her room, disguised sometimes as a nun and sometimes as a gardener. When the death of the Président de Monnier released her, she chose to live in a house at the monastery gates, conducting a liaison with the lieutenant of the local police, and finally committing suicide after sending a farewell letter to her old lover as he sat in the National Assembly, where the debates were in progress which would leave no convents available to house unwilling guests, and end the royal power to send them.[75]

V

The institutions caring for the sick, the infirm, the poor, the home-less, and orphans in eighteenth-century France were the compara-tively recent creation of the zeal of Counter-Reformation piety, seconded by the power of the royal government. They were mainly in the towns, for throughout the seventeenth and most of the eighteenth century, the bias of State organization was towards centralization, and the endowments of so many of the rural charit-able foundations of the Middle Ages were confiscated for the big urban establishments. Yet some of the local 'hospitals' in villages and tiny market towns survived: in 1789, of the 2,189 organizations listed under this name in an official enquiry, a quarter had fewer than ten beds. Some were well run. At Avallon (population 4,311) three *économes* with only informal vows of religion were in charge of a ward with twenty-four beds; the old endowments yielding 5,000 livres a year were ample. The governing committee was proud of its nursing sisters, and in 1781 provided them with uniforms: brown and dark blue, with round hats, a black silk neckerchief and a pectoral cross.[76] At Saint-Cales in the province of Maine, four sisters, not belonging to any Order, were on renewable three-year contracts under a governing body of the mayor, the curé, the prior of the nearby monastery, and two elected notables.[77] But places removed from the critical scrutiny of a wider public tended to inefficiency. The 2,000 inhabitants of Trets had 'ignorant artisans' as the recteurs of their hospital, and these officials misappropriated the funds or lent them to each other free of interest.[78] The traveller Richeprey found the hospital of Marcilhac a veritable 'stable', and the sight of the three straw palliasses made him feel ill.[79] In mitigation of such horror stories, it should be said that the beds of country hospitals were not normally occupied by sick persons, for the nurses preferred to treat their patients at home.[80] The institution would shelter pilgrims, indigent travellers, and homeless folk. A dictionary of 1680 defined 'hospital' as 'a place to which the poor who do not have means to live retire, and where a particular care is taken of their souls'.[81] The care of souls was important: the chapel attached to the filthy room at Marcilhac was in good order and well decorated.

By 1700, every sizeable town in France had two major charitable institutions: the *hôtel-Dieu* and the *hôpital général*. The first was a hospital in our sense, with wards where the sick were under medical care; the second was a multi-purpose building—almshouse, work-house, orphanage, staging-point for poor travellers, prison for incorrigible vagabonds. Very often, the *hôtel-Dieu* was the successor to a medieval foundation, while the *hôpital général* was a recent creation. Just after the mid-seventeenth century, the puritanical group of upper-class zealots, the Compagnie du Saint-Sacrement, had set up a prototype in Paris, and in 1662 a royal decree ordered every town to follow suit. This order was reinforced by the preaching of Jesuits sent round as government emissaries: they would conduct a three-day mission, then urge the municipality to set up an 'hôpital à la capucine', that is, without endowments, in the hope that benefactors would be forthcoming.[82] There was a divergence between the aims of the king and the hopes of his preachers. The latter were concerned for the welfare of the poor: the object of the royal decree was to round up beggars and 'instruct them in the ways of piety', thereby preventing crime and providing recruits for the army, the navy, and the colonies.

The structure of charitable organization in the towns, being dependent on the vagaries of individual generosity, was inevitably a patchwork, yet there was a common pattern. At Aix-en-Provence, a metropolis of Church and Law, the old foundations of Saint-Lazare for lepers and Saint-Eutrope for the dropsical were gone, and by the end of the sixteenth century the scene was dominated by the *hôtel-Dieu* (1519) and La Miséricorde (1591), an association of great ladies distributing alms to the 'pauvres honteux'—respectable folk who had fallen on hard times. Later on came the *hôpital général*, called La Charité, the Petit Bethléem for orphans, La Pureté to help poor girls preserve their virginity, and committees concerned with prison visiting and legal aid.[83] At Montpellier, with 30,000 inhabitants, about the same size as Aix, though with a manufacturing suburb alongside the splendid façades marking the headquarters of an intendancy and a bishopric, the main institutions were the same.[84] In the mid-century, the *hôtel-Dieu* had 200 patients, and the *hôpital général* over 700 inmates, as well as a clientele dependent on its food distributions outside the gates. La Miséricorde, an exclusive club recruited by co-option from the wives of the intendant, military governor, magistrates of the *cour des aides*, and others who were very rich, directed activities which elsewhere might have been independent—a manufactory to put the poor to work, the Bon Pasteur for prostitutes, schools, prison visiting, the provision of dowries for poor girls, and medical attention at home. Outside this nexus, there was an institution found in only a few cities—a military hospital for venereal disease. In Paris, as befitted its size, the standard institutions were bigger than elsewhere.[85] The *hôpital général* was a complex of ten buildings, including the grim Salpêtrière for erring or lunatic women, the Bicêtre for madmen, and the vast sad Enfants Trouvés for abandoned children. In place of a Miséricorde, there was the Grand Bureau des Pauvres, attended by magistrates of the parlement and high officials; individual parishes had their charitable committees linked to it. There were many smaller foundations, like the Hospice des Quinze-Vingts, a refuge for 300 blind 'brothers', who were a familiar sight outside churches, with their copper fleur-de-lis badges and collecting boxes, four houses of the Frères Hôpitaliers de Saint-Jean-de-Dieu, and the various parish charities, like the old folks' home founded in the mid-eighteenth century by curé Cochin of Saint-Jacques-du-Haut-Pas out of his private fortune.

The jurists did not regard the hospitals as ecclesiastical institutions, but as secular foundations in the position of minors under the tutelage of the government.[86] In 1505 the parlement of Paris ousted the canons of Notre-Dame from control of the *hôtel-Dieu* and substituted lay administrators. In 1579 a royal ordinance excluded ecclesiastics and nobles from hospital boards. Something of a change was made in 1698, for Louis XIV then decreed a mixed régime for any new foundations, the mayor, an alderman, the chief judicial officer of the place, and elected representatives of the inhabitants were to be joined by a single parish priest and have the bishop as president— honour to the clergy, but lay control. The letters patent setting up a hospital at Versailles in 1720 embodied the same principle in a rather different formula. The archbishop of Paris and the curé were to be in charge of the spiritual, while all temporal affairs would be run by the military governor, the *bailli*, the *procureur du roi*, and three elected inhabitants.[87] This pressure towards uniformity and lay control did not prevail everywhere. In remote areas hospitals would be run as they had always been, even by the local feudal seigneur. The *hôtel-Dieu* in Chartres remained under the control of the cathedral chapter. At Lisle-Noé the chapter of Auch had built a hospital and continued to own it—though it had the buildings knocked down in 1727, and the local community, after fifty years of litigation, compelled the canons to rebuild it. At Orléans, the three canons and six laymen on the board of the *hôtel-Dieu* were locked in disputes over precedence.[88] But the usual pattern in the bigger towns conformed to royal ordinances: control by a lay body with the bishop presiding. There might be another ecclesiastic or two among the administrators (for example, a representative of the cathedral chapter as one of the great local corporations), but this could not alter the lay dominance. For the most part, the *cahiers* of 1789 are not concerned with questions of hospital management (though the Tiers of Paris made the anticlerical point strongly), but many of them proposed the diversion of monastic wealth for their maintenance.[89] The general eighteenth-century view of the hospitals was that they were lay institutions, but the Church had the duty, whether by direct contribution or by exhorting the faithful to generosity, to raise money for them.

Most charitable institutions had wholly inadequate endowments. A town faced desperate problems in maintaining its *hôpital général*—being new, it had continually to be sustained by new funds. The work done by inmates was a limited resource, generally inefficiently done, and if efficiently, arousing the wrath of the local workers who resented the competition. Orphans sent out to work in the fields by some rural institutions were welcome to local farmers, but if they succeeded by dint of deft fingers and long hours at weaving silk or knitting woollen stockings, the local guildsmen would organize opposition.[90] Municipal contributions were grudging, though a small percentage might be given from the *octroi* on foodstuffs entering the city gates, or a levy on theatre tickets, or the profits of selling meat in Lent (to those who had medical certificates). Charitable gifts and legacies were a major resource, though variable and tending to decline.[91] At Aix-en-Provence, from 1710 to 1770, the annual collection fell from 4,000 to 1,000 livres, and from bequests in 80 per cent of the wills, the figure fell to 30 per cent. In Montpellier, half the wills in 1740–1 gave legacies to the *hôpital général*, and in 1782–6 only a quarter. People were switching their gifts to the Miséri-corde.[92] La Charité at Lyon had a system of enforced generosity by appealing to pride in a way approaching blackmail. On co-option as a recteur, a gift of 4,000 livres was due and an interest-free loan of 10,000, while the *trésorier*, the most prestigious figure of all, was expected to lend vast sums—which were never repaid. From 1776 to 1784, three held office and lost sums ranging from half a million to well over two million.[93] For a while, it was impossible to find a successor, and the citizen who eventually took over was bankrupted. In most places, the diocesan bishop was generous, though the well-intentioned craft of the recteurs at Lyon failed to penetrate the thick skin of their archbishop (Tencin, of Council of Embrun notoriety). They commissioned a marble bust from Coustou to be his memorial, but when he died, everything was left to his married sister. The bust was thrown on a rubbish heap, and rescued from a shop sometime later with the nose missing.

Everywhere, debts accumulated. In 1760 the *hôtel-Dieu* of Marseille[94] owed 3,500,000 livres, and the like institution at

Toulouse faced a bill for 700,000 livres interest, with only 196,000 available. Similar crises of debt occurred in Aix and many other places. Three years later the *hôtel-Dieu* of Autun was closed altogether, and its nuns pensioned off.[95] The creditors were mostly middling and little people who had invested their savings in return for a retirement income. The law courts intervened to compel municipalities to subsidize their collapsing institutions, but the activities of hospitals had to be curtailed, and the creditors suffered savage cuts in their annuities. Government policy and public opinion switched course. There was an end to annexing small charitable endowments to the big urban institutions; indeed, some such confiscations were reversed. Free food distributions were wound up. Private generosity turned to supporting the *miséricordes* and *bureaux de charité* dispensing help at home to the poor who could be identified as deserving.[96] The Enlightenment saw a switch from 'charité' to 'bienfaisance', a change in ideological approach, no doubt, but triggered by the spectacular and tragic bankruptcies of the 1760s.

VI

The 'hospitals' of every kind were run by women dedicated to the religious life. Some had vocations without formal engagements, as at La Charité at Lyon where the staff were recruited from the widows and orphans who came there for refuge. Others took permanent vows to care for the sick without belonging to any religious Order, as at Saint-Cales; here, the four ladies were engaged on short-term contracts, yet their families none the less had to provide them with dowries (including furniture, uniforms, and table silver) as if they were ordinary nuns.[97] There were numerous religious Orders to care for the sick, mostly founded in the seventeenth century—the Filles de la Charité de Saint-Vincent de Paul, the Sœurs de l'Annonciation, the Sœurs grises du Tiers Ordre de Saint-François, and sisterhoods under the invocation of Saint-Louis, Saint-Thomas de Villeneuve, Saint-Charles de Nancy, Saint-Maurice de Chartres, Sainte-Marthe, and Saint-Joseph. Small local initiatives could still arise in the eighteenth century, like Jeanne Delanoue's Servantes des Pauvres de la Providence de Saumur.[98] All had their peculiar ethos deriving from the rule of their founder. Some had educational work or the administering of outdoor charity as well as nursing on their charter. Some took temporary vows, some permanent, and the daily routines of work and prayer varied. The sisters of Saint-Joseph took lifelong vows, and by their constitution of 1686 fulfilled a complete round of liturgical offices; they made three visits a day to the wards, but the actual care of the sick was in the hands of the 'sœurs domestiques' (who had no voice in chapter) and the paid servants under them. By contrast, the sisters of Sainte-Marthe took only temporary vows, and looked after the sick themselves; there was a dispute in 1695 when an attempt was made to push them up to gentility, with daily devotions to take them out of constant attendance in the wards, and their families required to pay dowries of 1,500 livres for entrance to profession.[99]

The biggest nursing order of all was the Filles de la Charité de Saint-Vincent de Paul, the Order which broke through the practice of keeping nuns cloistered from the world. They took 'simple vows', voluntarily renewed annually, lived in 'houses', not 'convents', and were ruled not by 'superiors', but by 'sœurs servantes'. Their time was not spent in liturgical observances or in exercises of mortification; they offered silent individual prayer twice a day, otherwise they worked to respond to the cry of the poor, 'leaving God for God'. There was no question of their finding a niche near home and family, like so many nuns; for after central training in Paris, they were not allowed to serve in their own region. Thus Sœur Marguerite who in 1779 became head of the new hospital built by the bishop of Dax had qualified at the Paris noviciate twenty years earlier, followed by eight different postings, triangulating France from Pau to Autun to Brest; when stationed at Fontainebleau, she had become famous when chosen by Marie Antoinette to nurse Mlle de Fleury through the smallpox.[100] The Filles de la Charité had an exacting and in some ways lonely existence, but within their community they were well looked after. The food was good, the dress allowance reasonable, and in old age and infirmity they were made comfortable. Recruitment was from the lower-class majority, but from the élite within it. Voltaire,[101] who praised them unstintingly, thought, probably mistakenly, that many girls from distinguished families joined; a visitor to the *hôtel-Dieu* of Besançon described the sisters as 'well born (*bien nées*) and well educated'.[102] This was the impression they gave. But whatever their background, there was no doubt about their sterling character. 'A sister of charity', writes Colin Jones, their historian, 'was patient, saintly, laborious, discreet, committed—and tough.'[103]

By 1700, these dedicated women had taken control of 200 institutions, and expansion was continuing. 'One of the greatest predicaments in administering this community', said its governing sister in Paris in 1769, 'is to know how it can manage not to agree to the most energetic solicitations that are made nearly every day for new establishments.'[104] By preference, the Filles de la Charité would take over the *hôtel-Dieu* in a town, though sometimes they were constrained to accept the direction of the *hôpital général*, in which case they might stipulate that care of infants, the aged, and vagabonds would not be their responsibility, except in cases of illness—a limitation which in practice could rarely be enforced. The keynote of their organization was strong and simple central control, allied to informality and individual initiative below. Headquarters in Paris drew up a detailed contract with the municipality when a hospital was taken over. On the one hand, the sisters would accept obligations to keep a register of admissions, make an annual audit on St John's Eve, account for the drugs, perhaps look after the bakery, laundry, and livestock or even, in an *hôpital général*, supervise the work of the orphans. On the other hand, their individual dress allowances (about 80 livres in the 1780s) were guaranteed; they were assured of absolute control over the servants and of freedom from responsibility for lodging the chaplains or doing their laundry; and they would have the right of deciding who could be admitted as a patient—the doctors would check for venereal disease, but not rule on eligibility. Posting orders also came from Paris, each sister being moved every five years or so, and the *sœurs servantes* every eight or ten. The superior of the Congrégation de la Mission, the male foundation of Saint-Vincent de Paul, appointed confessors and nominated visitors; if occasion demanded, he would use his influence at Versailles to defend the sisters against local attempts to whittle down their rights. In a society where sinecures, inefficiency, and privilege were rampant, and hampered every government proposal to help the poor, the Filles de la Charité showed how selfless devotion and clear-headed organization could make a difference.

Conditions in an *hôtel-Dieu* were grim. Budgets were tight in comparison with ever growing needs. Everyone knew that patients ought to be one to a bed: in practice, it had to be two or three, with mattresses on the floor and in the corridors as well. Given the overcrowding, surgical operations, terrifying affairs in this age before anaesthetics, might take place in view, or at least within earshot, of the next batch of victims. Infections were general, and every scratch tended to become gangrenous. The mortality rate was high. In the *hôtel-Dieu* of Paris, one in every four entering left on the mortuary cart. But it is a myth that hospitals everywhere were death-traps.[105]

At Montpellier in the 1780s, deaths were at the rate of one in ten; it had been double a century earlier, so things were improving. Statistics need interpretation, however. From 1740 to 1785, the overall mortality figure for Nîmes was 11.7 per cent; however, this total is 'improved' by the fact that roughly a quarter of the admissions were soldiers, whose mortality rate was only 2–5 per cent, and that others swelling the total number of patients were vagabonds from outside the city, mostly younger people taking refuge, not because they were ill, but because they were starving. The various groups of nursing sisters had a common policy in refusing to accept anyone suffering from venereal disease, on moral grounds as well as because of the danger of infection, and anyone suffering from small-pox, because it was a killer impossible to contain. Some also rejected pregnant women. This was not so at Paris—here, in the year 1757, the maternity ward was responsible for 1,508 deliveries.[106] While in theory, through their contracts and their protests, the sisters would try to keep an *hôtel-Dieu* a hospital of the modern kind for the treatment of the sick exclusively, in practice they might have to put up with intruders. At Nîmes, beggars took refuge; at Montpellier, from 1770 to 1786 the *hôtel-Dieu* had to accept them by order of the intendant, who by government policy had to intern vagabonds somewhere; in crises of famine, a tide of starving humanity surged into every place where there was hope of support. In the grim winter of 1789, 30,000 of them swamped the resources of the *hôtel-Dieu* of Paris, camping in the courtyards, hopeless in their misery.[107]

Lunatics, who were not so much treated for illness as chained up or locked behind grilles or in cells, were not a suitable clientele; but where else could they be accommodated? At Paris, within the general orbit of the *hôtel-Dieu*, there were specific institutions for them. In the Salpêtrière, madwomen were chained or confined in airless, low-ceilinged rooms, five to a bed; at the Bicêtre, soldiers handed out food to the madmen at the point of the bayonet. In provincial towns, there was sometimes an establishment also called a *bicêtre*, a multi-purpose sink for the misfits who would cause disruption in hospitals proper. Alongside the *hôtel-Dieu* at Alençon there was one of them, described by a visitor as accommodating 'madmen, dangerous characters, abandoned children, criminals whose crimes cannot be documented by enough evidence for a trial, but about whom there is a moral certainty, and debauchees'.[108] Failing a *bicêtre*, however, lunatics would have to be confined in one of the existing hospital-type institutions. A man ran berserk at Montpellier in 1713, killing his wife and setting fire to their house. This led to an agreement to build twelve cells for madmen in the *hôtel-Dieu*, financed partly by the institution itself, partly by the bishop, and partly by the municipality and its police bureau.[109] Three years later a tenth sister was appointed to the staff to look after the new department and take charge of the wine-cellar, a joint task in which one duty may have provided some compensation for having to do the other. By 1789, the number of cells had risen to twenty-five, six belonging to the diocese (which had the right to nominate candidates for confinement) and six to the municipality and the police.

It was scarcely possible for sisters, however dedicated, to do all the chores of a hospital, though in small country places they might have to do so. At Montpellier in 1779, the *sœur servante* exercised general supervision, kept the registers, inventoried and stored the personal possessions of the patients, and ran some profit-making ventures, including selling the effects of the deceased and the bran extracted from the flour. Two sisters ran the pharmacy, three the kitchen, one the bakery, two the laundry, one the wine-cellar and the madhouse, and each of the remaining six was in charge of a ward. The wards and the other departments all had their lay auxiliaries—men as gaolers for the lunatics and doing the heavy portering, women as cleaners and assistant nurses. The *hôtel-Dieu* at Paris, run by the Sœurs Augustines, was a masterpiece of large-scale organization. As it existed before the great fire of 1772, there were seven lay doctors and one master surgeon, with thirteen other surgeons also coming in occasionally without pay. The department for bulk buying of corn, wood, and other commodities, the bakery, the kitchen (with ten cooks), and the *sommellerie* for buying and storing wine were all in lay hands. The 140 sisters had under them *emballeurs* (sweepers and porters), *garçons*, and women *servantes*. The mother superior herself and her deputy, with three other sisters, supervised the storehouse where the linen and dresses of the sisters were kept, and where jams, delicacies, and soap for the use of the patients were made. The entrance lodge with two sisters (assisted by two janitors) checked comings and goings and visitors to the sick. The laundry was a huge affair. In the Grande Lavanderie four sisters supervised thirty-six lay helpers. Eight thousand sheets had to be taken to the river, then back to be boiled in coppers, then to the river again, then up to the roof for drying, a continually repeated operation taking five days. Work in the Petite Lavanderie—the most revolting jobs in the hospital, for here the contaminated bandages were washed—was done by eight women and twelve boys directed by two sisters. Another department with three sisters and their helpers mended and stored the shirts of the patients, and went round weekly to change them; they also supervised the annual refilling of the mattresses, which took three months. The most agreeable post to hold was that of one of the two specialists in the pharmacy. The twenty-one wards were grouped into ten *offices*, each in charge of a sister called the *cheftaine*, elected for a three-year period to be in charge of the ward sisters and their teams of auxiliaries. At night, a force of fifteen sisters came in to relieve them all as *veilleresses*. These night nurses had keys for the side door leading to the Petit Pont, and through it sent out the bodies of the sick who had died that day; *emballeurs* pulled them on a cart, and, preceded by a priest in surplice with a server with bell and lantern, they went out into the night.

The *hôpital général* was a portmanteau institution combining in one a workhouse, reformatory, prison, old people's home, crèche, orphanage, hospice for travellers, and a bureau for outdoor relief. It might also include cells for lunatics and a surgery ward. From the mid-seventeenth century, government policy concerning vagabonds and beggars was 'enfermement', shutting up. It was a police measure to stop the tides of misery from surging dangerously around the towns, allied to the mercantilist rule of having no idlers in the commonwealth, and the drive of the Compagnie du Saint-Sacrement to regiment the poor into the observances of religion. In 1718, there was an overall plan to stage rootless and shiftless people in the *hôpitaux généraux* until they could be transported overseas to the Mississippi—but the colonists would not have them.[110] In 1724, a royal declaration ordered the incarceration of the unemployed, defined as those who had been given a fortnight to find work and had failed to do so. This was absurd—there was simply nowhere to put them all. In 1767, the government tried a new policy, setting up new institutions, *dépôts de mendicité*; later on, it was charity work-shops, *ateliers de charité*.[111] These workshops were flooded with applicants within a few months of opening. Any charitable refuge in eighteenth-century France, once established, was sure to be used by everyone in authority to clear the streets of nuisances, criminals and lunatics included. This had been the fate of the *hôpitaux généraux*, hopelessly underfunded, chaotic unpredictable places. It is obvious why the Filles de la Charité and the other nursing sisters did not wish to run them, and also why they so often had to do so, since nobody else would.

The range of the *hôpital général* was from the very old to the very young. Not all old people could hope to gain admission. At Lyon, the conditions were: to have lived in the town continuously for ten years, to be 70 years of age or over, and in possession of a certificate of indigence from the curé.[112] Some of the old people were supported by contributions from relatives or from former employers, and depending on the amount paid, conditions might be correspondingly better than were generally available. But it was the very young who took up the most space and presented the greatest problem. The eighteenth century, the age of the evolution of a new, affectionate attitude towards children, was also the age of abandoned infants. A modern estimate for the whole country in the single year 1784 is 50,000. It was an urban phenomenon. In Bordeaux there were 300 waifs left annually in charge of the municipality early in the century, rising to 600 later on.[113] In Paris there were 1,738 in 1700, 3,150 in 1740 (this was a fifth of all births in the capital), and 6,419 in 1776 (this was a third). At Metz in this latter year, a winter of sheer starvation, there were 900, an even greater proportion of total births than in the capital. 'Within a century all children will be without fathers and mothers,' observed a contemporary, extrapolating the figures.[114] Most of the abandoned victims were illegitimate, and probably half their mothers were girls in domestic service, a prey in their loneliness to seducers or to male members of the family exercising the 'droit de cuissage'. In years of economic disaster, however, desperate families would place their legitimate babies in municipal care, often leaving identification tokens in the hope of reclaiming them. If they did so and could afford it, they might be asked to pay a search fee and maintenance.[115] Jean-Jacques Rousseau, the prophet of sympathetic understanding of children, abandoned his five without distinguishing marks—he was ashamed of Thérèse, his ignorant mistress, and did not see how he could go on writing his masterpieces surrounded by squalling brats. In a prize essay of 1780, the abbé de Malvaux observed, darkly, that the provision of refuges for children was an invitation to get rid of them: 'l'hospice des Enfants Trouvés est le tombeau de l'amour maternel'.

Yet refuges there had to be, and in most places it was the all-purpose *hôpital général*. Paris—as also Nîmes[116] and Bordeaux—was exceptional in having a specialist foundling hospital, though it was in alliance with the great *hôtel-Dieu* in its various ramifications. The Enfants Trouvés of Paris, founded by royal edict in 1670, was a vast place. In addition to the 3,000 (rising to 6,000) babies coming in annually from the city itself, another 2,000 or so were carted in from the provinces, from as far afield as Angers. The procedure, here as elsewhere, was to send out the babies as soon as possible to wet-nurses in the countryside. Most of the children died quickly:

only one or two out of ten survived. In a poor state to begin with, probably starving or disease-ridden, they had to face a long trip out to their wet-nurses—the foster mothers in the nearer villages were pre-empted by bourgeois families of the town. Those carried from Angers to Paris had an even more dangerous preliminary ride, in charge of carriers who got the same fee for a dead body as a living one. And there were plenty of sinister mercenary wet-nurses caring only to draw the fee. Contemporaries lamented this tragic mortality, whether from sympathy with suffering or from the mercantilist belief in the importance of an increasing population. Yet the system worked only because death was its accomplice. As a nursing sister of the Enfants Trouvés of Paris told a visiting Genevan doctor: we must be glad the children are going to eternal happiness and not wish for them to live longer, 'because the revenues would not be sufficient to feed them all'.[117]

What happened to the survivors? At the age of 5 or so, they came back to the *hôpital général* (in Paris to the terrible Salpêtrière). Since they might be kept there for anything up to a dozen years, they would crowd the institution: at Montpellier, in mid-century, of the 600–750 inmates, two-thirds were children. These orphans spent their days sewing or spinning and, by all accounts, under a heartless discipline, alleviated only by excursions to parade the streets with billboards or to walk in the funeral processions of the rich, thus earning a fee towards their keep.[118] No wonder the Filles de la Charité were reluctant to have the running of orphanages imposed on them. At the age of 18, or possibly earlier, the young people were sent out to apprenticeship, domestic service, or casual labour (in coastal areas boys could go to sea)—or simply to become beggars and vagrants, thus qualifying to return to the crowded dormitories of the *hôpital-général* in a different capacity.

To complete the heterogeneous incongruity of life in an *hôpital général*, the gatherings of vagabonds, old people, helpless babies, and mobile orphans might be diversified by a special wing or corridor for prostitutes and other fallen women—though most often there was a house of correction for them. Originally, the government rule had been that prostitutes must be committed to the *hôpital général* nearest to the place of their arrest. The judicial regulations were codified in 1684, with a savage additional penalty to protect soldiers from the pox: a prostitute found within two leagues of a military camp would be condemned to nose slitting before imprisonment in the *hôpital général*. The concern of the government was to protect the public, rather than to reform the sinner—this was left to religious inspirations. In 1657, the Sœurs de Notre-Dame de Charité du Refuge were founded—a branch of the congregation of women already set up at Caen by Jean Eudes; its members took an additional fourth vow, to care for fallen women. About the same time came the Madelonnettes in Paris, Rouen, and Bordeaux. Then—the most significant development of all—in 1686, Mme de Combe, a converted Dutch Protestant, established, in Paris, the first house of the Bon Pasteur. She made astonishing demands on the sisters she persuaded to join her—they were to share the work equally with the girls, perform the same penances, and observe the almost perpetual silence of the rest of the inmates. It was an experiment in suffering shared, the just joining the unjust in their humiliation. This inspiration proved too demanding, and it was abandoned in the institutions under the invocation of 'the Good Shepherd' which were subsequently founded in many provincial towns. The initiative in setting up a house of the Bon Pasteur normally came from the wives of the leading citizens—leagued together in the Miséricorde, they would find a suitable building and recruit staff, possibly by calling in an existing religious Order. At Montpellier, they did this and more, for by their contacts and vigilance they identified the ladies of the night and for some years were responsible for more detentions than the *bureau de police* itself.[119] It was not just pharisaical delation; often they paid the fees to maintain a girl in whom they had taken an interest. In other places, the municipality itself took the lead, or an individual acting alone—as Mme Pugin at Rennes, to the wrath of her heirs.[120]

At the same time as refuges to reform prostitutes were being set up, preventive institutions were being founded, houses of safety for girls subjected to temptation. There were two in Lyon, both dating from the mid-seventeenth century, founded by members of the severely devout Compagnie du Saint-Sacrement and their wives. The Filles Pénitentes accepted fallen girls of good family, whether at the request of the parents or the girls themselves; after twelve years of repentance, they could be professed as sisters. La Providence was for the poor, for girls whose virtue was in danger because of sheer starvation. They were taken in until a job, probably as a domestic servant, could be found for them.[121] At Marseille there was another house of La Providence, but the annual fee was 195 livres—as the regulations not surprisingly stated, 'only girls of a status above that of the artisan class are admitted'.[122]

There had always been two aspects to society's view of prostitutes: they were lost sheep to be led back to the fold—the Bon Pasteur idea—and they were criminals to be locked up and disciplined. In the course of the eighteenth century, the latter concept was winning. At Montpellier, charitable contributions to the Bon Pasteur, which had once been half the revenues, fell to 3 per cent, while charitably sponsored detentions fell from a quarter of the total to 2 per cent. Prostitutes came to be classed as criminals, serving a formal sentence of three to five years, whether they repented or not. Their first weeks were spent in a punishment cell; thereafter they had to work gainfully, under strict discipline, though well fed and well housed. Life was much the same at the Recluses of Lyon under the Sœurs de Saint-Joseph—here, the prostitutes served a two-year sentence in prison cells, working at sewing shirts for the army. The corresponding institution in Paris was the fearsome Salpêtrière, a vast building formerly a saltpetre factory, and now a place of confinement for women. A visitor in 1787[123] described how a dozen sisters of Sainte-Catherine (no doubt with numerous auxiliaries) ruled over 2,400 *filles de joie* clad in shapeless sacks, herded together for eight hours a day on rows of backless seats, eternally sewing, then sleeping at night in tightly packed, low-ceilinged dormitories. If disobedient, they were punished by being pushed in with the senile and insane. In better conditions were kept *pensionnaires* confined at the expense of their families and prisoners of the Crown (including Mme de la Motte, notorious for having impersonated the queen in the diamond necklace affair). There were also the good-time girls who had incurred the wrath of some powerful protector to whom they had been disloyal. In kennels behind an iron grille madwomen were chained, deep in filth. Under the *ancien régime* charity or family subscriptions had to maintain all the social institutions: only for the rare individual case did the king's government pay.

In all the charitable institutions, the routines of religion were enforced. The chaplain was an indispensable member of staff: the hospital of Saint-André at Bordeaux had three of them, as against four physicians and two surgeons.[124] The doctors themselves, in theory at least, were under strict religious obligations. Those who took their degrees at Paris had to swear to defend the Catholic, apostolic, and Roman religion 'usque ad effusionem sanguinis'.[125] By a royal declaration of 1712, on the second day of a serious illness, the doctor had to warn the patient of the duty of confession, and if he refused, call in the parish priest. Apart from the *hôtel-Dieu* at Paris, hospitals had a religious test for entry. At the *hôpital général* of Orléans a *billet* of confession had to be produced within a fortnight, otherwise the fare was bread and water.[126] The ceremony of admission at Montpellier consisted of an interview by the board of management, shaving of the head, and confession. At La Charité of Lyon, an entrant began with a month of instruction: duties to God, the obligations of religious practice, the obedience due to the recteurs, reverence due to the memory of benefactors, the necessity to live in peace and work hard. Applicants for outdoor relief had to produce a certificate from their curé that they knew the principal articles of the faith, and ecclesiastics went round with one of the recteurs annually to check that they had not forgotten them.[127] There might be a rule for monthly communion; at Fougères, this could be enforced only by the chaplain calling in the constables (*archers*) to march the poor to the altar, 'most of them being so depraved and idle that he cannot oblige them to do their duty'.[128] The institutional life of orphan children was a monotonous catalogue of work and piety. In the *hôpital général* of Orléans the boys in the dormitory of Saint-Louis and the girls in that of Sainte-Agnès were awoken at 5 or 5.30 a.m. for prayer, mass, and breakfast, then three hours' work with half an hour off for catechism; there was silence at dinner to listen to the 'spiritual reading', then prayers and half an hour's recreation. Then six hours' work with a catechism break, supper at 6.30 p.m., half an hour's recreation, then off to bed preceded by the Angelus, Pater, Ave, prayers for benefactors, the *De Profundis*, and *In Manus tuas Domine*. There was no contact with the world except when getting outside the walls for street sweeping, carrying advertisement boards, or walking in funeral processions (thus getting a fee for the institution).[129] The Comité de Mendicité of the Constituent Assembly of 1790 was to wax angry at the exclusion of non-Catholics, 'as if charitable help should not be given to all, whatever their creed', and ironic about the pious precociousness of children who knew all about funerals and church services and could explain how the way for Christ had been prepared by the patriarchs and prophets.[130] The Revolution abolished the insupportable religious obligations attached to charity; also, in spite of grandiose schemes on paper, it abolished most of the charity as well.

The nursing sisters in an *hôtel-Dieu* would let no one forget that they were in charge. They insisted on supervising the meals, and, said the medical experts, overfed the patients. They would not allow any interference with the pharmacy and the supply of drugs; they monopolized the right to admit the sick and give them the good news that they could go; they defended the privacy of the sick 'pour ménager l'amour propre des pauvres', excluding students and curious visitors from the wards.[131] In Montpellier, they would not allow the doctors to take corpses away for dissection, on the ground that this offended the susceptibilities of local people; clinical researches had to be conducted in the morgues of prisons, the military hospital, and the Protestant one.[132] As the medical profession in the second half of the century developed an interest in precise observations to build up case histories, tensions between the doctors and the nursing sisters increased: in 1788, relations in the *hôtel-Dieu* of Paris reached crisis point, and the bureau of administration had to intervene.[133] The great Desault wanted his surgical patients two in a bed instead of four, while the sisters pointed out that this would halve the number which could be treated: he put on his anatomical lessons at times disrupting meals and visiting hours; also—a perennial problem—the sisters wanted the surgeon's apprentices excluded from the women's wards, where they flirted with the *servantes* and better-looking patients, and indulged in licentious discourses among themselves.

Other difficulties for the nursing sisters arose from the interventions of the lay administrators. The notables and oligarchs who held office in towns were proverbially self-important and parsimonious, and while they or their predecessors had been anxious to get the good ladies to take the sick off their hands, they were never happy with the stiff contracts they had signed. At Caen, the administrators tried to get rid of the Filles de la Madeleine altogether—'ces femmes inutiles, incapables, dépensières'—and habitually let their salaries fall into arrears.[134] Things were different at Nantes, the contract being so strict that the sisters did as they pleased and ran their house deep into debt. The bureau at Montpellier would not agree to their *sœur servante* taking time off to act as an inspector of hospitals in other towns, and refused to pay wages to young recruits still in training. In 1718 and 1723, authoritarian intervention from Versailles defeated the laymen, but in 1785, they scored a victory and had the *sœur servante* dismissed.[135] The Hôpital-Mage (the name of the *hôtel-Dieu*) at Béziers was a scene of guerrilla warfare in which the Dames de la Charité de Notre-Dame proved the most ingenious tacticians: orders from the bureau about admissions were ignored, new recruits were accepted without the customary dowry, thus diminishing the revenues, the archives were hidden from inspection, and meetings of the administrators with the nurses fixed at awkward times.[136] When Louis XV set up the Infirmerie Royale at Versailles for his servants and bodyguards, he naturally called on the Filles de la Charité to take charge (there were four of them in 1721, twenty-two in 1789). There was no management committee here; the royal institution was under the rule of a single administrator, the military governor.

In 1787, the maréchal de Rouchy wanted more discipline; the sisters were 'to sweep out the wards twice a day' in person. They are 'servants of the poor', said this crusty old soldier—besides, Mme Louise, the king's daughter, had done sweeping duties at the Carmelites. And he was not going to let the Filles have their contractual half-bottle of wine a day—'I don't drink any more myself'. It ended with the wine staying as before and the sisters undertaking 'to ensure that the wards are swept out', not necessarily doing it themselves.[137] When complaints of dubious conduct are made against hospital sisters, the source is—almost always—disgruntled municipal officers, wanting more for their money and less money to pay.[138] In one place they accused the sisters of treating rich bourgeois in preference to the poor, in another of taking in soldiers rather than local people because the government paid 13 sous a day for military men; or they were charging a small fee for the preferential treatment of a single bed and a private chamber-pot. At Provins, the sisters had a fine garden adorned with 'immodest statues' and a marquee in which they held garden parties and, in the house, a billiard-table. It all adds up to: the sisters had to earn money to keep their hospitals going, and they sometimes organized for themselves the relaxation they deserved.

19

THE COMMISSION DES RÉGULIERS

I *The Commission*

The Jesuits, useful to both Church and State, had been disbanded—
what then of the other religious Orders? The deliberations of the
Assembly of Clergy of 1765 were overshadowed by this question.
The bishops present knew of examples of misapplied wealth and lax
conduct in their dioceses, and two specific questions giving cause for
immediate concern were raised. One was the abuse of the translation
ad laxiorum, easily available from the Roman bureaucracy, allowing
a monk to transfer to a less rigorous Order and, skilfully used, a
device for escaping the cloister and slipping quietly into lay society.
The other was the proliferation of lawsuits of monks against their
superiors by use of the *appel comme d'abus*. In a famous case of 1760,
the parlement of Paris had overturned a sentence of three years'
imprisonment passed by the general of the Prémontrés on one of his
canons regular, awarding a pension on the revenues of an abbey as
damages.[1] A report to the Assembly listed lawsuits pending within six
different Orders, the Benedictines of Saint-Maur having three *appels
comme d'abus* before three different parlements.[2] Anything bringing
in the secular magistrates was dangerous: litigation before the parlement of Paris had led to the suppression of the Society of Jesus.

It was important to do something and to be seen to be doing it.
The Assembly therefore accepted a proposal from Loménie de
Brienne, archbishop of Toulouse, to ask the Pope, through the king,
to name a commission of enquiry and reform. Brienne was acting in
concert with Choiseul, Louis XV's anticlerical minister, and must
have known that the court of Versailles would not allow Rome to
exercise such authority over the Gallican Church. Nor would the
parlement of Paris. The magistrates vetoed recourse to the Pope, and
insisted on lay members being appointed to the commission as well
as ecclesiastics. On 31 July 1766 a royal order set up the Commission
des réguliers. The members were to be the archbishops of Reims,
Arles, Bourges, Narbonne, and Toulouse (zealots like the archbishops of Paris and Tours being excluded), and, as lay commis-

sioners, four luminaries of the great legal families of France, with six *avocats* and four theologians as technical advisers. Loménie de Brienne was rapporteur and in charge of all the business. Men of piety distrusted Brienne, but even from the narrowly ecclesiastical point of view, he was an excellent choice. A prelate with little in the way of Christian belief and devoured by ambition, he was concerned to promote the interests of the Church as an institution, and he was an indefatigable worker. 'He is ambitious,' said the abbé Véri, 'but in his eyes ambition is best furthered by duties zealously performed.'[3] Nothing could be done in eighteenth-century France without the conciliation of vested interests, and he was an arch-manipulator.

The files of the Commission accumulated denunciations.[4] Curés —though surprisingly few of them—complained of the honorific rights of the great abbeys in their parishes, and of the contrast between monastic wealth and their own poverty. Laymen volunteered picturesque delations, like the story of Dom Villemur of Saramon returning to his monastery 'dressed like a sailor' because the skirts of his cassock had been cut off by an angry citizen who caught him philandering with his sister. Local authorities admitted their interest in the confiscation of monastic property: the Cordeliers of Châteaudun are irreproachable, said the municipality, but there are only three of them, and their house would make a barracks for the garrison.[5] Rank-and-file monks and their superiors also told their conflicting stories.

But the reports that mattered came from the bishops responding to a questionnaire from Brienne in August 1766. Whether from idleness or conscientious objection, thirty did not reply. The bishops of Brittany sent a collective letter expressing reservations: 'in a destructive century like ours, one cannot be too careful to respect the rights of property and the intentions of founders'. Six older bishops said as little as possible, suspecting the use to which their answers would be put. Of the others, some waxed eloquent, the best-informed, incisive criticisms coming from worldly prelates like Jacques de Grasse of Angers, who for years had refused to pay his share of clerical taxation and spent most of his time in Paris. The bishops had their idiosyncratic bias. As aristocrats, they did not see the *commende* as the abuse it was; the archbishop of Reims, president of the Commission, and Brienne, its chief executive, drew as much income from abbeys held *in commendam* as they did from their episcopal sees. Their chief concern was to extend their jurisdiction to the regular as well as the secular clergy; in our dioceses, said one of them, there are 'as many little individual dioceses as there are monasteries, in which the bishop has no right of access for inspection'. Their chief criterion for approval was usefulness to the parishes; a fairly common observation was to praise a particular monastic house for its regularity, but to note its irrelevance to the needs of the pastoral ministry. They had an interest to promote suppressions to release income and buildings which could be used for diocesan projects. Though their reports give circumstantial details, they do not seem to be based on the formal procedure of *de commodo et incommodo* used by the jurisprudence of the day; their facts had not been verified by adversarial procedures. They were reporting what was said in the upper-class circles in which they moved or coming to them through their vicars-general, archdeacons, and curés. Even so, as representatives of the pastoral mission of the Church, the bishops' views were important, and their practical proposals for reform were realistic: they wished to close thinly populated houses and to raise the age for taking monastic vows—changes which the Commission was to implement.

Generalizations about monastic life in a particular country and century are likely to be falsified by the inevitably unequal distribution of evidence. Orders with a practical role in Church and society have a history; those dedicated to contemplation and prayer in the silence of the cloister have no history to speak of, unless things go wrong. The bishop of Bayeux praised the Trappists, the Chartreux, and the nuns of Sainte-Claire and of the Carmelite Order as austerely conforming to their ideals—what else was there for him or anyone else to say?[6] To describe French monasticism in the eighteenth century from the papers of an inquisitorial commission compounds the injustice, for behind so many complaints lie legacies of the past and pressures of local circumstance, while reformers naturally work from the formal concept of the monastic ideal rather than from a view of actual vocations in their accepted social context. In what follows, an impressionistic view of the diversity of monastic institutions will be given, broadening out in the case of some Orders into an account with the circumstantial detail which is needed to temper criticism with sympathy.

II *The Chartreux (Carthusians) and Grandmontins*

According to the files of the Commission,[7] there were 26,674 monks in France (this does not include lay brothers, possibly 8,000 of them). The mendicant Orders furnished half the total (14,388), the Benedictines one-fifth (4,647), the canons regular one-sixth (3,521).

Of the remaining groups the Carthusians were the most numerous (1,004). This left a few others with a limited number of houses, thinly populated—La-Merci, Grandmont, the Servites, the Barnabites, the Brigittines, and the Théatins.

Of these smaller Orders, two—the Carthusians and the Grandmontins—had originated as refuges for men who wished to follow the lonely disciplines of the hermit's life. The sixty-six houses of the Carthusians were beyond reproach. The bishops praised them, the only reservation coming from one who thought they were too fervent: their regime of absolute silence (except for saying the offices) was impossible for human nature to bear; they became prematurely aged, and their sanity was undermined.[8] The account-books of their house at Boserville in Lorraine show no wine or meat, no luxuries except tobacco and seed to feed cage-birds, and a dark entry 'for the carriage of a package of hair shirts from Lyon, 10 livres'.[9] An English traveller describes their house in Paris, the cells around a grassy quadrangle, each with a hatch for the delivery of meals and a private walled garden on the other side. Mercier forgot his journalistic irreverence when he visited this quiet spot: 'The trees are humble and bowed like the monks who salute you without looking at you; here is the noviciate of eternity.'[10]

Without being poor, the Carthusians kept the rules of eremetical discipline; by contrast, Grandmont, originally a fraternity of hermits forbidden to own property or deal in worldly affairs, had become a monastic Order like any other. From the start, the Commission seems to have had in mind the suppression of its thirty houses and the pensioning off of their 114 inmates, who were said to spend their days hunting and fishing. The accusation does not square with petitions from the villages around the mother-house of Grandmont in the diocese of Limoges, which talked of charitable contributions of 20,000 livres a year, and priests being sent out to help with parish duties and teach in schools. Essentially, two things were wrong with the Order.[11] First, the superior-general, Abbot René-Pierre François de la Guerinière, who died in 1744, had burdened his communities with crushing debts by embarking on an ostentatious building programme; at the mother-house, he had pulled down almost everything, including the medieval church, and rebuilt in the modern style, and at Paris he had enlarged the Collège Mignon, intending to make it a centre of learning. When Dom Mondain, simple and unworldly in spite of his name, became head of the Order in 1748, he had to fight Dom Vitecoq, the *procureur général* in charge of the finances and director of the Paris reconstruction project, to try to enforce economies. Nine years of litigation followed, with Vitecoq backed by the University and Parlement and Mondain by the Crown. Finally, in 1755, a general chapter accepted retrenchment, but the huge debts remained.

The second disastrous factor was the decline of Grandmontin recruitment. There were only forty-two monks in eight houses in the Strict Observance and seventy-two in twenty-two houses in the Common Observance. Behind the back of his superior-general, Dom Razat, the new *procureur général* of the finances, recommended to Loménie de Brienne the disbandment of the Order with pensions for himself and his colleagues, since they had not the numbers to keep going, and the faction fighting at general chapters would prevent any agreement on reform. The nineteenth-century historian of Grandmont calls this treachery; as between debts and depopulation, perhaps it was just realism. Dom Nicod, vicar-general of the Strict Observance, recommended suppressing four out of the eight houses to gain a reasonable quorum in the surviving ones. The question was not likely to be examined impartially, for D'Argentré, the bishop of Limoges, had the ear of the Commission and was pressing for the confiscation of the property of the mother-house for the benefit of his diocese. He was engaged in building a new episcopal palace, and the ill-disposed suggested it was this, and not concern for his parishes, which was inspiring his quest for supplementary funds.

III *The Mendicants*

The mendicants constituted more than half the total of male religious, and the Franciscans more than half the total of mendicants (1,001 houses with 8,870 inmates).

Of the five main Franciscan branches, three met with episcopal approval. The Picpus friars (the Tierçaires de Saint-François, called Picpus from the name of the village where their principal house was situated), a small group numbering 494 and running sixteen houses, were engaged in the care of lunatics—in their establishment at Saint-Omer they had no fewer than 200 of them. This dismal task made them indispensable. Then there were the Récollets, the result of a reform which arose in France at the beginning of the seventeenth century (222 houses with 2,491 friars). The bishops gave them an overwhelming vote of confidence, thirty-three for, and only three against.[12] Such criticisms as there were could be reversed and interpreted as reluctant praise. Many friars were from humble origins, 'peasants driven into religion by necessity and hunger', it was said. They specialized in the work of chaplains to the army and the navy, and those doing so were recalcitrant to ecclesiastical authority and affected an air of unspiritual toughness. The friars at Bergerac, where half the population was Calvinist, were censured for their tolerance, educating the children without trying to convert them to Catholicism and giving out 'certificates of Catholicity' (to obtain employment or admission to a hospital) without making an inquisition into details of belief. The majority of bishops praised the Récollets as active in the parochial ministry and welcome to the people, being 'well educated', 'peaceful', and 'laborious'. From within the Order itself the reports of the provincials and submissions from the rank and file do not suggest the tensions evident in the other mendicant Orders. A few scandals came to light, though one might forgive the *gardien* of the friary at Sainte-Foy his silk dressing-gown and house in the country, since he was a famous preacher and moved in high society.[13] 'We are not angels,' wrote the head of the Orléans province, 'but no abuse of any consequence has as yet arisen among us.' And he pointed out—an important consideration when passing judgement on mendicants—that those who are obliged to live by the collecting box are thereby involved in the rough-and-tumble of lay society, and are subject to continual temptations.[14]

The third group winning approval were the Capuchins, who had separated from the rest of the Franciscans by the reform which began in Italy in 1529. They were the biggest mendicant organization in France, having 3,497 friars in 418 establishments grouped in fourteen provinces covering the whole country. Sixty-five bishops praised them. Only five complained, saying their begging was a nuisance, they were ignorant, and competed with the curés for the allegiance of their parishioners. True enough, there were complaints about the continual rattle of collecting boxes, and the popular word for an obscurantist pious diatribe was a 'capucinade'. But behind the proverbial ridicule, the Capuchins had won a place in the affections of the people. In their white habits with pointed cowls, sandals, and obligatory beards, they were picturesque figures. 'Ils ont le don de fasciner.' As beggars, they acquired the arts of insinuation, appearing at the gates of a seigneur silent, with downcast eyes, at the door of a parish priest with modest deference, and calling at a farmhouse with the utmost affability.

He pats the dog, calls back the children who are running away, familiarizes them with his long beard and gives them pious images; he offers great compliments to the mistress of the house, and enters into discussions with the farmer in which he appears almost learned; you'd imagine that he had not come to ask for anything, but his request is forestalled, they offer him something and he accepts benignly.[15]

Partly by inclination, partly to alleviate their poverty, the Capuchins volunteered for parish work. Their house of Sollies near Toulon was typical: miserably poor, as the inventory of their battered furniture shows, they kept going from 350 livres a year for acting as vicaires in the parish of Saint-Michel, a smaller fee for a chaplaincy in a country mansion, and the municipality doing their repairs on condition of being allowed to use their buildings as a staging-point for conscripts to the coastguard service.[16] As Paris expanded, a new parish in the Chaussé d'Antin was needed, so the government moved the Capuchins of the rue Saint-Honoré to run it, building them a new friary.[17] Learned Capuchins specialized as preachers of Lent and Advent sermons, and the less learned in conducting evangelical missions, allying pastoral solicitude with hell-fire declamation. In time of plague, the friars were expected to risk their lives in the danger zone to help the dying and hear their confessions.[18] In popular mythology a cudgel-swinging Capuchin was the recognized exponent of muscular Christianity; the friar who knocked out a pistol-carrying highwayman was living up to the public image.[19] In most towns, the Capuchins were the fire brigade. The Parisian diarists record their exploits; one of Restif de la Bretonne's journalistic set pieces describes them effecting a hazardous rescue.[20] At the conflagration at the fair of Saint-Germain in 1763, soldiers formed a cordon to keep out looters, the seminarists of Saint-Sulpice rescued private possessions, and the Capuchins 'flew to the spot (the expression is no exaggeration) where peril and charity beckoned them, we saw them in teams, cowl over head, robes hitched up to the knees, carrying buckets, dragging their water pumps, rushing to seek danger and to perish as martyrs to their . . . love for their fellow citizens'.[21] More than other regulars, they were regarded as useful, and in a variety of activities. Père Antoine, Mme de Genlis remembered, was chaplain to the château, reading pious literature to the family after dinner; he ran the parish when the curé was away, and 'had shown his valour in several fires'.[22]

There was trouble in the Capuchin camp, however: corruption at the top, evident in the complaints of the rank and file which came in to the commissioners. The *gardiens* of the individual houses rigged the elections of the provincial superiors, and these superiors rigged the appointments of the *gardiens*. Thus secure in their despotic authority by 'ruse and cabal', they could live worldly lives at the top of the pyramid of mendicity and poverty. Intriguers aspiring to posts of command worked hard to ingratiate themselves with those who held them. An anonymous friar of Lyon described the mentality:

Men . . . brought up to be ploughmen or shop assistants join an Order where they pass their early years in extreme poverty under superiors who live comfortably, but treat them with a harshness no decent man would use towards a servant; they swear to themselves that they will go to any lengths to escape from their unhappy state, and they can contrive this all the more easily because official places are not awarded either by seniority or merit.[23]

This combination of despotism and self-indulgence at the top was characteristic, in greater or lesser degree, of most of the mendicant Orders. Just as aristocratic churchmen intrigued for the bishoprics reserved to their class, the bishop of Toul declared in a frank comparison, so, too, plebeians of the mendicant Orders strove to become 'provincials' and 'dominants'.[24] It was so with the Cordeliers. These were the original branch of the Franciscan tree, called 'Cordelier' in France because of the knotted cord of their girdles. There were two groups, the Observants (288 houses, 2,077 friars) and the Conventuals (57 houses, 311 friars). Thirty-nine bishops approved of the Observants, with twenty against; only six approved of the Conventuals, with fourteen against. Yet, whatever else was wrong with the Cordeliers, they certainly co-operated in the pastoral ministry. In the ports they did specialist work with seafaring families.[25] They volunteered to go to Protestant areas where it was difficult to find curés willing to face hostile parishioners. The bishop of Cahors praised their 'indefatigable zeal . . . I'd be in serious difficulties without them.' Complaints from the rank and file, however, tell the same story of corruption at the top as with the Capuchins. The dominants of the provinces of Aquitaine, Franche Comté, Touraine, and Provence are accused of 'despotism' and of accepting bribes from families to allow entry to the Order of army deserters and drunkards. Since they virtually appointed their own successors, the three-year term of office did not limit their depredations—all they needed were a few accomplices to keep the rotation going. Nineteen friars of Provence revealed how Père Julian, their retired dominant, had done well for himself, now living in his house in the country and owning another nearby for two girls 'he passes off as his nieces'. Others had doubts about the accounts of the four friars of the Commissariat of the Holy Land, who collected alms for the guardians of the Holy Sepulchre. There were also a few picturesque scandals in individual houses: the Cordeliers of Alise-Sainte-Reine drinking, womanizing, and playing cards all night to the outrage of the pilgrims who came to their shrine, the students in the Grand Couvent at Paris who indulged in drinking bouts and fisticuffs when the friars were away preaching their Lent and Advent courses.[26] These were not typical, but they were signs of a lack of inspection and oversight, which the discredited dominants could not hope to exercise.

The history of the mendicants had been one of periods of declining ideals followed by periods of regeneration by the separation of new, reformed observances from the old. Inevitably, the effects of the reform would fade, but there was always a residue of improvement preserved. It had been so with the Franciscans: the Capuchins and the Récollets of 1768 were better than the Cordeliers, and within the Cordeliers the Observants were better than the Conventuals.

This was equally true of the Augustinian and the Carmelite friars,[27] each group having its reformed offshoot. The Grands Augustins (with 123 houses and 844 inmates) had their stricter colleagues, the so-called Petits Pères (34 houses, 323 inmates). As against the Grands Carmes (129 houses, 1,194 inmates) there were the Carmes déchaussés—the 'discalced Carmelites'—who had separated to follow a more severe rule at the end of the sixteenth century (62 houses, 750 inmates). The limited number of comments made by the bishops about the two reformed observances, the Petits Pères and the Carmes déchaussés, were favourable. But their attitude was very different to the larger, unreformed branches. The Grands Augustins had fifteen bishops against, and only eleven for; the Grands Carmes were approved by twenty-two bishops, with those in Protestant areas being enthusiastic, but there were eleven against. In both cases, the rank and file were feuding with their superiors—the almost universal flaw in the mendicant Orders. The dominants ruling the provinces kept themselves (or each other) in office, and, ruling abusively, they lacked the moral authority to exercise discipline. The Toulouse province of the Grands Carmes had been under Père Sérapion for forty years, while the friary at Albi fell into ruin and the buildings at Béziers were rented out for shops, with the friars in both places living in town and doing what they pleased. In the Grands Augustins the divisions between rulers and ruled were exacerbated by the favours shown from on high to the aristocracy of doctors of theology, who received greater dress allowances and were excused from some of the rules of austerity. The moral accusations against the seven provincials were also more serious than in other Orders. Some were said to grow rich by trading and taking bribes for accepting novices, and, as for one of them, 'his mistress is known by all the province'. These accusations came from below, and were countered by accusations of insubordination; neither side should be implicitly believed in details, though the bitter divisions between them are clear.

In none of the mendicant Orders was election rigging developed to a finer art than with the Minims,[28] the friars who owed their origin to the other St Francis, Francis of Paola, in the fifteenth century. Yet to all appearances, their constitution was democratic, the local superiors (*correcteurs*) being elected and ruling for only a single year, and the provincials being elected by the deputies to the general chapter, with their term of office strictly triennial. This egalitarian system was subverted, however, by the operation of little groups who monopolized the office of provincial by rotating in power: in the provinces of Lorraine and Aquitaine, two brothers played this game over long periods. The election of the deputies to general chapter was manipulated. In houses where the friars showed independence, their opposition was overcome either by declaring the place a 'vicariate' (in which case the provincial had the right of naming the *correcteur* over the head of the community) or by adding to the nominal roll the names of friars from other houses, which entitled them to vote, though they never came into residence.

Yet the effect of these practices was less disastrous than in other Orders. Twenty-two bishops gave the Minims their approval, and the twelve who had reservations were complaining about atypical houses in which discipline had collapsed. Apart from the Trappists, the Minims had the most severe rule of all the monastic Orders. Eggs and cheese, as well as meat and fish, were excluded from their diet— they lived on bread, water, and vegetables. Their routine of daily devotions, sung without musical ornamentation with slow, strict concentration on meaning, was carried on in a perpetual Lent. To join them required a more than conventional vocation. Hence, their generally good conduct—and also their declining numbers. Many of their 153 houses (they had 975 friars) were already scheduled for closure before the Commission des réguliers met. Another factor— paradoxically perhaps—worked to preserve the Minims from decadence: their ownership of property.[29] Fees for saying masses and for burial in their chapels, the profits of annuities, and property rents kept them solvent, though modestly so. They were preserved from the temptations of wealth, on the one hand, and from those of the

rough-and-tumble of continual begging, on the other. This conferred a freedom, not only to observe their routines of prayer, but
also to indulge in scholarly pursuits—at the end of the seventeenth
century the Order had Mersenne the mathematician and polymath,
Maignen the engineer, Plumer the zoologist, and other scientific
writers. A third factor helping to preserve standards among the
Minims was their associated Third Order of pious laymen, who met
in their chapels and bound themselves to a strict rule of life, including the famous penance of standing with arms outstretched every
Friday for the space of five Paters and five Ave Marias, to share the
agony of the cross. They were, said Père Antoine Masson, the 'kingdom of God in its discipline established here on earth'.[30] As such,
they provided a continual example, an ever-watching lay censorship
on the monks who were charged with their spiritual oversight.

The Dominicans—the 'Black Friars' so called from the black
mantle they wore over their white habits, or, in France, the
'Jacobins', from their principal house in Paris in the rue Saint-
Jacques—fared worst of all the mendicants in the episcopal assize:
thirty-seven bishops condemned them, and of the twenty-eight who
approved, some were lukewarm. The severity of the indictment
owed something to the suspicion that the Black Friars (1,432 of them
in 179 houses) retained a continuing allegiance to Jansenist opinions;
hence they were described as 'republicans', 'infected with the spirit
of revolt which for long they have shown against all legitimate
authority'. Their institute, said one bishop, is 'a serpent which we
have nourished in our bosom'. But in other ways, apart from
doctrinal remissness, they were a threat to the orderly administration
of dioceses, for the free and easy nature of their organization
encouraged eccentricity and indiscipline.

The law of corporate poverty imposed by St Dominic in the
thirteenth century had been revoked in 1475. Thereafter, the various
houses had come by endowments, enough to involve them in
worldly affairs, but not enough to allow them the independence and
scope which a comfortable income might have provided. The
Dominican answer to the pressures of poverty was an unusual one.
Trappists dug, Capuchins begged, but the Black Friars paid their way
as individuals, whether by bringing with them a personal pension
furnished by their family, or by earning money, principally from fees
for their sermons (after all, preaching was the chief duty of their
institute). From their *pécule*, invested with some theoretical supervision from their superiors, they contributed to their meals and other
communal expenses. At Angers[31] in 1737, the prior ruled that those

who gave as much as 100 livres would be entitled to an extra pair of shoes and four pounds of candles a year more than the others. In the following year, a friar loaned the house 533 livres to pay off its debts. Later on, another friar died, and the community inherited his investment income of 55 livres a year. There was a nice—and dis-putatious—balance between the corporate life and individual inde-pendence. When the new buildings at Angers were completed in 1769, the friars chose their rooms in order of seniority, and the furniture was pooled for re-allocation. Thereafter, individuals were responsible for maintaining their own window-glass and keys and for providing their own firewood, though the house would provide a communal fireplace for those who needed it.

Informal arrangements of this kind undermined discipline.[32] Visitation reports speak of tonsures too small and hair too long and curled and powdered, of highly polished shoes and fancy leather hats, with accompanying attitudes of 'impudence', and conversation in 'disdainful terms' airing the sentiments of sceptical 'philosophy'. Those who were in nominal authority proved incapable of impos-ing reforms. Some priors and provincial officials did well for them-selves: there are stories of their mirrors and marble-topped tables, carriages and junketings, while in nearby priories the inmates are reduced to collecting their drinking water in chamber-pots from leaks in the roof and staying in bed while their breeches are mended. As was their wont, the doctors of theology claimed privileges, rang-ing from exemptions from the daily offices to a monopoly, along with the priors, of acting as deputies to provincial chapters. As in all the mendicant Orders, there was no effective central direction over the ten Dominican provinces of France. The general in Rome, by special permission of the French court and the parlement, enjoyed exclusive power over the Paris noviciate, and it was a model of decent conduct. The visitation reports about the state of the other houses went to him, but what could he do? The Gallican liberties prevented him from intervening. When the Commission des régu-liers met, the Roman general was being sued before the parlement of Toulouse by one of his provincials and in 1766 the court declared his decrees to be invalid in France unless confirmed by royal letters patent registered at law.[33] When in 1774 the government yielded on the issue of principle and called in the general to reform the college of the rue Saint-Jacques, it was with so many reservations that nothing effective was done.[34]

The Dominicans were unlucky. By the standard contemporary tests of monastic discipline, they were decadent. But if their establishments are accepted for what they really were, boarding-houses for preachers, confessors, and students, their local, non–monastic usefulness can be recognized. The Black Friars preached a great deal (they had to), and made an unregimented contribution to the life of the Church. The prior and the four Jacobins at Grasse were described by their enemies as running a gambling school, but when, in 1771, orders for the suppression of their house arrived, the mayor wrote in their defence. Their conduct is edifying, he said, and their masses 'provide us with a second parish'; they are all of honourable families of the town, 'finding there a comfortable and decent refuge without getting out of touch with their families and their native locality'.[35] A consideration of the activity of individuals goes some way to mitigating the severity of visitation reports. Amid the scandalous confusions of the house of the rue Saint-Honoré, Père Charles-Louis Richard, the librarian, published four volumes of sermons, six volumes of a *Dictionnaire universel des sciences ecclésiastiques* and sixty-three other tomes; the four Black Friars at Vitré were described by the parishioners as indispensable because of their exactitude in saying the offices, their care for the sick and the poor, and 'their elegant, moving, frequent and continuous preaching'.[36]

IV *The Canons Regular*

The bishops might have been expected to be tolerant of the seven branches of the Augustinian canons regular, since their main task was to man parochial cures. Yet approval was given to only two branches, the reformed Augustinians of Chancelade (six houses, 173 canons) and the canons of Saint-Antoine, the Antonins (thirty-eight houses, 242 canons). The abbey of Chancelade in Périgord,[37] with its five dependencies, had kept the right to elect its own abbot, and was fairly rich. It was therefore independent in running its own affairs, and had resources enough to undertake scholarly projects, especially in the writing of provincial history. As a result, young men of good families and intellectual inclinations were glad to join. From 1762, there was a further incentive, as the abbey branched out into superior journalism, founding the *Éphémérides du Citoyen*, a publication to which Mirabeau and Dupont de Nemours were to contribute. The Antonins were another small group (indeed, some of their houses were now deserted), but they too were able to attract recruits from notable families. The bishop of Belley was delighted with their seminary and their work in the parishes. Only one of his colleagues was critical, and he had to be inventive to find a grievance: they were not fulfilling their original purpose 'to care for the indigent sick afflicted by a malady very little known today'— which made it hardly surprising that they were doing something different. The Congrégation de Notre-Sauveur (seventeen houses and 169 canons, all in Lorraine) was detested by the bishops, but their assessment cannot be trusted—nowhere else was there such a lively nest of Jansenists.

This left four other branches of canons regular under condemnation: the forty-nine houses of those directly under diocesan authority, the Prémontrés (fifty-two houses of the Old Observance and forty of the Reformed), the Trinitaires (seventy-four houses of the Old Observance and seven of the Reformed), and the Génovéfains, or Congrégation de France (106 houses). Altogether, these four branches totalled about 3,000 canons. There were individual exceptions to the general allegations of decadence: notably all seven establishments of the reformed Trinitaires, the so-called *déchaussés*. There would have been more if the bishops had enquired more closely and been fair. Truth was, far from appreciating this particular monastic contribution to parish work, many of them objected to it. To be both a canon regular and a curé, it was argued, is to fulfil neither duty satisfactorily. 'They think they are independent of bishops because they are regulars, and independent of their monastic superiors because they are curés.'[38] Many young men who join the canons regular of Sainte-Geneviève, said the bishop of Orléans, are lacking in ability and deficient in morals, seeking a back-door entrance to the ranks of the parochial ministry, where they have independence and an assured income.

This was a libel, coming ill from a courtier of dubious morals. The Genovéfains had to study for seven years—two of literature, two of philosophy, and three of theology. Those who desired the pastoral ministry had then to teach for two years in a seminary and complete five years in priestly orders; thereafter, on consideration of reports from superiors and visitors, the triennial general chapter could put the candidate on the list for appointment to one of the 600 parishes in the gift of the congregation.[39] Yet only six bishops approved of their seminaries and parish work, while nineteen were dissatisfied. The real reason is not far to seek—the canons regular were not amenable to diocesan discipline. A *prieur-curé* was secure in his tenure; only the abbot, acting with the consent of both his council and the bishop and able to prove 'just cause' could revoke his title. Even so, while secure, he was under no obligation, for he could leave the pastoral vocation to teach or administer in a house of his Order. The Genovéfains regarded themselves as gentlemen-monks. They were resplendent in their white cassocks and well-creased cambric surplices, and the decrees of general chapters show how they affected silver watches and snuff-boxes, hair-powder, and shining buckles, and how they moved too freely in society. There were some strict houses, but most were inclined to comfort and sociability, which suited well-off families who liked the idea of establishing their sons in religious clubs rather than monasteries.[40] The congregation was in debt, yet insolvency did not seem to affect this superior life-style. Young men seeking a career in scholarship would join without a religious vocation, drawn to the Parisian abbey of Sainte-Geneviève with its prestigious library of over 100,000 volumes—like Mongez, elected to the Académie des Inscriptions at the age of 38, and Barthélemy Mercier, the librarian. Unmoved by the spectacle of St Augustine trampling on heresies depicted on the library dome, others of the canons regular of Paris ventured into dangerous speculation: there was Pingré, the astronomer, both a Jansenist and a freemason; Joseph Barre, who wrote anonymously in favour of Protestants; and Pierre François Courayer, who published various works in 1723 and 1726 to prove Anglican orders valid and in the end fled to England and obtained a sinecure in the Anglican Church.[41]

The bishops were alarmed by this sort of learning. The scholarly activities of the Prémontrés were also under suspicion. They published a great deal[42] on history, music, campanology, poetry, chronology, liturgiology, and casuistry; after twenty years' work, one of them produced a 'dictionary of the origin of all things'. These were mostly unexceptionable books, but what of Remacle Lissoir, the head of an abbey, who in 1766 published an attack on papal claims in the vein of Febronius? Later on there was J.-B.-A. Hédouin, who issued an appreciative study of the subversive writings of the abbé Raynal, and was rescued from dire consequences only by the heroic conduct of a relative, Captain Hédouin de Pons Luden, already in jail for libertinage, who wrote to the police claiming authorship. Independence, a free and easy life-style, and opinions ranging from Jansenism to sympathy with Protestants and philosophes ensured the condemnation of the Genovéfains and the Prémontrés, their work in the parishes largely forgotten.

V *The Anciens Bénédictins, Cluny and Cîteaux*

The great Benedictine family had 660 houses and about 6,000 monks. Of the seventy monasteries of the Anciens Bénédictins, the bishops approved of eighteen, condemned twenty-six and gave no verdict on the other twenty-six. Two broad conclusions may be inferred from the Commission's enquiry into these houses of the Old Observance. First, the prevailing temper in clerical and lay society was a major factor in maintaining or undermining monastic morale, for the houses where the rule was decently—sometimes fervently—observed were in the pious northern boundary zone, the dioceses of Arras, Boulogne, Cambrai, Saint-Omer, Tournai, and Ypres. Secondly, the rule tended to fall into abeyance and the monks slink off into a quasi-lay existence in houses with few inmates. There were exceptions either way: Troarn, in the diocese of Bayeux, was one of the few abbeys described as utterly scandalous, and it had fourteen monks, while the prior of Saint-Sever (Coutances) was proud of his tiny community, three of the four having previously served in the parochial ministry, and the other as a chaplain to the East India Company in Senegal. And small communities sunk in decadence could be engaging in their worldliness. One prior, with only three monks, admitted that they lived a 'purely secular life', and wondered why their house was permitted to survive. The prior of Chemillé (the diocese of Angers) said that he and his three monks each had a little house in which they lived privately, though they fasted and recited the offices.

Is our way of life an abuse? I would not be certain. All I will say, Monseigneur, is that I am edified by the conduct of my brethren. In truth, our duties are not burdensome, being indistinguishable from those of secular canons. We were instructed in these duties as novices, and we fulfil them. If they had been more onerous, perhaps we would not have undertaken them and our vocations would have been different.

This is revealing: taking vows was not forsaking the world in entire self-dedication; it was entering into a contractual relationship to hold an ecclesiastical sinecure on certain conditions. The ultimate logic of the idea was seen at Maurs (Aurillac), where the buildings had collapsed long ago and only the vestiges of the foundations remained. The twelve monks lived at home like secular priests, and, as their prior said, 'they support their families who, without them, would be in abject poverty'.

Brienne thought these old Benedictine houses ought to be

grouped together with the eleven houses of the so-called Exempts under the rule of a general chapter. But would this have improved them? The Exempts already had their chapter meetings to rule them, and the bishops condemned seven of their abbeys and approved only one.

The bishops who gave positive approval to only a quarter of the monasteries of the Anciens Bénédictins and the Exempts gave their warrant to even fewer of the Cluniac branch, sixteen houses out of eighty-eight. True, some escaped without notice, and of those condemned, few met with such severe and circumstantial censures as the bishop of Rodez directed against Sévérac and the bishop of Mâcon against Charlieu. In the first, the four monks put the parish clergy in fear of their lives and endangered the chastity of the local girls; in the second, there were female servants and every night, after the prior retired to bed, the brethren ran a gambling school. The great abbeys were decorous and proudly expending their wealth in splendid building programmes.[43] At Cluny itself, the head of the Order, the solemn routines of liturgical life rolled on, while all around new conventual buildings were being erected, their severe classical façades adorned with balconies and stair rails in cast iron designed by Frère Placide. At Saint-Martin-des-Champs in Paris, construction went on under the direction of the architect Soufflot the younger, nephew of the great one.[44] Here was the research centre of the order, where its history was being compiled by a team under Dom Claude Baudinot—nearly a thousand manuscript volumes of copies of documents were accumulated. It was not entirely disinterested history, for the general chapter of 1716 had resolved to print the basic charters 'serving to sustain the cause of the Strict Observance against the attacks of the commendatory abbot of Cluny'.[45]

This resolution is a pointer to the feuds which made the order incapable of reforming itself. Cluny was always held *in commendam* by a prelate of the court aristocracy, who would sometimes exercise his right to preside over general chapters and would sometimes interfere with the internal business of monasteries, which was not his right at all. The monks were not united against the incursions of their abbots. There were two observances, the 'old' (fifty houses with 296 monks) and the 'strict' (thirty-eight houses with 333 monks). The first tended to let the abbot have his way, the second to battle against him and his 'violation of our most sacred maxims'. Each observance had seven *définiteurs* at the triennial general chapters; they met separately for business concerning their own affairs and jointly for common interests.[46] When Louis XIV annexed

Franche Comté in 1684, he united the Benedictine houses of the province to Cluny, with a *définiteur* to represent them in the general chapter. From the start, the new arrival aligned himself with the old observance, which left the abbot's party dominant. This might have been the moment for the commendatory abbot, Cardinal Bouillon, to press home his advantage decisively, but he quarrelled with the king, who prevented him from subverting the right of the *définiteurs* to appoint the priors of monasteries.

In this continuing quarrel, neither side would allow the other to take the initiative in making major changes; nor would they agree to anyone else doing so. In 1730 a papal brief appointed Cardinal Bissy, archbishop of Rouen, as apostolic commissioner to reform Cluny; the commendatory abbot, Henri Oswald de la Tour d'Auvergne, archbishop of Vienne, refused to co-operate. Nothing was done, though twenty-two years later the lay magistrates of the Grand Council issued a regulation to keep priors of houses in order—they had to have permission from the abbot of Cluny to be away for more than a month, and if they went to Paris, they had to lodge in one of three named institutions. The Commission des réguliers in its turn was reticent about making proposals for action, leaving decisions to the abbot, Dominique de la Rochefoucauld, archbishop of Rouen— a sure formula for immobility.[47]

The Cluniacs had become an independent branch of the Benedictine family over eight centuries ago; the Cistercians had followed them to independence rather less than two centuries later. Both Orders were wracked with debilitating internal divisions. Strife between Cîteaux and its first four daughter-houses (each with the attendant train of the monasteries it had founded) was almost as old as the Order itself.[48] During the reign of Louis XIV, the abbot-general (a genuine abbot, not a commendatory one), ruling from Cîteaux, was backed in his authoritarian designs by the authoritarian king, and achieved a dominance over the proto-abbots of La Ferté, Pontigny, Morimond, and Clairvaux which continued after the great monarch died. General chapters were no longer called, so what little was done was done despotically, while the constraints which a common opinion might have exercised against abuses in individual houses were absent. The proto-abbots had two possible manœuvres for edging themselves out of their position of inferiority. According to their argument, the final authority in the Order should be vested in the steering committee, the *Definitorum*, on which they had a majority. By an old papal ruling, the abbot-general named four members, and the proto-abbots named five—though of these five only four could actually sit, for the abbot-general could exercise a veto against any one of them, a nice refinement of electoral procedure invented by the court of Rome; the abbot-general could easily be outvoted, but he need not put up with harassment by the most extreme of his enemies. However, the dominance of the *Definitorum* was never conceded at Cîteaux, where it was considered to be a 'subsidiary tribunal' capable of executive action only on matters specifically referred to it by a general chapter.

The other line of attack for the proto-abbots was to insist on the calling of the supposedly triennial general chapter. This would give them a forum in which to air their grievances, but the trouble was, they were not likely to win a vote. Half the Cistercian houses which had survived the Reformation were outside France, and the contingent of abbots coming from Germany voted solidly for authority. The Germans had political leverage: they could intrigue with the Austrian ambassador in Paris, and hold over the French court the threat of a schism in the Order, rejecting the generalship of a Frenchman. When, finally, in 1738, a general chapter did meet, the votes of the foreign abbots ensured the reaffirmation of the abbot of Cîteaux's authority.

There was an election for a new abbot-general in 1748. It was a glittering office to hold, conferring entitlement to a seat in the parlement of Dijon and in the provincial estates of Burgundy.[49] Anticlericals made the usual allegations of bribery by the various candidates.[50] Victory went to François Trouvé, a doctor of the Sorbonne and a man of character, of bourgeois origin and only 37 years of age. Sensing possible weakness, the proto-abbots renewed their claims, and finally, in 1760, took their case to the Grand Conseil. In the following year, the court gave its ruling: decisions of Trouvé taken without due consultation were illegal.[51] The issue came before the general chapter of 1765, the Germans once again swinging the vote to reject the proto-abbots' argument that final authority must rest with the *Definitorum*. The proto-abbots walked out and appealed to the king; the abbot-general went to the parlement of Dijon, where the magistrates reaffirmed his authority, a finding influenced by the lawyers of the German abbots, who declared that they would not attend assemblies of the Order if they were to be subject to a 'despotic committee'. So, when the Commission des réguliers met, the Cistercians were in chaos.

It would have been well if, as some had proposed, the Cistercian Order had split up, with each proto-abbot becoming independent, with his own general chapter to direct him. Smaller groupings were less prone to divisions, and more amenable to discipline. A break-away of this kind had taken place at the end of the sixteenth century, when the Feuillants had escaped from the control of Cîteaux. Their twelve houses in France (and their equal number in Italy) were a manageable group under coherent direction, and even the censorious bishops found no fault with them, though they still asked their usual questions about usefulness. But the vast main complex of Cistercian monasteries (288 of them) was too big, and the confusions of the government of the Order prevented the monks from reforming themselves, whether by authoritarian dictation or by communal inspiration.

The results were evident in the files of the Commission des réguliers.[52] Of the fifty bishops recording an opinion, eighteen praised the Order, thirty-six condemned it, and six were neutral. Few houses received the unreserved praise bestowed by the bishop of Lavaur on La Rode: there were only six monks, but they served in parishes, gave alms, provided employment, and had such a high reputation that the sons of the nobility were glad to join them. Praise, when it was given, tended to be qualified. The bishop of Agen said that the monks' conduct was 'fairly good . . . but they are useless'. Some houses were said to have nothing in their favour but their alms and the employment they provided. One was generous in times of disaster, another was custodian of the fragment of the Holy Shroud, and the local people made a living from the pilgrims who came to revere it. Of the four abbeys of his diocese, the bishop of Châlons-sur-Marne said, they recite the offices with dignity, give limited hospitality, and, above all, provide work—'that is the use they are and this usefulness is genuine'.

Great constructors of palaces themselves, the bishops did not complain of the building programmes of the richer Cistercian establishments. They ought to have done so, for there was a wasteful failure of central oversight. The abbey of Châlis was allowed to run up an astonishing debt of a million livres on its extension programme, an amount which could never be repaid, and led to bankruptcy and closure. Meanwhile the fabric of the Collège de Saint-Bernard at Paris was decaying all through the century. The great Gothic hall and the fourteenth-century church (adorned with the high altar salvaged from Port-Royal-des-Champs when Louis XIV demolished it) echoed empty, as a handful of students struggled through an exacting curriculum in the few viable rooms. Even selling the garden to speculators setting up a cattle market in 1772 barely paid off half the collegiate debt.[53]

There were many Cistercian houses with few inmates. The average was eight per house; 191 monasteries had nine monks or fewer, and of these, forty-four had three or less. Only thirty-seven had ten monks or more, the biggest being Cîteaux (60), Clairvaux (54), and Morimond (30). Smaller institutions were always in danger of slipping into the life of lay society, especially when they were in the depths of the countryside. The bishop of Poitiers accused the monks of the six priories in his diocese of doing nothing but ride around supervising their property. The archbishop of Bourges had eleven houses with only thirty-three monks in all of them together. He saw no hope of increasing their number, as the only recruits coming forward were 'of low birth and ignorant'—the idea that the uneducated mass of people might be a good recruiting ground for the cloisters never struck this great aristocrat. Only one house had a library, the others having merely their choir-books and lives of St Bernard; when not supervising their tenants, the monks read 'old gazettes and newspapers'. Of his four abbeys, each with only five or six monks in it, the bishop of Angers declared they did nothing but sing the offices, go hunting, and play cards with the locals. These reports generally stop short of total condemnation as scandalous; only one house in ten was accused of either neglect of duty or immorality. The general impression is of a lack of fervour and only a marginal contribution to the life of the Church.[54]

There were a few Cistercian houses which were astonishing exceptions, places where ruthless austerity, far beyond any rational interpretation of the rule, reigned supreme. In every case, the trans-formation was the achievement of a charismatic abbot. Orval[55] in the Low Countries was reformed by Charles de Bentzeradt (dd. 1707), but his task was made easy by the secret inspiration of the place, which was Jansenist. Here was one of the covert refuges for disciples of Quesnel and an *entrepôt* for the importation of Jansenist books. When a papal representative made a visitation in 1725, no fewer than twelve monks had to flee lest they were recognized. Orval was rich—so did not need to make the compromises with the world which poverty engenders—but disciplined; so the riches did not corrupt, though there was a splendid building programme. The abbey of Sept-Fons[56] in the diocese of Autun was reformed by Dom Eustache de Beaufort in a long reign which lasted from 1656 to 1707. A mixture of almost feminine tenderness and grim severity (he wept if he had to send a novice away, but put a sardonic thrust into the obituary notice of an old colleague), he had that strange personal magnetism which has the power to draw men to the ways of complete self-sacrifice. Throughout the eighteenth century, the harshness of the régime, with its perpetual silence, was proverbial: a father with noisy children would set them to play the game of 'aux pères de Sept-Fons' where everything was done by gestures. Yet there was no lack of recruits, and many had to be turned away: from 1701 to 1722, of 461 postulants or novices, only 99 were accepted for final profession.[57]

Orval, Sept-Fons, and a few other monasteries—Laigle, Verneuil, and Soligny—were also reformed in imitation of (though without coming into dependence upon) the most famous and grimly austere house of them all, La Trappe, in the diocese of Sées in Normandy. Here, from 1664 to his death in 1700, Armand-Jean de Rancé had ruled.[58] A scholar, courtier, dilettante churchman, and absentee holder of rich benefices, he had been converted by the death of Mme de Montbazon, a warning of the transience of earthly things. From commendatory abbot of La Trappe, he transformed himself into the regular one. The way of life which he imposed was designed to annihilate every pleasure, of both the body and the mind. The brethren lived in perpetual silence, doing arduous work in the fields and singing the offices with slow measured deliberation. Study was banned. They slept on straw mattresses placed on boards. Meat, fish, eggs, and seasonings such as thyme or garlic were excluded from their diet, the one meal of the day coming from the range of roots, beans, lentils, cereals, fruit, nuts, and black bread. Rancé was not a fanatic. His way was destined only for the few who had a special vocation to it, and the hardships were not meaningful except as being necessary to direct the mind solely to God: 'Dieu ne veut point de partage'. Dom Chabon, a later abbot of La Trappe, spoke of monks as 'successors of the martyrs . . . irreproachable witnesses . . . guardian angels of the world by the fervour of their prayer . . . models to the human race by the saintliness of their lives'.[59] Rancé would have seen dangers of pride lurking in this proclamation, for he was haunted by the shadow of the *amour propre* which feeds upon self-abasement. He would have been gratified by the men of the eighteenth century who regarded his foundation with contempt, denouncing useless austerities, anti-social renunciation of fatherland and family.[60] What would have alarmed him was the procession of fashionable courtiers who came to spend a night or two at his monastery, and the pilgrims who flocked— between 4,000 and 5,000 of them every year—to gape at the wild surroundings and the silent figures in their white habits, sleeves sweeping the ground, and shudder at the sight of the cells without light or fire, adorned with a skull and pictures of deathbeds and hell.[61]

The severe regime cut short the life span of those who accepted its rigours.[62] Yet, like Sept-Fons, La Trappe had no dearth of applicants: towards the end of the century, it was said that of the fifty novices who joined every year, only four or five were taken.[63] Visitors found it a frightening place, but serene. Revolutionary officials interviewing the monks noted how they appeared to be happy: 'with the exception of five or six, who seemed to be of limited intelligence, the monks are men of strong and well-balanced personality, not weakened by their fasts and austerities . . . It seemed to us they loved their state in the depths of their hearts.'[64]

VI *The Congregations of Saint-Vanne and Saint-Maur*

The Congrégation de Saint-Vanne was founded at the beginning of the seventeenth century, and it eventually drew into its orbit forty-nine of the old Benedictine houses, all in the provinces of Champagne, Lorraine, and Franche Comté. They were better-populated monasteries than most, for the total of monks in 1765 was over 600. The fourteen bishops of the dioceses where these houses were found faced a dilemma when they made their reports. The Vannists for the most part were Jansenists, yet—or because of the fact—their conduct was hard to fault. The episcopal reports, which covered thirty-six houses, described the monks as morally irreproachable, but deplored their mental attitudes. 'Their studies are perverted . . . they teach "Quesnelism",' said the bishop of Toul. 'It is much to be desired that they become more submissive to the bishops and the laws of the Church,' said the bishop of Verdun.

It was a learned congregation. Dom Calmet, the indefatigable biblical commentator, renowned for his learning and notorious for his naïveté, was one of theirs. His devotion to scholarship extended to inviting Voltaire to study at his abbey of Senones, and at the age of 80 climbing ladders to get down volumes for him; his reward was to have his commentaries plundered for dubious anecdotes to discredit the Scriptures and to have unpleasant suggestions made about his motives for writing about them.[65] There was Dom Sinsart, controversialist against Protestants and an expert on the topography of Hell; Dom Petitdidier, who had once given refuge to Quesnel, but ended up writing anti-Jansenist polemics; Dom Chardon, banned from teaching by the general chapter of 1730 because of his opposition to *Unigenitus*, who published a famous six-volume history of the sacraments fifteen years later.[66] As time went on, the Jansenist writers were silenced, but their *frondeur* spirit lived on in the brothers Cajot, Dom Charles writing a learned study of the Benedictines to recommend their suppression, and Dom Joseph publishing 'a critical history of monastic cowls', ridiculing the habit and those who wore it, himself included.[67]

Special problems arose in a congregation with a tradition of devotion to scholarship. One concerned the government of houses where so many of the inmates were absorbed in their own researches. Dom Sébastien Dieudonné wrote a snide report to Loménie de Brienne in 1774,[68] complaining of how superiors and *procureurs* were left to rule as they pleased, so they travelled round agreeably under pretext of looking after the estates and awarded themselves handsome suites of apartments, habits of fine cloth, and fancy snuff-boxes. (It is remarkable how often snuff-boxes figure in the inventories of misdemeanours in allegations of monastic decadence.) Brienne took this seriously, and feared the rise of 'a vicious aristocracy'. Another problem was the degree of allowable comfort. Reformers held up their hands in horror at the thought of monks with fireplaces in their cells. Dom Ignace de Courcelle pointed out the fallacy of freezing to be holy—if monks gathered round the communal fire, they would gossip and cabal, rather than concentrating on their studies. Even so, concessions to scholars by way of comfort or absence from the choir offices inevitably had the effect of separating them from the rest of the confraternity, a division and breach of community feeling which was to bedevil the most learned congregation of them all, the Benedictines of Saint-Maur.

The Congrégation de Saint-Maur was founded in 1618, in accordance with Gallican prejudice, as a purely French federation. When papal bulls of authorization were issued in 1621, five houses belonged to it; by 1667 there were 161, by 1766, 191—containing a total of 2,456 monks.[69] At the general chapter of 1684, a programme of research and publication, including every aspect of monastic history and editions of the Greek and Latin Fathers, was adopted. Thus, the great Maurist historical enterprise began. The monks received an extensive basic education: two years of classics, two of philosophy, three of theology, and another of 'recollection'. During their studies they were observed by their priors, who reported outstanding talent to the superior-general, who made the final choice of those who were to devote their lives to scholarship. Each established scholar named an assistant (as Mabillon co-opted Dom Germain and after him Dom Ruinart), and as their enterprise proceeded, they could call on the various houses of the congregation for help in locating manuscripts, transcription and translation, indexing, and handling the other chores leading to publication.

Was a lifetime of research a suitable occupation for monks? Rancé, abbot of La Trappe, denounced the idea as an infiltration of worldliness into the cloister. From Saint-Germain-des-Prés, the headquarters of the Maurists, came Jean Mabillon's[70] famous reply, the *Traité des études monastiques* (1691). A Jansenist by intellectual inclination and austerity of life, but not by partisanship, Mabillon distrusted theological studies in the scholastic vein as 'base chicanery'; as for philosophy, Christianity has abridged its subject-matter by 'settling definitively the final end of man and the methods which will bring us to it', leaving only themes for inconclusive wrangling. 'The disputes will go on for ever and men will remain the same, always in error and uncertainty.' So monks must concentrate their studies on the Bible, the Councils, the Fathers, and the developing history of the Church. These were necessary investigations in which certainty could be achieved. Erudition would lead to truth, and truth to charity, thus 'forming in us and others the new man whose likeness was revealed to us in the person of our Saviour'. The controversy was not all it seemed: Rancé had the art of using erudition while concealing it, and Mabillon would have followed learning even if its spiritual advantages had been proved non-existent.

When Mabillon died in 1707, the principles of Maurist research had been established.[71] His *De liturgica gallica* (1685) had made liturgiologists aware of the processes of development and adaptation which had layered over the practices of primitive antiquity: he showed, for example, how the custom of administering extreme unction after the last sacrament rather than before was a thirteenth-century innovation with superstitious overtones. His six volumes of the lives of the Benedictine saints were serene and reverent expositions of verifiable truth, scorning hagiography. And the greatest achievement of all was the *De re diplomatica* (1681), which created the science of authenticating and dating charters and other manuscripts; the many volumes of documents he edited were examples of its application.

Mabillon's work at Saint-Germain-des-Prés was carried on by Bernard de Montfaucon,[72] a soldier-turned-monk who, with military discipline, worked thirteen hours a day, accumulating a knowledge of six ancient and three modern languages, and publishing forty-four vast surveys—in folios—of the monuments of antiquity and of the early centuries of France, a catalogue of European manuscripts, and a pioneering work on Greek palaeography. Around him gathered a band of collaborators, united in scholarly endeavour, even though they differed on 'les affaires du temps', Montfaucon and Dom Martin being hostile to the Jansenists, while Dom Bouquet, who began the *Recueil des historiens des Gaules*, was an appellant and re-appellant. They held a learned discussion group attended by intellectuals from outside the congregation, including Rollin, the Jansenist recteur of the university; Père Tournemine, the editor of the Jesuit *Mémoires de Trévoux*; and Canon Gédoyn of Notre-Dame, author of dilettante essays on 'the urbanity of the Romans' and 'the pleasures of the table among the ancient Greeks'. In 1713, the abbey began to build a new library for its scholars with a gallery extension in the cloister to house manuscripts. Its fame attracted substantial acquisitions—bequests from bishops and magistrates of the parlement and the books of the abbey of Corbie and the chapter of Saint-Maur-des-Fossés (the secular canons here accepting money and a golden monstrance for their chapel in exchange).

Up to the Revolution, the Maurists produced more than 800 volumes: catalogues of manuscripts, descriptions of ancient monuments, collections of source material, grammars (Dom Guérin's Hebrew grammar leading to a splendidly acerbic dispute with canon Masclef of Amiens over the necessity of the Masoretic points[73]), and editions of the Fathers, some of which remained standard texts until our own century. They also turned to French history in a spirit not only of religion, but of patriotism, 'to illustrate the glory of France, to encourage the present generation to emulation lest the race degenerate'. From their indefatigable pens came the early volumes of the *Gallia Christiana*, the *Recueil des historiens des Gaules et de la France*, and, above all, the *Histoire littéraire de la France*, a project 'the mere idea of which makes slothful humanity tremble'. Exceptionally, it was produced, not at Paris, but at Le Mans, for Dom Rivet, its originator, was excluded from the capital as a Jansenist. When he died in 1749, the first eight volumes were in print, and Poncet, Colomb, and Duclou, still working from Le Mans, continued the next four.

In the course of the seventeenth century, the history of half a dozen French abbeys had been written. With Mabillon, the project was advanced by the systematic ransacking of the provincial archives. He himself travelled widely, searching and inspiring others to search, and his assistant, Dom Claude Estiennot, wandered everywhere, expanding the enquiries. One of their successors was Dom Jacques Boyer,[74] who from 1710 to 1714 was riding along the Pyrenees and the southern margins; his journal records some good dinners he enjoyed and the astonishing spectacle of the charter-house of the abbey of Obezine, all the manuscripts missing and a cluster of 300 bats on the ceiling, their dung on the floor a foot deep. The Maurist research tours went on throughout the century, and local antiquaries dropped their pens in despair in face of the competition of the Benedictine machine exhaustively accumulating every scrap of evidence. 'There can be no limit', wrote a canon of Paris in his memoirs, 'to the achievements of those who are so clever and industrious and who always have 400,000 crowns available in their coffers. This was said long ago about the congregation of Saint-Maur.'[75]

Meanwhile, each province had been allotted an official historian. The first to publish was Dom Lobineau on Brittany. A team of five researchers had worked for seven years before him; the first draft was put together at the abbey of Saint-Vincent in Le Mans; and the final version was polished by experts at Saint-Germain-des-Prés; it was presented—a volume of narrative and another of supporting documents—to the estates of Brittany in 1707. Historians being a prickly tribe the world over, there were controversies. From Le Mans, Dom Liron attacked the account of the early invasions of the province; what he said was sound sense, but he was denouncing phantom errors derived from the sight of an earlier version never put into circulation. The Rohan family, which had nagged Lobineau to constrain him to put in their legendary ancestor King Conan, were enraged to find him omitted, and tried to dissuade the estates of Brittany from paying the expenses of publication. Dom Morice, who took over on Lobineau's death in 1727, proved more amenable, and Conan rode again. 'Even if it was demonstrably false, which I do not admit,' wrote Rohan, bishop of Strasbourg, to Morice about the spurious charter on which the claim was grounded, 'it is not for you to say so, still less to prove it, on the contrary, it is fitting for us to defend it as far as it can be.'[76] It was not just the revenues of the abbeys which the aristocracy claimed to appropriate, but also the consciences of the monastic historians.

The estates of Languedoc,[77] burning to catch up with the Bretons, tried to persuade Lobineau to take over their history; he refused, though he sent a memorandum detailing his methodology. The work was done—five volumes by mid-century—by Dom Vaissète and Dom de Vic, the first being a Jansenist, protected against persecution by his collaborator, who was a supporter of *Unigenitus*. But if zeal for research could be a bond of union, it could also be divisive: just as Liron had attacked Lobineau, so Dom Marchard attacked the two historians of Languedoc, ridiculing their prospectus and publishing a rival one of his own, an unfriendly manœuvre among colleagues, which had the covert support of the superior-general. When the general chapter met in 1737, it had before it the first two volumes of the Languedoc history, Morice's revision of Lobineau's Brittany, and the manuscript of the first volume of a history of Burgundy. The meeting decided to press on, concentrating on Normandy, Touraine, Anjou, Maine, Gascony, and Dauphiné, provinces where there were numerous houses of the congregation, and as far as possible appointing local monks as the historiographers.

Yet the research drive was losing impetus. In 1746 Dom Morice wrote to a fellow monk at the abbey of Saint-Florent in Saumur: 'our rulers are vastly indifferent to what has up to now been the glory of the congregation; it is useless to talk to them about our provincial histories'. Sixteen years later another Maurist complained of the abandonment of the history of the province of Berry, researchers being in short supply as a result of 'the crass ignorance and idleness of the recruits who are now joining us'.[78] Even so, the government saw the congregation as its hope for the fulfilment of the plan of the royal historiographer Moreau to create a national archival depository by bringing in collections from all over the country. The general chapter of 1766 agreed to help, declaring: 'we are proud to be called Frenchmen, we wish to be useful to our country'. The work would be put in hand by twelve monks at Saint-Germain-des-Prés and another twelve at the Blancs-Manteaux, all dispensed from the night offices and other duties, with the right to call on help from auxiliaries in the provincial monasteries; for its part, the government promised to pay 1,200 livres annually for each historian seconded to the task. A committee was set up to meet weekly at Saint-Germain-des-Prés under Moreau. The project ran to 1787, when it merged into another of Moreau's creations, a 'Society of French History'. Yet, as organization became formalized, effectiveness declined. There were never more than eighteen historians available for the archival project, and they could not shake off the writing assignments they had already undertaken. The urgency faded from the provincial history ventures. The research teams amassed notes (299 volumes survive for Picardy), but failed to press on to publication. There was a deal of quiet torpid scholarship with no evident public achievement, like Dom de Gennes's fantastically detailed nine-volume catalogue of the 25,000 volumes at the library at Le Mans.[79] (A typical librarian, when the monks proposed to take some of the books away when the Revolution ousted them, he rushed off to give the keys to the municipality, to keep the collections intact.) Dom Rousseau, taking over the history of Champagne at the abbey of Saint-Rémy in Reims from 1752, failed to put his mass of accumulated materials in order; while Dom Housseau, coming in about the same time to direct the four historians working on Anjou, Touraine, and Maine, succeeded in frightening off local historians with rival schemes and in gathering a cartload of notes, but never published a line.[80] Even so, when in 1787 the government asked the superior-general for a list of the works on French history which his monks had produced in the last 150 years, the total was impressive—more than 200.[81]

The erudite productions of the Maurists were to win more approval from the generations of historians who succeeded them than from their own contemporaries. The Enlightenment wanted lively and readable history pointing a humanistic moral. 'The madness to get into print is an epidemic plague which continues unabated,' wrote Voltaire; 'the indefatigable and ponderous Benedictines have just published ten volumes of their *Histoire littéraire de la France*—I won't read them.'[82] In the second half of the century, Dom Colomb complained of the lack of interest in the succeeding volumes of the series: 'a work like ours is not to the taste of our century, it is too serious'. 'Frivolous literature stifles erudition,' wrote another monk; 'people want to read only books that are amusing.'[83] The congregation published the Fathers and monastic history at its own expense, but expected the provinces to pay the historians who wrote their secular chronicles, and laymen in France were notoriously stingy towards clerics—not surprisingly, considering the spectacle of ecclesiastical wealth so ill-distributed. In 1720, Dom Lobineau wrote to the mayor of Nantes saying he was no longer being paid, so he was laying down his pen; henceforward he would do only the duties of his 'office de moine moinant de moinerie'.[84] In 1770, Turgot, the intendant of Limoges, wanted his provincial history written, provided the archbishop of Rouen gave Dom Col a benefice to support his researches.[85] Six years later, Sénac de Meilhan, intendant of Hainault, declared that Dom Bévys would get nothing more than free accommodation in monasteries which were willing to put him up. The province would give nothing, though once a history appeared in print, a 'gratification' might be forthcoming. 'I have seen in several provinces similar enterprises which produced no results, and the most part of the monks who addressed themselves to the task did so with no aim other than to travel and escape for a while from the rule of their monasteries.'[86] Detractors of the Maurists drew attention to the disproportion between the total numbers in the congregation and the limited number of genuine scholars: according to a seventeenth-century critic, 'scarcely forty of them'. This was a strict count of actual writers, not taking into the reckoning researchers, indexers, and other auxiliaries; including all these, there would have been, say, 200.[87] In the mid-eighteenth century the congregation was about 2,500 strong, so the famous works of erudition were the production of a minority. But there were many others who, from the secular and utilitarian point of view, were usefully employed, whether as teachers or administrators, in the *collèges* established in thirty of the abbeys—schools very like those run by the Jesuits and other religious Orders, though the original aim had been to be severely selective, and take only the sons of the nobility.[88] In 1776, when the royal government set up a dozen military academies to improve the quality of candidates for commissions in the army, no fewer than five of these institutions were entrusted to the Maurists. It was partly a question of where spacious buildings and grounds were available, and partly a recognition of the Benedictines' willingness to experiment with a modernized curriculum adapted to practical ends, for the general chapter of 1759 had agreed to make Latin an optional subject and to teach it without the composition of themes and verses, and with a minimum of grammar. The great Benedictine military academies at Sorèze (diocese of Lavaur), Pontlevoy (Blois), and Beaumont (Lisieux) became famous, concentrating on history, geography, modern languages, music, gymnastics, fencing, and riding, with the performance of plays and ballets as a standard recreation. By 1788, Sorèze had forty-six monks engaged in teaching, with numerous lay auxiliaries, and there were 400 boarders. 'What would Saint Benedict say', asked a scandalized academic of the University of Paris, 'if he could come back and see a prize-giving there, with drums and bugles, drill and dancing?' Dom Ferlus made a reply which, in its frank acceptance of Enlightenment values, contrasts sharply with Mabillon's answer to Rancé a century earlier:

If our founder returned to earth, he would begin by looking for us in desert places. Then, finding them now cultivated and populated, with towns in place of rocks and forests and men in place of wild beasts, he would acclaim us as his disciples. He would say, 'Oh my children . . . you have enlarged the work whose foundations I laid, you have spread literacy and enlightenment, you have brought about an educational revolution.'[89]

Monks not engaged in education or teaching—about half the congregation—were left to get on with what Lobineau had contemptuously called 'moinant de moinerie', saying the day and night offices, training the novices, looking after the aged, managing the corporate possessions, and running the domestic affairs of the various houses, dispensing hospitality and contributing to local activities, ecclesiastical and secular, as individuals felt inclined. When we catch glimpses of the life they led, even in unsympathetic observations by anticlericals, it seems to have been generally decorous, though often lacking in fervour, and always comfortable. With revenues rising from the late seventeenth century, the great abbeys spent their surplus on rebuilding programmes.[90] Amid trim formal gardens, neo-classical façades in harmonious local stone arose (there was none of the baroque and rococo exhibitionism of the South German and Italian abbeys). Long ago dormitories had been abandoned, and the individual cells which were built exceeded the modest dimensions officially prescribed. From the beginning of the century, they were being fitted with fireplaces, and new chimney-stacks arose along the skylines of the abbeys. Recruitment did not keep pace with build-ing programmes, and by 1789, in many houses an individual monk had two rooms, and priors sometimes three. There were fine stair-cases, vestibules, galleries for promenading, and panelled reception rooms for recreation and entertaining. Monks dressed well, their standard habits well tailored, worn with black silk stockings and elegant shoes; they enjoyed hands at cards, games of billiards and tric-trac, and attended concerts and soirées. They dined well, even if the fasts were technically observed, and sometimes they evaded the fasting rules by posting themselves for a while to the infirmary table. The Jansenist Chevalier de Folard,[91] visiting Saint-Germain-des-Prés to receive help with his writing on Polybius, enjoyed intellectual conversation from 11 a.m. to 1 p.m., followed by a dinner which still had not reached the stage of coffee by 5 p.m. (Our knowledge of monastic cuisine comes from laymen who enjoyed the hospitality, then made puritanical remarks about it afterwards.) This was life in an agreeable religious club. 'If I am on the road to heaven,' wrote one of its members, 'I find the carriage very comfortable.'[92]

Though the vows of the Benedictines did not exclude reasonable comforts, they ought to have imposed discipline, and this was lack-ing in the eighteenth century. The *Unigenitus* quarrel brought strife and bitterness into the life of the community. Most of the Maurists sympathized with the Jansenist cause. Their studies of Church history in the centuries before papal claims were formulated inclined them to Gallicanism, as also their pride at being a purely French con-gregation. They had quarrelled with the Jesuits over the editing of the works of St Augustine, and there were recurrent aggravations over royal warrants annexing Benedictine priories to bolster the revenues of Jesuit houses. By 1713, intrigues and counter-intrigues in Rome had reached the point that the Pope urged Louis XIV to suppress the congregation altogether.[93] This was an astonishing proposal to put to a Gallican ruler; even so, in his last two years, the ageing king cracked down on the Maurists: a few were imprisoned (one fled to Canada, and one to Holland, to escape this fate[94]); others were exiled to the provinces; and three priors were deposed. Orders were issued to deploy some of the researchers to write in favour of *Unigenitus* (the monks evaded the command by ironically declaring their unwillingness to infringe the prior rights of the better-qualified Jesuits). During the brief thaw under the Regency, most of the monks in most of the abbeys signed the appeal to a General Council (Saint-Nicaise at Reims being a notable exception). At Saint-Germain-des-Prés, the only abstention was by Dom Coustant, a Jansenist, but just about to publish a book on the decretals which he wished to dedicate to the Pope. At the general chapter of 1720, Dom Denis de Sainte-Marthe, an appellant, was elected as superior-general. Then came the years of repression. Chapters were dominated by royal commissioners who excluded Jansenists and dictated the voting; appellants were kept out of official posts, excluded from monastic benefices, and sent off to isolated provincial abbeys. In 1763, of the 193 superiors of houses elected by the general chapter, only one or two were appellants.[95] The Jansenists, silenced, kept in touch with one another through clandestine correspondence.

Repression was effective, but its side-effects were disastrous. Priors imposed on houses received no respect, feuds abounded, and in the poisoned atmosphere latent vices of character emerged, revealing masochistic fanatics, servile hypocrites, boasters, and informers. As the commissioners of the great monastic enquiry of 1765 put it, on the one side were 'Jansenists who pride themselves on their regularity to accredit their party', and on the other, 'Constitutionals who affect submission to the Bull to dispense themselves from the observances'. To the commissioners, most of the monks were unsatisfactory, and of the others, a very few were 'saints', but they were 'isolated and without influence', while rather more were 'upright in their lives but negligent and lacking in fervour'.[96] In this same year when the Commission des réguliers was set up, the state of the congregation came to public notice in a resounding dispute over 'mitigations'.[97] On 15 June, twenty-eight monks of Saint-Germain-des-Prés (all except the prior and two others) petitioned the king for changes in rules and organization, and circulated their request to the other houses asking for adhesions. Their proposals were at once realistic and high-minded. They wanted to bring back free elections, both for officers in individual abbeys and for representatives from the six provinces to the general chapter. They also wished to rationalize arrangements by setting aside certain named houses for specialist tasks: two to receive novices, one for teaching canon law, one for learned languages, one for retired scholars, with Saint-Germain-des-Prés and the Blancs-Manteaux remaining as the centres of erudition. In each province, they proposed to turn one abbey into a seminar where a few young nobles would be given a theological education. Learning was to be encouraged by sending monks to study in the universities of Paris and of Reims, and by setting up a special committee to allot funds for research. As for 'mitigations', all they asked was to return to the old Benedictine monastic dress, to limit fasting to Lent, Advent, and three days a week at other seasons, and to make bedtime and getting up time two hours later, saying matins earlier, to avoid the nocturnal pilgrimage to chapel. A few vexatious trivialities were to be abandoned, like the prescription of an exact contour for the tonsure or the obligation to hold the cup in both hands when drinking. There was nothing in their petition against the spirit of St Benedict. 'Better a less severe rule with general conformity than a severe one ill observed' sums up their object.[98] The twenty-eight signatories included most of the established scholars—the editors of the *Gallia Christiana* and the other great collections and the writers of the provincial histories. As scholars, they were already exempt from matins and other time-consuming routines; they wished to get monastic communities together, themselves included, for the saying of all the offices.

Alas! with the incautious exaggeration of academic polemicists, they presented their case in a form calculated to arouse opposition and misrepresentation. They denounced 'despotism', thus alarming all in authority, and they referred to the 'minute practices' and 'pointless austerities' which 'keep away recruits from the nobility', giving the impression that they merely wished to make life easier for themselves. Their petition raised an outcry. The archbishop of Paris got the king to forbid Saint-Germain-des-Prés asking the houses for support. The superior-general sent round a circular denouncing this 'work of darkness', this 'yearning for the flesh-pots of Egypt. We must praise the Lord more especially in the silence of the night,' he said, 'when all nature seems buried in oblivion of its Creator.' He also forwarded a protest to the king, which 800 monks joined in signing. Some signed twice, and others came back from the dead to add their names. With the Commission des réguliers investigating discipline and some abbeys in danger of suppression, this was no time to conceal one's zeal under a bushel. The Blancs-Manteaux, jealous of the priority given to Saint-Germain-des-Prés more than a century ago, joined in the attack. Midnight psalmody, they said, was a practice of the earliest Christians, as attested by Pliny, and Peter the Venerable had described monks who break abstinence as crows, wolves, and bears. Three years later, long after the proposal for mitigations had been withdrawn, they were still thundering self-righteously against this apostasy.[99] The rank and file of monks seem to have agreed with one of the more temperate censures levelled against the petitioners by their superior-general—they were trying to make the congregation 'a society of men of letters, free and almost independent'. Most monks, not being concerned with scholarly activity, wished life to go on as usual. This meant supporting a régime of austerity which in practice they would ignore: as Tocqueville said, here was the essence of the *ancien régime*: 'règle rigide, pratique molle'. The defeat of the 'mitigations' was a victory for orthodoxy and unreality.

By now, the bitter divisions inherited from the Jansenist quarrel were ingrained and permanent, even as the original issues were coming to be forgotten. The general chapter at Saint-Denis in 1766 told the Commission des réguliers that the principal 'abuse' was 'the spirit of independence' which set the rank and file against authority—as the deputies to the chapter were heads of houses, the observation was predictable. The Commission itself thought the fault lay with the superiors.[100] By their thriftless inefficiency, they had allowed the congregation to run up a debt of nine million—so much for their right to rule. As for relations with their monks, they were too harsh to make the rule loved and too lax in their own conduct to make it respected.

Against the spectacle of decadence and feuding in the Congregation of Saint-Maur should be set the worthiness of so many individuals. They should be judged not by the monastic ideal as represented in pious handbooks and the sermons addressed to them at their profession, but by the notion of 'my station and its duties' which their families and society expected of them. There were the learned heroes of the Jansenist cause:[101] Dom Gesvres, who died at the age of 48, worn out by working fourteen hours a day in defence of the theology of Antoine Arnauld; Dom Gerberon, exile in

Holland, prisoner in the fortress of Vincennes, and writer of a vast number of polemics, the list of them occupying twenty-four pages in the *Histoire littéraire* of the congregation; Dom Massuet, who produced a digest of the Greek Fathers whose writings supported predestination; Dom Martienay, who published his translation of the New Testament in defiance of the censors; Dom Coustant, who never received visitors, never used a fire, and whose only relaxation from learning was an annual five days' walking tour. Their lives were austere; but austerity was not a Jansenist monopoly—Dom Charles de l'Hostallerie, superior-general from 1714 to 1720, ate sparingly, drank only water, devoted himself to prayer, and passed his final year of retirement at the age of 80 in teaching his servant to read.[102]

As the Jansenist propagandists died off or were silenced, the historical researchers dominated the work of the congregation. No others achieved the greatness of Mabillon and Montfaucon, but there were many who rivalled them in exactitude of conduct and indefatigable industry. Some come alive to us in their correspondence—above all, Dom Lobineau. Angular and legalistic, as befitted a descendant of an old legal family of Rennes, offering good value and demanding good money for it, with a sardonic wit which did not exclude self-mockery (as over his disastrous donkey ride on a Breton beach), given to wine and overwork, he toiled on, striving to complete his quota of writing before fate thrust him down 'into that damned worm-hole by which we have to go to Paradise'. And whatever sins he may have had to account for, obsequiousness to the great was not one of them, as the anger of the Rohan family bore witness. His older contemporary, Dom Denys Briant, another Breton, provides an interesting contrast, being a historian *malgré lui*, 'leafing through old books which so often tell me nothing, seeking out the names of the abbots no one cares about, amid an impenetrable confusion of old papers'. This research he hated; his real interest was in accumulating ideas to compose the definitive treatise on moral philosophy, 'how to live and how to die', a work which he never completed.[103]

The tradition of scholarship continued to produce dedicated characters right up to the Revolution, like Jean-Pierre Deforis,[104] who edited the works of Bossuet, not without controversy. He died heroically on 25 June 1794, standing on the platform of the guillotine, insisting on going last under the blade so that he could exhort the younger victims to fortitude. But in the last generation of the *ancien régime*, a new kind of learning became fashionable in the congregation, in the form of the contributions to controversy and competitions of wit which characterized the provincial culture of the Enlightenment. Such were the satires, odes, and essays which won Dom Maugier[105] so many prizes of the Academy of Caen, and the disquisitions on electricity, mesmerism, the physiological problem of the 'fluide nerveux', and the proof that republicanism was the best form of government which made Dom Gourdin the oracle of the academy of Rouen.[106] There was a Maurist who died in 1763 as prior of the minor benefice of Gennes, who published more than any of them, and in his own right was a major figure of the literature of the Enlightenment. From the first he had been unsure of his call to the monastic life. A priest and working in Saint-Germain-des-Prés on the *Gallia Christiana*, he knew his vocation was gone: 'my books were my faithful friends, but like me, they were dead'. In his cell he wrote the four volumes of the *Mémoires d'un homme de qualité*, a novel in which he described his superior-general and colleagues under the guise of the monks of the Escurial. He fled to England, came back, and was absolved and reintegrated into the congregation, remaining nominally a member even when chaplain to the Prince de Conti. All the while his hallucinatory imagination moved on, creating worlds which to him were more substantial than everyday reality.[107]

Those who publish, whether *Manon Lescaut*, like the abbé Prévost, or the *Histoire de Bretagne*, like Dom Lobineau, survive in historical memory; so too do many of those who indulge in intrigue and faction fights. But information is lacking about the ordinary majority who, with how strong a vocation we know not, joined in the natural course of things and led uneventful lives. Dom Benoît de Monceau d'Anvoile,[108] of a noble family, joined the Maurists with two of his brothers, ruled four houses successfully as prior, then in 1717, at the early age of 48, retired to Saint-Denis, where he ran the business affairs of the abbey; five years later he died, heroically ministering to the sick in an outbreak of smallpox. Others had more modest careers. Dom Benoît Dassac[109] followed his elder brother into the congregation, looked after the novices at Grasse, then became sub-prior at Avignon. Until the Revolution, nothing more startling is recorded in his journal than the cutting down of meals to a single course during the harsh winter of 1788–9 so as to be able to give more to the poor. Dom Pierre Chastelain, son of a cooper at Reims, joined the Maurists there and towards the end of his life succeeded in getting posted back to end his days in familiar surroundings. He had a few troubles because of his Jansenist connections, but nothing more serious than a malicious librarian locking up some books he needed. The brightest pages of his record concern the four days' holiday the abbey of Saint-Denis allowed him in 1733, at the age of 24. With a fellow monk and a small allowance of pocket-money, he spent a night at the Cordeliers of Noisy, saw the Trianon and the menagerie at Versailles, and the famous water-pumping machine at Marly, dined on the last day at Saint-Germain-des-Prés, and got back 'in a cart that charges five *sous* a seat to Saint-Denis in time for compline, very pleased to have seen such fine things. *Sic transit Gloria mundi*.'[110]

The young in their naïveté can scorn the glories of the world and believe that they will continue to do so. The abbé Prévost knew from the start the fickleness and ambiguity of vocation. Shortly after he was professed, he wrote:

I know the weakness of my heart, and I understand how important it is for my peace not to apply myself to sterile studies which will leave my heart dry and enfeebled. If I want to be happy in religion, I must conserve in all its force the inspiration of the grace which brought me to it. I know only too well—I realize it daily—how far I can sink if I lose the great rule from sight for a single moment, or even if I look with the least complaisance on certain images which all too often intrude into my mind.[111]

As with the individual, so too with the institution itself, the inspiration of grace faded as the monasteries became integrated into the social order, with the monastic vocation an ordinary way of life along with all the others.

VII *The Achievements of the Commission*

The working of the Commission des réguliers and the limited nature of its achievements is an illustration of the impossibility of radical reform under the *ancien régime*. As often, there was a change of ministry: in 1770, Brienne's backer, Choiseul, fell from power. The parlements, defending liberty as they saw it, stood by to protect the monks from arbitrary interventions; letters patent registered by the law courts were needed for the setting up of a monastic Order in France, so the magistrates considered themselves entitled to exercise a watching brief over them. Soon they were declaring the Commission 'an illegal tribunal', concerned with 'destroying rather than reforming'. The general assemblies of the clergy were a forum for episcopal complaint. The Pope was dissatisfied, and resort to extreme courses of action would have driven him to refuse the bulls of reform or suppression which—in the end—he usually conceded. Some Orders had foreign generals stationed in Rome, jealous of their rights and objecting to proposed changes in France because of their international implications. Other Orders, with their higher command in France, had foreign dependencies inaccessible to coercion from Versailles, their abbots threatening to secede if their interests were infringed. And above all, there was the play of aristocratic influence at court and of agitation by local notables in the provinces. Influence ruled much of what was done in eighteenth-century France, and dictated a great deal of what could not be done.

To end disputes between monks and their superiors and to adjust the rules, whether towards severity or towards mitigation, Brienne proposed to revise the existing monastic constitutions. He wished to promote 'democracy' by having more ordinary monks elected as conventuals at general chapters, to have superiors holding office for only limited periods, and to tie up provincials by compelling them to consult a committee of assessors, a 'définitoire'. He proceeded by authoritarian means, despatching royal commissioners (usually two, generally bishops) to the meetings of general chapters, if necessary arming them with *lettres de cachet* to exclude potential opponents. These authoritarian measures prevailed with seven congregations. Reforms in a 'democratic' direction were imposed on the Génovéfains, the Trinitaires, Picpus, and the Grands Carmes. Some mitigations were allowed to the Récollets, but none to Picpus; the separate Orders of the Trinitaires were united, and the provinces of Picpus increased from four to six for convenience of administration. Saint-Vanne did not need constitutional change, for its general chapters already had an equal number of elected monks and priors voting; certain games (*jeux*) were allowed as 'better than useless conversation', and priors holding independent benefices had to surrender their income to their monastery. By contrast, Saint-Maur was a prime example of 'despotism', with general chapters composed only of superiors. New rules therefore added twelve conventuals to the thirty-three existing ones, and superiors were limited to a reign of seven years. But it was not long before all the old feuding broke out again. General chapters continued to be scenes of chaos and of bleak authoritarian intervention. The royal commissioners at the meeting of 1778 reported the six provinces to be acting like independent congregations competing against each other for offices and power. In 1783, the parlement of Paris made the opposite complaint about the extraordinary chapter held at Saint-Denis: the prelates attending as commissioners in the king's name had used *lettres de cachet* to dragoon the voters into fraudulent unanimity. The Maurists, said the magistrates, 'will soon be just an incoherent assembly of individuals, strangers to one another'. In the following year, a lay observer complained of the lawsuits against abbots and priors which were bringing some houses to the brink of insolvency. The superior-general himself, in March 1788, wrote despairingly to the government. The education of novices was being neglected, since those who ought to teach them were more concerned with intrigues to draw them into partisan allegiances, while honest men were no longer prepared to accept office and responsibility, given the impossibility of doing any good. 'C'en est fait de la Congrégation de Saint-Maur,' he said; 'it's all up with the congregation if the reign of anarchy goes on much longer.'[112]

Other congregations refused changes, or delayed them. Monks whose conduct was irreproachable and who were not divided proved impregnable: the Feuillants, Chancelade, and the Carthusians retained their existing organization unchanged. Brienne accepted the rule of a general for life in the Congregation of Le Sauveur; its monks were austere and Jansenist—far be it from him to give them a *définitoire* as a discussion forum for their dying heresy. Cluny, left to its commendatory abbot, the archbishop of Rouen, did not have a new constitution approved in Rome until May 1789.

Cîteaux had 'foreign' houses, which helped to prevent change. The feud between the abbot-general and the proto-abbots had brought the Order near to ruin; the Commission decided to bring dissension to an end by a new and definitive constitution. Two royal commissioners (the bishop of Senlis and the intendant of the province of Burgundy) attended the general chapter of 1768[113] to compel action. A committee was set up to draft new statutes, but it was chosen to reflect the balance of the assembly, which was thirty-one for the general and twenty-three for the proto-abbots. So it was a committee of five, dividing three against two, though the representatives of the minority, the abbots of Chaloche and La Trappe were tough characters. Predictably, there were two rival projects presented to the general chapter of 1771. Royal policy was indecisive; Versailles was pressed towards the side of the proto-abbots by the bishop of Senlis, the papal nuncio, and Mme Louise, the king's pious daughter, and towards the abbot-general's side by Mercy d'Argenteau, the Austrian ambassador. After wrangling for a month, the longest meeting ever, the representatives dispersed with nothing decided. The deadlock was insuperable so long as the Germans came, but at the general chapter of 1783 there were only four, since the anticlerical Emperor Joseph II had refused travel permits to the rest. So, by twenty-one votes to fifteen, a royal decree proclaiming a new constitution was accepted. The *Definitorum* would be the supreme authority, its decisions binding unless overturned by a unanimous vote of the general chapter. These chapters would meet triennially at fixed dates without the need for formal summons, and the proto-abbots were to have authority over their affiliated abbeys independent of general headquarters at Cîteaux.

At the next assembly in 1786, with the defeated abbot-general and the victorious proto-abbots at last working in harmony, a belated programme of reform was agreed. It was decided to go along with the times and win public approval by running free boarding-schools for the 'sons of nobles and poor but deserving commoners'. The abbey of Morimond opened such a school for twenty boys in the very same year,[114] and other abbots announced their preparations. The Order resolved to pay off the debts of the Collège de Saint-Bernard in Paris and put the buildings in order to house a central seminary to train monks as teachers. Men of the Enlightenment wondered why something like this had not been done a century ago.

The generals of the Capuchins, the Dominicans, and the Discalced Carmelites held up reforms. The Capuchins were ruled from Rome by a Frenchman, P. Aimé de Lamballe; his letter of protest was given by Mme Louise, the king's Carmelite daughter, to her father when he visited her convent. The Spanish general of the Grands Augustins raised no overt difficulties, but he may have pulled strings behind the scenes, for Rome never approved the 1772 revision. The Commission wished to unite the two observances of the Cordeliers and make the rule of life stricter; the friars outwitted the reformers by agreeing at once to a union in which the practices of the lax observance were preserved, a change promptly accepted by the Franciscan Pope Clement XIV in 1771.

Some Orders were suppressed. In almost every case the monks wanted to go, and Brienne encouraged them with the offer of generous pensions, as he said, 'making bridges of gold for whoever wishes to give up his rights'. The canons of Saint-Ruf had already asked for a bull of secularization in 1760, and the Brigittins (only two houses in existence) in 1762. From 1742, the Servites de Marie had been forbidden to take novices, and now had only fourteen priests, all old. The canons of Saint-Antoine voted their own demise. The Commission delayed implementing it in the hope (vain, as it turned out) of keeping their property for ecclesiastical use—it went to the Order of Malta. There were only 168 Célestins, and all except eight wanted to be secularized. The rule of 1670 had not been observed within living memory, they said, and the vows which they had taken were to the comfortable way of life which they had seen. Their Italian general opposed them, and it was not until 1776 that they began drawing their generous pensions. The argument of the Célestins—that the *status quo* was the implied condition of the vows they had taken—was respectable by the standards of the day; the fervent Camaldolese also used it. Faced with an order to unite their six houses into one, they decided to abandon the monastic life altogether, since their 'peace of mind' amid familiar companions and in familiar surroundings would be lost.

Loménie de Brienne ruthlessly made sure that this same argument for leaving their monasteries was forced upon the monks of Grand-mont. Attending as royal commissioner at their general chapter of 1768, he ruled that only those monks who undertook to go back to the original rule of the twelfth century would be allowed to stay. This meant a diet of bread and vegetables and a life in silence. Recruitment was cut off by banning the taking of novices, and the bishops were instructed to close houses as they fell empty, allocating pensions to the monks and appropriating the rest of the property for diocesan works. But there were legal formalities which could be invoked as barriers against arbitrary action, and old Dom Mondain quickly learned how to make use of them. Not until his death in 1787 was the bishop of Limoges able to take over the mother-house, having lost a lot of money in legal fees during the intervening years. The episcopal palace was completed, while the abbey of Grandmont was demolished, the lead from the roof and the enamels from the altars sold, and the manuscripts disposed of by weight for use as wrapping paper.[115]

By contrast, the Order of La-Merci, with only 120 monks, raised no legal objections, but authorized its nineteen houses to negotiate with the local bishops for suppression. Even so, there were difficulties with the foreign general and the king of Spain, so that in 1788, seven houses were still in existence. The Benedictine congre-gation so-called of the Exempts (eleven houses and sixty-eight monks) refused to change its statutes or to name houses for suppres-sion, so royal letters patent were issued to pension them off (which the parlement suspended to allow the general chapter to vote its own end). It was discovered that two of their abbeys had no buildings, the monks simply living at home and drawing their money.[116]

The winding up of small and moribund Orders was not much more than a tidying-up operation on the margins of the monastic problem. The Commission hoped to achieve more by the suppression of individual houses. The criterion for the decision was to be a new rule of 'conventuality': the minimum number in a house which was part of a congregation was to be ten, and fifteen in isolated ones. Merely to keep the liturgical offices going and to administer the property would need as many, and small numbers encouraged somnolent conspiracies of idleness, and facilitated absorption into the secular world outside the gates. This was a fact of observation, but churchmen challenged the limitation on grounds of theology, canon law, tradition, and utility.[117] 'Where two or three are gathered together, there I am in the midst,' Jesus had said. Some rural areas would be deprived of spiritual support, and with a plenteous harvest the labourers would be few. Early councils of the Gallican Church had defined conventuality as consisting in six monks, or even three. The wishes of founders were being ignored; so too were the wishes of the present generation, for by the strict legal procedures for an 'alienation' of ecclesiastical property, the local inhabitants and the monks ought to be consulted, and the agreement of the bishop and of the Roman Curia obtained. What would happen to the employees of a suppressed house, to those who relied on its alms, to travellers who expected hospitality in difficult terrain?

Enforcing conventuality was not easy. Saint-Vanne and the Feuillants, for good reasons, and the Cistercians, for bad ones, escaped unscathed. Cluny suffered little until 1787–8, when a final revival of the reforming impulse caused the closure of the forty-four houses of the old observance. The story of the suppressions among the Anciens Bénédictins (37) and in Saint-Maur (only 21 out of 191 houses) is a revelation of the operation of the web of influences over provincial France. There were petitions to preserve pilgrimage sites and famous relics, orders from parlements prohibiting action, bishops wanting to retain help in parishes, and parishes wanting to retain schoolmasters, peasants revolting with sticks and muskets, intrigues by duchesses, marshals of France, and magistrates. The abbey of Troarn survived in spite of the vote of all its monks to leave; Brienne wrote to the bishop of Bayeux to say that he could not find where the opposition came from. Significantly, when an abbey was suppressed and its revenues diverted to worthy diocesan projects, the commendatory abbot still continued to draw his abusive revenues; real abbots and priors could be evicted, but the absentee, nominal ones had their pensions for life.

The canons regular suffered little, since the king insisted that the parochial cures they served must all be maintained. Only fifteen houses of Génovéfains were closed, fifteen of the Augustinians, one of Prémontrés and none of Chancelade. The Trinitaires lost sixteen establishments; the official total was double this, but half of these were empty already. Mostly the mendicants were allowed to keep their tiny groups of friars scattered over the land, since the bishops required their help in the parishes. The Récollets lost about a hundred friaries, but many of them were virtually empty already. The Cordeliers lost only 51 out of 345, the Capuchins only 22 out of 451. The Discalced Carmelites preserved all but four of their sixty-two establishments by acting quickly and drafting their members around to fill depleted contingents. The Grands Carmes with only 67 friars and 129 houses to maintain seemed in a hopeless position, but they lost only 22 establishments—Mme Louise, the king's daughter, was a Carmelite nun.

Even the worldly Dominicans lost only 20 friaries out of 179. When it came to the crunch, their preachers were needed. But the careless life-style in their friaries continued. A report of 1778 on the Parisian house on the rue Saint-Honoré spoke of 'dissipation and worldliness; everyone arrogates to himself the liberty to act as he thinks good'. Across in the rue Saint-Jacques a prior specially installed by a commission of reform was writing to the general in Rome asking to be released; the place, he said, 'is less a monastic community than a boarding-house where practically everyone is concerned with his own affairs'.[118] A new prior was sent, and was confronted by a rival prior illegally elected by the community. And both these Parisian houses were virtually bankrupt. The *collège* in the rue Saint-Jacques was in terminal disrepair, the chapel having been closed eight years ago as dangerous. The prior thanked Providence for the crumbling façade when mobs began to search other monasteries for hoarded food supplies—they did not trouble the obviously penurious Jacobins. In this same revolutionary year the other Parisian house (in the rue Saint-Honoré) sold its silver to keep solvent, and rented out its refectory to the Club Breton, later to be called the Jacobin Club. 'Thus, for 200 francs had been created the most terrible and powerful instrument of the Revolution,' wrote Lenôtre.

The Commission's most effective interventions were embodied in two royal edicts which could have been issued without any preliminary investigations, by the sole light of nature. The first, in March 1768, made a change which was much applauded by lay society. The age for taking monastic vows was raised from 16 for both sexes to 21 for men and 18 for women. As Joly de Fleury insisted, it was impossible to marry without parental consent before the age of 25, or to proceed to holy orders before 22. Celibacy, he said, is against nature, therefore extra years are required for mature consideration. The second edict, that of February 1773, was a Gallican document designed to increase the powers of bishops over the monasteries in their dioceses, and to codify the powers they had already.[119] A monastery could not accept foundation masses or sponsor a lay confraternity, and a monk could not be ordained, preach, or hear confessions without formal diocesan permission. Houses not under a general chapter were to be under episcopal tulelage, requiring approvals for their elections of priors, administrators of property, and masters of novices. In these and all other houses the bishop was authorized to intervene to suppress scandal, provided he gave the monks six months' warning and then conducted his visitation in person. Foreign generals could continue to exercise their jurisdiction, but not from Rome: the case had to be heard in France, and the verdict needed validation by royal letters patent.

The Assembly General of the clergy of France had no grievances against the edict of 1773, but it regarded that of 1768 on the age of taking vows as disastrous. There was an immediate gap in the flow of vocations, and once this mathematical hiatus ended, the psychological effect continued, for in the five years between 16 and 21 young men could so easily decide to follow worldly ambitions and affections. According to the archbishop of Arles, the trend of declining vocations predicted the end of all the mendicant Orders within forty years and of all the others after another thirty. The protests of the assemblies of clergy in 1770, 1772, 1775, and 1780 helped to bring the Commission des réguliers to an end. In 1780, it was transformed into a committee with a different name and limited powers, and Brienne left the scene. The proposed reform had achieved little, but had stirred up lay opinion, intensifying doubts about the usefulness of monks and whetting desires to appropriate monastic property.

20

VOCATION AND THE ART OF
OBTAINING A BENEFICE

I

'Before the foundation of seminaries', said Godeau, bishop of Grasse in the mid-seventeenth century, 'the doctrine of the divine vocation to the ecclesiastical state was practically unknown.'[1] He was using the word 'doctrine' in the technical sense of an officially formulated statement of belief; vocation—the thing in itself—was evident everywhere in the Old and New Testaments, whether it was the calling of Israel as a nation and the Pauline election of the people of God to salvation, or the special calling of individuals to service— Abraham, Samuel, the prophets, Jesus himself, and his disciples. The problem with the individual vocation was: how to authenticate it. The onlooker might be sceptical, and the person called would wonder how to be certain—has God spoken to me in a dream, or did I dream God spoke to me? With the advent of the seminary, it became important to have criteria to judge authenticity, if only to help and encourage the candidates for ordination. Antoine Godeau, learned, dwarf-like, with an ear for poetry and (in his younger days) an eye for women, visiting and reforming his mountain diocese, was a realist about the sort of clergy the Counter-Reformation needed. He did not want readers of Plato and Aristotle, but men who knew their New Testament and were expert at giving advice in the con-fessional; and they must have conviction. 'In a seminary,' he wrote, 'the matter to which particular attention must be paid is the testing of the vocation of the young clerics.'[2] In his *Discours de la vocation ecclésiastique* (1651), he laid down the questions to be asked, codify-ing the ideas current in the first half of the century. A candidate for ordination must ask himself, he said: 'Am I living a moral life?' 'Are my intentions pure?' 'Do I possess the requisite ability?' 'Am I pray-ing to God daily to help me to remain unswervingly loyal to the ecclesiastical profession in the depths of my mind?'[3]

With elaborations, these questions formed the basis for later dis-cussions of vocation. Louis Habert (1708) made more specific the tests for purity of intention—they were to include a disinclination to pursue the things of this world, a devotion to the discipline of the Church, and zeal for the glory of God. 'Discipline'—in Habert and in Sevoy's *Devoirs ecclésiastiques* (1763) there was a greater emphasis on objective tests imposed by the Church. A vocation is justified if the confessor approves it, the bishop accepts it, and the testimony of the people confirms it—though this testimony is unadventurously defined as 'evidence of a good reputation'.[4] While the casuists were ruthless in condemnation of anyone who actually sought promotion in the Church, they emphasized that when the Church in its wisdom offered high office, it ought not to be refused. Humility, fear, distrust of the worldly manœuvres of relatives, were not adequate motives for refusing a bishopric; indeed, there was an obligation to accept when 'the Pope or another legitimate superior orders'.[5]

To us, something seems lacking in these analyses: what of sheer 'attraction', the impulse in the soul, the hearing of God's voice— 'Magister adest et vocat te'? But we should not judge the eighteenth-century idea of vocation in the context of our own social order, in which the Church is a marginal community, and in the light of more complex ideas of psychological motivation reached through recent controversies.[6] Given the ordinariness of a career in the Church, and the rewards which such a career might offer, stern moralists at the end of the seventeenth and the beginning of the eighteenth centuries were inclined to reject 'attraction' as a dangerous concept. M. Olier (in a treatise posthumously published in 1675) and Louis Habert saw a sentimental attraction to the ecclesiastical life and the ardent desire for priestly office as dangerous; they could well be superficial, or arise from 'interest'. Later, however, the eighteenth century's rehabilitation of 'happiness' and its reconciliation of the human desire for self-fulfilment with the will of God for man seem to have had their effect, in a cautious way, on the idea of ecclesiastical vocation. This is evident in Sevoy, and in the anonymous *Conduite des âmes dans la voie du salut* (1750), where it is stated that 'L'inclination est la principale marque de la vocation de Dieu'. Given the requisite qualities and being in a state of grace and under the direction of ecclesiastical authority, a man was free to follow his impulses.

Maybe so, but one thing was certain to all the casuists and spiritual writers. A man must not seek any sort of comfort or pre-eminence from his vocation to the ministry; nor was he allowed to procure advantages of any kind for his family and friends. It was wrong to apply for a position of dignity and honour, even if worthy of it; as for rewards, a priest should ask only for enough to live on decently (*l'honnête subsistance*).[7] Relatives were not to be supported from an income derived from ecclesiastical sources; the most that was allowed was the giving of a very small sum to fathers or mothers to preserve them from utter destitution. If the sight of aged parents in poverty was too harrowing, a cleric must move away from them, lest he be tempted to liberality.[8] Whatever promotion came along, it must be freely offered, never solicited, even indirectly. Hence Tronson's subtle grounds of reproach to Fénelon when he became tutor to the duc de Bourgogne—sophisticated self-interest lurks behind our conviction that we are disinterested: we do not seek to exercise influence, but we remove obstacles; we do not solicit the great, but we take care to show ourselves to them in the best light; 'no one can be entirely certain that he has not called himself', instead of waiting for the calling of God.[9]

This was the ideal of an ecclesiastical vocation as the theologians defined it and as it was taught in the seminaries—a vocation based on the honest conviction (after all advice was taken) that one's life was pure, one's intentions disinterested, and one's abilities adequate; a vocation sustained by prayer for lifelong steadfastness, emphasizing allegiance to the Church, and, indeed, closely supervised by ecclesiastical authority; a vocation within which all worldly desires, including even affection for parents, were virtually annihilated. The object of this chapter is to test the theoretical ideal by looking at sources other than ecclesiastical, principally at the handbooks of the lawyers, and to see what had to be done in practice to get ordained and established in a benefice.

II

The first step on the way to a clerical career was the taking of the tonsure. According to the Council of Trent, 7 was the minimum age, though French bishops were inclined to set a rather later time.[10] Confirmation was usually a prerequisite, but not, apparently, First Communion.[11] No spiritual power or office was conferred by the tonsure ceremony—which consisted of little more than the snipping off of a lock of hair—and no clerical obligations were undertaken.[12] The essential point was: the tonsure admitted its recipient to the order of the clergy, and made possible the holding of benefices (provided no cure of souls was involved). Next came the four minor orders (porter, lector, exorcist, acolyte); again, no indelible clerical character was conferred, and the way back to a lay vocation remained open.[13] The decisive commitment came with admission to the subdiaconate, for which the minimum age was 21 (or, according to some ecclesiastical lawyers, 22). At this stage, a vow of perpetual chastity was taken, and a sort of banns were called in church beforehand, asking if the candidate had made some previous promise of marriage.[14] A year later, promotion to the diaconate was allowable, and at the age of 25, ordination to the priesthood. Before admission to the subdiaconate, the candidate had to demonstrate that he would not become a burden to the Church which he was undertaking to serve in perpetuity: hence the necessity for a 'clerical title'. This meant that he had to prove the possession of a permanent income, whether from his patrimony or from a benefice. In the diocese of Paris, 150 livres[15] annually was required; it was less—80 to 100, in the provinces.

A family of the poorer sort would have to reflect on ways and means—possibly all clubbing together—to produce the necessary capital; it was roughly about the amount which would be required to buy a minor judicial office.[16] A father making provision for his sons in his will might lay aside a sum to pay fees at a seminary and a 'pension sacerdotale' for any who might choose to seek ordination; this was done by a bourgeois of Nantes, Carrier, and one of the sons was the future terrorist, the inventor of the infamous *noyades*.[17] A clerical title was supposed to be inalienable, but in practice, a clause was sometimes inserted in the contract specifying that the endowment would revert to the family once a benefice of a suitable income had been acquired.[18] The contract, formally drawn up by a notary, would be witnessed by three or four persons, who engaged to make good, out of their own pockets, any deficiency in the property or other investments which were meant to yield the income of the 'title'.[19] The whole document had to be read out in Church on three successive Sundays, at the time of calling marriage banns and giving notices. The formula of publication ended with: 'If anyone knows that the possessions enumerated in the aforesaid contract are not of the value therein declared, or that they are not in full ownership quit of all other obligations, or that they do not belong [to the donor], let him so declare to me that all occasion of fraud may be avoided.'[20] Occasionally, there would be an objection: Père Coudrin, later to become famous for his austere spirituality, found his right to proceed to the subdiaconate challenged by creditors of his father, a pious man whose zeal to further his son's vocation was not matched by strict accountability in the affairs of the market-place.[21] A certificate that the contract had been published unopposed was required, along with the standard attestation of faith and morals, when a candidate for the subdiaconate presented himself to his bishop.

In addition to ordination *sub titulo patrimonii* or *sub titulo beneficii* there was a third way—*sub titulo paupertatis*.[22] A monk who had taken a vow of poverty could be so accepted, and the privilege was extended to the 'prêtres hibernois', the miserable Irish clerics who hung around so many towns doing odd jobs in churches and hiring themselves out to families to walk in funeral processions. The fact was: the bishop was the judge of who could be ordained, irrespective of all other considerations. When Fleury was bishop of the tiny, poverty-stricken diocese of Fréjus, he made up the numbers of his clergy by ordaining some whose title was 'la mense commune'—he would see to their support, provided they were at his disposal to be sent to take parish services.[23] Or a bishop might bestow the subdiaconate on someone with the understanding that a benefice would be following soon—probably the job of vicaire in some grim rural parish. One such cleric in November 1790 wrote to the Constituent Assembly asking that priests of this sort be not overlooked in the awarding of pensions now that Church property was to be sold. He himself had come in this way in 1788, 'sub titulo ab ordinario approbando'; this was Joseph Le Bon, the future terrorist.[24]

Long before ordination, the search for benefices had begun—something to support a course of study, to contribute towards the clerical 'title,' and to form a supplement to income in the longer-term future. France was full of 'chapels', 'prebends', and 'priories', minor benefices without care of souls, available to ecclesiastics once they had received the tonsure. These *bénéfices simples*, reformers always said, should be secularized or abolished;[25] indeed, search was made among them for income that could be confiscated whenever a new seminary, hospital, or *collège* was founded. Local officials (consulted, as the law prescribed, about these 'unions') were torn between the desire to accumulate endowments for a public amenity and regret at the prospect of supplements to the incomes of their sons being lost. Some 'chapels' had minor duties attached to them, like teaching Latin to local children; others were outright sinecures, like the one that the prince de Beauvau gave to a young theological student, son of his business manager.[26] Even sinecures, however, needed a certain amount of work put into them to collect and improve their revenue; repairs were an eternal problem, litigation was always a possibility, and research among old charters to safeguard rents and dues was a necessary precaution.[27] A curé, M. Marquis-Ducastel, has left a record of his father's unavailing attempts to get

him a benefice to pay for his seminary and university education. The
father, a minor official on the staff of the dauphin at Versailles,
pondered long on how best to enlist the aid of the great prince he
served. Finally he wrote to him, and the dauphin sent the petition
to Cardinal de La Rochefoucauld, who held the royal *feuille des
bénéfices*. Success seemed certain, but eight days later, on 29 April
1757, the cardinal died. A hard-up student in his seminary, Marquis-
Ducastel became friendly with a young man who gave up his ecclesiastical vocation and turned over to him a chapel in the jurisdiction
of the cathedral of Mâcon. Alas! its income turned out to be
exiguous, and he found himself in the ridiculous position of having
a useless benefice which he dared not surrender, as there was a
considerable bill for repairs which would have to be settled before
handing over to a successor. At Versailles, his father was still trying.
Long ago, he had been kind to a lackey, who had now become
secretary to a duke who was a friend of the archbishop of Paris. A
word passed along this chain of influence, and the archbishop came
up with an exhibition of 500 livres a year in one of the colleges of
the University of Paris. But the previous holder of this substantial
bourse had embarked on a lawsuit against the head of the college,
who refused to pay a sou to the new exhibitioner while the dispute
lasted. So Marquis-Ducastel completed his theological education
without subsidy: it was left to him to try to make it up to his parents
later.[28] After ordination to the priesthood, the search for supplementary benefices went on; vicaires and curés pursued chapels and
priories as before. In the rural deanery of Évron in the diocese of Le
Mans, a parish priest listed in his diary the opportunities he came
across; he recorded forty-four chapels, with incomes ranging from
10 to 500 livres, their average income being 102.[29] During the
Revolution, when Church property was confiscated and pensions
were arranged for the clergy, allotting a basic sum together with half
the income which had been derived from supplementary benefices,
the true story of the incomes of the curés under the *ancien régime*
began to appear. Some had been better off than their complaints had
implied. In the town of Angers,[30] the curé of Saint-Jacques had a
single extra benefice worth a mere 100 livres. But his confrère at
Saint-Aignan, whose living yielded only a derisory income, had
eight chapels bringing in 1,500 livres annually. Three other city
curés had extras totalling over 1,000 livres each. At least two vicaires,
both from well-known families, had begun their accumulation of
chapels; less well-connected ecclesiastics might have to wait for forty
years for something to turn up—if at all.

Furnished with an ecclesiastical income, a clerk might stop short of ordination and become a footloose abbé adventuring on the fringes of the Parisian literary bohemia or, more respectably, acting as a tutor in a noble household. If he became ordained, he might still do these sorts of things or, more prosaically, stay at home as a *prêtre habitué*, with his name inscribed on the list of those eligible to receive fees for helping at the offices of his church. More ambitiously and usefully, he might become a vicaire, serving an apprenticeship under a curé until he was ripe for promotion to a parish of his own. Perhaps, with appropriate influence, he might hope to annex a canonry in some local collegiate church. How long must he wait? Anything from a couple of years to a lifetime, depending on family connections, friendships, contacts, and luck. The great objective was to attract the notice of a patron. Concerning promotion to the office of curé, it might be supposed that the bishop would be the best judge of the worthiness of a vicaire, and some bishops had ample patronage at their disposal. This was so in Brittany.[31] In the South, rather more than half the parishes of the diocese of Tarbes had the bishop as collator, and rather less than half those of Agen; the archbishop of Auch disposed of seventeen out of every twenty livings, and the archbishop of Bordeaux of three out of every five. But some bishops had very little to give. Those of Alsace were ill provided, the bishop of Metz, for example, with 600 parishes under his jurisdiction had only 50 to which he nominated the incumbent—and these included some which came his way as abbot of Saint-Arnould. Of 234 parishes of the see of Dijon, the chief pastor appointed to only 47; in Angers to 102 out of 400; in Bourges, to 134 out of 802; in Coutances, to 30 out of 489; in the vast diocese of Rouen, to 135 out of 1,460. In many dioceses, a vicaire bent on promotion would do better to look towards a chapter, more especially a cathedral; the metropolitan church of Besançon had 24 parishes, Langres 8, Autun 26, Angers 60. In the diocese of Bourges, the cathedral and the chapters together exercised patronage in 144 parishes, seven more than the bishop. Contacts with great abbeys and their dependent priories were even more valuable; of the 802 parishes of Bourges, 344 belonged to monastic foundations. The abbot of Cluny nominated to 35 parishes in the diocese of Autun, the abbey of Saint-Martin to 11, and other monasteries to 36 more. Two abbeys of Dijon had 46 parishes; five monastic institutions of Angers had 99.

All in all, the great majority of parochial livings in France were in the gift of ecclesiastical persons and institutions. There were, however, some lay patrons—few in most dioceses,[32] but many in

Normandy and Alsace; in the diocese of Coutances, 215 parishes out of 489 had a lay collator; in that of Metz, 170 out of 600. The Law and the Gallican liberties protected these lay patrons: they did not lose their right of presentation, as ecclesiastics sometimes did, by the exercise of 'prevention' (except after a long interval), the 'expectations of graduates', and the 'papal months'.[33] Nor had the diocesan bishop much control over their presentations, since if he declared their candidates unworthy, they could go to the metropolitan, or to another bishop, to ask for institution, as well as appeal to the parlements.[34] The high-water mark of the magistrates' defence of lay patronage came with a judgment of 1774 declaring that a Jew who had bought a seigneurie was entitled to take with his purchase the seigneur's right of nominating canons in the local collegiate foundation.[35] (True, this was a deliberately provocative verdict; the numerous Protestant seigneurs of Alsace retained their rights of presenting to livings, but had to exercise it through a Catholic delegate.) Among the lay patrons of the land, the Crown was the chief. By the Concordat, the Pope had granted the king the right to name to the 'consistorial benefices', that is, the bishoprics and the abbacies *in commendam* of the 1,092 great abbeys; along with these went 552 priories. There were, too, stalls in collegiate churches which had been founded by monarchs in the Middle Ages—the Sainte-Chapelle in Paris and its sister church in Bourges. Also, certain prebends had come to the Crown as successors to the rights of individual seigneurs, or by papal concessions allowing the king to alternate with canons of a chapter in filling its vacant places, as at Nîmes.[36] But the Crown also had some humble parishes in its gift—as many as 137 in the diocese of Bourges, though this was exceptional. In addition, the king was sometimes entitled to appropriate a patron's turn to appoint as a sort of dignified perquisite on special occasions; these windfalls will be considered later. All in all, the Crown possessed a great deal of varied ecclesiastical patronage—not just the bishoprics and the commendatory abbacies which aristocratic families angled for at Versailles, but canonries, parochial livings, and minor benefices without cure of souls. Most of these were awarded by the prelate who held the royal *feuille des bénéfices*—hence the scene described by a pamphleteer in the antechamber of Marbeuf, bishop of Autun, minister of the *feuille* at the end of the *ancien régime*:

A bizarre collection of monks, abbés, curés, soldiers, women. They all want bread. 'Pension, abbey!' Monseigneur has promises and consolation for everyone. 'M. le chevalier . . . these are hard times, but do not get impatient, all will be arranged.' 'M. le curé you know my intentions; use them as a pillow for your repose, and believe me, the moment of happy awakening is not far away. I foresee . . . yes, go along, do not worry.' 'My dear abbé, you are angry, so am I; the queen is getting hold of everything, I am master of nothing. But leave it to me, I have my plan. Good day, be discreet, and rely on me.'

No doubt the insistence of the applicants matched the cynicism of their reception.[37]

III

So far, we have considered benefices solely as they were in the gift of their patrons: the whole pattern was complex, but it was predictable, and the earnest benefice-hunter could map out the field with some assurance. But over this pattern of predictable patronage was superimposed a whole web of incidental rights capable of ousting the ordinary collator on particular occasions. The Crown, for example, in addition to its patronage of the ordinary kind, had certain opportunities of privileged intervention. When a bishopric was vacant, benefices in episcopal patronage could be filled at royal discretion. When a new bishop was consecrated (or translated), the king could nominate a cleric, by the so-called *brevet de serment de fidélité*, to be given the first vacant stall in the cathedral. There were two similar *brevets* which the Crown could issue; one was on the occasion of the monarch's accession, the *brevet de joyeux avènement*, and the other when the king entered in person into certain churches, the *brevet de joyeuse entrée*.[38] These nominations were resented, bishops and cathedral chapters trying their best to defeat the royal intruders by presenting them with a *fait accompli*. At six o'clock on the morning of 7 January 1732, a canon of Montpellier died. At seven o'clock the bishop named one of his own *protégés*, a doctor of the Sorbonne. At eight o'clock, too late for the moment, the abbé Morel arrived, flourishing his *brevet de joyeux avènement*. A month passed, then the senior *gradué nommé* arrived, and as he had put down his name formally on the official waiting-list, he had priority for appointment in the graduate month of January, and the doctor of the Sorbonne was evicted. But Morel, the royal nominee, won in the end.[39] Another splendid race to take possession occurred at Sisteron on 11 January 1728. At nine o'clock at night, a canon died. The chapter met at once to circumvent Balthasar Barle de Curban, a vicar-general of the diocese, who was known to have a *brevet de joyeux avènement*. At 10.30 p.m., M. de Réal, captain of infantry, maternal uncle of Barle de Curban, arrived, accompanied by a royal notary and an apostolic notary and witnesses, and bearing copies of the *brevet* to serve on the chapter. After a tumult, at 11.30 p.m., the chapter elected its own candidate, and the canons went off to bed. But Barle de Curban beat them eventually—the king could not so easily be flouted.[40]

Like the Crown, magistrates of the parlement of Paris enjoyed a right of intervention in the award of benefices. This was by the so-called *droit d'indult*,[41] conceded by feeble Popes in the days of the Avignon schism. Then, there had been a dozen magistrates to enjoy the privilege: in the eighteenth century there were 352.[42] A *conseiller* of the parlement who sought a benefice for a friend (as Turgot did for the abbé Morellet) would put his name down (through the chancellor) with some ecclesiastical patron, who would thereby be obliged to hand over the next vacant benefice in his gift.[43] There were strict rules. Each magistrate could exercise the indult only once, and a particular collator could be subjected to such a requisition only once (if the patron was an institution, such as a chapter, once in the lifetime of the reigning monarch). The benefice had to be worth 600 livres or more, and the candidate had to be properly qualified to hold it. There were arguments as to whether the *droit d'indult* ran in provinces united to the Crown after the original bulls granting it; it certainly did not apply in Flanders and Artois, and it was much disputed in Brittany. But given compliance to all the rules, the indult was a powerful document indeed, overriding the rights of patrons and prevailing even over a royal *brevet de joyeux avènement*.

There were certain vacancies in benefices of the Gallican Church which fell as windfalls to the Pope. If a benefice holder died in the city of Rome or within two days' journey of it, the Pope could appoint his successor (though benefices in royal or lay nomination or which were elective were excluded from this provision, which operated almost exclusively at the expense of ecclesiastical patrons).[44] In the provinces of France which were united to the Crown after the Concordat of 1516, there were certain months of the year in which ecclesiastical patrons had to yield their right of appointment to the Pope; again, this did not apply to the rights of the Crown or of laymen.[45] In dioceses on the eastern frontier, in lands which had been under the old Germanic Concordat, most of the papal rights to appoint to benefices had been lost, surrendered to the French

Crown by various indults in the seventeenth century.[46] In Brittany, half the papal entitlement had been lost, but for a different reason, since, to encourage the bishops to reside in their dioceses, the Popes had allowed them to take over some of their 'apostolic months', provided always that there was not a single day of absence in any month in which an appointment was made (unless it was demonstrably for the urgent business of the king or the good of the Church). Arrangements of this kind left plenty of scope for litigation. A bishop who was a cardinal was exempt from the papal 'alternative' by right, not by grace. So too, according to the Gallican lawyers, was the collator of a Breton benefice who lived in the central area of France subject to the Concordat—a more doubtful proposition.[47] Just when did a month end? Officially at midnight, and this, said the standard law dictionary, was to be fixed by reference to the first chime of the public clock of the place where the benefice was situated; if there was no such clock, 'recourse must be had to the testimony of those who are experts in the interpretation of the course of the stars or of the crowing of the cock'.[48] Precise information was also required about the time when a Pope died, for then, all the rules of the Roman chancellery lapsed, and ordinary collators in the provinces of France could appoint to benefices until a new pontiff was elected.[49] It was not easy, then, for the Popes to reward French ecclesiastics for loyalty to the Roman cause. But it was done. In the memoirs of Le Gendre, a canon of Notre-Dame of Paris at the end of the seventeenth century, we read how Dr Gaillaud, a zealot for the bull *Unigenitus*, got himself a lucrative sinecure in Brittany this way.[50] Père Timothée de la Flèche tells how a canonry at Vannes was his for the asking, since it fell vacant in one of the months reserved for the Pope, but how he recommended some other priest of unimpeachable orthodoxy, to the edification of the town and the wrath of the bishop.[51]

For the encouragement of learning, and to raise intellectual standards among the clergy, there were rules giving preference to graduates for appointment to benefices. In theory, all curés in 'walled towns' and all dignitaries of cathedrals must have university qualifications.[52] In practice, in cathedrals only the canons holding the offices of *théologale* and of *pénitencier* had to be graduates; as for walled towns (defined as those which had walls standing in the fifteenth and sixteenth centuries), the simple *maîtrise ès arts*, with two years' university study, sufficed.[53] There was also a rule which was supposed to ensure that a third of all parishes in the patronage of ecclesiastics (lay patrons were exempt) had a scholarly curé. To this end, vacancies falling in the months of January, April, July, and October were reserved for graduates. Two of these months, April and October, were 'mois de faveur', when the patron chose as he pleased from whatever graduates were available (*gradués simples*). January and July were 'mois de rigueur', when the senior graduate of all those who had formally put themselves on the waiting-list (the *gradués nommés*) had to be appointed. In 1745, a royal declaration amended the law concerning the 'rigorous months'; in January and July the patron was to be allowed a modest margin of personal preference, provided always no applicant of lower status was promoted over a more distinguished one.[54] The order to be observed was: first, doctors of theology; second, the holders of master's degrees who had been academic teachers for at least seven years (*professeurs septenaires*);[55] third, the doctors of faculties other than theology; then *licenciés* and *bacheliers* (with those whose theses had been on theological topics preferred). If more than one graduate of a particular academic category was listed, the patron's choice determined between them.

No doubt these regulations improved the intellectual content of sermons: they certainly sharpened the wits and lined the purses of the lawyers. Once a graduate had aligned his sights on a particular benefice, a check had to be made to be sure that the 'expectation' really applied to it. Generally, in provinces united to the Crown after 1516, graduates did not enjoy special favours, but clever lawyers could find exceptions.[56] The collator had to have more than two benefices at his disposal; if not, he was exempt from requisition.[57] The graduate's own case had to be carefully organized, so that no flaws were evident. Benefices already held had to be manipulated for the record, lest disqualification arose from being too well provided (*rempli*).[58] The rules prescribed a minimum time to be spent at the university for each degree (ten years for a doctorate of theology, and so on); this was a favourite subject for investigation by *dévolutaires*, the bounty hunters of the Church, who hoped to be rewarded for making a delation of irregularities. A canon of Lyon, one of the splendid aristocratic 'chanoines-comtes', lost the dignity of *chamarier* in his great foundation because a colleague revealed that his doctorate from the University of Valence had been obtained without residence.[59] To become a *gradué nommé*, your legal representative had to give notice of your degrees and titles (baptismal extract, letters of tonsure, letters of ordination, diplomas of degrees, certificate of the duration of university courses) to the collator whose benefice was targeted—notification to be renewed annually at the end of Lent. When the actual vacancy occurred, formal requisition had to be made, and all the documents deposited at the diocesan registry. The slightest defect or omission nullified the application.[60] Entangling reluctant patrons in the web of graduate priorities was not an easy process, and could be an unedifying one. And so many of the degrees solemnly recorded in the dossiers of candidates were virtu-ally worthless. The abbé Paul-Louis de Mondran was admitted to the *maîtrise ès arts* at Toulouse in 1751; after three years' idleness, he reflected, an examination lasting twenty minutes, and the payment of a fee, four pistoles, he had obtained 'a fine parchment . . . I was a graduate, *ergo*, invited by the Concordat to put in for benefices in the four months reserved for us'.[61] And what an affair it was waiting, and hoping for the benefice holder to die in the right month! The abbé Raguenet, says a Parisian diarist in 1723, committed suicide on the first day of February, having postponed the deed throughout January to ensure that his rich priory was left in the gift of the arch-bishop of Vienne rather than falling to a graduate.[62] In January 1721, Jansenists had gathered round the deathbed of M. Bouret, curé of Saint-Paul, trying to persuade him to resign the parish to a fellow Jansenist, lest it fall into the hands of M. de Châlon, the senior graduate applicant, a fervent supporter of the bull *Unigenitus*. Bouret refused. 'It does not befit me', he said, 'who am about to be judged before God not many days hence, to criticize the morals or doctrine of my brother. The Providence of God is great, and it will dispose things as pleases Him.' So it was: he survived until 2 February, out of the graduate month of January, and Châlon was disappointed.[63] Sometimes, a graduate had long to wait. On 27 July 1762, a canon of Le Mans died, and his stall fell to Jacques Loppé de Mesnil, the oldest graduate of the diocese. He was 61 years of age, and had waited for thirty-seven years. On 6 May 1765, canon Loppé de Mesnil died in his turn, without having had time to remedy his life-long penury. 'As he had no fortune,' a fellow canon records, 'he was buried with only the second-class display of candles.'[64]

Another device for awarding benefices according to merit was to settle the conflicting claims of anxious vicaires for parishes of their own by examination. A bishop was always free to institute such a system of selection, as the prelate of Le Mans did in 1783. Graduates who had served as vicaires for six years and non-graduates who had served for eight were eligible to try. Thirty-three candidates came to the seminary one day and wrote papers from 8 a.m. to 3 p.m.; a dozen qualified, and were promised the next vacant parishes. A canon noted in his diary that the experiment would not last: the bishop had too few cures at his disposal to reward all the successful examinees.[65] This was a competition, putting the candidates in order of merit. There was a different way of proceeding: a bishop could tighten up his rules for testing the worthiness of priests who were put forward by patrons, subjecting them to a 'pass' examination to qualify. In the diocese of Bâle (which had some French parishes) the examination *pro cura* lasted a whole week, spent in the seminary. (There was an unusual system of marking; 'O' was *insigniter*, which was top; running down to 4½, *vix mediocriter*, and to 6, *nihil*, presumably consigning the candidate to outer darkness.[66])

In certain dioceses, there was a more general system of examination for the office of curé. According to the Council of Trent, the rights of patrons were to be transferred to the Pope for eight months of the year, on the understanding that vacancies occurring then would be filled strictly by merit. The decrees of Trent had not been accepted by the French monarchy, but they ran in the peripheral provinces which had conformed to them before being brought into union with the Crown.[67] As was usual, it was only benefices in the patronage of ecclesiastics which were subject to this reforming pre-emption, though there were exceptions. In the dioceses of Toul, Nancy, and Saint-Dié (the complication of the separating of these dioceses did not affect the system), a cure in the gift of an ecclesiastical patron which fell vacant in the months of January, February, April, May, July, August, October, or November was awarded to the winner of a competition held in the episcopal town within twenty days. The dossier of the victor was sent to Rome, from whence, in about two months' time, bulls of appointment would arrive—the parlement of Nancy checked these before granting permission to take over the temporalities.[68] In the diocese of Cambrai, there was an annual examination in Scripture, dogma, moral theology, preaching, and Gregorian chant, open to vicaires who had served at least three years in the diocese.[69] There were similar arrangements in the province of Roussillon, in Gex, Bugey, and Volromey, in the diocese of Tournai, and in Flanders and Artois.[70] In the diocese of Arras, the system left some latitude of choice to the patron: a priest who was admitted to examination on the certificate of his curé and rural dean, and passed in doctrine, moral theology, the administration of the sacraments, the conduct of ceremonies, sermon writing, and chanting, was put on the *feuille du concours*, which was sent to the patron, who chose one from those who had qualified.[71] In Brittany, the eight papal months were reduced to four, since Rome rewarded bishops who kept residence by allowing them to present to cures in the 'alternative months'. In the four 'apostolic months' retained by the Pope, benefices were awarded on the results of an examination held in Rome (or at least, assessed there). In 1740, however, the bishops of Brittany asked Pope Benedict XIV to allow them, for convenience sake, to take over the examination; this was granted by the bull *In apostolicae potestatis plenitudine*, registered by the parlement at Rennes in February 1741. A royal declaration drew up the rules in detail: six examiners, two at least being graduates; candidates must have been vicaires within the province, for a minimum of two years in the actual diocese, or of four years in one of the others; they must know the language, French or Breton, commonly spoken in the parish to which they sought appointment; the examination to consist of three written answers, a viva voce interrogation and the composition of a homily on a passage of Scripture.[72] There were fears about the fairness of the marking in dioceses where the Jansenist battle had raged. Bishop Fagon, a promoter of the doctrines of Quesnel, held the first examination in the diocese of Vannes in August 1741. There were twenty-one candidates competing for three vacancies, submitting solid essays in Latin to a high-powered jury of two vicars-general, one dignitary of the cathedral, the superior of the seminary, an expert theologian, and the incumbent of a city parish. All members of the jury (except one, and he did not attend) were Jansenistically inclined. Even so, the verdict seems to have been honest: three moderates were appointed.[73] Fagon died on 16 February 1742, and the cathedral chapter, in charge during the vacancy, put Archdeacon Dondel, an ally of the Jesuits, in charge of a new jury, with other members to match. At the examination of August 1742, twenty-five candidates competed for two livings (one rich). Severely orthodox supporters of the bull *Unigenitus* topped the list. Yet for the most part, the examiners seem to have been conscientious. Charles-Jean de Bertin, bishop of Vannes from 1746 to 1755, presided at all examinations in person (except in 1751 when the business of the Clergy of France called him to Paris).[74] In the diocese of Dol, there were no fewer than four fixed examinations annually, on the first day (if not a major feast) of March, June, September, and December.[75] Not surprisingly, it was universally said that parish priests were of higher quality in those areas where appointment was by competitive assessment. There were hard cases, of course—worthy vicaires who lacked the quickness of wit to dash off plausible answers presenting themselves again and again to the humiliation of failure. A curé of Lorraine noted in his journal, in 1782, how fate had been unkind to a vicaire of his acquaintance. 'M. Colvis d'Averaille, s'est présenté au concours pour la dix-neuvième fois, mais, sur le point de répondre, il a eu une extinction de voix.'[76] Perhaps, of his nineteen attempts, this was the only one when they asked him a question to which he knew the answer.

Churchmen and ecclesiastical institutions could, then, lose their right to appoint to a benefice on a particular occasion in various ways—the issue of a royal *brevet* of, say, *joyeux avènement*, a magistrate using his indult, the requisition of a graduate in an appropriate month, the papal entitlement in certain provinces to the 'apostolic months'. But the most frequently used legal device which clipped the patron's prerogative was the right of the titular of a benefice to resign to a cleric of his own choosing. The 'resignation in favour' had to be approved at Rome, but by the Gallican liberties, the application to the Pope was purely formal: no delay, let alone a refusal, was allowed.[77] As might be expected, since ecclesiastical superiors had little control over such resignations, the rules were strict. Bishoprics and other consistorial benefices and those in lay patronage could not be handed on by such agreements. Deathbed transfers were forbidden. If the resigning cleric had been in poor health and he died within twenty days of his signature, the benefice was vacant in the usual way, though if the attestations attached to the legal instruments of the transaction proved him to have been in perfect health when he signed, the transfer stood.[78] The son of a doctor who treated a *résignant* could not be the beneficiary, though oddly enough, by a decision of 1777, the parlement of Paris seemed to agree that a confessor could be.[79] The procuration which was sent to Rome had to be drawn up in the presence of two notaries (or one and two other witnesses), and all the documents had to be registered by the diocesan *greffier des insinuations ecclésiastiques*.[80] The law gave ample protection to the resigning cleric, affording him various grounds for revocation—undue pressure, recovery of health, and so on. This power of revocation, variously called the right of *regrès* or *regrets* (with contrasting, but equally plausible, etymological derivations) could be irresponsibly used with exasperating consequences. In the diocese of Nîmes in 1739, the aged curé of Villevielle resigned, but when his successor arrived from another diocese, did not like the look of him, so stayed on for ten years, when he finally resigned in favour of someone else.[81] In 1774, in another parish of Nîmes, Antoine Valette, feeling ill, resigned to his nephew, a neighbouring vicaire. Somewhat recovered, he revoked, and the nephew had to make do with a less agreeable parish ceded to him by another *résignant*. Five years later, Valette's health had declined again, so he permuted cures with his nephew.[82] No doubt, behind the changing medical verdicts lies some history of family relationships to complicate the explanation. Another case, in the diocese of Sens, about the same time, has sombre undertones. The curé of Saint-Sulpice de Moulon fled when a serving-girl who had killed her illegitimate child accused him of having seduced her; as he departed, he resigned his cure to an acquaintance. On the scaffold, the girl withdrew her accusation, and since the new incumbent of the parish unsportingly refused to withdraw, the unlucky curé used the proceedings by *regrès* to try to get back into his vicarage.[83] There were also rules to protect the incoming benefice holder, or rather, to prevent him from striking a bargain tainted with simony. The *résignant* was not to be given a pension unless he had served for a minimum of fourteen years (or was in failing health); the sum must not be more than a third of the revenues; and if the benefice was a parish on the *congrue*, no pension was allowed at all.[84] Once the pension was agreed, however, it was sacrosanct: the titular who failed to meet his obligations to his predecessor incurred automatic excommunication thirty days after falling into default.[85]

According to the standard eighteenth-century dictionary of canon law, resignations in favour were so common that they were no longer regarded as an abuse, provided the 'formalities inimical to simony and fraud' were observed.[86] How many benefices changed hands in this fashion? The records of the diocese of Lisieux suggest that one in five of the parish priests throughout the eighteenth century named his own successor.[87] In some dioceses, the proportion was higher. Certainly, resignation in favour was a general phenomenon, one which anticlericals seized on to cry scandal. There were anecdotes of benefices changing hands during drinking bouts:

> When Esau sold his birthright,
> it was because he hungered,
> When he signed away his cure,
> he'd dined before he blundered.[88]

There were tales of monstrous pensions illegally accorded to persuade incumbents to hand over; Mme du Deffand tells of a vicaire of Saint-Sulpice who agreed to pay his curé 15,000 livres a year for the succession.[89] In another Parisian parish, the agreement was for a pension of 2,500 livres to the heirs of the dying curé—which was dubiously allowable.[90] In 1718, Romain de la Forest, holder of a prebend in the cathedral of Strasbourg, was going round after dark to visit potential candidates for his stall, bearing his accounts with him as the basis of a sort of auction.[91] There was plenty of litigation. There was a lawsuit lasting six years after the curé of La Madeleine in Paris resigned to his nephew in 1732.[92] In 1783, the cathedral chapter of Saint-Flour appointed a new curé to its parish of Ternes, acting promptly, eight hours after the old one died. Fourteen months later, another claimant appeared, flourishing the resignation of the previous holder, accepted at Rome on the very day of his death. Another lengthy lawsuit ensued.[93]

But the essential abuse—and, paradoxically, the redeeming grace—of the resignation in favour was that it was the instrument used by families to obtain places in the ministry of the Church for their sons. 'People regard benefices as a patrimony', sighed Fleury, the great Church historian, 'that can be given by personal preference, and to which relatives have more right than others.'[94] 'A benefice', said a curé, 'is a piece of real property that ought not to be allowed to go out of the family.'[95] Christophe La Come resigned his living to a nephew in 1764, and went off to be a canon of Lescar; he moved again in 1778, in his turn succeeding an uncle.[96] Pierre Thuin, of a Parisian merchant family, had the good fortune to be tutor to the son of an influential man; his former pupil, rising in the Church ahead of him, resigned to him a canonry at Montereau, then in 1790 passed on to him the rich cure of Dontilly.[97] This was the way things were done. Certain desirable benefices were annexed more or less permanently. Eleven of the incumbents of parishes in the diocese of Auch in 1729 had the same name as their predecessors in 1672.[98] Two parishes of the diocese of La Rochelle were in the hands of the same family all through the seventeenth and eighteenth centuries; there were two parishes of this kind in the diocese of Autun.[99] It was a noble eccentricity when Joseph Chevassu, curé of Rousses in the Jura mountains, in 1743 put his parish at the disposal of the bishop, 'even though he had ecclesiastical nephews of great merit'.[100] Rousses was a harsh place, where snow lay all the year round. Had it been less forbidding, family pressures might have overcome pious scruples. Not surprisingly, it was the most lucrative benefices which changed hands by resignation. A family would cling to a rich prize, once one of its members had been lucky in the lottery. Besides, large incomes provided the larger pensions, enough for a retired ecclesiastic to live on in comfort. It was said of the parish of Andrezal-en-Brie, ten miles from Paris, with its income of 1,200 livres, that it was 'an excellent morsel', so much so that the canons who held the patronage could never exercise it unless the curé died suddenly.[101] Henry de Tristan enjoyed the cure of Gan, the richest in

Béarn, for forty years. Belatedly, in 1721, he decided to resign it to a nephew, and as the family nominee was in Paris, gave it to another nephew as a bridgeman, who, a year later, resigned to his brother. It was a risky procedure, challenged by a *dévolutaire*; but once the long lawsuit was won, Daniel de Tristan held office for twenty-three years.[102] Another parish with a substantial income was Saint-Merry in Paris. Curé Jean Vivant resigned it to his nephew Louis Métra in 1717. In 1744, on the day Métra died, the chapter of Notre-Dame hastened to appoint his successor, Artaud, brother of one of the canons. In 1757, Artaud became bishop of Cavaillon in the papal enclave of the comté Venaisson, his native country, so he resigned the parish to his nephew for a pension of 2,000 livres. The nephew, Donzeaud de Saint-Pons, died in 1773, and the chapter of Notre-Dame appointed the abbé de Vienne. Then appeared Louis Esprit Viennet, a curé from the distant diocese of Narbonne, smugly displaying the resignation documents of Donzeaud, duly countersigned by the Pope on the very day the old curé had died. Viennet took over the parish, and from his newly enhanced income was able to provide for his brother and give his three sisters dowries of 3,000 livres each.[103]

Bishops were angry to find the best livings in their nominal gift so rarely available to reward their most deserving clergy. They also regretted that a curé who was paying a pension to his predecessor had so much less left to give to the poor. On these grounds, the bishop of Le Mans did his best to stop resignations in favour. His tactics, he said, in a letter of 1784,[104] were to enforce strictly the rules governing pensions: anyone with less than fourteen years' service was disqualified. In 1785, when the richest cure in his diocese went by resignation to the abbé Bonnouvrier, his wrath knew no bounds, and with no justification he refused the worthy abbé the necessary attestation of faith and morals. In the end, the bishop had to withdraw from his untenable position; Bonnouvrier moved in and proved an excellent pastor—and he was able to help his poverty-stricken family: his mother, a bankrupt innkeeper, and his two sisters, seamstresses, who came to live with him, and he provided occasional refuge for his brothers, itinerant cooks, who were often out of employment.[105]

Like some other abuses of the *ancien régime*, the resignation in favour had much to be said for it in the overall social context. Favour, influence, family contacts, and intrigue ruled almost universally in appointments, even in the Church, and it might be supposed that a curé nominating his own successor was as likely to care for the interests of his parishioners as the usual patron—unless, maybe, this was some austere reforming bishop. The candidates a curé favoured—generally a nephew or a vicaire, occasionally a friend from seminary days, or a neighbour in a less favoured parish—were as likely to be reliable pastors as others brought from further afield, and they would have the advantage of knowing the local scene. There is an edifying story of François Feu, the Jansenist curé of Saint-Gervais in Paris, who in 1699 resigned into the hands of his archbishop, judging his nephew, at 28, too young to succeed him. The archbishop promptly appointed the nephew, François Feu II, to the parish, where he reigned in the odour of sanctity for sixty-two years.[106] No doubt there were many examples of a nephew brought up and trained in the hope of succeeding to a particular parish, carrying on the good work of his uncle. In the countryside, parishioners tended to be suspicious of outsiders and to prefer to carry on—grumbling, maybe—with someone they had come to appreciate. And peasants well understood the system of handing over to a relative—the younger people taking over the farm after making a contract with their parents to support them for the rest of their days.[107] From the point of view of the curé, what alternative was there? A parish priest growing old and feeble was in a difficult position: few dioceses had arrangements to care for him in his retirement, and by its very nature, the exercise of a celibate and authoritarian ministry would have left him with few close relatives and with friendships that stopped short of intimacy. Yet the only world he would know would be his parish. He could stumble on ineffectively as curé (a cynical parish priest said, postpone your resignation as long as you can, for once you do so, no one will court you—if your younger clergy have expectations, they will run your parish for you and even bring your chamber-pot).[108] Or, he could put some relative or friend into the vicarage, take a pension from him and potter round doing a few sacerdotal chores amid familiar faces for the rest of his days. And if the benefice stayed in the family, continuing to provide dowries for virtuous nieces and a refuge for ailing mothers and aunts, what was the harm in that?

IV

There was a further complexity in French benefice law: where there was dispute and confusion, an application might have to be taken before the court of Rome. In any case, the papal chancellery was concerned when dispensations were required before a candidate could qualify, and after an appointment had been made, lack of such authorization might be made a ground for eviction. Dispensation would be required for receiving holy orders below the fixed minimum age—22 for the subdiaconate, 23 for the diaconate, and 25 for the priesthood; similarly, for obtaining benefices—7 for one without cure of souls, 10 for an ordinary canonry, and 14 for a stall in a cathedral. There were also certain disqualifications for ordination which the Pope could overrule—bodily mutilation, illegitimate birth, and, in the case of a widower, a history of two marriages. In all these cases, dispensation would normally be forthcoming, but it would have to be applied for in Rome or at Avignon.[109] All resignations of ecclesiastics involving the transfer of the benefice to some other person, whether *in favorem*, with or without a pension, or an exchange, or *causa concordiae*, to settle a dispute with appropriate financial arrangements, had to be certified by the papal bureaucracy. Provided there was no defect in the application, there was nothing the officials in Rome could do to prevent these transactions going through (the parlements saw to that[110]), but the rigmarole had to be complied with all the same, and the procuration *ad resignandum*, sent by courier from France, circulated to the departments of the 'Concessum', the 'Consens', the 'de Missis', the 'little dates', the first and second 'Revisors', the 'Registry', and the 'Chancellery'.[111] Rome was also involved in the affairs of French benefices by the operation of the rules favouring *prévention*. These were calculated to penalize the negligence of collators. If there was undue delay in making an appointment, the Pope could issue provisions awarding the benefice to whatever French applicant presented himself.[112] The rules for the exercise of prevention were strictly drawn. The benefice must be genuinely vacant, and enough time must have elapsed for the news to have reached Rome by ordinary courier. Lay patrons had a full four months' grace (six months in Normandy) before their rights lapsed. Benefices in the collation of cardinals, consistorial benefices, those subject to the 'alternative' papal months, those under requisition by indult of the parlement of Paris, and the elective dignitaries of collegiate churches were exempt from Roman intervention. If the Pope and a bishop conferred the same benefice simultaneously, the ordinary's nomination prevailed.[113] Subject to these exceptions and safeguards, benefice hunters had a fine field for their operations. Given a negligent collator or an official candidate who was complacent, a pirate might get in first at Rome or Avignon and bear off the spoils. These operators in the art of prevention were not the most dedicated of ecclesiastics, but they were models of respectability compared with another sort of applicant at the Roman Curia, the *dévolutaires*. By the rule of *dévolut*,[114] an informer who could demonstrate that a benefice had been irregularly obtained was entitled to papal provisions transferring it to him—or at least, providing him with a prima-facie case to ask the royal tribunals to put him in possession. Bishoprics, abbacies, and benefices in lay patronage were exempt from such challenges; so too was an ecclesiastic who had held undisturbed possession for three years, except when his offence had been simony or fraud. *Dévolutaires* were universally hated and despised; the law-books describe them as 'odious', as 'pirates'. According to the Clergy of France, by very definition, they must be as bad as the ecclesiastics they displaced.[115] The courts required from them a deposit of 500 livres to guarantee any costs to which they might be condemned if they failed, a sum which was raised, in 1776, to 1,200 at the instance of the Assembly of the Clergy.[116] Generally, a benefice holder who was evicted by a *dévolutaire* was not a heretic, a pluralist, or guilty of simony, misconduct, or marriage; most often, it was a question of some error in legal title, some omission of protocol—for after all, these minor careless accidents were the easiest things to prove.[117]

In all these affairs of resignations, preventions, and devolutions, the Roman Curia had little scope for the exercise of judgement. By the Gallican liberties, the Pope was obliged to agree to the requisition of a benefice by a French ecclesiastic, provided it was put forward in due form; what is more, the consent had to be given the very day the application was received (even though half a dozen officials reviewed the documents). 'Date retenue, grâce accordée' was the formula.[118] The date was vital. Not infrequently, two candidates were after the same benefice, and other things being equal, it was first come, first served. Since simultaneous applications were regarded as cancelling each other, and since the Roman bureaucracy kept these transactions secret, it was sound policy to pay for the reservation of several dates, in the hope of hitting on the first clear one. This race for dates was complicated by the existence of a Daterie in the Vice-legation of Avignon[119] as an alternative resort for papal provisions for the neighbouring ecclesiastical provinces of Arles, Vienne, and Embrun. Thus, no amount of spying at either centre of papal officialdom could guarantee that no rival date buyer was on the trail. At Avignon, the registers recorded not only the day on which an application was made (as at Rome), but also the hour and minute,[120] so candidates there ran no danger of cancelling each other's applications. Also, by a not entirely logical rule, the exact time was taken as superior to the day pure and simple—an unjust advantage enjoyed by Avignon which the Assembly of the Clergy persuaded the king to cancel by a declaration issued in 1748.

The strict formalities of the Roman system (not unconnected with collecting fees) were paralleled by equally strict regulations on the French side. All applications for provisions, dispensations, and graces from Rome (though not from Avignon) had to go through the *banquiers expéditionnaires*, liaison agents.[121] Legislation of the second half of the seventeenth century prescribed that these officials must be laymen, at least 25 years of age, not servants or employees of ecclesiastics, sworn to strict secrecy, and forbidden to use extraordinary couriers to favour particular clients. There were twenty of these *banquiers expéditionnaires* in Paris, four in Lyon, three each in Toulouse and Bordeaux, and so on in the other parlement cities.[122] An ecclesiastic might be resident himself in Rome or Avignon, have friends there, have some ally willing to ride breakneck to get there— all to no avail, since no arrangement was legal unless it was recorded in the registers of the *banquiers* and verified by their signatures.[123] Their registers would show how, at a precise date after the benefice really fell vacant, the application was sent off—the name of the courier and the time of his departure were recorded. The documents brought back from Rome must have the signatures of two *banquiers* on the back, the name of the Roman agents, and the date of final delivery in France.[124] If the papal bureaucrats cancelled some clause or other in the French application, the *banquiers* could certify that the grace could be obtained only in this form, and their signature sufficed to reinstate the clause in question so far as the French courts were concerned.[125]

Legal pitfalls yawned on every side of the unwary candidate for Roman graces. When should dates reserved at the Daterie be transferred (at a stiff extra fee) to the permanent registers, bearing in mind that the officials burned all other records at yearly intervals?[126] In Brittany and other provinces outside the Concordat, the system of reserving dates did not apply, yet in Provence the custom of making a reservation at Avignon had arisen—did one follow the rule, or the custom?[127] The Roman chancellery began the year on 25 March, while the chamber began it on 25 December.[128] Rescripts of the court of Rome concerning private individuals were free from the formalities of publication required for briefs on public affairs— except in Artois, Flanders, Franche Comté, and Provence, where *lettres d'attache* from the magistrates were required.[129] And everywhere in France the Roman provisions had to be followed up with the visa of the diocesan bishop, which included a certificate of having been examined and found capable, and a mandate authorizing taking possession. If the bishop refused his visa, legal representations had to be made to him to extract a written statement of his reasons—to be used in an appeal to the metropolitan archbishop and to the parlement.[130] And when all documentation was complete and the take-over took place, the local curé must be asked to publish the event at mass or in an assembly of inhabitants, with the names of four reputable witnesses recorded. A move into a benefice without all these formalities made the careless ecclesiastic into an *intrus*, automatically disqualified from holding it, and open to eviction by the *dévolut* or prevention at Rome by some jealous rival.[131] Let no one therefore venture on the benefice quest without having an apostolic notary (*notaire apostolique*) engaged, a lawyer who knew all the niceties of the trade of the *banquiers expéditionnaires* and of the bureaucrats at Rome and Avignon, as well as the jurisprudence of the parlements.

No doubt there were many uncontroversial and reputable sets of provisions forwarded from Rome to worthy French ecclesiastics as a matter of routine. But the writers of law-books, the diarists, and anticlericals generally relished the comic and outrageous cases. Above all, everyone hated the *dévolutaires*, and longed for their downfall. Marais tells a story of the scandalous ousting of a Jansenist from a priory by an orthodox adventurer.[132] Barbier gloats over the parlement throwing out the abbé Baudry for simony, yet refusing to let the *dévolutaire*, his old tutor, profit by his delation.[133] The law-books applauded the monk with a defective title who quickly permuted his benefice to outwit his accuser; they approved also of the archbishop of Vienne who delayed granting a visa to a *dévolutaire* just long enough to allow a second bounty hunter to oust him on grounds of the delay in taking possession.[134] Where prevention was concerned, jurists loved to record how rivals took up astronomical numbers of dates in Rome; there were cases of 500 to 600 duly paid for before one outflanked the other. In 1772, a dispute over a priory in the Vexin ended in a draw, each claimant having taken up eighty-five dates, which, it so happened, exactly cancelled out.[135] The *prévôté*, the highest dignity in the cathedral of Auch, vacant in March 1742, was annexed by the abbé Palerue by Roman provisions dated 27 May, beating the archbishop's nominee by four days; but the archbishop's man won, since Palerue's date had also been taken by the abbé d'Orvalle (doubtfully, as the Roman registers did not show it, but the parlement was glad of an excuse to oust a 'pirate').[136] In 1749, the archbishop of Arles gave the priory of Charlotte-la-Petite in the diocese of Sens to a canon of Vannes—this grant was null, for the priory ought to have gone to a regular priest, not a secular. Three days after, the *grand vicaire* of the archbishop gave it to Dom le Prévôt—this was null because no one is entitled to usurp the episcopal prerogative. The abbé Chaumont, who had reserved 150 dates in Rome, thought he was home and dry, but he had not reckoned with the abbé Marion, who had taken up 372. In the end, the parlement awarded the priory to le Prévôt: at least he was properly qualified to hold it.[137] One confrontation of this kind is well known through having aroused Diderot's ironical and unfraternal contempt: the five years of to-ing and fro-ing to Rome by the agents of Didier Pierre Diderot, secretary of the bishop of Langres and brother of the philosophe, on the one hand, and the chevalier de Piolanc, a tonsured clerk of the Order of Malta, on the other. In the end, in 1757, the abbé Diderot got the priory after paying the 1,200 livres legal expenses of his rival, and accepting responsibility for repairs—all this for a benefice worth only 458 a year.[138]

One device available to operators by prevention was to guess the day on which a failing benefice holder would die, add on the standard time it took for news to get to Rome, then reserve a strategic run of dates around the crucial point. If this fraud was detected—the crime of *de impetrantibus Beneficia viventium*—the penalty was total disqualification.[139] Another device was to conceal the death of the benefice holder while the application to succeed him was speeding to Rome in the courier's saddle-bag; if found out, the crime involved excommunication by canon law as well as penalties by state law. Royal magistrates were entitled to make a search for ecclesiastics in poor health who had not been seen around recently; relatives, servants, and nurses were under orders to have the church bells rung immediately a benefice holder died, while bell-ringers were constrained to answer their call, even in the middle of the night. If suspicions of fraud were subsequently raised, an exhumation might be held to see if the corpse had been pickled in brine or otherwise artificially preserved.[140] These legislative precautions seem to have been effective, for in the eighteenth century the crime of 'recèlement du corps mort d'un bénéficier' was rare; the standard law dictionary found only one good example to quote—a commendatory priory of Le Mans, obtained in 1750 on the strength of forty-five dates reserved by one Bernard, lost by him to one Correard who convicted him of 'recèlement', then lost by Correard because the abbé Gobier had been lurking all the while in the wings with a better date up his sleeve.[141] In 1785, the dean of a great Parisian foundation died on a holiday in Montpellier, which left the way open for a rush to Avignon by one of the local clergy. The archbishop of Arles then made his famous protest to the Assembly General of the Clergy:

One of the most distinguished chapters of the kingdom lives in the fear that it will soon have as its dean an unknown character who happened to ask for and obtain provisions in the court of Rome a few days before the chapter elected. What mysteries of iniquity would appear to the light of day if we were allowed to ransack the registers of the *banquiers expédition- naires?*

He therefore asked for a month's delay before prevention could be allowed to operate.[142] Some of the *cahiers* of the clergy in 1789 echo this demand: two ask for a month's delay, one for two months', and another wanted to end applications to Rome altogether.[143]

V

An aspirant for the office of curé, consulting his local almanac, would be able to list a diversity of patrons to be courted—bishops, chapters, abbeys, laymen. Within each ecclesiastical institution there might well be complex arrangements for making appointments to livings, and it was important to know just how they worked. Some senior ecclesiastic of the diocese might be acting on behalf of an absentee commendatory abbot; some particular monastic official—a cellarer or a treasurer—might have peculiar rights. In a cathedral, the holder of a certain prebend would sometimes control a living, or the whole chapter might elect, or the canon in residence at the time of the vacancy would be in charge. Or there might be, for some parishes, a system of rotating choices. The University of Paris, for example, exercised its patronage in the parish of Saint-André des Arts in a pattern of seven turns: the Faculties of Theology, Law, and Medicine, then each of the four 'Nations' of the Faculty of Arts, 'France', 'Normandy', 'Germany', and 'Picardy'.[144]

Having completed his list of local patrons, the earnest benefice hunter then had to reflect upon possible accidents and interventions—those he might organize himself, or those that might be engineered against him. Was a *brevet* from the Crown or an indult from a magistrate a possibility? He might not have the standing to get one himself, but he could be ousted, after all his expenditure of time and money, by someone more influential. Should he register as a *gradué nommé*, and if so, with what patron or patrons? If, unexpectedly, something fell vacant in the appropriate month, what about coming forward as a *gradué simple*? Some neighbouring ecclesiastic had gone off on a pilgrimage to Rome; was it worth covering the remote possibility that he would fall mortally ill near to the Eternal City? Of the patrons near at hand, was any likely to be slow in making a nomination? If so, his candidate might be beaten by the exercise of 'prevention'. Was there a benefice holder who had got into office by dubious means or with defective qualifications, and therefore vulnerable to deposition by invoking the *dévolut* against him? And above all, there was the question, 'What friends have I who might offer me a resignation in favour?' This was the best bet of all. The very existence of the possibility helped to prevent the parochial ministry from becoming subservient to the great holders of patronage. A vicaire's best policy was to keep in with the local curés and with his own ecclesiastical uncles and other relatives. Whatever manœuvres the aspirant to a parochial charge embarked on, one thing was certain: speed was essential. The patron, or whoever was supposed to influence the patron, might make a promise to someone else, or a rival might get in an early application to Rome or Avignon. Possession was nine-tenths of the law. Immediately a curé died, there was a rush of applications for his benefice, with supporting letters from influential backers.[145]

'The curé of Dolgueville is dangerously ill: the priests of Épinal have been on the watch, and they are paying solicitous social calls on the chapter of Épinal, which is the patron of this good benefice.'[146] 'The Parish of Crouaï, which your brother was wanting for one of his protégés, is not vacant just yet: the curé is still alive. Mgr the duc d'Orléans also asked for it, thinking the curé was dead.'[147] These reports are typical. It was a standard ploy of applicants to anticipate the medical verdict and to transform grievous illness into death when asking a patron for his nomination. In 1781, the bishop of Le Mans condemned this 'ambitious practice'; he would refuse to promise a living to anyone, he declared in a diocesan circular, until he received an assurance from the local rural dean that the curé in question was well and truly dead.[148]

The picture of the way benefices were obtained in eighteenth-century France as given in the law-books is an unedifying one, far removed from the pious clichés of the theological treatises on 'vocation'. One is tempted to regard the whole process of favouritism, family interest, and chicanery as totally worldly and unspiritual. True enough, there were those whose vocation to the ecclesiastical state was simply a vocation to draw an easily earned income. It was the only profession, said a cynic at the beginning of the eighteenth century, which made its members rich instantaneously. 'A man gets up in the morning a chaplain or a mediocre abbé, and goes to bed a wealthy benefice-holder.'[149] Marmontel, seeking a literary career, took the tonsure to placate his family, who were trying to force him into a trade, and later, he even proposed to go on to ordination.[150] The abbé Pollin, in 1792, when over-frank admissions were welcomed by revolutionary officialdom, confessed that his vocation had been settled by a consideration of 'the delicacy of my health, my natural laziness which I cannot vanquish', and 'a secret attraction towards the first Order in the State, its majesty, and the distinction which it conferred upon its members'.[151] Vergniaud, the future Girondin, studied theology at Paris because his father at Limoges had gone bankrupt. He left his seminary in disillusionment, but was willing to go back if it was the only way to earn a decent living. 'If I thought that the ecclesiastical state would provide me with the existence that I cannot obtain through any other profession, I'd take it up again,' he wrote to his brother-in-law on 1 January 1780, 'and don't think that this would be by inconstancy: I took it up the first time without knowing what I was doing, I left because I didn't like it, and I'd only take it up again out of necessity.' His chief contact in the Church was an uncle, prior of a Cistercian monastery, who had made his way as a monk after serving as a soldier. The shrewd old prior discouraged his nephew's self-interested vocation: 'One priest in the same family is enough,' he declared, and Vergniaud became a successful *avocat* at Bordeaux.[152] Sometimes, an individual was manœuvred into a sense of vocation by his family, who pushed him into the ministry of the Church because there was no other way of providing for him. This was the accusation commonly made by the austere authors of handbooks of spirituality. A boy is physically unfit or deficient in intelligence—'fathers then usually imitate Cain, offering to Jesus Christ the worst of their children as candidates for the ecclesiastical condition'.[153] Or, it might simply be a younger son who was got rid of, to leave the inheritance intact for the eldest.

A child is destined for the ecclesiastical state from his mother's womb. The family is not well off, and it is numerous. He is not the eldest or, if he is, he has no talent for a worldly career. Uncle dear has a canonry which has been in the family, as if by inheritance, for more than a century . . . That settles it, his vocation is decided. He is taught parrot-wise what the tonsure means so that he can receive it just as soon as they can hoodwink the bishop about his motives. The first *bénéfice simple* that falls vacant will go to him, and pray God that they do not procure it by simony. You say that taking the tonsure and accepting a benefice is not a commitment. True—except that it is a commitment concerning his parents' eternal salvation.[154]

Undeniably, a worldly attitude to an ecclesiastical career predominated, but the austere censures of spiritual men and cynical admissions by unspiritual ones do not fairly reflect the atmosphere in which the decision to seek ordination was made. Religion then was so woven into all the affairs of ordinary life that it could hardly be regarded as an aspect of human thought and action which could be considered in isolation, in its own right. The assumptions behind the social complex are revealed in the games of children. 'If a mission is preached', said a novelist, 'all the children play at processions; if a regiment marches through, they all do drill.'[155] André Chénier, who was to become a poet and a priest-hater later, described how he had played at 'chapels':

I said mass, I preached: they listened to me and made the sign of the cross. And when, in the evening, at *salut*, by the light of 100 tiny candles, after many genuflexions and anthems, I elevated a toy 'Host' made of lead, my old nurse took her bonnet off and my aunt Juliette and her friends knelt down.[156]

In the eyes of most families, the choice of the ministry of the Church was an ordinary everyday matter, one of those commonplace reasonable decisions that did not need an explanation. An ecclesiastical career was self-justifying. This remained so, often, for those who came to have doubts about revelation. Rousseau was not the only one who did not see why intellectual reservations should withhold a young man from accepting a useful office of moral direction in the community. The standard logical progression in which the question of vocation would be approached today—Do I really believe? Am I willing to commit myself? Am I prepared to separate myself from the world?—did not prevail in the eighteenth-century mind. Ordination, like marriage, was 'arranged'—not necessarily in a bad sense of the word—within the family context. The Church provided places for so many sons of lower and middling bourgeois families who would otherwise have had no fortune, as well as offering the only opportunity for betterment to the clever sons of the poor. The Roland family of Thizy-en-Beaujolais—the father being a magistrate of the *bailliage* court and the mother from a poor noble family—had two sons in secular careers; one, Jean-Marie, became Minister of the Interior in the revolutionary government in 1792. The four other sons were ecclesiastics in comfortable situations. Planning was needed to make such successful provision for one's children.[157] A notary who settled in Gay in 1745 knew what he was doing: his sons, if he had any, would be eligible for places in the chapter there or in the *familiarité* of the priests who earned fees for helping at the parish church; this was a family that looked back with satisfaction to an ancestor who had one son inheriting the farm, one a curé, and six in monastic life—'they couldn't have organized things better if it had been a question of maintaining intact the lands of a duchy'.[158]

The family obligation worked both ways: the successful churchman would look after his aged parents and the lame ducks of the family. The abbé Brendel, professor in the seminary of Strasbourg at the end of the *ancien régime*, supported his 90-year-old father, a sister who had been left with seven children, and a nephew completing his studies.[159] When Mme de Grange Berthelot died in 1787, her four daughters had nowhere to go. Their brother, a canon of Le Mans, came fifty leagues to collect them in a broken-down old cabriolet, and walked all the way back on foot ahead of them to save expense. Another prebendary of Le Mans died: 'he leaves behind him a niece and a nephew who have lost everything.'[160] We have followed the tribulations of Marquis-Ducastel whose education cost his parents so much. Finally, he took a dogsbody job with the curé of Saint-Laurent in Paris: 'c'est que je cessai par là d'être à charge à ma famille'. The dauphin died in 1765, thus putting an end to another intrigue of his father to win him promotion. But in the following year, the bishop of Vannes sent for him to assist in the work of his *officialité* (the ecclesiastical court of the diocese). Why? His uncle, the curé of Belle-Île, had shown heroism five years before when the English had bombarded that port, and a vicar-general of the bishop, visiting Paris, had noted the efficient way in which Marquis-Ducastel ran routine parish business for the hypochondriacal curé of Saint-Laurent. Promptly, Marquis-Ducastel's father and mother came to Vannes to join him, and rejoiced when the commendatory abbot of Évron gave him the rich cure of Sainte-Suzanne in the diocese of Le Mans. What a rush there was for the new curé mounted on a hired horse, to take possession, lest some rival forestall him by prevention at the court of Rome! At last, Marquis-Ducastel reflected, 'I can provide a comfortable existence for my parents'. Alas! on 11 September 1771, his father, aged 67, painfully afflicted by the 'stone', died, having had only a few months to enjoy his son's new status and enhanced income.[161]

Looking back from his comfortable canonical stall in the cathedral of Rouen, the abbé Baston reflected on the chain of circumstances that had made his modest fortune possible. Son of the collector of municipal taxes at Pont-Audemar—an office of some standing, but small income—and the eldest of eleven children, he was lucky to attract the interest of a priest who ran a little private boarding-school; he thus learned Latin. His mother scoured Rouen to try to find someone who would contribute towards fees at *collège* and seminary. A prosperous canon who had the reputation of 'liking to make priests' failed her. Mme X, who had been helped by Baston's father to make a marriage of affection, said she could have obtained one of the exhibitions financed by the duc d'Orléans, had he been of noble birth: 'without *noblesse*—solid noble standing—the thing can't be done'. The marquise de X said: pass the hat round among your relatives—'you get him ordained priest, then I'll get him a rich living'. She was over 60. His mother left, expressing the hope that she'd live long enough to fulfil her promise. Finally, an old seam-stress gave him free lodgings in town on condition he did some errands; and, belatedly, another canon chipped in with a contribu-tion. At 17, he took the tonsure. 'It's not irrevocable,' he mused; 'even so, it is an engagement, a weight unreflectively placed on the scales on the opposite side to liberty'—'but I thought I could assume the ecclesiastical state with the same indifference as anyone else, not having the least tincture of what they call vocation.' He regretted not being able to go to the theatre, however. Then came five happy years of study at the seminary of Saint-Sulpice in Paris. He was allowed home for two months in each year—'feted by everybody. They all said I looked "very well" in the *petit collet*.' The best houses invited him; the curé put him on the *feuille des gagnants de l'office*, those who were paid for attending certain services in church; and a cleric who had stayed in minor orders told him how to know which services these were by the way in which the bells were rung. Then came the great, serious decision—should he become a sub-deacon? Two considerations encouraged him to do so: he had no interest in women, and he would be able to help his family. 'It certainly came into my mind that, as a priest, I would be able to help my respectable parents in their old age; surely religion would not condemn such a warm natural sentiment (*un sentiment si cher à la nature*).' He never regretted it, and after twelve years of teaching in seminaries and *collèges*, he became a canon of Rouen in 1778.[162]

'Pray to the Lord that in his majesty he will deign to shed upon me some rays of his beneficent light, without which study and toil are but grain sown on stony ground,' wrote a young theological student, the abbé Coudrin, to his father in 1786. Three years later, he was exhorting all his family to be edifying in their conversation and 'to say nothing but . . . what has the odour of sanctity'. He also exhorted his father, ruined in a lawsuit, to accept suffering in a religious spirit, while, by contrast, he himself was 'so happy to be right with God that I cannot prevent myself speaking of it'.[163] All this is most unlike our canon of Rouen's straightforward choice of a useful career with an assured income which would help his parents, but there are those who would not regard the comparison as unfavourable to Baston. How can the historian assess the 'vocations' of the past? In actual language and in secret thoughts, our minds work in clichés: we are conditioned by our social and religious environment to ascribe to ourselves not only avowable motives, but those that we can formulate intelligibly and convincingly. In an age when service in the ministry of the Church was at once a useful and, often enough, a well-paid career, and also a matter of spiritual and sacrificial decision, a man was not obliged to force the two things apart so that he could assess them for conscience' sake. To live means deciding, and decisions are normally made not by looking at all the evidence, but by looking at sufficient to produce the conviction that leads to action. Ordinations, like the marriages of the century, were arranged in the family context, but just as the world of arranged marriages had its detours of romance and vagaries of individual choice and could lead to lifelong devotion, so, too, the highest inspirations of spirituality could flourish amid the conformities and pressures arising from family interests. By our standards, there is something wrong with Canon Baston's scholarly complacency and the abbé Coudrin's fanatical insensitivity. The task of the historian is to set both within the cadre of the assumptions of the age so that we can at least accord them sympathetic understanding.

ABBÉS

I

'Abbé' originally meant abbot, the ruler of a monastery, and the term was extended to cover the nominal churchmen who, by virtue of the tonsure as the minimum qualification, held abbatial revenues *in commendam*.[1] There was a certain incongruity in using the word for a beneficiary of monastic income otherwise totally outside the life of the cloister: it would take six months, said Montesquieu, for a visitor from India or China to understand 'ce que c'est qu'un abbé commendataire qui bat le pavé de Paris'. There were other ecclesiastical benefices—priories, chapels, foundations—resembling the titular headships of abbeys in having no cure of souls and no duties to perform and capable of being enjoyed by *tonsurés*; by a further extension, the term 'abbé' was applied to their holders. Finally, by a quirk of semantic evolution, a word covering clerics living off the Church without working for it widened in meaning to become an honorific form of address for canons, curés, and all other ecclesiastics short of the rank of bishop, provided they were not monks or friars. The process was complete by the end of the seventeenth century. The Jansenist society of Port-Royal still used 'abbé' in its distant, original sense of the ruler of a monastic house,[2] but it was an archaic, strait-laced usage.

The ceremony of the tonsure signified, said a solemn liturgiologist, separation from the laity and renunciation of the world, a demonstration of the willingness to wear the crown of thorns, to suffer with Christ.[3] Often, the candidate being tonsured was very young, perhaps 9 or 10 years of age; it would have been unreasonable to expect him to grasp these lofty implications. His family was moving him into position to obtain an ecclesiastical income if he turned out to be willing; as the opera singer Sophie Arnould said in 1790 about her grown-up son by a great nobleman, 'we made him an abbé because we had sufficient influence to contrive the little fellow's fortune (in this state of life we'd have made him Pope—or, anyway, a holder of a big benefice). But heaven ruled otherwise . . . he is a soldier'.[4] Just short of the age of 13, Diderot's family had him tonsured; an uncle was supposed to be resigning a canonry in his favour, but died too soon—'eighteen hundred livres income lost', complained his father. All the same, the adolescent wore ecclesiastical dress for two years, and had a crisis of religious devotion, before realizing his unsuitability.[5] The same family policy, however, encouraged his brother into orders, becoming a sincere and intolerant archdeacon. Among those who were older, some had already chosen to proceed to the ministry of the Church, and would reflect seriously on the meaning of the ceremony. But many others would take the tonsure as a staging-point, moving into the status, and possibly an income, without knowing what opportunities would present themselves or what their sentiments would be in a few years' time. An illegitimate boy, of good family and recognized by his father, but with no hope of inheriting, paid for as a permanent boarder at the Collège de Lisieux in Paris, naturally took the tonsure and the distinctive dress going with it. However, it turned out that there was no need for Jacques Delille to seek a career in the Church; he won all the scholastic prizes, became an academic teacher, and with his translation of the *Georgics* in 1769 achieved financial security and membership of the Academy—the poet of nature and the darling of the salons at the end of the *ancien régime*.[6] François de Neufchâteau, whose precocious brilliance earned him election to the academy of Dijon at the age of 15, was tonsured because the bishop of Toul, hoping to recruit his talent, became his patron, 'the respectable benefactor I will never forget'. Soon he realized the clerical life was not for him, and left the seminary.[7] Another case was Marmontel, a tonsured prize-winner of the academy of Toulouse. Without wealth or influence to promote a career, he finally decided to ask for ordination, but his archbishop turned him down, saying (Marmontel records), 'I was just a gay young abbé, quite taken up with poetry, paying my court to the ladies and writing pastorals and songs for them—nay, sometimes at dusk I went to the public promenades to take the air with pretty girls.'[8] These three had socially conditioned provisional vocations, Delille for want of an alternative, François de Neufchâteau conforming to flattering episcopal patronage, Marmontel moving towards reluctant commitment to a profession, but compelled to face the superficiality of his sentiments by a stern prelate. Rightly for all of them, their tonsure took them no further in the Church.

As against these young men of ability with provisional vocations, there were other *tonsurés*, who from the start had no shred of vocation but simply wanted the qualification to hold a benefice without cure of souls, no work involved. For these, the relevant words of their initiation ceremony were those of the psalm: 'the Lord himself is the portion of mine inheritance and my cup; thou shalt maintain my lot. The lot is fallen to me in a fair ground: Yea, I have a goodly heritage.' Given the mores of the day, taking the tonsure without vocation may be allowed, but going on to the priesthood was cynical. Chamfort would not stoop to it: for a time he wore the clerical *petit collet* of the abbé, but he told the principal of the Collège des Grassins that he would never be ordained, 'liking repose, philosophy, women and honour too much'.[9] By contrast to this scrupulosity, the abbé Pollin in his autobiography (1792) confessed naïvely, in the manner of his idol Rousseau, how he became a priest for a livelihood, intrigued to try to get office as a minor chaplain at Versailles, then reverted to the status of abbé when he fell in love, 'au pied des autels', with a girl attending his mass.[10] Such vocation as he had was worldly, and the sight of a girl ended it, and he became one of the abbés by default, drop-outs from the established clergy, secular or regular.

Another variant of this category of abbé consisted of those who had the status as the aftermath of a failed vocation; they had joined a religious Order, gone through the noviciate and, possibly, further, then obtained their release. The late age for final profession in the Jesuits made a return to lay society more evidently available to their recruits, and some of them, well educated, experienced in writing and teaching, made their mark in the Parisian milieux of scholarship and literature. 'You are fortunate in having been [a Jesuit],' wrote a friend to Desfontaines, 'and fortunate in having left them; you have retained the inimitable characteristics and attributes which have made you so well-known in the world.'[11] Desfontaines always recognized his debt: the Jesuits, he said, had taught him to study, to reason, to argue, and to satirize, 'l'honneur que lui font ses ouvrages rejaillit sur eux'. Marsy left because of a homosexual relationship with an aristocratic pupil, and La Motte because he seduced a female penitent; but most parted amicably with their Institute.[12] Some— Olivet, the exponent of Ciceronian scepticism; Fraguier, of the Academy and the *Journal des Savants*; Gédoyn, Le Mascrier, Millot, Le Grand d'Aussy, and Grosier pursued scholarly activities away from the constraints of claustral discipline; others followed their poetic muse, as Gresset did, or embarked on journalism, controversy, and the precarious career of authorship—Fréron, Desfontaines, Lambert, Raynal, La Touche, and La Porte.[13] Except for La Touche, who denounced his former colleagues as fanatics, all showed respect and a certain affection for the teachers and the system which had formed them. Raynal exempted the Society of Jesus from his anti-clerical censures; La Motte continued to take the Jesuit side against the Jansenists; and even the disreputable Lambert's novel, *Anecdotes jésuitiques* (1740), the story of the amorous adventures of a renegade, showed admiration for the rebarbative discipline which was only for the few. Fréron, who resigned from the Society early in his teaching career (perhaps because his escapade at the theatre in lay dress got him banished to the provinces), was looked after by two ex-Jesuits when he came to Paris to earn his living by his pen: the abbé Boismorand gave him lodgings and introduced him to Desfontaines, who employed him on his literary journal, *Observations sur les écrits modernes*. The vocation of Desfontaines, said an admirer, was to 'guard the gates of the *Temple du Goût* to prevent the invasion of ignorance or pseudo-wit', and this mission he passed on to Fréron, who fulfilled it with irony and critical insight in the pages of his *Année littéraire*.[14]

Considering the diversity of its membership, and the gulf between actuality and terminology, contemporaries found the category of 'abbé' hard to define.[15] The *Encyclopédie* simply says 'the superior of a monastery of monks established at an Abbey', being 'a title derived from the Hebrew for father (Syriac *abba*)'. The article goes on to give the history of the institution, including the rise of the *commende*. There is nothing about the swarm of abbés on the contemporary scene, and no censure, unless it be the irony of noting how the bulls of appointment still include the archaic provisions conferring spiritual jurisdiction over the monks and the obligation of proceeding from the tonsure to holy orders in due course. Given that the *Encyclopédie* faced a threat of suppression, the early pages of the first volume were hardly the place for anticlerical irony or reflections on the greed of the aristocracy. Guyot's vast repertory of jurisprudence and Durand de Maillaine's dictionary of canon law had articles of a similar sort, without sardonic undertones, unless it be in pointing out how a commendatory abbot can take possession of his church with book, holy water, and incense like a regular one. Bergier's theological dictionary does not complain about the abuses of the system except to say that the 'best-regulated dioceses' do not accept candidates for the tonsure under the age of 14. (An example could have been the diocese of Paris under Noailles: in his synod of 1697 he had laid down a minimum age of 15, with a certificate from the curé that the candidate had been essaying his vocation for six months under supervision.[16]) Indeed, Bergier defends the *commende* as an ever present resource (as appointments fall vacant) for the king to make grants for schemes of 'public utility' or to pension useful servants—there is no reference to the scandal of the dispositions actually made. These were definitions in terms of the vast old traditional edifice, ignoring the interest groups operating within and around it, adapting and plundering. A novelist in 1739 describes the abbés as 'having the rank of those who have none, and the profession of those who do not propose to work at one'[17]—they were a motley crew, moving in to annex funds lying around to reward the performance of a ritual gesture of allegiance. According to another eighteenth-century description, 'the abbé does not enjoy a position in life (*état*), but simply wears a costume'.[18] This covers not only those lucky enough to get a benefice, but also those who were tonsured and adopted clerical garb while waiting for Fortune to smile on them, or simply to gain standing and consideration. This came with the dress. Canon Baston, who received the tonsure in 1760, tells how he forthwith donned the ecclesiastical habit and went round calling on his relatives, being surprised to find with what respect they now treated him.[19] When in Venice, Grossley adopted the dress for this reason, and to be able to turn out respectably without having to buy expensive clothes.[20]

A standard costume had evolved among the abbés, distinguishing them from monks and the pastoral clergy (though canons and curés on holiday might borrow it). Instead of, or supplementary to, the broad *rabat* ('bands') was the *petit collet*, a white collar of linen or lace, and instead of the cassock there was a short coat, generally brown in colour, with gold buttons. The ensemble would be surmounted by a wig.[21] True, the law of the Church banned the *perruque*, citing Tertullian, 'non amat falsum auctor veritatis'; but the abbés of the mid-seventeenth century broke through the prohibition, the other clergy following. In 1685 even the severe Tronson of Saint-Sulpice conceded wigs might be worn, though only in rare circumstances when celebrating mass, and always provided the bishop had given permission and the false hair was short.[22] Thereafter, two sorts of churchmen took up the fashion. There were the bald, concealing their handicap or just trying to keep warm, and if they were serious-minded (or affectedly scrupulous), having a hole in the middle to simulate a tonsure, perhaps with a fill-in of flesh-coloured silk or pigskin ('an unclean animal rejected from the sacrifices of antiquity', said a censorious Jansenist). The other class of wig wearers were the modish and frivolous, hiding their tonsure or lack of it. For abbés, the fashion was a wig of short hair, powdered and crowned with a recognizably ecclesiastical hat. Up to the end of the seventeenth century, it was the calotte, a round, shiny, black skull-cap, but from then onwards it became the standard wear of a doctor of theology, while the abbés turned to the three- or four-cornered *bonnet carré*.[23] According to Mercier, by the end of the *ancien régime* in Paris, they had dispensed with both *collet* and *rabat* and let the short 'Prussian' coat and the hat indicate their clerical status, while the wig would be 'impertinently curled'. There would be accompanying affectations, a favourite being the flaunting of a snuff-box.[24]

Some of these vocationless benefice holders stayed at home and did nothing. The *cahier* of the Tiers of Saint-Sulpice de Roumagnac in Périgord, in 1789, complaining of abbés, divided them into two types: one, with a considerable income, would go off to the city to live 'en homme du siècle'; the other, with a small income, would stay at home—'il végète dans sa famille'.[25] Cournot described 'mon oncle l'abbé':

an amiable and courteous man, a connaisseur of books, interested especially in literary curiosities, though without great expertise, writing verses in Latin and French and, even, publishing a few of them. While still a boy, he was already called 'l'abbé' because he had been tonsured in the customary way to enjoy a tiny benefice (I believe it had an income of 200 livres) depending on the patronage of a friend of the family, and because he had a singularly beautiful voice which was presumed to give him prospects in a clerical career. Of vocation, that was all he had, and he readily agreed this was so. The ecclesiastical state had seemed to him the means to have a more agreeable and comfortable existence.[26]

Occasionally, provincial abbés like Cournot's uncle emerged from leisured anonymity to read papers at the local academy—on some archaeological find, a curiosity of classical antiquity like the Amazons, an amateur scientific speculation, as on perpetual motion. At Besançon, an abbé, having failed to gain election to the academy, founded his own 'Société littéraire et militaire' (it was a garrison town), but was defeated by the jealous academicians, who obtained a royal *lettre de cachet* against him. An idyllic non-achieving or dilet-tante life-style like this depended on having a niche with well-off relations. Down-at-heel clerics without such a base eked out a sub-sistence doing small jobs around churches, like walking in funeral processions or keeping vigil over the corpse the night before the funeral.[27] In the end, said another *cahier* of 1789, 'they wander round in indigence and die at the Bicêtre'.[28] A sad case in the 1770s was an abbé of Saint-Malo grown old in poverty, excluded from office by his Jansenism; the bishop met him in the street and took him to dinner—he abandoned the resistance of a lifetime, and signed the Formulary.[29] The provincial abbés, whether well-beneficed, comfortable with their relatives, or miserably threadbare, for the most part escape the historical record. But there were those who ventured forth into the secular world, especially in Paris, and made contributions to literature, invention, and intellectual progress, to teaching and administration, and to the chronicle of scandal and the gaiety of the nation.

A particular group of abbés should be set aside from the rest: the aristocrats of old families who enjoyed huge incomes from the spoils of the great abbeys, pensions on the revenues of bishoprics, and the like; Blondel's *Des hommes tels qu'ils sont et doivent être* (1758) provided a name for them—those with at least 25,000 livres a year from ecclesiastical sinecures are 'abbés de cour'.[30] The most outrageous example of the century was Louis de Bourbon-Condé, who drew the abbatial income of Bec, Marmoutier, Saint-Claude, and Saint-Germain-des-Prés, each enough to furnish a life-style of the utmost luxury. Some *abbés de cour* did indeed frequent Versailles, making the life of a courtier their career. There was the abbé de Broglie,[31] raw-boned, tall, scruffily dressed, and outrageously witty, a familiar of Louis XV, to whom he retailed scandalous anecdotes, and of the queen and her pious circle, because he entertained them with sanitized ones. He drew the abbatial revenues of Mont-Saint-Michel, and apart from a 'retreat' every year in the sea air of his monastic domain, he never left the Court. While promoting the military careers of his brother and nephews, he asked for nothing for himself—he was, said Hénault, 'an intriguer without ambition and indecent with irreproachable morals'. In the following reign, the abbé de Véri was continually at Versailles, knowing everyone and observing everything.[32] He could have been a bishop, having studied at the Sorbonne and served as a *grand vicaire* at Bourges, but he chose to accept a prestigious legal office at Rome, one well known to attract the gift of benefices. After ten years he had over 100,000 livres of ecclesiastical income, and established himself at Court, advising the ministers, all the while realizing that disaster lay ahead, and confiding 'republican' sentiments to his journal—the king was just 'l'homme d'affaires de la nation'. He liked to think he could influence events, and encouraged Turgot towards reform, and discouraged Marie Antoinette from frivolity. But his only real success was in helping to ensure that Louis XV received the last sacraments before it was too late: he pressed Mme du Barry to leave Versailles, letting her and the king think it was revokable, and Mme Adélaïde and the archbishop of Paris assume it was definitive.

Other *abbés de cour* had the entrée to Versailles, but used it infrequently, having found more interesting things to do. The abbé de Dangeau, subject of a contemptuous notice by Saint-Simon when he died in 1723 at the age of 80, had bought the office of *lecteur* to have status at court if he wished to go there, but preferred living at ease in his 'joli prieuré' in agreeable countryside near Paris.[33] Scholarly activity was the vocation of the abbé de Bignon of the Académie Française and the Académie des Sciences, royal censor and librarian, editor of the *Journal des Savants*, enjoying 55,000 livres a year from two abbeys, as befitted the nephew of a chancelier of France.[34] So too, but in seclusion, was the abbé de Marolles immersed in his books in his apartment in the faubourg Saint-Germain or in his abbatial mansion in Touraine. The abbé de Radonvilliers, a former secretary to the embassy in Rome, came to Court as Latin tutor to the future Louis XVI, but his chief interest was in translating the ancient authors and compiling a guide to learning languages by the 'direct' method.[35] In spite of the scandal of a duel in his youth, the abbé de Voisenon could have hoped to be a bishop if, in Turgot's phrase, he had been 'willing to wear a mask for the rest of his life'; but he had been realistic about his suitability to lead the people of God: 'comment veut-on que je les conduise, lorsque j'ai tant de peine à me conduire moi-même?'[36] So he turned to monastic revenues, the writing of plays and novels, and the society of the actresses of the Comédie-Italienne. These and other sons of great aristocratic families stood apart from the common run of abbés: their share of monastic plunder was so much greater.

At the margin of the class of the *abbés de cour* were others, lacking the high birth which made the abbatial revenues of the great foundations available, but by their talents enjoying Court favour and in line for sinecures, the editorship of official journals, and the holding of canonries with permission not to reside. These, a sort of fluctuating artificial aristocracy at the summit of the 'republic of letters', will be considered later. Not entirely distinct from them was another class of abbé, prosperous and distinguished, the grandees of the University of Paris. Early in the century there was the abbé Renaudot, professor of Oriental languages, translator of the narratives of Muslim travellers to China, member of the Académie, and editor of the *Gazette de France*—he did not need to publish for profit. Batteux the aesthetician, a professor in the Collège de Navarre, had influential connections which got him into the Academy and appointed to devise the new syllabus for the École Militaire; he was well off, witness his 500 livres every year to the curé of the parish for the poor.[37] Nollet was an internationally renowned expounder of Newton's cosmology and of the wonders of electricity, dukes and duchesses and foreign royalty attending the Collège de Navarre to see his demonstrations, and he lectured at the artillery school at La Fère and the school of military engineering at Mézières.[38] Pluquet, writer of essays on fatalism and on luxury, in confutation of the philosophes, was a professor at the Collège de France, a former *grand vicaire* of Albi, and drew the income of a canonry at Cambrai. These academics moved in a lofty milieu far above the multitude of abbés who were Grub Street hacks, journalists, and the like; they had their professorial dignity to maintain, and one of them, the abbé Sigorne, fell into disgrace for publishing light-hearted trifles, 'unworthy of his profession and habit'.[39]

In the novels, correspondence, and memoirs of the age, there was a stereotype of the footloose, vocationless abbé involved in dubious adventures. It was a creation of public opinion hostile to a privileged class. Serious clergy and devout laymen saw the abbés as parasites on the Church, their income unearned and their leisure blameworthy. The mass of folk who had to work for their living envied them: law clerks, errand-boys, and porters whistled at them on the streets and in the theatres. Besides, whenever a secular cleric came to notice by a crime or a folly, he was commonly reported as an 'abbé', without reference to his standing as, say, a canon or a vicaire. The abbé de Moncrif, locked up in the Bastille, then in the fortress of Vincennes in the mid-eighteenth century, for an accumulation of mis-demeanours—claiming descent from Scottish royalty, boasting of knowing State secrets, running up huge debts, seducing a girl com-mitted to his charge, causing riots in the various monastic houses where his family had him confined—was a doctor of theology and of canon and civil law, and dean of the cathedral of Autun, yet it was not as a doctor or a dean that he was censured, but as an abbé.[40]

There were a few wearers of the *petit collet* who brought intelli-gence to the enterprises of the Parisian underworld. In 1749, the abbé de Flers was hanged in the Place de Grève for forging lottery tickets; he refused the ministrations of the attendant confessor, and clung to the ladder complaining that they would not accept his money to buy a pardon.[41] Four years later, the abbé Abbadie was broken on the wheel for a confidence trick leading to the attempted murder of a jeweller.[42] In 1760, the abbé de la Coste was sent to the galleys for life for another lottery fraud.[43] These were not penniless adventurers: Flers had an income of 10,000 livres from inheritance and benefices; Abbadie was a canon of a minor chapter in Bordeaux (though the judicial writ for his execution concealed the fact); while La Coste had been the 'homme de confiance' of the farmer-general La Riche de la Pouplinière, and had just negotiated his master's marriage to a girl in Toulouse whose fame as a beauty and a musician had inspired the old financier to seek simultaneous gratification for his two ruling passions. The forgery tradition carried on: when the Revolution printed the *assignats* as currency, the biggest-scale counterfeiter was another marginal churchman, and the police spy who informed on him was an ex-abbé already notorious for having stolen the silver from the garrison chapel when the mob stormed the Bastille.[44]

These were unusual cases; criminality did not figure in the stereotype of the dubious abbé, though sexual licence did.[45] Outrageous examples come from the dissolute age of the Regency. In the 'Société du Temple' (the Temple being an enclave immune from police intervention), the abbé de Chaulieu held court, 'a smug, libidinous, parasitic old reprobate . . . a disgrace to his cloth and to society'.[46] With him were two other nominal clerics pilloried in Saint-Simon's rogues' gallery: the fat and gluttonous Courtin, 'who took orders because of sloth and debauchery', and Servien, who publicly ridiculed the cult of deference to Louis XIV, 'was still a debauchee at the age of 65', and died 'surprised' in the company of a male dancer of the Opéra.[47] These were imitators of the old *libertin* tradition, without its intellectual awareness and irony, finding justification only in the commonplaces of Chaulieu's elegant verse. After Servien's death, the most notorious sodomist in Paris was the ex-Jesuit, the abbé Desfontaines,[48] an indefatigable translator from Latin, English, and Italian, a prolific commentator on the theatrical and literary scene, and the historian of Paris, Portugal, and the dukes of Brittany. Among his contemporaries were a group of rich and dissolute abbés haunting the theatrical world. Voisenon, the Court aristocrat, held an abbey and a priory bringing him 30,000 livres a year. Asthmatic, little, and simian, yet effervescent and charming, he was described by Grétry as 'much in society, where his smiling expression masked the signs of death . . . employing in his remarks to the ladies all the roses of love and the most amiable gallantry'.[49] His scope as a writer was wide, his style epigrammatic, the content insubstantial, his comic invention tedious; he wrote plays and religious oratorios, a *conte* teaching the vanity of pleasures, and an obscene fable on the vicissitudes of characters changed by wicked

fairies into animals and chamber-pots, 'l'ordure mise en calem-
bours'.⁵⁰ Aunillon was a lesser noble who had been envoy at The
Hague before settling down as the 'curé of the Comédie'.⁵¹ La Garde
was a secretary to Pompadour and organizer of fêtes at Versailles,
writing verses for royal occasions, theatrical criticism, reviews of
exhibitions of paintings, as well as novels, the most successful being
the *Mémoires d'une jeune demoiselle de province pendant son séjour à Paris*
(1739). Another protégé of Pompadour and tutor to her brother was
Leblanc, son of a prison warder, come to Paris from the provinces,
a playwright, a popularizer of English cultural ideas, and, in later life,
a correspondent of Buffon.⁵² All four were in the police reports for
their mistresses from the Opéra and the theatre, Aunillon with
special mention of his venereal disease, Voisenon for his *ménage à
trois* with Mme Favart, and Leblanc for his penchant for three in a
bed. Other abbés of the alcove figured in the chronicle of scandal of
the reign of Louis XV: a composer of erotic fables who was a boon
companion in debauchery of the maréchal d'Estrées, the librarian of
a royal prince dying of pox, two reckless characters who dared to
be lovers of wives of magistrates of the parlement,⁵³ and—less
culpably—the son of a duke and ambassador running off to Italy to
marry a jeweller's daughter.⁵⁴ The type of dissipated abbé was well
established, hence a young man new to the streets of Paris was not
surprised when propositioned by one, 'an effeminate character with
the face of a satyr';⁵⁵ hence too the joke in the *Encyclopédie* about the
abbé who was so alarmed at the news of the falling population of
France that 'he devoted a day a week to propagation'. Abbés of great
families sowing their wild oats before moving on to become *grands
vicaires* occasionally came to the notice of the police of Paris; but, by
the reign of Louis XVI, sexual escapades had become a disqualification for promotion in the Church, and even in the days of the
Regency they could be a disadvantage; Orléans warned his illegitimate son, in the presence of the outraged bishop of Soissons, to
avoid womanizing as an abbé and wait until he had been safely
awarded his mitre.⁵⁶

The great found the wearers of the *petit collet*, with their entrée
to polite society and, often, their verbal facility, useful to forward
their designs—sometimes sinister ones; there was the hunchback
employed by the duchesse de Bouillon to administer a potion to the
actress Adrienne Lecouvreur to make her fall out of love with the
maréchal de Saxe,⁵⁷ and the vicious pamphleteer hired by the
enemies of Marie Antoinette to write the *Lever de l'aurore* against
her.⁵⁸ By contrast, there was the heroic plotter who revealed to the

Jesuits Choiseul's hostile designs against them, and had to flee, escaping to England by holding a pistol to the head of a captain of a sailing boat.[59] Accused of conspiracy, though guilty only of naïveté, was the son of an intendant of Bordeaux sent to the Bastille for verses against the king—no one had told him how the police opened letters.[60] Another subversive versifier was the abbé Bon, tutor to the son of the duc de Chaulnes, who produced bitter lines on the subservience of the government to England in expelling the Pretender at the peace of 1748: 'tout est vil, Roi, ministre, maîtresse'. He kept them to himself, except for Turgot, who told the abbé Sigorgne of the University, who dictated them to his class. For his remaining years, Bon lived in terror, hiding in refuges provided by friends of Sorbonne days (after all, another poet on the same subject spent three years in the iron cage at Mont-Saint-Michel).[61] Other abbés made a name by eccentricity. One, a gambler, threatened God with the betrayal of a divine secret if he lost the next throw, and when he did, announced: 'There is no Purgatory'. An Irishman borrowed money to promote his career, then used it to go to Turkey to become a Muslim. A libertine collected papal medals; an egalitarian fanatic told the duchesse d'Harcourt that he was as well-born as her husband, being the son of a 'maréchal ferrant' (farrier), while the duke was the son of a 'maréchal de France' (field marshal). Another, an earnest patriot, concerned about the failure of the royal pair to produce an heir to the throne, pressed a paper into the hand of Louis XVI recommending a particular position to improve the chances of conception.[62]

Socially viable by education, status, and formal costume, abbés of the respectable sort were welcome in polite society. The sons of noble families needed tutors, and almost always these were ecclesiastics. Most parents would consider a modicum of religious instruction was necessary, though not all, for Saint-Simon tells of a magistrate of the parlement of Paris and his wife who wanted 'a tutor who had no religion, and who on principle would bring up their son carefully ensuring he did not have any'.[63] Even so, there were abbés to fit this unusual requirement. By contrast, the princesse de Rohan-Guémené wanted a serious theologian for her two sons. Mallet, later to be a professor of theology in the University of Paris, was appointed, but soon left; the princess was haughty and irregular in paying, and one of the sons was spoilt and unteachable—the future Cardinal Rohan, of diamond necklace notoriety.[64] So often, aristocrats had little time to spend with their children, and they would require the tutor to live continually with his charge and, maybe, in the end accompany him to the university, on the grand tour, and, at least in one case, on the battlefield.[65] Enquiries would be made as to character and religion—the abbé Du Parquet of the marquis de Sade's imaginings would never have qualified. Good salaries were offered. Morellet, as tutor to the son of Chaumont de La Galaizière, chancellor to King Stanislas of Lorraine, received maintenance, lodging, and 1,000 livres a year as he accompanied the young man during his studies in Paris and on a tour of Italy.[66] If the employer had contacts with patrons of benefices, ecclesiastical revenues might augment the stipend. The abbé Belley, tutor to a daughter of the regent, had an apartment at the Palais Royal, 400 livres salary, and a priory worth 900 livres a year.[67] The rewards for educating the son of Prince Ferdinand of Parma (the boy, through his mother, being a grandson of Louis XV) were splendid—Condillac was made for life by the appointment, his salary of 8,000 livres a year continuing as a pension, while the king of France gave him an abbey in the diocese of Toul with a similar income.[68] For a personable young man, the costume of abbé led to contacts, and contacts to offers of employment. In 1738 a young abbé of Nantes decided to throw over his parents' expectations and go to Paris to join the royal bodyguard. Once there, he found he could not afford to serve the necessary apprenticeship of two years as an unpaid supernumerary; but he stayed on, retaining his ecclesiastical dress, 'which will give me an entrée to society and a sort of standing'; social engagements followed, and the duc de Richelieu got him taken on as tutor to the sons of the duc d'Aumont.[69] Two noblemen have left lively portraits of the abbés who gave them their manifestly good education. The baron de Frénilly tells of M. Giraudet, who hated being regarded as an ecclesiastic and being called 'M. l'abbé', and was so ashamed of his position as tutor that, when walking with his pupil, he would cross the street to avoid being recognized.[70] By contrast, the prince de Ligne remembered the abbé Verdier as the only teacher he ever had who believed in God, a man of piety, like the best sort of country curé.[71] An absence of vocation is not to be assumed, even when it was not necessary.

Being a tutor gave the opportunity to join in the life of a great household, with the possibility of rising to high office within it. There was an engaging example at the court of Lorraine, where the wit in residence was the dapper little abbé Porquet, who had gone there as tutor to the second son of King Stanislas by his mistress Mme de Boufflers, and stayed on as chaplain and social ornament, though only after a year's probation to enable him to make up his mind to believe in God.[72] After educating the young duc de Penthièvre, the son of the comtesse de Toulouse, the abbé Quesnel was rewarded with a charming retreat in the Tuileries garden, and spent his days as a companion to the countess—when he took her invitations round to her lady-friends, his stock joke was to urge them to bring their husbands, as 'without him you would be bored and you'd be a bore yourself'. For the learned, there were posts as librarians and archivists with great aristocrats like the comte de Saint-Florentin and the duc d'Orléans, or as a keeper of the royal collections of books, coins, and medals. The king's library in the first half of the century was newly catalogued by Sallier, professor of Hebrew at the Collège Royal, member of the Académie des Inscriptions, the Académie Française, and the Royal Society of London.[73] Or learning might be encouraged by a household sinecure. Vertot, who died in his apartments in the Palais Royal in 1735, had written the histories of the 'revolutions' of the Roman Republic, of Portugal and Sweden, and the story of the knights of Malta, in a flowing style untramelled by lust for accuracy (he refused to correct his manuscript of the siege of Malta: 'mon siège est fait'); he had been a friar and a curé, but had finally achieved leisure for learning in the office of *secrétaire des commandements* to the duchesse d'Orléans. For abbés with administrative talents, there were supervisory appointments, keeping accounts, directing the servants, running the estates. Before settling down to preside over his licentious circle in the Temple, Chaulieu had run the household of the duc de Vendôme, feathering his own nest while doing so, according to Saint-Simon, and brazening it out when detected.[74] During the Regency, Law, the financier, had Coetlogeon as his 'âme damnée', and rewarded him with an estate bought with the notorious *billets* before their value collapsed. Having gone on to the subdiaconate, Coetlogeon had incurred the obligation of celibacy, preventing him from retiring there with a wife—until he got a dispensation from Rome enabling him to marry his mistress.[75] At that time, the household of Cardinal Rohan was run by the abbé de Ravenes, who could be seen 'going round the corridors and apartments finding dust everywhere and lamenting the state of the furniture'.[76] In 1725, the entourage of the cardinal was joined by another nominal ecclesiastic, Huber, tiny, deformed, agreeable, and witty, a convert from Protestantism, brother of the Marie Huber who wrote works of spirituality overthrowing grim, unethical notions of Hell. He went on to join the staff of a financier and become the agent of the farmers-general in America, negotiating for direct supplies of tobacco, and then in London, making a contract on their behalf, at the same time engaging in industrial espionage on textile machinery. When he died in 1744, he left his carriage and pair and the bulk of his fortune to La Tour, the Court painter, together with legacies to good causes, without enough money to pay them.[77] The abbé de Villemont, secretary to the prince de Croÿ, was sent to Turin to negotiate a marriage with a princess of the lineage of Carignan, a mission doomed to failure, for the family restricted its alliances to sovereign houses.[78] The great Orléans dynasty employed abbés to direct its affairs; in 1761, Breteuil was *chancelier* to the duke, and refused to allow his master to give Collé, the dramatist, a sinecure as one of his 'secretaries'. When Collé was given a less prestigious appointment, it was another abbé, Omelanne, who welcomed him when he arrived at the Palais Royal to take up his nominal duties.[79] At the end of the *ancien régime*, the chaotic finances of the then duc d'Orléans (Égalité) were run by the abbé de Limon, while Mme de Genlis looked after social events, and Choderlos de Laclos conducted political intrigues.[80] Lower down the social scale, in bourgeois establishments, abbés would find a niche as administrative assistants. In many houses in Paris, said Mercier, they enjoyed the title of 'friend' and supervised the household, helped the master with his business affairs, and chatted with his wife at her *toilette*.[81] In humbler milieux they insinuated themselves with impressive talk and worldly-wise advice, like Anatole France's Jérôme, l'abbé Coignard, always welcome at the fireside and to a free meal at the sign of *La Reine Pédauque*.

II

Numerous publications came from the abbés, some using the leisure afforded by their sinecures, others striving to make a living by their pens. One day it may be possible to hazard a generalization about their multifarious writings, detecting a contribution of a specific kind to the thought of the Enlightenment, one corresponding to their ambiguous station between Church and world. This essay, however, goes no further than attempting an impressionistic view of the marginal churchmen who sought fame—or mere survival—in the harsh and brilliant Parisian literary milieu.

There is a problem of categorization. Anyone who had been tonsured could call himself 'abbé', perhaps ceasing to do so later on, or even formally renouncing the status; others might call him 'abbé', whether in accordance with present facts or harking back to the past, or merely in irony. Taking examples from the ex-Jesuits, scandalous figures like Raynal and Desfontaines were always so called, and Desfontaines wore the costume, at least sometimes—'quel homme pour un tel habit!', exclaimed Piron. Marsy, disgraced as he was, did not abandon the *petit collet*; Fréron wrote savagely against him

> Revêtu du manteau d'abbé
> Laisse là ton honneur flambé!

For his own part, Fréron called himself 'abbé' for the first seven years after leaving the Jesuits, until he started living with his niece in 1748, marrying her two years later. Similarly, Gresset renounced the ecclesiastical connection when he got married. As with the ex-Jesuits, so with the other abbés on the literary scene. Some kept the title all their days, hoping for a benefice; Coyer, endlessly composing treatises on subjects of public utility, expected that the Church, in which he had proceeded to priestly orders, would reward him; not so, his last will and testament is bitter—'I give nothing to the Church which has given nothing to me'.[82] Others abandoned the *petit collet*, yet their friends continued to intrigue to try to get ecclesiastical revenues for them (as did Marmontel's allies in high places).

A further complexity arises because canons and curés in formal pastoral office might spend their leisure in writing for publication, and figure as abbés on their title-pages (these, professionals in the Church, but amateurs in the republic of letters, ought to be excluded—when their standing can be identified). Even so, there were holders of benefices supposedly with cure of souls who were dispensed from residence and simply drew the emoluments—abbés indeed. Of those we meet in the literary world, Expilly had an inconsiderable canonry in the Midi, and Dubos had a considerable one in his native town of Beauvais—in the last ten years of his life he visited it twice. He scored smugly both ways when discussing his absenteeism: the chapter, he said, was guilty of 'cowardly indulgence' in breaking the rules, but all the same, his own merit 'put him above them'.[83] Batteux, a professor at the Collège de Navarre in Paris, was a canon of Reims, but did not reside there, having won a three-year-long lawsuit against the chapter to establish his right to absence.[84] Trublet drew the income of prebends at Nantes and Saint-Malo while occupying all his days in Parisian literary circles; however, he did go to stay in Saint-Malo from 1750 to 1753, and he retired there at the end of his life, from 1765 to 1770, in spite of frail health attending all the offices, leaning on the shoulder of his servant.[85] Towards the end of the century the abbés Gérard and

Maydieu published successful moralizing novels; one was a canon of Saint-Louis-du-Louvre, the other of a provincial chapter—did they do the duties? Numerous nominal churchmen moved in the end into the formal ecclesiastical establishment: there were Mallet and Yvon of the *Encyclopédie*, and Prades too, though his benefices were outside France. A tutor to the sons of the duc de Clermont-Tonnerre moved on to teach at the École Militaire, then became a curé, and finally, during the Revolution, was elected a constitutional bishop. Or the movement might be the other way. Vertot, the historian, had once been a curé. Outhier, who accompanied Maupertuis to Lapland, was a canon of both Bayeux and Arles; but, accused of seducing a penitent, he fled to Avignon, and earned his living by writing for the local *Courier*. The archetypal abbé, always so called, is Prévost, master of the novelist's art of interpreting the passions; yet, in his productive years he was a Benedictine monk, in and out of his Order twice, a soldier, an adventurer in exile, and chaplain to the prince de Conti. In his last years he was indeed an abbé, with no ecclesiastical duties, his benefices providing a comfortable house, a cook, a lackey, and 'a good-looking housekeeper', the great novels behind him, his literary reputation secure, and cherishing the unfulfilled design of writing a work of religious apologetics in his declining days.[86]

Fortunately, the distinction between abbés as nominal churchmen and those of the ecclesiastical establishment hardly needs to be drawn in the case of editors, journalists, translators, playwrights, and novelists. Most of them manifestly fall into the first category, and precision about status is rarely necessary. But where writings on the margins of religious apologetics are considered, it is useful to separate the ministers of the Church committed and commissioned to defend it from those who wrote for a living and properly belong to the republic of letters. It would be valuable, too, to divide the literary abbés into Christian believers and others. But the status of many will remain ambiguous. It is a sad comment on the mores of the age that the distinction between simple *tonsurés* and those who proceeded to the priesthood does not necessarily help. The abandonment of aspirations to an ecclesiastical career or loss of faith may have come after ordination, or ordination may have been sought because the richer benefices tended to be reserved for those who accepted the (supposedly) ultimate commitment. Saint-Pierre, the sardonic conformist; Raynal, the sceptical anticlerical; Voisenon, Aunillon, and La Garde, the lechers; Desfontaines, the sodomist, were in holy orders.[87] Condillac proceeded quite naturally to the priesthood, while his brother Mably stayed in minor orders. Pellegrin was a hack playwright, but he composed hymns, carols, metrical psalms, and scriptural canticles, and he was proud of his ordination—'prêtre, poète et provençal', he boasted. No doubt the acid test of vocation would be the dutiful saying of mass (except that the hard-up might volunteer to acquit foundations for the fees). By this criterion, Pellegrin qualifies, for he said mass until Archbishop Noailles banned him because of his theatrical connections. Prévost, however, is excluded; the prince de Conti, offering him the post of chaplain, gave the warning that he never attended mass—'Monseigneur, I never say it'. But for most abbés, there is no evidence. Breaking the rules of the priestly life does not mean that belief is lacking. Deduction from publications is hazardous, unless religion is attacked in an unbelieving spirit. A writer was not bound to take the official line of the clerical hierarchy; certainly, the literary abbés tended to advocate toleration. Works reflecting the haunted or enthusiastic deism of the age do not exclude the underlying acceptance of revelation: a man is not obliged to state everything he believes when composing a book to sell. Behaving carelessly, yet intending to finish in the allegiance implied in the original tonsure, is an understandable attitude for those with a living to make in a morally dangerous milieu—the dyer's hand betrays his trade, but not his inmost thoughts. Desfontaines, given to unnatural vice and bitter feuding, had the Jesuits Segaut and Berthier at his deathbed: 'he died a good Christian, fortified by the Sacraments of our Mother the Church,' and edified his weeping friends 'with deeply religious protestations'.[88]

A convenient starting-point in considering the literary abbés is one where contemporary opinion has passed down to us the categorization—there was a stereotype of the age, 'the abbé philosophe', routinely denounced by serious churchmen. Though the denunciation was a commonplace, those who were effective writers accepted into the confraternity of the philosophes were comparatively few. There was Saint-Pierre, the optimistic, improving rationalist, deviser of proposals for utilitarian government and international order; Terrasson, whose *Séthos* (1731) exalted the efficacy of humanistic morality; Morellet, who wrote on theological subjects for the *Encyclopédie* with the detachment he would use for reviewing the doctrines of Muslims or Brahmins; Mably, the Rousseauistic 'republican' vaunting the austerity and equality of Sparta and ancient Rome; Raynal, cataloguing the cruelties of fanaticism and prophesying the decline of Christianity through deism to atheism; Condillac, drawing all thought and reasoning from the prompting of the senses; Marmontel, the apostle of toleration and hedonism. Perhaps only Raynal, ex-priest and ex-Jesuit, was a hater of religion; and even then, some of his savage observations were written for him by Diderot and other gleeful mischief makers. (And how serious were his extreme poses? In 1791, at the age of 78, he threw away his popularity with the new order, and went to Paris to denounce all the works of the Revolution.) The rest, if not deists, at least took a conventional attitude towards religion. Saint-Pierre recommended insincere conformity to the religion of one's own country; he died with the last sacraments, though telling his curé afterwards it was only a concession to decorum.[89] According to Grimm, Terrasson died without the sacraments, though he made a deathbed confession to a priest all the same (with the famous asides to his housekeeper for verification).[90] During his life, he had always worn the costume of an abbé (he was a *tonsuré*, not a priest). Except to clerical readers panicking at the idea of deism as a sufficiently effective promoter of morality, his Egyptian prince devising a universal code of conduct was harmless, and his account of ancient Egypt was safely packaged in the learned solemnity appropriate for the professor of Greek philosophy at the Collège Royal and author of a critical discourse on the *Iliad*.[91] Mably, a *tonsuré*, avoided attacks on the Church, a natural policy for a writer whose political views could be regarded as extreme; his brother, Condillac, had studied theology for eight years before proceeding to priestly orders, and his morals and religion were formally certified before his tutorship with the reigning house of Parma was confirmed; as for his philosophical writings, he hoped they would establish the proof of the existence of God, at least as the celestial clock maker.[92] After his early bid for ordination, Marmontel no longer used the title of abbé, except during the four years he spent as a tutor in the household of a farmer-general; thereafter he lived without religion (according to a malicious acquaintance, he had forgotten the words of the Creed), but in his later years he pontificated as if he had always been on the side of the angels. Morellet was a campaigner for toleration, ironically compiling a *Manuel des Inquisiteurs* (1762), but he had completed four years' theology at the Sorbonne, and he never renounced his title of abbé or his Catholic allegiance; in d'Holbach's atheistic circle he stood out as a deist. Mme Necker described him as a man 'of candour and probity . . . with enough religion to suspect there may be a God and to avow the fact sometimes to friends he knows are discreet and won't give him away'.[93]

These seven are clearly philosophes, by contemporary acceptance and subsequent agreement. More nominal churchmen could be included in the group, depending on the criteria chosen for its definition.[94] For reformist social opinions, there is the abbé Coyer, the utilitarian opponent of aristocratic and ecclesiastical privilege, also the abbé Badeau, the physiocrat, who had just enough religion to be given a deanery in Poland, but not enough to prevent him ogling the ladies at the Opera in Warsaw.[95] No doubt a sceptical and critical attitude to religion is one of the criteria; indeed, with obsessive emphasis, the *Dictionnaire de Trévoux* defined the philosophes as 'ces prétendus esprits forts'. In this respect the abbé Dulaurens would qualify with *Le Compère Mathieu* (1766), not because it is scabrous, but because it ridicules Christianity. Surely, however, something more than irreverence and anticlericalism is needed: a positive, shared ideology, however difficult to define, a self-conscious sense of mission. There are bound to be marginal cases, admirers or hangers-on who in the last resort were not really accepted as full members of the club. The case of the abbé de Prades was to show how risky it could be to manœuvre between the religious establishment and its sceptical critics; it was possible to gain a reputation and a living by brinkmanship, but it was also possible to be disowned by both sides.

Until the solemn determination to eradicate abuses took over during the last generation before the Revolution, *écrasez l'infâme* was less typical of the warfare of 'ces prétendus esprits forts' against religion than the contriving of entrapments into untenable positions and public ridicule. One was the affair of the thesis of the abbé de Prades in 1751–2. The story as fixed in the mind of the public by the philosophes had Prades writing it with unbelieving collaborators, putting it forward, as Helvétius said, as a dove sent out from the ark to see if the ocean of prejudices had abated. The writing being hard to decipher, the candidate read extracts to the chief examiner over dinner, and was certified as qualifying 'entre la poire et le fromage'.[96] The truth of the matter was otherwise.[97] Prades, of a noble family of the Midi, had hopes of a genuinely ecclesiastical career, and was being considered for a canonry at Montauban. He had translated Huet's Latin defence of the Scriptures against Hobbes and Spinoza into French, and his first three theses at the Sorbonne, the *tentative*, the *sorbonique*, and the *mineur* were praised by the examiners as effective presentations of the 'proofs of religion'. The final thesis, agreeably entitled 'Jerusalem coelesti', had to be printed and distributed to all the doctors before the oral examination, and as time was short, Dr Hooke had a hurried meeting with Prades, instructed him to change three expressions, and allowed publication. There-after, eight doctors in a day-long *soutenance* passed the thesis (true, it was printed in type so small that the faint-hearted might have been discouraged from attentive perusal). Concerning the Bible, the candidate's opinions were conservative: he said that the Pentateuch was entirely by Moses, the ark was a literal reality and all the animals could have boarded it, and the events of the life of Christ were predicted in the Old Testament. The only derogation from the Scriptures was the acceptance of Chinese chronology as correcting the time span commonly deduced from Genesis.[98] Though Prades believed in toleration, he made no concessions to the idea in the thesis, where he affirmed the right of the exponents of the true religion to establish their faith in Oriental countries. The Chinese annals apart, the complaints against the thesis concerned atmosphere and emphasis. The Latin was Ciceronian, not ecclesiastical (a style the archbishop of Paris called 'obscure and shocking'); the Fathers were cited only infrequently; the proofs of deism were more co-gently put than those of revelation (except in a Barthian theology, surely this is inevitable); though Christ's miracles were affirmed as proofs of his mission, they were cavalierly compared with pagan ones, and the fulfilment of prophecy was taken as superior evidence (as with the ark, the critics suspected difficult propositions were being blandly affirmed, to invite ridicule); equality among men was proclaimed to be in accordance with reason (a cliché of theological discourse, but a convenient allegation to alarm the civil authorities).

The attack on Prades began with two Jansenistically inclined doctors putting forward two objections to the award of the degree. First, the Chinese chronology; the Jesuits had been the impresarios introducing Chinese civilization to the West, and here was a com-plaint to bring in all their enemies in defence of the Scriptures. Second, Prades was a contributor to the *Encyclopédie*. Together with the abbé Yvon he had just produced the article 'Certitude' for volume ii, a blameless piece approved by the professors of the Collège de Navarre, but all the same inexcusable as written for editors whose design was supposed to be the propagation of doubts about religion. The thesis also echoed ideas in the preface to the first volume of the *Encyclopédie*, notably in accepting Locke's epistemo-logy. There was enough here to bring in the parlement of Paris; and facing the wrath of the magistrates, the Faculty of Theology, after eleven stormy sessions, cravenly condemned the thesis by a vote of 105 out of the 146 doctors present (21 January 1752). The arch-bishop of Paris weighed in with a pastoral letter, a Roman condem-

nation was fulminated on 22 March, and on 7 February the Royal
Council suppressed the first two volumes of the *Encyclopédie*. Far
from there having been a philosophic hoax against the theologians,
it looks as if there was a disorganized effort by enemies of the
philosophes to stop the *Encyclopédie*, with Prades a genuine apologist
for religion clumsily trying to contrive arguments acceptable to the
Enlightenment. All the same, the affair finished up as a triumph for
the philosophes, Diderot taking the opportunity for a powerful
diatribe he craftily tacked on to the 'apology' Prades issued from
exile in Berlin, and Voltaire and others wrote comic pieces on the
Sorbonne. True, the first two volumes of the *Encyclopédie* were suspended for the moment, but with a maximum of publicity, and the
Sorbonne was covered with ridicule.

Another triumph of the opponents of the Church came when
Marmontel, an undoubted philosophe and once an abbé aspiring to
ordination, published his *Bélisaire* in 1767, notable for a forceful
chapter on toleration. The Sorbonne issued a condemnation, a
reactionary fulmination the doctors regretted almost as soon as they
released it. They were out of tune with the age, and had gone
further than the defence of Catholicism required, incurring hostile
criticism from all sides. In fact, they deserved a certain sympathy, for
they had been unsure and divided, and while they argued, the printing press clattered on, so the book was on the streets before they had
time to devise a more sophisticated demurrer. The higher clergy had
been anxious to avoid a confrontation, for while they wanted to preserve the formulas of Catholic monopoly, they were aware of the
inevitability of concessions in practice. The message of *Bélisaire*[99] was
reform by an enlightened ruler, Marmontel having lost faith in his
earlier hope of a 'creeping virtue' spreading from a solid bourgeois
culture to improve the morals of the rest of society. It was important
not to have intolerance prominent on the list of evils to be eradi-
cated by the new-look monarchy which the philosophes were
asking for—the future was to show, indeed, that the conversion of
the king and his closest advisers to liberal sentiments would enable
the Protestants to break through the clergy's monopoly of presiding
over births, marriages, and deaths. The archbishop of Paris invited
Marmontel to a conference with a group of doctors of theology at
his country house at Conflans, and the bishops of Noyon and Autun
made a separate effort to influence him.[100] Their attempts to persuade
him to retract failed; the public rushed to buy the book to a total,
prodigious for the time, of 40,000 copies; and the Sorbonne issued
ineffective statements in self-exculpation.

While few *tonsurés* were publishing members of the philosophic élite, many were admirers or clients, not necessarily sharing in sceptical opinions, but basking in the acquaintance of literary lions,[101] seeking their advice or recommendation, publishing minor works in their shadow, and popularizing their ideas. Amid the extensive literature evoked by *L'Esprit des Lois*, the first refutation was by an abbé, while two others issued commentaries explaining and approving. They were effective journalists parasitic on greatness; there was, however, another churchman who had anticipated Montesquieu and provided him with a key idea which he annexed, simplified, and adorned with epigram. In 1743, the abbé Espiard, of a family of the *noblesse de robe* of Besançon, published in three volumes *Essais sur le génie et le caractère des nations*.[102] Montesquieu took over his aphorism, 'le climat est, de toutes les causes, la plus universelle, la plus puissante', and, dispensing with the abbé's cautious insistence on the complex of other factors combining to create a natural environment, elaborated brilliantly on the more limited theme. Espiard's work passed almost unnoticed, and when he published a revised edition in 1752, he was blamed for plagiarizing Montesquieu, who had published in 1748 with all the éclat of apparent originality. On the lower slopes of Parnassus, where stentorian voices and broad shoulders were aids to promote victories of the Enlightenment, abbés could be recruited to support the philosophic cause. When the philosophes mounted their attack on Fréron in 1760, by staging the *Écossaise*, with Diderot in person directing the claque of 'the printers, booksellers and their errand boys', he was assisted by two battered abbés of the literary bohemia leading their battalions to boo and cheer, one at the back of the theatre, and the other at the front as 'strategic reserve'.[103] There were others who did odd jobs for Voltaire on the business side, organizing money transfers, passing on manuscripts to publishers. It was the abbé Cordier de Saint-Firmin who presented him to the masonic lodge of the Neuf-Sœurs to be an apprentice member, and the abbés Millot and de Boismont who were the only clergy who attended when he was received in triumph at the Academy (of the latter, D'Alembert observed that he had none of the attributes of a priest save the eligibility to hold benefices). Some of Rousseau's most devoted admirers were found among the wearers of the *petit collet*, whether recognizing themselves in his 'Savoyard vicaire', or trying to put the theories of *Émile* into practice when tutoring the sons of the nobility.

A conspectus of abbés moving on the margins of the philosophic movement, and their diversity of attitudes and allegiances, can be

seen in the contributors to the *Encyclopédie*.[104] Of the eleven churchmen, seven may be classed as abbés—that is, omitting two ex-Jesuits
and one ex-Oratorian who left their Institutes in their early twenties
and the curé who wrote the article on 'eau-de-vie'. For a time, one
of the major theological contributors, Mallet, had been a parish
priest, and at the end of his life he was awarded a canonry; but most
of his active years were spent as a literary abbé and a professor. He
was a Christian believer, censored by Voltaire for his article affirming
the reality of 'Hell', though praised for his enthusiasm for religious
toleration. The abbé Pestres earned his living by tutoring the sons of
bankers and businessmen; he became suspect because he shared
lodgings with Prades and Yvon, though in fact he wrote his contributions on philosophical topics with the avowed aim of 'upholding
the morals and religion of J. C., our Legislator and also our God'.
Sauvages spent most of his life in minor orders, but in 1771, at the
age of 61, he was ordained priest and showed himself a zealous
pastor. La Chapelle, a brilliant mathematician, a Fellow of the Royal
Society of London and for forty years a royal censor of publications,
had been a devout Christian, but lost his faith in middle age. From
then on he indulged in agreeable eccentricities. In 1765 he invented
a cork life-jacket, and entertained Parisians by demonstrating it in
the Seine (when the king came to see, the current swept him away
just before the royal party arrived). Seven years later, he published a
manual on the art of ventriloquism, suggesting that it explained the
pagan oracles and, maybe, some of the Christian ones. The historian
Lenglet du Fresnoy, a doctor of theology of the Sorbonne, maintained a façade of religious belief while being a free-thinker, having
to take out religious insurance to cover his suspect political
opinions.[105] On several occasions he was imprisoned in the Bastille,
and in 1751, four years before he died, the police described him as
'a dangerous man . . . who could overthrow a kingdom'. The two
friends, Prades and Yvon, both priests, have long been taken as
the archetypal 'abbés philosophes', as distinct from the respectable
clerical contributors to the *Encyclopédie*, who were 'flags to cover the
contraband'.[106] They were, in fact, ambiguous figures. The outcry
against the notorious thesis of Prades was not justified by its actual
content; he always maintained he was orthodox in religion, and
finished up accepted as such by the Pope and the University of Paris
and holding benefices in Eastern Europe. Even in his comfortable
exile there were question marks over him:[107] how did he win so
much in an uncharacteristic venture into gambling? Did he spy for
France against his protector Frederick the Great? (No, but he would

not write accounts of Prussian victories against a French army in which his uncle, brother, and nephew served.) Yvon, like Prades, claimed to be writing in defence of religion: he excluded atheists from his pleas for toleration; he backed the condemnation of *Émile* by the archbishop of Paris, and after a lifetime of penury, ended up a benefice holder of the diocese of Tours, a canon of Coutances, and historiographer to the comte d'Artois. Believers and unbelievers of various hues, the ecclesiastics of the *Encyclopédie* seem to have had one thing in common: their acceptance of religious toleration. One might guess this was a fairly general trait among the literary abbés; certainly, when pamphleteers were urging the government of Louis XVI towards the liberal edict of 1787, two of the most effective, Guidi and Besoigne, were wearers of the *petit collet.*

There were disadvantages in alliance with the philosophes. Prades prospered on the income of benefices; but in a distant, colder climate, Diderot unsportingly added a section of extreme opinions to his 'apology', and Voltaire, far from showing gratitude to one who had been persecuted for the cause, was quick to accept the tale of his treachery to his Prussian protector. The corresponding advantages, however, were favourable reviews, invitations to certain salons, and the pulling of strings in high places—say, enlisting support from Mme de Pompadour. Churchmen conforming to the shibboleths of the Enlightenment might go far enough in brink-manship to be granted the philosophic accolade of a chair in the Academy; this was how the historian, the abbé Millot, was elected in 1778.[108] Conversely, the abbé Trublet was kept out because of his apologies for Christianity, until the *dévot* party at Court took up his cause and circumvented the ban. Yet he remained a friend of Voltaire and Helvétius, as did the abbé Pluquet (a professor at the Collège de France) after his defence of orthodoxy in his *Examen du fatalisme* (1757). In matters religious, feuds within the republic of letters tended to be single-issue affairs, not personal and lasting, though many a reckless blow was struck and misrepresentation and ridicule were standard weapons.

The philosophes had their inner ring and outer circle, but most of the literary abbés were in neither, writing without sceptical over-tones, unless some daring flourish occurred to them, or there was an accidental slip into a prevailing fashion. Their object was to earn a living. Those with contacts and influence would angle for nomina-tion to one of the government posts in the literary world, managerial offices in the republic of letters. There were appointments as official censors, with a salary of 6,000 livres, the right to be dispensed from the obligation of residence in benefices like canonries where it was normally required, and the intangible deference accorded to those with power to hinder publication. By the same token, it was possible to incur odium—the abbé Riballier, unpopular with the philosophes for his severity, contrived to fall out with the pious as well, by banning a biography of a general of the Capuchins because of its naïve acceptance of edifying anecdotes. The editorship of government-sponsored journals was more lucrative still—10,000 livres a year for the *Gazette de France*.[109] The abbé Arnauld, author of articles on the philosophy of the Etruscans, Greek tragedy, Roman eloquence, and Italian poetry, had the dauphin and Choiseul promoting his interests, was elevated to the Academy, and made director of the Foreign Ministry's *Gazette littéraire de l'Europe*, and when it folded, of the *Gazette de France*.

There were also sinecures at Court, not prestigious enough for great aristocrats, but suitable for literary men. Mme de Pompadour tried to get the abbé Leblanc elevated to the Academy in 1748; she failed, but ensured he was compensated by the office of *historiographe des bâtiments du Roi*.[110] The abbé Robin, who published a collection of the lives of great Christians in 1787 and another of great women the year after and settled down to write a history of the Estates General, was *secrétaire de la vénerie* of the comte d'Artois.[111] Two abbés patronized by Choiseul were given sinecures of this kind—men of solid learning, Le Grand d'Aussy and Barthélemy. The former, an ex-Jesuit and a collaborator in the medieval researches of La Curne de Sainte-Palaye, had earned his living by tutoring the sons of financiers until, in 1770, Choiseul, who was on the verge of leaving office, made him *secrétaire de la Direction de l'École Militaire*; from this secure base he published highly readable works on the margins of scholarship, old fables retold, a *Histoire de la vie privée des Français* and the *Voyages d'Auvergne*.[112] Jean-Jacques Barthélemy,[113] of the Académie des Inscriptions, curator of the Cabinet des Médailles, orientalist, classical scholar, and numismatist, was given another nominal secretarial office, that of the Gardes Suisses at Versailles, at 15,000 livres a year. He was a scholar of Christian convictions, for when Bausset, bishop of Béziers, sent for him to be his *grand vicaire*, Barthélemy, though in despair at the prospect of leaving the world of learning, offered to go if the bishop felt it was his duty; fortunately, Mgr de Bausset did not accept the 'sacrifice'. After thirty years' research, accumulating 20,000 *fiches* of quotations, in 1780, the abbé published his masterpiece, *Les Voyages du jeune Anacharsis en Grèce*, a fictional account of a young Scythian wandering over

Greece between 363 and 337 BC, meeting everyone and seeing everything recorded in the author's bank of quotations. The four volumes were well received by the intellectuals, because of the interest in classical antiquity aroused by the excavations at Herculaneum and Pompei, and by the wider public, because of the revolutionary political ferment of the day—here was a celebration of the supreme cultural achievements of the human spirit in a civilization ruled by 'les mœurs républicaines'. Versailles had its conventions about sinecures: they went to the high-born irrespective of merit, and to others through contacts, with merit borne in mind, but sheer sycophancy did not qualify. Hence the discomfiture of a certain abbé Petity, 'auteur obscur de plusieurs mauvais livres', who in 1775 went to the palace to present his two-volume study *La Sagesse de Louis XVI*; the king was tempted to throw it in his face, and Turgot banned the journals from reviewing it.[114]

In this age of enthusiasm for scientific experiment and invention, one way of coming to the notice of the Court—or, failing the Court, the Académie des Sciences—was to make useful discoveries. Abbés who published on mathematical subjects were invited by the Academy to go on prestigious expeditions—to Lapland to measure the width of a degree of latitude near the Pole, to observe the transit of Venus in Siberia in 1761 and in California in 1769, to the Cape of Good Hope in 1780 to report on the stars of the southern hemisphere. (From information gathered on his Siberian trip, the abbé Chappe d'Auteroche published a travel book on Russia, denouncing the dead hand of despotism, and thus arousing the wrath of Catherine II, who had grown used to the flattery of the philosophes.)[115] The invention of a diving suit and of a visual telegraph brought recognition from the Court, and of a bronze talking head from the sightseeing public in Paris. Even quicker profits were made by the two abbés who charged three livres a head for spectators to come into their enclosure in the Luxembourg gardens to see their ascent in a Montgolfière balloon; it took fire before take-off, to the rage of the crowd, especially when they found that the promoters had decamped with the takings.[116] When Turgot was minister, substantial rewards came to the nominal churchmen who produced handbooks on wine-making, silk production, the cultivation of beetroot, and the rectifying of hail damage. But ecclesiastical revenues were hard to come by when it was a question of merit without an immediate utilitarian contribution and unbuttressed by influential connections. Expilly, who compiled the monumental *Dictionnaire des Gaules et de la France* (6 vols., 1762–70) based on questionnaires filled in by local inhabitants, mostly the curés, waited long for government bounty, and when it came, it was meagre.[117] Nollet's invention of a device for projecting images earned him a present of books from the queen, but Boyer of the *feuille des bénéfices* refused to make an ecclesiastical sinecure available, 'the research not being of such a nature as to be recompensed from the property of the Church'. (Later experiments, making a chain of monks leap in the air by an electric shock and a study of the generative process by putting condoms on frogs, were even less eligible for ecclesiastical funding.)[118] Another devotee of experimental science turned down by Boyer was the abbé de Saint-Elier, naturalist and vivisectionist. His brother, the mathematician Maupertuis, put him forward for a benefice, and was told that 'the property of the Church ought to belong to those who serve it; if the abbé de Saint-Elier wishes to qualify, let him work for the salvation of souls, instead of amusing himself by mutilating cats'. However, influence intervened in the form of a letter from Frederick II of Prussia to the king, and a monastic sinecure had to be conferred. The abbé then gave further proof of his unworthiness by publishing a treatise anticipating La Mettrie in making men into machines, as well as warning women not to breast-feed children, advice capable of doing more harm than his philosophical rejection of moral responsibility.[119]

Life could be hard without a benefice, a sinecure, or a patron. For those who had to write saleable books or starve and who lacked the inspiration to produce works of the imagination, useful resorts were translation and compilation. Masterpieces of classical antiquity brought only modest profits, except to Jacques Delille; it was better to offer translations from newly fashionable English works (Desfontaines did well out of *Gulliver's Travels*, *Joseph Andrews*, and the *Essay on Man*). As for compilation, this was the century of encyclopedias, with the public avid for packaged information. From the abbés came dictionaries, whether conventional or of languages, neologisms, or technical terms, of notable French women and contemporary poets, of books classified for recommended reading. They also turned out anthologies—of fraud stories and of ghostly visitations, of jokes and epigrams, of extracts concerning matters of controversy or the religious Orders, of the writings of Rousseau and other luminaries, travellers' tales, literary anecdotes, and military ones. Plagiarism was the order of the day—reducing the *Encyclopédie* to five volumes for easy reference, reprinting an illustrated Dutch compendium of the religious ceremonies of all nations (taking out the sardonic references to Catholicism of the original Protestant

editors), producing a manual of military science lifting the information from the handbooks of the Prussian army (this was the abbé
Raynal's device to get a subvention out of the Foreign Office in his
earlier, penurious days). To encourage sales, the trick was to assure
the public that they were making an investment on the way to
becoming a well-informed and witty conversationalist, and to choose
intriguing titles—like 'arrows from Apollo's quiver', 'impostors
unmasked', *Almanach astronomique, géographique et qui plus est, véritable*[120]—and if the adjective 'curious' could be introduced, its
ambiguous nuances would extend the range of potential buyers still
further. The master of the compiler's art was the ex-Jesuit, the abbé
Joseph Delaporte (1713–79),[121] who always had a volume at the press,
yet found time to pour out expert reviews of plays, ballets, exhibitions of paintings, and books of every kind.[122] According to Grimm,
he produced a reference work every week and enjoyed 6,000 livres a
year—a comic exaggeration of output, but an underestimation of
earnings. Though he had the best-stocked mind in Paris, he saw
(as his play *L'Antiquaire* demonstrated) the comic side of the mania
for information which gave him his living, and he regretted that his
trade of purveyor of ephemera doomed him to remain a 'commoner'
in the world of literature, disqualifying him from election to the
aristocracy of the Academy.

While translating, editing, and compilation were natural resorts
for the abbés adventuring into the republic of letters, it might seem
unlikely that they would seek a living in writing for the theatre. Yet
one in fifty of the plays put on in Paris during the century came from
their pens.[123] Perhaps some training in the casuistry of the confessional had promoted an interest in the working of the passions, and
in an age when actors spoke in a formalized declamatory style, stints
of composing sermons for sale had given some of them a flair for the
language of the stage. Not that the subjects of their plots bore much
affinity with their erstwhile ecclesiastical vocation: Aunillon,
Allainval, and Voisenon wrote frivolous comedies with titles like *Les
Amants déguisés* (1728), *Le Mari curieux* (1731) and *La Coquette fixée*
(1746), and another abbé, an adventurer from the provinces, Pierre
Rousseau, succeeded to their speciality of amorous intrigue—calling
himself 'Rousseau de Toulouse' to be distinguished from Jean-
Jacques of Geneva, thereby causing more laughter than any of his
farcical situations.[124] Pellegrin, the widest-ranging of all the tonsured
playwrights, scored his greatest successes in tragedy, especially when
he turned from the heroes of antique Greece and Rome to the
exotic fringes, with Artaxerxes and Bajazet. The abbé Leblanc also

recognized the appeal of settings in the cruel and colourful confines of Asia, and his *Aben Said*, with its background of Persia under the successors of Genghis Khan, won applause from Voltaire and earned him 1,000 livres, a large sum for the day.[125] Perhaps abbés of the tragic stage should have turned more often to the Old Testament for themes of violence and pathos, following the way shown by the abbé Boyer's *Judith* (1695), which reduced the ladies to tears but not the men, except one who wept for Holofernes.[126] Aubert's *Mort d'Abel* (1765) did well, and Pellegrin's *Jephthe* (1732) was printed in four editions within the year, with five more to follow; while Voisenon's greatest triumphs were his oratorios on the *Madness of Saul* and the *Israelites on Mount Horeb*; he was less concerned with the severities engraved on the tablets of stone than with the thunder and lightning, and Mondonville composed suitably dramatic music.

III

A phalanx of formal apologists for Christianity replied for the establishment to the attacks of the sceptics and anticlericals of the Enlightenment; these are not counted here as abbés. Bergier, Nonnotte, Guénée, Barruel, Dom Calmet, Gros de Besplas, and the others were more tolerant, and had more common ground with their opponents than has been supposed. On points of logic and scholarly precision, they often had the better of the argument; but they could not repel the assaults on the weakest points in their defences—the concept of eternal punishment in Hell, the literal veracity of the Scriptures and miracles overturning the laws of Nature; and they lacked the extrovert talent to reply in kind to the wits and ironists operating against them.

It is not necessarily a disadvantage for an apologist to be dependent on his book sales for a living: those literary abbés who rallied to the defence of Christianity at least had the trick of being lively and readable. A few took the way of defending the faith not by joining the garrison in the ill-sited defences, but by sorties from the citadel to harass the enemy. Fréron's[127] guerrilla raids threatened the enormous reputation enjoyed by Voltaire and the deference accorded to the coterie arrogating to themselves the title of 'philosophe'. Against them he set his idol, Boileau, and the doctrines of classicism and, contrastingly, the example of Shakespeare, Young, Richardson, Prévost, and Rousseau, who recognized the spark of the divine in the doings of men and had deep resources of sympathy. '*Candide*

excites laughter,' he said, 'but leaves despair in the heart.' Combining acceptance of the Enlightenment with 'a virulent conservatism',[128] courageous to endure every insult, his standing enhanced by
his choice of lay status independent of the Church and its rewards,
Fréron was the philosophes' most dangerous adversary. He swayed
opinion not only by his triumphs, but in his defeats, for the persecution unleashed against him by scurrilous innuendo and influence
on the government revealed for all to see a strain of malice and
injustice in his would-be high-minded foes.

There was only one Fréron, but his school of counter-attack was
joined, in 1757, by a rumbustious abbé who struck a notable blow
against the philosophes, as it were by accident. This was Odet Giry
de Saint-Cyr, who in the *Mercure de France* warned against the
'Cacouacs', a tribe waging war with a venomous poison in their
tongues and by weaving illusionist spells. His pedestrian comic
invention would soon have been forgotten, but his legendary tribe
was brought to vivid life by an account of a voyage to their land
published two months later by Moreau—lawyer, historian, and royal
pensioner—embarking on satire in the cause of religion and political conservatism. Coded into his account of the illusions conjured up
by the Cacouacs were references to Diderot's materialism, Voltaire's
scepticism, and Rousseau's egalitarianism, tied together in a single
subversive design. The abbé de Saint-Cyr tried to reclaim his
property by publishing a 'catechism and manual of casuistry for the
use of the Cacouacs'; but it was Moreau who won the applause of
the public and the glory of inflicting a rare defeat on the philosophic
confraternity.[129]

In contrast to these adversarial tactics, the abbé Pluche had been
annexationist, taking the most evocative ideas of the age and combining them to present a world-view in harmony with Christian
belief. His naïve and glowing *Spectacle de la Nature* (1736) was a best-
seller: Mornet found more copies in eighteenth-century libraries
than any other work save Buffon's natural history. At once a
glorification of scientific enquiry and a precursor of Rousseauistic
deism, it is the work of a Christian believer—indeed, of a principled
Jansenist, who lost his teaching post for refusing to take the
Formulary. His preferred argument for supporting the faith is mini-
malist, irrefutable because not presenting a target area: the Church is
one of those institutions we accept as given, imposing themselves by
'l'éclat de leur notoriété'.[130] With Jansenist severity, he insists on the
Fall and the curse of unremitting toil laid upon mankind, yet he sub-
scribes to the optimism of the Enlightenment, for God has counter-

balanced the curse with the gift of sociability.[131] At the same time
Pluche was writing, the Jesuits were emulating his design to make
apologetics readable by presenting the sacred drama of redemption
as an epic tale, and in so doing had fallen foul of ecclesiastical
authority. In 1753 the abbé La Baume followed by publishing a
sequel to Milton, *La Christiade, ou le Paradis reconquis*. It came to its
crisis when Christ, triumphant over death, visits Hell. 'Adam, where
art thou?' The question that struck fear in Eden after the first transgression is now an offer of reconciliation: 4,000 years of penitence
are over. Unmoved, the parlement of Paris condemned the epic as
treating the gospel mysteries too familiarly.

Less obviously, and for the intellectual minority, apologetical
issues were involved in one of the more rarefied controversies of the
century—concerning aesthetics. Three of the literary abbés were
involved; indeed, as a formal discipline, aesthetics was their creation.
As befitted such an Olympian subject, they were not professional
authors with an eye on the market, but scholars of sophistication,
well provided with ecclesiastical benefices and enjoying an entrée to
high society; they were respectful to the Church, and one of them,
Trublet, was a zealous and committed apologist. There was already
a controversy concerning the concept of beauty, whether as an
absolute or as existing in the mind of the beholder,[132] and the abbé
Dubos, an intellectual of universal scope, diverted it into new and
more enlightening courses. Under Louis XIV and the Regency he
had been a diplomat, rewarded with a pension, an abbey, and a
canonry where he did not reside, and thereafter he wrote on archaeology, numismatics, Homer, the contrasting virtues of the Ancients
and Moderns, and finally, in later life, produced a voluminous
history of the origins of the French monarchy.[133] In 1719, soon after
his diplomatic career ended, he published his *Réflexions critiques sur la
poésie et la peinture*. There were abbés who were connoisseurs of the
visual arts (Louis Gougenot, consultant on the composition of
monuments to Pigalle, and Saint-Non, a familiar of Fragonard and
Hubert Robert);[134] Dubos did not have their expertise, but he was
widely read and a knowledgeable reviewer of theatrical performances.[135] His *Réflexions critiques* was concerned, not with artistic
techniques, but with mental attitudes: looking into the mind, he
detected a 'sixth sense' by which beauty was recognized. In the
classical tradition, he took beauty as objectively given, and he
excluded reason from challenging the findings of the sixth sense—
faced with its verdict, 'reason tells us not to reason'. A deficiency in
this sense is like blindness, an affliction incurable by thought or

application. These principles were modified by two other literary abbés, Trublet and Batteux, who sensed a lurking danger to Christianity; for what if religious feeling and devotion are similarly inspired, say, by a 'seventh sense', with some men for ever blind, incapable of conversion? Trublet rehabilitated reason in a supporting role, allowing education to play a part in developing aesthetic appreciation and, by analogy, in religious conviction; Batteux, in *Les Beaux-Arts réduits à un même principe* (1747), described the intelligence as seeing things according to their essence (that is, he makes reason all-embracing), and *goût* as seeing things in their relationship to us, bringing inspiration. Though aesthetics moved on into greater subtleties, the abbés had founded the discipline, especially Dubos. D'Alembert's *éloge* indicated dissent from Dubos' conclusions, but admitted his influence: 'il a le mérite de faire beaucoup penser . . . il a répandu la semance qui a fait naître les idées'.[136] Apart from this courteous hat doffing, there seems almost to have been a conspiracy to ignore Dubos. For all his learning, he lacked style; his presentation was formless, repetitive, and boring. Batteux, the *Encyclopédie*, and Diderot annexed his themes without acknowledgement, an author not to be praised but plagiarized.

A further theme favoured by the abbés—and this was a popular one—was the working of the mind in matters of conscience. Some wrote as apologists for Christianity, some as advocates of deism: all were high-minded, but it could not be denied that this was a lucrative genre; there was a market for improving books on moral issues—a fashion established by the end of the reign of Louis XIV, when the abbé Jean Richard's voluminous *Discours moraux* had earned him eight times what Molière got for *Tartuffe* and fifty times what Claude Fleury got for the first volume of his ecclesiastical history.[137] Some of their writing provided an entertaining reworking for lay amusement of the dour manuals of the confessional. Between 1741 and 1767 four of them published treatises, and another a novel, to wean their readers from the selfish pursuit of pleasure: separate the true pleasures from the false, recognize those pleasures recommended to us by the obligations of society, do not pursue enjoyment obsessively to hide the inner void behind personal gratification. Chaudon,[138] compiler of a successful *Dictionnaire anti-philosophique* (1767), produced a solemn work in the tradition of reconciling Christianity with worldly *savoir-faire*, *L'Homme du monde éclairé* (1774). Inclining rather to the arguments of the Enlightenment were Sauri's *La Morale du citoyen du monde, ou la morale de la raison* and Duval Pirrau's *Code de la raison*.[139] In them, Christian morality was equated with the dictates of reason, with the unavoidable implication that even if revelation was abandoned, the moral code would remain intact.[140]

From discussion of morality in general, the literary abbés inevitably moved into the long-running controversy over whether works of the imagination, particularly novels, ought to have a moral content. The Jesuit *Mémoires de Trévoux* continually expressed the case for constraints, pugnaciously summed up in 1736 in an oration by Père Porée: the unfettered working of the imagination can threaten morals and be aesthetically disastrous, overthrowing the classical ideal of 'a controlled reworking of nature'.[141] The abbés who joined in the controversy were sufficiently influenced by the notion to hedge their approval of the novel with conditions. The most liberal was Granet, who in 1730 declared that the 'only rule' was 'to please and to amuse', though he insisted on realism of plot and setting—no need to moralize, but foster no illusions, present things as they really are.[142] The test of a novel for Desfontaines was to ask if it presented 'un tableau de la vie humaine', though anything dangerous to religion must be excluded.[143] According to Leblanc, the fault of romances was their all-too-frequent superficiality, and he unchivalrously blamed the ladies for creating the demand for frivolous literature. The reactionary clerical line was taken by the abbé Jaquin, in his *Entretiens sur les romans, ouvrage moral et critique* (1758); it was wrong to present a picture of manners without adding criticism, and he complained especially of romances implying marriage to be the 'self-giving of hearts', independent of 'vain ceremonies', an attack on Prévost's *Cleveland* and Rousseau's *Nouvelle Héloïse*. Further solemnities came from the abbé Chasles in 1785, in his *Timanti*,[144] denouncing authors who rise in the world by writing without serious purpose; he rose himself in consequence, for the archbishop of Tours rewarded him with a canonry. Two examples of the serious purpose which Chasles was demanding had just been published by churchmen, masterpieces of didactic fiction, best-selling and saccharine: Gérard's *Le Comte de Valmont ou les égarements de la raison* (1774), and Maydieu's *Histoire de la vertueuse portugaise, ou le modèle des femmes chrétiennes* (1779). They used the current vogue of *sensibilité* to recommend Christian doctrine and morality, though perhaps they involuntarily contributed to the evolution of fashion towards sentimental deism.

The intellectual warfare between the Christian apologists and the philosophes, in spite of its complexities, is straightforward to chronicle; but almost insuperable difficulties arise concerning an allied, but less tangible, issue in the literature of the Enlightenment—how to define the relationship of traditional Christianity to the tide of Rousseauism which swept on to the cult of 'sensibilité' at the end of the *ancien régime*. Directly or deviously, all the roads of the century lead to this destination, innumerable writers being involved in the creation of an optimistic deism incorporating the magic and wonder of nature and excluding the darkness of sin and the harsh necessity of redemption. Did the abbés play a significant role, whether by tacitly limiting apologetical arguments to the more defensible frontiers of belief, or by airing religious convictions allied to scepticism about revelation, or, like Delille,[145] according respect to the old convictions but reserving enthusiasm for the new? An impressionistic sketch of the eighteenth-century abbés can do no more than pose the question. It could be that it is from the *sensibilité* of those years and its associated 'culte des tombeaux'[146] that the 'religion populaire' of today arises, a creedless hope of reunion beyond the grave, a lingering residue of an abandoned Christianity, all that is left to cling to in the shadow of death. Perhaps the abbés, masters of the art of balancing between Church and world, played a part in shaping this last decadent compromise of all.

Everywhere in the towns of eighteenth-century France, wearers of the *petit collet* and the *bonnet carré* were to be seen, sauntering in the streets, showing off in salons and provincial academies, leading claques in the theatres or at ease in the boxes, tutoring the sons of the rich, administering households, their exploits enlivening the newsletters and figuring in novels, their names on the title-pages of books, successful or remaindered. They were a unique phenomenon on the margins of a Church whose dominance over men's minds faltered even as its power in social relationships remained, whose wealth was out of proportion to its needs and in contradiction to its ideals, which was so completely absorbed into the life of the nation that vocation to its service was a routine. The abbés were utterly diverse in their activities, a disparate group defying generalization; their common defining characteristics were eligibility to wear a costume and assume a title and to qualify for an ecclesiastical income without duties to perform. Their cloth gained them a modicum of consideration, though they thereby made the cloth of others, the serious clergy, less respected. Their presence blurred the boundaries between Church and world. A composite picture derived from examples over the space of three generations makes them look more interesting than they were; so many whose doings were not recorded were provincial nonentities or Parisian failures. But a collage of the more noteworthy figures at least gives a fair reflection of the impression the abbés made on public opinion. They provided amusement, inspired gossip, brokered ideas, and could be useful; but taken together, they constituted an abuse, a picturesque excrescence on society too expensive to be allowed continued maintenance as the nation slid towards bankruptcy. By their accepted status as drones, they were an incitement to anticlericals to propose the confiscation of the ecclesiastical wealth so many of them so cheerfully misappropriated.

NOTES

CHAPTER I

With the permission of the Clarendon Press I have used my chapter from *Christian Authority: Essays in Honour of Henry Chadwick*, ed. G. L. Evans (1988), as the first section here.

1. Blue coats, white breeches, red stockings, red facings on waistcoats, white belts ('Les Gardes Françaises à Versailles', *Rev. Versailles* (1915), 10). Other details in Claude Manceron, *Les Hommes de la liberté* (2 vols., 1972), i. 208, and P. de Nolhac, *La Reine Marie-Antoinette* (1948), 97–102.
2. The abbé J.-A. de Véri, *Journal*, ed. J. de Witte (2 vols., n.d.), i. 68. Cf. Mme du Deffand to the duchesse de Choiseul, 25 Feb. 1772. *Correspondance complète de Mme du Deffand avec la duchesse de Choiseul, l'abbé Barthélemy et M. Craufort*, ed. Sainte-Aulaire (3 vols., 1880), ii. 138.
3. J. Gog, *A Reims, le sacre des rois de France* (1980), 95.
4. The maréchal de Croÿ, *Journal 1718–1784*, ed. le vicomte de Grouchy and P. Cottin (4 vols., 1906), iii. 173.
5. L. S. Greenbaum, *Talleyrand Statesman-Priest* (1970), 18.
6. *Mémoires du prince de Talleyrand*, ed. the duc de Broglie (5 vols., 1891–2), i. 24. Otherwise, just the vague 'tout était amour! tout était fêtes!'
7. Account in the *Correspondance secrète*, conveniently given in A. Chéruel, *Dictionnaire historique des institutions, mœurs et coutumes de la France* (2 vols., 1855), ii. 1118.
8. Ibid. 1119.
9. See H. Jadart (ed.), 'Journal anonyme', *Trav. Acad. nat. Reims* (1902), 269–315. For description of the sacred object and for its final fate, G. Laurent, 'Le Conventionnel Rühl à Reims: la destruction de la Sainte Ampoule', *Ann. hist. Rév. fr.* (1926), 26.
10. Full wording in Chéruel, *Dictionnaire*, ii. 1119.
11. Gog, *A Reims*, 65.
12. Croÿ, *Journal*, iii. 184; A. N. Duchesne, 'Relation d'un voyage à Reims à l'occasion du Sacre', *Trav. Acad. nat. Reims* (1902), 48.
13. Chéruel, *Dictionnaire*, ii. 1120. The archaic titles had been annexed to the Crown, and the king nominated the six relatives who were to bear them (*Encyclopédie, ou dictionnaire raisonné des Sciences, des Arts et des Métiers*, xiv (1765), 476, s.v. 'Sacre'). The sardonic comment is Manceron's, *Les Hommes*, 215.
14. In fact, a crown made in the late twelfth century for a queen. An identical one for the king had been stolen.
15. H. Destainville, 'La Jeunesse de Danton', *Ann. hist. Rév. fr.* (1928), 427–8.

16. Nolhac, *Marie-Antoinette*, 102; Duchesne, 'Relation', 47; Croÿ, *Journal*, iii. 188.

17. Marie-Antoinette, in *Correspondance secrète entre Marie-Thérèse et le Cte de Mercy-Argenteau avec les lettres de Marie-Thérèse et Marie-Antoinette*, ed. A. d'Arneth and M. A. Geffroy (3 vols., 1875), ii. 343. For the queen's tears etc. see Mercy d'Argenteau's letter, p. 346.

18. F. Masson, *Le Cardinal de Bernis depuis son ministère, 1758–94* (1884), 193 n.

19. Manceron, *Les Hommes*, 223–5.

20. Croÿ, *Journal*, iii. 203–5.

21. Liturgy given in full in Gog, *A Reims*, 61–88.

22. Chéruel, *Dictionnaire*, ii. 1120.

23. M. Bloch, *Les Rois thaumaturges*, trans. J. E. Anderson, *The Royal Touch* (1973), 126–8.

24. J.-J. Chifflet, *Tractatus de sancta Ampulla Remensi*, cited by Gog, *A Reims*, 20. For others, see J. W. Merrick, *The Desacralization of the French Monarchy in the 18th Century* (1990), 21.

25. Letter of 18 June 1740 to Frederick II, in *Corresp.* x (1954), 161 (letter 2110).

26. B. Plongeron, *Théologie et politique au siècle des lumières, 1770–1820* (1973), 64–5.

27. For a defence of the royal power see E. Regnault, *Dissertation touchant le pouvoir accordé aux Rois de France de guérir les Escroüelles, accompagnée de preuves touchant la vérité de la Sainte Ampoule* (1722). Regnault was a canon of Saint-Symphorien of Reims.

28. Bloch, *Les Rois*, 224. See also Voltaire, *Mœurs*, introduction. No less a celebrity than Jansenius had pointed out that the curing of king's evil demonstrated only God's gifts, not a king's right to rule. Balaam's ass had prophesied, but had no right to dominate other animals: R. E. Mousnier, *The Institutions of France under the Absolute Monarchy, 1598–1789*, i, trans. B. Pearce (1974), 675.

29. Luynes, i. 116–17, 154, 426. Barbier, iii. 167. For Louis XV's statement that he did not exercise his healing power because he was not in a state of grace see Merrick, *Desacralization*, 19.

30. Durand de Maillane, *Dictionnaire de droit canonique et de pratique bénéficiale*, 3rd edn. (1776), v. 225, s.v. 'Sacre'.

31. D'Aguesseau (H.-F. Chancelier), *Essai d'une institution du droit public*, ed. L. Rigaud (1955), 123.

32. *Encyclopédie*, xiv. 476.

33. K. M. Baker, 'French Political Thought at the Accession of Louis XVI', *J. Mod. Hist.* (1978), 279–81. For Baker's view of the background, the 'new political culture' arising at the end of the *ancien régime*, see his 'On the Problem of the Ideological Origins of the French Revolution', in D. La Capra and S. L. Kaplan (eds.), *Modern European Intellectual History* (1982), 197–219.

34. *Correspondance secrète*, in Chéruel, *Dictionnaire*, ii. 1120.

35. D. Bien, 'Catholic Magistrates and Protestant Marriage', *Fr. Hist. St.* (1962), 409–25. For the neat legal arguments used, see Guyot, iii, 318–39.

36. D. Dakin, *Turgot* (1939), 217–21.

37. M. C. Peronnet, 'Les Assemblées du Clergé de France sous le règne de Louis XVI, 1775–1788', *Ann. hist. Rév. Fr.* (1962), 29, 31.

38. Ch. Robert, *Urbain de Hercé, dernier évêque de Dol* (1900), 162–3, 183.
39. R. A. Schneider, *The Ceremonial City: Toulouse Observed, 1738–80* (1995), 161–5. For the more general picture, Schneider cites M. Fogel, *Les Cérémonies de l'information dans la France du XVIᵉ au XVIIIᵉ siècle* (1989).
40. For these events in Paris see Barbier, ii. 77, 49–54; iii. 547, 551; Marais, i. 477, 499–500; Barbier, ii. 366–8.
41. A. Delahante, *Une Famille de finance au XVIIIᵉ siècle* (2 vols., 1881), i. 197.
42. A. Bernard, *Le Sermon au XVIIIᵉ siècle, 1715–89* (1901), 276–7.
43. Merrick, *Desacralization*, 125.
44. *Sur les devoirs des Rois*, Palm Sunday, 1662, in *Sermons* (9 vols., 1772), vii. 220–55.
45. A. Sicard, *L'Ancien Clergé de France: les évêques avant la Révolution* (1912), 185.
46. Oath in full in Masson, *Le Cardinal de Bernis*, 37.
47. Guyot, xiv. 254.
48. *Sermon sur les écueils de la piété des grands* (Petit Carême), Massillon, *Œuvres* (14 vols., 1822) vi. 151–76.
49. Cited by A. Mathiez, *Rome et le clergé français sous la Constituante* (1911), 460.
50. Plongeron, *Théologie*, 64–5.
51. Ibid. 115–19.
52. P. Quesnel, *La Discipline de l'Église tirée du Nouveau Testament* (1689), and idem, *La Souveraineté des Rois défendue contre l'Histoire Latine de Melchior Leydecker* (1704), in R. Taveneaux, *Jansénisme et politique* (1965), 124–33.
53. *P.V. Ass.* vii. 1886 (1745).
54. Bossuet, *Politique tirée des propres paroles de l'Écriture Sainte*, ed. J. Lebrun (1967), p. i.
55. Bossuet, *Œuvres Oratoires*, ed. J. Lebarq (6 vols., 1921), iv. 356. Cf. *Politique*, viii (i).
56. Mousnier, *Institutions*, 312–31.
57. J. Rogister, 'The Crisis of 1753–4 in France and the Debate on the Nature of the Monarchy and of the Fundamental Laws', in R. Vierhaus (ed.), *Herrschaftsverträge, Wahlkapitulationen, Fundamentalgesetze* (1977), 105–20. Cf. the gifts of ecclesiastical ornaments the king had to give to the chapter of Reims and to the tomb of Charlemagne at Aix-la-Chapelle: Papillon de la Ferté, *Journal, 1756–80*, ed. E. Boysse (1887), 383–5.
58. M. Antoine, *Le Conseil du Roi sous la règne de Louis XV* (1970), 7–8.
59. Ibid., 15–17.
60. R. Bickart, *Les Parlements et la notion de souveraineté nationale au XVIIIᵉ siècle* (1932), is devoted to this theme.
61. Baker, 'French Political Thought', 279–83.
62. R. L. Herbert, *David, Voltaire, Brutus and the French Revolution: An Essay in Art and Politics* (1972), 15–61, 71–4.
63. L. Voyer de Boutigny (1682), cited by H. Leclerq, *Histoire de la Régence* (3 vols., 1921), vol. i, p. xvi.
64. Marais, iv. 288.
65. D'Aguesseau, *Mémoire* (1718), in J. Carreyre, *Le Jansénisme durant la Régence* (3 vols., 1929–33), ii. 41.
66. Gerbier (*avocat*), cited by L. M. Raison, 'Le Jansénisme à Rennes', *Ann. Bretagne* (1941), 255–6.
67. Guyot, ix. 302.

68. Mousnier, *Institutions*, 315.
69. Gerbier, cited by Raison, 'Le Jansénisme'.
70. Guyot, lxiv. 5–14.
71. The argument that First Estate means 'the Church' rather than 'the Clergy' was not discussed outside clerical circles.
72. Guyot, xi. 290–1; xlvii. 187–92.
73. Père H. Griffet, *Mémoires pour servir à l'histoire de Louis, Dauphin de France* (2 vols., 1777), i. 124–6.
74. *P.V. Ass.* viii/2. 421 (1765).
75. Ibid.
76. Ibid., 425–6.
77. Dom Rémi Carré, *Recueil curieux et édifiant, sur les cloches de l'Église, avec les cérémonies de leur bénédiction* (1759), 67–8.
78. *P.V. Ass.* viii/2. 429.
79. D. Van Kley, 'Church, State and the Ideological Origins of the French Revolution: The Debate over the General Assembly of the Gallican Clergy in 1765', *J. Mod. Hist.* (1979), 629–51.
80. *P.V. Ass.* viii/1. 102–7.
81. Ibid., viii/2. 2313 (1775).
82. J.-M. Goulemot, *Discours, histoire et révolution* (1975), 259–70.
83. Cited by G. Weulersse, *Les Physiocrates* (1931), 311.
84. Maugard, *Remarques sur la noblesse dédiées aux assemblées provinciales* (1787), cited by Y. Durand, *Les Fermiers Généraux au XVIIIᵉ siècle* (1971), 227.
85. *Journal de l'Assemblée des Notables de 1787 par le comte de Brienne, et Loménie de Brienne, archevêque de Toulouse*, ed. P. Chevallier (1960), 149.

CHAPTER 2

1. Guyot, iv. 60–2.
2. Ibid. x. 365.
3. Luynes, xi. 389; iv. 84; viii. 437, 440, 137; iii. 298; v. 288; E. Lavaquery, *Le Cardinal de Boisgelin* (2 vols., 1920), i. 316; Mme du Hausset, *The Private Memoirs of Louis XV* (Eng. trans. 1895), 20–1; the maréchal de Croÿ, *Journal, 1718–84*, ed. the vicomte de Grouchy and P. Cottin (4 vols., 1906), i. 439–40.
4. The actual office gave revenues of 14,400 livres, of which 6,000 was as a commander of the Ordre du Saint-Esprit (Guyot, iv. 62). He named chaplains of regiments, and had the hospital of the Quinze-Vingts and the convent of the Assumption under his jurisdiction (Luynes, vi. 260).
5. A. Sicard, *L'Ancien Clergé de France: les évêques avant la Révolution* (1912), 209–13.
6. Georgel, *Mémoires pour servir à l'histoire de la fin du 18ᵉ siècle* (6 vols., 1820), ii. 5–6, 11–18.
7. Sicard, *L'Ancien Clergé*, 209–15.
8. Luynes, ii. 410–12; iv. 100; viii. 469.
9. L. Bassette, *Jean de Caulet, évêque de Grenoble* (1946), 16–17. Cf. *Mémoires de la duchesse de Brancas*, ed. E. Asse (1890): 'La chapelle du Roi était, pour les jeunes ecclésiastiques, une autre espèce de séminaire qui les préparait à entrer dans le monde, comme les mousquetaires en étaient une pour ceux

qui se destinaient au service.'

10. F. Masson, *Le Cardinal de Bernis depuis son ministère, 1758–94* (1884), 426.

11. Luynes, iii. 423; vii. 298. For the importance of the office see Saint-Simon (Pléiade), iii. 447–8.

12. J. Levron, *La Vie quotidienne à la Cour de Versailles* (1965), 40–53, 135. Saint-Simon's account (iv. 1081–92) of Louis XIV's religious observances in his pious later years differs somewhat.

13. Luynes, i. 228–31; iv. 114.

14. Ibid. i. 235; iv. 115.

15. Ibid. i. 345; iv. 116–17; vi. 405; ix. 77.

16. Mme de Campan, *Mémoires* (2 vols., 1822), i. 316.

17. Luynes, iii. 367; iv. 13; vii. 283.

18. Ibid. i. 427–8; vii. 276.

19. Strictly, the rules of the Lazarists forbade any of their members to take episcopal rank.

20. E. Houth, *Versailles, la paroisse royale* (1962), 36–8, 46, 59, 63, 111–14, 138. Similar figures from the archbishop's visitation of 1784: 45,000 parishioners, 14 priests (A. Joly, 'La Paroisse de Notre-Dame de Versailles pendant la Révolution', *Rev. Versailles* (1973–5), 33).

21. Saint-Simon, iv. 1094.

22. Luynes, ii. 176; M. Leroy, 'Une Visite à l'église Notre-Dame de Versailles', *Rev. Versailles* (1912), 215.

23. Houth, *Versailles*, 42–4. He was also there for a Te Deum on 4 Sept.

24. Luynes, v. 458.

25. Ibid. xiii. 2. The last *fête-Dieu* at the parish with the Court present was on 11 June 1789. The procession for the opening of the Estates General started here, 4 May 1789 (*Gazette de France*, 12 May 1789).

26. Y. Bezard, 'L'Assistance à Versailles sous l'ancien régime', *Rev. Versailles* (1919), 67–80, 242–51.

27. P. Bienvenue, 'La Manufacture royale de dentelles et de blondes établie pour l'instruction des enfants pauvres de Versailles', *Rev. Versailles* (1954), 18.

28. C. Kunstler, *La Vie quotidienne sous la Régence* (1960), 185.

29. Signing himself 'curé' (E. Mennet de Goutel, 'L'Exposition de Marie-Antoinette à la bibliothèque de Versailles', *Rev. Versailles* (1929), 107). See also the list of baptisms, weddings, and funerals of the royal family, and the families of Orléans, Condé, Conti, Bourbon, Maine, and Penthièvre in L.-A. Gatin, 'Les Anciens Registres de l'état civil de Versailles', *Rev. Versailles* (1913), 27–31.

30. P. de Nolhac, *Louis XV et Marie Leczinski* (1922), 80.

31. Saint-Simon, iii. 845.

32. Luynes, iii. 208.

33. Ibid. xi. 399–402.

34. P. Fromageot, 'La Mort et les obsèques de Mme de Pompadour', *Rev. Versailles* (1902), 275–87; M. Tourneux, 'Un Mot célèbre qui n'a jamais été prononcé', *Rev. Versailles* (1903), 25–6.

35. The queen went to Paris, Sept. 1728, to Notre-Dame and Sainte-Geneviève to pray for a male heir (Nolhac, *Louis XV et Marie Leczinski*, 143–7).

36. Saint-Simon, iii. 644.

37. Luynes, viii. 361–3.

38. Saint-Simon, vii. 262–4.
39. Luynes, i. 228; vi. 213; vii. 277; viii. 167–70. (For duchesses claiming the monopoly of parasols at the Corpus Christi procession, see v. 35.)
40. Luynes, vii. 358–9; xi. 411.
41. Ibid. i. 436–7; ii. 3.
42. Ibid. vi. 138–9.
43. Guyot, xv. 295–6. *P.V. Ass.* vi. 1769–75 (1723). Other clashes: ibid. vi. 1493, 1169, 1232–4.
44. Luynes, vii. 51–2.
45. Ibid. ix. 74 n.
46. Ibid. ix. 73.
47. Ibid. i. 111–12.
48. Ibid. vii. 357.
49. 'Les Obsèques de Louis XIV et de Louis XV', *Rev. Versailles* (1907), 70–3. Cf. the plot of bishops to get better chairs at the dauphin's funeral in 1712 (Saint-Simon, iii. 1190–1).
50. Saint-Simon (Pléiade), iv. 531.
51. Luynes, i. 107–8.
52. E. Oroux, *Histoire ecclésiastique de la Cour de France* (2 vols., 1777), ii. 633–4.
53. François-Joachim de Pierre, cardinal de Bernis, *Mémoires et lettres*, ed. F. Masson (2 vols., 1878), i. 45.
54. Sicard, *L'Ancien Clergé*, 209.
55. A. Bernard, *Le Sermon au XVIIIᵉ siècle, 1715–89* (1901), 42–3.
56. Ibid. 119.
57. Ibid. 120; Luynes, v. 53.
58. Luynes, iii. 129; iv. 88; xiii. 148; xvi. 354. See also iv. 15; xi. 392; xiv. 405–6, and D'Argenson, viii. 265–6.
59. Luynes, iv. 114.
60. Ibid. iv. 263–4.
61. Ibid. xi. 392.
62. Ibid. viii. 21–2. (For a canon of Sens who had not prepared an alternative, see vii. 139.)
63. Ibid. ix. 7.
64. Ibid. iv. 15.
65. Barbier, ii. 456–7.
66. D'Argenson, vi. 370, 378 (Mar. 1751).
67. Ibid. viii. 265–6; Luynes, xiii. 228.
68. Luynes, xiv. 405–6.
69. E. and J. de Goncourt, *La du Barry* (1880), 178.
70. J. Levron, *Un Libertin fastueux, le maréchal de Richelieu* (1971), 383–5.
71. A. Rosne, *M. de Beauvais, évêque de Senez, 1731–1790* (1883), 35–7.
72. Bachaumont, vii. 114 (7 Feb. 1774).
73. J. Truchet, *La Prédication de Bossuet* (2 vols., 1960), ii. 219–21.
74. Ibid. ii. 223.
75. P. Girault de Coursac, *L'Éducation d'un Roi. Louis XVI* (1972), 252–3.
76. Métra, vi. 181–2 (23 Apr. 1778). (Voltaire was in Paris, and the abbé de Beauregard had attacked him in his Lenten sermons (ibid. vi. 183).)
77. Sicard, *L'Ancien Clergé*, 209.
78. Luynes, ii. 227.

79. G. Minois, *Le Confesseur du roi* (1988), 493–7.
80. Ibid. 508.
81. According to Hardy, *Mes loisirs*, ed. M. Tourneux and M. Vitrac (1912), 7, the Jesuits helped his father, a grocer of the faubourg Saint-Antoine, when he went bankrupt, then promoted his own ecclesiastical career by taking him on as a sacristan. For the story that the Jesuits even wanted to have the dauphin's *valet de chambre* as one of theirs, see 'Mémoires de Marc-Antoine Thierry, baron du ville d'Auray', *Rev. Versailles* (1908), 84.
82. R. Roux, 'L'Abbé Madier archiprêtre de Paris, confesseur de Mesdames, 1725–1799', *Rev. Versailles* (1924), 21–39.
83. Montesquieu, *Lettres persanes*, letter 107, ed. L. Versini (1995), 215. The two powers are rivals under a young king, allies under an old.
84. J. Sareil, *Les Tencin: histoire d'une famille au XVIIIᵉ siècle* (1969), 362–5.
85. Bernis, *Mémoires*, ii. 70–1. For Desmaretz's appointment in 1753 see E. Regnault, *Christophe de Beaumont, archevêque de Paris, 1703–81* (2 vols., 1882), i. 247–8.
86. Girault de Coursac, *L'Éducation*, 214–15; Minois, *Le Confesseur*, 511–15.
87. See L. Dussieux, *Le Château de Versailles* (2 vols., 1881), ii. 108–12, and L. Deshàirs, 'Documents inédits sur la chapelle du château de Versailles, 1689–1772', *Rev. Versailles* (1905), 241–62.
88. Deshàirs, 'Documents', 261–2.
89. La Bruyère, *Les Caractères*, viii. 74, ed. R. Barthes (1965), 240.
90. Luynes, v. 95 (June 1743).
91. Ch. Hirschauer, 'Les Premières Expériences aérostatiques à Versailles', *Rev. Versailles* (1916), 39–40.
92. Bachaumont, xiii. 251–2 (12 Jan. 1779). Taken as a plot to hint that Louis XVI was not the father by G. Walter, *Le Comte de Provence* (1950), 97.
93. P. de Nolhac, *Marie-Antoinette, Dauphine* (1896), 102; A. N. Duchesne, 'Relation d'un voyage à Reims à l'occasion du Sacre de Louis XVI', *Trav. Acad. nat. Reims* (1902), 47.
94. J. Flammermont, *La Journée du 14 Juillet 1789* (1892), pp. clxxv–vi.
95. Ascribed to Mme de Lafayette.
96. F. Evrard, 'Les Mœurs à Versailles sous Louis XVI', *Rev. Versailles* (1928), 95–204.
97. Mme de Campan, *Mémoires*, i. 12–13.
98. P. de Nolhac, *Louis XV à Versailles* (1934), 19–28.
99. L. Madelin, *Le Crépuscule de la monarchie* (1936), 112.
100. Cited by G. Poisson, *M. de Saint-Simon* (1973), 187.
101. Y. Coirault, *L'Optique de Saint-Simon* (1965), 302, 465–6, 576–7. For the injustice to Le Tellier, see P. Bliard, *Les Mémoires de Saint-Simon et le père le Tellier* (1891).
102. Mme du Hausset, *Private Memoirs*, 42.
103. Croÿ, *Journal*, i. 353.
104. J. N. Dufort, comte de Cheverny, *Mémoires sur les règnes de Louis XV et Louis XVI* (2 vols., 1886), i. 173 (date *c.*1755).
105. Mme du Hausset, *Private Memoirs*, 44.
106. Levron, *La Vie quotidienne*, 132.
107. See J. McManners, *Death and the Enlightenment* (1981), for the qualifications made by the theologians.

108. Croÿ, *Journal*, iii. 88, 109.

109. If gossip is to be believed, Louis insisted that the teenage girls he kept in his harem at the Parc aux Cerfs, attend mass, and say their prayers before going to bed with him ([J. L. Soulavie], *Mémoires historiques et anecdotes de la cour de France pendant la faveur de la marquise de Pompadour* (1802), 237–8).

110. Nolhac, *Marie-Antoinette*, 323, says his last Easter duty was in 1736. Luynes, however (i. 350), says in 1737 that the king's custom is to communicate five times yearly.

111. Croÿ, *Journal*, iii. 97.

112. Luynes, vi. 47–8, 85.

113. Croÿ, *Journal*, i. 366; Dufort, *Mémoires*, i. 182, 188.

114. D'Argenson, ix. 196–8; Luynes, xv. 324–5; Croÿ, *Journal*, iii. 335–8.

115. G. Desnoiresterres, *Voltaire et la société française au XVIIIe siècle*, 2nd edn. (8 vols., 1867–76), v. 196–7.

116. E. and J. de Goncourt, *Mme de Pompadour* (1888), 124. Soubise called on her husband to warn him not to.

117. Croÿ, *Journal*, ii. 137.

118. Luynes, i. 113–14; vi. p. iii; x. 19. D'Argenson, viii. 77 (19 July 1753).

119. D'Argenson, vii. 16–17.

120. Luynes, vi. 419; vii. 91. Girault de Coursac, *L'Éducation*, 19–20.

121. E. and J. de Goncourt, *Marie-Antoinette* (1875), 34–5.

122. Luynes, xi. 423. Cf. Mme de Campan, *Mémoires*, i. 29.

123. Girault de Coursac, *L'Éducation*, 33; D'Argenson, vii. 100–1, 130, 179–80.

124. [J. L. Soulavie], *Mémoires historiques et politiques du règne de Louis XVI* (6 vols., 1801).

125. Ph. Mansel, *Louis XVIII* (1981), 12.

126. Police report of 1765 that du Barry slept with her daily but also farmed her out to the great, on this particular day to the maréchal de Richelieu and the marquis de Villeroy (cited by M. Mansergh, 'The Revolution of 1771' (Oxford Ph.D. thesis, 1973), 90–100).

127. Walter, *Le Comte de Provence*, 15–16.

128. Campan, *Mémoires*, i. 336 ff.; Nolhac, *Marie-Antoinette*, 323–5; E. and J. de Goncourt, *La du Barry*, 1–2.

129. Nolhac, *Marie-Antoinette*, 326.

130. Croÿ, *Journal*, iii. 100–1.

131. Nolhac, *Marie-Antoinette*, 328.

132. Croÿ, *Journal*, iii. 104.

133. Sicard, *L'Ancien Clergé*, 202.

134. *Lettre de Voltaire à M. de Beauvais, évêque de Senez*, in App. X of A. de Coulanges, *La Chaire française au 18e siècle* (1901), 524.

135. R. Metz, *La Monarchie française et la provision des bénéfices ecclésiastiques en Alsace, 1648–1789* (1947), 65 ff. The Crown collected the revenues of these benefices in the vacancies (ten months was the limit of vacancy, and once a nomination was made, only one-third of the revenue was appropriated until the taking of possession). There was a bureau, the *Œconomats*, of six *conseillers d'État* and four *maîtres des requêtes* to handle these revenues—they went to pension converted Protestants and to support new parishes in which the king had an interest (e.g. Saint-Louis at Versailles). See Luynes, xvi. 472–3 (June 1758).

136. See Ch. 20 below.

137. *Relation de la Cour de France en 1690, par Ézéchiel Spanheim, envoyé . . . de Brandenbourg*, ed. M. Ch. Schefer (Soc. de l'histoire de France, 1882), 278–9.

138. M. Antoine, *Le Conseil du Roi sous le règne de Louis XV* (1970), 61.

139. Dom H. Leclercq, *Histoire de la Régence* (3 vols., 1921), i. 403.

140. Métra, vi. 199–200 (1778).

141. Bernis, *Mémoires et lettres*, i. 40.

142. Marais, i. 36–7, 49–51.

143. Bernis, *Mémoires*, Masson's Introduction, i. p. xxvii.

144. E. Appolis, *Le Jansénisme dans le diocèse de Lodève* (1952), 72–3.

145. Luynes, xi. 3 (Jan. 1751).

146. Bernis, *Mémoires*, i. 73–4.

147. Ibid. i. 81; Luynes, vii. 269–70: Sicard, *L'Ancien Clergé*, 496.

148. D'Argenson, iv. 213. (Cf. the Jansenist Pavie de Fourquevaux, *Catéchisme historique et dogmatique* (1768), iii. 259–60; cited by Appolis, *Le Jansénisme*, 239.)

149. D'Argenson, iv. 214.

150. Bernis, *Mémoires*, i. 81–2. For his severity—refusing a bishopric to the nephew of a bishop because of a madrigal—see C. Collé, *J. hist.* (1911), 193–4.

151. Letter to Tercier, 3 Feb. 1764, in *Correspondance secrète inédite de Louis XV sur la politique étrangère*, ed. E. Boutaric (2 vols., 1866), i. 311–12.

152. To the duchesse de Choiseul, 25 Feb. 1772: *Correspondance complète de Mme du Deffand avec la duchesse de Choiseul*, ed. M. de Sainte-Aulaire (3 vols., 1877), ii. 138.

153. P. Vial, 'L'Église de France vue par le nonce en 1766', *Cahiers hist.* (1963), 109.

154. Louis d'Illiers, *Deux prélats de l'ancien régime: les Jarente* (1948), 29–32.

155. Ibid. 32.

156. Sicard, *L'Ancien Clergé*, 508 n.

157. To the duchesse de Choiseul, 25 Feb. 1772 (cf. n. 152).

158. J.-A. de Véri, *Journal*, ed. J. de Witte (2 vols., n.d.), ii. 68–9.

159. Ch. Monternot, *Yves-Alex. de Marbeuf, . . . archevêque de Lyon, 1734–99* (1911), 11–19.

160. Bachaumont, xxii. 296–7 (May 1783). The abbé de Bourbon, son of Mlle de Romans, wandered in Italy and died at Naples in 1787.

161. Métra, v. 261–2 (11 Nov. 1777).

162. Mme de Campan, *Mémoires*, i. 237 (a secret agreement at Court to keep all priories for nobles; she was censured by Vermond because she obtained a priory for a curé).

163. D'Argenson, iv. 213; viii. 453.

164. Vial, 'L'Église', 109.

165. F. de Saint-Just, *Témoins de quatre siècles* (1962), 194.

166. *Lettres de Turgot à la duchesse d'Enville, 1764–74, 1777–80*, ed. J. Rowet (Travaux de la Faculté de Philosophie et des Lettres de l'Université Catholique de Louvain, 1976), 148.

167. Voltaire, *Corresp.* lxxxi. 139–40 (Mar. 1772).

168. The baron A. de Maricourt, 'Lettres de l'abbé Le Gouz au baron de Gémeaux', *Rev. quest. hist.* (1914), 120–1.

169. A Sicard, *La Nomination aux bénéfices ecclésiastiques avant 1789* (1896), 12.

CHAPTER 3

1. H. Doniol, *Le Comte de Vergennes et F. M. Hennin* (1898), 89–90.
2. *Éloge de Reinhard*, cited by F. Masson, *Le Cardinal de Bernis, la suppression des Jésuites* (1884), i. p. xi.
3. François-Joachim de Pierre, cardinal de Bernis, *Mémoires et lettres*, ed. F. Masson (2 vols., 1878), ii. 88.
4. His reports in A. de Saint-Priest, *Histoire de la chute des jésuites* (1846), app. V.
5. Bernis, *Mémoires*, i. 77.
6. The abbé J.-A. de Véri, *Journal*, ed. J. de Witte (2 vols., n.d.), i. 2–3, 5–8, 33, 37.
7. For these two see Bernis, *Mémoires*, Masson's notes at i. 275, 171.
8. Guyot, ix. 252–9; J. F. Bluche, *L'Origine des magistrats du Parlement de Paris au XVIIIe siècle, 1715–71* (1956), 58, 61, 96–7, 194–5, 218, 221–4, 361, 367–8; G. Desnoiresterres, *Voltaire et la société française au XVIIIe siècle*, 2nd edn. (8 vols., 1867–76), vii. 388–90; B. de Lacombe, *La Résistance janséniste: l'abbé Nigon de Berty, 1704–77* (1948). A new study of the *conseillers-clercs* has just appeared: W. Doyle, 'Secular Simony: The Clergy and the Sale of Offices in 18th-Century France', in N. Aston (ed.), *Religious Change in Europe, 1650–1914* (1997), 135–47.
9. A. Tuetey, *Répertoire général des sources manuscrites de l'histoire de Paris pendant la Révolution* (11 vols., 1890–1914), i. 296, 328.
10. J. McManners, *Death and the Enlightenment* (1981), 381–9.
11. Mme de Sévigné, *Lettres*, ed. G. Gailly (3 vols., Pléiade, 1953), i. 573 (20 June 1672).
12. F. de Dainville, *La Géographie des humanistes* (1940), 257–8.
13. M.-C. Varachaud, 'La Formation des aumôniers de la Marine du Roi Soleil', *Rev. hist. Église Fr.* (1994), 65–83.
14. Guyot, iv. 65.
15. M. Giraud, 'La Crise de conscience et l'autorité à la fin du règne de Louis XIV', *Ann.* (1952), 294–7.
16. A. Carré, 'Notes sur l'histoire de la médecine du travail et l'ergomanie dans la marine', *Rev. hist. écon. sociale* (1969), 271–3; A. Cabantous and J. Messiaen, *Gens de mer à Dunkerque aux XVIIe et XVIIIe siècles* (1979), 31–8.
17. P. M. Conlon, *Jean-François Bion et sa relation des tourments soufferts par les forçats Protestants* (1960), 14, 25, 18, 86–7.
18. A. Cabantous, *Le Ciel dans la mer: Christianisme et civilisation maritime, XVIe–XIXe siècle* (1990), 222–3, 234–5. For the Irish seminary at Nantes see C. Berthelot du Chesnay, *Les Prêtres Séculiers en Haute-Bretagne au XVIIIe siècle* (1974), 169–71.
19. Ibid., 236–7.
20. Guyot, iv. 64.
21. Marriages conducted by army chaplains were suspect (L. Châtellier, *Tradition chrétienne et renouveau catholique dans les cadres de l'ancien diocèse de Strasbourg, 1650–1770* (1981), 253).
22. A. Babeau, *La Vie militaire sous l'ancien régime,* i: *Les Soldats* (1889), 225.

23. A. Redier and G. Hénocque, *Les Aumôniers militaires français* (1940), 124–8, basic for all this section.
24. E. Regnault, *Christophe de Beaumont, archevêque de Paris, 1703–81* (2 vols., 1882), ii. 336; F. Masson, *Le Cardinal de Bernis depuis son ministère* (1884), 342.
25. *Les Invalides: trois siècles d'histoire* (Musée de l'Armée, 1974), 163–5, 176, 191–4, 197, 210–11.
26. See J.-P. Bois, *Les Anciens Soldats dans la société française au XVIIIe siècle* (1990).
27. Germain Brice, *Description nouvelle de la ville de Paris* (3 vols., 1713), cited in *Les Invalides*, 211. For another testimony to the 'sincere piety of these defenders of the fatherland', by the abbé Hébert, 'Dix jours à Paris, 1791', ed. J.-A. des Retours, *Rev. quest. hist.* (1937), 70.
28. A. Corvisier, *L'Armée française de la fin du XVIIIe siècle au ministère de Choiseul: le soldat* (2 vols., 1964), ii. 866.
29. François de Chennevières, *Détails militaires dont la connaissance est nécessaire aux officiers* (4 vols., 1742), ii. 147; cited by Redier and Hénocque, *Les Aumôniers*, 126.
30. Babeau, *La Vie militaire*, i. 227; A. Corvisier, 'La Mort du soldat depuis la fin du Moyen Âge', *Rev. hist.* (1975), 10.
31. Corvisier, *L'Armée française*, ii. 865–7.
32. J. Godefroy, 'Dom Chardon', *Rev. Mabillon* (1944), 82–3.
33. J.-M. Alliot, *Le Clergé de Versailles pendant la Révolution* (1912), 30–1.
34. 'Le Journal de guerre de M. Nicolas Segretier', ed. 'P.G.', *Bull. Soc. Orléanais*, NS 1 (1959), 170–6. For another chaplain see G. Robert, 'La Vie d'un aumônier militaire au 18e siècle', *Rev. hist. armée* (1972), 23–37.
35. Bachaumont, xxi. 156–7 (Oct. 1782).
36. J. Gaudemet, 'Législation canonique et attitudes séculaires à l'égard du lien matrimonial au XVIIe siècle', *XVIIe Siècle* (1974), 15–24.
37. B. Plongeron, *Théologie et politique au siècle des lumières, 1770–1820* (1973), 200–16.
38. Ibid. 211.
39. Ibid. 225–34.
40. M. Marion, *Dictionnaire des institutions de la France aux XVIIe et XVIIIe siècles* (2 vols., 1923), i. 215.
41. J. Brunet, *Le Parfait Notaire apostolique*, rev. Durand de Maillane, rev. edn. (2 vols., 1775), i. 215.
42. A. Dupuy, 'La Collégiale de Notre-Dame de la Fosse', *Ann. Bretagne* (1889–90), 604. The resentment of the curés was evident when the intendant asked them for population statistics in 1785. They referred him to the *greffe* where they had to deposit copies of their registers (C. Berthelot du Chesnay, *Les Prêtres séculiers en Haute-Bretagne* (1974), 550).
43. A duty of curés, according to one who did not do so himself (J. Salvini, 'Clergé rural en Haut-Poitou à la veille de la Révolution', *Bull. Soc. Ouest* (1957–8), 240).
44. L. Cahen, 'La Question de l'état civil à Paris au 18e siècle', *Rév. fr.* (1909), 193–202.
45. D. Diderot, *Correspondance*, ed. G. Roth and J. Varloot (16 vols., 1955–70), viii. 212 (Nov. 1768).
46. Dupy, 'La Collégiale', 476.
47. C. L. Chassin, *Les Cahiers des curés* (1921), 180.

48. M. Delamare, *Traité de la Police* (4 vols., 1722), i. 287.

49. Ibid. i. 240, 221–2.

50. O. Christin, 'Sur la condamnation du blasphème (XVIᵉ–XVIIᵉ siècles)', *Rev. hist. Église Fr.* (1994), 43–65. See also A. Cabantous, 'Du blasphème au blasphémateur', in P. Dartevelle (ed.), *Blasphèmes et libertés* (1993), 11–31.

51. N. Rateneau, 'Les Peines capitales et corporelles en France sous l'ancien régime', *Ann. internat. crim.* (1963), 303.

52. F. Hildesheimer, 'La Répression du blasphème au XVIIIᵉ siècle', *Mentalités* (1989), 70.

53. Guyot, vi. 210.

54. Ibid. vi. 209.

55. E. Appolis, *Le Jansénisme dans le diocèse de Lodève au XVIIIᵉ siècle* (1952), 200.

56. McManners, *Death*, ch. 11.

57. P. Rétat *et al.*, *L'Attentat de Damiens: discours sur l'événement au XVIIIᵉ siècle*, Centre d'Études du XVIIIᵉ siècle, Univ. Lyon, 2 (1979); Barbier, ii. 421 (29 Aug. 1733). At this time, Barbier says, such a theft in a church would have been punished with a flogging only.

58. Guyot, lvii. 145.

59. J. P. Gutton, *La Société et les pauvres: l'exemple de la généralité de Lyon, 1534–1789* (1971), 202.

60. O. H. Hufton, *The Poor of Eighteenth-Century France, 1750–1789* (1974), 251. For two sentences of perpetual slavery on the galleys for blasphemy, see R. Demogue, 'La Criminalité . . . en Champagne', *Trav. Acad. nat. Reims* (1904), 137.

61. Dom Pierre Chastelain, *Journal, 1709–1782*, ed. M. Jadert (1902), year 1725.

62. T. J. Schmitt, *L'Organisation ecclésiastique et la pratique religieuse dans l'archidiaconé d'Autun de 1650 à 1750* (1957), p. lxxxiii.

63. G. Bouchard, *Le Village immobile: Sennely-en-Sologne au XVIIIᵉ siècle* (1972), 278.

64. Barbier, i. 95 (Dec. 1720). The soldier was executed by burning.

65. L. Baloche, *L'Église Saint-Merry de Paris* (2 vols., 1911), i. 488.

66. P. Chevallier, *La Première Profanation du temple maçonnique, ou Louis XV et la Fraternité, 1737–1755* (1968), 52.

67. Guyot, lvii. 144–5.

68. S. T. McCloy, *The Humanitarian Movement in 18th-Century France* (1937), 174.

69. Guyot, lvii. 144–5; there were burnings for sacrilege at Mende in 1787 and at Montpellier in 1789 (Hufton, *Poor*, 251). Did the parlements and the other 'sovereign courts' tend to a greater strictness than inferior courts? This was the case in Lorraine in the early eighteenth century (A. Logette, 'La Peine capitale devant la cour souveraine de Lorraine et Barrois à la fin du règne de Louis XIV', *XVIIᵉ Siècle* (1980), 14).

70. A. Dinaux, 'Sacrilège à Lille en 1713', *Archives historiques et littéraires du nord de la France et du midi de la Belgique*, 2e sér. 5 (1844), 82–5.

71. Montesquieu, *L'Esprit des Lois*, xxvi. 8 (Pléiade (2 vols., 1951), ii. 758).

72. Ibid. xii. 4 (Pléiade, ii. 433).

73. Voltaire, 'Blasphème', in *Dictionnaire philosophique*, in *Œuvres*, xvii. 3.

74. Voltaire, *Prix de la justice et de l'humanité*, in *Œuvres*, xxx. 554.

75. Guyot, vi. 210.

76. McManners, *Death*, 375.

77. M. Chassaigne, *Le Procès du Chevalier de la Barre* (1920), 154–5.
78. Ibid. 41.
79. Ibid. 181.
80. Martial-Levé, *Louis-François-Gabriel d'Orléans de la Motte, évêque d'Amiens, 1683–1774* (1962), 130.
81. Voltaire, *Relation de la mort du Chevalier de La Barre*, in *Œuvres*, xxv. 503–6.
82. Voltaire, *Prix de la justice*, in *Œuvres*, xxx. 556.
83. Voltaire, *Relation de la mort*, in *Œuvres*, xxv. 542–5.
84. J.-B. Thiers, *Traité des jeux et des divertissements qui peuvent être permis, ou qui doivent être défendus aux chrétiens* (1686), 413.
85. Guyot, xxiv. 526–31.
86. P. Crousaz-Crétet, *Paris sous Louis XIV* (2 vols. 1922–3), ii. 237; A. Rébillon, 'Recherches sur les anciennes corporations . . . de Rennes', *Ann. Bretagne* (1902–3), 424.
87. Y. Brisset de Morcour, *La Police séculière des dimanches et fêtes dans l'ancienne France* (1938), 84.
88. Ibid. 78–84.
89. Ibid. 69–70.
90. Restif de la Bretonne, *L'École des Pères* (3 vols. 1776).
91. Guyot, xxiv. 526–33.
92. Brisset de Morcour, *La Police*, 71.
93. P. Wolff, *Histoire de Toulouse* (1974), 360.
94. P. de Saint-Jacob, *Documents relatifs à la communauté villageoise en Bourgogne* (1962), 60–1.
95. F. Baqué and A. Rouquette, *Un Village du littoral au cours des siècles: Bouziques* (1960), 121–2.
96. Brisset de Morcour, *La Police*, 60.
97. Ibid. 61–7.
98. J.-B. Lyonnet, *Histoire de Mgr d'Aviau-du-Bois-de-Sanzay, archevêque de Vienne et de Bordeaux* (2 vols. 1847), i. 129.
99. R. Mandrou, *De la culture populaire aux 17ᵉ et 18ᵉ siècles* (1964), 126.
100. Reports that Sunday is observed in country areas: Bouchard, *Sennely*, 288–9; J. Déchelette, 'Visites pastorales des archiprêtrés de Charlieu par Mgr De Lort de Sérignan de Valras, évêque de Mâcon, 1745–64', *Ann. Acad. Mâcon* 3ᵉ ser., 6 (1901), 422. Reports that it is not: Hubrecht, 'La Région, Sedanaise à la veille de la Révolution', *Ann. hist. Rév. fr.* (1936), 324.
101. J. de Viguerie, 'Les Missions intérieures des Doctrinaires Toulousains au début du XVIIIᵉ siècle: un missionnaire, le père Jean-Baptiste Badou', *Rev. hist.* (1969), 48.
102. J. Delumeau, *Histoire du diocèse de Rennes* (1979), 128.
103. M. C. Péronnet, *Les Évêques de l'ancienne France* (2 vols., 1977), ii. 779–80.
104. Thomas Bentley, *Journal of a Visit to Paris, 1776*, ed. P. France (1977), 34–5. Cf. Voltaire on the gloom of the English Sunday, *Lettres philosophiques*, 6ᵉ lettre in *Mélanges* (Pléiade, 1901), 17.
105. H. C. Payne, *The Philosophes and the People* (1976), 122.
106. Voltaire, *Œuvres*, xxviii. 312.
107. The abbé C. I. C. Saint-Pierre, *Œuvres* (7 vols. 1735–41), vi. 73–5.
108. A. Sicard, *Les Études classiques avant la Révolution* (1887), 265.
109. H. Grange, *Les Idées de Necker* (1974), 193–4.

110. Marion, *Dictionnaire*, i. 72.
111. M. Marais, iv. 7.
112. Luynes, xiii. 183 (Mar. 1754).
113. Ibid. xi. 59 (Feb. 1751).
114. Guyot, vii. 435.
115. D'Argenson, viii. 394.
116. M. Fosseyeux, 'Le Cardinal de Noailles et l'administration du diocèse de Paris', *Rev. hist.* (1913), 267.
117. Guyot, vii. 437.
118. R. Laprune, *Histoire religieuse de Montier-sur-Saulx* (1969), ii. 47.
119. C. Port, *Inventaire analytique des archives anciennes de la Mairie d'Angers* (1861), 274–5.
120. G. Cormary, *Loménis de Brienne à Toulouse, 1763–1788* (1935), 14.
121. Voltaire, 'Carême', in *Dictionnaire philosophique*, in *Œuvres*, xviii. 53–4.
122. Guyot, vii. 433.
123. G. Avenel, *Anarcharsis Cloots* (2 vols., 1865), i. 10–11.
124. Voltaire, *Requête à tous les magistrats* (1770), in *Œuvres*, xviii. 342–5.
125. Grimm, viii. 33–4. Cf. Bachaumont on the abbé Georgel's composition for the Lenten pastoral of the Court, xxxi. 201–3.
126. M. Vallery-Radot, *Un Administrateur ecclésiastique à la fin de l'ancien régime: le Cardinal de Luynes, archevêque de Sens (1753–88)* (1966), 50.
127. Cited by A. Monod, *De Pascal à Chateaubriand: les défenseurs français du Christianisme de 1670 à 1802* (1916), 214.
128. G. Maugras, *La Fin d'une société: le duc de Lauzan et la cour intime de Louis XV* (1895), 17.
129. Getting butter sent up from Brittany to Paris, a basket of twelve 'pots' every week. Letter of 13 Jan. 1787 in A. Le Moy, *Le XVIIIᵉ siècle breton . . . correspondance inédite de M. M. de Robian et de la Bellangerais, 1765–91* (n.d.), 253.
130. Mme de Campan, *Mémoires sur la vie de Marie Antoinette*, ed. F. Barrière (1886), 28–9.
131. Voltaire, *Corresp.*, lxxiii. 86 (27 Sept. 1769).
132. Ibid. xxix. 183 (22 Apr. 1756).
133. M. Bouchard, *De l'humanisme à l'Encyclopédie: essai sur l'évolution des esprits dans la bourgeoisie bourguignonne sous les règnes de Louis XIV et Louis XV* (1929), 62.
134. A. Bernard, *Le Sermon au XVIIIᵉ siècle, 1715–89* (1901), 78.
135. Yves Besnard, *Souvenirs d'un nonagénaire*, ed. C. Port (2 vols., 1880), i. 196.
136. L.-S. Mercier, *Tableau de Paris*, new edn. (12 vols., 1782–8), v. 213.
137. Ch. Collas, *Saint-Louis d'Antin et son territoire* (1932), 53; Bachaumont, ix. 52–3 (24 Feb. 1776).
138. Thiery, *Guide des amateurs et des étrangers à Paris* (2 vols., 1787), i. 25.
139. Bachaumont, iii. 324 (30 Mar. 1768).
140. Ibid. vii. 134 (4 Apr. 1774); Métra, i. 313–16 (15 Apr. 1775).
141. Britsch, *La Jeunesse de Philippe-Égalite* (1926), 392; Bachaumont, xv. 15 (Mar. 1780).
142. Bachaumont, xxv. 56–7 (30 Apr. 1787).
143. J. Dupâquier, 'Sur la population française aux 17ᵉ et 18ᵉ siècles', *Rev. hist.* (1968), 70–2. There are innumerable references in the literature of demography to the Lenten low.

144. Guyot, iii. 198.
145. A. Forrest, *Society and Politics in Revolutionary Bordeaux* (1975), 13.
146. L. de Loménie, *Beaumarchais et son temps* (2 vols., 1880), ii. 67–9.
147. Guyot, i. 442.
148. F. Duine, 'Les Généraux des paroisses Bretonnes—Saint-Martin de Vitré', *Ann. Bretagne* (1907–8), 16–17. Some *cahiers* of 1789 asked for the charge for private notices to be limited to one sol (E. Dupont, 'La Condition des paysans dans la sénéchaussée de Rennes d'après les cahiers', *Ann. Bretagne* (1900–1), 59). For announcing stolen horses, see R. Plessix, 'Les *Affiches* du Mans, 1787', *Bull. Soc. Sarthe* (1973–4), 241.
149. A. Mathiez, *La Lecture des décrets au prône* (1907), 36–9.
150. Ibid.
151. *P.V. Ass.* viii. 2 (1775), 2390–2.
152. P. de la Gorce, *Histoire religieuse de la Révolution française* (3 vols., 1909), i. 379–80.
153. Guyot, xl. 209–26.
154. *Le Parfait Notaire apostolique*, i. 689.
155. A. Schaer, *Le Clergé paroissial catholique en Haute-Alsace sous l'ancien régime, 1648–1789* (1966), 203.
156. For an effective one, T. Leuridan, *Histoire de Linselles* (1883), 214 (in 1740, diocese of Tournai). In some areas, where there was a Mafia-like code of silence, the *monitoire* might give an informer a feeling of respectability (Y. Castan, *Honnêteté et relations sociales en Languedoc, 1715–80* (1974), 94–5).
157. J. McManners, *French Ecclesiastical Society under the Ancien Régime: A Study of Angers* (1960), 21.
158. J. Meyer, *La Noblesse bretonne au XVIIIe siècle* (2 vols., 1966), i. 569.
159. T. Tackett, *Priest and Parish in 18th-Century France* (1977), 212–13. The cases in O. Hufton, 'Le Paysan et la loi en France au XVIIIe siècle', *Ann.* (1983), 695–6.
160. P. Gosset, 'Scandales littéraires rémois au xviiie siècle,' *Nouv. Rev. Champagne et Brie* (1936), 88–9; McManners, *Angers*, 21; G. Walter, *Hébert et le Père Duchesne* (1946), 16.
161. M. Forestier, 'Une Exécution manquée', *Ann. Bourgogne* (1960), 60.
162. G. Aubry, *La Juridiction criminelle du Châtelet* (1971), 30.
163. E. G. Léonard, *Mon Village sous Louis XV* (1941), 335–6.
164. Roualt (curé), *Traité des monitoires* (1740), 149.
165. A. Coquerel, *Jean Calas et sa famille* (1869), 91–2.
166. Voltaire, *Lettre d'un membre du conseil de Zurich* (1767), in *Œuvres*, xxvi. 106.
167. Duine, 'Les généraux', 12.
168. Chassin, *Les Cahiers des curés*, 194–5; Marion, *Dictionnaire*, i. 583.
169. Cit. A. Babeau, *Le Village sous l'ancien régime* (1883), 128.

CHAPTER 4

1. Ph. Sagnac, *La Formation de la société française moderne* (2 vols., 1945–6), i. 32.
2. G. Frêche, *Toulouse et la région Midi-Pyrénées au siècle des Lumières* (1975), 531.
3. G. Lizerand, *Le Régime rural de l'ancienne France* (1942), 173–5.
4. Barbier, iii. 208.

5. P. de la Gorce, *Histoire religieuse de la Révolution française* (5 vols., 1909–23), i. 10.

6. A. Rébillon, 'La Situation économique du clergé à la fin de l'ancien régime', *Rév. fr.* (1929), 328–30.

7. G. Lefebvre, 'The Evolution of Peasant Society', in E. M. Acomb and Brown (eds.), *French Society and Culture* (1961), 44.

8. P. Wolff, *Histoire de Toulouse* (1974), 316; A. Thouroude, *La Vente des biens nationaux particulièrement dans le District de Revel* (thèse droit, Toulouse, 1912), 110–15; A. Guillon, 'La Vente des biens nationaux dans l'ancienne commune de Fougerai', *Ann. Bretagne* (1908–9), 338–9.

9. G. Lefebvre, 'Recherches relatives à la répartition de la propriété et de l'exploitation foncière à la fin de l'ancien régime', *Rev. hist. mod. contemp.* (1928), 110.

10. J. Lestocquoy, *Le Diocèse d'Arras* (1949), 173.

11. T. Bentley, *Journal of a Visit to Paris in 1776*, ed. P. France (1972), 25–6.

12. C.-G. Porée, 'La Vente des biens nationaux dans le district de Sens', *Rév. fr.* (1914), 88.

13. A. Meynier, 'La Terre et le paysan de la Révolution à l'Empire', *Rév. fr.* (1936), 126.

14. D. Dakin, *Turgot and the Ancien Régime* (1939).

15. Lefebvre, 'Recherches', and Meynier, 'La Terre'.

16. A. Degert, 'La Propriété ecclésiastique dans le Gers à la veille de la Révolution', *Rev. Gascogne* (1913), 267.

17. J. Bascou, 'Les Paysans de Béarn en 1789', *Ann. hist. Rév. fr.* (1940), 12.

18. A. Rébillon, *Ann. Bretagne* (1910–11), 463.

19. C. Port, *La Vendée angevine* (2 vols., 1888), ii. 1–21.

20. Lizerand, *Le Régime rural*, 172–4.

21. J. Loutchisky, 'Régime agraire et populations agricoles dans les environs de Paris à la veille de la Révolution', *Rev. hist. mod. contemp.* (1933), 106–12.

22. R. H. Andrews, *Les Paysans des Mauges au XVIIIᵉ siècle* (1935), 15–17. A more sophisticated calculation comes to almost exactly the same conclusion: clergy 5.1 per cent, nobles 59.8 per cent, peasants 17.2 per cent (C. Tilly, *The Vendée* (1964), 74).

23. G. Michaux, 'Les Abbayes Bénédictines de Metz à la veille de la Révolution', *Ann. Est* (1979), 259.

24. M. Vallery-Radot, *Un Administrateur ecclésiastique à la fin de l'ancien régime: le cardinal de Luynes, archévêque de Sens* (1966), 159.

25. P. Goubert, 'Disparités de l'ancienne France rurale', *Cahiers hist.* (1967), 58–9.

26. Ch. Girault, *Les Biens de l'église dans la Sarthe à la fin du XVIIIᵉ siècle* (1953), 359.

27. R. Caisso, *La Vente des biens nationaux de première origine dans le district de Tours* (1967), 38.

28. Girault, *Les Biens*, 358–71. The *cahiers* say that these capitalist *fermiers* treat their subtenants 'comme des nègres qui ne doivent travailler que pour les enrichir'.

29. O. H. Hufton, *The Poor of 18th-Century France* (1974), chs. 3 and 4.

30. G. Lecarpentier, 'La Propriété foncière du clergé et la vente des biens ecclésiastiques dans la Seine-Inférieure', *Rev. hist.* (1901), 73–5.

31. Girault, *Les Biens*, 376.

32. Caisso, *Tours*, 42.
33. M. Chamboux, *Les Paysans dans la Creuse à la fin de l'ancien régime* (1955), 26.
34. G. Lefebvre, *Questions agraires au temps de la Terreur* (1932), 61.
35. M. M. Kovelevsky, *La France économique et sociale à la veille de la Révolution* (2 vols., 1909–11), i. 12.
36. C. Bournisien, 'La Vente des biens nationaux', *Rev. hist.* (1909), 39. But see Caisso, *Tours*, 51. Basing estimated prices on the leases was to forget that the *fermier* also had to make a profit.
37. Bournisien, 'La Vente', 39. For communities claiming an immemorial right to cultivate the curé's land see L. Châtellier, *Tradition chrétienne et renouveau catholique dans l'ancien diocèse de Strasbourg, 1650–1770* (1981), 116.
38. F. D. Mathieu, *L'Ancien Régime dans la province de Lorraine et Barrois* (1879), 324–5.
39. J. McManners, *French Ecclesiastical Society under the Ancien Régime: A Study of Angers* (1960), 115–16.
40. M. Marion, *Histoire financière de la France depuis 1715* (2 vols., 1933), ii. 43.
41. Lefebvre, *Questions agraires*, 81.
42. G. Robert, 'La Seigneurie de Givry-sur-Aisne', *Trav. Acad. nat. Reims* (1913), 307–8.
43. G. Lefebvre, *Les Paysans du Nord pendant la Révolution française* (1924), 264.
44. L. Fournier, 'Les Paysans de l'ancien régime en Picardie', *Rév. fr.* (1884), 185–6.
45. M. Marion, *Dictionnaire des institutions de la France au XVIIe et XVIIIe siècles* (2 vols., 1923), i. 31.
46. Alexis de Tocqueville, *L'Ancien régime et la Révolution* (1856), ch. 11.
47. Girault, *Les Biens*, 374–7.
48. F. Rozier, *Démonstration élémentaire de botanique* (2 vols., 1766; 3 vols., 1789); *De la Fermentation des vins, et de la meilleure manière de faire l'eau-de-vie* (1770); *Traité sur la meilleure manière de cultiver la navette* (1776); *Mémoire sur la culture du chanvre* (1787); *Cours complet d'agriculture . . . et de médecine rurale et vétérinaire* (9 vols., 1781–96).
49. L. Froger, *Institutions d'agriculture et d'économie pour les habitans de la campagne* (1769), 16.
50. O. Festy, *L'Agriculture pendant la Révolution française: l'utilisation des jachères, 1789–1795* (1950), 92.
51. The abbé de Commerell, *Mémoire sur l'amélioration de l'agriculture par la suppression des jachères* (1788); *Instruction sur la culture, l'usage et les avantages de la betterave champêtre* (1786, 1788), and other essays on the cultivation of 'la racine de disette' and the 'chou à faucher' in 1786 and 1789.
52. François de la Rochefoucauld, *Voyages en France*, ed. J. Marchand (1933), 123. Cf. Arthur Young, *Travels in France during the years 1787, 1788, and 1789* (1792), 2 Aug. 1789 (ed. T. Okey (1934), 183).
53. F. Cognel, *La Vie parisienne sous Louis XVI* (1882), 5.
54. Fr. Crouzet, R. Pijassou, and J.-P. Poussou, in F. G. Pariset (ed.), *Bordeaux au XVIIIe siècle* (1968), 160.
55. Ibid. 181.
56. A. Chaulac, *Histoire de l'abbaye de Sainte-Croix*, Archives de la France monastique (1910), 284.
57. B. Gille, *Les Forges françaises en 1772* (1960), 41–66, 98–9, 154–9.

58. J. Peter, 'Un Curieux Procès du XVIIIe siècle, 1723–6', *Rev. Nord* (1937), 243–59.

59. R. Dauvergne, *Les Résidences du maréchal de Croÿ, 1718–84* (1950), 56.

60. J.-F.-H. de Richeprey, *Journal des voyages en Haute-Guienne*, ed. H. Guilhamon (1952), 240–1.

61. E. Préclin, 'La Situation ecclésiastique et religieuse de la Franche Comté à la veille de la Révolution', *Bull. Féd. Socs. Franche Comté* (1955), 19–20; J. Faivre, 'Le Bas-clergé franc-comtois au milieu du XVIIIe siècle', *Ann. rév.* (1914), 10.

62. E. Appolis, *Le Diocèse civil de Lodève* (1951), 48–50, 64–66.

63. J. Savina, *Le Clergé de Cornouaille à la fin de l'ancien régime et sa convocation aux États-Généraux* (1926), 27.

64. M. Fosseyeux, 'Le Cardinal de Noailles et l'administration du diocèse de Paris', *Rev. hist.* (1913), 44, 272–3; *Le Gendre, chanoine de Notre-Dame, Mémoires*, ed. M. Roux (1863), 126–8. For the revenue in 1746, N. Ravitch, *Sword and Mitre: Government and Episcopate in France and England in the Age of Aristocracy* (1960), 219.

65. A. Soboul, 'La Révolution française et la féodalité', *Rev. hist.* (1968), 53.

66. G. Laurent, *Reims et la région rémoise à la veille de la Révolution* (1930), pp. vii–x. For the bishop of Beauvais as comte and *haut justicier* see P. Goubert, *Familles marchandes sous l'ancien régime: les Danse et les Motte, de Beauvais* (1959), p. ii.

67. McManners, *Angers*, 97–8, 64–7.

68. R. Métivier, *Les Anciennes Institutions judiciaires de l'Anjou* (1851), 5–10.

69. Rébillon, 'La Situation économique', 341.

70. A. Soboul, 'De la pratique des terriers à la veille de la Révolution', *Ann.* (1964), 1063.

71. Richeprey, *Journal*, 69–70.

72. Lefebvre, *Paysans du Nord*, 159.

73. J. Chétail, 'Pierre Louis de Leyssin, archevêque d'Embrun', *Bull. Acad. Delp.* (1958–9), 96–9.

74. Richeprey, *Journal*, 60–70.

75. Laurent, *Reims*, pp. xlvii–xlviii, lxxiv–lxxx, 108–9.

76. L. Trénard, 'La Crise sociale lyonnaise à la veille de la Révolution', *Rev. hist. mod. contemp.* (1955), 26.

77. McManners, *Angers*, 116.

78. G. Hubrecht, 'La Région sedanaise à la veille de la Révolution', *Ann. hist. Rév. fr.* (1937), 19–49.

79. Lizerand, *Le Régime rural*, 176.

80. J. Q. C. Mackrell, *The Attack on Feudalism in 18th-Century France* (1973), 6, 33, 119.

81. H. Sée, 'Les Classes rurales en Bretagne du XVIe siècle à la Révolution', *Ann. Bretagne* (1905), 15–25; L. Dubreuil, 'L'Usement de quevaise dans le domaine de Penlan, évêché de Tréguier', *Ann. Bretagne* (1961), 403.

82. L. Barbedette, 'La Terre de Luxeuil à la veille de la Révolution', *Ann. hist. Rév. fr.* (1927), 157–9.

83. Voltaire, *Précis du siècle de Louis XV*, in *Œuvres*, 427.

84. G. Demante, *Étude sur les gens de condition mainmortable en France au XVIIIe siècle* (1894), 20, 31–2.

85. Voltaire, *La Voix du curé*, in *Œuvres*, xviii. 567–74. Other references in Voltaire on this subject in G. Desnoiresterres, *Voltaire et la société française au XVIIIe siècle*, 2nd edn. (8 vols., 1867–76), vii. 479.

86. Demante, *Étude*, 39–49.

87. Marion, *Dictionnaire*, i. 508–9.

88. G.-L. Chassin, *L'Église et les derniers serfs* (1880), 113.

89. Ibid. 263.

90. Barbedette, 'Luxeuil', 159.

91. Ph. Sagnac, *La Révolution et le concept de la propriété, 1789–1804* (1946), 35 ff.

92. Guyot, ii. 74–5.

93. Durand de Maillaine, *Dictionnaire de droit canonique et de pratique bénéficiale* (2 vols., 1776), i. 127.

94. G. de la Véronne, 'Une Aliénation de biens ecclésiastiques', *Rev. quest. hist.* (1914), 490–4.

95. R. Tallegrain, *Du Temporel des bénéfices ecclésiastiques sous l'ancien régime* (1909), 87–9.

96. Maillaine, *Dictionnaire*, i. 150.

97. F.-A. Isambert, *Recueil des anciennes lois françaises* (29 vols., 1822–33), xxii. 226–35, and interpretive declaration in 1762 at 323–8.

98. McManners, *Angers*, 119.

99. D'Argenson, vi. 46 (24 Sept. 1749).

100. L. Antoine, *Le Conseil du roi sous le règne de Louis XV* (1970), 465.

101. S. T. McCloy, *Government Assistance in 18th-Century France* (1946), 377.

102. E. Vaillé, *Histoire générale des Postes françaises* (6 vols., 1953), v. 232.

103. F. Braesch, *La Commune du dix août, 1792* (1911), 869.

104. C. Carrière, M. Courdurié, and F. Rebuffat, *Marseille, ville morte: la peste de 1720*, ed. Courdurié (1968), 27–9; R. Forster, *The Nobility of Toulouse in the 18th Century* (1960), 22; E. Esmonin, 'Un Recensement de la population de Grenoble en 1725', *Cahiers hist.* (1957), 266; A. Babeau, *Histoire de Troyes pendant la Révolution* (1873), 6; Laurent, *Reims*, p. lxviii; G. Aubert, 'La Révolution à Douai', *Ann. hist. Rév. fr.* (1935), 316; E. Palanque, *Le Diocèse d'Aix-en-Provence* (1975), 124–6.

105. N. Wraxall, *A Tour through the Western, Southern and Interior Provinces of France* (3 vols., 1777), ii. 198.

106. E. Charpentier, 'La Loge maçonnique de Montreuil-sur-Mer, 1761–1809', *Rév. fr.* (1894), 533.

107. P. Tartat, *Avallon au XVIIIe siècle* (2 vols., 1951–3), i. 34–42.

108. F. Le Lay, *Histoire de la ville et communauté de Pontivy* (1911), 13, 16, 18, 35–8.

109. Descriptions of the town in Arthur Young, *Travels in France*, and in Legrand d'Aussy, *Voyage fait en Auvergne en 1787 et 1788*.

110. L. and G. Trénard, *Belley*, Histoire des diocèses de France (1978), 108–9.

111. A. Babeau, *La Ville sous l'ancien régime* (2 vols., 1884), ii. 102–29; generally, see J.-C. Perrot, 'Rapports sociaux et villes au XVIIIe siècle', *Ann.* (1968), 252 ff.

112. McManners, *Angers*, 117–28.

113. E. Martin, 'La Population de la ville de Vannes au début et à la fin du XVIIIe siècle', *Ann. Bretagne* (1921–3), 613.

114. P. Chevallier, *Loménie de Brienne et l'ordre monastique, 1766–89* (2 vols., 1959–60), i. 83–4.

115. M. Bouchard, *De l'humanisme à l'Encyclopédie: essai sur l'évolution des esprits dans la bourgeoisie bourguignonne sous les règnes de Louis XIV et Louis XV* (1929), 6–7; D. Ligou, 'Population, citoyens actifs et élections à Dijon, 1790–1', in *Actes du 88e Congrès des Sociétés savantes* (Clermont-Ferrand, 1963) (1964), 243–7; M. Garden, 'Niveaux de fortune à Dijon', *Cahiers hist.* (1964), 140.

116. Cognel, *La Vie parisienne*, 75.

117. McManners, *Angers*, 253.

118. O. Hufton, *Bayeux in the Late 18th Century* (1967), 40.

119. H. Prentout, 'Les Tableaux de 1790 en réponse à l'enquête du Comité de mendicité, Calvados', *Rév. fr.* (1907), 425–6.

120. J. McManners, *Death and the Enlightenment* (1981), ch. 10.

121. McManners, *Angers*, 120.

122. J. Thibaut-Payen, *Les Morts, l'Église et l'État dans le ressort du Parlement de Paris aux XVIIe et XVIIIe siècles* (1977), 375, 379–81, 396.

123. e.g. the article 'Biens d'Église' in the *Dictionnaire philosophique* (1764).

124. Montesquieu, *Lettres persanes*, letter 117, in *Œuvres complètes*, ed. R. Caillois (2 vols., 1951), i. 305–7; *L'Esprit des lois*, xxv. 5, ibid. ii. 740–1.

125. J. A. Clarke, 'Turgot's Critique of Perpetual Endowments', *Fr. Hist. St.* (1963–4), 495–501.

126. Étienne Mignot, *Traité des droits de l'État et du prince sur les biens possédés par le Clergé* (6 vols., 1755–7) (Bibl. Nat. 8° Ld4 2831); id., *Histoire du démêlé de Henri II, roi d'Angleterre, avec Thomas Becket, archevêque de Cantorbéry* (1756) (Bibl. Nat. 8° NF. 43). For his Jansenism see P. Feret, *La Faculté de Théologie de Paris et ses docteurs les plus célèbres* (7 vols., 1900–10), vii. 49–50.

127. Bachaumont, vi. 148–51 (13 Aug. 1770).

128. Métra, v. 281–7 (Nov. 1777).

129. I am grateful to Cambridge University Press for permission to use my essay in *History, Society and the Churches: Essays in Honour of Owen Chadwick* (1985), 147–68.

130. H. Marion, *La Dîme ecclésiastique en France au 18e siècle et sa suppression* (1912), 116.

131. Arthur Young, *Travels*, Fr. trans. H. Sée (3 vols., 1931), with excellent notes, iii. 1038.

132. P. Gagnol, *La Dîme ecclésiastique en France* (1910), 137–51; M. Marion, *Dictionnaire*, i. 174.

133. A. Poitrineau, *La Vie rurale en Basse-Auvergne au XVIIIe siècle, 1726–1789* (2 vols., 1965), i. 351.

134. Lefebvre, *Paysans du Nord*, 108.

135. Gagnol, *La Dîme ecclésiastique*, 151–3.

136. Appolis, *Lodève*, 124–5; Poitrineau, *Basse-Auvergne*, i. 353.

137. Appolis, *Lodève*, 124–5.

138. Gagnol, *La Dîme ecclésiastique*, 35–9; Marion, *Dictionnaire*, i. 174.

139. Potier de la Germondaye, *Introduction au gouvernement des paroisses suivant la jurisprudence du Parlement de Bretagne* (1777), 146–8.

140. M. Faucheux, *Un Ancien Droit ecclésiastique perçu en Bas-Poitou: le boisselage*, (1953), 19–21, 44, 57, 63, 66; J. Deharge, *La Bas-Poitou à la veille de la Révolution* (1963), 102.

141. Appolis, *Lodève*, 126; Sée, 'Les Classes rurales', 507.

142. Voltaire, *Dictionnaire philosophique*, 'Impôt', *Œuvres*, xix. 444.
143. F. Caussy, 'Voltaire et ses curés. Lettres sur les dîmes', *Rev. hist.* (1909), 254–6, 619–35. (His parish priest was not the one in the tithe dispute.)
144. Guyot, xix. 509–17. L. Michel, 'La Dîme et les revenus du clergé d'Anjou à la fin de l'ancien régime', *Ann. Bretagne* (1979), 570.
145. See Ch. 50 below.
146. Hubrecht, 'La Région sedanaise', 33.
147. Mathieu, *Lorraine et Barrois*, 140.
148. Frêche, *Toulouse*, 521.
149. Marion, *La Dîme*, 20.
150. Girault, *Les Biens*, 379.
151. Guyot, xix. 429–32.
152. Laurent, *Reims*, pp. cclxiv–cclxviii.
153. Michel, 'La Dîme', 572.
154. F. Évard, 'Les Dîmes dans le parc de Versailles', *Rév. fr.* (1928), 115.
155. E. Le Roy Ladurie, *Les Paysans de Languedoc* (1966), 480.
156. Frêche, *Toulouse*, 527–30.
157. J. Rives, *Dîme et société dans l'archidiocèse d'Auch au XVIIIe siècle* (1976), 57–60.
158. Michel, 'La Dîme', 571.
159. Gagnol, *La Dîme ecclésiastique*, 124–5.
160. Poitrineau, *Basse-Auvergne*, i. 352.
161. A. Saramon (ed.), *Les Paroisses du diocèse de Comminges en 1786* (1968), 23.
162. R. Laprune, 'Histoire religieuse de Montiers-sur-Saulx' (5 vols., dupl. thesis, Bibl. Nat. 4° Lk7 58305 (1–5), 1967), i. 25–6.
163. Gagnol, *La Dîme ecclésiastique*, 86–9.
164. Marion, *La Dîme*, 76–7.
165. M. Pialès, *Traité des réparations* (4 vols., 1762), ii. 22.
166. A. Playoust-Chaussis, *La Vie religieuse dans le diocèse de Boulogne au XVIIIe siècle* (1976), 60.
167. Marion, *La Dîme*, 154–5.
168. Ibid. 148.
169. Guyot, x. 50.
170. Évard, 'Versailles', 122–3.
171. Pialès, *Traité*, ii. 133, 191–210.
172. Guyot, xi. 112–27.
173. Marion, *La Dîme*, 73.
174. Gagnol, *La Dîme ecclésiastique*, 113.
175. Ibid. 114–15.
176. E. Sol, *La Vie en Quercy à l'époque moderne (le mouvement économique)* (1948), 99.
177. Gagnol, *La Dîme ecclésiastique*, 15.
178. C. Bloch, *L'Assistance et l'État en France à la veille de la Révolution* (1908), 273–6.
179. Laurent, *Reims*, pp. ccxlv–ccxlvii.
180. Marion, *La Dîme*, 35–8.
181. Poitrineau, *Basse-Auvergne*, I, 352.
182. Évard, 'Versailles', 58–9.
183. P. de Saint-Jacob, *Les Paysans de la Bourgogne du nord au dernier siècle de l'ancien régime* (1960), 271.

184. P. de Saint-Jacob, *Documents relatifs à la communauté villageoise en Bourgogne* (1962), 146–8.

185. Gagnol, *La Dîme ecclésiastique*, 128; Marion, *La Dîme*, 97.

186. Trénard, *Belley*, 114.

187. Marion, *La Dîme*, 144.

188. Guyot, xix. 404–7.

189. G. Coolen, *Helfaut: essai sur l'administration d'une paroisse sous l'ancien régime*, Méms. Soc. Morinie, 37 (1939), 24.

190. P. de Vaissière, *Curés de campagne de l'ancienne France* (1933), 88–9.

191. G. Guillot and A. Amic, 'Le Dernier Abbé de la Ferté-sur-Grosne', *Rev. Mabillon* (1907), 367–9.

192. Voltaire, *Corresp.* rev. edn. (1971), 299–30, 312 (nos. D7996 of 25 Dec. 1758 and D8011 of 29 Oct. 1758). When the curé got into a fracas, Voltaire got his revenge by stirring up a legal inquiry (F. Caussy, *Voltaire, seigneur de village* (1912), 53–6).

193. P. Lemarchand, 'Journal d'un curé de campagne au 18ᵉ siècle', *Bull. méms. Soc. Côtes-du-Nord* (1960), 63–4.

194. Restif de la Bretonne, *La Vie de mon père*, in *Œuvres*, ed. M. Bachelin (9 vols., 1930–2), iv. 81.

195. V. Gourdet, 'Saint-Hilaire-de-Briouze', *Bull. Soc. Orne*, 13 (1894), 78–9.

196. Guyot, xix. 421–6, and for what follows.

197. Marion, *La Dîme*, 48–53.

198. G. Weulersse, *Le Mouvement Physiocratique en France de 1756 à 1770* (2 vols., 1910), i. 462. See ii. 185–6, where it is said that most dioceses had accepted.

199. J. Rives, 'Dîme et défrichements en Gascogne et Quercy au XVIIIᵉ siècle', *Ann. Midi* (1980), 57–66.

200. P. de Vaissière, *Gentilshommes campagnards de l'ancienne France* (1928), 356–7.

201. Marion, *La Dîme*, 112–13.

202. Sée, 'Les Classes rurales', 506–7.

203. Marion, *La Dîme*, 10–13; Gagnol, *La Dîme ecclésiastique*, 49–50.

204. Richeprey, *Journal*, 300.

205. P. Goubert, *Beauvais et le Beauvaisis de 1600 à 1730* (2 vols., 1960), i. 180.

206. L. Ampoulange, *Le Clergé et la convocation aux États Généraux de 1789 dans la sénéchaussée principale de Périgord* (1912), 47–9.

207. Lizerand, *Le Régime rural*, 175. Cf. register of the commune of Artiguelouve, 'Une Commune rurale des Pyrénées au début de la Révolution', *Rev. hist.* (1889), 97.

208. Marion, *La Dîme*, 117–22.

209. Duhamel du Monceau, *Éléments d'agriculture* (2 vols., 1763), i. 200.

210. Châtellier, *Tradition chrétienne*, 287.

211. F. Mourlot, 'La Convocation des États Généraux de 1789 dans le bailliage de Vire', *Rév. fr.* 31 (1896), 421.

212. Lefebvre, *Paysans du Nord*, 112.

213. Hubrecht, 'La Région sedanaise', 33–4; Girault, *Les Biens*, 318.

214. Gagnol, *La Dîme ecclésiastique*, 122.

215. *Vie de M. Marquis-Ducastel, doyen rural d'Évron et du Sonnois*, ed. E. Pichon (1873), 57–8.

216. *Journal d'un curé de campagne au XVIIIᵉ siècle*, ed. M. Platelle (1965), 88.

217. P. Viard, 'La Dîme en France au 17ᵉ siècle', *Rev. hist.* (1927), 243.

218. Guyot, xix. 399–400; L. F. Dejouy, *Principes et usages concernant les dixmes* (1761), 4.
219. Guyot, xlvii. 162–7.
220. Montesquieu, *L'Esprit des Lois*, xxxi. 12, in *Œuvres complètes* (Pléiade, 2 vols., 1966), ii. 960–2.
221. Voltaire, *Dictionnaire philosophique*, 'Curé de campagne', in *Œuvres*, xviii. 303–5.
222. J.-A. de Véri, *Journal*, ed. J. de Witte (2 vols., n.d.), i. 255–6.
223. Weulersse, *Le Mouvement physiocratique*, i. 454–5.
224. E. Lavaquerie, *Le Cardinal de Boisgelin, 1732–1804* (2 vols., 1920), i. 230–1.
225. Marion, *Dictionnaire*, i. 175.
226. Marion, *La Dîme*, 141–3. In fact, so far as the great were concerned— bishops and chapters—the parlement was often inclined to favour them (Frêche, *Toulouse*, 539–40).
227. A. Degert, 'Les Assemblées provinciales du Clergé Gascon', *Rev. Gascogne* (1925), 87–184.
228. Saramon (ed.), *Les Paroisses*, 66.
229. Rives, *Dîme et société*, 147–56.
230. Marion, *La Dîme*, 140–1.
231. Saint-Jacob, *Bourgogne*, 374–6.
232. It was then resolved that arrangements for buying off tithe would be made. Earlier proposals would have made tithe a permanent tax, see [G.-F.-R. Molé, *avocat*], *Vœu d'un citoyen pour la conversion des dîmes en un impôt territorial qui sera perçu au profit de l'État* (1788). For the injustice to *métayers* involved in this gift to landowners see S. Aberdam, 'La Révolution et les luttes des métayers', *Études rurales*, 59 (1975), 73 ff.
233. Condorcet (M. J. A. N. marquis de), *Sur les Assemblées provinciales*, in *Œuvres*, ed. M. L. S. Caritat *et al.* (21 vols. 1804), viii. 160. The fluctuations in the yield of tithe are being studied as an indicator of agricultural progress (E. Le Roy Ladurie and J. Goy, *Les Fluctuations du produit de la dîme. Conjoncture décimale et domaniale de la fin du Moyen Âge au XVIII* siècle (1972)). For the eighteenth century, the findings are: around Toulouse and Bordeaux and along the Pyrenees, the tithe yield was rising slowly, but there was no improvement in Brittany (summary in E. Le Roy Ladurie and J. Goy, 'La Dîme et le reste, XIVᵉ–XVIIIᵉ siècles', *Rev. hist.* (1978), 123–38; but the whole thesis of growth is denied by M. Morineau, in *Les Faux-semblants d'un démarrage économique: agriculture et démographie en France au XVIII* siècle (1971); see also 'La Dîme et l'enjeu', *Ann. hist. Rév. fr.* (1980), 162–80). In some areas, the rise of population must have cancelled out any improvement of living standards which might have been expected from the increased yield of agriculture, in contrast to the extra income which ecclesiastical institutions received from the tithe; it would be interesting to know if these were areas of more intense rural anticlericalism. But at the moment the whole subject bristles with difficulties and disagreements.

CHAPTER 5

1. *P.V. Ass.* i, Préface.
2. M. C. Peronnet, *Les Évêques de l'ancienne France* (2 vols., Univ. Lille III, 1977), ii. 732. For the early history of the assemblies, see L. Serbat, *Les Assemblées du Clergé de France, origines, organisation, développement* (1906), and P. Blet, *Le Clergé de France et la Monarchie. Études sur les Assemblées du Clergé de 1615 à 1666* (2 vols., 1957).
3. The abbé Dangeau (1693), in F. de Dainville, *Cartes anciennes de l'église de France* (1956), 282–91.
4. A. Cans, *La Contribution du Clergé de France à l'impôt, 1689–1715* (1910), 75–6.
5. G. Lepointe, *L'Organisation politique et financière du Clergé de France sous le règne de Louis XV* (1923).
6. Luynes, xiv. 177 (June 1755).
7. M. Marion, *Histoire financière de la France depuis 1715*, i (1914), 131.
8. Lepointe, *L'Organisation politique*, 7.
9. A. Cans, *L'Organisation financière du Clergé de France à l'époque de Louis XIV* (1910), 197.
10. Guyot, vii. 45.
11. Up to 1719 there were provincial *receveurs* also, acting as intermediaries. These were unnecessary officials created by the Crown merely to have jobs to sell; they were abolished in 1719.
12. Lepointe, *L'Organisation politique*, 106.
13. V. Dufour, 'État du diocèse de Paris en 1789', *Bull. Com. Paris*, 1 (1883), 329.
14. J. McManners, *French Ecclesiastical Society under the Ancien Régime: A Study of Angers* (1960), 191.
15. [M. Jousse], *Traité de la juridiction des Officiaux et autres juges d'église, tant en matière civile que criminelle* (1769), 457–8.
16. *P.V. Ass.* vii. 2062–7. Cf. the dispute at Chalon-sur-Saône, 1726–40, ibid. vi. 1720–1.
17. Ibid. vi., p. viii; viii 2. 2512.
18. According to Jousse, *Traité*, 46, Pau should be added.
19. McManners, *Angers*, 190.
20. A. Degert, 'Les Assemblées provinciales du clergé Gascon', *Rev. Gascogne* (1924), 174, 63, 177, 210, 214; 20 (1925), 81–5, 89, 183, 187–8.
21. Peronnet, *Les Évêques*, ii. 741–4.
22. P. Guillaume, *Essai sur la vie religieuse dans l'Orléanais de 1789 à 1801* (3 fasc., 1958), i. 9. Things were worse at the end of the seventeenth century. One deputy from the province of Aix was a boy under the charge of his tutor (*Mémoires de l'abbé Le Gendre, chanoine de Notre Dame*, ed. M. Roux (1863), 99–100).
23. *P.V. Ass.* viii 2. 2615–36.
24. Peronnet, *Les Évêques*, ii. 748–56.
25. Luynes, vi. 294, 304 (1745).
26. Peronnet, *Les Évêques*, 734, 726.
27. J. Boswell, *Life of Johnson* (6 vols., 1901), iii. 234. In 1775 the *receveur général* claimed 132,000 livres in costs and fees.
28. J. F. Bosher, *French Finances, 1770–1795* (1970), 165–93. *P.V. Ass.*, vii.

92–158, 331–70. Ogier, the *receveur*, had lost them 471,776 livres, 6 deniers.

29. E. Besnier, *Les Agents généraux du Clergé de France, spécialement de 1780 à 1785* (1939), 16593.
30. M. Antoine, *Le Conseil du roi sous le règne de Louis XV* (1970), 239. See also J. Coudy, *Les Moyens d'action de l'ordre du Clergé au conseil du Roi* (1956).
31. *P.V. Ass.* vii. 1853.
32. Ibid. viii/1. 109–12.
33. Ibid. vi. 1356–66. Additional room added in 1725, ibid. (vii. 61).
34. Ibid. viii/2. 1765, 2601–2 (1775).
35. L. S. Greenbaum, 'Talleyrand as agent-général', *Cath. Hist. Rev.* (1963), 475.
36. Besnier, *Les Agents généraux*, 76–132.
37. Ibid. 57.
38. Ch. Robert, *Urbain de Hercé, dernier évêque et comte de Dol* (1900), 76–7.
39. Guillaume, *Essai*, i. 11–12.
40. Guyot, ii. 547–9.
41. *P.V. Ass.* viii/2. 1328–30.
42. Ibid. viii/1. 952–7.
43. Ibid. viii/2. 1331–3. Similar cases: viii/2. 1336, 1566–75.
44. Ibid. vii. 1307, 1439 (1735); vii. 1675–81 (1740); vii. 1785–6, 1834–6 (1742); vii. 2007–9 (1745); viii/1. 327–30 (1750); viii/1. 505–14 (1750); viii/1. 828, 1705 (1760); viii/2. 1308, 1311 (1765); viii/2. 2590–3 (1770–5).
45. Cans, *L'Organisation financière*, 189.
46. T. J. Schmitt, *L'Organisation ecclésiastique et la pratique religieuse dans l'archidiaconé d'Autun de 1650 à 1750* (1957), 150.
47. *P.V. Ass.* vi. 1749–50 (1723); vii. 1181–9 (1730); vii. 1464–5 (1739); vii. 1740 (1752); vii. 2073–5 (1745); vii/1. 375–90 (1750).
48. Lepointe, *L'Organisation politique*, 243–6.
49. *P.V. Ass.* viii/1. 536–7 (1755).
50. Ibid. vii. 412–13 (1725); vii. 778 (1726); vii. 1766–9 (1740); viii/1 527 (1755).
51. Ibid. viii/1. 525, 529 (1755).
52. Ibid. viii/1. 851–6 (1760). The full story of the new system is at viii/2. 1790 ff. (1770).
53. Ibid. vii. 1842 (1742); viii/1. 71–8 (1747); viii/1. 392–3 (1750); Grenoble alone, viii/2. 2462–3 (1775); Provence alone, viii/1. 673 (1758); viii/2. 2434 (1775).
54. Ibid. viii/1. 79–82 (1747); viii/2. 1086 (1762).
55. Ibid. vii. 1450–4 (1735).
56. Rodez case of 1772, ibid. viii/2. 2574–8 (1775).
57. Ibid. viii/2. 1423–9, 1515–23 (1765).
58. Ibid. viii/2. 2347–51 (1775).
59. Ibid. vii. 1115 (1730); viii/2. 1075 (1762).
60. Ibid. vii. 454–6 (1725).
61. Ibid. vii. 1082–99 (1730).
62. Ibid. viii/1. 102–11 (1752).
63. Ibid. vii. 2016–23 (1745); viii/1. 339–45 (1750); viii/1. 675 (1758); viii/2. 2219 (1775).
64. Ibid. viii/1. 405–7 (1750).
65. Ibid. viii/2. 2527–44.

66. Ibid. viii/2. 2527–44.
67. Ibid. vii. 1691–1706 (1740). Other cases at vii. 186–90 (1726), 433–5 (1725).
68. Ibid. viii/2. 2374–6 (1775). Cf. vi. 1223–7 (1711).
69. Ibid. vii. 1110 (1730); viii/2. 1078 (1762).
70. Ibid. vi. 1123–6 (1710); vi. 1218–19 (1711); vi. 1466 (1715); vi. 1703–7 (1723); vii. 426, 478–9 (1725); vii. 1463 (1735); vii. 1717–18, 1724–5, 1727–8 (1740); vii. 2027–31 (1745); viii/1. 706–7 (1758); viii/2. 2319–20 (1775).
71. Ibid. viii/2. 1053 (1762); viii/2. 1961–2011 (1772); viii/2. 2241–60 (1775).
72. Ibid. vi. 597 (1700).
73. Ibid. vii. 415–18 (1725); vii. 1063–73 (1730).
74. Ibid. viii/2. 1394–7 (1765). For the argument that the Assembly was a sort of 'Concile National' see J. M. Gres-Gayer, *Théologie et pouvoir en Sorbonne: la Faculté de Théologie de Paris et la Bulle Unigenitus* (1991), 188, citing Ellies Du Pin, *Traité de la puissance ecclésiastique et temporelle* (1707).
75. *P.V. Ass.* vi. 315–16, 345–7 (1700).
76. Ibid. vi. 1243 (1713–14).
77. Ibid. vii. 23–4 (1725).
78. Ibid. vi. 842 (1705); viii/2. 1441–2 (1765); vii. 476–7 (1725); vii. 1490 (1735); viii/2. 1448 (1765).
79. For what follows, see Lepointe, *L'Organisation politique*, and Marion, *Histoire financière*.
80. *P.V. Ass.* vii. 1–4, 65, 81–9, 577, 614–15.
81. A 'despotic' speech: Luynes, x. 425 (22 May 1750).
82. V. Durand, *Les Évêques au XVIIIe siècle en Languedoc* (1907), 68–72.
83. Luynes, x. 463.
84. L. Bassette, *Jean de Caulet, évêque de Grenoble, 1693–1771* (1946), 167.
85. D'Argenson, vi. 145.
86. A. Mathiez, 'Les Philosophes et le pouvoir au milieu du XVIIIe siècle', *Ann. hist. Rév. fr.* (1935), 1.
87. Voltaire, *Extrait du décret de la sacrée Congrégation de l'Inquisition de Rome*, in *Œuvres*, xxiii. 463.
88. D'Argenson, vi. 166, 280, 391, 23.
89. *P.V. Ass.* viii/2. 1123, 1169, show both clergy and king recognizing that there had been 'few examples of such a delay'.
90. J. McManners, *The French Revolution and the Church* (1970), 3.
91. Luynes, vi. 292–3; iii. 193–9.
92. *P.V. de l'Assemblée générale extraordinaire du Clergé de l'année 1782* (1783), 17, 34, 333, 99–101, 146, 131–2, 297, 86–7, 261–2. On the 'bourses de jetons' see C. Florange, *Les Assemblées du Clergé de France avant 1789 et leurs jetons commémoratifs* (1927).
93. Marion, *Histoire financière*, i. 40.
94. A. Guth, 'Les Impositions du clergé d'Alsace', *Arch. Église Alsace* (1956), 164–201; (1958), 120–89; (1959), 152–78.
95. M. Fosseyeux, 'Le Cardinal de Noailles et l'administration du diocèse de Paris', *Rev. hist.* (1914).
96. H. Antoine, 'Recherches sur la paroisse et sur l'église de Saint-Pierre-de-Montsort', *Rev. Maine*, 6 (1879), 183–4.
97. René-Pierre Nepveu de la Manoullière, *Mémoires*, ed. G. Esnault (3 vols., 1877–9), i. 51.

98. See J. Marchal, *Le Droit d'oblat* (1955).
99. McManners, *Angers*, 193–4.
100. Guyot, i. 282–7. For its enforcement, Antoine, *Le Conseil du roi*, 507. For the following examples, *P.V. Ass.* viii. 1129–36, 1296, 1458.
101. Durand de Maillane, *Dictionnaire de droit canonique et de pratique bénéficiale* (1776), 150.
102. *P.V. Ass.* vii. 1719 (1740).
103. Guyot, iv. 467.
104. *P.V. Ass.* viii/1. 674 (1758).
105. Ibid. vii. 1139 (1742); viii/2. 2039 (1772).
106. J.-A. de Véri, *Journal*, ed. J. de Witte (2 vols., n.d.), ii. 339.
107. Lepointe, *L'Organisation politique*, corrects a lot of older estimates here.
108. Bosher, *French Finances*, 128.
109. Cited by E. Lavaquery, *Le Cardinal de Boisgelin, 1732–1804* (2 vols., 1920), i. 216–17.
110. Véri, *Journal*, ii. 330–9.
111. R. Chevallier, 'Les Revenus des bénéfices ecclésiastiques au 18ᵉ siècle', *Bull. Soc. hist. mod.* (1921).
112. E. Sévestre, *Les Idées gallicanes et royalistes du haut clergé . . . la correspondance de Pierre-Augustin Godert de Belbeuf, évêque d'Avranches, 1762–1803* (1917), 58–63.
113. J. Letaconnoux, 'Le Régime de la corvée en Bretagne', *Ann. Bretagne* (1906–7), 604.
114. M. Pialès, *Traité des Collations* (1753), pp. i–viii; Guyot, vi. 71–6.
115. Cerfvol, *Du Droit du souverain sur les bien fonds du clergé et des moines* (1770), cited by C. Bloch, *L'Assistance et l'État en France à la veille de la Révolution* (1908), 372.
116. Guyot, i. 143.
117. Ibid. xxx. 162.
118. Ibid. i. 140.
119. Cans, *La Contribution*, 8–10.
120. Barbier, iv. 469–70.
121. R. Tattegrain, *Du Temporel des bénéfices ecclésiastiques sous l'ancien régime* (1909), 56–7; for the eighteenth century see M. Laubry, *Traité des unions* (1778), 159.
122. [J.-L. Brunet, rev. Durand de Maillane], *Le Parfait Notaire apostolique*, rev. edn. (2 vols., 1775), ii. 2–3.
123. Guyot, xxx. 140.
124. Ibid. 147.
125. Ibid. i. 139.
126. Cans, *La Contribution*, i. 139.
127. Guyot, i. 139.
128. *Très humbles Remontrances présentées au Roi par l'assemblée générale du clergé de Bourgogne*, in Luynes, x. 469–70; D'Argenson, vi. 162–3.
129. Guyot, xvii. 160–9.
130. They pay 'quasi-rien', says Le Gendre (*Mémoires*, ed. M. Roux (1863), 43) in 1690.
131. McManners, *Angers*, 206.
132. E. Préclin, 'La Situation ecclésiastique et religieuse de la Franche Comté à la

veille de la Révolution', *Bull. Féd. Franche Comté* (1955), 3–27; L. Bourgain, 'La Contribution du clergé à l'impôt sous la monarchie française', *Rev. quest. hist.* (1890), 103.

133. McManners, *Angers*, 201.

134. J. Savina, *Le Clergé de Cornouaille à la fin de l'ancien régime et sa convocation aux États Généraux* (1926), 101.

135. *Procès-verbal de l'assemblée générale du clergé de France . . . en l'année 1782* (1783), 99–101, 104, 141–6, 219–21, 307–11.

136. Ibid. 225–78. For the history of the dispute, *Mémoires du prince de Talleyrand*, ed. the duc de Broglie (5 vols., 1891), i. 21, and *Précis . . . des matières contenues dans la Nouvelle Collection des P.V. des Ass. Gén. du . . . Clergé* (1780), 1129–59.

137. *P.V. Ass.* viii/1. 352–5.

138. Ibid. viii/2. 2292.

139. *Mémoires pour le Clergé de France dans l'affaire des foi et hommages, et réponses de l'inspecteur du domaine* (1785) (Bibl. Nat. Fo. L⁵d529), 73, 133, 249–96, 9–59.

CHAPTER 6

1. See H. Marion, *Dictionnaire des institutions de la France aux XVIIᵉ et XVIIIᵉ siècles* (2 vols., 1923), i. 177 ff., and F. de Dainville, *Cartes anciennes de l'Église de France* (1956).

2. F.-J. Casta, *Le Diocèse d'Ajaccio* (1974).

3. The bishop, driven out by the infidels, followed a duke of Nevers to France, and was given the administration of the hospital there (Luynes, xiii. 236).

4. M. Vovelle, *Piété baroque et déchristianisation en Provence au XVIIIᵉ siècle* (1973), 436.

5. J. Chétail, 'Notice sur les limites du diocèse de Glandève et son dernier évêque', *Actes 86ᵉ Congrès national des Sociétés savantes: Montpellier, 1961* (1962), 27–8.

6. No map of the dioceses as a whole was available before 1790, though individual dioceses and provinces had theirs (J. Dubois, 'La Carte des diocèses de France avant la Révolution', *Ann.* (1945), 681–6).

7. Ch. Berthelot du Chesnay, 'Le Clergé diocésain français et les registres des insinuations ecclésiastiques', *Rev. hist. mod. contemp.* (1963), 261–2.

8. Ch. Robert, *Urbain de Hercé, dernier évêque et comte de Dol* (1900), 14–15.

9. A. Brette, 'Papiers et correspondance du prince Emmanuel de Salm-Salm', *Rev. hist.* (1899), 67.

10. F. Glasson, 'Le Rôle politique du Conseil Souverain d'Alsace', *Rev. hist.* (1900), 37–8.

11. A. Schaer, *Le Clergé paroissial catholique en Haute-Alsace sous l'ancien régime, 1648–1789* (1966), pp. v–viii; A. Guth, 'Les Impositions du clergé d'Alsace', *Arch. Église Alsace* (1956), 163.

12. G. Gatherot, 'Gobel, évêque constitutionnel de Paris', *Rev. quest. hist.* (1909), 493–9.

13. R. Collier, *La Vie en Haute Provence de 1600 à 1850* (1973), 322–4.

14. D. Andreis, 'Le Rôle du Sénat de Nice, 1614–1792', *Nice historique* (1973), 25–49; L. and G. Trénard, *Histoire des diocèses de France: Belley* (1978), 114–15,

126; A. Bergier, *Des Libertés de l'Église savoyarde, 17ᵉ–18ᵉ siècle* (thèse droit, Paris, 1942).

15. J. Chétail, 'La *Réduction* du temporel de Mgr Caulet, évêque de Grenoble', *Cahiers hist.* (1960), 417–20.

16. V. Durand, *État religieux des trois diocèses de Nîmes, d'Uzès et d'Alais à la fin de l'ancien régime* (1909), 6; Th. Puntous, *Un Diocèse civil de Languedoc: les États particuliers du diocèse de Toulouse aux XVIIᵉ et XVIIIᵉ siècles* (1909), 37–61, 107.

17. L. Ampoulange, *Le Clergé et sa convocation aux États-Généraux de 1789 dans la sénéchaussée principale de Périgord* (1912), 30.

18. G. Stivil, *Le Régime administratif du Roussillon* (1927), 41–2.

19. See J.-F. Soulet, *Tradition et réformes religieuses dans les Pyrénées centrales au XVIIᵉ siècle* (1974).

20. T. J. Schmitt, *L'Organisation ecclésiastique et la pratique religieuse dans l'archidiaconé d'Autun de 1650 à 1750* (1957), 4.

21. For the proposal to unite Digne and Senez see L. Ventre. 'L'Ancien Diocèse de Senez', *Bull. Soc. Basses-Alpes* (1930), 23 ff. On the legal requirements, Guyot, xix. 241–2; lxii. 87–91.

22. J. Gallerand, 'L'Érection de l'évêché de Blois', *Rev. hist. Église Fr.* (1956), 184–201.

23. R. Sauzet, *Contre-réforme et réforme catholique en Bas-Languedoc: le diocèse de Nîmes au XVIIᵉ siècle* (1979), 45–8.

24. G. Dumary, 'Les Évêques de Dijon', *Mêms. Comm. Côte-d'Or*, 12 (1899–90), 2–11.

25. B. Hours, 'La Création du diocèse de Saint-Claude', *Rev. hist. Église Fr.* (1984), 322.

26. E. Martin, *Histoire des diocèses de Toul, de Nancy et de Saint-Dié* (3 vols., 1900–3), ii. 386–625; iii. 6–7, 15–18, 24–37. For problems of organization in the diocese of Nancy, see *Répertoire des visites pastorales de la France (anciens diocèses)*, ed. D. Julia and M. Venard, iii, (1983), 243. See also Roussel, 'L'Érection de l'évêché de Saint-Dié', *Bull. Soc. phil. vosgienne* (1932).

27. M. Braure, *Lille et la Flandre wallonne au XVIIIᵉ siècle* (2 vols., 1932), ii. 619.

28. L. Welter, 'Projet de l'érection d'un évêché de Moulins, 1787–90', *Bull. Auvergne* (1944), 73–82. Comment in E. Champion, *Rév. fr.* (1888), 591–2.

29. V. Durand, *Le Jansénisme au XVIIIᵉ siècle et Joachim Colbert* (1907), 312–13.

30. A. Cans, *L'Organisation financière du Clergé de France à l'époque de Louis XIV* (1901), 69 n.

31. *Mémoires de l'abbé Le Gendre, chanoine de Notre Dame*, ed. M. Roux (1863), 296.

32. M. Jousse, *Traité de la juridiction des officiaux* (1769), 35, 52, 57; Guyot, ii. 551.

33. A. Degert, 'L'Ancien Diocèse d'Aire', *Rev. Gascogne* (1907), 177–8.

34. François-Joachim, cardinal de Bernis, *Mémoires et lettres*, ed. F. Masson (2 vols., 1878), ii. 57–8; Jousse, *Traité*, 454–5; M.-L. Rostagnet-Latreille, 'Le Primat des Gaules et Louis XIV', *Cahiers hist.* (1958), 155.

35. *Mémoires de Le Gendre*, 313.

36. E. Regnault, *Christophe de Beaumont, archevêque de Paris, 1763–81* (2 vols., 1882), i. 437; for Saint-Sulpice see the Duc de Croÿ, *Journal, 1718–84*, ed. the vicomte de Grouchy and P. Cottin (4 vols., 1906), ii. 190–1; he was a parishioner.

37. M. C. Peronnet, *Les Évêques de l'ancienne France* (2 vols., 1977), ii. 744 ff.

38. Dainville, *Cartes*, 191.
39. For Reims see G. Laurent, *Reims et la région rémoise à la veille de la Révolution* (1930), pp. clxxii–iii; for Quimper, J. Savina, *Le Clergé de Cornouaille à la fin de l'ancien régime* (1926), 7; for Paris, L. Longon, 'L'Ancien Diocèse de Paris et ses subdivisions', *Bull. Com. Paris*, 1 (1883), 16–17.
40. Schmitt, *L'Organisation*, 1, 2, 5.
41. [J.-L. Brunet, rev. Durand de Maillane] *Le Parfait Notaire apostolique* (2 vols., 1775), i. 641–3.
42. P.-T. Durand de Maillane, *Dictionnaire de droit canonique et de pratique bénéficiale* (2 vols., 1776), i. 207.
43. Berthelot du Chesnay, 'Le Clergé', 248–50. (There were 20 sols to the livre.)
44. Potier de la Germondaye, *Introduction au gouvernement des paroisses* (1777), 62.
45. Dom P. Piolin, *L'Église du Mans durant la Révolution* (4 vols., 1868), i. 454.
46. Potier de la Germondaye, *Introduction*, 61.
47. L. Marcel, *Le Frère de Diderot* (1913), 119–20.
48. A. Playoust-Chaussis, *La Vie religieuse dans le diocèse de Boulogne au XVIIIe siècle, 1725–90* (1976), 134–6.
49. *Répertoire des visites pastorales*, iii. 226–32.
50. G. Viard, 'Les Visites pastorales dans l'ancien diocèse de Langres', *Rev. hist. Église Fr.* (1977), 253–70.
51. *Répertoire des visites*, iv (1985), 478.
52. Berthelot du Chesnay, 'Le Clergé', 247.
53. Peronnet, *Les Évêques*, ii. 744.
54. Schmitt, *L'Organisation*, 5–6.
55. Berthelot du Chesnay, 'Le Clergé', 247.
56. Jousse, *Traité*, 366–8. For Saintes, L. Audiat, *Deux victimes des Septembriseurs, Pierre-Louis de la Rochefoucauld, dernier évêque de Saintes, et son frère, évêque de Beauvais* (1897).
57. J. Grente and O. Havard, *Villedieu-les-Poêles: sa commanderie, sa bourgeoisie, ses métiers* (2 vols., 1898), i. 241–2.
58. Jousse, *Traité*, 117–20.
59. Guyot, xliii. 239–40.
60. Durand, *État religieux*, 18.
61. Berthelot du Chesnay, 'Le Clergé', 242.
62. Brémond d'Ars Migré, *Un Collaborateur de Buffon: l'abbé Bexon* (1936), 33–4.
63. Jousse, *Traité*, 124–6.
64. V. Dufour, 'État du diocèse de Paris en 1789', *Bull. Comm. Paris*, 1 (1883), 48–53.
65. Jousse, *Traité*, 224–68.
66. Ibid. 251–87.
67. Guyot, xi. 243 ff.
68. R. Phillips, *Family Breakdown in 18th-Century France: Divorce in Rouen 1792–1803* (1980), 4–7; A. Lottin, 'Vie et mort du couple . . . dans le Nord de la France aux XVIIe et XVIIIe siècles', *XVIIe siècle* (1974), 65–8. For Cambrai, Guyot, xliii. 267–9. The *officialité* of Strasbourg had only 144 applicants from 1685 to 1719, two-thirds of them being women: 48 applications were granted (L. Châtellier, *Tradition chrétienne et renouveau catholique dans les cadres de l'ancien diocèse de Strasbourg, 1650–1770* (1981), 251).
69. V. Durand, *Les Évêques au XVIIIe siècle en Languedoc* (1907), 190.

70. M. Briffaut, 'Incident tumultueux dans l'église de Saint-Géry en 1758', *Méms. Soc. Cambrai* (1970), 215–24.

71. Barbier, ii. 71–2 (July 1729).

72. P. L. Varaigne, 'Justice royale et justice ecclésiastique au XVIIIe siècle', *Rev. Soc. Villiers-sur-Marne*, 22e ann., NS 2 (1969–70), 7–12.

73. B. Plongeron, *La Vie quotidienne du clergé français au XVIIIe siècle* (1974), 65–8; René-Pierre Nepveu de la Manoullière, *Mémoires*, G. Esnault ed. (3 vols., 1877–9), ii. 87; G. Doublet, *Le Jansénisme dans l'ancien diocèse de Vence* (1901), 290–1.

74. The basic authority is A. Degert, *Histoire des séminaires français* (2 vols., 1912). Also indispensable is G. Bonnenfant, *Les Séminaires normands du XVIe au XVIIIe siècle* (1915).

75. Bonnenfant, *Les Séminaires normands*, 156–8, 182, 167, 173, 199, 288–9.

76. Ibid. 393–7, 334.

77. Degert, *Histoire*, ii. 347–8.

78. Ibid. ii. 458–505.

79. Ibid. ii. 508–10. Toulouse had three seminaries (Lazarist, Oratorian, and Jesuit); there was also an Irish one (Cl. Tournier, *Histoire des séminaires toulousains* (1942)).

80. P. R. Harris, *Douai College Documents, 1639–1794* (1992), 148–9.

81. P. Boyle, *The Irish College in Paris, 1578–1901* (1901).

82. C. Mooney, *The Irish Franciscans in France* (1964).

83. H. Fleming, OP, *The Undoing of the Friars of Ireland: A Study of the Noviciate Question in the 18th Century* (1972), 109–16, 191.

84. The view as angrily described by the bishop of Ossory (ibid. 115).

85. *P.V. Ass.* vii. 1753 (23 Aug. 1740).

86. Degert, *Histoire*, ii. 337–8, 346. There is a life of Claude-François Pouillart by le Floch (1904).

87. J. Ferté, *La Vie religieuse dans les campagnes parisiennes, 1622–95* (1962), 161–70.

88. L. Dantin, *François de Gain-Montagnac évêque de Tarbes, 1782–1801* (1908), 25–8.

89. P.-D. Bernier, *Essai sur le tiers état rural: les paysans de Basse-Normandie au XVIIIe siècle* (1891), 233–4.

90. Bonnenfant, *Les Séminaires normands*, 368–73.

91. Ch. Robert, *Urbain de Hercé*, 57, 94.

92. One year for ordination at Auch (J. Bénac, 'Le Séminaire d'Auch', *Rev. Gascogne* (1907), 216–38).

93. J. Charrier, *Histoire religieuse du département de la Nièvre* (2 vols., 1936), i. 12.

94. J. Daranatz, 'Les Ordinations sacerdotales du diocèse de Bayonne au XVIIIe siècle', *Bull. Soc. Bayonne* (1931), 143.

95. F.-G. Pariset (ed.), *Bordeaux au XVIIIe siècle* (1968), 132.

96. 'Mémoires inédits de M. Lebay, curé de Veules, 1761–1834', *La Semaine religieuse de Rouen*, 10 (1876), 460 ff.

97. J. Leflon, *M. Emery* (2 vols., 1943), i. 33; J. Delumeau, *Le Diocèse de Rennes* (1979), 135; Degert, *Histoire*, ii. 19; Bonnenfant, *Les Séminaires normands*, 410.

98. Reminiscences of his early days by Cardinal Fesch, Napoleon's uncle (A. Latreille, *Napoléon et le Saint-Siège* (1935), 47).

99. F. Lebrun (ed.), *Histoire des catholiques en France du XVe siècle à nos jours* (1980), 151–2.

100. Bonnenfant, *Les Séminaires normands*, 264, 391, 379; Degert, *Histoire*, ii. 512; F. D. Mathieu, *L'Ancien Régime en Lorraine et Barrois* (1879), 335–6; A. H. Van der Weil, *Paul-Louis de Mondran, un chanoine homme d'esprit* (1944), 13.

101. J.-J. Gautier, *Essai sur les mœurs champêtres* (1787), ed. X. Rousseau (1935), 21–2.

102. The abbé Dinouart, in A. Bernard, *Le Sermon au XVIIIᵉ siècle, 1715–89* (1901), 369.

103. P. Sage, *Le Bon Prêtre dans la littérature française d'Amadis de Gaule au Génie du Christianisme* (1951), 148 n.

104. R. Darricau, *La Formation des professeurs de séminaire au début du XVIIIᵉ siècle d'après un directoire de M. Jean Bonnet* (1966), 4–12.

105. Detail in Degert, *Histoire*, ii. 148–300.

106. A. Degert, 'L'Enseignement de l'histoire dans les anciens séminaires français', *Rev. quest. hist.* (1910), 125–9.

107. Van der Weil, *Paul-Louis de Mondran*, 11.

108. Ch. Berthelot du Chesnay, 'Études ecclésiastiques et formation du clergé en Bretagne au XVIIIᵉ siècle', *Ann. Bretagne* (1976), 659.

109. Y. Poulet and J. Roubert, 'Les Assemblées secrètes des XVIIᵉ et XVIIIᵉ siècles en relation avec l'Aa de Lyon', *Divus Thomas* (1967), 165–92.

110. The Lazarists took lifelong vows, but they were 'vows simple'—they could withdraw (J. W. Carver, *Napoleon and the Lazarists* (1974), 74–5).

111. Leflon, *M. Emery*, i. 11.

CHAPTER 7

1. R. Darricau, 'Louis XIV et le Saint-Siège: les indults de nomination aux bénéfices consistoriaux', *Bull. litt. ecclés.* (1905), 16–34, 107–31. Durtelle de Saint-Sauveur, *Les Pays d'obédience dans l'ancienne France* (1908).

2. Recorded by the abbé de Dangeau in 1690 (in F. de Dainville, *Cartes anciennes de l'Église de France* (1956), 280–1).

3. L. S. Greenbaum, 'Ten Priests in Search of a Mitre: How Talleyrand became a Bishop', *Cath. Hist. Rev.* (1964), 305–7.

4. J. Blampignon, *L'Épiscopat de Massillon* (1884), 32–4.

5. L. Tronson, *Correspondance*, ed. L. Bertrand (3 vols., 1904), iii. 389–90; Mme de Sévigné, *Lettres*, ed. Gérard-Gailly (3 vols., 1995), ii. 813. Even if the six nominated but not yet consecrated bishops she refers to are added, the number falls short of Nicea.

6. G. Namer, *L'Abbé Le Roy et ses amis* (1964), 58.

7. All this section is based on the indispensable work of M.-C. Peronnet, *Les Évêques de l'ancienne France* (2 vols., 1977).

8. J. Godel, 'Le Cardinal des montagnes: Etienne le Camus, évêque de Grenoble, 1671–1707', *Actes Colloque le Camus, Grenoble, 1971* (1974), 24.

9. Luynes, viii. 208–9.

10. Peronnet (*Les Évêques*, i. 154–9) takes the strict line about *preuves*, and counts these two as *roturiers*. This is what the genealogists would have said, but it does not accord with eighteenth-century social usage.

11. Pioneer work here by N. Ravitch, *Sword and Mitre: Government and Episcopate in France and England in the Age of Aristocracy* (1966).

12. Peronnet, *Les Évêques*, i. 580.

13. Marais, i. 145–6.

14. A. Rosne, *M. de Beauvais, évêque de Senez, 1731–90* (1883), 13–41. For the miserable diocese, M. Vovelle, *Piété baroque et déchristianisation en Provence au XVIIIe siècle* (1973), 463 ff.

15. P. Feret, *La Faculté de Théologie de Paris et ses docteurs les plus célèbres* (7 vols., 1909), vii. 358.

16. Examples in the Oxford thesis of Dr Nigel Aston, 'The Politics of the French Episcopate, 1786–91' (1985).

17. Ch. Robert, *Urbain de Hercé* (1900), 14–15; L. Alloing, *Le Diocèse de Belley* (1938), 276–7.

18. Peronnet, *Les Évêques*, i. 347–9.

19. Ibid. i. 576–7.

20. C. Bianchi, 'L'Application de la constitution civile du clergé dans l'ancien diocèse de Grasse', *Ann. Soc. Cannes* (1951–4), 98.

21. J. Eich, *Histoire religieuse du département de la Moselle pendant la Révolution* (1964), i. 4.

22. J. Loth, *Histoire du cardinal de la Rochefoucauld et du diocèse de Rouen* (1893), 24.

23. J. Carreyre, *Le Jansénisme durant la Régence* (3 vols., 1929–33), iii. 369.

24. Peronnet, *Les Évêques*, i. 612 ff.

25. E. Appolis, *Le Diocèse civil de Lodève au milieu du XVIIIe siècle* (1951), 72–3; C. Cézérai, 'A propos de la nomination de Mgr de Latour-Dupuis à l'évêché d'Auch', *Rev. Gascogne* (1903), 357.

26. E. Sévestre, *Les Idées gallicanes et royalistes du haut clergé. Pierre-Augustin Godart de Belbeuf, évêque d'Avranches, 1762–1803* (1917), 44–5.

27. J. Meyer, *La Noblesse bretonne au XVIIIe siècle* (2 vols., 1966), ii. 1101–3. Only one Breton succeeded to the see of Rennes between 1642 and 1789 (J. Delumeau, *Le Diocèse de Rennes* (1979), 131–2).

28. Luynes, vii. 381–2.

29. Peronnet, *Les Évêques*, i. 337.

30. François-Joachim, cardinal de Bernis, *Mémoires et lettres*, ed. F. Masson (2 vols., 1878), ii. 211–13, 218–19.

31. T. Tackett, *Priest and Parish in 18th-Century France, 1750–91* (1977), 30.

32. N.-J. Chaline, *Rouen-Le Havre* (Histoire des diocèses de France) (1976), 127–8.

33. A. Sicard, *L'Ancien Clergé de France: les évêques avant la Révolution*, 5th edn. (1912), 279; Luynes, x. 350, xiii. 387–8.

34. H. Lancelin, *Histoire du diocèse de Cambrai* (1946), 248.

35. Peronnet, *Les Évêques*, i. 353.

36. *Dictionnaire portatif des cas de conscience*, 2nd edn. (2 vols., Lyon, 1761), i. 421.

37. Tronson, *Correspondance*, iii. 301.

38. R. Daon, *Conduite des âmes dans la voie du salut* (1750).

39. *Dictionnaire portatif*, i. 422.

40. L. de Sambucy Saint-Estève, *Vie de Mgr de Beauvais, ancien évêque de Senez* (1843), 55.

41. Cited by Ravitch, *Sword and Mitre*, 118–19 (though the preacher added that the Gallican Church was burdened with prelates 'without learning or virtue').

42. Voltaire, *Instruction pastorale de l'humble évêque d'Alétopolis* (1763), in *Œuvres*, xxv. 2 ff; P. Sage, *Le 'Bon prêtre' dans la littérature française* (1951), 379.

43. J. F. Marmontel, 'La Mauvaise Mère', in *Contes Moraux* (3 vols., 1765), ii. 101.

44. P. de Vaissière, *Gentilshommes campagnards de l'ancienne France* (1903), 372. (Cf. G. Gilot and A. Amic, 'Le Dernier Abbé de la Ferté-sur-Grosse', *Rev. Mabillon* (1907), 239 ff.)

45. M. Vallery-Radot, *Un Administrateur ecclésiastique à la fin de l'ancien régime: le cardinal de Luynes, archevêque de Sens, 1753–88* (1966), 12–13.

46. G. Vavasseur, 'L'Abbé Souquet de Latour', *Bull. Soc. Orne* (1895), 309–38; C. de Lacroix, *Souvenirs du comte de Montgaillard*, cited by Fabre de Massaguel, *L'École de Sorèze de 1758 au 19 fructidor, an IV* (1958), 155.

47. Chateaubriand, *Mémoires d'outre-tombe*, ed. M. Levaillant and G. Moutinier (2 vols., 1958), i. 135, 203.

48. *Mémoires du duc des Cars* (2 vols., 1890), i. 8.

49. J. Perrin, *Le Cardinal de Loménie de Brienne, archevêque de Sens* (1896), 3–6.

50. P. Coste, *Le Grand Saint du grand siècle: M. Vincent* (3 vols., 1932), ii. 426.

51. Sévestre, *Les Idées*, 29–45.

52. E. Lavaquery, *Le Cardinal de Boisgelin, 1732–1804* (2 vols., 1920), i. 24, 31, 41.

53. F. Lorin, 'Les Trois Derniers Abbés de Vaux-de Cerney', *Méms. Soc. Rambouillet* (1913), 445.

54. L. Audiat, *Deux victimes des Septembriseurs, Pierre-Louis de la Rochefoucauld, dernier évêque de Saintes, et son frère, évêque de Beauvais* (1897), 178 ff.

55. V. Dubaret, 'Notice historique sur les évêques d'Oloron, 506–1792', *Bull. Soc. Pau*, 2ᵉ sér. 17 (1881–2).

56. A. Degert, 'L'Ancien Diocèse d'Aire', *Rev. Gascogne* (1907), 119–69.

57. Ch. Monternot, *Yves-Alexandre de Marbeuf . . . archevêque de Lyon, 1734–99* (1911), 2.

58. P. Parfouru, *Les Comptes d'un évêque et les anciens manoirs épiscopaux de Rennes et de Bruz au XVIIIᵉ siècle* (1895), 6.

59. L. W. B. Brockliss, *French Higher Education in the 17th and 18th Centuries* (1987), 236. Details of the examination in J.-J. Pialès, *Traité des gradués* (6 vols., 1757), i. 432–8.

60. Alloing, *Le Diocèse de Belley*, 274.

61. The king could send letters asking for dispensation from theses (Feret, *La Faculté*, vi. 44).

62. *Mémoires de l'abbé Baston, chanoine de Rouen*, ed. J. Loth and C. Verger (3 vols., 1897) i. 101–2.

63. Feret, *La Faculté*, vi. 194–6.

64. Baston, *Mémoires*, i 115–18.

65. Tronson, *Correspondance*, i. p. ix, ii. 143, iii. 158, 200–1, 257–8, 305; J. Ferté, *La Vie religieuse dans les campagnes parisiennes, 1622–95* (1962), 154.

66. P. Boissard, *Issy, le séminaire et la communauté de Saint-Sulpice* (1942), 19–34.

67. Talleyrand, *Mémoires*, ed. the duc de Broglie (5 vols., 1891–2), i. 22.

68. J. Leflon, *M. Emery* (2 vols., 1943), i. 115 ff.

69. Baston, *Mémoires*, i. 119.

70. Cited by P. Pisani, *L'Église de Paris et la Révolution* (4 vols., 1908–11), i. 65–6.

71. C. Laplatte, *Le Diocèse de Coutances* (1942), 47; Degert, 'L'Ancien Diocèse

d'Aire', 221–2; P. Pérez and S. Daugé, 'Nomenclature des prêtres et religieux de la famille de Daignon de Sendat', *Bull. Soc. Gers* (1932), 280–1.

72. Eich, *Histoire religieuse*, i. 15–16.

73. Fr. de la Rochefoucauld, *Voyages en France*, ed. J. Marchand (1933), 12–13; A. Degert, 'Un Vicaire-général aérostatier', *Rev. Gascogne* (1903), 373–4.

74. V. Durand, *État religieux des trois diocèses de Nîmes, d'Uzès et d'Alais à la fin de l'ancien régime* (1909), 36.

75. See Bernard de Brye, *Un évêque d'ancien régime à l'épreuve de la Révolution: le cardinal A.L.M. de la Fare* (1985).

CHAPTER 8

1. D'Argenson, v. 246–8.

2. A. Sicard, *L'Ancien Clergé de France: les évêques avant la Révolution*, 5th edn. (1912), 306.

3. P. Vial, 'L'Église de France vue par le nonce en 1766', *Cahiers hist.* (1963), 112.

4. The Véri MSS, *cahier* 128, arch. dép. Drôme, cited by J. Hardman, 'Ministerial Politics from the Accession of Louis XVI to the Assembly of Notables' (Oxford thesis, 1972).

5. J. Leflon, *M. Emery* (2 vols., 1943), i. 39.

6. D'Argenson, v. 246–8.

7. P. Parfouru, *Les Comptes d'un évêque et les anciens manoirs épiscopaux au XVIIIe siècle* (1895), 11–12.

8. F. Baboin, 'L'Application de la Constitution Civile du Clergé dans la Drôme', *Rév. fr.* (1899), 228.

9. C. Port, *La Vendée angevine* (2 vols., 1888), i. 153. Dr Nigel Aston tells me he was being treated by doctors in Paris.

10. L. Bassette, *Jean de Caulet, évêque de Grenoble, 1725–71* (1946), 38–43.

11. J. Eich, *Histoire religieuse du département de la Moselle pendant la Révolution* (2 vols., 1964), i. 11.

12. L. Desgraves and J.-P. Poussou, in F.-G. Pariset (ed.), *Bordeaux au XVIIIe siècle* (1968), 122–4.

13. M. C. Peronnet, *Les Évêques de l'ancienne France* (2 vols., 1977), ii. 966–8.

14. H. Espitalier, *Les Évêques de Fréjus* (1898), 225–6.

15. E. Lavaquery, *Le Cardinal de Boisgelin, 1732–1804* (2 vols., 1920), i. 258.

16. J. Blampignon, *L'Épiscopat de Massillon* (1884), 38.

17. D'Argenson, v. 379 (Feb. 1749).

18. E. Appolis, *Le Jansénisme à Lodève* (1952), 14–16.

19. G. Lizerand, *Le Duc de Beauvillier, 1648–1714* (1933), 308–10; G. Poisson, *M. de Saint-Simon* (1973), 245–6.

20. D'Argenson, vi. 282, viii. 398–9.

21. Vial, 'L'Église', 110.

22. Moreau de Jonnès, 'Mémoires', *Rév. fr.* (1890), 34–5; J. Flammermont, 'La Banqueroute Rohan-Guémené', *Rév. fr.* (1898), 140–7; Ch. Collas, *Saint-Louis d'Antin* (1932), 47; H. Carré, *La Noblesse de France et l'opinion publique au XVIIIe siècle* (1920), 258–9.

23. According to Doppet's solemn *Traité du fouet et de ses effets sur le physique de*

l'amour (1788), 31, cited by R. Mauzi, *L'Idée du bonheur au XVIIIe siècle* (1960), 427–8.

24. J.-A. Dulaure, *La Vie privée des ecclésiastiques qui n'ont point prêté leur serment sur la Constitution civile du clergé* (1791), 81–3.

25. M. G. Coolen, 'Le Duel de Mgr de Conzié', *Bull. Soc. Morinie* (1938), 46–61.

26. For all that follows, masterly analysis in Peronnet, *Les Évêques*, ii. 1013–20.

27. See S. Brugal, *Le Schisme constitutionnel dans l'Ardèche: Lafont-Savine, évêque jureur de Viviers* (1889).

28. G. Maugras, *Lauzun and the Court of Marie-Antoinette* (E.T. 1896), 369–76; the marquise de la Tour-du-Pin, *Journal d'une femme de cinquante ans, 1778–1815* (2 vols., 1913), i. 3, 27, 29, 30.

29. L. S. Greenbaum, *Talleyrand, Statesman Priest. The Agent General of the Clergy and the Church of France at the End of the Old Régime* (1970); and id., 'Ten Priests in Search of a Mitre: How Talleyrand became a Bishop', *Cath. Hist. Rev.* (1964), 307–31.

30. B. de Lacombe, *Talleyrand évêque d'Autun* (1903), 75–118.

31. Vial, 'L'Église', 108.

32. E. S. Mercier, *Tableau de Paris*, new edn. (12 vols., 1782–8), iv. 110. The 1st edn. was 1781.

33. Péronnet, *Les Évêques*, ii. 1006–8.

34. Luynes, iii. 321 (Feb. 1741); *Correspondance complète de la marquise du Deffand*, ed. M. de Lescure (2 vols., 1865), i. 273–4.

35. Bachaumont, x. 172 (Mar. 1778), x. 186 (Apr.).

36. Mme de Sévigné, *Lettres*, ed. Gérard-Gailly (3 vols., 1953), ii. 465 (6 Oct. 1679).

37. Sicard, *L'Ancien Clergé*, 101–3.

38. L. Châtellier, *Tradition chrétienne et renouveau catholique dans les cadres de l'ancien diocèse de Strasbourg, 1650–1770* (1981), 56–8.

39. J. Savina, *Le Clergé de Cornouaille à la fin de l'ancien régime et sa convocation aux États-Généraux de 1789* (1926), 27.

40. M. Fosseyeux, 'Le Cardinal de Noailles et l'administration du diocèse de Paris', *Rev. hist.* (1913), 44–6, 272–3; *Mémoires de l'abbé Le Gendre, chanoine de Notre-Dame*, ed. M. Roux (1863), 126–8.

41. B. Gille, *Les Forges françaises en 1777* (1960), 91, 99, 157–8.

42. V. Durand, *Les Évêques au XVIIIe siècle en Languedoc* (1907), 3.

43. Deffand, *Correspondance*, ii. 522–3 (3 Jan. 1776).

44. Luynes, iii. 99, vii. 451.

45. L. Charpentier, 'Un Inventaire épiscopal à Alet en 1764', *Méms. Soc. Carcassonne* (1904), 3–40.

46. Ch. Monternot, *Yves-Alexandre de Marbeuf . . . archevêque de Lyon, 1734–99* (1911), 47.

47. A. Degert, *Histoire des évêques de Dax* (1903), 379.

48. Ch. Robert, *Urbain de Hercé* (1900), 83–4; J. Chétail, 'Notice sur le diocèse de Glandève', *Actes 86e Congrès national des Sociétés savantes; Montpellier* (1961), 25.

49. Luynes, i. 140, 150; J.-J. Pialès, *Traité des réparations* (4 vols., 1762), ii. 459.

50. *Vie de M. Marquis-Ducastel, curé de Sainte-Suzanne*, ed. F. Pichon (1873), 36–9; A. Vidal, *L'Ancien Diocèse d'Albi* (1913), 54–7.

51. E. Esmonin, 'La Société grenobloise au temps de Louis XV d'après les

Miscellanea de Letourneau', in *Études sur la France des XVIIe et XVIIIe siècles* (1964), 490.

52. Bachaumont, xxxiv. 239–40.
53. Lavaquery, *Boisgelin*, i. 183.
54. L. Tronson, *Correspondance*, ed. L. Bertrand (3 vols., 1904), iii. 88–93.
55. J.-A. Dulaure, *Nouvelle Description de Paris* (2 vols., 1787), i. 127.
56. Sicard, *L'Ancien Clergé*, 80–1.
57. M. Vallery-Radot, *Un Administrateur ecclésiastique à la fin de l'ancien régime: le cardinal de Luynes, archevêque de Sens, 1753–88* (1966), 21–3.
58. 'Un Pèlerinage à la campagne et à la cathédrale de Bossuet en 1775', *Méms. Acad. nat. de Caen* (1899), 20.
59. Luynes, vii. 38.
60. J.-F.-H. de Richeprey, *Journal des voyages en Haute-Guienne*, ed. H. Guilhamon (1952), 78.
61. Parfouru, *Les Comptes*, 40–4.
62. E. Appolis, *Le Diocèse civil de Lodève* (1951), 244–5.
63. Sicard, *L'Ancien Clergé*, 98.
64. G. Couarraze, *Lombez, évêché rural, 1317–1861* (1973), 212.
65. E. Vivier, 'La Condition du clergé séculier dans le diocèse de Coutances au XVIIIe siècle', *Ann. Normandie* (1952), 3–4.
66. Guyot, ii. 369. See also R. Metz, *La Monarchie française et la provision des bénéfices ecclésiastiques en Alsace, 1648–1789* (1947), 43, 65 ff.
67. F. Bluche, *Les Magistrats du Parlement de Paris au XVIIIe siècle* (1960), 49.
68. P. Goubert, *Beauvais et le Beauvaisis de 1600 à 1730* (2 vols., 1960), i. 283–9.
69. Marais, i. 159–60.
70. Ibid. ii. 89.
71. F.-X.-J. Droz, *Histoire du règne de Louis XVI* (3 vols., 1839–42), i. 120.
72. Guyot, *Traité des droits . . . annexés en France à chaque dignité* (4 vols., 1787), ii. 138 ff.
73. Marais, iv. 281–4.
74. Piron, *Lettres*, ed. E. Lavaquery (1920), 31–2.
75. Th. Besterman, *Voltaire* (1965), 558.
76. J. McManners, *Abbés and Actresses: The Church and the Theatrical Profession in 18th-Century France*, Zaharoff Lecture (1986), 12–13.
77. Piron, *Lettres*, 32.
78. Lavaquery, *Boisgelin*, 258.
79. Sicard, *L'Ancien Clergé*, 60 ff.
80. P. Tallez, 'Mgr Claude-Marc Antoine d'Apochon, archevêque d'Auch', *Rev. Gascogne* (1926), 220–4.
81. Bassette, *Jean de Caulet*, 43–6.
82. e.g. Christophe de Beaumont when bishop of Bayonne (E. Regnault, *Christophe de Beaumont, archevêque de Paris, 1763–81* (2 vols., 1882), i. 78–83).
83. Espitalier, *Les Évêques*, 198–270.
84. A. Babeau, *La Ville sous l'ancien régime* (2 vols., 1889), i. 23.
85. e.g. Appolis, *Le Diocèse civil de Lodève*, 33, 48–53, 66, 72, 76, 82, 108.
86. F. Masson, *Le Cardinal de Bernis depuis son ministère, 1758–94* (1884), 42–3.
87. Sicard, *L'Ancien Clergé*, 74.
88. E. Laurent, *Reims et la région rémoise à la veille de la Révolution* (1930), pp. xx–xxiv.

89. Durand, *Les Évêques*, 25, 49, 50.
90. E. Laurès, *La Municipalité de Béziers à la fin de l'ancien régime* (1926), 18, 45–7, 50.
91. Bassette, *Jean de Caulet*, 126; Guyot, ix. 297–8.
92. Desgraves and Poussou, in Pariset (ed.), *Bordeaux*, 129.
93. A. Le Moy, *Le Parlement de Bretagne et le pouvoir royal au XVIIIe siècle* (1909), 14–15.
94. J. Pandellé, 'Une Grande Figure épiscopale, Jean-François de Montillet', *Rev. Gascogne* (1937), 113–16.
95. *Lettres secrètes sur l'état actuel de la religion et du clergé*, in Métra, xiii. 366.
96. Sicard, *L'Ancien Clergé*, 75.
97. C. Cézérac, 'A propos de la nomination de Mgr de Latour-Dupin à l'archevêché d'Auch, 1783', *Rev. Gascogne* (1903), 357.
98. J. Thibaut-Payen, *Les Morts, l'Église et l'État dans le ressort du Parlement de Paris aux XVIIe et XVIIIe siècles* (1977), 334–5.
99. On the exaggerations in the outcry about administrative bishops see F. Dumont, 'Les Prélats administrateurs au XVIIIe siècle', in *Études d'histoire et du droit canonique dédiées à Gabriel Le Bras* (1965), 513 ff.
100. M.-R. Vilette, *Les États-Généraux du Cambrésis de 1677 à 1790* (thesis, Lille, 1950), 44–70.
101. T. J. Schmitt, *L'Organisation ecclésiastique et la pratique religieuse dans l'archidiaconé d'Autun de 1650 à 1750* (1957), 7; Sicard, *L'Ancien Clergé*, 203.
102. J. Roussot, *Le Mâconnais* (1937), 111–24.
103. Savina, *Le Clergé*, 18–19.
104. Luynes, iii. 74 (Nov. 1739).
105. Lavaquery, *Boisgelin*, i. 130–5, 150–2.
106. Roussot, *Le Mâconnais*, 189–90, 195–6.
107. Robert, *Urbain de Hercé*, 128, 153, 162–3, 195, 215.
108. J. Meyer, *La Noblesse bretonne au XVIIIe siècle* (2 vols., 1966), ii. 1101. For their part the bishops did not conceal their contempt for the drunken conduct of the nobles (ibid. ii. 1081; A. Le Moy, *Le XVIIIe Siècle breton: correspondance . . . de M.M. de Robien et de la Bellangerais, 1769–91* (1931), 180).
109. G. Cormary, *Loménie de Brienne à Toulouse, 1763–88* (1935), 86 ff.
110. Durand, *Les Évêques*, 80–1.
111. Lavaquery, *Boisgelin*, 340–77.
112. Masson, *Le Cardinal de Bernis*, 61–2.

CHAPTER 9

1. R. J. Palanque, *Le Diocèse d'Aix en Provence* (1975), 123.
2. F. de Dainville, *Cartes anciennes de l'Église de France* (1956), 52–7.
3. For Reims, G. Hubrecht, 'Les Droits seigneuriaux dans la région sedanaise', *Nouv. Rev. Champagne et Brie* (1936), 35–49. For Cambrai, P. Bourgard, 'Dénombrement de la population du Cambrésis', in M. Lachiver *et al.* (eds.), *Hommage à Marcel Reinhard* (1973), 73. For Tarbes, L. Dantin, *François de Gain Montagnac, évêque de Tarbes, 1782–1801* (1908), 22. For Comminges, A. Sarramon, *Les Paroisses du diocèse de Comminges en 1786* (1987), 13–15.

4. C. Daur, 'L'État du diocèse de Montauban à la fin de l'ancien régime', *Rev. quest. hist.* (1914), 495–7.
5. M. C. Peronnet, *Les Évêques de l'ancienne France* (2 vols., 1977), i. 945–60.
6. Voltaire, *Correspondance*, ed. Th. Besterman, i. 322 (Aug. 1725).
7. Grimm, vi. 456–7 (Jan. 1760).
8. J. Dautry, 'Sébastien Lacroix', *Ann. hist. Rév. fr.* (1933), 50.
9. Voltaire, *Écrivains français du siècle de Louis XIV*, in *Œuvres*, xiv. 89.
10. G. Cholvy, *Le Diocèse de Montpellier* (1976), 161–2.
11. Bachaumont, vii. 81–2 (Nov. 1773).
12. J. Droz, *Histoire du règne de Louis XVI* (3 vols., 1839), i. 447.
13. Marais, iv. 428 (Oct. 1732).
14. Details in R. Suadeau, *L'Évêque inspecteur administratif sous la monarchie absolue* (2 vols., 1940), i. 7–17.
15. Potier de la Germondaye, *Introduction au gouvernement des paroisses* (1777), 66.
16. J. Lovié, 'La Vie paroissiale dans le diocèse de Dié à la fin de l'ancien régime', *Bull. Soc. Drôme* (1931–2), 358 ff.
17. Martial-Levé, *Louis-François-Gabriel d'Orléans de la Motte, évêque d'Amiens, 1683–1774* (1902), 18.
18. E. Appolis, 'Entre jansénistes et constitutionnaires', *Ann.* (1951), 160.
19. R. Darricau and B. Peyrous, 'Les Visites pastorales dans le Midi aquitain: bilan d'une enquête', *Ann. Midi* (1977), 398. See also the same two authors, 'Les Visites pastorales des évêques d'Aire et des évêques de Dax', *Bull. Soc. Borda* (1977), 107–21, and 'Les Visites pastorales des évêques de Bazas', *Cahiers Bazadais* (1977), 3–15.
20. M. A. Coulandres, 'Journal de Bernard-Laurent Soumille', *Mems. Soc. Alais* (1879), 157; L. Boisse, 'Les Chapelles anciennes de Grange-Gontard', *Bull. Soc. Drôme* (1931–2), 118–22; M.-C. Guibert, *Mémoires pour servir à l'histoire de la ville de Dieppe*, ed. M. Hardy (2 vols., 1878), i. 97.
21. M. Dommanget, *Le Curé Meslier* (1965), 33–8, 62.
22. A. Sicard, *L'Ancien Clergé de France: les évêques avant la Révolution* (1912 edn.), 360–70. Another case in M. Riollet, 'Le Journal d'un curé de campagne, 1768–90', *Rev. Lyon* (1911). Grimaldi's successor at Le Mans immediately set out on a confirmation tour (A. Durand, *Une Paroisse mayennaise: Fougerolles sous la Révolution, 1789–1800* (1960), 130).
23. H. Lancelin, *Histoire du diocèse de Cambrai* (1946), 237–42; L. G. Trénard, 'Les Visites pastorales dans le diocèse de Cambrai', *Rev. Nord* (1970), 473.
24. A. Kleinclausz, *Histoire de Lyon* (1948), i. 196; Raison, 'Le Jansénisme à Rennes', *Ann. Bretagne* (1940), 186–7; C. Laplatte, *Le Diocèse de Coutances* (1942), 44.
25. R.-P. Nepveu de la Manoullière, *Mémoires*, ed. G. Esnault (3 vols., 1877–9), ii. 60.
26. D. Julia and M. Vénard (gen. eds.), *Répertoire des visites pastorales de la France (anciens diocèses)*, iii (1983), 300–5.
27. F. Lebrun, *Le Diocèse d'Angers* (1981), 128.
28. L. Pérouas, *Le Diocèse de la Rochelle de 1648 à 1724: sociologie et pastorale* (1964).
29. J. Blampignon, *L'Épiscopat de Massillon* (1884), 39–44, 55–60.
30. Julia and Vénard (eds.), *Répertoire*, iii. 326–32.
31. Ibid. iv (1985), 366–76.
32. Ibid. iv. 211 ff.

33. M. Vallery-Radot, *Un Administrateur ecclésiastique à la fin de l'ancien régime: le cardinal de Luynes* (1966), 25, 103; L. Audiat, *Deux victimes des Septembriseurs, Pierre-Louis de la Rochefoucauld, dernier évêque de Saintes, et son frère, évêque de Beauvais* (1897), 21, 35; P. Pisani, *L'Église de Paris et la Révolution* (4 vols., 1908–11), i. 79.

34. E. Houth, *Versailles, la paroisse royale* (1962), 64–5; A. Kwantan, 'Antoine Elénore-Léon Le Clerc de Juigné, évêque de Châlons, 1764–82', *Méms. Soc. Marne* (1973), 168.

35. Martial-Levé, *Louis-François-Gabriel*, 37, 38; V. Durand, *État religieux des trois diocèses de Nîmes, d'Uzès et d'Alais à la fin de l'ancien régime* (1909), 45; L. Alloing, *Le Diocèse de Belley* (1938), 274; G. Minois, 'Les Visites épiscopales du diocèse de Tréguier, 1700–80', *Méms. Soc. Côtes-du-Nord* (1978), 18.

36. L. Bassette, *Jean de Caulet, évêque de Grenoble, 1725–71* (1946), 123.

37. Pérouas, *Le Diocèse de la Rochelle*, 353–4.

38. J.-T. Lasserre, *Recherches historiques sur la ville d'Alet et son ancien diocèse* (1877), 192–3.

39. Durand, *Fougerolles*, 130; *Vie de M. Marquis-Ducastel, curé de Sainte-Suzanne*, ed. F. Pichon (1873), 99–100.

40. The following examples in M.-H. Froeschlé-Chopard, 'Les Visites pastorales de Provence orientale', *Rev. hist. Église Fr.* (1977), 273–4; S. Bonnet, *Notice biographique sur Guillaume-Louis du Tillet, évêque d'Orange* (1880), 45; A. Degert, *Histoire des évêques de Dax* (1900), 379; H. Espitalier, 'Les Évêques de Fréjus', *Bull. Soc. Draguignan* (1898–9), 188–9, 192, 197, 220, 241, and 'Pouillé historique, 1743', ibid. (1869), 360; M.-H. Froeschlé-Chopard, *La Religion populaire en Provence orientale au XVIIIe siècle* (1980), 37–8.

41. F.-G. Pariset (ed.), *Bordeaux au XVIIIe siècle* (1968), 127; E. Alain, 'Un Grand Diocèse d'autrefois', *Rev. quest. hist.* (1894), 513–18; M. Bordes, *Contribution à l'étude de l'enseignement et de la vie intellectuelle dans les pays de l'intendance d'Auch au XVIIIe siècle* (1958), 21–2; G. Le Bras, 'L'État religieux et moral du diocèse de Châlons au dernier siècle de l'ancien régime', *Nouv. Rev. Champagne et Brie* (1935), 162–4.

42. G. Viard, 'Les Visites pastorales dans l'ancien diocèse de Langres', *Rev. hist. Église Fr.* (1977), 234–70.

43. Julia and Vénard (eds.), *Répertoire*, iii. 222–42.

44. Darricau and Peyrous, 'Les Visites', 389.

45. Suadeau, *L'Évêque*, i. 136.

46. Ibid. i. 107.

47. Le Bras, 'L'État religieux', 165–6.

48. B. Peyrous, 'La Vie religieuse dans le pays Bordelais: les visites pastorales durant le XVIIIe siècle', *L'Information hist.* (1975), 73–4; R. Darricau, 'Les Formulaires des visites pastorales dans l'archidiocèse de Bordeaux, 1600–1789', *Bull. Soc. Guyenne* (1968), 131–49.

49. H. Jadart, *Nicolas Dumont, curé de Villers-devant-le-Thour* (1885), 35.

50. E. G. Léonard, *Mon Village sous Louis XV* (1941), 236.

51. C. Laplatte, *Le Diocèse de Coutances* (1942), 46.

52. J. Déchelette, 'Les Visites pastorales des archiprêtrés de Charlieu et du Rousset par Mgr de Lort de Sérignan de Valras, évêque de Mâcon', *Ann. Acad. Mâcon*, 3e sér. iii (1898), 446–9.

53. F. Baqué and A. Rouquette, *Un Village: Bouziges* (1960), 145–6.

54. Halaussère, *L'Évolution d'un village frontalier de Provence: Saint-Jeanret* (1909), 333–6.

55. J.-F. Soulet, *Tradition et réformes religieuses dans les Pyrénées centrales au XVIIᵉ siècle: Le diocèse de Tarbes de 1602 à 1716* (1974).

56. Boisse, 'Les Chapelles', 122.

57. Suadeau, *L'Évêque*, i. 126–7.

58. Durand, *État religieux*, 46.

59. Vallery-Radot, *Un Administrateur ecclésiastique*, 104.

60. e.g., at Lormont in 1766 (F. Lemoing, *Ermites et reclus du diocèse de Bordeaux* (1953), 80).

61. Martial-Levé, *Louis-François-Gabriel*, 73.

62. Déchelette, 'Les Visites', 449–53.

63. Martial-Levé, *Louis-François-Gabriel*, 49–50.

64. 'Visites pastorales dans les Hauts de Gironde aux XVIIᵉ et XVIIIᵉ siècles', *Cahiers Vitrezais* (1975), 35, 46; Vallery-Radot, *Un Administrateur ecclésiastique*, 109.

65. R. Poulle, *Histoire de l'église paroissiale de Notre-Dame et Saint-Michel à Draguignan* (1865), 360–5.

66. T. J. Schmitt, *L'Organisation ecclésiastique et la pratique religieuse dans l'archidia-coné d'Autun de 1650 à 1750* (1957), 112; A. Schaer, *Le Clergé paroissial catholique en Haute-Alsace sous l'ancien régime, 1648–1789* (1960), 44–7.

67. P. Cattin, 'La Visite pastorale de Mgr Claude de Saint-Georges en 1700', *Bull. Belley* (1973), 40, 63–6.

68. Blampignon, *Massillon*, 42–3.

69. Kwanten, 'Antoine-Léon', 170–1.

70. J. McManners, *Death and the Enlightenment* (1981), ch. 10.

71. Suadeau, *L'Évêque*, i. 49–57; Maugis, 'L'enquête du Parlement sur la tenue des registres de l'état civil', *Rev. hist. droit fr.* (1922), 637.

72. Suadeau, *L'Évêque*, i. 56–7; E. Houth, *Versailles, la paroisse royale* (1962), 644.

73. J.-F.-H. de Richeprey, *Journal des voyages en Haute-Guienne*, ed. H. Guilhamon (1952), 96–7.

74. Froeschlé-Chopard, 'Les Visites', 282–8; Minois, 'Les Visites', 19; Déchelette, 'Les Visites', *Ann. Acad. Mâcon* (1898) 468–587, (1899) 576, (1900) 47, 422, 448, (1902) 322, 355–6.

75. Ch. Robert, *Urbain de Hercé* (1900), 45–9.

76. M. Vénard and D. Julia, 'Le Répertoire des visites pastorales', *Rev. hist. Église Fr.* (1977), 232–3.

77. Peronnet, *Les Évêques*, i. 934.

78. Pérouas, *Le Diocèse de la Rochelle*, 372.

79. Lasserre, *Recherches historiques*, 193.

80. A. Frézet, 'Guillaume Desmarets, curé de Courville, 1682–1765', *Nouv. Rev. Champagne et Brie* (1936), 185–6.

81. Suadeau, *L'Évêque*, i. 34. A 'contre-visite' by the archbishop of Auch in person in 1745, in J. Pandellé, 'Une Grande Figure épiscopale, Jean-François de Montillet', *Rev. Gascogne* (1937), 177–8.

82. Peronnet, *Les Évêques*, i. 935.

83. J.-M. Gouesse, 'Synodes et conférences ecclésiastiques dans le diocèse de Coutances aux XVIIᵉ et XVIIIᵉ siècles', *Ann. Normandie* (1974), 37–66.

84. E. Appolis, 'Les Assemblées spirituelles du clergé dans un diocèse de France

aux XVIIe et XVIIIe siècles', in *Liber Memorialis Antonio Era*, International Commission for the History of Representative and Parliamentary Institutions, 26 (1963), 212–20.

85. W. R. V. Brade, *The Diocesan Synod, being some Chapters from the Treatise by Pope Benedict XIV* (1926), 32.

86. J. Ferté, *La Vie religieuse dans les campagnes parisiennes, 1622–95* (1962), 26–7.

87. P.-D. Bernier, 'Les Synodes du diocèse de Paris de 1715 à 1790', in *Études d'histoire du droit canonique dédie à Gabriel Le Bras* (2 vols., 1965), i. 33–40.

88. Peronnet, *Les Évêques*, i. 924. Case of an *appel comme d'abus* against a bishop's synodal ordinances in 1726 (Schmitt, *L'Organisation*, 9).

89. Kwanten, 'Antoine-Léon', 163–7.

90. L. Marcel, *Le Frère de Diderot* (1913), 120–30.

91. Peronnet, *Les Évêques*, i. 922–3.

92. F. Lebrun, *Histoire des catholiques en France du XVe siècle à nos jours* (1981), 153.

93. Appolis, 'Les Assemblées spirituelles', 221–6.

94. Allain, 'Un Grand Diocèse', 513–19.

95. Schmitt, *L'Organisation*, 36–7.

96. L. Charpentier, *Un Évêque de l'ancien régime: Louis Joseph de Grignan, 1650–1722* (1899), 80–4.

97. J.-M. Mioland (ed.), *Actes de l'Église d'Amiens: recueil de tous les documents relatifs à la discipline du diocèse, 811–1849* (2 vols., 1849), i. 346.

98. Vallery-Radot, *Un Administrateur ecclésiastique*, 346.

99. Gouesse, 'Synodes', 37–66.

100. The marquis de Ferrières, *Théisme* (1790), cited by L. Salvini, 'Le Clergé rural en Haut-Poitou à la veille de la Révolution', *Bull. Soc. Ouest* (1957–8), 250.

101. Peronnet, *Les Évêques*, i. 925.

102. R. Daon, *La Conduite des âmes dans la voie du salut* (1750), 343. The first edition was 1738.

103. F.-H. Sevoy, *Devoirs ecclésiastiques* (3 vols., 1770), i. pp. iii–v.

104. Daon, *Conduite des âmes*, p. xxvi.

105. Robert, *Urbain de Hercé*, 43.

106. Nepveu de la Manoullière, *Mémoires*, i. 359; J. Loth, *Le Cardinal de la Rochefoucauld, archevêque de Rouen* (1893), 50.

107. *Mémoires de l'abbé Baston, chanoine de Rouen*, ed. J. Loth and C. Verger (3 vols., 1897–8), i. 234–7.

108. V. Dufour, 'L'État du diocèse de Paris en 1789', *Bull. Com. Paris* (1883), 194–432.

109. E. Millet, 'La Tour Saint-Gélin, vicissitudes d'un curé au XVIIIe siècle', *Les Amis du vieux Chinon, Bulletin* (1912), 349.

110. Sicard, *L'Ancien Clergé*, 349.

111. e.g. Urbain de Hercé, bishop of Dol.

112. E. Lavaquery, *Le Cardinal de Boisgelin, 1732–1804* (2 vols., 1920), i. 192.

113. J. Eich, *Histoire religieuse du département de la Moselle pendant la Révolution* (2 vols., 1964), i. 12–13.

114. Blampignon, *Massillon*, 162.

115. V. Durand, *Les Évêques au XVIIIe siècle en Languedoc* (1907), 62–5; S. Pillorget, *Provence historique* (1967), 253–5.

116. Luynes, xi. 37 (Feb. 1751).

117. Durand, *État religieux*, 8, 31.

118. E. Esmonin, 'La Société grenobloise au temps de Louis XV d'après les *Miscellanea* de Letourneau', in his *Études sur la France des XVIIe et XVIIIe siècles* (1964), 482–3.

119. J. Charrier, *Histoire du Jansénisme dans le diocèse de Nevers* (1920), 38–40.

120. S. Bonnet, *Notice biographique sur Guillaume-Louis du Tillet, évêque d'Orange* (1880), 41.

121. See Sicard, *L'Ancien Clergé*, 386, 415.

122. Loth, *Le Cardinal*, 83, 118–19.

123. Robert, *Urbain de Hercé*, 115–16.

124. Levé, *Louis-François-Gabriel*, 132; M. Bruyère, *Le Cardinal de Cabrières, 1820–1921* (1926), 89.

125. Curé A. Plassard, 'Journal', ed. J. Joachim, *Ann. Acad. Mâcon* (1954–5), 101; *Rev. Gascogne* (1927), 39–44; Richeprey, *Journal*, 93; L. Pingaud, *Les Saulx-Tavannes* (1876), 265 (in Rouen, 1740–1).

126. Sicard, *L'Ancien Clergé*, 387–9.

127. Pisani, *L'Église de Paris*, i. 80.

128. Th. Bérengier, 'Journal du maître d'hôtel de Mgr Belsunce durant la peste de Marseille', *Rev. quest. hist.* (1878), 567–76. See also McManners, *Death*, 43 ff.

129. From Sicard, *L'Ancien Clergé*, except for Rennes (in S. T. McCloy, *Government Assistance in 18th-Century France* (1946), 88).

130. E. Esmonin, 'La Fortune du cardinal Le Camus', in his *Études sur la France des XVIIe et XVIIIe siècles* (1964), 391–2.

131. P. Vaillant, 'La Fondation de la bibliothèque de Grenoble', *Cahiers hist.* (1963), 286.

132. G. Armigon, *Banquiers des pauvres* (n.d.), 83–8.

133. Saint-Simon (Pléiade), vii. 325–6.

134. Sicard, *L'Ancien Clergé*, 377–9.

135. Pingaud, *Les Saulx-Tavannes*, 269.

136. Luynes, xiii. 116.

137. Ibid. vi. 139–41 (Nov. 1744).

CHAPTER 10

1. McManners, *French Ecclesiastical Society under the Ancien Régime: A Study of Angers* (1960), 130; J. Meyer, *La Noblesse bretonne au XVIIIe siècle* (2 vols., 1966), ii. 1151.

2. P. Pisani, *L'Église de Paris et la Révolution* (4 vols., 1908), i. 3–14. See also the grading of the 52 parishes of Paris by the number of priests (Saint-Eustache 80, Saint-Nicolas-des-Champs and Saint-Roch 60 etc.) in D. Garrioch, *Neighbourhood and Community in Paris, 1740–90* (1986), 153.

3. A. Babeau, *Le Village sous l'ancien régime*, 3rd edn. (1882), 115–16; E. Champion, *La France d'après les cahiers* (1921 edn.), 185.

4. F. de Dainville, *Cartes anciennes de l'Église de France* (1956), 195.

5. E. Chevrier, 'Notice sur les églises de Sablé', *Rev. Maine* (1876), 415–16.

6. A. Friedmann, 'Les Circonscriptions paroissiales de Paris avant la Révolution', *L'Année canonique* (1960), 33–40.

7. T. J. Schmitt, *L'Organisation ecclésiastique et la pratique religieuse dans l'archidiaconé d'Autun de 1650 à 1750* (1957), 104.

8. Ibid. 101–2, 261.
9. Dainville, *Cartes anciennes*, 196.
10. Ch. Berthelot du Chesnay, 'Le Clergé diocésain . . . au XVIIIᵉ siècle et les registres des insinuations ecclésiastiques', *Rev. hist. mod. contemp.* (1963), 244; E. Sévestre, *L'Organisation du clergé . . . corresp. du curé de Saint-Nicolas de Coutances, 1784–8* (1911), 189.
11. L. Ampoulange, *Le Clergé et la convocation des États Généraux dans la sénéchaussée principale de Périgord* (1912), 65–6.
12. E. Millet, 'La Tour Saint-Gélin: vicissitudes d'un curé au XVIIIᵉ siècle', *Amis Chinon* (1957–8), 27.
13. J.-F.-H. de Richeprey, *Journal des voyages en Haute-Guienne*, ed. H. Guilhamon (1952), 44.
14. M. Reinhard, *Paris pendant la Révolution* (dupl. Sorbonne lectures, n.d.), i. 26.
15. Ibid., i. 205.
16. V. Durand, *État religieux des trois diocèses de Nîmes, d'Uzès et d'Alais à la fin de l'ancien régime* (1909), 88–9; A. Playout-Chaussis, *La Vie religieuse dans le diocèse de Boulogne au XVIIIᵉ siècle, 1725–90* (1976), 50–2.
17. J. Daranatz, 'Les Ordinations sacerdotales du diocèse de Bayonne au XVIIIᵉ siècle', *Bull. Soc. Bayonne*, NS 7 (1931), 363–5.
18. Guyot, xvi. 635–7.
19. V. Dubaret, *Études d'histoire locale et religieuse* (2 vols., 1889–92), ii. 190–230.
20. X. Azéma, 'Évangélisation populaire sous l'ancien régime: le faubourg Boutonnet à Montpellier', *Ann. Midi* (1970), 399–408.
21. Potier de la Germondaye, *Introduction au gouvernement des paroisses* (1777), 1.
22. Guyot, xliv. 414–15.
23. McManners, *Angers*, 152–3.
24. A. Dupuy, 'L'Administration municipale de Bretagne au XVIIIᵉ siècle', *Ann. Bretagne* (1887–8), 560–1.
25. E. Lafforgue, *Histoires des Fabriques des églises de Tarbes sous l'ancien régime* (1923), 61, 64, 87.
26. L. Brochard, *Saint-Gervais: histoire de la paroisse* (1950), 242–3.
27. P. de Saint-Jacob, *Documents relatifs à la communauté villageoise en Bourgogne* (1962), 148.
28. Ibid. 51–3.
29. Babeau, *Le Village*, 31–45.
30. McManners, *Angers*, 153–4.
31. G. Lefebvre, *Les Paysans du Nord et la Révolution Française* (1924), 320; A. Babeau, *La Ville sous l'ancien régime* (2 vols., 1884), i. 35.
32. A. Lottin, 'Mémoire des Curez de la ville de Lille . . . contre le magistrat . . .', *Rev. Nord* (1971), 25.
33. Lafforgue, *Histoire*, 64. In Brittany, in small places with no municipal officers, the *général* was said to be responsible for the rights and duties of all citizens (F. Duine, 'Les Généraux des paroisses Bretonnes', *Ann. Bretagne* (1907–8), 4).
34. Following Guyot, xliv. 413–14, and Lafforgue, *Histoire*, 57–9.
35. G. Robert, 'La Seigneurie de Givry-sur-Aisne', *Trav. Acad. nat. Reims*, 133 (1913), 364–5.
36. Babeau, *Le Village*, 28–30, 55.
37. Guyot, xliv. 415.
38. Dupuy, 'L'Administration' (1887–8), 577.

39. Guyot, xliv. 415. In Brittany, discussion was in Breton, but the transcription of the resolutions was in French (D. Bernard, 'Le Breton dans les actes publics', *Ann. Bretagne* (1921–3), 23–49).
40. Guyot, xliv. 416.
41. H. Antoine, 'Recherches sur la paroisse . . . Saint-Pierre de Montsort', *Rev. Maine*, 6 (1879), 175–80.
42. Dupuy, 'L'Administration', *Ann. Bretagne* (1889–90), 665–6.
43. M. Marion, *Dictionnaire des institutions de la France aux XVIIe et XVIIIe siècles* (2 vols., 1923), i. 363, 229; Lafforgue, *Histoire*, 14–20; J. Boyreau, *Le Village en France au XVIIIe siècle* (1955), 99–102.
44. Saint-Jacob, *Documents*, 148.
45. Lafforgue, *Histoire*, 15–16.
46. Ibid.
47. M. Vimont, *Histoire de l'église et de la paroisse Saint-Leu-Saint-Gilles à Paris* (1932), 101.
48. M. Brongniart, *La Paroisse Saint-Médard* (1951), 65.
49. Saint-Jacob, *Documents*, 121, 148.
50. Babeau, *Le Village*, 134; Schmitt, *L'Organisation*, 119.
51. Babeau, *Le Village*, 133–4.
52. L. Brochard, *Saint-Gervais, histoire de la paroisse* (1950), 242. Cf. Potier de la Germondaye, *Introduction*, pt. 3, 1.
53. Dupuy, 'L'Administration', *Ann. Bretagne* (1887–8), 572–3.
54. E. Houth, *Versailles, la paroisse royale* (1962), 119.
55. Dupuy, 'L'Administration', 573.
56. Guyot, xxxix. 139–49, 13.
57. J.-J. Gautier, *Essai sur les mœurs champêtres* (1787), ed. X. Rousseau (1935), 15.
58. For what follows, Lafforgue, *Histoire*, 25, 47–53, 56; Babeau, *Le Village*, 136–40; A. Dupuy, 'L'Administration', *Ann. Bretagne* (1887–8), 57–121; (1889–90), 184–5; Duine, 'Les Généraux', 9.
59. McManners, *Angers*, 156–7.
60. La Poix de Fréminville, *Dictionnaire de la police*, cited by Babeau, *Le Village*, 141.
61. Boyreau, *Le Village*, 115.
62. A. Lesort, 'Particularité liturgique de la paroisse Saint-Germain-l'Auxerrois', *Bull. Soc. Paris* (1942–3), 14–15.
63. Lafforgue, *Histoire*, 17.
64. Ibid. 28.
65. Barbier, ii. 250–1; Marais, iv. 358–61.
66. Brochard, *Saint-Gervais*, 159, 162, 227–8, 230–2, 242–3, 288, 296–7, 300.
67. Lafforgue, *Histoire*, 29.
68. G. Minois, 'La Situation matérielle des paroisses du diocèse de Tréguier dans la première moitié du XVIIIe siècle d'après les visites pastorales', *Ann. Bretagne* (1977), 44.
69. Guyot, xxiv. 283–4.
70. Lafforgue, *Histoire*, 96–9; L. Froger, 'De l'organisation et de l'administration des fabriques au diocèse du Mans', *Rev. quest. hist.* 63 (1898), 406. The parish of Rémalard had eight meadows, one piece of arable land, and its principal confraternity had a meadow, a field, and nine houses (M. Lecoq, 'La Vie paysanne dans un coin du Perche', *Ann. hist. Rév. fr.* (1949), 62).

71. Froger, 'De l'organisation', 423.
72. Dupuy, 'L'Administration', *Ann. Bretagne* (1889–90), 182.
73. Ibid. 177–80.
74. L.-S. Mercier, *Tableau de Paris*, new edn. (12 vols., 1782–8), ii. 87–9.
75. Dupuy, 'L'Administration', 171–2.
76. J. McManners, *Death and the Enlightenment* (1981), ch. 9.
77. Guyot, viii. 396–7.
78. Lecoq, 'La Vie paysanne', 42; McManners, *Angers*, 153; C. Baloche, *L'Église Saint-Merry de Paris: histoire de la paroisse et de la collégiale, 700–1910* (2 vols., 1911), i. 566. Cf. 5,400 livres in Saint-Leu-Saint-Giles (Vimont, *Histoire*, 87) and 13,000 in the royal parish of Notre-Dame at Versailles (Houth, *Versailles*, 131).
79. Guyot, v. 48–53; Isambert, *Recueil des anciennes lois françaises* (29 vols., 1822–33), xx. 504.
80. M. Maréchal and M. J. A. Serieux, *Traité des droits honorifiques des patrons et des seigneurs dans les églises* (2 vols., 1772), i. 77.
81. Guyot, v. 50–4. In another case, a notary gets back his pew after threatening litigation (A. Pioger, 'Thorigné-le-Reneaulme au XVIIIᵉ siècle', *Bull. Soc. Sarthe* (1973–4), 98–9).
82. Dupuy, 'L'Administration', *Ann. Bretagne* (1889–90), 160–5; *Vie de M. Marquis-Ducastel*, ed. F. Pichon (1873), 86–8.
83. Dupuy, 'L'Administration', 166–7.
84. Houth, *Versailles*, 131; Luynes, xiii. 11–12.
85. Vimont, *Histoire*, 87.
86. Baloche, *L'Église Saint-Merry*, i. 515.
87. Dupuy, 'L'Administration', *Ann. Bretagne* (1887–8), 586.
88. Ibid. 594–8.
89. G. Bouchard, *Prieur de la Côte d'Or* (1940), 179.
90. Dupuy, 'L'Administration', 592–3.
91. G. Coolen, *Helfaut: essai sur l'administration d'une paroisse sous l'ancien régime*, Méms Soc. Morinie (1939), 76.
92. Baloche, *L'Église Saint-Merry*, i. 300.
93. Babeau, *Le Village*, 101–2; Saint-Jacob, *Documents*, 153.
94. Legal position in J.-J. Pialès, *Traité des réparations* (2 vols., 1762), i. 215–43; La Poix de Fréminville, *Traité général du governement des biens des communautés d'habitans des . . . paroisses* (1760).
95. Babeau, *Le Village*, 47.
96. Saint-Jacob, *Documents*, 134.
97. As, for example, in law enforcement.
98. 'Visites pastorales dans les Hauts de Gironde aux XVIIᵉ et XVIIIᵉ siècles', *Cahiers Vitrezais* (1975), 31–2; P. Caffin, 'La Visite pastorale de Mgr Charles de Saint-Georges en 1700', *Bull. Belley*, 49 (1974), 28.
99. Marion, *Dictionnaire*, i. 175.
100. Playoust-Chaussis, *La Vie religieuse*, 53–4.
101. Dupuy, 'L'Administration', *Ann. Bretagne* (1889–90), 668.
102. Saint-Jacob, *Documents*, 152.
103. F. Baqué and A. Rouquette, *Un Village du littoral au cours des siècles: Bouzigues* (1960), 137; A. Hawtin, 'Le Testament d'un Prémontré en 1792', *Rev. Nord* (1962), 304.

104. A. Krieger and L. Ruffin, *La Madeleine* (1937), 50.

105. Ch. Joathan, 'Le Journal inédit d'un curé de Saint-Vincent de Mâcon au XVIIIe siècle', *Ann. Acad. Mâcon* (1954–5), 104.

106. L. Ledeur, 'La Difficile Reconstruction de l'église Saint-Pierre: un problème d'urbanisme à Besançon au XVIIIe siècle', *Méms. Soc. Doubs*, 13 (1971), 1–43.

107. M. Vénard, 'Les Églises paroissiales, XV–XVIIIe siècles', *Rev. hist. Église Fr.* (1987), 7–39.

108. P. Maloubier-Tournier, 'Les Rétables du XVIIe et du XVIIIe siècle en Ille-et-Vilaine', *Ann. Bretagne* (1962), 93–137.

109. L. Lery, 'Une Visite à l'église Notre-Dame de Versailles', *Rev. Versailles* (1912), 219–20.

110. Baloche, *L'Église Saint-Merry*, i. 537, 541, 571–3.

111. Barbier, ii. 140–1 (Dec. 1730), 333 (Aug. 1732); C. Hamel, *Saint-Sulpice* (1900), 176–86.

112. Guyot, xi. 323.

113. In a case of 1717, the intendant punished the village by putting it to the expense of 'having the bells taken down and flogged by the public executioner' (Babeau, *Le Village*, 118).

114. Ibid. 117–18; H. Carré, *Recueil curieux et édifiant sur les cloches de l'Église, avec les cérémonies de leur bénédiction* (1757), 29.

115. P. Dop, 'L'Église de Saint-Jean-de-Luz', *Bull. Soc. Bayonne* (1932), 404.

116. M. Yvart, 'La Vie d'un écolier au séminaire Saint-Nicaise et au collège royal de Rouen de 1786 à 1792: Eloi Pigré', *Rev. Socs. Haute-Normandie*, 3e trim. (1957), 37. The weight in Carré, *Recueil*, 4.

117. Duine, 'Les Généraux', 477.

118. J. B. Pelt, *Études sur la cathédrale de Metz* (1853), 264.

119. R. Charles, 'Les Chroniques de la paroisse et du collège de Courdemanche au Maine', *Rev. Maine*, i (1876), 298–9.

120. L. Paris, *Histoire de l'abbaye d'Avenay*, i (1879), 497–8.

121. F. Duine, 'Guipel: les communes rurales en Bretagne', *Ann. Bretagne* (1924–5), 260–1; René-Pierre Nepveu de la Manouillère, *Mémoires*, ed. G. Esnault (3 vols., 1877–9), i. 326–7.

122. Houth, *Versailles*, 37, 57, 69–70; Luynes, xiv. 339, vii. 100–2, 175.

123. Duine, 'Les Généraux', 484–5.

124. Antoine, 'Recherches', 182.

125. M. L. Legros, 'Le Fessier et "Son Bérus", 1764–91', *Rev. Anjou* (1916), 190.

126. J. E. Malaussène, *Saint-Jeannet: l'évolution d'un village frontalier de Provence* (1969), 336.

127. Carré, *Recueil*, 314.

128. e.g., at Saint-Jeannet, the first bell-founder was from Piedmont, the second a German from Lorraine.

129. Coolen, *Helfaut*, 64.

130. Dop, 'Saint-Jean-de-Luz', 404.

131. C. Torchet, *Histoire de l'abbaye royale de Notre-Dame de Chelles* (2 vols., 1881), ii. 182.

132. See Pialès, *Traité*; Guyot, xlvi. 565–6, liv. 7.

133. M. Louis, *Trav. Acad. nat. Reims* (1902), 199–200.

134. Ch. Girault, *Les Biens d'église dans la Sarthe à la fin du XVIIIe siècle* (1953), 377.

135. Guyot, xlvi. 565.

136. Ibid.
137. Pierre de Vaissière, *Curés de campagne de l'ancienne France* (1933), 178–86.
138. Malaussène, *Saint-Jeannet*, 331–6.
139. Schmitt, *L'Organisation*, 135.
140. Baqué and Rouquette, *Bouzigues*, 143.
141. L. de Montfalcon, 'Querelle autour d'un presbytère à Flaxie au XVIIIe siècle', *Bull. Belley* (1966), 35.
142. A. Kwantan, 'Antoine-Elénore-Léon Le Clerc de Juigné, évêque de Châlons (1764–82)', *Méms. Soc. Marne* (1973), 171.
143. P. de Saint-Jacob, *Les Paysans du Bourgogne du nord au dernier siècle de l'ancien régime* (1960), 533.
144. Dupuy, 'L'Administration', *Ann. Bretagne* (1887–8), 578–80.
145. Marquis-Ducastel, *La Vie*, 704.

CHAPTER 11

1. A. Playoust-Chaussis, *La Vie religieuse dans le diocèse de Boulogne au XVIIIe siècle, 1725–1790* (1976), 153.
2. E. Buchez, 'Le Clergé paroissial du diocèse de Reims d'après l'enquête de 1774', *Trav. Acad. nat. Reims* (1911), 128.
3. Dom P. Piolin, *L'Église du Mans durant la Révolution* (4 vols., 1868), i. 4.
4. P. Goubert, *Beauvais et le Beauvaisis de 1600 à 1730* (2 vols., 1960), i. 198.
5. D. Julia, 'Le Clergé paroissial du diocèse de Reims à la fin du XVIIIe siècle', *Rev. hist. mod. contemp.* (1966), 195–216.
6. Ch. Berthelot du Chesnay, 'Le Clergé diocésain français au XVIIIe siècle et les registres des insinuations ecclésiastiques', *Rev. hist. mod. contemp.* (1963), 263.
7. T. Tackett and Ch. Langlois, 'Ecclesiastical Structures and Clerical Geography on the Eve of the French Revolution', *Fr. Hist. St.* (1978–80), 364.
8. Playoust-Chaussis, *La Vie religieuse*, 142.
9. L. Châtellier, *Tradition chrétienne et renouveau catholique dans l'ancien diocèse de Strasbourg* (1981), 379.
10. L. Pérouas, *Le Diocèse de La Rochelle de 1648 à 1724: sociologie et pastorale* (1964), 200, 444.
11. J. de Font-Réaulx, 'Études administratives et financières du diocèse de Valence', *Bull. Soc. Drôme* (1931–2), 277.
12. E. Appolis, *Le Jansénisme dans le diocèse de Lodève au XVIIIe siècle* (1932), 83.
13. Tackett and Langlois, 'Ecclesiastical Structures', 369.
14. T. J. A. Le Goff, *Vannes and its Region: A Study of Town and Country in Eighteenth-Century France* (1981), 251–3.
15. Châtellier, *Tradition chrétienne*, 373–9.
16. T. Tackett, 'Le Clergé de l'archidiocèse d'Embrun à la fin de l'ancien régime', *Ann. Midi* (1976), 181–3.
17. M. Reinhard, *Paris pendant la Révolution française* (dupl.), fasc. i. 38–9.
18. B. Guillemin, *Le Diocèse de Bordeaux* (1979), 151–3, 197.
19. F. G. Pariset (ed.), *Bordeaux au XVIIIe siècle* (1968), 131. The town of Metz shows a similar recruitment: of twenty-nine curés and vicaires, twelve were

born in the town itself (J. Eich, *Histoire religieuse du département de la Moselle pendant la Révolution* (2 vols., 1964), i. 22–4).

20. Cited by B. Peyrous, reporting on his thesis, in *L'Information hist.* (1975), 76.
21. Ph. Loupès, 'Le Clergé paroissial du diocèse de Bordeaux d'après la grande enquête de 1772', *Ann. Midi* (1971), 21. See also Loupès' 'Les Ecclésiastiques Irlandais dans le diocèse de Bordeaux sous l'ancien régime', *Rev. Bordeaux* (1974), 181–200.
22. T. Tackett, 'L'Histoire sociale du clergé diocésain dans la France du XVIIIᵉ siècle', *Rev. hist. mod. contemp.* (1979), 211.
23. G. Minois, 'Les Vocations sacerdotales dans le diocèse de Tréguier au XVIIIᵉ siècle', *Ann. Bretagne* (1979), 52.
24. J. R. Palanque (ed.), *Le Diocèse d'Aix-en-Provence* (1975), 97.
25. J. F. Soulet, *Tradition et réformes religieuses dans les Pyrénées centrales au XVIIᵉ siècle* (1974), 120–7.
26. Le Goff, *Vannes*, 250.
27. Berthelot du Chesnay, 'Le Clergé diocésain', 48–9.
28. D. Julia, 'Le Clergé paroissial', 199.
29. Châtellier, *Tradition chrétienne*, 378–82.
30. J. Richard, 'L'Élaboration d'un cahier de doléances: Pierre-Claude Perrot, curé de Brazey-en-Plaine', *Ann. Bourgogne* (1960), 10.
31. E. Vivier, 'La Condition du clergé séculier', *Ann. Normandie* (1952), 15–23.
32. P. Boucher, *Charles Cochon de Lapparent* (n.d.), 15.
33. C. Hamel, *Histoire de l'église de Saint-Sulpice* (1900), 161–212.
34. V. Lespy, *Un Curé béarnais au 18ᵉ siècle: correspondance de l'abbé Tristan* (1879), 1–39.
35. A. Leveille, 'Les Revenus du clergé breton avant la Révolution', *Rev. quest. hist.* (1912), 467.
36. J. Meyer, *La Noblesse bretonne au XVIIIᵉ siècle* (2 vols., 1966), ii. 1107.
37. The vicomte de Motey, 'Saint-Germain-de-Clairefeuille', *Bull. Soc. Orne* (1894), 200–1.
38. C. Marcilhacy, *Le Diocèse d'Orléans au milieu de XIXᵉ siècle, les hommes et leurs mentalités* (1964), 432.
39. J.-M. Alliot, *Le Clergé de Versailles pendant la Révolution française* (1913), 41.
40. A. Sarramon (ed.), *Les Paroisses du diocèse de Comminges en 1786* (1968), 334–5.
41. J.-J. Gautier, curé, *Essai sur les mœurs champêtres* (1787), ed. X. Rousseau (1935), 33.
42. A. Durand, *Une Paroisse mayennaise: Fougerolles sous la Révolution, 1789–1800* (1960), 121–7.
43. J. McManners, *French Ecclesiastical Society under the Ancien Régime: A Study of Angers* (1960), 135, 186.
44. H. de Sarrau, 'Un Poète libournais inconnu, l'abbé Léglise, curé de Pomerol', *Rev. Libournais* (1961), 106.
45. L'abbé Baston, *Mémoires*, ed. S. Loth and C. Verger (3 vols., 1897), i. 53.
46. C. Berthelot du Chesnay, *Les Prêtres Séculiers en Haute-Bretagne au XVIIIᵉ siècle* (1974), 52–4.
47. Verlac, *Nouveau Plan pour toutes les classes* (1789), cited by A. Sicard, *Les Études classiques avant la Révolution* (1887), 325–6.
48. Meyer, *La Noblesse*, ii. 1151. For the same recruiting problem in the nearby

diocese of Quimper see J. Savina, *Le Clergé de Cornouaille à la fin de l'ancien régime et sa convocation aux États-Généraux* (1926), 38.

49. Goubert, *Beauvais*, i. 199–200.
50. P. de Saint-Jacob, *Les Paysans de la Bourgogne du nord au dernier siècle de l'ancien régime* (1960), 532–3.
51. Ch. Joathan, 'Le Journal inédit d'un curé de Saint-Vincent de Mâcon au XVIII⁰ siècle', *Ann. Acad. Mâcon* (1954–5), 7.
52. 'Trois Lettres inédites de l'abbé Jallet', *Ann. hist. Rév. fr.* (1950), 326; G. Tardy, *Notice sur l'abbé J. Jallet* (1882), 2–4.
53. McManners, *Angers*, 135–6.
54. Ibid.
55. Tackett and Langlois, 'Ecclesiastical Structures', 352–70.
56. Le Goff, *Vannes*, 250–4.
57. For Coutances, H. Nédelec, summarized in *Rev. hist. droit fr.* (1962), 500. For Tréguier, Minois, 'Les Vocations sacerdotales', 52.
58. Playoust-Chaussis, *La Vie religieuse*, 149–52.
59. Julia, 'Le Clergé paroissial', 200. The administrative and liberal professions provided one out of every nine in the diocese of Viviers (J. Charay, *Petite histoire de l'église diocésaine de Viviers* (1977), 160–1).
60. Cf. the cloth makers of Lodève (Appolis, *Le Jansénisme*, 834).
61. Berthelot du Chesnay, 'Le Clergé diocésain', 256–7.
62. T. Tackett, *Priest and Parish in Eighteenth-Century France: A Political and Social Study of the Curés in a Diocese of Dauphiné, 1750–1791* (1977), 59–67.
63. Ch. Girault, *Les Biens d'église dans la Sarthe à la fin du XVIII⁰ siècle* (1953), 374–5. Note: the livre was 20 sous or sols, and there were 12 deniers in each. The pistole was 10 livres commonly. The écu was an actual coin whose value varied up to 1762, but thereafter was fixed at 6 livres. The louis was a gold coin originally worth 10 livres, but had risen to 36 by 1718; finally, in 1720, it was fixed at 36.
64. Saint-Jacob, *Les Paysans*, 534–5. For France generally, J. Loutchisky, *L'État des classes agricoles en France à la veille de la Révolution* (1911), 22.
65. P. de Vaissière, *Curés de campagne de l'ancienne France* (1933), 143–50, 109–14.
66. The Assembly General of the Clergy took up this issue in 1745, and in 1747 a royal declaration stated that the *taille* fell on the *fermier*'s own profits alone. But in fact, this remission was not observed.
67. L. Lex, 'Histoire de Saint-Point', *Ann. Acad. Mâcon*, 3⁰ Sér. 3 (1898), 307–9. The law courts had awarded the possession of the field to the curé, over-riding her claim.
68. J. Rombault, 'Un Curé de campagne au 18⁰ siècle', *Bull. Soc. Orne*, 12 (1893), 21–32.
69. Curé Barbotin, *Lettres*, ed. A. Aulard (1910), 18, 40, 19, 65, 13–14, 70.
70. M. Lecoq, 'La Vie paysanne dans un coin du Perche', *Ann. hist. Rév. fr.* (1949), 67.
71. G. Mandou, 'Les Revenus des vicaires perpétuels du chapitre de Périgueux au XVIII⁰ siècle', *Ann. Midi* (1980), 50.
72. H. M. Riollet, 'Le Journal d'un curé de campagne, 1768–1790', *Rev. Lyon* (1911), 283.
73. Vaissière, *Curés*, 128.
74. P. Gagnol, *La Dîme ecclésiastique en France* (1910), 124–5.

75. F. Duine, 'Les Communes rurales en Bretagne: Guipel', *Ann. Bretagne* (1924–5), 243.

76. G. Roches, 'La Commune des Rieux (Manche) pendant la Révolution', *Rév. fr.* (1914), 339–40.

77. Durand, *Fougerolles*, 17. Cf. a parish with 2,450 livres income has to pay 750, the salary of two vicaires; see F. Lemeunier, 'Bazouges', *Province du Maine* (1978), 51.

78. Lespy (ed.), *Un Curé béarnais*, 36.

79. G. Robert, 'Le Prieuré de Saint-Thomas en Argonne', *Nouv. Rev. Champagne et Brie* (1936), 246.

80. E. Millet, 'La Tour Saint-Gélin: vicissitudes d'un curé au XVIIIe siècle', *Amis Chinon* (1957–9), 27–32.

81. P.-D. Bernier, *Essai sur le tiers état rural ou les paysans de Basse-Normandie au XVIIIe siècle* (1891), 120–1.

82. Gagnol, *La Dîme ecclésiastique*, 159.

83. G. Desnoiresterres, *Voltaire et la société française au XVIIIe siècle*, 2nd edn. (8 vols., 1867–76), vi. 43–4.

84. See above, ch. 4 (Tithe).

85. Durand, *Fougerolles*, 14.

86. F. D. Mathieu, *L'Ancien Régime dans la province de Lorraine et Barrois* (1879), 196.

87. Gagnol, *La Dîme ecclésiastique*, 162–9.

88. L. Ampoulange, *Le Clergé et la convocation aux États Généraux de 1789 dans la sénéchaussée principale de Périgord* (1912), 51–2.

89. Vaissière, *Curés*, 159–75.

90. Ibid. 169–70.

91. P. Perceveaux, 'La Portion congrue: aumône ou minimum vital? Notes sur les conditions de vie du bas clergé en Valromey aux 17e et 18e siècles', *Bull. Belley* (1967), 89. Cf. an agreement of the curé with the inhabitants of Mornay in H. Cottin, *La Liquidation des biens du clergé à Is-sur-Tille* (1911), 37.

92. P. Janvier, 'Histoire religieuse du district de Rennes sous la Constituante', *Ann. Bretagne* (1908–9), 352.

93. R. H. Andrews, *Les Paysans des Mauges au 18e siècle* (1935), 180.

94. H. Marion, *Dictionnaire des insitutions de la France aux XVIIe et XVIIIe siècles* (2 vols., 1923), i. 412.

95. Sarrau, 'Un Poète libournais', 109–13, also *Rev. Libournais* (1961), (1972), 65–9.

96. C. Torchet, *Histoire de l'abbaye royale de Notre-Dame de Chelles* (2 vols., 1889), ii. 218–19.

97. E. Hubert, *Inventaire sommaire des archives départementales de l'Indre*, Sér. A, Apanage du comte d'Artois (1901), 143–4.

98. Ch. Berthelot du Chesnay, 'Le Clergé diocésain', 251.

99. Mandou, 'Les Revenus'. (They used the *novales* as a lever.)

100. Vaissière, *Curés*, 76; H. Marion, *La Dîme ecclésiastique en France au 18e siècle et sa suppression* (1912), *passim*, give general figures. Add E. Sévestre, *L'Organisation du clergé paroissial à la veille de la Révolution. Correspondance du curé de Saint-Nicolas de Coutances, 1784–88* (1911), 14; Tackett, *Priest and Parish*, 120; Eich, *Histoire religieuse*, i. 44–5; T. J. Schmitt, *L'Organisation ecclésiastique et la pratique religieuse dans l'archidiaconé d'Autun de 1650 à 1750* (1957), 144.

101. Tackett cites the figures in A. Nat. G^8 499–516 as published by Ch. Léouzon Le Duc, 'La Fortune du clergé sous l'ancien régime', *Journal des économistes*, 4e sér. 15 (1881), 228–30.

102. Vaissière, *Curés*, 220 ff.

103. E. Lavaquery, *Le Cardinal de Boisgelin, 1732–1804* (2 vols., 1920), i. 225.

104. J.-P. Desaive, 'Clergé rural et documents fiscaux. Les revenus et charges des prêtres de campagne au nord-est de Paris, d'après les enquêtes fiscales des XVIIe et XVIIIe siècles', *Rev. hist. mod. contemp.* (1970), 941–52.

105. A. Huguenin, *Un Village bourguignon sous l'ancien régime* (1893), 43.

106. Berthelot du Chesnay, 'Le Clergé diocésain', 250.

107. L. Brochard, *Saint-Gervais, histoire de la paroisse* (1950), 170.

108. M. Vimont, *Histoire de l'Église et de la paroisse Saint-Leu-Saint-Gilles à Paris* (1932).

109. F. de Saint-Just, *Témoins de quatre siècles* (1962), 183.

110. J. McManners, *Death and the Enlightenment* (1981), 281–4 (quoted in various places in this para.).

111. G. Hardy, 'L'Anticléricalisme paysan', *Ann. rév.* (1912), 607–8.

112. Schmitt, *L'Organisation*, 146.

113. J.-M. Mioland (ed.), *Actes de l'Église d'Amiens: recueil de tous les documents relatifs à la discipline du diocèse, 811–1849* (2 vols., 1849), i. 367–72.

114. Details from the Parisian table of fees in C. Baloche, *L'Église Saint-Merry de Paris: histoire de la paroisse et de la collégiale, 700–1910* (2 vols., 1911), i. 445–6.

115. E. Préclin, 'La Situation ecclésiastique et religieuse de la Franche Comté à la veille de la Révolution', *Bull. Féd. Franche Comté* (1955), 10.

116. McManners, *Death*, 284.

117. Préclin, 'La Situation ecclésiastique', 10.

118. Playoust-Chaussis, *La Vie religieuse*, 279.

119. E.-G. Léonard, *Mon village sous Louis XV* (1941), 83–4.

120. Gagnol, *La Dîme ecclésiastique*, 100.

121. E. Esmonin, 'La Société grenobloise au temps de Louis XV d'après les Miscellanea de Letourneau', in his *Études sur la France des XVIIe et XVIIIe siècles* (1964), 485–7.

122. Sarramon (ed.), *Les Paroisses*, 21, 60, 90, 126, 128, 138, 302, 307, 331, 332.

123. McManners, *Angers*, 139–41.

124. A. Dupuy, 'L'Administration municipale de Bretagne au 18e siècle', *Ann. Bretagne* (1887–8), 580–1.

125. J. Déchelette, 'Visites Pastorales des archiprêtrés de Charlieu par Mgr De Lort de Sérignan de Valras, évêque de Mâcon, 1745–64', *Ann. Acad. Mâcon*, 3e sér. 3 (1898), 474; 5 (1900), 442.

126. C. Lafforgue, 'Charges et revenus d'un curé de campagne en 1790', *Rev. Gascogne* (1905), 278–81.

127. M. Jousse, *Temporel et spirituel des paroisses* (1769), 79.

128. Dupuy, 'L'Administration' (1889–90), 180–1.

129. McManners, *Angers*, 141.

130. Cottin, *La Liquidation*, 51.

131. Brochard, *Saint-Gervais*, 307, 298.

132. *La Vie de M. Marquis-Ducastel*, ed. F. Pichon (1873), 129.

133. Borthelot du Chesnay, *Les prêtes séculiers*, 259.

134. Desaive, 'Clergé rural', 940–3.

135. L. Michel, 'La Dîme et les revenus du clergé d'Anjou à la fin de l'ancien régime', *Ann. Bretagne* (1979), 576–7; Savina, *Le Clergé de Cornouaille*, 44–5; Mathieu, *L'Ancien Régime*, *passim*; Eich, *Histoire religieuse*, i. 44–5.

136. G. Dumay, 'Pouillé du diocèse de Dijon', *Méms. Comm. Côte-d'Or* (1889–95), 81–100. V. Durand, *État religieux des trois diocèses de Nîmes, d'Uzès et d'Alais à la fin de l'ancien régime* (1909), 111–12.

137. E. Allain, 'Un Grand Diocèse d'autrefois', *Rev. quest. hist.* (1894), 531–4.

138. R.-P. Nepveu de la Manoullière, *Mémoires*, ed. G. Esnault (3 vols., 1877–9), i. 333. (He thought his benefice the richest in the diocese—but see one at 10,122 livres, in Piolin, *L'Église du Mans*, i. 5.)

139. Rennes 22 : 143; Anjou 23 : 328; Bordeaux 20 : 336; Metz 14 : 397; Quimper 6 : 171; the Sarthe 59 : 444.

140. Marquis-Ducastel, *La Vie*, 102–8.

141. P. de Crousaz-Crétet, *Paris sous Louis XVI* (2 vols., 1922), ii. 11.

142. Dumay, 'Pouillé', 81–100.

143. See Ch. 50, sect. III. Even a standard legal handbook joins in: M. Pialès, *Traité des réparations* (3 vols., 1761), ii. 258.

144. Goubert, *Beauvais*, 202–3; Saint-Jacob, *Bourgogne*, 531.

145. Diderot, *Jacques le fataliste*, in *Œuvres* (Pléiade, 1935), 33. How to be happy in the simple life, with a bed, table, a few chairs, and simple food in a non-expensive area—200 livres is needed, says Paradis de Raymondi, *Traité de la morale et du bonheur* (1784), cited by R. Mauzi, *L'Idée du bonheur dans la littérature et la pensée françaises au XVIIIe siècle* (1960), 177. Voltaire's 'quarante écus' is 240 livres.

146. F. Bridoux, *Histoire religieuse du département de Seine-et-Marne pendant la Révolution* (2 vols., 1953), i. 42.

147. Lavaquery, *Boisgelin*, i. 226–7.

148. *Œuvres* (1734), xvi. 80, cited by P. Sage, *Le Bon Prêtre dans la littérature française d'Amadis de Gaule au Génie du Christianisme* (1951), 203–4.

149. Gagnol, *La Dîme ecclésiastique*, 104. In the Mauges, they asked 1,200–2,500 livres (Andrews, *Les Paysans des Mauges*, 180).

150. *Moniteur*, 169 (17 June 1790), 690.

151. *Mémoires* of the abbé Fabry, cited by G. Lefebvre, *Ann. hist. Rév. fr.* (1935), 70.

152. M. Jusselin, *Recherches sur les cahiers de 1789 en Eure-et-Loir: paroisse de Saint-Germain-les-Alluyes, cahiers des curés* (1934), 58–9.

153. J. Leuffour, 'L'Édict de 1768 et le clergé du diocèse d'Auch', *Rev. Gascogne* (1903), 489–90.

154. Ibid.

155. Diocese of Auch, 200 livres; curés of Nantes, 400 livres for a farm worker and a cook; L. E. Pouchet, *Traité sur la fabrication des étoffes* (1788), 7, says that in the pays de Caux a woman servant costs 80 livres plus the cost of her food (cited by J. Marchand (ed.), *Voyages en France de François de la Rochefoucauld, 1781–83* (1933), 48–9).

156. Auch and Nantes, 200; Orléans, 100.

157. Vaissière, *Curés*, 216–18.

158. Assuming the 30 per cent on the *congrue* comes down to 25 per cent when 'extras' are considered.

159. P. Collet (prêtre de la Congrégation de la Mission), *Traité des devoirs d'un Pasteur* (1758), 32–68.

160. See the lists of the Congrégation académique de Molsheim (omitting Jesuit works after 1770), in Châtellier, *Tradition chrétienne*, 389–91. For the bishop of Agde's list of 1673, very Jansenist, see X. Azéma, *Un Prélat janséniste, Louis Foucquet, évêque et comte de Agde, 1656–1702* (1963), 87. Lists of the bishops of Autun in Schmitt, *L'Organisation*, 132–3. For the diocese of Bâle in 1716, see A. Schaer, *Le Clergé paroissial catholique en Haute-Alsace sous l'ancien régime, 1648–1789* (1966), 158.

161. J. Quéniart, *Culture et société dans la France de l'Ouest au XVIIIᵉ siècle* (1978), 112–16. From here to ibid. 224 the information is essential for this paragraph.

162. Pérouas, *Le Diocèse de La Rochelle*, 203.

163. L. Salvini, 'Le Clergé rural en Haut-Poitou à la veille de la Révolution', *Bull. Soc. Ouest* (1957–8), 249. (For the little reading of the curés of the diocèse of Lodève *c.*1735 see Appolis, *Le Jansénisme*, 84.) A. Babeau, *La Vie rurale dans l'ancienne France* (1883), 158 (citing Gazier's *Lettres à Grégoire*, 146).

164. H. J. Martin, *Livre, pouvoir et société à Paris au 17ᵉ siècle, 1598–1701* (1969), 927.

165. Quéniart, *Culture*, 193–221. For a vicaire, not well off, who in 1789 had 105 books, see Berthelot du Chesnay, *Les Prêtres Séculiers*, 557. For a focused view on a single town see Quéniart, 'Les Bibliothèques ecclésiastiques à Rennes au XVᵉ siècle', *Rev. hist. Église Fr.* (1997), 203–14.

166. Meyer, *La Noblesse bretonne*, ii. 1160–1.

167. Bridoux, *Histoire religieuse*, i. 39.

168. Quéniart, *Culture*, 224.

169. La Louptière, *Poésies* (1768), i. 203, cited by Babeau, *La Vie rurale*, 276.

170. W. Coleman, 'The People's Health: Medical Themes in 18th-Century French Popular Literature', *Bull. Hist. Med.* (1977), 65–8.

171. In what follows, I am using my *Death*, 27–8.

172. Report of 1786 in Bernier, *Essai*, 146–7.

173. Salvini, 'Le Clergé rural', 259, 238; A. Brette, 'Les Dépenses des assemblées électorales en 1789', *Rév. fr.* (1897), 113.

174. Nepveu de la Manoullière, *Mémoires*, i. 223.

175. Duhamel du Monceau, *Éléments d'agriculture* (2 vols., 1763), i. p. x.

176. A. Rigaudière, 'La Haute-Auvergne face à l'agriculture nouvelle au XVIIIᵉ siècle', in *Études d'histoire économique rurale au XVIIIᵉ siècle*, Trav. Fac. Droit Paris, 6, 47; Duhamel de Monceau and Tillet, *Hist. d'un insecte qui dévore les grains de l'Angoumois avec les moyens que l'on peut employer pour le détruire* (1762), 9, cited by Eich, *Histoire religieuse*, i. 24–5. For curés in Societies of Agriculture—at Alençon, two curés, one monk, the intendant and eighteen laymen; at Falaise, one curé, two monks, twenty-four laymen (H.-L. de la Sicotière, 'La Société royale de la généralité d'Alençon', *Bull. Soc. Orne*, 13 (1894), 488–93).

177. L. Froger, *Instructions d'agriculture et d'économie pour les habitans de la campagne* (1769), 6–11.

178. Ibid. 248–59, 223–40.

179. E. Salliard, *Trois petits constitutionnels de province, les frères Pressac de Civray, 1789–1815* (1922).

180. J.-T. Lasserre, *Recherches historiques sur la ville d'Alet et son ancien diocèse* (1877), 355–7.

181. Bachaumont, xxi. 147–9 (21 Oct. 1782).

182. G. Bonnenfant, *Les Séminaires normands du XVIᵉ au XVIIIᵉ siècle* (1915), 241.

183. 'Cassanyes et ses mémoires inédits, 1758–1843', *Rév. fr.* (1888), 968.

184. F. Vermale, 'La Jeunesse de Mounier', *Ann. hist. Rév. fr.* (1939), 3.

185. McManners, *Angers*, 188.

186. Y. Leblanc, 'Pierre Buquet, bibliothécaire de l'Université de Caen et curé de Saint-Sauveur du Marché', *Bull. Soc. Normandie* (1956), 640.

187. For Cotelle de la Blandinière, see McManners, *Angers*, 199–200. Bergier, curé of Flangebouche, then principal of the *collège* of Besançon, 1767; then canon of Notre-Dame (A. Sicard, *L'Ancien Clergé de France: les évêques avant la Révolution*, 5th edn. (1912), 398–9).

188. J.-M. Ory, 'Les Curés du diocèse de Toul en 1733, d'après les notes de l'abbé Chatrian, secrétaire de l'évêque', *Ann. Est* (1977), 39.

189. 'Les Affiches du Mans', *Bull. Soc. Sarthe* (1973–4), 251.

190. McManners, *Angers*, 44–56. Others elsewhere, e.g. Dr Charles Trignan, curé of Digoville, diocese of Coutances (P. Feret, *La Faculté de Théologie de Paris et ses docteurs les plus célèbres* (7 vols., 1909–10), vii. 152); Pierre Lespine, curé of Montagnac-la-Crempse (L. de Lanzac de Laborie, 'La Révolution à Périgord . . . d'après les notes et correspondance de l'abbé Lespine', *Rev. quest. hist.* (1895), 97).

191. McManners, *Angers*, 56.

192. P. Gache, 'Curés et registres paroissiaux de Souppes au XVIIIe siècle', *Bull. Soc. Montargis*, 3e ser. 43 (1978), 74. Date 1740.

193. Froger, *Instructions*, 243–4.

194. S. Dontenvîde, 'Les Crises démographiques à Charlieu, 1690–1720', *Cahiers hist.* (1969), 125.

195. McManners, *Angers*, 150.

196. 'Travaux et recherches', *Ann. Bourgogne* (1962), 71.

197. A. Dupuy and Charvot, 'Journal d'un curé de campagne, 1712–1765', *Ann. Bretagne* (1889–90), 407.

198. C. Port, *Inventaire analytique des archives anciennes de la Mairie d'Angers* (1861), 270–1.

199. McManners, *Angers*, 150.

200. Joathan, 'Le Journal inédit', 98–104.

201. Ricommard, *La Lieutenance générale de police à Troyes au XVIIIe siècle* (1934), 143.

202. L. Dautheuil, 'Louis Sallentin, 1746–1821, curé de Mouy, puis membre du Directoire du District de Clermont', *Comptes Clermont-en-Beauvaisis* (1957–9), 28–44.

203. See E. Vaillé, *Histoire générale des Postes françaises* (6 vols., 1949–55), vi. 222–75.

204. Bachaumont, xxiii. 131 (29 Aug. 1783).

205. Jean Roux, curé of la Balne, near Lyon (Riollet, 'Le Journal', 302).

206. De Lamarre, curé of Saint-Denoual, in P. Lemarchand, 'Journal d'un curé de campagne au XVIIIe siècle', *Bull. méms. Côtes-du-Nord* (1960), 54–97.

207. *Mercure de France* (1755), cited by P. Girault de Coursac, *L'Éducation d'un roi: Louis XVI* (1972), 37.

208. A. Lantoine, *Histoire de la franc-maçonnerie française: la franc-maçonnerie dans l'État* (1935), reviewed by G. Lefebvre, *Ann. hist. Rév. fr.* (1936), 175.

209. L. Charpentier, 'La Loge maçonnique de Montreuil-sur-Mer, 1761–1809', *Rév. fr.* (1895–6), 536–7; J.-J. Gautier, *Essai sur les mœurs champêtres*, ed. X. Rousseau (1935, orig. pub. 1787), pp. iii–x.

210. Ch. Gérin, 'Les Francs-maçons et la maçonnerie française au XVIIIe siècle', *Rev. quest. hist.* (1875), 553.
211. R. Pomeau, *La Religion de Voltaire* (1956), 434; Riollet, 'Le Journal', 298–91.
212. P. de La Gorce, *Histoire religieuse de la Révolution française* (5 vols., 1924–34), i. 25; R. Darnton, *The Business of Enlightenment: A Publishing History of the Encyclopédie, 1775–1800* (1979), 293.
213. La Gorce, *Histoire*, i. 64.
214. See my comments in *Angers*, 37–45.
215. The marquis de Mirabeau, cited by I. O. Wade, *The Clandestine Organization and Diffusion of Philosophic Ideas in France from 1700 to 1750* (1938), 23. For Meslier see below, ch. 50.
216. Saint-Just, *Témoins*, 195–8.
217. Sarrau, 'Un Poète libournais', *Rev. hist. arch. du Libournais* (1961), 105–14, (1962), 65–71, 115–21, (1963), 15–21.
218. E. Guitton, *Jacques Delille, 1731–1813, et la poésie de la nature* (1976), 365–6.
219. P.-M. Masson, *La Religion de Rousseau* (3 vols., 1916), i. 103–4.
220. J. Lestrade, 'Les Poésies de M. Bordages', *Rev. Gascogne* (1903), 127. (Curé of Estancarbon, diocese of Comminges.)
221. J. F. Marmontel, *Mémoires*, ed. J. Renwick (2 vols., 1972), i. 48. He was staying with the curé of Saint-Bonet after his father died.
222. Gautier, *Essai*, pp. iii–x.
223. Grimm, iii. 60–3, 71 (Aug. 1755). A. Wilson, *Diderot: The Testing Years* (1972), 182.

CHAPTER 12

1. P. Sage, *Le Bon Prêtre dans la littérature française d'Amadis de Gaule au Génie du Christianisme* (1951), 113–14.
2. Rousseau, *Émile*, in *Œuvres complètes* (Pléiade, 1964), iv. 629.
3. Diderot, *Lettres à Sophie Volland*, ed. A. Babelon (2 vols., 1948), ii. 109–10 (30 Sept. 1760).
4. R. Hubert, *D'Holbach et ses amis* (1928), 59.
5. See p. 356.
6. Voltaire, *Corresp.*, i. 336–7.
7. Voltaire, 'Catéchisme du curé', in *Dictionnaire philosophique*, *Œuvres*, xviii. 80.
8. L.-R. de Caradeuc de la Chalotais, *Essai d'éducation nationale* (1763), 145–6.
9. Rousseau, *Correspondance*, ed. Th. Dufour (1924), i. 291–2 (Aug.–Sept. 1749).
10. Restif de la Bretonne, *La Vie de mon père*, in *Œuvres*, ed. M. Bachelin (9 vols., 1930–2), iv. 95–8, 174–80.
11. Ch. Demia, *Trésor clérical, ou conduites pour acquérir et conserver la sainteté ecclésiastique* (1694).
12. Document in H. M. Legros, 'Assassinat du curé de Gesves-le-Gandelain', *Rev. Anjou* (1920), 185.
13. Guyot, xvi. 563–4.
14. C. Berthelot du Chesnay, 'Le Clergé diocésain français au XVIIIe siècle et les registres des insinuations ecclésiastiques', *Rev. hist. mod. contemp.* (1963), 245.

15. A. Schaer, *Le Clergé paroissial catholique en Haute-Alsace sous l'ancien régime, 1648–1789* (1966), 77.

16. Berthelot du Chesnay, 'Le Clergé diocésain', 244; J. McManners, *French Ecclesiastical Society under the Ancien Régime: A Study of Angers* (1960), 226; M. Vallery-Radot, *Un Administrateur ecclésiastique . . . le cardinal de Luynes, archevêque de Sens, 1753–88* (1966), 84–5; F. de Dainville, *Cartes anciennes de l'Église de France* (1956), 197. In the archdiocese of Sens there were sixty canons regular, twelve *prémontrés*, four *frères prêcheurs*, and one Lazarist.

17. P. Furet, *L'Abbaye de Sainte-Geneviève* (2 vols., 1883), ii. 774–5.

18. M. Chartier, 'Un Procès à l'officialité de Cambrai en 1788', *Rev. Nord* (1965), 295–300.

19. e.g., P. Gaffarel, 'Les Lettres de cachet en Provence', *Rev. hist.* (1914), 14–15. The curés referred to in n. 45 were removed by *lettres de cachet*.

20. E. Martin, *Histoire des diocèses de Toul, de Nancy et de Saint-Dié* (3 vols., 1900–3), iii. 58; F. D. Mathieu, *L'Ancien Régime dans la province de Lorraine et Barrois* (1879), 121–3.

21. L. Audiat, *Deux victimes des Septembriseurs: Pierre-Louis de la Rochefoucauld, dernier évêque de Saintes, et son frère, évêque de Beauvais* (1897), 50–4. For the intendant, see Ch. Berthelot du Chesnay, *Les Prêtres séculiers en Haute-Bretagne au XVIIIᵉ siècle* (1984), 443–6.

22. Guyot, xvi. 610–11; M. Jousse, *Traité de la juridiction . . . des Officiaux et autres juges d'église, tant en matière civile que criminelle* (1769), 397. Complaints against the bishops' power of imprisoning in a seminary in the *cahiers* of the curés of Beauvais and of Bigorre (E. Champion, *La France d'après les cahiers* (1921), 89).

23. Luynes, iv. 217–19 (Sept. 1742).

24. Ibid. ii. 255.

25. Barbier, ii. 286–7 (June 1732).

26. Guyot, xvi. 605–6.

27. Ibid. 593.

28. Ibid. ii. 479–80, xvi. 600–3.

29. Complex legal situation: synodal statutes of a particular diocese might make a difference to the findings of the courts (Guyot, lxiii. 251–65, xvi. 594–7).

30. The bishop was also the judge of the legitimacy of the cause which would allow a curé to be absent from the parish (Guyot, xvi. 588, 592).

31. J. Savina, *Le Clergé de Cornouaille à la fin de l'ancien régime et sa convocation aux États-Généraux* (1920), 59–60.

32. M. Pialès, *Traité des gradués* (2 vols., 1757), i. 211. In 1766, the papal nuncio reports that the curés of Paris were excellent (P. Vial (ed.), 'L'Église de France vue par le nonce en 1766', *Cahiers hist.*, viii (1963), 113–14).

33. A. Aulard (ed.), 'Relation sommaire . . . de ce qui s'est passé dans l'Assemblée du clergé de Paris intra muros', *Rév. fr.* (1894), 75.

34. A. Mousset, *L'Étrange Histoire des convulsionnaires de Saint-Médard* (1953), 91.

35. McManners, *Angers*, 184.

36. L. Pérouas, *Le Diocèse de La Rochelle de 1648 à 1724: sociologie et pastorale* (1964), 452.

37. T. J. Schmitt, *L'Organisation ecclésiastique et la pratique religieuse dans l'archidiaconé d'Autun de 1650 à 1750* (1957), 134; Mme H.-L. Rostagnet, 'Les Visites pastorales de Mgr Camille de Neufville dans le diocèse de Lyon au XVIIᵉ siècle, 1654–1662', *Cahiers hist.* (1960), 271–5.

38. As in various cases 1691–1700 in the diocese of Cambrai. See G. Deregnaucourt, 'Scandale et religion au XVIIe siècle: aspects de l'image du prêtre dans les campagnes cambrésiennes', *Rev. Nord* (1976), 451–61.

39. J. Ferté, *La Vie religieuse dans les campagnes parisiennes, 1622–95* (1962), 187.

40. Schmitt, *L'Organisation*, 140–1.

41. G. Minois, 'Les Visites épiscopales dans le diocèse de Tréguier de 1700 à 1750', *Méms. Soc. Côtes-du-Nord* (1978), 19–20.

42. Pérouas *La Rochelle*, 449–51.

43. M. Join-Lambert, 'Pratique religieuse dans le diocèse de Rouen de 1707 à 1787', *Ann. Normandie* (1953), 250–60 (1955), 39.

44. L. Châtellier, *Tradition chrétienne et renouveau catholique dans l'ancien diocèse de Strasbourg, 1650–1770* (1981), 172–80, 388–9.

45. Savina, *Le Clergé*, 60–3. Of the forty-six *lettres de cachet* issued against secular priests in the five dioceses of Haute-Bretagne from 1735 to 1788, only ten were for sexual offences, fifteen for drunkenness, seven for violence (Berthelot du Chesnay, *Les Prêtres séculiers*, 455).

46. Pierre de Vaissière, *Curés de campagne de l'ancienne France* (1933), 230.

47. J.-M. Ory, 'Les Curés du diocèse de Toul en 1773, d'après les notes de l'abbé Chatrian, secrétaire de l'évêque', *Ann. Est* (1979), 33–8, 43, 45, 48, 51, 53, 58–9, 62–3.

48. V. Durand, *État religieux des trois diocèses de Nimes, d'Uzès et d'Alais à la fin de l'ancien régime* (1909), 115–17.

49. J. de Font-Réaulx, 'Études administratives et financières du diocèse de Valence', *Bull. Soc. Drôme* (1931–2), 276.

50. R. Collier, *La Vie en Haute-Provence de 1600 à 1850* (1973), 360.

51. E. Martin, *Histoire*, ii. 346–7.

52. Métra, xv. 72–3 (Aug. 1783); cf. Bachaumont, xxxii. 3–4 (28 Apr. 1786); Voltaire, *Corresp.* xlii. 226 (July 1760).

53. G. Hardy, 'L'Anticléricalisme paysan dans une province française avant 1789', *Ann. rév.* (1912), 613. Cf. J. Faivre, 'Le Bas-clergé Franc-Comtois au milieu du 18e siècle', *Ann. rév.* (1914), 1–7, arguing on limited evidence, that the *bon curé* is a legend.

54. C. Marcilhacy, *Le Diocèse d'Orléans au milieu du XIXe siècle* (1964), 432.

55. A. Monglond, *Le Préromantisme français* (2 vols., 1930), ii. 319.

56. L. Trénard, 'Les Visites pastorales dans le diocèse de Cambrai', *Rev. Nord* (1976), 473.

57. C. Port, *La Vendée angevine* (2 vols., 1888), i. 62.

58. Savina, *Le Clergé*, 60–3.

59. Schaer, *Le Clergé*, 221.

60. Schmitt, *L'Organisation*, 131; J. Lovie, 'La Vie paroissiale dans le diocèse de Die à la fin de l'ancien régime', *Bull. Soc. Drôme* (1941–2), 376, 378.

61. Schmitt, *L'Organisation*, 130.

62. Vallery-Radot, *Un Administrateur ecclésiastique*, 87.

63. J. Eich, *Histoire religieuse du département de la Moselle pendant la Révolution* (2 vols., 1964), i. 27; Durand, *État religieux*, 115–17; F.-Y. Besnard, *Souvenirs d'un nonagénaire*, ed. C. Port (2 vols., 1880), i. 285.

64. Faivre, 'Le Bas-clergé', 10; E. Préclin, 'La Situation ecclésiastique . . . de la Franche-Comté à la veille de la Révolution', *Bull. Féd. Franche Comté* (1955), 19–20.

65. P. Belne, 'Démêlés du curé de Saint-Cirgues de Clermont avec un de ses paroissiens, 1764–9', *Bull. Auvergne* (1961), 25–32.
66. Hardy, 'L'Anticléricalisme', 616.
67. Ibid. 610; Faivre, 'Le Bas-clergé', 3.
68. T. J. A. Le Goff, *Vannes and its Region: A Study of Town and Country in 18th-Century France* (1981), 263.
69. Voltaire, *Corresp.* xlv. 9 (3 Jan. 1761), 30 (12 Jan.), 92–3 (29 Jan.); xlvi. 300–1.
70. O. H. Hufton, *The Poor of Eighteenth-Century France, 1750–1789* (1974), 292–6.
71. G. Gautier, 'La Contrebande du sel en Bretagne', *Méms. Soc. Bretagne* (1957), 105–82.
72. E. Guieysse-Frère, *Sedaine: ses protecteurs et ses amis* (n.d.), 123–4.
73. J.-M. Mioland (ed.), *Actes de l'Église d'Amiens* (2 vols., 1849), i. 134, 216–17, 444, 452, 479, 526.
74. *Souvenirs d'A. Cournot, 1760–1860*, ed. E. P. Bottinelli (1912), 210.
75. McManners, *Angers*, 144.
76. Schaer, *Le Clergé*, 23 (date 1771).
77. Marmontel to Beaumarchais, cited by L. de Loménie, *Beaumarchais et son temps* (2 vols., 1880), ii. 34–5.
78. F. Guérin, 'Un Original Curé de campagne au XVIIIᵉ siècle', *Bull. Soc. Meuse* (1972), 115–27.
79. E. G. Léonard, *Mon village sous Louis XV* (1941), 149, 151.
80. F.-G. Pariset (ed.), *Bordeaux au XVIIIᵉ siècle* (1968), 133; Monglond, *Le Préromantisme*, ii. 308–9; Besnard, *Souvenirs*, i. 295, 311–12.
81. C. Port, *Dictionnaire historique, géographique et biographique de Maine et Loire* (3 vols., 1878), i. 446. This was in 1764.
82. In the diocese of Vannes, the average age in 1789 was 57. In that of Bordeaux, 83 per cent were over 40 years of age, and 23 per cent over 60. In that of Reims, two-thirds were between 40 and 59 years of age; here, curé du Chesne of L'Echelles resigned in 1769 at the age of 105, and in 1774 he was still living with his successor, 'hearing the confessions of those who wished to address themselves to him' (Ph. Loupès, 'Le Clergé paroissial du diocèse de Bordeaux d'après la grande enquête de 1772', *Ann. Midi* (1971), 5–24; E. Bouchez, 'Le Clergé paroissial du diocèse de Reims d'après l'enquête de 1774', *Trav. Acad. nat. Reims* (1911), 128). For Vannes, see Le Goff, *Vannes*, 259.
83. A. Sarramon (ed.), *Les Paroisses du diocèse de Comminges en 1786* (1968), 16, 411, 71, 343.
84. A. Zink, *Azereix: la vie d'une communauté rurale à la fin du XVIIIᵉ siècle* (1969), 26–30, for details.
85. J. Boyreau, *Le Village en France au XVIIIᵉ siècle* (1955), 122; Schaer, *Le Clergé*, 266–7; M. M. Legros, 'Le Fessier et son Bérus, 1761–1791', *Rev. Anjou* (1916), 26.
86. [J.-L. Brunet, rev. Durand de Maillane], *Le Parfait Notaire apostolique* (2 vols., 1775), i. p. vii.
87. T. J. Schmitt, *L'Assistance dans l'archidiaconé d'Autun au XVIIᵉ et XVIIIᵉ siècles* (1952), 323; S. T. McCloy, *Government Assistance in 18th-century France* (1946), 303; J. P. Gutton, *La Société et les pauvres: l'exemple de la généralité de Lyon, 1534–1789* (1971), 194.

88. Métra, v. 5–6 (1777).

89. Hufton, *Poor*, 83–4.

90. McManners, *Angers*, 146.

91. L. Lallemand, *De l'organisation de la bienfaisance publique et privée dans les campagnes au XVIIIᵉ siècle* (1895), 16.

92. J. Villain, *Le Recouvrement des impôts directs sous l'ancien régime* (1952), 48.

93. Monglond, *Le Préromantisme*, ii. 56.

94. J. A. Dulaure, *Nouvelle Description de Paris* (1787), ii. 257.

95. L. Lallemand, *Un chapître de l'histoire des Enfants trouvés: la Maison de la Couche à Paris, XVIIᵉ–XVIIIᵉ siècles* (1889), 54–5.

96. D. Dakin, *Turgot and the Ancien Régime* (1939), 58–9.

97. J.-J. Gautier, *Essai sur les mœurs champêtres*, ed. X. Rousseau (1935), 43–4; M. de Broc, 'Une Famille de province au XVIIIᵉ siècle', *Bull. Soc. Orne* (1890), 195–200.

98. M. Riollet, 'Le Journal d'un curé de campagne, 1768–1790', *Rev. Lyon* (1911), 286, 298.

99. J. Buvat, *Journal de la Régence*, ed. E. Campardon (2 vols., 1865), ii. 92.

100. E. Esmonin, *Études sur la France des XVIIᵉ et XVIIIᵉ siècles* (1964), 253, 297.

101. Dainville, *Cartes anciennes*, 62–91.

102. P. Collet, *Traité des devoirs d'un pasteur* (1758), 91–114.

103. L. Michard and G. Couton, 'Les Livres d'états des âmes', *Rev. hist. Église Fr.* (1981), 261–9.

104. J. A. T. Dinouart, *Abrégé de l'embryologie sacrée* (1766), 200–2.

105. E. Barbotin, *Lettres de l'abbé Barbotin, député à l'Assemblée Constituante*, ed. A. Aulard (1910), 54.

106. G. Lenôtre, *Vieilles maisons, vieux papiers* (1930), 31–4.

107. See the plot of La Harpe's *Mélanie*.

108. Rousseau, *Correspondance*, iii. 299 (3 Mar. 1758).

109. The fermier général La Pouplinière was dissatisfied when he met her—so gave her a dowry of 130,000 livres and married her to an officer of the *gardes suisses* (Mme de Genlis, *Mémoires* (2 vols., 1825), i. 81–2).

110. Restif de la Bretonne, *La Vie de mon père*, pt. 2, bk. 3. For the wise curé in another novel, F. C. Green, *La Peinture des mœurs de la bonne société dans le roman français de 1715 à 1761* (1924), 121.

111. M. de Broc, 'Une famille' (consists of the memoirs of Michel Le Prince, 1737–1815).

112. M. Maréchal, rev. M. J. A. Serieux, *Traité des droits honorifiques des patrons et seigneurs dans les Eglises* (2 vols., 1772), i. 37.

113. P.-J. Guyot, *Observations sur le droit des patrons* (1751), 15.

114. P.-J. Guyot, *Dictionnaire*, xxi. 271. He says *seigneur haut justicier*—there were, in fact, many complexities in definition (265–6).

115. Ibid. xxi. 296–310. (As against Maréchal, who is for the patrons—because, says Guyot, he was a patron himself in various churches.)

116. Ibid. xxi. 342–4.

117. Guyot, *Observations*, 329–30.

118. Guyot, *Dictionnaire*, xxi. 369–70; id., *Observations*, 279, 387–8; Maréchal, *Traité*, i. 73–6.

119. Guyot, *Dictionnaire*, xlviii. 5; id., *Observations*, 240 ff., 331.

120. Guyot, *Observations*, 153, 161, 232.

121. McManners, *Angers*, 311.
122. Collet, *Traité*, 39.
123. Guyot, *Observations*, 350–61; id., *Dictionnaire*, xxi. 346–60.
124. Maréchal, *Traité*, i. 287–9.
125. Guyot, *Observations*, 373; id., *Dictionnaire*, xi. 301.
126. Champion, *La France*, 140–1.
127. P. de Saint-Jacob, *Les Paysans de la Bourgogne du nord au dernier siècle de l'ancien régime* (1960), 248.
128. Barbier, i. 190 (Feb. 1722).
129. P. Le Marchand, 'Journal d'un curé de campagne au XVIIIᵉ siècle', *Soc. Côtes-du-Nord: Bull. et Mém.* (1960), 75–89.
130. Gautier, *Essai*, 13–14, 44.
131. J. Salvini, 'Le Clergé rural en Haut-Poitou à la veille de la Révolution', *Bull. Soc. Ouest* (1957–8), 240.
132. G. Desnoiresterres, *Voltaire et la société française au XVIIIᵉ siècle*, 2nd edn. (8 vols., 1867–76), vi. 132, 65, 119.
133. Collet, *Traité*, 148.
134. Salvini, 'Le Clergé rural', 245–8. Ferrières says so in his *Théisme* (2 vols., 1790).
135. P. Massé, *Varennes et ses maîtres, 1779–1842* (1956), 62.
136. Léonard, *Mon village*, 82, 88.
137. L. N. Berthe, *Dubois de Fosseux, secrétaire de l'Académie d'Arras, 1785–92* (1969), 82–7.
138. H. Beauchet-Filleau, *Pièces inédites . . . concernant le Poitou* (2 fasc., n.d.), i. 16–19.
139. L. N. Berthe, 'La Fin de l'ancien régime à Fosseux, d'après les lettres du curé au seigneur', *Mélanges sc. relig.* (1955), 51–8.
140. E. Bouley, 'Nobles et paysans Picards à la fin de l'ancien régime', *Rev. hist. mod. contemp.* (1969), 606–10.
141. Gautier, *Essai*, 11.
142. Guyot, *Dictionnaire*, xi. 325.
143. Vaissière, *Curés*, 295–9; Guyot, xxi. 266–7; H. Carré, *La Noblesse de France et l'opinion publique au XVIIIᵉ siècle* (1920), 317–18.
144. Vaissière, *Curés*, 294.
145. Marais, iv. 516 (16 Aug. 1733).
146. J. Grente and O. Havard, *Villedieu-les-Poêles: sa commanderie, sa bourgeoisie, ses métiers* (2 vols., 1898), i. 244.
147. Guyot, xxi. 266–7.
148. Ibid.
149. Carré, *La Noblesse*, 318.
150. Collier, *La Vie en Haute-Provence*, 87.
151. Ch. du Bus, *Stanislas de Clermont-Tonnerre et l'échec de la révolution monarchique 1757–1792* (1931), 39.
152. J. Camoreyt, 'Une Lettre de Mgr de Montillet', *Rev. Gascogne* (1927), 226–7.
153. Vaissière, *Curés*, 301–2.
154. Schmitt, *L'Organisation*, 136; Riollet, 'Le Journal', 290; Carré, *La Noblesse*, 318; Vaissière, *Curés*, 303.
155. Carré, *La Noblesse*, 317.
156. Riollet, 'Le Journal', 283–90.

157. C. Hippeau, *Les Cahiers de 1789 en Normandie* (2 vols., 1869), i. 148.

158. J. Bindet, *L'Évêque constitutionnel de la Manche, François Bécherel, 1732–1802* (1934), 12.

159. G. LeFebvre, *La Grande Peur de 1789* (1932), 123.

160. Carré, *La Noblesse*, 399–400.

161. A. Aulard, 'La Féodalité sous la Révolution', *Rév. fr.* (1913), 112.

162. Le Monnier (1778), cited by Sage, 288.

163. Sarramon (ed.), *Les Paroisses*, 23, 26.

164. P. Gagnol, *La Dîme ecclésiastique en France* (1910), 101.

165. E. Sévestre, *Les Idées gallicanes et royalistes du haut clergé . . . d'après la correspondance de Pierre-Augustin Godert de Belbeuf, évêque d'Avranches, 1762–1803* (1917). Letter of 18 Jan. 1786.

166. Praise of the charity of the curés of Paris in [Seguier de Saint-Brisson], *Lettre à Philopémas, ou réflexions sur le régime des pauvres* (1764), cited by P. M. Masson, *La Religion de Rousseau* (3 vols., 1916), iii. 65.

167. Grimm, iii. 416 (Sept. 1757); see also Luynes, ix. 126 (Nov. 1748), and C. Hamel, *Histoire de l'église de Saint-Sulpice* (1900), 169.

168. *Journal de Paris*, 3 Dec. 1777, cited by Masson, *La Religion*, iii. 208–9.

169. A. Krieger and L. Raffin, *La Madeleine* (1937), 57–8.

170. Bachaumont, xi. 73–5 (28 Jan. 1778).

171. Saint-Jacob, *Bourgogne*, 534.

172. E. Dupont, 'La condition des paysans dans la sénéchaussée de Rennes d'après les cahiers des paroisses', *Ann. Bretagne* (1900–1), 59; 58; G. Hubrecht, 'La Région sedanaise à la veille de la Révolution', *Ann. hist. Rév. fr.* (1937), 129–32; id. '*Cahier* of Tiers of Verdun', *Rév. fr.* (1900), 452; Port, *La Vendée angevine*, 61–2, 105.

173. Le Goff, *Vannes*, 261–2.

174. F. Clérembray, 'Le Comté d'Eu au moment de la convocation des États Généraux de 1789', *Rév. fr.* (1894), 144.

175. A. Dupuy, 'Les Épidémies en Bretagne au XVIIIe siècle', *Ann. Bretagne* (1886–7), 28.

176. Salvini, 'Le Clergé rural', 238; A. Brette, 'Une Lettre de l'abbé Jallet à Necker', *Rév. fr.* (1893), 83.

177. McCloy, *Government Assistance*, 78–9.

178. Gilbert van de Louw, *Baculard d'Arnaud, romancier ou vulgarisateur* (1972), 71.

179. A. Corvisier, *L'Armée française de la fin du XVIIe siècle au ministère de Choiseul*, 2 vols. (1964), i. 105–6.

180. Barbotin, *Lettres*, 18–19, 71, 83, 70.

181. E. Chevrier, 'Notice sur les églises de Sable', *Rev. Maine* (1876), 403–6.

182. A. Dupuy and Charvot, 'Journal d'un curé de campagne, 1712–1765', *Ann. Bretagne* (1889–1907), 407.

CHAPTER 13

1. J.-J. Pialès, *Traité des réparations* (3 vols., 1762), ii. 10; E. and L. Delonca, *Un Village en Roussillon* (1947), 234.

2. J. McManners, *French Ecclesiastical Society under the Ancien Régime: A Study of Angers* (1960), 141–2.

3. J. Déchelette, 'Visites pastorales des archiprêtres de Charlieu par Mgr De Lort de Sérignan de Valras, évêque de Mâcon, 1745–64', *Ann. Acad. Mâcon*, 3ᵉ sér. iii (1898), 522–3.

4. J. Savina, *Le Clergé de Cornouaille à la fin de l'ancien régime et sa convocation aux États-Généraux* (1926), 41.

5. L. de Montfalcon, 'Querelle autour d'un presbytère à Flaxien au XVIIIᵉ siècle', *Bull. Belley* (1965), 29, 36.

6. J. Charrier, *Histoire religieuse du département de la Nièvre pendant la Révolution* (2 vols., 1920), i. 19.

7. P. Feret, *L'Abbaye de Sainte-Geneviève et la Congrégation de France* (2 vols., 1883), ii. 261–8.

8. A. Sarramon (ed.), *Les Paroisses du diocèse de Comminges en 1786* (1968), 269, 147, 228, 296, 346.

9. Ibid. 374.

10. Comic observations about a curé's sister, very fat and always sacking the servants (E.-G. Léonard, *Mon Village sous Louis XV* (1941), 81–3).

11. e.g. G. Coolen, *Helfaut: essai sur l'administration d'une paroisse sous l'ancien régime* (1939), 85; A. Frézet, 'Guillaume Desmarets, curé de Courville, 1682–1765', *Nouv. Rev. Champagne et Brie* (1936), 186.

12. They saved and made up the dowries to him later, Restif de la Bretonne tells us (*Vie de mon père*). The curé was Foudriat's predecessor.

13. Stories in J. A. Dulaure, *Nouvelle Description de Paris* (2 vols., 1787), ii. 26–34, and in C. du Povey, 'Un Épisode sensationnel de la vie de l'abbé Torné exhumé des casiers d'un greffe', *Ann. rév.* (1913), 127. (Both took place in 1766.)

14. T. J. Schmitt, *L'Organisation ecclésiastique et la pratique religieuse dans l'archidiaconé d'Autun de 1650 à 1750* (1957), 128; M. Vallery-Radot, *Un Administrateur ecclésiastique . . . le cardinal de Luynes, archevêque de Sens, 1753–88* (1966), 55.

15. A. Playoust-Chaussis, *La Vie religieuse dans le diocèse de Boulogne . . . 1725–90* (1976), 180.

16. As the curés of Le Mans argue in synod (A. Babeau, *La Vie rurale dans l'ancienne France* (1883), 160). Cf. V. Durand, *L'État religieux des trois diocèses de Nîmes, d'Uzès et d'Alais à la fin de l'ancien régime* (1909), 115–17 (Nîmes).

17. e.g. Sarramon (ed.), *Les Paroisses*, 201, 219.

18. J.-J. Gautier, *Essai sur les mœurs champêtres*, ed. X. Rousseau (1935, orig. pub. 1787), 47.

19. P. de Vaissière, *Curés de campagne de l'ancienne France* (1933), 117–24. The advantage of a job with the curé was that it might be used to avoid militia service.

20. Verses of Poisson de la Chabeaussière in L. Johanet, *Bull. Soc. Orléanais* (1942), 286.

21. See the abbé A. Prévost, *L'Ordre moral*, in *Œuvres* (39 vols. 1810–16), xxxix. 3–5, 153, 156.

22. Curé E. Barbotin, *Lettres*, ed. A. Aulard (1910), 36, 46, 79, 85–6.

23. M. Chartier, 'A travers les papiers Caprara', *Rev. Nord* (1921), 121 ff.

24. L. Dantin, *Le Diocèse de Tarbes* (1908), 33.

25. McManners, *Angers*, 132. The clergy of Anjou in 1760 said the optimum size for a compact town parish was 3,000 souls.

26. Ibid. 131–2.

27. E. Sévestre, *L'Organisation du clergé paroissial à la veille de la Révolution: correspondance du curé de Saint-Nicolas de Coutances, 1784–88* (1911), 113.

28. *Vie de M. Marquis-Ducastel*, ed. F. Pichon (1873), 27–8 (date 1763).

29. M. Baurit and J. Hillairet, *Saint-Germain-l'Auxerrois* (1955), 103. (The parish where Boucher was buried, where Danton was married.)

30. Alençon, population 18,000 (Sévestre, *L'Organisation*, 113).

31. Guyot, xlvi. 558–9.

32. Payment of 72 livres only (P. Perceveaux, 'La Portion congrue: aumône ou minimum vital? Notes sur les conditions de vie du bas clergé en Valromey aux 17ᵉ et 18ᵉ siècles', *Bull. Belley* (1967), 88). Plot of common land, H. Cottin, *La Liquidation des biens du clergé à Is-sur-Tille* (1911), 36, 41.

33. A. Dupuy, 'L'Administration municipale en Bretagne', *Ann. Bretagne* (1887–8), 579–80.

34. P. de Saint-Jacob, *Documents relatifs à la communauté villageoise en Bourgogne* (1962), 144–6. In 1749 the inhabitants refused to go on paying it.

35. Ch. Berthelot du Chesnay, 'Le Clergé diocésain français au XVIIIᵉ siècle et les registres des insinuations ecclésiastiques', *Rev. hist. mod. contemp.* (1963), 253.

36. T. Leuridan, *Histoire de Linselles* (1883), 143–50.

37. R. Desreumaux, 'À propos d'un arpentage au 18ᵉ siècle, Vaux-Vraucourt, Pas-de-Calais', *Ensemble d'Écoles supérieures et des Facultés catholiques, Lille* (1977), 227–35.

38. Sévestre, *L'Organisation*, 7–8, 14, 55–78.

39. A. Laveille, 'Les Revenus du clergé breton avant la Révolution', *Rev. quest. hist.* (1912), 462–3.

40. E. Bouchez, 'Le Clergé paroissial du diocèse de Reims d'après l'enquête de 1774', *Trav. Acad. nat. Reims* (1911), 282–6.

41. Gautier, *Essai*, 27.

42. Léonard, *Mon village*, 84–9.

43. T. Tackett and Cl. Langlois, 'Ecclesiastical Structures and Clerical Geography on the Eve of the French Revolution', *Fr. Hist. St.* (1980), 715–45.

44. In the diocese of Vannes, the average waiting time was eight years; in that of Bordeaux half the vicaires had achieved their ambition within eight years, and nearly all the others in a further four years. In the town of Bordeaux, where the parishes were regarded as superior, the average wait was ten years from ordination.

45. Le Maire, 'Le Placet d'un vicaire . . . 1760', *Bull. Soc. Orléanais* (1943), 440–58.

46. Mme Roland, *Lettres*, NS, ed. Cl. Perroud (2 vols., 1913–15), ii. 83.

47. Chateaubriand, *Mémoires d'outre-tombe*, ed. M. Levaillant (2 vols., 1947), i. 86.

48. In April 1790 this fate befell a vicaire who had served in a parish for twenty-two years and was the support of his aged parents (Sévestre, *L'Organisation*, 26).

49. Gautier, *Essai*, 30. Cf. J. Charrier, *Claude Fauchet* (1909), 51. In a funeral oration Fauchet praises the archbishop of Bourges for closing such a home for aged clergy and giving them pensions instead. 'Men who are used to long years of freedom must not, at the end of their days, be subjected to a monastic discipline nor, old themselves, be limited to the company of the old.'

50. R. Mousnier, Sorbonne lecture course, duplicated (n.d.), 54.
51. P. D. Bernier, *Paysans de Basse-Normandie* (1891), 104–8.
52. Gautier, *Essai*, 25–6.
53. P. Pisani, *L'Église de Paris et la Révolution* (4 vols., 1908), i. 29–33.
54. 'Obsèques d'une grande dame à Saint-Sulpice à Paris', *Bul. Com. Nîmes* (1959), 33.
55. F.-G. Pariset (ed.), *Bordeaux au XVIIIᵉ siècle* (1968), 131.
56. J.-M. Alliot, *Le Clergé de Versailles pendant la Révolution française* (1913), 47–8.
57. Dupuy, 'L'Administration', 586–9.
58. Sévestre, *L'Organisation*, 27–8.
59. R. Suadeau, *L'Évêque inspecteur administratif sous la monarchie absolue* (2 vols., 1940), ii. 66–7; Guyot, xiii. 196; L. Welter, 'Les Communautés de prêtres dans le diocèse de Clermont du XIIIᵉ au XVIIIᵉ siècle', *Rev. hist. Église Fr.* (1949), 9.
60. Schmitt, *L'Organisation*, 25–7.
61. E. Préclin, 'La Situation ecclésiastique . . . de la Franche Comté à la veille de la Révolution', *Bull. Féd. Franche Comté* (1955), 8–9.
62. Guyot, xxv. 201.
63. A. Cournot, *Souvenirs, 1760–1806*, ed. E. P. Bottinelli (1913), 9.
64. Semonsons, 'Communautés des prêtres à Cambraille', *Bull. Auvergne* (1959), 100–1.
65. Ibid. 101–10.
66. Sévestre, *L'Organisation*, 29–30, 61–2.
67. Ibid. 55.
68. Suadeau, *L'Évêque*, i. 70, ii. 8–10, 14–18.
69. Guyot, xiii. 197–9, 202.
70. L. Brochard, *Saint-Gervais, histoire de la paroisse* (1950), 156–6, 210, 299.
71. H. Manissadjan, 'La Communauté des prêtres de l'église de Sainte-Feyre', *Cahiers hist.* (1957), 227, 240.
72. Delonca and Delonca, *Un Village*, 234–5.
73. L. Pérouas, *Le Diocèse de La Rochelle de 1648 à 1724: sociologie et pastorale* (1964), 129, 445–6.
74. Schmitt, *L'Organisation*, 25.
75. Delonca and Delonca, *Un Village*, 234.
76. Manissadjan, 'Saint-Feyre', 240.
77. G. de Léotoing d'Anjouy, 'La Communauté des prêtres-filleuls de l'église Notre-Dame d'Aurillac', *Rev. Haute-Auvergne* (1952), 287–301.
78. J. Vinatier, *Histoire générale de Treignac-sur-Vézéré* (2 vols., 1974), ii. 34–6.
79. Pariset (ed.), *Bordeaux*, 131.
80. 'Une Paroisse rurale sous l'ancien régime: Raulhac-en-Caulades', *Rev. quest hist.* (1905), 210–17.
81. Brochard, *Saint-Gervais*, 285–6.
82. His journal is in the communal archives—see Léotoing d'Anjouy, 'Notre-Dame d'Aurillac', 455.
83. M.-C. Guibert, *Mémoires pour servir à l'histoire de la ville de Dieppe*, ed. M. Hardy (2 vols., 1878), pp. vii–xxi.

CHAPTER 14

1. Guyot, xii. 70–3.
2. Indispensable reading is Ph. Loupès, *Chapitres et chanoines de Guyenne aux XVIIᵉ et XVIIIᵉ siècles* (1985), ranging wider than its title.
3. M.-R. Vilette, *Les États-Généraux du Cambrésis de 1677 à 1790* (thèse droit, Lille, 1950), 86–126.
4. E. Jarry, 'Le Chapitre de Saint-Martin de Tours aux XVIIᵉ et XVIIIᵉ siècles', *Rev. hist. Église Fr.* (1961), 119–20.
5. G. Laurent, *Reims et la région rémoise à la veille de la Révolution* (1930), pp. xiv–xv. More details in *L'Église et les chapîtres de Reims avant 1790, par l'abbé Bauny*, published in *Le Bibliophile rémigeois* (1881), e.g. on incomes, p. 36.
6. M. Laubry, *Traité des unions* (1778), 93.
7. G. Cholvy, *Le diocèse de Montpellier* (1970), 163.
8. R. Collier, *La Vie en Haute-Provence de 1600 à 1800* (1973), 104, 184, 364.
9. L. É. Bellivière, *Jacobins du village: un bourg de Normandie pendant la Révolution* (1943), 16–18.
10. Loupès, *Chapitres*, 423.
11. T. J. Schmitt, *L'Organisation ecclésiastique et la pratique religieuse dans l'archidiaconé d'Autun de 1650 à 1750* (1957), p. xiii.
12. M. Vallery-Radot, *Un Administrateur ecclésiastique à la fin de l'ancien régime: le cardinal de Luynes, archevêque de Sens, 1753–88* (1966), 118–29.
13. A. Dupuy, 'La Collégiale de Notre-Dame de la Fosse', *Ann. Bretagne* (1888–9), 429–83. The Guéméné family were the patrons.
14. C. Daux, 'État du diocèse de Montauban à la fin de l'ancien régime', *Rev. quest. hist.* (1914), 499–500.
15. J. Denais, 'La Sainte-Chapelle royale du Gué de Maulny', *Rev. Maine* (1892), 379–99.
16. Laubry, *Traité*, 109–10.
17. See J. Meuret, *Le Chapitre de Notre-Dame de Paris en 1790* (1903), and E. Delmas, *Essai historique sur le chapitre de Saint-Germain l'Auxerrois* (1905).
18. Vallery-Radot, *Un Administrateur ecclésiastique*, 129–39.
19. Loupès, *Chapitres*, 298.
20. P. Bastid, *Siéyès et sa pensée* (1939), 39. For interesting details, N. Aston, 'The Abbé Siéyès before 1789: The Progress of a Clerical Careerist', *J. Ren. Mod. St.* (1989), 41–52.
21. F. D. Mathieu, *L'Ancien régime en Lorraine et Barrois* (1879), 130–1.
22. J. Eich, *Histoire religieuse du département de la Moselle pendant la Révolution* (2 vols., 1964), i. 118–19.
23. The appointment of a 23-year-old at Lombez before he had even proceeded to the subdiaconate, in J. Clermont, 'Louis Aygobère, 1765–1842, chanoine de Lombez', *Rev. Gascogne* (1936), 75–9.
24. R.-P. Nepveu de Manoullière, *Mémoires*, ed. G. Esnault (3 vols., 1877–9), i. pp. ix, 7, 10, 79, 140, 234–5; ii. 91, 106–7.
25. R. Poulle, *Histoire de l'église paroissiale de Notre-Dame et Saint-Michel à Draguignan* (1865), 372–3; Schmitt, *L'Organisation*, 12–13; A. V. Durand, *L'État religieux des trois diocèses de Nîmes, d'Uzès et d'Alais à la fin de l'ancien régime* (1909), 58–9.
26. J. Blampignon, *L'Épiscopat de Massillon* (1884), 23, 28.

27. E. Regnault, *Christophe de Beaumont, archevêque de Paris, 1763–81* (2 vols., 1882), i. 72–3 (he was a canon of Lyon at the time).

28. J. Meyer, *La Noblesse bretonne au XVIIIe siècle* (2 vols., 1966), ii. 878.

29. C. Van der Cruysse, *La Mort dans les mémoires de Saint-Simon* (1981), 249.

30. François-Joachim, cardinal de Bernis, *Mémoires et Lettres*, ed. F. Masson (2 vols., 1878), i. 122–3 n.

31. R. Reuss, *La Cathédrale de Strasbourg pendant la Révolution* (1885), 2–5.

32. J. McManners, *French Ecclesiastical Society under the Ancien Régime: A Study of Angers* (1960), ch. 4.

33. M. Vovelle, 'Un des plus grands chapitres de France à la fin de l'ancien régime: le chapitre cathédral de Chartres', *Actes 85e Congrès national des Sociétés Savantes, Section d'histoire moderne et contemporaine, 1960* (1961), 236–62; M.-M.-J. Compère, summary of thesis in *Bill. Soc. Eure-et-Loire* (1968), 28–32.

34. Loupès, *Chapitres*, 237–9.

35. Montesquieu, *Pensées*, in *Œuvres*, ed. H. Masson (3 vols., 1955), ii. 63.

36. Loupès, *Chapitres*, 224, 229, 277–8, 327.

37. Cited, ibid. 247.

38. Marais, ii. 191 (Sept. 1721); C. Marcilhacy, *Le Diocèse d'Orléans au milieu du XIXe siècle* (1964), 432; McManners, *Angers*, 61; A. Playoust-Chaussis, *La Vie religieuse dans le diocèse de Boulogne au XVIIIe siècle, 1725–90* (1976), 69. A few more cases in Bachaumont, xxviii. 229 (1785), xxvii. 157 (1774), xxxiv. 11 (1787), xxxi. 164 (1768).

39. E. Violet, 'Quatre Plaisantes Affaires judiciaires au XVIIIe siècle', *B.S.A.A.T.* (1958), cited in *Ann. Bourgogne* (1962), 69.

40. Dupuy, 'La Collégiale', 469–70.

41. P. Gosset, 'Scandales littéraires rémois au XVIIIe siècle', *Nouv. Rev. Champagne et Brie* (1936), 88–95.

42. Bernard-Laurent Soumille, 'Journal', ed. M. A. Coulondres, *Méms. Soc. Alais* (1879), 131, 153, 197.

43. G. Doublet, *Le Chapitre abbatial de Foix sous Louis XIV* (1890), 6–7; Deschamps de la Rivière, 'Un Braconnier dans le chapitre de Saint-Pierre de la Cour', *Bull. Soc. Sarthe* (1901–2), 277; J. Contrasty, *Histoire de la cité de Rieux-Volvestre et de ses évêques* (1936), 310.

44. Vallery-Radot, *Un Administrateur ecclésiastique*, 142–3.

45. Bremond d'Ars-Migré, *Un Collaborateur de Buffon: l'abbé Bexon* (1936), 183.

46. Dom P. Chastelain, *Journal*, ed. M. Jadert (1902), 89.

47. Guyot, xlv. 111–12.

48. Nepveu de la Manoullière, *Mémoires*, i. 115.

49. The following from Mathieu, *Lorraine*, 132; Doublet, *Foix*, 5; Luynes, ix. 16; Schmitt, *L'Organisation*, 16.

50. G. Bonnenfant, *Les Séminaires normands du XVIe au XVIIIe siècle* (1915), 430–3.

51. Regnault, *Christophe de Beaumont*, i. 32–5.

52. L'Abbé Baston, *Mémoires*, ed. J. Loth and C. Verger (3 vols., 1879), i. 271.

53. V. Dufour, 'État du diocèse de Paris en 1789', *Bull. Com. Paris*, 1 (1883), 41–2.

54. A. H. Van der Weil, *Paul-Louis Mondran, 1734–95, un chanoine homme d'esprit* (1942), 93–5.

55. McManners, *Angers*, ch. 2.
56. Soumille, 'Journal', 178; McManners, *Angers*, 24.
57. Bachaumont, xviii. 172–3 (1781).
58. Vovelle, 'Chartres', 256–8.
59. Marcel, *Le Frère de Diderot* (1913), 73.
60. Baston, *Mémoires*, i. 269.
61. McManners, *Angers*, 63; Schmitt, *L'Organisation*, 16.
62. Cl. Joly, *Traité historique des écoles épiscopales et ecclésiastiques* (1673). Joly was a canon of Notre-Dame of Paris.
63. L. Paris, *Histoire de l'abbaye d'Avenay* (2 vols., 1879), i. 18–19.
64. For the examples following: Vallery-Radot, *Un Administrateur ecclésiastique*, 85; E. Préclin, 'La Situation ecclésiastique de Franche-Comté à la veille de la Révolution', *Bull. Féd. Franche-Comté* (1955), 8; Schmitt, *L'Organisation*, p. xiv; Eich, *Histoire*, i. 20; P. de Crousaz-Crétet, *Paris sous Louis XIV* (2 vols., 1922), ii. 7; Daux, 'État du diocèse de Montauban', 500–1; Poulle, *Histoire*, 234–58.
65. Blampignon, *Massillon*, 281.
66. A. Faure, 'J.-B. Blain, chanoine de Rouen', *Rev. Socs. Haute Normandie* (1959), 39–42.
67. J. Savina, *Le Clergé de Cornouaille à la fin de l'ancien régime et sa convocation aux États-Généraux de 1789* (1926), 22–7.
68. Cl. Perroud, 'Une Entrée épiscopale en 1791', *Rév. fr.* (1896), 164.
69. Bachaumont, xix. 75 (Jan. 1778). For reclaiming the *landes*, ibid. xix. 239.
70. H.-L. de la Sicotière, 'La Société royale de la généralité d'Alençon', *Bull. Soc. Orne* (1894), 503.
71. A. Barnes, *Jean Leclerc et la république des lettres* (1938), 191–2.
72. For Trublet see the chapter on 'Abbés'.
73. Bremond d'Ars-Migré, 38, 75–82, 176–7, 181, 189.
74. Loupès, *Chapitres*, 312.
75. E. Chartraire, 'Trois recueils de la correspondance des abbés Fenel avec l'abbé Lebeuf et autres', *Bull. Soc. Sens* (1927), 118–26. The other abbé Fenel was his brother and the dean of his chapter.
76. The baron A. de Maricourt, 'Lettres de l'abbé Le Gouz', *Rev. quest. hist.* (1914), 96–126.
77. L. Welter, 'Le Chapitre cathédral de Clermont: sa constitution, ses privilèges', *Rev. hist. Église Fr.* (1955), 7–20.
78. Dufour, 'État', 34.
79. Loupès, *Chapitres*, 177–8.
80. Soumille, 'Journal', 124–9, 208.
81. Ibid., 141, 186.
82. Van der Weil, *Mondran*, 35–7.
83. A. Degert, *Histoire des évêques de Dax* (1903), 416.
84. C. Baloche, *L'Église Saint-Merry de Paris* (2 vols., 1911), i. 519, 548.
85. Jarry, 'Saint-Martin de Tours', 121.
86. Nepveu de la Manoullière, *Mémoires*, 101, 112.
87. Vovelle, 'Chapitres', 235 ff.
88. McManners, *Angers*, 57, 116.
89. M. Lhéritier, *L'Intendant Tourny, 1695–1760* (2 vols., 1920), ii. 94–5.
90. E. Laurès, *La Municipalité de Béziers à la fin de l'ancien régime* (1926), 144–7;

for Metz see J. B. Pelt, *Études sur la cathédrale de Metz* (1853), 334.

91. P. de la Haye, *Histoire de Tréguier, ville épiscopale* (1927), 287–8.

92. J. Carreyre, *Le Jansénisme durant la Régence* (3 vols., 1929–33), pp. xx, 218.

93. Barbier, i. 152; Luynes, v. 29–30, viii. 252–3 (June 1743, June 1747).

94. Guyot, ix. 420–62, and, generally, Ducasse, *Traité des droits et des obligations des églises cathédrales* (1706).

95. Contrasty, *Rieux-Volvestre*, 350–3.

96. D'Argenson, vi. 396.

97. L. Charpentier, *Un Évêque de l'ancien régime: Louis-Joseph de Grignon, 1670–1722* (1899), 130–8.

98. L. Pingaud, *Les Saulx-Tavannes* (1876), 267.

99. Bachaumont, vii. 144–5.

100. Letter of Dom Jean Colomb, 30 Mar. 1760, *Rev. Maine* (1877), 236–7; Nepveu de la Manoullière, *Mémoires*, i. 6–7, 53.

101. McManners, *Angers*, 178–9.

102. G. Courraze, *Lombez, évêché rural, 1312–1801* (1973), 135–9, 210–11.

103. G. Viard, 'Le Chapitre de Langres' (thesis), cited by Loupès, *Chapitres*, 365.

104. Nepveu de la Manoullière, *Mémoires*, 63–101.

105. M. Dommanget, *Le Curé Meslier* (1965), 283.

106. For a detailed account of this trouble in Angers, see McManners, *Angers* 162–89. The lawyers usually favoured the rights of the curés (Laubry, *Traité*, 86–7).

107. Summed up in *Lettres à un ami sur la dignité des curés et des chanoines* (1770) (Bibli. nat. F 6361), pp. v, 4, 113.

108. Bib. nat. LK3 114, pp. iv, vi, 3, 12, 19, 56, 143.

109. Loupès, *Chapitres*, 384–5.

110. Vovelle, 'Chapitres', 260–2.

111. Loupès, *Chapitres*, 403–5; J. Loth, *Histoire du cardinal de la Rochefoucauld et du diocèse de Rouen pendant la Révolution* (1893), 134–5.

CHAPTER 15

1. Ph. Loupès, *Chapitres et chanoines de Guyenne aux XVIIᵉ et XVIIIᵉ siècles* (1985), 58.

2. Guyot, xxi. 264–5.

3. J. McManners, *French Ecclesiastical Society under the Ancien Régime: A Study of Angers* (1960), 14; Clerval, *L'Ancienne Maîtrise de Notre-Dame de Chartres* (1899), 171, 186, 195.

4. L. Réau, *Histoire du vandalisme: les monuments détruits de l'art français* (2 vols., 1989), i. 13–14.

5. E. Champion, 'J.-J. Rousseau et le vandalisme révolutionnaire', *Rév. fr.* (1908), 163.

6. P. Feret, *L'Abbaye de Sainte-Geneviève* (2 vols., 1883), ii. 40–6; N. Jacquin, 'Louis XV pose la première pierre de la nouvelle église de Sainte-Geneviève', *La Montagne Sainte-Geneviève* (Mar. 1973), 58–61.

7. H. Tavernier, 'Gauthey, ingénieur en chef de la province de Bourgogne au XVIIIᵉ siècle', *Méms. Acad. Lyon*, 3ᵉ sér. 9 (1907), 226–7.

8. M.-A. Laugier, *Observations sur l'architecture* (1765), 84.

9. Voltaire, *Le Temple du goût* (1733), ed. E. Carcassonne (1938), 70.

10. R. Lanson, *Le Goût du Moyen Âge en France au XVIIIe siècle* (1926), 7–39; M. Jacoubet, *Le Genre troubadour et les origines du romantisme: La Curne de Sainte-Palaye* (1929); L. Gossman, *Medievalism and the Ideologies of the Enlightenment . . . La Curne de Sainte-Palaye* (1968).

11. J. Mondain Monval, *Soufflot, sa vie, son œuvre, son esthétique* (1918), 43, 431.

12. M.-A. Laugier, *Essai sur l'architecture* (1755), 173. Ten years later, he said 'Gothic' was best for interiors, 'Greek' for exteriors (*Observations*, 116–17).

13. Réau, *Histoire*, i. 110.

14. Montesquieu, *Essai sur le goût*, cited by Réau, *Histoire*, 111.

15. Grimm, v. 349–50 (Aug. 1765).

16. Cochin, *Doutes . . . d'un marguillier de la paroisse de Saint-Etienne du Mont sur le problème proposé par M. Patte, architecte* (1770), cited by Mondain Monval, *Soufflot*, 431.

17. F. Pupil, 'L'Architecture médiévale religieuse dans l'iconographie de l'époque révolutionnaire', in *Pratiques religieuses, Mentalités, Spiritualités. Actes du Colloque bicentenaire de la Révolution, Chantilly, 1986* (1988), 695.

18. J. Lestocquoy, 'La Persistance du style gothique aux XVIIe et XVIIIe siècles', *Rev. Nord* (1938), 103 ff.

19. M. Lévi, *Inventaire des papiers de Robert de Cotte, premier architecte du Roi, 1656–1735* (1906), p. xxvii.

20. G. Chénesseau, 'Un Essai d'alliance du *gothique* de l'*antique* par un architecte Orléanais au XVIIIe siècle', *Bull. Soc. Orléanais* (1936), 36–8. See also his *Sainte-Croix d'Orléans, histoire d'une cathédrale gothique réédifiée par les Bourbons, 1599–1829* (1921).

21. J. McManners, *Death and the Enlightenment* (1981), 305–6.

22. Laugier, *Essai* (1755), 156; J. Seznec, *Essais sur Diderot et l'antiquité* (1957), 113.

23. Diderot, *Salons*, ed. J. Seznec and J. Adhémar (4 vols., 1957–67), iii. 315–16, i. 244.

24. Grimm (Dec. 1752), cf. N. Wraxall, *A Tour through the Western, Southern and Interior Provinces of France* (3 vols., 1777), ii. 195.

25. Dom G. Givelet, 'L'Église abbatiale de Saint-Niçaise de Reims', *Trav. Acad. nat. Reims* (1897), 129–45.

26. J. Corblet, *Histoire dogmatique, liturgique et archéologique du sacrement de l'Eucharistie* (2 vols., 1886), i. 129.

27. L. Pingaud, *Les Saulx Tavannes* (1876), 267.

28. McManners, *Angers*, 35.

29. A. Babeau, *La Ville sous l'ancien régime* (2 vols., 1884), ii. 129–30.

30. For these, see Réau, *Histoire*. Up to then, no one had listened to J.-B. Thiers's arguments for a simple dome on classical columns as being the decoration over the first recognizable Christian altars (*Dissertations ecclésiastiques* (2 vols., 1688), ii. 39–60).

31. Réau, *Histoire*, 119–24.

32. 'Les Tombes royales de Saint-Denis à la fin du XVIIIe siècle', *Le Cabinet historique*, 22 (1876), 2–12.

33. J.-B. Thiers, *Dissertation sur les jubés* (1688), 29–40, 146. For Amiens see Laugier, *Observations*, 139–40. For Rieux, J. Contrasty, *Histoire de Rieux-Volvestre* (1930), 347.

34. Langlois, *Notes historiques . . . sur les jubés de l'Église métropolitaine de Rouen: Précis analytique* (1851), 244 ff.
35. Guide Bleu, *Île de France* (1968), 256–7.
36. F. Blondel, *Cours d'architecture* (1683), 236.
37. R. Farcy, *Les Travaux de Soufflot à Notre-Dame* (1930).
38. A. H. Van der Weil, *Paul-Louis Mondran, 1734–95, un chanoine homme d'esprit* (1942), 135.
39. Séroux d'Agincourt, a retired farmer-general (Y. Durand, *Les Fermiers Généraux au XVIIIᵉ siècle* (1971), 512–20). Also F. S. Mercier, *Tableau de Paris*, new edn. (12 vols., 1782–8), i. 240.
40. Some of the chant books used were of great antiquity, especially the big bound copies for the lectern.
41. Dr Charles Burney, *A Musical Tour of France and Italy*, ed. P. A. Scholes (2 vols., 1959), i. 5, 37.
42. D. Launay, in *The New Oxford History of Music* (10 vols., 1975), vol. 5: *Opera and Church Music, 1630–1750*, ed. A. Lewis and N. Fortune (1975), 418.
43. H. Carré, *Recueil curieux et édifiant sur les cloches de l'Église* (1757), 47–8.
44. M. Benoît, *Versailles et les musiciens du roi, 1661–1733* (1971), 46.
45. H. E. Smither, *A History of the Oratorio* (3 vols., 1977), i. 418.
46. Carré, *Recueil*.
47. Grimault, *Noëls angevins* (1876), cited by C. Port, *Dictionnaire hist. géog. biogr. de Maine-et-Loire* (3 vols., 1878), iii. 234; Van der Weil, *Mondran*, 16–17.
48. D. Launay and N. Dufourcq, in *New Oxford History of Music*, v. 418–20, 443.
49. A. Cellier, 'Les Motets de Michel-Richard de Lalande', *Rev. mus.* (1946), 20–3. It is estimated that over 1,000 *grands motets* from 1683 to 1789 have survived, mostly gathering dust in libraries (Ph. Beaussant, *Rameau de A à Z* (1982), 219). A Benedictine of Le Mans in 1719 wrote to Paris for music for motets—voices with bass accompaniment (W. P. Denis, *Rev. Mabillon* (1910), 521).
50. Jean Gilles, 1668–1705. His requiem was used for the funerals of Rameau and of Louis XV. See *The New Grove Dictionary of Music and Musicians*, S. Sadie (ed.) (20 vols., 1980), vii. 378–9. For Giroust see J. Brosset, *François Giroust, 1737–91* (1911), 14.
51. H. Prunières, review in *Rev. mus.* (1960), 566.
52. Clerval, *L'Ancienne Maîtrise*, 81–92.
53. Loupès, *Chapitres*, 169–70.
54. Van der Weil, *Mondran*, 57, 148–9.
55. *La Revue des maîtres de chapelle et musiciens de la Métropole de Rouen* (1850), 221.
56. F. J. Fétis, *Biographie universelle des musiciens* (8 vols., 1800–5), iv. 210.
57. J. Brosset, *Charles Hérissé, chanoine honoraire de l'Église d'Orléans, maître de chapelle de la cathédrale, 1737–1817* (1904), 9–18.
58. Clerval, *L'Ancienne Maîtrise*, 90–104. Cf. Coutances; in the first half of the century, two appointments from Paris, one from Caen, one from Marseille (J. Toussaint, *Feuilles détachées de l'histoire de Coutances—la maîtrise de la cathédrale* (1967), 12–131).
59. A. Prévost, 'Histoire de la maîtrise de la cathédrale de Troyes, *Mém. Soc. Aube*, 3ᵉ sér. 42 (1905), 258–65. There was no positive rule against marriage for someone who had not reached the subdiaconate. Toulouse appointed a married man in 1723 (R. Machard, 'Les Musiciens de la cathédrale Saint-

Étienne de Toulouse, 1682–1790', *Ann. Midi* (1976), 302. Concerning Deroussy, his crime may have been more than idleness. The *chant sur le livre*, said the abbé Lebeuf in 1729, 'is not singing at sight what the open book presents to view; it is to compose on the notes that are printed in the book harmonies corresponding to these notes'. He adds that the bass singers follow the book while the tenors improvise descants. There were variants and complexities, set forth in Henri Madin's *Traité du contrepoint simple ou du chant sur le livre* (1742). Madin, while appreciating the fantasy and 'joyful discord', admits there can be a collapse into confusion. For this reason, and from a distrust of unpredictable ornamentation, some French churches banned the genre—described later, in 1838, by La Fage, as 'that baroque and indecorous harmony'. See J. Prim, 'Chant sur le livre in French Churches in the Eighteenth Century', *JAMS* (1961), 37–49; and for the earlier history, Margaret Bent's erudite '*Resfacta* and *Cantare Super Librum*', *JAMS* (1984), 371–91.

60. Fétis, *Biographie*, v. 446; M. Brenet, 'Sébastien de Brossard', *Méms. Soc. Paris* (1896), 105–6.

61. J. Leflon, *Henri Hardouin et la musique du chapitre de Reims au XVIIIe siècle* (1933), 42, 52, 57.

62. C. Port, *Les Artistes angevins* (1881), 10–11; McManners, *Angers*, 28–9.

63. Benoît, *Versailles*, 245–6, 372.

64. O. Marcault, *Le Diocèse de Tours* (3 vols., 1918), ii. 579.

65. *Rouen*, 22.

66. Loupès, *Chapitres*, 181.

67. M. Brenet, *Les Musiciens de la Sainte-Chapelle du Palais* (1910), 309–10.

68. Prévost, 'Histoire . . . de Troyes', 349.

69. McManners, *Angers*, 30.

70. Machard, 'Les Musiciens . . . de Toulouse', 303–5.

71. Prévost, 'Histoire . . . de Troyes'; for Reims below, Leflon, *Hardouin*, 53.

72. Le Cerf de Viéville, *Comparaison de la musique italienne et de la musique française* (1705), 178.

73. Benoît, *Versailles*, 60–1, 48.

74. Garault, 'Instruments d'amour', *Rev. mus.* (1927), 105; A. Prévost, 'Instruments de musique', *Méms. Soc. Aube*, 3e sér. 41 (1904), 194–210.

75. Van der Weil, *Mondran*, 145–6.

76. B. Gérard and R. Machard, *La Grande Orgue et les organistes de Notre-Dame de Paris* (1980), 11.

77. N. Dufourcq, 'Coup d'œil sur l'histoire de la facture d'orgues', *Rev. mus.* (1929), 113–19, and id. 'L'Orgue de la chapelle de Versailles', *Rev. mus.* (1934), 288–9. See generally, P. de Fleury, *Dictionnaire biographique des facteurs d'orgues nés ou ayant travaillé en France* (1926).

78. E. Houth, *Versailles, la paroisse royale* (1962).

79. Port, *Les Artistes angevins*, 115. For the Dupont family, Fétis, *Biographie*, iii. 81.

80. A. Chaulieu, *Histoire de l'abbaye de Sainte-Croix* (1910), 201.

81. P. Dop, 'L'Église de Saint-Jean-de-Luz', *Bull. Soc. Bayonne* (1932), 395–8, 424–5.

82. Prévost, 'Instruments', 177.

83. R. Poulle, *Histoire de l'église paroissiale de Notre-Dame et Saint-Michel à Draguignan* (1865), 424–30.

84. J. Brosset, *L'Orgue et les organistes de l'Église Saint-Paul d'Orléans* (1909), 9–10.

85. E. and L. Delonca, *Un Village en Roussillon* (1947), 258.

86. Some of the great organists had female relatives who acted as 'stand-ins'—Armand-Louis Couperin's daughter, Calvière's sister, Bainville's wife.

87. D. H. Foster, *Jean-Philippe Rameau: A Guide to Research* (1989), 5–6. The anecdote about the Clermont contract originates with Maret, *Éloge historique de M. Rameau* (1766), who cites the secretary of the local academy as his source. More certainly, it is told of Rameau's brother. C. Girdlestone, *Jean-Philippe Rameau* (1957), accepts both stories. If one brother used the trick, why not the other in imitation?

88. W. Mellers, *François Couperin and the French Classical Tradition* (1957), 4–5; J. Tiersot, *Les Couperin* (1926), 115–18.

89. Gérard and Machard, *La Grande Orgue*, 30.

90. N. Dufourcq, 'De l'emploi du temps des organistes parisiens sous les règnes de Louis XIII et Louis XIV', *Rev. mus.* (1955), 35–8.

91. Burney, *Musical Tour*, i. 6, 15.

92. A. Tessier, 'Les Messes d'orgue de Couperin', *Rev. mus.* (1924), 37–47; N. Dufourcq, 'Les Grandes Formes de la musique d'orgue', *Rev. mus.* (1937), 89–91.

93. Mercier, *Tableau de Paris*, ii. 81.

94. G. Servais, 'Quelques organistes du grand siècle', *Rev. mus.* (1922), 198–200.

95. Dufourcq, 'Coup d'œil', 118–20.

96. P. C. C. Bogaerts, *Études sur les livres choraux qui ont servi de base dans la publication des livres de chant Grégorien édités à Malines* (1855), 118–20.

97. Cited in *New Oxford History of Music*, 288–9.

98. Voltaire, 'Sottisier', in *Œuvres*, xxxii. 577.

99. G. E. Bonnet, 'L'Œuvre de Philidor', *Rev. mus.* (1921), 226; G. de Froidcourt, *Correspondance générale de Grétry* (1962), 21. Other examples in Fétis, *Biographie*, i. 168, 387, 473; ii. 40, 172, 405, 456; iii. 10, 31, 200, 442, 451; iv. 91, 438–9; v. 170, 256, 265, 438; vi. 55–6, 333, 490–1; vii. 3, 92, 109, 337, 341. For the seventeenth century, Th. Gérold, *L'Art du chant en France au XVIIᵉ siècle* (thesis, Strasbourg, 1921), pp. xi, 189.

100. Cit. Marcault, *Tours*, ii. 286.

101. See the discussion from Couturier and Maritain in J. McManners, *The Oxford Illustrated History of Christianity* (1990), 13. For the assimilation of the music of church and theatre so that all music was 'profane', see J.-M. Duhamel, *La Musique dans la ville de Lully à Rameau* (1994), 254–63.

102. R. H. F. Scott, *Jean-Baptiste Lully* (1973), 65–7, 100–5.

103. L. de la Laurencie, 'André Campra, musicien profane', *Rev. mus.* (1913), 152, 195. See also his article on Campra's church music in *Recueil de la Société Internationale de Musique* (1909), 159 ff.

104. *Nouvelles ecclésiastiques*, 14 July 1734.

105. J. McManners, *Abbés and Actresses: The Church and the Theatrical Profession in 18th-Century France*, Zaharoff Lecture (1986), 3.

106. C. Kintzler, *Poétique de l'Opéra français de Corneille à Rousseau* (1991), 107–8.

107. A. B. Oliver, *The Encyclopedists as Critics of Music* (1947), 6–7.

108. M. Busson, *La Religion des classiques* (1948), 17.

109. La Bruyère, *Les Caractères*, xiv (19), ed. P. Kuentze (1969), 207.

110. L. Blond, *La Maison professe des Jésuites* (1956), 114.

111. E. Regnault, *Christophe de Beaumont, archevêque de Paris* (2 vols., 1882), i. 256. In 1721 the singers of the king's music sang a *Miserere* by Lalande at *Tenebrae* in the chapel of the Temple (Marais, ii. 118, 9 Apr.).

112. Van der Weil, *Mondran*, 137–46.

113. See the view of the church-goers of Saint-Merry about an organist, in opposition to their curé (C. Baloche, *L'Église Saint-Merry de Paris* (1911), 544–9).

114. *Des Églises et des temples chrétiens* (1706).

115. They took over the Te Deum entirely in Aug. 1752 (Luynes, xii. 101–2). For their organization, M. Benoît, *Musique de cour, chapelle, chambre, écurie, 1661–1733, Documents* (1971). For special occasions, the orchestra could be reinforced by the military drums and trumpets of the *écurie* (twelve trumpets, six oboes, fifes, and drums). The regiments of the palace guard also had trumpets (Benoît, *Versailles*, 48, 51–2).

116. F. Raugel, 'La Musique à la chapelle du château de Versailles sous Louis XV', *XVIIᵉ Siècle* (1957), 21–3.

117. Luynes, xiii. 390–1.

118. Ibid., vi. 436–7, vii. 280. A list of 1702 shows six Italian castrati and three French *hauts*. Strong high male voices were important to keep the boys firm in difficult passages.

119. Raugel, 'Versailles', 20.

120. Conducting the Te Deum with massed choirs in the church of the Feuillants on 8 Jan. 1687 killed him (gangrene from the conducting pole striking his foot).

121. She heard it at the funeral of Chancelier Séguier.

122. Luynes, vii. 9.

123. H. Prunières, *New History of Music* (E. T.), 97–112, 278. (Also influences from Saint-André des Arts.)

124. 'Arcangelo Corelli à Saint-Louis-des-Français à Rome', *Rev. mus.* (1922), 25–6. In Paris, St Louis was celebrated by the Académie royale de Musique in the garden of the Tuileries (G. Sadler, 'A Letter from Claude-François Rameau', *Music & Letters* (1978), 143–4.

125. E. Fubini, *The History of Music Aesthetics*, trans. F. M. Habwill (1962), 201–9.

126. For the link between Rousseau's view and his conviction of the decadence of society see A. Whittall, 'Rousseau and the Scope of Opera', *Music & Letters* (1964), 308.

127. S. Bonnet, *Histoire de la musique* (1725), cited in *New Oxford History of Music*, v. 288.

128. D. Tunley, *The 18th-Century French Cantata* (1974), 89.

129. F. Couperin, *Les Goûts réunis*, preface.

130. Marais, iv. 458.

131. Mme de Genlis, *Mémoires* (2 vols., 1825), i. 78 (1760).

132. Luynes, vii. 280 (1746); ix. 9 (1748).

133. Fétis, *Biographie*, i. 172. M. Pincherle, 'Le Peintre violiniste ou les aventures de l'abbé Robineau', *Rev. mus.* (1925), 232–9. He painted the portrait of the future George IV of England.

134. Brosset, *François Giroust*, 8.

135. C. Pierre, *Histoire du Concert spirituel* (1975), 220–2.

136. R. Viollier, 'Jean-Joseph Mouret', *Rev. mus.* (1938), 20–1.

137. Tunley, *French Cantata*, 29, 31, 72–89.

138. Smither, *Oratorio*, iii. 539–42.

139. E. Haeringer, *L'Esthétique de l'opéra en France au temps de Jean-Philippe Rameau* (1990), 23.

140. N. Dufourcq, *La Musique religieuse française de 1660 à 1781* (1954), 109–10.

141. Some written by Racine (L. Boulay, *Les Cantiques spirituels de Racine mis en musique au XVIIIe siècle* (1957), 79–92.

142. The baron A. de Maricourt, 'Lettres de l'abbé le Gouz', *Rev. quest. hist.* (1914), 30–1.

143. Thomas Bentley, *Journal of a Visit to Paris, 1776*, ed. P. France (1977).

CHAPTER 16

1. S. R. N. Chamfort, *Maximes et anecdotes*, with preface by A. Camus (1963), 63.

2. Voltaire, *Essai sur les mœurs*, in *Œuvres*, xi. 21.

3. C. Langlois and T. Tackett, in F. Lebrun (ed.), *Histoire des catholiques en France du XVe siècle à nos jours* (1980), 216–17.

4. L. Pérouas, *Le Diocèse de la Rochelle de 1648 à 1724: sociologie et pastorale* (1964), 187–9, 432–45.

5. Cl. Langlois, *Catholicisme au féminin: les congrégations françaises à supérieure générale au XIXe siècle* (1984), 136–8.

6. M. Vallery-Radot, *Un Administrateur ecclésiastique à la fin de l'ancien régime: le cardinal de Luynes, archevêque de Sens, 1753–88* (1966), 159; A. Chaulieu, *Histoire de l'abbaye de Sainte-Croix* (1910), 285; P. Goubert, 'Disparités de l'ancienne France rurale', *Cahiers hist.* (1967), 58.

7. Chaulieu, *Sainte-Croix*, 284. For Beaune, Fr. de la Rochefoucauld, *Voyages en France*, ed. J. Marchand (1933), 123.

8. R. Dauvergne, *Les Résidences du maréchal de Croÿ, 1718–84* (1950), 56.

9. J. Peter, 'Un Curieux Procès: l'abbaye de Liesses contre les maîtres de forges de Hainault', *Rev. Nord* (1937), 243–59.

10. J.-F.-H. de Richeprey, *Journal des voyages en Haute-Guienne*, ed. H. Guilhamon (1952), 240–1.

11. J.-J. Pialès, *Traité des réparations* (4 vols., 1762), i. 371 ff.

12. B. Pocquet du Haut-Jussé, 'La Vie temporelle des communautés de femmes au XVIIe et au XVIIIe siècle', *Ann. Bretagne* (1917), 540.

13. The baron A. de Maricourt and A. Briard, 'Une Abbaye de femmes au XVIIIe siècle: Gomerfontaine', *Rev. quest. hist.* (1907), 25–7.

14. T. J. Schmitt, *L'Organisation ecclésiastique et la pratique religieuse dans l'archidiaconé d'Autun de 1650 à 1750* (1957), 86–91.

15. L. Desgraves and J.-P. Poussou, 'La Vie religieuse', in F.-G. Pariset (ed.), *Bordeaux au XVIIIe siècle* (1968), 136.

16. J. Eich, *Histoire religieuse du département de la Moselle pendant la Révolution* (2 vols., 1964), i. 38–40; C. Michaux, 'Les Abbayes bénédictines de Metz à la veille de la Révolution', *Ann. Est* (1979), 257–70.

17. J. Savina, *Le Clergé de Cornouaille à la fin de l'ancien régime et sa convocation aux États-Généraux de 1789* (1926), 32.

18. J. McManners, *French Ecclesiastical Society under the Ancien Régime: A Study of Angers* (1960), ch. 5.

19. Guyot, i. 12, 16–17; xii. 358–404.

20. C. Pfister, 'Extrait d'un mémoire sur l'Alsace', *Rev. hist.* (1916), 85; J. Marchal, 'Remacle Lissoir', *Ann. Est* (1967), 29–30.

21. François-Joachim, cardinal de Bernis, *Mémoires et Lettres*, ed. F. Masson (2 vols., 1875), ii. 308, 326; G. Lizerand, *Le Duc de Beauvillier, 1648–1714* (1933), 83–4.

22. J. Thomas, *Le Concordat de 1516* (3 vols., 1910), ii. 73, 359.

23. Guyot, i. 41–7, xii. 402–4.

24. A. Sicard, *L'Ancien Clergé de France: les évêques avant la Révolution*, 5th edn. (1912), 22.

25. L'Abbé de Véri, *Journal*, ed. J. de Witte (2 vols., n.d.), i. 3.

26. Marais, ii. 61; the duc de Broglie, *Le Secret du roi: correspondance secrète de Louis XV et ses agents diplomatiques* (2 vols., 1886), i. 458–68.

27. Luynes, i. 324–5, 375; Barbier, iii. 69–70, 89, 341.

28. Luynes, vi. 403–4.

29. McManners, *Angers*, 76.

30. P.-L. Langlois, *Histoire du prieuré du Mont-aux-Malades-lès-Rouen, 1120–1820* (1951), 320–3.

31. A. de Cardevacque and A. Terninck, *L'Abbaye de Saint-Vaast* (3 vols., 1865–8), i. 47–8, ii. 57–69.

32. Luynes, vi. 402–3; D'Argenson, vi. 272; Pialès, *Traité*, iv. 4.

33. B. Bois, *La Vie scolaire et les créations intellectuelles en Anjou, 1789–99* (1929), 40.

34. J. Marchal, *Le Droit d'oblat* (1955), 234–53.

35. Luynes, xiii. 215, 406; i. 252, 324.

36. Guyot, lviii. 465–6.

37. Ibid. lxii. 349–87.

38. J. Gallerand, 'L'Érection de l'évêché de Blois, 1697', *Rev. hist. Église Fr.* (1956), 175–201.

39. A. Broutin, *Histoire du couvent de Montbrison avant 1793* (2 vols., 1874), ii. 65–70.

40. J. Blampignon, *L'Épiscopat de Massillon* (1884), 194–5.

41. R. Laulan, 'Aperçu sur les finances de l'École Royale Militaire, 1751–88', *Actès 86ᵉ Congrès National des Sociétés Savantes: Montpellier 1961* (1962), 228–32.

42. M. Cornereau, 'Les Hôpitaux du Saint-Esprit et de Notre-Dame de la Charité à Dijon', *Méms. Comm. Côte-d'Or* 12 (1889–95), 272.

43. P.-D. Bernier, *Essai sur le tiers état rural ou les paysans de Basse-Normandie au XVIIIᵉ siècle* (1891), 85–9.

44. Voltaire, 'Biens d'Église', in *Dictionnaire philosophique*, in *Œuvres* (50 vols., Firmin Didot, 1843), vii. 261–4. This entry is omitted from modern critical editions.

45. Pialès, *Traité*, iii for details, esp. 359–60.

46. A. Lombard, *L'Abbé Dubos* (1913), 163–4.

47. E. Jarossy, *Histoire de l'abbaye de Ferrières en Gâtinais* (1901), 426–7.

48. L. Deries, *La Vie monastique en Normandie* (1937), 49.

49. L. Côte, *Histoire du prieuré Clunisien de Souvigny* (1942), 276–81.

50. Luynes, xiv. 12; McManners, *Angers*, 77.

51. Jarossy, *Gâtinais*, 421–4.

52. See 'Lettres inédites de P.-D. Huet à son neveu', *Méms. Acad. nat. Caen*

(1900), 133–65; Deries, *Normandie*, 71–3.

53. Pialès, *Traité*, i. 268.
54. Chaulieu, *Sainte-Croix*, 238 ff.
55. J. Loth (ed.), *Histoire de l'abbaye royale de Saint-Pierre de Jumièges par un religieux de la Congrégation de Saint-Maur* (3 vols., 1885), iii. 201–3.
56. Deries, *Normandie*, 243–8; E. Goiffon, *Monographies paroissiales: paroisses de l'archiprêtré de Nîmes* (1898), 277–8.
57. X. Azéma, *Un Prélat janséniste: Louis Foucquet, évêque et comte d'Agde, 1656–1702* (1963), 131.
58. e.g. C. Hippeau, *Les Cahiers de 1789 en Normandie* (2 vols., 1869), i. 55.
59. Bachaumont, vii. 44–6 (Aug. 1773).
60. Barbier, iii. 89 (1737).
61. Bernis, *Mémoires*, i. 125.
62. Dom P. Denis, 'Un Projet . . . de Mgr Talleyrand-Périgord, archevêque de Rouen, 1787', *Trav. Acad. nat. Reims* (1910), 261–7.
63. Guyot, i. 41–2.
64. Deries, *Normandie*, 61–71.
65. See C.-É. Engel, *L'Ordre de Malte en Méditerranée, 1530–1798* (1957).
66. In 1789, to try to avert the confiscation of its lands in France, the Order threatened to hand over Malta to a foreign power (G. Saumade, 'La Révolution française et l'Ordre international de Malte', *Rév. fr.* (1937), 249).
67. G. Gangneux, 'Société nobiliaire et l'Ordre de Malte', *Cahiers hist.* (1975), 358–9.
68. Luynes, iv. 23–4.
69. G. Maugras, *Delphine de Sabran, marquise de Custine* (1912), 46.
70. G. Gangneux, 'Une Commanderie de l'Ordre de Malte aux XVIIe et XVIIIe siècles', *Cahiers hist.* (1962), 355–78.
71. Richeprey, *Journal*, 139–42.
72. A. Guelloni, 'L'Évolution de l'idée internationale dans les écrits de l'abbé de Saint-Pierre', in A. Viala and H. Labriolle (eds.), *La Régence, Colloque Aix-en-Provence, 1968* (1970), 333.
73. R. Cavalière, 'Le Bailli de Suffren', *Ann. Malte* (1962), 101–2.
74. Engel, *L'Ordre de Malte*, 292–3, 122, 175, 287.
75. A. Bouyal d'Arnaud, 'Un Gentilhomme provençal au 18e siècle', *Rev. hist. mod. contemp.* (1955), 59–60.
76. Engel, *L'Ordre de Malte*, 122.
77. Luynes, vii. 167–8.
78. Guyot, ix. 135.
79. Mme de Genlis, *Mémoires* (2 vols., 1825), i. 14–15.
80. Chateaubriand, *Mémoires d'outre-tombe* (Pléiade, 2 vols., 1955), i. 16.
81. Ch. du Bus, *Stanislas de Clermont-Tonnerre et l'échec de la révolution monarchique, 1757–1792* (1931), 23.
82. F. Boquilon, 'Gabrielle de Spada, abbesse d'Épinal, 1738–84', *Ann. Est* (1980), 243–56.
83. Mme de Chastenay, *Mémoires 1771–1815*, ed. A. Roderot (2 vols., 1896), i. 50–69.
84. P.-M. Masson, *Mme de Tencin* (1909), 7 n.
85. T. J. Schmitt, *L'Assistance dans l'archidiaconé d'Autun aux XVIIe et XVIIIe siècles* (1952), pp. xxix, 60.

86. Luynes, vi. 82 (1744).

87. E. Préclin, 'La Situation ecclésiastique . . . de la Franche Comté à la veille de la Révolution', *Bull. Féd. Franche Comté* (1955), 17–18.

88. F. D. Mathieu, *L'Ancien Régime en Lorraine et Barrois* (1879), 70–1.

89. Mme de Genlis, *Mémoires*, i. 14–18, 50.

90. Luynes, iv. 125 (1742); Président de Brosses, *Lettres à Ch. C. Loppin de Gemeaux* (1929), 41.

91. L. Trénard, *Le Diocèse de Belley* (1978), 116 ff.

92. Eich, *Histoire religieuse*, i. 20.

93. F. Masson, *Le Cardinal de Bernis depuis son ministère, 1758–94* (1884), 417–20.

94. L. Audiat, *Deux victimes des Septembriseurs: Pierre-Louis de la Rochefoucauld, dernier évêque de Saintes et son frère, évêque de Beauvais* (1897), 69–74.

95. L. Welter, 'Une Tentative pour redonner prospérité à l'abbaye de Saint-Pierre de Blesle', *Bull. Auvergne* (1945), 123–35.

96. Durand de Maillaine, *Dictionnaire de droit canonique* (4 vols., 1776), i. 30–1; Guyot, i. 12.

97. 'M. B.', 'Contribution à l'histoire de l'abbaye de Jouarre', *Rev. Mabillon* (1933), 47.

98. G.-M. Oury, 'Abbesse et moniales de Notre-Dame de Perrigne aux XVIIᵉ et XVIIIᵉ siècles', *Province du Maine* (1978), 315.

99. See C. Torchet, *Histoire de l'abbaye royale de Notre Dame de Chelles* (2 vols., 1889).

100. L. Paris, *Histoire de l'abbaye d'Avenay* (2 vols., 1879), i. 460–87; ii. 1.

101. See Dom Y. Chaussy *et al.*, *L'Abbaye royale de Notre Dame de Jouarre* (2 vols., 1961), ii. 312–45.

102. See S. Poignant, *L'Abbaye de Fontevrault et les filles de Louis XV* (1966).

103. J.-M. Alliot, *Histoire de l'abbaye . . . de Notre-Dame du Val de Gif* (1892), 235–6.

104. J. Levron, *Amours et drames du passé* (1976), 193–215.

105. La marquise du Deffand, *Correspondance complète*, ed. M. de Lescure (1865), p. ix; Bachaumont, vii. 36–7 (5 Aug. 1773).

106. Canon Uzureau, 'La Maréchale d'Aubeterre', in *Andegaviana* (1927), 145; J.-M. Alliot, *Histoire de l'abbaye de Notre-Dame d'Yerres* (1899), 276–9.

107. See M. Chassaigne, *Le Procès du chevalier de la Barre* (1920).

108. Marais, i. 163–4, 272, 320; Saint-Simon, xi. 310; Barbier, i. 42.

109. Deries, *Normandie*, 194.

110. F.-Y. Besnard, *Souvenirs d'un nonagénaire*, ed. C. Port (2 vols., 1880), i. 258 ff., 322–7.

111. Poignant, *Fontevrault*, 109–10, 116–17.

112. Guyot, xx. 488–97.

113. Paris, *Avenay*, i. 523.

114. Pocquet du Haut-Jussé, 'La Vie temporelle', 342–3.

115. P. de Vaissière, *Gentilshommes campagnards de l'ancienne France* (1925), 379–80.

116. J.-F. Soulet, *Traditions et réformes religieuses dans les Pyrénées centrales au XVIIᵉ siècle* (1974), 212–13.

117. L. Ampoulange, *Le Clergé et la convocation aux États Généraux de 1789 dans la sénéchaussée principale de Périgord* (1912), 101–2.

118. Diderot, *Jacques le fataliste*, in *Œuvres* (1935), 333.

119. McManners, *Angers*, 93; cf. L. Pérouas, 'Les Religieuses dans le pays

Creusois', *Cahiers hist.* (1979), 24.

120. D'Argenson, vi. 31; J. Bouchary, *Les Compagnies financières à Paris à la fin du XVIIIᵉ siècle* (3 vols., 1940), i. 12.

121. By Brunet de Bru (1720). See F. C. Green, *La Peinture des mœurs de la bonne société dans le roman français de 1715 à 1761* (1924), 92–6.

122. L. Pingaud, *Les Saulx-Tavannes* (1876), 292–305. For Mme de Tencin see P. M. Masson, *Mme de Tencin*, and J. Sareil, *Les Tencin* (1969).

123. Guyot, xlix. 81–2; E. Regnault, *Christophe de Beaumont, archevêque de Paris, 1763–81* (2 vols., 1882), i. 429–30.

124. L. de Loménie, *La Comtesse de Rochefort et ses amis* (1879), 190–2.

125. M. Cousin (ed.), *Souvenirs de la marquise de Créquy*, 2nd edn. (1865), 29.

126. Paris, *Avenay*, i. 489–90.

127. Guyot, xlix. 99–101, 110–11.

128. A nun released in 1750 (P. de la Haye, *Histoire de Tréguier, ville épiscopale* (1977), 272).

129. Guyot, lxiv. 63–6.

130. Ibid. xlix. 79–86, lxiv. 52–3.

131. R. Graham, 'The Married Nuns before Cardinal Caprara', in *Pratiques religieuses en l'Europe révolutionnaire. Colloque* (1986), 324–5.

132. Bernis, *Mémoires*, i. 5.

133. C. Charrier, *Héloïse dans l'histoire et dans la légende* (1933); R. Shackleton, 'The Cloister Theme in French Preromanticism', in N. Moore *et al.* (eds.), *The French Mind: Studies in Honour of Gustave Rudler* (1952), 173–7; A. Prévost, *Mémoires et aventures d'un homme de qualité*.

134. A. Mathiez, 'Les Prêtres révolutionnaires devant le cardinal Caprara', *Ann. hist. Rév. fr.* (1926), 8.

135. A. Chérel, *Un Aventurier religieux: André-Michel Ramsay* (1928), 63.

136. J. Verbier, 'Les Demoiselles de Beauvilliers à Montargis', *Bull. Soc. Montargis*, 3ᵉ sér., 47 (1979), 11–12.

137. Mme Roland (Marie-Jeanne Philipon), *Mémoires*, ed. Cl. Perroud (2 vols., 1905), ii. 69–70.

138. C.-L. Richard, *Dissertation sur les vœux en général et sur les vœux des religieux* (1771), 50.

139. Brunet de Brou (Green, *La Peinture*, 99).

140. e.g. Pingaud, *Les Saulx-Tavannes*, 294.

141. J. B. Bergier, *Histoire de la communauté des prêtres missionnaires de Beaupré* (1853), 198.

142. Marivaux, *La Vie de Marianne ou les aventures de Mme la comtesse de XX* (1736), ed. M. Gilot (1978), 402–3.

CHAPTER 17

1. G. Fleury, 'L'Abbaye cistercienne de Pereigne, 1145–1790', *Rev. Maine* (1878), 50.

2. Fr. de la Rochefoucauld, *Voyages en France, 1781–3*, ed. J. Marchand (1923), 157–9.

3. L. Vignols, 'Les Émigrants allemands cantonnés en Bretagne, 1763–6', *Bull. méms. Soc. Ille-et-Vilaine* (1894), 34; J. Mathorez, *Les Étrangers en France sous*

l'ancien régime (2 vols., 1919), ii. 151.

4. J. Salmon, *Morimond: les derniers jours de l'abbaye* (1961), 24–7.

5. 'L'Assistance publique au XVIIIᵉ siècle: l'enquête de 1775 dans le diocèse civil de Toulouse', *Rév. fr.* (1917), 157–64.

6. e.g. J. Meyer, *La Noblesse bretonne au XVIIIᵉ siècle* (2 vols., 1966), ii. 1108.

7. J.-F.-H. de Richeprey, *Journal des voyages en Haute-Guienne*, ed. M. Guilhamon (1952), 103–4, 51–2.

8. e.g. 2,400 livres in one parish, 60 in another (G. Lefebvre, *Les Paysans du Nord pendant la Révolution française* (2 vols., 1924), i. 294).

9. H. Prentout, 'Les Tableaux de 1790 en réponse à l'enquête du Comité de Mendicité (Calvados)', *Rév. fr.* (1907), 426.

10. L. Lallemand, *De l'organisation de la bienfaisance dans les campagnes au XVIIIᵉ siècle* (1893), 36–7; Lefebvre, *Les Paysans du Nord*, 36–7.

11. L. Jacob, 'La Grande Peur en Artois', *Ann. hist. Rév. fr.* (1936), 140–1.

12. La Rochefoucauld, *Voyages*, 51; Chateaubriand, *Mémoires d'outre-tombe* (2 vols., 1955), i. 85; N. Wraxall, *A Tour through the Western, Southern and Interior Provinces of France* (3 vols., 1777), ii. 242–3.

13. They sacked the abbey in 1789 (see A. Faure, 'L'Abbaye de Saint-Sulpice en Bugey', *Le Bugey* (1971–4), 517 ff.).

14. G. Macdonogh, *Brillat-Savarin, the Judge and his Stomach* (1992), 39–40 (a book throwing entertaining light on an aspect of French history neglected by solemn professionals).

15. J. Breval, *Remarks on Several Parts of Europe* (2 vols, 1738), ii. 50.

16. V. Durand, *État religieux des trois diocèses de Nîmes, d'Uzès et d'Alais à la fin de l'ancien régime* (1909), 153–4.

17. J. F. Bluche, *Les Magistrats du Parlement de Paris au XVIIIᵉ siècle, 1715–71* (1960), 346–7.

18. Marais, iii. 39 (1723); Loaisel de Tréogate, *Dolbreuse* (1783), cited by A. Monglond, *Le Préromantisme français* (2 vols., 1930; new edn., 1965), i. 81–2; J. McManners, *Death and the Enlightenment* (1981), 224–5.

19. F. D. Mathieu, *L'Ancien Régime en Lorraine et Barrois* (1879), 91–4.

20. M. Dubois, 'Documents . . . la Chartreuse de Notre-Dame de La Verne', *Rev. Mabillon* (1933), 131.

21. G. Lefebvre, *La Grande Peur* (1932), 294.

22. O. H. Hufton, *The Poor of 18th Century France, 1750–89* (1974), 125.

23. T. J. Schmitt, *L'Assistance dans l'archidiaconé d'Autun aux XVIIᵉ et XVIIIᵉ siècles* (1952), 323.

24. Lefebvre, *La Grande Peur*, 16.

25. L. Deries, *La Vie monastique en Normandie* (1933), 42, 59, 61–2; Lallemand, *De l'organisation*, 37.

26. J. Dehergne, *Le Bas Poitou à la veille de la Révolution* (1963), 107; Duhamel du Monceau, *Éléments d'agriculture* (2 vols., 1763), i. 251; L. Bertre, 'Moulins à blé et moulins à huile', *Rev. Nord* (1959), 164–5.

27. R. Gandilhon, *La Naissance du champagne: Dom Pérignon* (1968), 245, 92, 100; G. Laurent, *Reims et la région rémoise à la veille de la Révolution* (1930), p. ccxx.

28. E. Maury, 'L'Inventaire du cabinet d'histoire naturelle de l'abbaye de Clairvaux', *Ann. hist. Rév. fr.* (1924), 567.

29. E. Lery, 'Le Père Sébastien Truchet et ses travaux à Versailles et à Marly', *Rev. Versailles* (1929), 220–30. For monks as architects see F. Machelart,

'Religieux architectes en Cambrésis aux XVIIe et XVIIIe siècles', *Rev. Nord* (1980), 415–27.

30. Marais, i. 481.
31. G. Laurent and G. Boussinecq, *Histoire de Reims* (2 vols., 1933), ii. 170–5.
32. Bachaumont, xxi. 23–4 (18 July 1782).
33. Luynes, x. 51 (1751).
34. Voltaire, *Dictionnaire philosophique*, in *Œuvres*, xvii. 117.
35. C. Serpas, 'Les Esclaves chrétiens au Maroc', *Bull. hist. Prot. fr.* (1930), 243.
36. P. Delandres, *L'Ordre des Trinitaires pour le rachat des captifs* (2 vols., 1903), i. 124, 287; Guyot, xlii. 213.
37. See G. Lambert, *L'Œuvre de la rédemption des captifs à Toulon* (1882).
38. P. Chevallier, *Loménie de Brienne et l'Ordre monastique, 1766–89* (2 vols., 1959–61), i. 97.
39. H. de Gramont, 'Études algériennes', *Rev. hist.* (1885), 11.
40. Deslandres, *L'Ordre des Trinitaires*, i. 343–51.
41. L. Vignols, 'La Piraterie sur l'Atlantique au XVIIIe siècle', *Ann. Bretagne* (1889–90), 228.
42. Martial-Levé, *Louis-François-Gabriel d'Orléans de la Motte, évêque d'Amiens, 1683–1774* (1962), 143–4.
43. *P.V. Ass.* viii (2), cols. 1595–7.
44. See Vignols, 'La Piraterie', 231–3; Deslandres, *L'Ordre des Trinitaires*, i. 379–88, 406–7; Gramont, 'Études algériennes', 22–5; L. Pingaud, 'Les Captifs à Alger au XVIIIe siècle', *Rev. hist.* (1880), 335.
45. C.-E. Engel, *L'Ordre de Malte en Méditerranée, 1530–1798* (1957), 169–71.
46. J. G. Lydon, 'Thomas Jefferson and the Mathurins', *Cath. Hist. Rev.* (1963), 192–202.
47. Deslandres, *L'Ordre des Trinitaires*, i. 396.
48. Lambert, *L'Œuvre*, 82.
49. Moreau de Jonnes, 'Mémoires', ed. F.-A. Aulard, *Rév. fr.* (1890), 363; Bachaumont, xxx. 24 (Oct. 1785). For accounts of processions see S. Moreau-Rendu, *Les Captifs libérés: les Trinitaires de Saint-Mathurin à Paris* (1974); account of Le Chevalier, *avocat* of Rouen, in *La Semaine religieuse de Rouen* (1876), 629–30; A. Plassard, 'Journal', *Ann. Acad. Mâcon* (1954–5), 102; 'Notes et souvenirs d'Antoine Sabatier', *Bull. Lyon* (1922), 161–2.
50. E. Lequay, *Études historiques de l'Ordre de la Charité de Saint-Jean-de-Dieu et ses établissements en France* (1854), 33–4, 42–8, 54–5, 61, 111.
51. J. T. Murphy, *The History of Urology* (1972), 111–20.
52. Métra, ii. 197–8 (1775).
53. J.-B. Rousseau, *Œuvres*, ed. A. de La Tour (1869), 381 (epigram 17).
54. Diderot, *Correspondance*, ed. G. Roth and J. Varloot (16 vols., 1955–70), v. 197 (1765).
55. M. Giraud, 'Crise de conscience et d'autorité à la fin du règne de Louis XIV', *Ann.* (1952), 228–32.
56. C. Frostin, 'Les *Enfants perdus* de l'État, ou la condition militaire à Saint-Domingue au XVIIIe siècle', *Ann. Bretagne* (1973), 328–35.
57. F. X. Emmanuelli, 'Ordres du roi et lettres de cachet en Provence', *Rev. hist.* (1974), 358.
58. G. Lely, *Vie du Marquis de Sade* (2 vols., 1957), ii. 347–8.
59. Marquis de Sade, *Correspondance inédite*, ed. P. Bourdin (1926), 264.

60. G. Vauthier, 'La Maison du Charenton en 1790', *Ann. hist. Rév. fr.* (1926), 264–6.

61. Ibid. 267–70. In fairness to the nuns, it should be noted that they themselves led lives of grim severity—with an income of only 150 livres a head and penitential scourging every Friday and many other days (J. Jobin, 'Le Prieuré du Val d'Osne à Charenton, 1700–93', *Bull. Com. Paris* (1883), 105–37).

62. Ch. Gérin, 'Les Monastères franciscains et la Commission des réguliers', *Rev. quest. hist.* (1895), 95.

63. Deries, *Normandie*, 297–8; P. Grosclaude, *Malesherbes, témoin et interprète de son temps* (1961), 35; Y. Durand, *Les Fermiers Généraux au XVIIIe siècle* (1971), 589–90; P. Chevallier (ed.), *Journal de l'Assemblée des Notables* (1960), 51.

64. Wraxall, *Tour*, ii. 213–15 (in 1777).

65. Deries, *Normandie*, 97–104.

66. Emmanuelli, 'Ordres', 358–64; G. Gaffarel, 'Les Lettres de cachet en Provence', *Rev. hist.* (1914), 5–19.

67. For the Jesuits, see below, ch. 42.

68. P. Ricordel, 'Le Collège de Rennes après le départ des Jésuites, 1762–1803'. *Ann. Bretagne* (1936–7), 108.

69. A. Sicard, *Les Études classiques avant la Révolution* (1887), 413.

70. M. Garden, *Lyon et les Lyonnais au XVIIIe siècle* (1970), 371.

71. Maillard, *L'Oratoire d'Angers au XVIIIe siècle* (n.d.), 116–19; Jean de Viguerie, *Une Œuvre d'éducation sous l'ancien régime: les Pères de la Doctrine Chrétienne en France et en Italie, 1592–1792* (1970), 153–8, 276.

72. Viguerie, *Une Œuvre*, 270.

73. Ibid. 222–33.

74. Y. Besnard, *Souvenirs d'un nonagénaire*, ed. C. Port (2 vols., 1880), i. 102–3.

75. Canon Uzureau, 'Les Ballons en Anjou', *L'Anjou hist.* (1901–2), 30.

76. A. Queinot, 'Les Dieppois et la presse périodique à la fin du 18e siècle', *Ann. hist. Rév. fr.* (1938), 55.

77. A. Martin, 'Les Chambres littéraires de Nantes et la préparation de la Révolution', *Ann. Bretagne* (1926), 349.

78. 20 per cent of Doctrinaires, 19.8 of Oratorians (Viguerie, *Une Œuvre*, 425).

79. G. Guillaume, *Billaud Varenne* (1969), 4–24. His brother had been astonished when he joined the Oratory in the first place (Billaud Varenne, *Mémoires et Correspondance*, ed. A. Begis (1893), 4–5.

80. See L. Jacob, *Joseph Lebon* (2 vols., 1933), and L. Madelin, *Fouché* (1900).

81. R. Chartier, M.-M. Compère, and D. Julia, *L'Éducation en France du XVIe au XVIIIe siècle* (1976), 194–6.

82. M. Garden, 'Pédagogie et parents d'élèves au collège de La Trinité, Lyon, 1763–92', *Cahiers hist.* (1969), 308.

83. E. Dard, *Hérault de Séchelles, 1759–94* (1907), 20. For the Labordes, see J.-A. Dulaure, *Nouvelle Description de Paris* (2 vols., 1787), ii. 5.

84. Maillard, *L'Oratoire*, 108–10; P. Marchand, 'Le Collège de Lille', *L'Information hist.* (1975), 164.

85. A. Brun, 'Un Collège d'Oratoriens au XVIIIe siècle', *Rev. hist. Église Fr.* (1949), 207–9; Lallemand, *De l'organisation*, 70–1.

86. R. Collier, *La Vie en Haute-Provence, 1600–1850* (1973), 463.

87. Lallemand, *De l'organisation*, 41–3, 55, 68, 103, 105–6.

88. Maillard, *L'Oratoire*, 108–10.

89. F. de Dainville, 'Les Effectifs des collèges et scolarité aux 17ᵉ et 18ᵉ siècles', *Population* (1955), 455–88.

90. Dulaure, *Paris*, ii. 3.

91. Lallemand, *De l'organisation*, 194.

92. Restif de la Bretonne, *La Femme dans les trois états* (1775), in *Œuvres*, ed. M. Bachelin, iii. 153.

93. Mallet du Pan, *Mémoires et correspondance*, ed. A. Sayous (2 vols., 1851), ii. 491–2.

94. P. Haudrière, 'Mémoire' (1720), in *L'Information hist.* (1975), 200–1.

95. A. Franklin, *La Vie privée . . . les collèges* (1892), 220–1.

96. Moreau de Jonnes, 'Mémoires', 456–7.

97. G. Snyders, *La Pédagogie en France aux XVIIᵉ et XVIIIᵉ siècles* (1965), 60–4.

98. Chartier *et al.*, *L'Éducation*, 216–17.

99. Snyders, *La Pédagogie*, 413–14.

100. See G. Saillant, *La Fable en France* (1912).

101. P. Marchand, 'L'Enseignement de l'histoire et de la géographie au collège de Lille, 1765–1791', *Rev. Nord* (1968), 351–6.

102. J. Leflon, *Eugène de Mazenod* (2 vols., 1957), i. 67, 76.

103. M. Thiery, *Guide des amateurs et étrangers voyageurs à Paris* (2 vols., 1787), i. 8–10.

104. G. Bouchard, *Prieur de la Côte d'Or* (1948), 21.

105. A. Babeau, *La Vie militaire sous l'ancien régime* (2 vols., 1890), i. 72.

106. The Countess of Minto, *A Memoir of the Right Hon. Hugh Elliot* (1868), 4–6.

107. Maillard, *L'Oratoire*, 101; Lallemand, *De l'organisation*, 62–4.

108. W. Frijhoff and D. Julia, 'Deux pensionnats', *Cahiers hist.* (1970), 107–10.

109. Babeau, *La Vie militaire*, ii. 59.

110. Corresp. Acad. Anjou, 4 Dec. 1758 (Bibliothèque Municipale, Angers MS 611 (56 ff.)).

111. Chartier *et al.*, *L'Éducation*, 220–2; E. G. Léonard, *L'Armée au 18ᵉ siècle* (1958), 247.

112. J. Fabre de Massaguel, *L'École de Sorèze de 1758 au 19 Fructidor, an IV* (1958), 42–128.

113. A. Chuquet, *La Jeunesse de Napoléon* (3 vols., 1897–9), i. 114.

114. Definitive history by G. Rigault, *Histoire générale de l'Institut des Frères des Écoles Chrétiennes* (9 vols., 1937–53), i and ii.

115. Ibid. i. 292.

CHAPTER 18

1. H. Carré, *La Noblesse de France et l'opinion publique au 18ᵉ siècle* (1920), 197–8.

2. E. and J. de Goncourt, *La Femme au 18ᵉ siècle* (1862), 17.

3. C. Kunstler, *La Vie quotidienne sous Louis XVI* (1950), 272.

4. L. de Loménie, *Les Mirabeau* (5 vols., 1891), iii. 125.

5. Carré, *La Noblesse*, 183.

6. W. Doyle, *The Parlement of Bordeaux* (1973), 117.

7. L. Paris, *Histoire de l'abbaye d'Avenay* (2 vols., 1875), i. 513.

8. See S. Poignant, *L'Abbaye de Fontevrault et les filles de Louis XV* (1966).

9. R. Chartier, M.-M. Compère, and D. Julia, *L'Éducation en France du XVIᵉ au*

XVIIIe siècle (1976), 242–3; J. A. Dulaure, *Nouvelle Description de Paris* (2 vols., 1787), i. 143.

10. A. Le Moy, 'La Grande Prêtresse', *Ann. Bretagne* (1932–3), 77.

11. E. Catta, *La Vie d'un monastère sous l'ancien régime: La Visitation Sainte-Marie de Nantes, 1630–1792* (1954), 110–18.

12. Chartier *et al.*, *L'Éducation*, 236.

13. T. J. Schmitt, *L'Assistance dans l'archidiaconé d'Autun aux XVIIe et XVIIIe siècles* (1952), 80–2.

14. J. McManners, *French Ecclesiastical Society under the Ancien Régime: A Study of Angers* (1960), 92–3.

15. G. Desnoiresterres, *Voltaire et la société française au XVIIIe siècle*, 2nd edn. (8 vols., 1867–76), iii. 791–2.

16. Definitive history by Chantal Gueudré, *Les Monastères d'Ursulines sous l'ancien régime* (1960), being vol. ii of her *Histoire de l'Ordre des Ursulines en France*.

17. *Nouvelles ecclésiastiques*, 16 Jan. 1789.

18. E. Maxfield-Millar, 'Le "Tartuffe" joué par les religieuses', *Rev. hist. du théâtre* (1972), 383–5.

19. Fr. de Saint-Just, *Témoins de quatre siècles* (1962), 166.

20. Molière, *Les Femmes Savantes*.

21. McManners, *Angers*, 97.

22. Mme de Lambert, *Avis d'une mère à sa fille*, in A. Chérel, *Fénelon au XVIIIe siècle, 1715–1820* (1917), 317.

23. Gusdorf, in P. Hoffmann, *La Femme dans la pensée des Lumières* (1978), 12. See also E. Jacobs (ed.), *Women and Society in 18th-Century France* (1979). Further bibliography in J. McManners, *Death and the Enlightenment* (1981), ch. 13.

24. Voltaire, *Dialogue de l'éducation d'une fille* (1765), in *Œuvres*, xxiv. 285.

25. L. Versini, *Laclos et la tradition: essai sur les sources et la technique des 'Liaisons dangereuses'* (1968), 553.

26. Schmitt, *L'Assistance*, 83.

27. McManners, *Angers*, 97.

28. Gueudré, *Les Monastères d'Ursulines*, ii. 116, 379, 392.

29. An exception, the Congrégation de Notre-Dame in Lorraine (M.-E. Aubry, 'La congrégation de Notre-Dame de Nancy et l'éducation des filles aux XVIIe et XVIIIe siècles', *Ann. Est* (1974), 76–96).

30. Cl. Langlois and P. Wagret, *Structures religieuses et célibat féminin au XIXe siècle* (1972), 14–63. See also Th. Perrée, *Le Tiers Ordre de Notre-Dame du Mont Carmel d'Avranches* (1965).

31. Ch. Molette, *Guide des sources de l'histoire des Congrégations féminines françaises de vie active* (1974).

32. J.-P. Latrobe, 'Contribution à l'enseignement au XVIIIe siècle: les écoles des Sœurs d'Ernemont', *Cahiers hist. enseign.* (1978), 4–86.

33. Pierre de la Haye, *Histoire de Tréguier, ville épiscopale* (1977), 258–9.

34. G. Tavard, *Jean-Martin Moye, mystique et missionnaire* (1978).

35. Gueudré, *Les Monastères d'Ursulines*, ii. 201–3.

36. J. Vaudon, *Histoire générale de la Communauté des Filles de Saint-Paul de Chartres* (4 vols., 1922–31).

37. Cl. Langlois, *Catholicisme au féminin: les congrégations françaises à supérieure générale au XIXe siècle* (1984), 101–2, 139–42.

38. Cl. Langlois, *Histoire de la congrégation de la Providence d'Evreux* (2 vols., 1901).

39. J. Perrel, 'Les Écoles de filles dans la France d'ancien régime', in D. N. Baker and P. J. Harrigan (eds.), *The Making of Frenchmen: Current Directions in the History of Education in France, 1679–1979* (1980), 77.

40. Chartier *et al.*, *L'Éducation*, 239.

41. R. P. H. de Grèzes, *Histoire de l'Institut des écoles charitables du Saint-Enfant Jésus, dit de Saint-Maur, 1700–1877* (n.d.), 27–39.

42. Sr. Paul-Marie de Jésus, *Mère Marie-Louise de Jésus, première fille de la Sagesse, 1641–1759* (1947).

43. Perrel, 'Les Écoles', 78.

44. Chartier *et al.*, *L'Éducation*, 278.

45. M. Claeyssen, 'L'Enseignement de la lecture au 18ᵉ siècle', in Baker and Harrigan (eds.), *Making of Frenchmen*, 66–74.

46. L. Trénard, 'L'Enseignement de la langue nationale, 1750–90', in ibid. 107.

47. R. A. Weight, 'Le Meuble brodé de la Salle du Trône de Louis XIV à Versailles', *Rev. Versailles* (1930), 199–206.

48. J. P. Gutton, *La Société et les pauvres: l'exemple de la généralité de Lyon, 1534–1789* (1971), 388.

49. Grèzes, *Saint-Maur*, 592–3.

50. Chartier, *et al.*, *L'Éducation*, 244–5.

51. Grèzes, *Saint-Maur*, 89.

52. Chartier, *et al.*, *L'Éducation*, 245–6.

53. Perrel, 'Les Écoles', 79–82.

54. Schmitt, *L'Assistance*, 82; F. Bridoux, *La Fin du Lys* (1945), 25; B. Pocquet du Haut-Jussé, 'La Vie temporelle des communautés de femmes à Rennes au XVIIᵉ siècle et au XVIIIᵉ siècle', *Ann. Bretagne* (1917), 39, 44–5, 77–8.

55. Mme de Genlis, *Mémoires* (2 vols., 1825), i. 140, 125.

56. Mme Roland, *Mémoires*, ed. Cl. Perroud (2 vols., 1905), ii. 41–4.

57. E. and J. de Goncourt, *La Femme*, 8–10.

58. McManners, *Death*, 33–4.

59. D'Argenson, vi. 185.

60. La marquise du Deffand, *Correspondance complète*, ed. M. de Lescure (2 vols., 1865), ii. p. xlv.

61. Kunstler, *La Vie quotidienne*, 276.

62. L. de Loménie, *Beaumarchais et son temps* (2 vols., 1889), i. 279–83.

63. Diderot, *Correspondance*, ed. G. Roth and J. Varlot (16 vols., 1955–70), vi. 505.

64. Dom E. Lecroq, *Les Annoncionades de Fécamp 1618–1792* (1947), 160–72.

65. M. Fosseyeux, 'Le Cardinal de Noailles et l'administration du diocèse de Paris', *Rev. hist.* (1913), 282–3.

66. E. Lavaquery, *Le Cardinal de Boisgelin, 1732–1804* (2 vols., 1920), i. 57.

67. Gueudré, *Les Monastères d'Ursulines*, ii. 546–9.

68. Guyot, i. 416–18.

69. Deffand, *Correspondance*, i. 401–5 (1767); cf. ii. 468 (1777).

70. A. Lods, 'Les Luthériens d'Alsace devant la Constituante', *Rév. fr.* (1900), 532.

71. F.-X.-J. Droz, *Histoire du règne de Louis XVI* (3 vols., 1839–42), i. 31.

72. Barbier, i. 248–9, 321–3.

73. [Mlle d'Albert], *Confidences d'une jolie femme* (2 vols., 1777; 1st edn., 1775), ii. 214.

74. Choderlos de Laclos, *Les Liaisons dangereuses*.
75. Loménie, *Beaumarchais*, ii. 606, 619; P. Pinsseau, *Gien sous l'ancien régime et la Révolution d'après les mémoires inédits de l'abbé Vallet* (1922), 77–9.
76. P. Tartat, *Histoire de l'Avalonnais* (2 vols., 1958–60), ii. 46.
77. L. Froger, 'Les Établissements de charité à Saint-Cales', *Rev. Maine* (1878), 341.
78. G.-J. Sumeire, *La Communauté de Trets à la veille de la Révolution* (1960), 177–9.
79. J.-F.-M. de Richeprey, *Journal des voyages en Haute-Guienne*, ed. H. Guilhamon (1952), 367.
80. C. Bloch, *L'Assistance et l'État en France à la veille de la Révolution* (1908), 61.
81. C. Jones, *The Charitable Imperative: Hospitals and Nursing in Ancien Régime and Revolutionary France* (1989), 21.
82. Gutton, *La Société*, 394–9.
83. See C. C. Fairchilds, *Poverty and Charity in Aix-en-Provence, 1640–1789* (1976).
84. C. Jones, *Charity and 'Bienfaisance': The Treatment of the Poor in the Montpellier Region, 1740–1815* (1982), 86. The part played by lay charity—especially by pious aristocrats—is evident. See also the full details in K. Norberg, *Rich and Poor in Grenoble, 1600–1814* (1985).
85. P. Delaunay, *Le Monde médical parisien au 18ᵉ siècle*, 2nd edn. (1906), 72–6; A. Gobert, 'Le District des Enfants Trouvés au Faubourg Saint-Antoine', *Rév. fr.* (1936), 141–3; C. Ronan, 'Les Pauvres à Paris au XVIIIᵉ siècle', *Ann.* (1984), 750–2. (There were vast numbers of inmates—in 1788, 6,720 in the Salpêtrière, and 4,094 in the Bicêtre.)
86. Bloch, *L'Assistance*, 138–9.
87. Marais, i. 367.
88. Bloch, *L'Assistance*, 64.
89. J. Imbert, *Le Droit Hospitalier de la Révolution et l'Empire* (1954), 18–20.
90. For an example J. Vinatier, *Treignac-sur-Vévère* (2 vols., 1974), ii. 125.
91. Fairchilds, *Aix-en-Provence*, 134–5.
92. Jones, *Charity and 'Bienfaisance'*, 86.
93. G. Armigon, *Banquiers des pauvres* (n.d.), 82–6, 221.
94. M. Courdurié, *La Dette des collectivités publiques de Marseille au XVIIIᵉ siècle* (1975), 182–96.
95. Schmitt, *L'Assistance*, 310.
96. Gutton, *La Société*, 478; P. D. Bernier, *Essai sur le tiers état rural ou les paysans de Basse-Normandie au XVIIIᵉ siècle* (1891), 68–70.
97. Froger, 'Saint-Cales', 346.
98. See M.-C. Guillerand, *Les Servantes des pauvres de la Providence de Saumur de 1736 à 1814* (1989).
99. Schmitt, *L'Assistance*, 204, 306.
100. P. Coste, 'Une Victime de la Révolution', *Rev. Gascogne* (1904), 161–225.
101. Voltaire, *Essai sur les Mœurs*, in *Œuvres*, xii. 324.
102. *Voyage d'une Française en Suisse et en Franche-Comté* (2 vols., 1790), i. 223.
103. Jones, *Charitable Imperative*, 85.
104. Ibid. 169.
105. Ibid. 45–50, 123.
106. A. Chevallier, *L'Hôtel-Dieu de Paris et les sœurs augustines, 1680–1810* (1901), 416, 444, 463—the basic authority for what follows.

107. D. Roche, *Paris, capitale des pauvres*, European University Institute Working Paper 86/238 (1986), 21–2.
108. Fr. de la Rochefoucauld, *Voyages en France*, ed. J. Marchand (1923), 98.
109. Jones, *Charitable Imperative*, 278.
110. Bloch, *L'Assistance*, 51–2.
111. Y. Forado Cunéo, 'Les Ateliers de charité de Paris, 1788–91', *Rév. fr.* (1933), 322–9.
112. Gutton, *La Société*, 30.
113. J.-P. Poussou, in F.-G. Pariset (ed.), *Bordeaux au XVIIIe siècle* (1968), 365–6.
114. H. Bergues, P. Ariès, *et al.*, *La Prévention des naissances dans la famille: ses origines dans les temps modernes*, I.N.E.D. Cahier 35 (1960), 173, 179–81; M. Cl. Murtin, 'Les Abandons d'enfants à Bourg et dans le département de l'Ain', *Cahiers hist.* (1965), 135–43.
115. L. Lallemand, *Un Chapitre de l'histoire des Enfants Trouvés: la Maison de la Couche à Paris, XVIIe et XVIIIe siècles* (1885), 139–40; J.-J. Rousseau, *Correspondance complète*, ed. R. A. Leigh, ii (1963), 142–4.
116. V. A. Durand, *État religieux des trois diocèses de Nîmes, d'Uzès et d'Alais à la fin de l'ancien régime* (1909), 319–12.
117. R. Mercier, *La Réhabilitation de la nature humaine, 1700–50* (1960), 58.
118. McManners, *Death*, 284.
119. Jones, *Charitable Imperative*, 247 ff.
120. Pocquet du Haut-Jussé, 'La Vie temporelle', 335.
121. Gutton, *La Société*, 389–92.
122. Sumeire, *La Communauté de Trets*, 181–2.
123. F. Cognel, *La Vie parisienne sous Louis XVI* (1882), 49–50.
124. A. Forrest, *The Revolution and the Poor* (1981), 44–6.
125. Delaunay, *Le Monde médical parisien*, 349, 353.
126. Bloch, *L'Assistance*, 89, 116–17.
127. Gutton, *La Société*, 341–2.
128. J. Delumeau, *Le Diocèse de Rennes* (1979), 127.
129. Bloch, *L'Assistance*, 116–17.
130. Ibid. 61, 114.
131. Ibid. 74–5.
132. Jones, *Charitable Imperative*, 111.
133. See T. Gelfand, *Professionalizing Modern Medicine: Paris Surgeons and Medical Science and Institutions in the 18th Century* (1981), and M. Fosseyeux, 'L'Hôtel-Dieu de Paris sous la Révolution', *Rév. fr.* (1914), 41–3.
134. J. Musset, 'Administration hospitalière et l'anticléricalisme municipal à la fin du XVIIIe siècle', *Ann. Normandie* (1980), 318–19.
135. Jones, *Charitable Imperative*, 151–3.
136. E. Laurès, *La Municipalité de Béziers à la fin de l'ancien régime* (1926), 217–19.
137. Y. Bezard, 'L'Assistance à Versailles', *Rev. Versailles* (1919), 145–6.
138. Bloch, *L'Assistance*, 71–3.

CHAPTER 19

1. Guyot, i. 30–40.
2. *P.V. Ass.* viii(2), cols. 1407 ff.

3. J.-A. de Véri, *Journal*, ed. J. de Witte (2 vols., n.d.), i. 199–200.

4. P. Chevallier, *Loménie de Brienne et l'Ordre monastique, 1760–89* (1959), 73–85.

5. Ch. Gérin, 'Les Monastères franciscains et la Commission des réguliers, 1766–89', *Rev. quest. hist.* (1875), 99, 101.

6. Chevallier, *Loménie de Brienne*, i. 44.

7. For the statistics, see L. Lecestre, *Abbayes, prieurés et couvents d'hommes en France. Liste générale d'après les papiers de la Commission des réguliers* (1902).

8. Chevallier, *Loménie de Brienne*, i. 209–10.

9. F. D. Mathieu, *L'Ancien régime en Lorraine et Barrois* (1874), 91–4.

10. Thomas Bentley, *Journal of a Visit to Paris 1776*, ed. P. France (n.d.), 57–8; L. S. Mercier, *Tableau de Paris*, new edn. (12 vols., 1782–8), xii. 40–1.

11. A. Hutchinson, *The Hermit Monks of Grandmont* (1989), 204–74.

12. Chevallier, *Loménie de Brienne*, 214–15.

13. Ibid. i. 174–6.

14. Ibid. i. 137.

15. J. J. Gautier, *Essai sur les mœurs champêtres* (1787), ed. X. Rousseau (1933), 20.

16. P. Dubois, 'Les Capucins dans le Midi: Les Capucins de Varois-Sollies-Pont, 1650–1791', *Bull. Soc. Draguignan* (1965), 72–91.

17. Ch. Collas, *Saint-Louis d'Antin et son territoire* (1932), 64–5.

18. A. Babeau, *La Ville sous l'ancien régime* (2 vols., 1888), ii. 141–4.

19. Bachaumont, xvii. 320 (1767).

20. Restif de la Bretonne, 'Récit d'un incendie', in *Les Nuits de Paris*, ed. M. Bachelin, i. 65. Cf. Barbier, iii. 93–103.

21. L'Abbé Baston, *Mémoires*, ed. J. Loth and C. Verger (3 vols., 1879), i. 104–9, 141.

22. Mme de Genlis, *Mémoires* (2 vols., 1825), i. 38.

23. Chevallier, *Loménie de Brienne*, i. 167–8. For stories of hoarded riches at the top of the Capuchin hierarchy, see R. Reuss, *La Constitution civile du clergé et la crise religieuse en Alsace* (2 vols., 1927), i. 211–13.

24. Chevallier, *Loménie de Brienne*, i. 186–7.

25. A. Playoust-Chaussis, *La Vie religieuse dans le diocèse de Boulogne, 1725–50* (1969), 62.

26. L. Beaumont-Maillet, *Le Grand Couvent des Cordeliers de Paris* (1975), 175–80.

27. Chevallier, *Loménie de Brienne*, i. 123, 137–9, 153–8, 217, 139–41, 178–81, 218.

28. Ibid. i. 183–4, 219–20.

29. P. J. S. Whitmore, *The Order of Minims in 17th-Century France* (1969), 236.

30. Ibid. 32.

31. J. D. Levesque, *L'Ancien Couvent des Frères Prêcheurs d'Angers* (1961), 292–3, 308–9, 325–6.

32. Chevallier, *Loménie de Brienne*, i. 150–1.

33. R. P. Mortier, *Histoire des maîtres-généraux de l'ordre des Frères Prêcheurs* (8 vols, 1904–14), vii. 400–5.

34. Ch. Gérin, 'Les Augustins et Dominicains en France avant 1789', *Rev. quest. hist.* (1877), 79–93.

35. B. Cousin, 'Un Discours . . . l'histoire de Grasse de Père Crespy', *Ann. Midi* (1973), 290–2.

36. F. Duine, 'Les Généraux des paroisses Bretonnes: Saint-Martin de Vitré', *Ann. Bretagne* (1907–8), 481.

37. L. Ampoulange, *Le Clergé et la convocation aux États-Généraux de 1789 dans la sénéchaussée principale de Périgord* (1912), 90.

38. Chevallier, *Loménie de Brienne*, i. 68.

39. P. Feret, *L'Abbaye de Sainte-Geneviève et la Congrégation de France* (2 vols., 1883), ii. 136–9, 153, 163–5, 171–5.

40. L'Abbé Le Gendre, *Mémoires*, ed. M. Roux (1863), 367–8.

41. E. Préclin, *L'Union des Églises gallicane et anglicane: une tentative au temps de Louis XV—P.-F. Le Courayer et Guillaume Wake* (1928).

42. Goevaerts, *Écrivains et savants de l'Ordre de Prémontré* (4 vols., 1895–1917), i. 39, 110, 563–4, 556, 520–4, 362–3; ii. 59–60; iii. 110–29.

43. J. Evans, *Monastic Architecture in France from the Renaissance to the Revolution* (1964), 51–3.

44. Dom G. Charvin, *Statuts, chapitres-généraux et visites de l'Ordre de Cluny* (4 vols., 1965), i. 1–7.

45. G. Charvin, 'À propos d'un projet d'une histoire de l'Ordre de Cluny au XVIIIe siècle', in *Société des Amis de Cluny, Congrès* (1950), 183.

46. L. H. Champly, *Histoire de l'abbaye de Cluny*, rev. R. Champly (1930), 338.

47. G. Charvin, 'Frédéric-Jerôme de la Rochefoucauld, abbé de Cluny, 1747–57', *Rev. Mabillon* (1949), 31; id., 'L'Abbaye et l'Ordre de Cluny à la fin du XVIIIe siècle', ibid. 44–5.

48. L.-J. Lekai, *The Cistercian Ideal and Reality* (1972), 159–65.

49. Guyot, v. 517.

50. Bezard (ed.), *Lettres du président de Brosses à Ch. Loppin de Gémeaux* (1929), 202.

51. Guyot, xi. 114–17.

52. Chevallier, *Loménie de Brienne*, i. 196–200.

53. L.-J. Lekai, 'The Financial Status of the Parisian College of Saint Bernard, 1705–90', *Anal. cist.* (1969), 210–14; and id., 'Introduction à l'étude des collèges cisterciens en France avant la Révolution', ibid. 145–214.

54. L.-J. Lekai, 'Cistercian Monasteries and the French Episcopate on the Eve of the Revolution', *Anal. cist.* (1967), 79–84.

55. N. Tillière, *Histoire de l'abbaye d'Orval* (1967), 240–2, 274.

56. A. Krailsheimer, 'Les Débuts de la réforme de Sept-Fons', *Cîteaux* (1968), 210–11.

57. A. Krailsheimer, 'Sept-Fons de 1700 à 1723', *Cîteaux* (1987), 253.

58. A. Krailsheimer, *Armand-Jean de Rancé, abbot of La Trappe* (1974).

59. Ch. Gérin, 'Les Bénédictins français avant 1789', *Rev. quest. hist.* (1870), 470.

60. A. Morize, *L'Apologie du luxe au XVIIIe siècle: le 'Mondain' et ses sources* (1909), 42; F. Rousseau, *Moines bénédictins martyrs et confesseurs de la foi pendant la Révolution* (1926), 27–8.

61. Le maréchal duc de Croÿ, *Journal, 1718–84*, ed. le vicomte de Grouchy and P. Cottin (4 vols., 1906), ii. 109–15; Fr. de la Rochefoucauld, *Voyages en France*, ed. J. Marchand (1933), 101–2.

62. Up to 1739, more than half died within five years (Krailsheimer, *Rancé*, 92). Average age of death at Saint-Germain-des-Prés was 71, at La Trappe under 40 (M. Ultee, *The Abbey of St Germain des Prés in the 17th Century* (1981), 20).

63. Croÿ, *Journal*, ii. 113. A soldier tries his vocation in Oct. 1718, and is back in his regiment in Jan. 1719 (A. Corvisier, *L'Armée française de la fin du XVIIe siècle au ministère de Choiseul: le Soldat* (2 vols., 1964), ii. 870).

64. M. H. Jette, *La France religieuse au XVIIIe siècle* (1956), 25.

65. J. McManners, 'Voltaire and the Monks', in *Studies in Church History* (1985), 319–42.

66. J. L. Godefroy, 'Figures de moines: Dom Chardon', *Rev. Mabillon* (1944), 82–93.

67. See J. L. Godefroy, *La Congrégation de Saint-Vanne et la Révolution: Dom Charles* (1911).

68. Chevallier, *Loménie de Brienne*, i. 113–18.

69. Dom P. Schmitz, *Histoire de l'Ordre de Saint-Benoît* (7 vols., 1942–56), iv. 31–42.

70. See H. Leclercq, *Dom Mabillon* (2 vols., 1953–7).

71. E. de Broglie, *Mabillon et la société de l'abbaye de Saint-Germain-des-Prés à la fin du 17e siècle* (2 vols., 1888).

72. E. de Broglie, *Bernard de Montfaucon et les Bernardins* (2 vols., 1891), i. 27 ff.

73. Dom L. Deries, 'Dom Pierre Guérin et le chanoine Masclef', *Rev. Mabillon* (1908), 39–67, 151–87.

74. A. Vernière, *Journal de Voyage de Dom Jacques Boyer* (1886).

75. Le Gendre, *Mémoires*, 400.

76. A. de la Borderie, *Correspondance historique des Bénédictins Bretons* (1880), pp. xvii–xxiv, 249–56.

77. L. Lecomte, 'Les Bénédictins et l'histoire des provinces aux XVIIe et XVIIIe siècles', *Rev. Mabillon* (1927), 237 ff.; (1928), 39 ff.

78. L. Deries, 'Un Grand Sauveteur des documents . . . Dom Germain Poirier', *Rev. Mabillon* (1930), 62–6.

79. B. Hauréau, *Histoire littéraire du Maine* (4 vols., 1843), i. pp. xxiii–xxxvii.

80. J. McManners, *French Ecclesiastical Society under the Ancien Régime: A Study of Angers*, 53–4.

81. M. Laurais, 'Les Travaux d'érudition des Mauristes: origine et évolution', *Rev. hist. Église Fr.* (1957), 232.

82. Voltaire to Cideville, 6 May 1733, in Voltaire, *Corresp.* iii. 67 (no. 586).

83. Laurais, 'Les Travaux', 252.

84. Broglie, *Montfaucon*, i. 45–7.

85. J. Ruwet *et al.* (eds.), *Lettres de Turgot à la duchesse d'Enville, 1764–74 et 1777–80* (1976), 53, 57, 70.

86. Le Glay, *Mission historique de Dom Bévys, Spicilège . . . pour servir à l'histoire des sciences dans le Nord* (Lille, 1858), fasc. i. 45–53.

87. Dom B. Knowles, *Great Historical Enterprises* (1963), 41.

88. Schmitz, *Saint-Benoît*, v. 115–19.

89. *Réponse à la lettre d'un professeur émérite de l'Université de Paris au sujet des exercices de l'école militaire de Sorèz* (1777), cited by A. Sicard, *Les Études classiques avant la Révolution* (1887), 485.

90. A. Rostand, 'L'Œuvre architectural des Bénédictins de Saint-Maur en Normandie, 1616–1789', *Bull. Soc. Normandie* (1939), 88–222; M. Bugner, 'Les Constructions des Bénédictins de Saint-Maur au XVIIe et XVIIIe siècles', *Rev. hist. Église Fr.* (1987), 120–1.

91. J. L. Godefroy, 'Le Chevalier de Folard et les Bénédictins de Saint-Germain-des-Prés', *Rev. Mabillon* (1936), 128.

92. It was the abbé Prévost (E. Harrisse, *L'Abbé Prévost: histoire de sa vie et de ses œuvres* (1896), 250–1).

93. P. Timothée de la Flèche, *Mémoires et lettres . . . 1703–30*, ed. P. Ubald d'Alençon (1907), 73.

94. P. Denis, 'Un Bénédictin janséniste réfugié au Canada', *Rev. Mabillon* (1909), 208–12.

95. Schmitz, *Saint-Benoît*, iv. 50.

96. Chevallier, *Loménie de Brienne*, 120–2.

97. Dom P. Anger, 'Les Mitigations demandées par les moines de Saint-Germain-des-Prés en 1765', *Rev. Mabillon* (1908), 196–229.

98. Chevallier, *Loménie de Brienne*, i. 247–8.

99. Dom A. du Bourg, 'Vie monastique dans l'abbaye de Saint-Germain-des-Prés', *Rev. quest. hist.* (1905), 458.

100. Chevallier, *Loménie de Brienne*, i. 119–22.

101. Dom R.-P. Tassin, *Histoire littéraire de la Congrégation de Saint-Maur* (1770), 197–9, 314–47, 376, 394–5, 421.

102. Dom P. Denis, 'Dom Charles de l'Hostellerie', *Rev. Mabillon* (1909), 8 ff.; (1910), 429 ff.

103. A. de la Borderie, *Correspondance*, pp. xvi, 167–70, 220, 160–3.

104. Dom Th. Réjalot, 'Dom J. P. Deforis et l'abbé Mercier de Saint-Léger', *Rev. Mabillon* (1932), 38 ff.

105. Dom F. Lohier, 'Dom Étienne Maugier, 1753–94', *Rev. Mabillon* (1912–13), 345–9.

106. L. Deries, 'La Vie d'un bibliothécaire, Dom Gourdin, 1739–1825', *Rev. Mabillon* (1928), 211–15.

107. Harrisse, *Prévost*, 15–16, 19–24.

108. Ultee, *St Germain des Prés*, 16, 20–2.

109. 'La Congrégation de Saint-Maur d'après le Journal et les lettres de Dom Dassac, 1752–1826', *Rev. monde catholique* (1893), 59.

110. Dom Pierre Chastelain, 'Journal', ed. H. Jadert, *Trav. Acad. nat. Reims* (1902), 79–90.

111. Harrisse, *Prévost*, 15.

112. L. Deries, 'Poirier', *Rev. Mabillon* (1930), 52–3.

113. L.-J. Lekai, 'The Cistercian Order and the Commission des Réguliers', *Anal. cist.* (1976), 179–209.

114. J. Salmon, *Morimond: les derniers jours de l'abbaye* (1961), 28.

115. Hutchinson, *Grandmont*, 256–71.

116. Ch. Gérin, 'Les Monastères', *Rev. quest. hist.* (1876), 563.

117. S. Lemaire, *La Commission des réguliers* (1926), 92–100.

118. M. Gasnier, *Les Dominicains de la rue Saint-Honoré* (1942), 279–80; M. D. Chapotin, *Le Dernier Prieur du dernier couvent, 1736–1806* (1893), 116–21, 176–7.

119. Lemaire, *La Commission*, 110–23, 231–40.

CHAPTER 20

1. A. Degert, *Histoire des séminaires français jusqu'à la Révolution* (2 vols., 1912), ii. 359.

2. R. Darricau, in *Antoine Godeau, 1605–1672, de la galanterie à la sainteté*, ed. Y. Giraud, Acts et Colloques, Grasse, 17 (1972), 171.

3. Degert, *Histoire*, ii. 374–5. Discussion also of M. Olier, *Traité des saints Ordres* (1675) and L. Habert, *Theologia dogmatica et moralis* (7 vols., 1708), 369–74.

4. *Dictionnaire portatif des cas de conscience*, 2nd edn. (2 vols., Lyon, 1761), i. 422.

5. For Pius XII's rehabilitation of 'attraction' (1912) see E. Farrell, *The Theology of Religious Vocation* (1952), 17–18, 47, 103. I cite occasionally in this section my chapter 'The Bishops of France in the 18th Century', in D. Baker (ed.), *Religious Motivation*, Studies in Church History, 15 (1978), 305–7.

6. [R. Daon], *Conduite des âmes dans la voie du salut* (1750), 86.

7. P. Feret, *La Faculté de Théologie de Paris et ses docteurs les plus célèbres* (7 vols. 1900–9), vi. 142.

8. Mangin, *Science des confesseurs, ou décisions théologiques canoniques, domestiques et morales* (3 vols., 1757), iii. 258. See also the censures of family interests in P. Collet, *Traité des devoirs des gens du monde et surtout des chefs de famille* (1764), 201. A churchman, one should note, could dispose as he willed, within the boundaries of Christian responsibility, of the income coming to him from private sources.

9. L. Tronson, *Correspondance*, ed. L. Bertrand (3 vols., 1904) iii. 301.

10. [J.-L. Brunet, rev. de Maillane], *Le Parfait Notaire apostolique* (2 vols., 1775), i. 252–3.

11. 'Cassanyes et ses mémoires inédits (1758–1843)', *Rév. fr.* (1888), 979.

12. P.-A. Alletz, *La Discipline de l'église de France d'après ses maximes et ses décisions répandues dans la collection des Mémoires du Clergé* (1780), 79.

13. *Le Parfait Notaire*, i. 253. The standard treatise on the theology of minor and major orders in the church and on their ceremonies of initiation was A. Godeau, *Discours sur les Ordres sacrez, ou toutes les cérémonies de l'ordination selon le Pontifical Roman sont expliquées*, 2nd edn. (1658).

14. *Le Parfait Notaire*, i. 259.

15. C. Berthelot du Chesnay, 'Le Clergé diocésain français au XVIIIᵉ siècle et les registres des insinuations ecclésiastiques', *Rev. hist. mod. contemp.* (1963), 245, Autun, 90–200 livres (T. J. Schmitt, *L'Organisation ecclésiastique et la pratique religieuse dans l'archidiaconé d'Autun de 1650 à 1750* (1957), 128); Alsace, 100 livres (A. Schaer, *Le Clergé paroissial catholique en Haute-Alsace sous l'ancien régime, 1648–1789* (1960), 100; Amiens, 100 livres (P. Deyon, *Amiens: capitale provinciale* (1967), 364); Paris, 150 livres (M. Pialès, *Traité des collations et provisions de bénéfices* (8 vols. 1753–6), i. 148).

16. Le marquis de Roux, *Histoire religieuse de la Révolution à Poitiers et dans la Vienne* (1952), 24–5.

17. Leymarie, 'Documents . . . sur la jeunesse de J.-B. Carrier', *Rev. Haute-Auvergne* (1954), 443–4.

18. L. Bassette, *Jean de Caulet, évêque de Grenoble, 1693–1771* (1946), 16; Berthelot du Chesnay, 'Le Clergé diocésain', 255.

19. Berthelot du Chesnay, 'Le Clergé diocésain', 255.

20. *Le Parfait Notaire*, i. 306–11.

21. A. Lestra, *Le Père Coudrin, fondateur de Picpus* (1952), 30.

22. *Le Parfait Notaire*, i. 305.

23. H. Espitalier, 'Les Évêques de Fréjus', *Bull. Soc. Draguignan* (1898–9), 122.

24. 'Une Lettre de Joseph Le Bon', *Rév. fr.* (1913), 229–31.

25. e.g. M. Pialès, *Traité et la dévolution, du dévolut, et des variantes de plein droit* (3 vols., 1757), ii. 189.

26. F. D. Mathieu, *L'Ancien Régime dans la province de Lorraine et Barrois* (1879), 128.

27. A good example: the priory of Andresy, in E. Chartraire, 'Trois recueils de la correspondance des abbés Fenel avec l'abbé Lebeuf et autres', *Bull. Soc. arch. de Sens* (1927), 120.

28. *La Vie de M. Marquis-Ducastel, doyen rural d'Évron et Sonnois, curé de Sainte-Suzanne*, ed. F. Pichon (1873), 7, 11–13, 27. A very able youth might win a free place at a seminary by carrying off academic prizes (see M. Yvart, 'La Vie d'un écolier . . . 1784–92', *Rev. Socs. Haute-Normandie* (1957), 53–72.

29. Marquis-Ducastel, *La Vie*, 101, 107–8.

30. J. McManners, *French Ecclesiastical Society under the Ancien Régime: . . . A Study of Angers* (1960), 140.

31. In the dioceses of Dol, Nantes, Rennes, Saint-Brieuc, and Saint-Malo, a total of a fifth of the livings were at the bishop's disposal, two-fifths shared between bishop and Pope, one-fifth in the patronage of abbeys (C. Berthelot de Chesnay, *Les Prêtres séculiers en Haute-Bretagne au XVIIIᵉ siècle* (1974), 203–4).

32. Pialès, *Traité de la dévolution*, i. 221.

33. Guyot, xlv. 26.

34. Potier de la Germondaye, *Introduction au gouvernement des paroisses* (1777), 22.

35. A. Besnier, *Les Agents généraux du Clergé de France* (1939), 111.

36. Pialès, *Traité de la dévolution*, i. 368–95.

37. A. Sicard, *La Nomination aux bénéfices ecclésiastiques avant 1789* (1896), 12.

38. M. Marion, *Dictionnaire des institutions de la France aux XVIIᵉ et XVIIIᵉ siècles* (2 vols., 1923), i. 43; J.-B. Daranatz, 'Les Ordinations sacerdotales du diocèse de Bayonne au XVIIIᵉ siècle', *Bull. Soc. Bayonne* (1931), 360.

39. M. Pialès, *Traité de l'expectative des gradués, des droits et des privilèges des universités* (4 vols., 1757), iii. 224.

40. Ibid. ii. 451–2.

41. Marion, *Dictionnaire*, ii. 287.

42. For the working of the indult in detail, see Melchior Cochet de Saint-Vallier, *Traité de l'indult du Parlement de Paris* (3 vols., 1747; orig. pub. 1703).

43. Morellet had studied at the Sorbonne with Turgot.

44. Marion, *Dictionnaire*, i. 45.

45. *Le Parfait Notaire*, i. 537 ff. The months varied in different places. For the Trois Évêchés, see E. Martin, *Histoire des diocèses de Toul, de Nancy et de Saint-Dié* (3 vols., 1900–3), ii. 316.

46. Marion, *Dictionnaire*, 431; Pialès, *Traité de la dévolution*, i. 368–9.

47. Guyot, ii. 141–2.

48. Ibid. ii. 138–9.

49. Ibid. ii. 138.

50. Le Gendre, *Mémoires*, ed. M. Roux (1863), 372.

51. Timothée de la Flèche, *Mémoires et lettres, 1703–1730*, ed. P. Ubald d'Alençon (1907), 141.

52. Pialès, *Gradués*, iv. 2.

53. Ibid. iv. 31, 46; *Le Parfait Notaire*, i. 331–2.

54. Marion, *Dictionnaire*, i. 263.

55. Pialès, *Gradués*, iii. 363.

56. Ibid. i. 150–2, 159, 199–205.

57. Ibid. ii. 180–90.

58. Y. Leblanc, 'Pierre Buquet, bibliothécaire de l'Université de Caen . . .', *Bull. Soc. Normandie* (1961–2), 646.

59. Pialès, *Gradués*, iv. 214–18.

60. Ibid. ii. 420–1; *Le Parfait Notaire*, ii. 353–70.

61. A. H. Van der Weil, *Paul-Louis de Mondran, 1734–1795* (1962), 8–11.

62. Marais, ii. 431.

63. Ibid. ii. 62–3.

64. R.-P. Nepveu de la Manoullière, *Mémoires*, ed. G. Esnault (3 vols., 1877–9), i. 19–20.

65. Ibid. ii. 10; Marquis-Ducastel, *La Vie*, 112.

66. Schaer, *Le Clergé paroissial*, 79.

67. Guyot, xiv. 115–26.

68. Mathieu, *L'Ancien Régimen*, 114–15.

69. H. Lancelin, *Histoire du diocèse de Cambrai* (1944), 250.

70. For details on the various provinces, see Pialès, *Traité des commandes et des réserves ou des provisions des bénéfices* (3 vols., 1758), iii. 89–162.

71. B. Coolen, *Helfaut: Essai sur l'administration d'une paroisse sous l'ancien régime* (1939).

72. Guyot, xiv. 122.

73. J. Mahuas, 'Le Concours pour l'obtention des cures dans le diocèse de Vannes au XVIIIe siècle', *Méms. Soc. Bretagne* (1965), 41–52.

74. Ibid. 49–50.

75. Ch. Robert, *Urbain de Hercé, dernier évêque et comte de Dol* (1900), 44.

76. Mathieu, *L'Ancien Régime*, 115.

77. Guyot, lv. 138.

78. M. Perard-Castell, *Traité de l'usage et pratique de la Cour de Rome pour l'expédition des signatures et provisions des bénéfices de France* (2 vols., 1717), i. 70–1.

79. Guyot, iv. 144–6.

80. Pialès, *Traité des collations*, i. 436–7.

81. E. Goiffon, *Monographies paroissiales: paroisses de l'archiprêtré de Nîmes*, 2nd edn. (1898), 307.

82. Ibid. 175 ff.

83. M. Vallery-Radot, *Un Administrateur ecclésiastique à la fin de l'ancien régime: le cardinal de Luynes, archevêque de Sens, 1753–88* (1966), 89–90.

84. Guyot, xlv. 428–9, 441; Daranatz, 'Les Ordinations', 359, 368, 358.

85. Coolen, *Helfaut*, 146.

86. P.-T. Durand de Maillane, *Dictionnaire de droit canonique et de pratique bénéficiale* (2 vols., 1776), cited by L. Châtellier, 'Société et bénéfices ecclésiastiques: le cas alsacien (1670–1730)', *Rev. hist.* (1970), 76–9.

87. Berthelot du Chesnay, 'Le Clergé diocésain', 245.

88. 'Quand it vendit sa primogéniture | Esaü était affamé, | Mais quand il céda sa cure | C'est qu'il avait trop bien diné' (Marion, *Dictionnaire*, i. 45).

89. Letter to Voltaire, 29 May 1764, in la marquise du Deffand, *Correspondance complète*, ed. M. de Lescure (2 vols., 1865), i. 299.

90. A. Krieger and L. Raffin, *La Madeleine* (1937), 47.

91. Châtellier, 'Société', 76–9.

92. Krieger and Raffin, *La Madeleine*, 47–51.

93. Pierre de Vaissière, *Curés de campagne de l'ancienne France* (1933), 72.

94. Cited by Châtellier, 'Société', 81.

95. J.-J. Gautier, *Essai sur les mœurs champêtres* (1787), ed. X. Rousseau (1935), 49.

96. Ch. Bourgeat, 'À propos d'une lettre du comte de Noé', *Rev. Gascogne* (1938), 142.

97. F. Bridoux, *Histoire religieuse du département de Seine-et-Marne pendant la Révolution* (2 vols., 1953), i. 16.

98. Thesis of J. D'Audney, 'The Diocese of Auch, 1650–1730' (Bodl. Lib., 1971).

99. L. Pérouas, *Le Diocèse de la Rochelle de 1648 à 1724: sociologie et pastorale* (1964); T. J. Schmitt, *L'Organisation ecclésiastique et la pratique religieuse dans l'archidiaconé d'Autun de 1650 à 1750* (1957), p. lxvii.

100. J. R. Joly, *Histoire de la prédication* (1767), 519–22.

101. Th. Lhuillier, 'Un Curé de campagne à l'époque de la Révolution: Romain Pichonnier', *Rév. fr.* (1898), 493.

102. V. Lespay (ed.), *Un Curé Béarnais au 18ᵉ siècle: correspondance de l'abbé Tristan*, i (1879), 6–7, 85.

103. C. Baloche, *L'Église Saint-Merry de Paris: histoire de la paroisse et de la collégiale, 700–1910* (2 vols., 1911), i. 448, 563–5; ii. 4–5.

104. Marquis-Ducastel, *La Vie*, 112.

105. Nepveu de la Manoullière, *Mémoires*, ii. 118–19.

106. L. Brochard, *Saint-Gervais, histoire de la paroisse* (1950), 150–1, 154, 162.

107. Y. Castan, *Honnêteté et relations sociales en Languedoc, 1715–80* (1974), 277; A. Poitrineau, *La Vie rurale en Basse-Auvergne au XVIIIᵉ siècle* (1969), 114.

108. Gautier, *Essai*, 49.

109. Perard-Castell, *Traité*, i. 221–2.

110. Guyot, lv. 138; Perard-Castell, *Traité*, i. 210.

111. Pialès, *Traité des collations*, i. 355.

112. Guyot, xlvii. 425–41.

113. *Le Parfait Notaire*, ii. 224.

114. Guyot, xviii. 568 ff.

115. Ibid. xix. 3–4; Pialès, *Traité de la dévolution*, i. 316–18.

116. Guyot, xix. 23–8.

117. Ibid. xix. 3–4.

118. Ibid. xvii. 69.

119. Ibid. xvii. 71.

120. Ibid. xvii. 50–2.

121. Marion, *Dictionnaire*, i. 36–7.

122. Guyot, v. 144.

123. Ibid. xvii. 60–1.

124. Ibid. v. 150, xvii. 67.

125. Ibid. xvii. 63–4.

126. Ibid. xvii. 62.

127. Ibid. xvii. 69.

128. *Le Parfait Notaire*, i. 124.

129. Guyot, vi. 563; *Le Parfait Notaire*, i. 248.

130. Guyot, lxiii. 451–6.

131. Ibid. xxxiii. 424; *Le Parfait Notaire*, ii. 423–4.

132. Marais, i. 124–5.

133. Barbier, ii. 123–4.
134. Pialès, *Traité de la dévolution*, i. 437; Vaissière, *Curés*, 71.
135. Marion, *Dictionnaire*, i. 162.
136. Guyot, xvii. 36–8.
137. Ibid. xvii. 39–41.
138. L. Marcel, *Le Frère de Diderot* (1913), 53–62; Diderot, *Correspondance*, ed. G. Roth and J. Varloot (16 vols., 1955–70), i. 219–20.
139. Pialès, *Traité des collations*, i. 436–8.
140. Guyot, vii. 131–2, lii. 62–4.
141. Ibid. xvii. 41–2.
142. Marion, *Dictionnaire*, ii. 45–6.
143. E. Champion, *La France d'après les cahiers de 1789* (1921), 195–6.
144. C. H. G. B. Jourdain, *Histoire de l'Université de Paris aux XVIIe et XVIIIe siècles* (2 vols., 1888), i. 235. For a list of the patrons of the leading parishes of Paris, see P. de Crousaz-Crétet, *Paris sous Louis XIV* (2 vols., 1922), ii. 9.
145. e.g. Tronson, *Correspondance*, i. 454 (1681); Schaer, *Le Clergé paroissial*, 70.
146. Mathieu, *L'Ancien Régime*, 113.
147. Dom Malaret, prior of Saint-Denis, Paris, to the comte d'Angiviller, 16 Mar. 1788, in 'Les Tombes royales de Saint-Denis', *Le Cabinet historique*, 23 (1876), 144.
148. Marquis-Ducastel, *La Vie*, 110–11.
149. Le Noble, *L'École du monde* (4 vols., 1700), cited by G. Atkinson, *The Sentimental Revolution* (1965), 122.
150. J. F. Marmontel, *Mémoires*, ed. J. Renwick (2 vols., 1972) i. 35, 50–5, 83.
151. A. Monglond, *Le Préromantisme français* (2 vols., 1930), ii. 305.
152. E. Lintilhac, *Vergniaud* (1920), 1–5.
153. J.-B. Thiers, *Traité des superstitions qui regardent tous les Sacremens* (3 vols., 1704; 1st edn. 1696), iii. 403.
154. Collet, *Traité*, 201.
155. J. Brengues, *Charles Duclos* (1971), 396.
156. J. Fabre, *André Chénier* (1955), 14.
157. E. Bernstin, *Jean-Marie Roland et le Ministère de l'Intérieur 1792–93* (1964), 1.
158. A. Cournot, *Souvenirs 1760–1860*, ed. E.-P. Bottinelli (1913), 7–9.
159. R. Reuss, *La Constitution civile du clergé et la crise religieuse en Alsace* (2 vols., 1922), i. 158.
160. Pierre de Vaissière, *Gentilshommes campagnards de l'ancienne France* (1925, 1st edn. 1903), 377–8; Nepveu de la Manoullière, *Mémoires*, i. 22.
161. Marquis-Ducastel, *La Vie*, 26–56.
162. L'Abbé Baston, *Mémoires*, ed. J. Loth and Ch. Verger (3 vols., 1897–9), i. 10–38, 77–8, 152–4.
163. Lestra, *Père Coudrin*, 22, 25–6, 29–30.

CHAPTER 21

1. There were at least 770 abbeys available for the *commende* (P. T. Durand de Maillaine, *Dictionnaire de droit canonique* (4 vols., 1776), i. 2–8).
2. C. A. Sainte-Beuve, *Port-Royal*, ed. Leroy (7 vols., 1912), iii. 112.

3. J.-B. Thiers, *Histoire des perruques* (1777, orig. edn. 1689), 235–9.

4. E. and J. de Goncourt, *Sophie Arnould* (1877), 98–9.

5. M. Souvira, 'La Crise mystique du jeune Diderot', *XVIIIᵉ Siècle* (1987), 315–26.

6. Ph. Auserve, *Delille, poète français* (n.d. [1968]), 7–31; see generally E. Guitton, *Jacques Delille et la poésie de la Nature en France, 1750–1820* (1974).

7. P. Marot, *Recherches sur la vie de François de Neufchâteau* (1960), 49–53.

8. J. F. Marmontel, *Mémoires*, ed. J. Renwick (2 vols., 1972), i. 83.

9. M. Pellisson, *Chamfort* (1895), 17. (Was he the illegitimate son of an ecclesiastic? See C. Arnaud, *Chamfort* (1988), 9, 22–25.)

10. A. Monglond, *Le Préromantisme français* (2 vols., 1930), ii. 305–6.

11. T. Morris, 'L'Abbé Desfontaines et son rôle dans la littérature de son temps', *XVIIIᵉ Siècle* (1961), 20.

12. C. Northeast, *The Parisian Jesuits and the Enlightenment, 1700–1762* (1991), 204–5.

13. For the abbé de Fontenac (Louis-Abel Bonafons), who, after the Jesuits were suppressed, became a journalist and a right-wing propagandist during the Revolution, see W. J. Murray, *The Right-Wing Press in the French Revolution* (1986), 45–7.

14. J. Balcou, *Fréron contre les philosophes* (1975), 12–15; J. Biard-Millérioux, *L'Esthétique d'Eli-Catherine Fréron, 1739–76* (1983), 9.

15. *Encyclopédie ou dictionnaire raisonné des sciences, des arts et des métiers*, i (1751), 12–14 and xvi (1765), 'Tonsure', 413–14; L. Moréri, *Le Grand Dictionnaire historique* (1759), 17–18, copies the *Encyclopédie*; Guyot, i. 32–44; Durand de Maillaine, *Dictionnaire*, i. 42–4; A. Bergier, *Dictionnaire de théologie* (8 vols., 1830 edn.), i. 7–8, viii. 147.

16. For Noailles see B. de Lacombe, *La Résistance janséniste et parlementaire au temps de Louis XV: l'abbé Nigon de Berty, 1702–72* (1948), 24.

17. Bridard de la Garde, *Les Lettres de Thérèse*, in F. C. Green, *La Peinture des mœurs de la bonne société dans le roman français de 1715 à 1761* (1924), 112.

18. Ginguené, *Notice sur la vie de Chamfort*, in S.-R.-N. Chamfort, *Œuvres* (2 vols., 1808), i. 12.

19. L'Abbé Baston, *Mémoires*, ed. J. Loth and C. Verger (3 vols., 1897), i. 22.

20. A. Babeau (ed.), 'Lettres inédites de Grossley, 1758', *Bull. Soc. Aube* (1906), 221–5.

21. Thiers, *Histoire*, 235–9.

22. L. Tronson, *Correspondance*, ed. L. Bertrand (3 vols., 1904), i. 32.

23. B. Plongeron, *La Vie quotidienne du clergé français au 18ᵉ siècle* (1964), 81.

24. *Dictionnaire critique, pittoresque et sentencieux* (3 vols., 1768), i, 'abbé'.

25. L. Ampoulange, *Le Clergé et les élections aux États-Généraux de 1789 dans la sénéchaussée principale de Périgord* (1912), 39–46.

26. A. Cournot, *Souvenirs*, ed. E. P. Bottellini (1915), 31–2.

27. J. McManners, *Death and the Enlightenment* (1981), 270–1, 278.

28. *Archives parlementaires*, ed. J. Mavidal (82 vols., 1869–1913), v. 296 (art. 24). The Bicêtre at Paris was a combined gaol, house of correction, and poorhouse.

29. F. Tuloup, *Saint-Malo, histoire religieuse* (1975), 86.

30. Cited by R. Mauzi, *L'Idée du bonheur dans la littérature et la pensée française au XVIIIᵉ siècle* (1960), 167. The *Dictionnaire de Trévoux* treats all abbés as 'abbés

de cour'; so does B. Guy, 'Towards an appreciation of the Abbé de cour', *Yale Fr. St.* (1968), 71–88.

31. Le duc de Broglie, *Le Secret du roi: correspondance secrète de Louis XV et ses agents diplomatiques* (2 vols., 1886), i. 27–30.

32. J. A. Véri, *Journal*, ed. J. de Witte (2 vols., n.d.), i. 7, 87; ii. 115.

33. Saint-Simon, xviii. 271, xx. 346.

34. J. A. Clarke, 'J. P. de Bignon', *Fr. Hist. St.*, viii (1973–4), 215–27; J. Le Brun, 'Censure . . . et littérature religieuse', *Rev. hist. Église Fr.* (1975), 225; D. H. Jarry, 'Le Collège Royal en 1724', *XVIIIe Siècle* (1976), 357–67.

35. P. Girault de Coursac, *L'Éducation d'un roi, Louis XVI* (1972), 193–4.

36. R. Robert, *Contes parodiques et licencieux du 18e siècle* (1987), 22–3.

37. Batteux, *Les Beaux-Arts réduits à un même système*, ed. J. R. Mantou (1990), 267.

38. R. Taton (ed.), *L'Enseignement et la diffusion des sciences en France au XVIIIe siècle* (1964), 273, 586.

39. C. H. G. B. Jourdain, *Histoire de l'Université de Paris aux XVIIe et XVIIIe siècles* (2 vols., 1862–6), ii. 275–6.

40. E. Pease Shaw, *The Case of the Abbé de Moncrif* (1953), 9–47.

41. D'Argenson, vi. 95.

42. Ibid. vii. 396.

43. A. H. Van der Weil, *Paul-Louis de Mondran, 1734–1795* (1962), 27. As a girl, Mme de Genlis saw him, and thought he would end up there (*Mémoires* (2 vols., 1825), i. 69–70).

44. J. Bouchary, *Les Faux-monnayeurs sous la Révolution française* (1946), 10, 23.

45. For their portrayal in eighteenth-century literature, E. Van der Schveren, 'Les Petits Abbés dans la France du 17e et 18e siècle', in *Études sur le 18e siècle* (1991), 166–7.

46. R. Fargher, *Life and Letters in France in the 18th Century* (1970), 7–9.

47. Saint-Simon, x. 334, xi. 106.

48. H. Boivin, 'Les Dossiers de l'abbé Desfontaines aux archives de la Bastille', *Rev. hist. litt. Fr.* (1907), 55–72.

49. D. Charlton, *Grétry and the Growth of Opéra comique* (1986), 339.

50. These two novelettes printed in R. Trousson, *Romans libertins du 18e siècle* (1993), 490 ff. For the life of Voisenon, see Grimm, xi. 150–1 (Nov. 1775); Bachaumont, vi. 132 (Apr. 1772); W. d'Ormesson, *Le Clergé et l'Académie* (1965), 20; J. Comy, *Un Abbé de cour sous Louis XV: M. de Voisenon* (1959).

51. *Rev. rétrospective* (1885), 150 ff.

52. H. Monod-Cassidy, *Un Voyageur philosophe au 18e siècle: l'abbé Jean-Bernard le Blanc* (1941); D'Argenson, vi. 16, 25.

53. G. Gaillard, *Essai sur la fable en France* (1912); Bachaumont, xxvii. 49 (3 Dec. 1782); F. Bluche, *Les Magistrats du Parlement de Paris au 18e siècle* (1956), 369–71.

54. He resigned his benefices before crossing the frontier. Ch. de Brosses, *Lettres familières* (3 vols., 1991 edn.), ii. 717.

55. [Rutlidge], *La Quinzaine Angloise à Paris* (1776), ed. A. Franklin (1902), 51–2.

56. M. de Lescure, *Les Maîtresses du Régent* (1851), 57.

57. G. Rivollet, *Adrienne Lecouvreur* (1925), 102–5.

58. C. Kunstler, *La Vie privée de Marie-Antoinette* (1938), 89.

59. E. Regnault, *Christophe de Beaumont, archevêque de Paris, 1763–81* (2 vols.,

1882), i. 508–9.

60. D'Argenson, v. 392–5.

61. Véri, *Journal*, i. 190–4.

62. J. Dusaulx, *De la passion du jeu depuis les temps anciens jusqu'à nos jours* (2 vols., 1779), i. 216; P. Barbier and F. Vermillot, *Histoire de la France par les chansons: du Jansénisme au Siècle des Lumières* (1957), 192: Voltaire, *Corresp.* viii. 36 (Dec. 1758); Bachaumont, xi. 156–7 (31 Dec. 1776).

63. Saint-Simon, *Mémoires*, ed. A. de Boislisle (41 vols., 1879–1928), xxvii. 163.

64. R. Morel, 'Les Déboires d'un précepteur au XVIIIe siècle. L'abbé Edme Mallet et la princesse de Rohan-Guémené', *Bull. Soc. Seine-et-Marne* (1908–9), 191–203.

65. For the University, J. Nowinski, *Baron Dominique Vivant Denon, 1747–1825* (1970), 20, and Morellet, next note. For battlefield, the case of the prince de Montbarey, see H. Carré, *La Noblesse de France et l'opinion publique au XVIIIe siècle* (1920).

66. L'Abbé Morellet, *Lettres*, ed. D. Medlin *et al.* (2 vols., 1991), i. pp. xxxii–xxxv. The duchesse de la Trémouille gave the abbé Foucher 1,500 livres a year, and he already had an income from the Chastellux family (J.-N. Moreau, *Mes Souvenirs*, ed. C. Hermelin (2 vols., 1892), i. 20–30).

67. H. Duranton, 'Le Métier d'historien au XVIIIe siècle', *Rev. hist. mod. contemp.* (1976), 493–8. The advantage of employing an abbé was that no retirement pension was needed (Carré, *La Noblesse*, 211).

68. J. Sgard, *Corpus Condillac, 1714–80* (1981), 67–9, 81.

69. E. Colombet (ed.), *Revue des provinces de l'Ouest*, ii (1854–5), 259–61.

70. *Souvenirs du baron de Frénilly, 1768–1828*, ed. A. Chuquet (1908), 33–45.

71. Le prince de Ligne, *Mémoires*, ed. A. Lacroix (1861), 30.

72. G. Maugras, *La Cour de Lunéville au XVIIIe siècle* (1906), 195–9. For the abbé Quesnel, see Moreau, *Mes Souvenirs*, i. 18–19.

73. L. Quérard, *La France littéraire* (2 vols., 1827–50), iii. 553, iv. 362, viii. 407.

74. Saint-Simon, xviii. 209–10.

75. Marais, ii. 6, 235.

76. Charles de Mathei, marquis de Valfons, *Souvenirs, 1710–86*, ed. le marquis de Valfons and G. Maurin (1906), 64.

77. A. Rheinwald, 'L'Abbé Huber, la psychologie d'une conversion', *Genava* (1927), 93 ff.; H. Lüthy, *La Banque Protestante en France, de la révocation de l'édit de Nantes à la Révolution* (2 vols., 1961), ii. 68, 219–22.

78. *Journal du duc de Croy, 1718–84*, ed. le vicomte de Grouchy and P. Cottin (4 vols., 1906), ii. 86.

79. Ch. Collé, *Journal historique, 1761–3*, ed. A. J. van Bever (1911), 157–65.

80. E. Dard, *Le Général Choderlos de Laclos, auteur des 'Liaisons dangereuses', 1741–1803* (1936), 147–8.

81. E. S. Mercier, *Tableau de Paris* (12 vols., 1782–8), i. 268. There is an abbé at a lady's *lever* in Badouin's picture *Le Matin*. The puritanical curé Thiers has a diatribe against priests serving as 'domestiques'—business agents, household managers, valets, butlers, horse-dealers, huntsmen, and the mysterious and no doubt disreputable category of 'Quinola' (slang for the knave of hearts) (J. B. Thiers, *Superstitions anciennes et nouvelles* (2 vols., 1732), ii. 250).

82. Cited by J. Fabre, *Lumières et Romantisme* (1963), 142–7.

83. A. Lombard, *L'Abbé Dubos* (1913), 146, 168.

84. Batteux, *Les Beaux-Arts*, 256–7.

85. J. Jacquart, *L'Abbé Trublet, critique et moraliste, 1697–1770* (1926), 101, 121–2, 399.

86. E. Harrisse, *L'Abbé Prévost; histoire de sa vie et de ses œuvres* (1896), 61–2; P. Trahard, *Les Maîtres de la sensibilité française au XVIIIe siècle* (4 vols., 1931–3), i. 91–5. For Maydieu, a tutor, a canon of Troyes and correspondent of Rousseau, see P.-M. Masson, *La Religion de Rousseau* (3 vols., 1916), iii. 176–7.

87. For Saint-Pierre's ordination, J. Drouet, *The Abbé de Saint-Pierre* (1912), 15. For Raynal, H. Jürgen, Lüsebrock, and Tietz, *Lectures de Raynal*, S.V.E.C. (1991), introduction. When called 'ce bougre de prêtre', Desfontaines replied, 'Monsieur, je ne suis pas prêtre'. But this is contradicted by his formal statement to the police when he was arrested for homosexual rape in 1725 (Boivin, 'Les Dossiers').

88. Paul d'Estrée, 'La Mort de l'abbé Desfontaines', *Rev. hist. litt. Fr.* (1908), 126–8.

89. D'Argenson, iv. 65 (May 1743).

90. Grimm, ii. 453 (Dec. 1754). Terrasson died in 1750.

91. R. Granderoute, *Le Roman pédagogique de Fénelon à Rousseau* (2 vols., 1985), i. 305–6, 327; ii. 1070.

92. Sgard, *Corpus Condillac*, 39–68.

93. D'Haussonville, *Le Salon de Mme Necker* (2 vols., 1882), i. 139–40.

94. J. Lough, 'Who were the Philosophes?', in J. M. Fox *et al.* (eds.), *Studies in 18th Century French Literature . . . Robert Niklaus* (1975), 139 ff.

95. A. Jobert, *Magnats polonais et physiocrates français, 1762–1771* (1941), 29.

96. E. Lavaquery (ed.), *Lettres de Piron à Jean-François Le Vayer* (1921), 53 (29 Dec. 1751).

97. C. Daux, *Une Réhabilitation: l'abbé Jean-Martin de Prades* (1902); J. Spink, 'Un Abbé philosophe: l'affaire de l'abbé de Prades', *XVIIIe Siècle* (1971), 145–73; N. Noël, *Une Figure énigmatique parmi les encyclopédistes: l'abbé de Prades* (1973); J. Combes-Malaville, 'Vues nouvelles sur l'abbé de Prades', *XVIIIe Siècle* (1988), 377–97.

98. See V. Pinot, *La Chine et la formation de l'esprit philosophique en France* (1932), as corrected by Northeast, *Parisian Jesuits*, 119–23. Northeast shows the Jesuits facing the contradiction honestly; Prades could well have been following them.

99. J. Renwick, *Marmontel: The Formative Years* (S.V.E.C., 1970), 198–210. The Sorbonne was foolish to allow its list of condemned propositions to be published, for some were unexceptionable (id., 'Marmontel et *Bélisaire*', in J. Ehrard (ed.), *J.-F. Marmontel 1723–99: études* (1972), 63–4).

100. Marmontel, *Mémoires*, ii. 18–21.

101. A sad case of such hero worship in P. Dupont, *Un Poète philosophe: Houdar de la Motte* (1898), 188.

102. J. Ehrard, *L'Idée de Nature en France dans la première moitié du XVIIIe siècle* (2 vols., 1963), ii. 715–17.

103. Fréron's own account in G. Desnoiresterres, *Voltaire et la société française au XVIIIe siècle*, 2nd edn. (8 vols., 1867–76), v. 45–72, 489–90.

104. F. A. and S. L. Kafker, *The Encyclopedists as Individuals: A Biographical Dictionary of the Authors of the* Encyclopédie (1988).

105. L. A. Segal, 'Lenglet du Fresnoy: The Treason of a Cleric', *S.V.E.C.* (1973), 278.

106. R. Hubert, *Les Sciences sociales dans* l'Encyclopédie (1923), 18–19; J. Proust, *Diderot et* l'Encyclopédie (1967), 18–22.

107. J. F. Combes-Malaville, 'L'Incarcération de l'abbé de Prades à Magdebourg', *XVIIIᵉ Siècle* (1993), 338–53.

108. L. Gossman, *Medievalism and the Ideologies of the Enlightenment* (1968), 314; L. Brunel, *Les Philosophes et l'Académie* (1884), 341.

109. R. Darnton, *The Literary Underworld of the Old Régime* (1982), 5.

110. P. Grosclaude, *Malesherbes, témoin et interprète de son temps* (1961), 90–1.

111. J. Wogue, *J.-B.-L. Gresset* (1894), 222–3.

112. G. Wilson, *A Medievalist in the 18th Century: Le Grand d'Aussy and the Fabliaux* (1975), 3–4, 7.

113. M. Badolle, *L'Abbé Jean-Jacques Barthélemy, 1716–1795* (n.d. [1927]), 100, 230–53.

114. G. Bonno (ed.), *Correspondance littéraire de Suard avec le Margrave de Bayreuth*, University of California Publications in Modern Philology (1934), 225 (Oct. 1775).

115. F. de Dainville, *Cartes anciennes de l'Église de France* (1956), 75; Jourdain, *Histoire*, ii. 275–6; C. Chaudon-Adhémar, 'Le Voyage en Sibérie de Chappe d'Auteroche', *XVIIIᵉ Siècle* (1964), 274–94; J. M. Racault, 'L'Observation du passage de Vénus sur le soleil', *XVIIIᵉ Siècle* (1990), 107–20.

116. Bachaumont, iv. 106 (6 Sept. 1768); xxvi. 214–15 (27 Sept. 1784); xxvi. 82–108 (July 1784).

117. E. Esmonin, 'L'Abbé Expilly et ses travaux de statistique', in his *Études sur la France des 17ᵉ et 18ᵉ siècles* (1964), 274–94.

118. D. Mornet, *Les Sciences de la Nature en France au XVIIIᵉ siècle* (1911), 87; C. Kiernan, *The Enlightenment and Science in 18th Century France* (1973), 154–5.

119. A. Vartarnian, 'Le Frère de Maupertuis', *XVIIIᵉ Siècle* (1982), 305–22.

120. Quérard, *La France littéraire*, i. 32; ii. 158, 193; iii. 54; iv. 572; vii. 472–3.

121. Grimm, viii. 276.

122. D. Lynham, *The Father of Modern Ballet: The Chevalier Noverre* (1950), 55–6; J. Seznec and J. Adhémar, *Diderot, Salons I, 1759–61–63* (1957), 32.

123. Guy, 'Towards an Appreciation', 86. For Allainval see F.C.B.'s edn. of his *École des bourgeois* (1937).

124. Quérard, *La France littéraire*, viii. 191.

125. H. C. Lancaster, *French Tragedy . . . 1715–75* (2 vols., 1977), i. 219–20.

126. *Anecdotes dramatiques* (4 vols., 1775), i. 486–7. Racine first made the joke—to Boileau, 4 Aug. 1695. In the *Apocrypha*, Judith cuts off the head of the Assyrian general Holofernes.

127. *Année littéraire*, 1758, 1760, in C. Barthélemy, *Les Confessions de Fréron* (1876). See also Biard-Milléroux, *L'Esthétique*, 26, 517, 524 and Balcou, *Fréron*, 469. (I have counted the abbé d'Olivet of the Academy as an official apologist. His translation of Cicero's *De natura deorum* was accompanied by notes and an essay refuting its anti-Christian implications. See for him A. C. Kors, *Atheism in France, 1650–1729* (1990), 208–17.

128. Biard-Milléroux, *L'Esthétique*, 524.

129. D. Gembicki, *Histoire et politique à la fin de l'ancien régime: Jacob-Nicolas Moreau, 1717–1803* (1976), 71–3, 82–3. Moreau's *Nouveau mémoire pour servir*

à l'histoire des Cacouacs has been reprinted by Slatkine from the 1828 edn. (1968). The abbé de Saint-Cyr is said to have been a minor chaplain at Versailles.

130. Pluche, *Spectacle de la Nature* (9 vols., 1750 edn.), viii (2), 169 ff.

131. A. Viala, 'Les Idées de l'abbé Pluche sur la société', in A. Viala and M. Labriolle (eds.), *La Régence*, Colloque, Aix-en-Provence 1968 (1970), 308 ff.

132. W. Folkierski, *Entre le Classicisme et le Romantisme: étude sur l'esthétique et les esthéticiens du XVIIIᵉ siècle* (1969), 39 ff.

133. See Lombard, *Dubos*.

134. De la Brétèche, *Saint-Non et Fragonard* (1928); and L. Mascoli, 'Le *Journal du voyage* en Italie de l'abbé de Saint-Non, 1759–61', *XVIIIᵉ Siècle* (1989), 423–38.

135. Lombard, *Dubos*, 51. He was an austere critic, wanting opera shorn of its 'machines', suitable only to impress 'les garçons de boutique nouvellement arrivés à Paris'.

136. J. Chouillet, *La Formation des idées esthétiques de Diderot, 1745–63* (1973), 239, 283.

137. H. J. Martin, *Livre, pouvoir et société à Paris au XVIIᵉ siècle* (2 vols., 1969), ii. 909–19.

138. J. Lough, 'Chaudon's Dictionnaire anti-philosophique', in P. J. Howells *et al.* (eds.), *Studies . . . W. H. Barber* (1985), 307–27. For the *honnête homme* tradition see Ch. 31 below.

139. Mauzi, *L'Idée du bonheur*, 185–6, 387, 401.

140. Aubert, a *tonsuré*, taught much the same lesson in his eight volumes of fables, progressive in politics, prudential in morals. See J. N. Pascal (ed.), *La Fable au siècle des Lumières* (1991), 23 ff.

141. Northeast, *Parisian Jesuits*, 28. The basic discussion is in Cl. Labrosse, 'Les *Mémoires de Trévoux* et le roman, 1730–40', in H. Duranton (ed.), *Études sur la presse au XVIIIᵉ siècle* (1973).

142. Green, *La Peinture*, 20–7.

143. Morris, 'L'Abbé Desfontaines', 174–5, 178.

144. S. Etienne, *Le Genre romanesque en France depuis la parution de la 'Nouvelle Héloïse' jusqu'aux approches de la Révolution* (1922), 171–2, 337.

145. To Delille, the Christian hopes for resurrection, but the consoler is Nature: 'Eh qui n'a pas pleuré quelque perte cruelle? | Loin d'un monde léger, venez donc à vos pleurs, | Venez associer les bois, les eaux, les fleurs. | Tout devient un ami pour les âmes sensibles' (*Les Jardins, ou l'art d'embellir les paysages* (1782), in *Œuvres* (9 vols., 1825), i. 85–6).

146. McManners, *Death*, ch. 10.

GENERAL INDEX

and official ceremonial 16
and parishes 300
and property rights 114
and republicanism 22
and seigneurs 379–80
and taxation 164
and tithes 140
Frères des écoles Chrétiennes 198, 420,
    473, 475, 515, 529–33
Frères de Saint-Jean-de-Dieu 510, 513–14,
    515–16
Fréron, Élie-Catherine 649–50, 662, 669,
    676–7
Froger, L. 104, 349–50, 352
funerals 195, 308, 338–9, 367
    at sea 63–4
    royal 35, 36, 48
    and surplice-fees 337–40

gabelle (salt tax) 171, 181, 258, 299
Gallican Church:
    bureaucracy 143–4, 150–4, 156, 163,
        188
    central direction 143, 159, 185, 219
    and change 2
    and Four Gallican Articles 20
    and infallibility 205–6
    and interests of the monarchy 58, 121,
        141
    liberties 582, 622, 630, 636
    and primacy 186–8, 193
    and secular society 3–4
    and sovereignty 10, 12, 13, 14
    see also bishops; Church–State relations;
        dioceses; General Assemblies of the
        clergy; parishes; wealth
Gap diocese:
    and chapters 401
    and curés 92–3, 329–30, 337, 343
    and seminaries 201
Gautier, J.-J. 305, 356, 377–8, 393
General Assemblies of clergy 141–73
    agents généraux, see agent-general
    and appointments to benefices 636–7,
        640
    assemblée extraordinaire 146, 159, 162, 171
    and bishops 158, 186, 188, 237
    and *Bureau de l'agence* 151
    bureaucracy 143–4, 150–4, 156, 163,
        188
    and charitable donations 163
    and clerical ambition 148
    and *congrue* 335
    and decline of religion 157–8

and dioceses 216, 271
and doctrine 159–60
and freehold 361
Grande and *Petite Assemblée* 146, 150
and *grands vicaires* 147–8, 153, 192
and grievances 141, 156–7, 162, 188
and heresy 15
and Jansenism 157, 159, 160
and leadership 188
and monarchy 20–1, 24–6, 141, 143–4,
    148–9
procedure 149–50
and religious observance 82
and religious Orders 571, 607, 614
and representation 144–5, 146–8, 152,
    227
and rights of the Church 24–5
and sceptical literature 264
and taxation 141–6, 149, 150–1, 154–6,
    157, 158–9, 160–3, 166–7, 169–72,
    732 n. 66
and tithes 132, 138–9
see also *syndics*
Genlis, Stéphanie-Félicité du Crest, Mme
    de 489, 577, 661, 780 n.43
Génovéfains:
    and almsgiving 506
    and Commission des réguliers 584–5,
        608, 613
Gilles, Jean 447, 469
Girac, François Bareau de, bishop of
    Rennes 153, 248, 257, 271–2
Glandève diocese:
    and bishops 213, 220, 244
    and chapter 178, 399, 401
    and size 178, 180
    and taxation 155, 156
glass 440–1, 443, 444
godparents:
    and church bells 317
    and spiritual affinity 69, 195
Good Friday, Court ceremonies 31
Gossec, François-Joseph 469–70
grace, royal 36
grand aumônier 7, 29–30, 31, 33, 34, 43
    and Court factions 47
    and precedence 36
    and royal *lever* and *coucher* 29, 44
    and royal patronage 49
Grandmontins 166, 574–5, 611
grands jours 302
grands vicaires (vicars-general):
    aristocratic 211, 214, 215, 222, 225–7,
        232–4, 241, 287–8